THE FIREFLY SPANISH/ENGLISH VISUAL DICTIONARY

Jean-Claude **Corbeil**
Ariane **Archambault**

FIREFLY BOOKS

Published by Firefly Books Ltd. 2004

First Printing

Publisher Cataloging-in-Publication Data (U.S.)
Corbeil, Jean-Claude.
The Firefly Spanish - English visual dictionary / Jean-Claude Corbeil, Ariane Archambeault.–1st ed.
[592] p. : col. ill. ; cm.
Includes index.
Summary: A comprehensive general reference visual dictionary featuring terms in English and Spanish. Includes sections on astronomy, geography, the animal and vegetable kingdoms, human biology, the home, clothing and accessories, art and architecture, communication, transportation, energy, science, society and sports.
ISBN 1-55297-951-2
1. Picture dictionaries, Spanish. 2. Picture dictionaries, English. 3. Spanish language – Dictionaries – English. 4. English language – Dictionaries – Spanish. I. Archambeault, Ariane. II. Title.
463.21 dc22 PC4629.C67 2004

National Library of Canada Cataloguing in Publication
Corbeil, Jean-Claude, 1932-
The Firefly Spanish/English visual dictionary / Jean-Claude Corbeil, Ariane Archambault.
Text in English and Spanish.
Includes index.
ISBN 1-55297-951-2
1. Picture dictionaries, Spanish. 2. Picture dictionaries, English. 3. Spanish language–Dictionaries–English. 4. English language–Dictionaries–Spanish. I. Archambault, Ariane, 1936- II. Title.
AG250.C66378 2004 463'.17 C2004-901313-0

Published in the United States in 2004 by
Firefly Books (U.S.) Inc.
P.O. Box 1338, Ellicott Station
Buffalo, New York 14205

Published in Canada in 2004 by
Firefly Books Ltd.
66 Leek Crescent
Richmond Hill, Ontario L4B 1H1

Cover design: Gareth Lind

Printed in Singapore

ACKNOWLEDGMENTS

Our deepest gratitude to the individuals, institutions, companies and businesses that have provided us with the latest technical documentation for use in preparing *The Firefly Spanish/English Visual Dictionary*.

Arcand, Denys (réalisateur); Association Internationale de Signalisation Maritime; Association canadienne des paiements (Charlie Clarke); Association des banquiers canadiens (Lise Provost); Automobiles Citroën; Automobiles Peugeot; Banque du Canada (Lyse Brousseau); Banque Royale du Canada (Raymond Chouinard, Francine Morel, Carole Trottier); Barrett Xplore inc.; Bazarin, Christine;Bibliothèque du Parlement canadien (Service de renseignements); Bibliothèque nationale du Québec (Jean-François Palomino); Bluechip Kennels (Olga Gagne); Bombardier Aéronautique; Bridgestone-Firestone; Brother (Canada); Canadien National; Casavant Frères ltée; C.O.J.O. ATHENES 2004 (Bureau des Médias Internationaux); Centre Eaton de Montréal; Centre national du Costume (Recherche et de Diffusion); Cetacean Society International (William R. Rossiter); Chagnon, Daniel (architecte D.E.S. – M.E.Q.); Cohen et Rubin Architectes (Maggy Cohen); Commission Scolaire de Montréal (École St-Henri); Compagnie de la Baie d'Hudson (Nunzia Iavarone, Ron Oyama); Corporation d'hébergement du Québec (Céline Drolet); École nationale de théâtre du Canada (Bibliothèque); Élevage Le Grand Saphir (Stéphane Ayotte); Énergie atomique du Canada ltée; Eurocopter; Famous Players; Fédération bancaire française (Védi Hékiman); Fontaine, PierreHenry (biologiste); Future Shop; Garaga; Groupe Jean Coutu; Hôpital du Sacré-Cœur de Montréal; Hôtel Inter-Continental; Hydro-Québec; I.P.I.Q. (Serge Bouchard); IGA Barcelo; International Entomological Society (Dr. Michael Geisthardt); Irisbus; Jérôme, Danielle (O.D.); La Poste (Colette Gouts); Le Groupe Canam Manac inc.; Lévesque, Georges (urgentologue); Lévesque, Robert (chef machiniste); Manutan; Marriot Spring Hill suites; MATRA S.A.; Métro inc.; ministère canadien de la Défense nationale (Affaires publiques); ministère de la Défense, République Française; ministère de la Justice du Québec (Service de la gestion immobilière – Carol Sirois); ministère de l'Éducation du Québec (Direction de l'équipement scolaire- Daniel Chagnon); Muse Productions (Annick Barbery); National Aeronautics and Space Administration; National Oceanic and Atmospheric Administration; Nikon Canada inc.; Normand, Denis (consultant en télécommunications); Office de la langue française du Québec (Chantal Robinson); Paul Demers & Fils inc.; Phillips (France); Pratt & Whitney Canada inc.; Prévost Car inc.; Radio Shack Canada ltée; Réno-Dépôt inc.; Robitaille, Jean-François (Département de biologie, Université Laurentienne); Rocking T Ranch and Poultry Farm (Pete and Justine Theer); RONA inc.; Sears Canada inc.; Secrétariat d'État du Canada : Bureau de la traduction ; Service correctionnel du Canada; Société d'Entomologie Africaine (Alain Drumont); Société des musées québécois (Michel Perron); Société Radio-Canada; Sony du Canada ltée; Sûreté du Québec; Théâtre du Nouveau Monde; Transports Canada (Julie Poirier); Urgences-Santé (Éric Berry); Ville de Longueuil (Direction de la Police); Ville de Montréal (Service de la prévention des incendies); Vimont Lexus Toyota; Volvo Bus Corporation; Yamaha Motor Canada Ltd.

QA International wishes to extend a special thank you to the following people for their contribution to *The Firefly Spanish/English Visual Dictionary*:

Jean-Louis Martin, Marc Lalumière, Jacques Perrault, Stéphane Roy, Alice Comtois, Michel Blais, Christiane Beauregard, Mamadou Togola, Annie Maurice, Charles Campeau, Mivil Deschênes, Jonathan Jacques, Martin Lortie, Raymond Martin, Frédérick Simard, Yan Tremblay, Mathieu Blouin, Sébastien Dallaire, Hoang Khanh Le, Martin Desrosiers, Nicolas Oroc, François Escalmel, Danièle Lemay, Pierre Savoie, Benoît Bourdeau, Marie-Andrée Lemieux, Caroline Soucy, Yves Chabot, Anne-Marie Ouellette, Anne-Marie Villeneuve, Anne-Marie Brault, Nancy Lepage, Daniel Provost, François Vézina, Brad Wilson, Michael Worek, Lionel Koffler, Maraya Raduha, Dave Harvey, Mike Parkes, George Walker and Anna Simmons.

The Firefly Spanish/English Visual Dictionary was created and produced by
QA International
329, rue de la Commune Ouest, 3e étage
Montréal (Québec) H2Y 2E1 Canada
T 514.499.3000 F 514.499.3010
www.qa-international.com

EDITORIAL STAFF

Publisher: Jacques Fortin
Authors: Jean-Claude Corbeil and Ariane Archambault
Editorial Director: François Fortin
Editor-in-Chief: Serge D'Amico
Graphic Design: Anne Tremblay

PRODUCTION

Mac Thien Nguyen Hoang
Guylaine Houle

TERMINOLOGICAL RESEARCH

Jean Beaumont
Catherine Briand
Nathalie Guillo

ILLUSTRATIONS

Art Direction: Jocelyn Gardner
Jean-Yves Ahern
Rielle Lévesque
Alain Lemire
Mélanie Boivin
Yan Bohler
Claude Thivierge
Pascal Bilodeau
Michel Rouleau
Anouk Noël
Carl Pelletier

LAYOUT

Pascal Goyette
Janou-Ève LeGuerrier
Véronique Boisvert
Josée Gagnon
Karine Raymond
Geneviève Théroux Béliveau

DOCUMENTATION

Gilles Vézina
Kathleen Wynd
Stéphane Batigne
Sylvain Robichaud
Jessie Daigle

DATA MANAGEMENT

Programmer: Daniel Beaulieu
Nathalie Fréchette

REVISION

Marie-Nicole Cimon

PREPRESS

Sophie Pellerin
Kien Tang
Tony O'Riley

Jean-Claude Corbeil is an expert in linguistic planning, with a world-wide reputation in the fields of comparative terminology and socio-linguistics. He serves as a consultant to various international organizations and governments.

Ariane Archambault, a specialist in applied linguistics, has taught foreign languages and is now a terminologist and editor of dictionaries and reference books.

Introduction to *The Firefly Spanish/English Visual Dictionar*

A DICTIONARY FOR ONE AND ALL

The Firefly Spanish/English Visual Dictionary uses pictures to define words. With thousands of illustrations and thousands of specialist and general terms, it provides a rich source of knowledge about the world around you.

Designed for the general reader and students of language, *The Firefly Spanish/English Visual Dictionary* responds to the needs of anyone seeking precise, correct terms for a wide range of objects. Using illustrations enables you to "see" immediately the meaning of each term.

You can use *The Firefly Spanish/English Visual Dictionary* in several ways:

By going from an idea to a word. If you are familiar with an object but do not know the correct name for it, you can look up the object in the dictionary and you will find the various parts correctly named.

By going from a word to an idea. If you want to check the meaning of a term, refer to the index where you will find the term and be directed to the appropriate illustration that defines the term.

For sheer pleasure. You can flip from one illustration to another or from one word to another, for the sole purpose of enjoying the illustrations and enriching your knowledge of the world around us.

STRUCTURE

The Firefly Spanish/English Visual Dictionary is divided into CHAPTERS, outlining subjects from astronomy to sports.

More complex subjects are divided into THEMES; for example, the Animal Kingdom chapter is divided into themes including insects and arachnids, mollusks, and crustaceans.

The TITLES name the object and, at times, the chief members of a class of objects are brought together under the same SUBTITLE.

The ILLUSTRATIONS show an object, a process or a phenomenon, and the most significant details from which they are constructed. It serves as a visual definition for each of the terms presented.

TERMINOLOGY

Each word in *The Firefly Spanish/English Visual Dictionary* has been carefully chosen and verified. Sometimes different words are used to name the same object, and in these cases the word most commonly used was chosen.

COLOR REFERENCE

On the spine and back of the book this identifies and accompanies each theme to facilitate quick access to the corresponding section in the book.

TITLE

It is highlighted in English, and the Spanish equivalent is placed underneath in smaller characters. If the title runs over a number of pages, it is printed in gray on the pages subsequent to the first page on which it appears.

SUB-THEME

Most themes are subdivided into sub-themes. The sub-theme is given both in English and in Spanish.

NARROW LINES

These link the word to the item indicated. Where too many lines would make reading difficult, they have been replaced by color codes with captions or, in rare cases, by numbers.

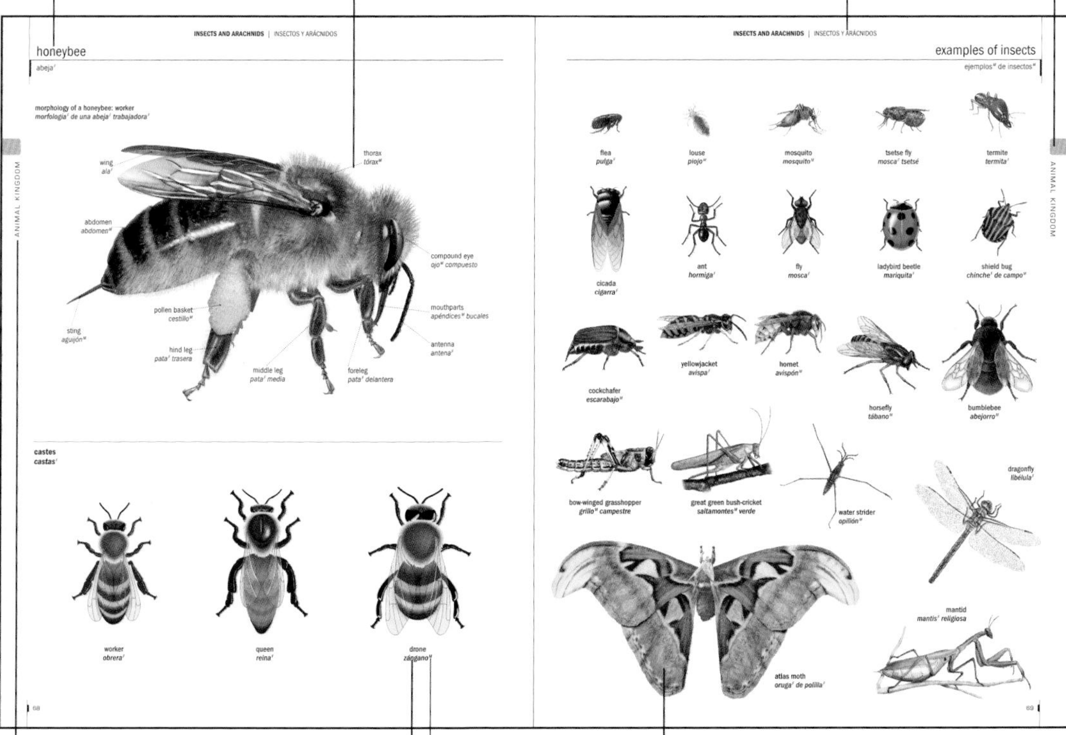

THEME

It is always unilingual, in English.

ILLUSTRATION

It serves as the visual definition for the terms associated with it.

GENDER INDICATION

F: feminine M: masculine N: neuter

The gender of each word in a term is indicated.

The characters shown in the dictionary are men or women when the function illustrated can be fulfilled by either. In these cases, the gender assigned to the word depends on the illustration; in fact, the word is either masculine or feminine depending on the sex of the person.

TERM

Each term appears in the index with a reference to the pages on which it appears. It is given in both languages, with English as the main index entry.

Contents

ASTRONOMY 2
- Celestial bodies 2
- Astronomical observation 7
- Astronautics 10

EARTH 14
- Geography 14
- Geology 26
- Meteorology 37
- Environment 44

VEGETABLE KINGDOM 50

ANIMAL KINGDOM 66
- Simple organisms and echinoderms 66
- Insects and arachnids 67
- Crustaceans 71
- Mollusks 72
- Fishes 74
- Amphibians 75
- Reptiles 76
- Birds 78
- Rodents and lagomorphs 82
- Ungulate mammals 83
- Carnivorous mammals 86
- Marine mammals 90
- Primate mammals 91

HUMAN BEING 92
- Human body 92
- Anatomy 96
- Sense organs 114

FOOD AND KITCHEN 120
- Food 120
- Kitchen 162

HOUSE 182
- Location 182
- Elements of a house 185
- Structure of a house 187
- Heating 192
- Plumbing 194
- Electricity 198
- House furniture 200

DO-IT-YOURSELF AND GARDENING 216
- Do-it-yourself 216
- Gardening 230

CLOTHING 238

PERSONAL ADORNMENT AND ARTICLES 264
- Personal adornment 264
- Personal articles 271

ARTS AND ARCHITECTURE 278
- Architecture 278
- Performing arts 290
- Music 295

COMMUNICATIONS AND OFFICE AUTOMATION 312
- Communications 312
- Office automation 329

TRANSPORT AND MACHINERY 342
- Road transport 342
- Rail transport 374
- Maritime transport 381
- Air transport 388
- Handling 396
- Heavy machinery 398

ENERGY 402
- Geothermal and fossil energy 402
- Hydroelectricity 406
- Nuclear energy 408
- Solar energy 410
- Wind energy 412

SCIENCE 414
- Chemistry 414
- Physics: electricity and magnetism 416
- Physics: optics 418
- Measuring devices 422
- Scientific symbols 426

SOCIETY 430
- City 430
- Justice 440
- Economy and finance 440
- Education 444
- Religion 446
- Politics 448
- Safety 454
- Health 460

SPORTS AND GAMES 468
- Games 468
- Track and field 472
- Ball sports 474
- Racket sports 490
- Gymnastics 496
- Combat sports 498
- Strength sports 500
- Precision and accuracy sports 502
- Winter sports 506
- Aquatic and nautical sports 516
- Cycling 522
- Motor sports 523
- Sports on wheels 526
- Outdoor leisure 528

List of chapters

2 ASTRONOMY

14 EARTH

50 VEGETABLE KINGDOM

66 ANIMAL KINGDOM

92 HUMAN BEING

120 FOOD AND KITCHEN

182 HOUSE

216 DO-IT-YOURSELF AND GARDENING

238 CLOTHING

264 PERSONAL ADORNMENT AND ARTICLES

278 ARTS AND ARCHITECTURE

312 COMMUNICATIONS AND OFFICE AUTOMATION

342 TRANSPORT AND MACHINERY

402 ENERGY

414 SCIENCE

430 SOCIETY

468 SPORTS AND GAMES

539 INDEX

solar system

sistema[M] solar

outer planets
planetas[M] externos

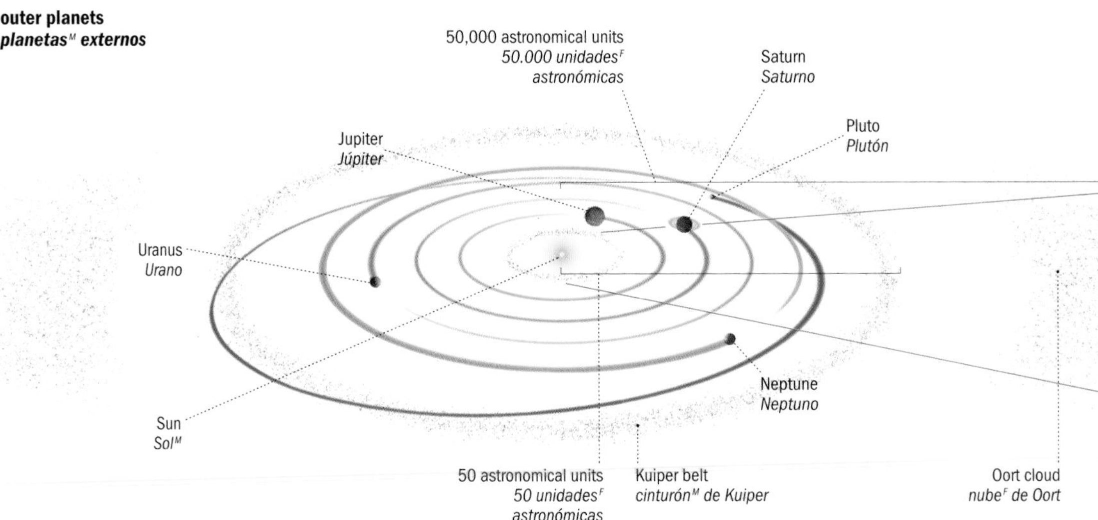

planets and moons

planetas[M] y satélites[M]

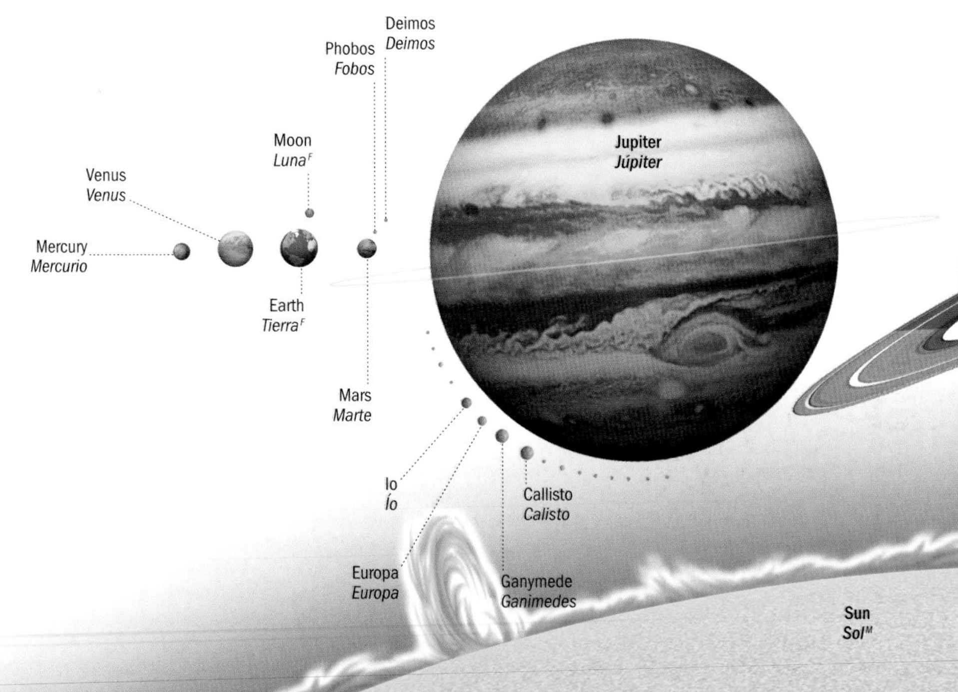

solar system

inner planets
planetas[M] internos

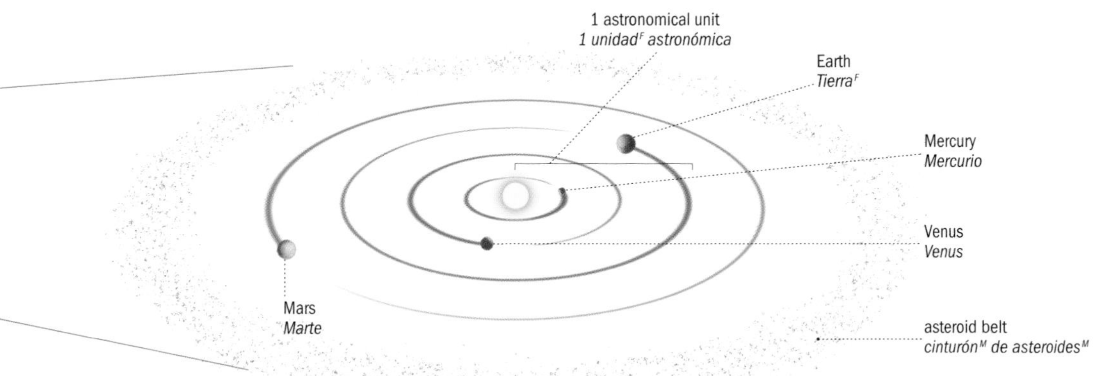

planets and moons

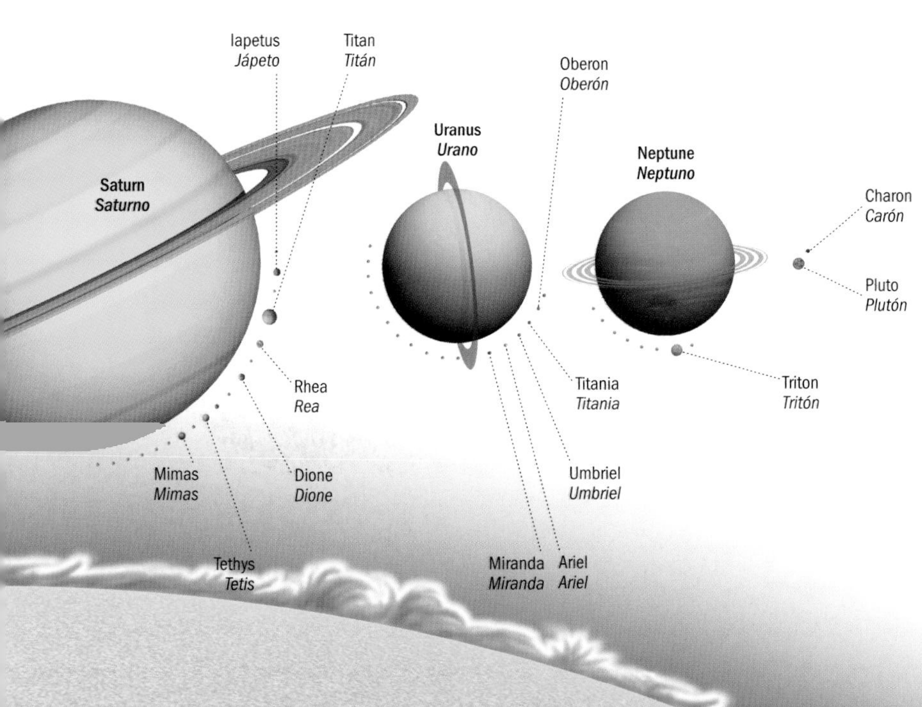

Sun

Sol[M]

structure of the Sun
estructura[F] del Sol[M]

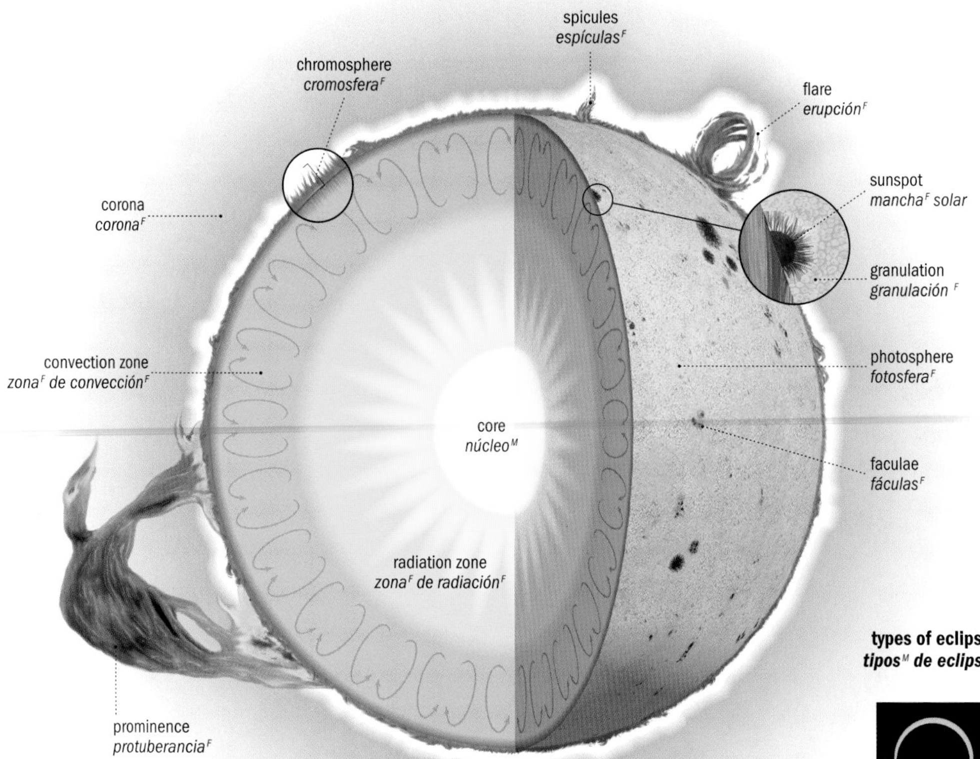

spicules
espículas[F]
chromosphere
cromosfera[F]
flare
erupción[F]
sunspot
mancha[F] solar
corona
corona[F]
granulation
granulación[F]
convection zone
zona[F] de convección[F]
photosphere
fotosfera[F]
core
núcleo[M]
faculae
fáculas[F]
radiation zone
zona[F] de radiación[F]
prominence
protuberancia[F]

types of eclipses
tipos[M] de eclipses[M]

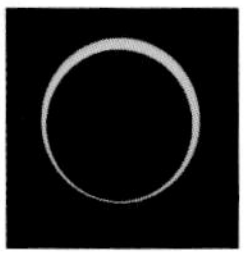

annular eclipse
eclipse[M] anular

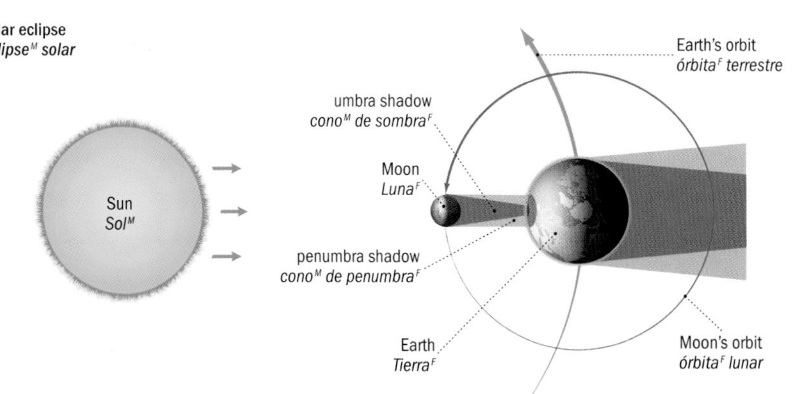

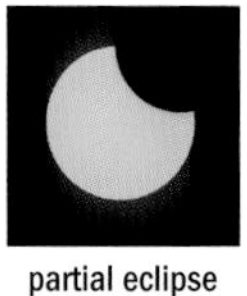

partial eclipse
eclipse[M] parcial

total eclipse
eclipse[M] total

solar eclipse
eclipse[M] solar

Earth's orbit
órbita[F] terrestre
umbra shadow
cono[M] de sombra[F]
Moon
Luna[F]
Sun
Sol[M]
penumbra shadow
cono[M] de penumbra[F]
Earth
Tierra[F]
Moon's orbit
órbita[F] lunar

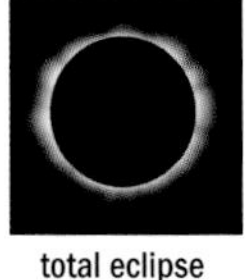

Moon

Luna[F]

types of eclipses
tipos[M] de eclipses[M]

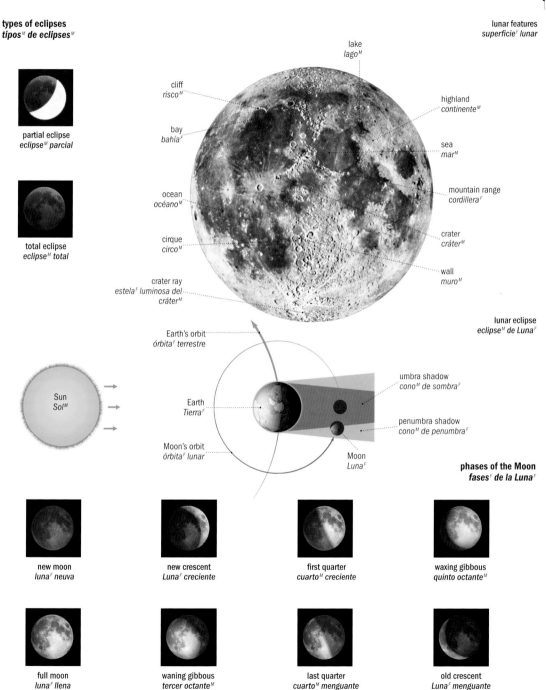

partial eclipse
eclipse[M] parcial

total eclipse
eclipse[M] total

lunar features
superficie[F] lunar

lake
lago[M]

cliff
risco[M]

highland
continente[M]

bay
bahía[F]

sea
mar[M]

mountain range
cordillera[F]

ocean
océano[M]

crater
cráter[M]

cirque
circo[M]

wall
muro[M]

crater ray
estela[F] luminosa del cráter[M]

lunar eclipse
eclipse[M] de Luna[F]

Earth's orbit
órbita[F] terrestre

Sun
Sol[M]

Earth
Tierra[F]

umbra shadow
cono[M] de sombra[F]

penumbra shadow
cono[M] de penumbra[F]

Moon's orbit
órbita[F] lunar

Moon
Luna[F]

phases of the Moon
fases[F] de la Luna[F]

new moon
luna[F] neuva

new crescent
Luna[F] creciente

first quarter
cuarto[M] creciente

waxing gibbous
quinto octante[M]

full moon
luna[F] llena

waning gibbous
tercer octante[M]

last quarter
cuarto[M] menguante

old crescent
Luna[F] menguante

galaxy

galaxia^F

Milky Way
Vía^F Láctea

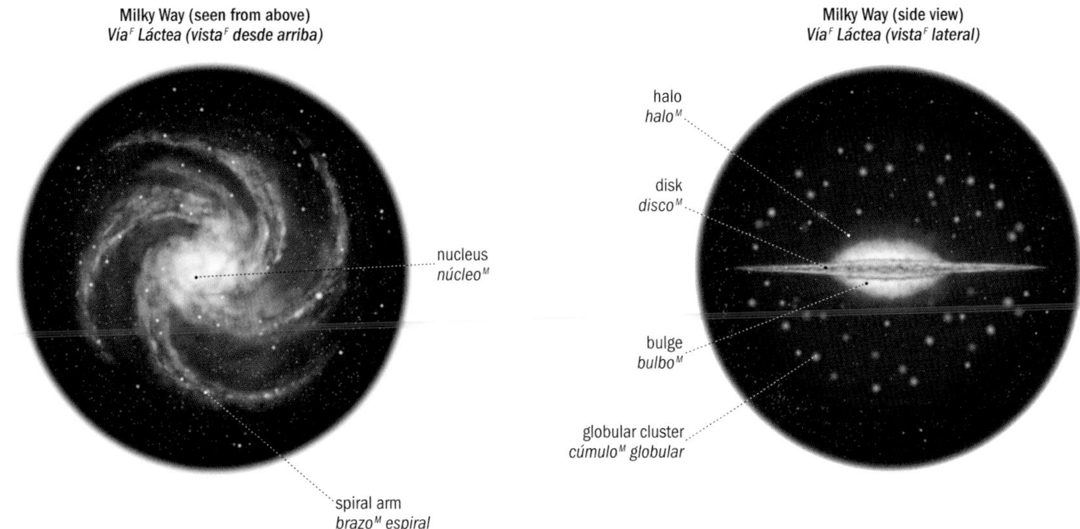

comet

cometa^M

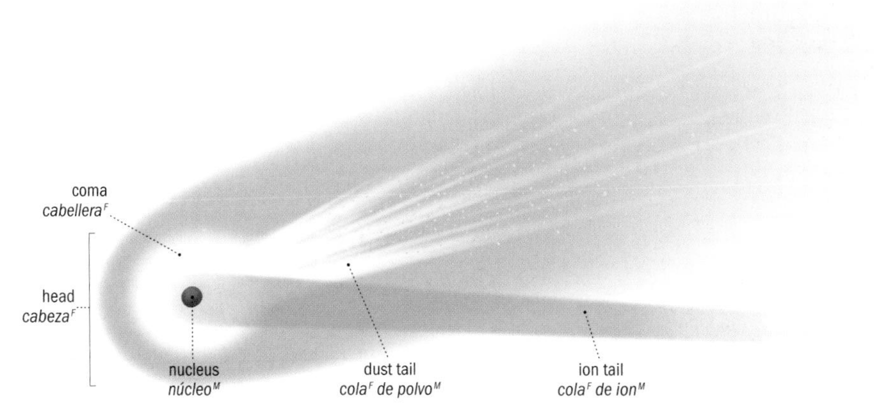

Hubble space telescope

telescopio[M] espacial Hubble

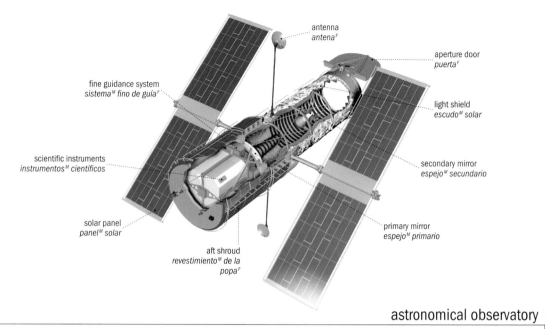

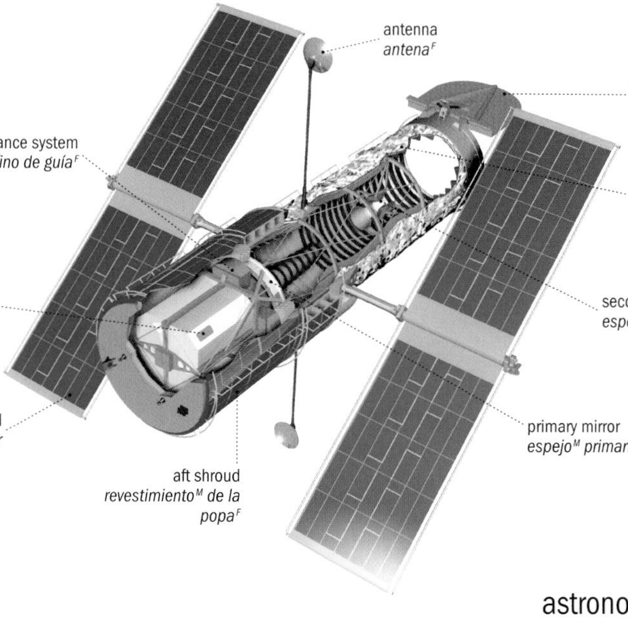

antenna
antena[F]

aperture door
puerta[F]

fine guidance system
sistema[M] fino de guía[F]

light shield
escudo[M] solar

scientific instruments
instrumentos[M] científicos

secondary mirror
espejo[M] secundario

solar panel
panel[M] solar

primary mirror
espejo[M] primario

aft shroud
revestimiento[M] de la popa[F]

astronomical observatory

observatorio[M] astronómico

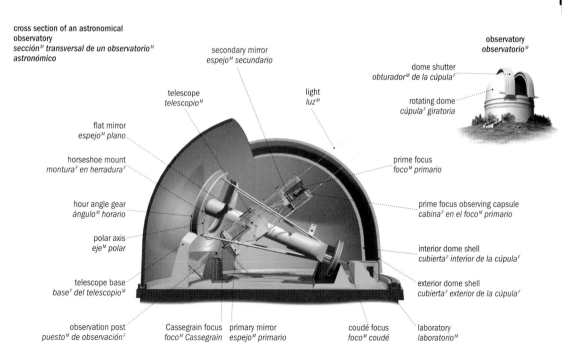

cross section of an astronomical observatory
sección[M] transversal de un observatorio[M] astronómico

secondary mirror
espejo[M] secundario

telescope
telescopio[M]

light
luz[M]

flat mirror
espejo[M] plano

horseshoe mount
montura[F] en herradura[F]

prime focus
foco[M] primario

hour angle gear
ángulo[M] horario

prime focus observing capsule
cabina[F] en el foco[M] primario

polar axis
eje[M] polar

interior dome shell
cubierta[F] interior de la cúpula[F]

telescope base
base[F] del telescopio[M]

exterior dome shell
cubierta[F] exterior de la cúpula[F]

observation post
puesto[M] de observación[F]

Cassegrain focus
foco[M] Cassegrain

primary mirror
espejo[M] primario

coudé focus
foco[M] coudé

laboratory
laboratorio[M]

observatory
observatorio[M]

dome shutter
obturador[M] de la cúpula[F]

rotating dome
cúpula[F] giratoria

refracting telescope

telescopio^{M} refractor

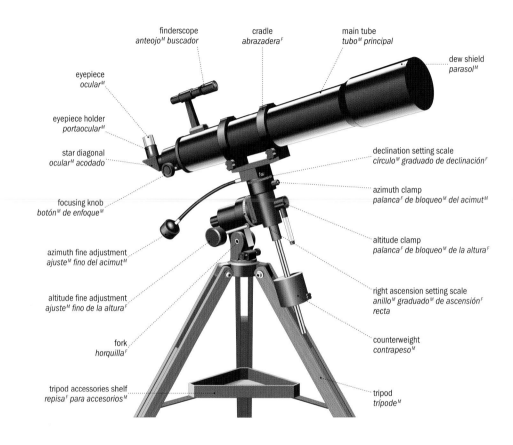

finderscope
anteojo^{M} buscador
cradle
abrazadera^{F}
main tube
tubo^{M} principal
dew shield
parasol^{M}
eyepiece
ocular^{M}
eyepiece holder
portaocular^{M}
star diagonal
ocular^{M} acodado
declination setting scale
círculo^{M} graduado de declinación^{F}
azimuth clamp
palanca^{F} de bloqueo^{M} del acimut^{M}
focusing knob
botón^{M} de enfoque^{M}
altitude clamp
palanca^{F} de bloqueo^{M} de la altura^{F}
azimuth fine adjustment
ajuste^{M} fino del acimut^{M}
right ascension setting scale
anillo^{M} graduado^{M} de ascensión^{F} recta
altitude fine adjustment
ajuste^{M} fino de la altura^{F}
counterweight
contrapeso^{M}
fork
horquilla^{F}
tripod accessories shelf
repisa^{F} para accesorios^{M}
tripod
trípode^{M}

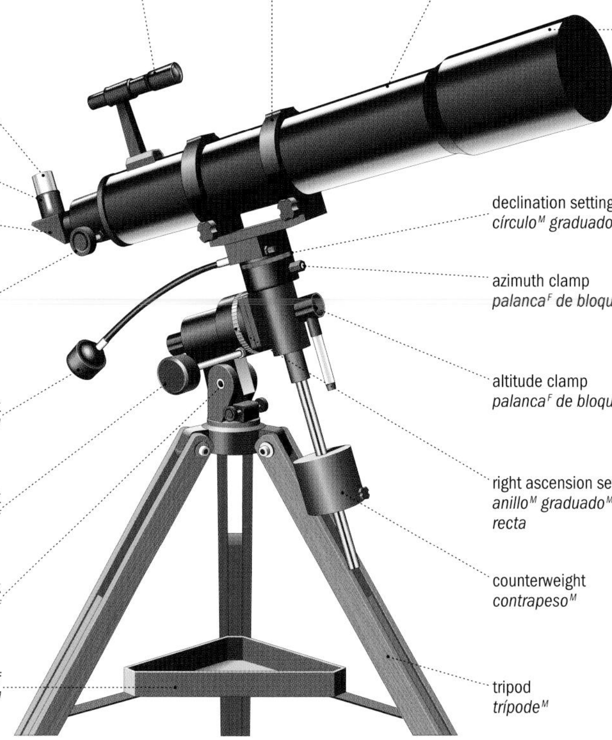

cross section of a refracting telescope
sección^{F} transversal de un telescopio^{M} refractor

light
luz^{F}
eyepiece
ocular^{M}
objective lens
objetivo^{M}
main tube
tubo^{M} principal

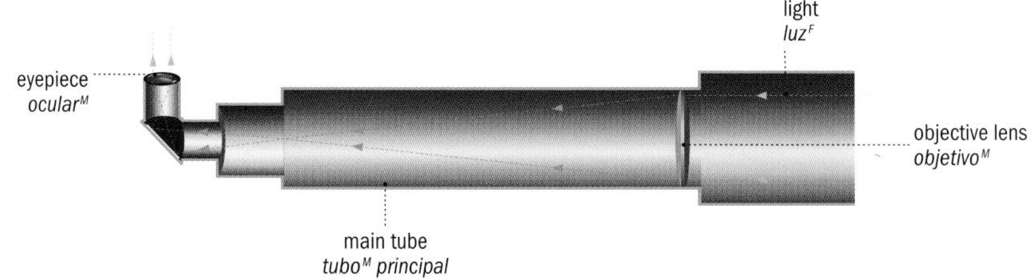

reflecting telescope

telescopio^{M} reflector

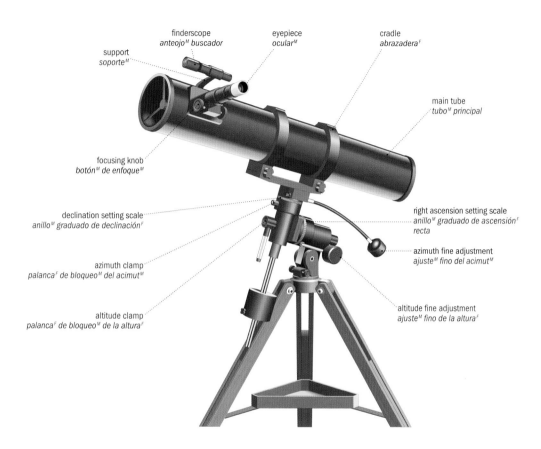

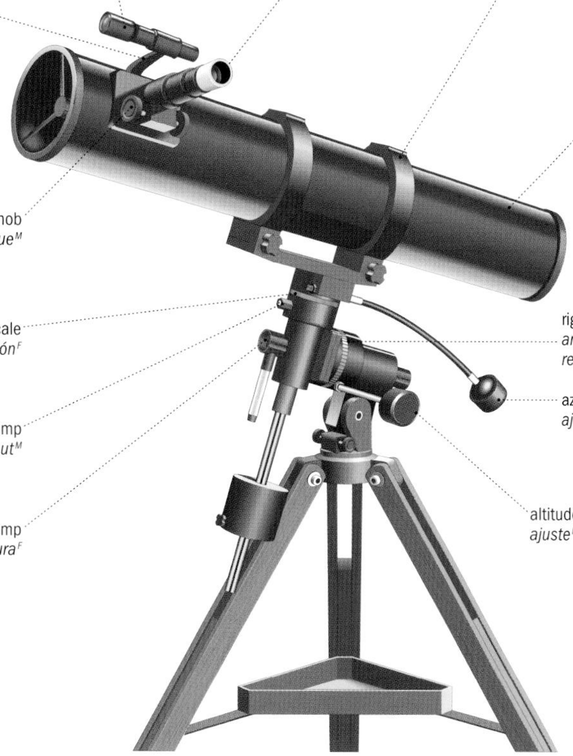

finderscope
anteojo^{M} buscador
eyepiece
ocular^{M}
cradle
abrazadera^{F}
support
soporte^{M}
main tube
tubo^{M} principal
focusing knob
botón^{M} de enfoque^{M}
declination setting scale
anillo^{M} graduado de declinación^{F}
right ascension setting scale
anillo^{M} graduado de ascensión^{F} recta
azimuth fine adjustment
ajuste^{M} fino del acimut^{M}
azimuth clamp
palanca^{F} de bloqueo^{M} del acimut^{M}
altitude fine adjustment
ajuste^{M} fino de la altura^{F}
altitude clamp
palanca^{F} de bloqueo^{M} de la altura^{F}

cross section of a reflecting telescope
sección^{F} transversal de un telecopio^{M} reflector

eyepiece
ocular^{M}
secondary mirror
espejo^{M} secundario
concave primary mirror
espejo^{M} cóncavo primario
light
luz^{F}
main tube
tubo^{M} principal

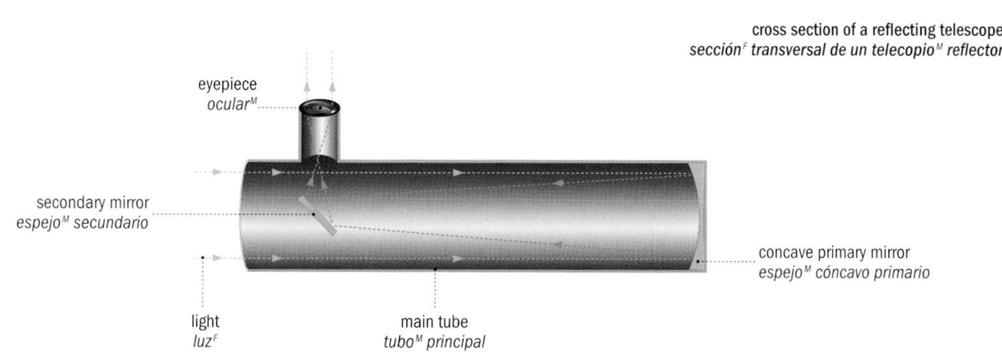

spacesuit

traje^M espacial

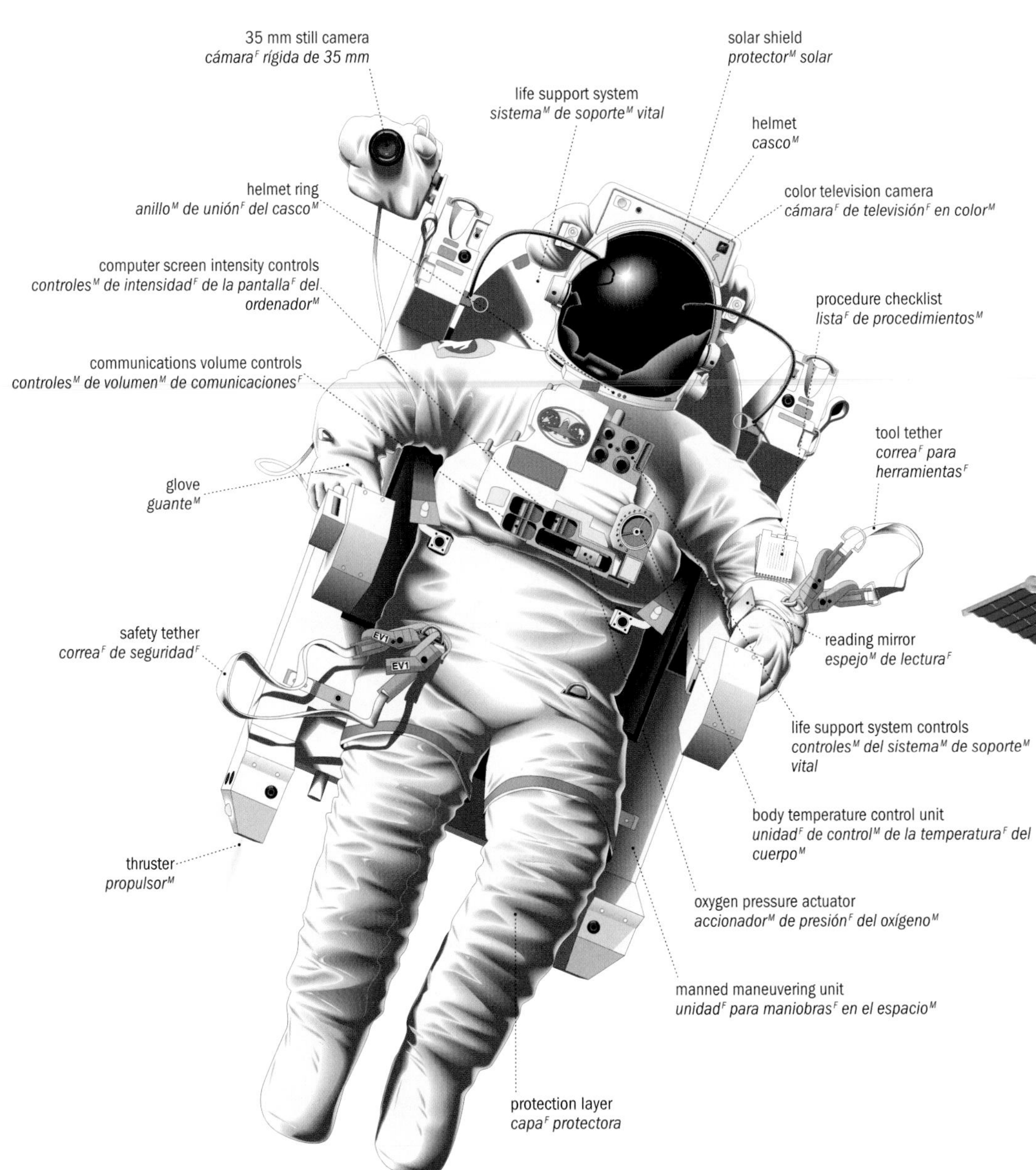
35 mm still camera
cámara^F rígida de 35 mm
solar shield
protector^M solar
life support system
sistema^M de soporte^M vital
helmet
casco^M
helmet ring
anillo^M de unión^F del casco^M
color television camera
cámara^F de televisión^F en color^M
computer screen intensity controls
controles^M de intensidad^F de la pantalla^F del ordenador^M
procedure checklist
lista^F de procedimientos^M
communications volume controls
controles^M de volumen^M de comunicaciones^F
tool tether
correa^F para herramientas^F
glove
guante^M
EV1
EV1
reading mirror
espejo^M de lectura^F
safety tether
correa^F de seguridad^F
life support system controls
controles^M del sistema^M de soporte^M vital
body temperature control unit
unidad^F de control^M de la temperatura^F del cuerpo^M
thruster
propulsor^M
oxygen pressure actuator
accionador^M de presión^F del oxígeno^M
manned maneuvering unit
unidad^F para maniobras^F en el espacio^M
protection layer
capa^F protectora

international space station

estación^F espacial internacional

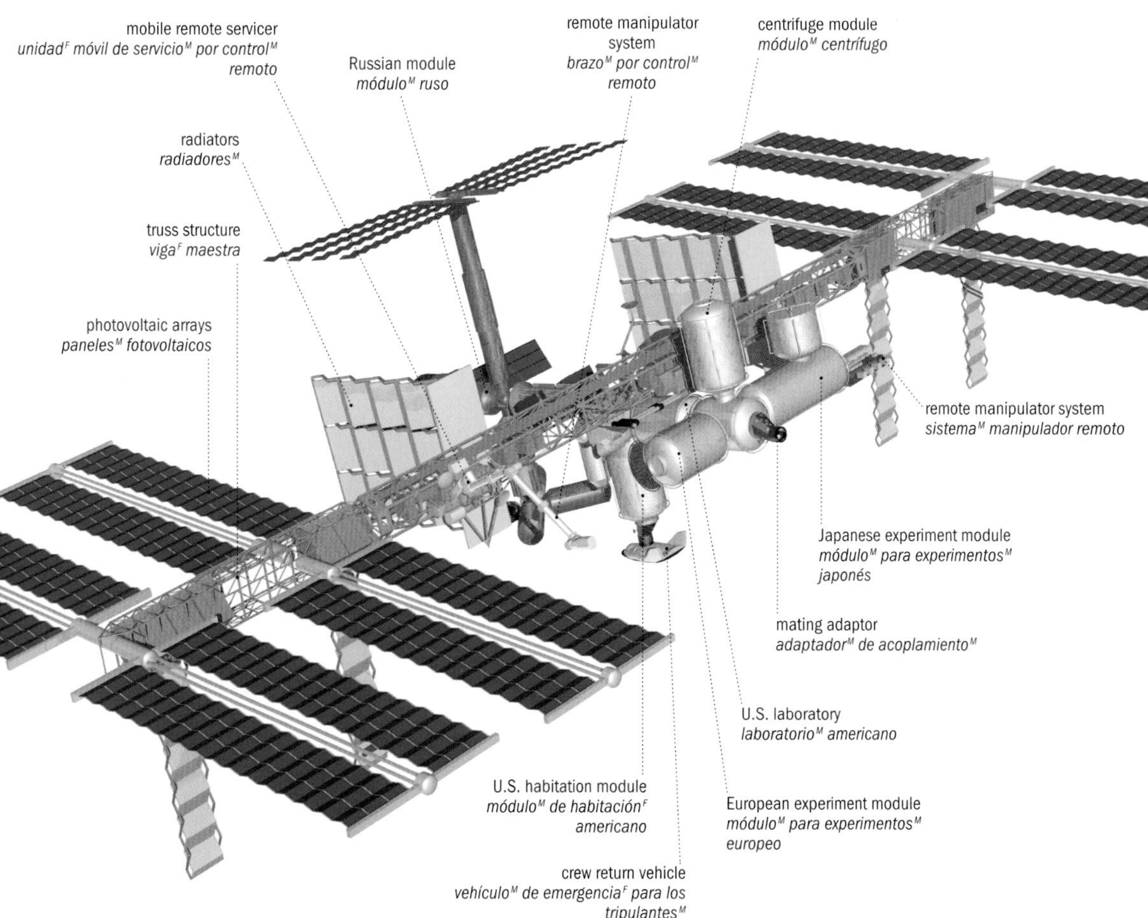
mobile remote servicer
unidad^F móvil de servicio^M por control^M remoto
Russian module
módulo^M ruso
remote manipulator system
brazo^M por control^M remoto
centrifuge module
módulo^M centrífugo
radiators
radiadores^M
truss structure
viga^F maestra
photovoltaic arrays
paneles^M fotovoltaicos
remote manipulator system
sistema^M manipulador remoto
Japanese experiment module
módulo^M para experimentos^M japonés
mating adaptor
adaptador^M de acoplamiento^M
U.S. laboratory
laboratorio^M americano
U.S. habitation module
módulo^M de habitación^F americano
European experiment module
módulo^M para experimentos^M europeo
crew return vehicle
vehículo^M de emergencia^F para los tripulantes^M

space shuttle

transbordador[M] espacial

space shuttle at takeoff
transbordador[M] espacial en posición[F] de lanzamiento[M]

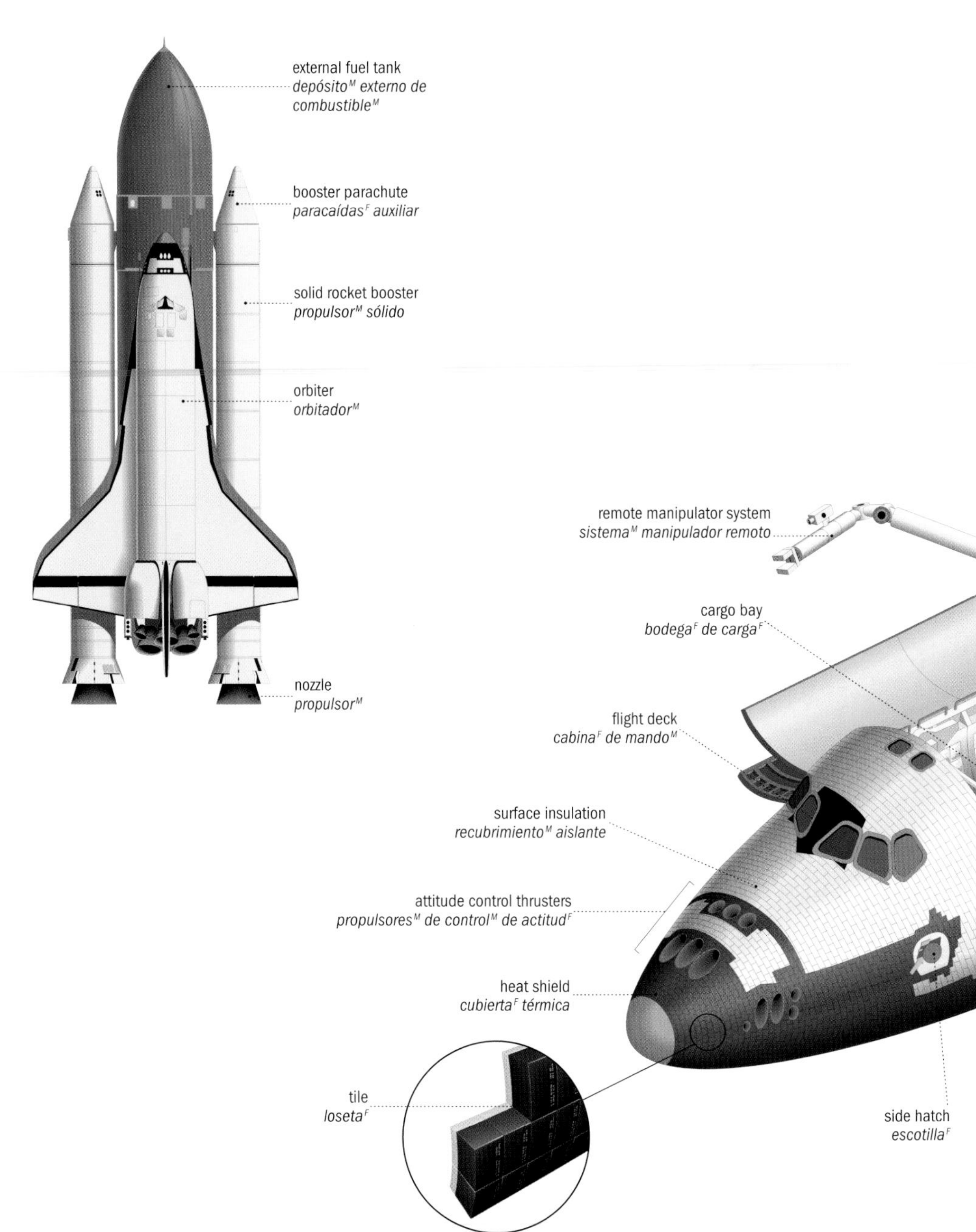

orbiter
orbitador^{M}

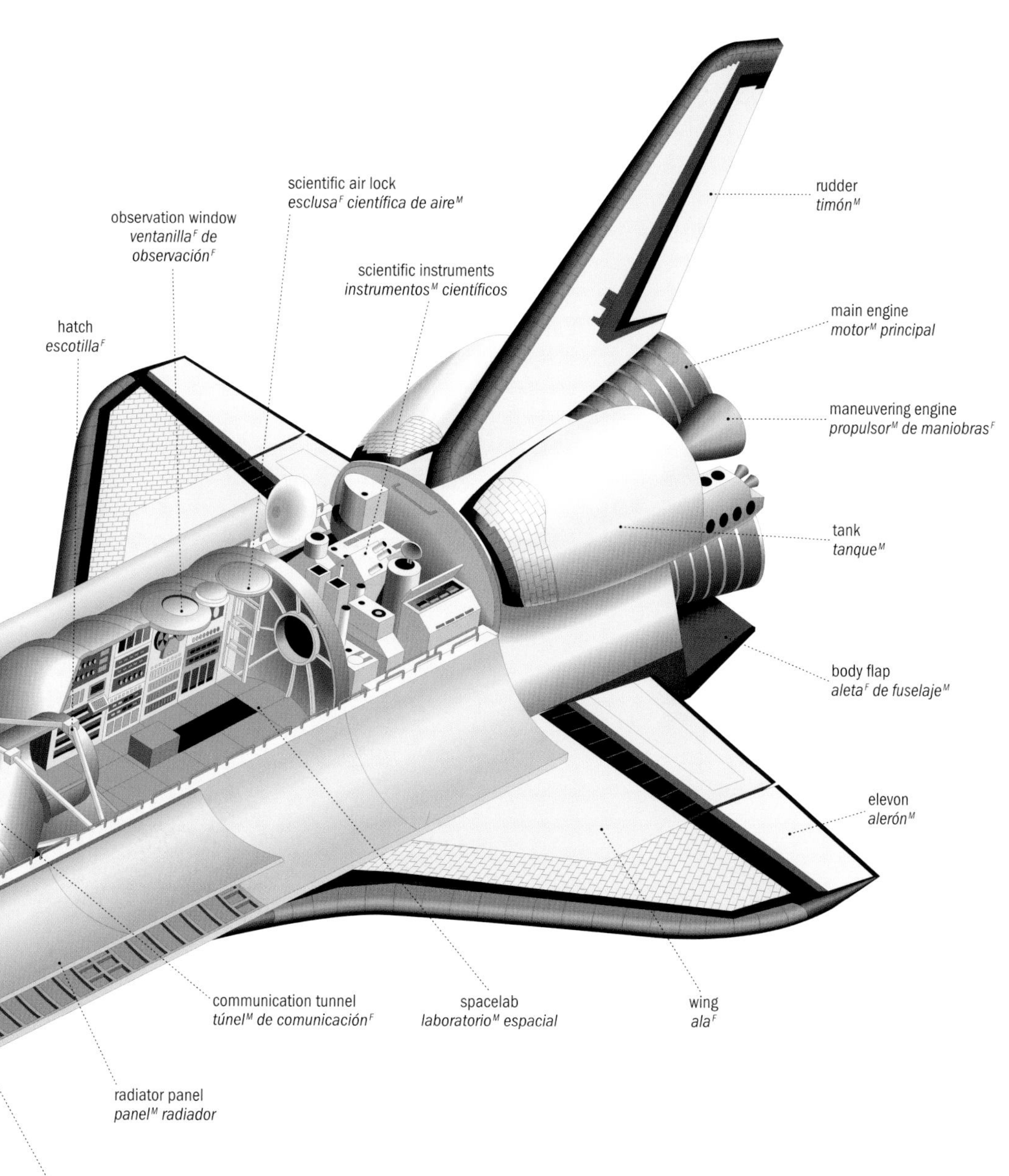
scientific air lock
*esclusa*ᶠ *científica de aire*ᴹ
observation window
*ventanilla*ᶠ *de observación*ᶠ
scientific instruments
*instrumentos*ᴹ *científicos*
hatch
*escotilla*ᶠ
rudder
*timón*ᴹ
main engine
*motor*ᴹ *principal*
maneuvering engine
*propulsor*ᴹ *de maniobras*ᶠ
tank
*tanque*ᴹ
body flap
*aleta*ᶠ *de fuselaje*ᴹ
elevon
*alerón*ᴹ
communication tunnel
*túnel*ᴹ *de comunicación*ᶠ
spacelab
*laboratorio*ᴹ *espacial*
wing
*ala*ᶠ
radiator panel
*panel*ᴹ *radiador*
cargo bay door
*puerta*ᶠ *de la bodega*ᶠ *de carga*ᶠ

configuration of the continents

configuración[F] de los continentes[M]

planisphere
planisferio[M]

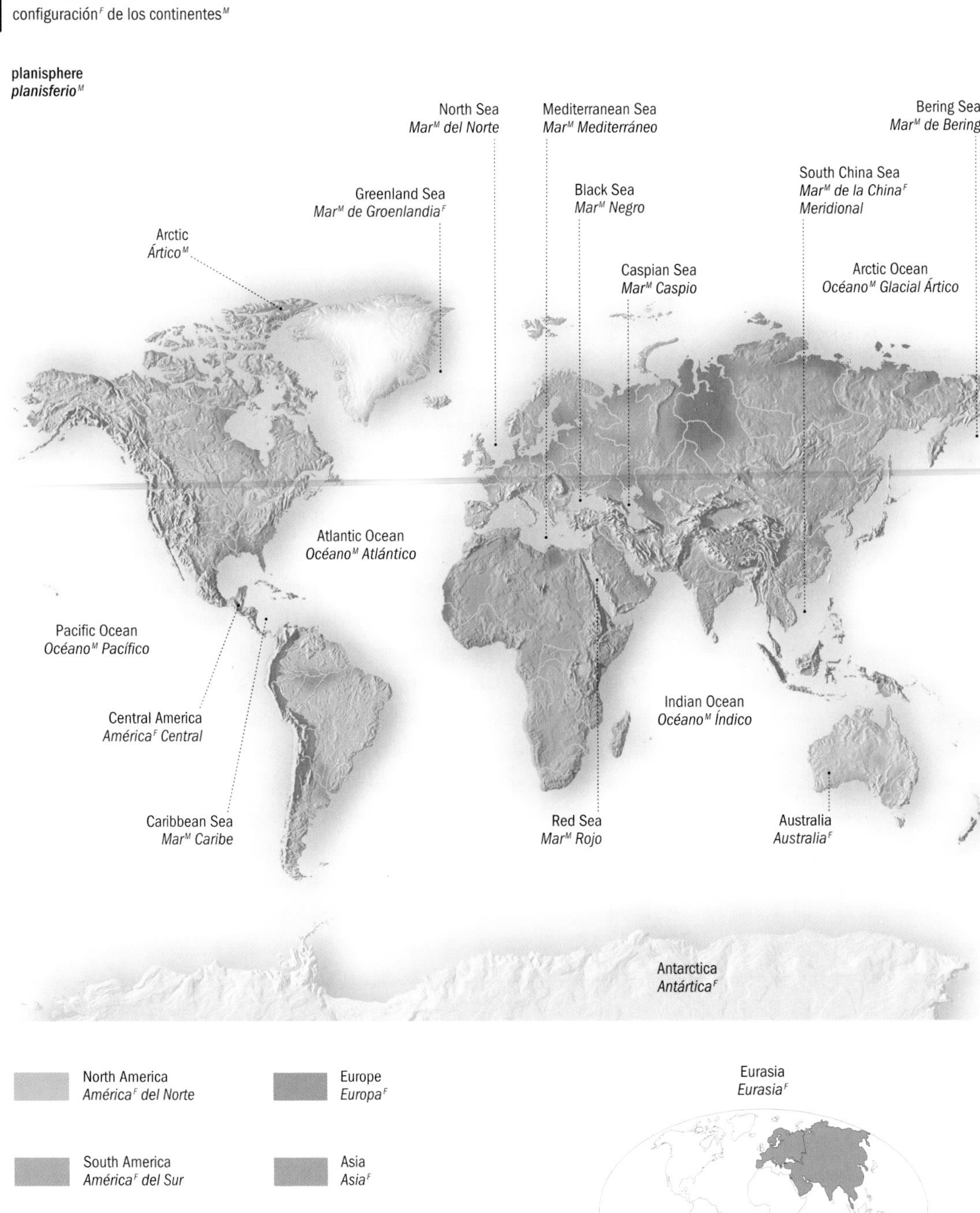

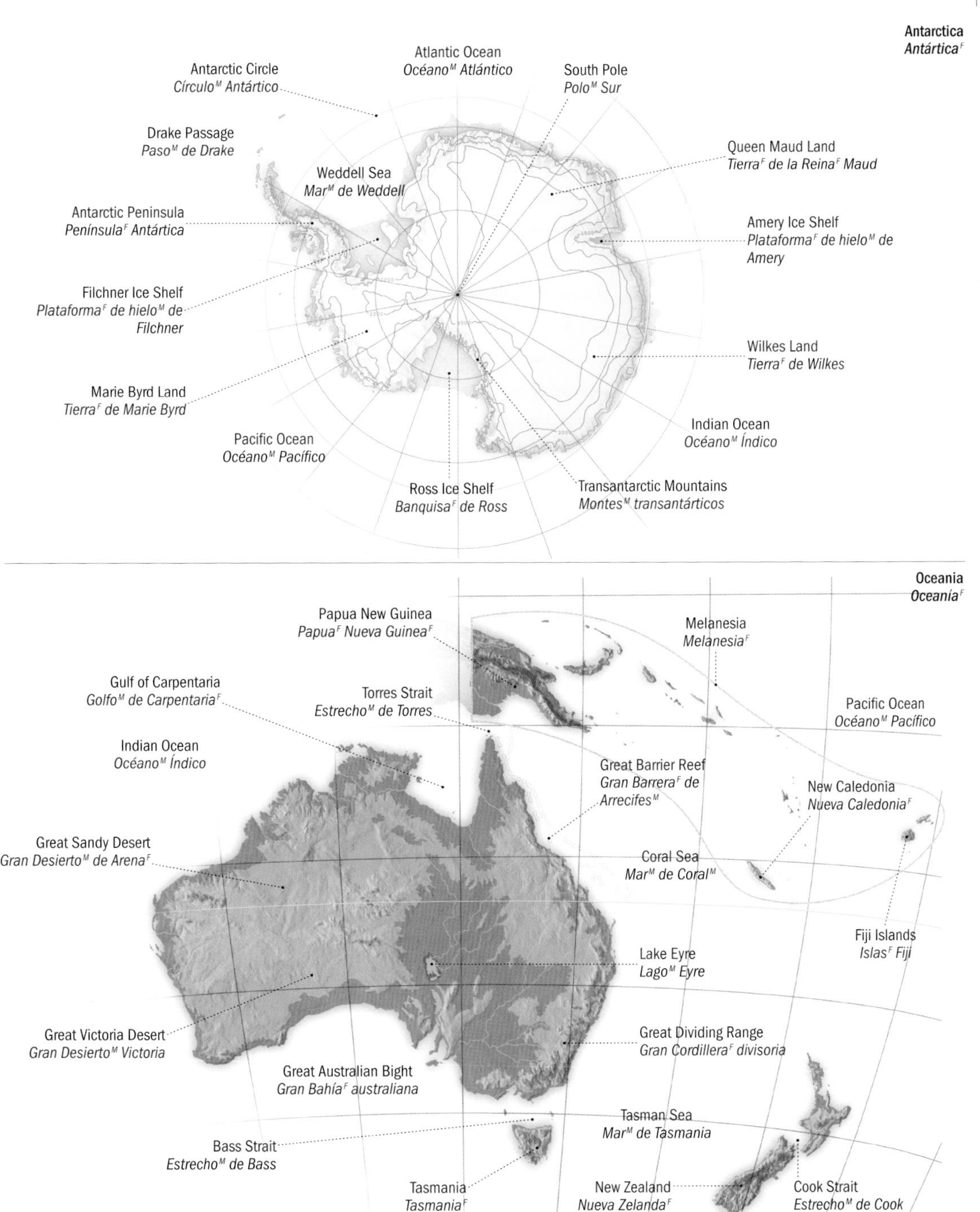
Antarctica
Antártica^F
Atlantic Ocean
Océano^M Atlántico
Antarctic Circle
Círculo^M Antártico
South Pole
Polo^M Sur
Drake Passage
Paso^M de Drake
Weddell Sea
Mar^M de Weddell
Queen Maud Land
Tierra^F de la Reina^F Maud
Antarctic Peninsula
Península^F Antártica
Amery Ice Shelf
Plataforma^F de hielo^M de Amery
Filchner Ice Shelf
Plataforma^F de hielo^M de Filchner
Wilkes Land
Tierra^F de Wilkes
Marie Byrd Land
Tierra^F de Marie Byrd
Indian Ocean
Océano^M Índico
Pacific Ocean
Océano^M Pacífico
Ross Ice Shelf
Banquisa^F de Ross
Transantarctic Mountains
Montes^M transantárticos
Oceania
Oceanía^F
Papua New Guinea
Papua^F Nueva Guinea^F
Melanesia
Melanesia^F
Gulf of Carpentaria
Golfo^M de Carpentaria^F
Torres Strait
Estrecho^M de Torres
Pacific Ocean
Océano^M Pacífico
Indian Ocean
Océano^M Índico
Great Barrier Reef
Gran Barrera^F de Arrecifes^M
New Caledonia
Nueva Caledonia^F
Great Sandy Desert
Gran Desierto^M de Arena^F
Coral Sea
Mar^M de Coral^M
Fiji Islands
Islas^F Fiji
Lake Eyre
Lago^M Eyre
Great Victoria Desert
Gran Desierto^M Victoria
Great Dividing Range
Gran Cordillera^F divisoria
Great Australian Bight
Gran Bahía^F australiana
Tasman Sea
Mar^M de Tasmania
Bass Strait
Estrecho^M de Bass
Tasmania
Tasmania^F
New Zealand
Nueva Zelanda^F
Cook Strait
Estrecho^M de Cook

North America
América*[F] *del Norte

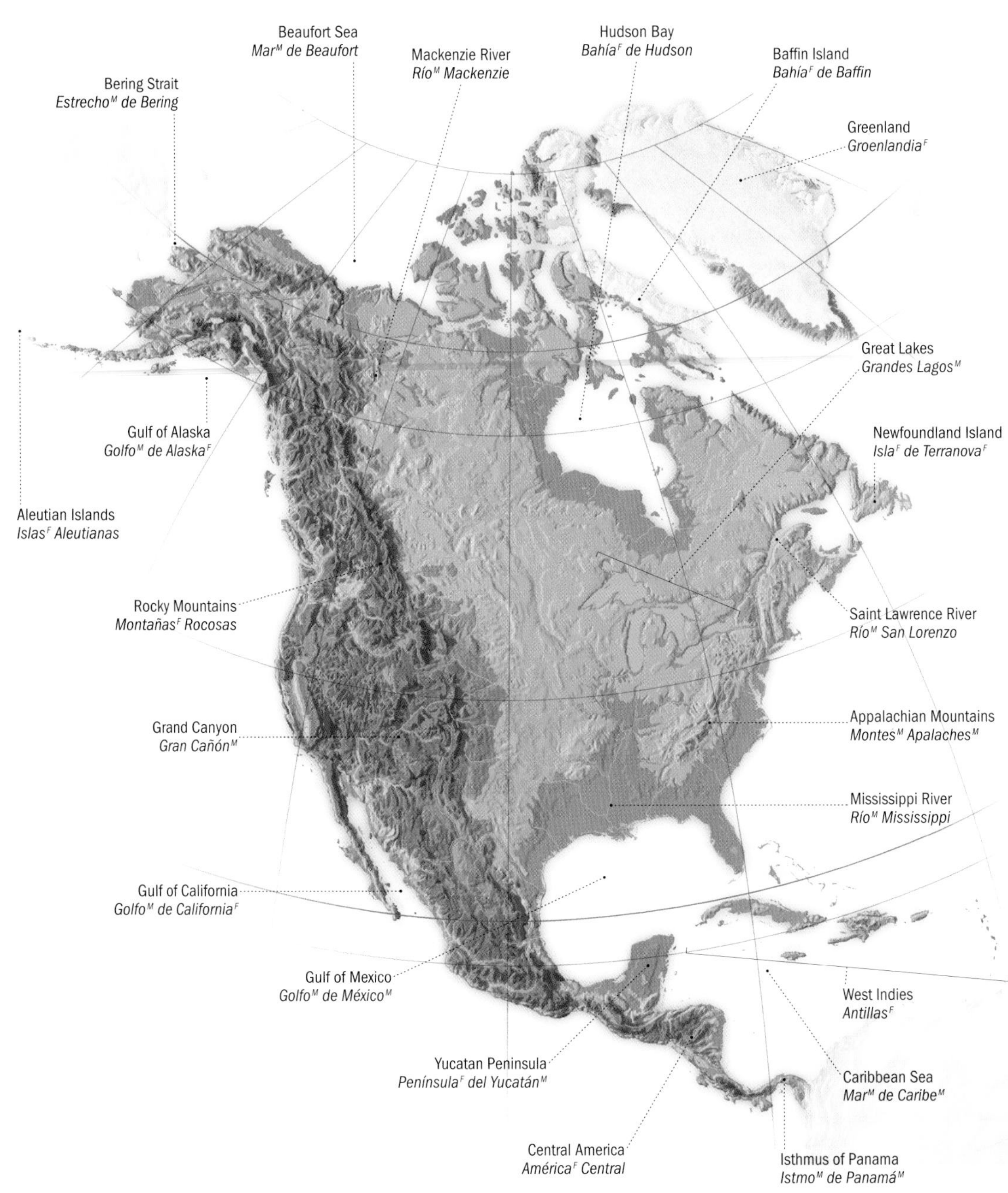

Beaufort Sea
Mar[M] de Beaufort
Mackenzie River
Río[M] Mackenzie
Hudson Bay
Bahía[F] de Hudson
Baffin Island
Bahía[F] de Baffin
Bering Strait
Estrecho[M] de Bering
Greenland
Groenlandia[F]
Great Lakes
Grandes Lagos[M]
Gulf of Alaska
Golfo[M] de Alaska[F]
Newfoundland Island
Isla[F] de Terranova[F]
Aleutian Islands
Islas[F] Aleutianas
Rocky Mountains
Montañas[F] Rocosas
Saint Lawrence River
Río[M] San Lorenzo
Grand Canyon
Gran Cañón[M]
Appalachian Mountains
Montes[M] Apalaches[M]
Mississippi River
Río[M] Mississippi
Gulf of California
Golfo[M] de California[F]
Gulf of Mexico
Golfo[M] de México[M]
West Indies
Antillas[F]
Yucatan Peninsula
Península[F] del Yucatán[M]
Caribbean Sea
Mar[M] de Caribe[M]
Central America
América[F] Central
Isthmus of Panama
Istmo[M] de Panamá[M]

South America
América*[F] *del Sur

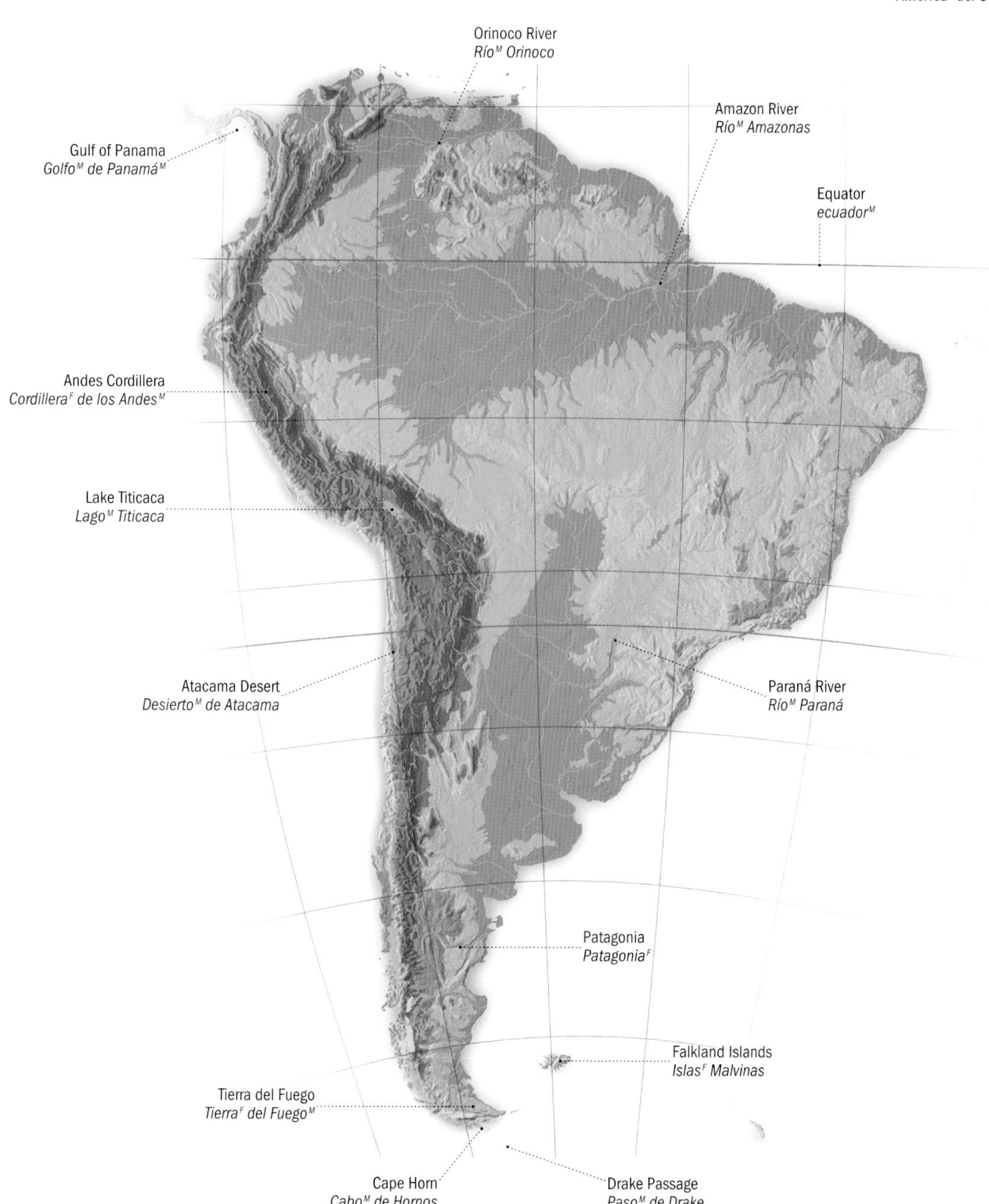
Orinoco River
Río[M] Orinoco
Amazon River
Río[M] Amazonas
Gulf of Panama
Golfo[M] de Panamá[M]
Equator
ecuador[M]
Andes Cordillera
Cordillera[F] de los Andes[M]
Lake Titicaca
Lago[M] Titicaca
Atacama Desert
Desierto[M] de Atacama
Paraná River
Río[M] Paraná
Patagonia
Patagonia[F]
Falkland Islands
Islas[F] Malvinas
Tierra del Fuego
Tierra[F] del Fuego[M]
Cape Horn
Cabo[M] de Hornos
Drake Passage
Paso[M] de Drake

configuration of the continents

Europe
EuropaF

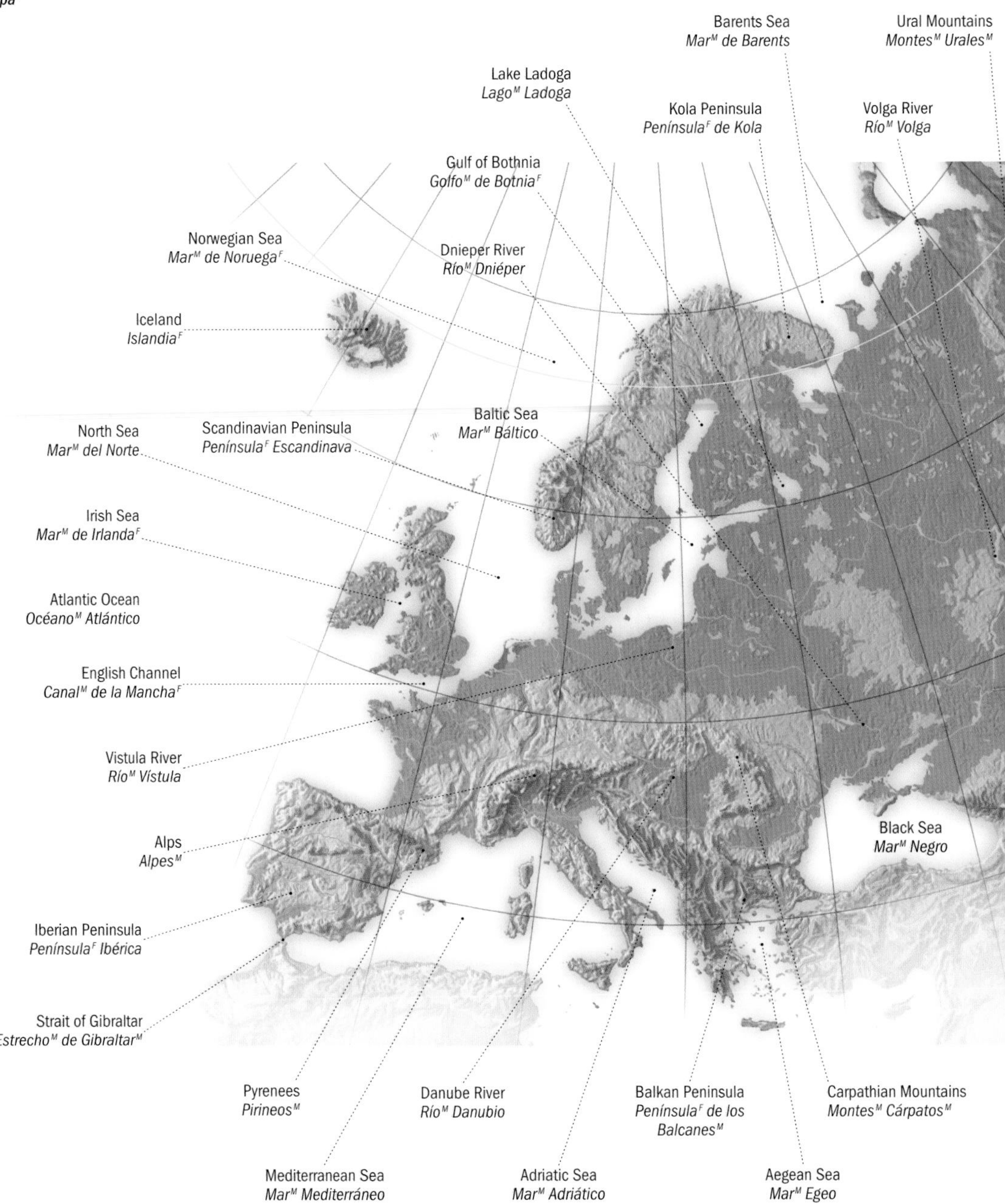
Barents Sea
MarM de Barents
Ural Mountains
MontesM UralesM
Lake Ladoga
LagoM Ladoga
Kola Peninsula
PenínsulaF de Kola
Volga River
RíoM Volga
Gulf of Bothnia
GolfoM de BotniaF
Norwegian Sea
MarM de NoruegaF
Dnieper River
RíoM Dniéper
Iceland
IslandiaF
North Sea
MarM del Norte
Scandinavian Peninsula
PenínsulaF Escandinava
Baltic Sea
MarM Báltico
Irish Sea
MarM de IrlandaF
Atlantic Ocean
OcéanoM Atlántico
English Channel
CanalM de la ManchaF
Vistula River
RíoM Vístula
Alps
AlpesM
Black Sea
MarM Negro
Iberian Peninsula
PenínsulaF Ibérica
Strait of Gibraltar
EstrechoM de GibraltarM
Pyrenees
PirineosM
Danube River
RíoM Danubio
Balkan Peninsula
PenínsulaF de los BalcanesM
Carpathian Mountains
MontesM CárpatosM
Mediterranean Sea
MarM Mediterráneo
Adriatic Sea
MarM Adriático
Aegean Sea
MarM Egeo

Asia
Asia^F

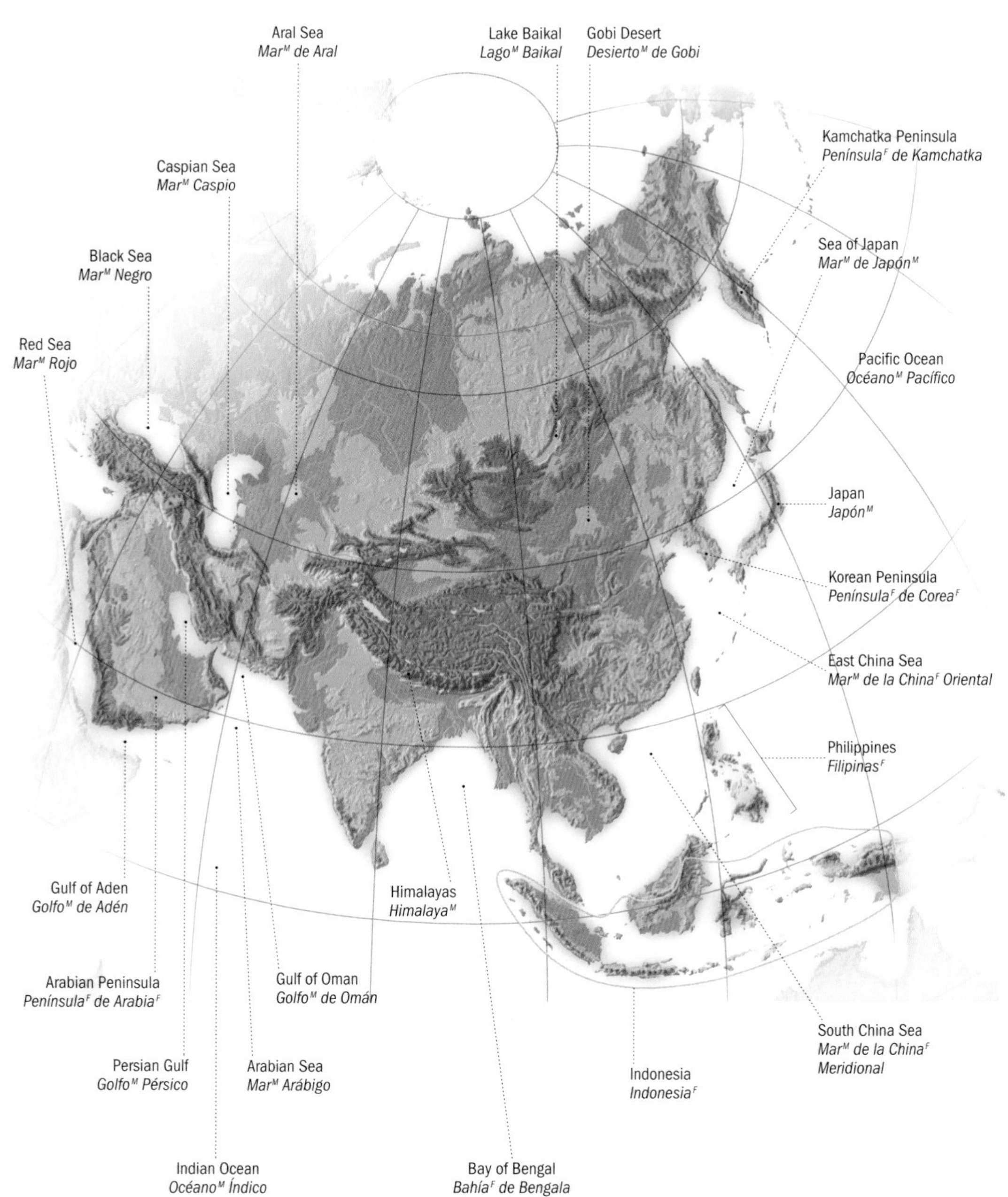
Aral Sea
Mar^M de Aral
Lake Baikal
Lago^M Baikal
Gobi Desert
Desierto^M de Gobi
Kamchatka Peninsula
Península^F de Kamchatka
Caspian Sea
Mar^M Caspio
Black Sea
Mar^M Negro
Sea of Japan
Mar^M de Japón^M
Red Sea
Mar^M Rojo
Pacific Ocean
Océano^M Pacífico
Japan
Japón^M
Korean Peninsula
Península^F de Corea^F
East China Sea
Mar^M de la China^F Oriental
Philippines
Filipinas^F
Gulf of Aden
Golfo^M de Adén
Himalayas
Himalaya^M
Arabian Peninsula
Península^F de Arabia^F
Gulf of Oman
Golfo^M de Omán
South China Sea
Mar^M de la China^F Meridional
Persian Gulf
Golfo^M Pérsico
Arabian Sea
Mar^M Arábigo
Indonesia
Indonesia^F
Indian Ocean
Océano^M Índico
Bay of Bengal
Bahía^F de Bengala

configuration of the continents

EARTH

Africa
África[F]

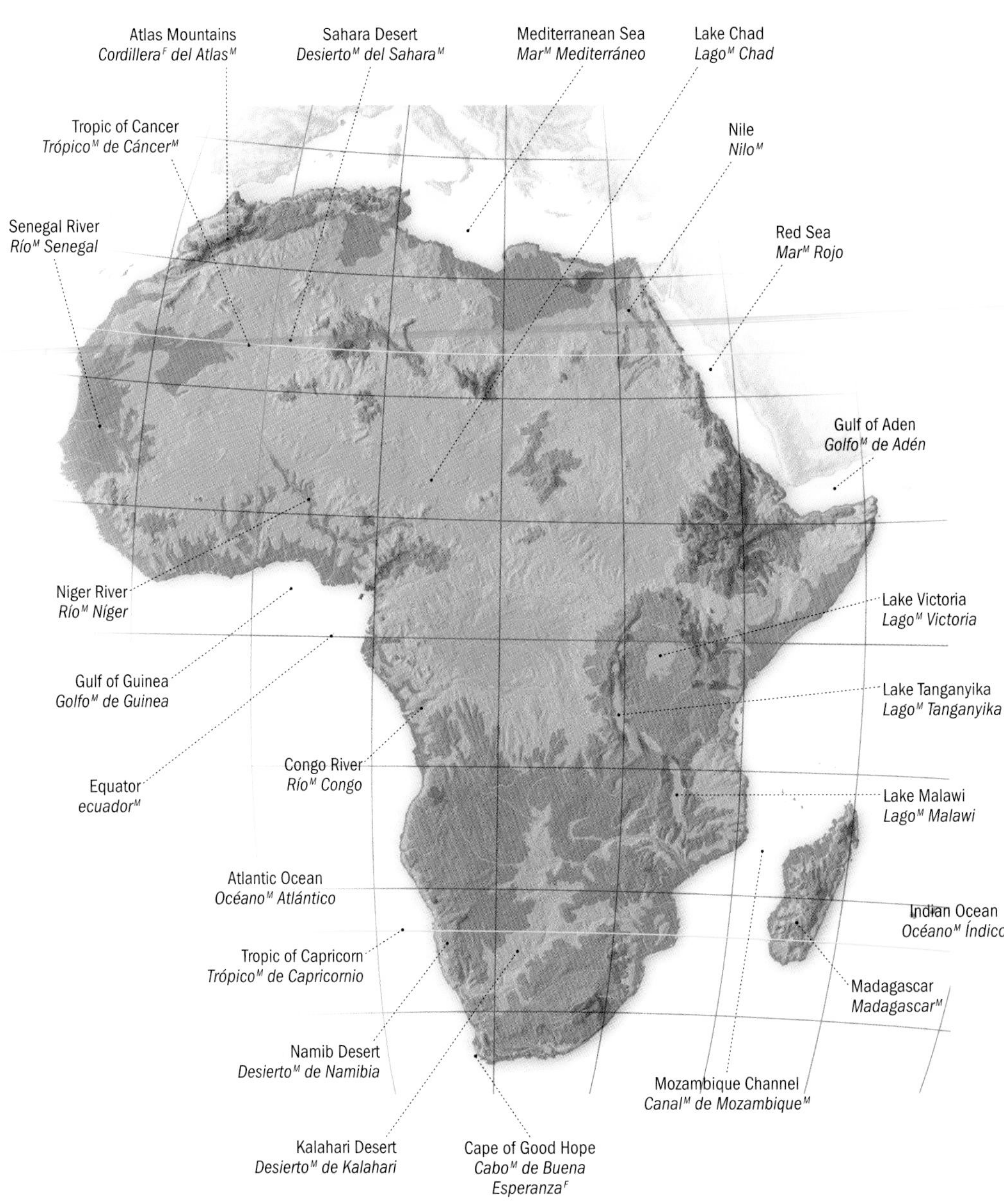
Atlas Mountains
Cordillera[F] del Atlas[M]
Sahara Desert
Desierto[M] del Sahara[M]
Mediterranean Sea
Mar[M] Mediterráneo
Lake Chad
Lago[M] Chad
Tropic of Cancer
Trópico[M] de Cáncer[M]
Nile
Nilo[M]
Senegal River
Río[M] Senegal
Red Sea
Mar[M] Rojo
Gulf of Aden
Golfo[M] de Adén
Niger River
Río[M] Níger
Lake Victoria
Lago[M] Victoria
Gulf of Guinea
Golfo[M] de Guinea
Lake Tanganyika
Lago[M] Tanganyika
Congo River
Río[M] Congo
Equator
ecuador[M]
Lake Malawi
Lago[M] Malawi
Atlantic Ocean
Océano[M] Atlántico
Indian Ocean
Océano[M] Índico
Tropic of Capricorn
Trópico[M] de Capricornio
Madagascar
Madagascar[M]
Namib Desert
Desierto[M] de Namibia
Mozambique Channel
Canal[M] de Mozambique[M]
Kalahari Desert
Desierto[M] de Kalahari
Cape of Good Hope
Cabo[M] de Buena Esperanza[F]

cartography
cartografía^F

Earth coordinate system
sistema^M de coordenadas^F terrestres

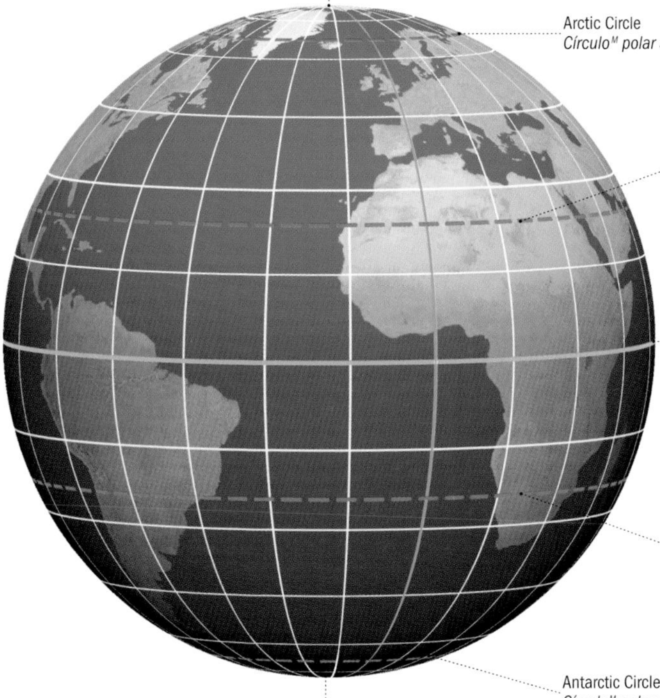

North Pole
polo^M Norte
Arctic Circle
Círculo^M polar ártico
Northern hemisphere
hemisferio^M Norte
Tropic of Cancer
Trópico^M de Cáncer
Equator
ecuador^M
Southern hemisphere
hemisferio^M Sur
Tropic of Capricorn
Trópico^M de Capricornio
Antarctic Circle
Círculo^M polar antártico
South Pole
polo^M Sur

hemispheres
hemisferios^M

Northern hemisphere
hemisferio^M Norte
Southern hemisphere
hemisferio^M Sur

Western hemisphere
hemisferio^M occidental
Eastern hemisphere
hemisferio^M oriental

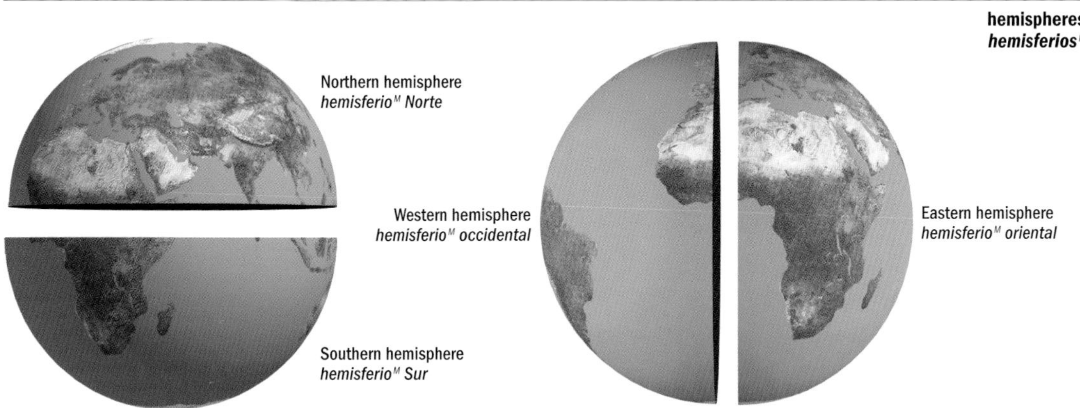

grid system
sistema[M] de retícula[F]

lines of latitude
líneas[F] de latitud[F]

lines of longitude
líneas[F] de longitud[F]

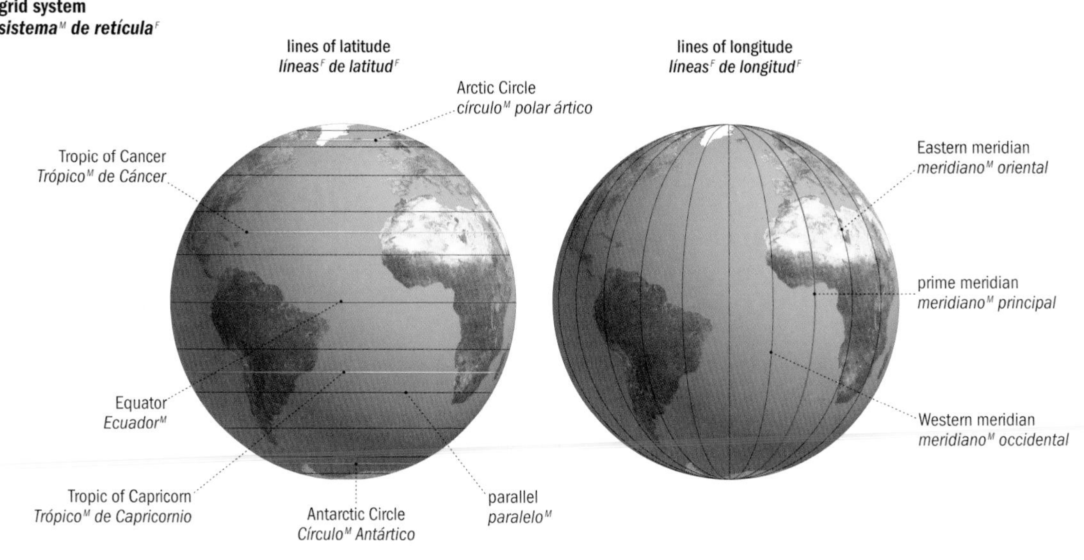

map projections
proyecciones[F] cartográficas

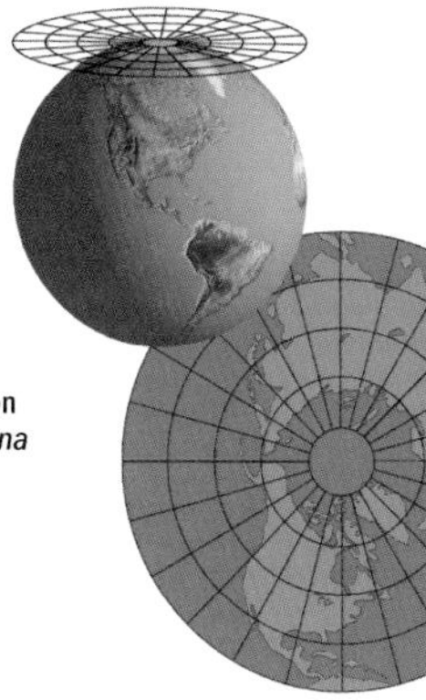

plane projection
proyección[F] plana

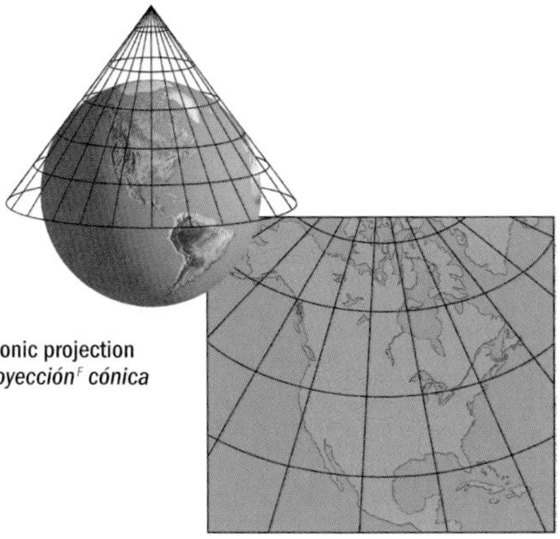

conic projection
proyección[F] cónica

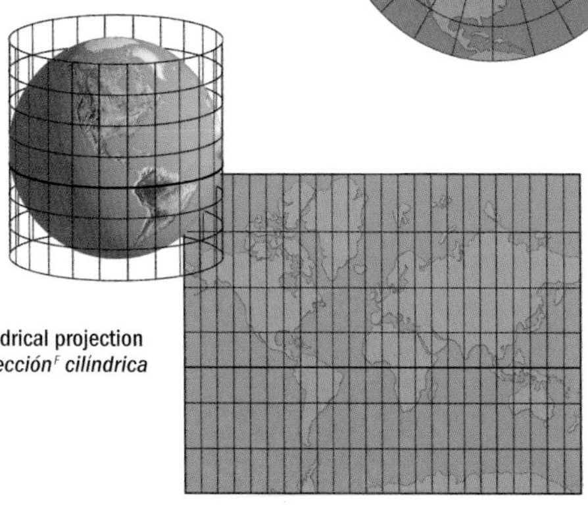

cylindrical projection
proyección[F] cilíndrica

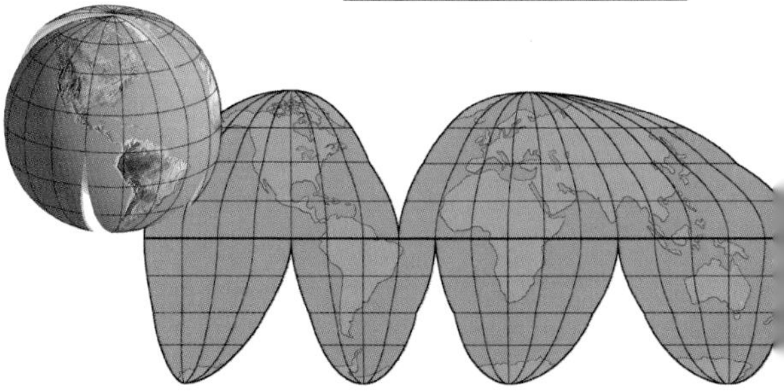

interrupted projection
proyección[F] interrumpida

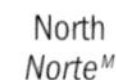

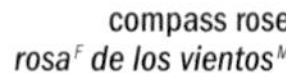

compass rose
rosa[F] de los vientos[M]

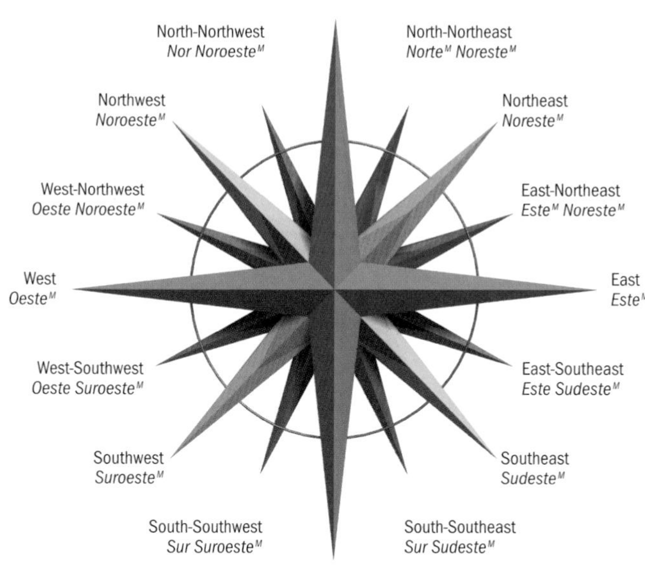
North
Norte[M]
North-Northwest
Nor Noroeste[M]
North-Northeast
Norte[M] Noreste[M]
Northwest
Noroeste[M]
Northeast
Noreste[M]
West-Northwest
Oeste Noroeste[M]
East-Northeast
Este[M] Noreste[M]
West
Oeste[M]
East
Este[M]
West-Southwest
Oeste Suroeste[M]
East-Southeast
Este Sudeste[M]
Southwest
Suroeste[M]
Southeast
Sudeste[M]
South-Southwest
Sur Suroeste[M]
South-Southeast
Sur Sudeste[M]
South
Sur[M]

political map
mapa[M] político

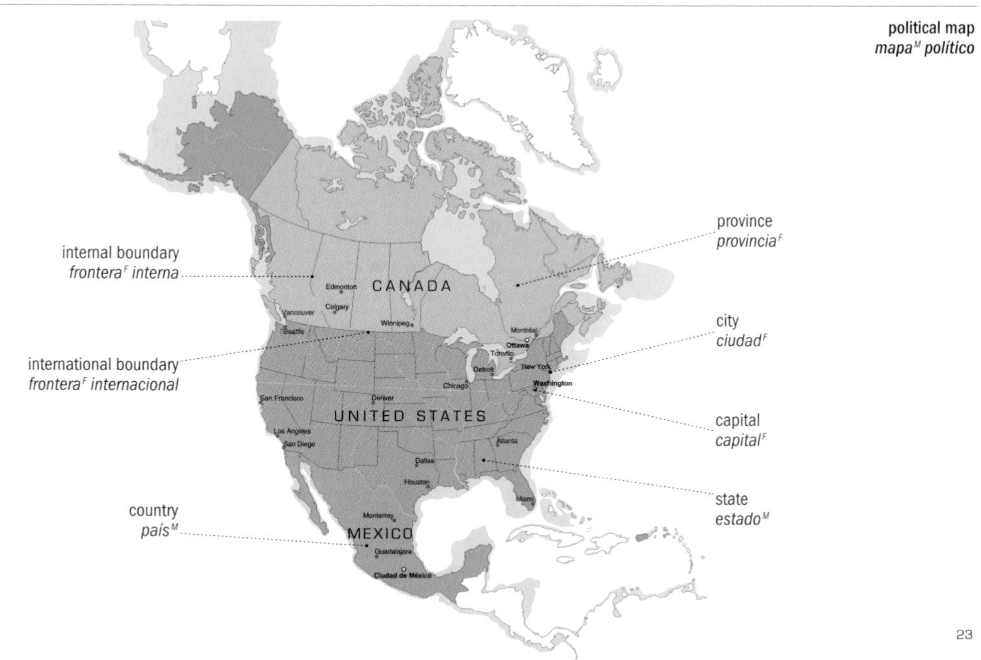
internal boundary
frontera[F] interna
province
provincia[F]
international boundary
frontera[F] internacional
city
ciudad[F]
capital
capital[F]
state
estado[M]
country
país[M]
CANADA
Edmonton
Calgary
Vancouver
Winnipeg
Seattle
Montréal
Ottawa
Toronto
New York
Detroit
Washington
Chicago
San Francisco
Denver
UNITED STATES
Los Angeles
San Diego
Atlanta
Dallas
Houston
Miami
Monterrey
MEXICO
Guadalajara
Ciudad de México

cartography

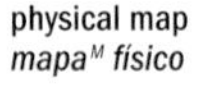

physical map
mapa**[M]* ***físico

sea
mar[M]

bay
bahía[F]

strait
estrecho[M]

mountain range
cordillera[F]

island
isla[F]

ocean
océano[M]

prairie
llanura[F]

mountain mass
macizo[M]

river estuary
estuario[M]

lake
lago[M]

river
río[M]

plateau
meseta[F]

archipelago
archipiélago[M]

gulf
golfo[M]

peninsula
península[F]

cape
cabo[M]

plain
planicie[F]

isthmus
istmo[M]

river
río[M]

urban map
mapa[M] urbano

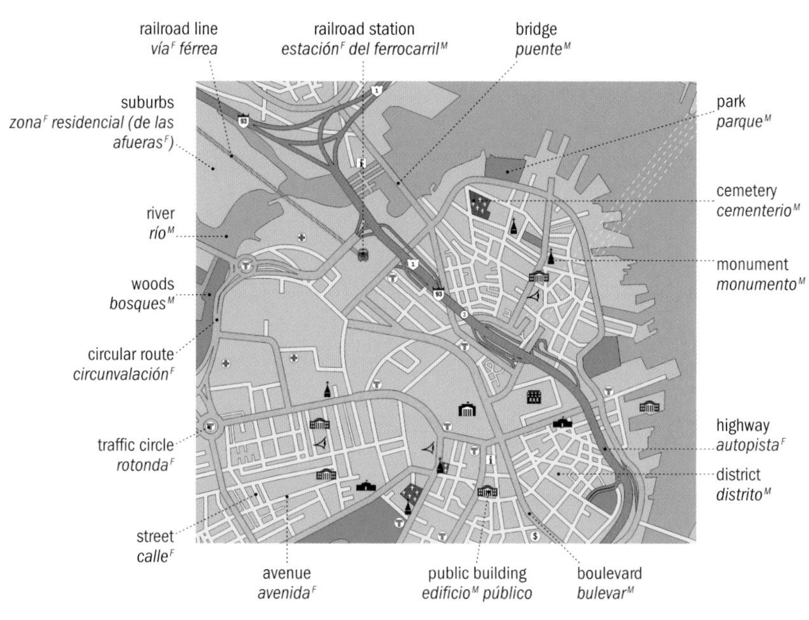
railroad line
vía[F] férrea
railroad station
estación[F] del ferrocarril[M]
bridge
puente[M]
suburbs
zona[F] residencial (de las afueras[F])
park
parque[M]
cemetery
cementerio[M]
river
río[M]
monument
monumento[M]
woods
bosques[M]
circular route
circunvalación[F]
highway
autopista[F]
traffic circle
rotonda[F]
district
distrito[M]
street
calle[F]
avenue
avenida[F]
public building
edificio[M] público
boulevard
bulevar[M]

road map
mapa[M] de carreteras[F]

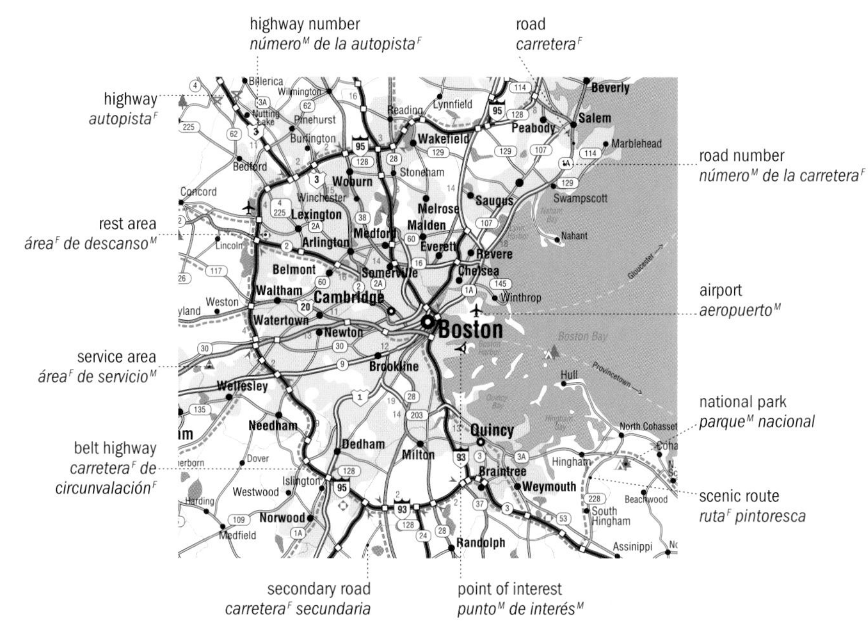
highway number
número[M] de la autopista[F]
road
carretera[F]
highway
autopista[F]
road number
número[M] de la carretera[F]
rest area
área[F] de descanso[M]
airport
aeropuerto[M]
service area
área[F] de servicio[M]
national park
parque[M] nacional
belt highway
carretera[F] de circunvalación[F]
scenic route
ruta[F] pintoresca
secondary road
carretera[F] secundaria
point of interest
punto[M] de interés[M]
Boston
Cambridge
Quincy
Beverly
Salem
Peabody
Wakefield
Woburn
Lexington
Arlington
Medford
Malden
Melrose
Everett
Revere
Chelsea
Somerville
Belmont
Waltham
Watertown
Newton
Brookline
Wellesley
Needham
Dedham
Milton
Braintree
Weymouth
Norwood
Randolph
Boston Bay

section of the Earth's crust

corte^M de la corteza^F terrestre

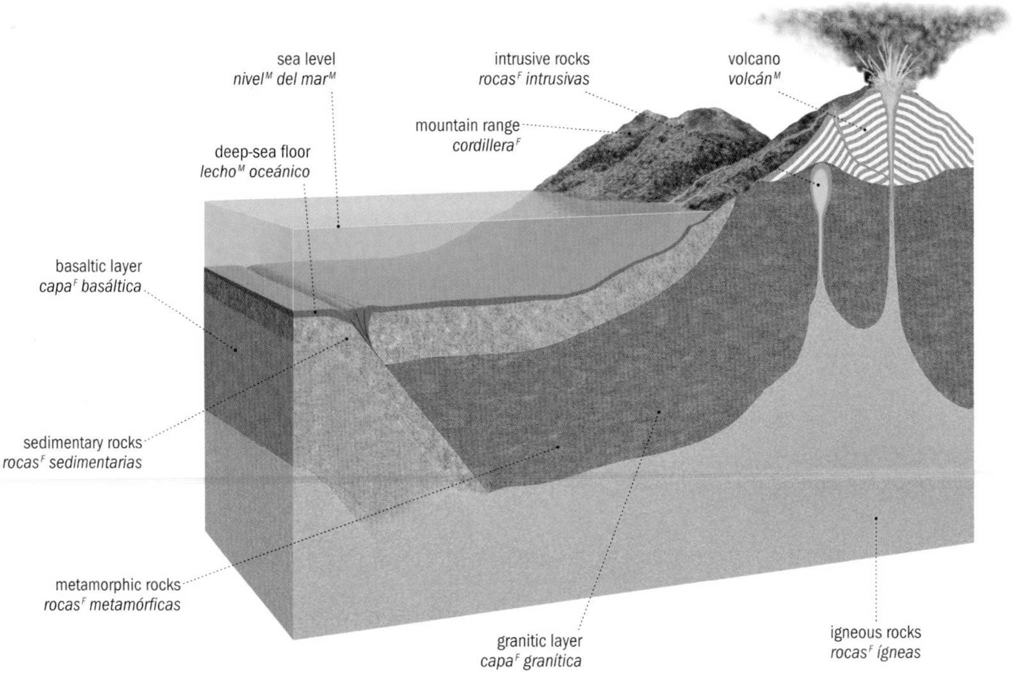

sea level
nivel^M del mar^M
intrusive rocks
rocas^F intrusivas
volcano
volcán^M
mountain range
cordillera^F
deep-sea floor
lecho^M oceánico
basaltic layer
capa^F basáltica
sedimentary rocks
rocas^F sedimentarias
metamorphic rocks
rocas^F metamórficas
granitic layer
capa^F granítica
igneous rocks
rocas^F ígneas

structure of the Earth

estructura^F de la Tierra^F

Earth's crust
corteza^F terrestre
oceanic crust
corteza^F oceánica
continental crust
corteza^F continental
lithosphere
litosfera^F
asthenosphere
astenosfera^F
Mohorovicic discontinuity
discontinuidad^F de Mohorovicic
upper mantle
manto^M externo
lower mantle
manto^M interno
Gutenberg discontinuity
discontinuidad^M de Gutenberg
outer core
núcleo^M externo
inner core
núcleo^M interno

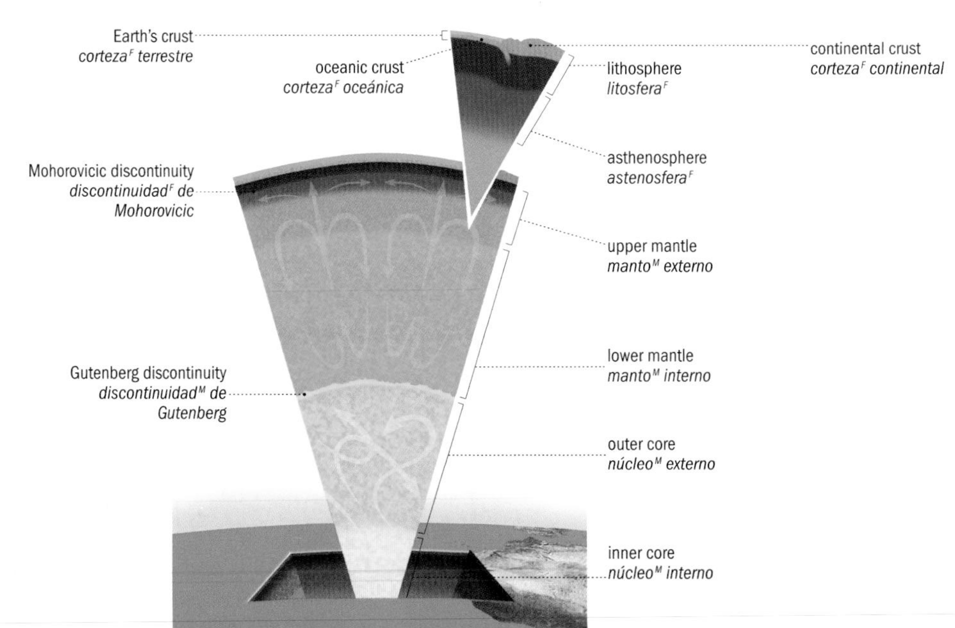

tectonic plates

placas^F tectónicas

North American Plate
placa^F norteamericana
Cocos Plate
placa^F de Cocos
Caribbean Plate
placa^F del Caribe
Pacific Plate
placa^F del Pacífico
Nazca Plate
placa^F de Nazca
Scotia Plate
placa^F de Escocia
South American Plate
placa^F sudamericana
African Plate
placa^F africana
Eurasian Plate
placa^F euroasiática
Philippine Plate
placa^F de Filipinas
Australian-Indian Plate
placa^F indoaustraliana
Antarctic Plate
placa^F antártica

subduction
subducción^M

divergent plate boundaries
placas^F divergentes

convergent plate boundaries
placas^F convergentes

transform plate boundaries
fallas^F transformantes

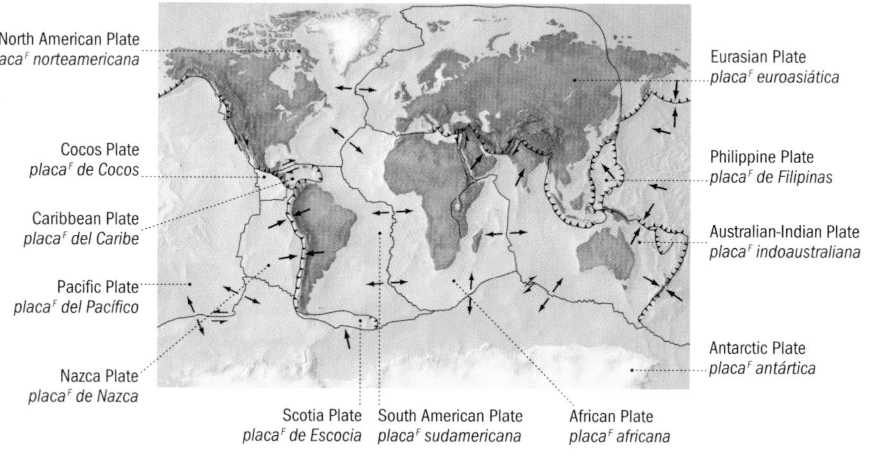

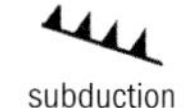

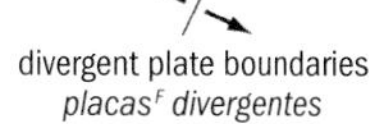

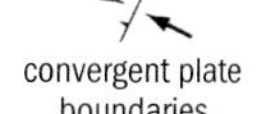

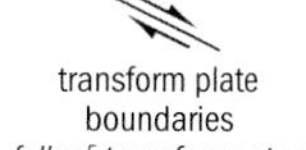

earthquake

terremoto^M

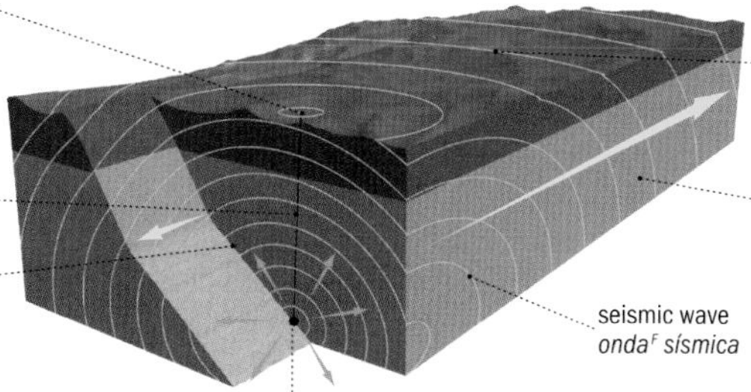

epicenter
epicentro^M
isoseismal line
isosista^F
depth of focus
profundidad^F del hipocentro^M
Earth's crust
corteza^F terrestre
fault
falla^F
seismic wave
onda^F sísmica
focus
hipocentro^M

seismographs
sismógrafos^M

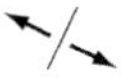

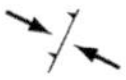

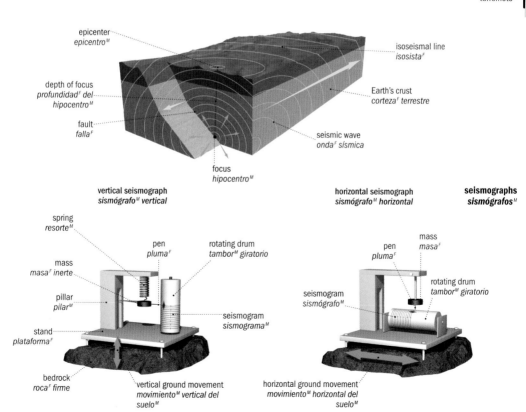

vertical seismograph
sismógrafo^M vertical

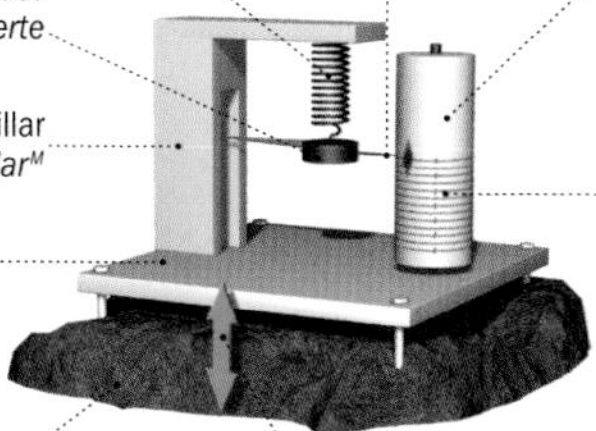

spring
resorte^M
pen
pluma^F
rotating drum
tambor^M giratorio
mass
masa^F inerte
pillar
pilar^M
seismogram
sismograma^M
stand
plataforma^F
bedrock
roca^F firme
vertical ground movement
movimiento^M vertical del suelo^M

horizontal seismograph
sismógrafo^M horizontal

mass
masa^F
pen
pluma^F
rotating drum
tambor^M giratorio
seismogram
sismógrafo^M
horizontal ground movement
movimiento^M horizontal del suelo^M

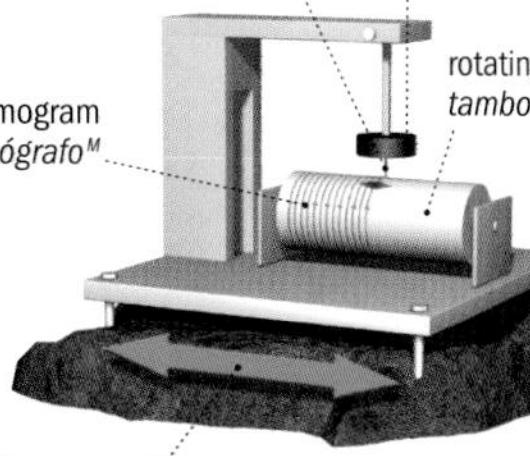

volcano

volcán[M]

volcano during eruption
volcán[M] en erupción[F]

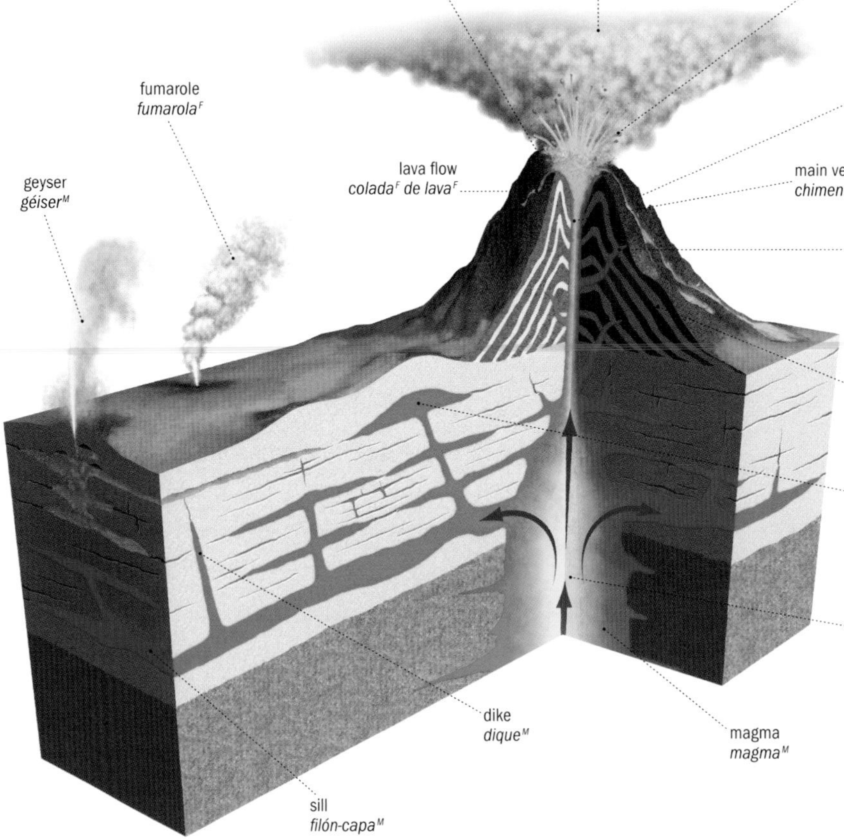

crater
cráter[M]
cloud of volcanic ash
nube[F] de cenizas[F]
volcanic bomb
bomba[F] volcánica
fumarole
fumarola[F]
lava layer
estrato[M] de lava[F]
geyser
géiser[M]
lava flow
colada[F] de lava[F]
main vent
chimenea[F] principal
side vent
chimenea[F] lateral
ash layer
estrato[M] de cenizas[F]
laccolith
lacolito[M]
magma chamber
cámara[F] de magma[M]
dike
dique[M]
magma
magma[M]
sill
filón-capa[M]

examples of volcanoes
ejemplos[M] de volcanes[M]

explosive volcano
volcán[M] explosivo

effusive volcano
volcán[M] efusivo

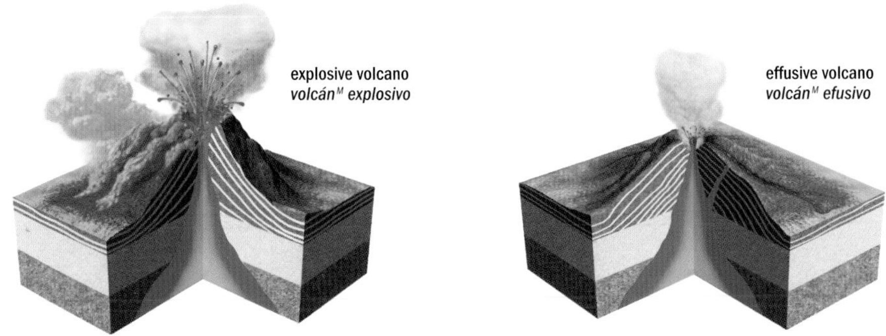

mountain

montaña^F

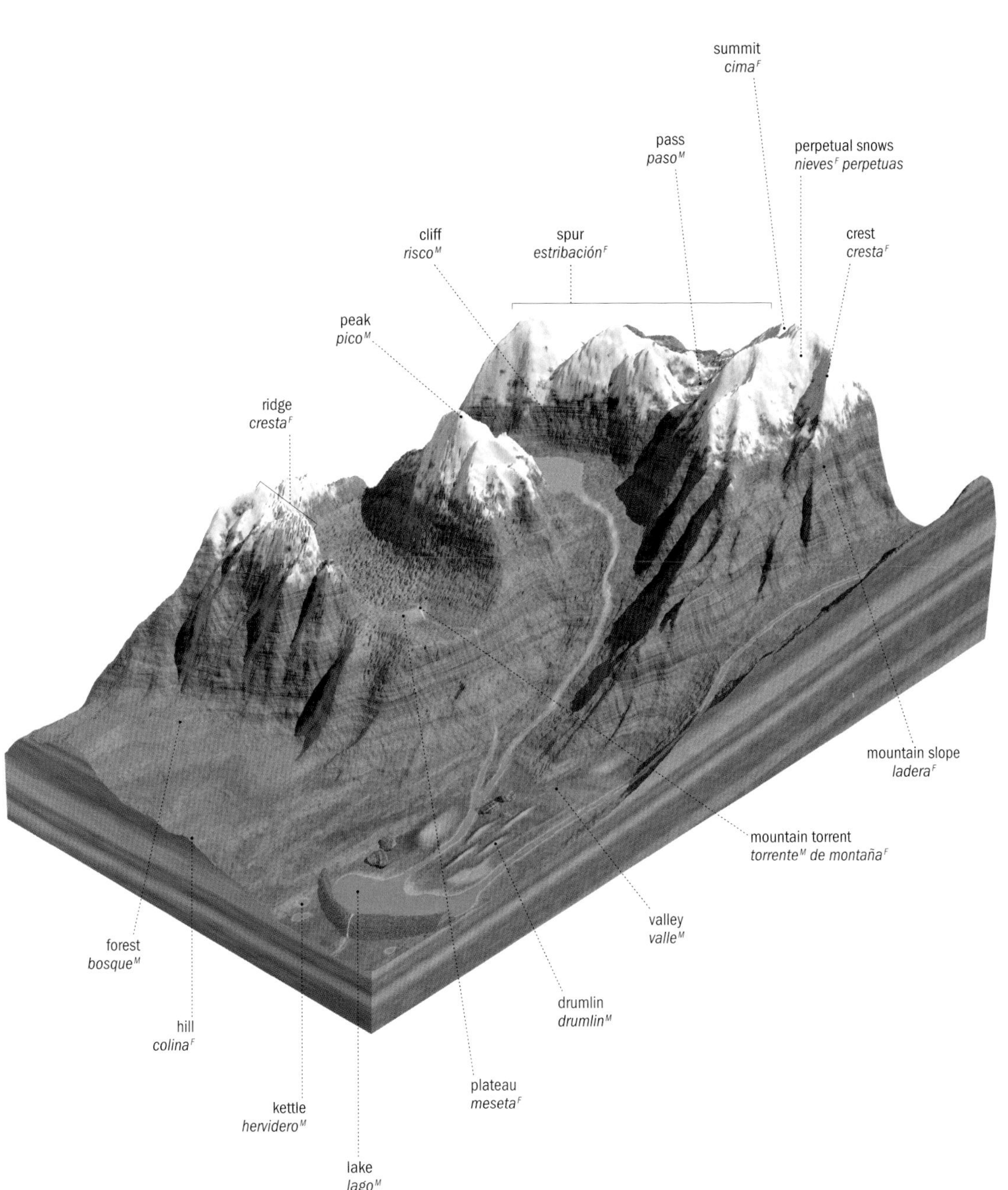
summit
cima^F
pass
paso^M
perpetual snows
nieves^F perpetuas
cliff
risco^M
spur
estribación^F
crest
cresta^F
peak
pico^M
ridge
cresta^F
mountain slope
ladera^F
mountain torrent
torrente^M de montaña^F
valley
valle^M
forest
bosque^M
drumlin
drumlin^M
hill
colina^F
plateau
meseta^F
kettle
hervidero^M
lake
lago^M

glacier

glaciar^M

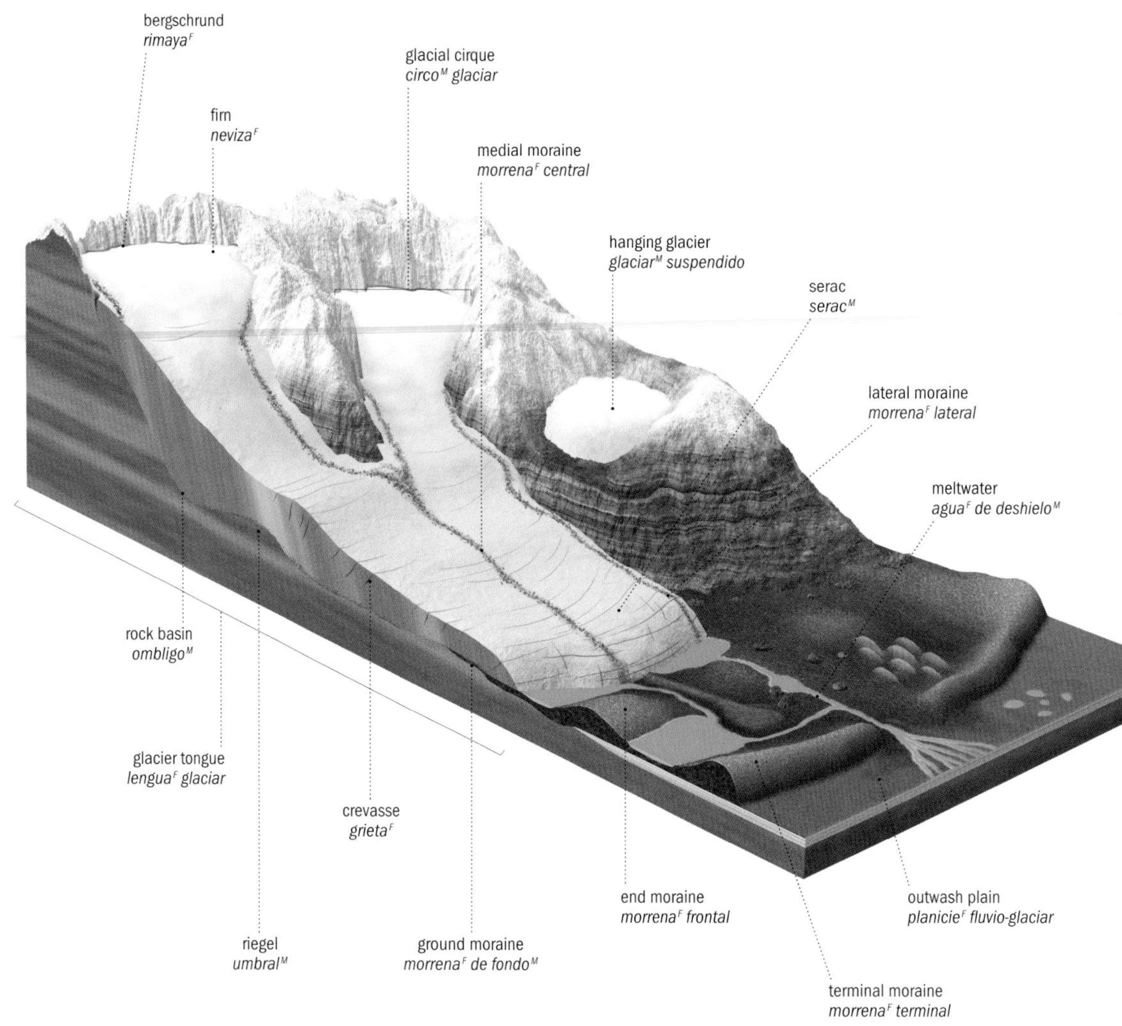
bergschrund
rimaya^F
firn
neviza^F
glacial cirque
circo^M glaciar
medial moraine
morrena^F central
hanging glacier
glaciar^M suspendido
serac
serac^M
lateral moraine
morrena^F lateral
meltwater
agua^F de deshielo^M
rock basin
ombligo^M
glacier tongue
lengua^F glaciar
crevasse
grieta^F
riegel
umbral^M
ground moraine
morrena^F de fondo^M
end moraine
morrena^F frontal
outwash plain
planicie^F fluvio-glaciar
terminal moraine
morrena^F terminal

cave

gruta[F]

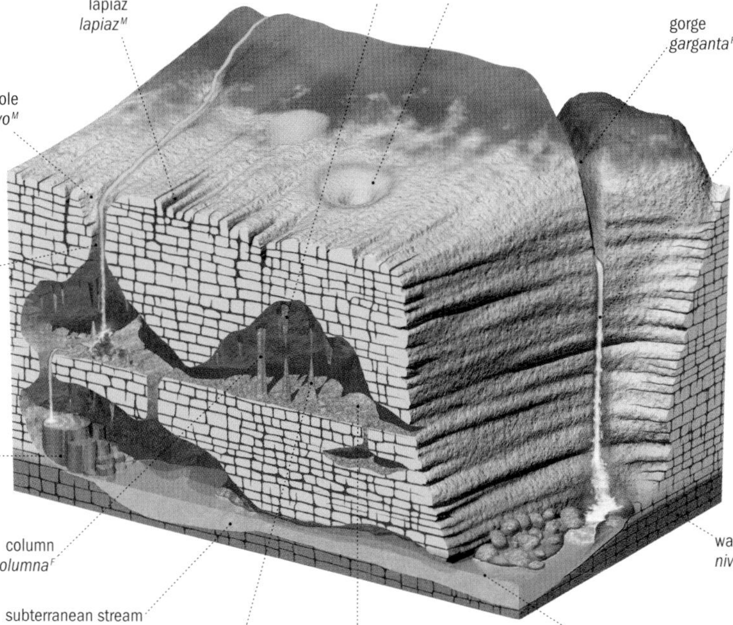

stalactite
estalactita[F]

sinkhole
torca[F]

lapiaz
lapiaz[M]

gorge
garganta[F]

pothole
hoyo[M]

waterfall
cascada[F]

swallow hole
tragadero[M]

gour
derrubios[M]

column
columna[F]

water table
nivel[M] freático

subterranean stream
corriente[F] subterránea

stalagmite
estalagmita[F]

dry gallery
galería[F] seca

resurgence
resurgencia[F]

landslides

desprendimientos[M] de tierras[F]

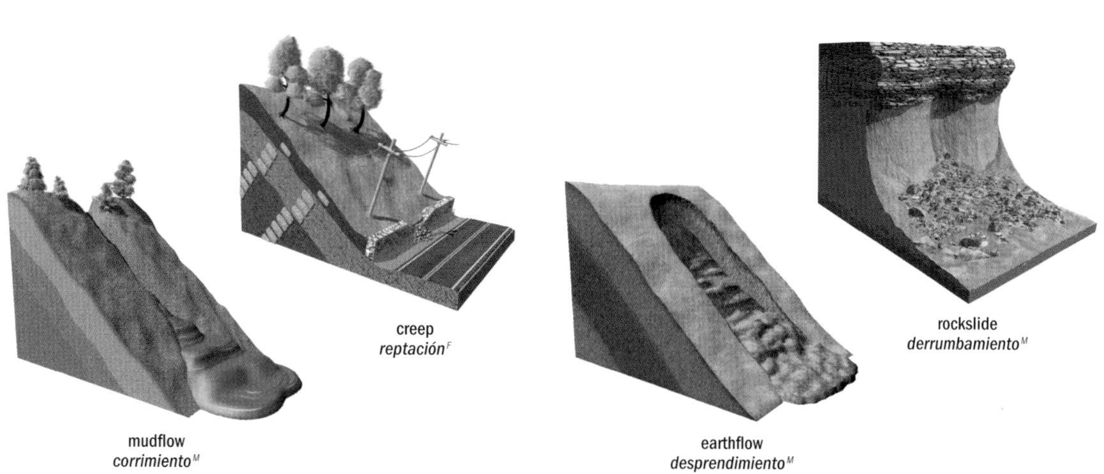

creep
reptación[F]

rockslide
derrumbamiento[M]

mudflow
corrimiento[M]

earthflow
desprendimiento[M]

watercourse

corriente[F] de agua[F]

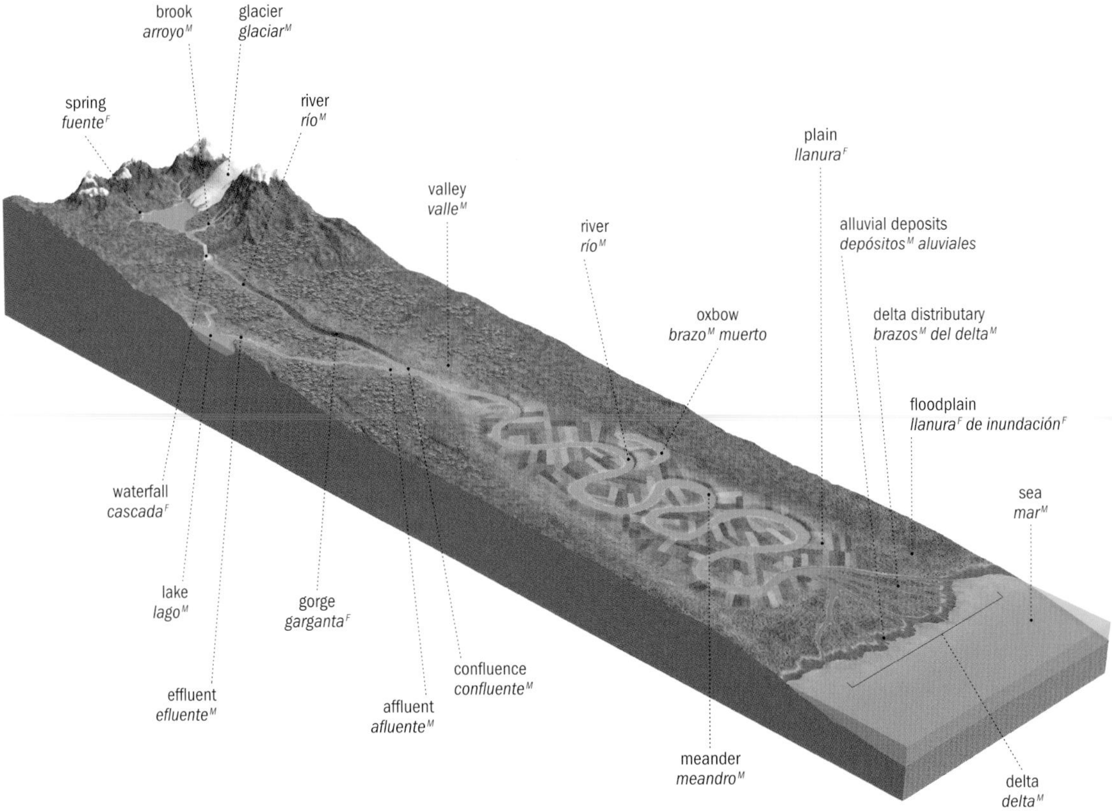

brook
arroyo[M]

glacier
glaciar[M]

spring
fuente[F]

river
río[M]

valley
valle[M]

plain
llanura[F]

river
río[M]

alluvial deposits
depósitos[M] aluviales

oxbow
brazo[M] muerto

delta distributary
brazos[M] del delta[M]

floodplain
llanura[F] de inundación[F]

waterfall
cascada[F]

sea
mar[M]

lake
lago[M]

gorge
garganta[F]

confluence
confluente[M]

effluent
efluente[M]

affluent
afluente[M]

meander
meandro[M]

delta
delta[M]

lakes

lagos[M]

glacial lake
lago[M] glaciar

volcanic lake
lago[M] volcánico

tectonic lake
lago[M] tectónico

oxbow lake
lago[M] de brazo[M] muerto

oasis
oasis[M]

artificial lake
embalse[M]

wave
ola[F]

wave height
altura[F] de la ola[F]
crest
cresta[F]
wave length
longitud[F] de la ola[F]
breaker
rompiente[M]
shore
costa[F]
wave base
base[F] de la ola[F]
still water level
nivel[M] de equilibrio[M] del agua[F]
trough
seno[M]
sand bar
banco[M] de arena[F]
foam
espuma[F]

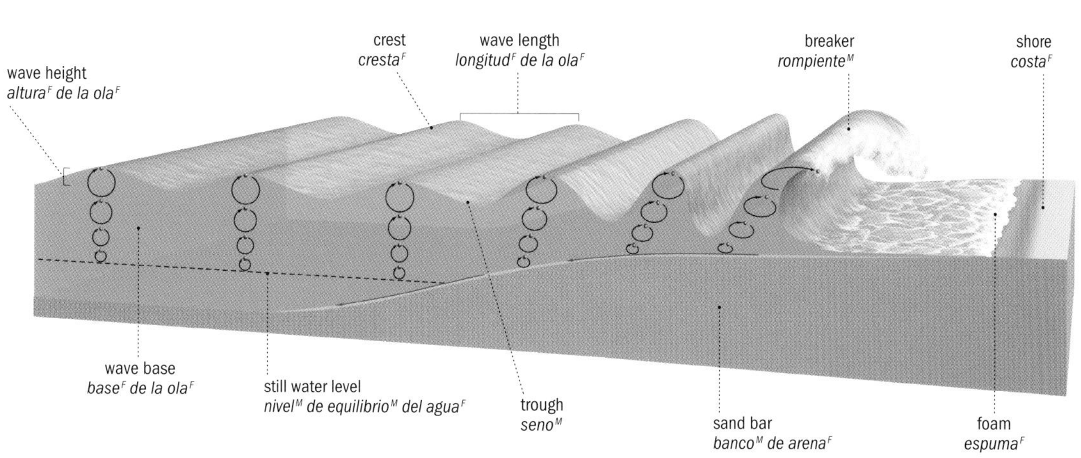

ocean floor
fondo[M] oceánico

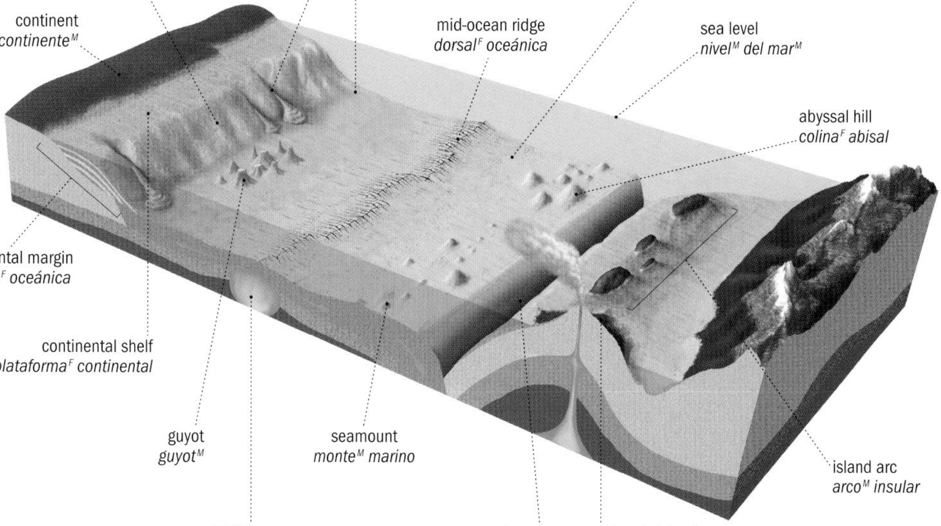

continental slope
talud[M] continental
submarine canyon
cañón[M] submarino
continental rise
elevación[F] continental
abyssal plain
llanura[F] abisal
continent
continente[M]
mid-ocean ridge
dorsal[F] oceánica
sea level
nivel[M] del mar[M]
abyssal hill
colina[F] abisal
continental margin
cuenca[F] oceánica
continental shelf
plataforma[F] continental
guyot
guyot[M]
seamount
monte[M] marino
island arc
arco[M] insular
magma
magma[M]
trench
fosa[F] abisal
volcanic island
isla[F] volcánica

ocean trenches and ridges

fosas^F y dorsales^F oceánicas

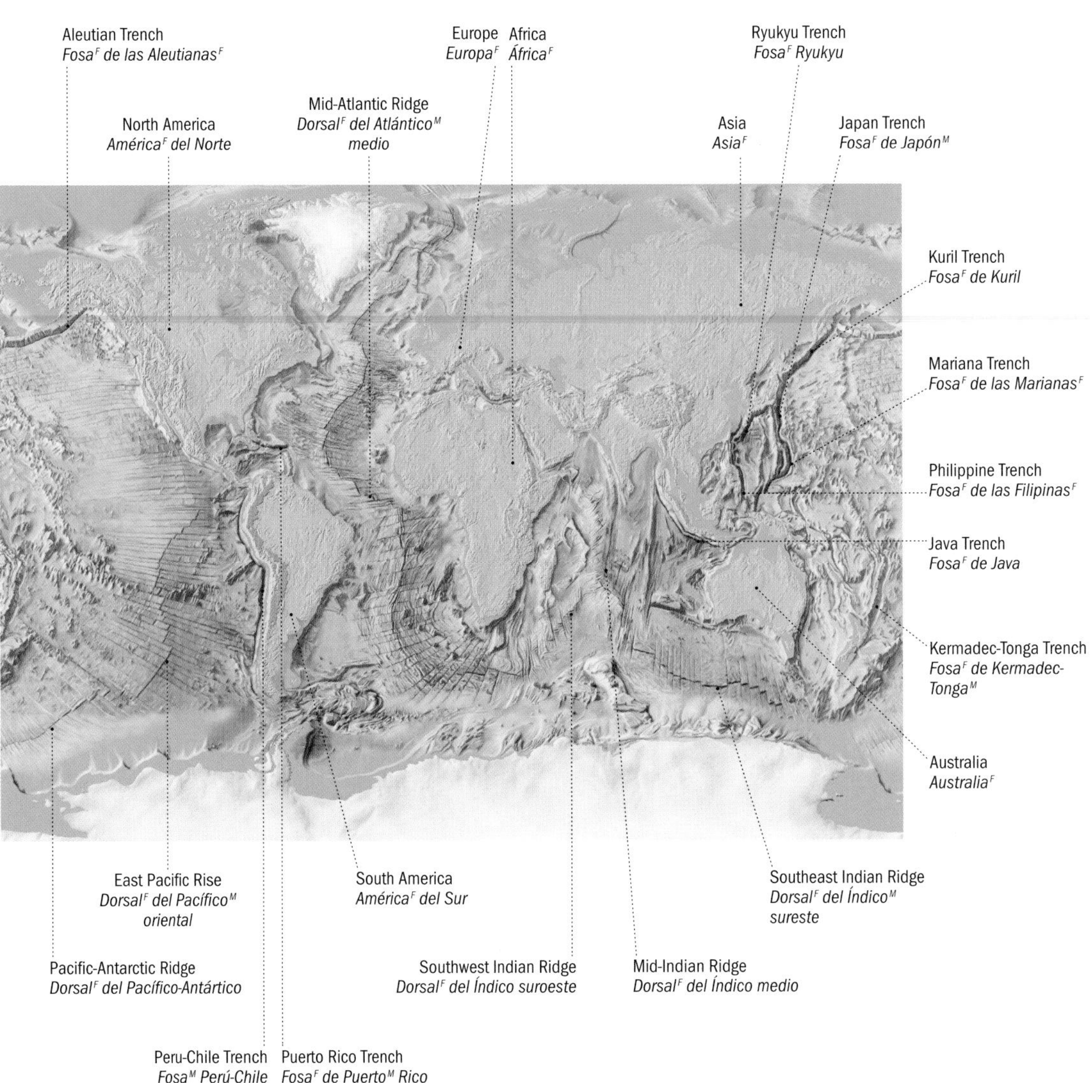
Aleutian Trench
Fosa^F de las Aleutianas^F
North America
América^F del Norte
Mid-Atlantic Ridge
Dorsal^F del Atlántico^M medio
Europe
Europa^F
Africa
África^F
Asia
Asia^F
Ryukyu Trench
Fosa^F Ryukyu
Japan Trench
Fosa^F de Japón^M
Kuril Trench
Fosa^F de Kuril
Mariana Trench
Fosa^F de las Marianas^F
Philippine Trench
Fosa^F de las Filipinas^F
Java Trench
Fosa^F de Java
Kermadec-Tonga Trench
Fosa^F de Kermadec-Tonga^M
Australia
Australia^F
East Pacific Rise
Dorsal^F del Pacífico^M oriental
Pacific-Antarctic Ridge
Dorsal^F del Pacífico-Antártico
Peru-Chile Trench
Fosa^M Perú-Chile
Puerto Rico Trench
Fosa^F de Puerto^M Rico
South America
América^F del Sur
Southwest Indian Ridge
Dorsal^F del Índico suroeste
Mid-Indian Ridge
Dorsal^F del Índico medio
Southeast Indian Ridge
Dorsal^F del Índico^M sureste

common coastal features

configuración^F del litoral^M

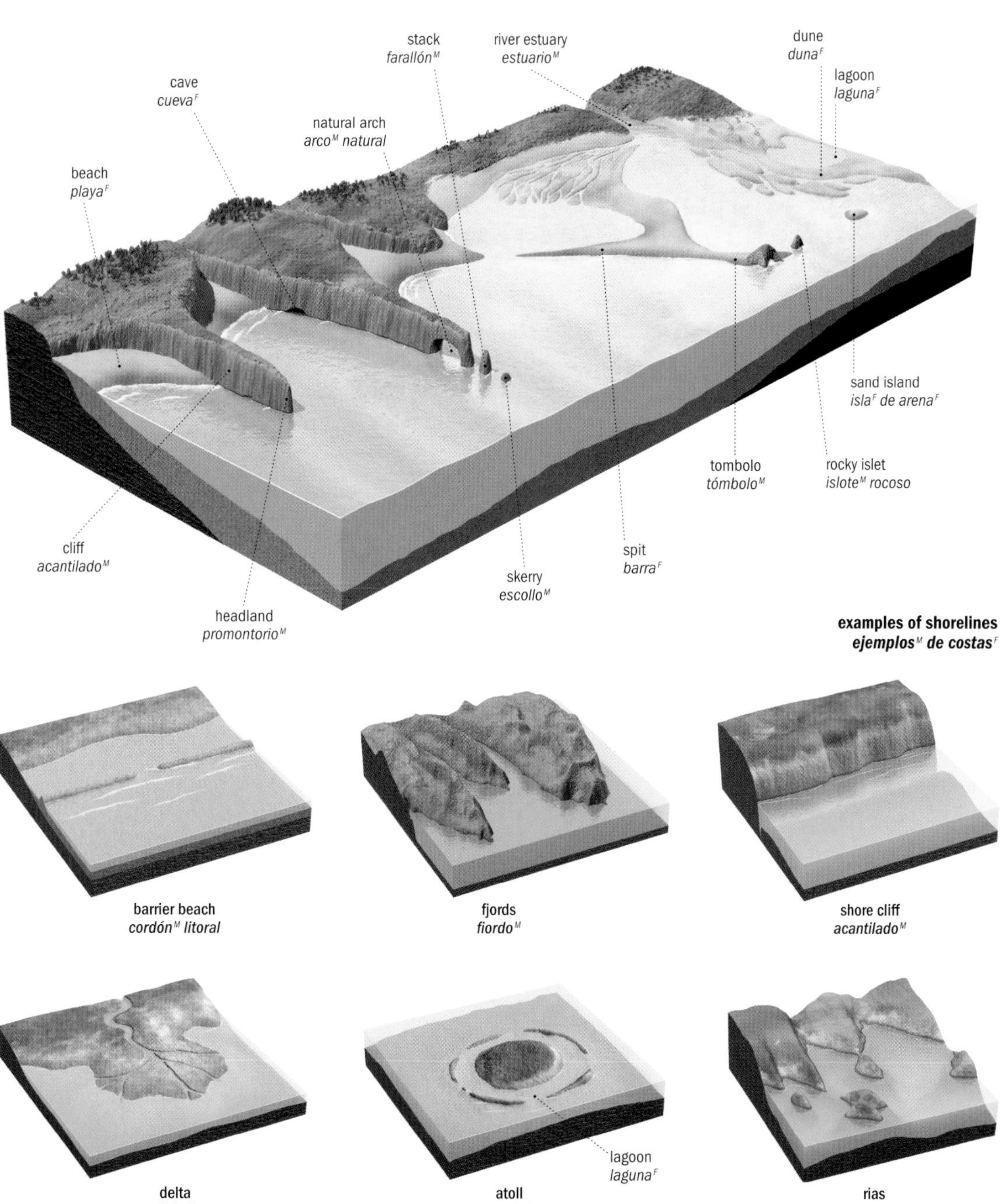

desert

desierto[M]

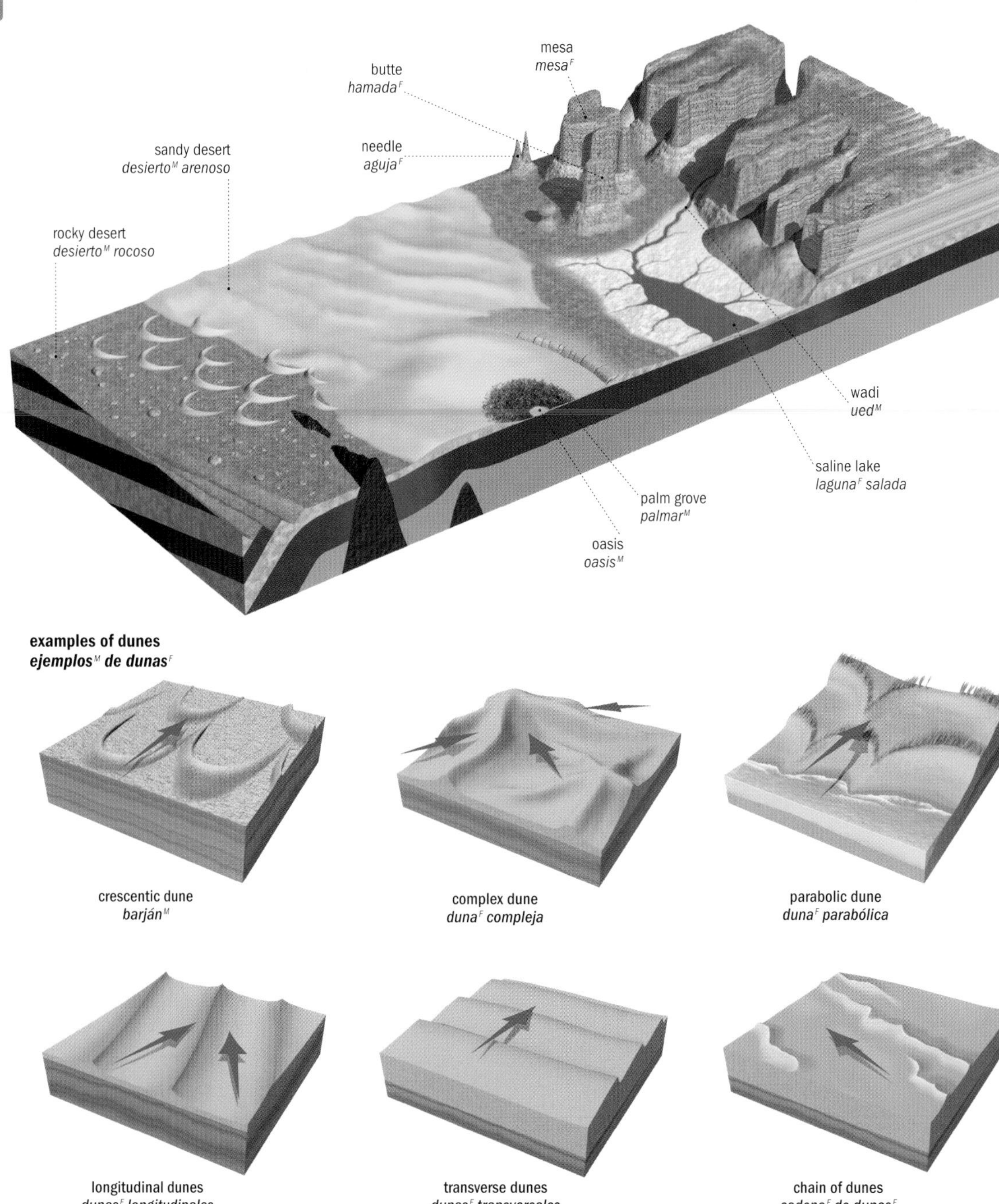
mesa
mesa[F]
butte
hamada[F]
sandy desert
desierto[M] arenoso
needle
aguja[F]
rocky desert
desierto[M] rocoso
wadi
ued[M]
saline lake
laguna[F] salada
palm grove
palmar[M]
oasis
oasis[M]
examples of dunes
ejemplos[M] de dunas[F]
crescentic dune
barján[M]
complex dune
duna[F] compleja
parabolic dune
duna[F] parabólica
longitudinal dunes
dunas[F] longitudinales
transverse dunes
dunas[F] transversales
chain of dunes
cadena[F] de dunas[F]

profile of the Earth's atmosphere

corte[M] de la atmósfera[F] terrestre

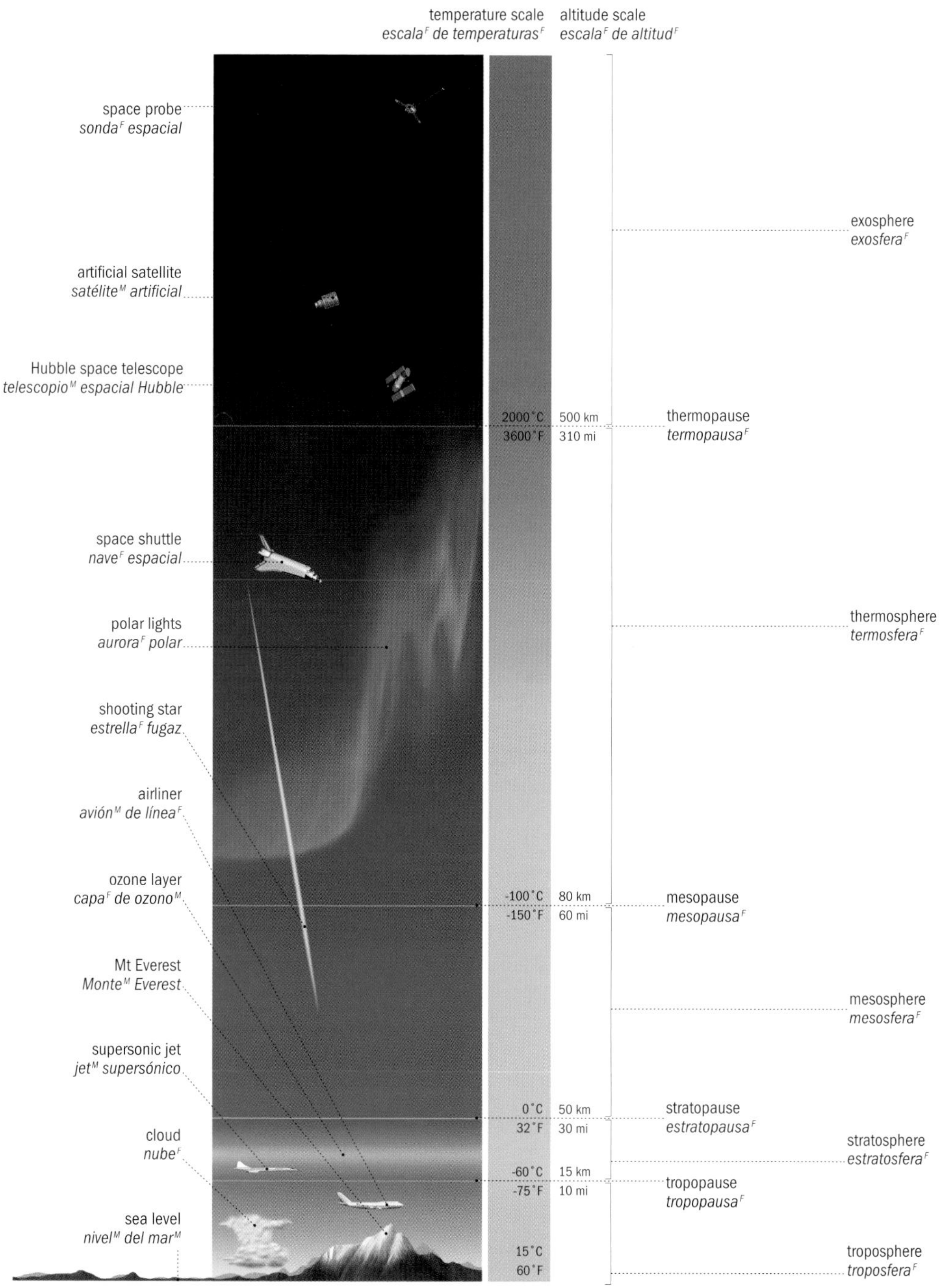

temperature scale
escala[F] de temperaturas[F]
altitude scale
escala[F] de altitud[F]
space probe
sonda[F] espacial
artificial satellite
satélite[M] artificial
Hubble space telescope
telescopio[M] espacial Hubble
space shuttle
nave[F] espacial
polar lights
aurora[F] polar
shooting star
estrella[F] fugaz
airliner
avión[M] de línea[F]
ozone layer
capa[F] de ozono[M]
Mt Everest
Monte[M] Everest
supersonic jet
jet[M] supersónico
cloud
nube[F]
sea level
nivel[M] del mar[M]
exosphere
exosfera[F]
2000°C
3600°F
500 km
310 mi
thermopause
termopausa[F]
thermosphere
termosfera[F]
-100°C
-150°F
80 km
60 mi
mesopause
mesopausa[F]
mesosphere
mesosfera[F]
0°C
32°F
50 km
30 mi
stratopause
estratopausa[F]
stratosphere
estratosfera[F]
-60°C
-75°F
15 km
10 mi
tropopause
tropopausa[F]
15°C
60°F
troposphere
troposfera[F]

seasons of the year

estaciones[F] del año[M]

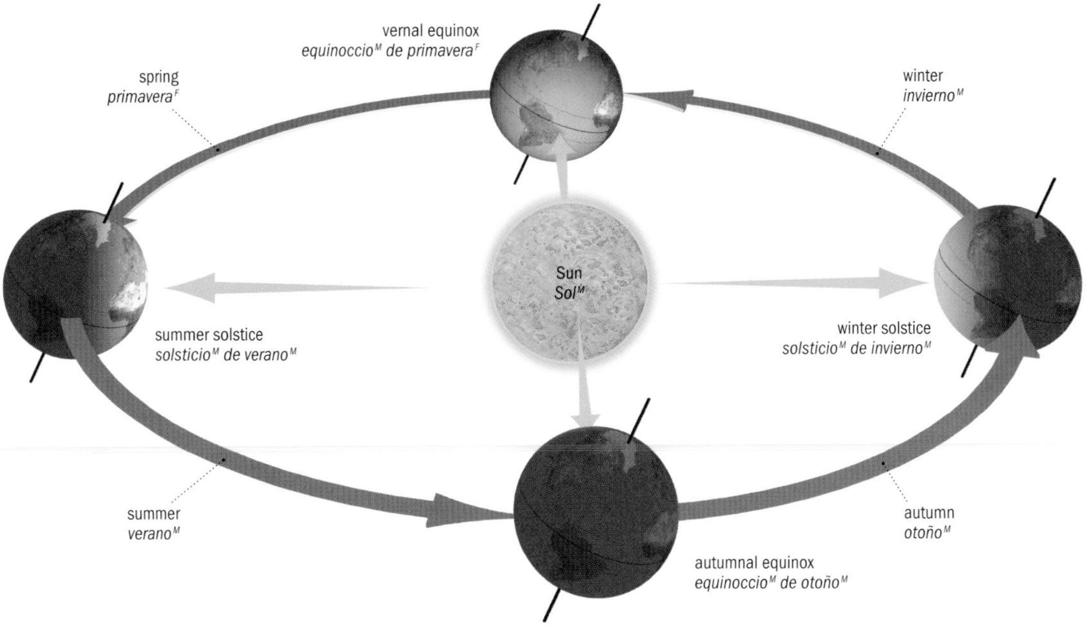

vernal equinox
equinoccio[M] de primavera[F]

spring
primavera[F]

winter
invierno[M]

Sun
Sol[M]

summer solstice
solsticio[M] de verano[M]

winter solstice
solsticio[M] de invierno[M]

summer
verano[M]

autumn
otoño[M]

autumnal equinox
equinoccio[M] de otoño[M]

meteorological forecast

previsión[F] meteorológica

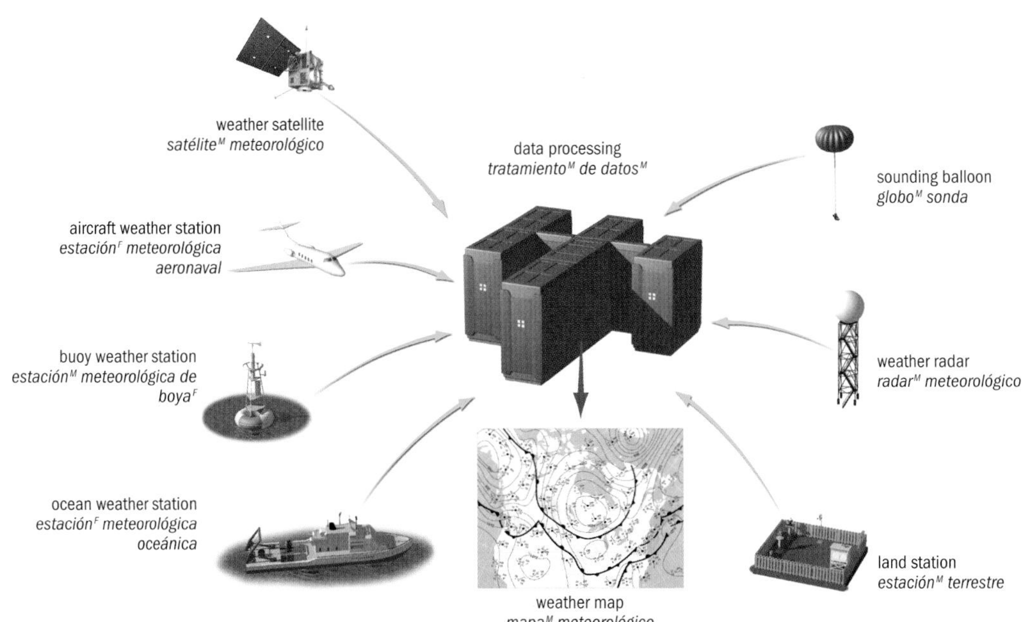

weather map

mapa^{M} meteorológico

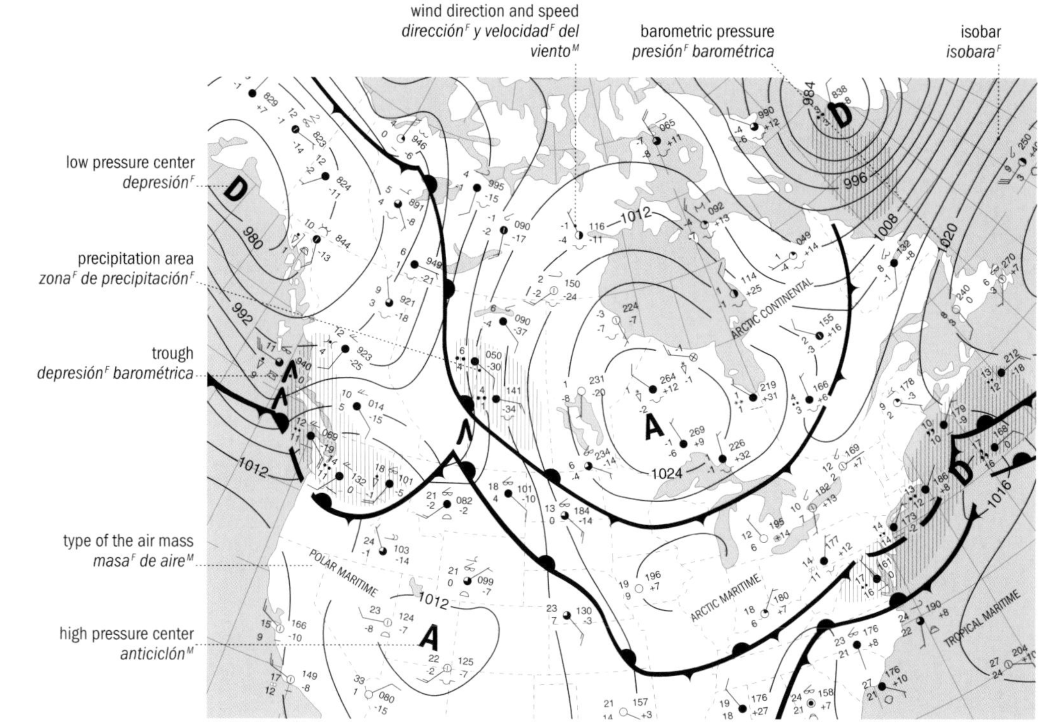

wind direction and speed
dirección^{F} y velocidad^{F} del viento^{M}
barometric pressure
presión^{F} barométrica
isobar
isobara^{F}
low pressure center
depresión^{F}
precipitation area
zona^{F} de precipitación^{F}
trough
depresión^{F} barométrica
type of the air mass
masa^{F} de aire^{M}
high pressure center
anticiclón^{M}
POLAR MARITIME
ARCTIC CONTINENTAL
ARCTIC MARITIME
TROPICAL MARITIME

station model

modelo^{M} de estación^{F}

type of high cloud
tipo^{M} de nube^{F} alta
type of middle cloud
tipo^{M} de nube^{F} media
wind speed
velocidad^{F} del viento^{M}
station circle
círculo^{M} de la estación^{F}
air temperature
temperatura^{F} ambiente
-2
995
sea-level pressure
presión^{F} barométrica a nivel^{M} del mar^{M}
sky coverage
proporción^{F} de nubes^{F}
wind direction
dirección^{M} del viento^{M}
+16
barometric tendency
tendencia^{F} barométrica
-6
present state of weather
estado^{M} actual del tiempo^{M}
temperature of dew point
temperatura^{F} del punto^{M} de rocío^{M}
type of low cloud
tipo^{M} de nube^{F} baja
pressure change
cambio^{M} de presión^{F}

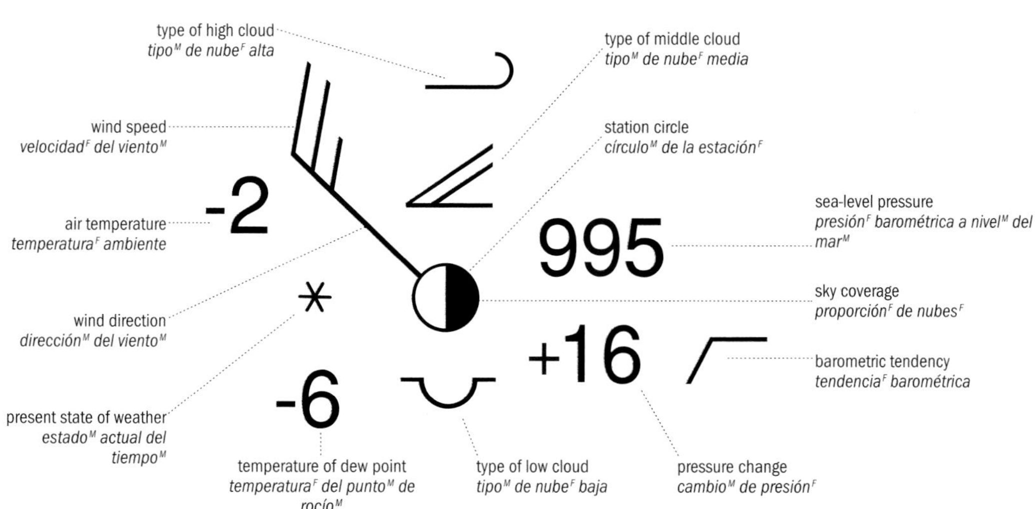

climates of the world

climas^M del mundo^M

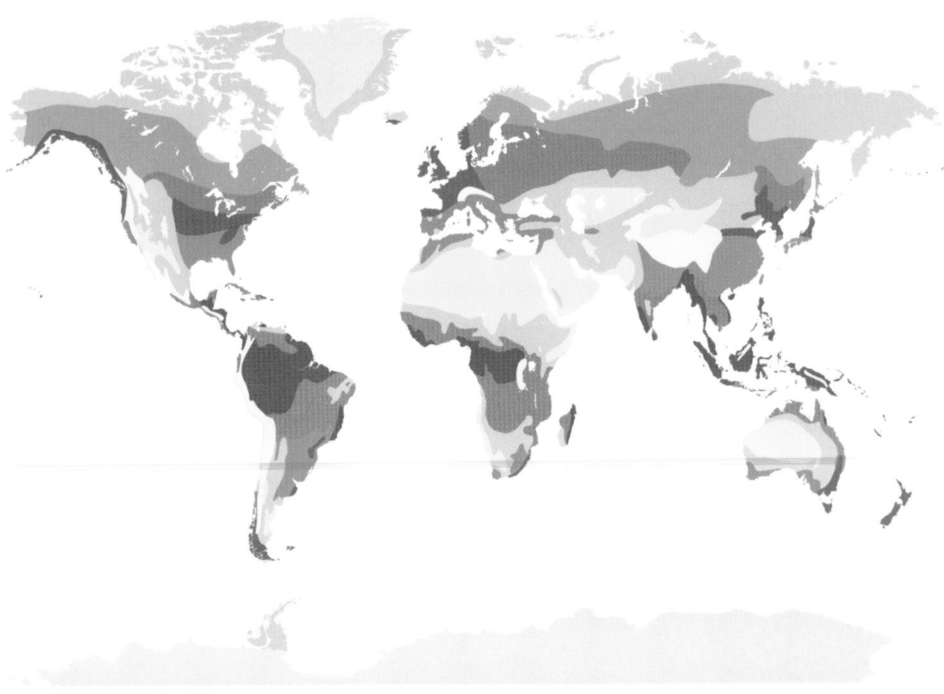

tropical climates
climas^M tropicales

tropical rain forest
tropical^M lluvioso

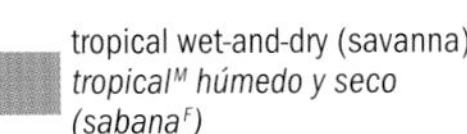
tropical wet-and-dry (savanna)
tropical^M húmedo y seco (sabana^F)

dry climates
climas^M áridos

steppe
estepario

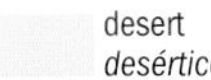
desert
desértico

cold temperate climates
climas^M templados fríos

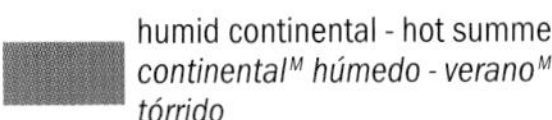
humid continental - hot summer
continental^M húmedo - verano^M tórrido

humid continental - warm summer
continental^M húmedo - verano^M fresco

subarctic
subártico^M

warm temperate climates
climas^M templados cálidos

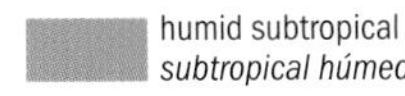
humid subtropical
subtropical húmedo

Mediterranean subtropical
subtropical mediterráneo

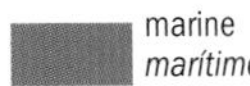
marine
marítimo

polar climates
climas^M polares

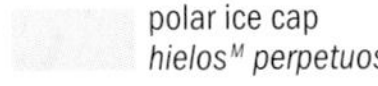
polar tundra
tundra^F

polar ice cap
hielos^M perpetuos

highland climates
climas^M de alta montaña^F

highland
climas^M de montaña^F

precipitation

precipitaciones[F]

winter precipitation
precipitaciones[F] invernales

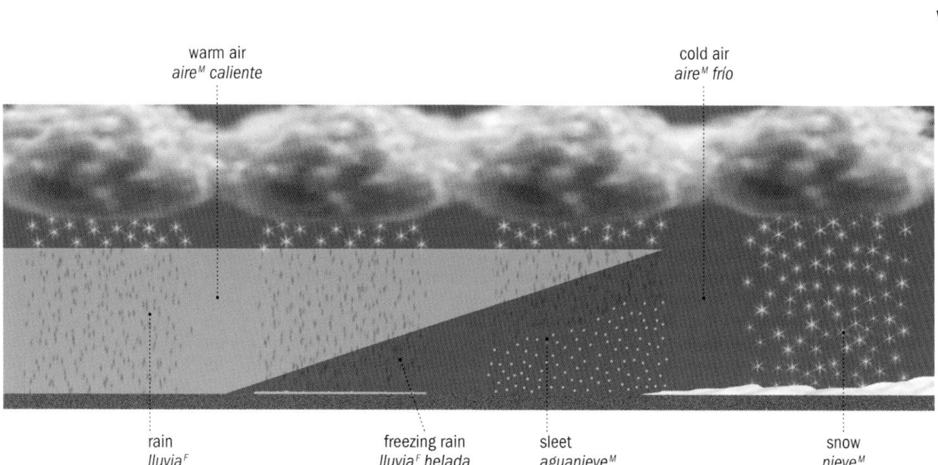

stormy sky
cielo[M] turbulento

dew
rocío[M]

mist
neblina[F]

fog
niebla[F]

frost
hielo[M]

rime
escarcha[F]

clouds

nubes^F

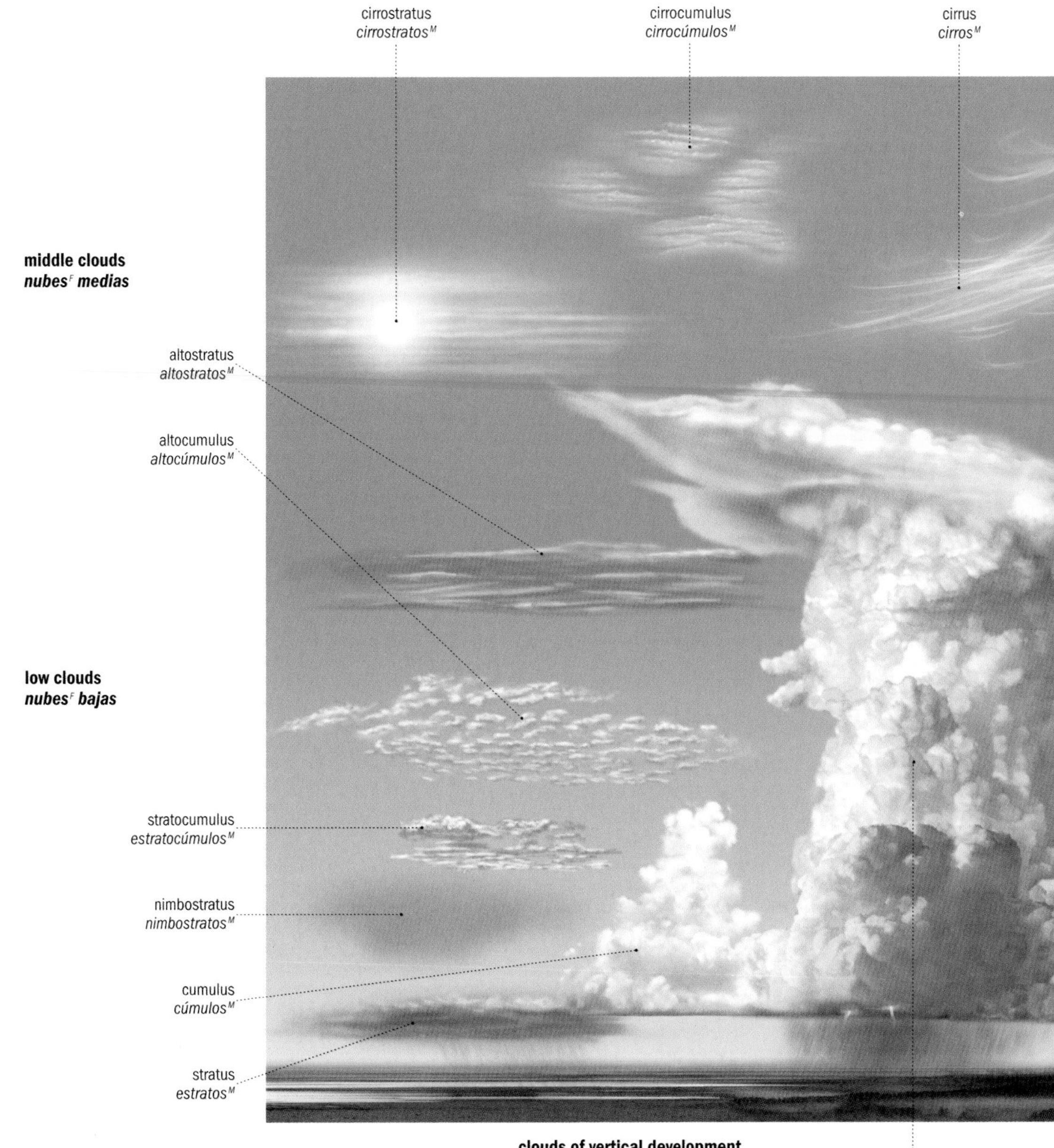
high clouds
nubes^F altas
cirrostratus
cirrostratos^M
cirrocumulus
cirrocúmulos^M
cirrus
cirros^M
middle clouds
nubes^F medias
altostratus
altostratos^M
altocumulus
altocúmulos^M
low clouds
nubes^F bajas
stratocumulus
estratocúmulos^M
nimbostratus
nimbostratos^M
cumulus
cúmulos^M
stratus
estratos^M
clouds of vertical development
nubes^F de desarrollo^M vertical
cumulonimbus
cumulonimbos^M

tornado and waterspout

tornado[M] y tromba[F] marina

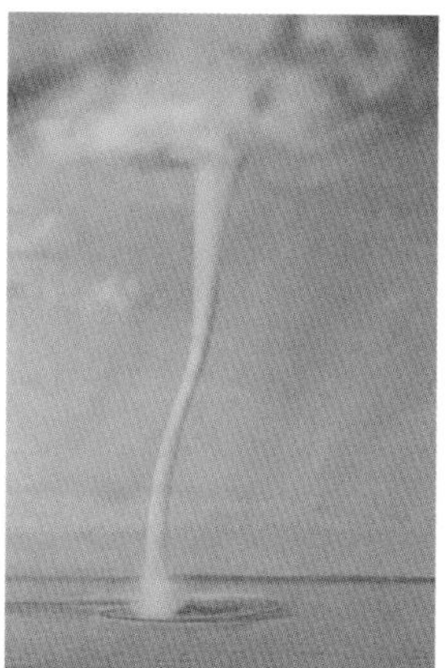

waterspout
tromba[F] marina

wall cloud
muro[M] de nubes[F]
funnel cloud
nube[F] en forma[F] de embudo[M]
debris
detritos[M]

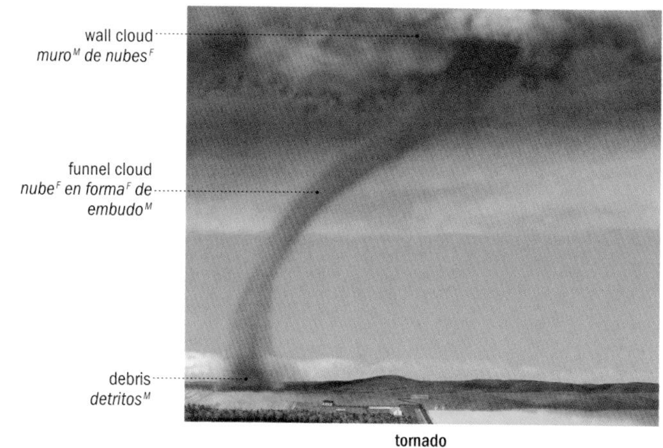

tornado
tornado[M]

tropical cyclone

ciclón[M] tropical

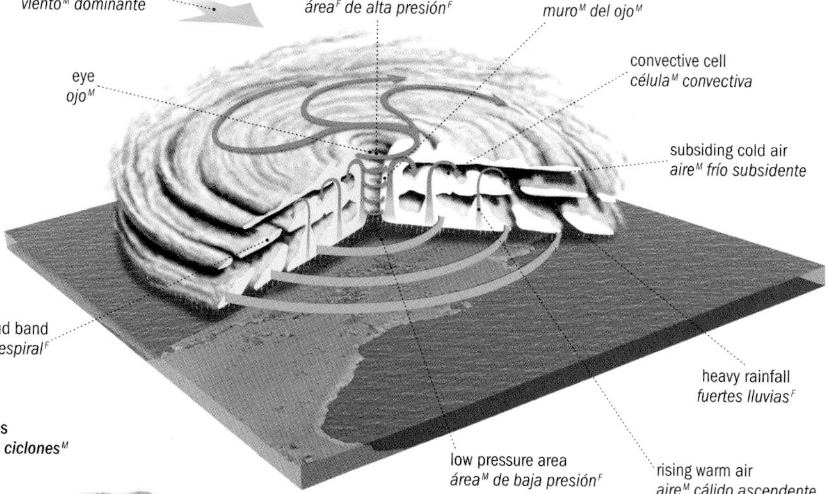

prevailing wind
viento[M] dominante
high pressure area
área[F] de alta presión[F]
eye wall
muro[M] del ojo[M]
convective cell
célula[M] convectiva
eye
ojo[M]
subsiding cold air
aire[M] frío subsidente
spiral cloud band
banda[F] nubosa en espiral[F]
heavy rainfall
fuertes lluvias[F]
low pressure area
área[M] de baja presión[F]
rising warm air
aire[M] cálido ascendente

tropical cyclone names
denominación[F] de los ciclones[M] tropicales

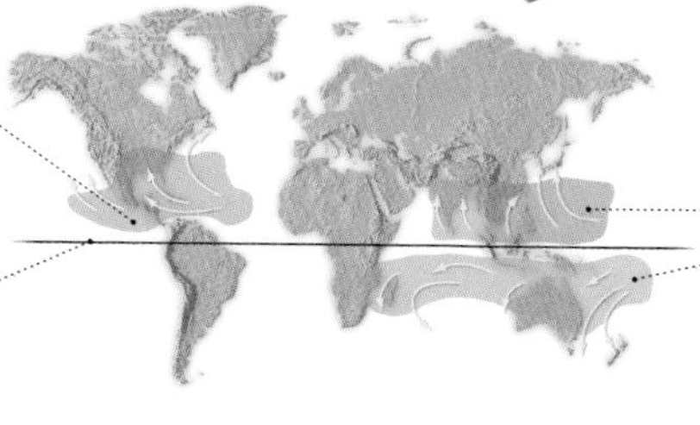

hurricane
huracán[M]
typhoon
tifón[M]
Equator
ecuador[M]
cyclone
ciclón[M]

vegetation and biosphere

vegetación[F] y biosfera[F]

vegetation regions
distribución[F] de la vegetación[F]

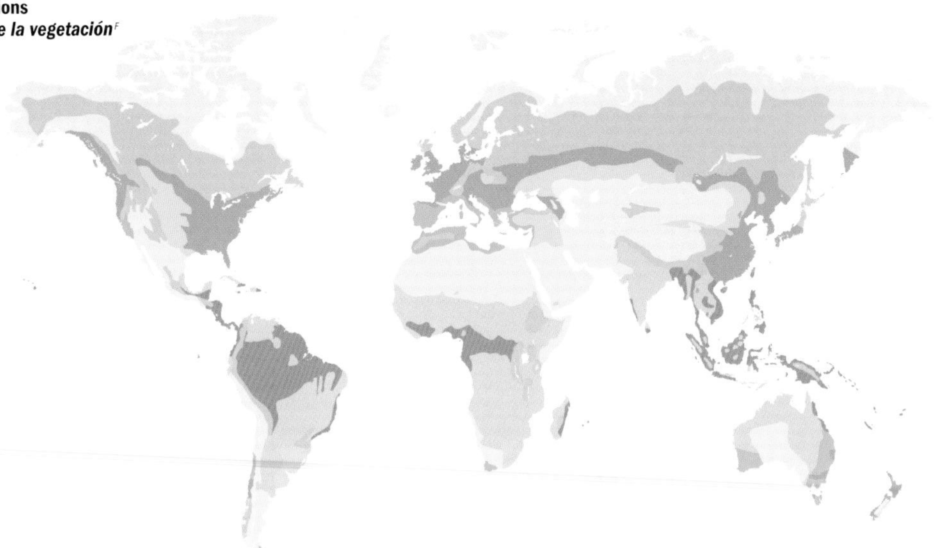

tundra
tundra[F]

temperate forest
bosque[M] templado

tropical rain forest
bosque[M] tropical húmedo

desert
desierto[M]

boreal forest
bosque[M] boreal

grassland
praderas[F]

savanna
sabana[F]

maquis
maquis[M]

elevation zones and vegetation
altitud[F] y vegetación[F]

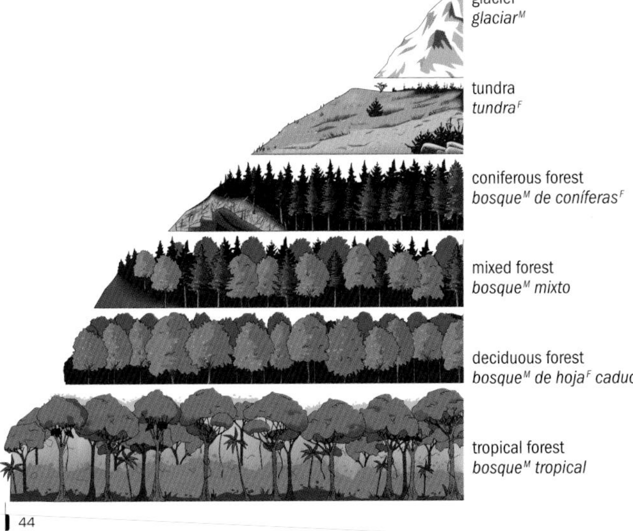

structure of the biosphere
estructura[F] de la biosfera[F]

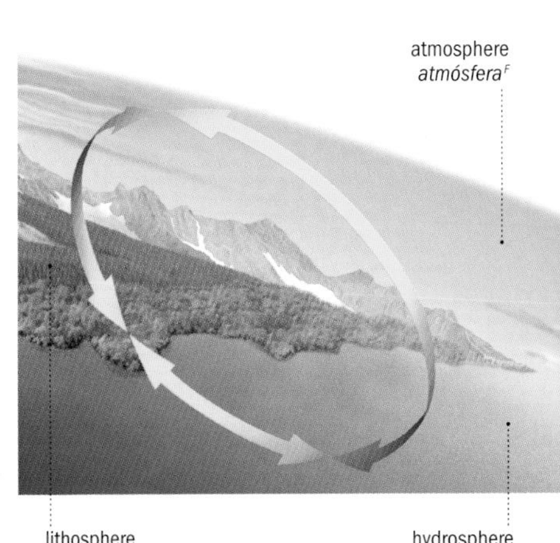

food chain

cadena^F alimentaria

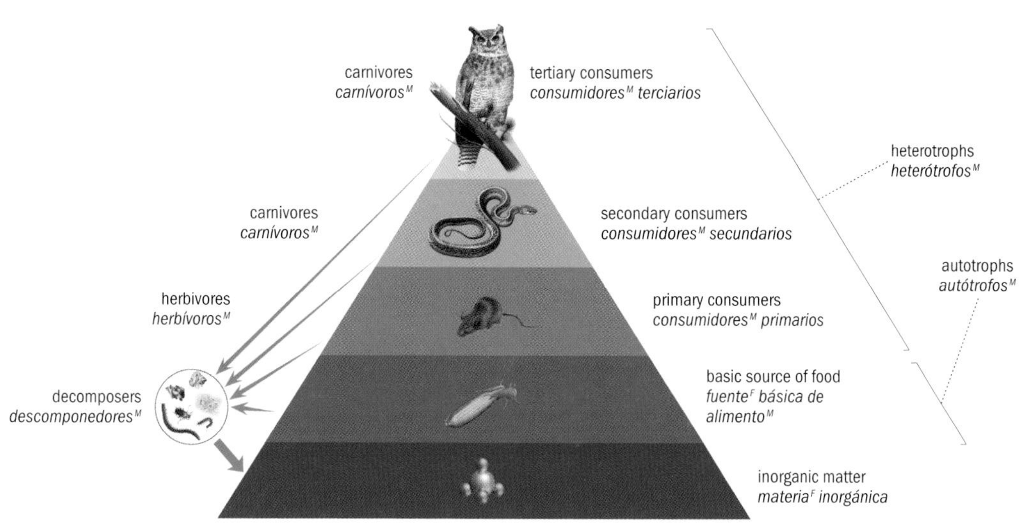

carnivores
carnívoros^M
tertiary consumers
consumidores^M terciarios
heterotrophs
heterótrofos^M
carnivores
carnívoros^M
secondary consumers
consumidores^M secundarios
autotrophs
autótrofos^M
herbivores
herbívoros^M
primary consumers
consumidores^M primarios
basic source of food
fuente^F básica de alimento^M
decomposers
descomponedores^M
inorganic matter
materia^F inorgánica

hydrologic cycle

ciclo^M hidrológico

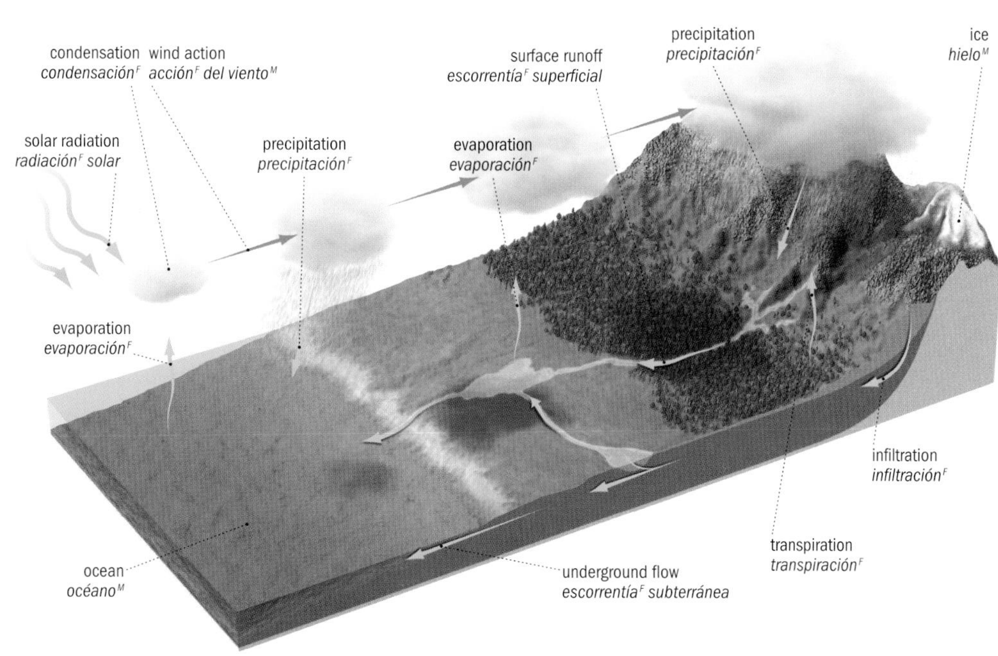

condensation
condensación^F
wind action
acción^F del viento^M
surface runoff
escorrentía^F superficial
precipitation
precipitación^F
ice
hielo^M
solar radiation
radiación^F solar
precipitation
precipitación^F
evaporation
evaporación^F
evaporation
evaporación^F
infiltration
infiltración^F
transpiration
transpiración^F
ocean
océano^M
underground flow
escorrentía^F subterránea

greenhouse effect

efecto[M] invernadero

natural greenhouse effect
efecto[M] invernadero natural

reflected solar radiation
radiación[F] solar refleja

heat loss
pérdida[F] de calor

tropopause
tropopausa[F]

greenhouse gas
gas[M] de efecto[M] invernadero[M]

solar radiation
radiación[F] solar

absorbed solar radiation
radiación[F] solar absorbida

absorption by clouds
absorción[F] por las nubes[F]

absorption by Earth's surface
absorción[F] por el suelo[M]

infrared radiation
radiación[F] infrarroja

heat energy
energía[F] calorífica

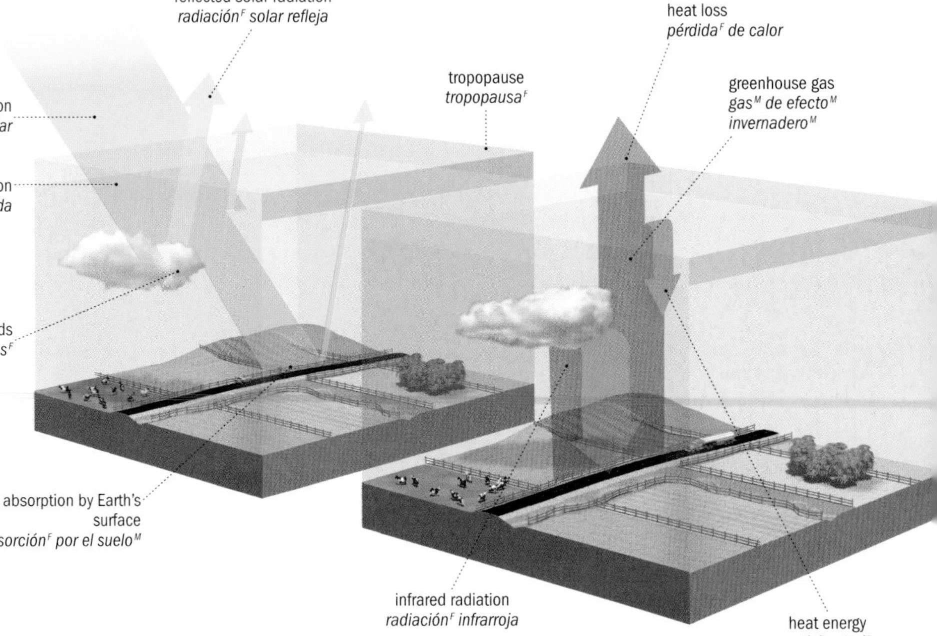

enhanced greenhouse effect
aumento[M] del efecto[M] invernadero

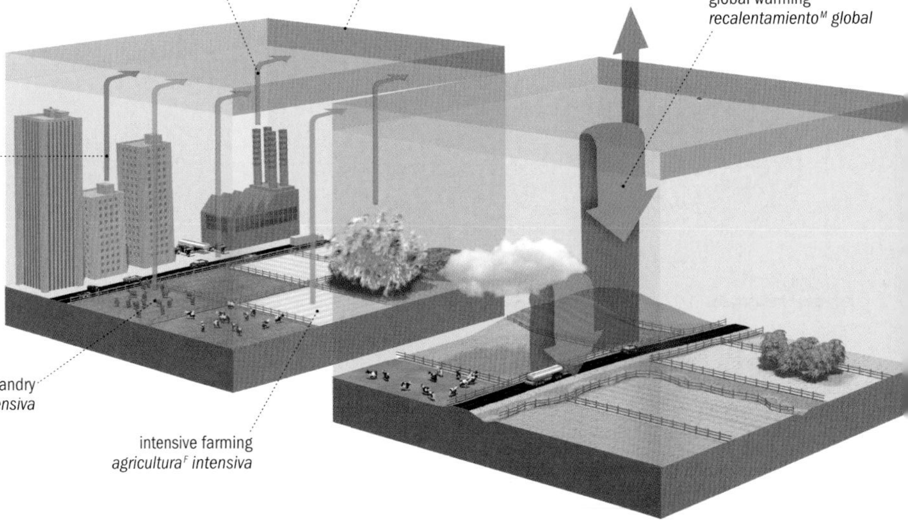

fossil fuel
combustible[M] fósil

greenhouse gas concentration
concentración[F] de gas[M] de efecto[M] invernadero[M]

global warming
recalentamiento[M] global

air conditioning system
sistema[M] de aire[M] acondicionado

intensive husbandry
ganadería[F] intensiva

intensive farming
agricultura[F] intensiva

air pollution

contaminación[F] del aire[M]

polluting gas emission
emisión[F] de gases[M] contaminantes
authorized landfill site
vertedero[M] autorizado
air pollutants
contaminantes[M] del aire[M]
smog
smog[M]/niebla[F] tóxica
wind
viento[M]
acid rain
lluvia[F] ácida
forest fire
incendio[M] forestal
industrial waste
residuos[M F] industriales
motor vehicle pollution
contaminación[F] de automóviles[M]
deforestation
deforestación[F]
paddy field
arrozal[M]
soil fertilization
fertilización[F] del suelo[M]
intensive husbandry
ganadería[F] intensiva

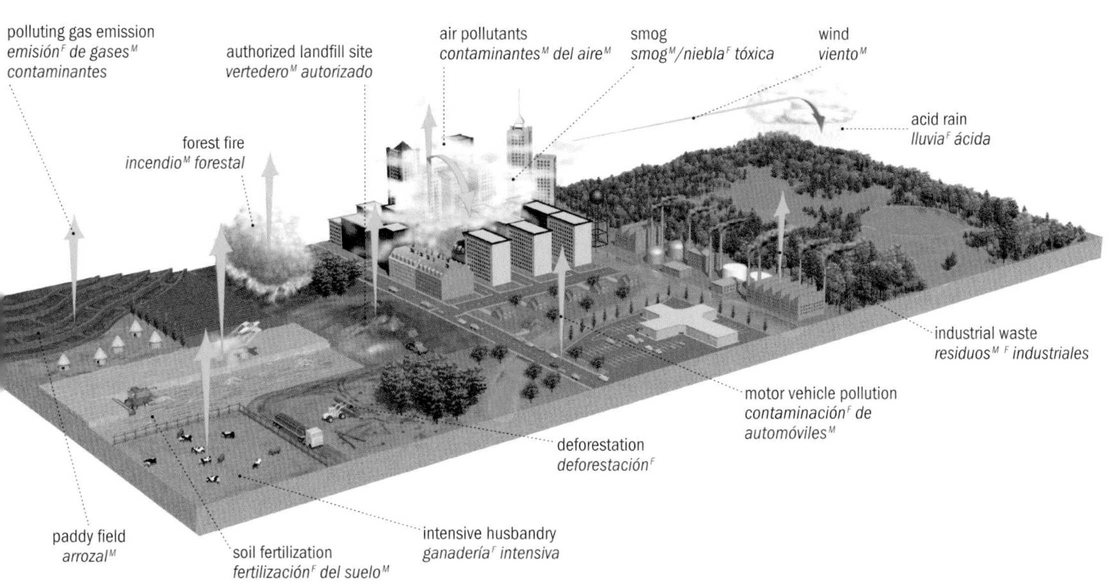

land pollution

contaminación[F] del suelo[M]

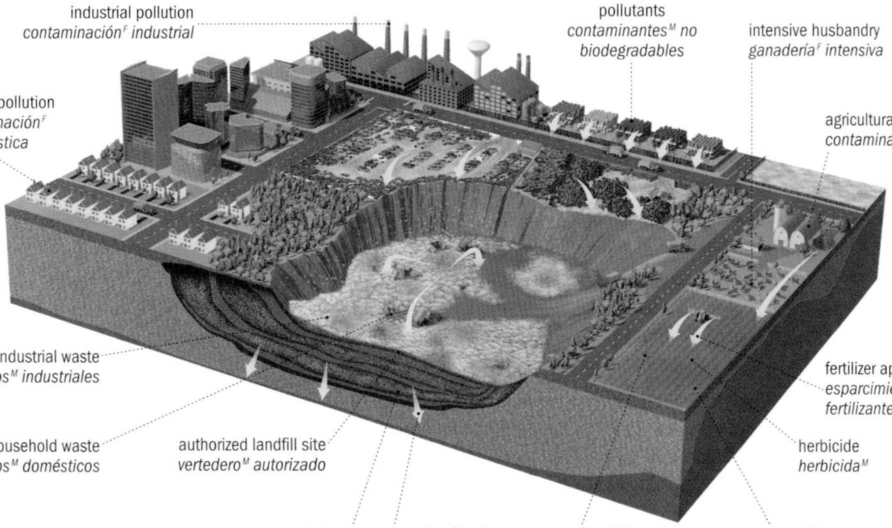

industrial pollution
contaminación[F] industrial
non-biodegradable pollutants
contaminantes[M] no biodegradables
intensive husbandry
ganadería[F] intensiva
domestic pollution
contaminación[F] doméstica
agricultural pollution
contaminación[F] agrícola
industrial waste
residuos[M] industriales
fertilizer application
esparcimiento[M] de fertilizante[M]
household waste
residuos[M] domésticos
authorized landfill site
vertedero[M] autorizado
herbicide
herbicida[M]
waste layers
capas[F] de residuos[M]
intrusive filtration
infiltración[F]
fungicide
funguicida[M]
pesticide
pesticida[M]

water pollution

contaminación^F del agua^F

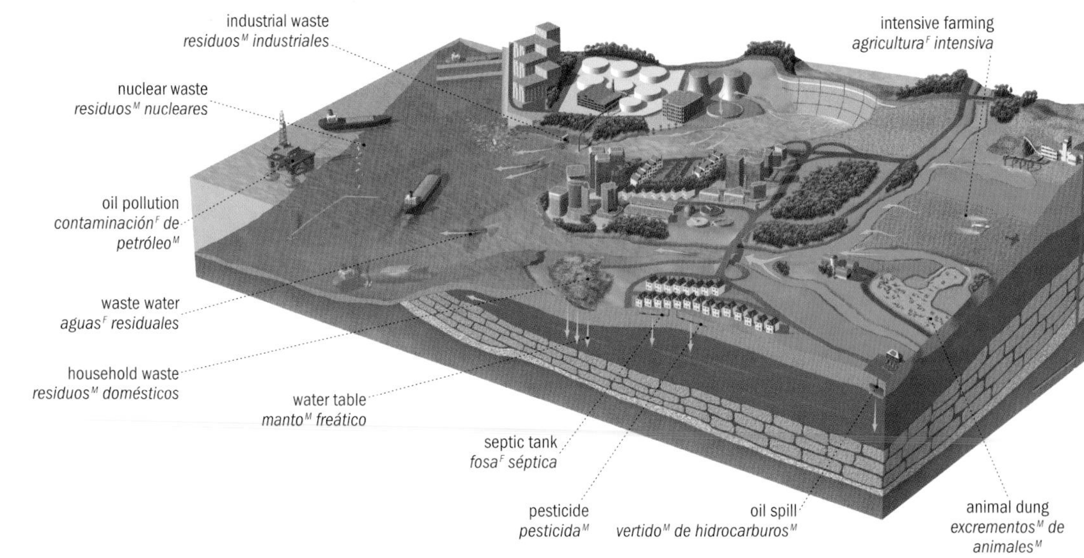
industrial waste
residuos^M industriales
nuclear waste
residuos^M nucleares
oil pollution
contaminación^F de petróleo^M
waste water
aguas^F residuales
household waste
residuos^M domésticos
water table
manto^M freático
septic tank
fosa^F séptica
pesticide
pesticida^M
oil spill
vertido^M de hidrocarburos^M
animal dung
excrementos^M de animales^M
intensive farming
agricultura^F intensiva

acid rain

lluvia^F ácida

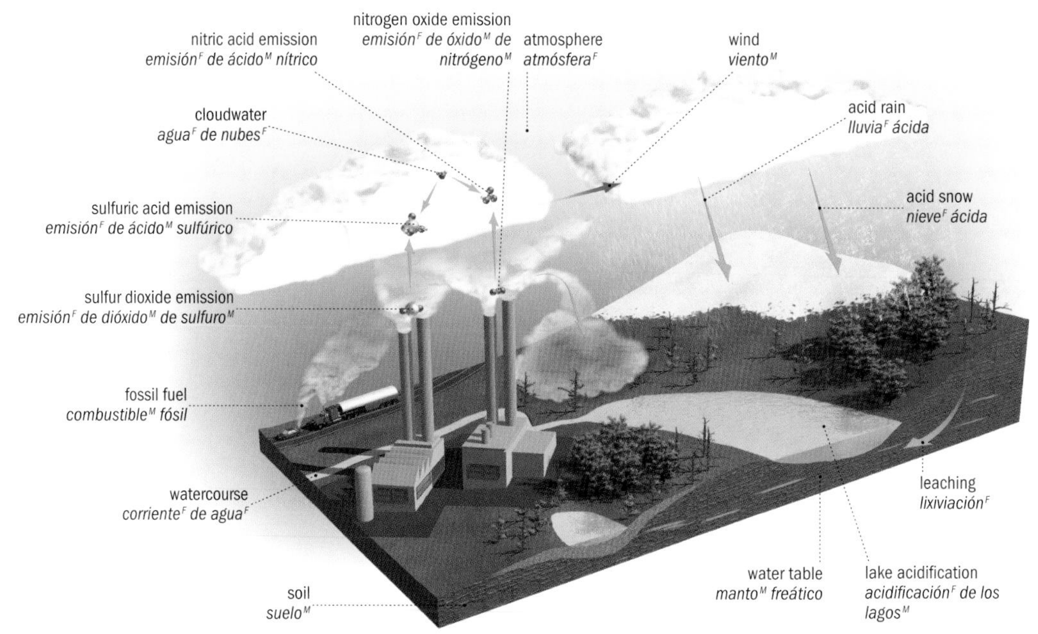
nitric acid emission
emisión^F de ácido^M nítrico
nitrogen oxide emission
emisión^F de óxido^M de nitrógeno^M
atmosphere
atmósfera^F
wind
viento^M
cloudwater
agua^F de nubes^F
acid rain
lluvia^F ácida
sulfuric acid emission
emisión^F de ácido^M sulfúrico
acid snow
nieve^F ácida
sulfur dioxide emission
emisión^F de dióxido^M de sulfuro^M
fossil fuel
combustible^M fósil
watercourse
corriente^F de agua^F
leaching
lixiviación^F
soil
suelo^M
water table
manto^M freático
lake acidification
acidificación^F de los lagos^M

selective sorting of waste

separación^{F} selectiva de residuos^{M}

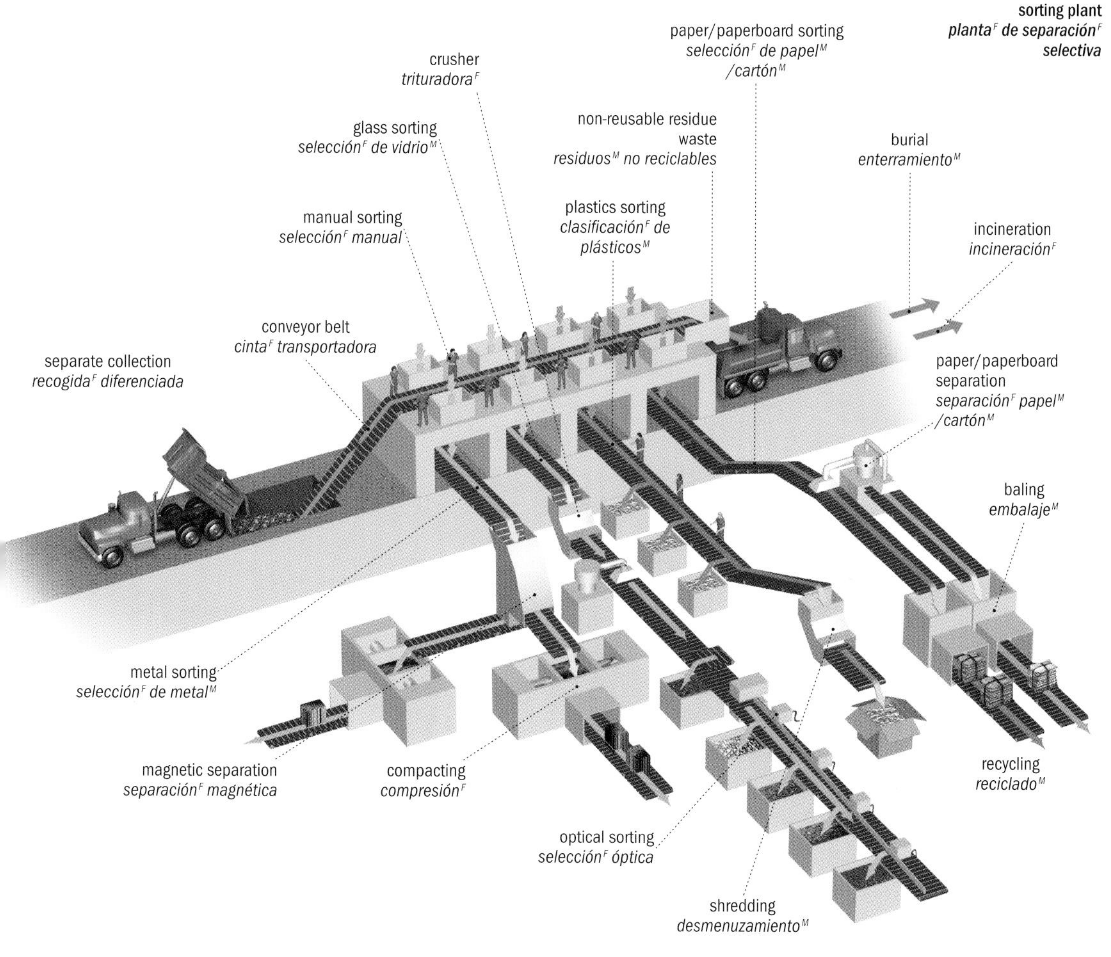

sorting plant
planta^{F} de separación^{F} selectiva

paper/paperboard sorting
selección^{F} de papel^{M} /cartón^{M}

crusher
trituradora^{F}

non-reusable residue waste
residuos^{M} no reciclables

glass sorting
selección^{F} de vidrio^{M}

burial
enterramiento^{M}

plastics sorting
clasificación^{F} de plásticos^{M}

manual sorting
selección^{F} manual

incineration
incineración^{F}

conveyor belt
cinta^{F} transportadora

separate collection
recogida^{F} diferenciada

paper/paperboard separation
separación^{F} papel^{M} /cartón^{M}

baling
embalaje^{M}

metal sorting
selección^{F} de metal^{M}

recycling
reciclado^{M}

magnetic separation
separación^{F} magnética

compacting
compresión^{F}

optical sorting
selección^{F} óptica

shredding
desmenuzamiento^{M}

recycling containers
contenedores^{M} de reciclaje^{M}

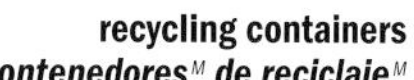

paper recycling container
contenedor^{M} de reciclado^{M} de papel^{M}

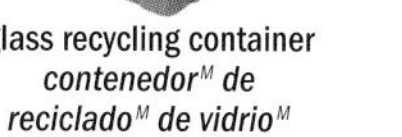

glass recycling container
contenedor^{M} de reciclado^{M} de vidrio^{M}

aluminum recycling container
contenedor^{M} de reciclado^{M} de aluminio^{M}

paper collection unit
contenedor^{M} de recogida de papel^{M}

glass collection unit
contenedor^{M} de recogida de vidrio^{M}

recycling bin
cubo^{M} de basura^{F} reciclable

plant cell

célula^F vegetal

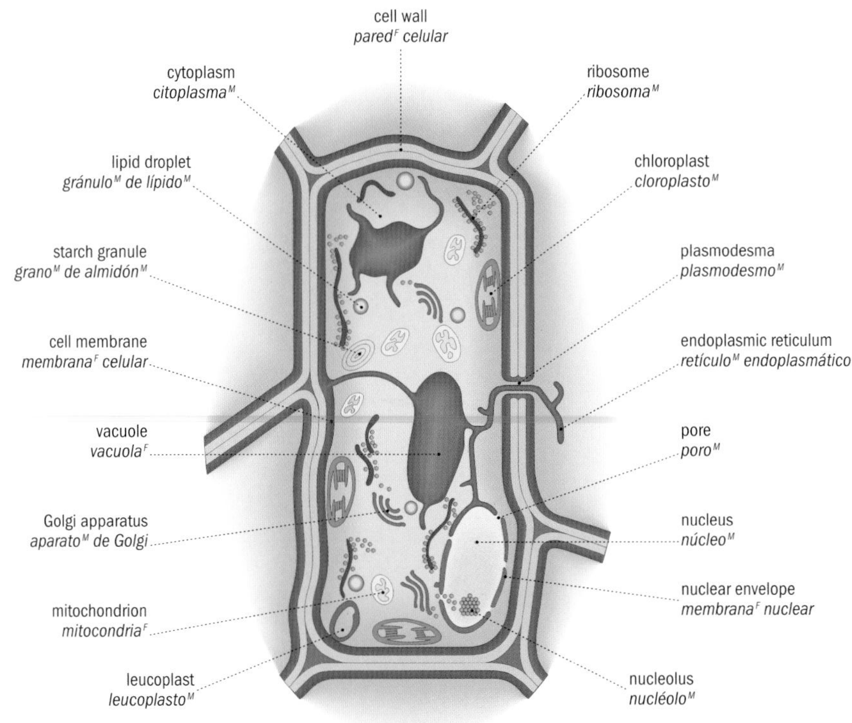

lichen

liquen

structure of a lichen
estructura^F de un liquen^M

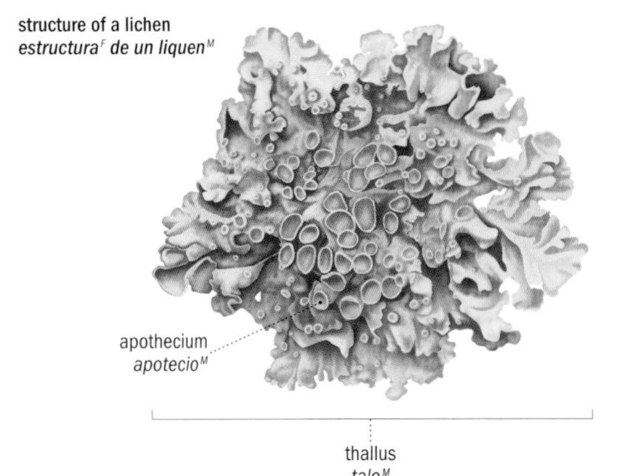

examples of lichens
ejemplos^M de líquenes^M

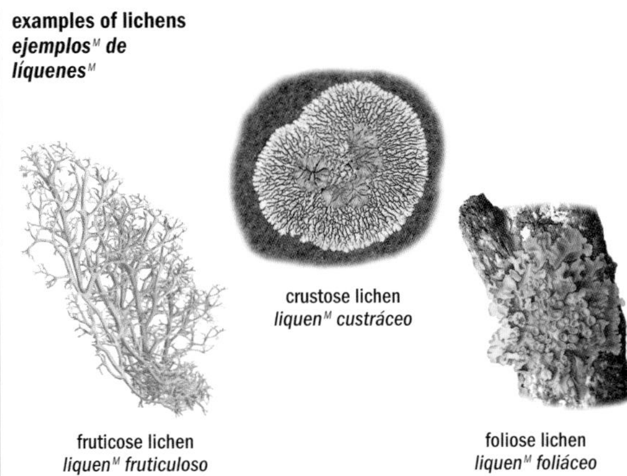

moss
musgo^M

structure of a moss
estructura^F de un musgo^M

capsule
cápsula^F
stalk
pedúnculo^M
leaf
hoja^F
stem
tallo^M
rhizoid
rizoide^M

examples of mosses
ejemplos^M de musgos^M

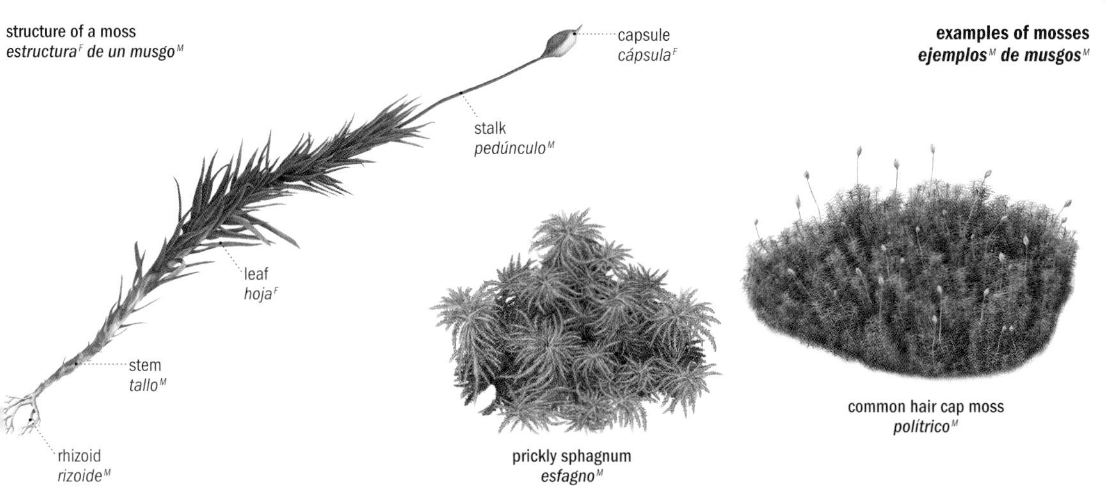

prickly sphagnum
esfagno^M

common hair cap moss
polítrico^M

algae
alga^F

structure of an alga
estructura^F de un alga^F

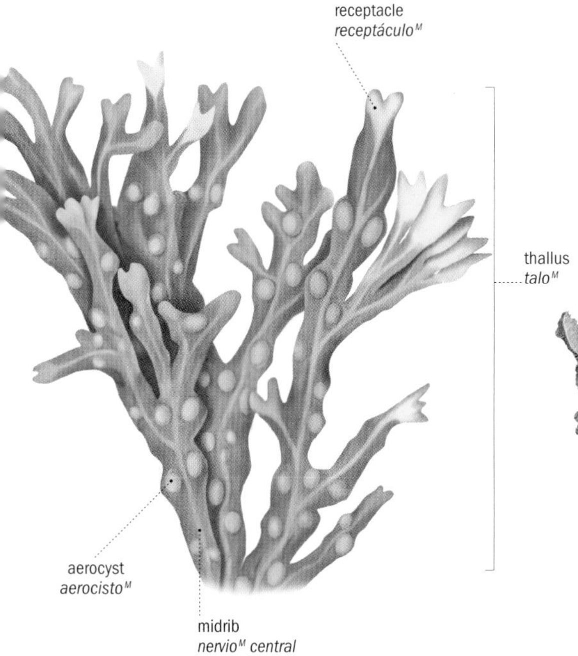

receptacle
receptáculo^M
thallus
talo^M
aerocyst
aerocisto^M
midrib
nervio^M central

examples of algae
ejemplos^M de algas^F

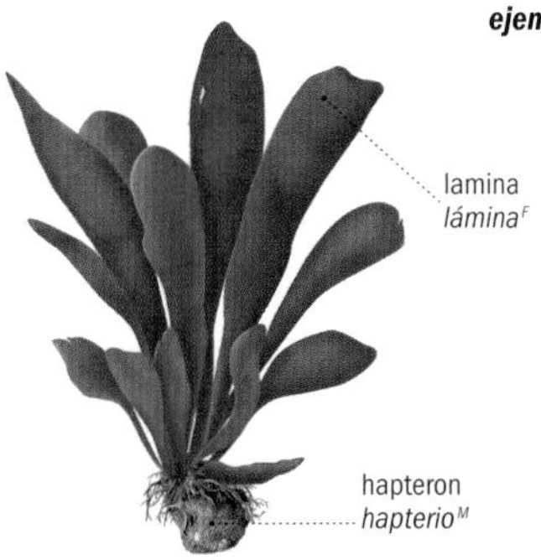

lamina
lámina^F
hapteron
hapterio^M

red alga
alga^F roja

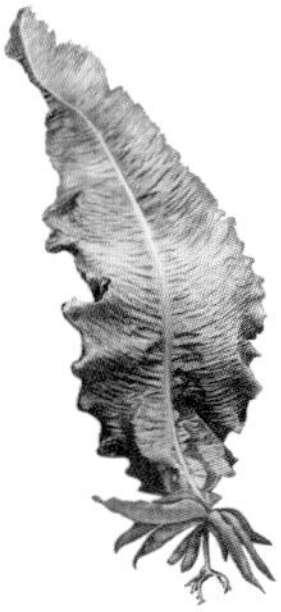

green alga
alga^F verde

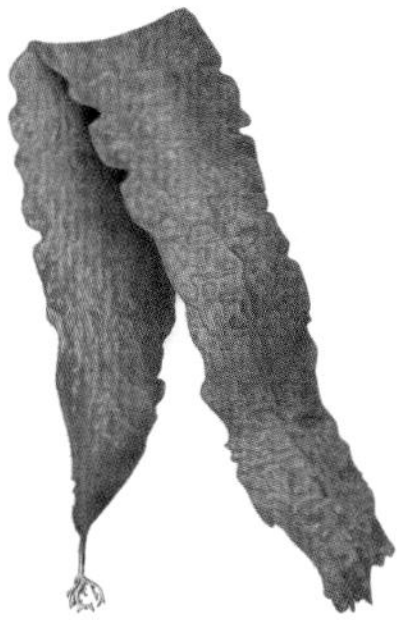

brown alga
alga^F parda

mushroom

hongo[M]

structure of a mushroom
anatomía[F] de un hongo[M]

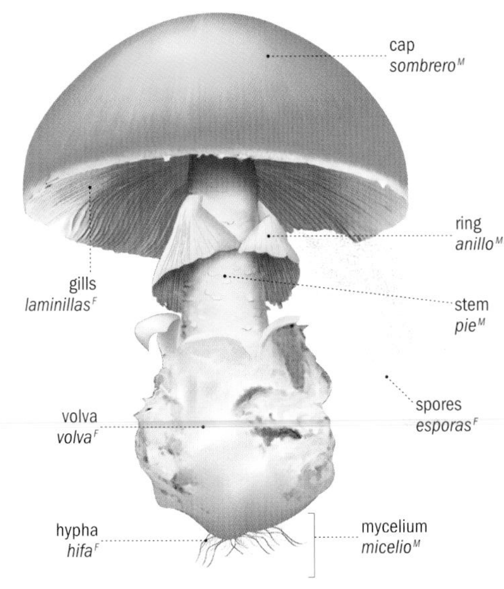

deadly poisonous mushroom
hongo[M] mortal

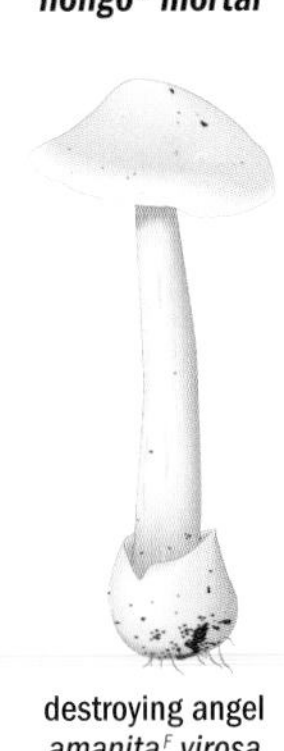

destroying angel
amanita[F] virosa

poisonous mushroom
hongo[M] venenoso

fly agaric
falsa oronja[F]

fern

helecho[M]

structure of a fern
estructura[F] de un helecho[M]

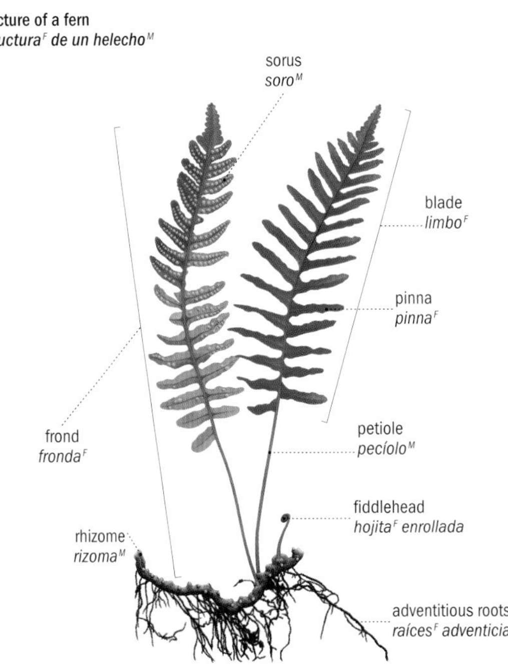

examples of ferns
ejemplos[M] de helechos[M]

structure of a plant
anatomíaF de una plantaF

germination
germinaciónF

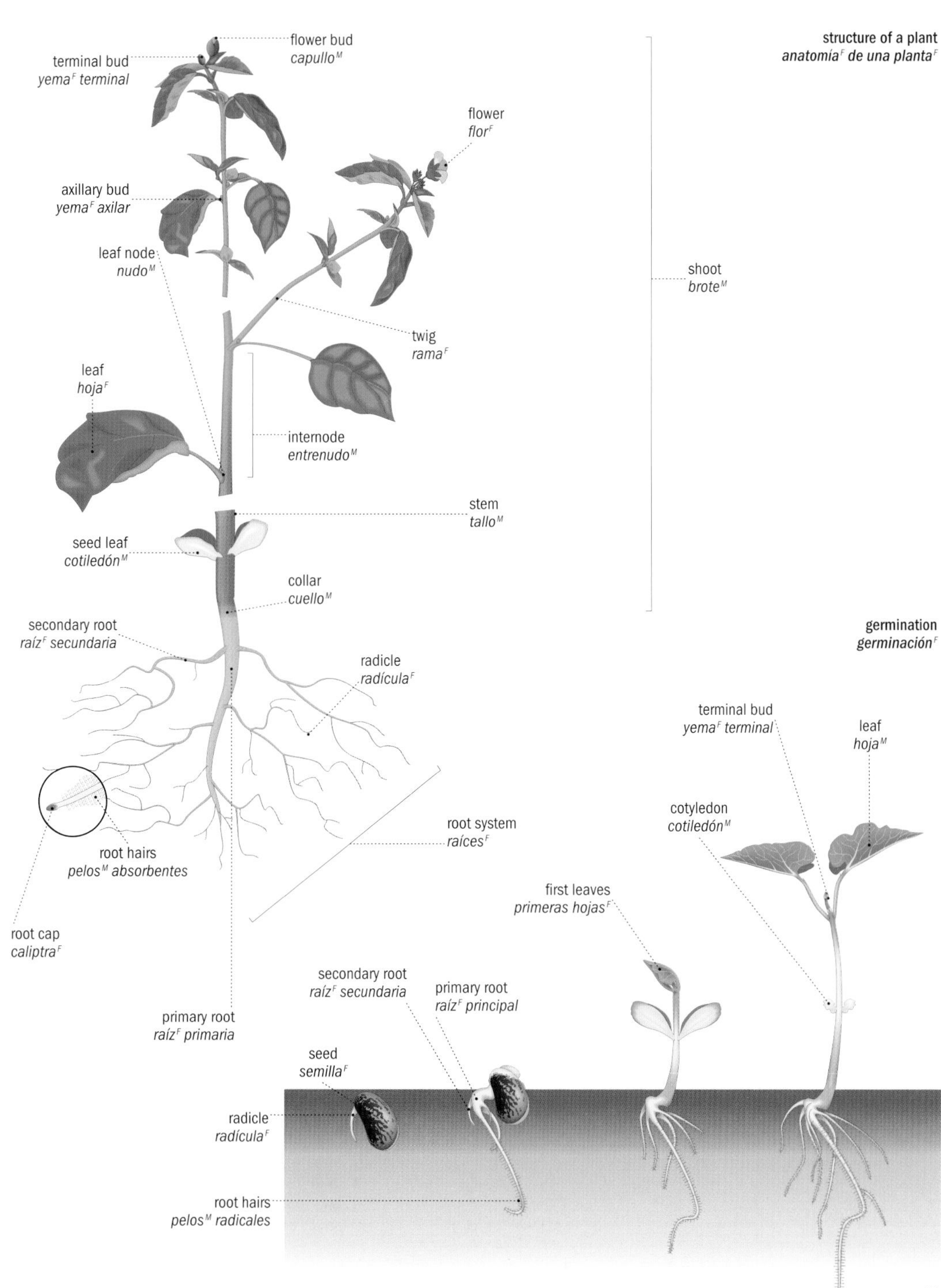

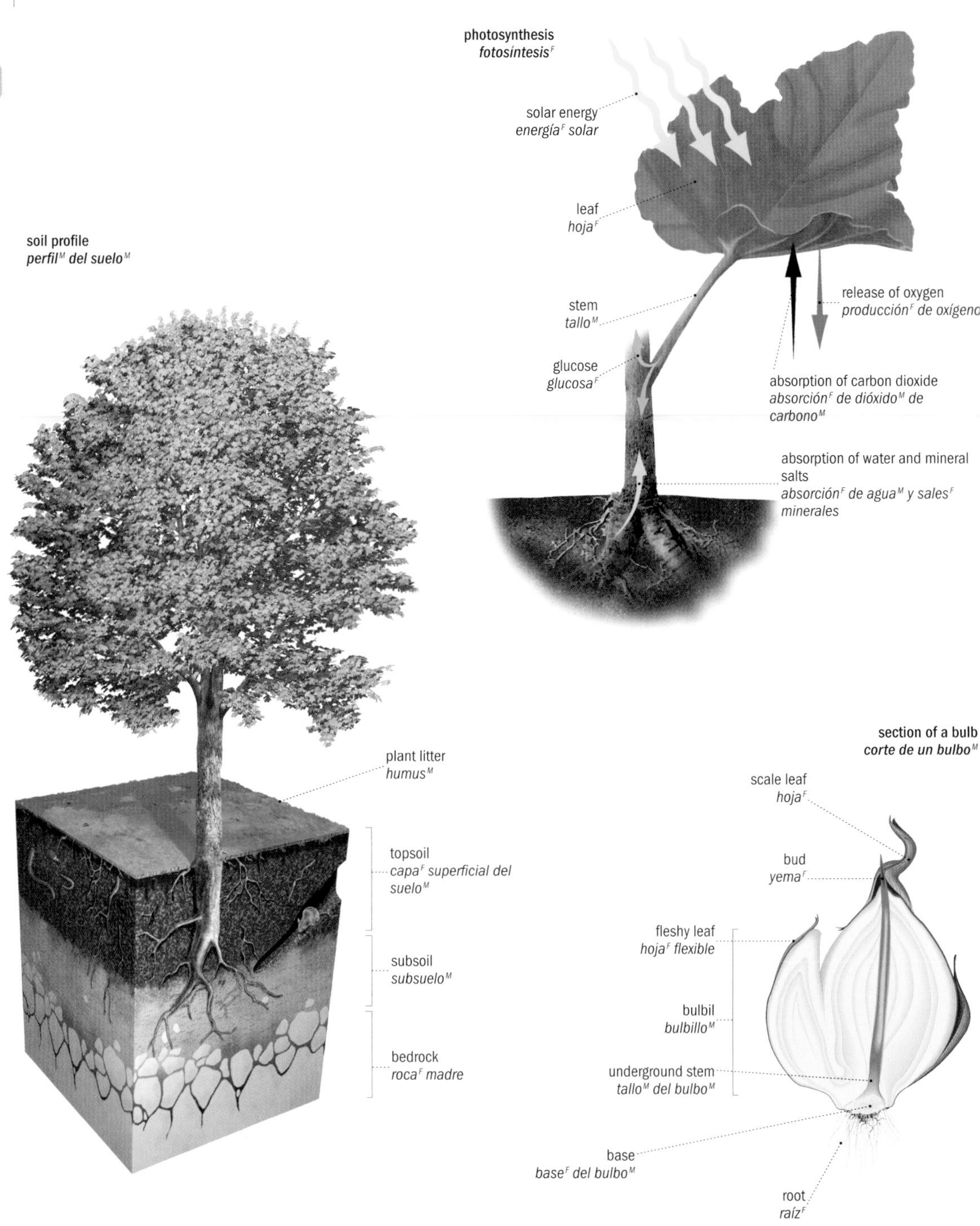
photosynthesis
fotosíntesis^F
solar energy
energía^F solar
leaf
hoja^F
stem
tallo^M
glucose
glucosa^F
release of oxygen
producción^F de oxígeno
absorption of carbon dioxide
absorción^F de dióxido^M de carbono^M
absorption of water and mineral salts
absorción^F de agua^M y sales^F minerales
soil profile
perfil^M del suelo^M
plant litter
humus^M
topsoil
capa^F superficial del suelo^M
subsoil
subsuelo^M
bedrock
roca^F madre
section of a bulb
corte de un bulbo^M
scale leaf
hoja^F
bud
yema^F
fleshy leaf
hoja^F flexible
bulbil
bulbillo^M
underground stem
tallo^M del bulbo^M
base
base^F del bulbo^M
root
raíz^F

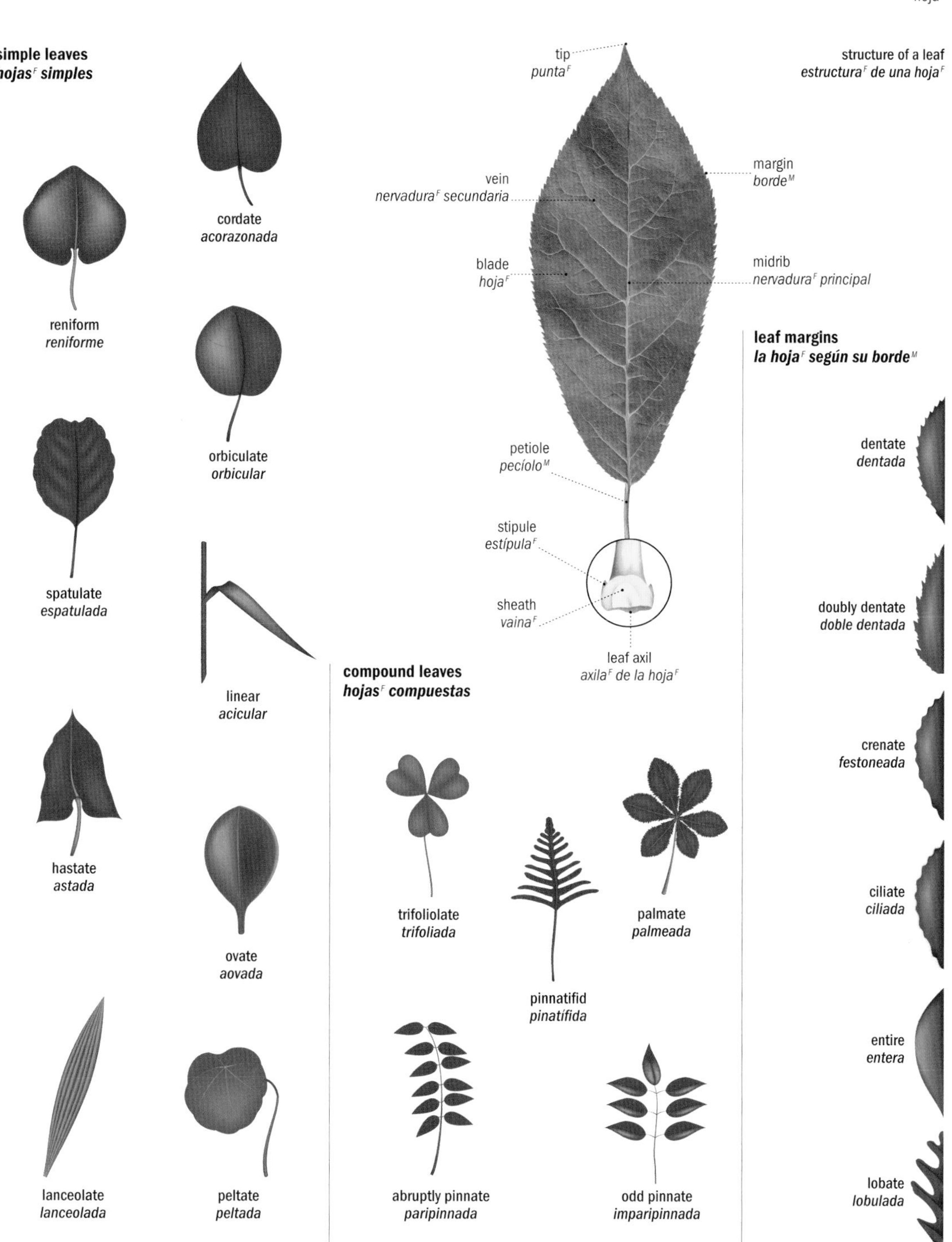
simple leaves
hojas^F simples
reniform
reniforme
cordate
acorazonada
orbiculate
orbicular
spatulate
espatulada
linear
acicular
hastate
astada
ovate
aovada
lanceolate
lanceolada
peltate
peltada
tip
punta^F
vein
nervadura^F secundaria
blade
hoja^F
petiole
pecíolo^M
stipule
estípula^F
sheath
vaina^F
leaf axil
axila^F de la hoja^F
structure of a leaf
estructura^F de una hoja^F
margin
borde^M
midrib
nervadura^F principal
compound leaves
hojas^F compuestas
trifoliolate
trifoliada
pinnatifid
pinatífida
palmate
palmeada
abruptly pinnate
paripinnada
odd pinnate
imparipinnada
leaf margins
la hoja^F según su borde^M
dentate
dentada
doubly dentate
doble dentada
crenate
festoneada
ciliate
ciliada
entire
entera
lobate
lobulada

flower

flor^{F}

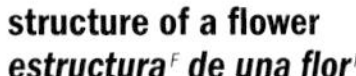

structure of a flower
estructura^{F} de una flor^{F}

pistil
pistilo^{M}

corolla
corola^{F}

stamen
estambre^{M}

calyx
cáliz^{M}

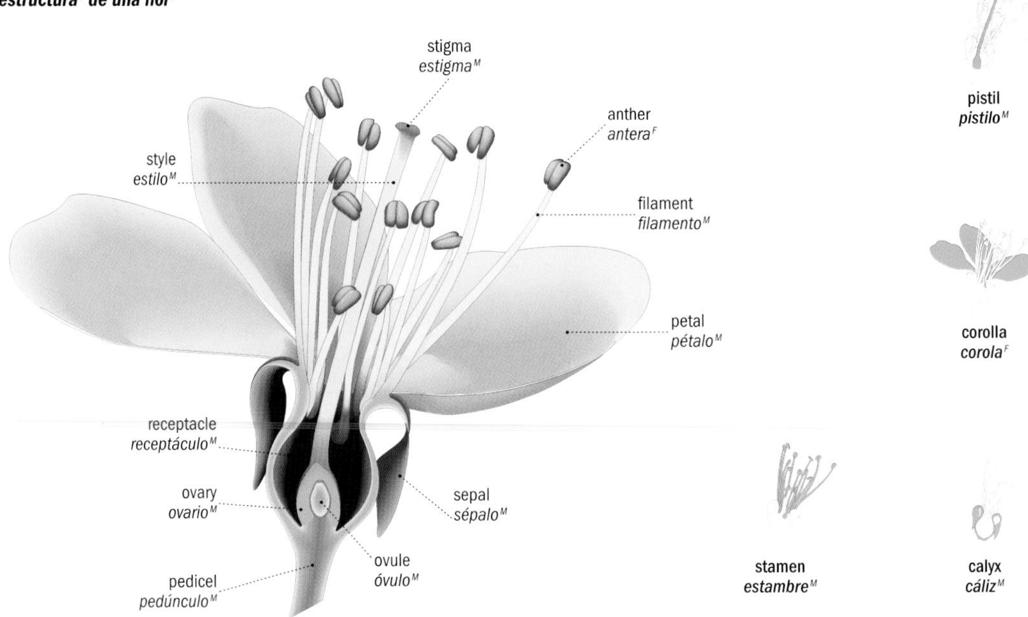

examples of flowers
ejemplos^{M} de flores^{F}

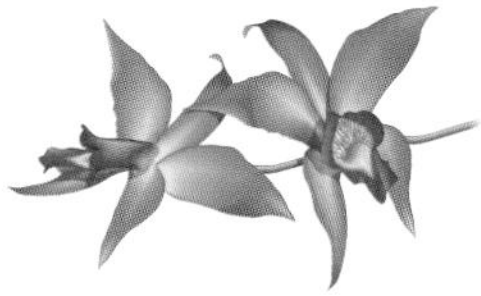

orchid
orquídea^{F}

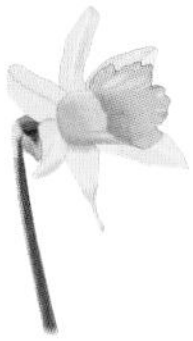

daffodil
narciso^{M}

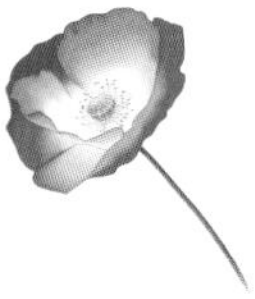

poppy
amapola^{F}

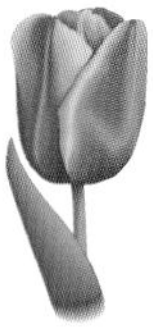

tulip
tulipán^{M}

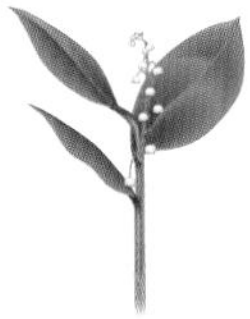

lily of the valley
muguete^{M}

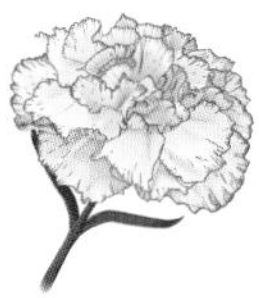

carnation
clavel^{M}

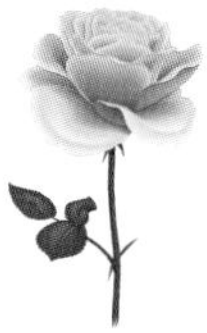

rose
rosa^{F}

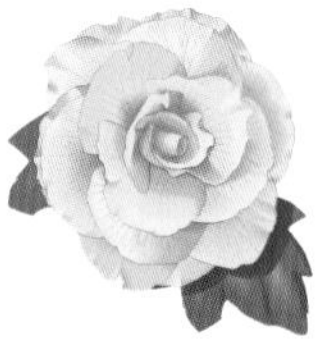

begonia
begonia^{F}

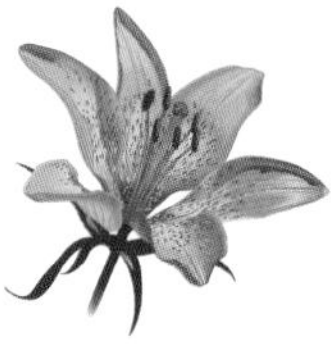

lily
azucena^{F}

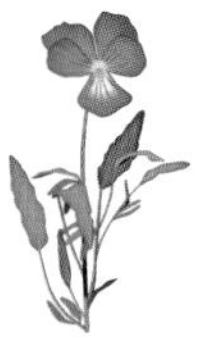

violet
violeta^{F}

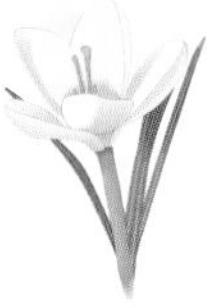

crocus
croco^{M}

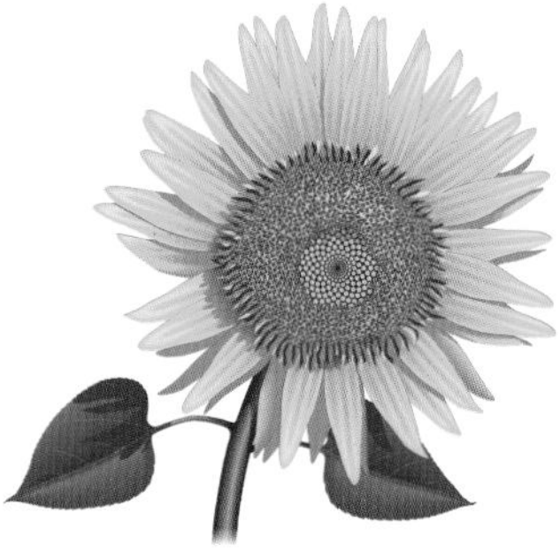

sunflower
girasol^{M}

types of inflorescences
variedades[F] de inflorescencias[F]

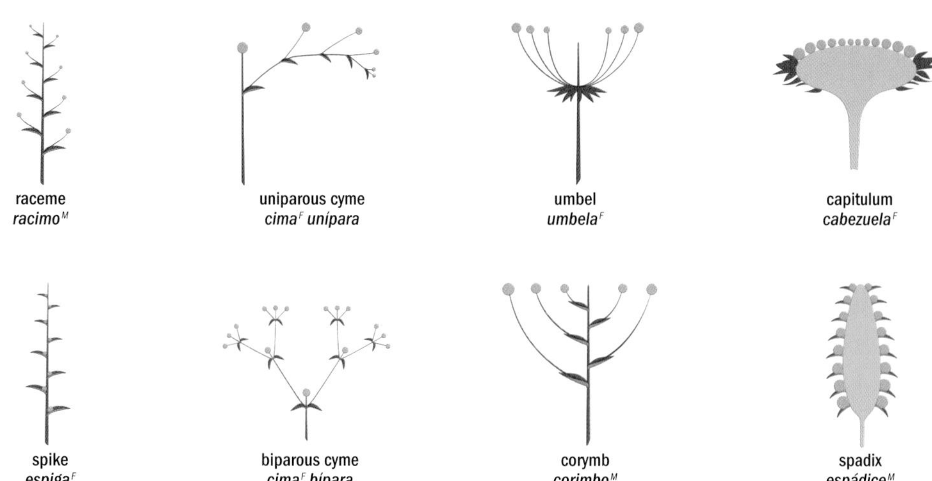

fruit

frutos[M]

fleshy fruit: stone fruit
drupa[F]

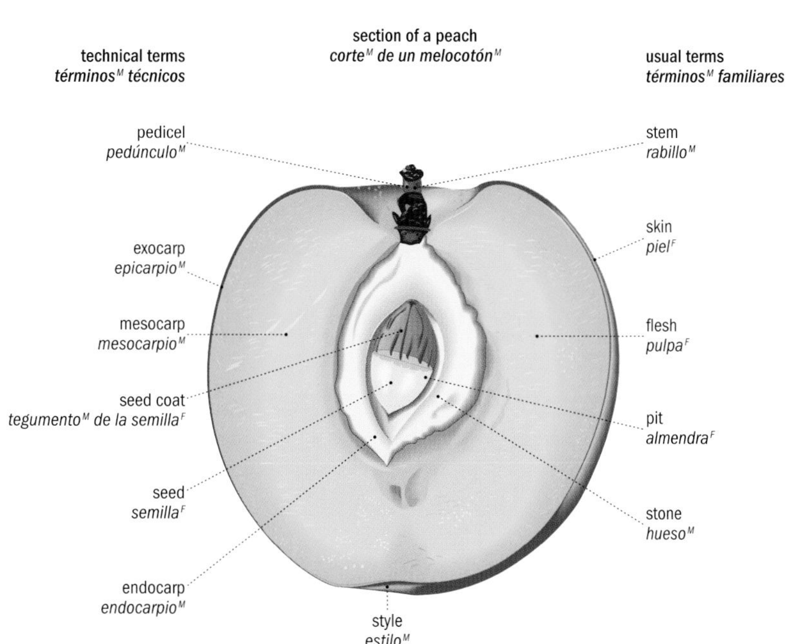

fleshy fruit: pome fruit
pomo^M carnoso

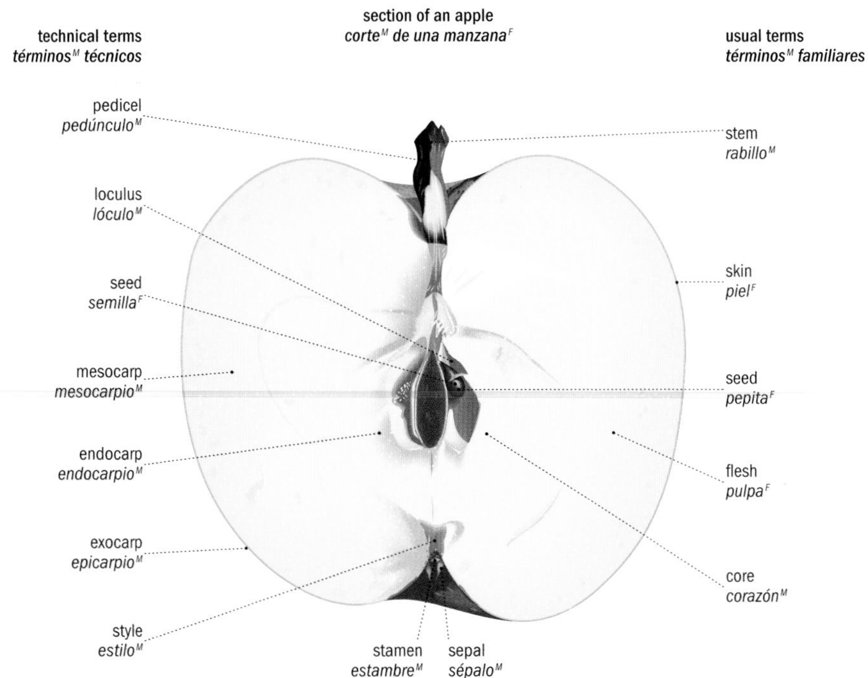

fleshy fruit: citrus fruit
fruto^M carnoso: cítrico^M

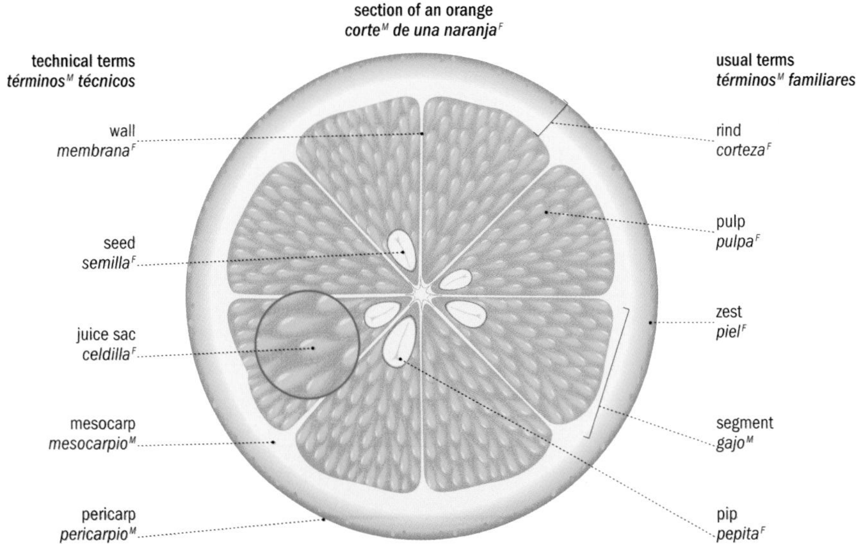

fleshy fruit: berry fruit
fruto^F carnoso: baya^F

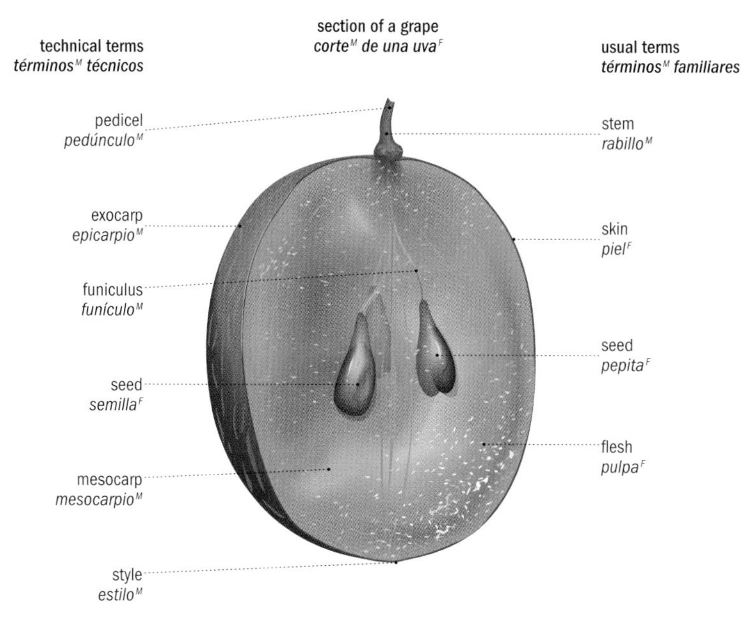
section of a grape
corte^M de una uva^F
technical terms
términos^M técnicos
usual terms
términos^M familiares
pedicel
pedúnculo^M
stem
rabillo^M
exocarp
epicarpio^M
skin
piel^F
funiculus
funículo^M
seed
pepita^F
seed
semilla^F
flesh
pulpa^F
mesocarp
mesocarpio^M
style
estilo^M

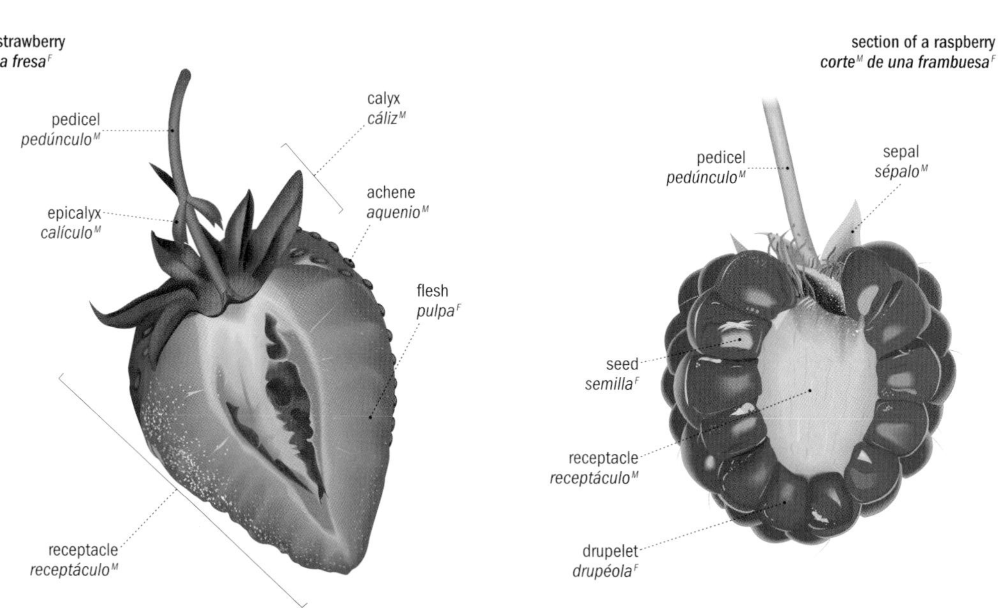
section of a strawberry
corte^M de una fresa^F
pedicel
pedúnculo^M
calyx
cáliz^M
epicalyx
calículo^M
achene
aquenio^M
flesh
pulpa^F
receptacle
receptáculo^M
section of a raspberry
corte^M de una frambuesa^F
pedicel
pedúnculo^M
sepal
sépalo^M
seed
semilla^F
receptacle
receptáculo^M
drupelet
drupéola^F

dry fruits
frutos*^M *secos

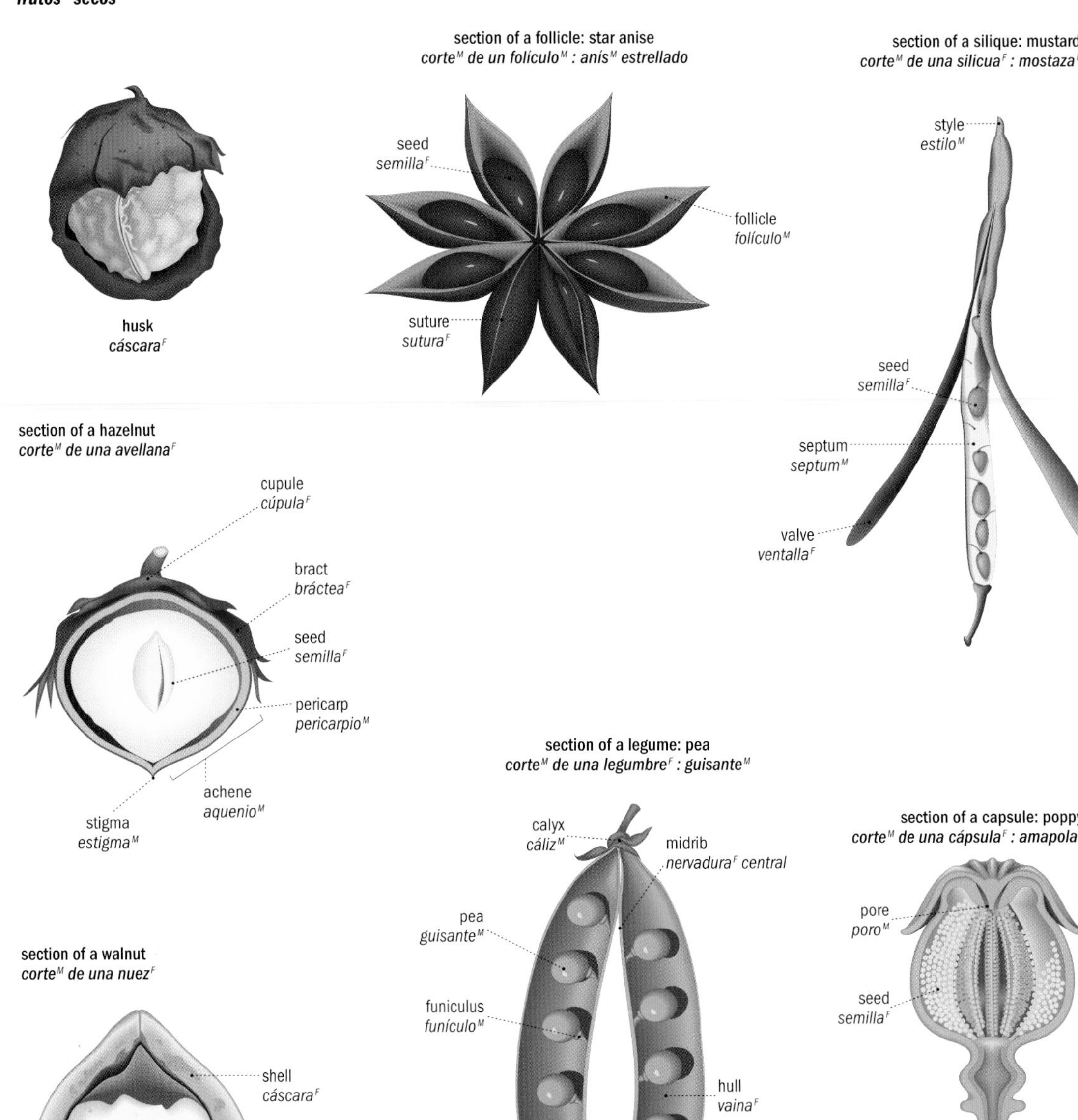
husk
cáscara^F
section of a follicle: star anise
corte^M de un folículo^M : anís^M estrellado
seed
semilla^F
follicle
folículo^M
suture
sutura^F
section of a silique: mustard
corte^M de una silicua^F : mostaza^F
style
estilo^M
seed
semilla^F
septum
septum^M
valve
ventalla^F
section of a hazelnut
corte^M de una avellana^F
cupule
cúpula^F
bract
bráctea^F
seed
semilla^F
pericarp
pericarpio^M
achene
aquenio^M
stigma
estigma^M
section of a legume: pea
corte^M de una legumbre^F : guisante^M
calyx
cáliz^M
midrib
nervadura^F central
pea
guisante^M
funiculus
funículo^M
hull
vaina^F
suture
sutura^F
style
estilo^M
section of a capsule: poppy
corte^M de una cápsula^F : amapola^F
pore
poro^M
seed
semilla^F
section of a walnut
corte^M de una nuez^F
shell
cáscara^F
green walnut
nuez^F verde
partition
bizna^F

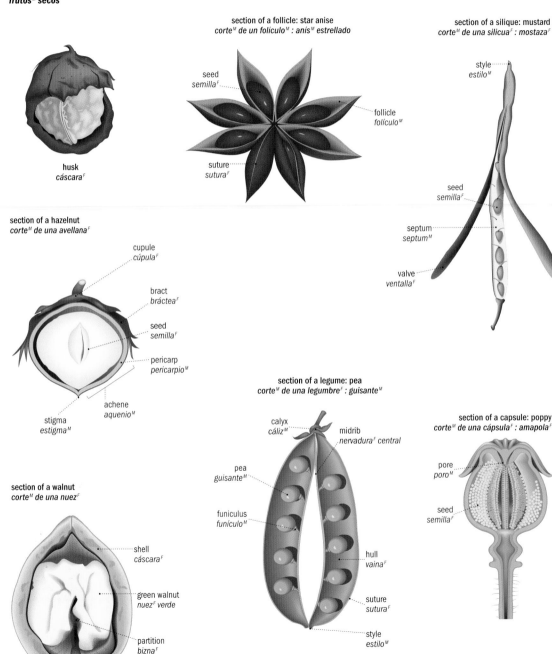

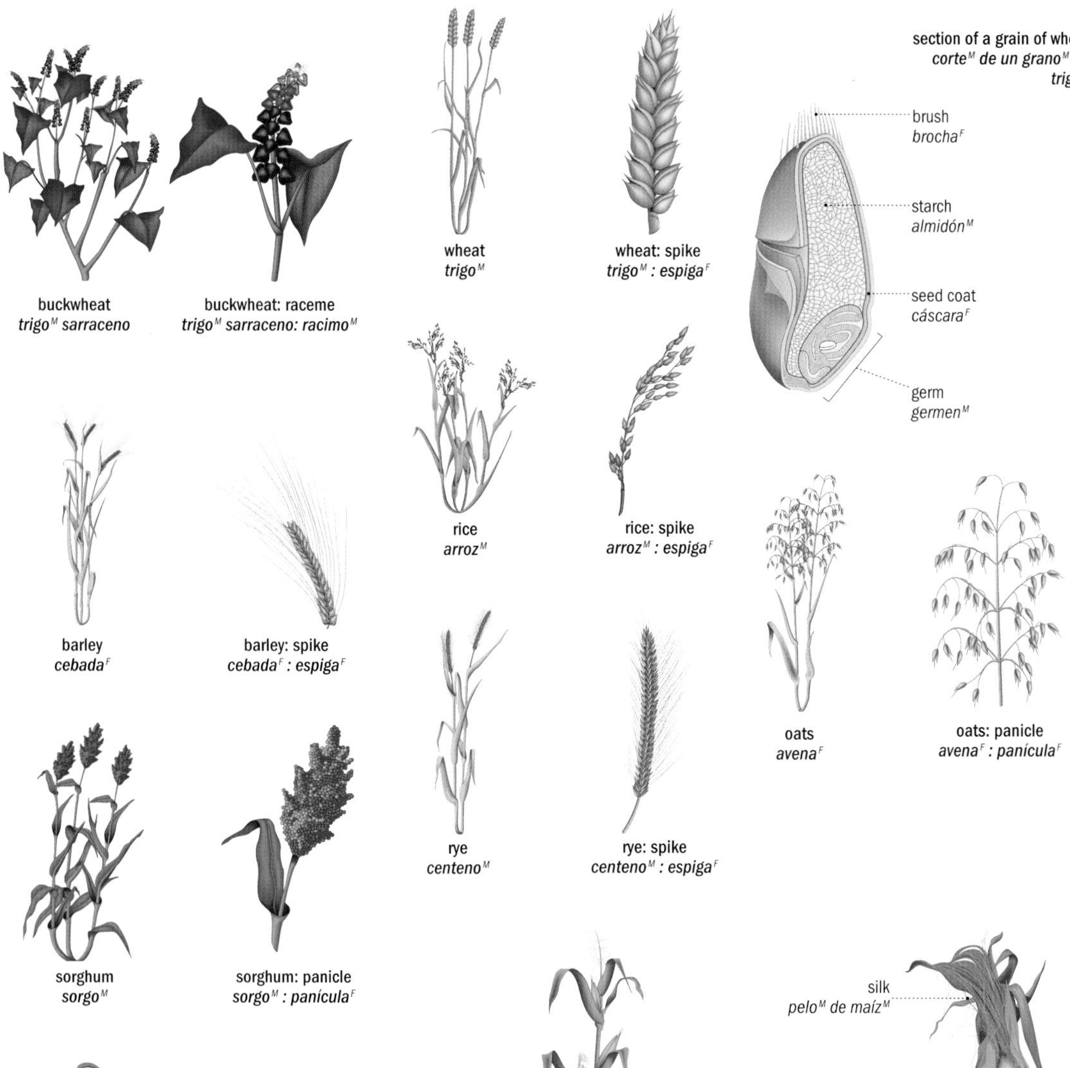

millet
mijo[M]

millet: spike
mijo[M] : espiga[F]

corn
maíz[M]

silk
pelo[M] de maíz[M]

cob
mazorca[F]

husk
hoja[F]

kernel
grano[M]

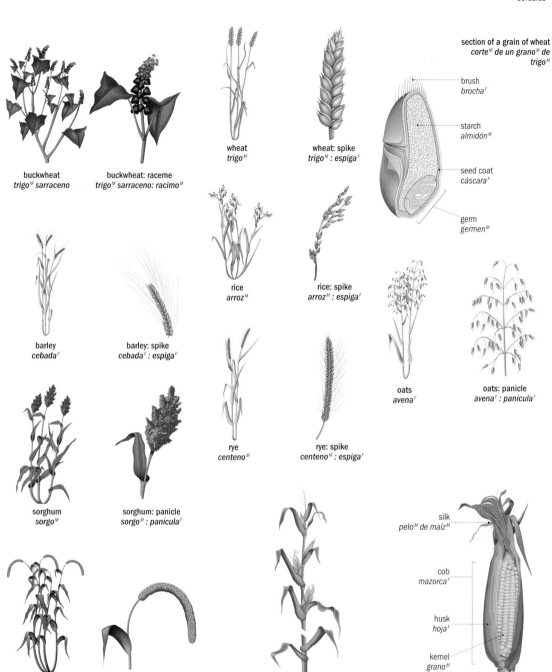

corn: cob
maíz[M] : mazorca[F]

grape

uva[F]

bunch of grapes
racimo[M] de uvas[F]

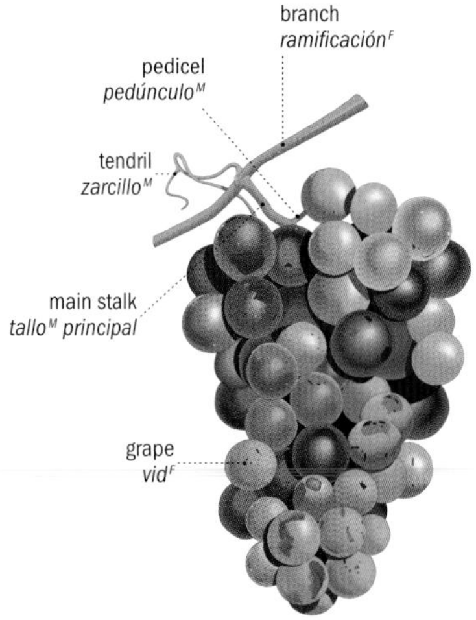

branch
ramificación[F]

pedicel
pedúnculo[M]

tendril
zarcillo[M]

main stalk
tallo[M] principal

grape
vid[F]

vine stock
cepa[F] de vid[F]

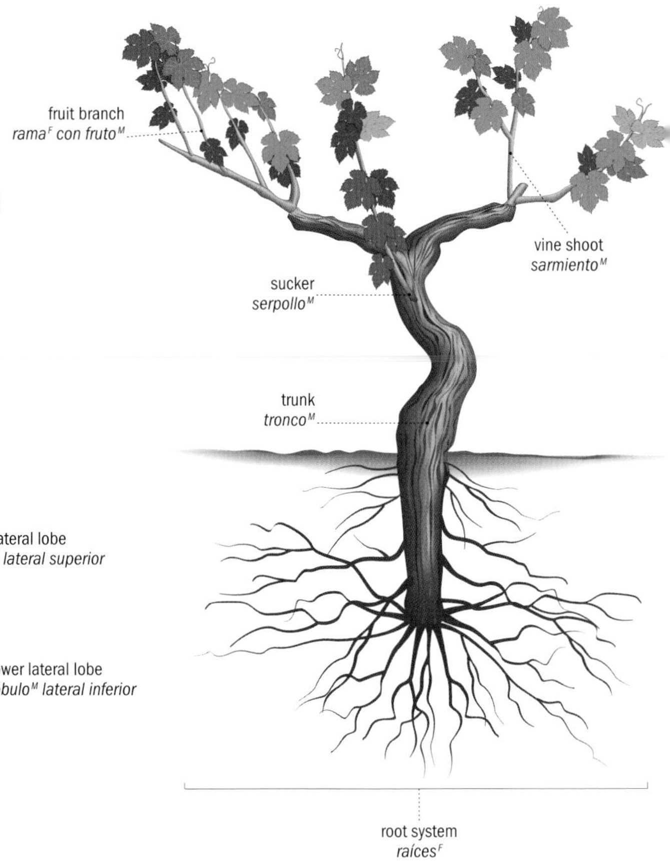

fruit branch
rama[F] con fruto[M]

vine shoot
sarmiento[M]

sucker
serpollo[M]

trunk
tronco[M]

root system
raíces[F]

grape leaf
hoja[F] de la vid[F]

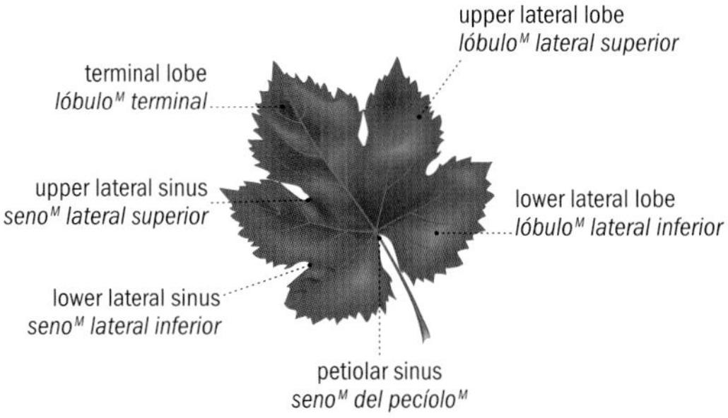

upper lateral lobe
lóbulo[M] lateral superior

terminal lobe
lóbulo[M] terminal

upper lateral sinus
seno[M] lateral superior

lower lateral lobe
lóbulo[M] lateral inferior

lower lateral sinus
seno[M] lateral inferior

petiolar sinus
seno[M] del pecíolo[M]

steps in maturation
etapas[F] de la maduración[F]

flowering
floración[F]

fruition
fructificación[F]

ripening
envero[M]

ripeness
madurez[F]

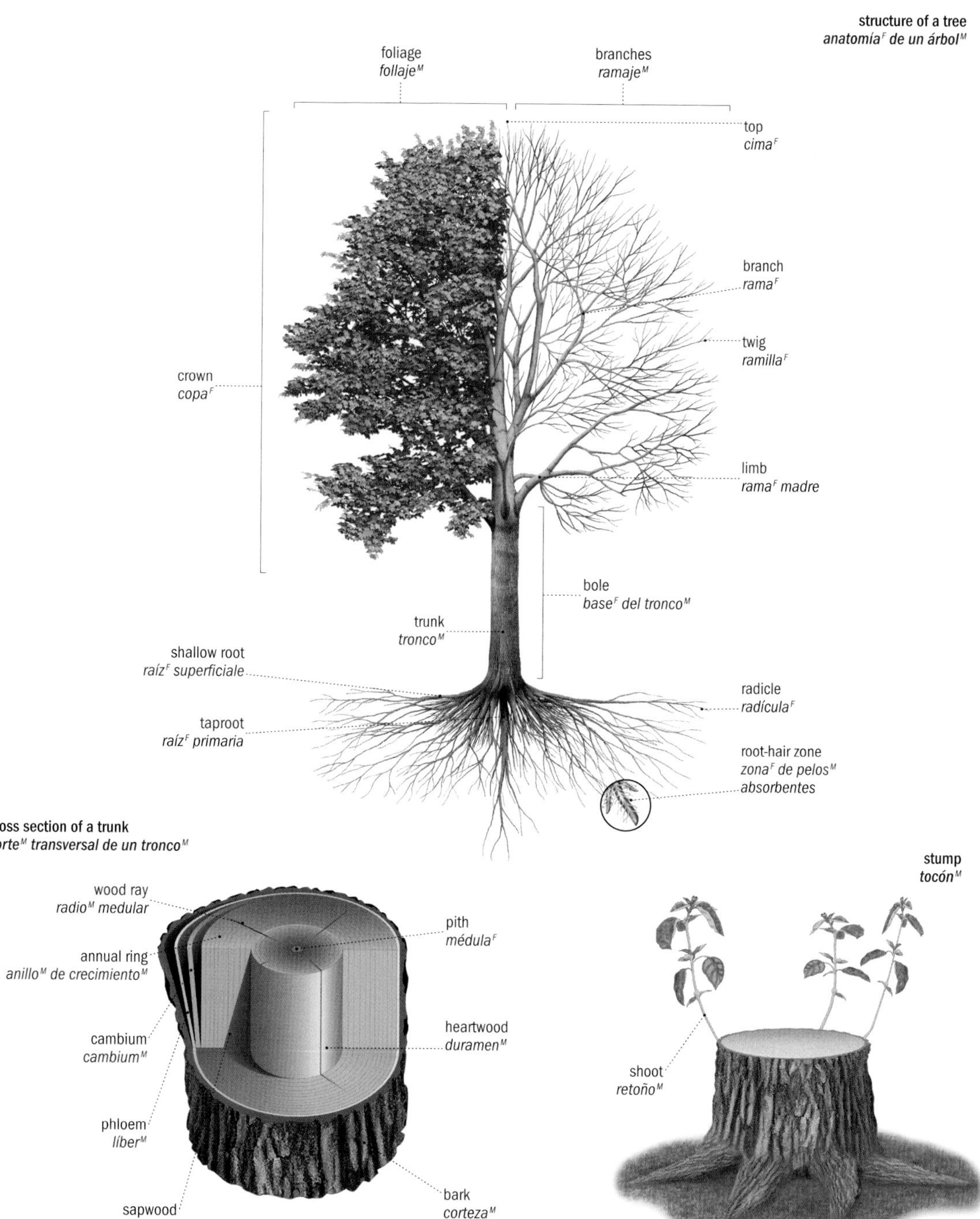
structure of a tree
anatomía[F] de un árbol[M]
foliage
follaje[M]
branches
ramaje[M]
top
cima[F]
branch
rama[F]
twig
ramilla[F]
crown
copa[F]
limb
rama[F] madre
bole
base[F] del tronco[M]
trunk
tronco[M]
shallow root
raíz[F] superficiale
radicle
radícula[F]
taproot
raíz[F] primaria
root-hair zone
zona[F] de pelos[M] absorbentes
cross section of a trunk
corte[M] transversal de un tronco[M]
wood ray
radio[M] medular
pith
médula[F]
annual ring
anillo[M] de crecimiento[M]
heartwood
duramen[M]
cambium
cambium[M]
phloem
líber[M]
sapwood
albura[F]
bark
corteza[M]
stump
tocón[M]
shoot
retoño[M]

examples of broadleaved trees
***ejemplos*[M] *de latifolios*[M]**

cone
piña[F]

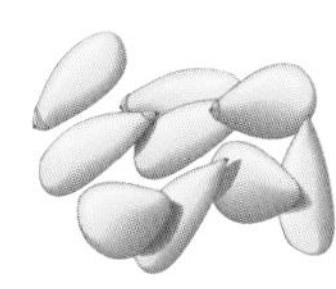

pine seed
piñón[M]

branch
rama[F]

examples of leaves
***ejemplos*[M] *de hojas*[F]**

fir needles
agujas[F] *del abeto*[M]

pine needles
agujas[F] *del pino*[M]

cypress scalelike leaves
hojas[F] *escamadas del ciprés*[M]

examples of conifers
***ejemplos*[M] *de coníferas*[F]**

umbrella pine
pino[M] *piñonero*

cedar of Lebanon
cedro[M] *del Líbano*[M]

spruce
pícea[F]

larch
alerce[M]

fir
abeto[M]

animal cell

célula[F] animal

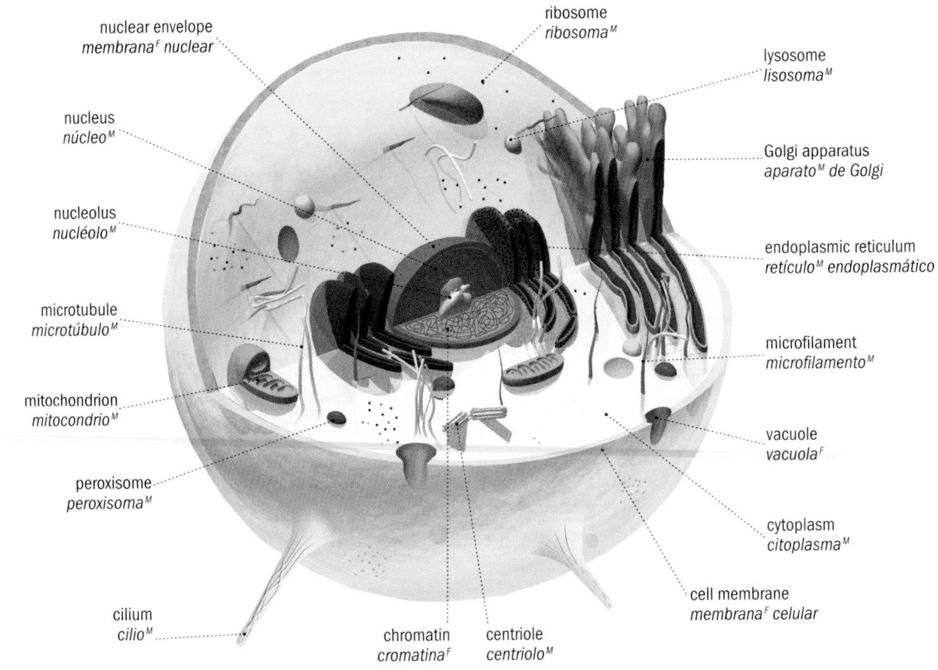

nuclear envelope
membrana[F] nuclear
ribosome
ribosoma[M]
lysosome
lisosoma[M]
nucleus
núcleo[M]
Golgi apparatus
aparato[M] de Golgi
nucleolus
nucléolo[M]
endoplasmic reticulum
retículo[M] endoplasmático
microtubule
microtúbulo[M]
microfilament
microfilamento[M]
mitochondrion
mitocondrio[M]
vacuole
vacuola[F]
peroxisome
peroxisoma[M]
cytoplasm
citoplasma[M]
cell membrane
membrana[F] celular
cilium
cilio[M]
chromatin
cromatina[F]
centriole
centriolo[M]

unicellulars

unicelulares[M]

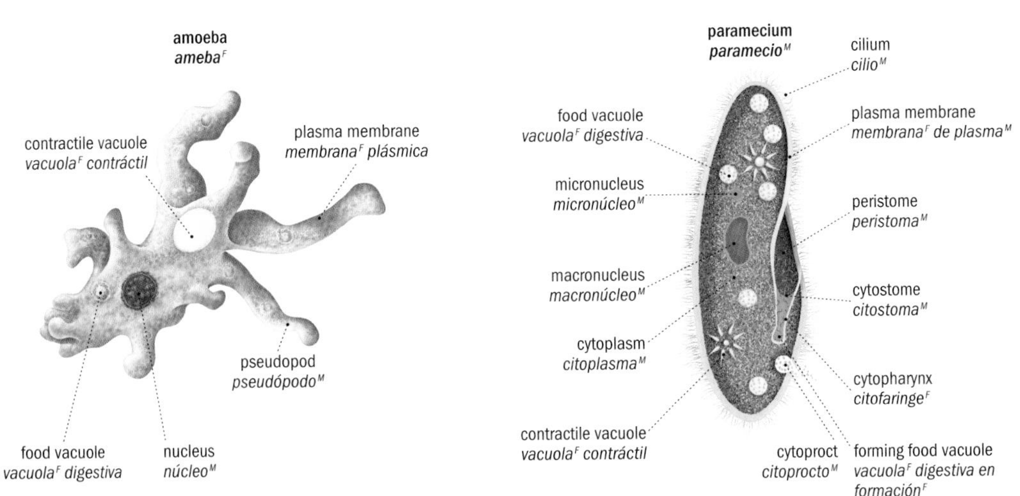

amoeba
ameba[F]
contractile vacuole
vacuola[F] contráctil
plasma membrane
membrana[F] plásmica
pseudopod
pseudópodo[M]
food vacuole
vacuola[F] digestiva
nucleus
núcleo[M]
paramecium
paramecio[M]
cilium
cilio[M]
food vacuole
vacuola[F] digestiva
plasma membrane
membrana[F] de plasma[M]
micronucleus
micronúcleo[M]
peristome
peristoma[M]
macronucleus
macronúcleo[M]
cytostome
citostoma[M]
cytoplasm
citoplasma[M]
cytopharynx
citofaringe[F]
contractile vacuole
vacuola[F] contráctil
cytoproct
citoprocto[M]
forming food vacuole
vacuola[F] digestiva en formación[F]

butterfly
mariposa^F

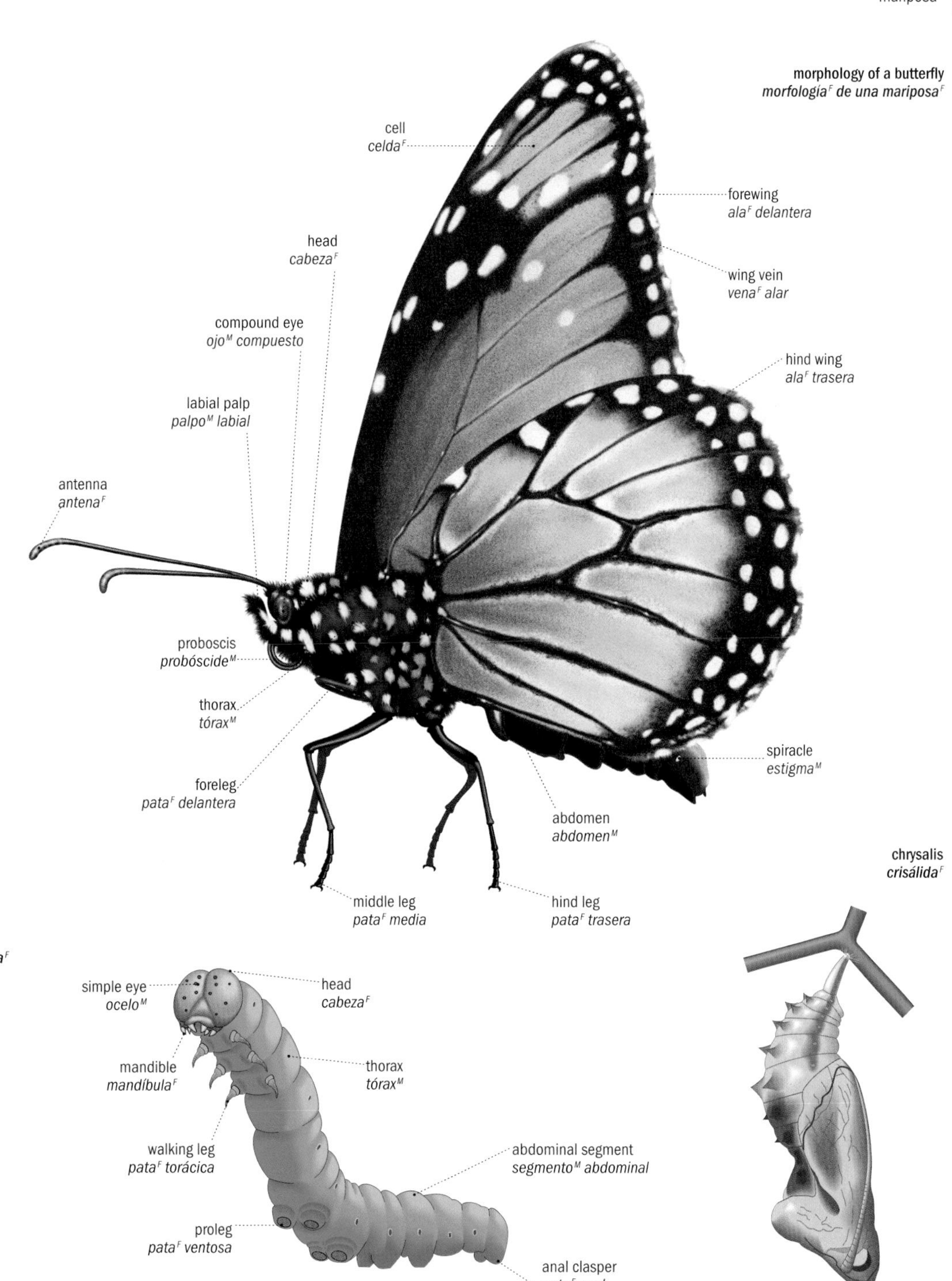
morphology of a butterfly
morfología^F de una mariposa^F
cell
celda^F
forewing
ala^F delantera
head
cabeza^F
wing vein
vena^F alar
compound eye
ojo^M compuesto
hind wing
ala^F trasera
labial palp
palpo^M labial
antenna
antena^F
proboscis
probóscide^M
thorax
tórax^M
spiracle
estigma^M
foreleg
pata^F delantera
abdomen
abdomen^M
chrysalis
crisálida^F
middle leg
pata^F media
hind leg
pata^F trasera
larva
oruga^F
simple eye
ocelo^M
head
cabeza^F
mandible
mandíbula^F
thorax
tórax^M
walking leg
pata^F torácica
abdominal segment
segmento^M abdominal
proleg
pata^F ventosa
anal clasper
pata^F anal

honeybee

abeja^F

ANIMAL KINGDOM

morphology of a honeybee: worker
morfología^F de una abeja^F trabajadora^F

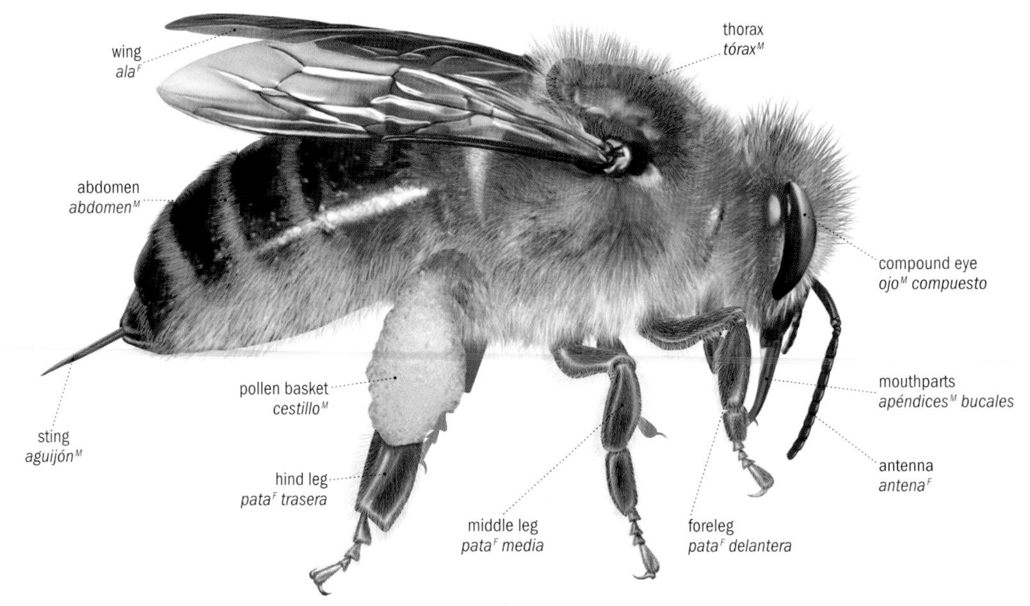

castes
castas^F

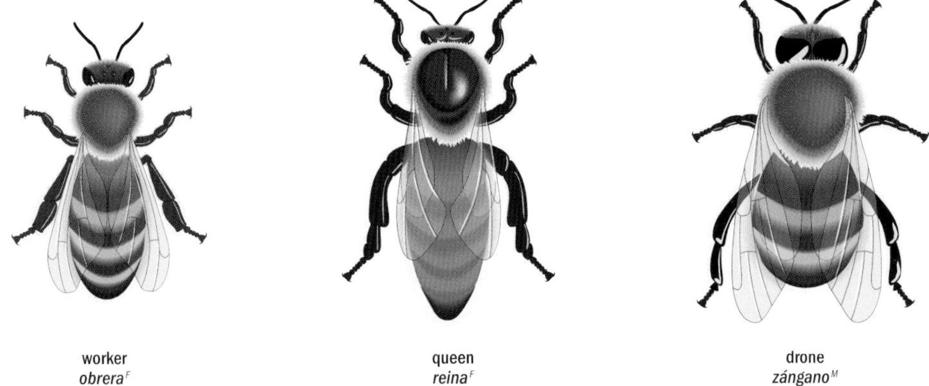

examples of insects

ejemplos[M] de insectos[M]

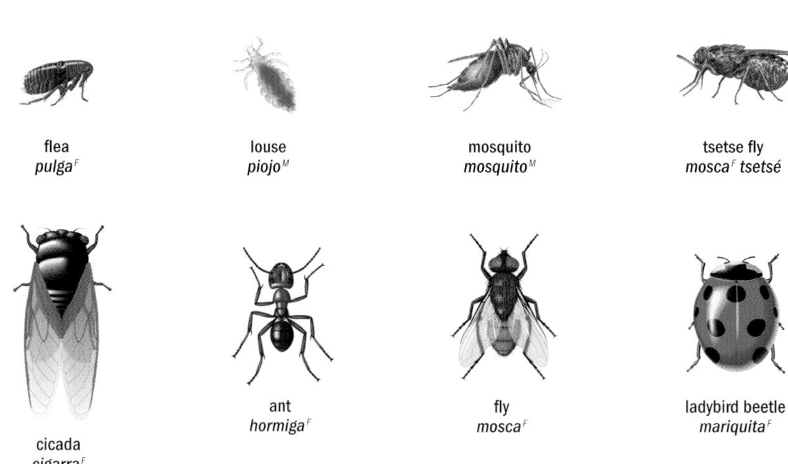

flea
pulga[F]

louse
piojo[M]

mosquito
mosquito[M]

tsetse fly
mosca[F] *tsetsé*

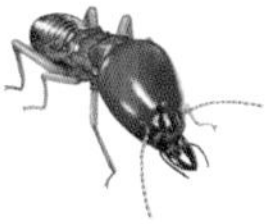

termite
termita[F]

cicada
cigarra[F]

ant
hormiga[F]

fly
mosca[F]

ladybird beetle
mariquita[F]

shield bug
chinche[F] *de campo*[M]

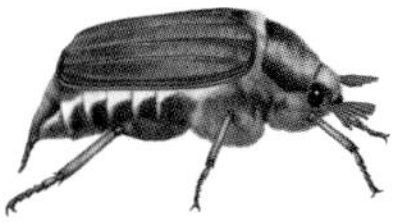

cockchafer
escarabajo[M]

yellowjacket
avispa[F]

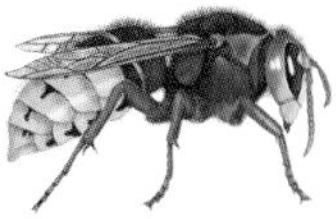

hornet
avispón[M]

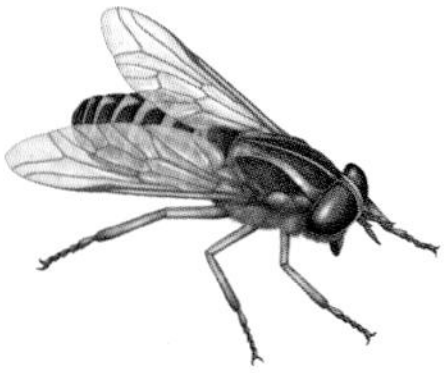

horsefly
tábano[M]

bumblebee
abejorro[M]

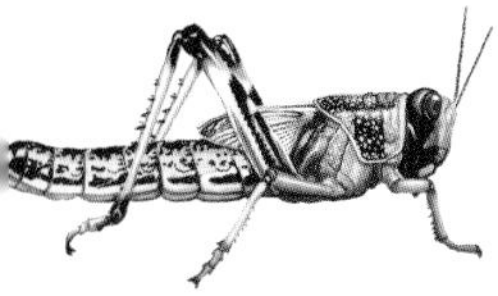

bow-winged grasshopper
grillo[M] *campestre*

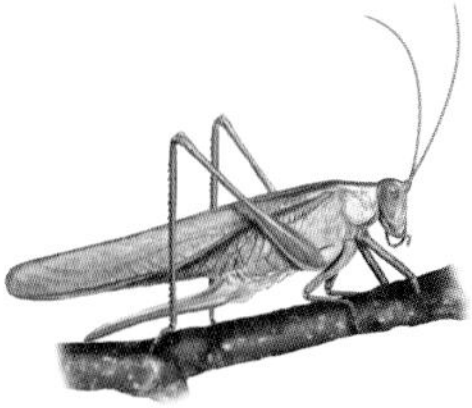

great green bush-cricket
saltamontes[M] *verde*

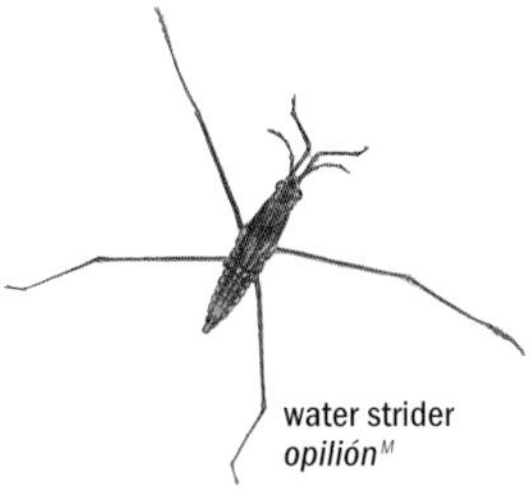

water strider
opilión[M]

dragonfly
libélula[F]

atlas moth
oruga[F] *de polilla*[F]

mantid
mantis[F] *religiosa*

spider

araña[F]

spider web
tela[F] de araña[F]

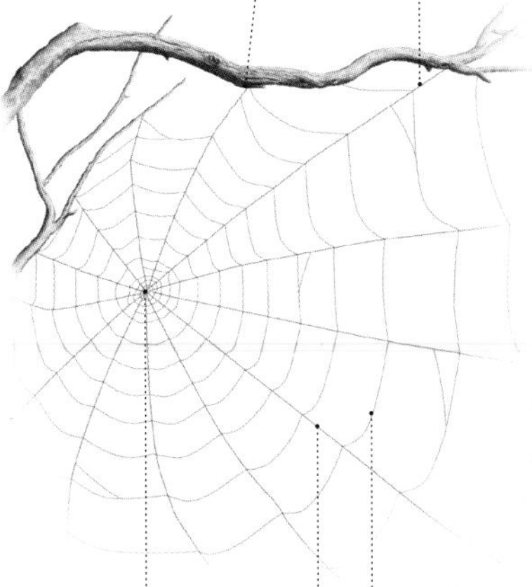

anchor point
punto[M] de apoyo[M]
support thread
cabo[M] de soporte[M]
hub
espiral[F] central
spiral thread
espiral[F]
radial thread
radio[M]

morphology of a spider
morfología[F] de una araña[F]

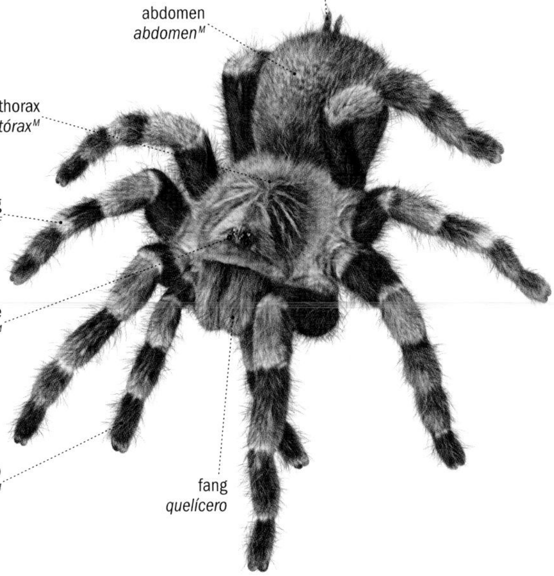

spinneret
hileras[F]
abdomen
abdomen[M]
cephalothorax
cefalotórax[M]
leg
pata[F] de locomoción[F]
eye
ojo[M]
pedipalp
pedipalpo[M]
fang
quelícero

examples of arachnids

ejemplos[M] de arácnidos[M]

crab spider
araña[M] cangrejo

tick
garrapata[F]

water spider
araña[F] de agua[F]

garden spider
epeira[F]

red-kneed tarantula
migala[F]

scorpion
escorpión[M]

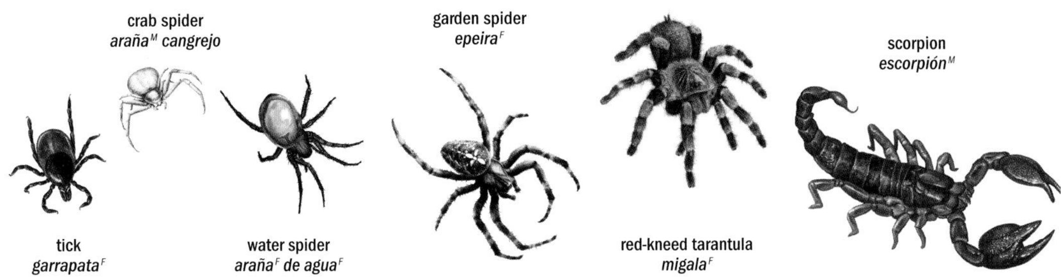

lobster

bogavante^M

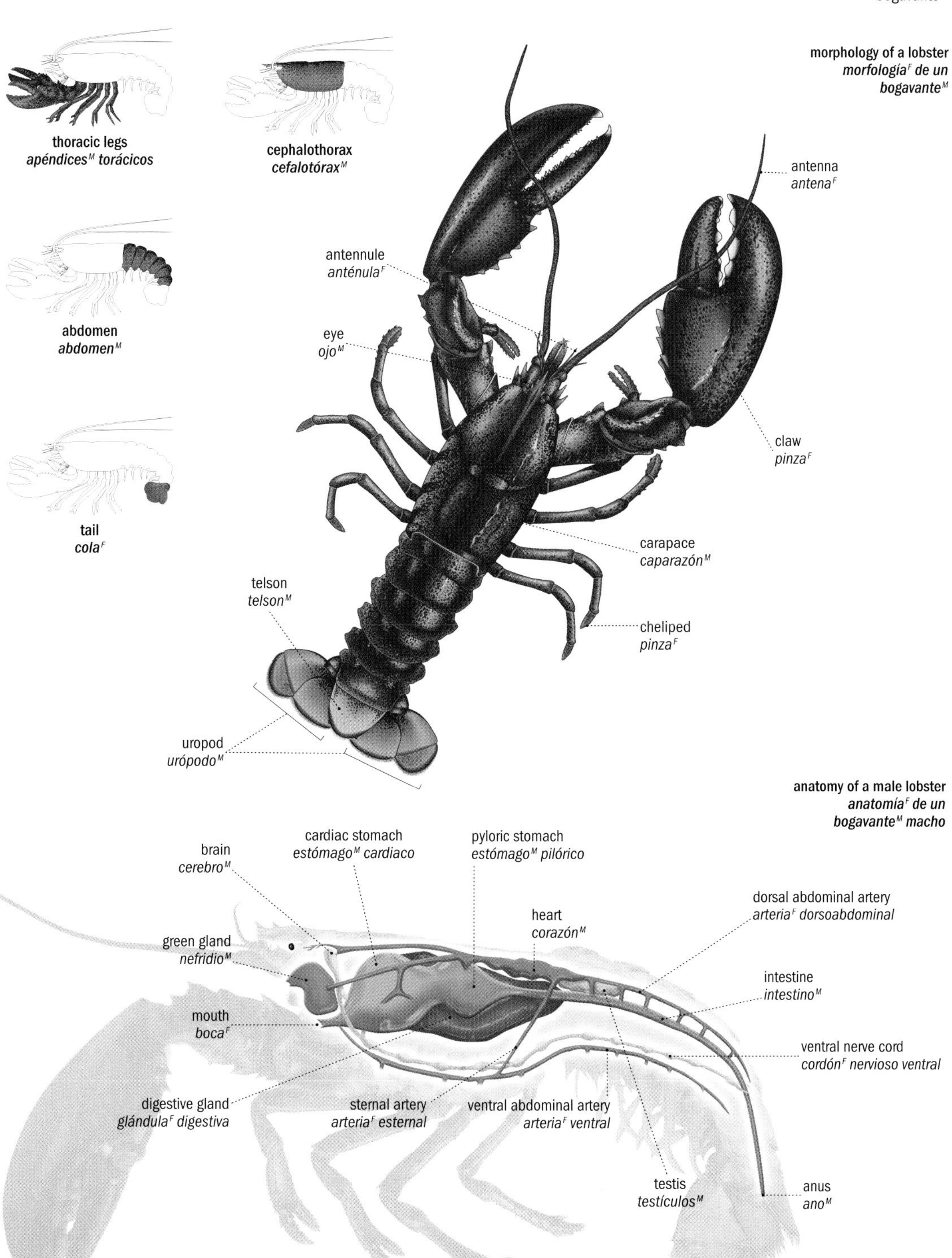
thoracic legs
apéndices^M torácicos
cephalothorax
cefalotórax^M
abdomen
abdomen^M
tail
cola^F
morphology of a lobster
morfología^F de un bogavante^M
antenna
antena^F
antennule
anténula^F
eye
ojo^M
claw
pinza^F
carapace
caparazón^M
telson
telson^M
cheliped
pinza^F
uropod
urópodo^M
anatomy of a male lobster
anatomía^F de un bogavante^M macho
brain
cerebro^M
cardiac stomach
estómago^M cardiaco
pyloric stomach
estómago^M pilórico
heart
corazón^M
dorsal abdominal artery
arteria^F dorsoabdominal
green gland
nefridio^M
intestine
intestino^M
mouth
boca^F
ventral nerve cord
cordón^F nervioso ventral
digestive gland
glándula^F digestiva
sternal artery
arteria^F esternal
ventral abdominal artery
arteria^F ventral
testis
testículos^M
anus
ano^M

ANIMAL KINGDOM

snail

caracol^M

morphology of a snail
morfología^F de un caracol^M

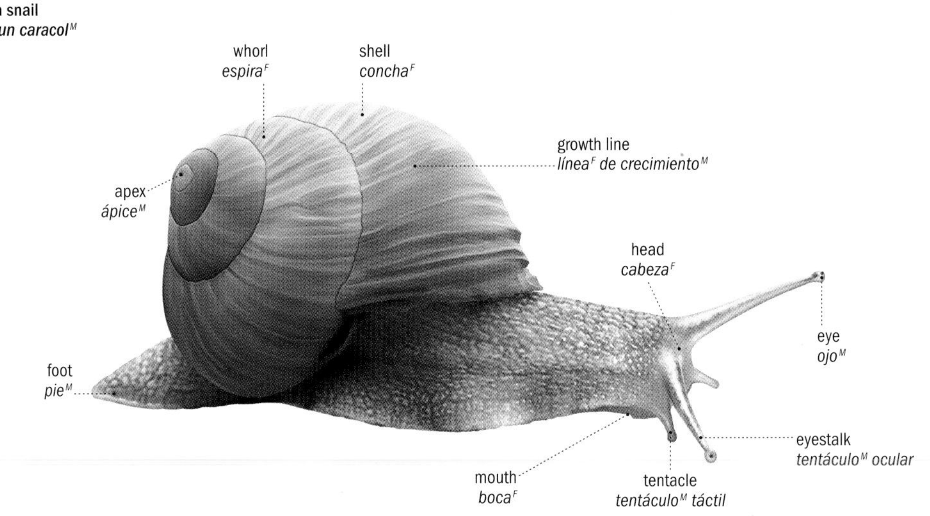

octopus

pulpo^M

morphology of an octopus
morfología^F de un pulpo^M

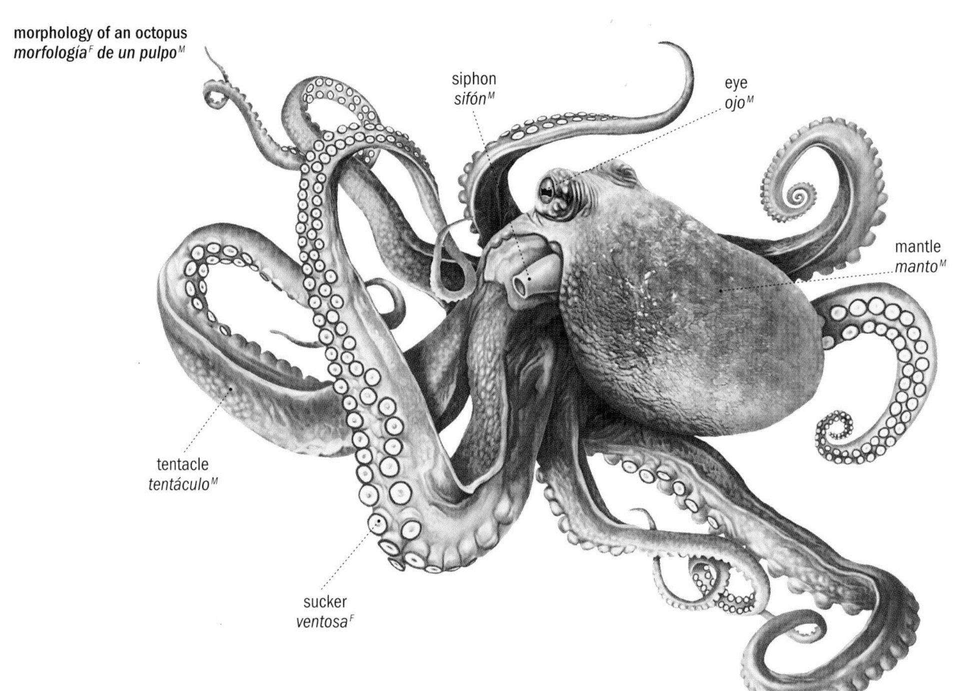

univalve shell

concha^F univalva

morphology of a univalve shell
morfología^F de una concha^F univalva
apex
ápice^M
nuclear whorl
espiral^F embrionaria
columella
columela^F
whorl
espiral^F
axial rib
costilla^F axial
suture
sutura^F
spiral rib
costilla^F espiral
aperture
apertura^F terminal
outer lip
labio^M externo
columella fold
pliegue^M de la columela^F
inner lip
labio^M interno
siphonal canal
canal^M del sifón^M

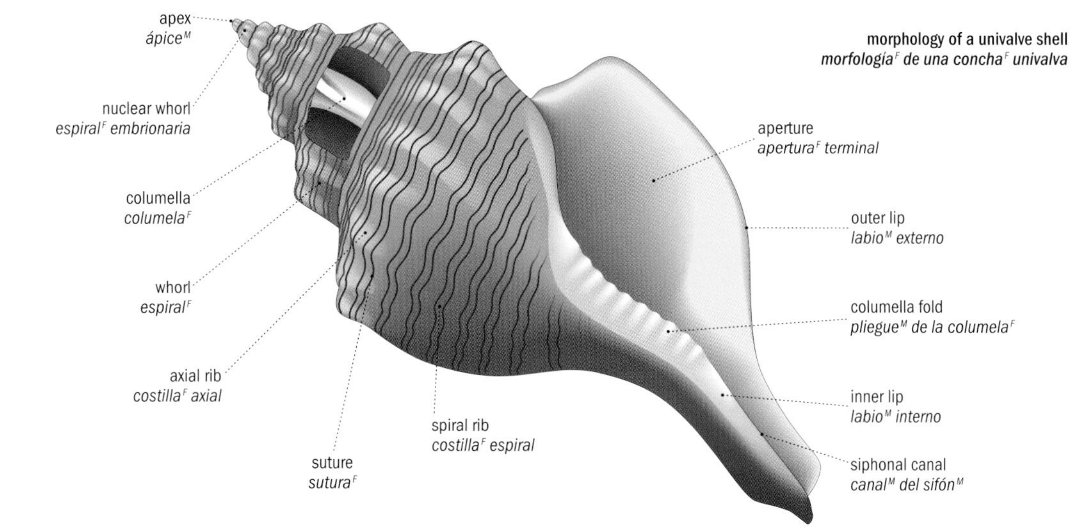

bivalve shell

concha^F bivalva

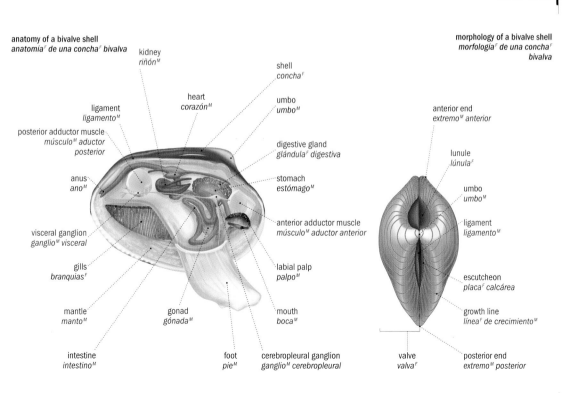

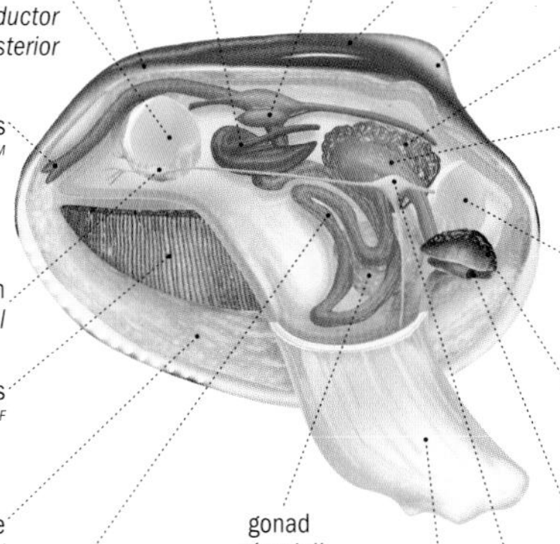

anatomy of a bivalve shell
anatomía^F de una concha^F bivalva
kidney
riñón^M
shell
concha^F
heart
corazón^M
umbo
umbo^M
ligament
ligamento^M
posterior adductor muscle
músculo^M aductor posterior
digestive gland
glándula^F digestiva
anus
ano^M
stomach
estómago^M
anterior adductor muscle
músculo^M aductor anterior
visceral ganglion
ganglio^M visceral
gills
branquias^F
labial palp
palpo^M
mantle
manto^M
gonad
gónada^M
mouth
boca^M
intestine
intestino^M
foot
pie^M
cerebropleural ganglion
ganglio^M cerebropleural

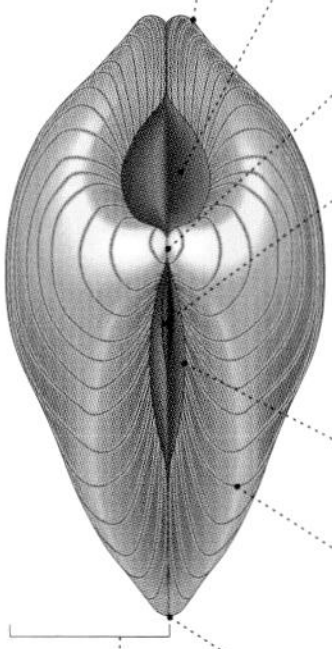

morphology of a bivalve shell
morfología^F de una concha^F bivalva
anterior end
extremo^M anterior
lunule
lúnula^F
umbo
umbo^M
ligament
ligamento^M
escutcheon
placa^F calcárea
growth line
línea^F de crecimiento^M
valve
valva^F
posterior end
extremo^M posterior

ANIMAL KINGDOM

cartilaginous fish

pez^M cartilaginoso

morphology of a female shark
morfología^F de un tiburón^M hembra
first dorsal fin
primera aleta^F dorsal
carina
carena^F
second dorsal fin
segunda aleta^F dorsal
caudal fin
aleta^F caudal
snout
hocico^M
nostril
narina^F
tooth
diente^M
pelvic fin
aleta^F pélvica
gill slits
aberturas^F branquiales
pectoral fin
aleta^F pectoral
anal fin
aleta^F anal

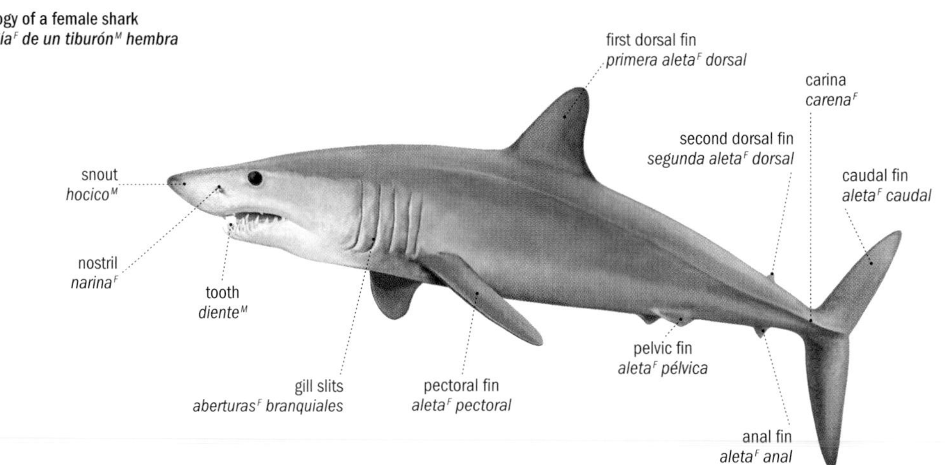

bony fish

pez^M óseo

morphology of a perch
morfología^F de una perca^F
spiny ray
radio^M espinoso
soft ray
radio^M blando
nostril
narina^F
lateral line
línea^F lateral
premaxilla
premaxilar^M
caudal fin
aleta^F caudal
mandible
mandíbula^F
maxilla
maxilar^M
pectoral fin
aleta^F pectoral
anal fin
aleta^F anal
operculum
opérculo^M
pelvic fin
aleta^F abdominal
scale
escama^F

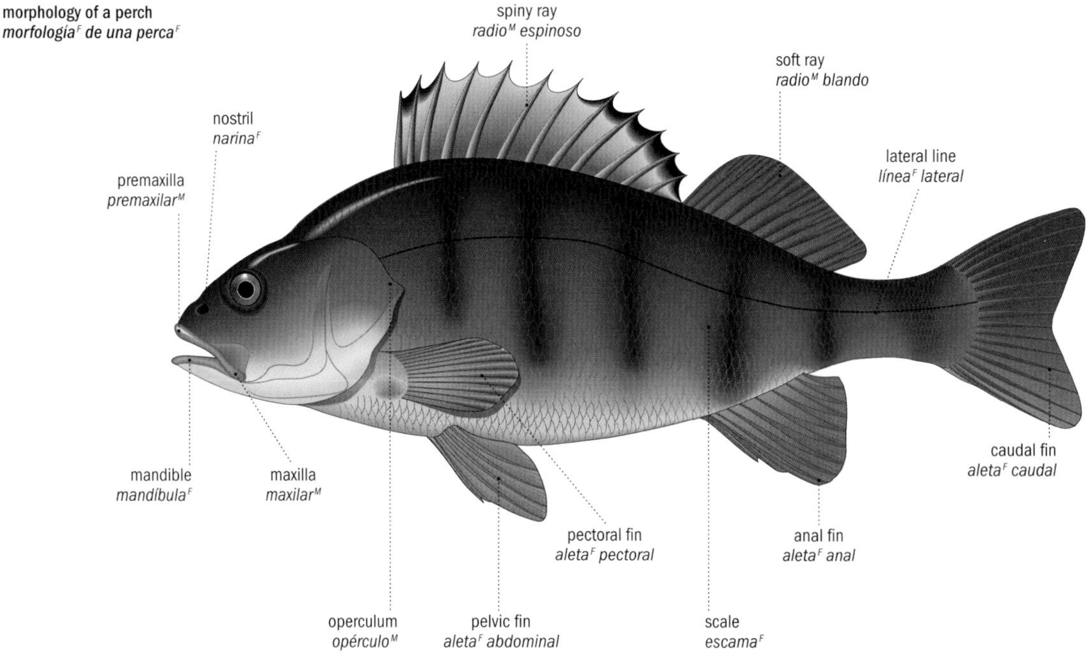

frog

rana[F]

morphology of a frog
morfología[F] de una rana[F]

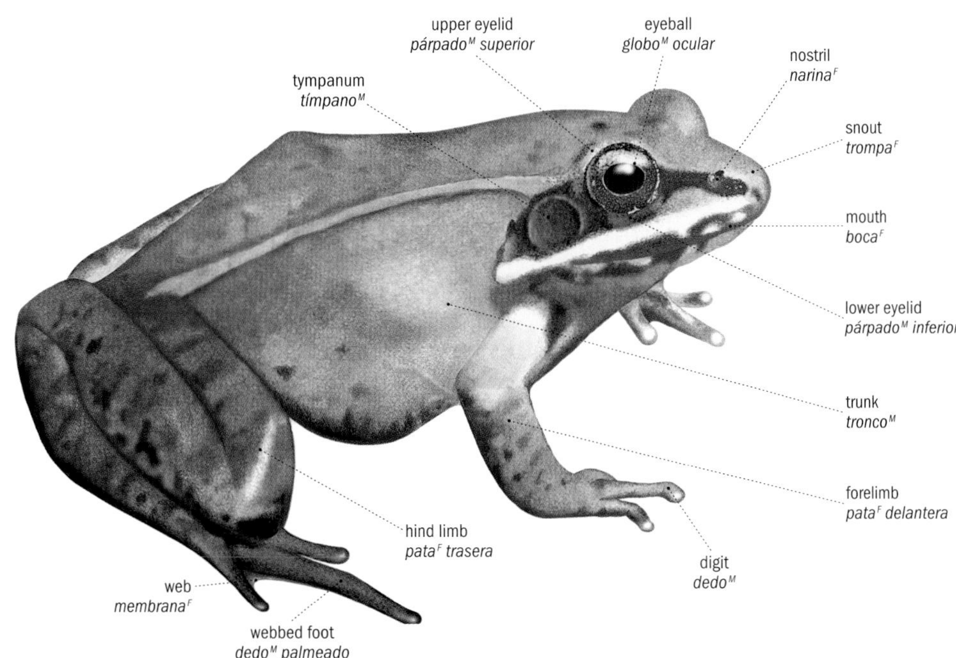

examples of amphibians

ejemplos[M] de anfibios[M]

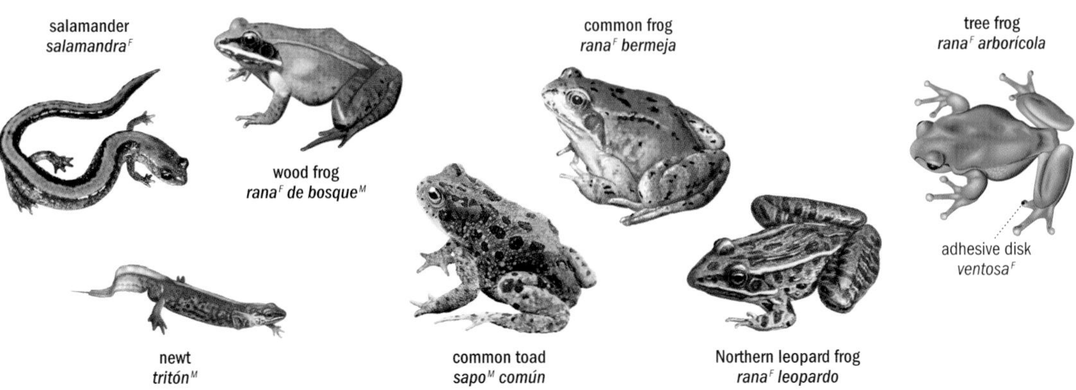

snake

serpiente[M]

ANIMAL KINGDOM

morphology of a venomous snake: head
morfología[F] de una serpiente[F] venenosa: cabeza[F]

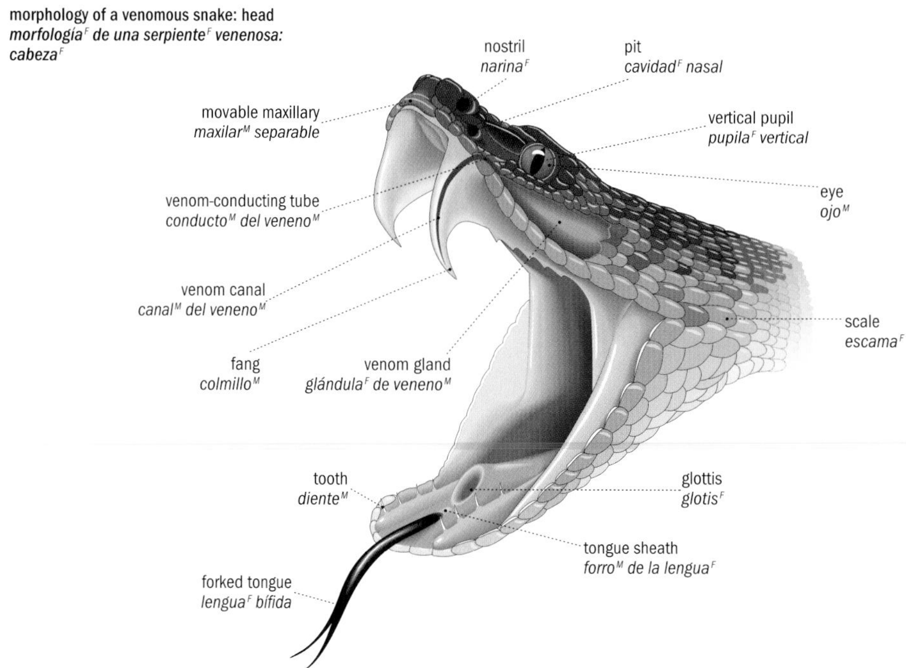

turtle

tortuga[F]

morphology of a turtle
morfología[F] de una tortuga[F]

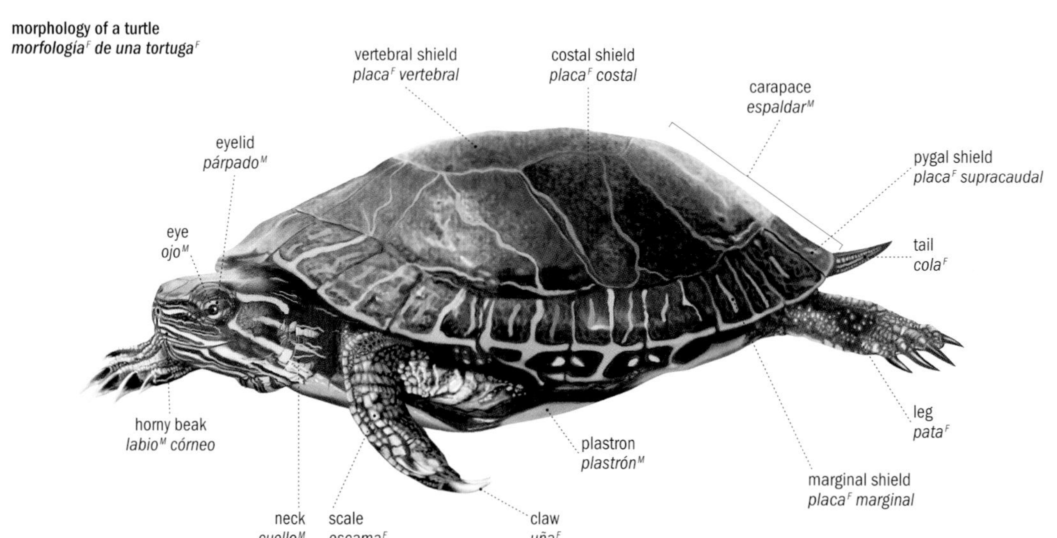

examples of reptiles

ejemplos[M] de reptiles[M]

viper
víbora[F]

garter snake
serpiente[F] *de jarretera*[F]

chameleon
camaleón[M]

lizard
lagarto[M]

rattlesnake
serpiente[F] *de cascabel*[M]

cobra
cobra[F]

coral snake
serpiente[F] *coral*

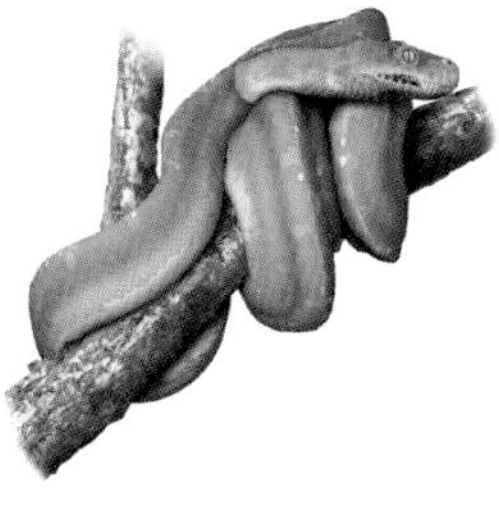

python
pitón[F]

monitor lizard
varano[M]

iguana
iguana[F]

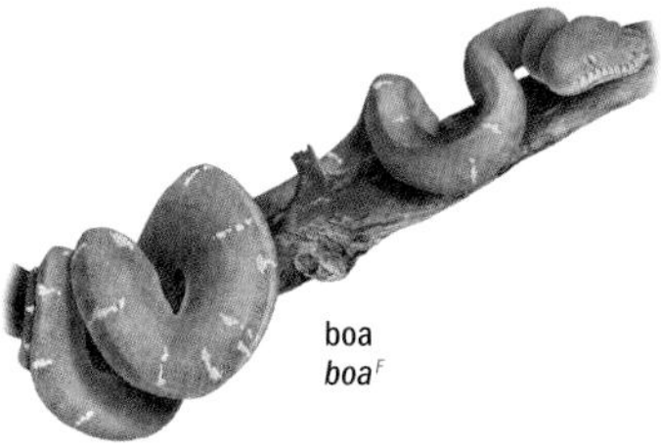

boa
boa[F]

alligator
aligátor[M]

crocodile
cocodrilo[M]

caiman
caimán[M]

bird

ave^F

morphology of a bird
morfología^F de un pájaro^M

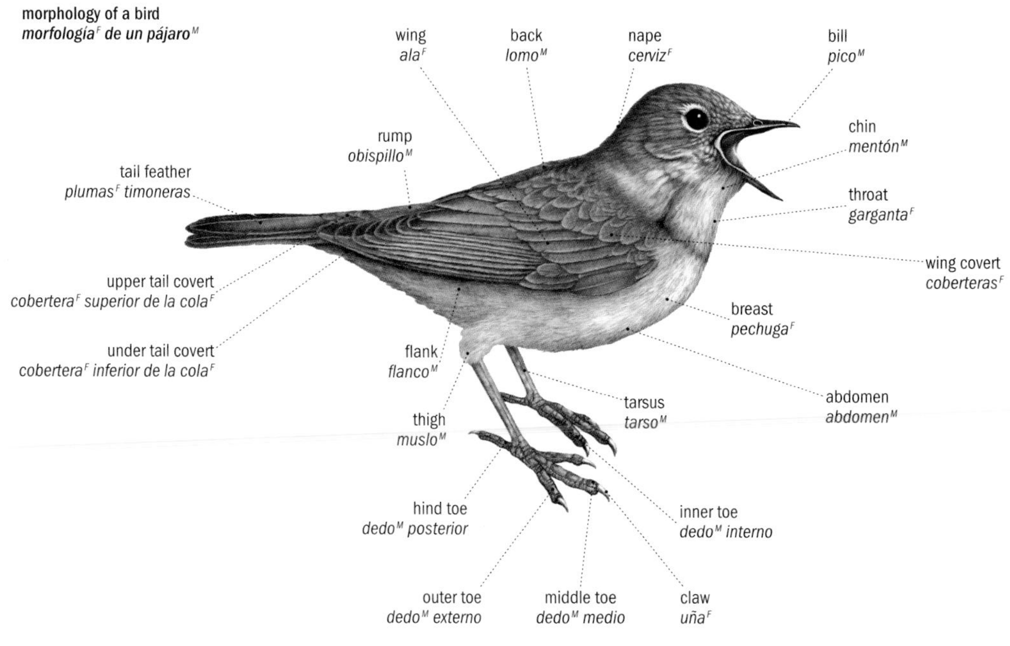
wing
ala^F
back
lomo^M
nape
cerviz^F
bill
pico^M
rump
obispillo^M
chin
mentón^M
tail feather
plumas^F timoneras
throat
garganta^F
wing covert
coberteras^F
upper tail covert
cobertera^F superior de la cola^F
breast
pechuga^F
under tail covert
cobertera^F inferior de la cola^F
flank
flanco^M
tarsus
tarso^M
abdomen
abdomen^M
thigh
muslo^M
hind toe
dedo^M posterior
inner toe
dedo^M interno
outer toe
dedo^M externo
middle toe
dedo^M medio
claw
uña^F

head
cabeza^F

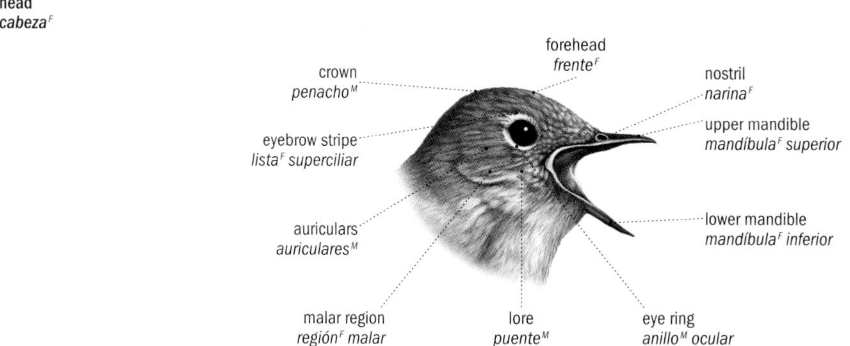
forehead
frente^F
crown
penacho^M
nostril
narina^F
upper mandible
mandíbula^F superior
eyebrow stripe
lista^F superciliar
auriculars
auriculares^M
lower mandible
mandíbula^F inferior
malar region
región^F malar
lore
puente^M
eye ring
anillo^M ocular

wing
ala^F

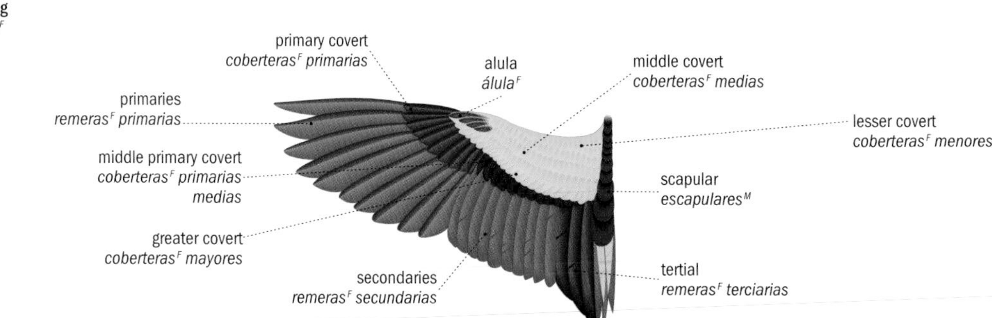
primary covert
coberteras^F primarias
alula
álula^F
middle covert
coberteras^F medias
primaries
remeras^F primarias
lesser covert
coberteras^F menores
middle primary covert
coberteras^F primarias medias
scapular
escapulares^M
greater covert
coberteras^F mayores
secondaries
remeras^F secundarias
tertial
remeras^F terciarias

bird

egg
huevo[M]

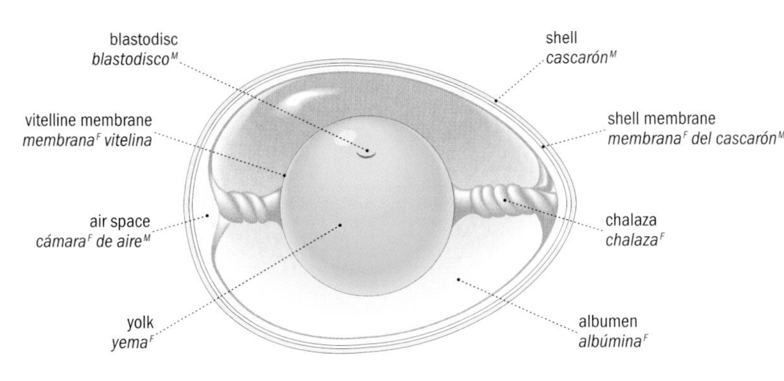

examples of bills
***ejemplos*[M] *de picos*[M]**

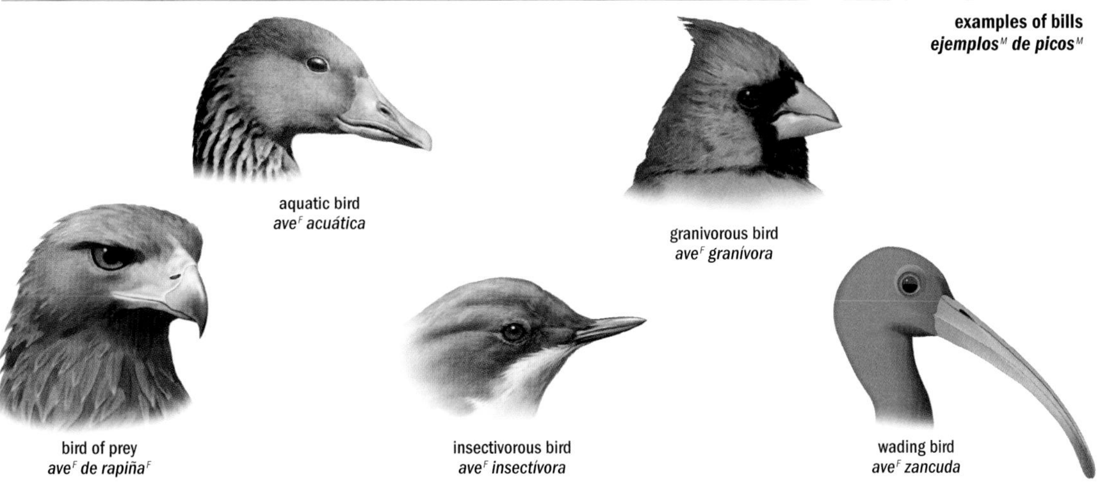

examples of feet
***ejemplos*[M] *de patas*[F]**

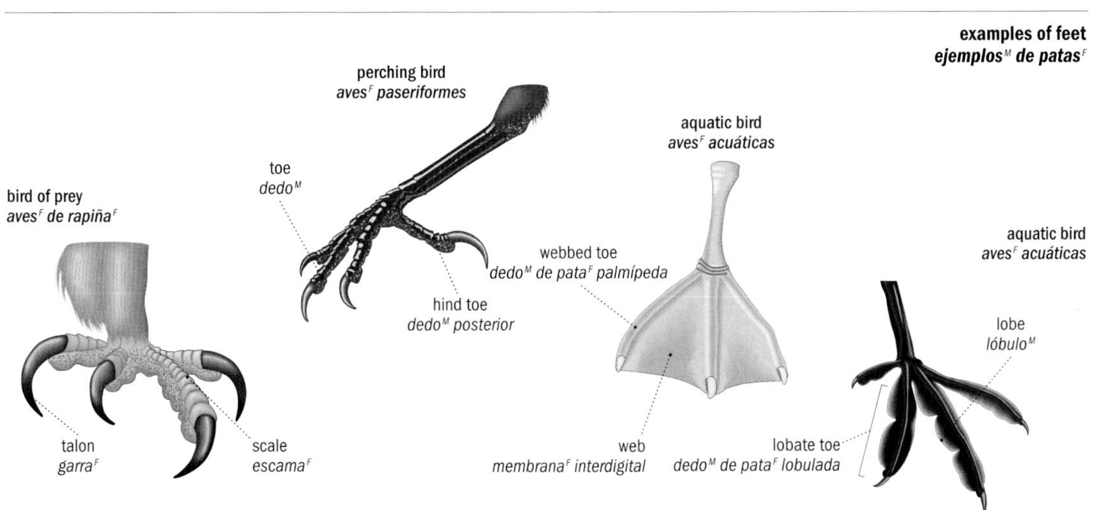

examples of birds

ejemplos[M] de pájaros[M]

hummingbird
colibrí[M]
European robin
petirrojo[M]
finch
pinzón[M]
kingfisher
martín[M] *pescador*
nightingale
ruiseñor[M]
sparrow
gorrión[M]
swallow
golondrina[F]
starling
estornino[M]
jay
arrendajo[M]
cardinal
cardenal[M]
swift
vencejo[M]
partridge
perdiz[F]
condor
cóndor[M]
macaw
guacamayo[M]
woodpecker
pájaro[M] *carpintero*
raven
cuervo[M]
toucan
tucán[M]
vulture
buitre[M]
penguin
pingüino[M]
albatross
albatros[M]
heron
garza[F]
pelican
pelícano[M]
stork
cigüeña[F]

examples of birds

pheasant
faisán[M]
great horned owl
búho[M] *real*
falcon
halcón[M]
quail
codorniz[F]
eagle
águila[F]
duck
pato[M]
hen
gallina[F]
pigeon
paloma[F]
turkey
pavo[M]
guinea fowl
pintada[F]
goose
oca[F]
rooster
gallo[M]
ostrich
avestruz[F]
peacock
pavo[M] *real*
flamingo
flamenco[M]

rodent

roedor[M]

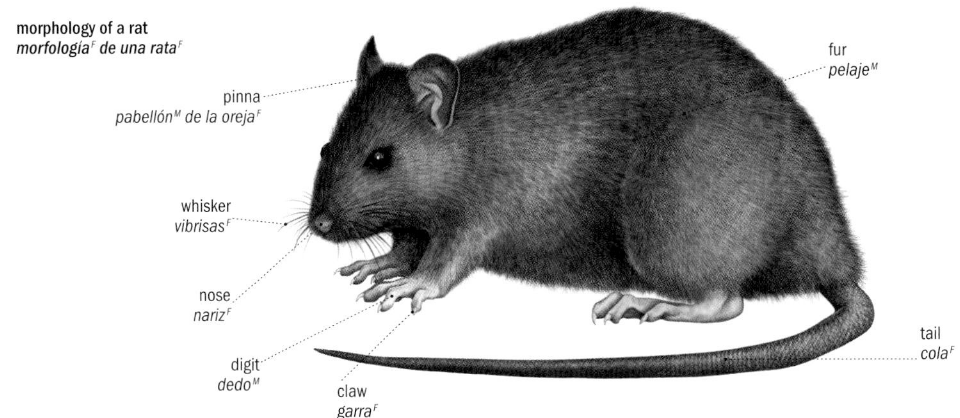

examples of rodents

ejemplos[M] de roedores[M]

examples of lagomorphs

ejemplos[M] de lagomorfos[M]

pika
pica[F]

rabbit
conejo[M]

hare
liebre[F]

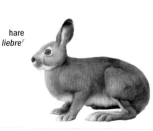

horse
caballo[M]

morphology of a horse
morfología[F] de un caballo[M]

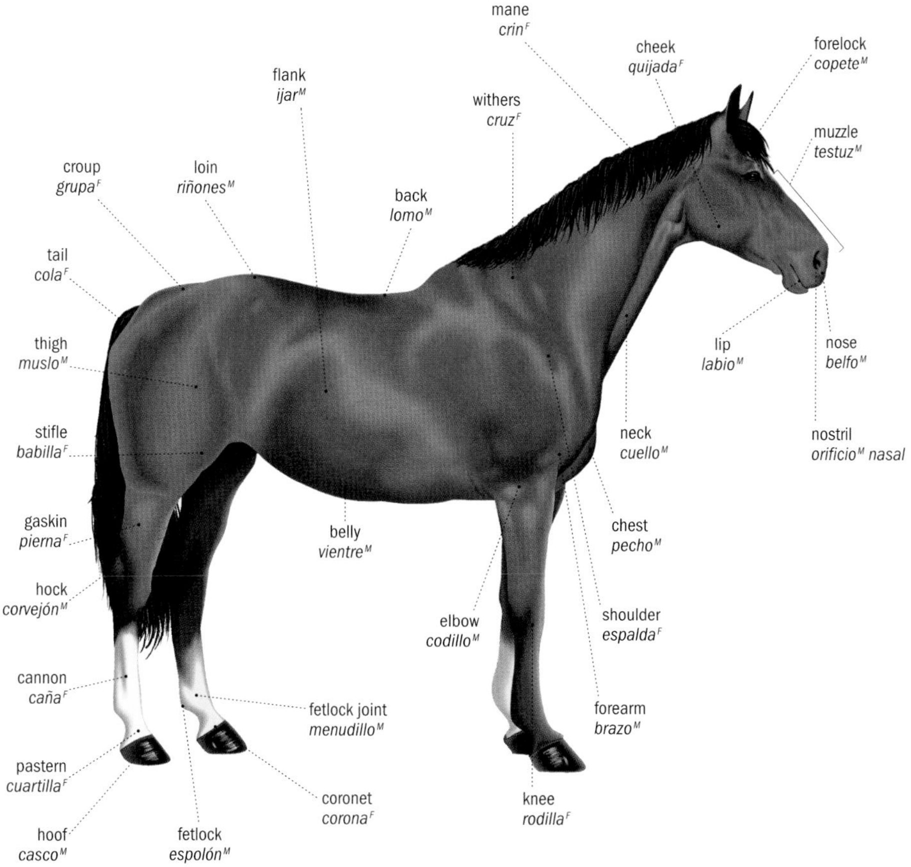

mane
crin[F]

cheek
quijada[F]

forelock
copete[M]

flank
ijar[M]

withers
cruz[F]

muzzle
testuz[M]

croup
grupa[F]

loin
riñones[M]

back
lomo[M]

tail
cola[F]

thigh
muslo[M]

lip
labio[M]

nose
belfo[M]

stifle
babilla[F]

neck
cuello[M]

nostril
orificio[M] nasal

gaskin
pierna[F]

belly
vientre[M]

chest
pecho[M]

hock
corvejón[M]

elbow
codillo[M]

shoulder
espalda[F]

cannon
caña[F]

fetlock joint
menudillo[M]

forearm
brazo[M]

pastern
cuartilla[F]

coronet
corona[F]

knee
rodilla[F]

hoof
casco[M]

fetlock
espolón[M]

gaits
andaduras[F]

walk
paso[M]

pace
portante[M]

trot
trote[M]

gallop
galope[M]

examples of ungulate mammals

ejemplos^{M} de mamíferos^{M} ungulados

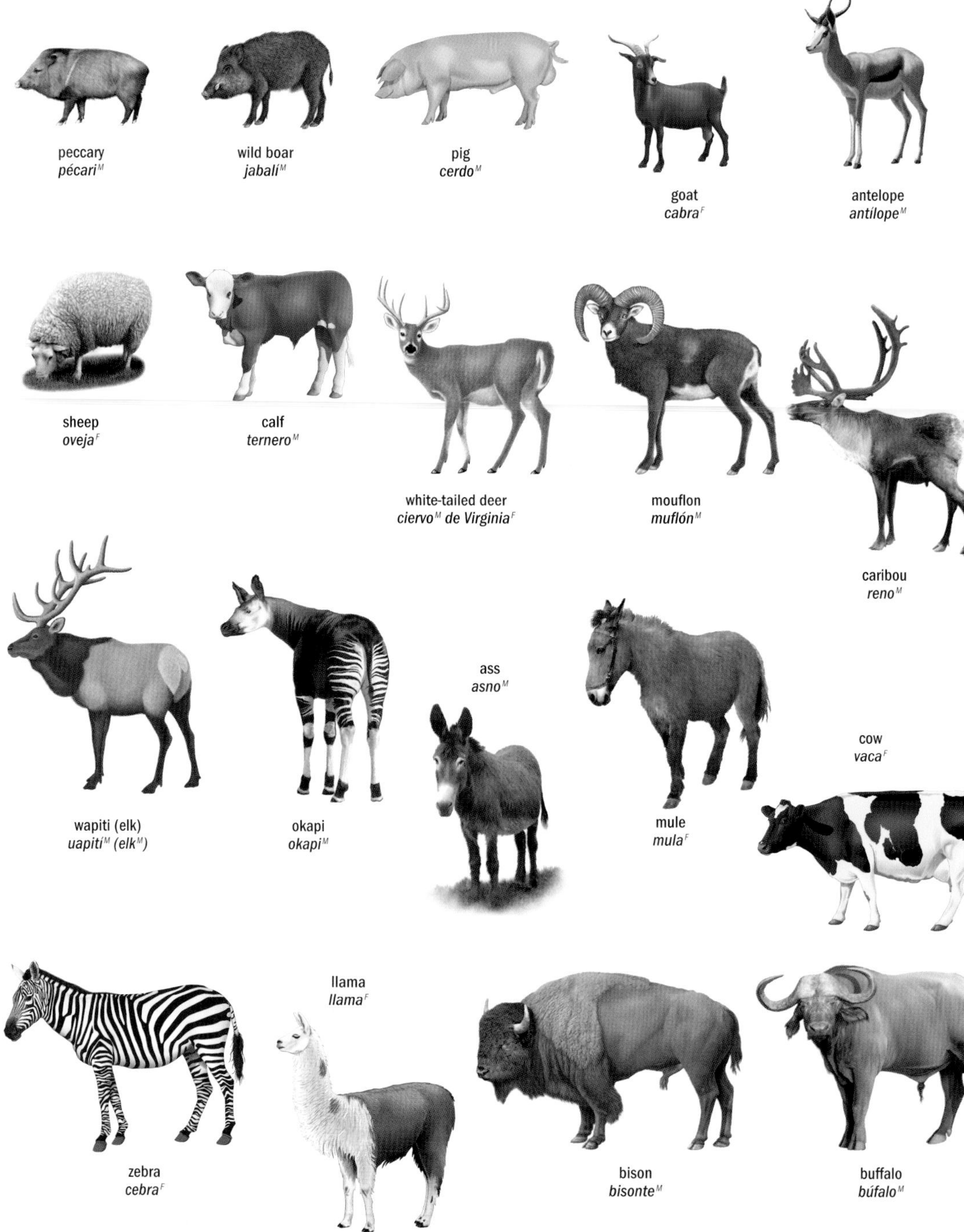

examples of ungulate mammals

ox
buey[M]

yak
yak[M]

horse
caballo[M]

moose
alce[M]

bactrian camel
camello[M]

dromedary camel
dromedario[M]

rhinoceros
rinoceronte[M]

hippopotamus
hipopótamo[M]

giraffe
jirafa[F]

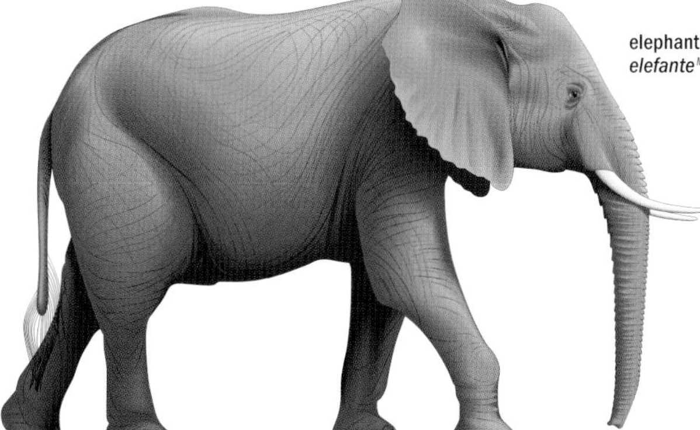

elephant
elefante[M]

dog

perro[M]

morphology of a dog
morfología[F] de un perro[M]

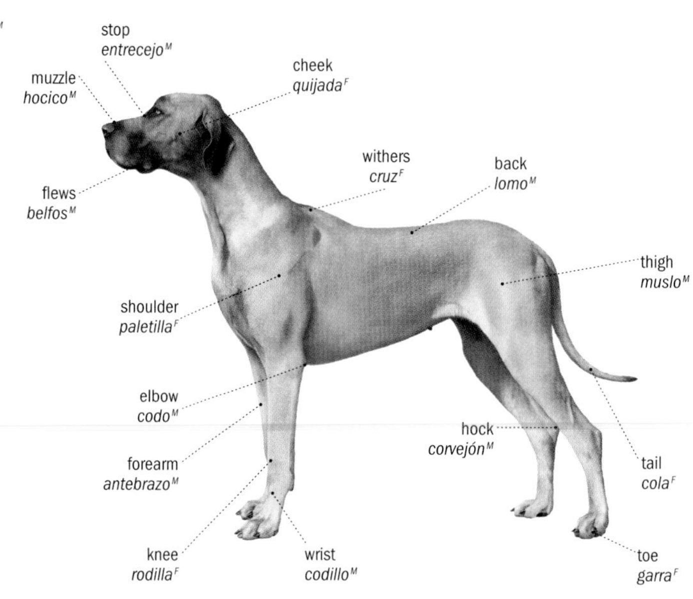

examples of dog breeds

razas[F] de perros[M]

bulldog
buldog[M]

collie
collie[M]

Dalmatian
dálmata[M]

poodle
caniche[M]

schnauzer
schnauzer[M]

Great Dane
gran danés[M]

German shepherd
pastor[M] alemán

Saint Bernard
San Bernardo[M]

cat

gato^{M} doméstico

cat's head
***cabeza**^{F}*

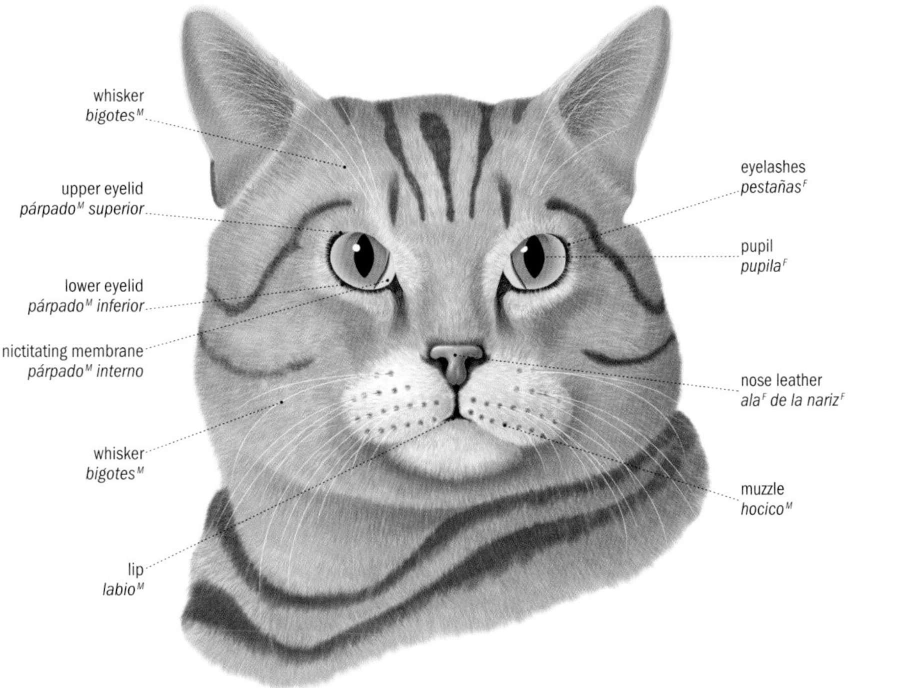

examples of cat breeds

razas^{F} de gatos^{M}

examples of carnivorous mammals

ejemplos[M] de mamíferos[M] carnívoros

cheetah
*guepardo*ᴹ
leopard
*leopardo*ᴹ
lion
*león*ᴹ
jaguar
*jaguar*ᴹ
tiger
*tigre*ᴹ
polar bear
*oso*ᴹ *polar*
black bear
*oso*ᴹ *negro*

dolphin

delfín[M]

morphology of a dolphin
morfología[F] de un delfín[M]

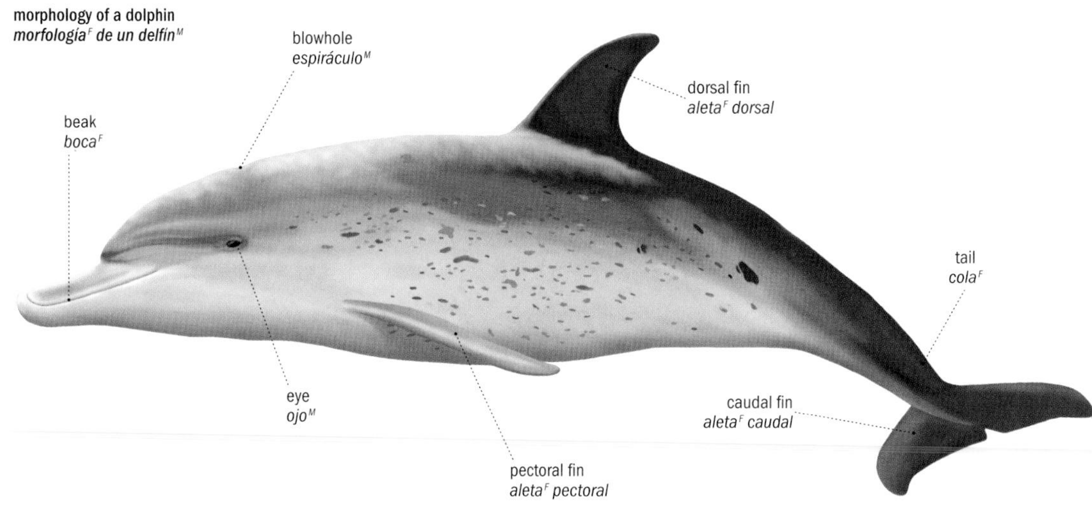

examples of marine mammals

ejemplos[M] de mamíferos[M] marinos

killer whale
orca[F]

seal
foca[F]

humpback whale
rorcual[M]

northern right whale
ballena[F] boréale

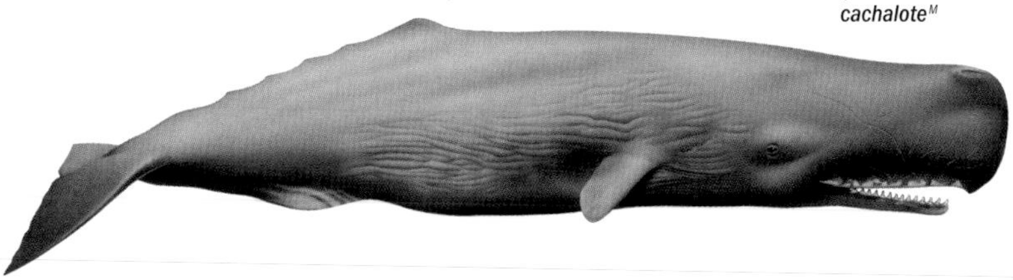

sperm whale
cachalote[M]

sea lion
otaria[F]

gorilla

gorila[M]

morphology of a gorilla
morfología[F] de un gorila[M]

face
cara[F]
fur
pelaje[M]
prehensile digit
dedos[M] prensiles
opposable thumb
pulgar[M] oponible
arm
brazo[M]
hand
mano[F]
leg
pata[F]
foot
pie[M]

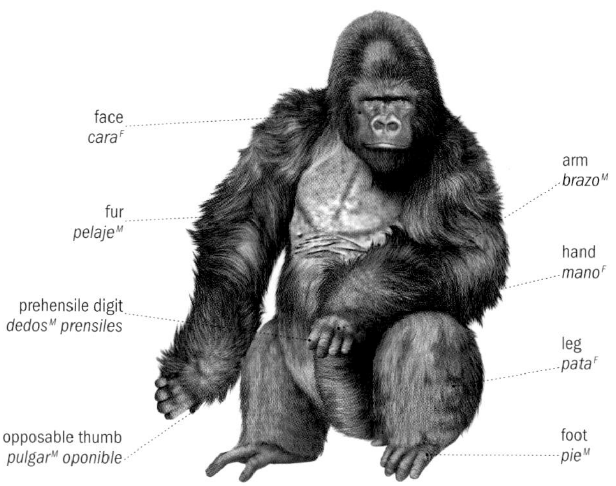

examples of primates

ejemplos[M] de primates[M]

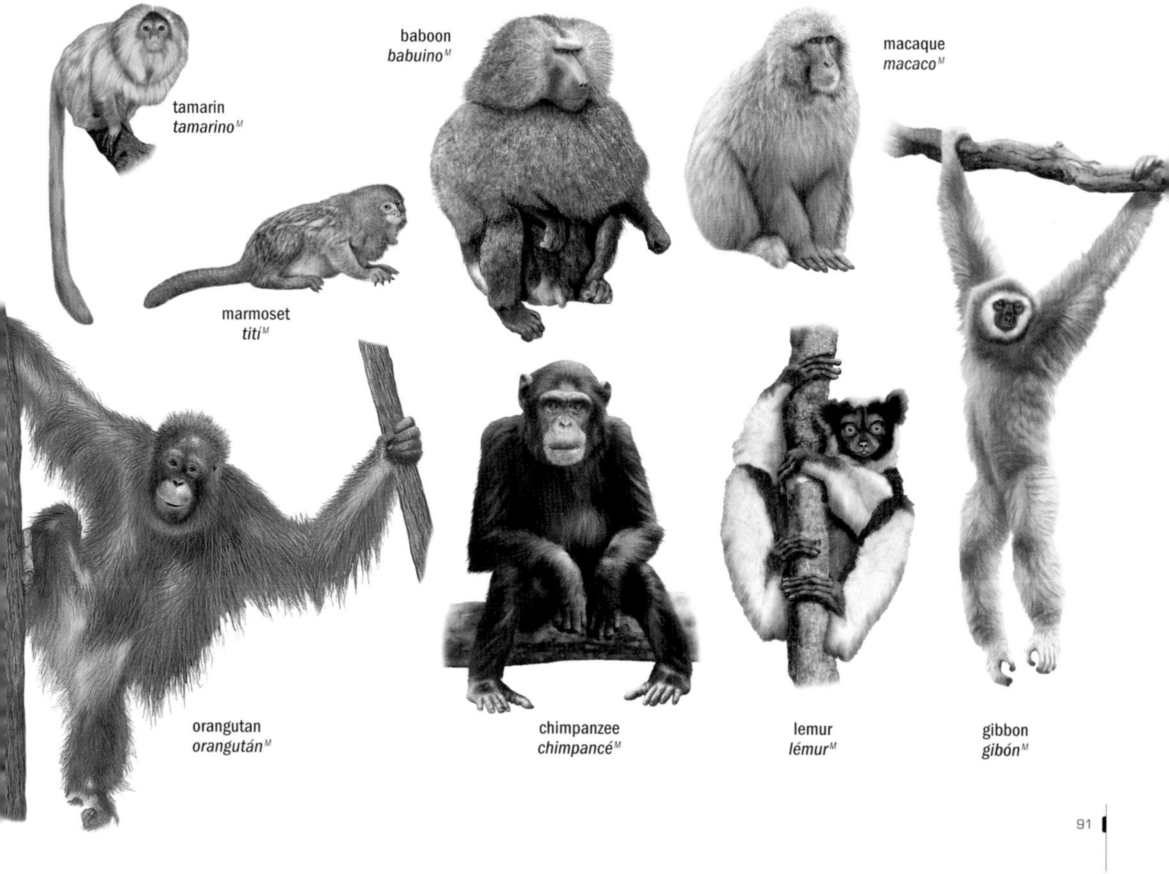

tamarin
tamarino[M]
baboon
babuino[M]
macaque
macaco[M]
marmoset
tití[M]
orangutan
orangután[M]
chimpanzee
chimpancé[M]
lemur
lémur[M]
gibbon
gibón[M]

man

hombre^{M}

anterior view
vista^{F} anterior

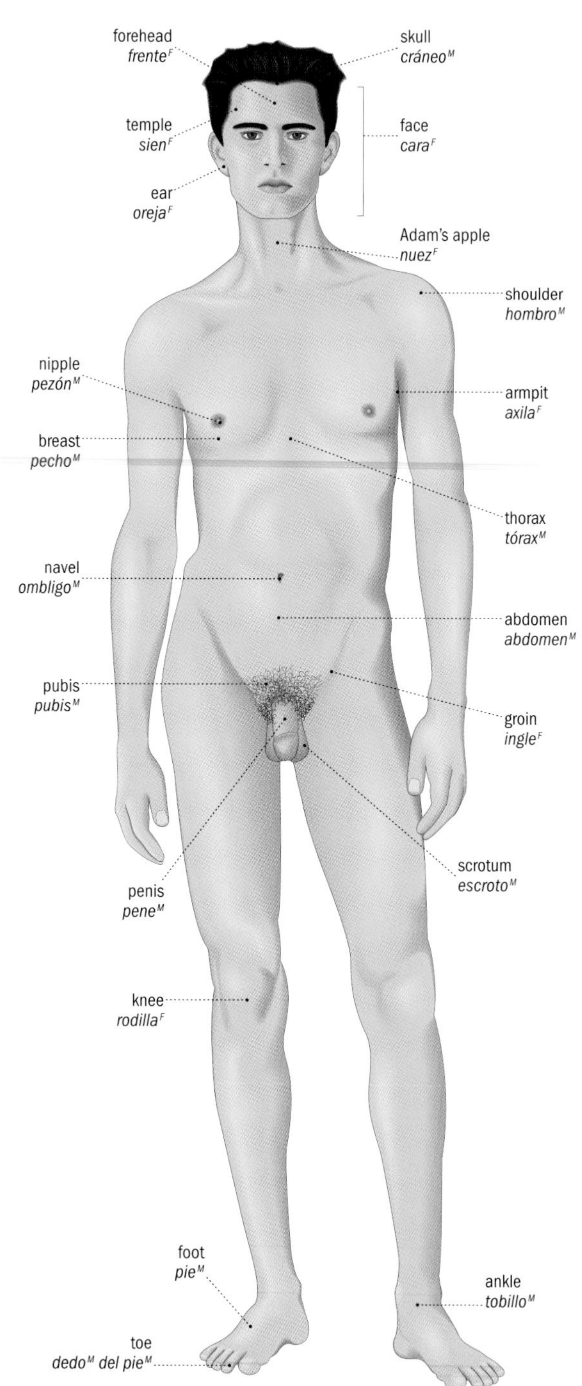

posterior view
vista[F] *posterior*

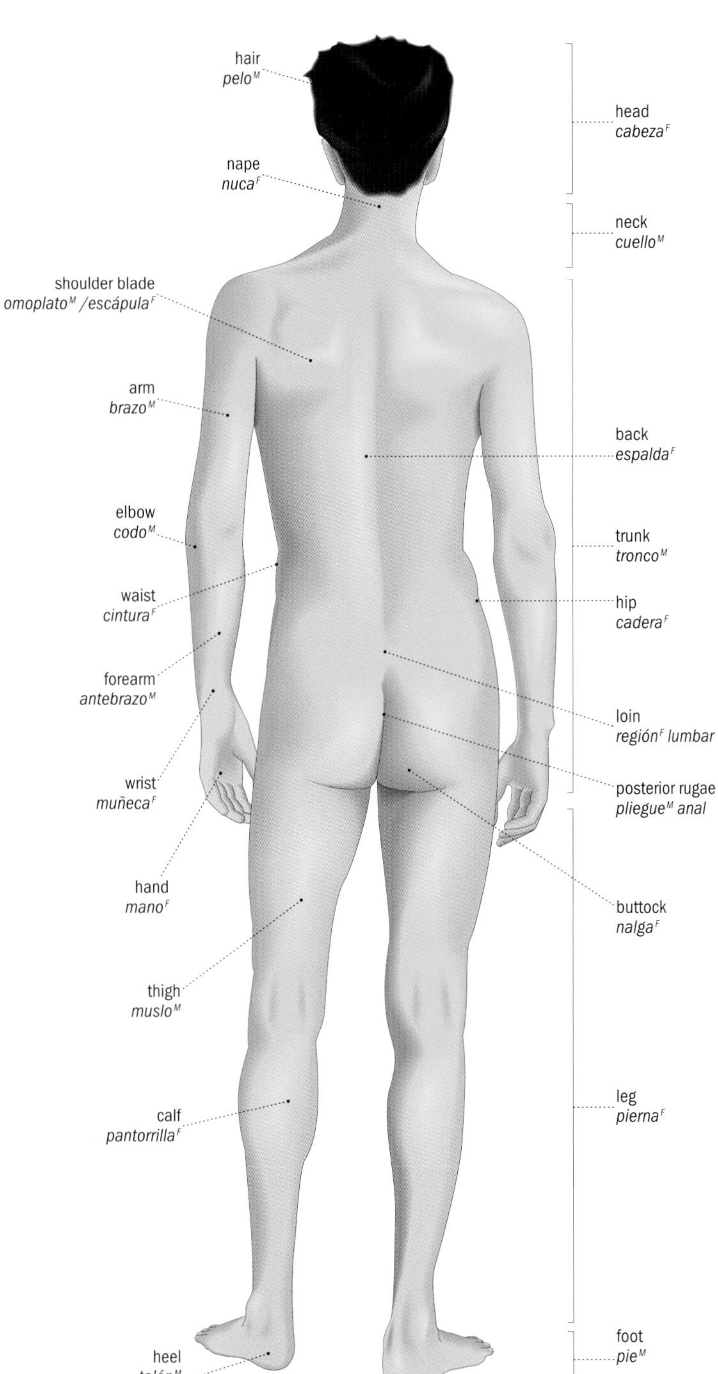
hair
pelo[M]
nape
nuca[F]
shoulder blade
omoplato[M] /escápula[F]
arm
brazo[M]
elbow
codo[M]
waist
cintura[F]
forearm
antebrazo[M]
wrist
muñeca[F]
hand
mano[F]
thigh
muslo[M]
calf
pantorrilla[F]
heel
talón[M]
head
cabeza[F]
neck
cuello[M]
back
espalda[F]
trunk
tronco[M]
hip
cadera[F]
loin
región[F] lumbar
posterior rugae
pliegue[M] anal
buttock
nalga[F]
leg
pierna[F]
foot
pie[M]

woman

mujer[F]

anterior view
vista[F] anterior

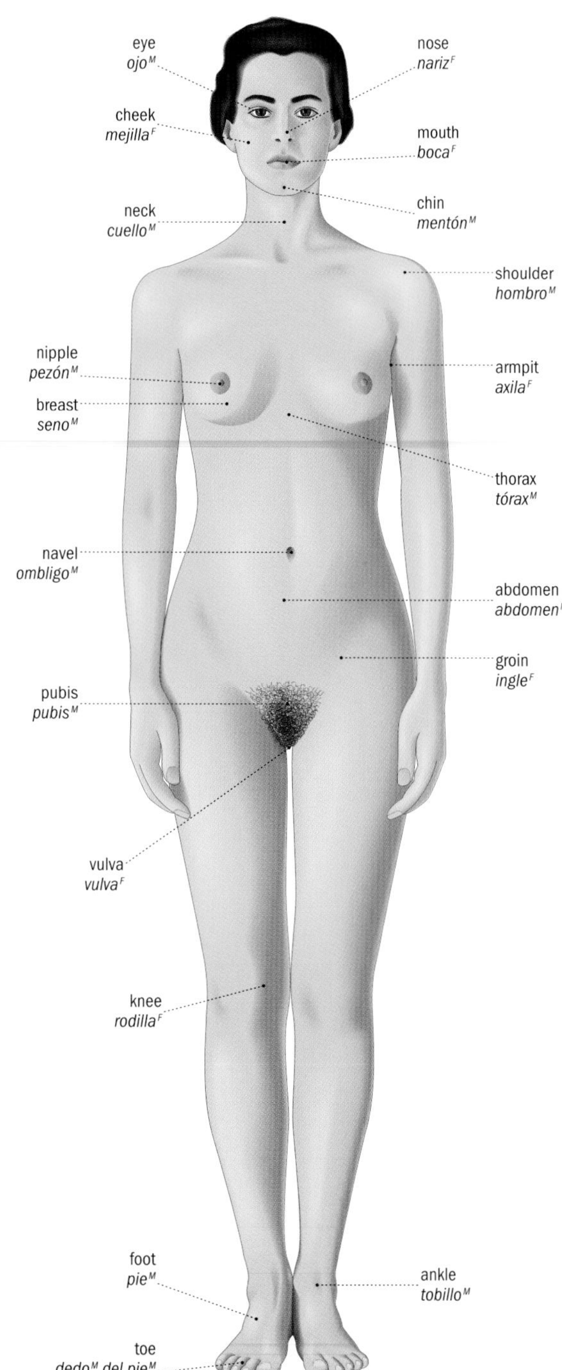

posterior view
vista*[F] *posterior

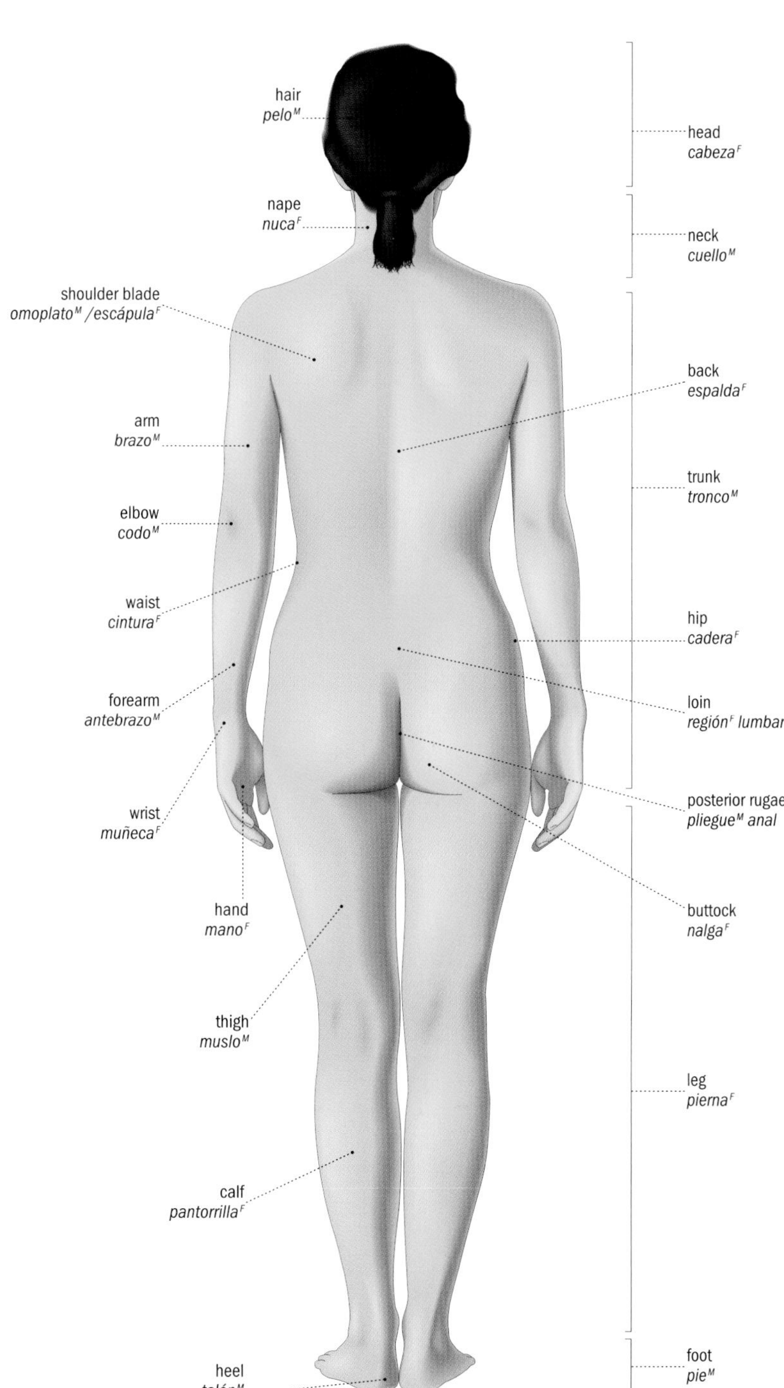
hair
pelo[M]
head
cabeza[F]
nape
nuca[F]
neck
cuello[M]
shoulder blade
omoplato[M] */escápula*[F]
back
espalda[F]
arm
brazo[M]
trunk
tronco[M]
elbow
codo[M]
waist
cintura[F]
hip
cadera[F]
forearm
antebrazo[M]
loin
región[F] *lumbar*
wrist
muñeca[F]
posterior rugae
pliegue[M] *anal*
hand
mano[F]
buttock
nalga[F]
thigh
muslo[M]
leg
pierna[F]
calf
pantorrilla[F]
heel
talón[M]
foot
pie[M]

muscles

músculos[M]

anterior view
vista[F] anterior

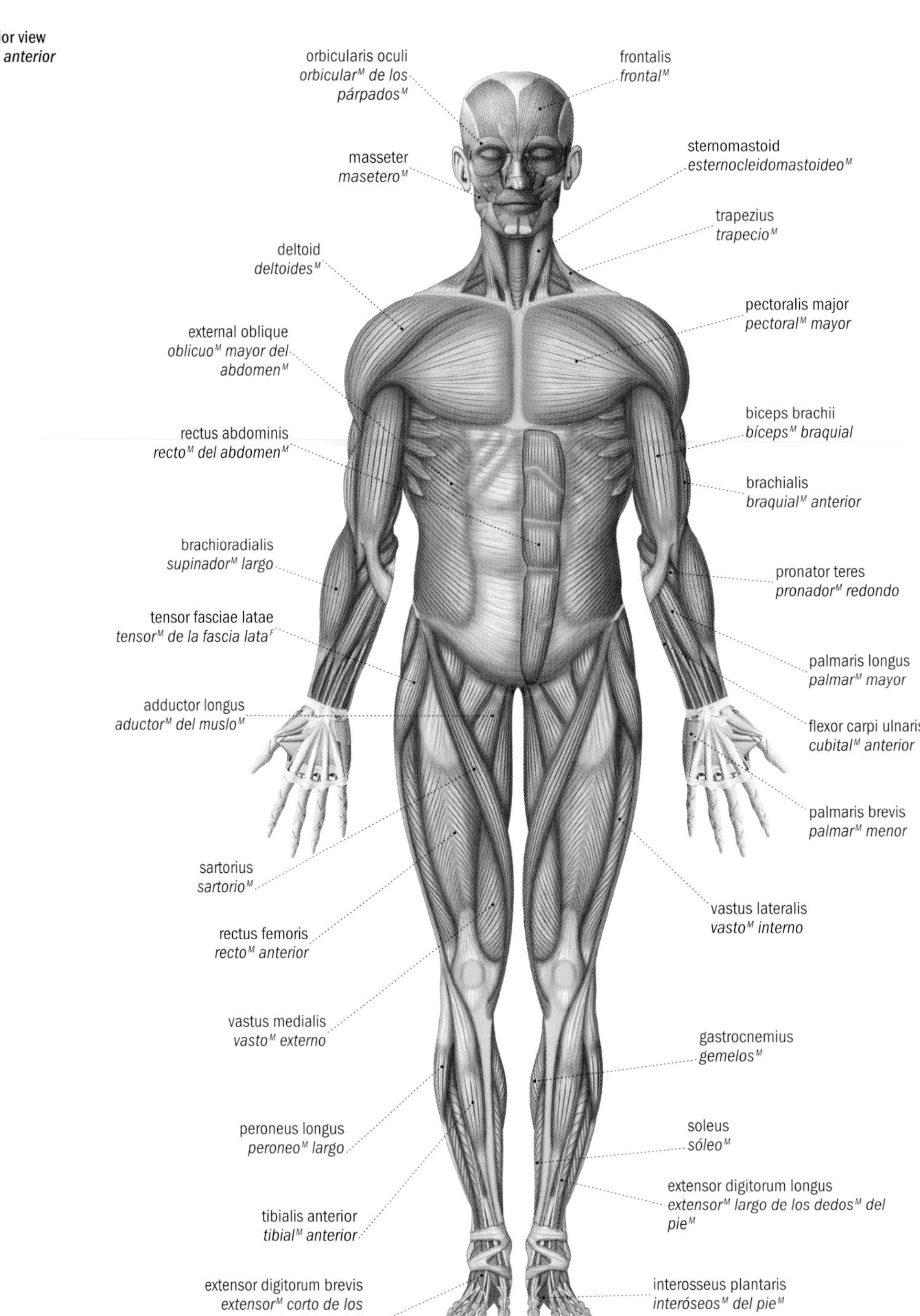
orbicularis oculi
orbicular[M] de los párpados[M]
frontalis
frontal[M]
masseter
masetero[M]
sternomastoid
esternocleidomastoideo[M]
trapezius
trapecio[M]
deltoid
deltoides[M]
pectoralis major
pectoral[M] mayor
external oblique
oblicuo[M] mayor del abdomen[M]
biceps brachii
bíceps[M] braquial
rectus abdominis
recto[M] del abdomen[M]
brachialis
braquial[M] anterior
brachioradialis
supinador[M] largo
pronator teres
pronador[M] redondo
tensor fasciae latae
tensor[M] de la fascia lata[F]
palmaris longus
palmar[M] mayor
adductor longus
aductor[M] del muslo[M]
flexor carpi ulnaris
cubital[M] anterior
palmaris brevis
palmar[M] menor
sartorius
sartorio[M]
vastus lateralis
vasto[M] interno
rectus femoris
recto[M] anterior
vastus medialis
vasto[M] externo
gastrocnemius
gemelos[M]
peroneus longus
peroneo[M] largo
soleus
sóleo[M]
extensor digitorum longus
extensor[M] largo de los dedos[M] del pie[M]
tibialis anterior
tibial[M] anterior
extensor digitorum brevis
extensor[M] corto de los dedos[M] del pie[M]
interosseus plantaris
interóseos[M] del pie[M]

posterior view
vista^F posterior

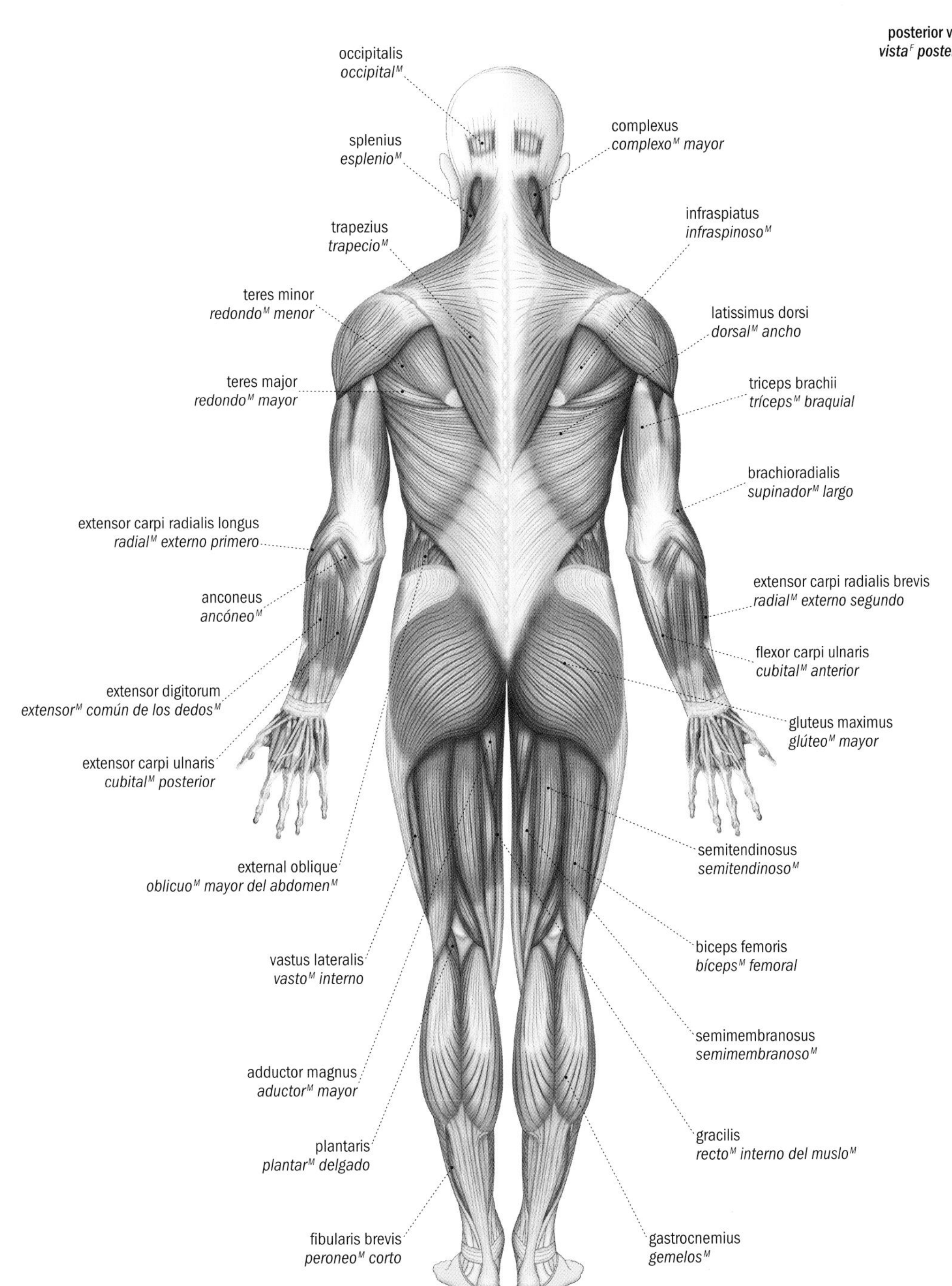
occipitalis
occipital^M
splenius
esplenio^M
trapezius
trapecio^M
teres minor
redondo^M menor
teres major
redondo^M mayor
extensor carpi radialis longus
radial^M externo primero
anconeus
ancóneo^M
extensor digitorum
extensor^M común de los dedos^M
extensor carpi ulnaris
cubital^M posterior
external oblique
oblicuo^M mayor del abdomen^M
vastus lateralis
vasto^M interno
adductor magnus
aductor^M mayor
plantaris
plantar^M delgado
fibularis brevis
peroneo^M corto
complexus
complexo^M mayor
infraspiatus
infraspinoso^M
latissimus dorsi
dorsal^M ancho
triceps brachii
tríceps^M braquial
brachioradialis
supinador^M largo
extensor carpi radialis brevis
radial^M externo segundo
flexor carpi ulnaris
cubital^M anterior
gluteus maximus
glúteo^M mayor
semitendinosus
semitendinoso^M
biceps femoris
bíceps^M femoral
semimembranosus
semimembranoso^M
gracilis
recto^M interno del muslo^M
gastrocnemius
gemelos^M

skeleton

esqueleto[M]

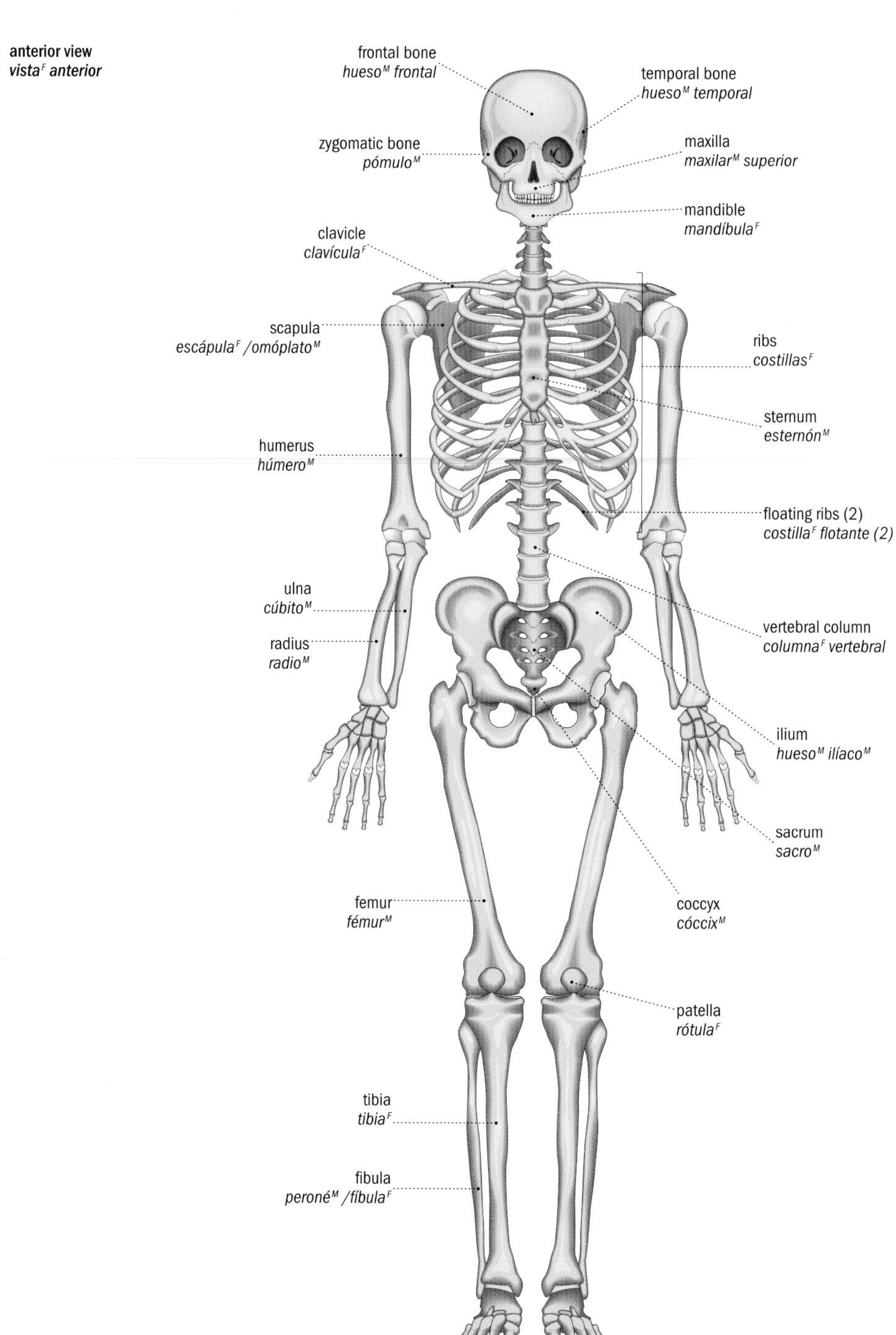
anterior view
vista[F] anterior
frontal bone
hueso[M] frontal
temporal bone
hueso[M] temporal
zygomatic bone
pómulo[M]
maxilla
maxilar[M] superior
mandible
mandíbula[F]
clavicle
clavícula[F]
scapula
escápula[F] /omóplato[M]
ribs
costillas[F]
sternum
esternón[M]
humerus
húmero[M]
floating ribs (2)
costilla[F] flotante (2)
ulna
cúbito[M]
vertebral column
columna[F] vertebral
radius
radio[M]
ilium
hueso[M] ilíaco[M]
sacrum
sacro[M]
femur
fémur[M]
coccyx
cóccix[M]
patella
rótula[F]
tibia
tibia[F]
fibula
peroné[M] /fíbula[F]

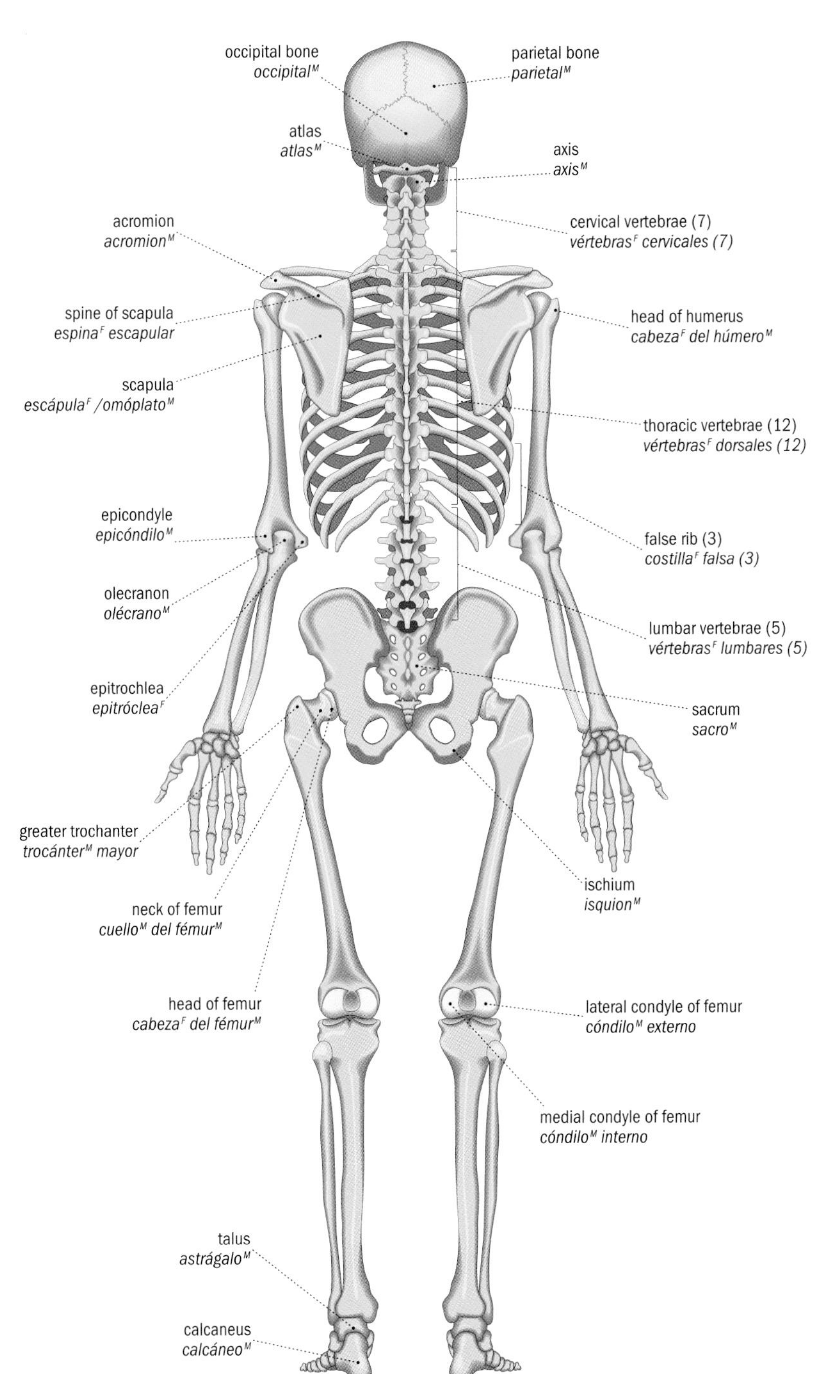

posterior view
vista^F posterior
occipital bone
occipital^M
parietal bone
parietal^M
atlas
atlas^M
axis
axis^M
acromion
acromion^M
cervical vertebrae (7)
vértebras^F cervicales (7)
spine of scapula
espina^F escapular
head of humerus
cabeza^F del húmero^M
scapula
escápula^F /omóplato^M
thoracic vertebrae (12)
vértebras^F dorsales (12)
epicondyle
epicóndilo^M
false rib (3)
costilla^F falsa (3)
olecranon
olécrano^M
lumbar vertebrae (5)
vértebras^F lumbares (5)
epitrochlea
epitróclea^F
sacrum
sacro^M
greater trochanter
trocánter^M mayor
ischium
isquion^M
neck of femur
cuello^M del fémur^M
head of femur
cabeza^F del fémur^M
lateral condyle of femur
cóndilo^M externo
medial condyle of femur
cóndilo^M interno
talus
astrágalo^M
calcaneus
calcáneo^M

lateral view of adult skull
vista[F] lateral del cráneo[M] adulto

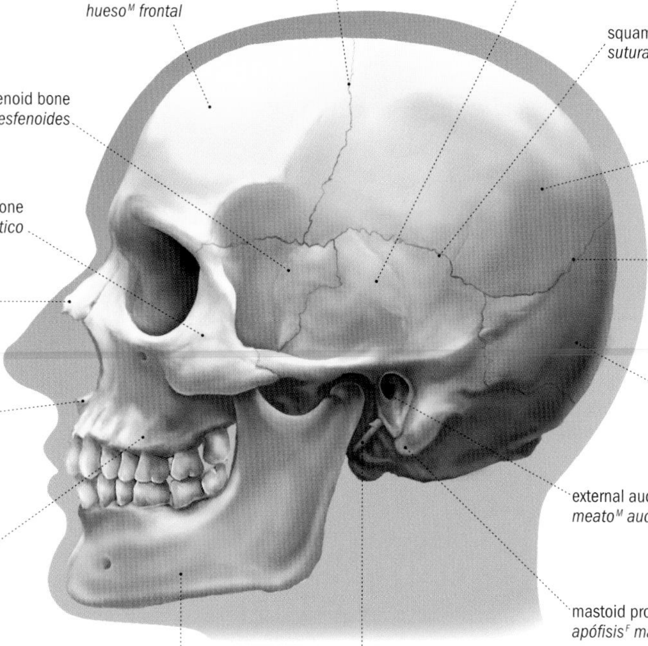

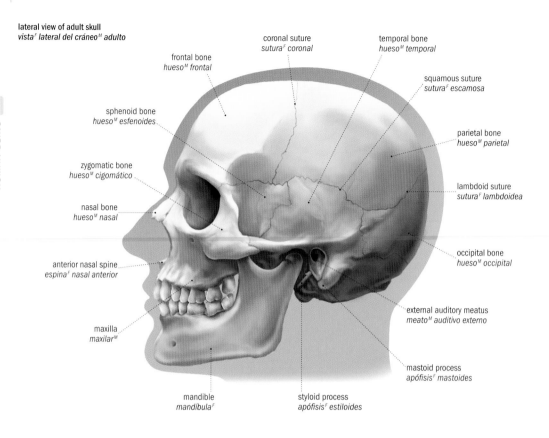

coronal suture
sutura[F] coronal
temporal bone
hueso[M] temporal
frontal bone
hueso[M] frontal
squamous suture
sutura[F] escamosa
sphenoid bone
hueso[M] esfenoides
parietal bone
hueso[M] parietal
zygomatic bone
hueso[M] cigomático
lambdoid suture
sutura[F] lambdoidea
nasal bone
hueso[M] nasal
occipital bone
hueso[M] occipital
anterior nasal spine
espina[F] nasal anterior
external auditory meatus
meato[M] auditivo externo
maxilla
maxilar[M]
mastoid process
apófisis[F] mastoides
mandible
mandíbula[F]
styloid process
apófisis[F] estiloides

lateral view of child's skull
vista[F] lateral del cráneo[M] de un niño[M]

anterior fontanelle
fontanela[F] anterior
parietal bone
hueso[M] parietal
coronal suture
sutura[F] coronal
posterior fontanelle
fontanela[F] posterior
frontal bone
hueso[M] frontal
occipital bone
hueso[M] occipital
sphenoidal fontanelle
fontanela[F] esfenoidal
mastoid fontanelle
fontanela[F] mastoidea

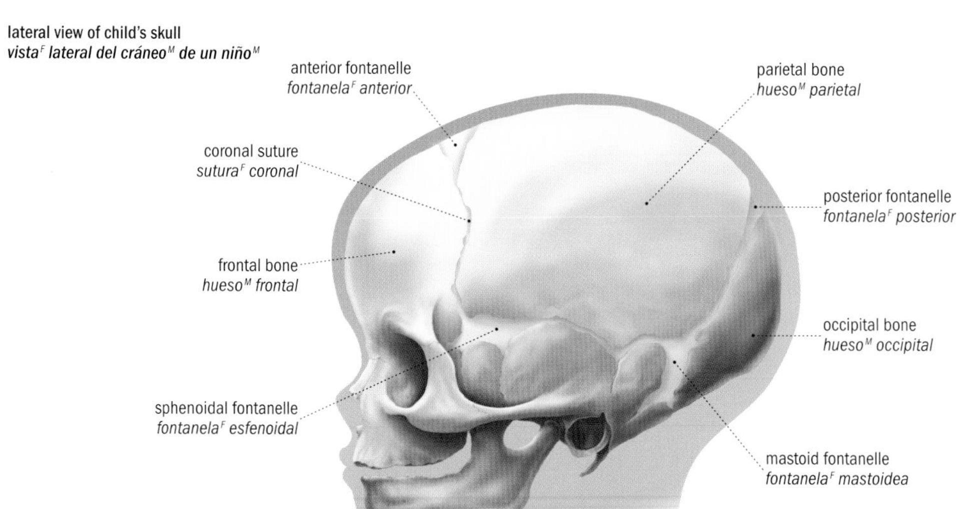

teeth

dientes[M]

human denture
dentadura[F] humana

incisors
incisivos[M]
canine
colmillo[M]
premolars
premolares[M]
molars
molares[M]
first molar
primer molar[M]
third molar
muela[F] del juicio[M]
central incisor
incisivo[M] central
lateral incisor
incisivo[M] lateral
first premolar
primer premolar[M]
second premolar
segundo premolar[M]
second molar
segundo molar[M]

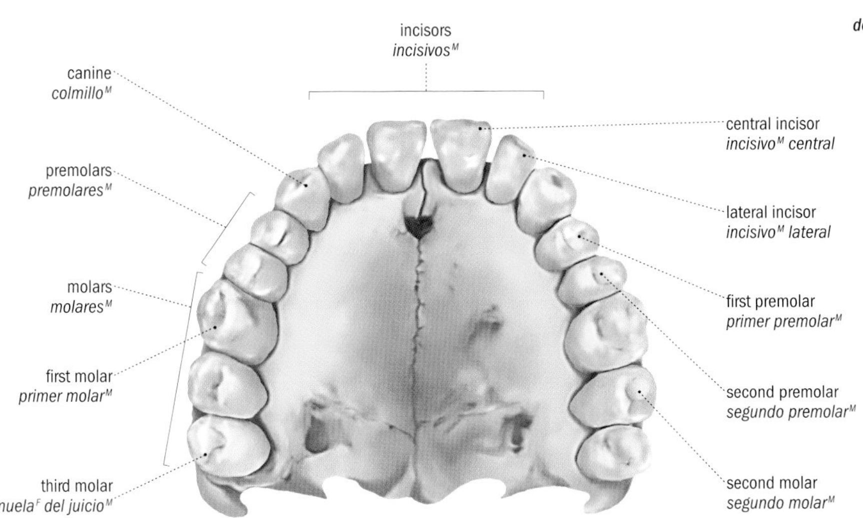

cross section of a molar
corte[M] transversal de un molar[M]

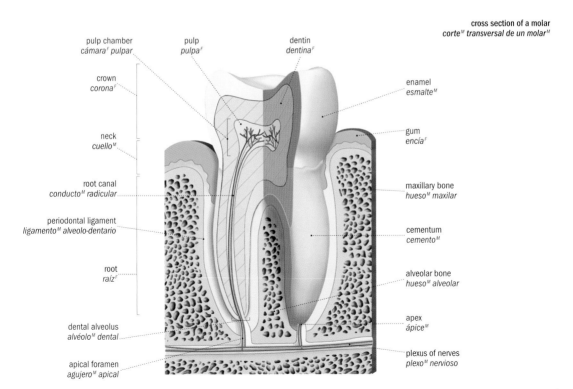

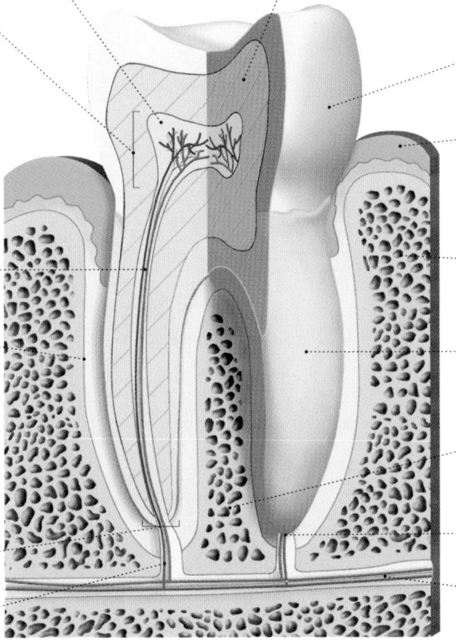

pulp chamber
cámara[F] pulpar
pulp
pulpa[F]
dentin
dentina[F]
crown
corona[F]
neck
cuello[M]
root canal
conducto[M] radicular
periodontal ligament
ligamento[M] alveolo-dentario
root
raíz[F]
dental alveolus
alvéolo[M] dental
apical foramen
agujero[M] apical
enamel
esmalte[M]
gum
encía[F]
maxillary bone
hueso[M] maxilar
cementum
cemento[M]
alveolar bone
hueso[M] alveolar
apex
ápice[M]
plexus of nerves
plexo[M] nervioso

blood circulation

circulación[F] sanguínea

principal veins and arteries
principales venas[F] y arterias[F]

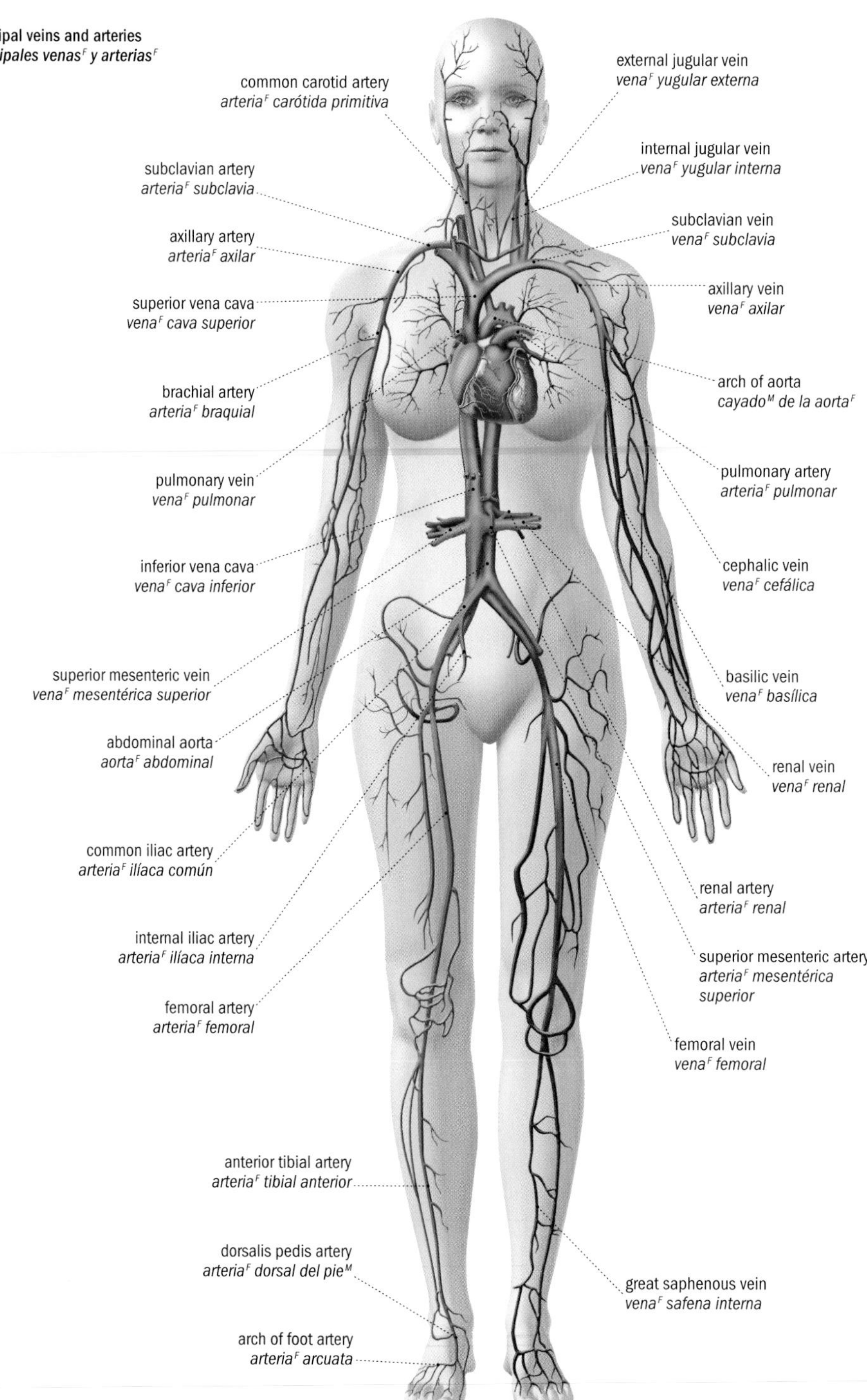
common carotid artery
arteria[F] carótida primitiva
subclavian artery
arteria[F] subclavia
axillary artery
arteria[F] axilar
superior vena cava
vena[F] cava superior
brachial artery
arteria[F] braquial
pulmonary vein
vena[F] pulmonar
inferior vena cava
vena[F] cava inferior
superior mesenteric vein
vena[F] mesentérica superior
abdominal aorta
aorta[F] abdominal
common iliac artery
arteria[F] ilíaca común
internal iliac artery
arteria[F] ilíaca interna
femoral artery
arteria[F] femoral
anterior tibial artery
arteria[F] tibial anterior
dorsalis pedis artery
arteria[F] dorsal del pie[M]
arch of foot artery
arteria[F] arcuata
external jugular vein
vena[F] yugular externa
internal jugular vein
vena[F] yugular interna
subclavian vein
vena[F] subclavia
axillary vein
vena[F] axilar
arch of aorta
cayado[M] de la aorta[F]
pulmonary artery
arteria[F] pulmonar
cephalic vein
vena[F] cefálica
basilic vein
vena[F] basílica
renal vein
vena[F] renal
renal artery
arteria[F] renal
superior mesenteric artery
arteria[F] mesentérica superior
femoral vein
vena[F] femoral
great saphenous vein
vena[F] safena interna

schema of circulation
***diagrama*[M] *de la circulación*[F]**

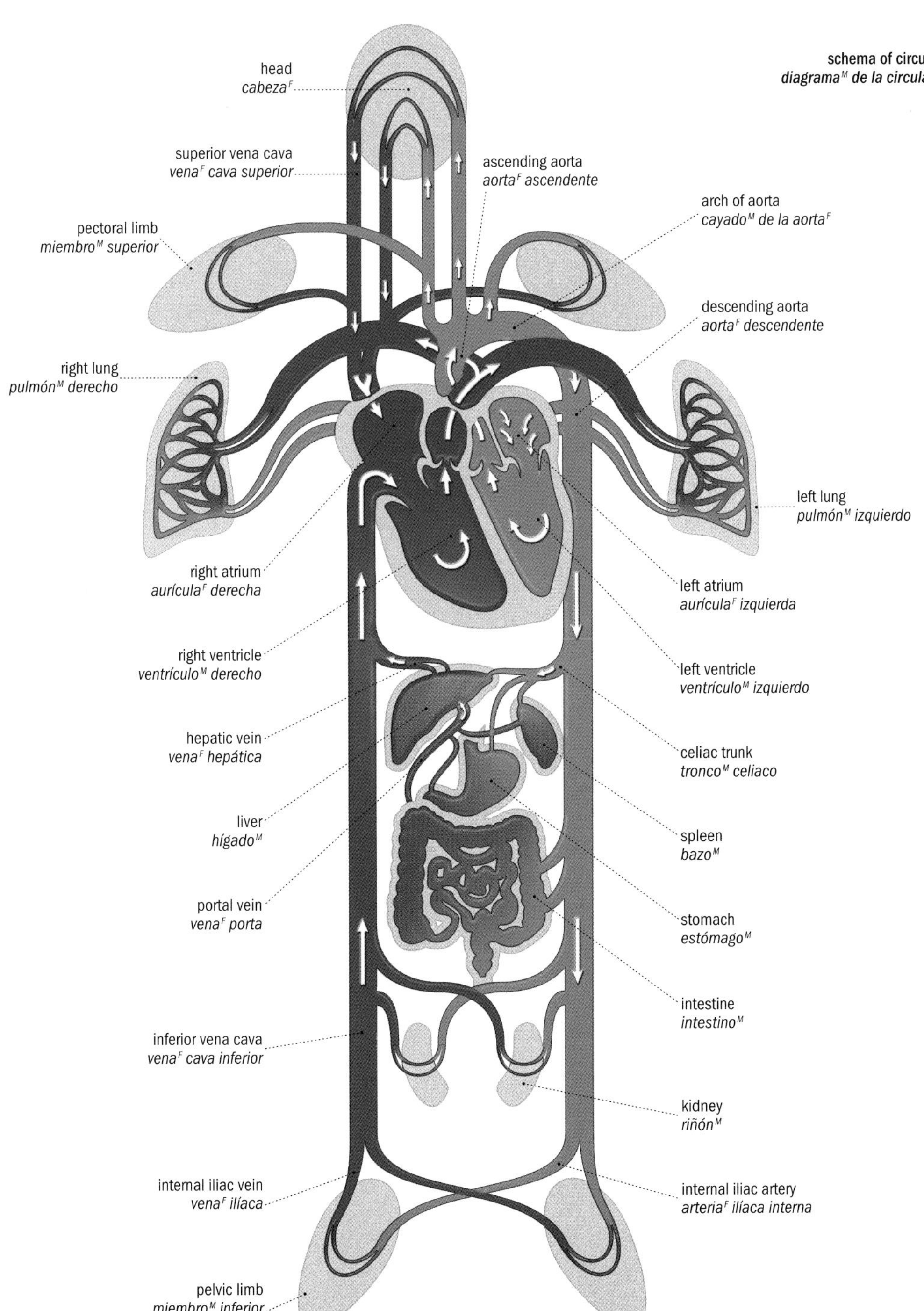
head
cabeza F
superior vena cava
vena F cava superior
ascending aorta
aorta F ascendente
arch of aorta
cayado M de la aorta F
pectoral limb
miembro M superior
descending aorta
aorta F descendente
right lung
pulmón M derecho
left lung
pulmón M izquierdo
right atrium
aurícula F derecha
left atrium
aurícula F izquierda
right ventricle
ventrículo M derecho
left ventricle
ventrículo M izquierdo
hepatic vein
vena F hepática
celiac trunk
tronco M celiaco
liver
hígado M
spleen
bazo M
portal vein
vena F porta
stomach
estómago M
intestine
intestino M
inferior vena cava
vena F cava inferior
kidney
riñón M
internal iliac vein
vena F ilíaca
internal iliac artery
arteria F ilíaca interna
pelvic limb
miembro M inferior

blood circulation

composition of the blood
composición[F] de la sangre[F]

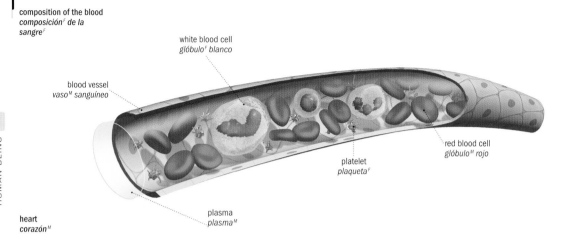

white blood cell
glóbulo[F] blanco

blood vessel
vaso[M] sanguíneo

red blood cell
glóbulo[M] rojo

platelet
plaqueta[F]

plasma
plasma[M]

heart
corazón[M]

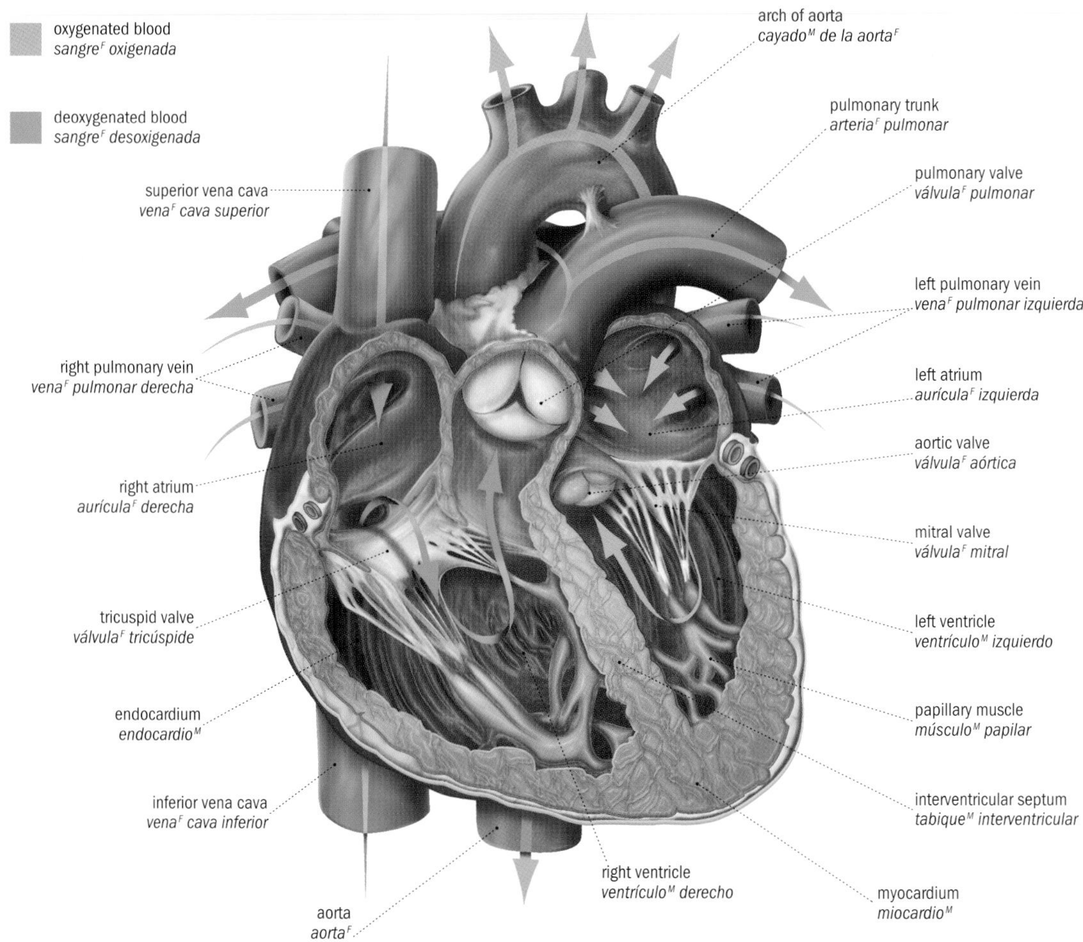

respiratory system

aparato[M] respiratorio

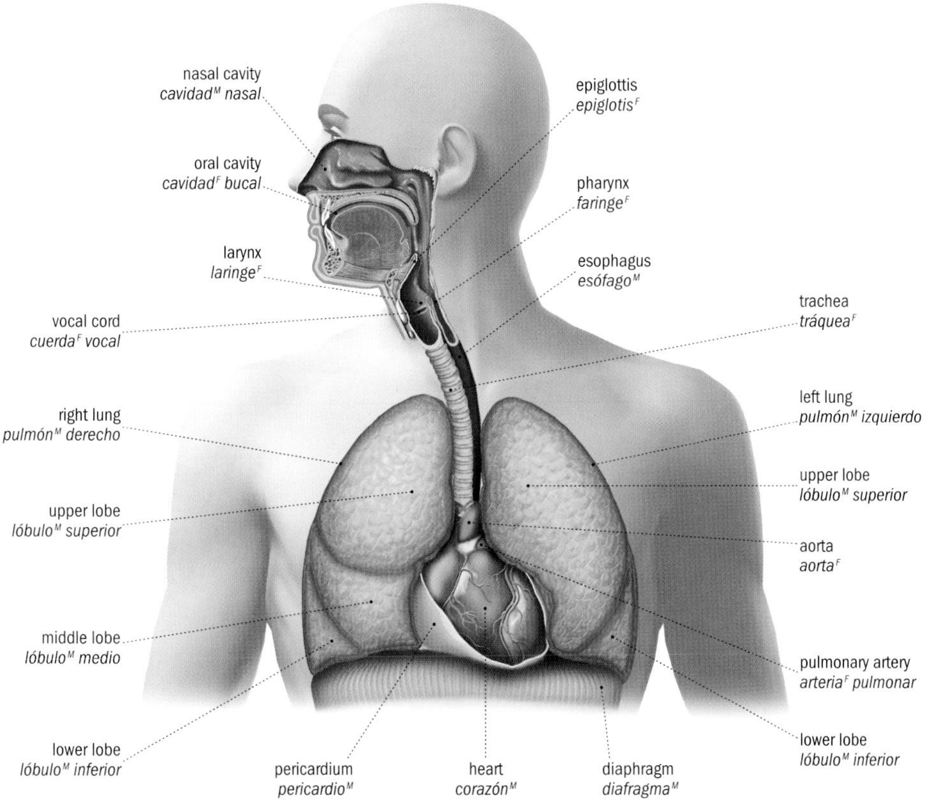

nasal cavity
cavidad[M] nasal
oral cavity
cavidad[F] bucal
larynx
laringe[F]
vocal cord
cuerda[F] vocal
right lung
pulmón[M] derecho
upper lobe
lóbulo[M] superior
middle lobe
lóbulo[M] medio
lower lobe
lóbulo[M] inferior
pericardium
pericardio[M]
heart
corazón[M]
diaphragm
diafragma[M]
epiglottis
epiglotis[F]
pharynx
faringe[F]
esophagus
esófago[M]
trachea
tráquea[F]
left lung
pulmón[M] izquierdo
upper lobe
lóbulo[M] superior
aorta
aorta[F]
pulmonary artery
arteria[F] pulmonar
lower lobe
lóbulo[M] inferior

lungs
pulmones[M]

upper lobe
lóbulo[M] superior
trachea
tráquea[F]
main bronchus
bronquio[M] principal
lobe bronchus
bronquio[M] lobular
terminal bronchiole
bronquiolo[M] terminal
parietal pleura
pleura[F] parietal
pleural cavity
cavidad[F] pleural
visceral pleura
pleura[F] visceral
oblique fissure
cisura[F] oblicua
lower lobe
lóbulo[M] inferior

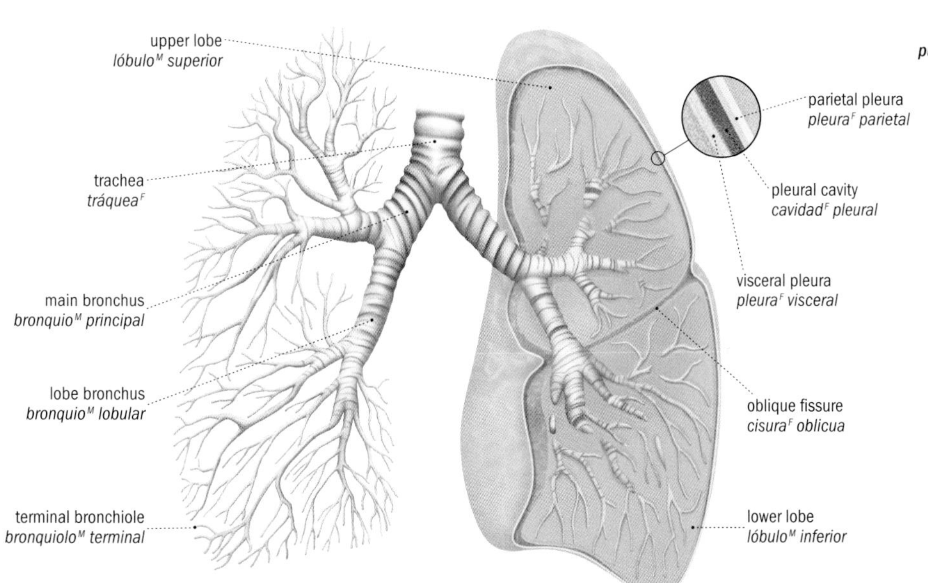

digestive system

aparato[M] digestivo

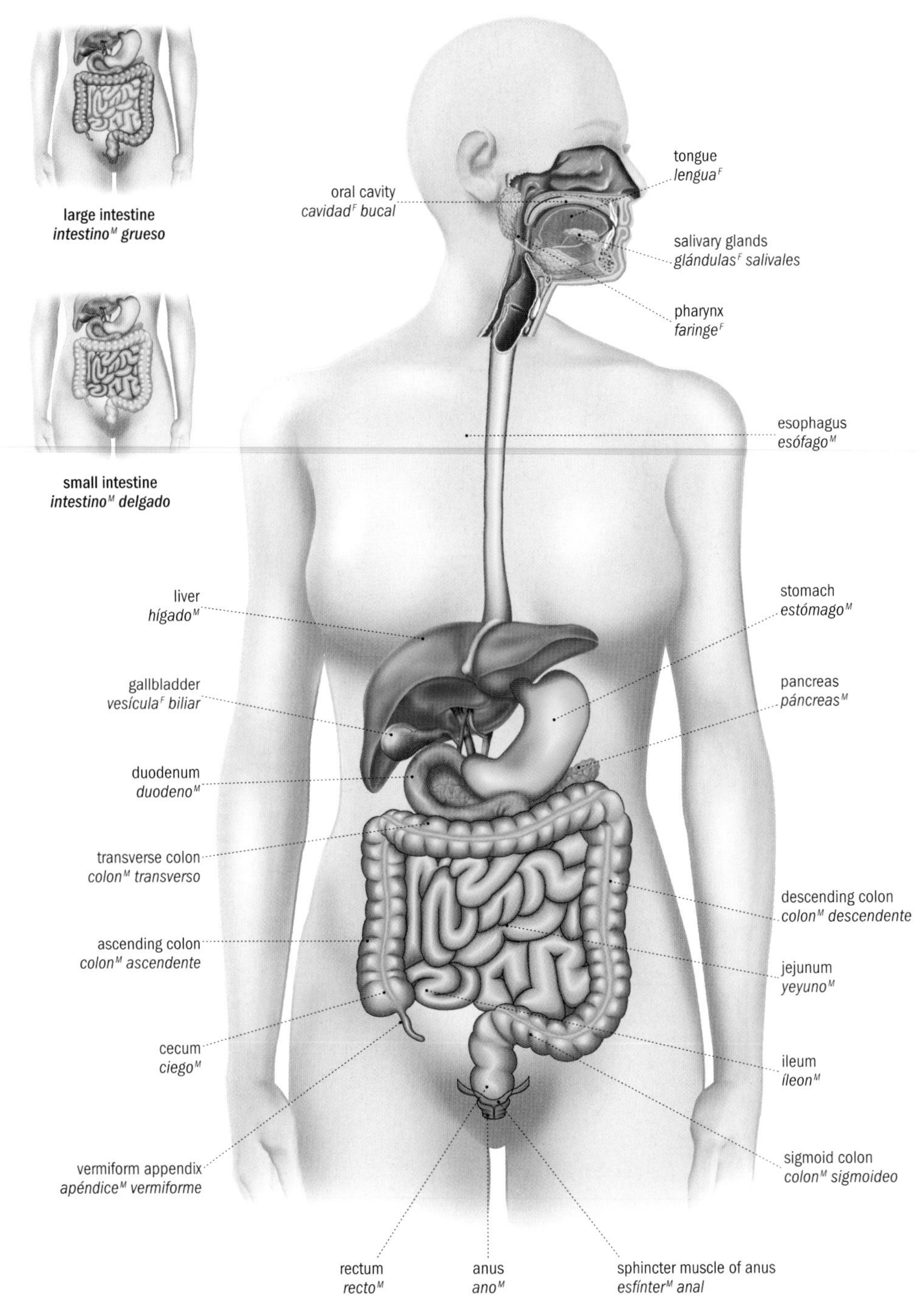
large intestine
intestino[M] grueso
small intestine
intestino[M] delgado
oral cavity
cavidad[F] bucal
tongue
lengua[F]
salivary glands
glándulas[F] salivales
pharynx
faringe[F]
esophagus
esófago[M]
liver
hígado[M]
stomach
estómago[M]
gallbladder
vesícula[F] biliar
pancreas
páncreas[M]
duodenum
duodeno[M]
transverse colon
colon[M] transverso
descending colon
colon[M] descendente
ascending colon
colon[M] ascendente
jejunum
yeyuno[M]
cecum
ciego[M]
ileum
íleon[M]
vermiform appendix
apéndice[M] vermiforme
sigmoid colon
colon[M] sigmoideo
rectum
recto[M]
anus
ano[M]
sphincter muscle of anus
esfínter[M] anal

urinary system

aparato[M] urinario

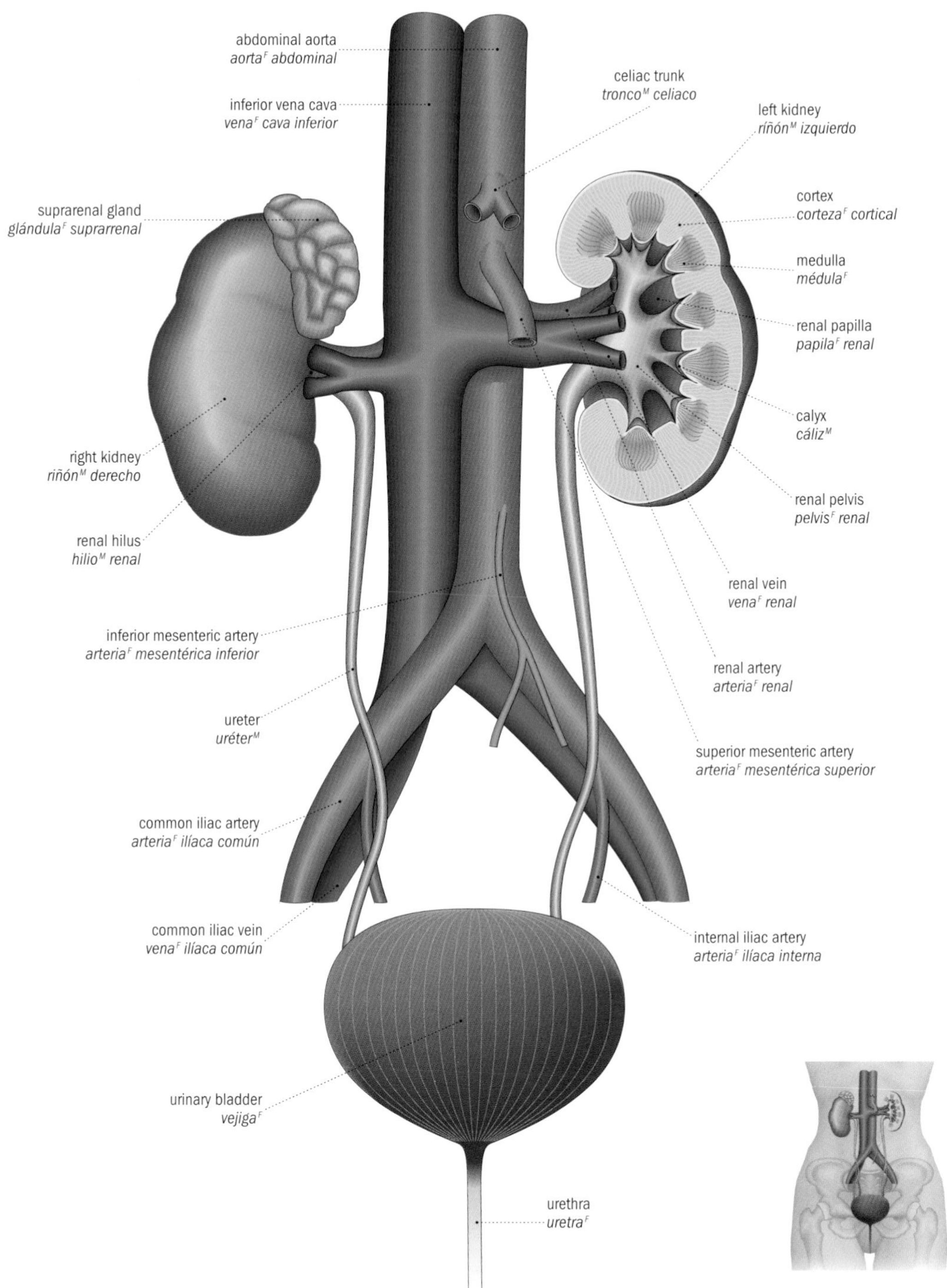
abdominal aorta
aorta[F] abdominal
inferior vena cava
vena[F] cava inferior
celiac trunk
tronco[M] celiaco
left kidney
riñón[M] izquierdo
suprarenal gland
glándula[F] suprarrenal
cortex
corteza[F] cortical
medulla
médula[F]
renal papilla
papila[F] renal
calyx
cáliz[M]
right kidney
riñón[M] derecho
renal pelvis
pelvis[F] renal
renal hilus
hilio[M] renal
renal vein
vena[F] renal
inferior mesenteric artery
arteria[F] mesentérica inferior
renal artery
arteria[F] renal
ureter
uréter[M]
superior mesenteric artery
arteria[F] mesentérica superior
common iliac artery
arteria[F] ilíaca común
common iliac vein
vena[F] ilíaca común
internal iliac artery
arteria[F] ilíaca interna
urinary bladder
vejiga[F]
urethra
uretra[F]

nervous system

sistema[M] nervioso

peripheral nervous system
sistema[M] nervioso periférico

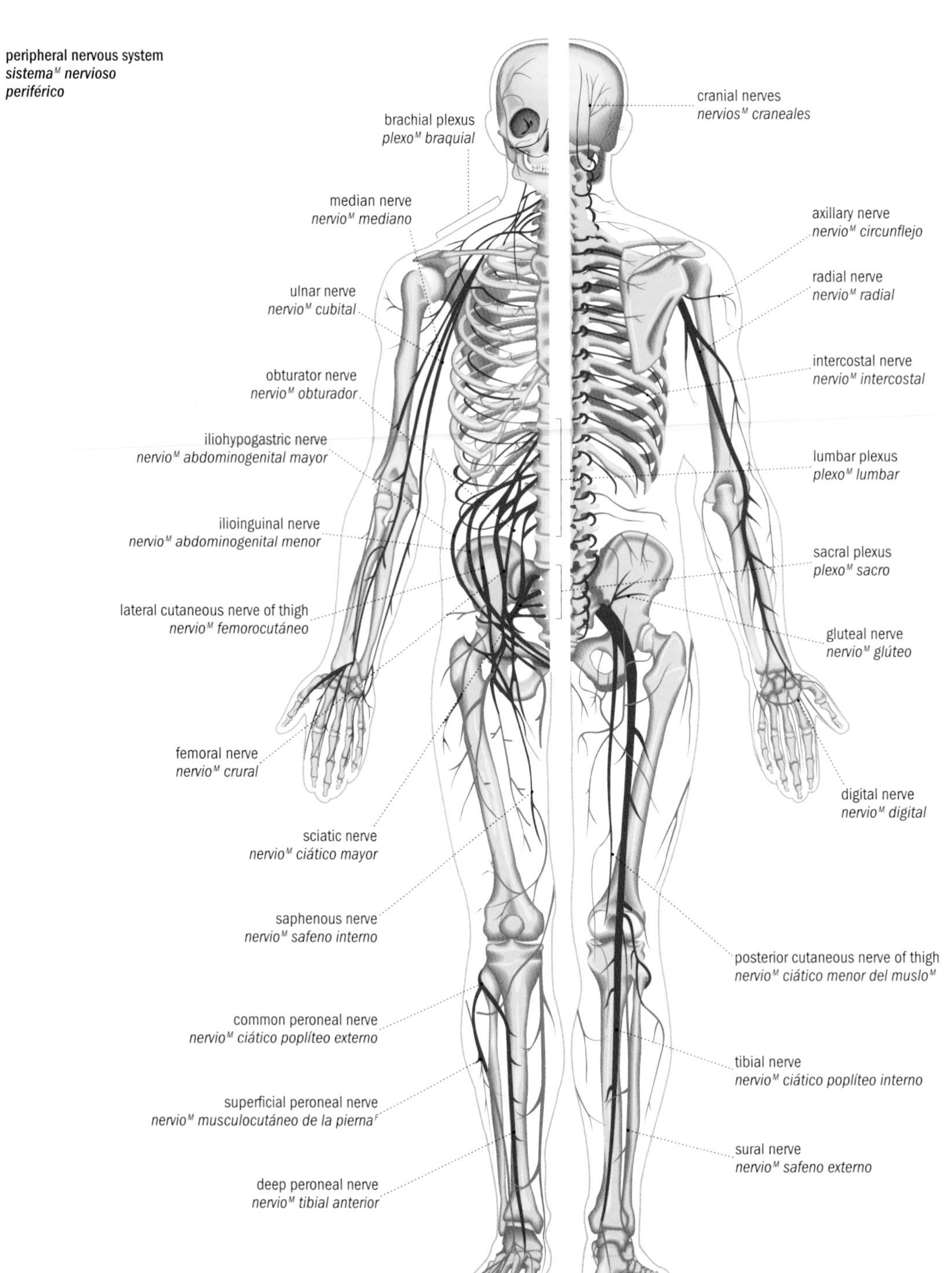

brachial plexus
plexo[M] braquial
cranial nerves
nervios[M] craneales
median nerve
nervio[M] mediano
axillary nerve
nervio[M] circunflejo
radial nerve
nervio[M] radial
ulnar nerve
nervio[M] cubital
intercostal nerve
nervio[M] intercostal
obturator nerve
nervio[M] obturador
iliohypogastric nerve
nervio[M] abdominogenital mayor
lumbar plexus
plexo[M] lumbar
ilioinguinal nerve
nervio[M] abdominogenital menor
sacral plexus
plexo[M] sacro
lateral cutaneous nerve of thigh
nervio[M] femorocutáneo
gluteal nerve
nervio[M] glúteo
femoral nerve
nervio[M] crural
digital nerve
nervio[M] digital
sciatic nerve
nervio[M] ciático mayor
saphenous nerve
nervio[M] safeno interno
posterior cutaneous nerve of thigh
nervio[M] ciático menor del muslo[M]
common peroneal nerve
nervio[M] ciático poplíteo externo
tibial nerve
nervio[M] ciático poplíteo interno
superficial peroneal nerve
nervio[M] musculocutáneo de la pierna[F]
sural nerve
nervio[M] safeno externo
deep peroneal nerve
nervio[M] tibial anterior

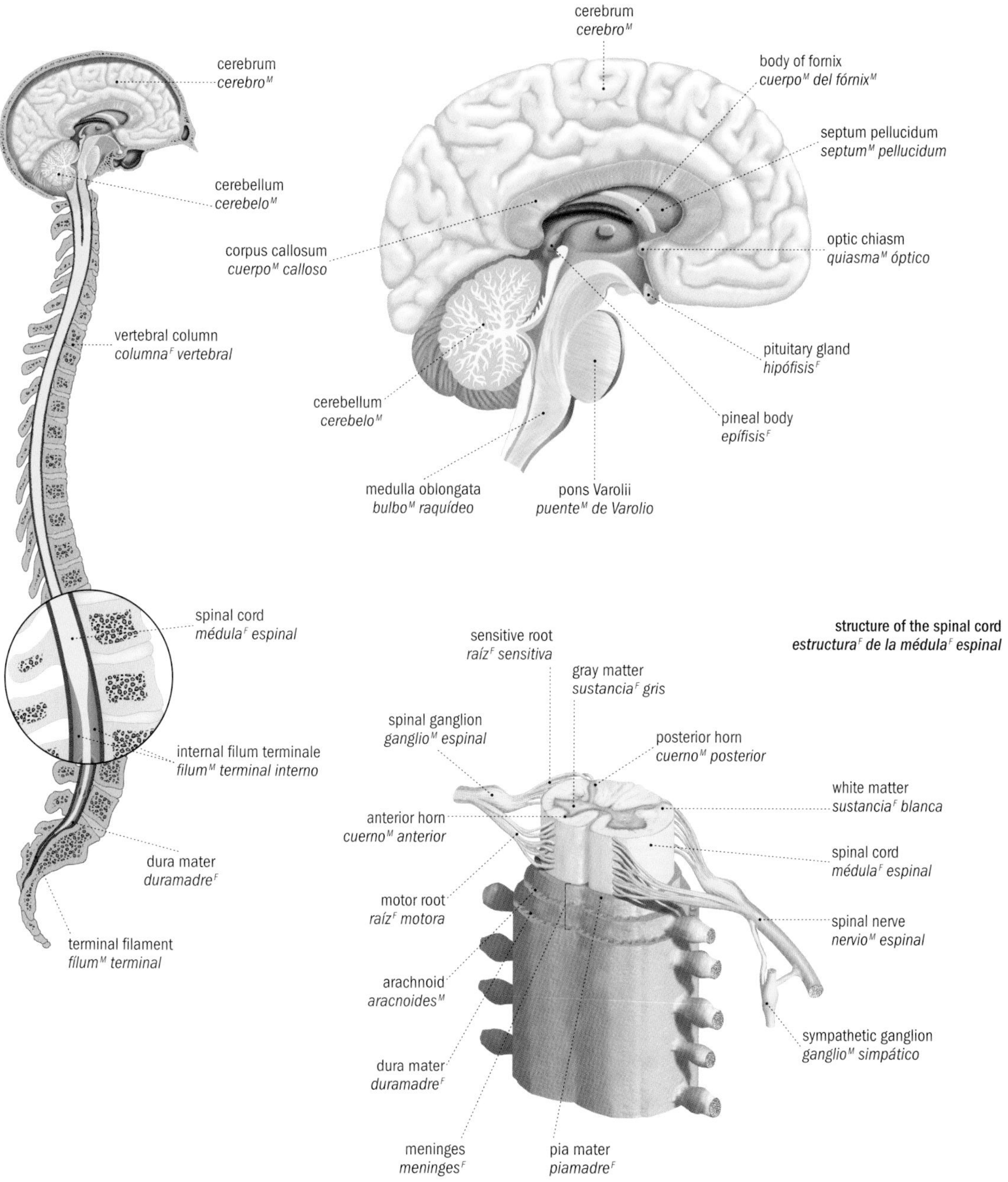
central nervous system
sistema^M nervioso central
cerebrum
cerebro^M
cerebellum
cerebelo^M
vertebral column
columna^F vertebral
spinal cord
médula^F espinal
internal filum terminale
filum^M terminal interno
dura mater
duramadre^F
terminal filament
filum^M terminal
cerebrum
cerebro^M
body of fornix
cuerpo^M del fórnix^M
septum pellucidum
septum^M pellucidum
corpus callosum
cuerpo^M calloso
optic chiasm
quiasma^M óptico
pituitary gland
hipófisis^F
cerebellum
cerebelo^M
pineal body
epífisis^F
medulla oblongata
bulbo^M raquídeo
pons Varolii
puente^M de Varolio
structure of the spinal cord
estructura^F de la médula^F espinal
sensitive root
raíz^F sensitiva
gray matter
sustancia^F gris
spinal ganglion
ganglio^M espinal
posterior horn
cuerno^M posterior
white matter
sustancia^F blanca
anterior horn
cuerno^M anterior
spinal cord
médula^F espinal
motor root
raíz^F motora
spinal nerve
nervio^M espinal
arachnoid
aracnoides^M
sympathetic ganglion
ganglio^M simpático
dura mater
duramadre^F
meninges
meninges^F
pia mater
piamadre^F

nervous system

chain of neurons
cadena[F] de neuronas[F]

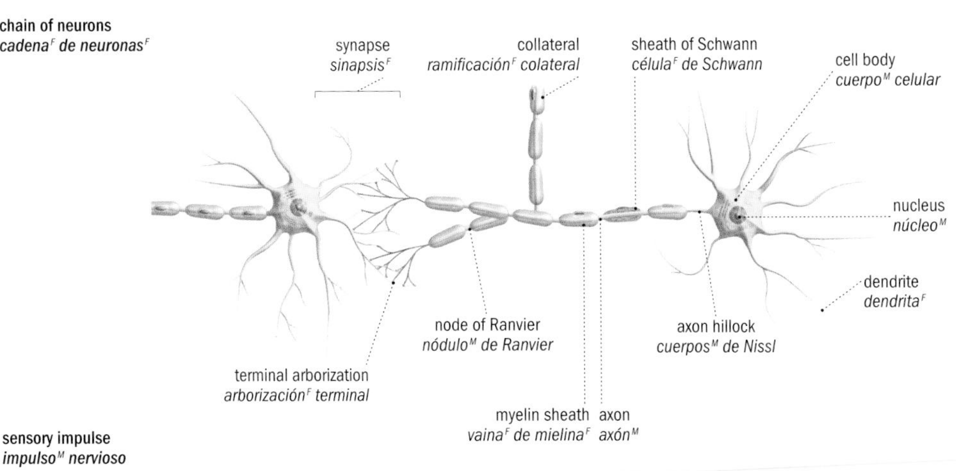

sensory impulse
impulso[M] nervioso

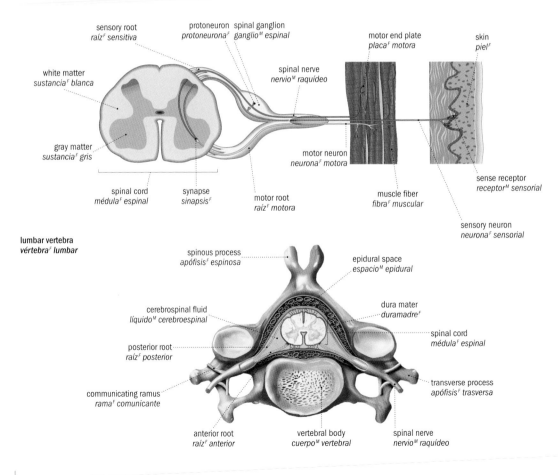

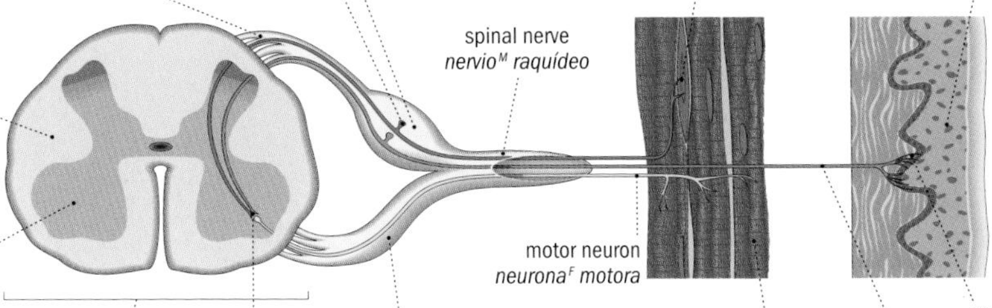

sensory root
raíz[F] sensitiva

protoneuron
protoneurona[F]

spinal ganglion
ganglio[M] espinal

motor end plate
placa[F] motora

skin
piel[F]

white matter
sustancia[F] blanca

spinal nerve
nervio[M] raquídeo

gray matter
sustancia[F] gris

motor neuron
neurona[F] motora

sense receptor
receptor[M] sensorial

spinal cord
médula[F] espinal

synapse
sinapsis[F]

motor root
raíz[F] motora

muscle fiber
fibra[F] muscular

sensory neuron
neurona[F] sensorial

lumbar vertebra
vértebra[F] lumbar

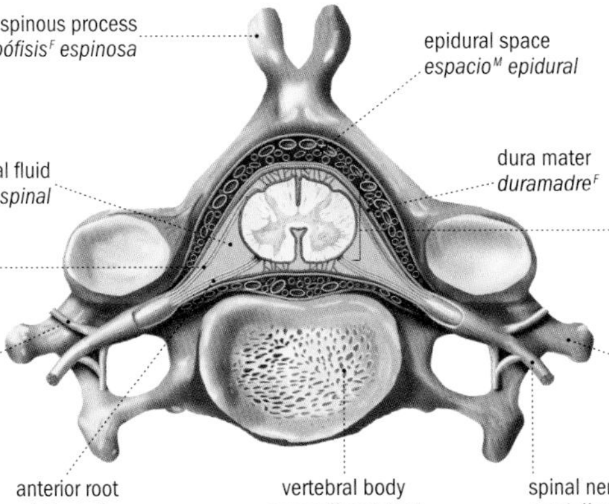

spinous process
apófisis[F] espinosa

epidural space
espacio[M] epidural

cerebrospinal fluid
líquido[M] cerebroespinal

dura mater
duramadre[F]

spinal cord
médula[F] espinal

posterior root
raíz[F] posterior

transverse process
apófisis[F] trasversa

communicating ramus
rama[F] comunicante

anterior root
raíz[F] anterior

vertebral body
cuerpo[M] vertebral

spinal nerve
nervio[M] raquídeo

male reproductive organs

órganos^{M} genitales masculinos

sagittal section
sección^{F} sagital

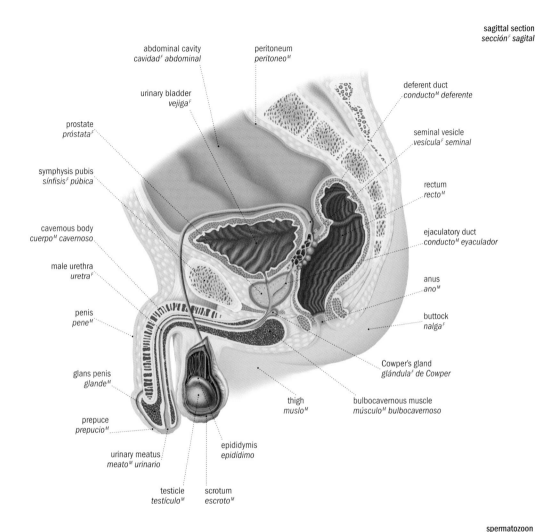

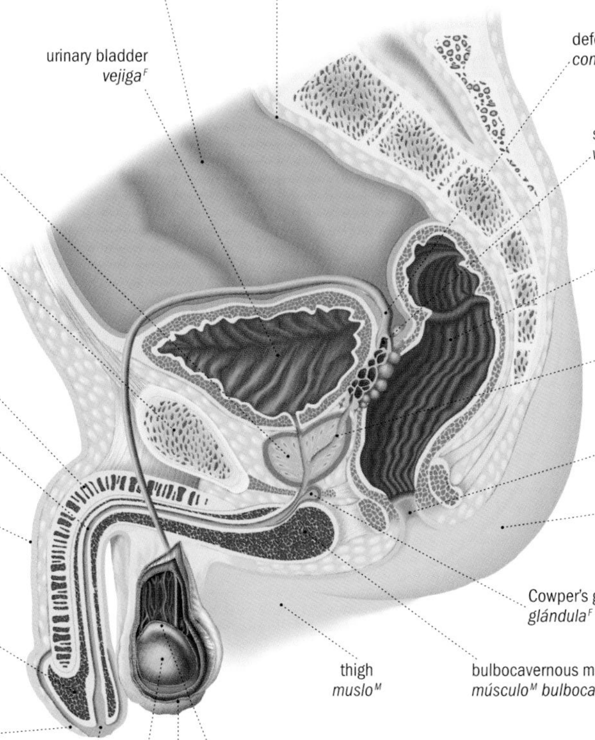

abdominal cavity
cavidad^{F} abdominal
peritoneum
peritoneo^{M}
urinary bladder
vejiga^{F}
prostate
próstata^{F}
symphysis pubis
sínfisis^{F} púbica
cavernous body
cuerpo^{M} cavernoso
male urethra
uretra^{F}
penis
pene^{M}
glans penis
glande^{M}
prepuce
prepucio^{M}
urinary meatus
meato^{M} urinario
testicle
testículo^{M}
scrotum
escroto^{M}
epididymis
epidídimo
thigh
muslo^{M}
bulbocavernous muscle
músculo^{M} bulbocavernoso
Cowper's gland
glándula^{F} de Cowper
buttock
nalga^{F}
anus
ano^{M}
ejaculatory duct
conducto^{M} eyaculador
rectum
recto^{M}
seminal vesicle
vesícula^{F} seminal
deferent duct
conducto^{M} deferente

spermatozoon
espermatozoide^{M}

head
cabeza^{F}
end piece
segmento^{M} terminal
tail
cola^{F}
neck
cuello^{M}
middle piece
segmento^{M} intermedio

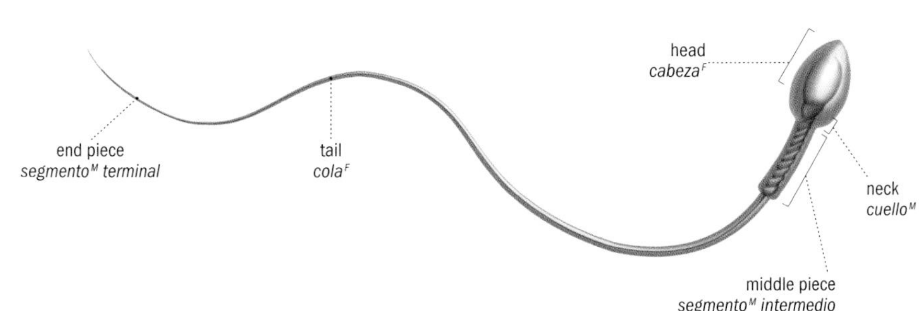

female reproductive organs

órganos[M] genitales femeninos

sagittal section
sección[F] sagital

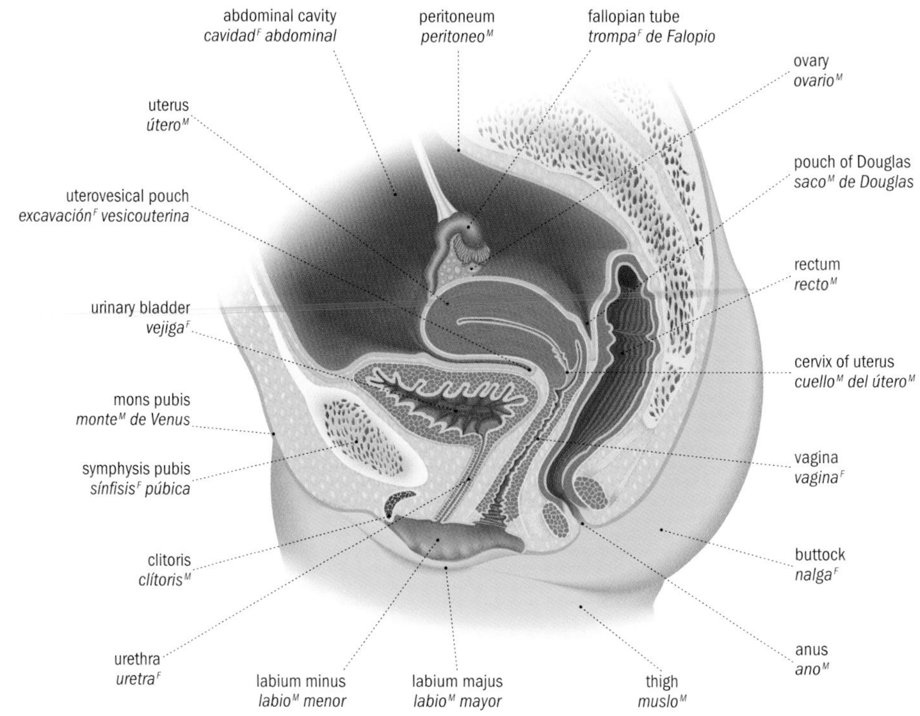

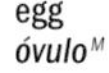

egg
óvulo[M]

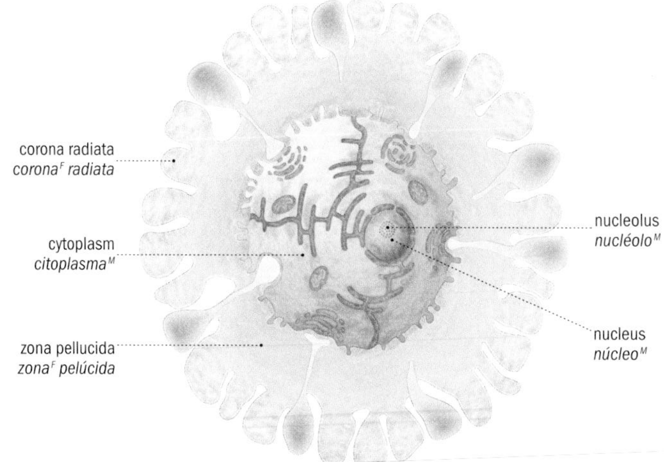

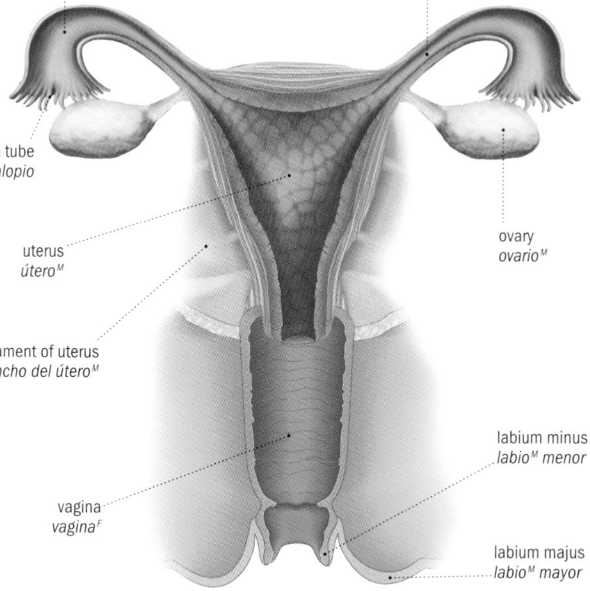

female reproductive organs

posterior view
vista[F] posterior

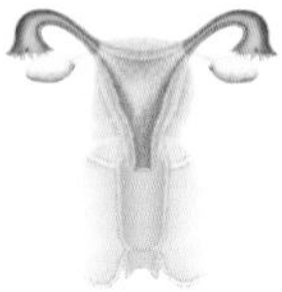

ampulla of fallopian tube
ampolla[F] de la trompa[F] uterina

isthmus of fallopian tube
istmo[M] de la trompa[F] de Falopio

infundibulum of fallopian tube
pabellón[M] de la trompa[F] de Falopio

uterus
útero[M]

ovary
ovario[M]

broad ligament of uterus
ligamento[M] ancho del útero[M]

labium minus
labio[M] menor

vagina
vagina[F]

labium majus
labio[M] mayor

fallopian tubes
trompas[F] de Falopio

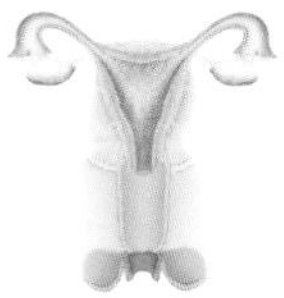

vulva
vulva[F]

breast

seno[M]

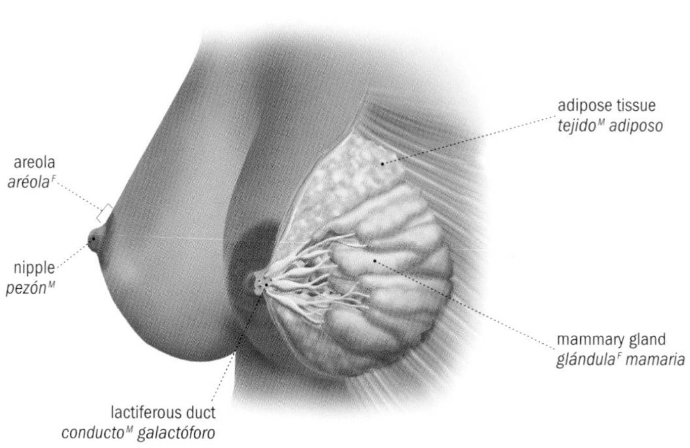

touch

tacto[M]

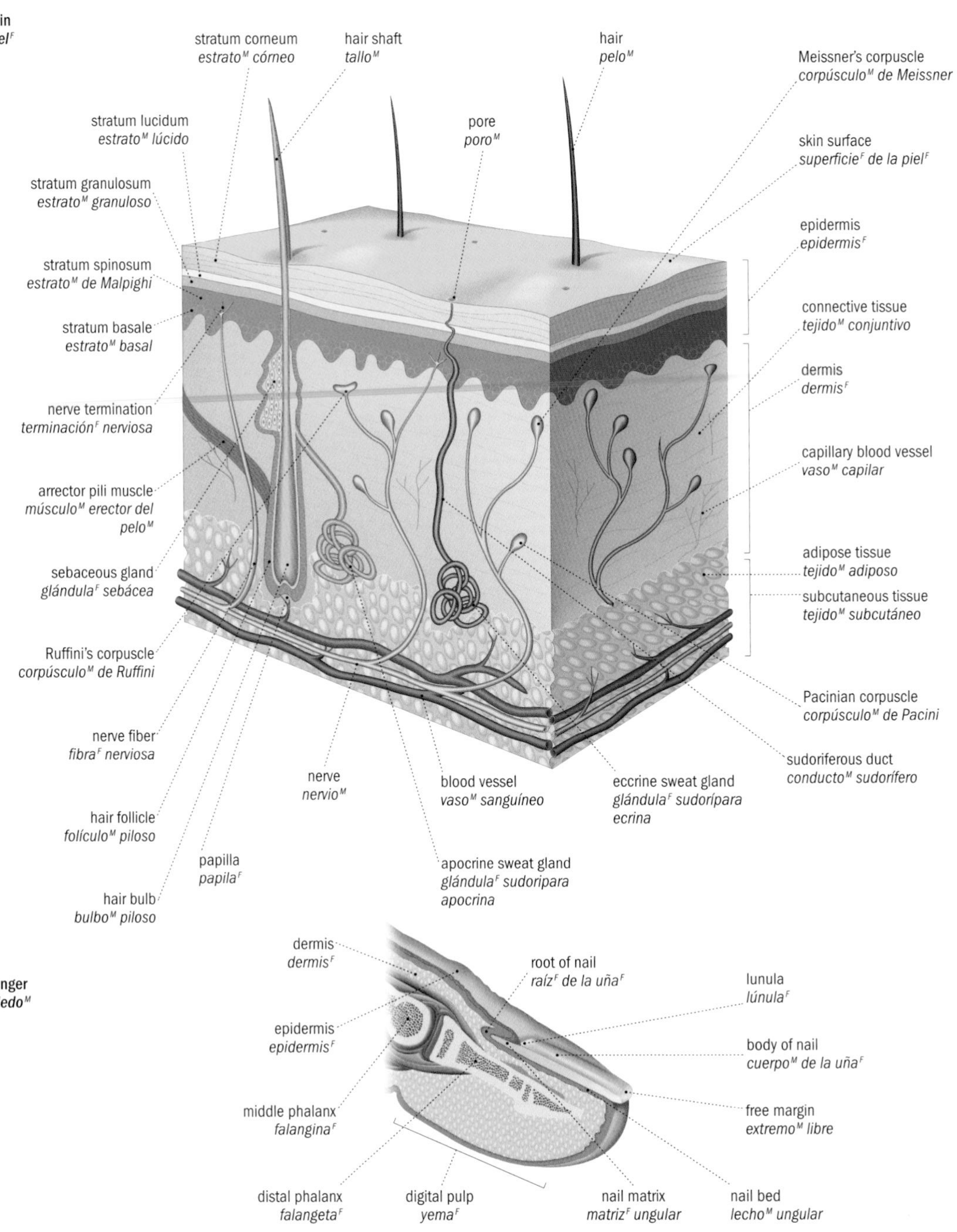
skin
pielF
stratum corneum
estratoM córneo
hair shaft
talloM
hair
peloM
Meissner's corpuscle
corpúsculoM de Meissner
stratum lucidum
estratoM lúcido
pore
poroM
skin surface
superficieF de la pielF
stratum granulosum
estratoM granuloso
epidermis
epidermisF
stratum spinosum
estratoM de Malpighi
connective tissue
tejidoM conjuntivo
stratum basale
estratoM basal
dermis
dermisF
nerve termination
terminaciónF nerviosa
capillary blood vessel
vasoM capilar
arrector pili muscle
músculoM erector del peloM
adipose tissue
tejidoM adiposo
sebaceous gland
glándulaF sebácea
subcutaneous tissue
tejidoM subcutáneo
Ruffini's corpuscle
corpúsculoM de Ruffini
Pacinian corpuscle
corpúsculoM de Pacini
nerve fiber
fibraF nerviosa
sudoriferous duct
conductoM sudorífero
nerve
nervioM
blood vessel
vasoM sanguíneo
eccrine sweat gland
glándulaF sudorípara ecrina
hair follicle
folículoM piloso
papilla
papilaF
apocrine sweat gland
glándulaF sudoripara apocrina
hair bulb
bulboM piloso
dermis
dermisF
root of nail
raízF de la uñaF
lunula
lúnulaF
finger
dedoM
epidermis
epidermisF
body of nail
cuerpoM de la uñaF
middle phalanx
falanginaF
free margin
extremoM libre
distal phalanx
falangetaF
digital pulp
yemaF
nail matrix
matrizF ungular
nail bed
lechoM ungular

touch

hand
manoF

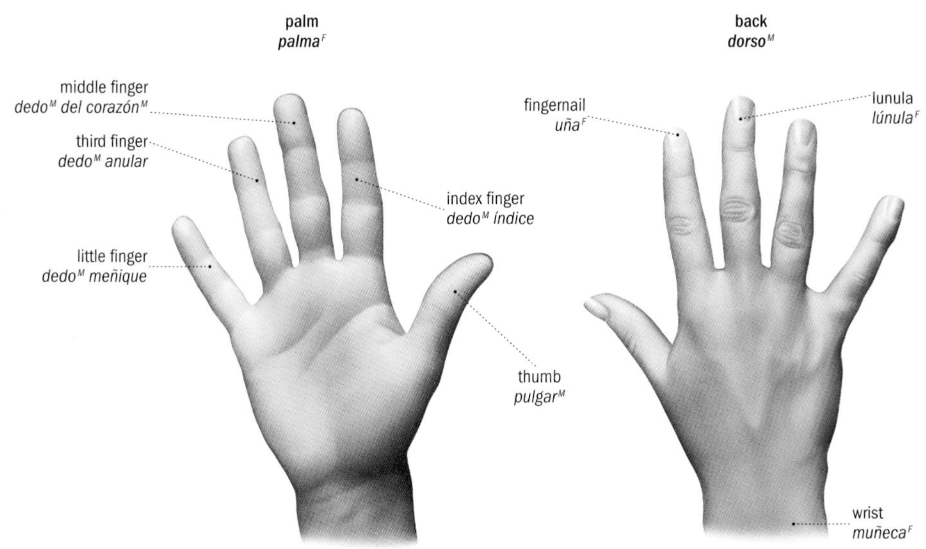

hearing

oídoM

auricle
pabellón*M *auricular

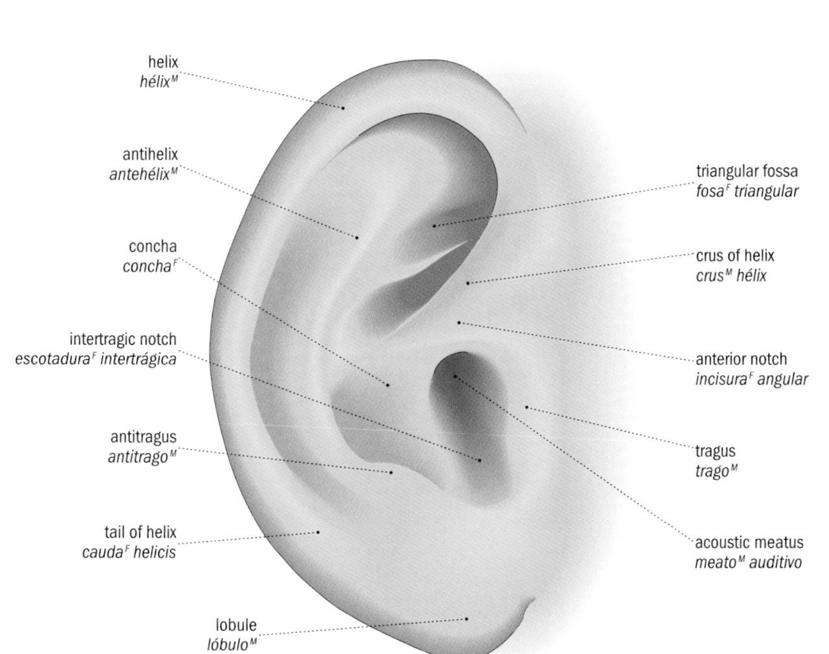

hearing

structure of the ear
estructura^F^ del oído^M^

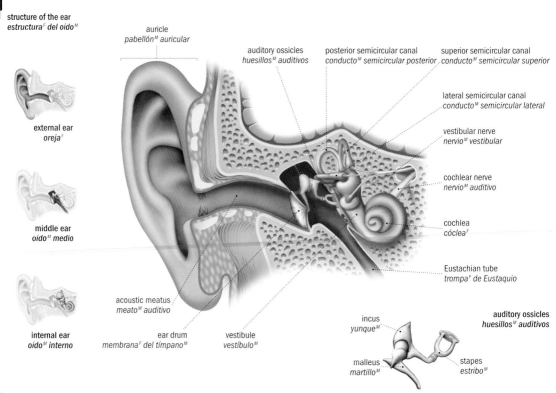

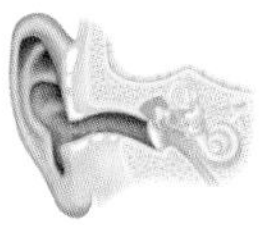

external ear
oreja^F^

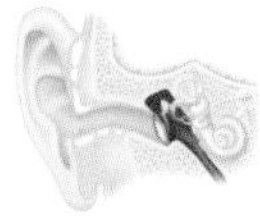

middle ear
oído^M^ medio

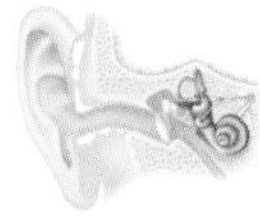

internal ear
oído^M^ interno

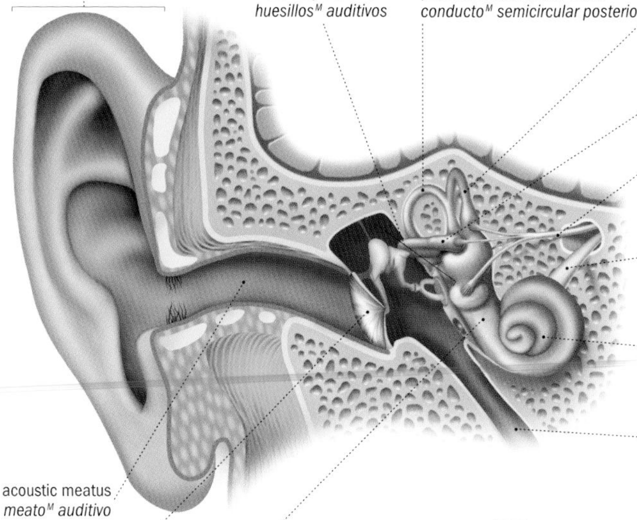

auricle
pabellón^M^ auricular
auditory ossicles
huesillos^M^ auditivos
posterior semicircular canal
conducto^M^ semicircular posterior
superior semicircular canal
conducto^M^ semicircular superior
lateral semicircular canal
conducto^M^ semicircular lateral
vestibular nerve
nervio^M^ vestibular
cochlear nerve
nervio^M^ auditivo
cochlea
*cóclea^F^*
Eustachian tube
trompa^F^ de Eustaquio
acoustic meatus
meato^M^ auditivo
ear drum
*membrana^F^ del tímpano^M^*
vestibule
*vestíbulo^M^*

incus
*yunque^M^*
malleus
*martillo^M^*
stapes
*estribo^M^*

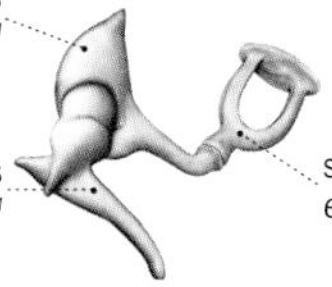

auditory ossicles
huesillos^M^ auditivos

smell and taste

olfato^M^ y gusto^M^

mouth
boca^F^

upper lip
labio^M^ superior
gum
*encía^F^*
superior dental arch
arco^M^ dentario superior
hard palate
bóveda^F^ palatina
isthmus of fauces
*istmo^M^ de las fauces^F^*
soft palate
*velo^M^ del paladar^M^*
commissure of lips of mouth
comisura^F^ labial
palatoglossal arch
*pilar^M^ anterior del velo^M^ del paladar^M^*
tongue
*lengua^F^*
tonsil
*amígdala^F^*
uvula
*úvula^F^*
inferior dental arch
arco^M^ dentario inferior
lower lip
labio^M^ inferior

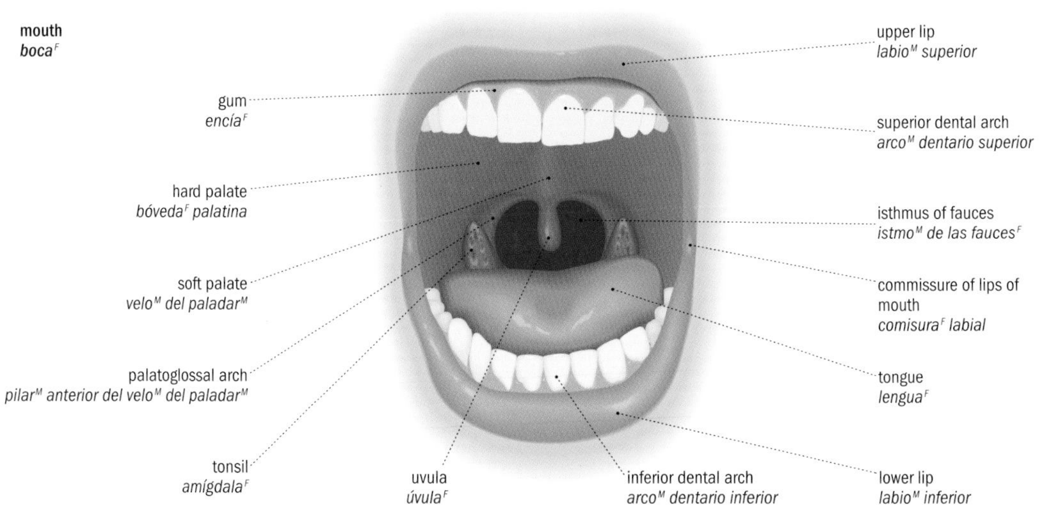

external nose
nariz^F

root of nose
puente^M de la nariz^F
dorsum of nose
dorso^M de la nariz^F
tip of nose
lóbulo^M
septum
tabique^M nasal
ala
aleta^F de la nariz^F
nostril
ventana^F de la nariz^F
philtrum
surco^M nasolabial

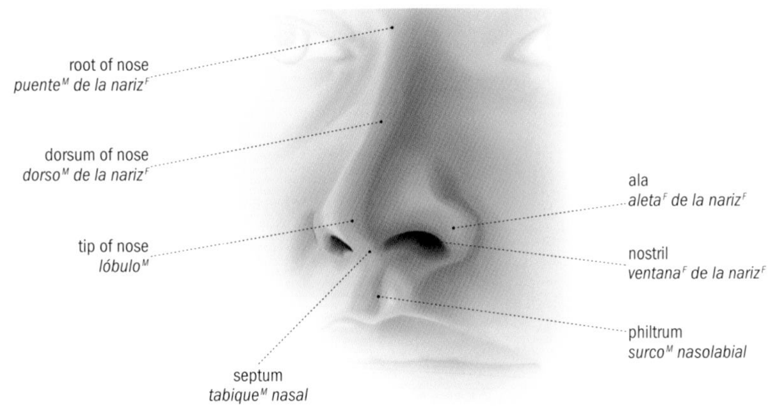

nasal fossae
fosas^F nasales

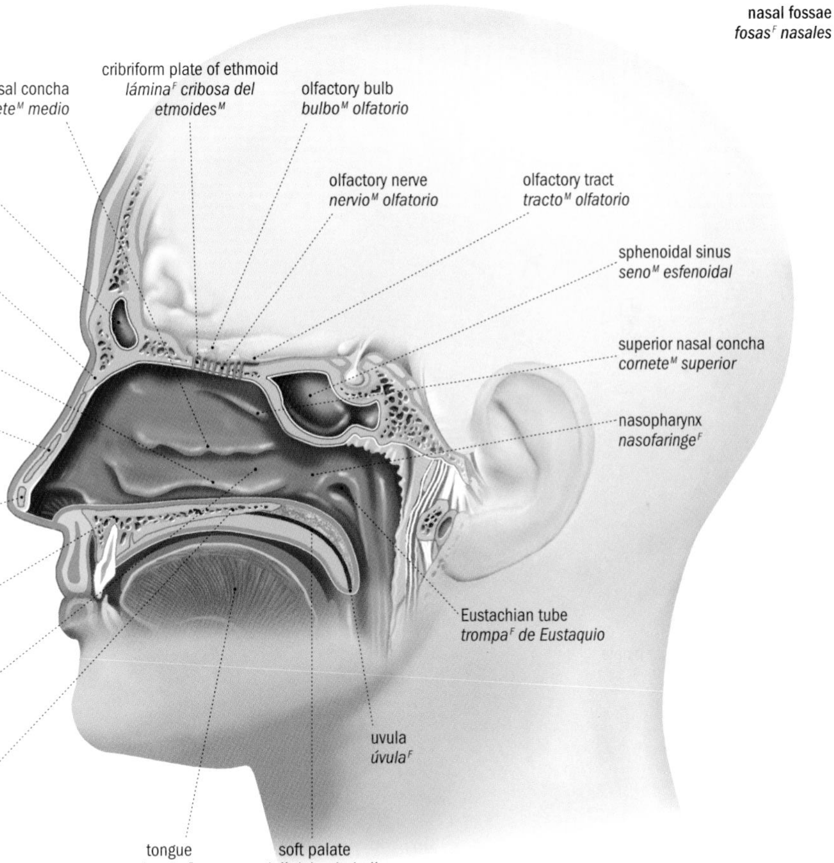

middle nasal concha
cornete^M medio
cribriform plate of ethmoid
lámina^F cribosa del etmoides^M
olfactory bulb
bulbo^M olfatorio
frontal sinus
seno^M frontal
olfactory nerve
nervio^M olfatorio
olfactory tract
tracto^M olfatorio
nasal bone
hueso^M nasal
sphenoidal sinus
seno^M esfenoidal
inferior nasal concha
cornete^M inferior
superior nasal concha
cornete^M superior
septal cartilage of nose
cartílago^M nasal del tabique^M
nasopharynx
nasofaringe^F
greater alar cartilage
cartílago^M alar mayor
maxilla
maxilar^M
Eustachian tube
trompa^F de Eustaquio
olfactory mucosa
mucosa^F olfatoria
uvula
úvula^F
hard palate
bóveda^F palatina
tongue
lengua^F
soft palate
velo^M del paladar^M

smell and taste

dorsum of tongue
lengua ^F^

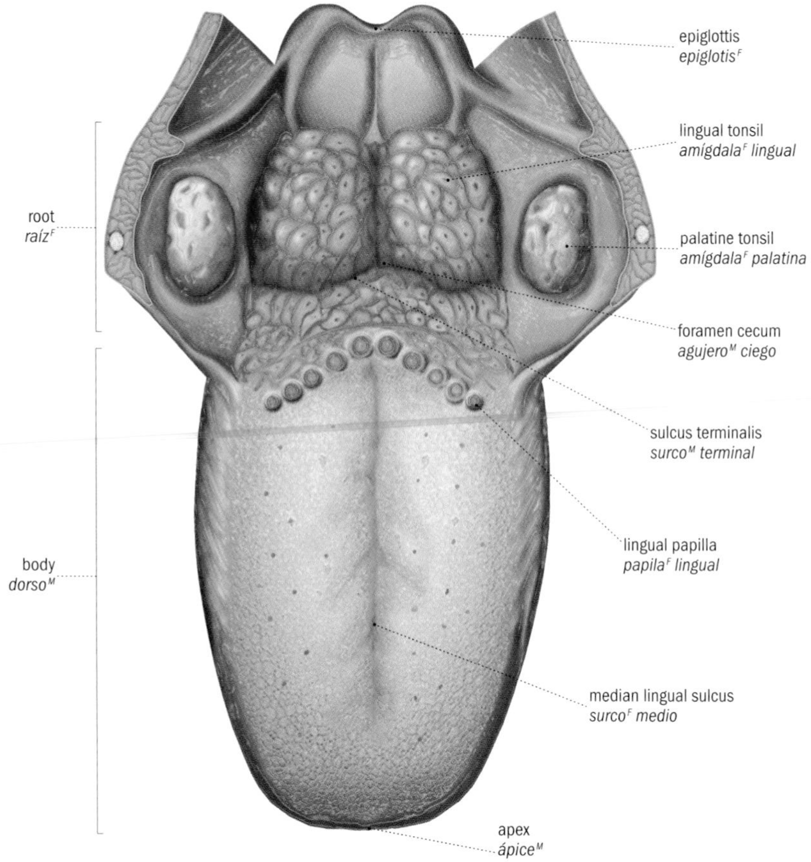

epiglottis
epiglotis F
lingual tonsil
amígdala F lingual
root
raíz F
palatine tonsil
amígdala F palatina
foramen cecum
agujero M ciego
sulcus terminalis
surco M terminal
lingual papilla
papila F lingual
body
dorso M
median lingual sulcus
surco F medio
apex
ápice M

taste receptors
receptores ^M^ ***gustativos***

fungiform papilla
papila F fungiforme
filiform papilla
papila F filiforme
salivary gland
glándula F salival
circumvallate papilla
papilla F circunvalada
foliate papilla
papila F foliada
furrow
surco M
taste bud
papila F gustativa

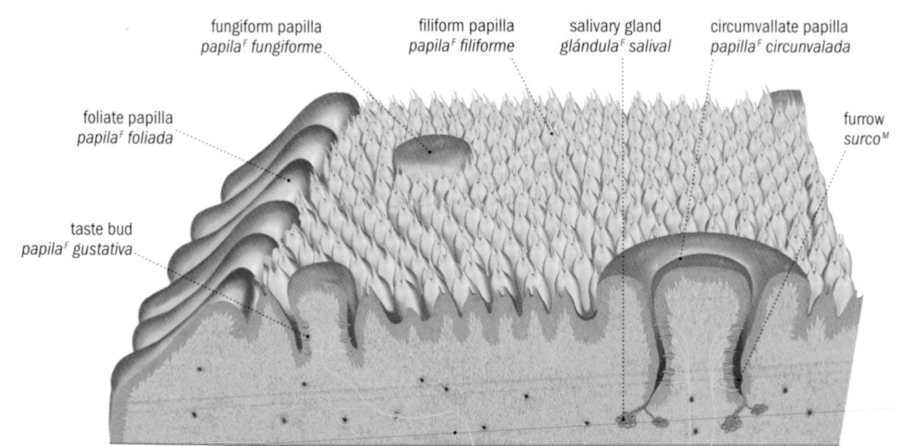

sight
vista[F]

eye
ojo[M]

upper eyelid
párpado[M] superior
eyelash
pestaña[F]
lachrymal duct
conducto[M] lacrimal
lachrymal canal
canal[M] lacrimal
iris
iris[M]
lower eyelid
párpado[M] inferior
sclera
esclerótica[F]
pupil
pupila[F]
lachrymal gland
glándula[F] lacrimal

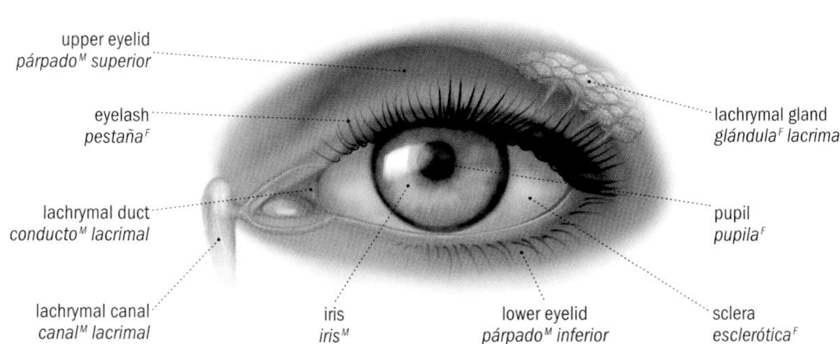

eyeball
globo[M] ocular

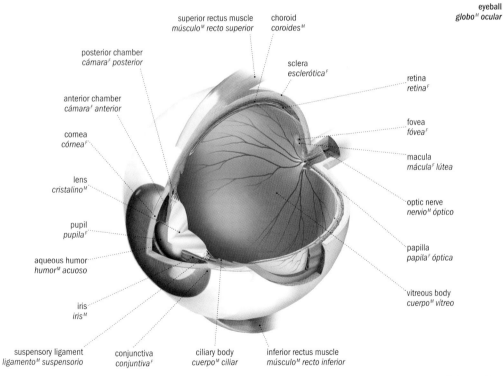

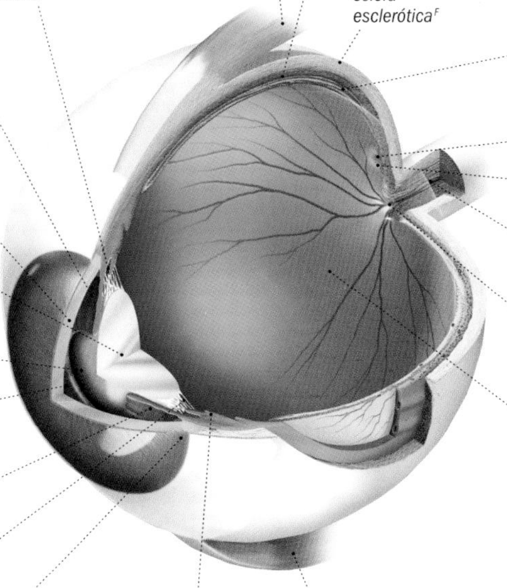

superior rectus muscle
músculo[M] recto superior
choroid
coroides[M]
posterior chamber
cámara[F] posterior
sclera
esclerótica[F]
retina
retina[F]
anterior chamber
cámara[F] anterior
fovea
fóvea[F]
cornea
córnea[F]
macula
mácula[F] lútea
lens
cristalino[M]
optic nerve
nervio[M] óptico
pupil
pupila[F]
papilla
papila[F] óptica
aqueous humor
humor[M] acuoso
vitreous body
cuerpo[M] vítreo
iris
iris[M]
suspensory ligament
ligamento[M] suspensorio
conjunctiva
conjuntiva[F]
ciliary body
cuerpo[M] ciliar
inferior rectus muscle
músculo[M] recto inferior

photoreceptors
fotorreceptores[M]

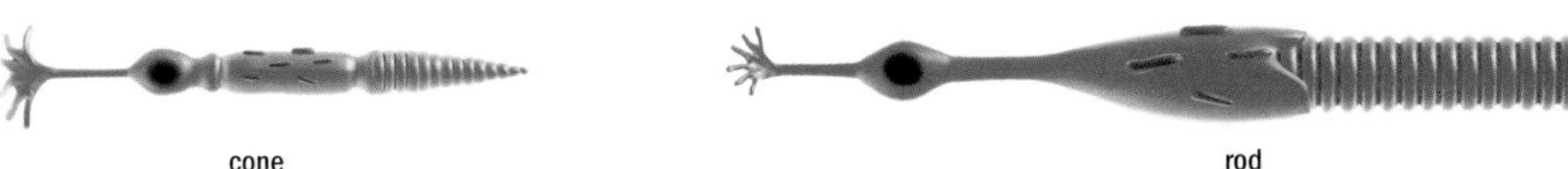

cone
cono[M]

rod
bastoncillo[M]

supermarket

supermercado^M

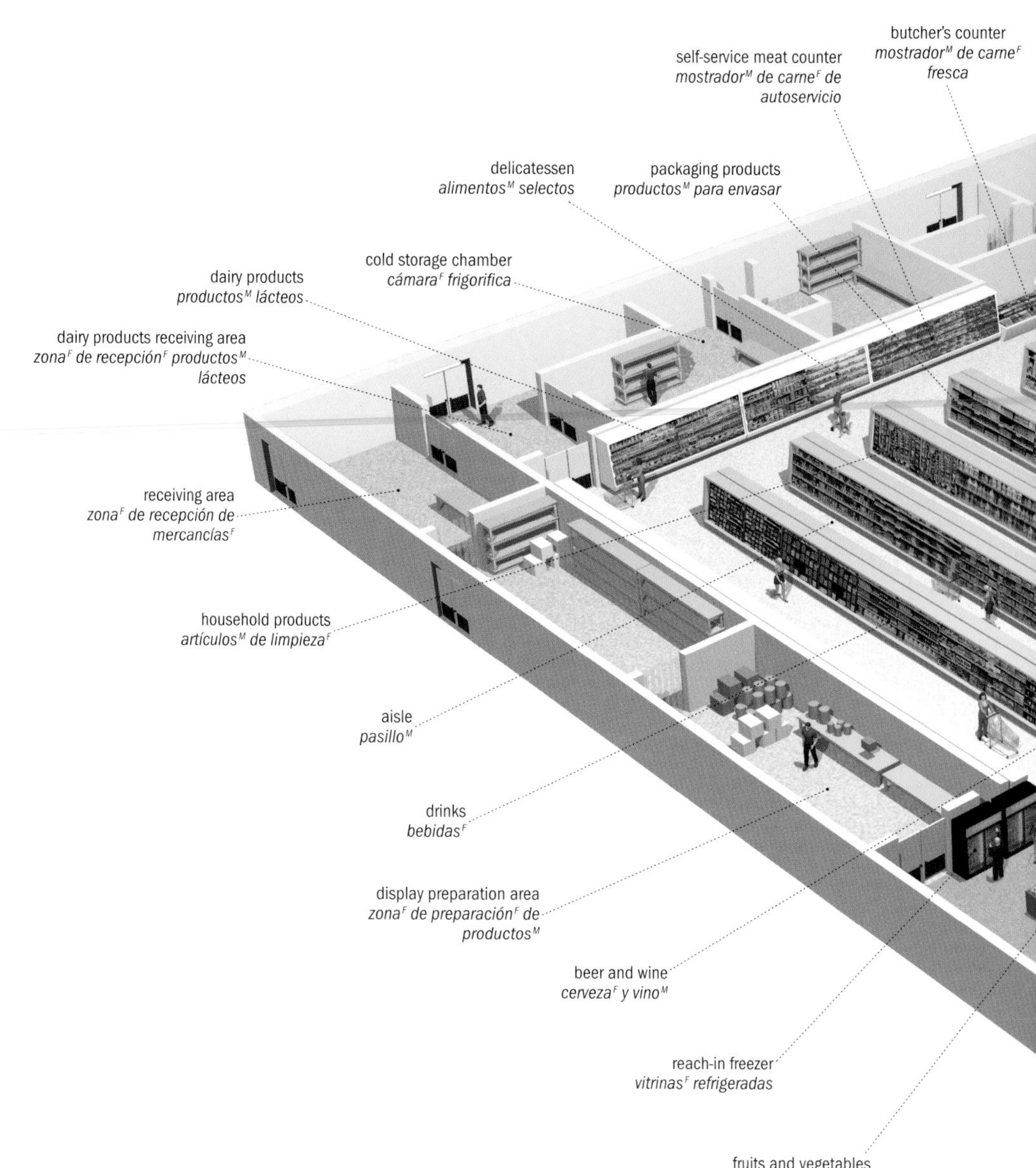
butcher's counter
mostrador^M de carne^F fresca
self-service meat counter
mostrador^M de carne^F de autoservicio
delicatessen
alimentos^M selectos
packaging products
productos^M para envasar
cold storage chamber
cámara^F frigorífica
dairy products
productos^M lácteos
dairy products receiving area
zona^F de recepción^F productos^M lácteos
receiving area
zona^F de recepción de mercancías^F
household products
artículos^M de limpieza^F
aisle
pasillo^M
drinks
bebidas^F
display preparation area
zona^F de preparación^F de productos^M
beer and wine
cerveza^F y vino^M
reach-in freezer
vitrinas^F refrigeradas
fruits and vegetables
frutas^F y verduras^F

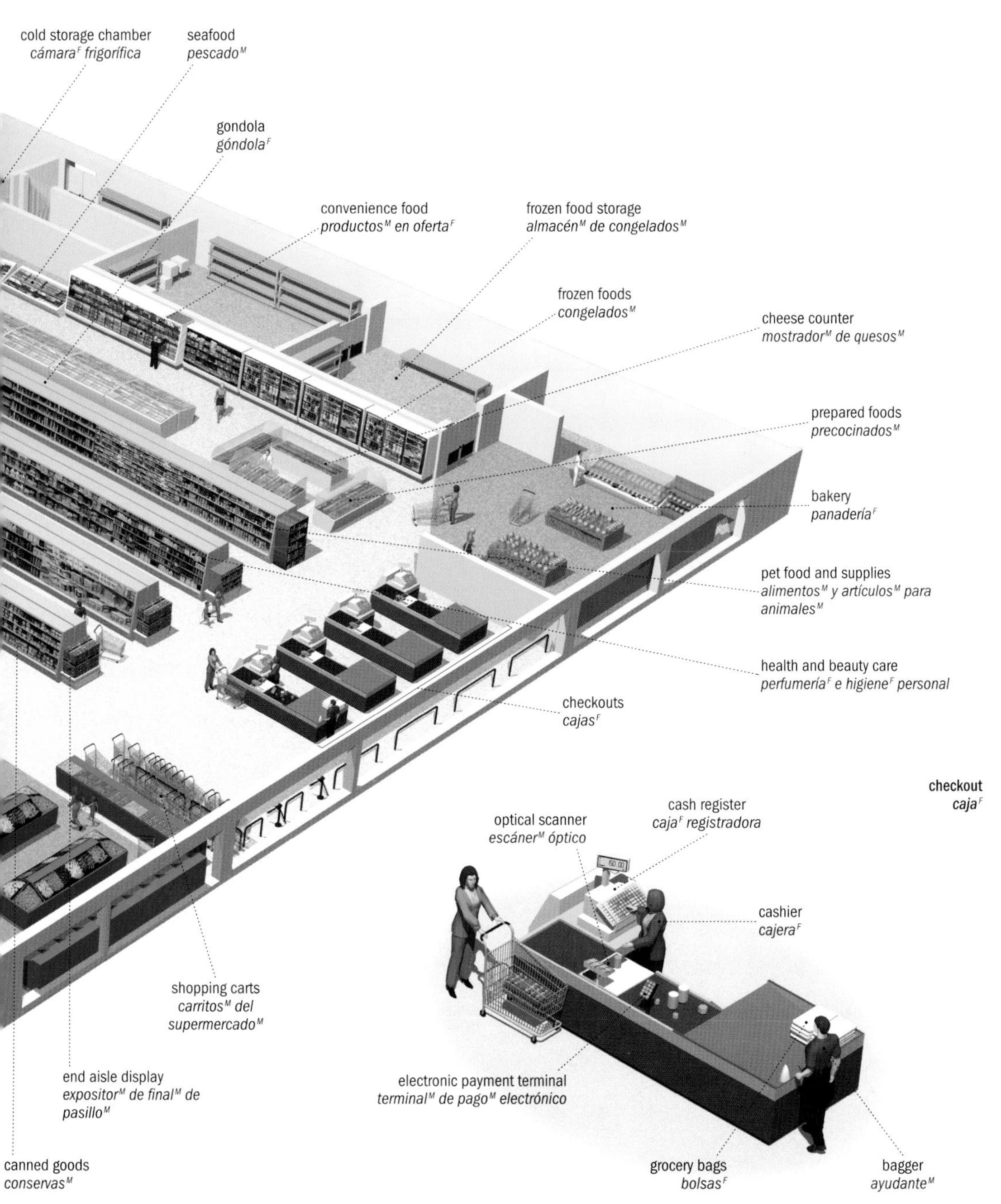
cold storage chamber
cámara[F] frigorífica
seafood
pescado[M]
gondola
góndola[F]
convenience food
productos[M] en oferta[F]
frozen food storage
almacén[M] de congelados[M]
frozen foods
congelados[M]
cheese counter
mostrador[M] de quesos[M]
prepared foods
precocinados[M]
bakery
panadería[F]
pet food and supplies
alimentos[M] y artículos[M] para animales[M]
health and beauty care
perfumería[F] e higiene[F] personal
checkouts
cajas[F]
shopping carts
carritos[M] del supermercado[M]
end aisle display
expositor[M] de final[M] de pasillo[M]
canned goods
conservas[M]
checkout
caja[F]
cash register
caja[F] registradora
optical scanner
escáner[M] óptico
cashier
cajera[F]
electronic payment terminal
terminal[M] de pago[M] electrónico
grocery bags
bolsas[F]
bagger
ayudante[M]

farmstead

granja^F

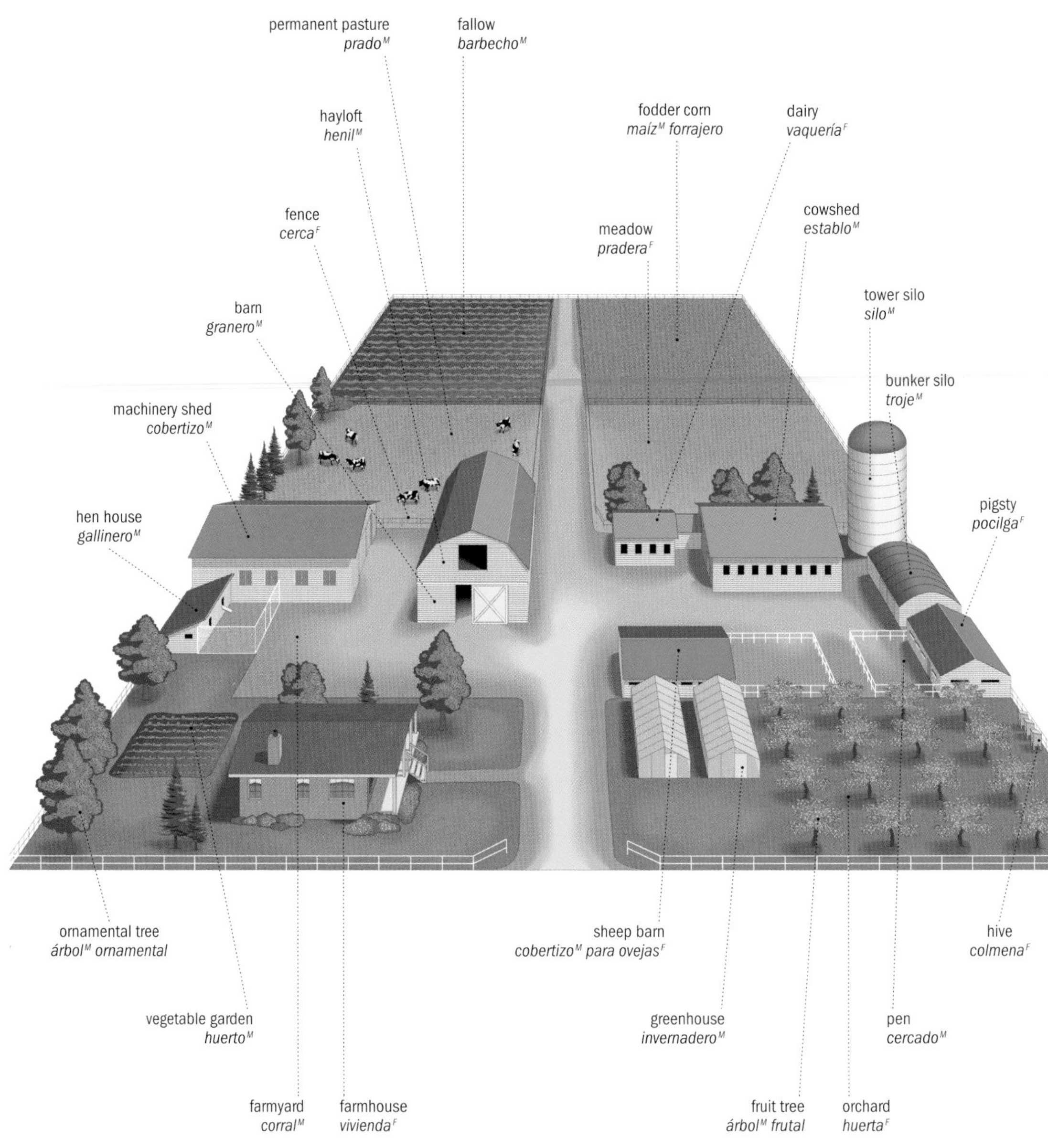
permanent pasture
prado^M
fallow
barbecho^M
hayloft
henil^M
fodder corn
maíz^M forrajero
dairy
vaquería^F
fence
cerca^F
meadow
pradera^F
cowshed
establo^M
barn
granero^M
tower silo
silo^M
bunker silo
troje^M
machinery shed
cobertizo^M
pigsty
pocilga^F
hen house
gallinero^M
ornamental tree
árbol^M ornamental
sheep barn
cobertizo^M para ovejas^F
hive
colmena^F
vegetable garden
huerto^M
greenhouse
invernadero^M
pen
cercado^M
farmyard
corral^M
farmhouse
vivienda^F
fruit tree
árbol^M frutal
orchard
huerta^F

mushrooms
hongos^{M}

truffle
trufa^{F}

wood ear
oreja^{F} *de Judas*

royal agaric
oronja^{F}

delicious lactarius
mízcalo^{M}

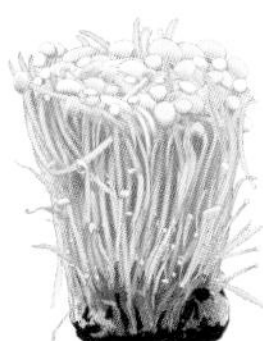
enoki
seta^{F} *enoki*

oyster
orellana^{F}

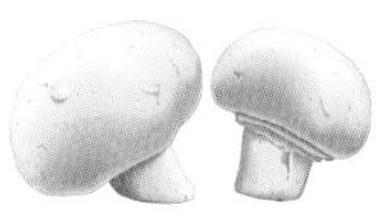
cultivated mushrooms
champiñón^{M}

green russula
rusula^{F} *verde*

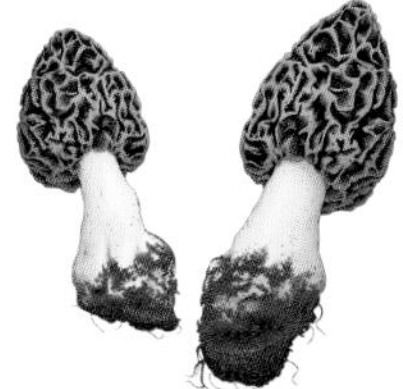
morels
morilla^{F}

edible boletus
boleto^{M} *comestible*

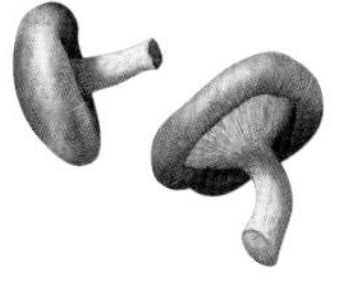
shitake
shiitake^{M}

chanterelles
rebozuelo^{M}

seaweed
algas^{F}

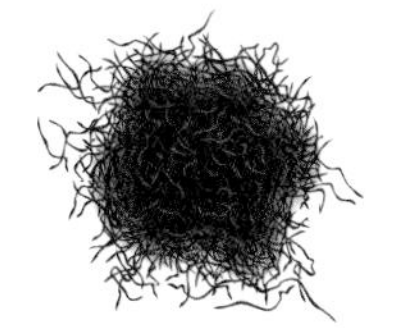
arame
arame^{M}

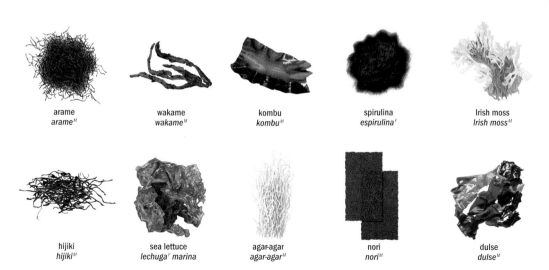

wakame
wakame^{M}

kombu
kombu^{M}

spirulina
espirulina^{F}

Irish moss
Irish moss^{M}

hijiki
hijiki^{M}

sea lettuce
lechuga^{F} *marina*

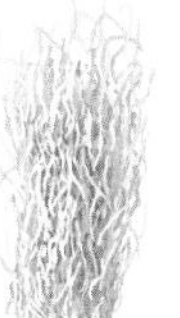
agar-agar
agar-agar^{M}

nori
nori^{M}

dulse
dulse^{M}

vegetables

hortalizas[F]

bulb vegetables
bulbos[M]

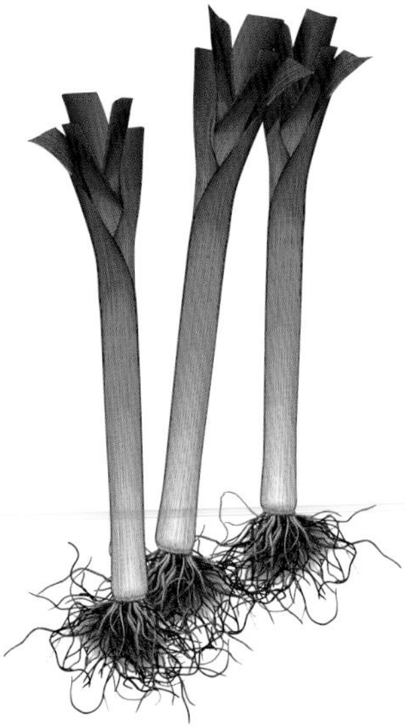

shallot
chalote[M]

water chestnut
castaña[F] *de agua*

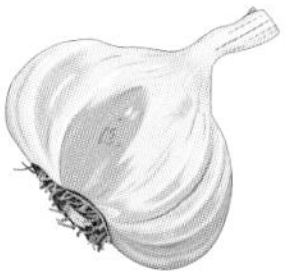

green onion
cebolla[F] *tierna*

scallion
cebolla[F] *tierna*

garlic
ajo[M]

chives
cebollino[M]

leeks
puerros[M]

yellow onion
cebolla[F] *amarilla*

red onion
cebolla[F] *roja*

white onion
cebolla[F] *blanca*

pickling onions
cebolletas[M]

tuber vegetables
tubérculos[M]

cassava
mandioca[F]

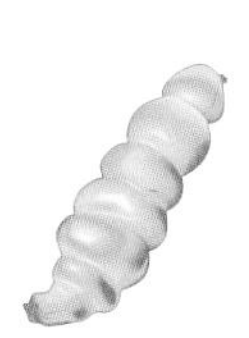

crosne
crosne[M]

taro
taro[M]

jicama
jícama[F]

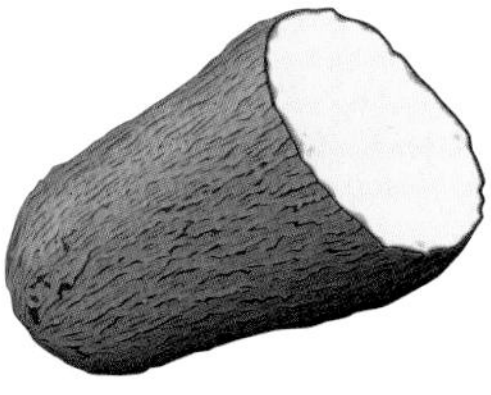

tropical yam
batata[F]

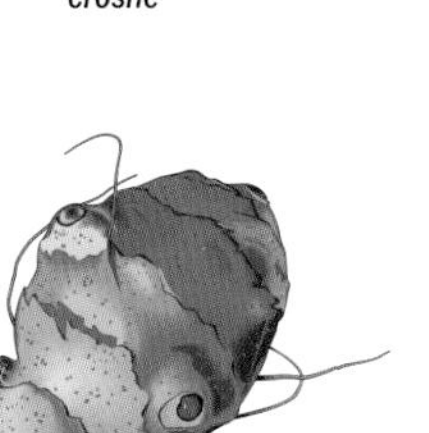

Jerusalem artichoke
aguaturma[F]

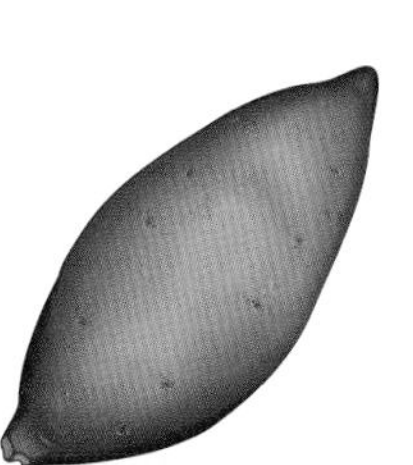

sweet potato
batata[F]

potatoes
patatas[F]

stalk vegetables
hortalizas[F] de tallos[M]

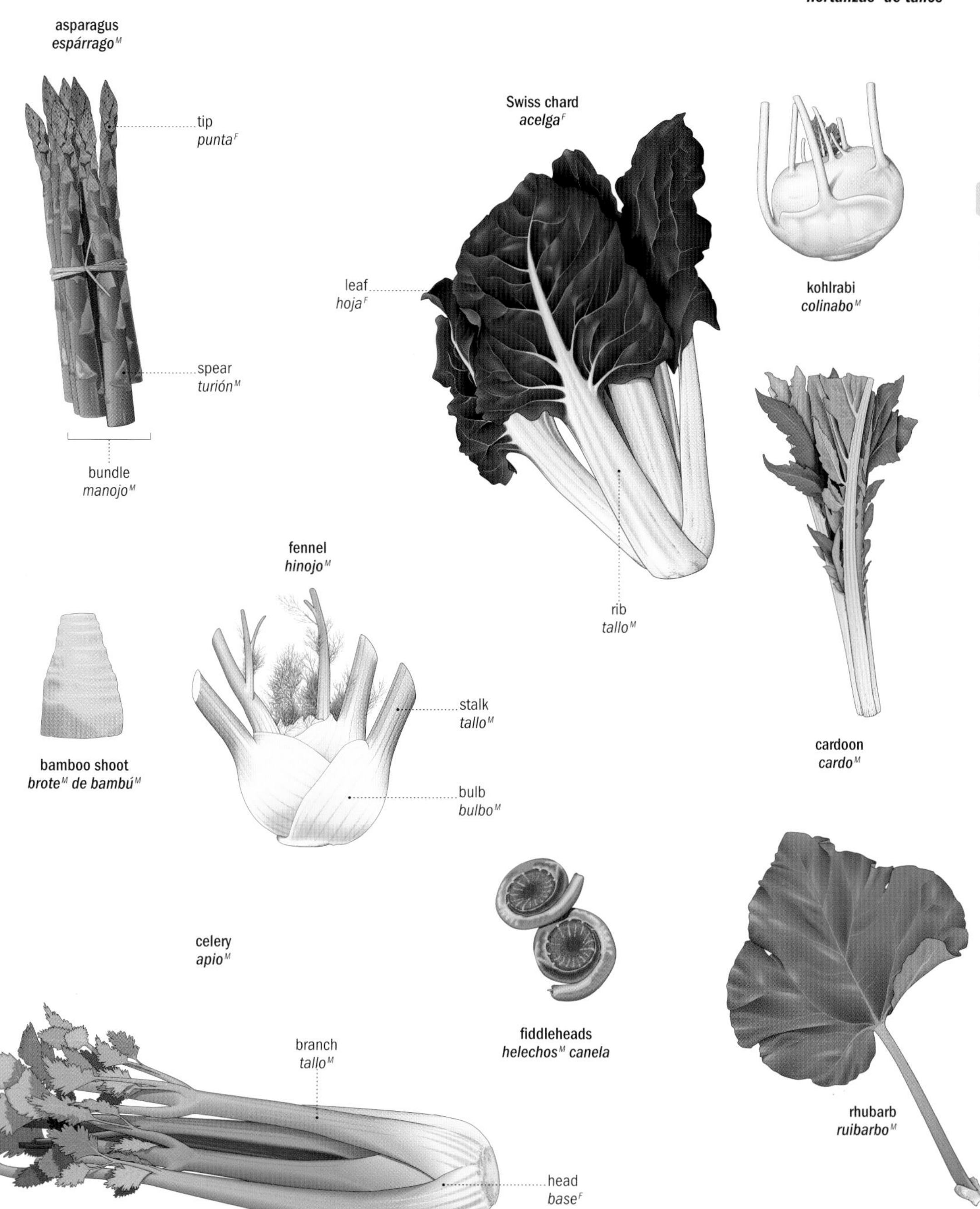

leaf vegetables
verduras^F de hojas^F

leaf lettuce
lechuga^F rizada

romaine lettuce
lechuga^F romana

celtuce
lechuga^F de tallo^M

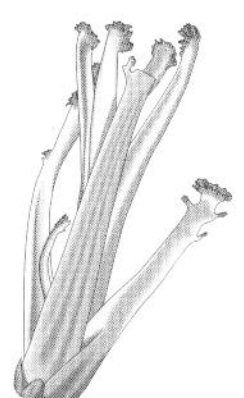

sea kale
col^F marina

collards
berza^F

escarole
escarola^F

butter lettuce
lechuga^F de cogollo^M

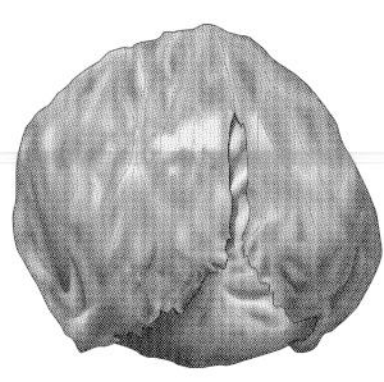

iceberg lettuce
lechuga^F iceberg

radicchio
achicoria^F de Treviso

ornamental kale
col^F ornamental

curly kale
col^F rizada

grape leaves
hoja^F de parra^F

brussels sprouts
coles^F de Bruselas

red cabbage
col^F lombarda

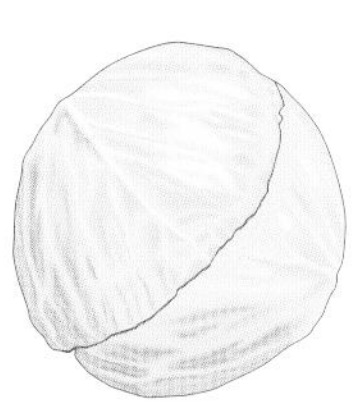

white cabbage
col^F/repollo^M

savoy cabbage
col^F rizada de otoño^M

green cabbage
col^F verde/repollo^M verde

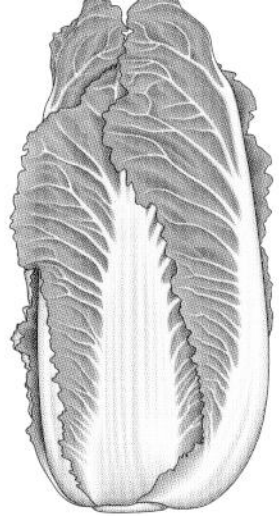

pe-tsai
col^M china

bok choy
pak-choi^M

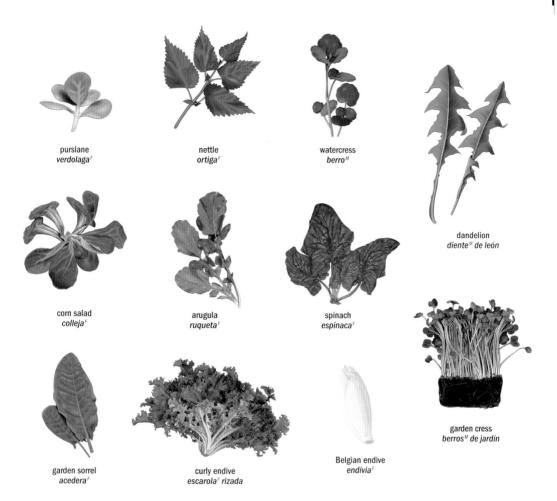

purslane
verdolaga[F]

nettle
ortiga[F]

watercress
berro[M]

dandelion
diente[M] *de león*

corn salad
colleja[F]

arugula
ruqueta[F]

spinach
espinaca[F]

garden cress
berros[M] *de jardín*

garden sorrel
acedera[F]

curly endive
escarola[F] *rizada*

Belgian endive
endivia[F]

inflorescent vegetables
inflorescencias[F]

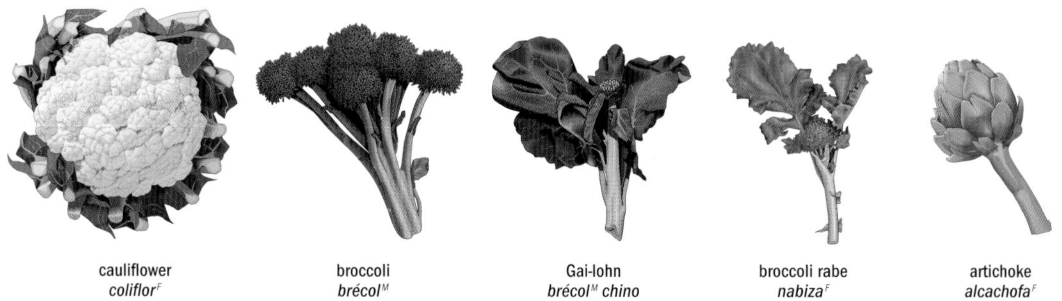

cauliflower
coliflor[F]

broccoli
brécol[M]

Gai-lohn
brécol[M] *chino*

broccoli rabe
nabiza[F]

artichoke
alcachofa[F]

vegetables

fruit vegetables
hortalizas[F] de fruto[M]

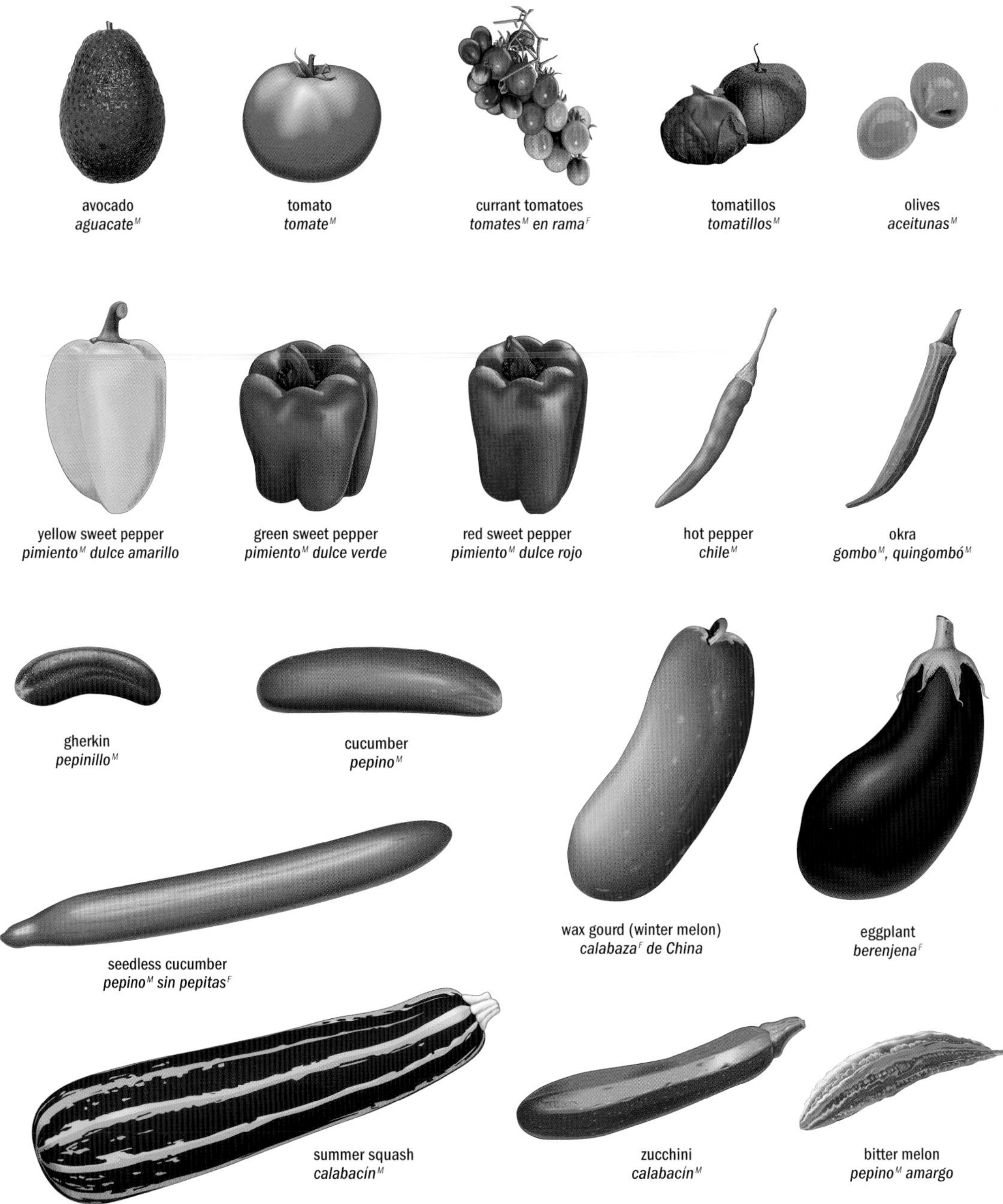
avocado
aguacate[M]
tomato
tomate[M]
currant tomatoes
tomates[M] en rama[F]
tomatillos
tomatillos[M]
olives
aceitunas[M]
yellow sweet pepper
pimiento[M] dulce amarillo
green sweet pepper
pimiento[M] dulce verde
red sweet pepper
pimiento[M] dulce rojo
hot pepper
chile[M]
okra
gombo[M], quingombó[M]
gherkin
pepinillo[M]
cucumber
pepino[M]
wax gourd (winter melon)
calabaza[F] de China
eggplant
berenjena[F]
seedless cucumber
pepino[M] sin pepitas[F]
summer squash
calabacín[M]
zucchini
calabacín[M]
bitter melon
pepino[M] amargo

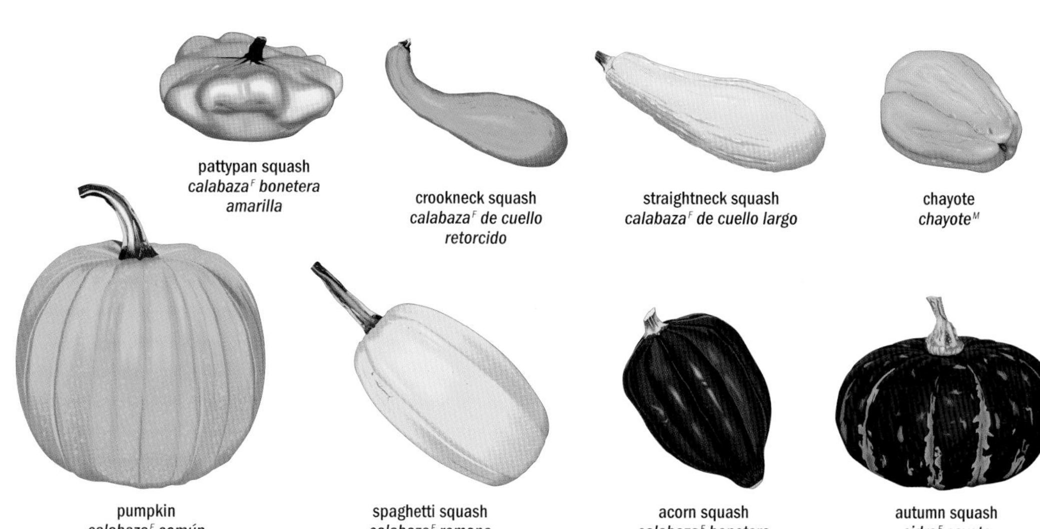

pattypan squash
calabaza[F] bonetera amarilla

crookneck squash
calabaza[F] de cuello retorcido

straightneck squash
calabaza[F] de cuello largo

chayote
chayote[M]

pumpkin
calabaza[F] común

spaghetti squash
calabaza[F] romana

acorn squash
calabaza[F] bonetera

autumn squash
cidra[F] cayote

root vegetables
raíces[F]

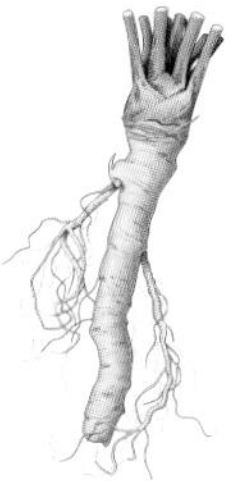

horseradish
rábano[M] blanco

black radishes
rábanos[M] negros

radish
rábano[M]

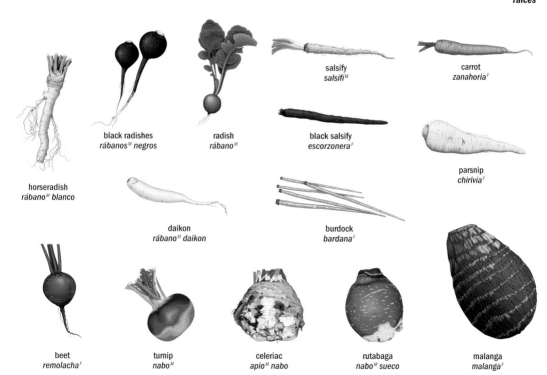

salsify
salsifí[M]

carrot
zanahoria[F]

black salsify
escorzonera[F]

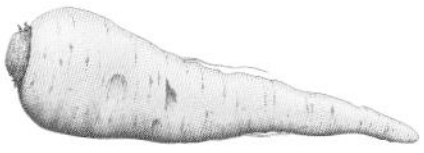

parsnip
chirivía[F]

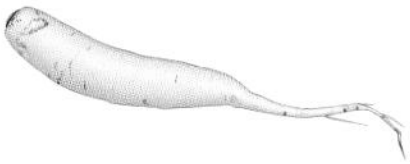

daikon
rábano[M] daikon

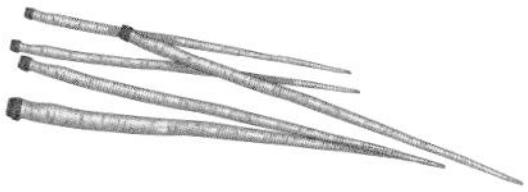

burdock
bardana[F]

beet
remolacha[F]

turnip
nabo[M]

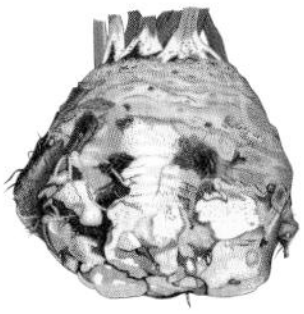

celeriac
apio[M] nabo

rutabaga
nabo[M] sueco

malanga
malanga[F]

legumes

legumbres^F

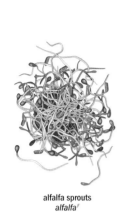

lupines
altramuz^M

peanut
cacahuete^M

alfalfa sprouts
alfalfa^F

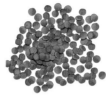

lentils
lentejas^F

broad beans
habas^F

peas
guisantes^M

chick peas
garbanzos^M

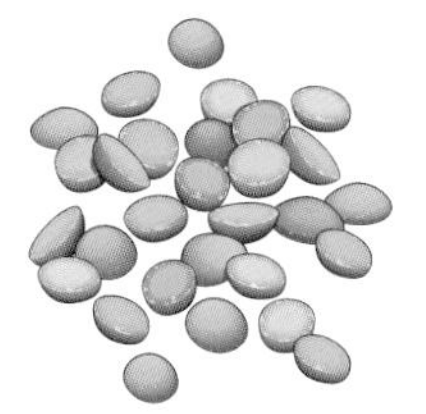
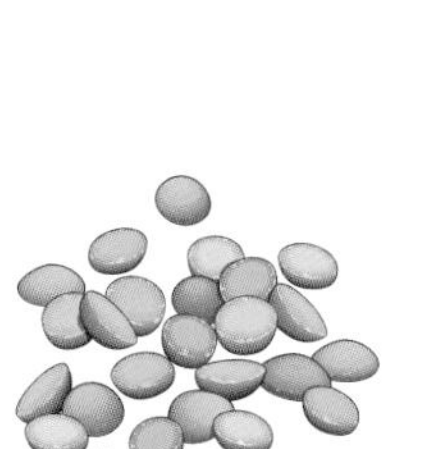
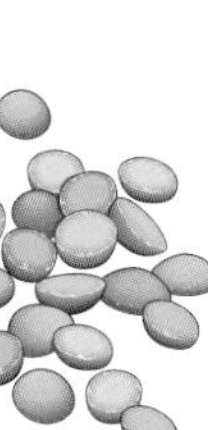

split peas
guisantes^M partidos

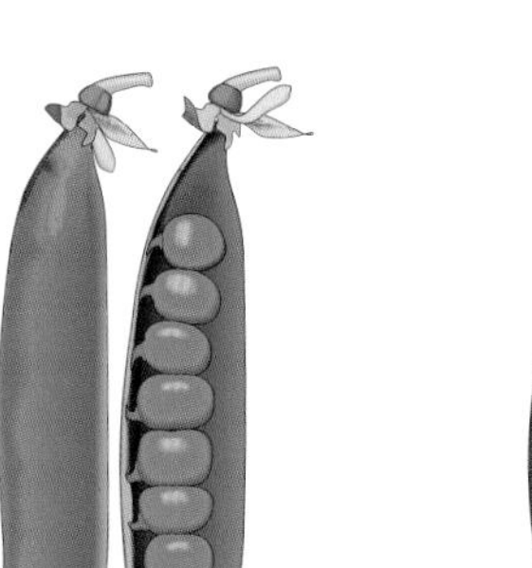

green peas
guisantes^M

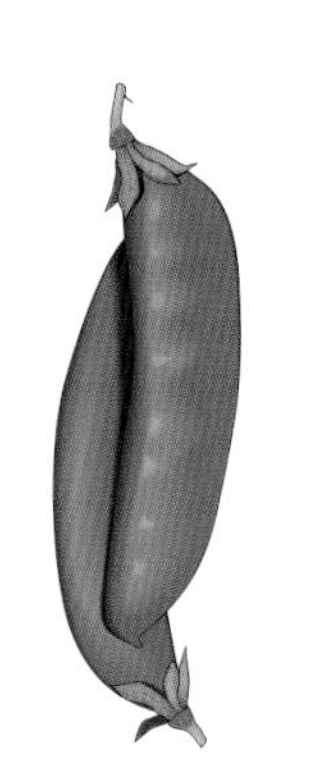
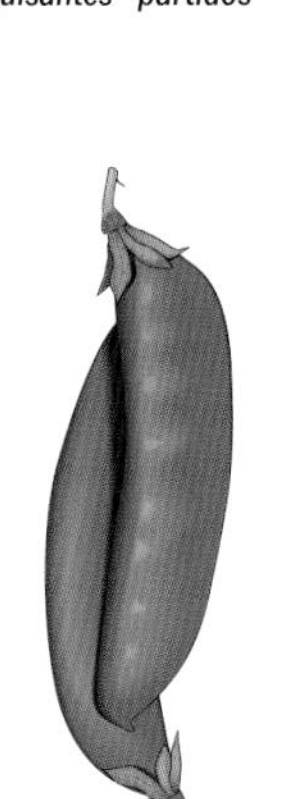

snow peas
guisantes^M mollares

dolichos beans
dolichos^M

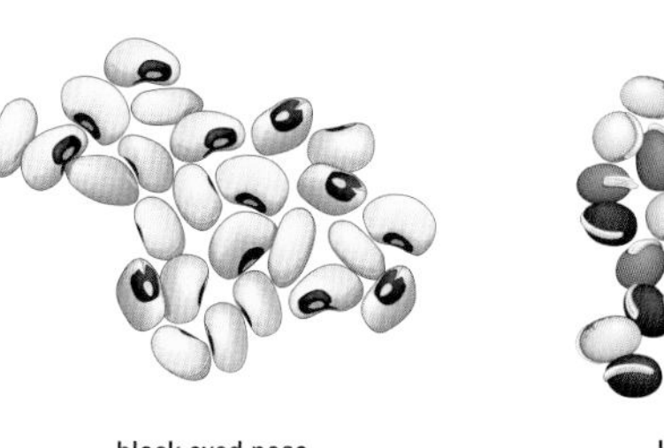
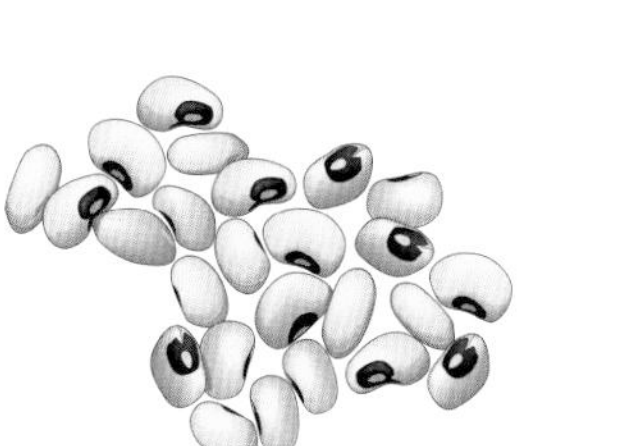

black-eyed peas
judías^F de ojo

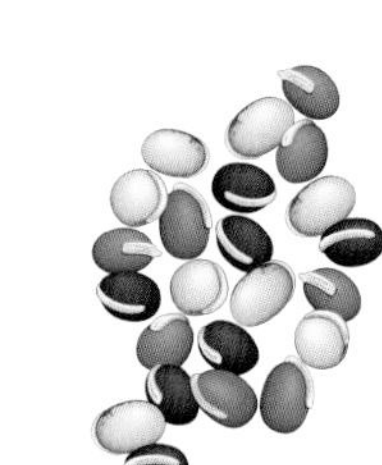

lablab beans
judía^F de Egipto

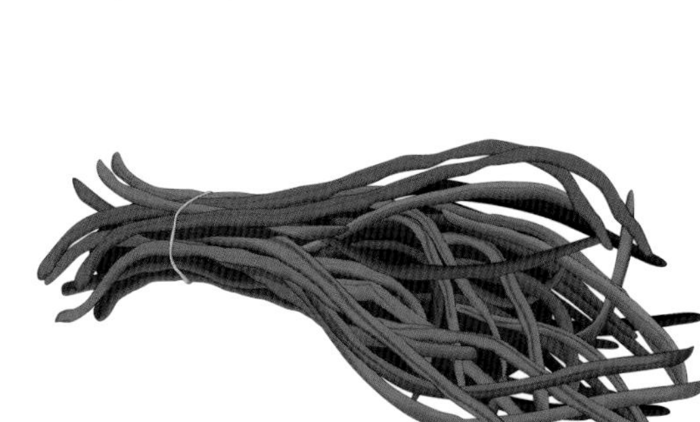
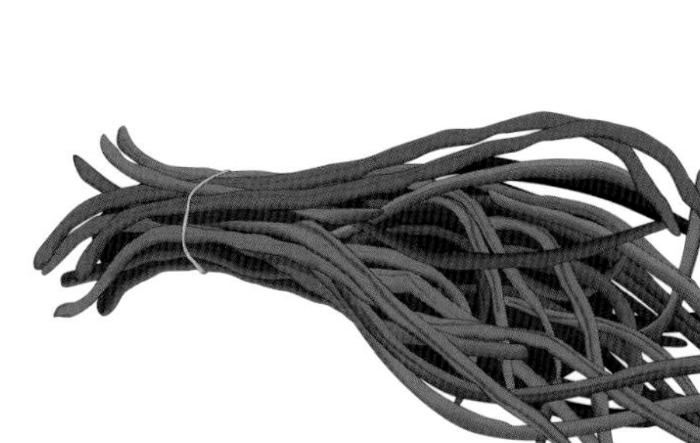

yard-long beans
judía^F china larga

beans
judías[F]

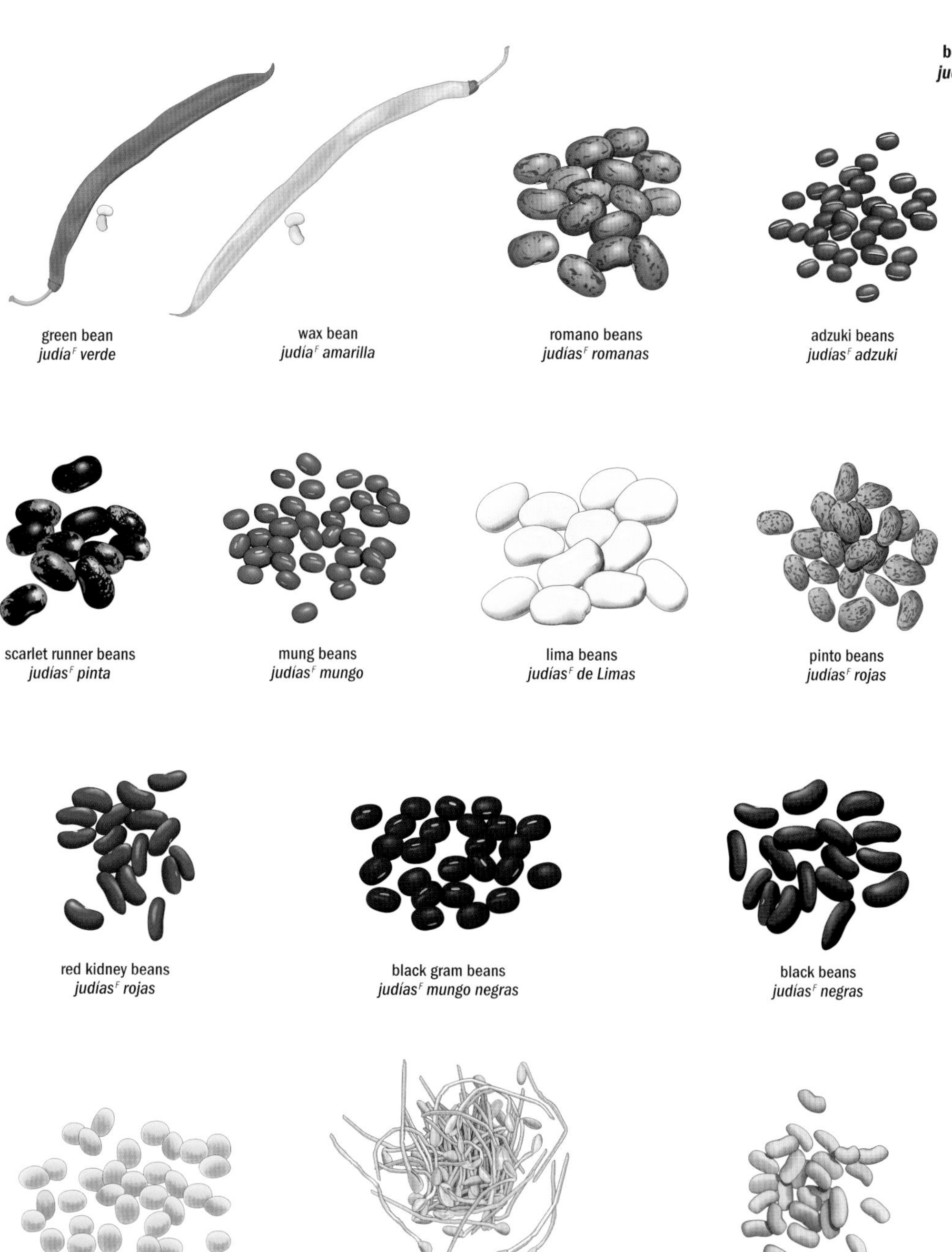

green bean
judía[F] *verde*

wax bean
judía[F] *amarilla*

romano beans
judías[F] *romanas*

adzuki beans
judías[F] *adzuki*

scarlet runner beans
judías[F] *pinta*

mung beans
judías[F] *mungo*

lima beans
judías[F] *de Limas*

pinto beans
judías[F] *rojas*

red kidney beans
judías[F] *rojas*

black gram beans
judías[F] *mungo negras*

black beans
judías[F] *negras*

soybeans
semillas[F] *de soja*[F]

soybean sprouts
brotes[M] *de soja*[F]

flageolets
frijoles[M]

fruits

frutas[F]

berries
***bayas*[F]**

currants
grosellas[F]

black currants
grosellas[F] *negras*

gooseberries
grosellas[F] *espinosas*

grapes
uvas[F]

blueberries
arándanos[M]

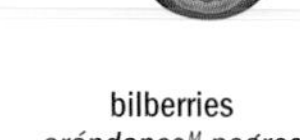

bilberries
arándanos[M] *negros*

red whortleberries
arándanos[M] *rojos*

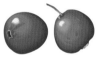

alkekengi
alquequenje[M]

cranberries
arándanos[M] *agrios*

raspberries
frambuesas[F]

blackberries
moras[F]

strawberries
fresas[F]

stone fruits
***drupas*[F]**

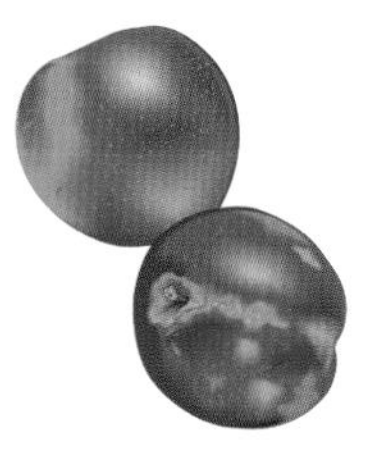

plums
ciruelas[F]

peach
melocotón[M]

nectarine
nectarina[F]

apricot
albaricoque[M]

cherries
cerezas[F]

dates
dátiles[M]

dry fruits
frutas^{F} secas

macadamia nuts
nuezes^{F} de macadamia^{F}

ginkgo nuts
nuezes^{F} de ginkgo

pistachio nuts
pistachos^{M}

pine nuts
piñónes^{M}

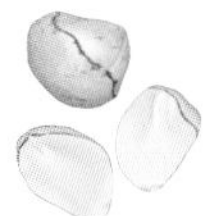

cola nuts
nuezes^{F} de cola

pecan nuts
pecanas^{F}

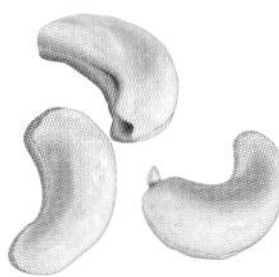

cashews
anacardos^{M}

almonds
almendras^{F}

hazelnuts
avellanas^{F}

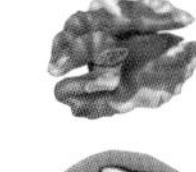

walnut
nuez^{F}

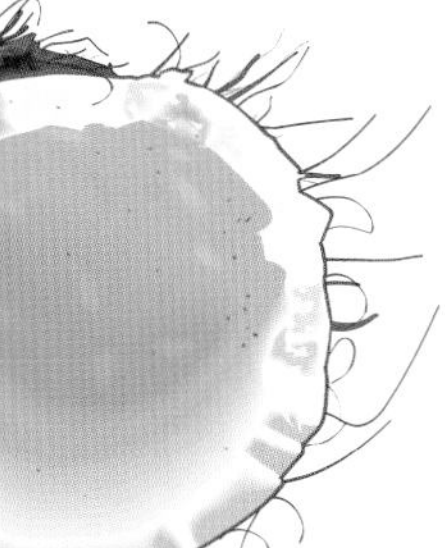

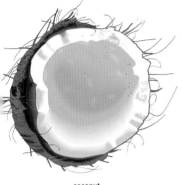

coconut
coco^{M}

chestnuts
castañas^{M}

beechnut
hayuco^{M}

Brazil nuts
neuzes^{F} del Brasil^{M}

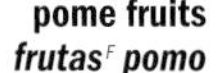

pome fruits
frutas^{F} pomo

pear
pera^{F}

quince
membrillo^{M}

apple
manzana^{F}

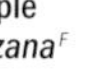

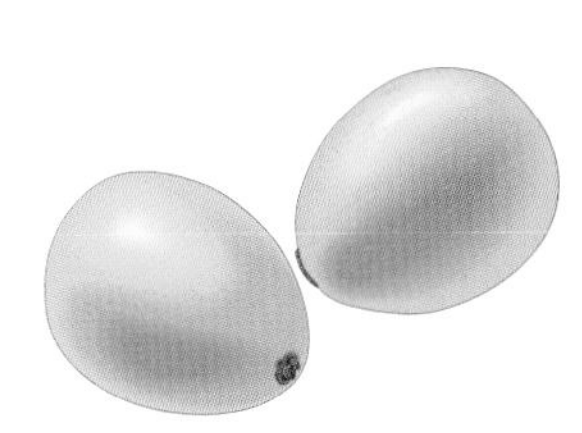

Japanese plums
nísperos^{M}

citrus fruits
cítricos[M]

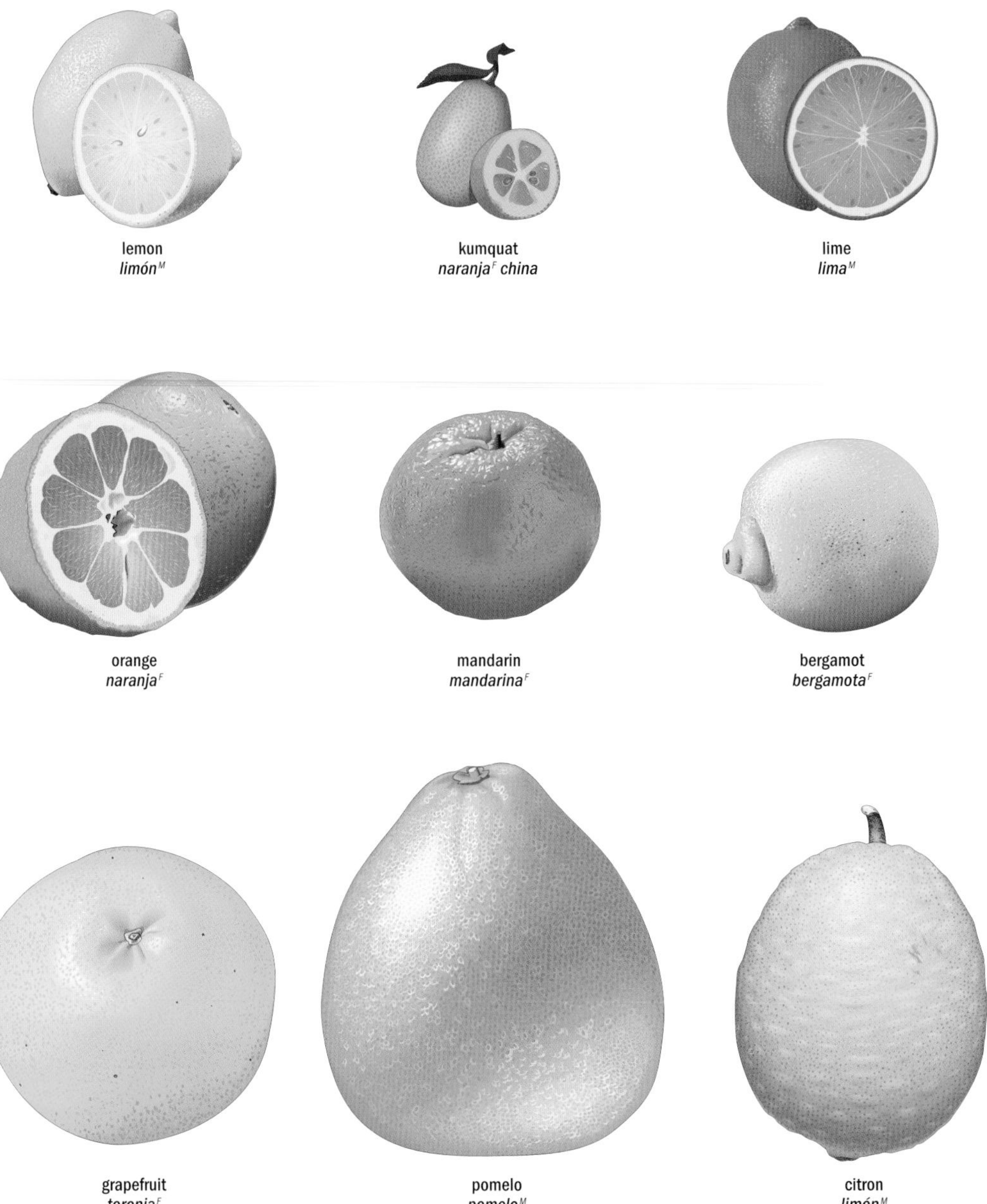

melons
melones[M]

cantaloupe
melón[M] *cantalupo*

casaba melon
melón[M] *invernal*

honeydew melon
melón[M] *de miel*

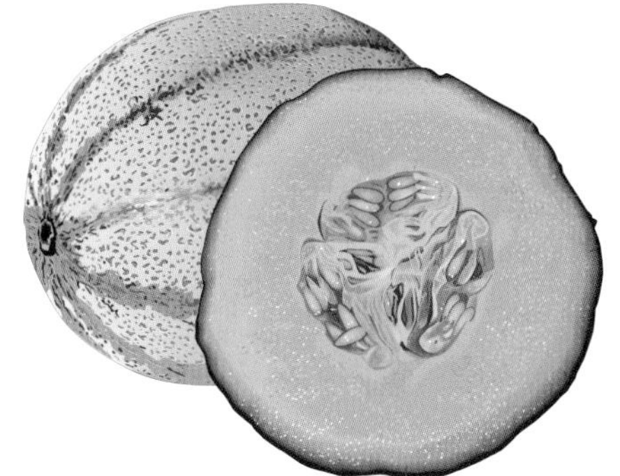
muskmelon
melón[M] *escrito*

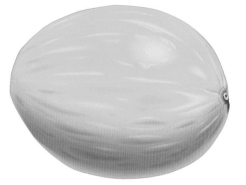

canary melon
melón[M] *amarillo*

watermelon
sandía[F]

Ogen melon
melón[M] *de Ogen*

tropical fruits
frutas*[F] *tropicales

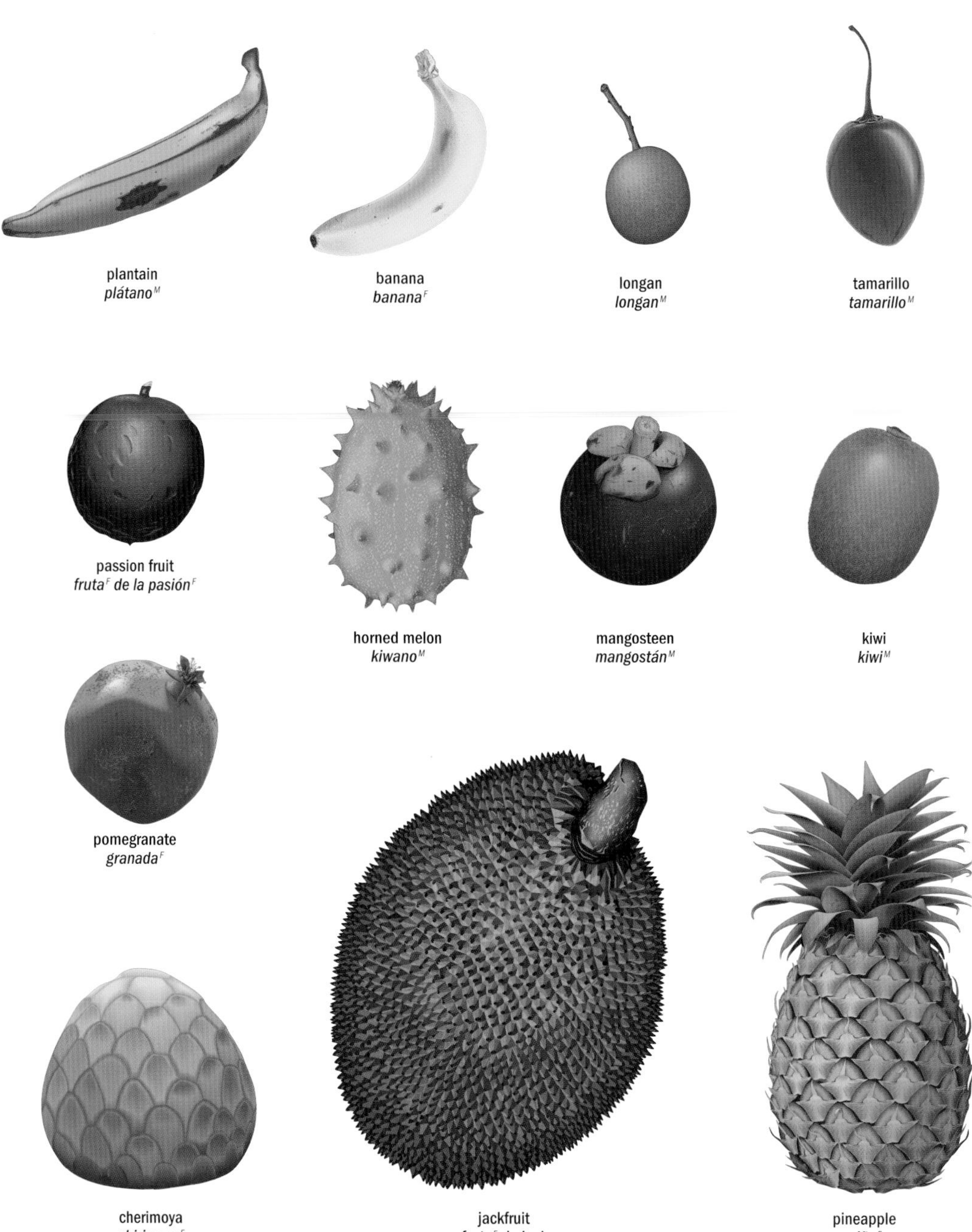

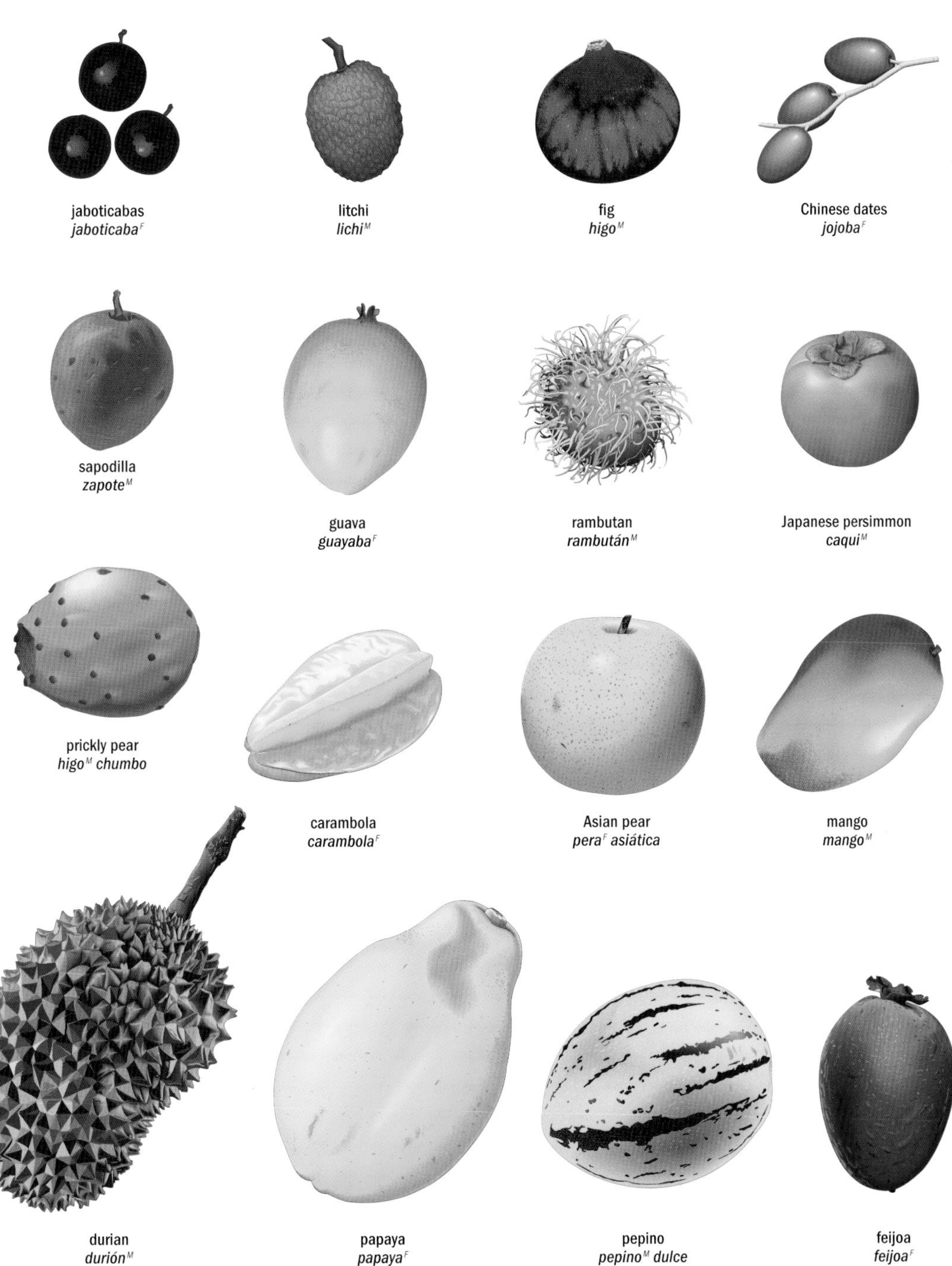
jaboticabas
jaboticaba[F]
litchi
lichi[M]
fig
higo[M]
Chinese dates
jojoba[F]
sapodilla
zapote[M]
guava
guayaba[F]
rambutan
rambután[M]
Japanese persimmon
caqui[M]
prickly pear
higo[M] *chumbo*
carambola
carambola[F]
Asian pear
pera[F] *asiática*
mango
mango[M]
durian
durión[M]
papaya
papaya[F]
pepino
pepino[M] *dulce*
feijoa
feijoa[F]

spices

especias[F]

juniper berries
bayas[F] de enebro[M]

cloves
clavos[M]

allspice
pimienta[F] de Jamaica

white mustard
mostaza[F] blanca

black mustard
mostaza[F] negra

black pepper
pimienta[F] negra

white pepper
pimienta[F] blanca

pink pepper
pimienta[F] rosa

green pepper
pimienta[F] verde

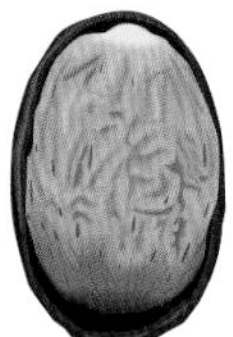
nutmeg
nuez[F] moscada

caraway
alcaravea[F]

cardamom
cardamomo[M]

cinnamon
canela[F]

saffron
azafrán[M]

cumin
comino[M]

curry
curry[M]

turmeric
cúrcuma[F]

fenugreek
fenogreco[M]

jalapeño chile
chile[M] jalapeño

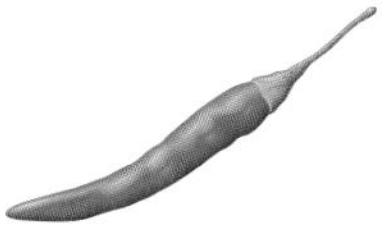

bird's eye chile
guindilla[F]

crushed chiles
guindilla[F] triturada

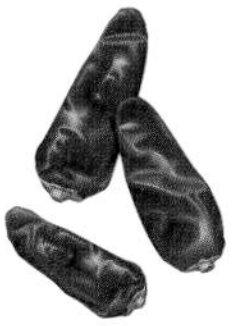

dried chiles
guindilla[F] seca[M]

cayenne pepper
pimienta[F] de cayena[F]

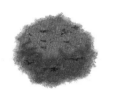

paprika
pimentón[M]

ajowan
ajowán[M]

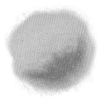

asafetida
asafétida[F]

garam masala
garam masala[M]

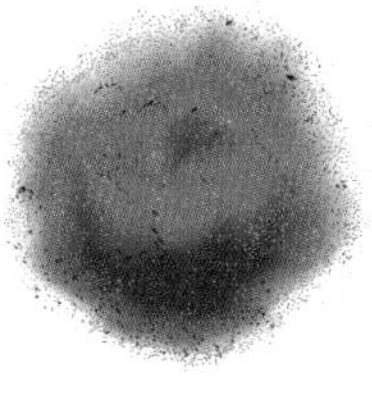

cajun spice seasoning
condimento[M] de especias[F] cajún

marinade spices
especias[F] para salmuera[F]

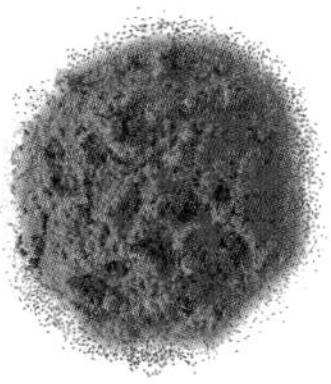

five spice powder
cinco especias[F] chinas

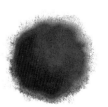

chili powder
guindilla[F] molida

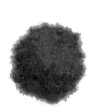

ground pepper
pimienta[F] molida

ras el hanout
ras el hanout[M]

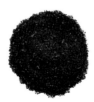

sumac
zumaque[M]

poppy seeds
semillas[F] de adormidera[F]

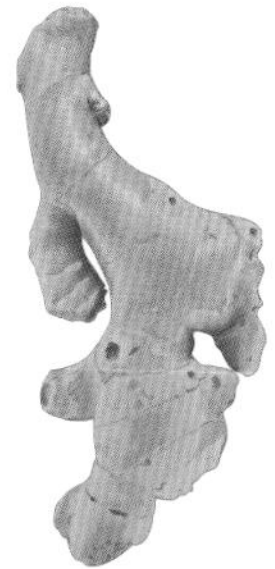

ginger
jengibre[M]

condiments

condimentos[M]

Tabasco® sauce
salsa[F] Tobasco®[M]

Worcestershire sauce
salsa[F] Worcertershire

tamarind paste
salsa[F] de tamarindo[M]

vanilla extract
extracto[M] de vainilla[F]

tomato paste
concentrado[M] de tomate[M]

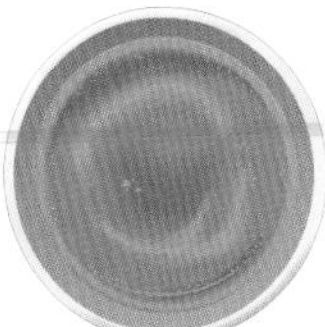

tomato sauce
salsa[F] de tomate[M]

hummus
hummus[M]

tahini
tajín[M]

hoisin sauce
salsa[F] hoisin

soy sauce
salsa[F] de soja[F]

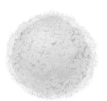

powdered mustard
mostaza[F] en polvo[M]

wholegrain mustard
mostaza[F] en grano[M]

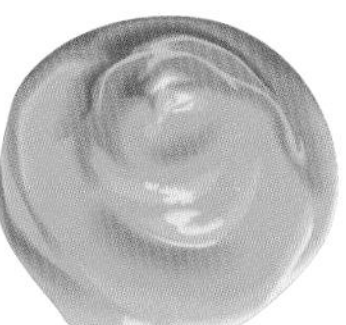

Dijon mustard
mostaza[F] de Dijon

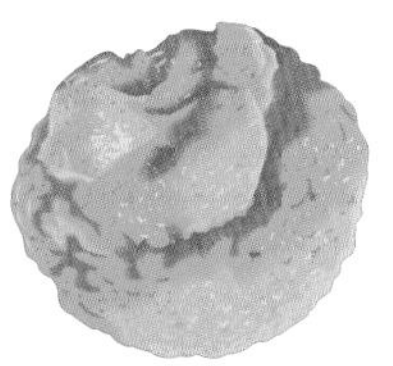

German mustard
mostaza[F] alemana

English mustard
mostaza[F] inglesa

American mustard
mostaza[F] americana

condiments

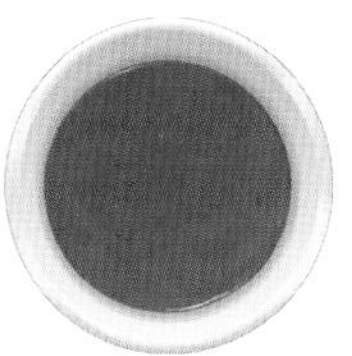

plum sauce
salsa[F] de ciruelas[F]

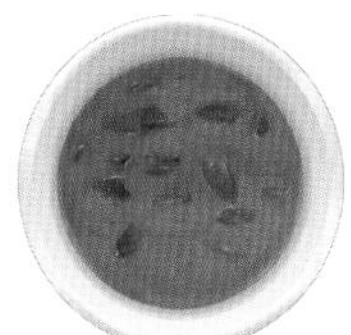

mango chutney
chutney[M] de mango[M]

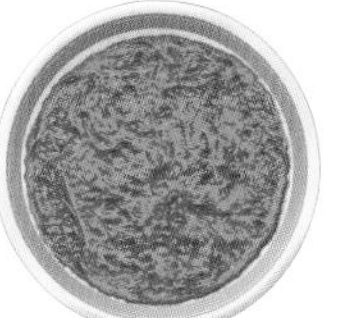

harissa
harissa[F]

sambal oelek
sambal oelek[M]

ketchup
ketchup[M]

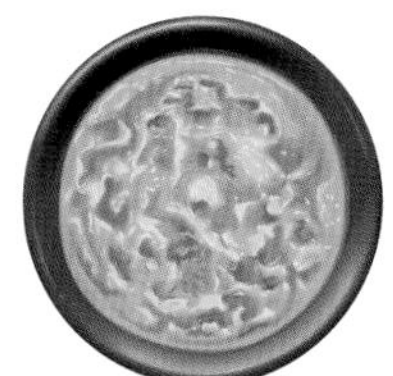

wasabi
wasabi[M]

table salt
sal[F] de mesa[F]

coarse salt
sal[F] gorda

sea salt
sal[F] marina

balsamic vinegar
vinagre[M] balsámico

rice vinegar
vinagre[M] de arroz[M]

apple cider vinegar
vinagre[M] de manzana[F]

malt vinegar
vinagre[M] de malta[F]

wine vinegar
vinagre[M] de vino[M]

herbs

hierbas[F] aromáticas

dill
eneldo[M]
anise
anís[M]
sweet bay
laurel[M]
oregano
orégano[M]
tarragon
estragón[M]
basil
albahaca[F]
sage
salvia[F]
thyme
tomillo[M]
mint
hierbabuena[F]
parsley
perejil[M]
chervil
perifollo[M]
coriander
cilantro[M]
rosemary
romero[M]
hyssop
hisopo[M]
borage
borraja[F]
lovage
alheña[F]
savory
ajedrea[F]
lemon balm
melisa[F]

cereal

cereales[M]

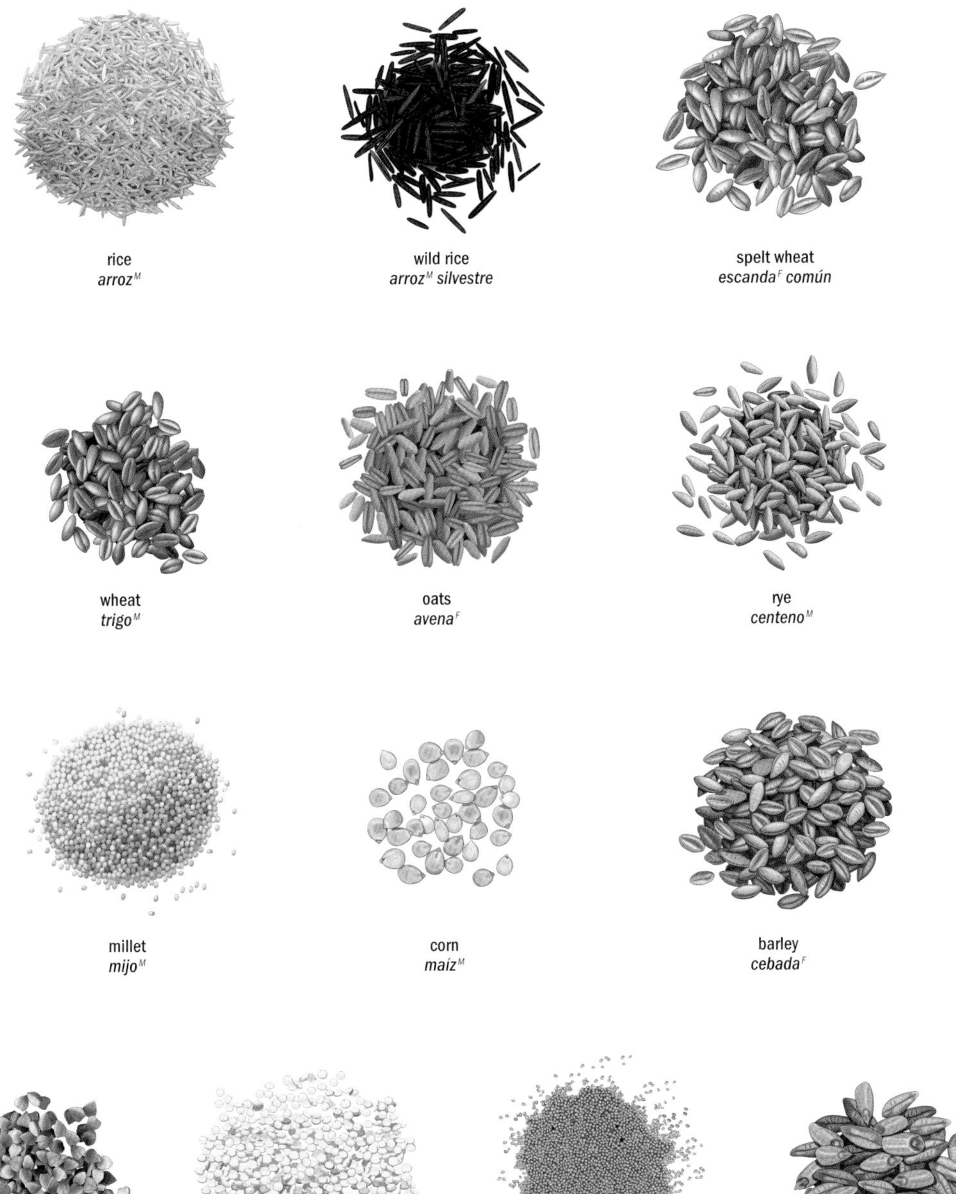

rice
arroz[M]

wild rice
arroz[M] *silvestre*

spelt wheat
escanda[F] *común*

wheat
trigo[M]

oats
avena[F]

rye
centeno[M]

millet
mijo[M]

corn
maíz[M]

barley
cebada[F]

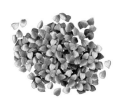

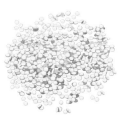

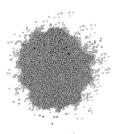

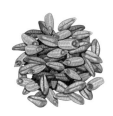

buckwheat
trigo[M] *sarraceno*

quinoa
quinua[F]

amaranth
amaranto[M]

triticale
triticale[M]

cereal products

cereales[M]

flour and semolina

harina[F] y sémola[F]

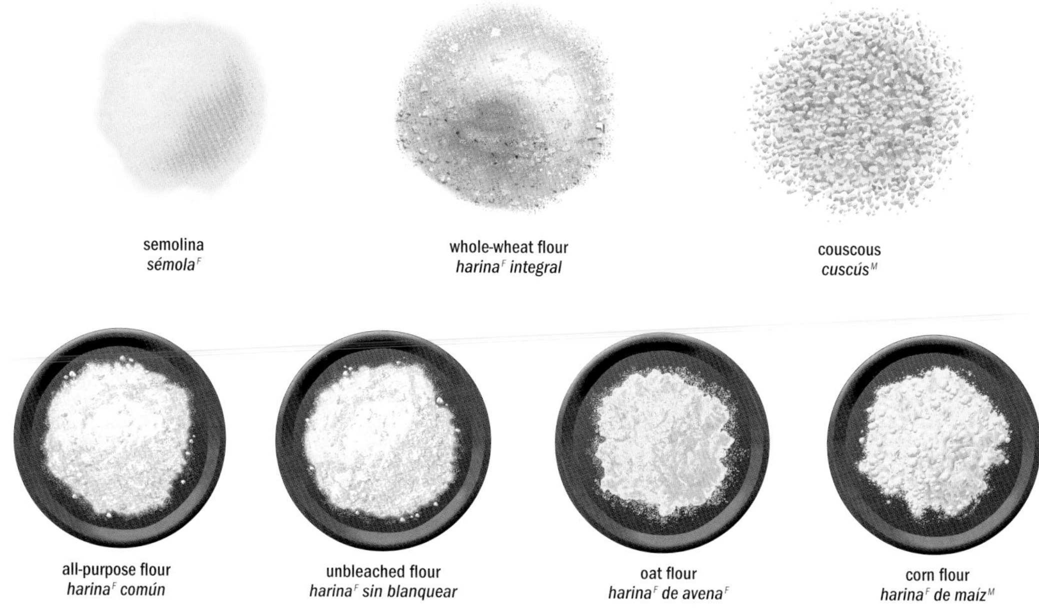

semolina
sémola[F]

whole-wheat flour
harina[F] integral

couscous
cuscús[M]

all-purpose flour
harina[F] común

unbleached flour
harina[F] sin blanquear

oat flour
harina[F] de avena[F]

corn flour
harina[F] de maíz[M]

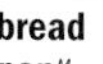

bread

pan[M]

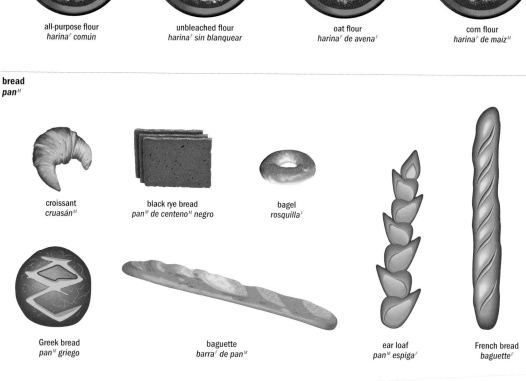

croissant
cruasán[M]

black rye bread
pan[M] de centeno[M] negro

bagel
rosquilla[F]

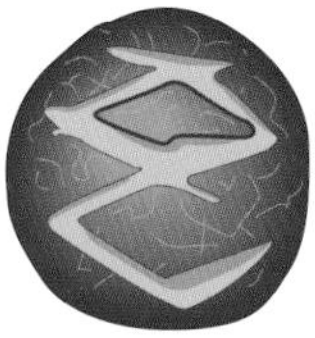

Greek bread
pan[M] griego

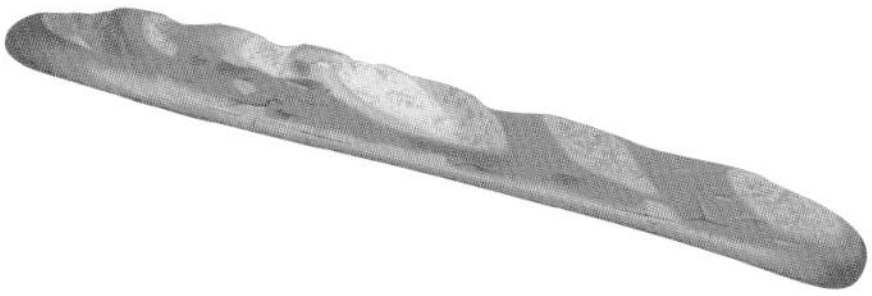

baguette
barra[F] de pan[M]

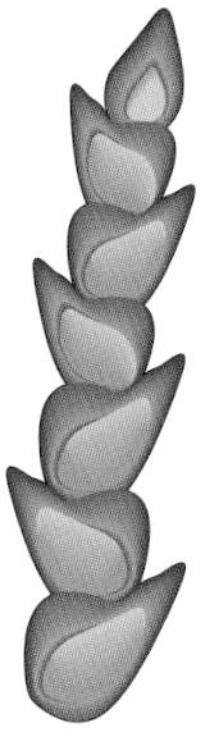

ear loaf
pan[M] espiga[F]

French bread
baguette[F]

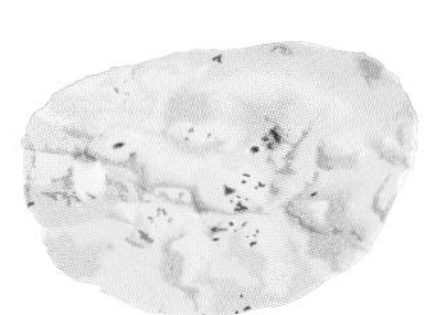
chapati
pan^M indio chapatí

tortillas
tortillas^F

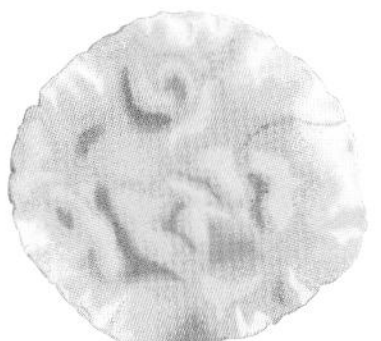
pita bread
pan^M de pita^F

naan
pan^M indio naan

cracked rye bread
galleta^F de centeno^M

phyllo dough
pasta^F de hojaldre^M

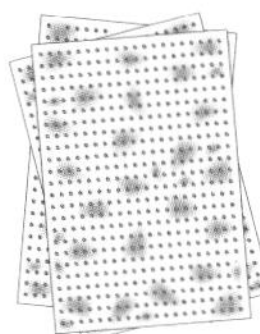
unleavened bread
pan^M ácimo

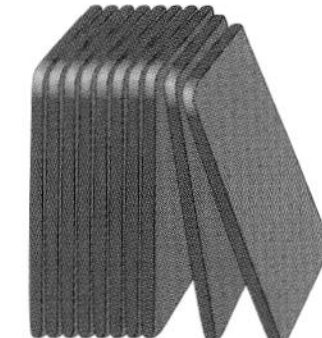
Danish rye bread
pan^M danés de centeno^M

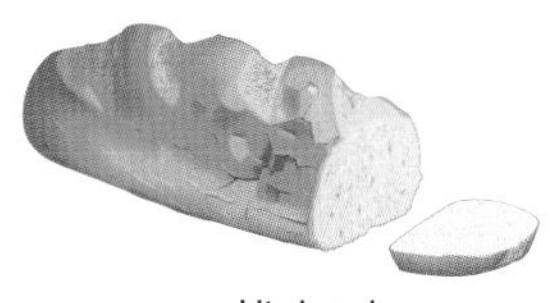
white bread
pan^M blanco

multigrain bread
pan^M multicereales

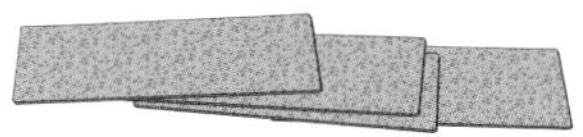
Scandinavian cracked bread
galleta^F escandinava

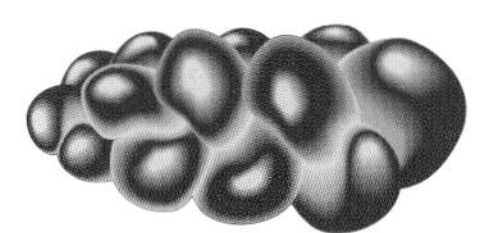
challah
pan^M judío hallah

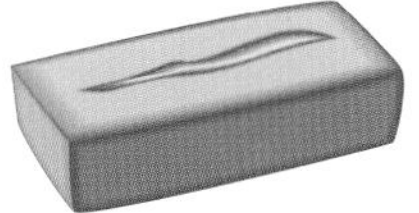
American corn bread
pan^M americano de maíz^M

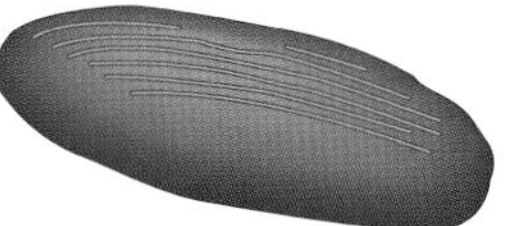
German rye bread
pan^M alemán de centeno^M

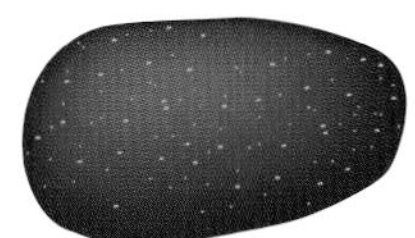
Russian pumpernickel
pan^M negro ruso

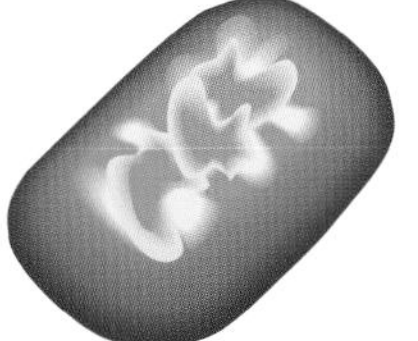
farmhouse bread
pan^M campesino

wholemeal bread
pan^M integral

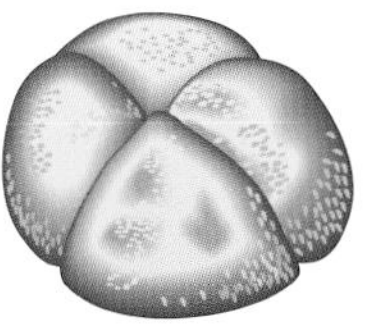
Irish soda bread
pan^M irlandés

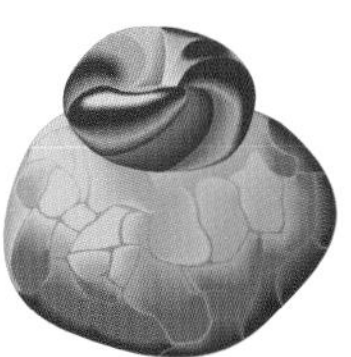
English loaf
pan^M de flor^F

pasta
pasta[F]

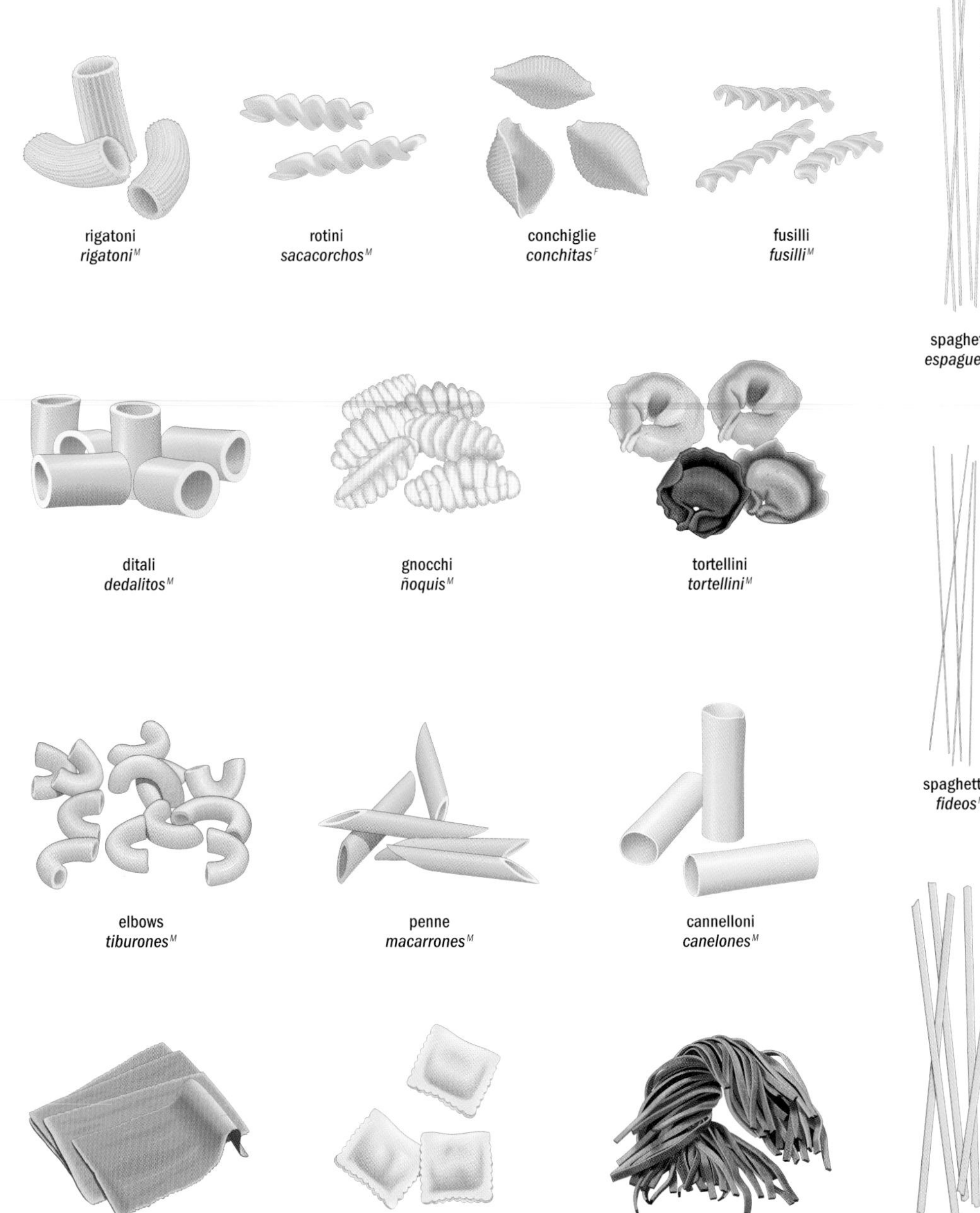

rigatoni
rigatoni[M]
rotini
sacacorchos[M]
conchiglie
conchitas[F]
fusilli
fusilli[M]
spaghetti
espagueti[M]
ditali
dedalitos[M]
gnocchi
ñoquis[M]
tortellini
tortellini[M]
spaghettini
fideos[M]
elbows
tiburones[M]
penne
macarrones[M]
cannelloni
canelones[M]
lasagna
lasañas[F]
ravioli
raviolis[M]
spinach tagliatelle
tallarines[M] *de espinacas*[F]
fettucine
fetuchinas[F]

Asian noodles
fideos[M] asiáticos

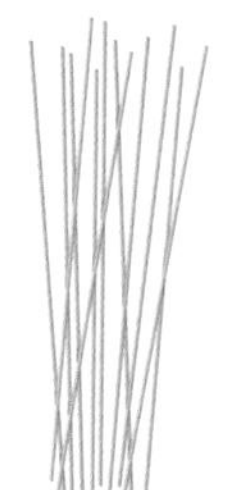
soba noodles
fideos[M] de soba[F]

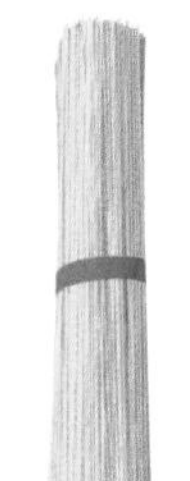
somen noodles
fideos[M] de somen[M]

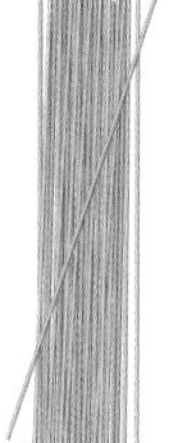
udon noodles
fideos[M] de udon[M]

rice paper
galletas[F] de arroz[M]

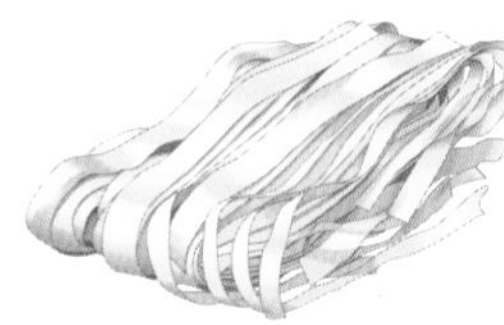
rice noodles
fideos[M] de arroz[M]

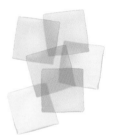

bean thread cellophane noodles
fideos[M] de judías[F] mungo

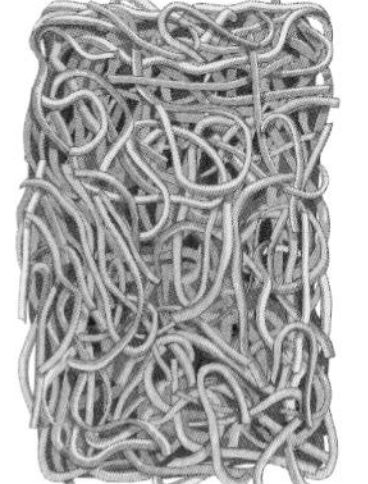
egg noodles
fideos[M] de huevo[M]

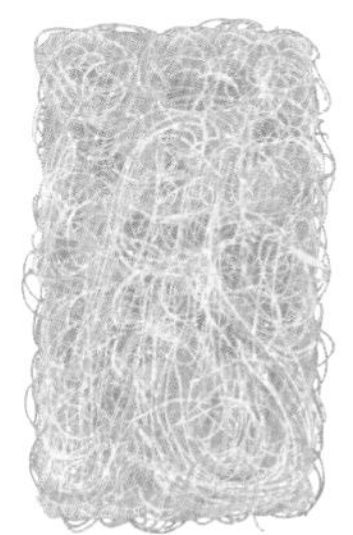
rice vermicelli
vermicelli[M] de arroz[M]

won ton skins
pasta[F] won ton

rice
arroz[M]

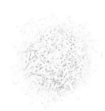

white rice
arroz[M] blanco

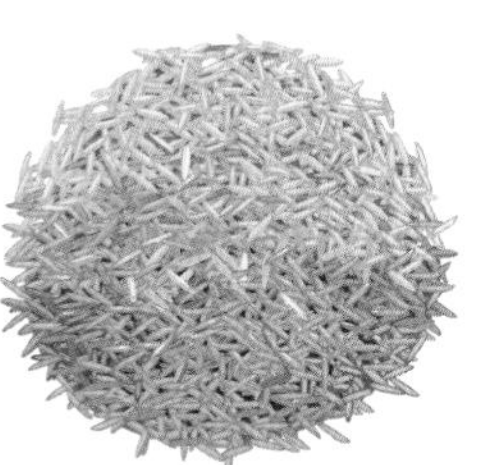
brown rice
arroz[M] integral

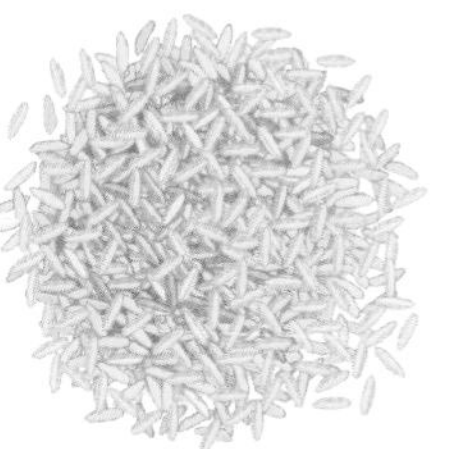
parboiled rice
arroz[M] vaporizado

basmati rice
arroz[M] basmati

coffee and infusions

café^M y infusionnes^F

coffee
café ^M

green coffee beans
granos^M verdes de café^M

roasted coffee beans
granos^M torrefactos de café^M

herbal teas
tisanas ^F

linden
tila^F

chamomile
manzanilla^F

verbena
verbena^F

tea
té ^M

green tea
té^M verde

black tea
té^M negro

oolong tea
té^M oolong

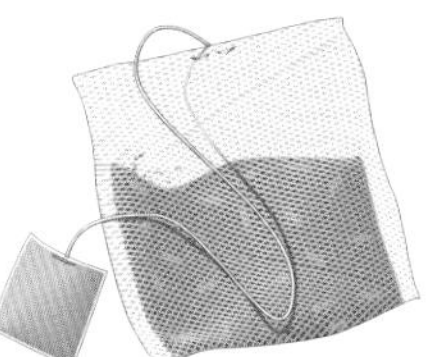

tea bag
bolsita^F de té^M

chocolate

chocolate^M

dark chocolate
chocolate^M amargo

milk chocolate
chocolate^M con leche^F

cocoa
cacao^M

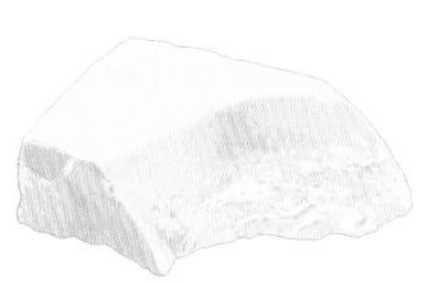

white chocolate
chocolate^M blanco

sugar

azúcar[M]

granulated sugar
azúcar[M] granulado

powdered sugar
azúcar[M] glas

brown sugar
azúcar[M] moreno

rock candy
azúcar[M] candi

molasses
melazas[F]

corn syrup
jarabe[M] de maíz[M]

maple syrup
jarabe[M] de arce[M]

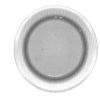

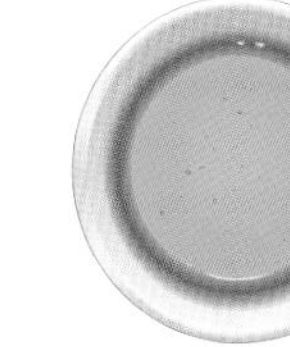
honey
miel[M]

fats and oils

grasas[F] y aceites[M]

corn oil
aceite[M] de maíz[M]

olive oil
aceite[M] de oliva[F]

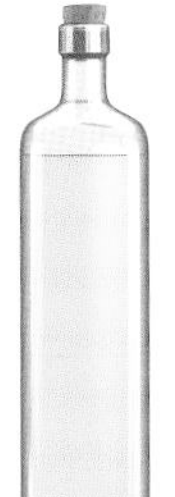
sunflower-seed oil
aceite[M] de girasol[M]

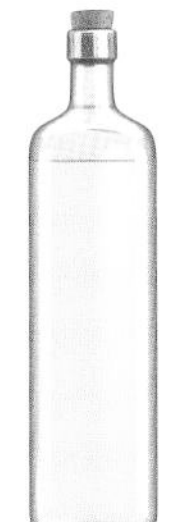
peanut oil
aceite[M] de cacahuete[M]

sesame oil
aceite[M] de sésamo[M]

shortening
grasa[F] para cocinar

lard
manteca[F] de cerdo[M]

margarine
margarina[F]

dairy products

productos[M] lácteos

yogurt
yogur[M]

ghee
mantequilla[F] *clarificada*

butter
mantequilla[M]

cream
nata[F]

whipping cream
nata[F] *de montar*

sour cream
nata[F] *agria*

milk
leche[M]

homogenized milk
leche[F] *homogeneizada*

goat's milk
leche[F] *de cabra*

evaporated milk
leche[F] *evaporada*

buttermilk
suero[M] *de la leche*[F]

powdered milk
leche[F] *en polvo*[M]

fresh cheeses
quesos[M] ***frescos***

cottage cheese
queso[M] *cottage*

mozzarella
mozzarella[F]

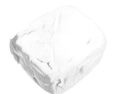

ricotta
ricotta[F]

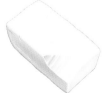

cream cheese
queso[M] *cremoso*

goat's-milk cheeses
quesos[M] ***de cabra***[F]

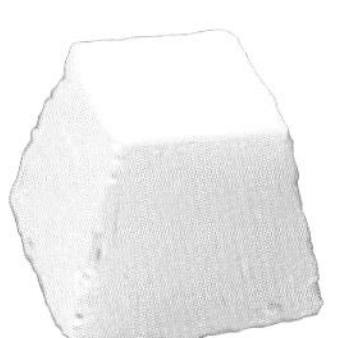

chèvre cheese
queso[M] *chèvre*

Crottin de Chavignol
Crottin[M] *de Chavignol*

pressed cheeses
*quesos*ᴹ *prensados*

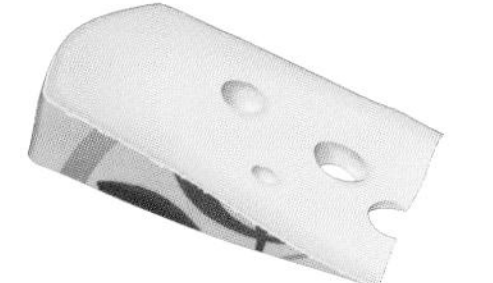
Jarlsberg
jarlsberg[M]

Emmenthal
emmenthal[M]

raclette
raclette[F]

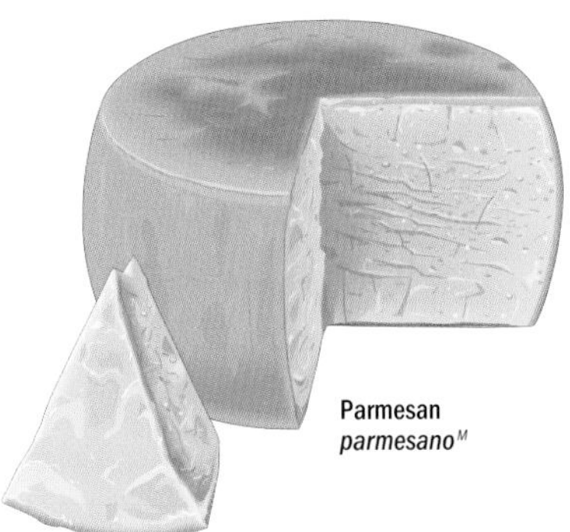
Parmesan
parmesano[M]

Gruyère
gruyère[M]

Romano
pecorino romano[M]

blue-veined cheeses
quesos[M] *azules*

Roquefort
roquefort[M]

Stilton
stilton[M]

Gorgonzola
gorgonzola[M]

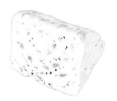

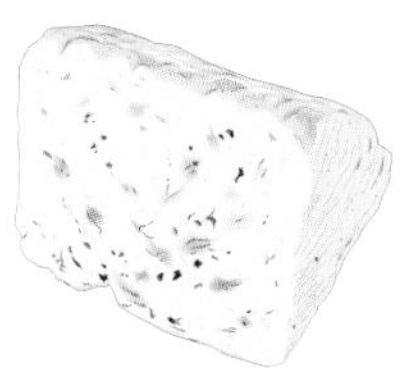
Danish Blue
azul danés[M]

soft cheeses
quesos[M] *blandos*

Pont-l'Évêque
Pont-l'Éveque[M]

Coulommiers
coulommiers[M]

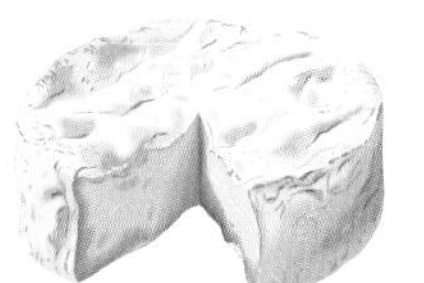
Camembert
camembert[M]

Brie
brie[M]

Munster
munster[M]

meat

carne^F

cuts of beef
cortes^M de vacuno^M

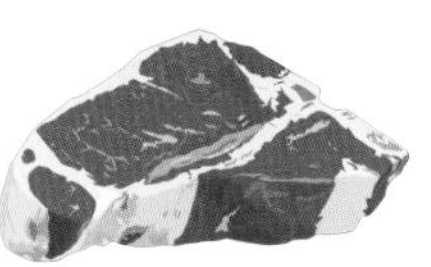

steak
bistec^M

beef cubes
carne^F de vacuno^M troceada

ground beef
carne^F picada

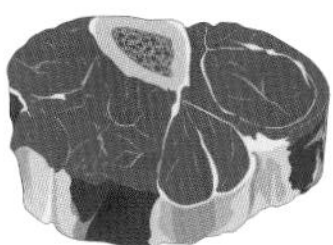

shank
morcillo^M

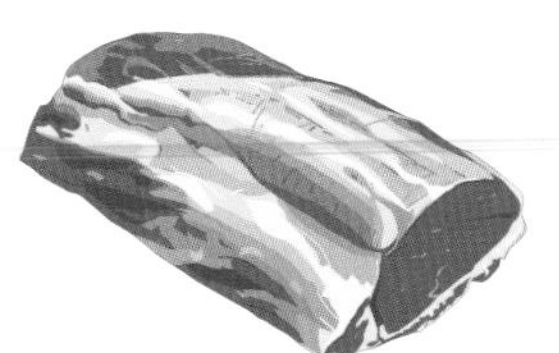

tenderloin roast
lomo^M

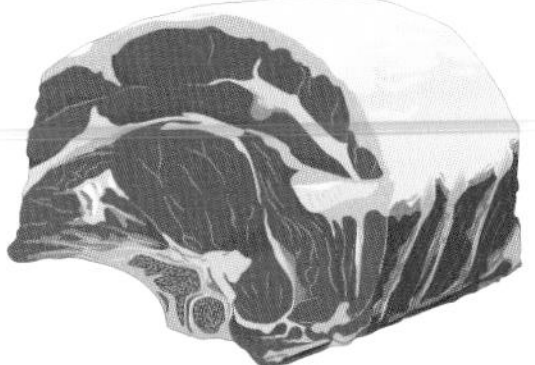

rib roast
chuletón^M

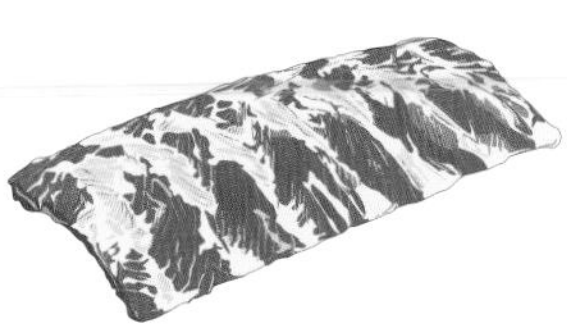

back ribs
costillar^M

cuts of veal
cortes^M de ternera^F

veal cubes
carne^F de ternera^F troceada

ground veal
carne^F picada de vacuno^M

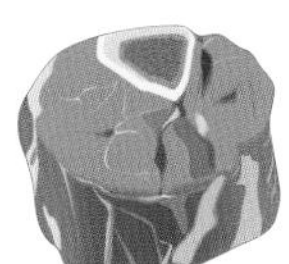

shank
paleta^F

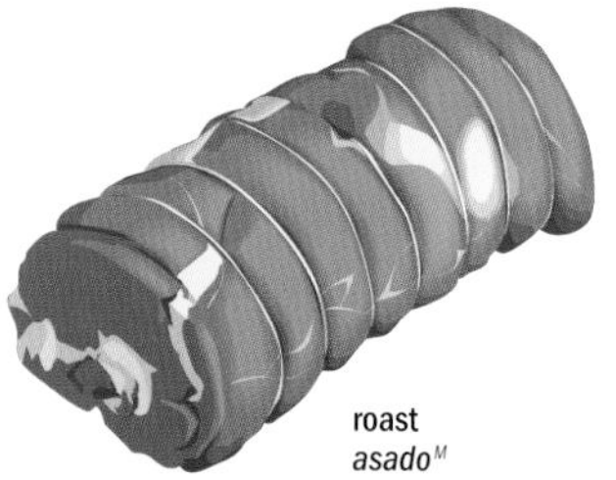

roast
asado^M

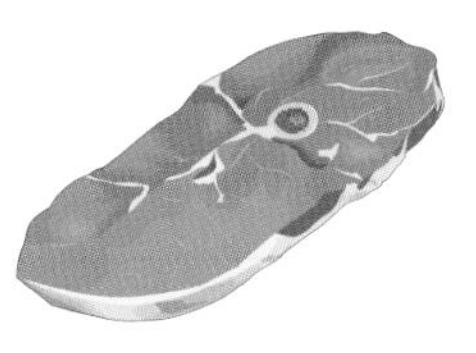

steak
bistec^M

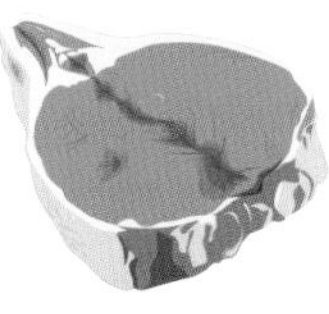

chop
chuleta^F

cuts of lamb
cortes [M] ***de cordero*** [M]

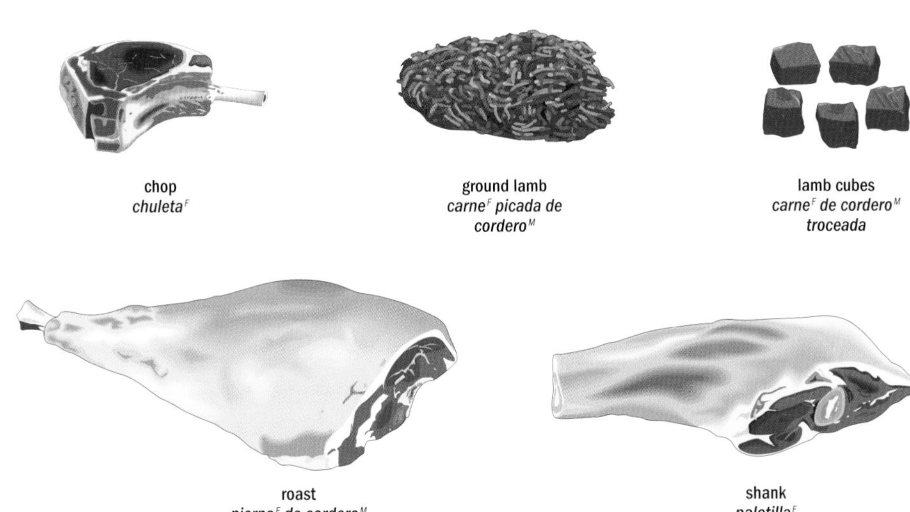

chop
chuleta [F]

ground lamb
carne [F] *picada de cordero* [M]

lamb cubes
carne [F] *de cordero* [M] *troceada*

roast
pierna [F] *de cordero* [M]

shank
paletilla [F]

cuts of pork
cortes [M] ***de cerdo*** [M]

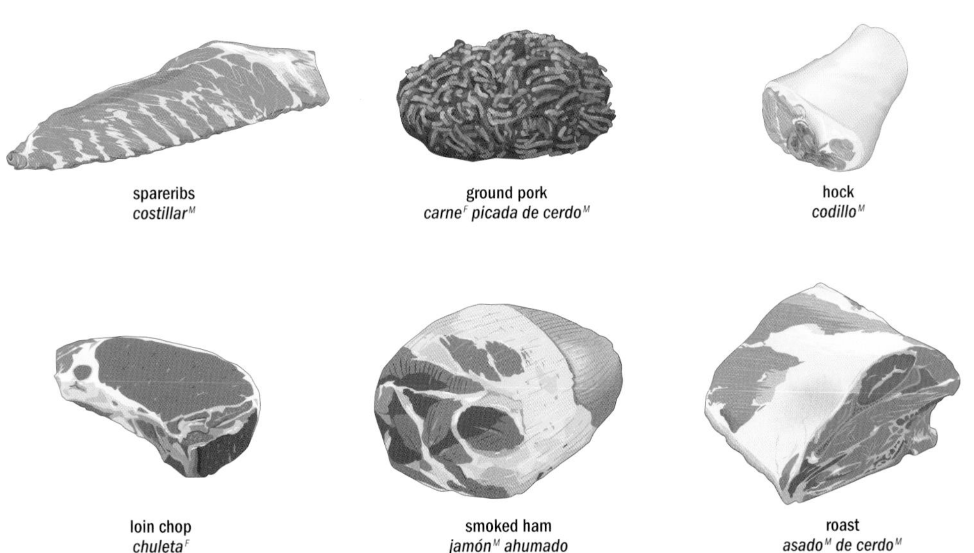

spareribs
costillar [M]

ground pork
carne [F] *picada de cerdo* [M]

hock
codillo [M]

loin chop
chuleta [F]

smoked ham
jamón [M] *ahumado*

roast
asado [M] *de cerdo* [M]

organ meat

despojos[M]

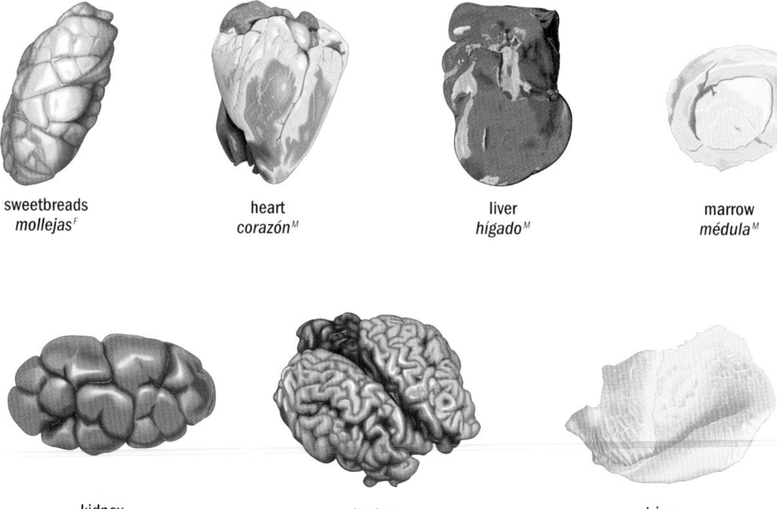

sweetbreads
mollejas[F]

heart
corazón[M]

liver
hígado[M]

marrow
médula[M]

tongue
lengua[F]

kidney
riñones[M]

brains
sesos[M]

tripe
tripa[F]

game

caza[F]

quail
codorniz[F]

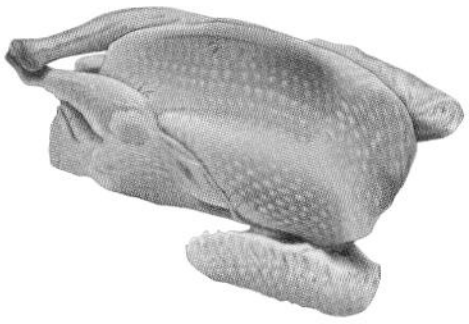

pigeon
pichón[M]

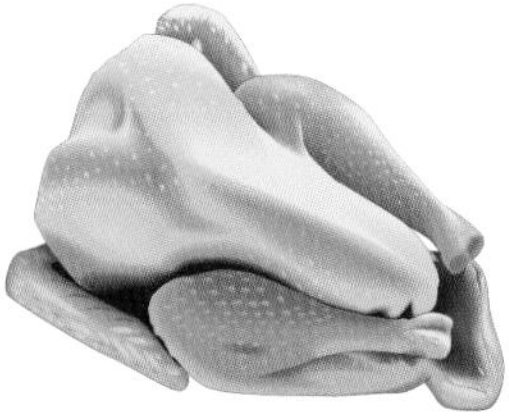

guinea fowl
pintada[F]

pheasant
faisán[M]

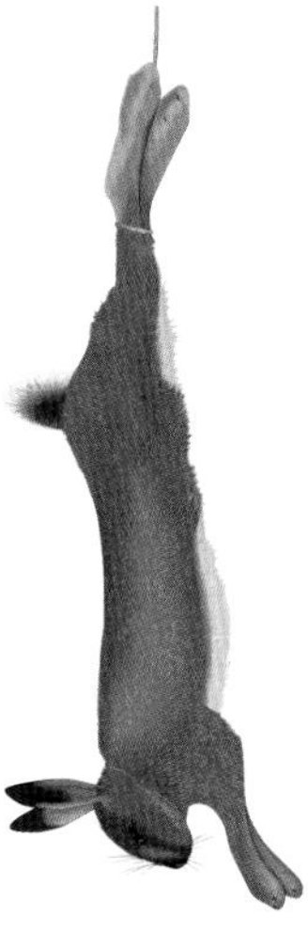

hare
liebre[F]

rabbit
conejo[M]

poultry

aves[F] de corral[M]

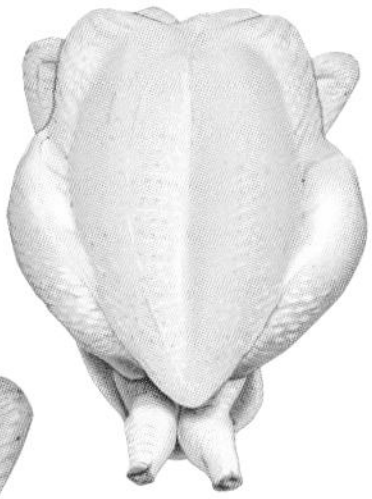

chicken
pollo[M]

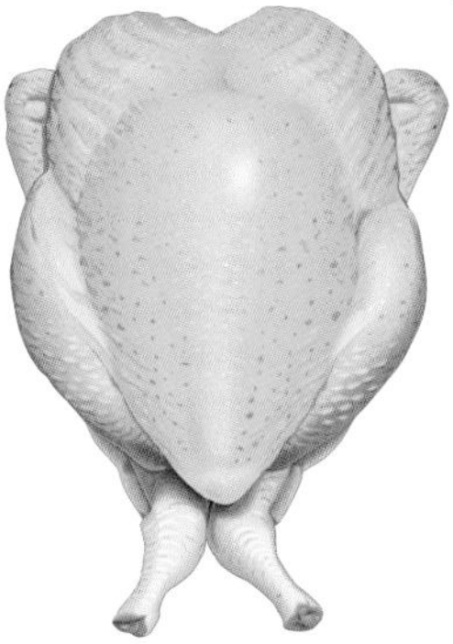

capon
capón[M]

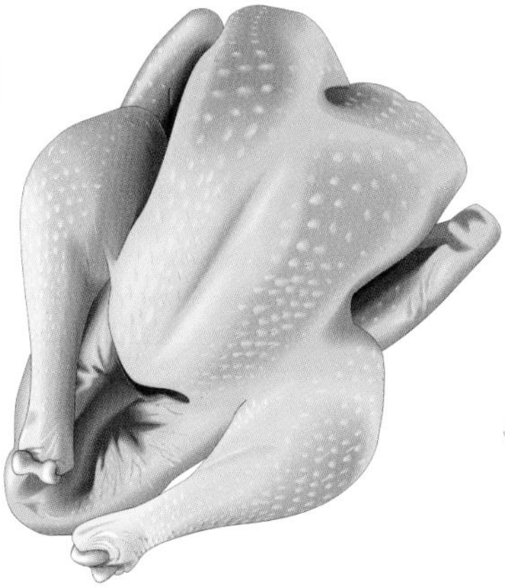

turkey
pavo[M]

duck
pato[M]

goose
oca[F]

eggs

huevos[M]

ostrich egg
huevo[M] *de avestruz*[M]

goose egg
huevo[M] *de oca*[F]

quail egg
huevo[F] *de codorniz*[F]

pheasant egg
huevo[M] *de faisán*[M]

duck egg
huevo[M] *de pato*[M]

hen egg
huevo[M] *de gallina*[F]

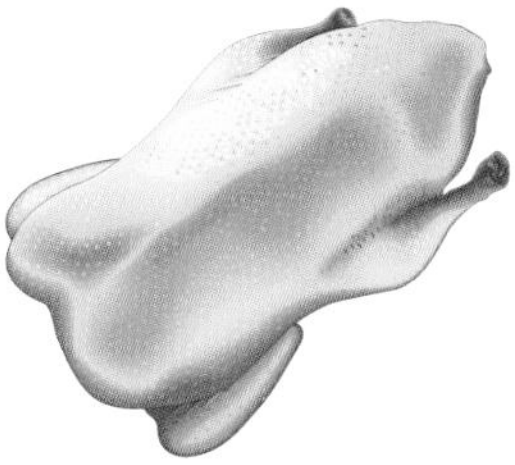

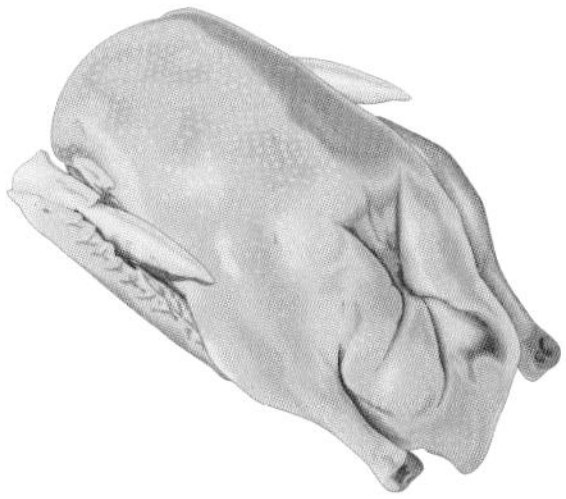

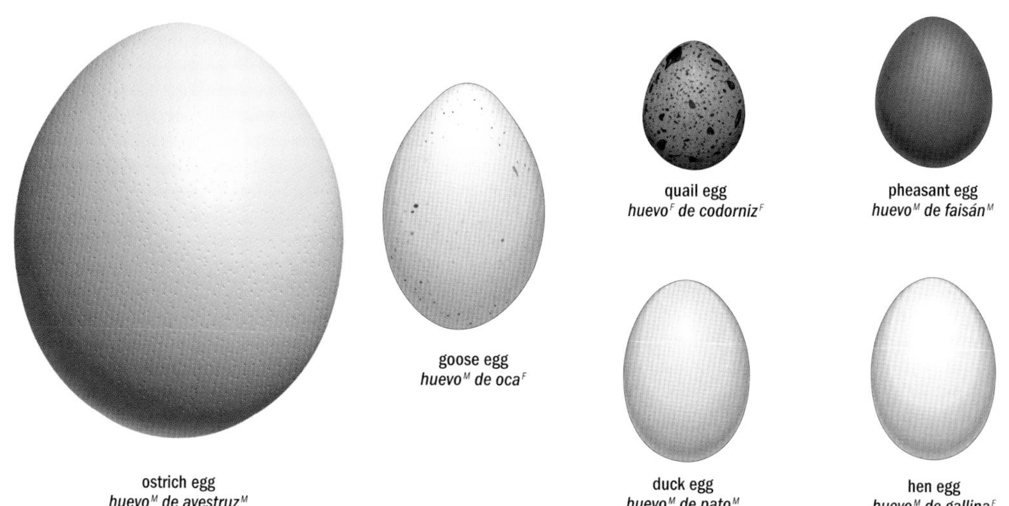

delicatessen

charcutería[F]

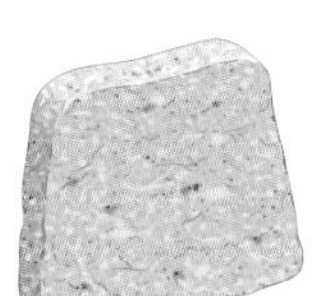

rillettes
rillettes[F]

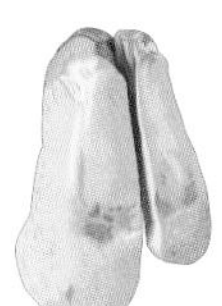

foie gras
foie-gras[M]

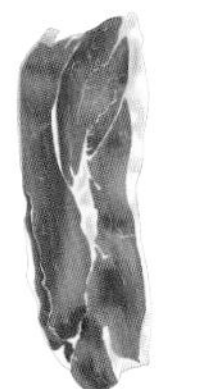

prosciutto
jamón[M] *serrano*

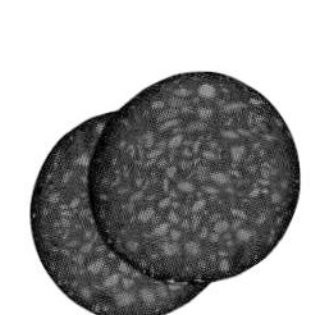

kielbasa sausage
salchicha[F] *kielbasa*

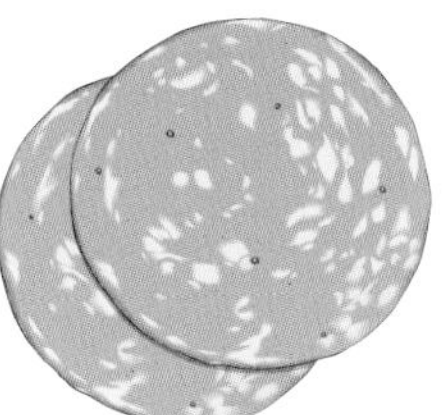

mortadella
mortadela[F]

blood sausage
morcilla[F]

chorizo
chorizo[M]

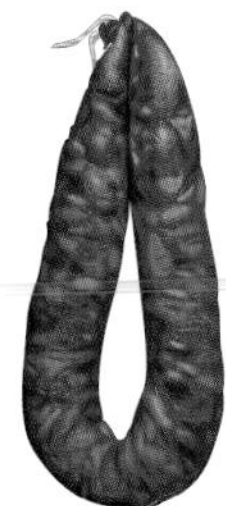

pepperoni
pepperoni[M]

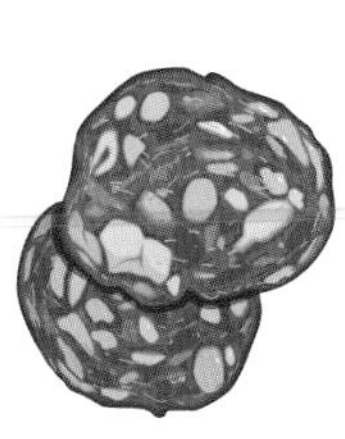

Genoa salami
salami[M] *de Génova*

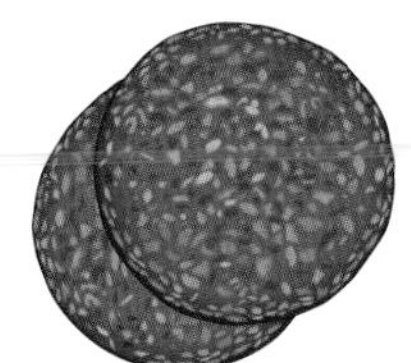

German salami
salami[M] *alemán*

Toulouse sausages
salchicha[F] *de Toulouse*

merguez sausages
salchicha[F] *merguez*

andouillette
andouillete[F]

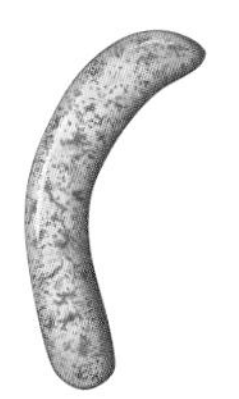

chipolata sausage
salchicha[F] *chipolata*

frankfurters
salchicha[F] *de Frankfurt*

pancetta
panceta[F]

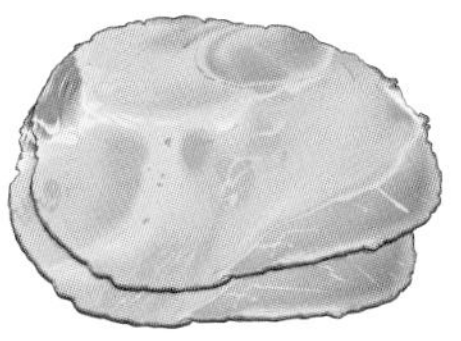

cooked ham
jamón[M] *de York*

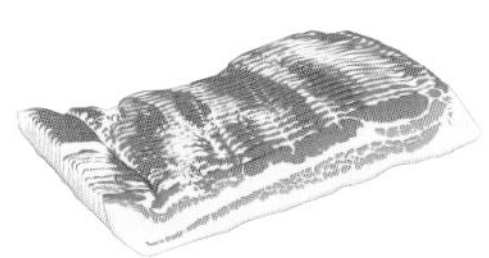

American bacon
bacón[M] *americano*

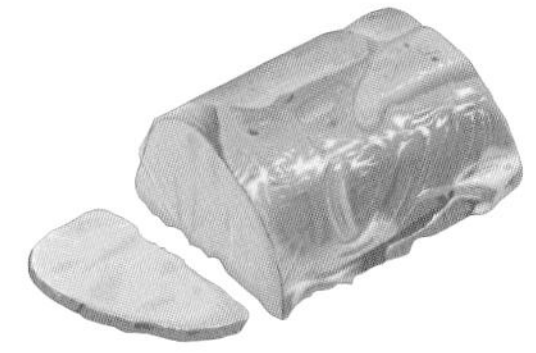

Canadian bacon
bacón[M] *canadiense*

mollusks

moluscos[M]

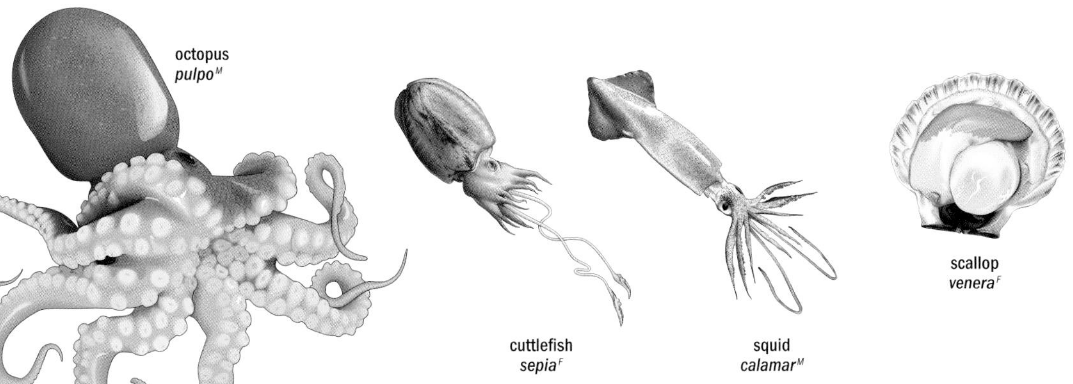

octopus
pulpo[M]

cuttlefish
sepia[F]

squid
calamar[M]

scallop
venera[F]

hard-shell clams
almeja[F]

soft shell clam
coquina[F]

abalone
oreja[F] *de mar*[M]

great scallop
vieira[F]

snail
caracol[M] *terrestre*

limpet
lapa[F]

common periwinkles
bígaros[M]

clams
almejas[F]

cockles
berberechos[M]

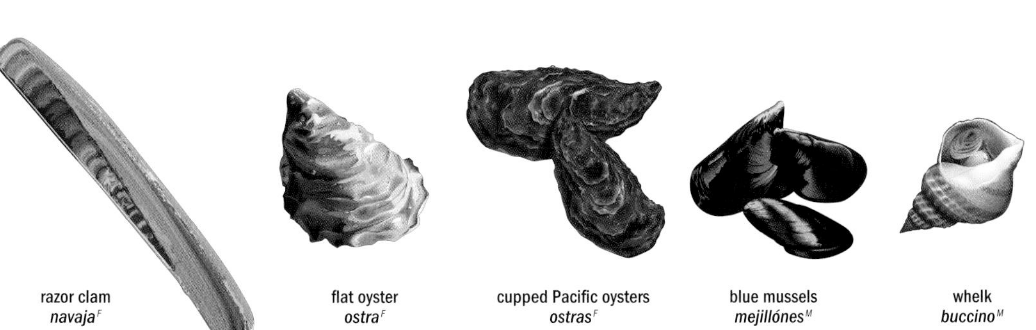

razor clam
navaja[F]

flat oyster
ostra[F]

cupped Pacific oysters
ostras[F]

blue mussels
mejillónes[M]

whelk
buccino[M]

crustaceans

crustáceos^M

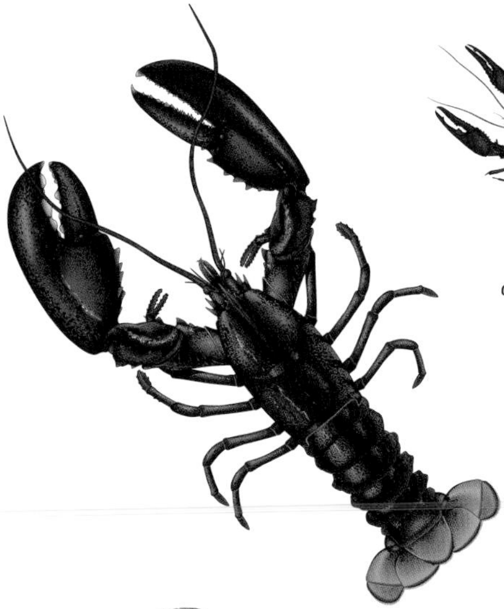

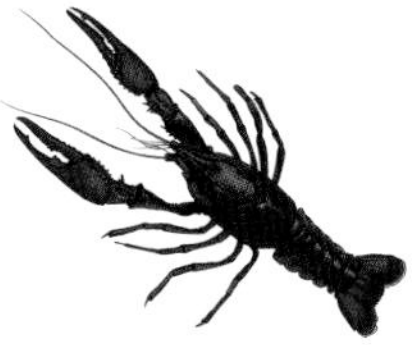

crayfish
cangrejo^M de río^M

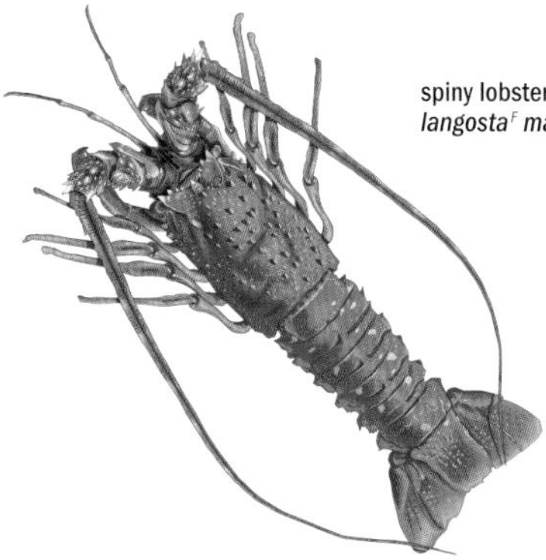

spiny lobster
langosta^F marina

lobster
bogavante^M

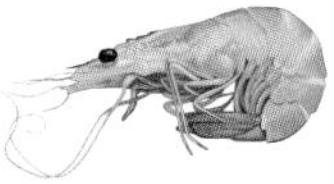

shrimp
gamba^F

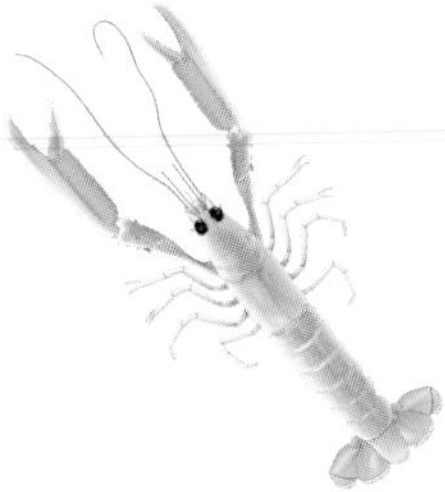

scampi
cigala^F

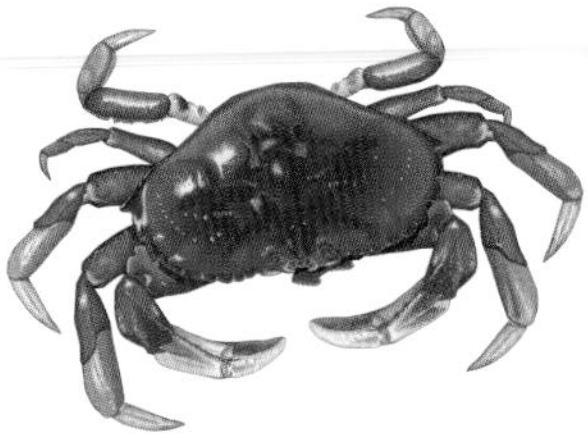

crab
cangrejo^M de mar^M

cartilaginous fishes

peces^M cartilaginosos

larger spotted dogfish
alitán^M

skate
raya^F

smooth hound
musola^F

sturgeon
esturión^M

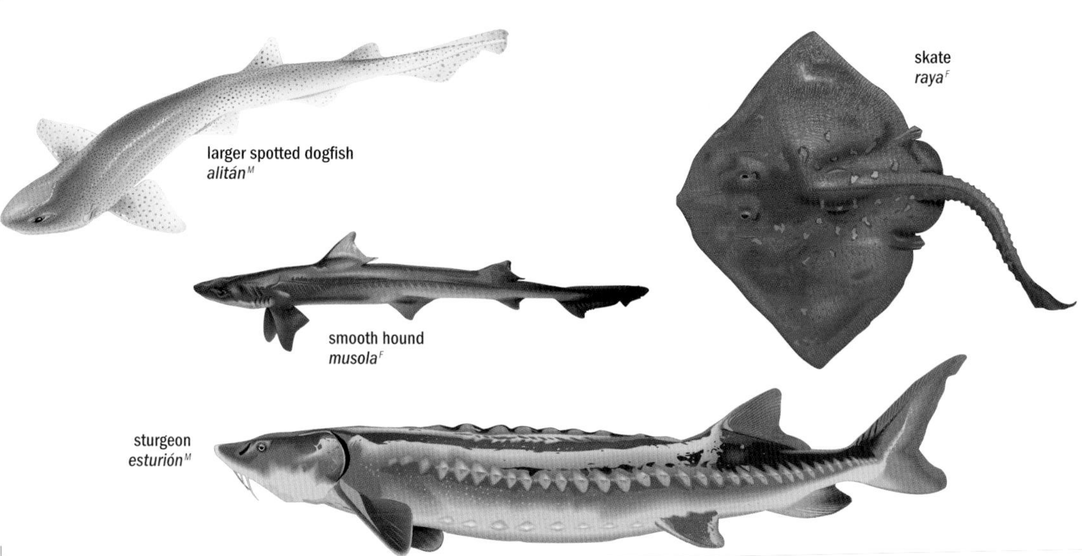

bony fishes

peces[M] óseos

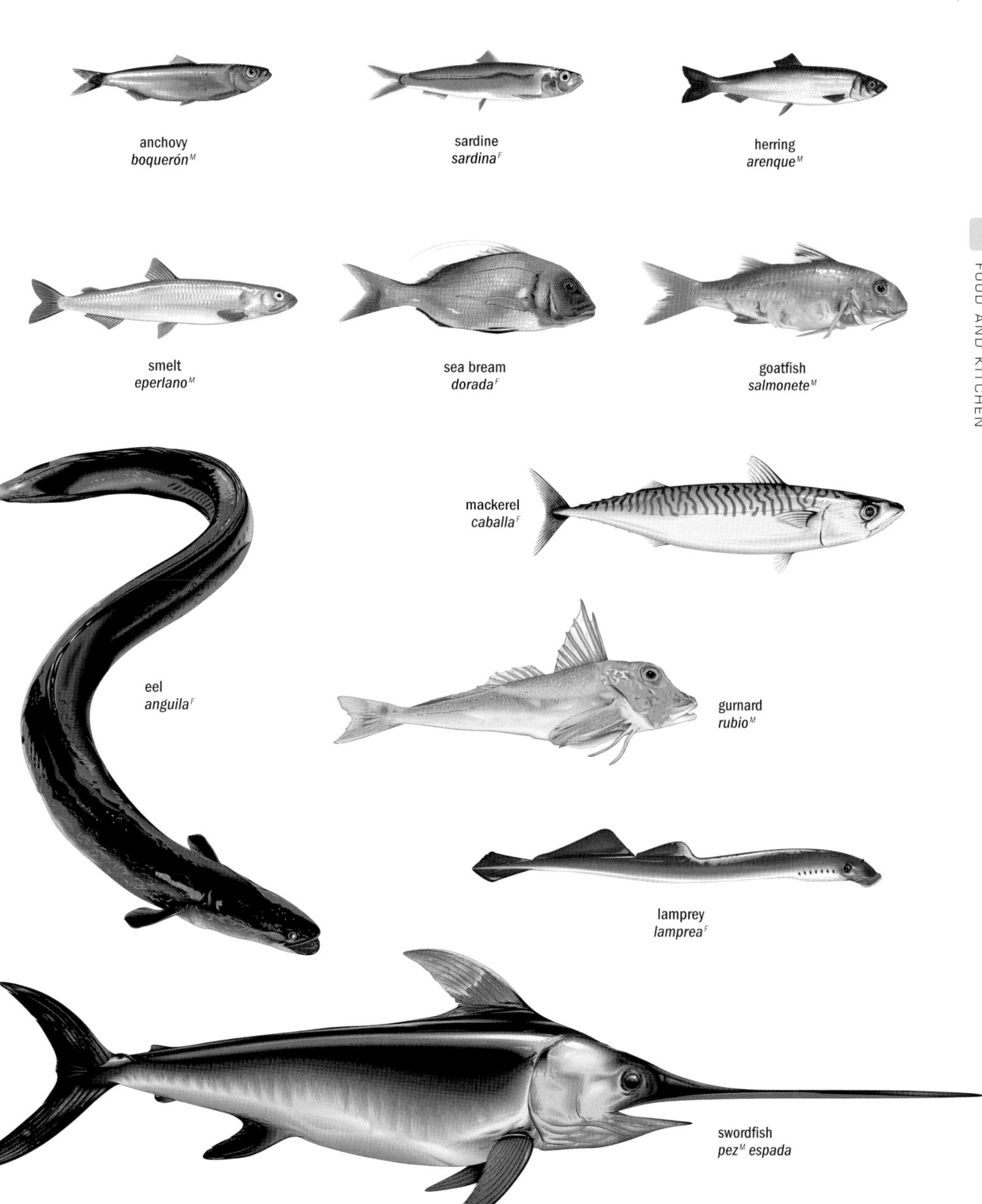

bony fishes

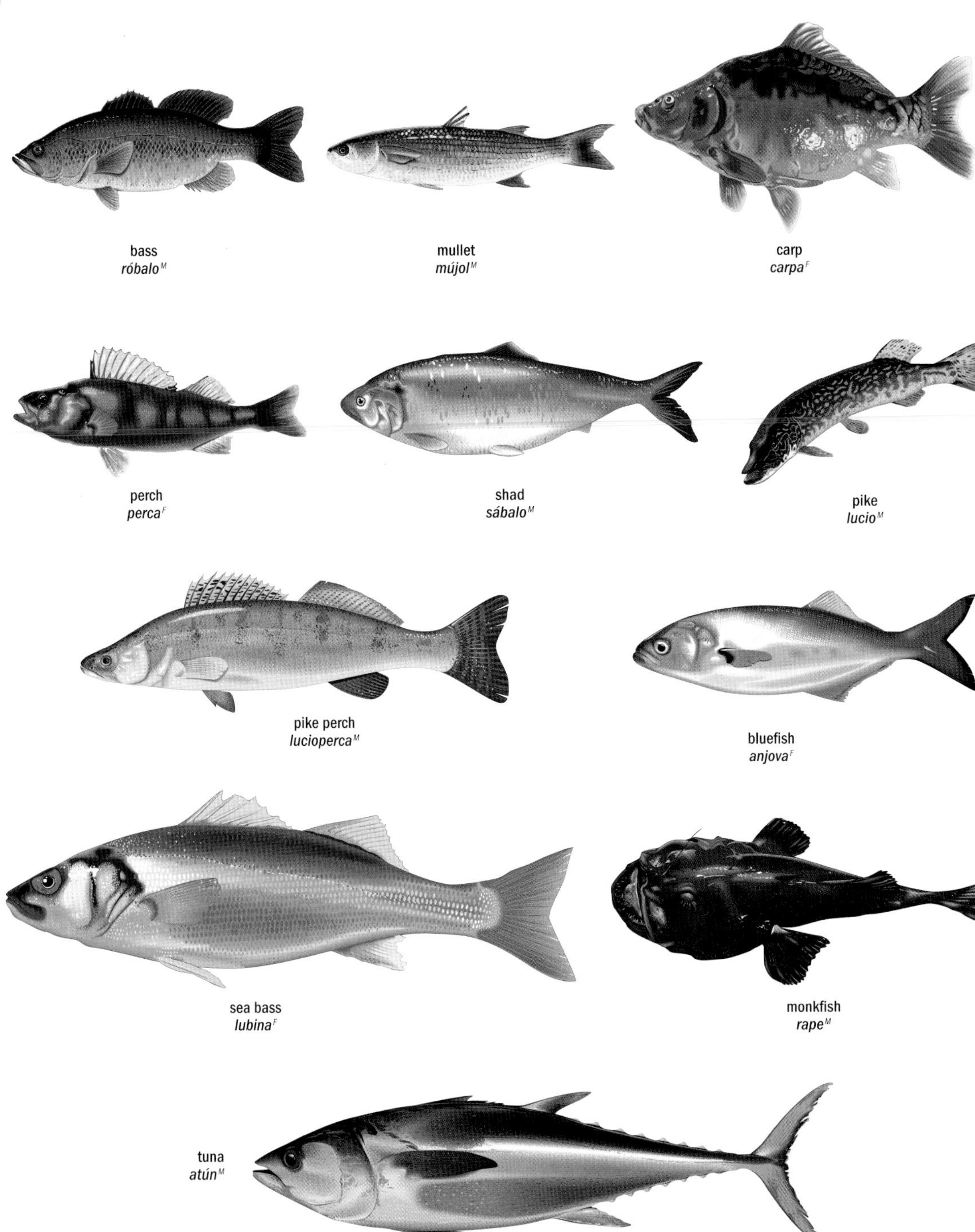

bass
róbalo[M]

mullet
mújol[M]

carp
carpa[F]

perch
perca[F]

shad
sábalo[M]

pike
lucio[M]

pike perch
lucioperca[M]

bluefish
anjova[F]

sea bass
lubina[F]

monkfish
rape[M]

tuna
atún[M]

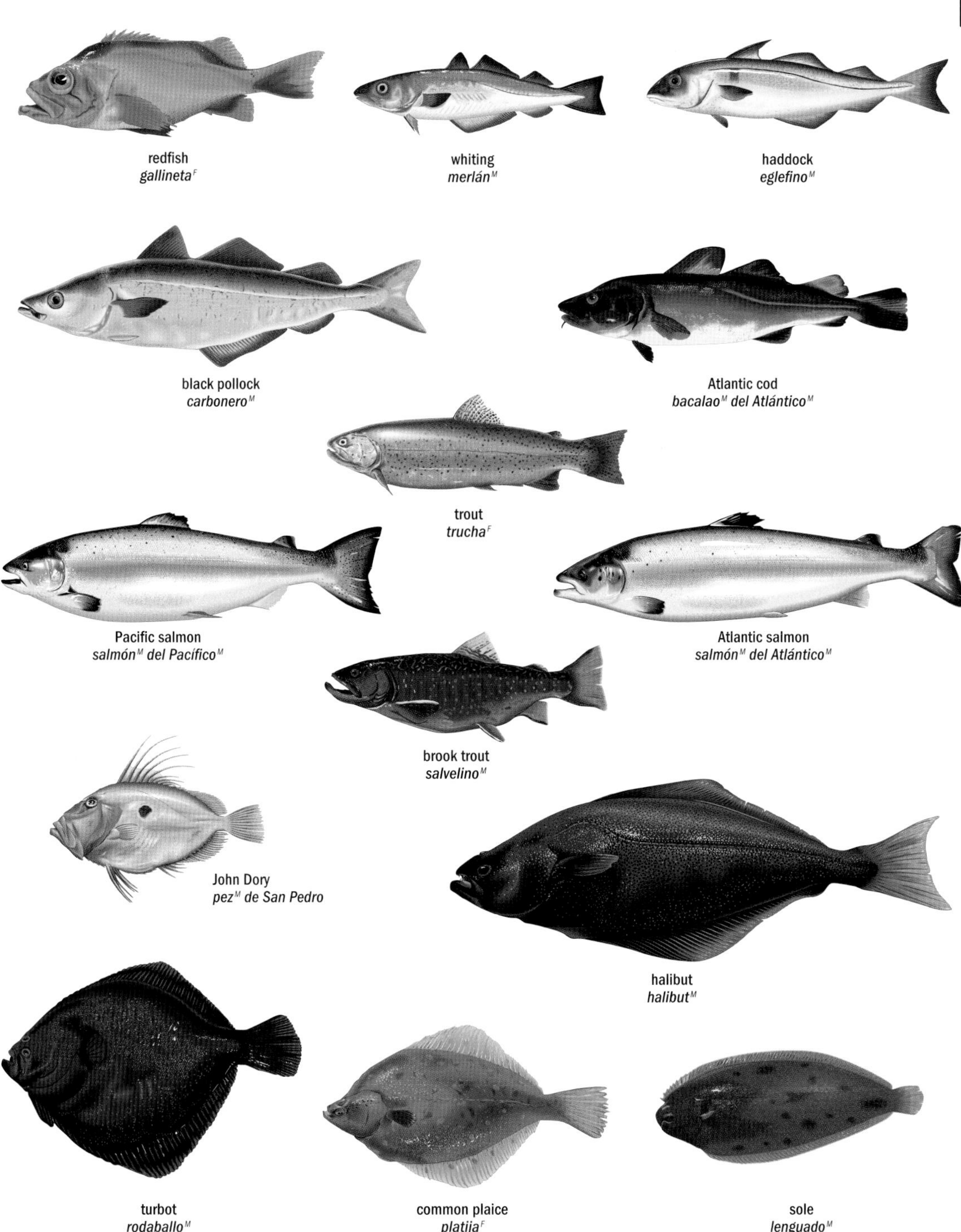
redfish
gallineta^{F}
whiting
merlán^{M}
haddock
eglefino^{M}
black pollock
carbonero^{M}
Atlantic cod
bacalao^{M} del Atlántico^{M}
trout
trucha^{F}
Pacific salmon
salmón^{M} del Pacífico^{M}
Atlantic salmon
salmón^{M} del Atlántico^{M}
brook trout
salvelino^{M}
John Dory
pez^{M} de San Pedro
halibut
halibut^{M}
turbot
rodaballo^{M}
common plaice
platija^{F}
sole
lenguado^{M}

packaging

envases[M]

pouch
bolsa[F]

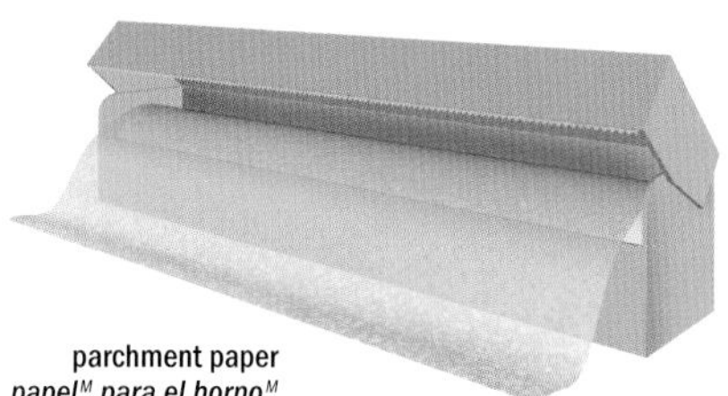

parchment paper
papel[M] para el horno[M]

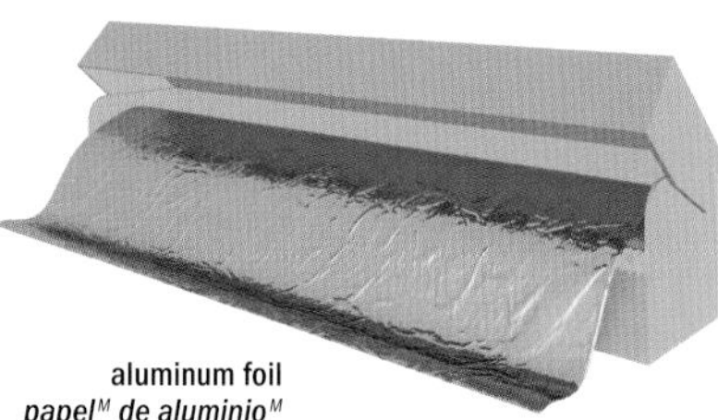

aluminum foil
papel[M] de aluminio[M]

freezer bag
bolsa[F] para congelados[M]

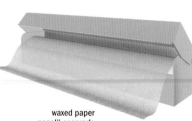

waxed paper
papel[M] encerado

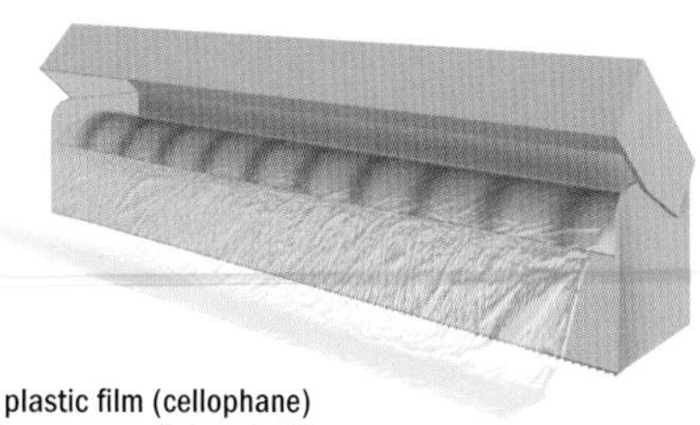

plastic film (cellophane)
papel[M] de celofán

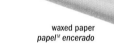

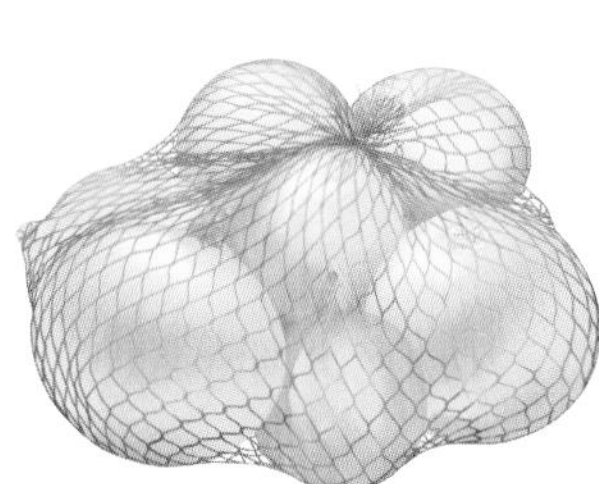

mesh bag
bolsa[F] de malla[F]

canisters
botes[M] herméticos

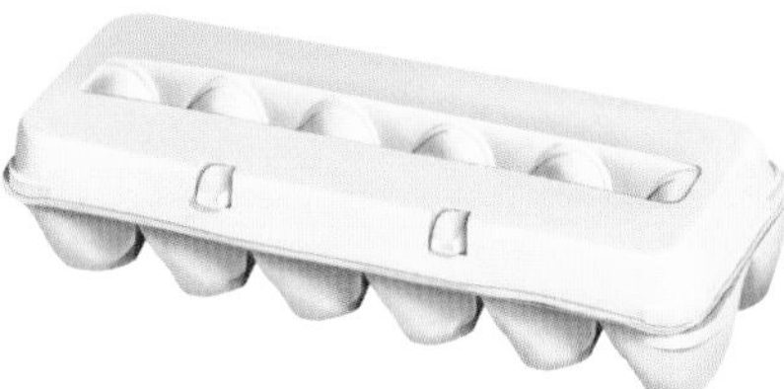

egg carton
cajas[F] de cartón[M] para huevos[M]

food tray
barqueta[F]

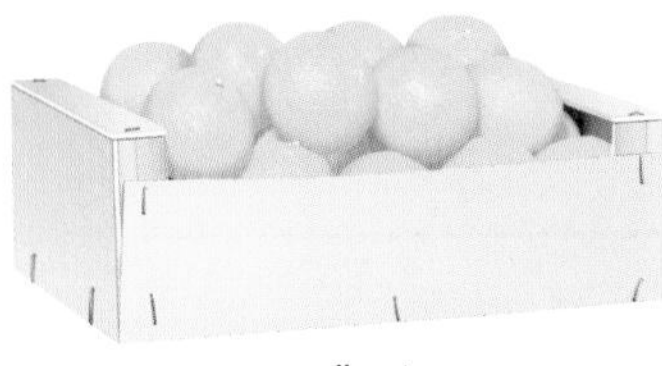

small crate
caja[F] pequeña

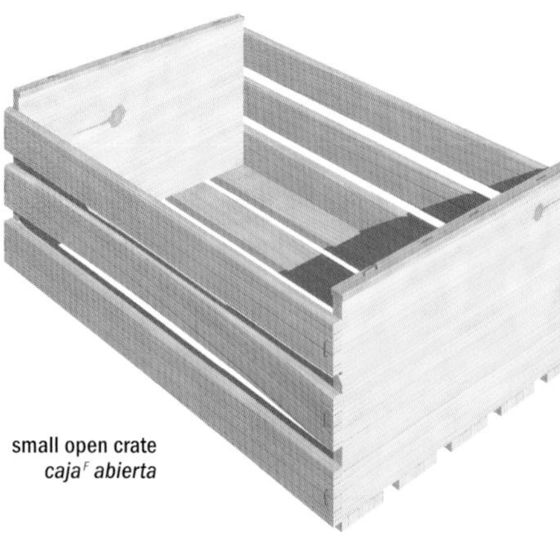

small open crate
caja[F] abierta

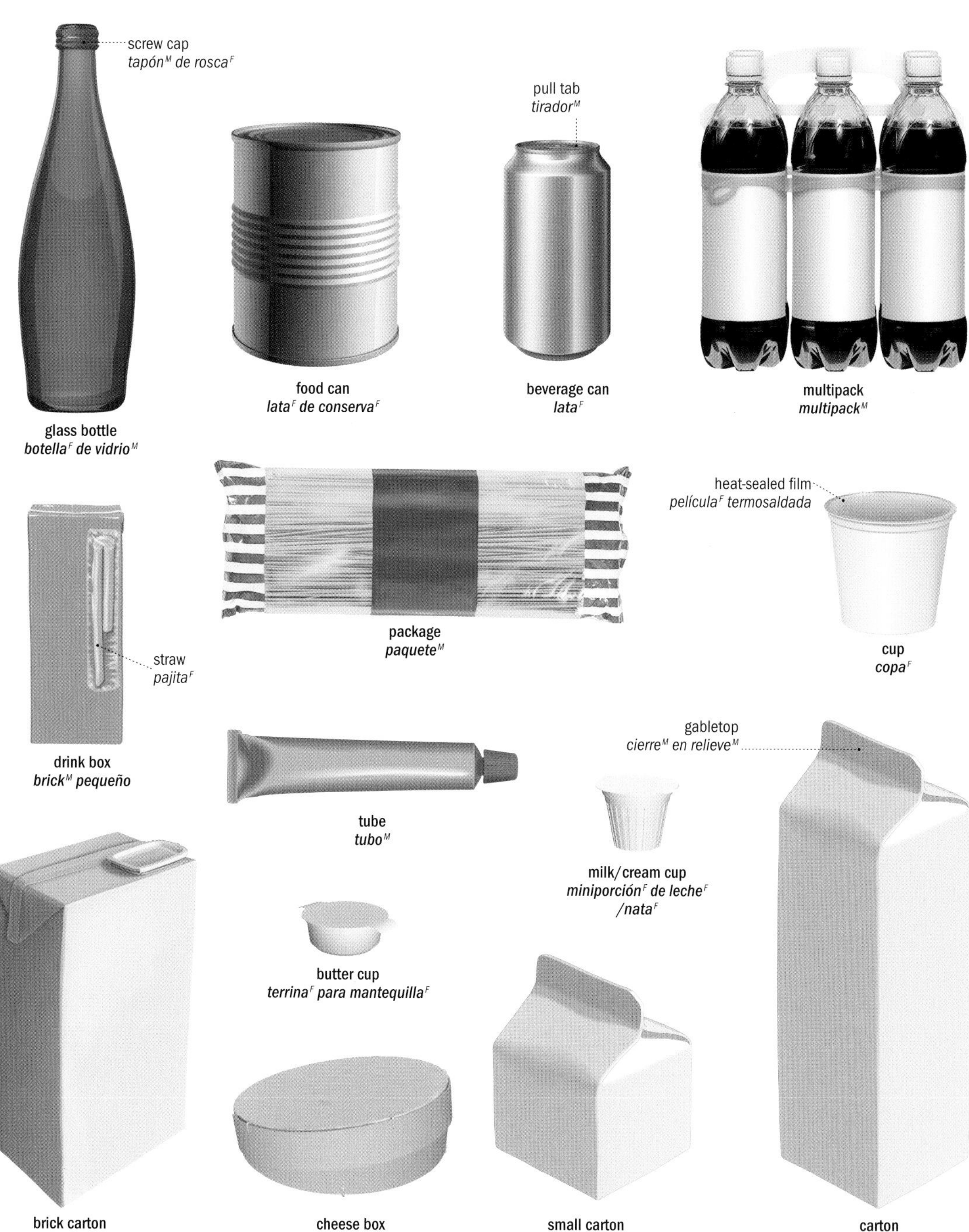
screw cap
tapón^M de rosca^F
glass bottle
botella^F de vidrio^M
food can
lata^F de conserva^F
pull tab
tirador^M
beverage can
lata^F
multipack
multipack^M
drink box
brick^M pequeño
straw
pajita^F
package
paquete^M
heat-sealed film
película^F termosaldada
cup
copa^F
tube
tubo^M
gabletop
cierre^M en relieve^M
milk/cream cup
miniporción^F de leche^F /nata^F
butter cup
terrina^F para mantequilla^F
brick carton
brick^M
cheese box
caja^F para queso^M
small carton
cartón^M pequeño
carton
cartón^M

kitchen

cocina[F]

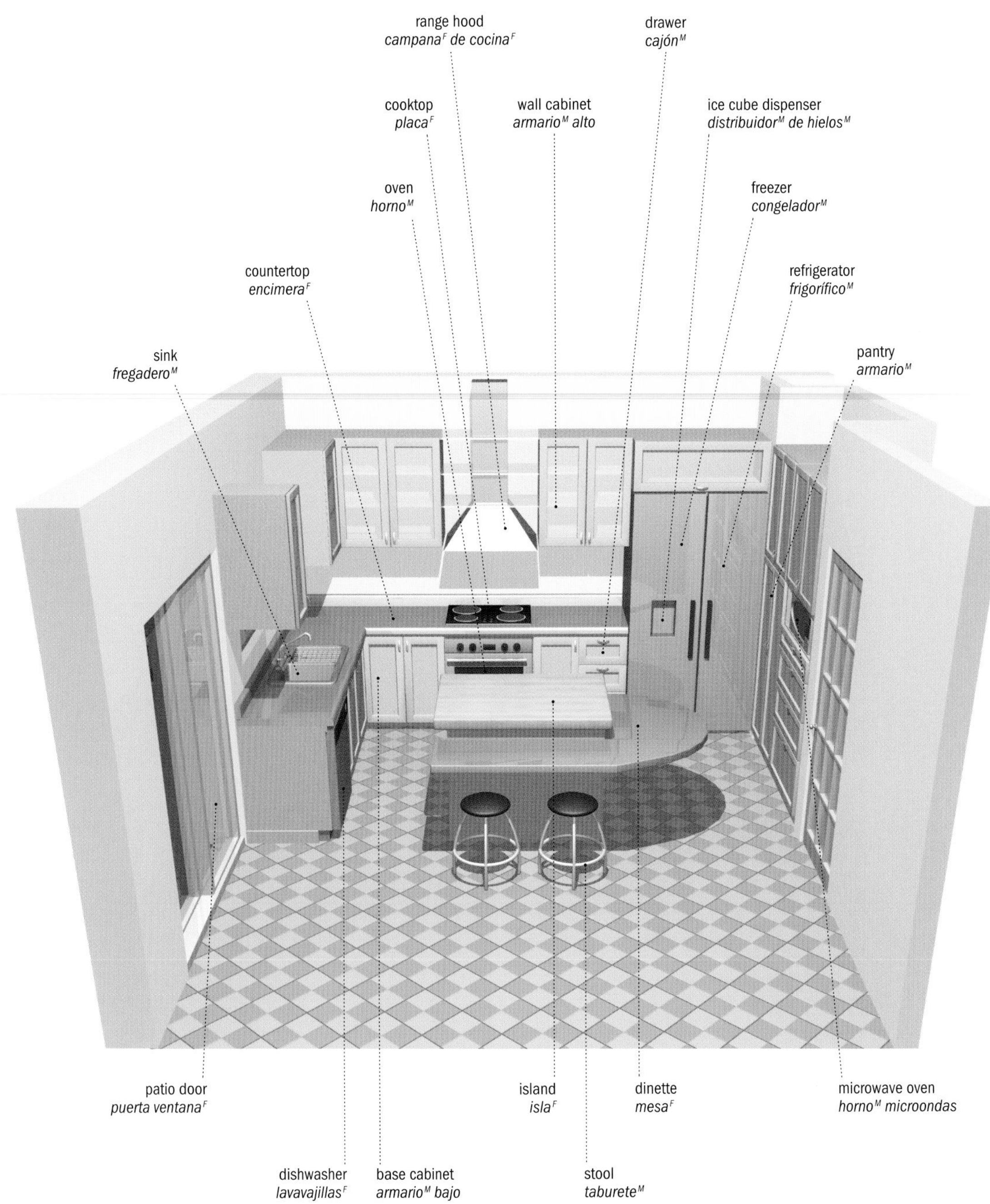

range hood
campana[F] de cocina[F]
drawer
cajón[M]
cooktop
placa[F]
wall cabinet
armario[M] alto
ice cube dispenser
distribuidor[M] de hielos[M]
oven
horno[M]
freezer
congelador[M]
countertop
encimera[F]
refrigerator
frigorífico[M]
sink
fregadero[M]
pantry
armario[M]
patio door
puerta ventana[F]
island
isla[F]
dinette
mesa[F]
microwave oven
horno[M] microondas
dishwasher
lavavajillas[F]
base cabinet
armario[M] bajo
stool
taburete[M]

glassware

cristalería[F]

liqueur glass
copa[F] para licores[M]

port glass
copa[F] para oporto[M]

sparkling wine glass
copa[F] de champaña[F]

brandy snifter
copa[F] para brandy[M]

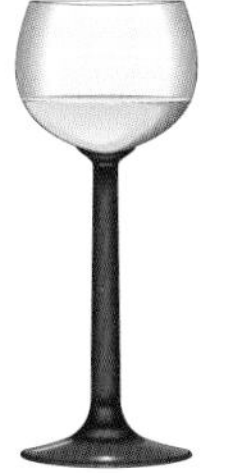

Alsace glass
copa[F] para vino[M] de Alsacia

burgundy glass
copa[F] para vino[M] de Borgoña

bordeaux glass
copa[F] para vino[M] de Burdeos

white wine glass
copa[F] para vino[M] blanco

water goblet
copa[F] de agua[F]

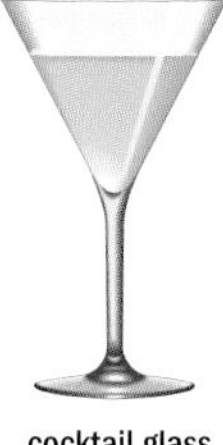

cocktail glass
copa[F] de cóctel[M]

highball glass
vaso[M] largo

old-fashioned glass
vaso[M] corto

beer mug
jarra[M] de cerveza[F]

champagne flute
copa[F] de flauta[F]

small decanter
decantador[M]

decanter
garrafa[F]

dinnerware

vajilla[F] y servicio[M] de mesa[F]

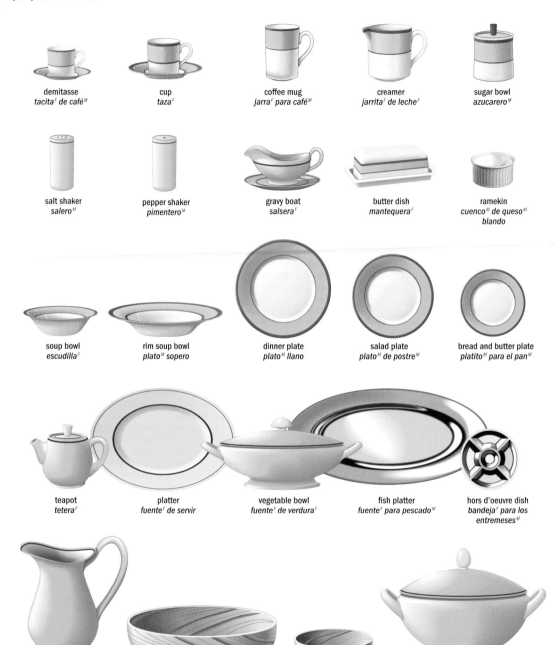

demitasse
tacita[F] de café[M]

cup
taza[F]

coffee mug
jarra[F] para café[M]

creamer
jarrita[F] de leche[F]

sugar bowl
azucarero[M]

salt shaker
salero[M]

pepper shaker
pimentero[M]

gravy boat
salsera[F]

butter dish
mantequera[F]

ramekin
cuenco[M] de queso[M] blando

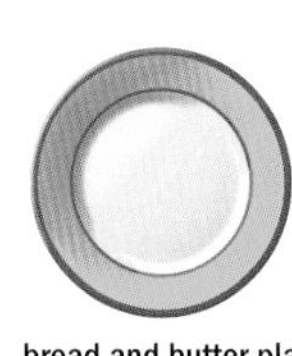

soup bowl
escudilla[F]

rim soup bowl
plato[M] sopero

dinner plate
plato[M] llano

salad plate
plato[M] de postre[M]

bread and butter plate
platito[M] para el pan[M]

teapot
tetera[F]

platter
fuente[F] de servir

vegetable bowl
fuente[F] de verdura[F]

fish platter
fuente[F] para pescado[M]

hors d'oeuvre dish
bandeja[F] para los entremeses[M]

water pitcher
jarra[F] de agua[F]

salad bowl
ensaladera[F]

salad dish
bol[M] para ensalada[F]

soup tureen
sopera[F]

silverware

cubertería[F]

knife
cuchillo[M]

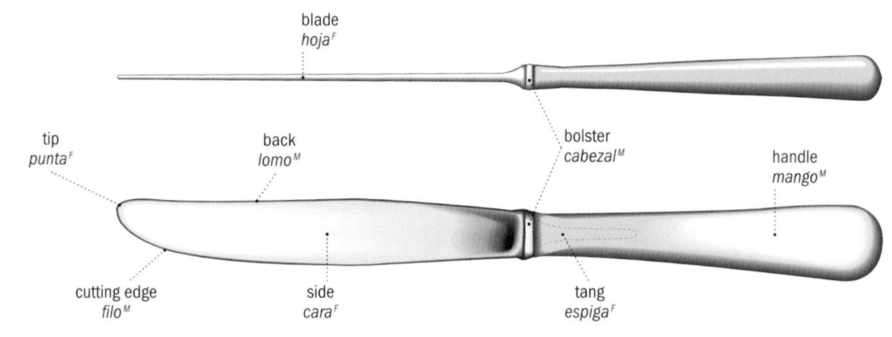

fork
tenedor[M]

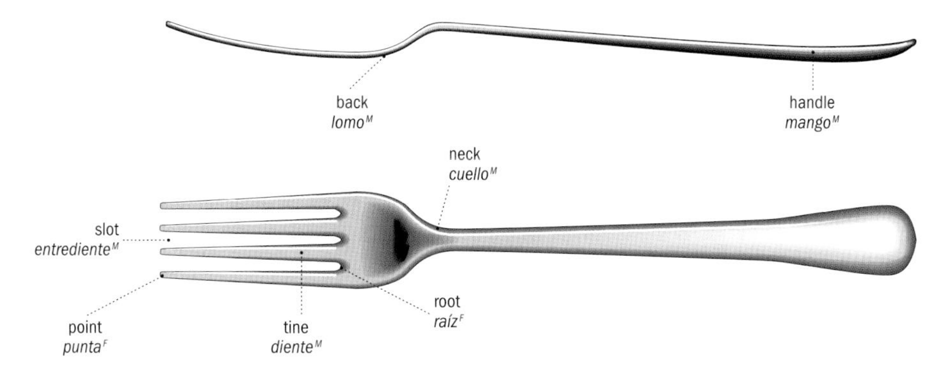

spoon
cuchara[F]

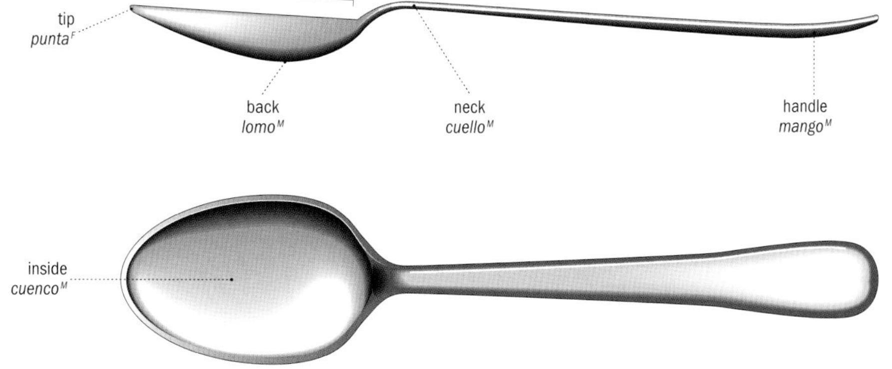

silverware

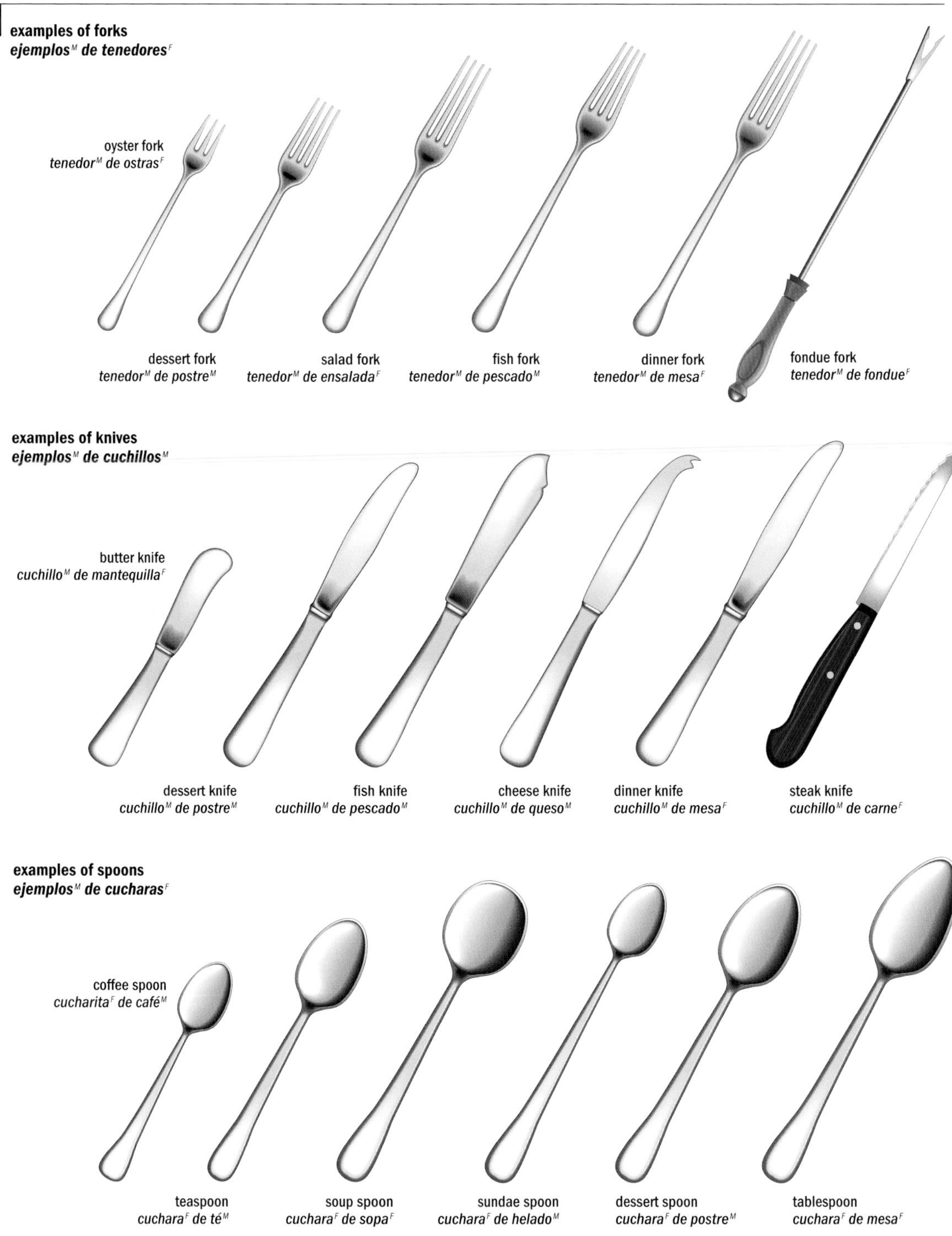

examples of forks
ejemplos[M] de tenedores[F]
oyster fork
tenedor[M] de ostras[F]
dessert fork
tenedor[M] de postre[M]
salad fork
tenedor[M] de ensalada[F]
fish fork
tenedor[M] de pescado[M]
dinner fork
tenedor[M] de mesa[F]
fondue fork
tenedor[M] de fondue[F]
examples of knives
ejemplos[M] de cuchillos[M]
butter knife
cuchillo[M] de mantequilla[F]
dessert knife
cuchillo[M] de postre[M]
fish knife
cuchillo[M] de pescado[M]
cheese knife
cuchillo[M] de queso[M]
dinner knife
cuchillo[M] de mesa[F]
steak knife
cuchillo[M] de carne[F]
examples of spoons
ejemplos[M] de cucharas[F]
coffee spoon
cucharita[F] de café[M]
teaspoon
cuchara[F] de té[M]
soup spoon
cuchara[F] de sopa[F]
sundae spoon
cuchara[F] de helado[M]
dessert spoon
cuchara[F] de postre[M]
tablespoon
cuchara[F] de mesa[F]

kitchen utensils

utensilios[M] de cocina[F]

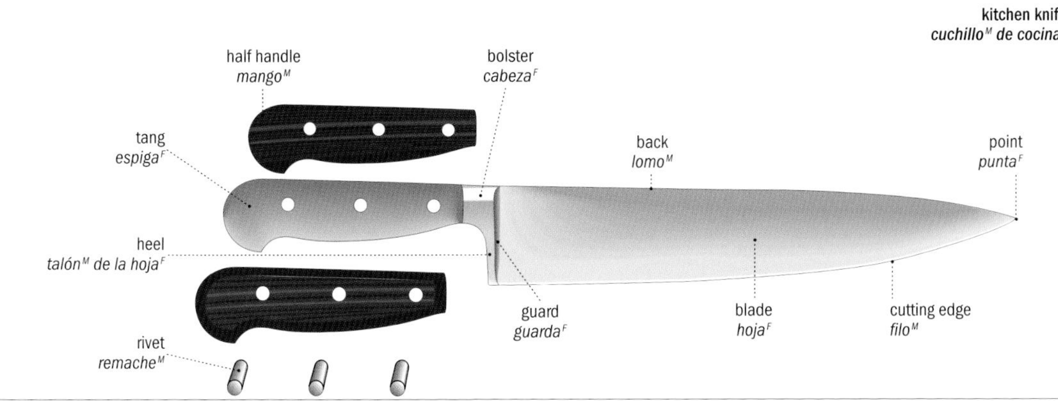

examples of utensils for cutting
ejemplos[M] de cuchillos[M] de cocina[F]

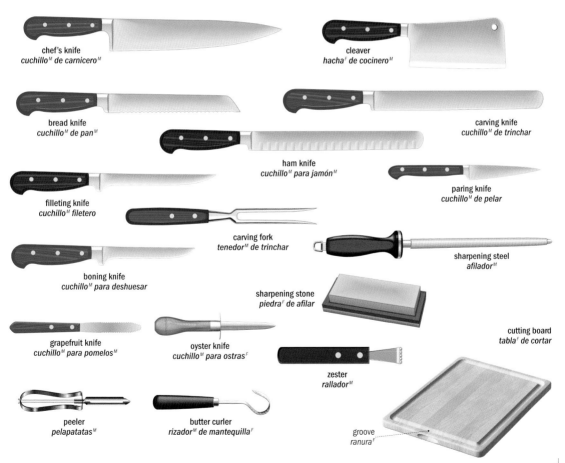

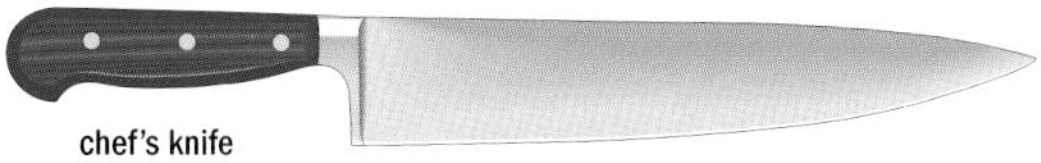

chef's knife
cuchillo[M] de carnicero[M]

cleaver
hacha[F] de cocinero[M]

bread knife
cuchillo[M] de pan[M]

carving knife
cuchillo[M] de trinchar

ham knife
cuchillo[M] para jamón[M]

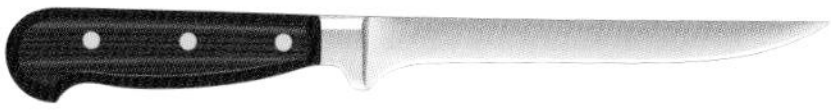

filleting knife
cuchillo[M] filetero

paring knife
cuchillo[M] de pelar

carving fork
tenedor[M] de trinchar

sharpening steel
afilador[M]

boning knife
cuchillo[M] para deshuesar

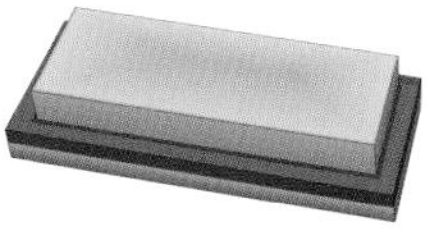

sharpening stone
piedra[F] de afilar

cutting board
tabla[F] de cortar

grapefruit knife
cuchillo[M] para pomelos[M]

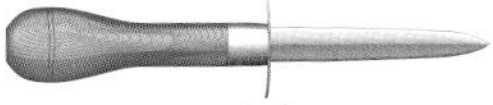

oyster knife
cuchillo[M] para ostras[F]

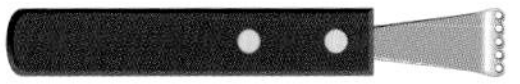

zester
rallador[M]

peeler
pelapatatas[M]

butter curler
rizador[M] de mantequilla[F]

groove
ranura[F]

kitchen utensils

for opening
para abrir y descorchar

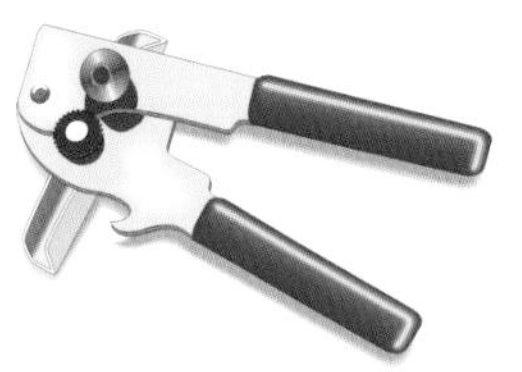

can opener
abrelatas^M

bottle opener
abrebotellas^M

waiter's corkscrew
sacacorchos^M

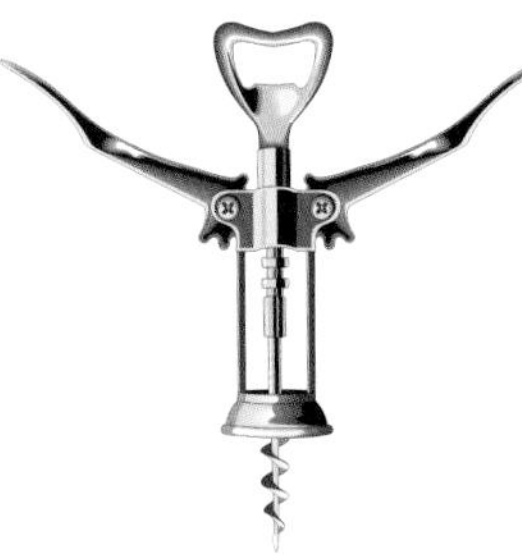

lever corkscrew
sacacorchos^M *con brazos*^M

for grinding and grating
para moler y rallar

nutcracker
cascanueces^M

mortar
almirez^M

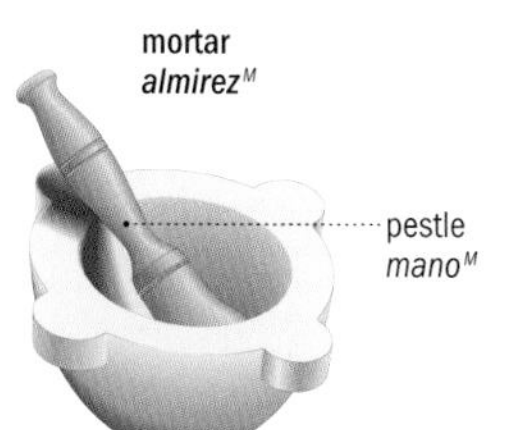

meat grinder
picadora^F *de carne*^F

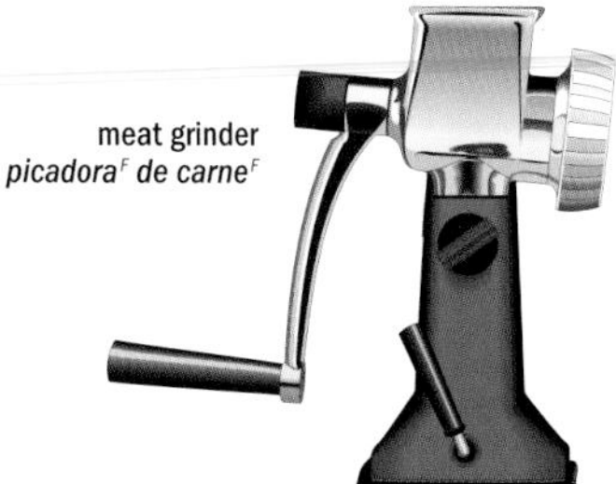

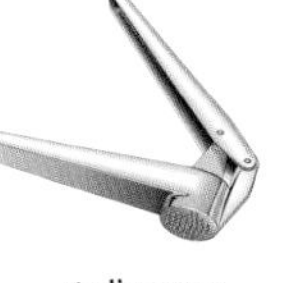

garlic press
triturador^M *de ajos*^M

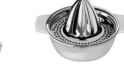

citrus juicer
exprimidor^M

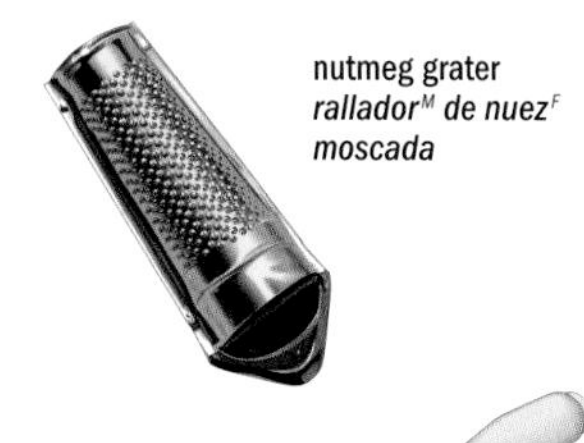

nutmeg grater
rallador^M *de nuez*^F *moscada*

grater
rallador^M

rotary cheese grater
rallador^M *cilíndrico de queso*^M

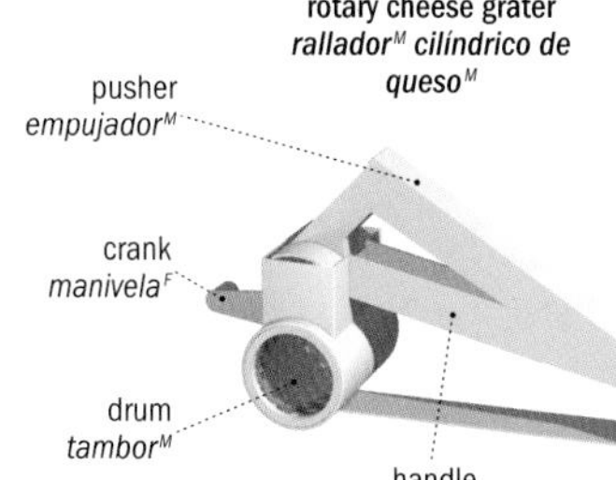

pasta maker
máquina^F *para hacer pasta*^F *italiana*

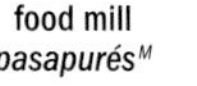

food mill
pasapurés^M

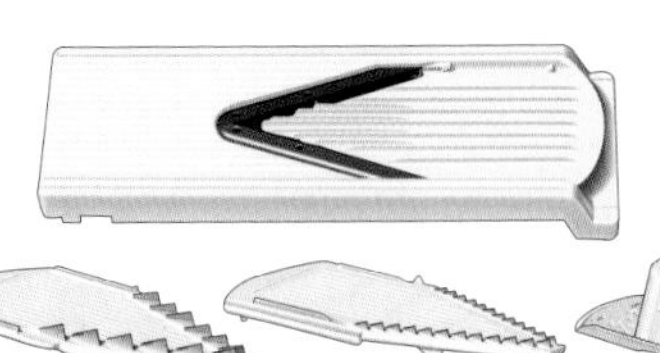

mandoline
mandolina^F

for measuring
utensilios^M para medir

measuring spoons
cucharas^F dosificadoras

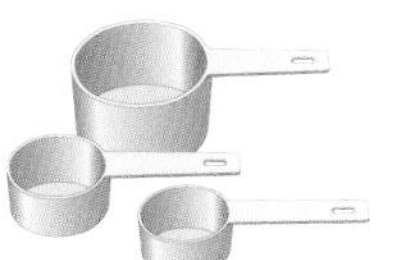

measuring cups
tazas^F medidoras

candy thermometer
termómetro^M de azúcar^M

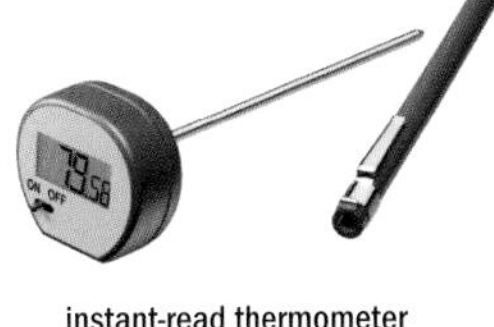

instant-read thermometer
termómetro^M de medida^F instantánea

measuring cup
jarra^F medidora

meat thermometer
termómetro^M para carne^F

oven thermometer
termómetro^M de horno^M

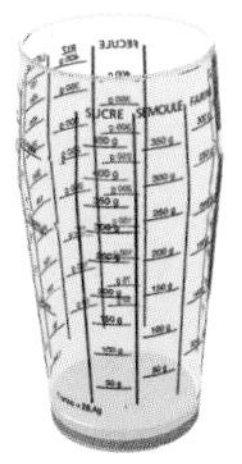

measuring beaker
vaso^M medidor

kitchen timer
minutero^M

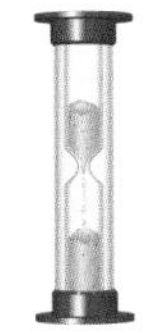

egg timer
reloj^M de arena^F

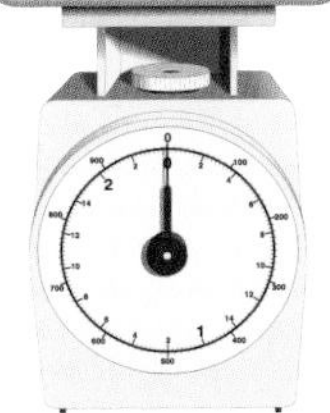

kitchen scale
báscula^F de cocina^F

for straining and draining
coladores^M y escurridores^M

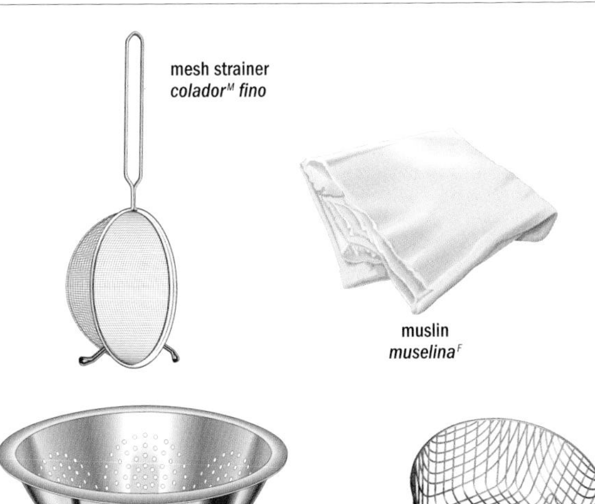

mesh strainer
colador^M fino

muslin
muselina^F

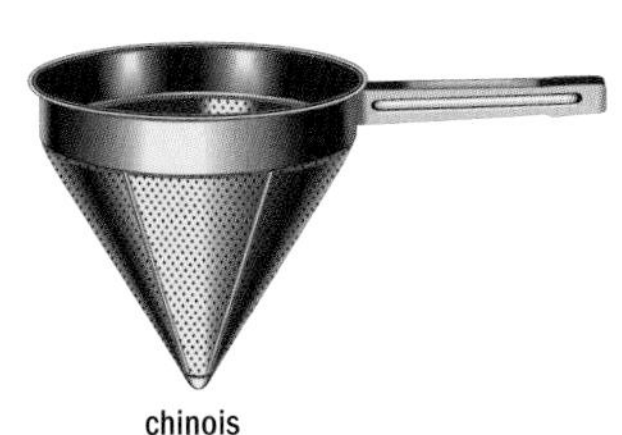

chinois
chino^M

funnel
embudo^M

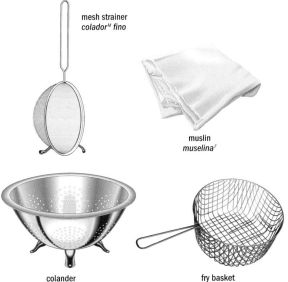

colander
escurridor^M

fry basket
cesta^F de freír

sieve
tamiz^M

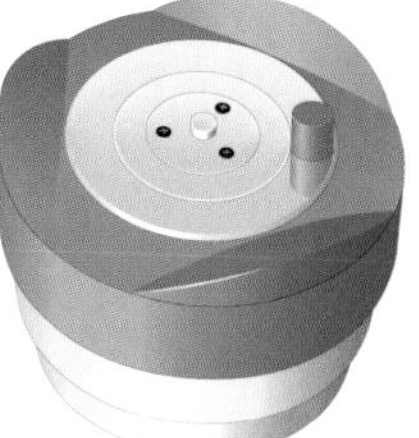

salad spinner
secadora^F de ensalada^F

baking utensils
utensilios[M] para repostería

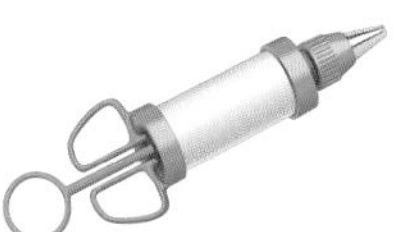
icing syringe
jeringa[F] de decoración[F]

pastry cutting wheel
cortapastas[M]

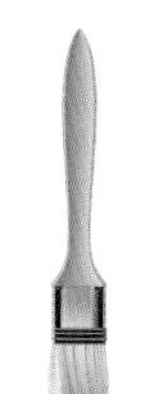
pastry brush
pincel[M] de repostería[F]

egg beater
batidor[M] mecánico

whisk
batidor[M]

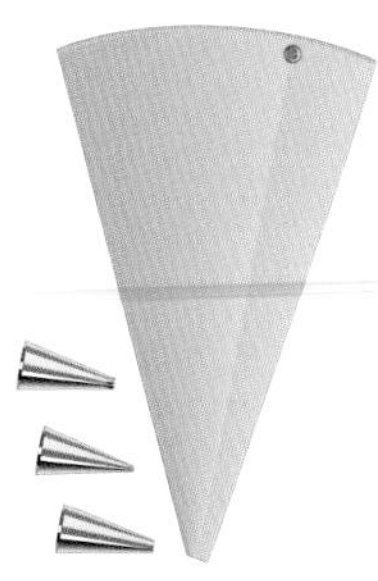
pastry bag and nozzles
manga[F] y boquillas[F]

sifter
tamiz[M]

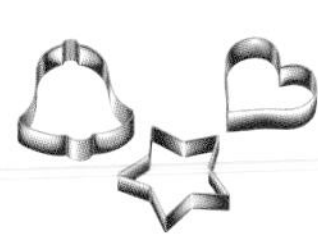
cookie cutters
moldes[M] de pastas[F]

dredger
espolvoreador[M]

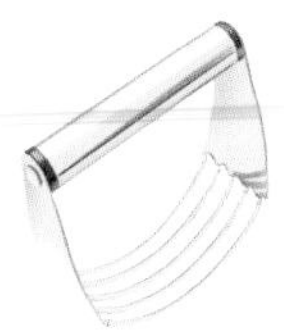
pastry blender
mezclador[M] de pastelería[F]

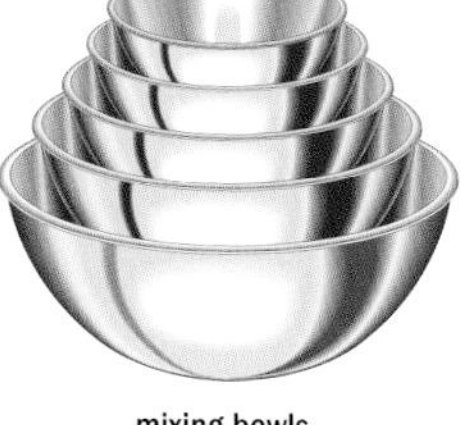

mixing bowls
boles[M] para batir

rolling pin
rodillo[M]

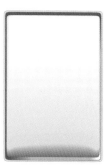

baking sheet
bandeja[F] de pastelería[F]

muffin pan
molde[M] para magdalenas[F]

soufflé dish
molde[M] de soufflé[M]

charlotte mold
molde[M] de carlota[F]

spring-form pan
molde[M] redondo con muelles[M]

pie pan
molde[M] para tartas[F]

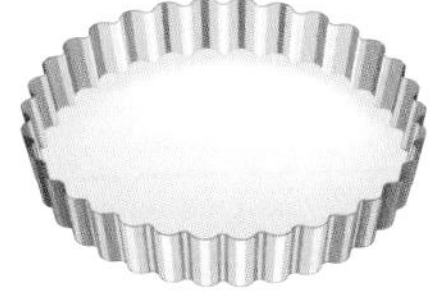
quiche plate
molde[M] acanalado

cake pan
molde[M] para bizcocho[M]

set of utensils
juego[M] de utensilios[M]

skimmer
espumadera[F]

draining spoon
escurridera[F]

spatula
espátula[F]

turner
paleta[F]

ladle
cazo[M]

potato masher
pasapuré[M]

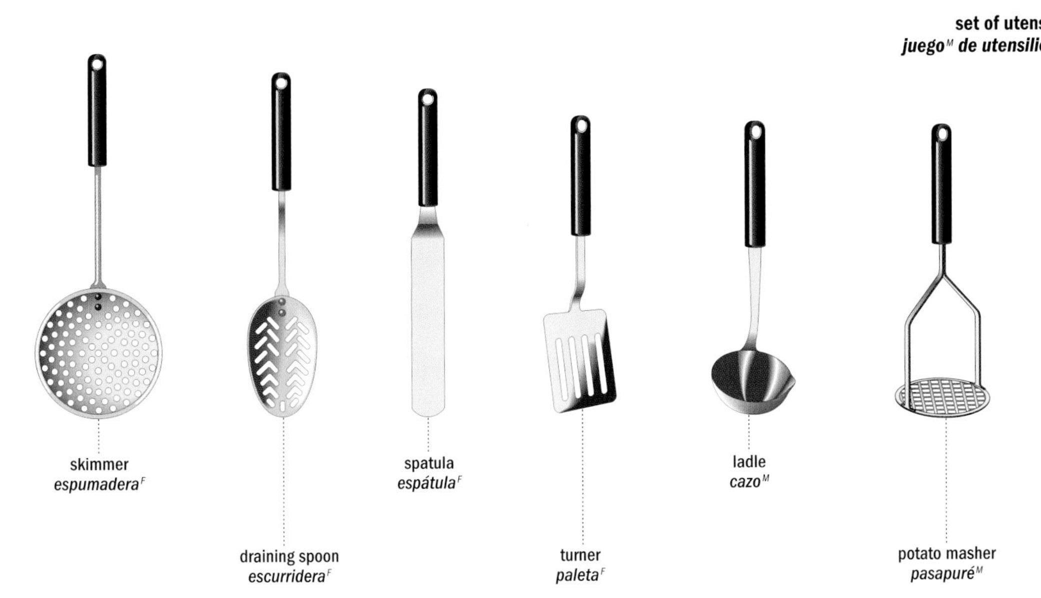

miscellaneous utensils
utensilios[M] diversos

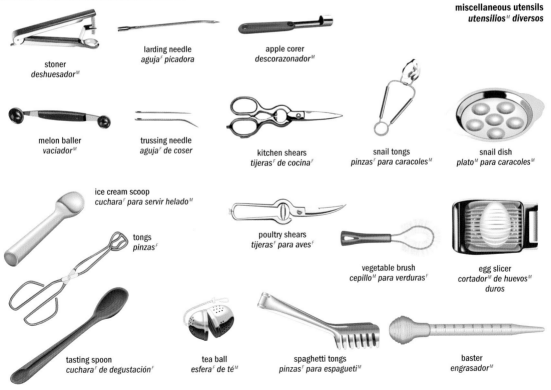

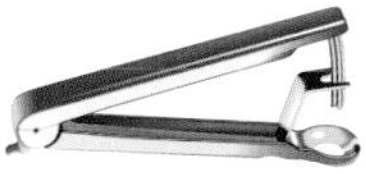

stoner
deshuesador[M]

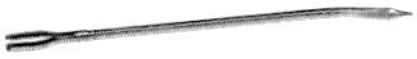

larding needle
aguja[F] picadora

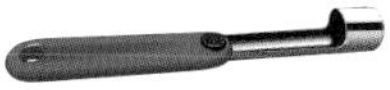

apple corer
descorazonador[M]

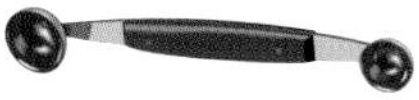

melon baller
vaciador[M]

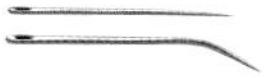

trussing needle
aguja[F] de coser

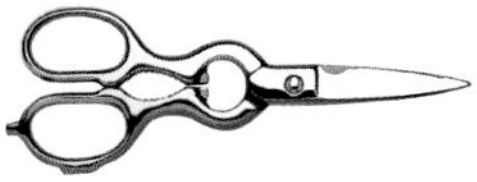

kitchen shears
tijeras[F] de cocina[F]

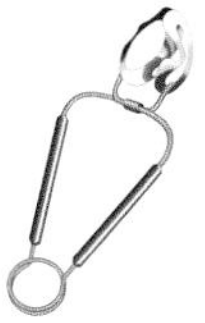

snail tongs
pinzas[F] para caracoles[M]

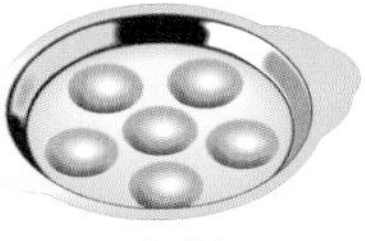

snail dish
plato[M] para caracoles[M]

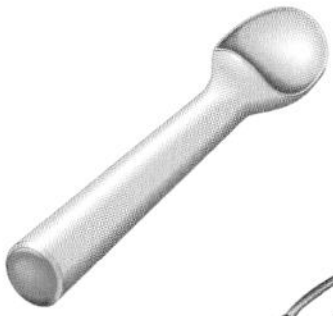

ice cream scoop
cuchara[F] para servir helado[M]

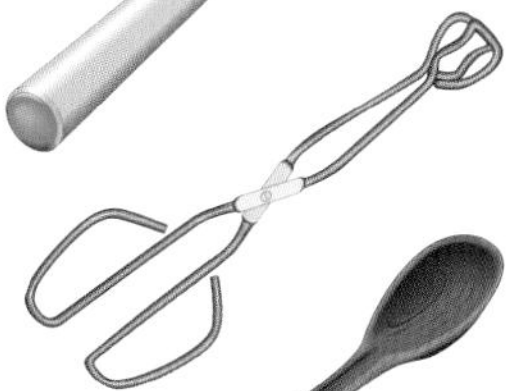

tongs
pinzas[F]

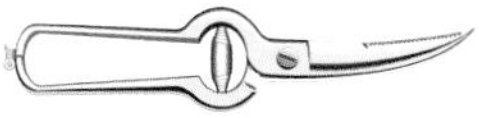

poultry shears
tijeras[F] para aves[F]

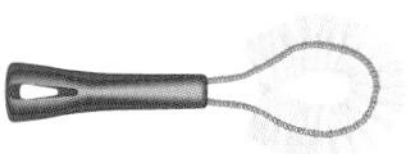

vegetable brush
cepillo[M] para verduras[F]

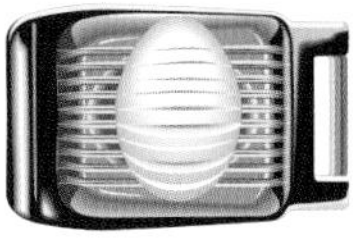

egg slicer
cortador[M] de huevos[M] duros

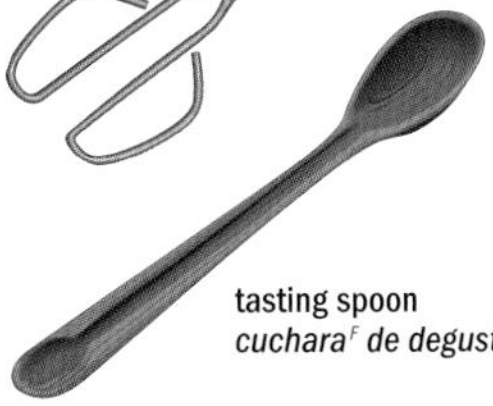

tasting spoon
cuchara[F] de degustación[F]

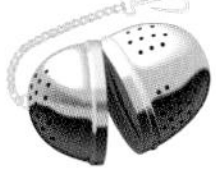

tea ball
esfera[F] de té[M]

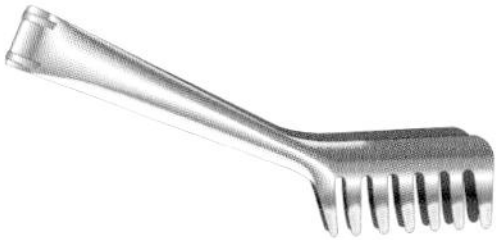

spaghetti tongs
pinzas[F] para espagueti[M]

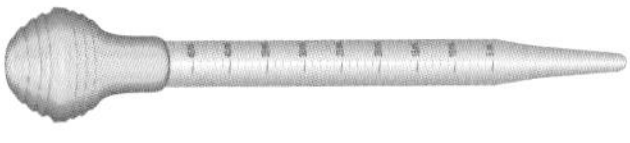

baster
engrasador[M]

cooking utensils

utensilios^M de cocina^F

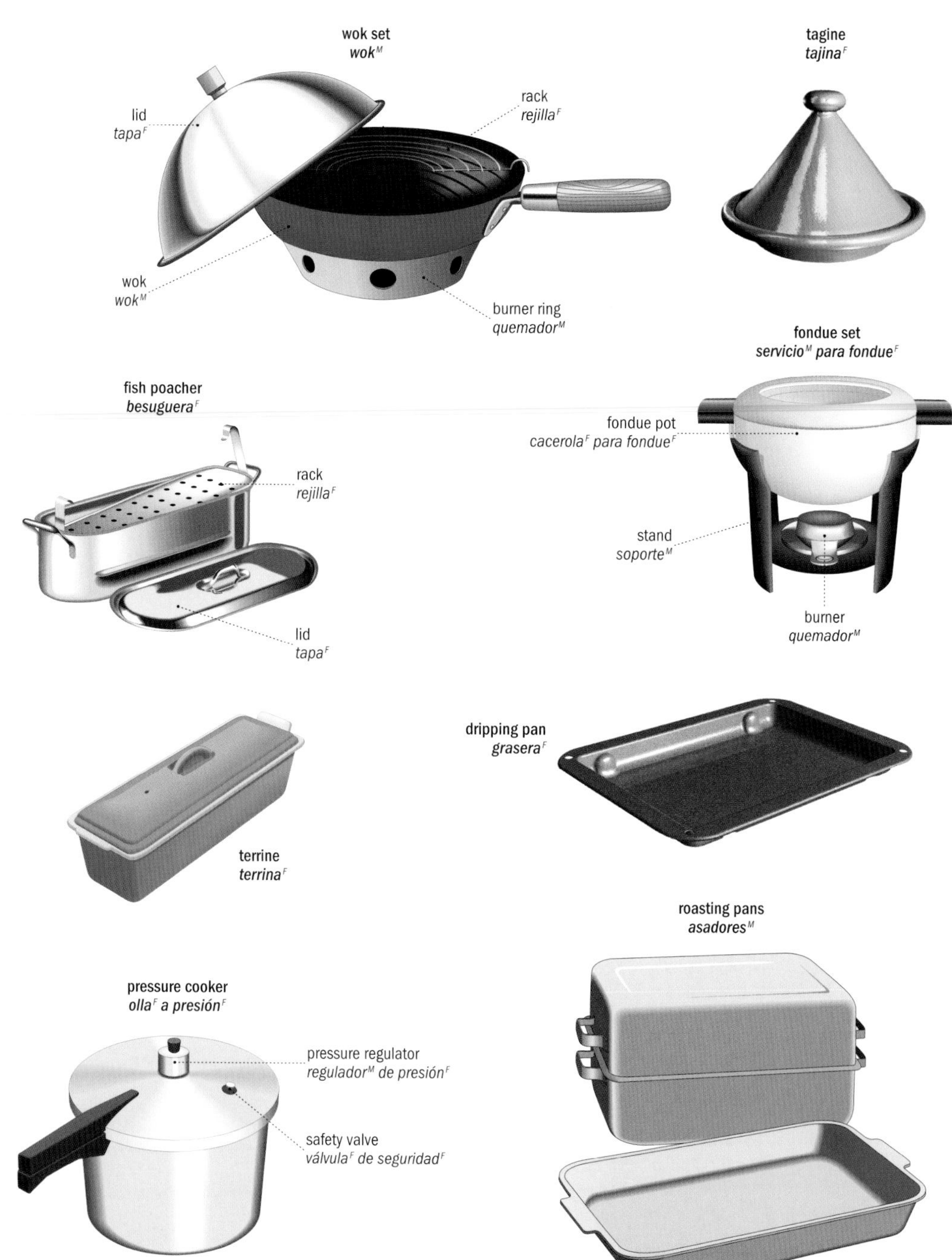
wok set
wok^M
lid
tapa^F
rack
rejilla^F
wok
wok^M
burner ring
quemador^M
tagine
tajina^F
fondue set
servicio^M para fondue^F
fish poacher
besuguera^F
rack
rejilla^F
lid
tapa^F
fondue pot
cacerola^F para fondue^F
stand
soporte^M
burner
quemador^M
dripping pan
grasera^F
terrine
terrina^F
roasting pans
asadores^M
pressure cooker
olla^F a presión^F
pressure regulator
regulador^M de presión^F
safety valve
válvula^F de seguridad^F

Dutch oven
cacerola^F refractaria

stock pot
olla^F

couscous kettle
olla^F para cuscús^M

frying pan
sartén^F

steamer
cazuela^F vaporera

egg poacher
escalfador^M de huevos^M

sauté pan
sartén^F honda

small saucepan
sartén^F pequeña

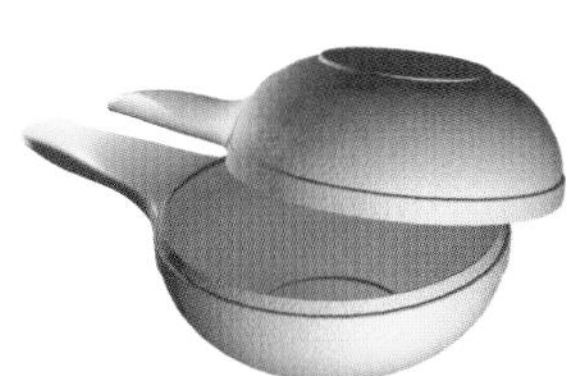

diable
sartén^F doble

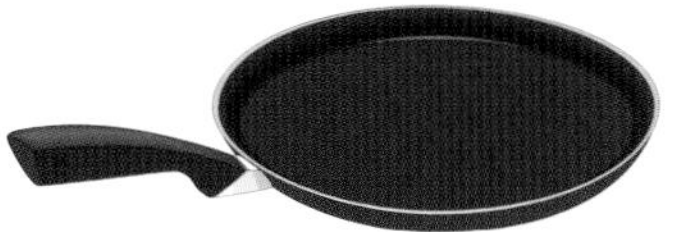

crêpe pan
sartén^F para crepes^M

steamer basket
cesto^M de cocción^M al vapor^M

double boiler
cacerola^F para baño^M de María

saucepan
cacerola^F

domestic appliances

aparatos[M] electrodomésticos

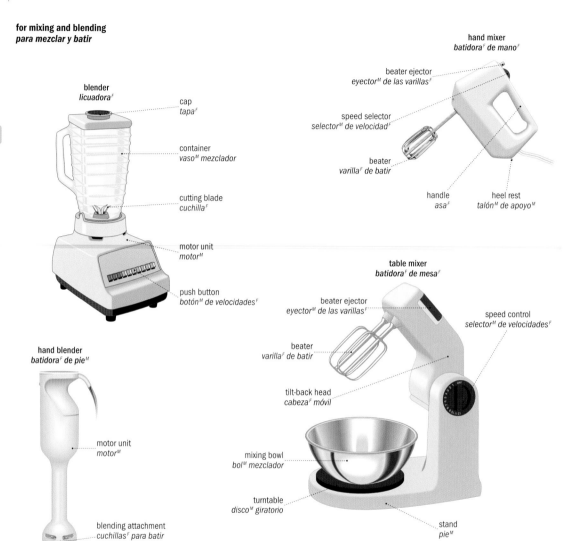

for mixing and blending
para mezclar y batir

blender
licuadora[F]

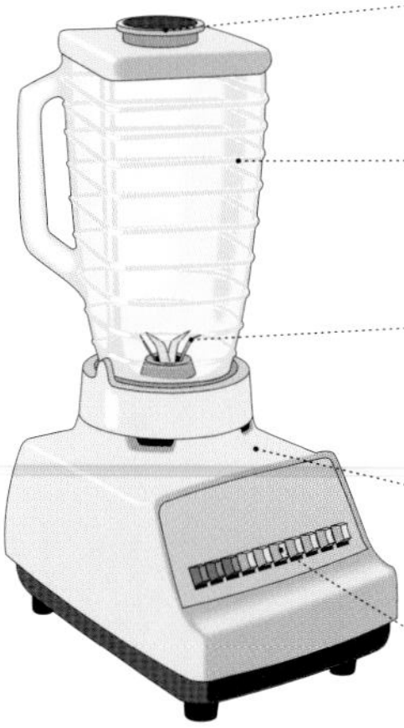

cap
tapa[F]

container
vaso[M] mezclador

cutting blade
cuchilla[F]

motor unit
motor[M]

push button
botón[M] de velocidades[F]

hand mixer
batidora[F] de mano[F]

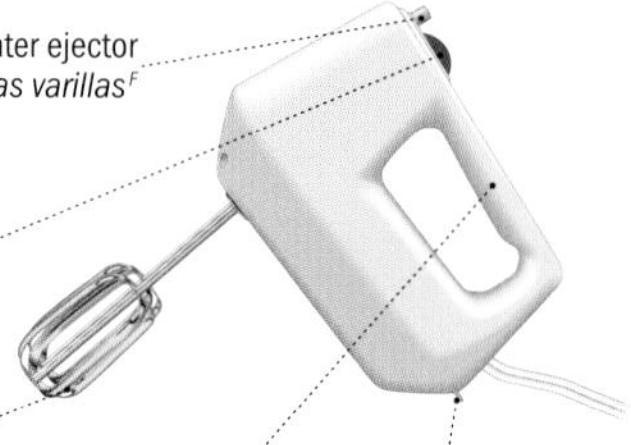

beater ejector
eyector[M] de las varillas[F]

speed selector
selector[M] de velocidad[F]

beater
varilla[F] de batir

handle
asa[F]

heel rest
talón[M] de apoyo[M]

hand blender
batidora[F] de pie[M]

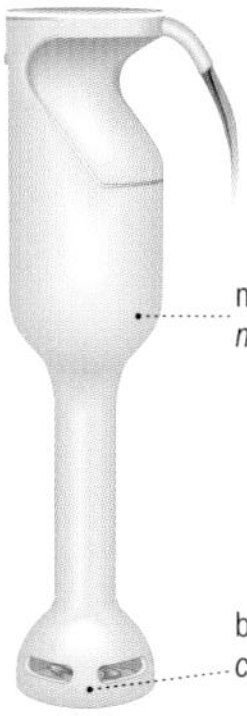

motor unit
motor[M]

blending attachment
cuchillas[F] para batir

table mixer
batidora[F] de mesa[F]

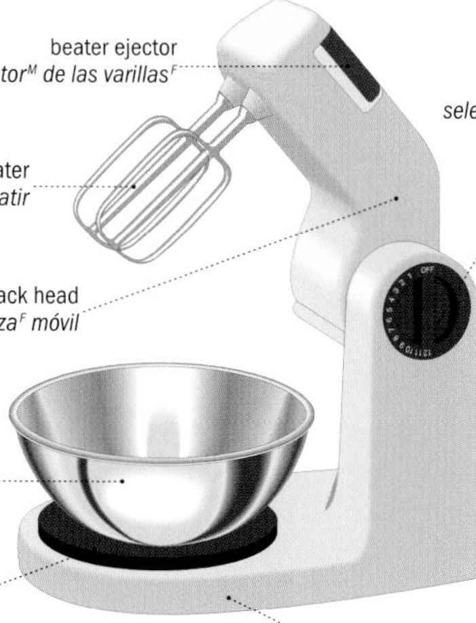

beater ejector
eyector[M] de las varillas[F]

speed control
selector[M] de velocidades[F]

beater
varilla[F] de batir

tilt-back head
cabeza[F] móvil

mixing bowl
bol[M] mezclador

turntable
disco[M] giratorio

stand
pie[M]

beaters
tipos[M] de varillas[F]

four blade beater
varilla de aspas[F]

spiral beater
varilla en espiral[F]

wire beater
varilla circular

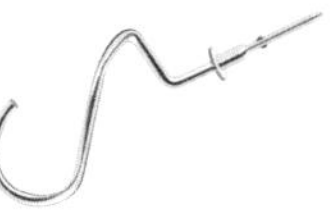

dough hook
varilla de gancho[M]

food processor
***robot*[M] *de cocina*[F]**

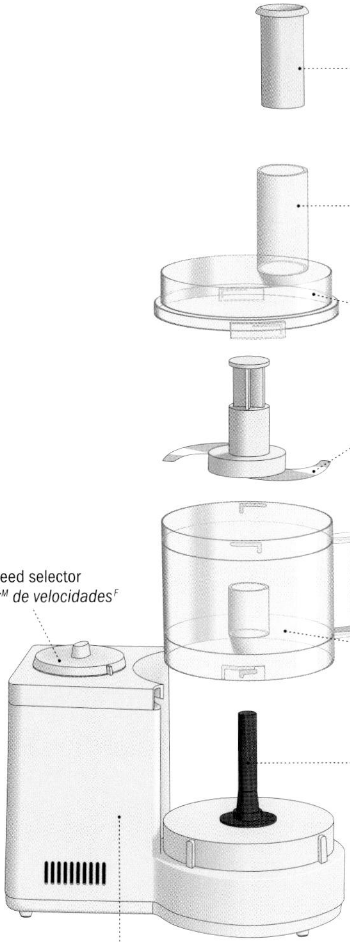

pusher
empujador[M]
feed tube
tubo[M] *de entrada*[F]
lid
tapa[F]
blade
cuchilla[F]
handle
asa[F]
speed selector
selector[M] *de velocidades*[F]
bowl
bol[M]
spindle
eje[M]
motor unit
motor[M]

for cutting
para cortar

disks
***discos*[M]**

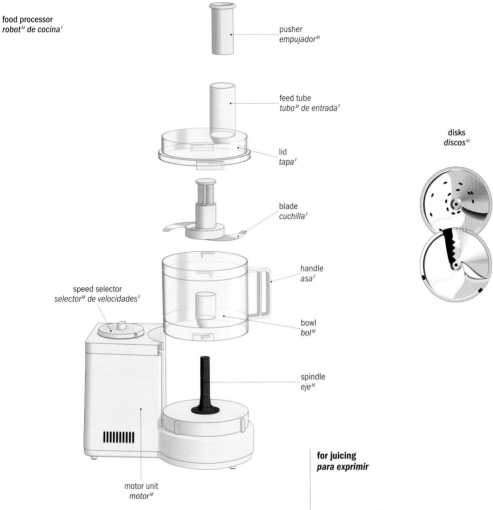

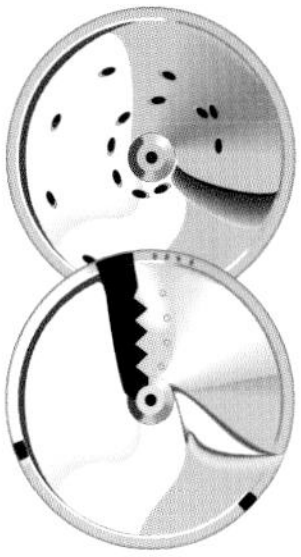

electric knife
cuchillo*[M] *eléctrico

power cord
cordón[M] *de alimentación*[F]
blade
cuchilla[F]
on-off switch
interruptor[M]

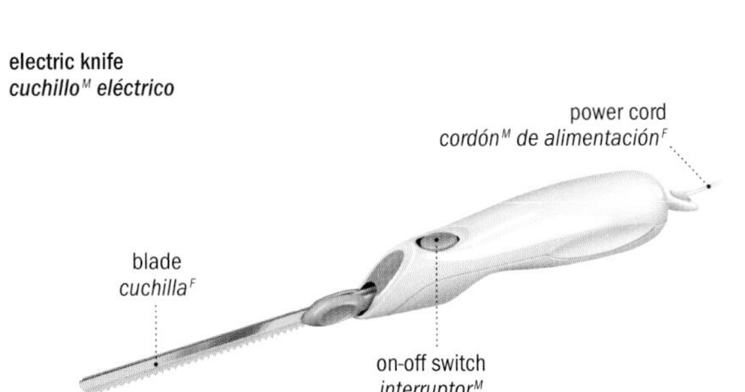

for juicing
para exprimir

citrus juicer
***exprimidor*[M] *de cítricos*[M]**

reamer
exprimidor[M]
strainer
colador[M]
bowl with serving spout
recipiente[M] *con vertedor*[M]
motor unit
motor[M]

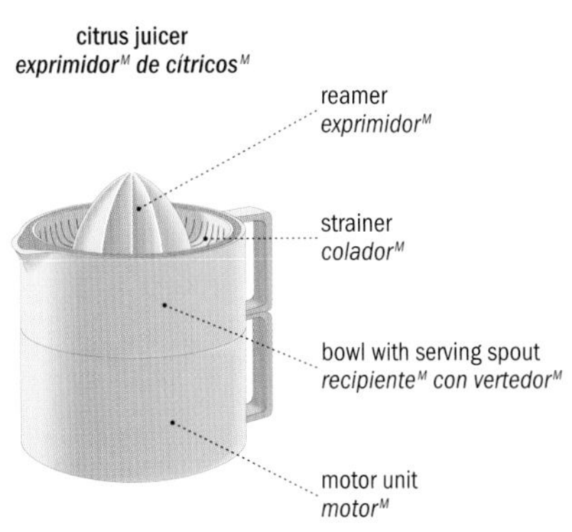

for cooking
para cocinar

microwave oven
horno[M] microondas

door
puerta[F]
sensor probe
sonda[F] térmica
probe receptacle
enchufe[M] del termómetro[M]
window
ventana[F]
clock timer
reloj[M] programador
latch
seguro[M]
control panel
panel[M] de mandos[M]
handle
asa[F]

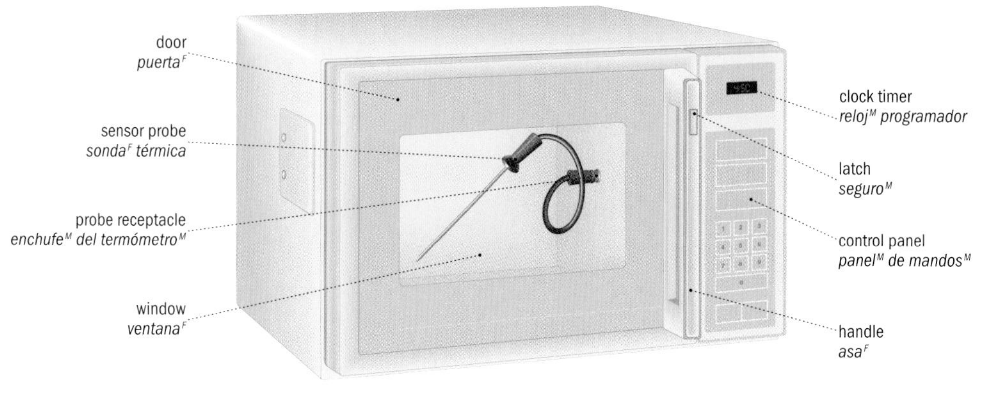

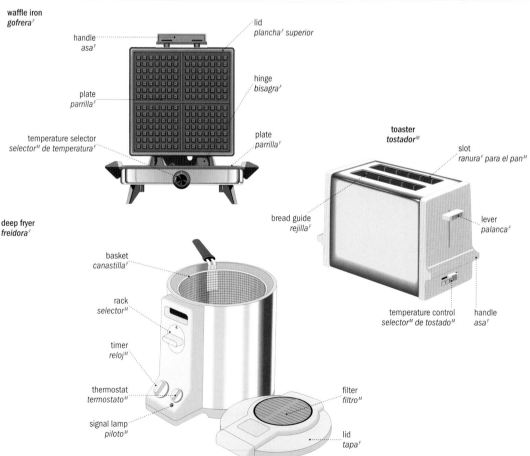

waffle iron
gofrera[F]

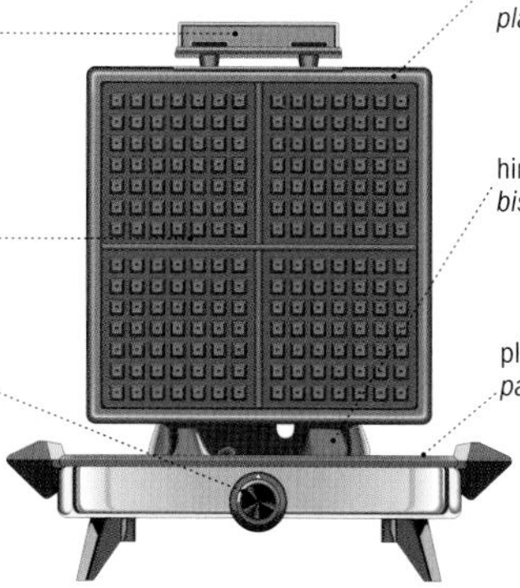

handle
asa[F]
lid
plancha[F] superior
hinge
bisagra[F]
plate
parrilla[F]
temperature selector
selector[M] de temperatura[F]
plate
parrilla[F]

toaster
tostador[M]

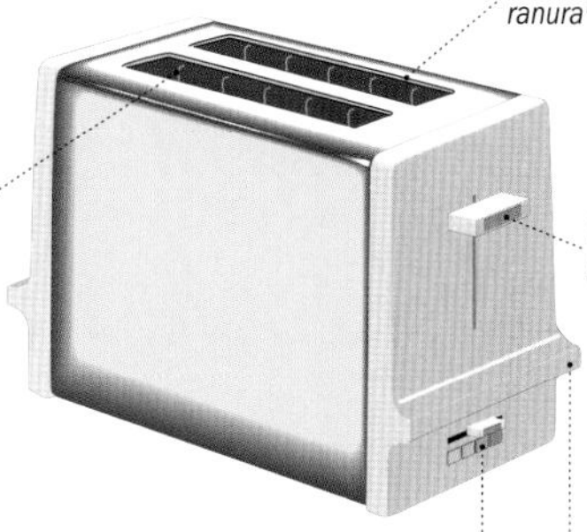

slot
ranura[F] para el pan[M]
bread guide
rejilla[F]
lever
palanca[F]
temperature control
selector[M] de tostado[M]
handle
asa[F]

deep fryer
freidora[F]

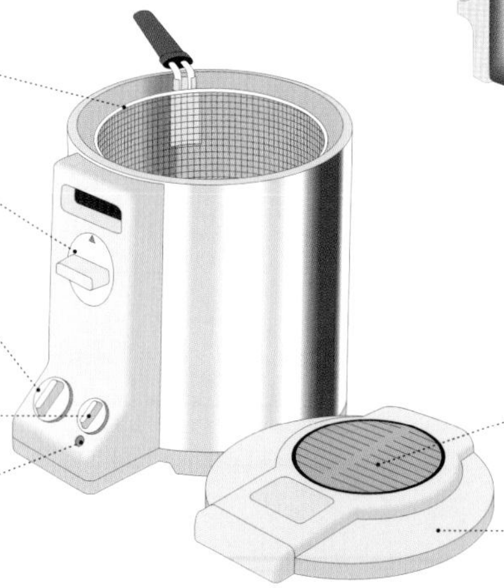

basket
canastilla[F]
rack
selector[M]
timer
reloj[M]
thermostat
termostato[M]
signal lamp
piloto[M]
filter
filtro[M]
lid
tapa[F]

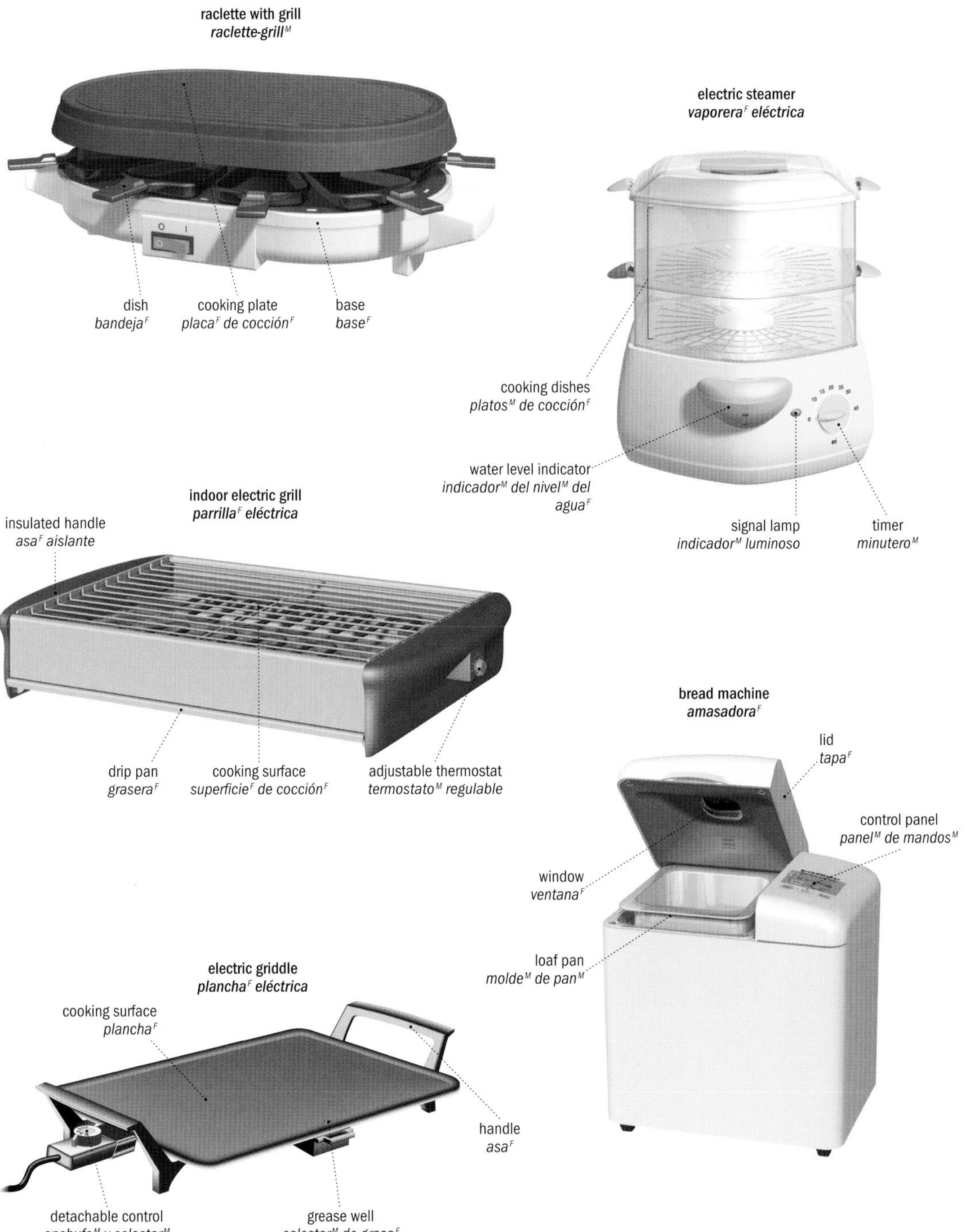
raclette with grill
raclette-grill^M
dish
bandeja^F
cooking plate
placa^F de cocción^F
base
base^F
electric steamer
vaporera^F eléctrica
cooking dishes
platos^M de cocción^F
water level indicator
indicador^M del nivel^M del agua^F
signal lamp
indicador^M luminoso
timer
minutero^M
indoor electric grill
parrilla^F eléctrica
insulated handle
asa^F aislante
drip pan
grasera^F
cooking surface
superficie^F de cocción^F
adjustable thermostat
termostato^M regulable
bread machine
amasadora^F
lid
tapa^F
control panel
panel^M de mandos^M
window
ventana^F
loaf pan
molde^M de pan^M
electric griddle
plancha^F eléctrica
cooking surface
plancha^F
handle
asa^F
detachable control
enchufe^M y selector^M desmontables
grease well
colector^M de grasa^F

miscellaneous domestic appliances

varios aparatos^M electrodomésticos

can opener
abrelatas^M

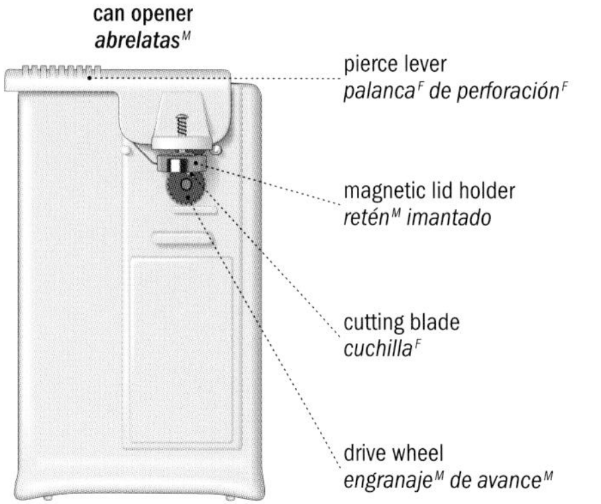

coffee mill
molinillo^M de café^M

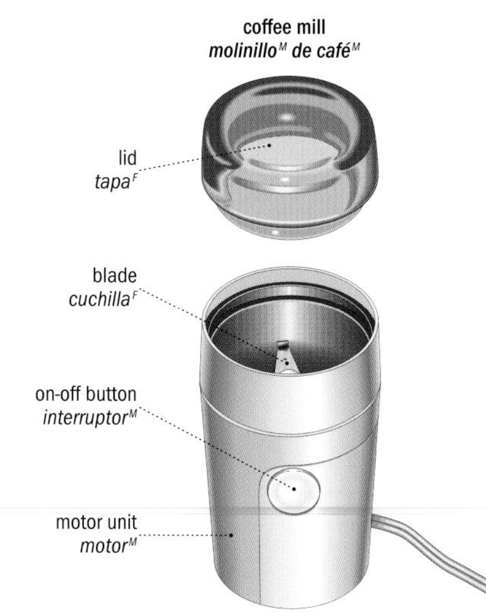

kettle
hervidor^M

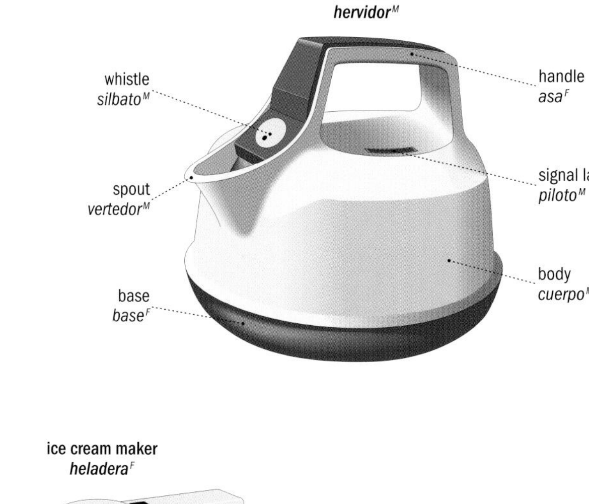

ice cream maker
heladera^F

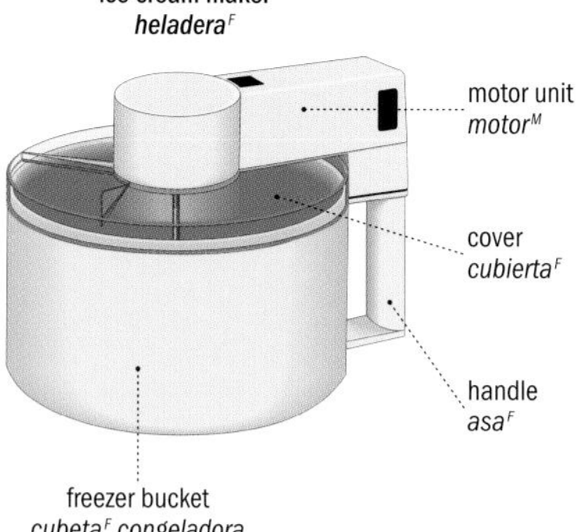

juicer
licuadora^F

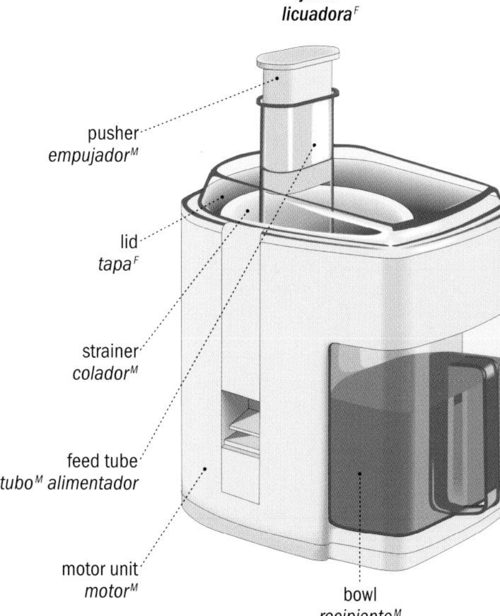

FOOD AND KITCHEN

coffee makers

cafeteras[F]

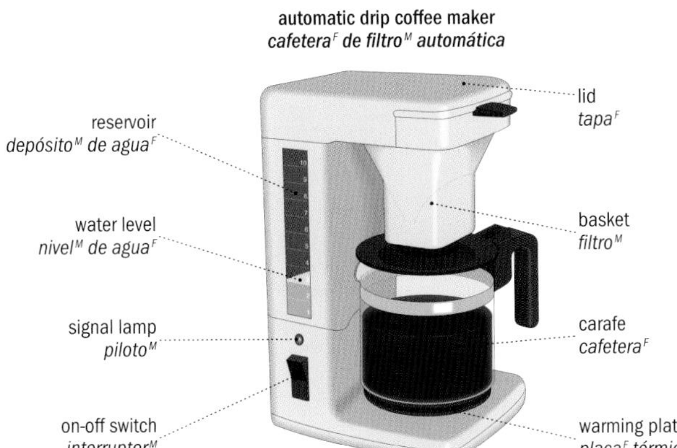
automatic drip coffee maker
cafetera[F] de filtro[M] automática
reservoir
depósito[M] de agua[F]
water level
nivel[M] de agua[F]
signal lamp
piloto[M]
on-off switch
interruptor[M]
lid
tapa[F]
basket
filtro[M]
carafe
cafetera[F]
warming plate
placa[F] térmica

Neapolitan coffee maker
cafetera[F] napolitana

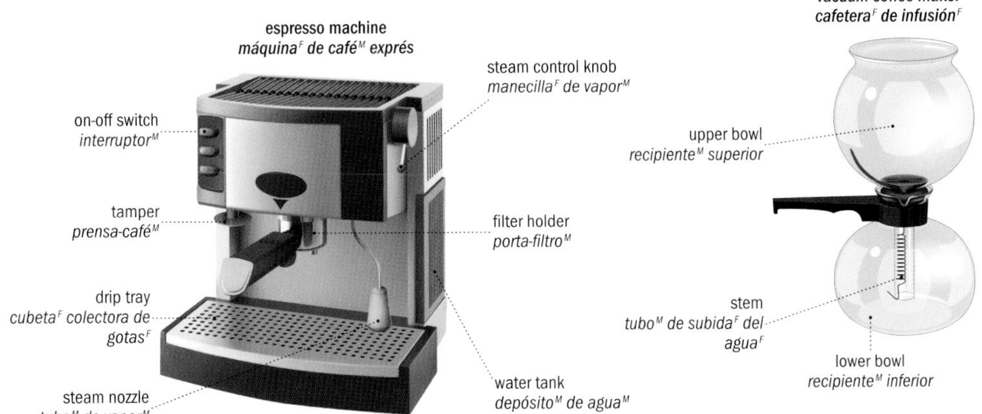
espresso machine
máquina[F] de café[M] exprés
on-off switch
interruptor[M]
tamper
prensa-café[M]
drip tray
cubeta[F] colectora de gotas[F]
steam nozzle
tubo[M] de vapor[M]
steam control knob
manecilla[F] de vapor[M]
filter holder
porta-filtro[M]
water tank
depósito[M] de agua[M]
vacuum coffee maker
cafetera[F] de infusión[F]
upper bowl
recipiente[M] superior
stem
tubo[M] de subida[F] del agua[F]
lower bowl
recipiente[M] inferior

French press
cafetera[F] de émbolo[M]
espresso maker
cafetera[F] italiana

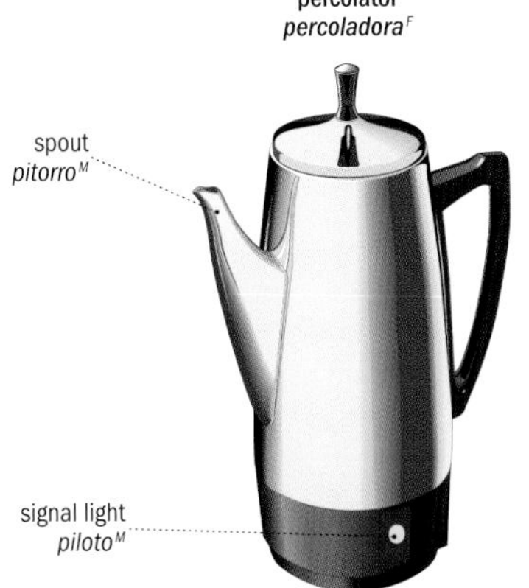
percolator
percoladora[F]
spout
pitorro[M]
signal light
piloto[M]

exterior of a house

exterior[M] de una casa[F]

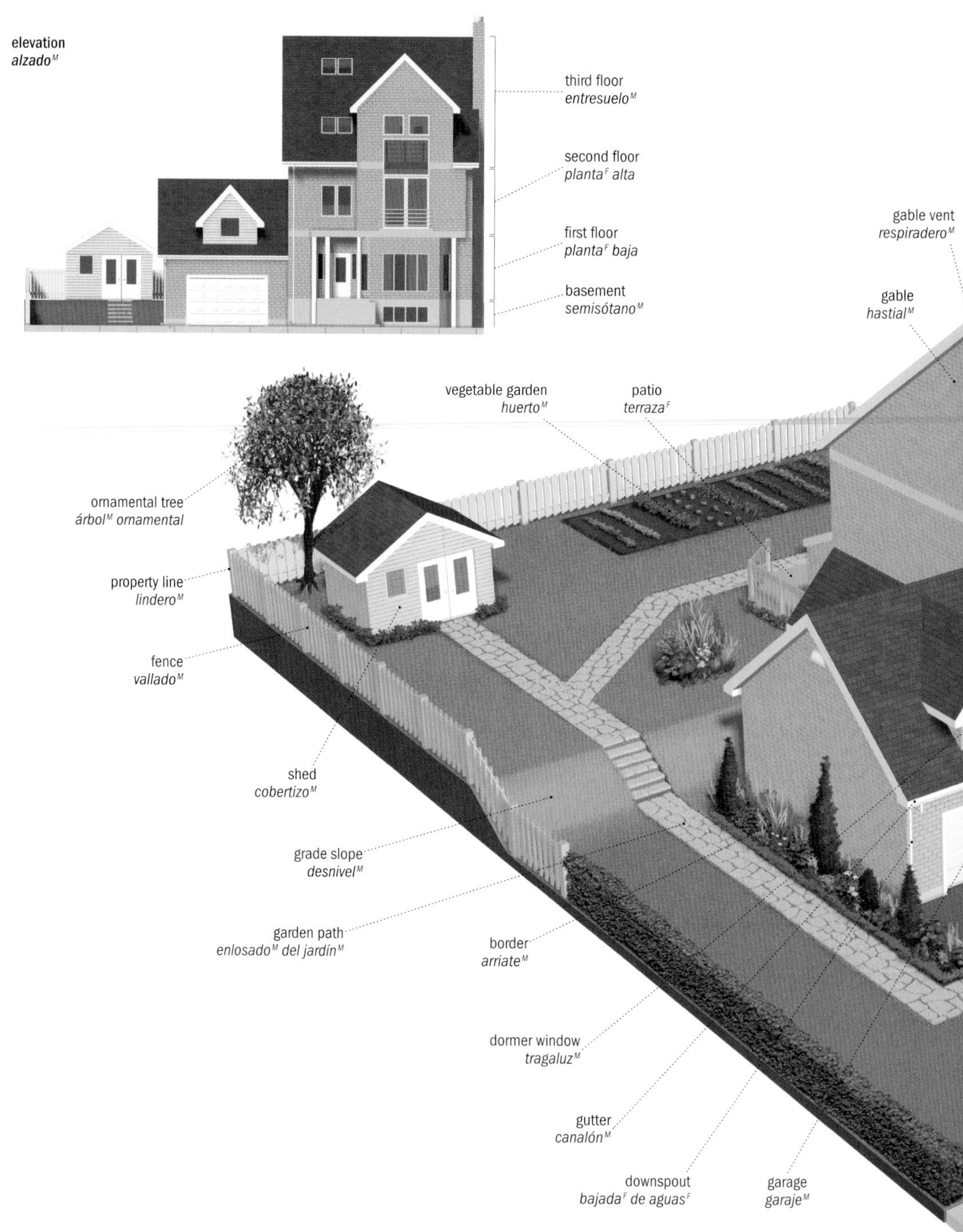
elevation
alzado[M]
third floor
entresuelo[M]
second floor
planta[F] alta
first floor
planta[F] baja
basement
semisótano[M]
gable vent
respiradero[M]
gable
hastial[M]
vegetable garden
huerto[M]
patio
terraza[F]
ornamental tree
árbol[M] ornamental
property line
lindero[M]
fence
vallado[M]
shed
cobertizo[M]
grade slope
desnivel[M]
garden path
enlosado[M] del jardín[M]
border
arriate[M]
dormer window
tragaluz[M]
gutter
canalón[M]
downspout
bajada[F] de aguas[F]
garage
garaje[M]

site plan
plano del terreno

HOUSE

pool

piscina^F

aboveground swimming pool
piscina^F elevada

skimmer
skimmer^M
filter
filtro^M
pump
bomba^F
upright
montante^M
wall
muro^M

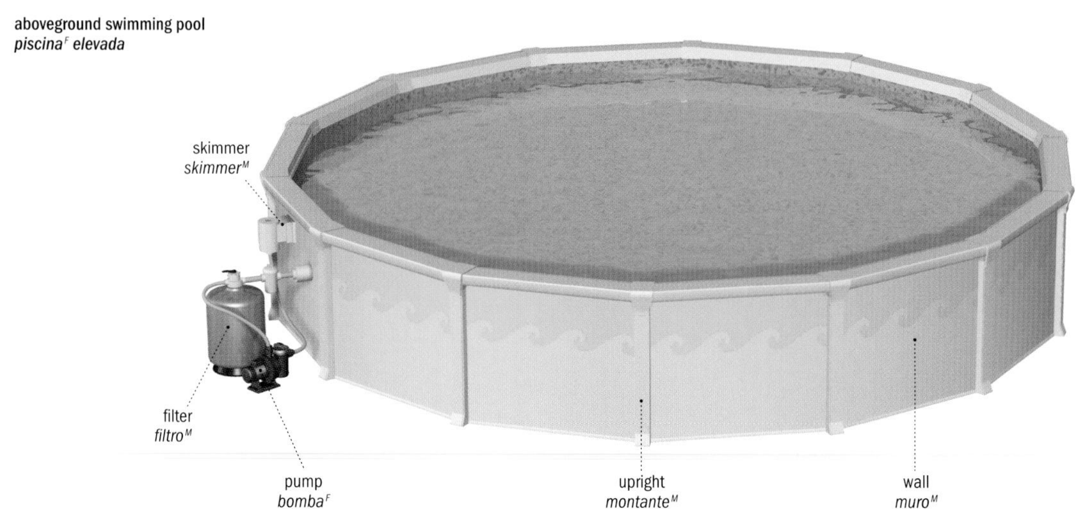

in-ground swimming pool
piscina^F enterrada

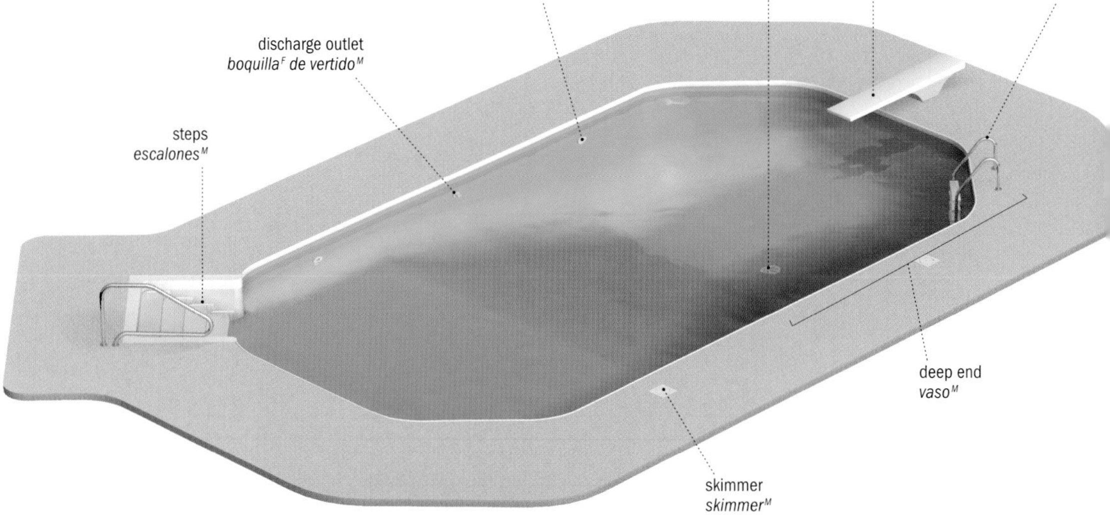

diving board
trampolín^M
main drain
desagüe^M de fondo^M
underwater light
foco^M subacuático
ladder
escalera^F
discharge outlet
boquilla^F de vertido^M
steps
escalones^M
deep end
vaso^M
skimmer
skimmer^M

exterior door

puerta^F de entrada^F

cornice
cornisa^F

entablature
entablamento^M

header
dintel^M

top rail
cabio^M alto

door jamb
jamba^F

panel
entrepaño^M vertical

muntin
montante^F central

shutting stile
montante^M de la cerradura^F

lock rail
peinazo^M de la cerradura^F

lock
cerradura^F

middle panel
entrepaño^M horizontal

doorknob
manilla^F

hanging stile
montante^M de la bisagra^F

hinge
bisagra^F

bottom rail
cabio^M bajo

weatherboard
vierteguas^M

threshold
umbral^M

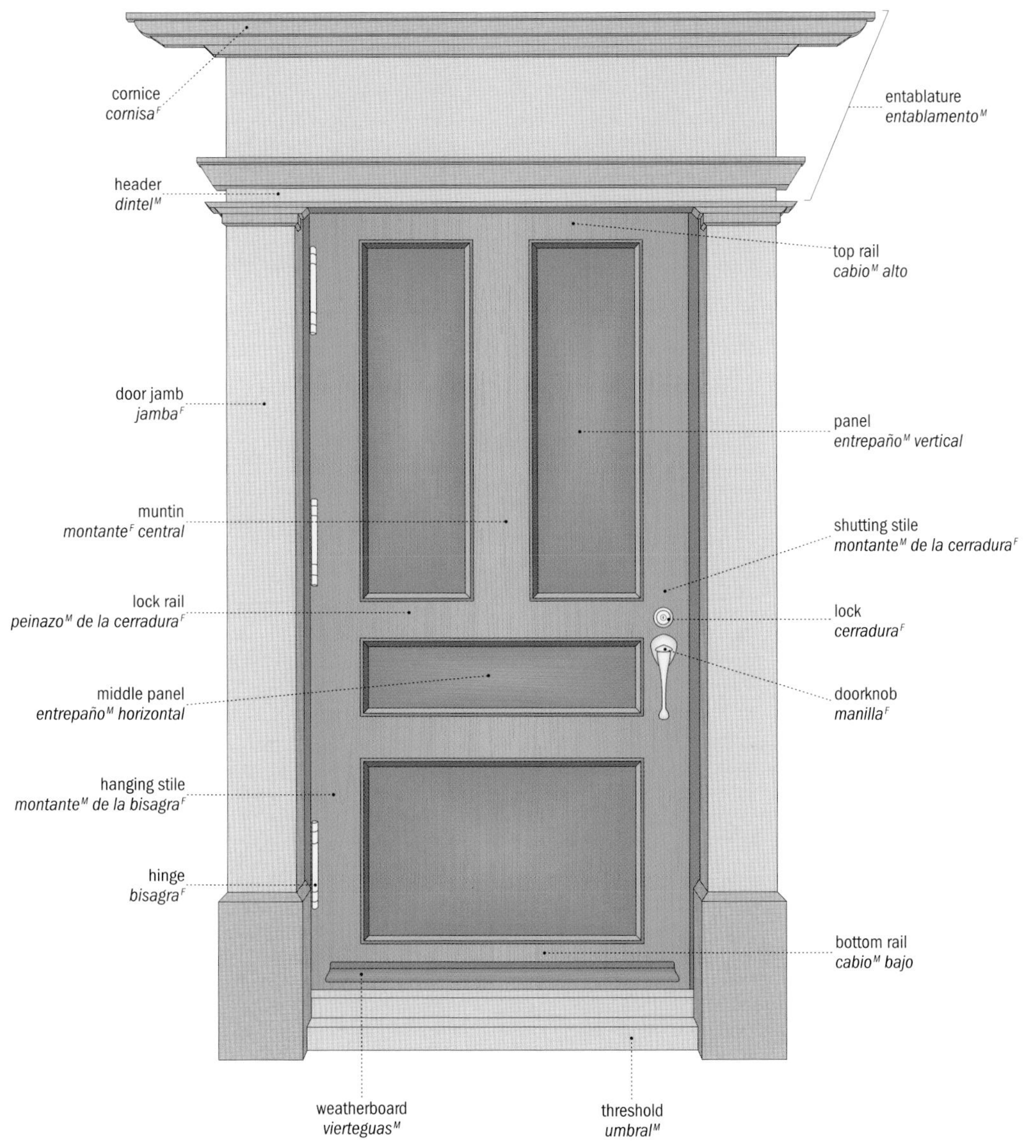

lock

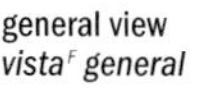

cerrajería[F]

general view
vista[F] general

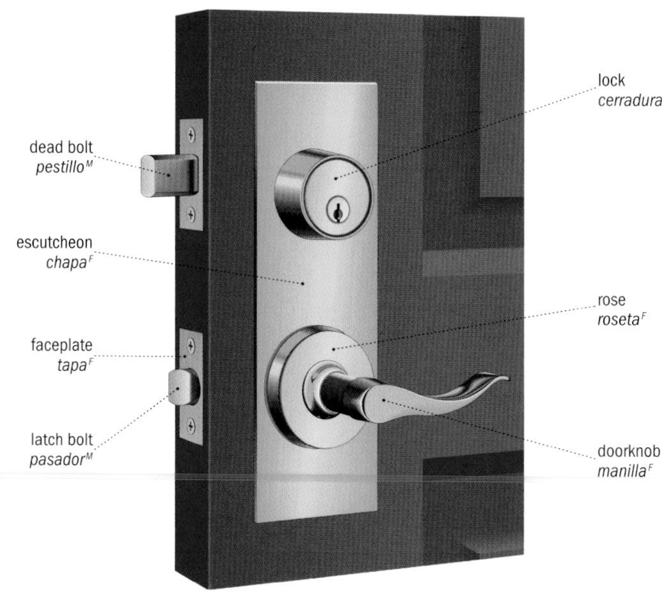

HOUSE

window

ventana[F]

structure
estructura[F]

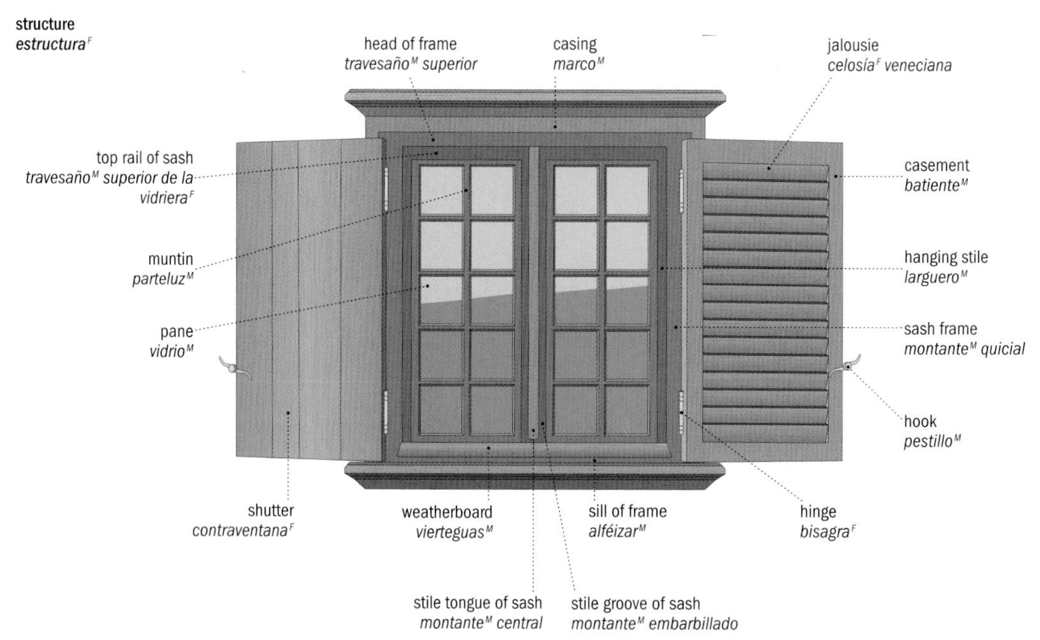

frame

armazón[M]

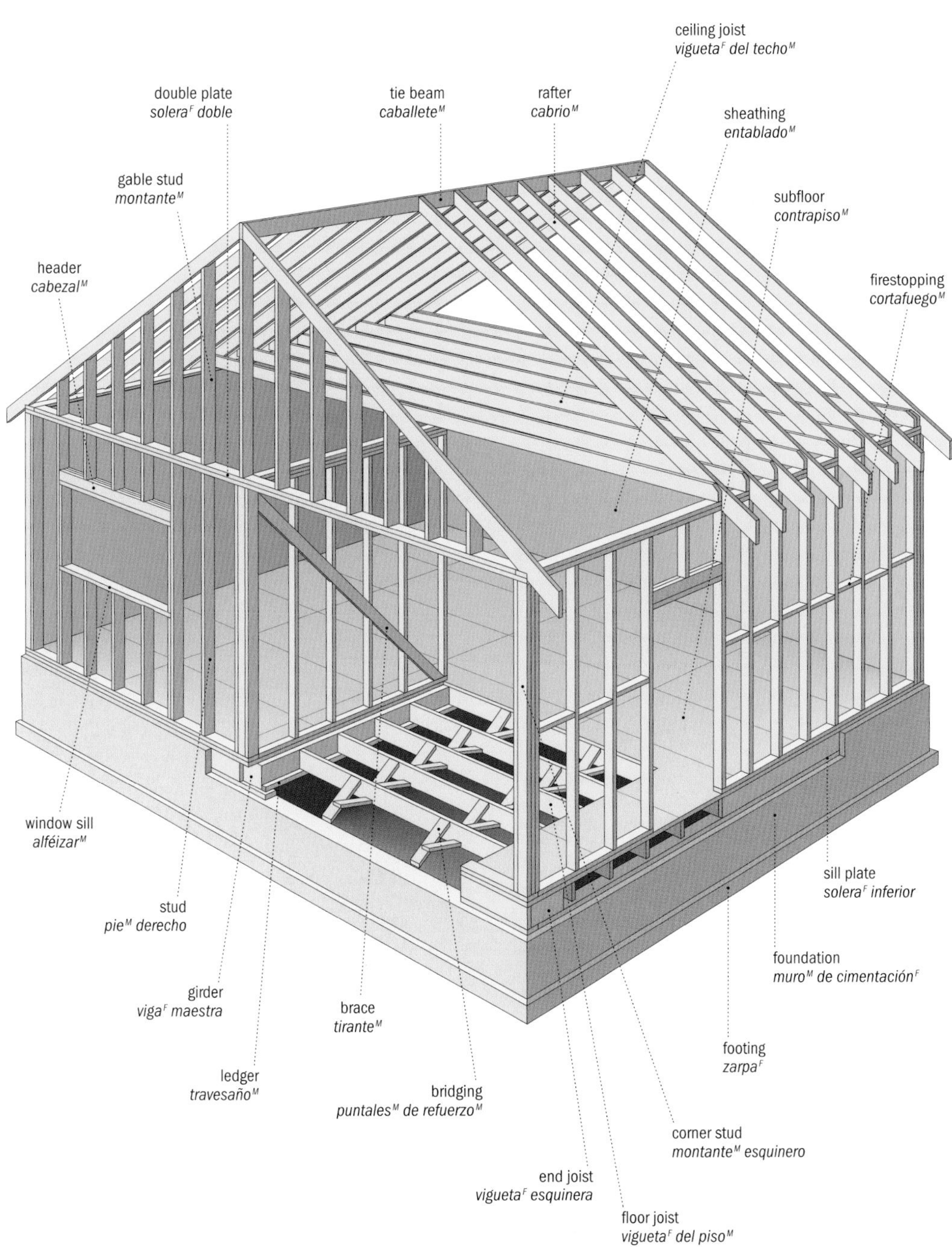

ceiling joist
vigueta^F del techo^M

double plate
solera^F doble

tie beam
caballete^M

rafter
cabrio^M

sheathing
entablado^M

gable stud
montante^M

subfloor
contrapiso^M

header
cabezal^M

firestopping
cortafuego^M

HOUSE

window sill
alféizar^M

sill plate
solera^F inferior

stud
pie^M derecho

foundation
muro^M de cimentación^F

girder
viga^F maestra

brace
tirante^M

footing
zarpa^F

ledger
travesaño^M

bridging
puntales^M de refuerzo^M

corner stud
montante^M esquinero

end joist
vigueta^F esquinera

floor joist
vigueta^F del piso^M

main rooms

habitaciones[F] principales

first floor
planta[F] baja

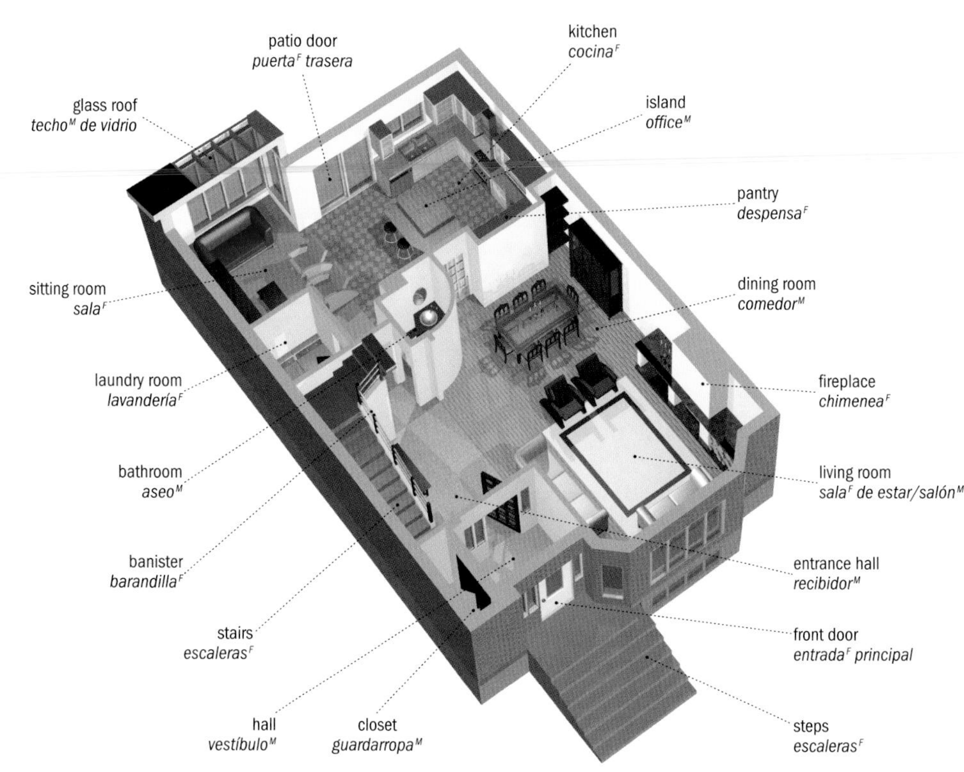

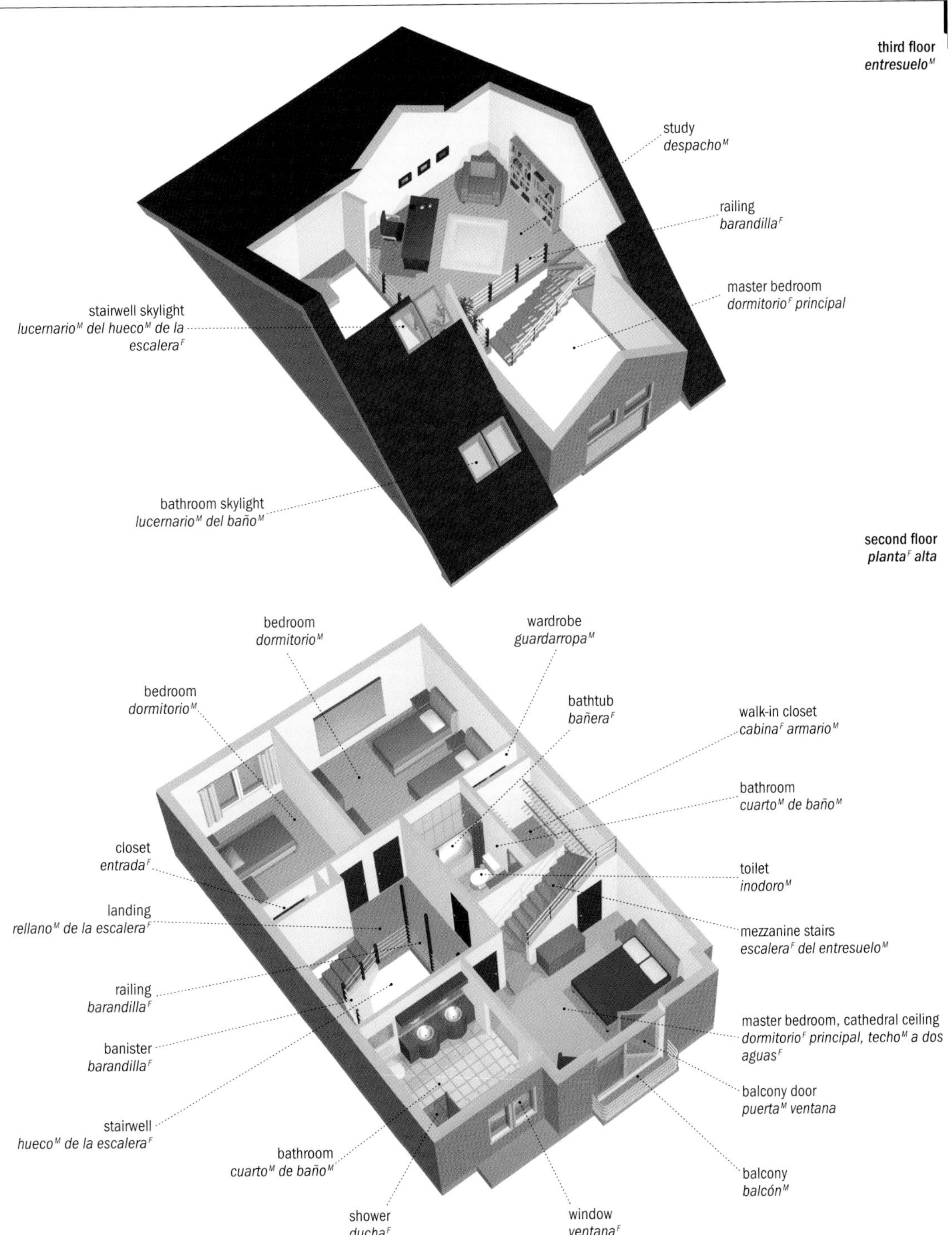
third floor
entresuelo[M]
study
despacho[M]
railing
barandilla[F]
master bedroom
dormitorio[F] principal
stairwell skylight
lucernario[M] del hueco[M] de la escalera[F]
bathroom skylight
lucernario[M] del baño[M]
second floor
planta[F] alta
bedroom
dormitorio[M]
wardrobe
guardarropa[M]
bedroom
dormitorio[M]
bathtub
bañera[F]
walk-in closet
cabina[F] armario[M]
bathroom
cuarto[M] de baño[M]
closet
entrada[F]
toilet
inodoro[M]
landing
rellano[M] de la escalera[F]
mezzanine stairs
escalera[F] del entresuelo[M]
railing
barandilla[F]
master bedroom, cathedral ceiling
dormitorio[F] principal, techo[M] a dos aguas[F]
banister
barandilla[F]
balcony door
puerta[M] ventana
stairwell
hueco[M] de la escalera[F]
bathroom
cuarto[M] de baño[M]
balcony
balcón[M]
shower
ducha[F]
window
ventana[F]

wood flooring

pisos^M de madera^F

wood flooring on cement screed
parqué^M sobre base^F de cemento^M

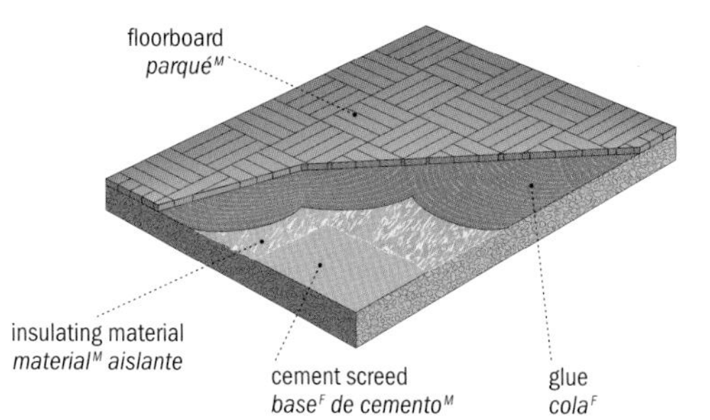

wood flooring on wooden structure
entarimado^M sobre estructura^F de madera^F

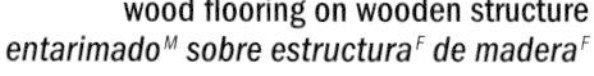

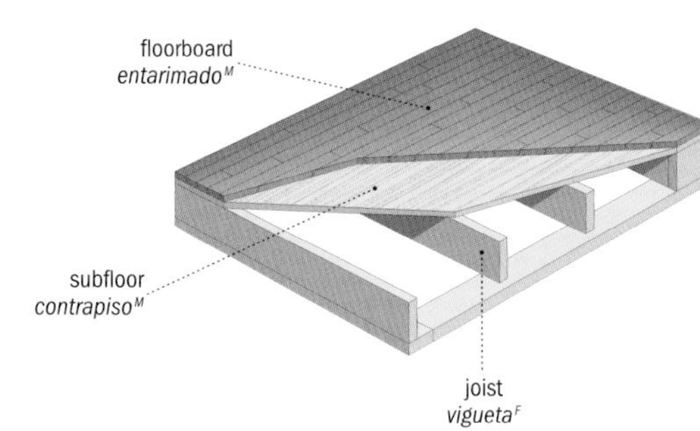

wood flooring arrangements
tipos^M de parqué^M

overlay flooring
parqué^M sobrepuesto

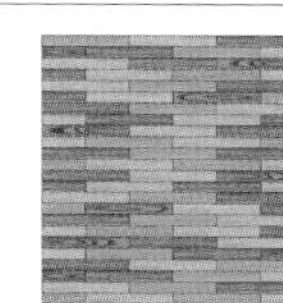

strip flooring with alternate joints
parqué^M alternado a la inglesa

herringbone parquet
parqué^M espinapez^M

herringbone pattern
parqué^M en punta^F de Hungría

inlaid parquet
parqué^M de mosaico

basket weave pattern
parqué^M de cestería^F

Arenberg parquet
parqué^M Arenberg

Chantilly parquet
parqué^M Chantilly

Versailles parquet
parqué^M Versalles

textile floor coverings

revestimientos^M textiles del suelo^M

rug
alfombra^F

pile carpet
moqueta^F

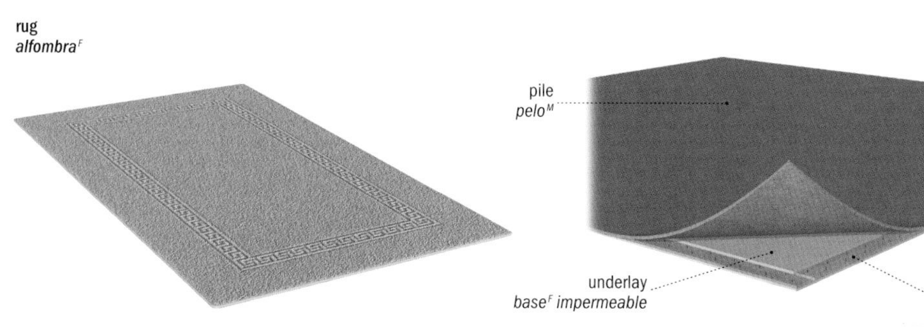

HOUSE

stairs

escalera[F]

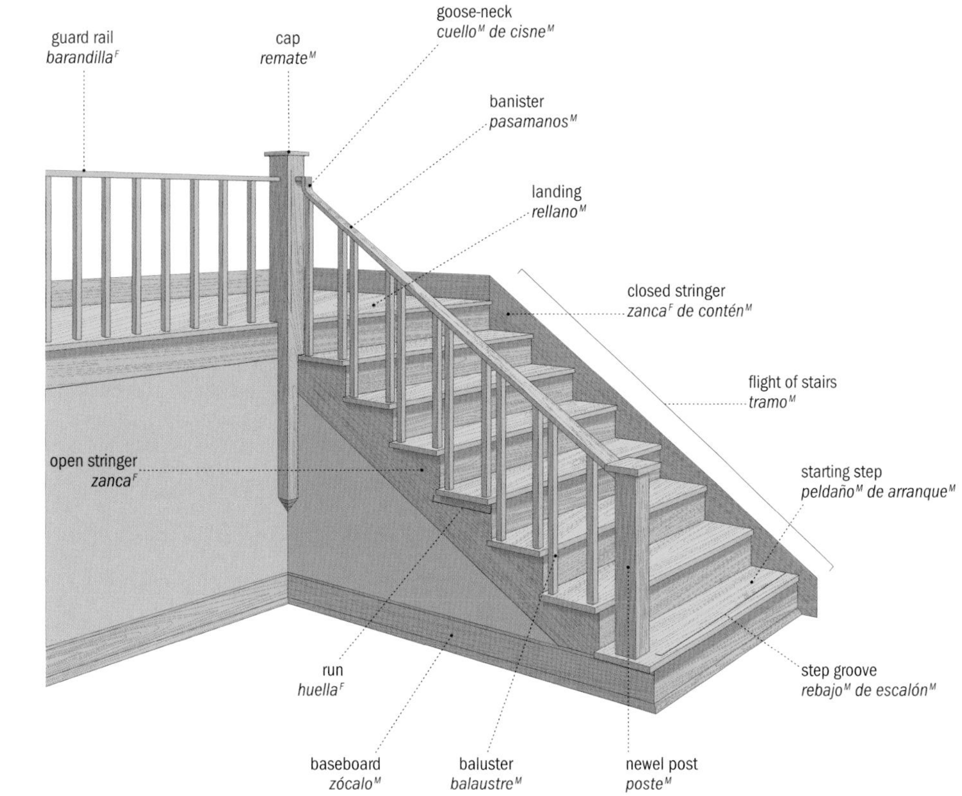

guard rail
barandilla[F]
cap
remate[M]
goose-neck
cuello[M] de cisne[M]
banister
pasamanos[M]
landing
rellano[M]
closed stringer
zanca[F] de contén[M]
flight of stairs
tramo[M]
open stringer
zanca[F]
starting step
peldaño[M] de arranque[M]
run
huella[F]
step groove
rebajo[M] de escalón[M]
baseboard
zócalo[M]
baluster
balaustre[M]
newel post
poste[M]

step

peldaño[M]

tread
peldaño[M]
riser
contrahuella[F]
rise
altura[F] del peldaño[M]
nosing
vuelo[M] del peldaño[M]

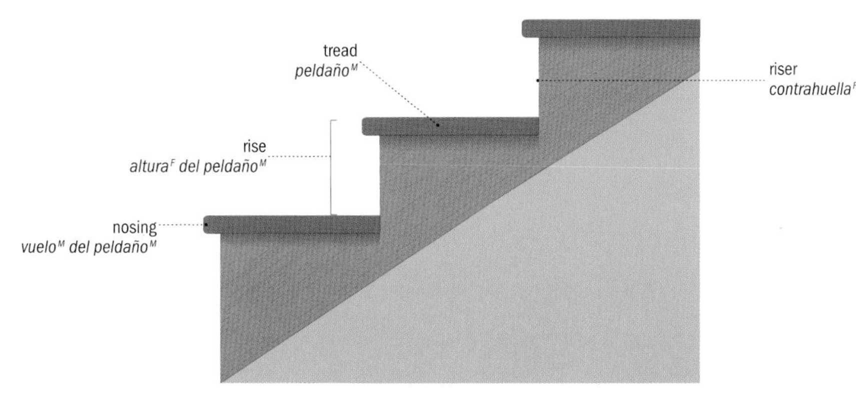

wood burning

calefacción^F de leña^F

fireplace
chimenea^F

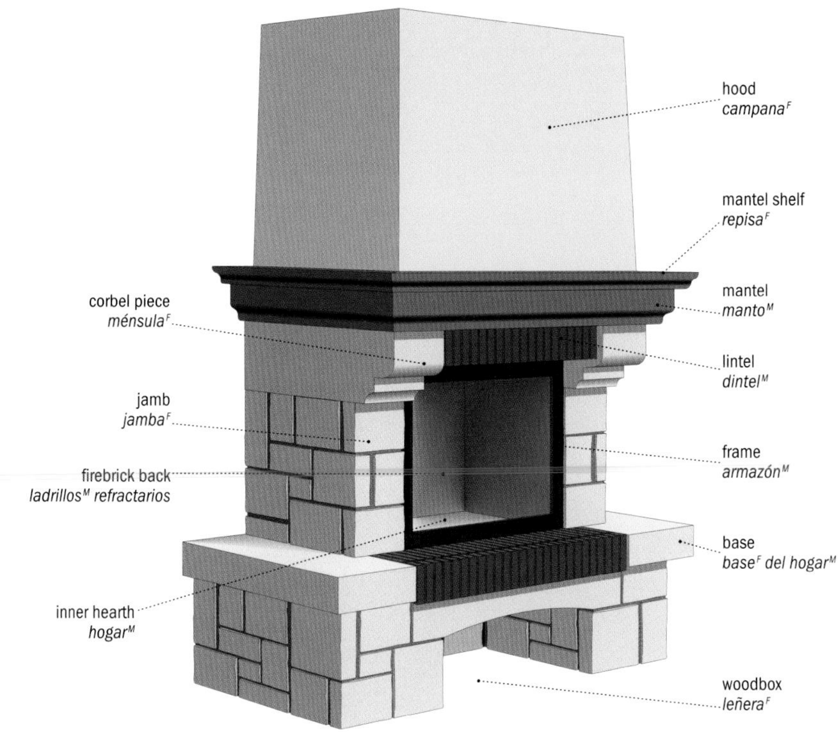

slow-burning wood stove
estufa^F de leña^F a fuego^M lento

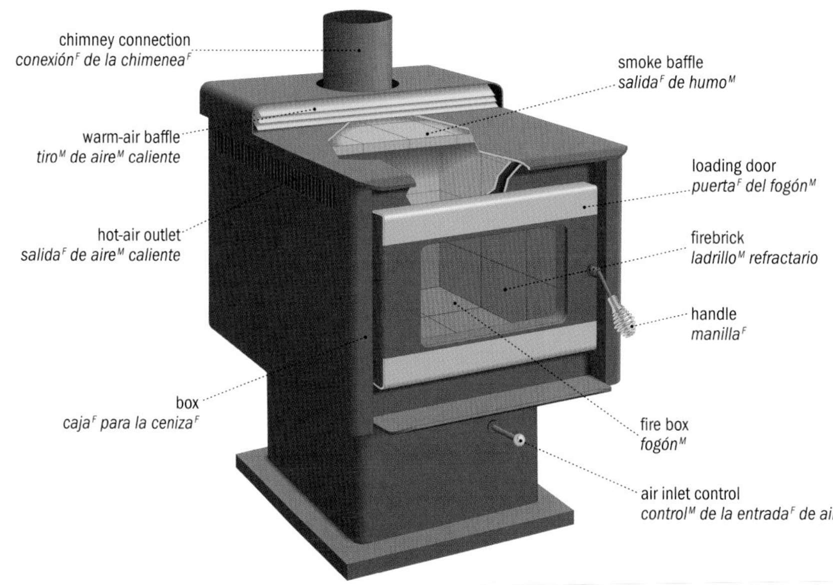

chimney
chimenea^F^

rain cap
caperuza^F^

roof
tejado^M^

storm collar
collarín^M^

flashing
vierteguas^M^

ceiling
techo^M^

ceiling collar
collar^M^ *cortafuego*

pipe section
sección^F^ *del cañón*^M^

ceiling collar
collar^M^ *cortafuego*

floor
piso^M^

capped tee
remate^M^ *en T*

fire irons
utensilios^M^ ***para la chimenea***^F^

plumbing system

cañerías^F

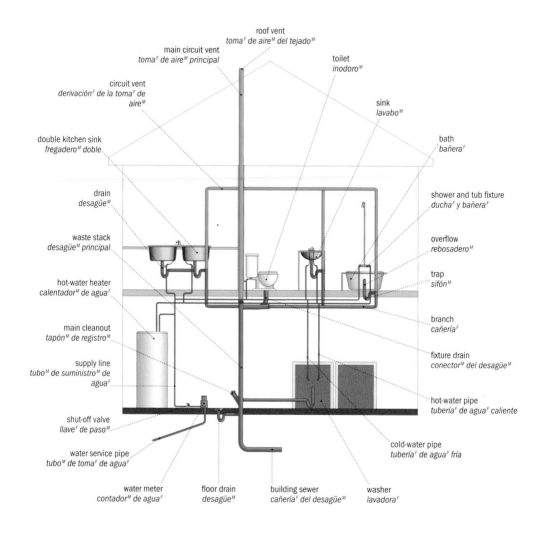

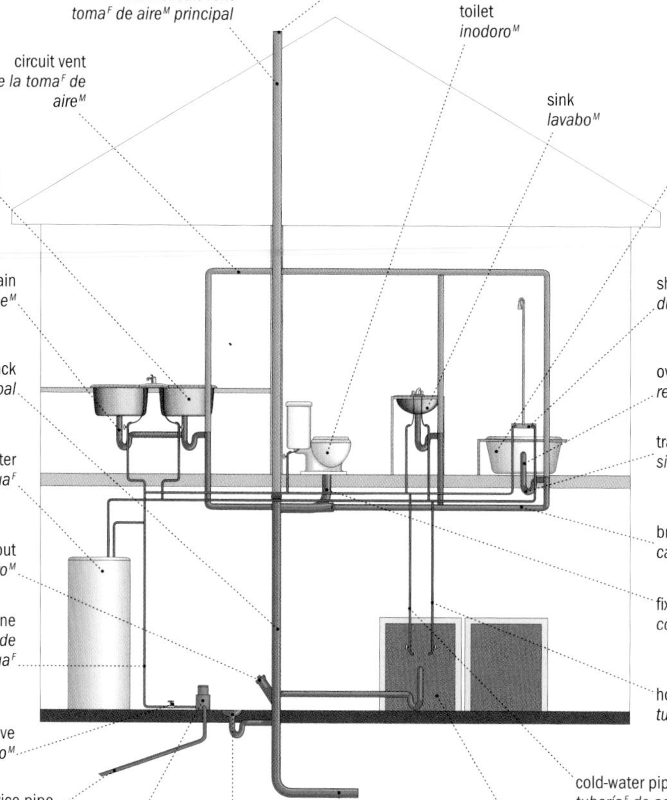

roof vent
toma^F de aire^M del tejado^M
main circuit vent
toma^F de aire^M principal
toilet
inodoro^M
circuit vent
derivación^F de la toma^F de aire^M
sink
lavabo^M
double kitchen sink
fregadero^M doble
bath
bañera^F
drain
desagüe^M
shower and tub fixture
ducha^F y bañera^F
waste stack
desagüe^M principal
overflow
rebosadero^M
trap
sifón^M
hot-water heater
calentador^M de agua^F
branch
cañería^F
main cleanout
tapón^M de registro^M
fixture drain
conector^M del desagüe^M
supply line
tubo^M de suministro^M de agua^F
hot-water pipe
tubería^F de agua^F caliente
shut-off valve
llave^F de paso^M
cold-water pipe
tubería^F de agua^F fría
water service pipe
tubo^M de toma^F de agua^F
water meter
contador^M de agua^F
floor drain
desagüe^M
building sewer
cañería^F del desagüe^M
washer
lavadora^F

ventilating circuit
circuito^M de ventilación^F

draining circuit
circuito^M de desagüe^M

cold-water circuit
circuito^M de agua^F fría

hot-water circuit
circuito^M de agua^F caliente

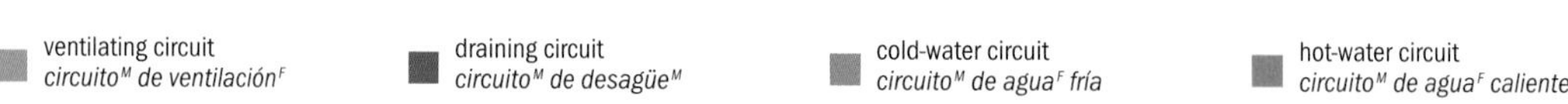

bathroom

cuarto^M de baño^M

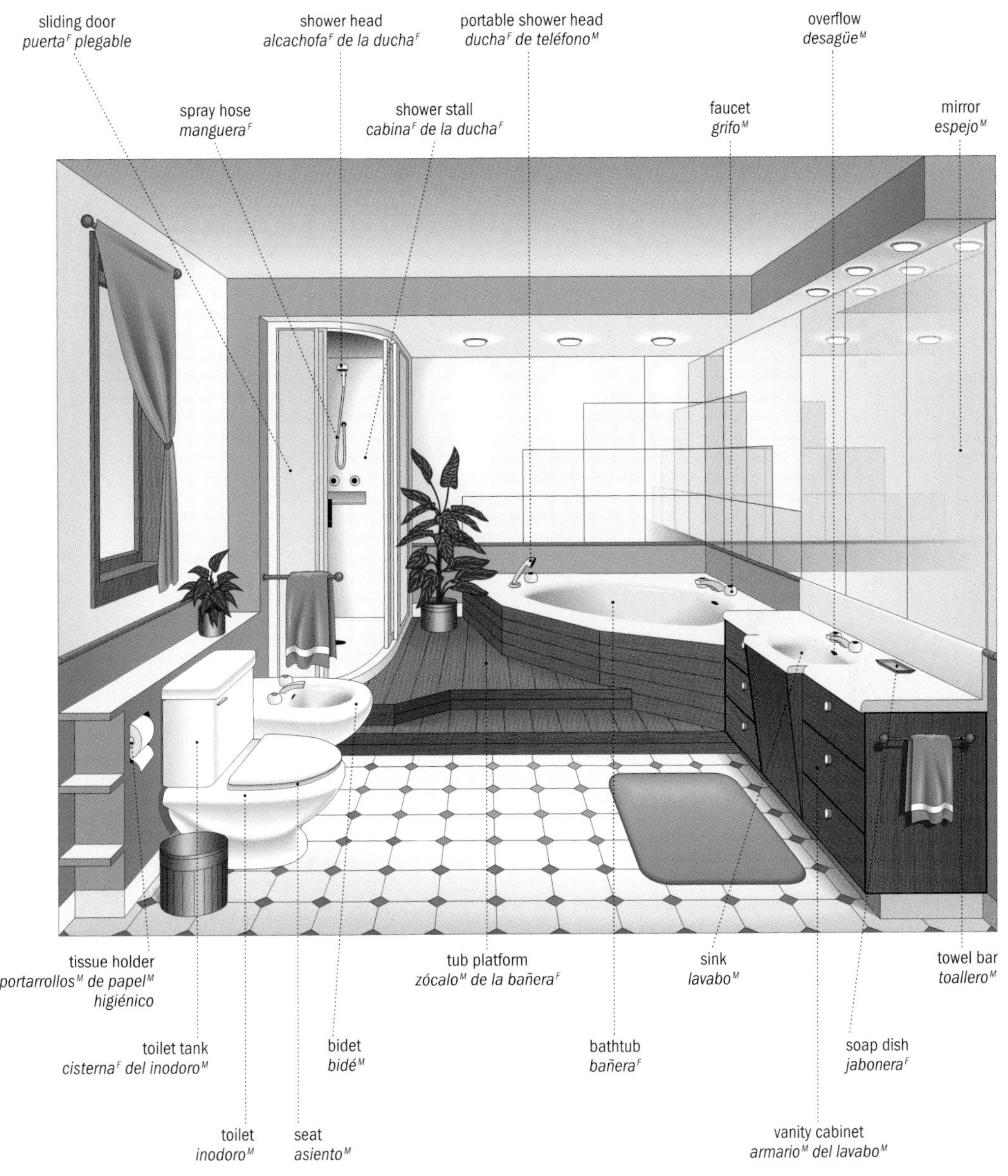
sliding door
puerta^F plegable
shower head
alcachofa^F de la ducha^F
portable shower head
ducha^F de teléfono^M
overflow
desagüe^M
spray hose
manguera^F
shower stall
cabina^F de la ducha^F
faucet
grifo^M
mirror
espejo^M
tissue holder
portarrollos^M de papel^M higiénico
tub platform
zócalo^M de la bañera^F
sink
lavabo^M
towel bar
toallero^M
toilet tank
cisterna^F del inodoro^M
bidet
bidé^M
bathtub
bañera^F
soap dish
jabonera^F
toilet
inodoro^M
seat
asiento^M
vanity cabinet
armario^M del lavabo^M

toilet

inodoro[M]

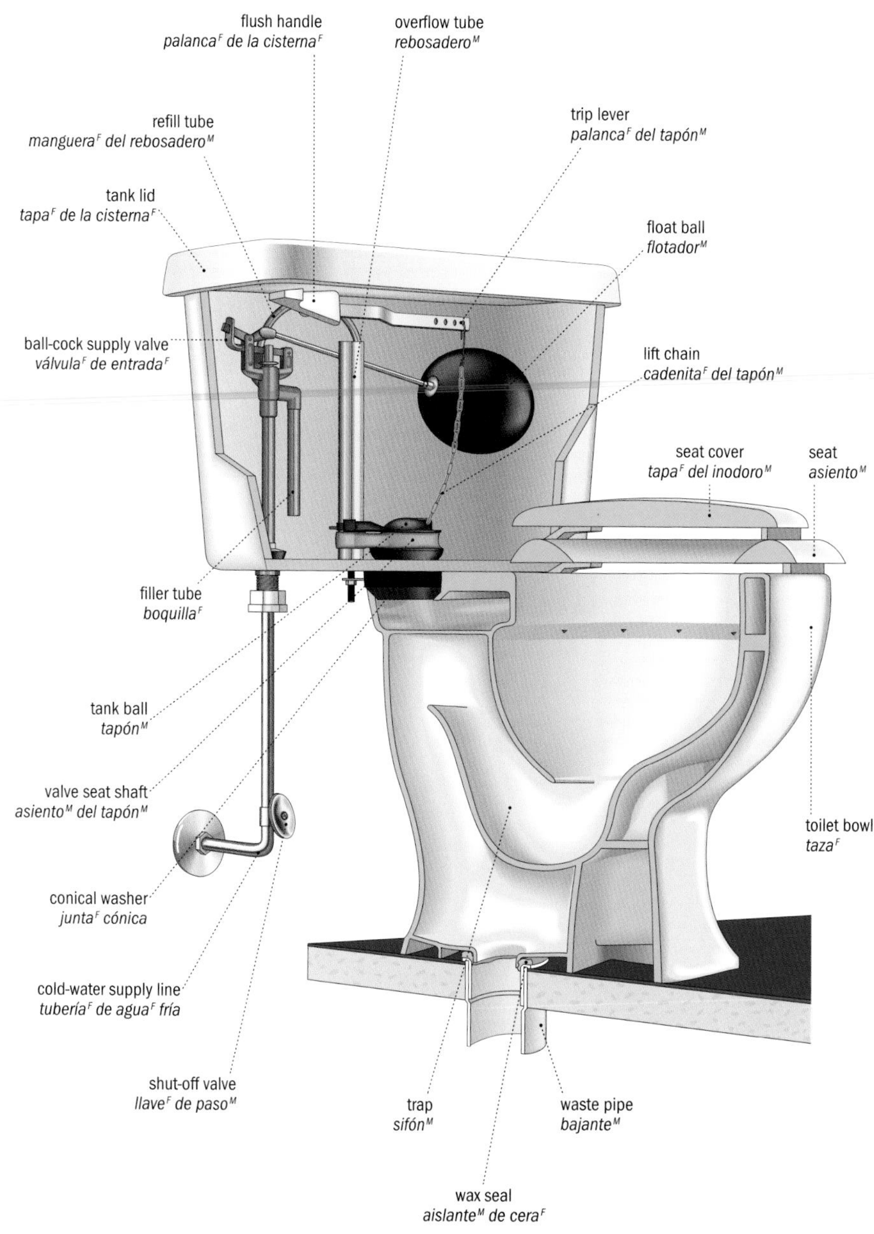
flush handle
palanca[F] de la cisterna[F]
overflow tube
rebosadero[M]
refill tube
manguera[F] del rebosadero[M]
trip lever
palanca[F] del tapón[M]
tank lid
tapa[F] de la cisterna[F]
float ball
flotador[M]
ball-cock supply valve
válvula[F] de entrada[F]
lift chain
cadenita[F] del tapón[M]
seat cover
tapa[F] del inodoro[M]
seat
asiento[M]
filler tube
boquilla[F]
tank ball
tapón[M]
valve seat shaft
asiento[M] del tapón[M]
toilet bowl
taza[F]
conical washer
junta[F] cónica
cold-water supply line
tubería[F] de agua[F] fría
shut-off valve
llave[F] de paso[M]
trap
sifón[M]
waste pipe
bajante[M]
wax seal
aislante[M] de cera[F]

examples of branching

ejemplos^M de conexiones^F

garbage disposal sink
fregadero^M con triturador^M de basura^F

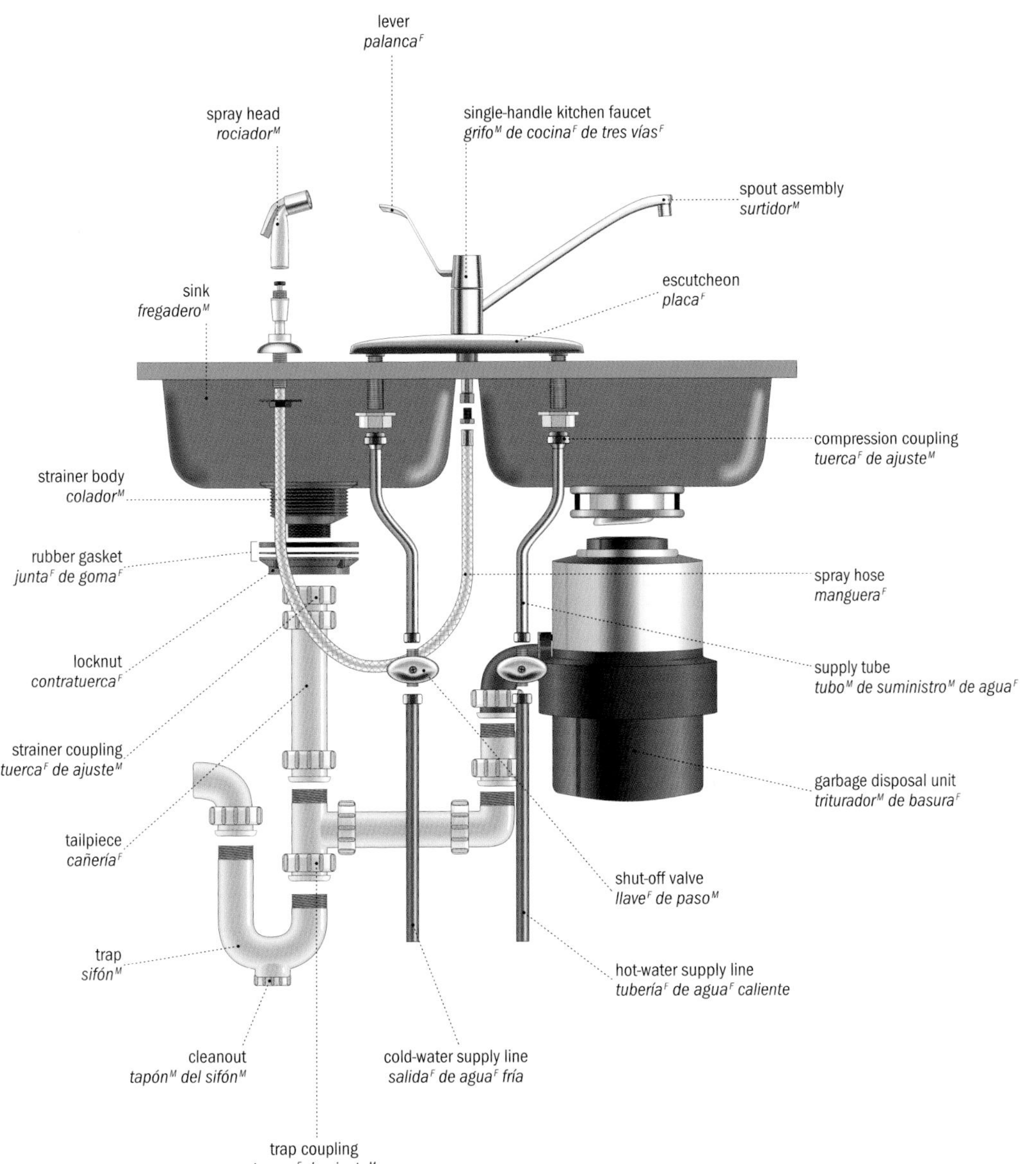

network connection

conexión[F] a la red[F]

supply point
cables[M] de suministro[M]
customer's service entrance
entrada[F] del suministro[M]
connection point
conexión[F]
phase conductor
conductor[M] de fase[F]
medium-tension distribution line
cables[M] de tensión[F] mediana
neutral conductor
conductor[M] neutral
low-tension distribution line
cables[M] de baja tensión[F]
ground wire
conexión[F] de tierra[F]
distributor service loop
cables[M] de conexión[F]
electricity meter
contador[M] eléctrico
main switch
interruptor[M] principal
service box
caja[F] de servicio[M]
distribution panel
tablero[M] de distribución[F]
fuse
fusible[M]

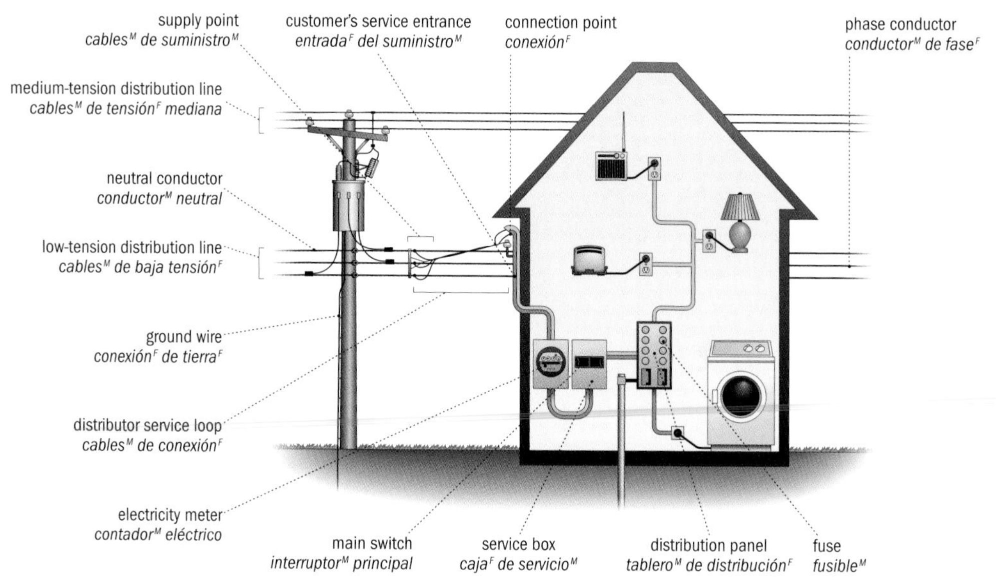

contact devices

dispositivos[M] de contacto[M]

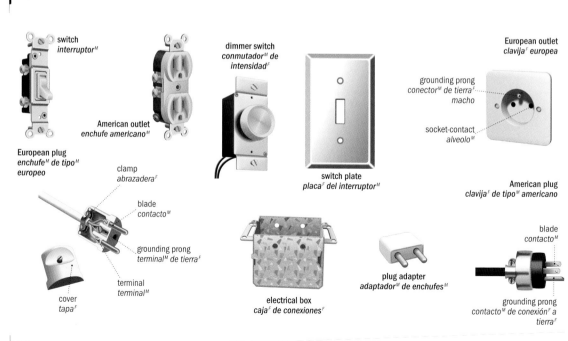

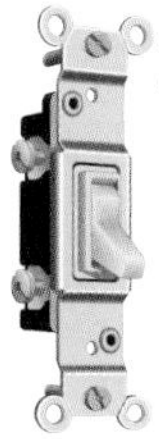

switch
interruptor[M]

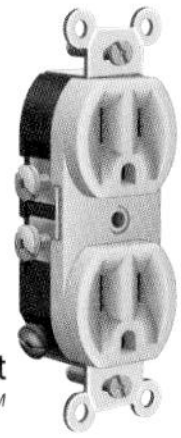

American outlet
enchufe americano[M]

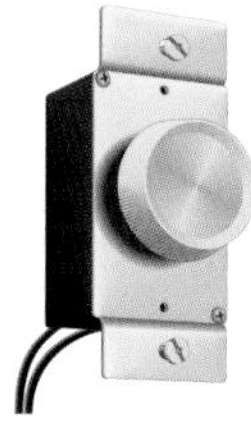

dimmer switch
conmutador[M] de intensidad[F]

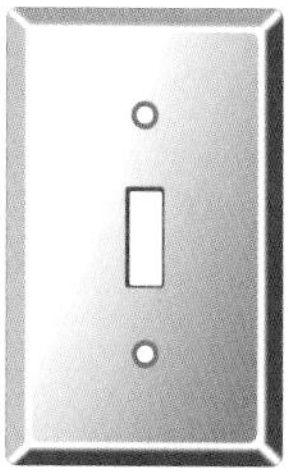

switch plate
placa[F] del interruptor[M]

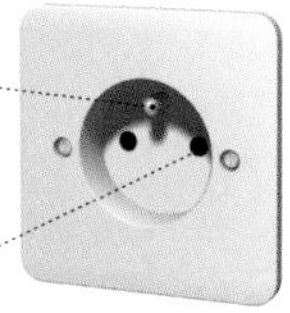

European outlet
clavija[F] europea
grounding prong
conector[M] de tierra[F] macho
socket-contact
alveolo[M]

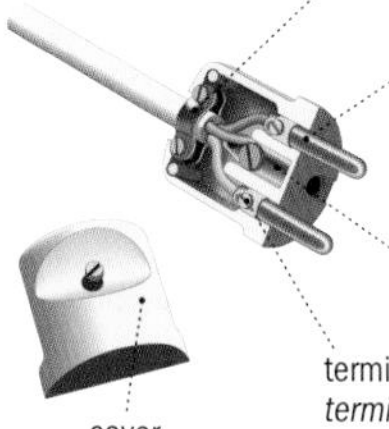

European plug
enchufe[M] de tipo[M] europeo
clamp
abrazadera[F]
blade
contacto[M]
grounding prong
terminal[M] de tierra[F]
terminal
terminal[M]
cover
tapa[F]

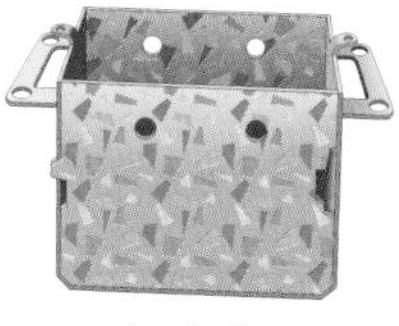

electrical box
caja[F] de conexiones[F]

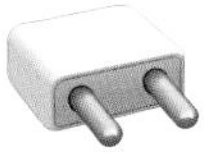

plug adapter
adaptador[M] de enchufes[M]

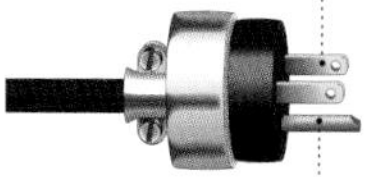

American plug
clavija[F] de tipo[M] americano
blade
contacto[M]
grounding prong
contacto[M] de conexión[F] a tierra[F]

lighting
iluminación[F]

incandescent lightbulb
bombilla[F] incandescente

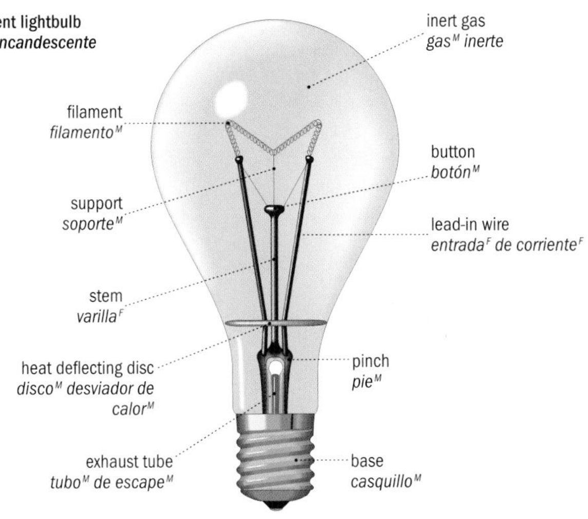

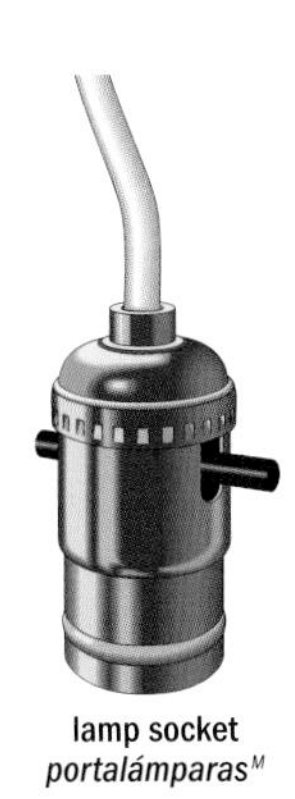

lamp socket
portalámparas[M]

bulb
ampolla[F] de vidrio[M]

energy-saving bulb
bombilla[F] de bajo consumo

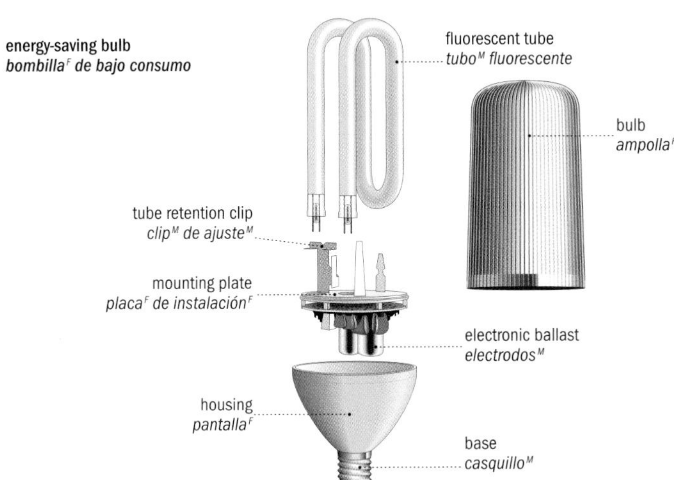

screw base
bombilla[F] de rosca[F]

bayonet base
bombilla[F] de bayoneta[F]

fluorescent tube
tubo[M] fluorescente

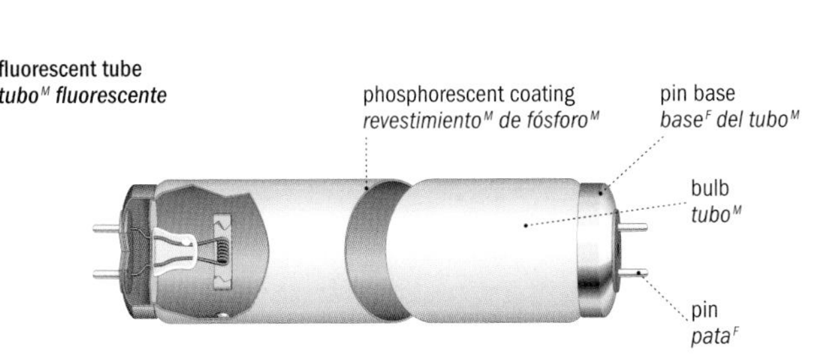

tungsten-halogen lamp
lámpara[F] halógena

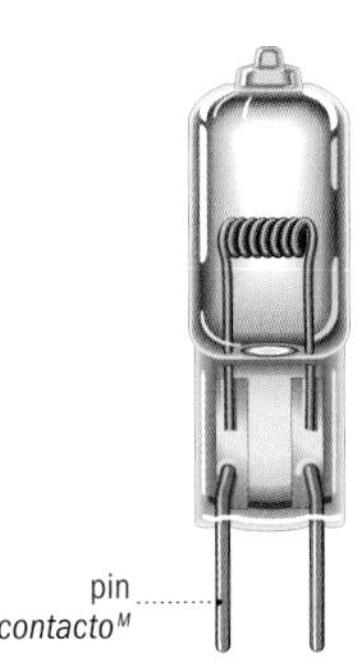

HOUSE

armchair

silla[F] de brazos[M]

parts
partes[F]

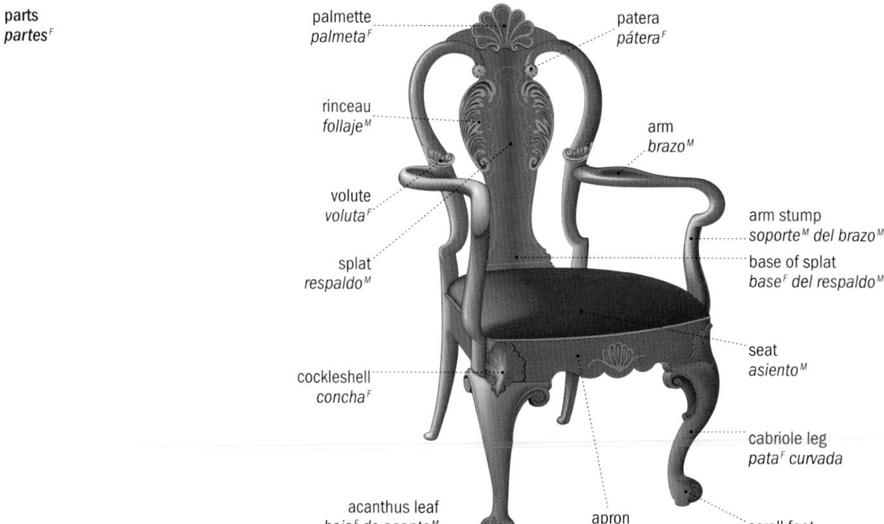

examples of armchairs
ejemplos[M] de divanes[M] y butacas[F]

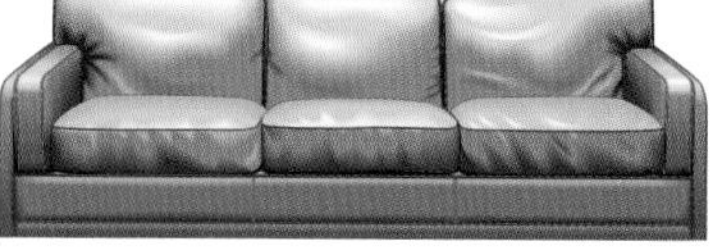

sofa
sofá[M]

love seat
sofá[M] de dos plazas[F]

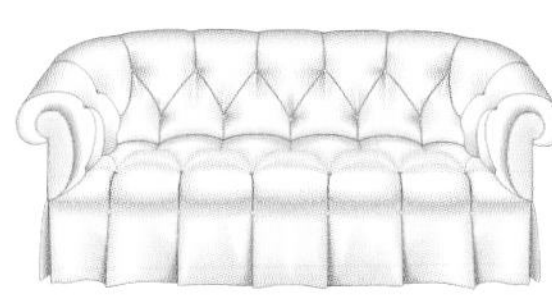

chesterfield
chesterfield[M]

side chair

silla[F] sin brazos[M]

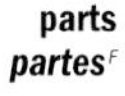

parts
partes[F]

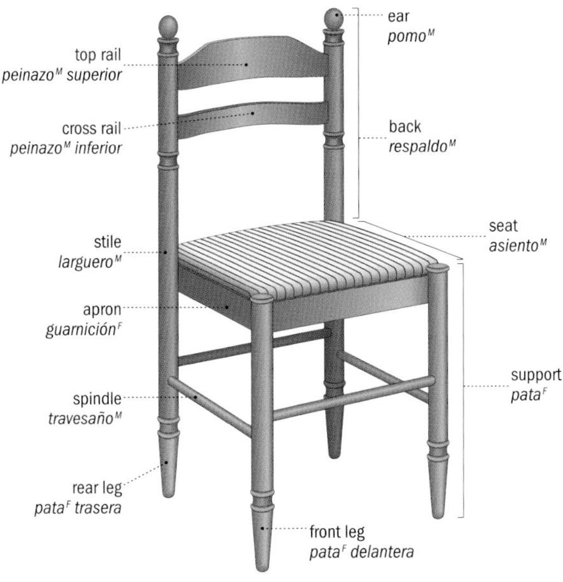

examples of chairs
ejemplos[M] de sillas[F]

rocking chair
mecedora[F]

stacking chairs
sillas[F] apilables

folding chairs
sillas[F] plegables

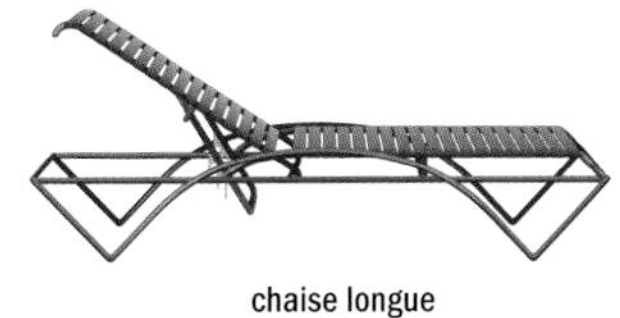

chaise longue
tumbona[F]

seats

asientos[M]

ottoman
puf[M]

bench
banco[F]

banquette
banqueta[F]

bean bag chair
silla[F] cojín[M]

step chair
silla[F] escalera[F]

footstool
escabel[M]

bar stool
taburete[M]

table

mesa^F

gate-leg table
mesa^F de hojas^F abatibles

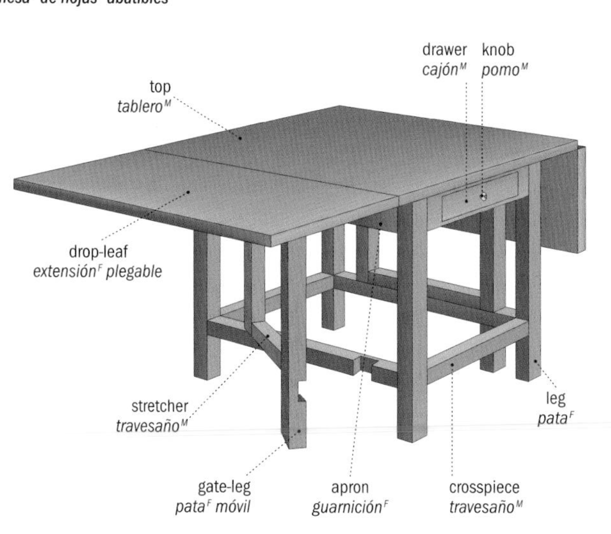

examples of tables
ejemplos^M de mesas^F

extension table
mesa^F plegable

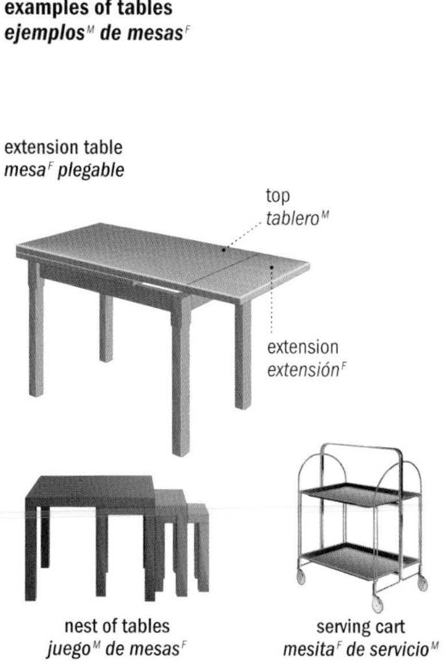

nest of tables
juego^M de mesas^F

serving cart
mesita^F de servicio^M

storage furniture

muebles^M contenedores

armoire
armario^M

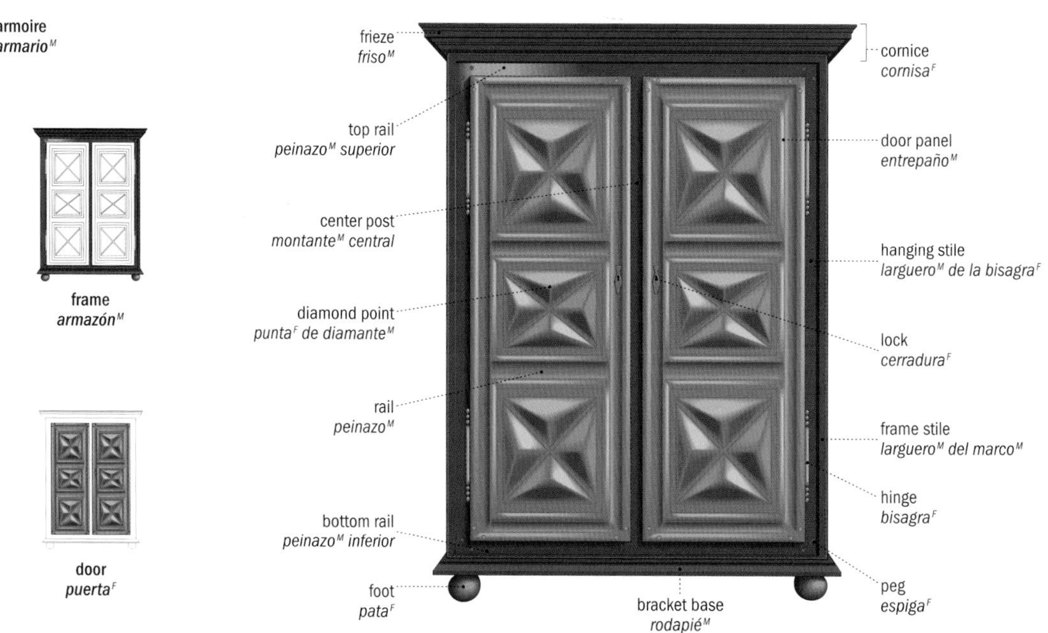

frame
armazón^M

door
puerta^F

linen chest
baúl[M]

secretary
bufete[M]

dresser
cómoda[F]

wardrobe
ropero[M]

chiffonier
chifonier[M]

display cabinet
vitrina[F]

corner cupboard
rinconera[F]

glass-fronted display cabinet
aparador[M] *con vitrina*[F]

buffet
aparador[M]

cocktail cabinet
mueble[M] *bar*[M]

bed

cama[F]

sofa bed
sofá cama[M]

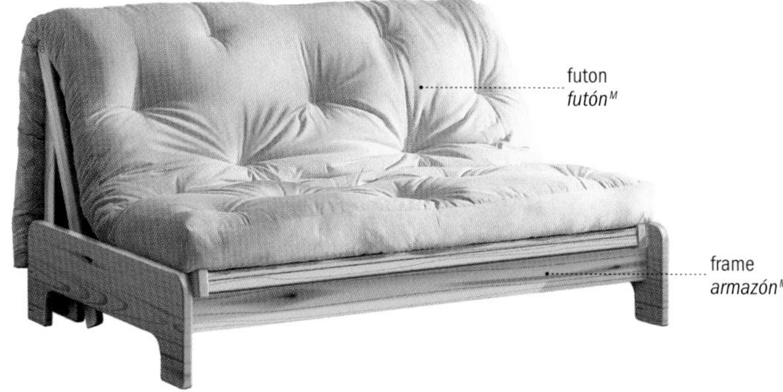

parts
partes[F]

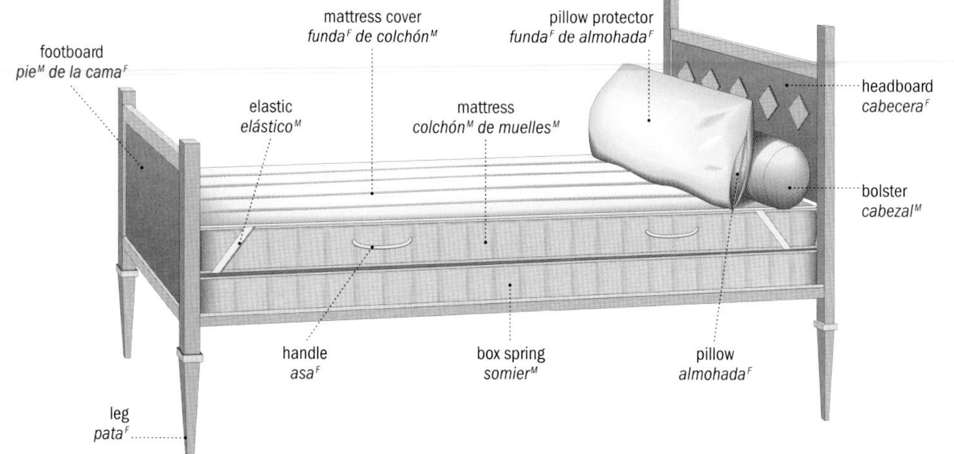

linen
ropa[F] de cama[F]

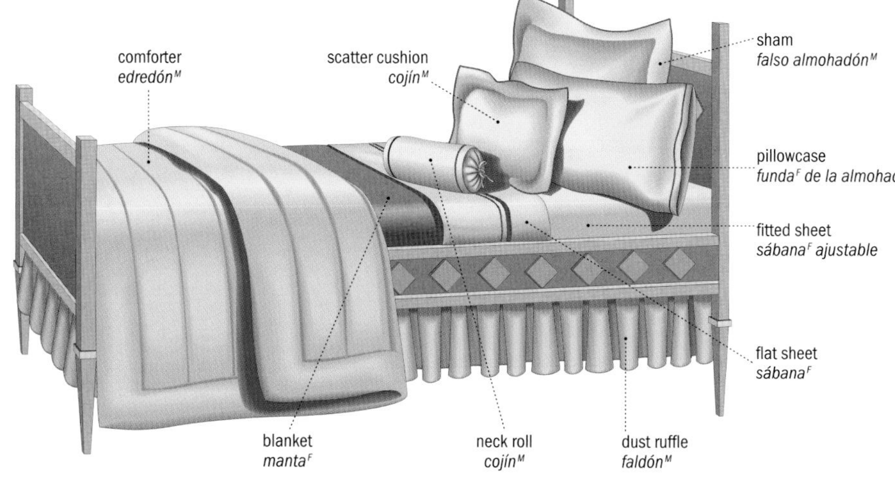

children's furniture

muebles[M] infantiles

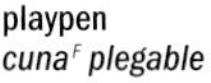

playpen
cuna[F] plegable

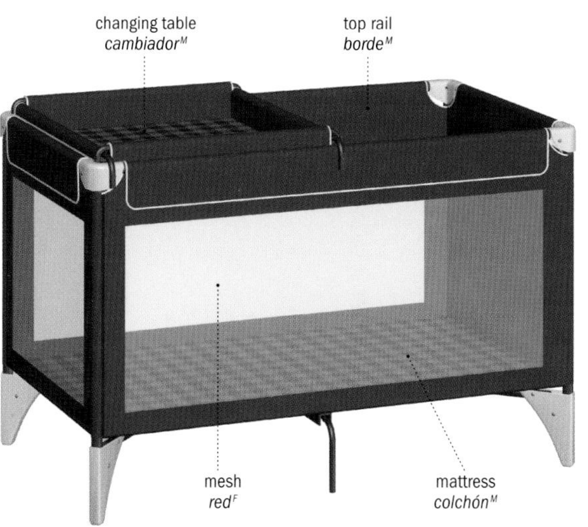

booster seat
silla[F] alzadora

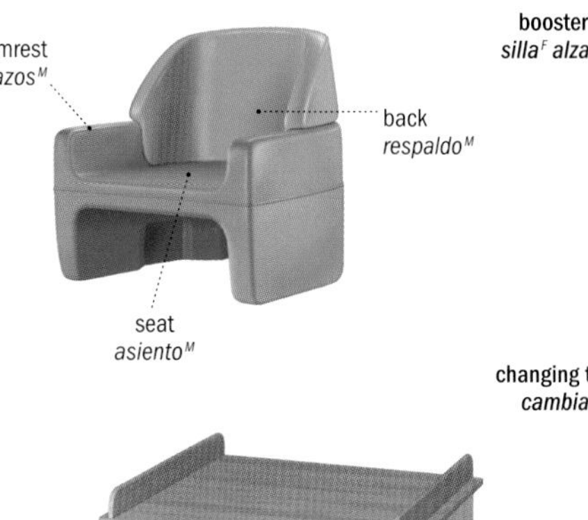

changing table
cambiador[M]

high chair
trona[F]

crib
cuna[F]

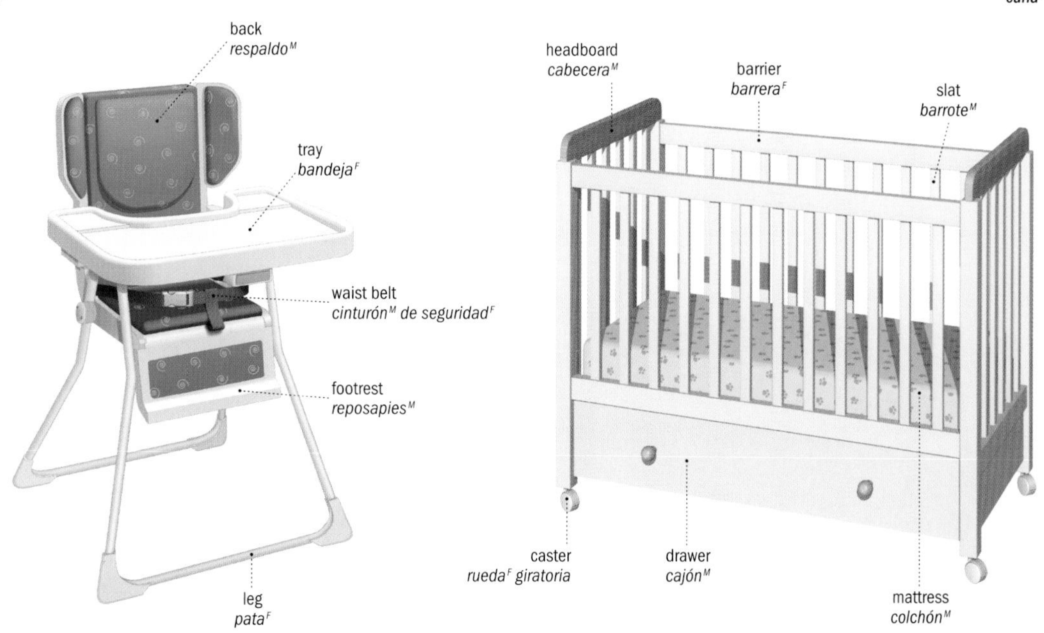

lights

lámparas^F

ceiling fixture
plafón^M
clamp spotlight
lámpara^F de pinza^F
hanging pendant
lámpara^F de techo^M
halogen desk lamp
lámpara^F de despacho^M halógena
arm
brazo^M
adjustable lamp
flexo^M
base
base^M
on-off switch
interruptor^M
arm
brazo^M
shade
pantalla^F
spring
resorte^M
reading lamp
lámpara^F de cabecera^F
adjustable clamp
tornillo^M de ajuste^M
shade
pantalla^F
base
base^F
stand
pedestal^M
floor lamp
lámpara^F de pie^M
table lamp
lámpara^F de mesa^F
desk lamp
lámpara^F de escritorio^M

chandelier
*araña*F
bobeche
*arandela*F
crystal drop
*colgante*M
crystal button
*gota*F
column
*columna*F
track lighting
*riel*M *de iluminación*F
bar frame
*armazón*M
transformer
*transformador*M
contact lever
*interruptor*M
spot
*foco*M
wall lantern
*farol*M
wall sconce
*aplique*M
swivel wall lamp
*lámpara*F *orientable de pared*F
strip lights
*lámparas*F *en serie*F
post lantern
*farola*F

domestic appliances

aparatos^M electrodomésticos

steam iron
plancha^F de vapor^M

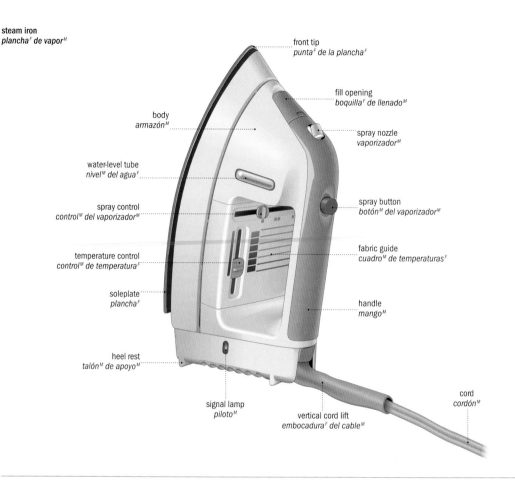

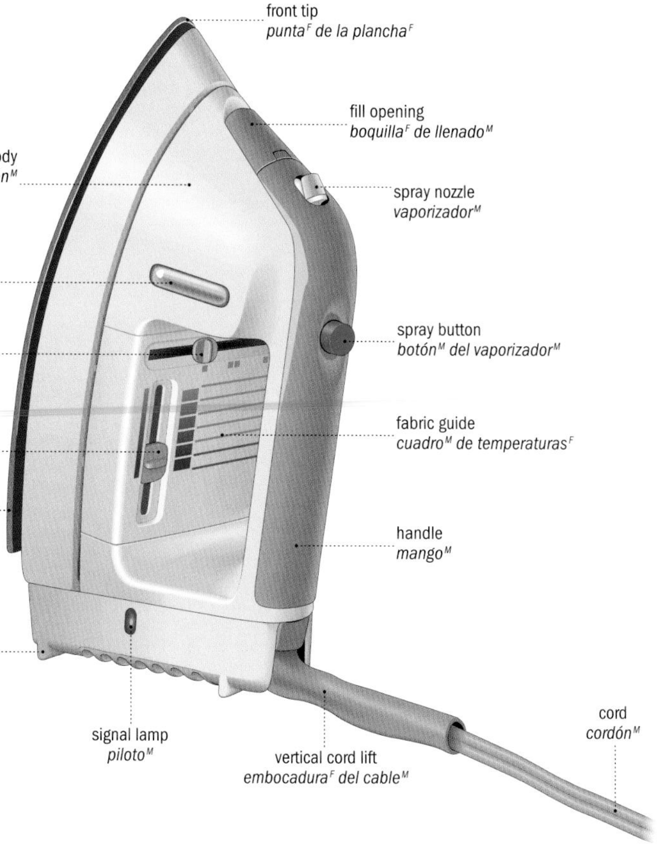

front tip
punta^F de la plancha^F
fill opening
boquilla^F de llenado^M
body
armazón^M
spray nozzle
vaporizador^M
water-level tube
nivel^M del agua^F
spray button
botón^M del vaporizador^M
spray control
control^M del vaporizador^M
fabric guide
cuadro^M de temperaturas^F
temperature control
control^M de temperatura^F
soleplate
plancha^F
handle
mango^M
heel rest
talón^M de apoyo^M
cord
cordón^M
signal lamp
piloto^M
vertical cord lift
embocadura^F del cable^M

hand held vacuum cleaner
aspirador^M manual

locking button
botón^M de cierre^M
on-off switch
interruptor^M
dust receiver
depósito^M de polvo^M
recharging base
cargador^M
motor unit
motor^M

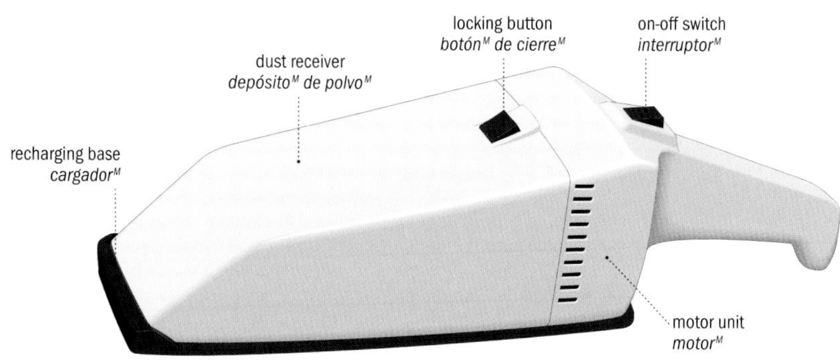

upright vacuum cleaner
escoba[F] eléctrica

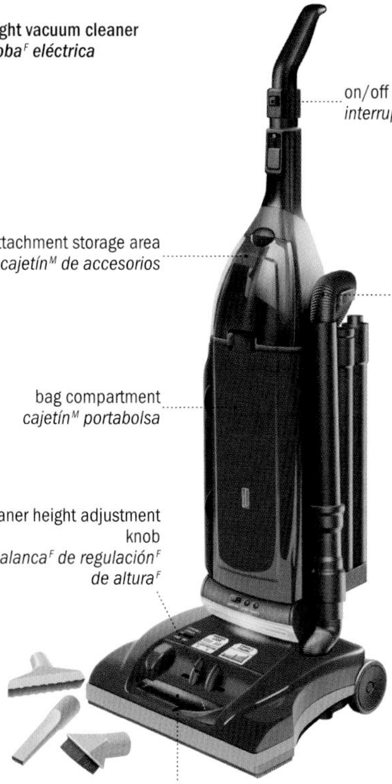

on/off switch
interruptor[M] on/off

attachment storage area
cajetín[M] de accesorios

hose
tubo[M] flexible

bag compartment
cajetín[M] portabolsa

cleaner height adjustment knob
palanca[F] de regulación[F] de altura[F]

attachments
accesorios[M]

brush
cepillo[M]

cylinder vacuum cleaner
aspirador[M]

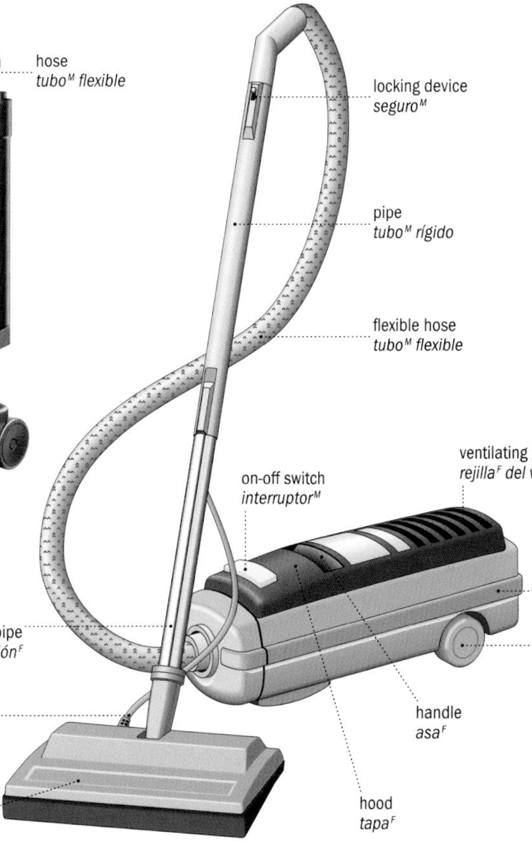

locking device
seguro[M]

pipe
tubo[M] rígido

flexible hose
tubo[M] flexible

ventilating grille
rejilla[F] del ventilador[M]

on-off switch
interruptor[M]

bumper
tope[M] amortiguador

caster
ruedecilla[F]

extension pipe
tubo[M] de extensión[F]

handle
asa[F]

cord
cordón[M]

rug and floor brush
boquilla[F] para suelos[M] y alfombras[F]

hood
tapa[F]

vacuum cleaner attachments
accesorios[M]

upholstery nozzle
boquilla[F] para tapicería[F]

dusting brush
cepillo[M]-plumero[M]

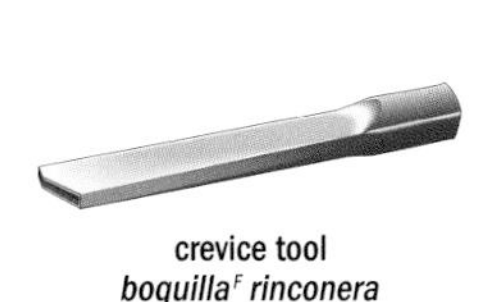

crevice tool
boquilla[F] rinconera

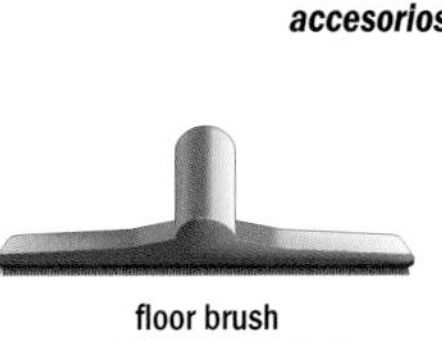

floor brush
cepillo[M] para suelos[M]

domestic appliances

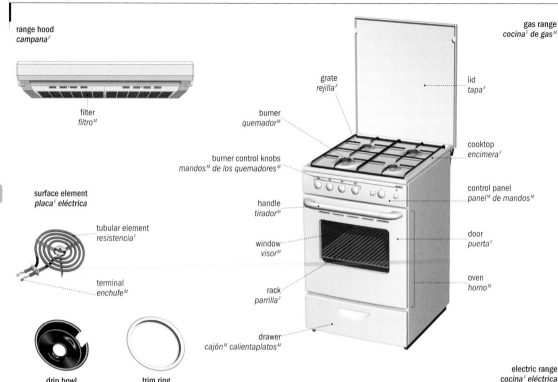

range hood
campana[F]

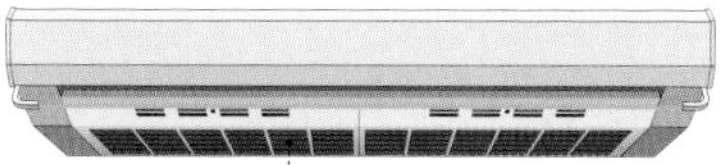

filter
filtro[M]

surface element
placa[F] eléctrica

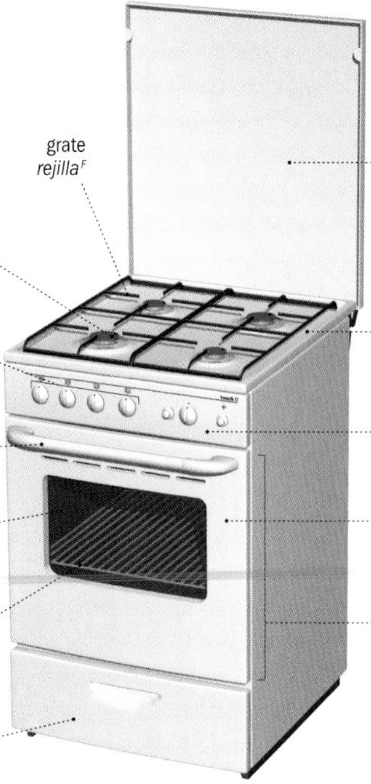

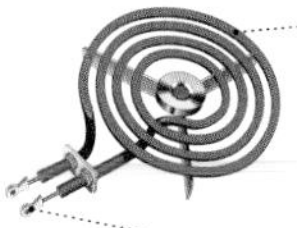

tubular element
resistencia[F]
terminal
enchufe[M]

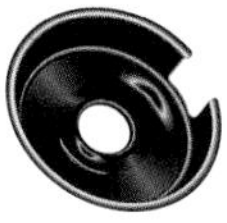

drip bowl
protector[M]

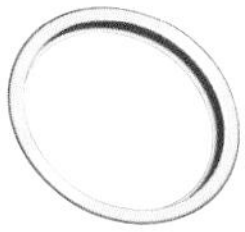

trim ring
arandela[F]

gas range
cocina[F] de gas[M]

grate
rejilla[F]
lid
tapa[F]
burner
quemador[M]
cooktop
encimera[F]
burner control knobs
mandos[M] de los quemadores[M]
control panel
panel[M] de mandos[M]
handle
tirador[M]
door
puerta[F]
window
visor[M]
oven
horno[M]
rack
parrilla[F]
drawer
cajón[M] calientaplatos[M]

electric range
cocina[F] eléctrica

oven control knobs
botón[M] del horno[M]
clock timer
reloj[M]
signal lamp
piloto[M]
backguard
panel[M] de mandos[M]
control knob
botón[M] de mando[M]
timed outlet
enchufe[M] con control[M] de tiempo[M]
control panel
panel[M] de mandos[M]
cooktop
encimera[F]
surface element
hornillo[M]
cooktop edge
borde[M]
rack
parrilla[F]
handle
asa[F]
oven
horno[M]
window
visor[M]
drawer
cajón[M] calientaplatos

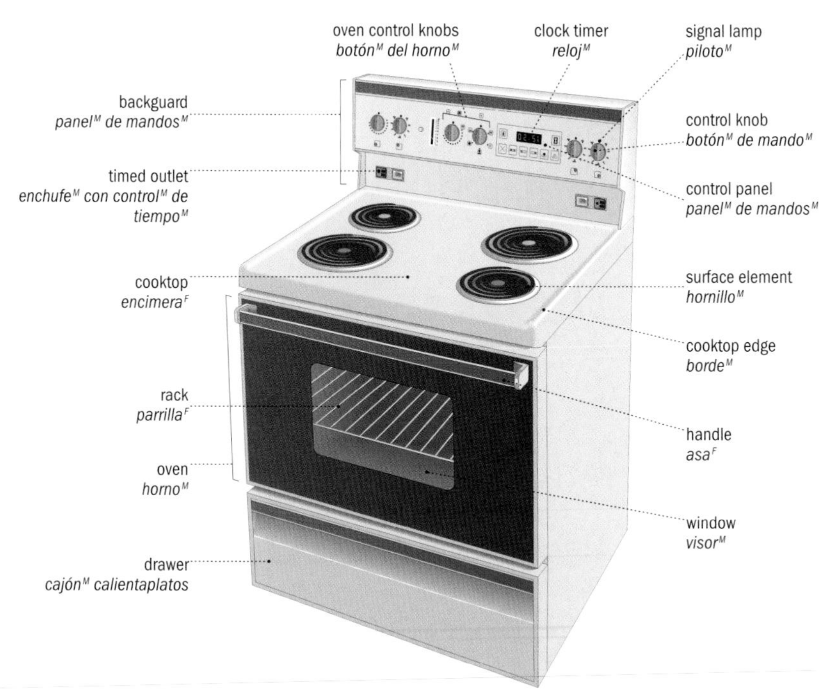

chest freezer
arcón*^M *congelador

lock
cierre^M
lid
tapa
basket
cesto^M
cabinet
cuba^F
temperature control
termostato^M
defrost drain
válvula^F *de drenaje*^M

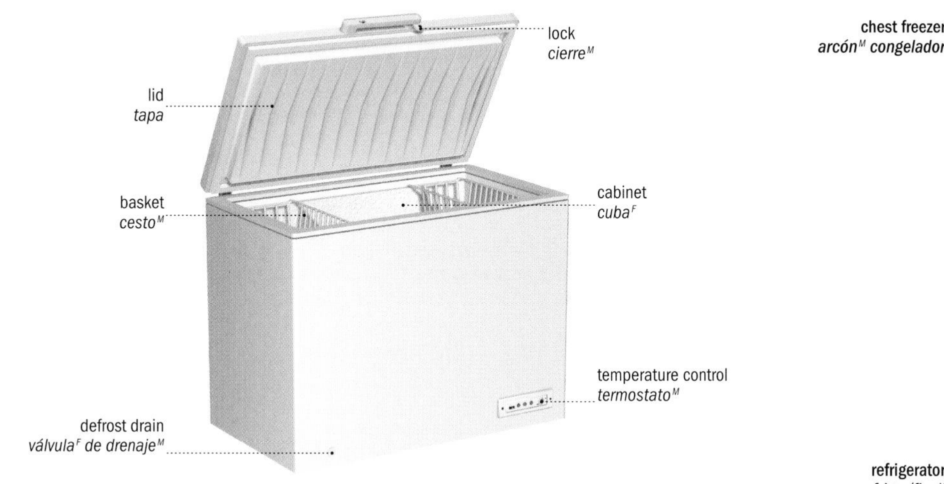

refrigerator
***frigorífico*^M**

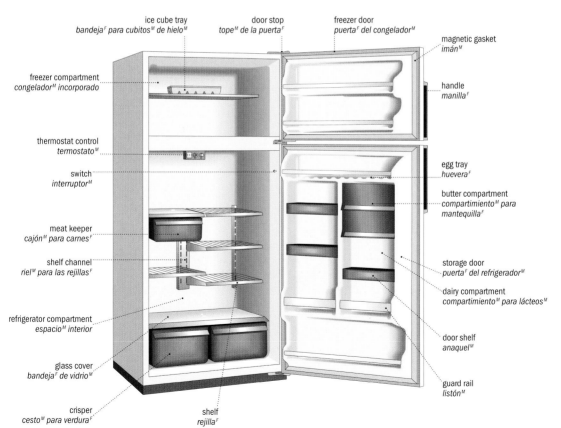

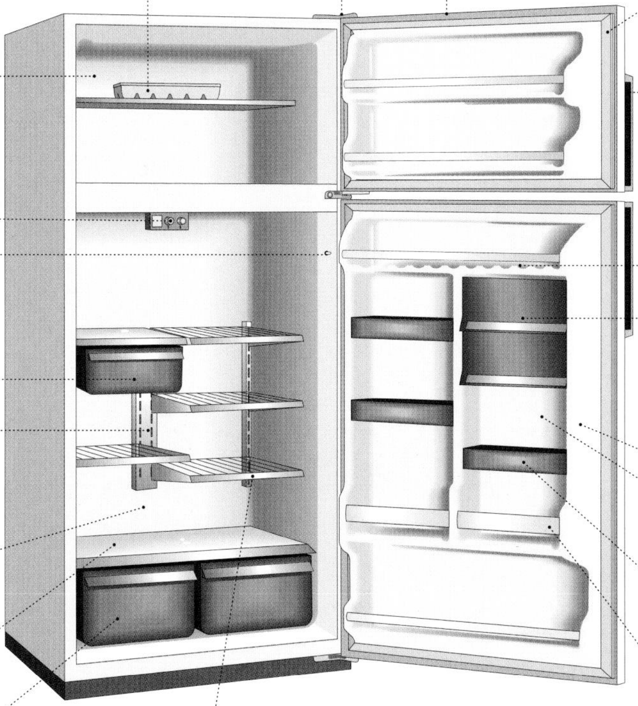

ice cube tray
bandeja^F *para cubitos*^M *de hielo*^M
door stop
tope^M *de la puerta*^F
freezer door
puerta^F *del congelador*^M
magnetic gasket
imán^M
freezer compartment
congelador^M *incorporado*
handle
manilla^F
thermostat control
termostato^M
switch
interruptor^M
egg tray
huevera^F
butter compartment
compartimiento^M *para mantequilla*^F
meat keeper
cajón^M *para carnes*^F
shelf channel
riel^M *para las rejillas*^F
storage door
puerta^F *del refrigerador*^M
dairy compartment
compartimiento^M *para lácteos*^M
refrigerator compartment
espacio^M *interior*
door shelf
anaquel^M
glass cover
bandeja^F *de vidrio*^M
guard rail
listón^M
crisper
cesto^M *para verdura*^F
shelf
rejilla^F

washer
lavadora[F]

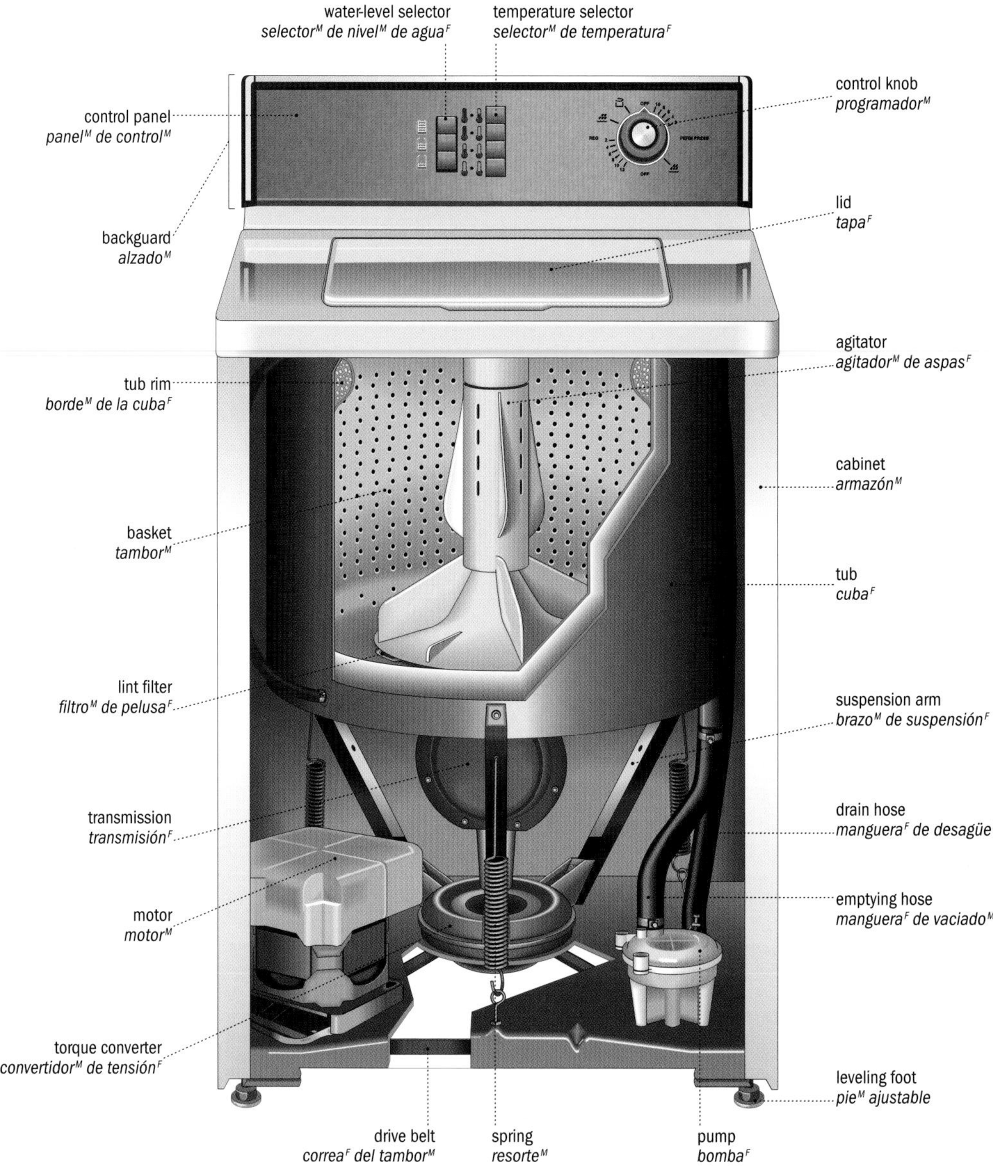
water-level selector
selector[M] de nivel[M] de agua[F]
temperature selector
selector[M] de temperatura[F]
control knob
programador[M]
control panel
panel[M] de control[M]
backguard
alzado[M]
lid
tapa[F]
agitator
agitador[M] de aspas[F]
tub rim
borde[M] de la cuba[F]
cabinet
armazón[M]
basket
tambor[M]
tub
cuba[F]
lint filter
filtro[M] de pelusa[F]
suspension arm
brazo[M] de suspensión[F]
transmission
transmisión[F]
drain hose
manguera[F] de desagüe[M]
motor
motor[M]
emptying hose
manguera[F] de vaciado[M]
torque converter
convertidor[M] de tensión[F]
leveling foot
pie[M] ajustable
drive belt
correa[F] del tambor[M]
spring
resorte[M]
pump
bomba[F]

dryer
***secadora*[F] *de ropa*[F]**

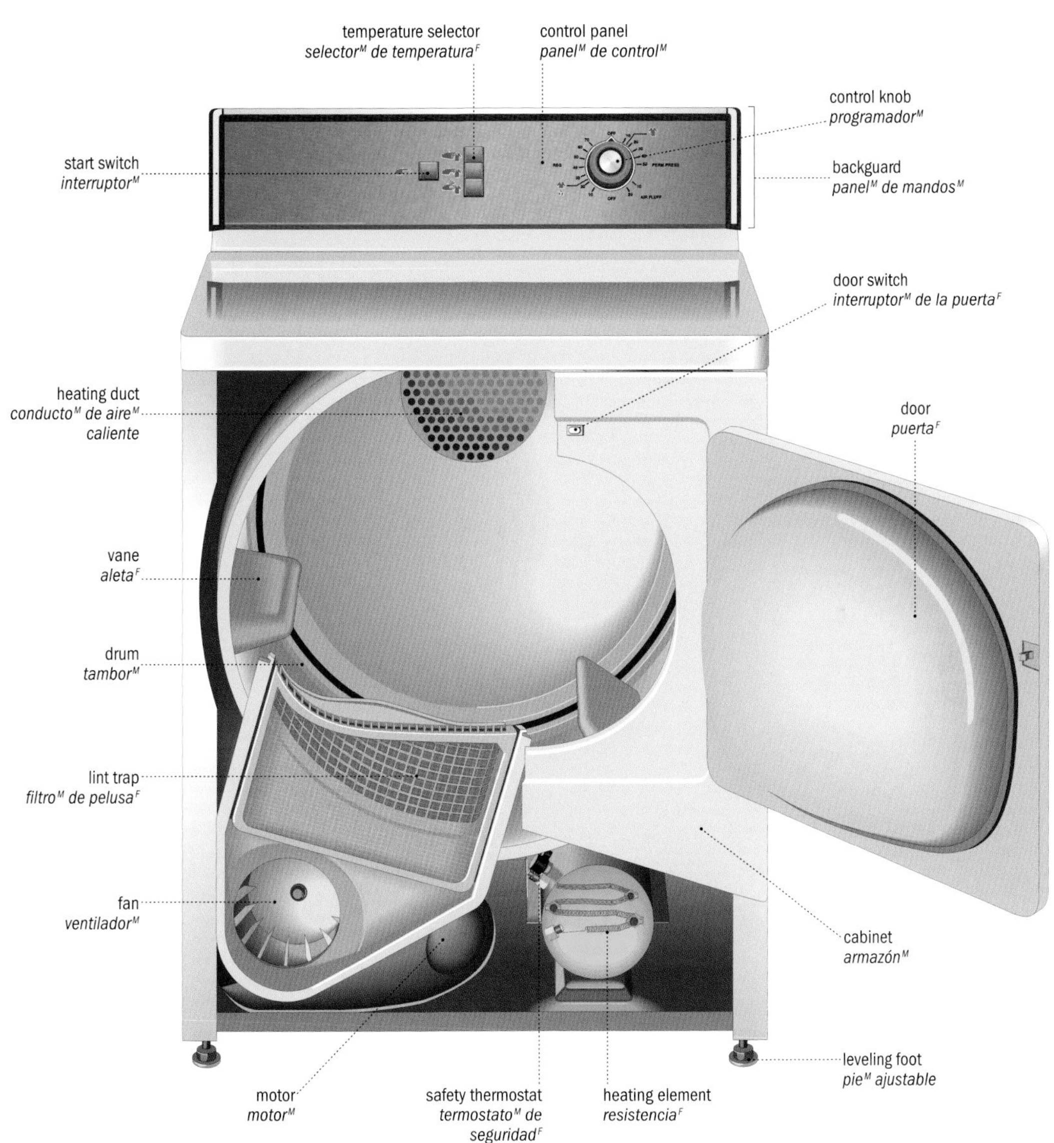
temperature selector
selector[M] *de temperatura*[F]
control panel
panel[M] *de control*[M]
control knob
programador[M]
start switch
interruptor[M]
backguard
panel[M] *de mandos*[M]
door switch
interruptor[M] *de la puerta*[F]
heating duct
conducto[M] *de aire*[M] *caliente*
door
puerta[F]
vane
aleta[F]
drum
tambor[M]
lint trap
filtro[M] *de pelusa*[F]
fan
ventilador[M]
cabinet
armazón[M]
leveling foot
pie[M] *ajustable*
motor
motor[M]
safety thermostat
termostato[M] *de seguridad*[F]
heating element
resistencia[F]

domestic appliances

control panel: dishwasher
panel[M] de control[M]

OFF
REG
ECONO
signal lamp
piloto[M]
control knob
programador[M]
push button
botón[M] selector
air vent
rejilla[F] de ventilación[F]
latch
palanca[F] de cierre[M]

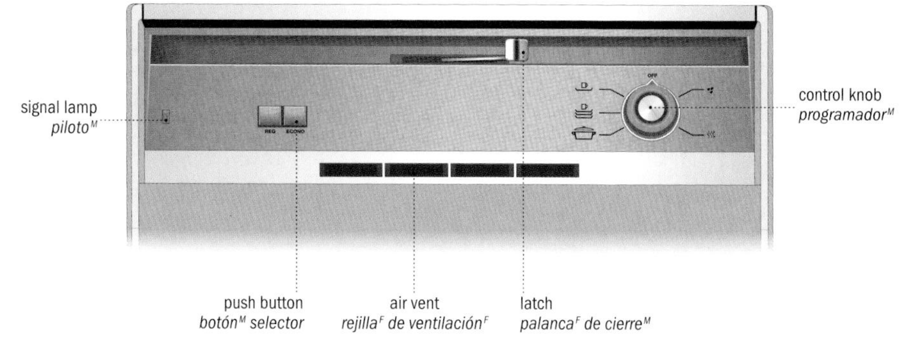

dishwasher
lavavajillas[M]

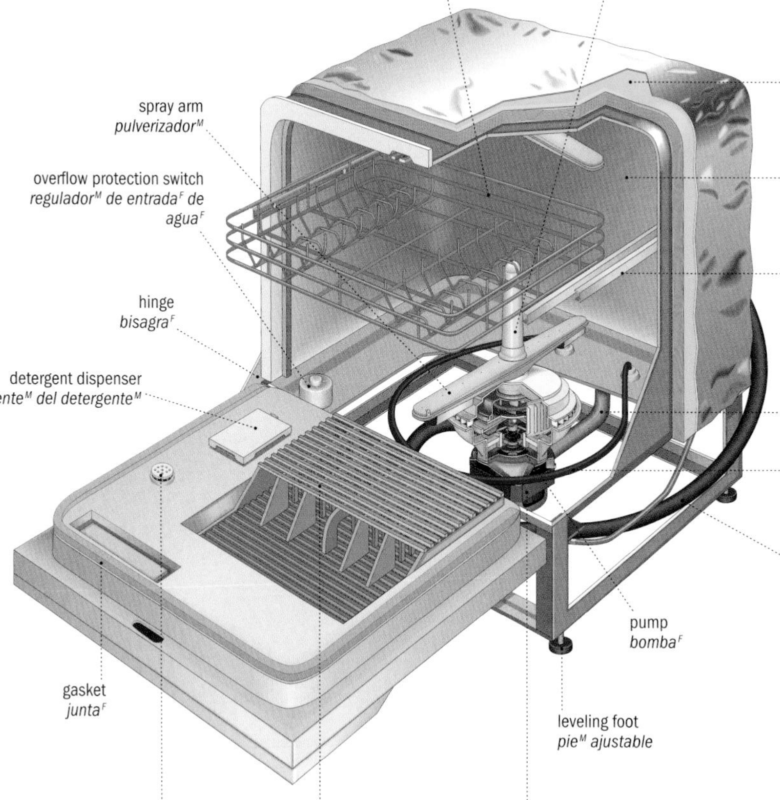

rack
cesto[M]
wash tower
torrecilla[F] de lavado[M]
insulating material
aislante[M]
spray arm
pulverizador[M]
overflow protection switch
regulador[M] de entrada[F] de agua[F]
tub
cuba[F] de lavado[M]
slide
riel[M] corredizo
hinge
bisagra[F]
detergent dispenser
recipiente[M] del detergente[M]
water hose
manguera[F] de alimentación[F]
heating element
resistencia[F]
drain hose
manguera[F] de desagüe[M]
pump
bomba[F]
gasket
junta[F]
leveling foot
pie[M] ajustable
rinse-aid dispenser
recipiente[M] del abrillantador[M]
cutlery basket
cesto[M] para cubiertos[M]
motor
motor[M]

household equipment

artículos^M de limpieza^F

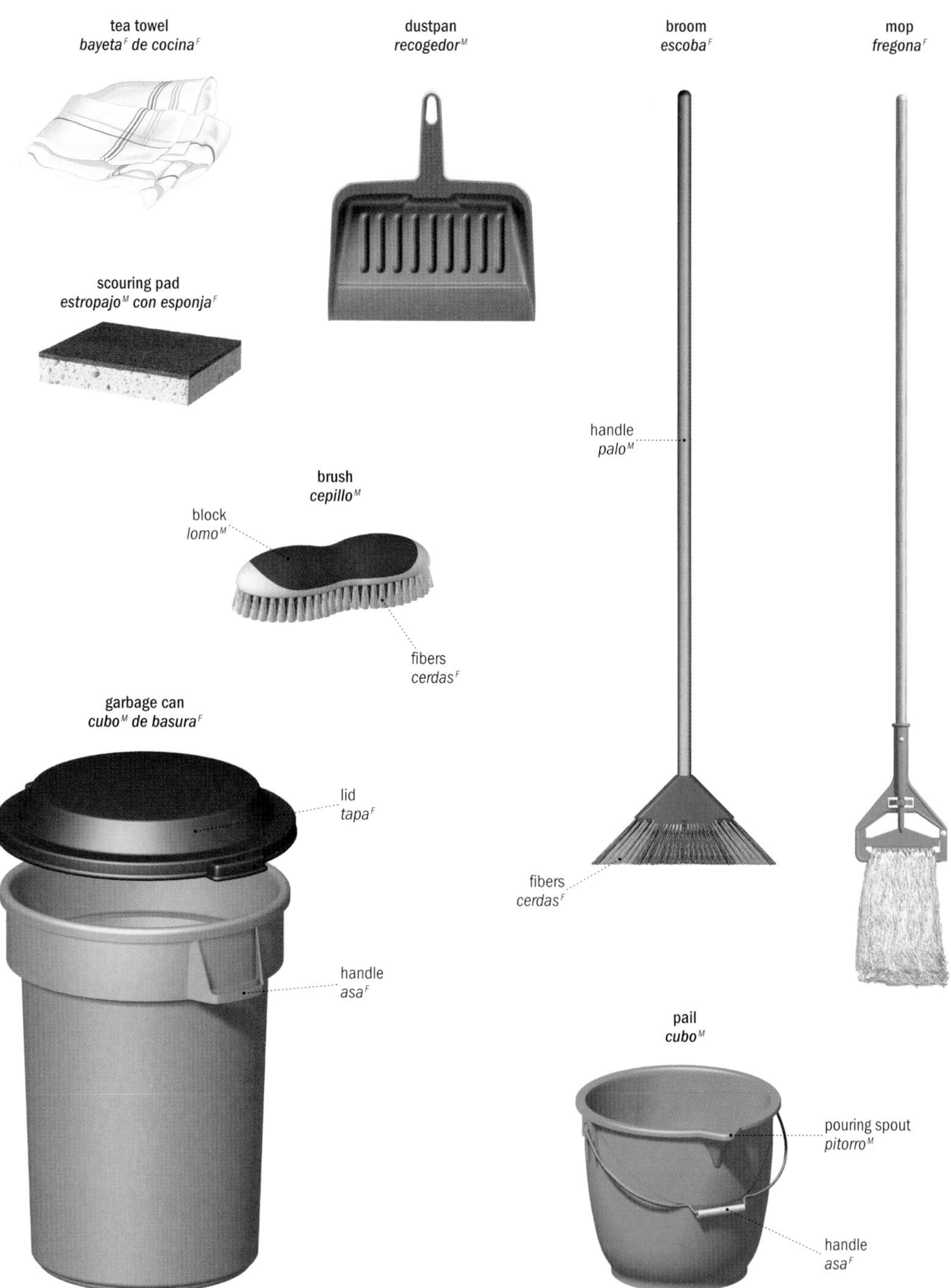

plumbing tools

fontanería[F] : herramientas[F]

plunger
desatascador[M]

plumber's snake
sonda[F] destapacaños[M]

Teflon tape
cinta[F] de teflón[M]

wrenches
llaves[F]

basin wrench
llave[F] de fontanero[M]

pipe wrench
llave[F] inglesa

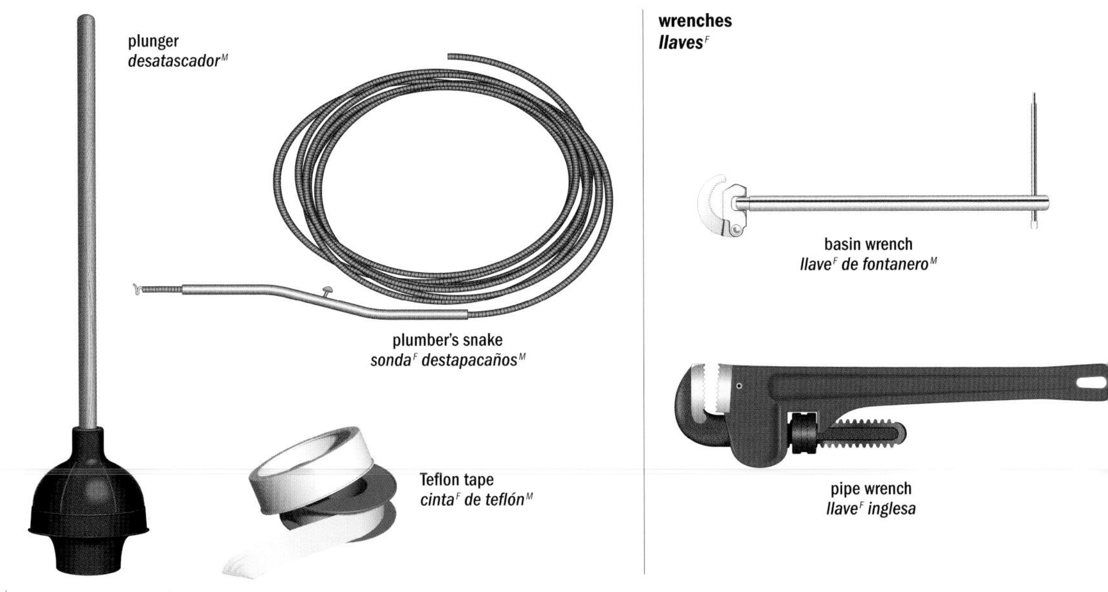

masonry tools

albañilería[F] : herramientas[F]

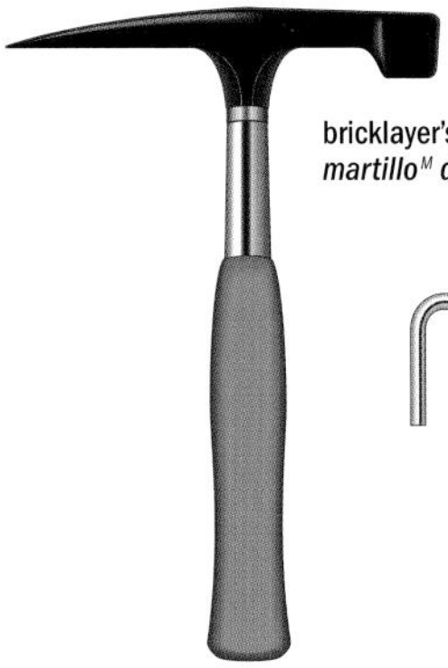

bricklayer's hammer
martillo[M] de albañil[M]

caulking gun
pistola[F] para calafateo[M]

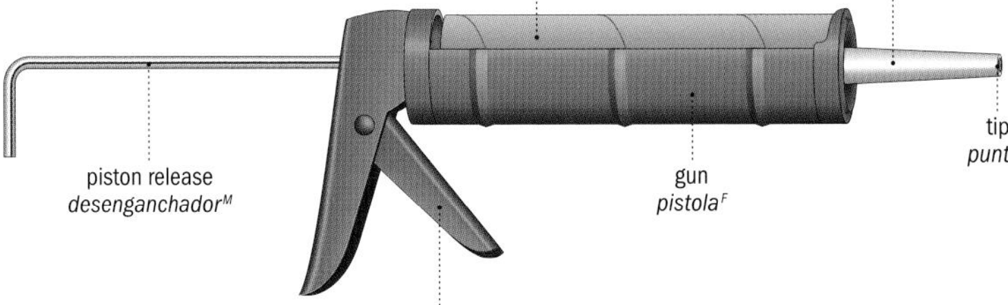

cartridge
cartucho[M]
nozzle
boquilla[F]
piston release
desenganchador[M]
gun
pistola[F]
tip
punta[F]
piston lever
gatillo[M]

mason's trowel
paleta[F] de albañil[M]

hawk
esparavel[M]

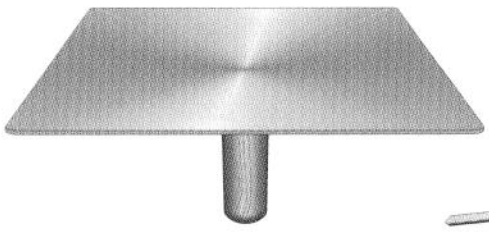

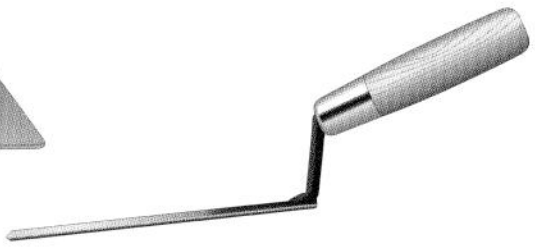

joint filler
paleta[F] de relleno[M]

square trowel
llana[F]

blade
hoja[F]
tang
espiga[F]
handle
mango[M]

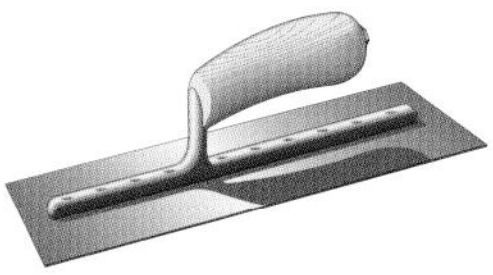

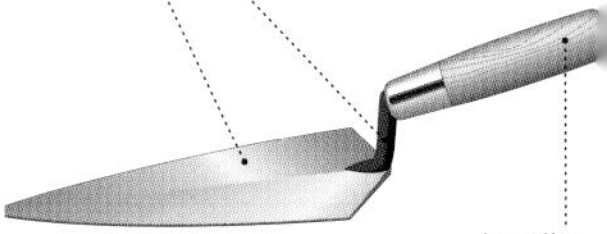

electricity tools

electricidad[F] : herramientas[F]

drop light
linterna[F] movible

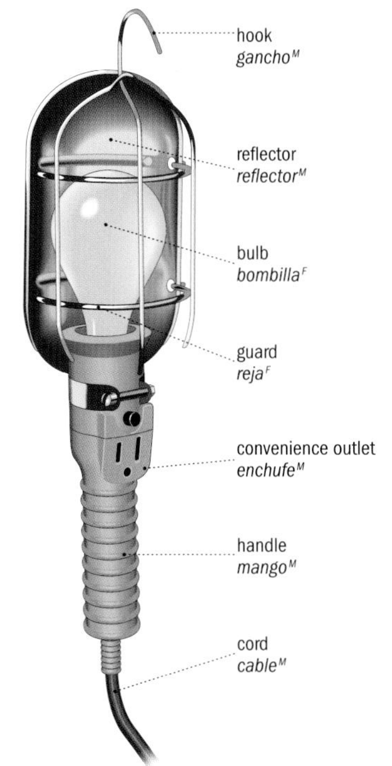

neon tester
lámpara[F] de prueba[F] de neón[M]

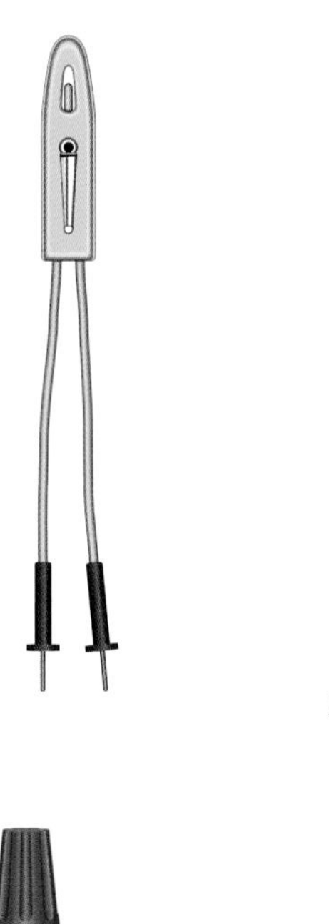

voltage tester
detector[M] de tensión[F]

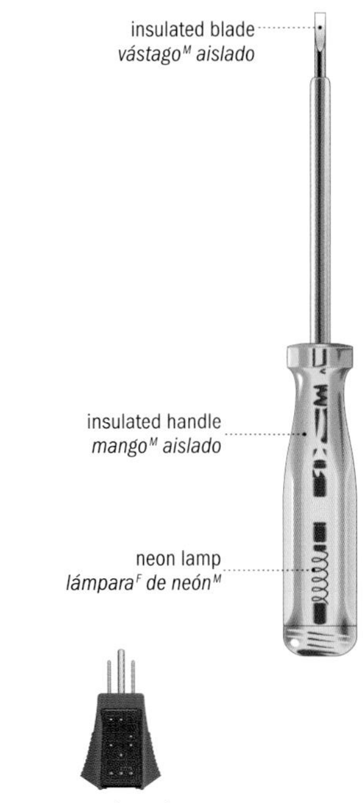

wire nut
capuchón[M] de plástico[M]

receptacle analyzer
probador[M] de contactos[M] con tierra[F]

multipurpose tool
pinzas[F] multiuso

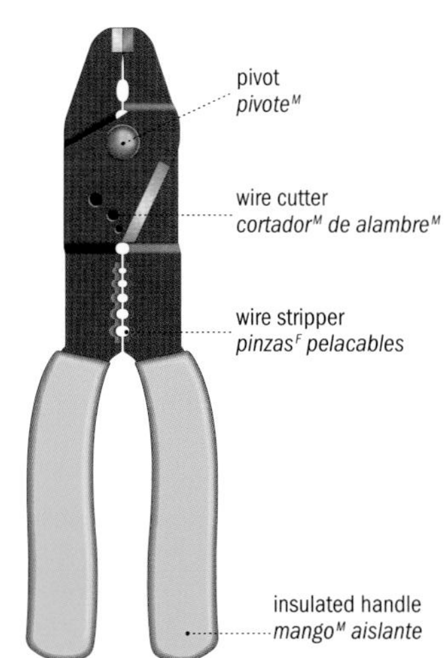

needle-nose pliers
alicates[M] de punta[F]

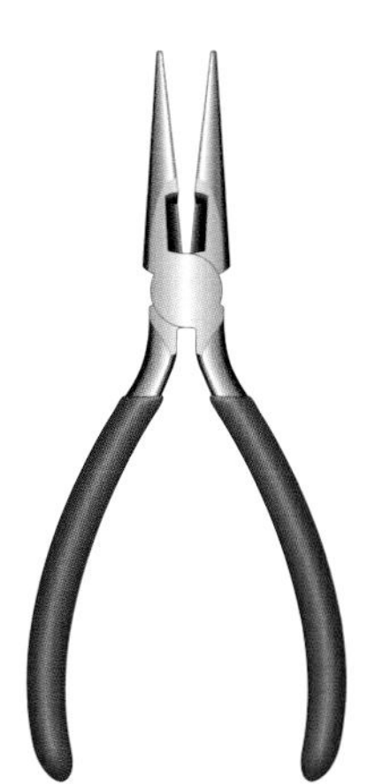

lineman's pliers
alicates[M] de electricista[M]

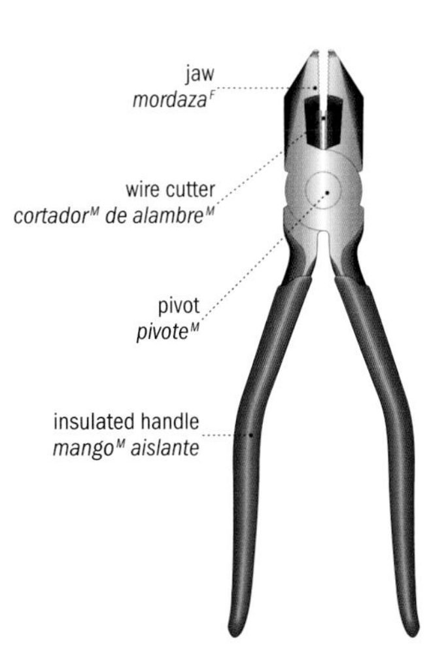

soldering and welding tools

herramientas[F] de soldadura[F]

soldering gun
pistola[F] para soldar

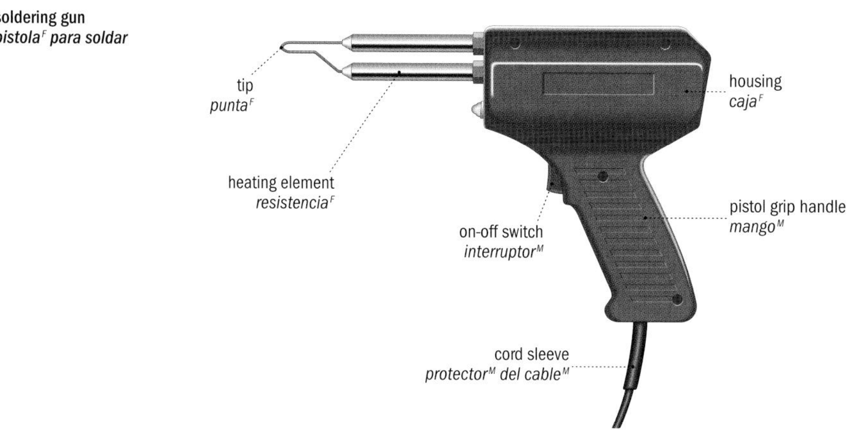

striker
encendedor[M]

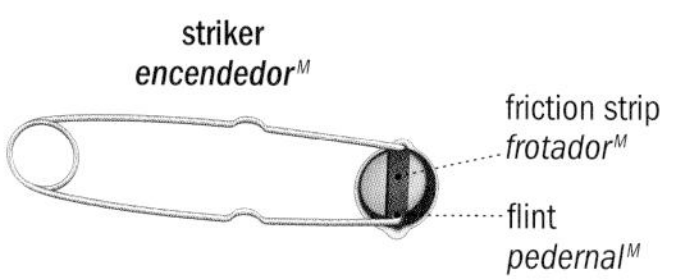

solder
estaño[M] de soldar

tip cleaners
limpiador[M] de boquillas[F]

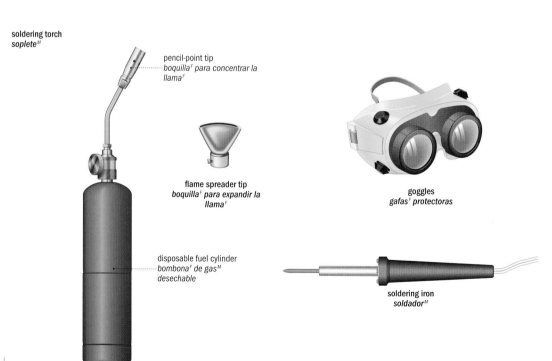

soldering torch
soplete[M]

pencil-point tip
boquilla[F] para concentrar la llama[F]

disposable fuel cylinder
bombona[F] de gas[M] desechable

flame spreader tip
boquilla[F] para expandir la llama[F]

goggles
gafas[F] protectoras

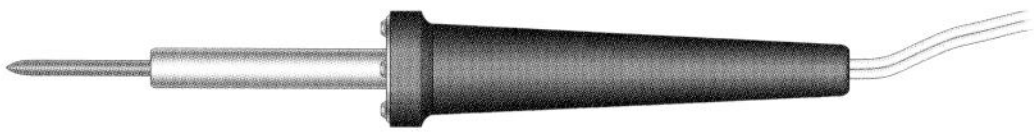

soldering iron
soldador[M]

painting

mantenimiento[M] de pinturas[F]

paint roller
rodillo[M] de pintor[M]

handle
mango[M]
roller frame
armazón[M]
roller cover
rodillo[M]

tray
bandeja[F] de pintura[F]

heat gun
pistola[F] de calor[M]

nozzle
boquilla[F]
switch
interruptor[M]

scraper
rasqueta[F]

knurled bolt
tornillo[M]
handle
mango[M]
blade
hoja[F]

brush
brocha[F]

handle
mango[M]
ferrule
collar[M]
bristles
cerdas[F]

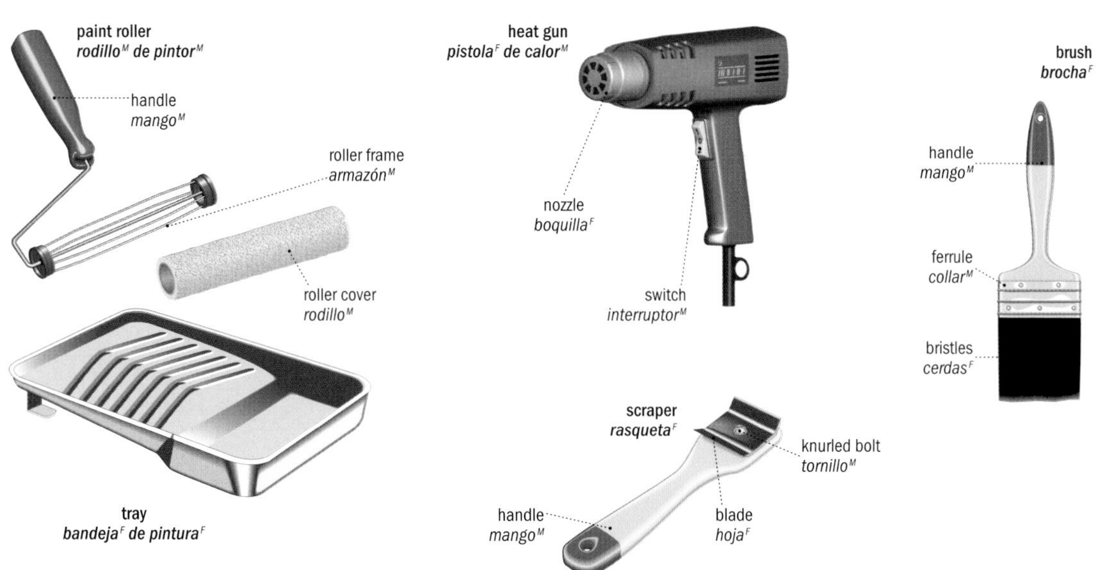

ladders and stepladders

escaleras[F] de mano[F]

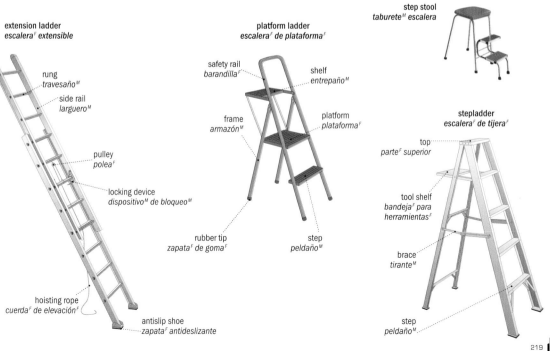

extension ladder
escalera[F] extensible

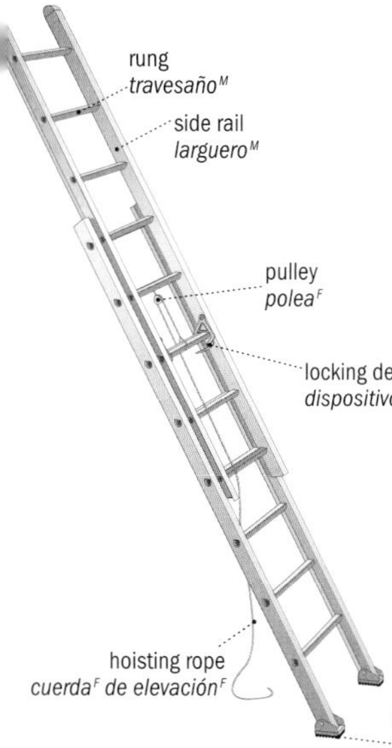

rung
travesaño[M]
side rail
larguero[M]
pulley
polea[F]
locking device
dispositivo[M] de bloqueo[M]
hoisting rope
cuerda[F] de elevación[F]
antislip shoe
zapata[F] antideslizante

platform ladder
escalera[F] de plataforma[F]

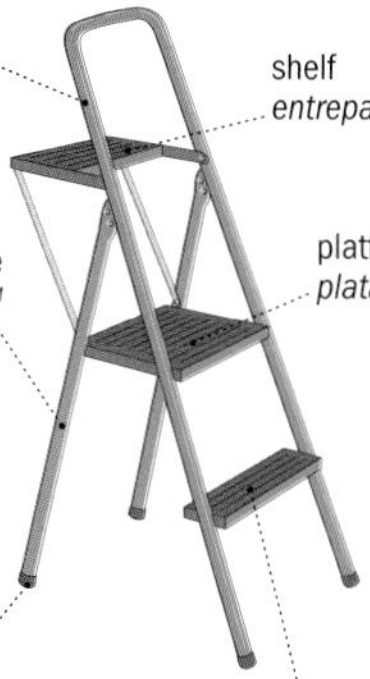

safety rail
barandilla[F]
shelf
entrepaño[M]
frame
armazón[M]
platform
plataforma[F]
rubber tip
zapata[F] de goma[F]
step
peldaño[M]

step stool
taburete[M] escalera

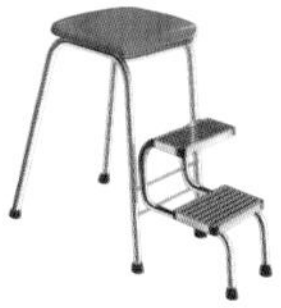

stepladder
escalera[F] de tijera[F]

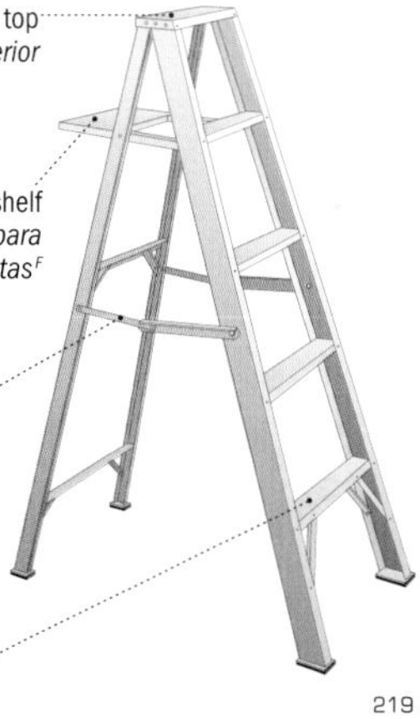

top
parte[F] superior
tool shelf
bandeja[F] para herramientas[F]
brace
tirante[M]
step
peldaño[M]

carpentry: nailing tools

carpintería: herramientas^F para clavar

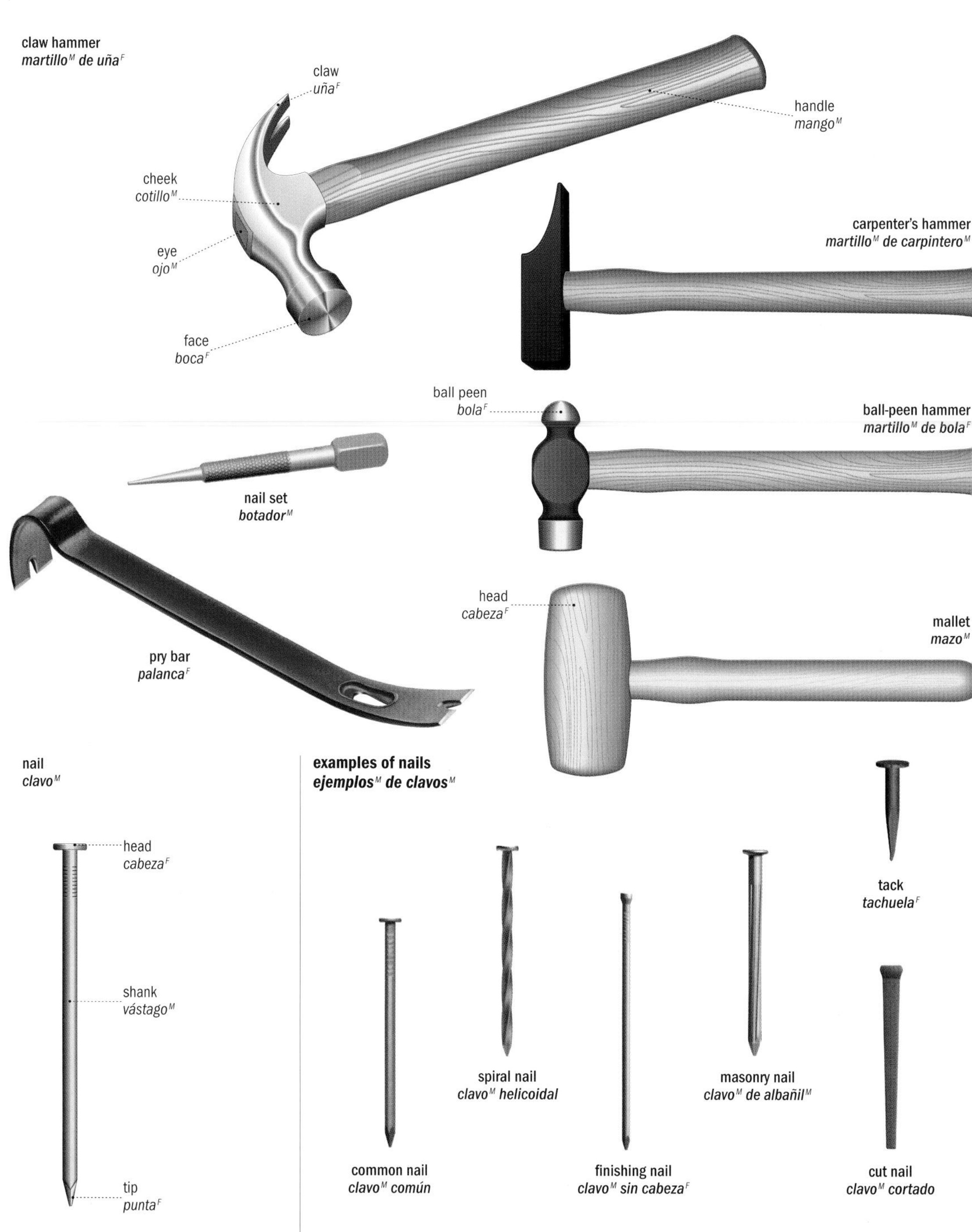

carpentry: screw-driving tools

carpintería[F] : herramientas[F] para atornillar

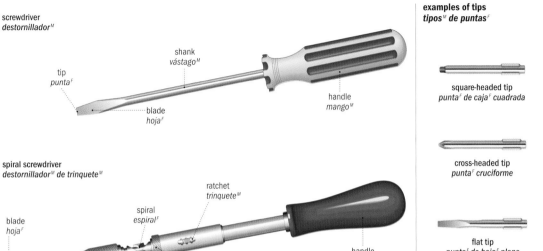

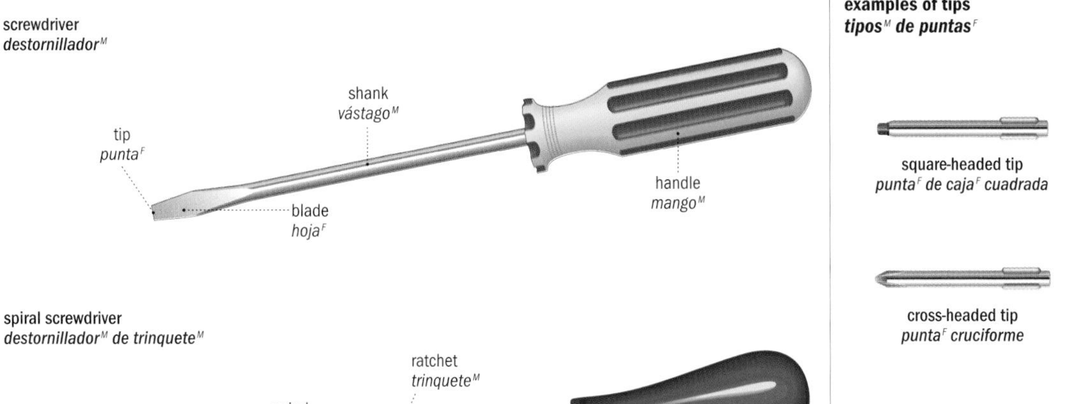
screwdriver
destornillador[M]
shank
vástago[M]
tip
punta[F]
blade
hoja[F]
handle
mango[M]
spiral screwdriver
destornillador[M] de trinquete[M]
ratchet
trinquete[M]
spiral
espiral[F]
blade
hoja[F]
handle
mango[M]
locking ring
anillo[M] de ajuste[M]
jaw
mordaza[F]
chuck
mandril[M]

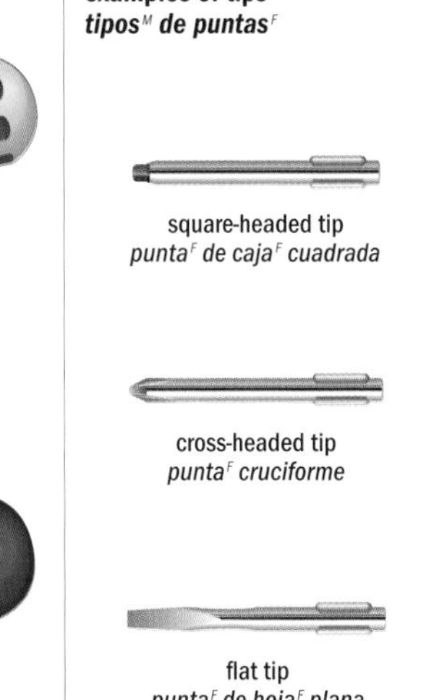
examples of tips
tipos[M] de puntas[F]
square-headed tip
punta[F] de caja[F] cuadrada
cross-headed tip
punta[F] cruciforme
flat tip
punta[F] de hoja[F] plana

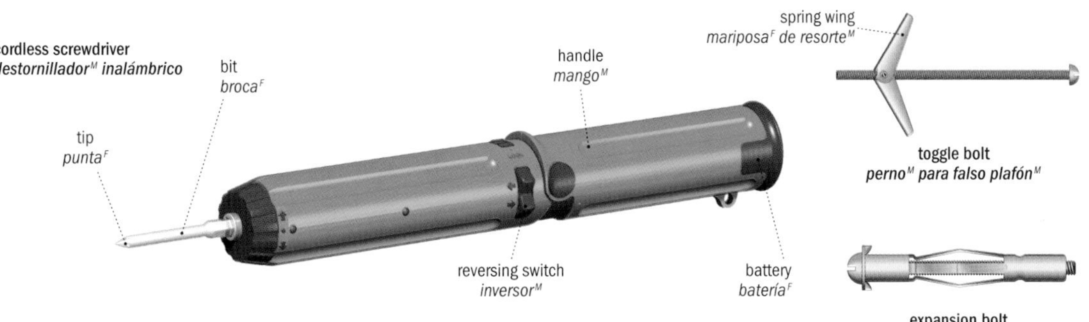
cordless screwdriver
destornillador[M] inalámbrico
bit
broca[F]
tip
punta[F]
handle
mango[M]
reversing switch
inversor[M]
battery
batería[F]
spring wing
mariposa[F] de resorte[M]
toggle bolt
perno[M] para falso plafón[M]
expansion bolt
perno[M] de expansión[F]

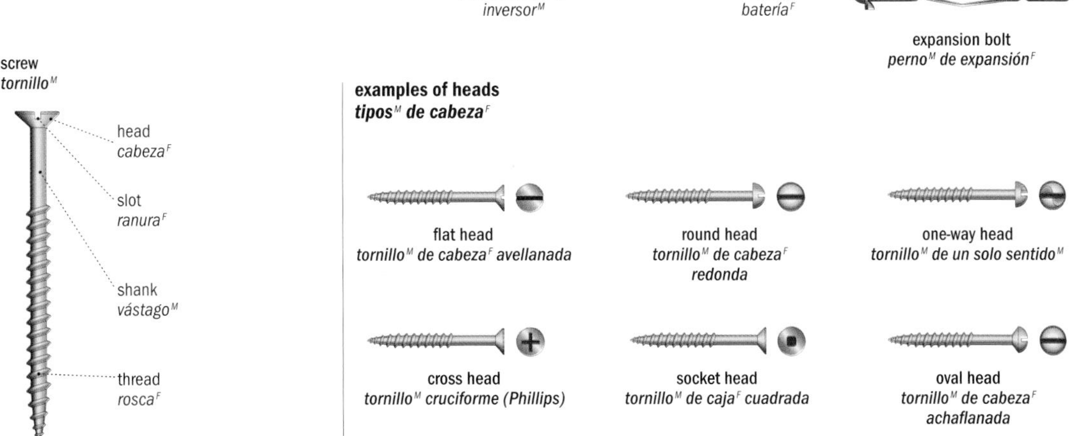
screw
tornillo[M]
head
cabeza[F]
slot
ranura[F]
shank
vástago[M]
thread
rosca[F]
examples of heads
tipos[M] de cabeza[F]
flat head
tornillo[M] de cabeza[F] avellanada
round head
tornillo[M] de cabeza[F] redonda
one-way head
tornillo[M] de un solo sentido[M]
cross head
tornillo[M] cruciforme (Phillips)
socket head
tornillo[M] de caja[F] cuadrada
oval head
tornillo[M] de cabeza[F] achaflanada

carpentry: gripping and tightening tools

carpintería^F : herramientas^F para apretar

pliers
***alicates**^M*

slip joint pliers
pinzas**^F **universales

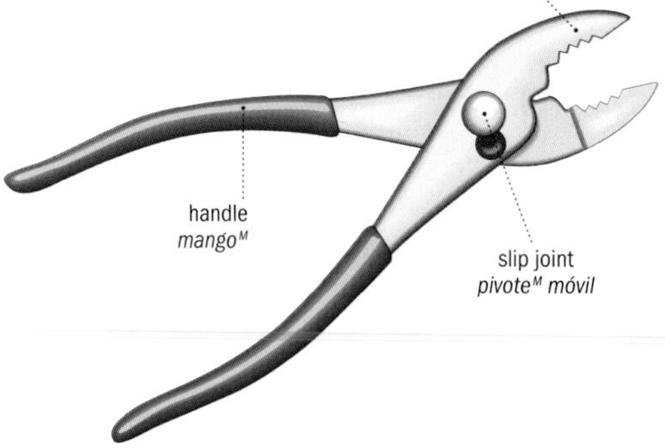

curved jaw
mordaza^F curva

handle
mango^M

slip joint
pivote^M móvil

rib joint pliers
***alicates**^M **pico**^M **de loro**^M*

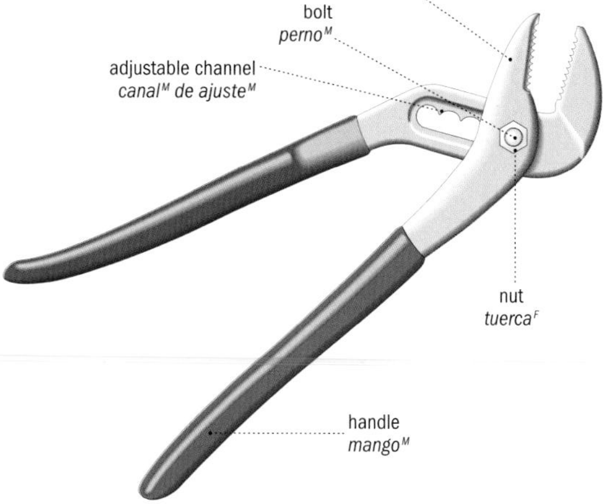

straight jaw
mordaza^F recta

bolt
perno^M

adjustable channel
canal^M de ajuste^M

nut
tuerca^F

handle
mango^M

locking pliers
***alicates**^M **de presión**^F*

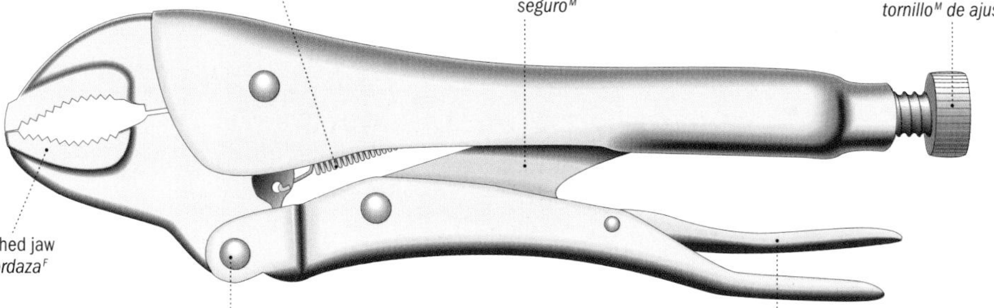

spring
resorte^M

lever
seguro^M

adjusting screw
tornillo^M de ajuste^M

toothed jaw
mordaza^F

rivet
remache^M

release lever
liberador^M del seguro^M

washers
***arandelas**^F*

flat washer
arandela**^F **plana

lock washer
***arandela**^F **de presión**^F*

external tooth lock washer
arandela**^F **de presión**^F **de dientes**^M **externos

internal tooth lock washer
arandela**^F **de presión**^F **de dientes**^M **internos

wrenches
llaves^{F}

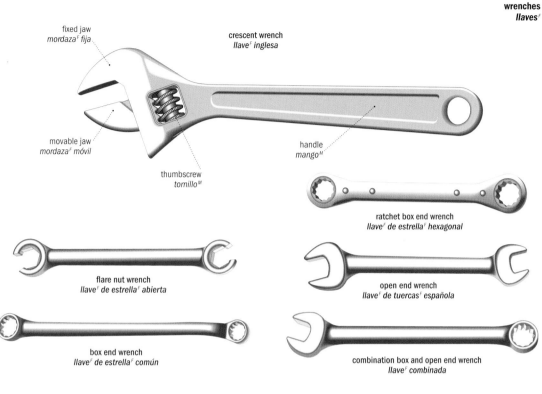

fixed jaw
mordaza^{F} fija

crescent wrench
llave^{F} inglesa

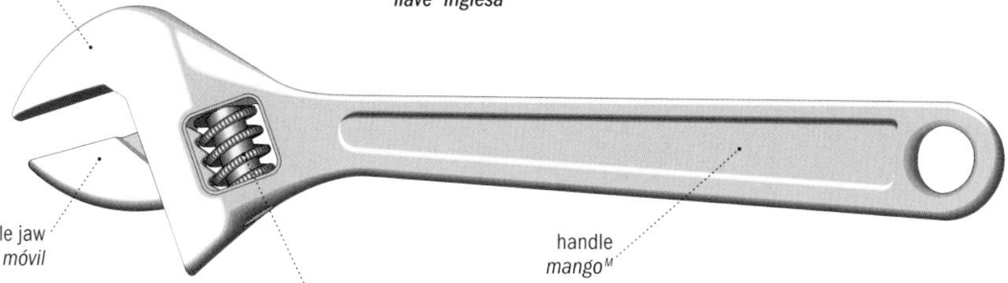

movable jaw
mordaza^{F} móvil

handle
mango^{M}

thumbscrew
tornillo^{M}

ratchet box end wrench
llave^{F} de estrella^{F} hexagonal

flare nut wrench
llave^{F} de estrella^{F} abierta

open end wrench
llave^{F} de tuercas^{F} española

box end wrench
llave^{F} de estrella^{F} común

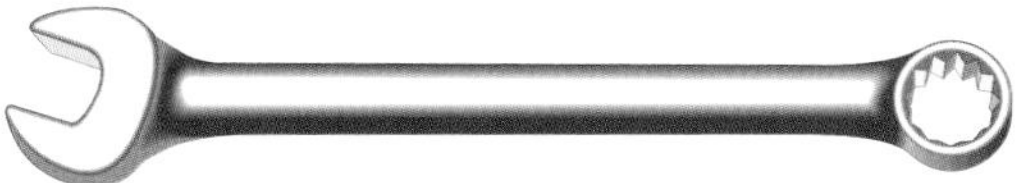

combination box and open end wrench
llave^{F} combinada

ratchet socket wrench
llave^{F} de carraca^{F}

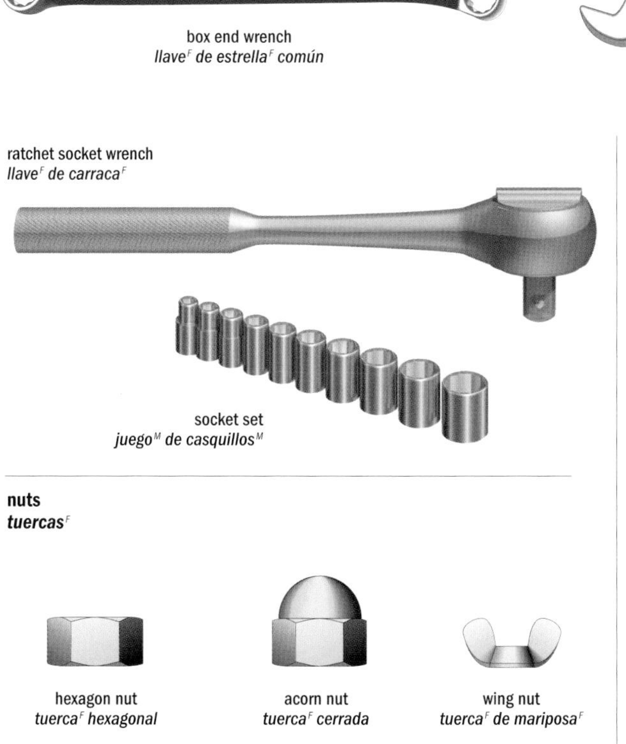

socket set
juego^{M} de casquillos^{M}

bolts
pernos^{M}

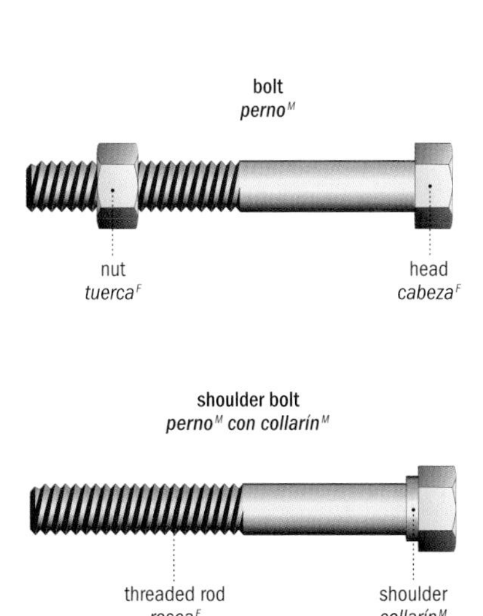

bolt
perno^{M}

nut
tuerca^{F}

head
cabeza^{F}

shoulder bolt
perno^{M} con collarín^{M}

threaded rod
rosca^{F}

shoulder
collarín^{M}

nuts
tuercas^{F}

hexagon nut
tuerca^{F} hexagonal

acorn nut
tuerca^{F} cerrada

wing nut
tuerca^{F} de mariposa^{F}

carpentry: gripping and tightening tools

C-clamp
prensa^M en C

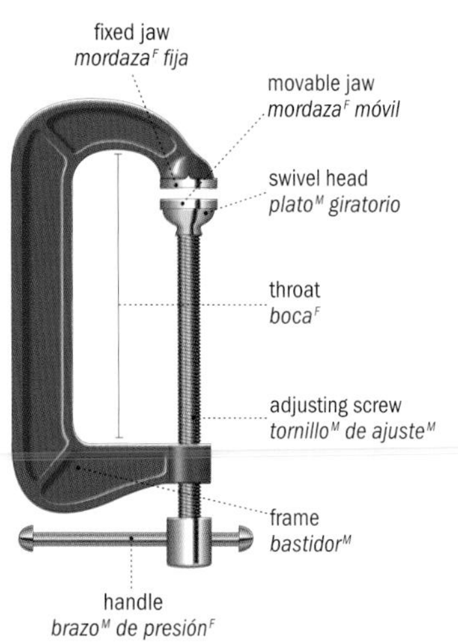

vise
torno^M de banco^M

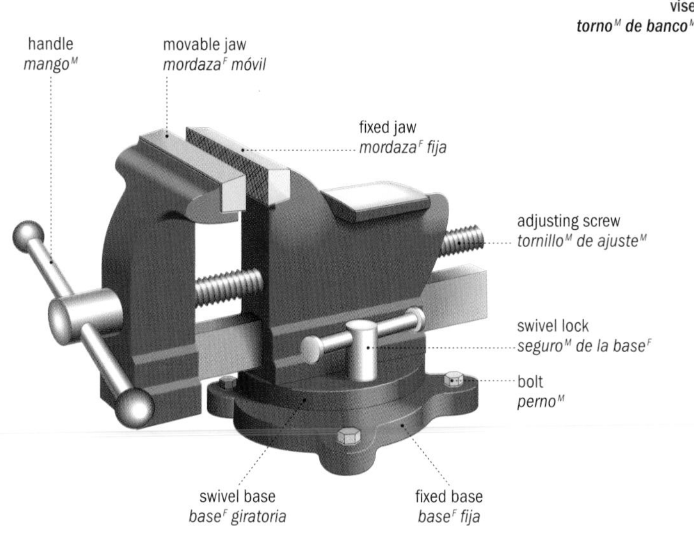

pipe clamp
sargento^M

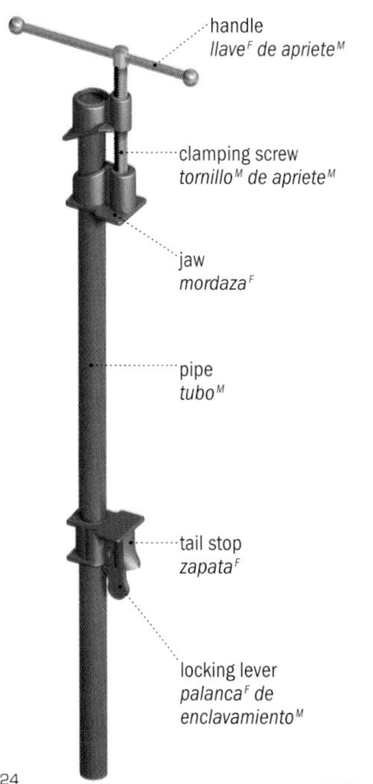

work bench and vise
banco^M de trabajo^M

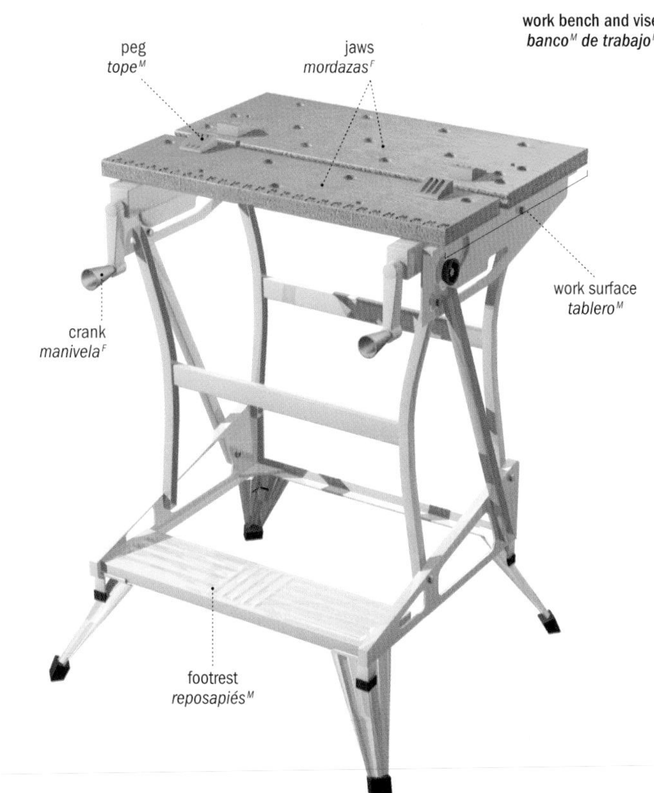

carpentry: measuring and marking tools

carpintería^{F} : instrumentos^{M} de trazado^{M} y de medición^{F}

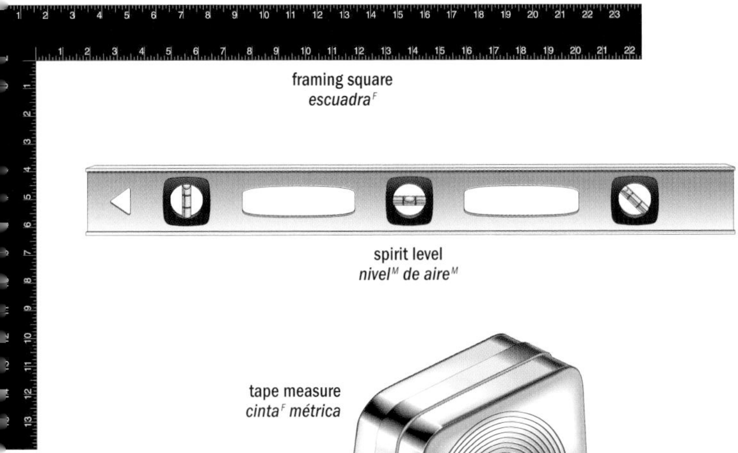

framing square
escuadra^{F}

spirit level
nivel^{M} de aire^{M}

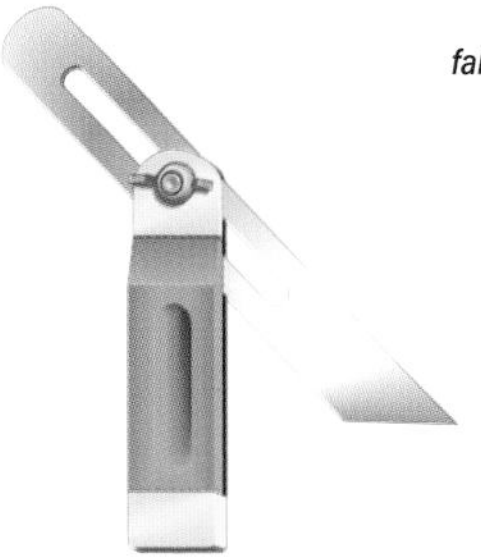

bevel square
falsa escuadra^{F}

tape measure
cinta^{F} métrica

tape lock
botón^{M} de bloqueo^{M}
scale
escala^{F}
hook
gancho^{M}
tape
cinta^{F}
case
estuche^{M}

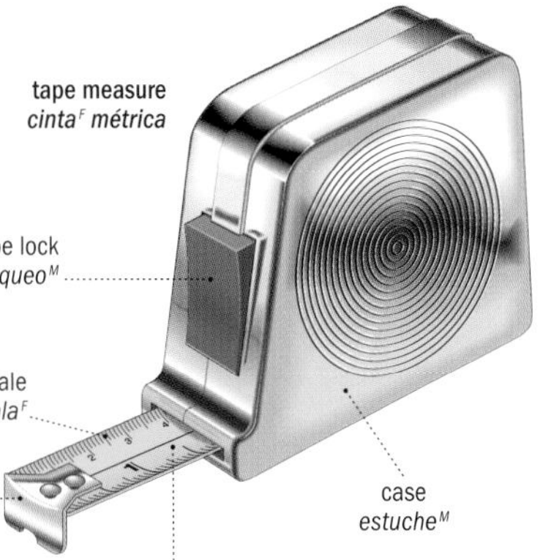

chalk line
cordón^{M} de trazar

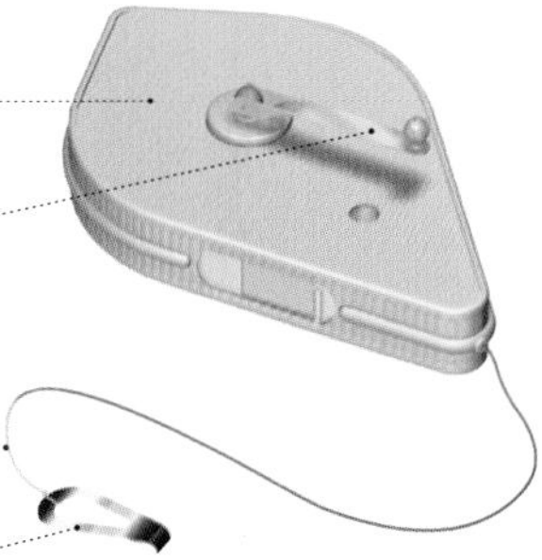

case
caja^{F}
crank handle
manivela^{F} de enrollado^{M}
line
cordón^{M}
hook
gancho^{M}

DO-IT-YOURSELF AND GARDENING

carpentry: miscellaneous material

carpintería^{F} : materiales^{M} varios

tool box
caja^{F} de herramientas^{F}

handle
asa^{F}
lid
tapa^{F}
tray
bandeja^{F}

tool belt
cinturón^{M} de herramientas^{F}

belt
cinturón^{M} de herramientas^{M}
hammer loop
porta martillo^{M}
pocket
bolsillo^{M}

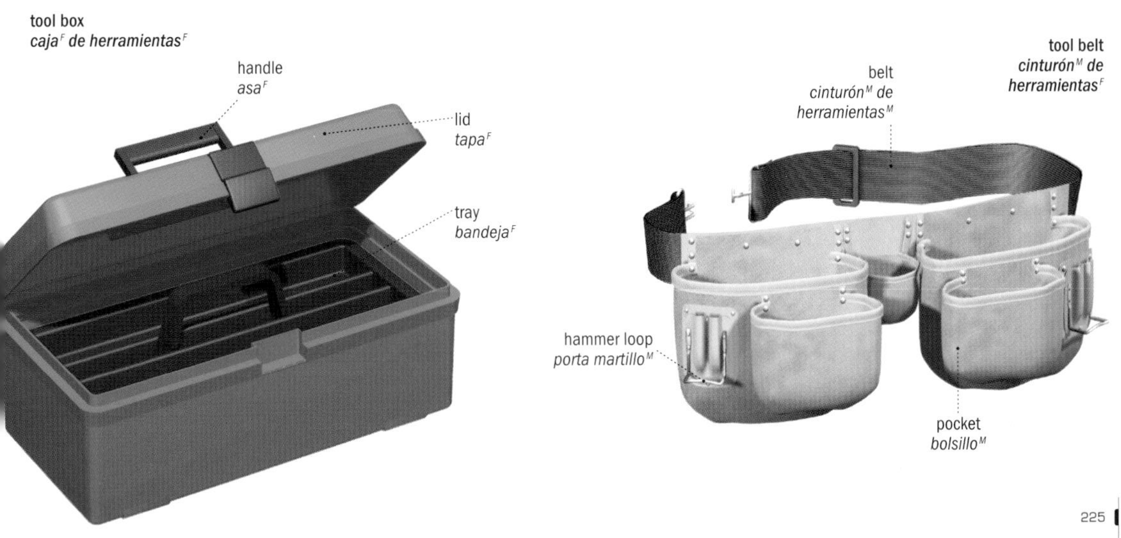

carpentry: sawing tools

carpintería[F] : herramientas[F] para serrar

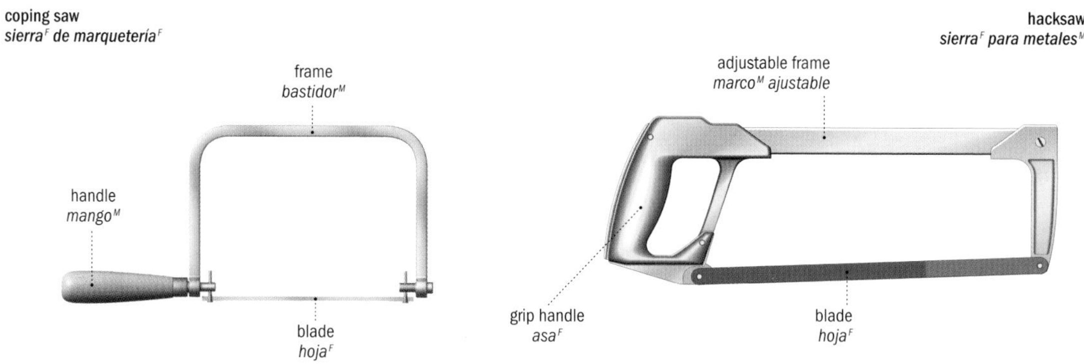

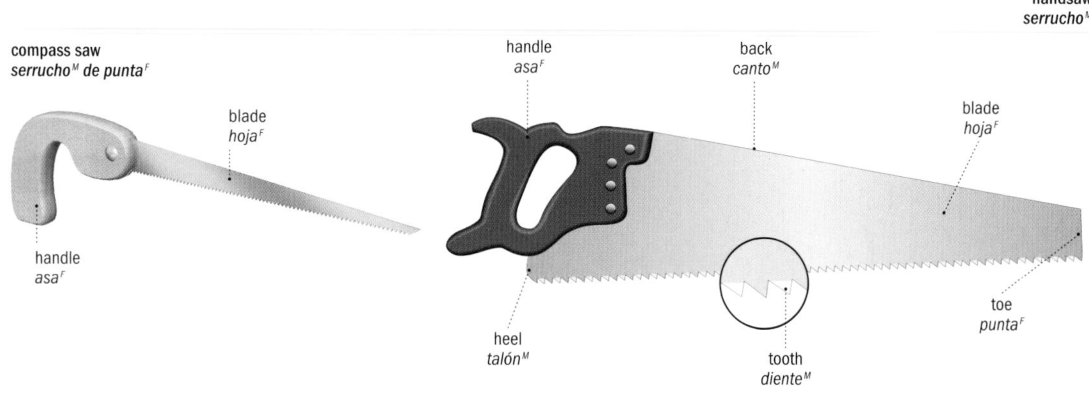

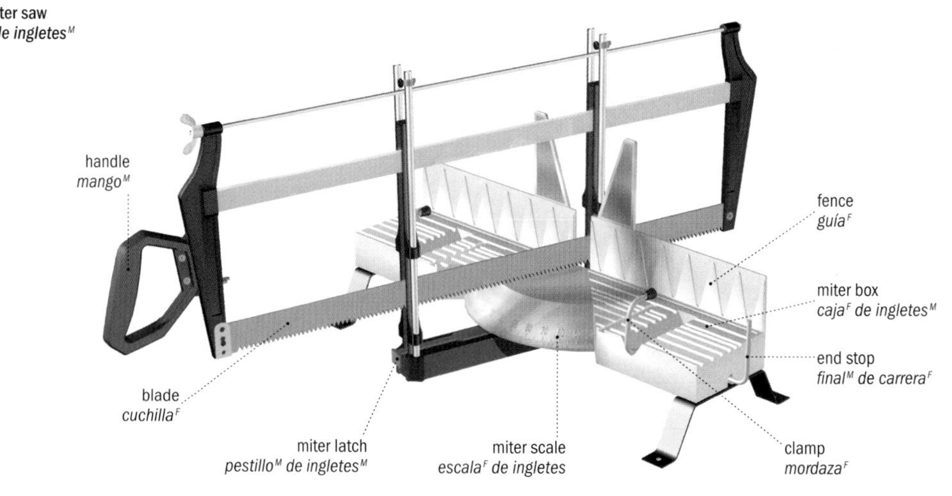

jig saw
sierra[F] de calar

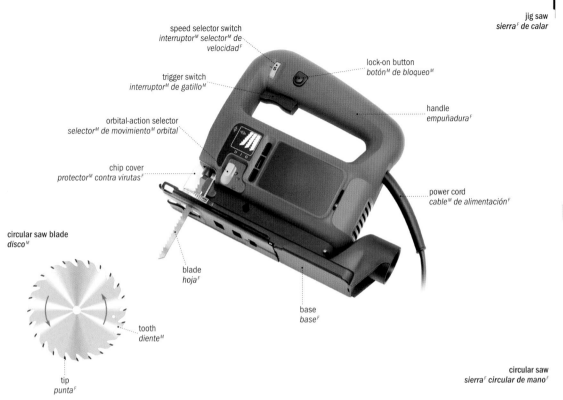

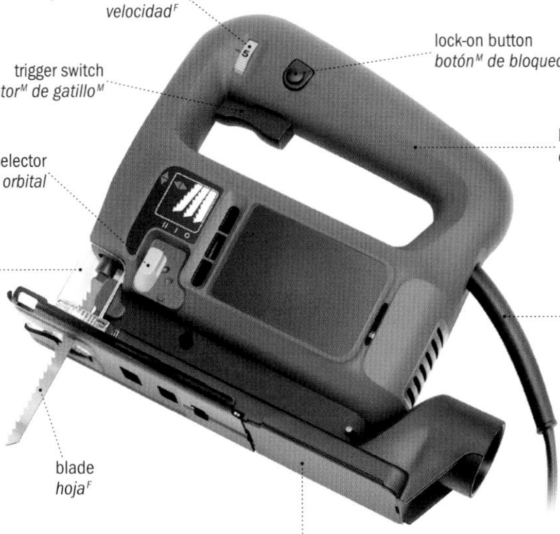

speed selector switch
interruptor[M] selector[M] de velocidad[F]
lock-on button
botón[M] de bloqueo[M]
trigger switch
interruptor[M] de gatillo[M]
handle
empuñadura[F]
orbital-action selector
selector[M] de movimiento[M] orbital
chip cover
protector[M] contra virutas[F]
power cord
cable[M] de alimentación[F]
blade
hoja[F]
base
base[F]

circular saw blade
disco[M]

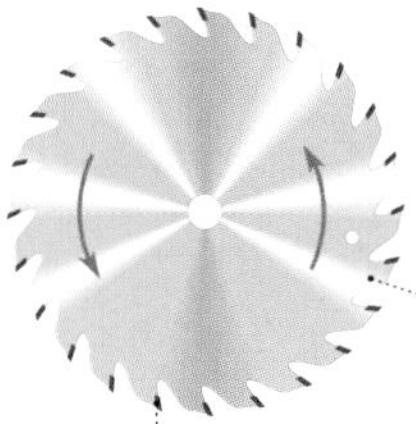

tooth
diente[M]
tip
punta[F]

circular saw
sierra[F] circular de mano[F]

handle
asa[F]
trigger switch
interruptor[M] de gatillo[M]
upper blade guard
guarda[F] fija del disco[M]
height adjustment scale
escala[F] de altura[F]
blade
disco[M]
motor
motor[M]
lower guard retracting lever
palanca[F] retráctil de la guarda[F] móvil
blade tilting mechanism
escala[F] de inclinación[F]
blade locking bolt
tornillo[M] de sujeción[F]
knob handle
perilla[F]
lower blade guard
guarda[F] móvil del disco[M]
blade tilting lock
seguro[M] de inclinación[F] del disco[M]
rip fence
guía[F] de corte[M]
base plate
soporte[M]

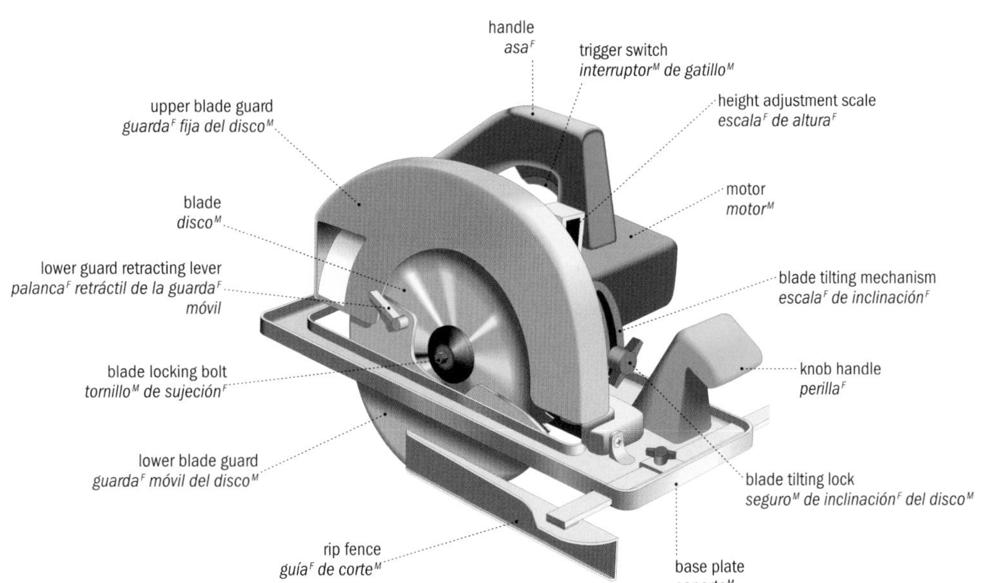

carpentry: drilling tools

carpinteríaᶠ : herramientasᶠ percutoras

cordless drill
taladroᴹ percutor inalámbrico

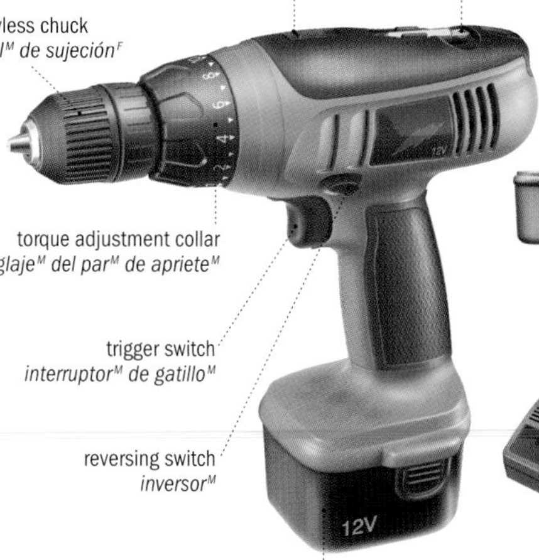

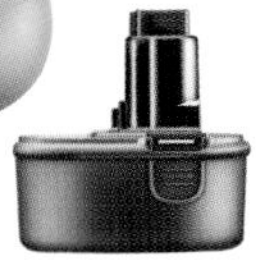

speed selector switch
selectorᴹ de velocidadᶠ
screwdriver bit
brocaᶠ de atornillado
keyless chuck
mandrilᴹ de sujeciónᶠ
torque adjustment collar
anilloᴹ de reglajeᴹ del parᴹ de aprieteᴹ
trigger switch
interruptorᴹ de gatilloᴹ
reversing switch
inversorᴹ
12V
battery pack
bateríaᶠ

battery pack
bateríaᶠ

charger
cargadorᴹ

chuck key
llaveᶠ del mandrilᴹ

electric drill
taladroᴹ eléctrico

name plate
placaᶠ de especificacionesᶠ
warning plate
placaᶠ de advertenciasᶠ
switch lock
seguroᴹ del interruptorᴹ
housing
cárterᴹ
chuck
mandrilᴹ
trigger switch
interruptorᴹ de gatilloᴹ
pistol grip handle
mangoᴹ
jaw
mordazaᶠ
cable sleeve
protectorᴹ del cableᴹ
auxiliary handle
mangoᴹ auxiliar
plug
enchufeᴹ
cable
cableᴹ

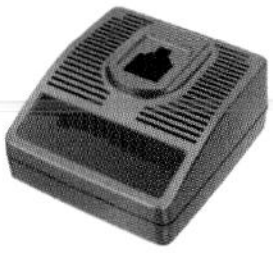

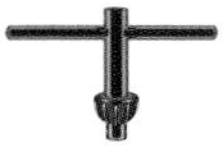

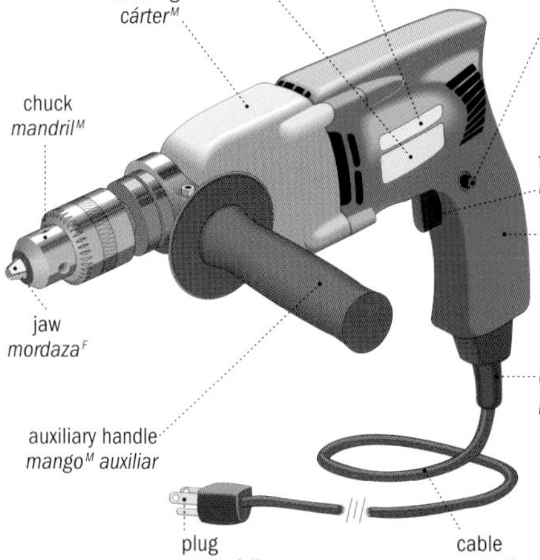

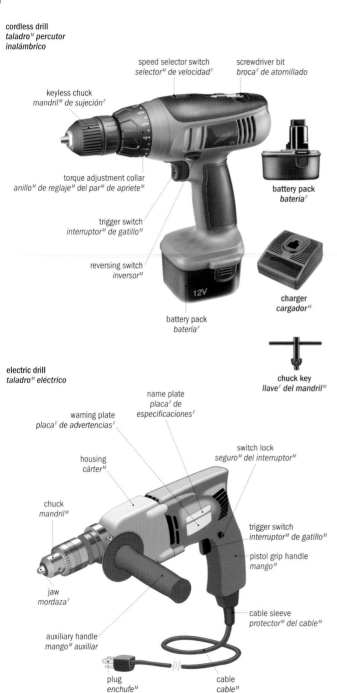

examples of bits and drills
ejemplosᴹ de brocasᶠ y barrenasᶠ

twist bit
brocaᶠ helicoidal

shank
talónᴹ
flute
canalᴹ
body
cuerpoᴹ
fluted land
lomoᴹ con canalᴹ
land
bordeᴹ del lomoᴹ
lead screw
bordeᴹ de la puntaᶠ

solid center auger bit
brocaᶠ helicoidal central

shank
talónᴹ
twist
torsiónᶠ
spur
espolónᴹ
lead screw
tornilloᴹ guía

masonry drill
barrenaᶠ de muroᴹ

twist drill
brocaᶠ helicoidal

spade bit
brocaᶠ de palaᶠ

double-twist auger bit
brocaᶠ salomónica de canalᴹ angosto

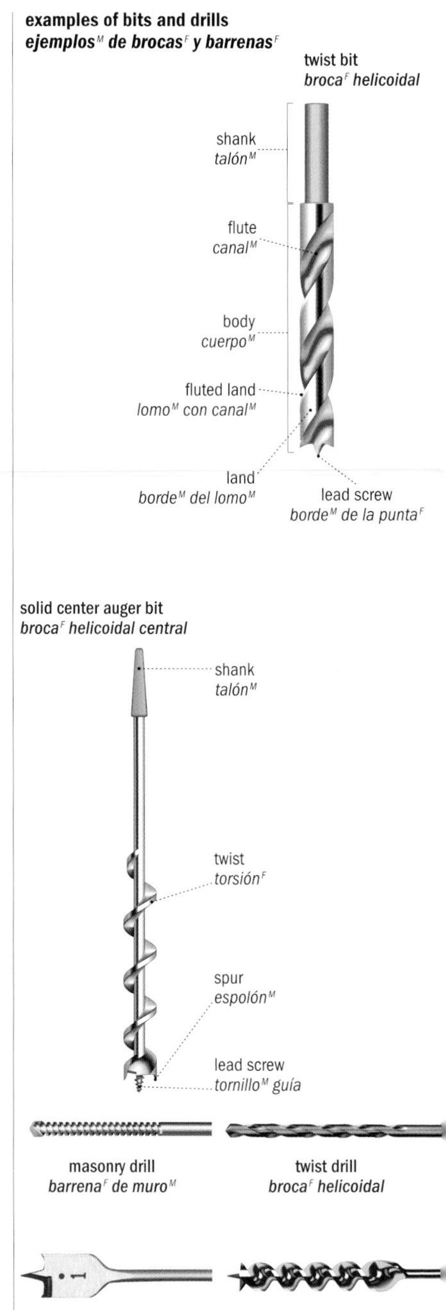

carpentry: shaping tools

carpintería[F] : herramientas[F] de perfilado[M]

plane
***cepillo*[M]**

lateral-adjustment lever
nivelador[M]
wedge lever
palanca[F] *de la cuña*[F]
handle
empuñadura[F]
lever cap
palanca[F] *de bloqueo*[M]
depth-of-cut adjustment knob
calibre[M] *de ajuste*[M] *de profundidad*[F] *de corte*[M]
knob
pomo[M]
heel
talón[M]
toe
puntera[F]
sole
suela[F]
frog-adjustment screw
tornillo[M] *de ajuste*[M] *de ranilla*[F]
blade
hoja[F]
cap iron
contrahoja[F]

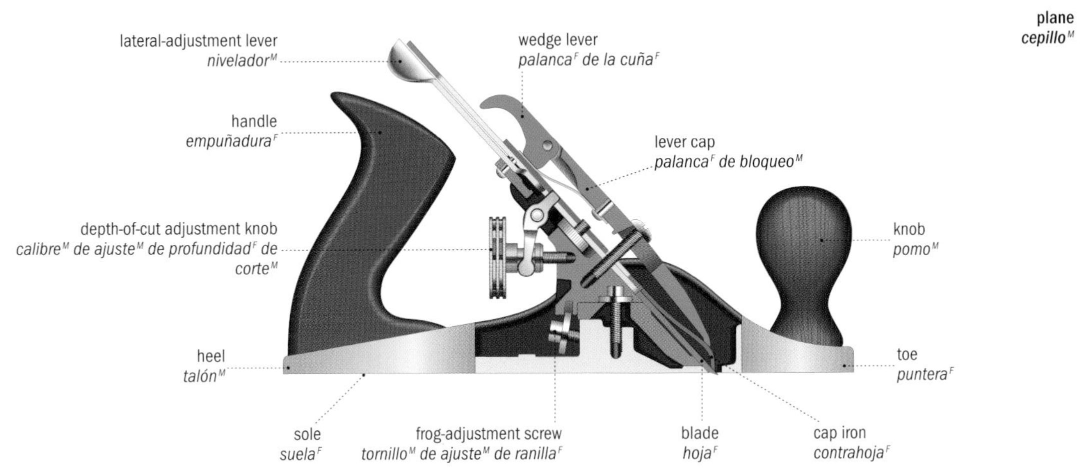

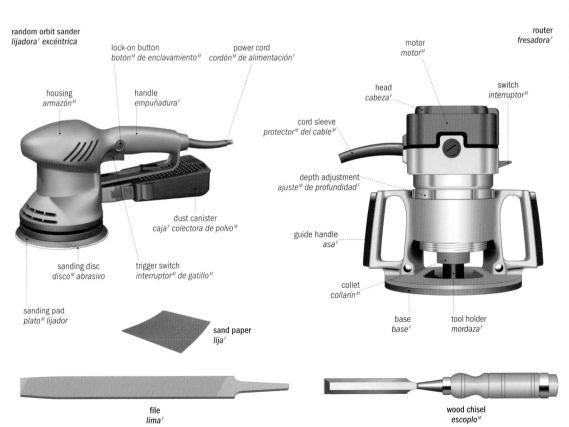

random orbit sander
lijadora*[F] *excéntrica

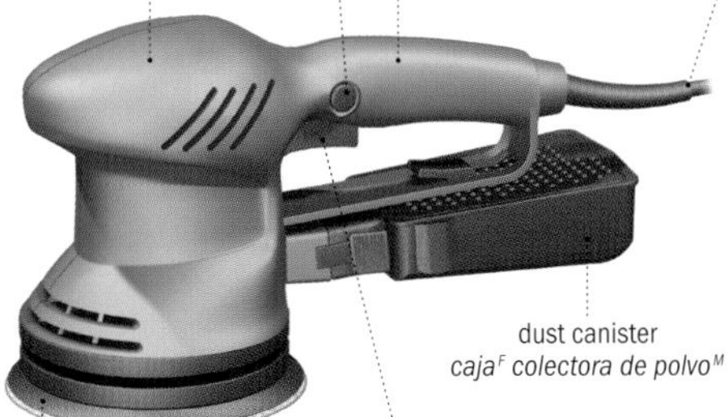

lock-on button
botón[M] *de enclavamiento*[M]
power cord
cordón[M] *de alimentación*[F]
housing
armazón[M]
handle
empuñadura[F]
dust canister
caja[F] *colectora de polvo*[M]
sanding disc
disco[M] *abrasivo*
trigger switch
interruptor[M] *de gatillo*[M]
sanding pad
plato[M] *lijador*

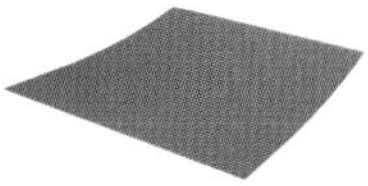

sand paper
***lija*[F]**

router
***fresadora*[F]**

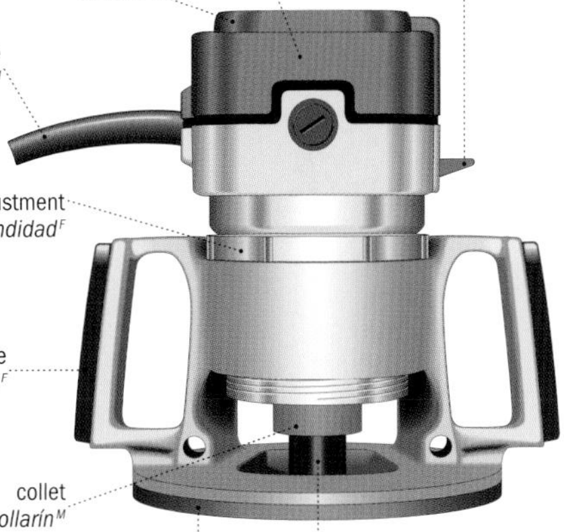

motor
motor[M]
head
cabeza[F]
switch
interruptor[M]
cord sleeve
protector[M] *del cable*[M]
depth adjustment
ajuste[M] *de profundidad*[F]
guide handle
asa[F]
collet
collarín[M]
base
base[F]
tool holder
mordaza[F]

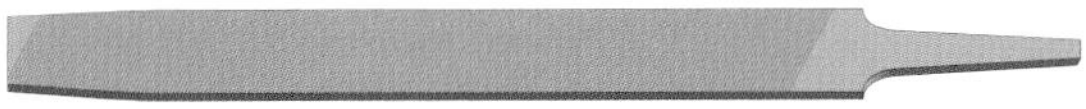

file
***lima*[F]**

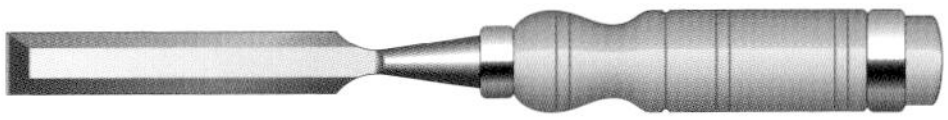

wood chisel
***escoplo*[M]**

pleasure garden

jardín^M

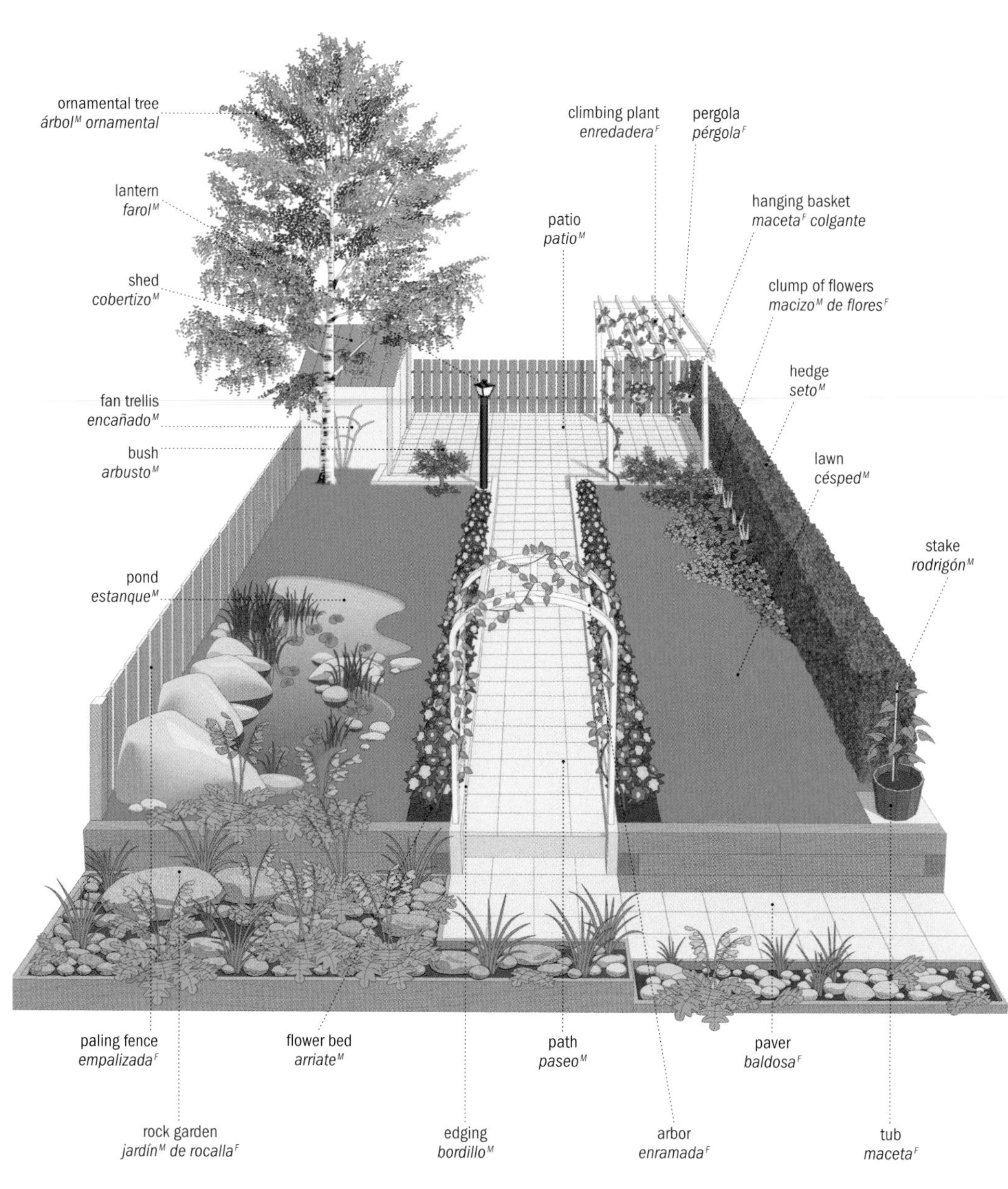
ornamental tree
árbol^M ornamental
lantern
farol^M
shed
cobertizo^M
fan trellis
encañado^M
bush
arbusto^M
pond
estanque^M
climbing plant
enredadera^F
pergola
pérgola^F
patio
patio^M
hanging basket
maceta^F colgante
clump of flowers
macizo^M de flores^F
hedge
seto^M
lawn
césped^M
stake
rodrigón^M
paling fence
empalizada^F
flower bed
arriate^M
path
paseo^M
paver
baldosa^F
rock garden
jardín^M de rocalla^F
edging
bordillo^M
arbor
enramada^F
tub
maceta^F

miscellaneous equipment

equipamiento[M] vario

compost bin
cajón[M] de abono[M] compuesto

wheelbarrow
carretilla[F]

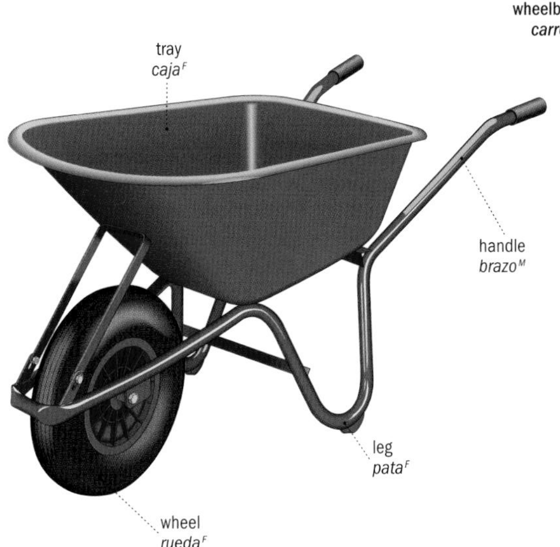

seeding and planting tools

herramientas[F] para sembrar y plantar

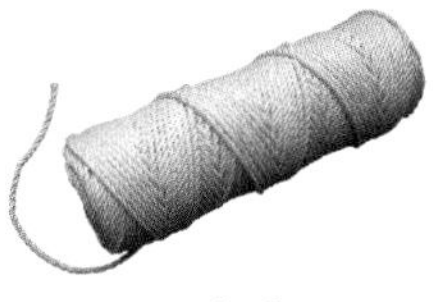

garden line
cuerda[F]

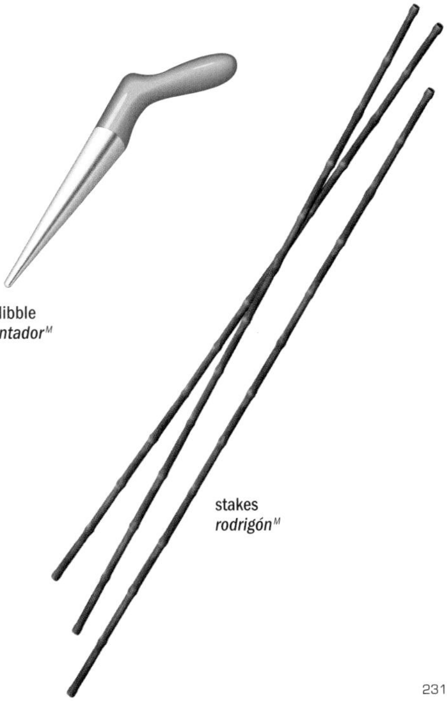

dibble
plantador[M]

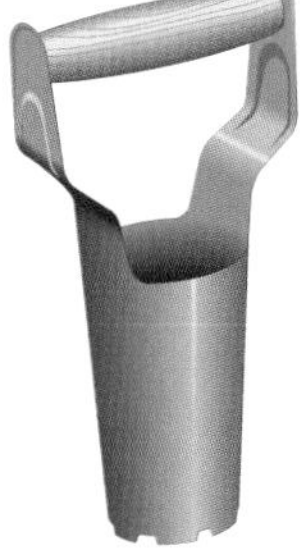

bulb dibble
plantador[M] de bulbos[M]

seeder
sembradora[F] de mano[F]

stakes
rodrigón[M]

hand tools

juego[M] de pequeñas herramientas[F]

small hand cultivator
cultivador[M] de mano[F]

trowel
desplantador[M]

weeder
desyerbador[M]

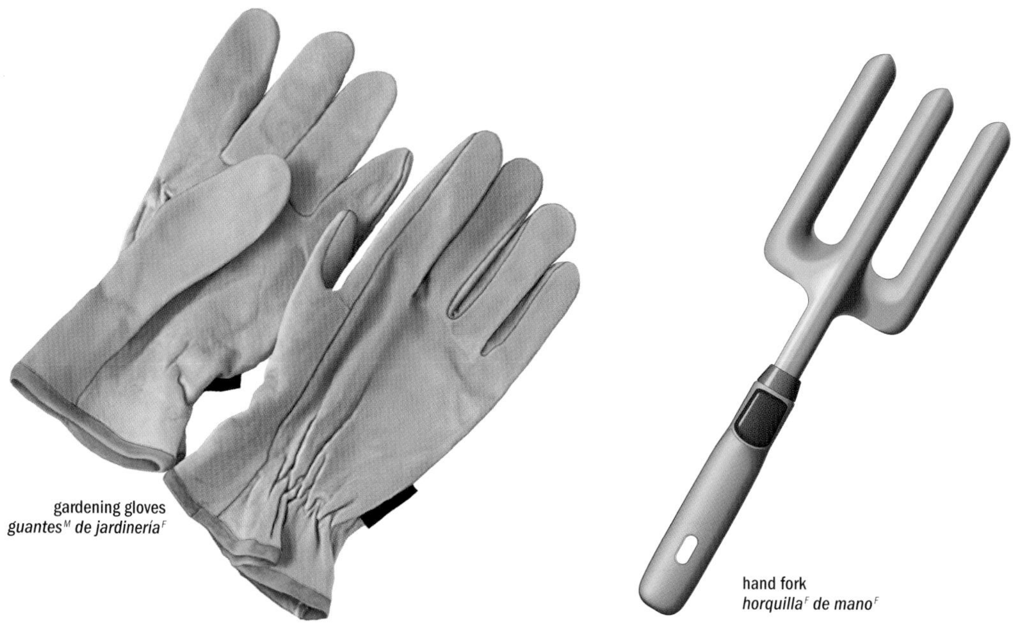

gardening gloves
guantes[M] de jardinería[F]

hand fork
horquilla[F] de mano[F]

tools for loosening the earth

herramientas[F] para remover la tierra[F]

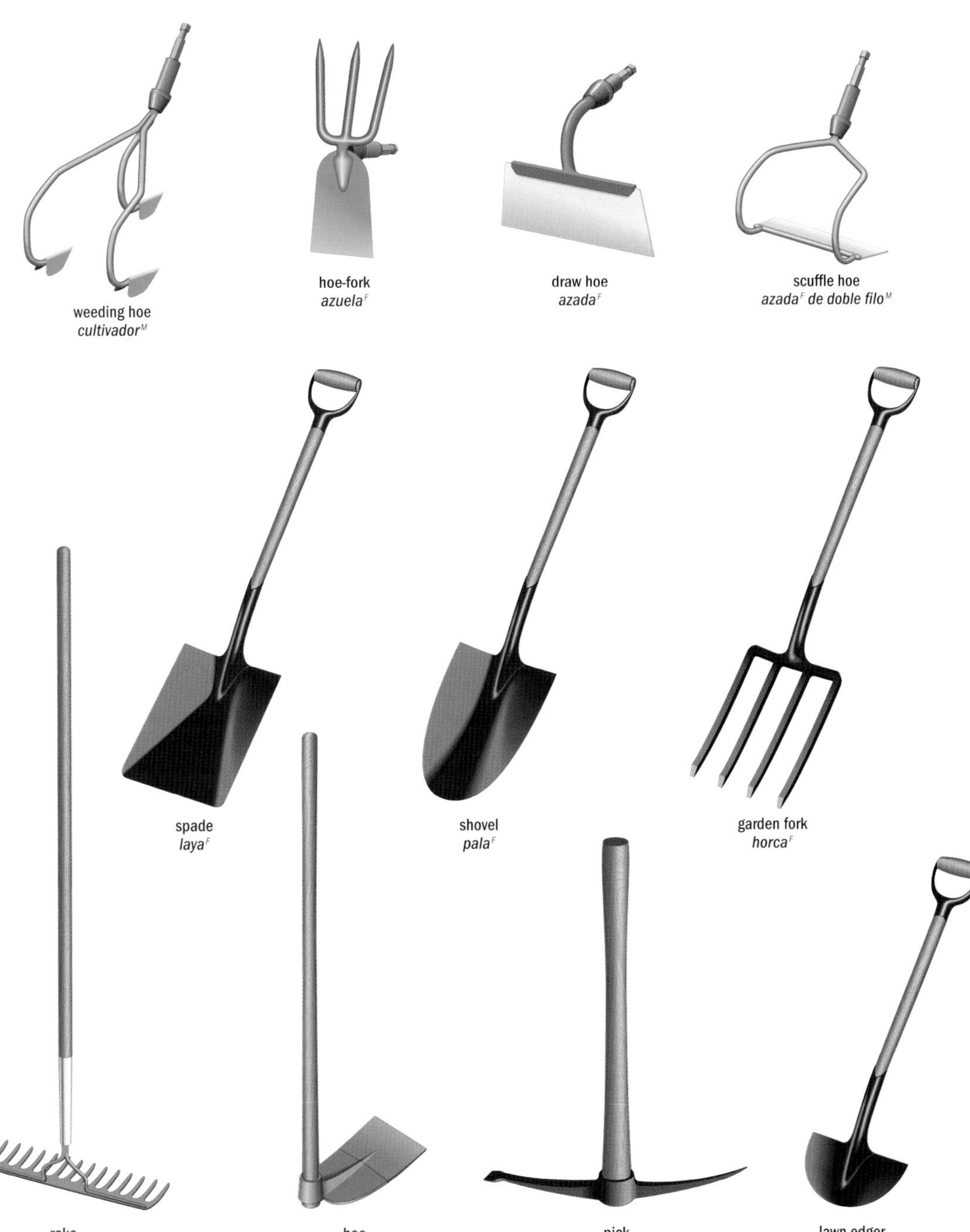

pruning and cutting tools

herramientas[F] para cortar

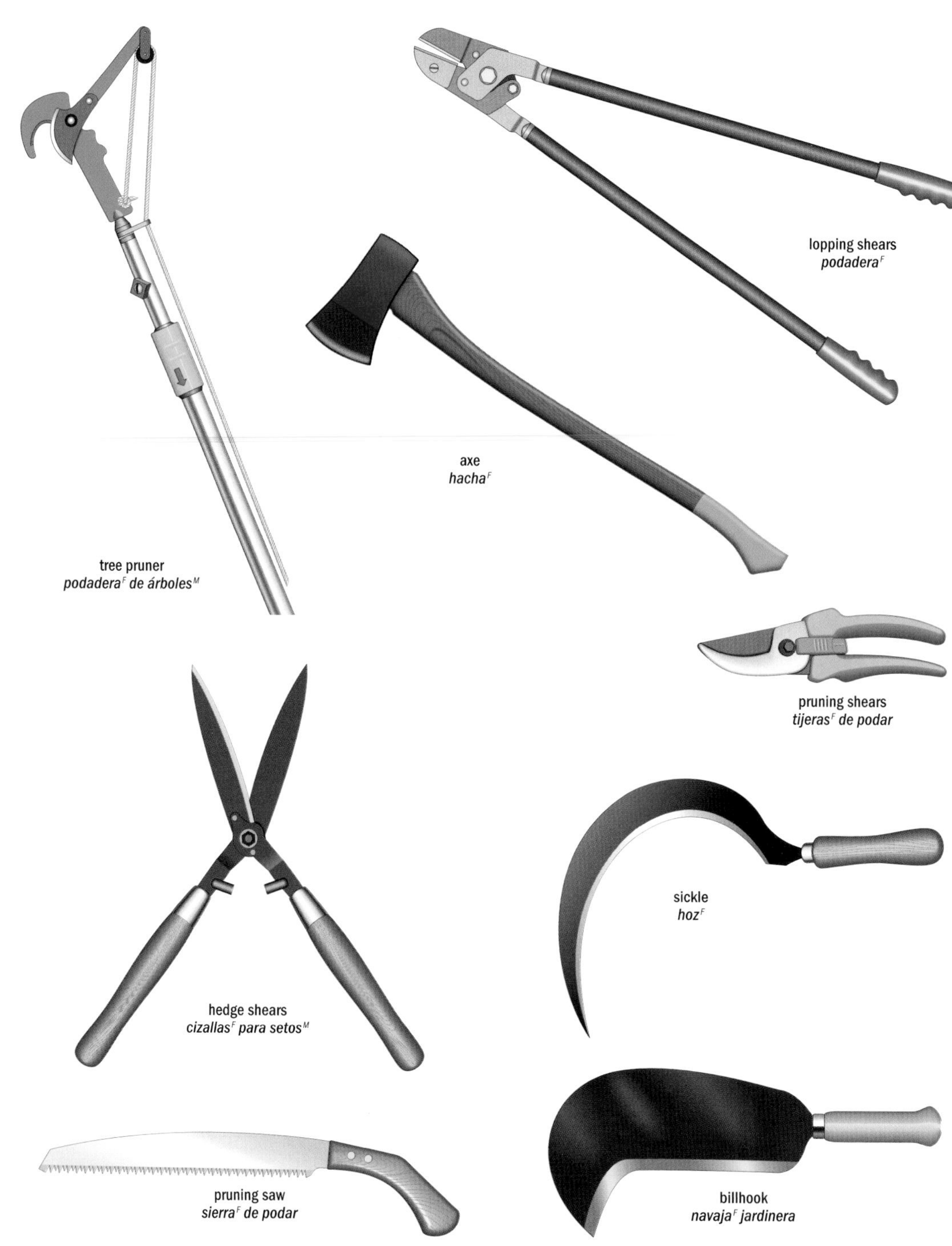

hedge trimmer
cortasetos*[M] *eléctrico

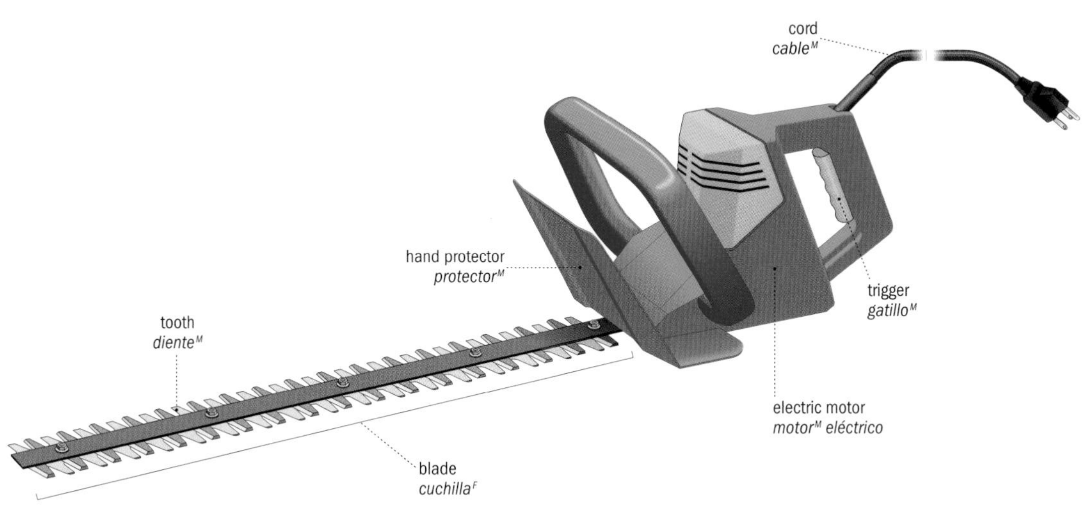

chainsaw
***sierra*[F] *de cadena*[F]**

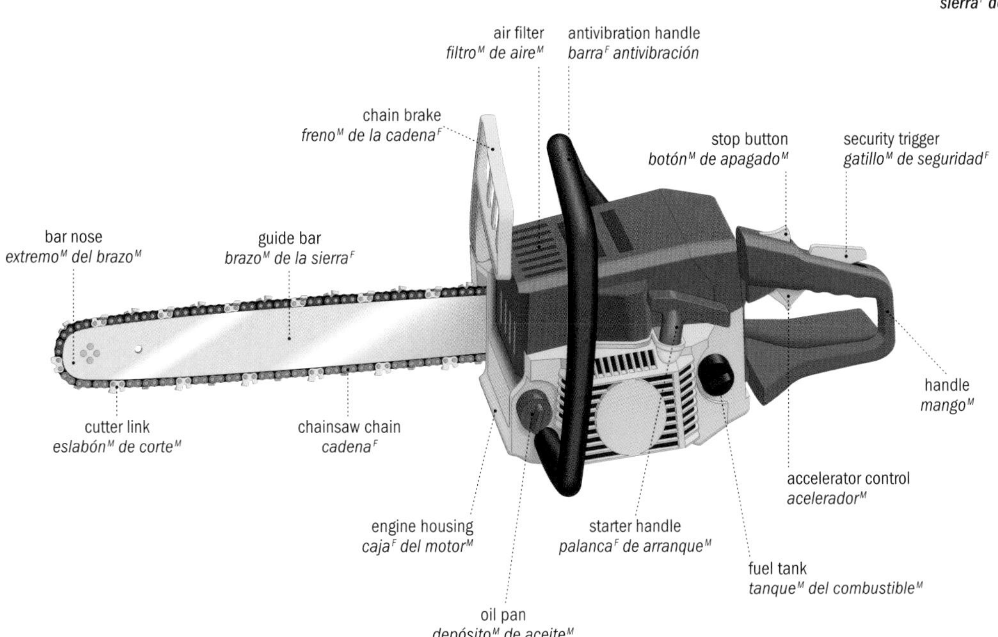

watering tools

herramientas[F] para regar

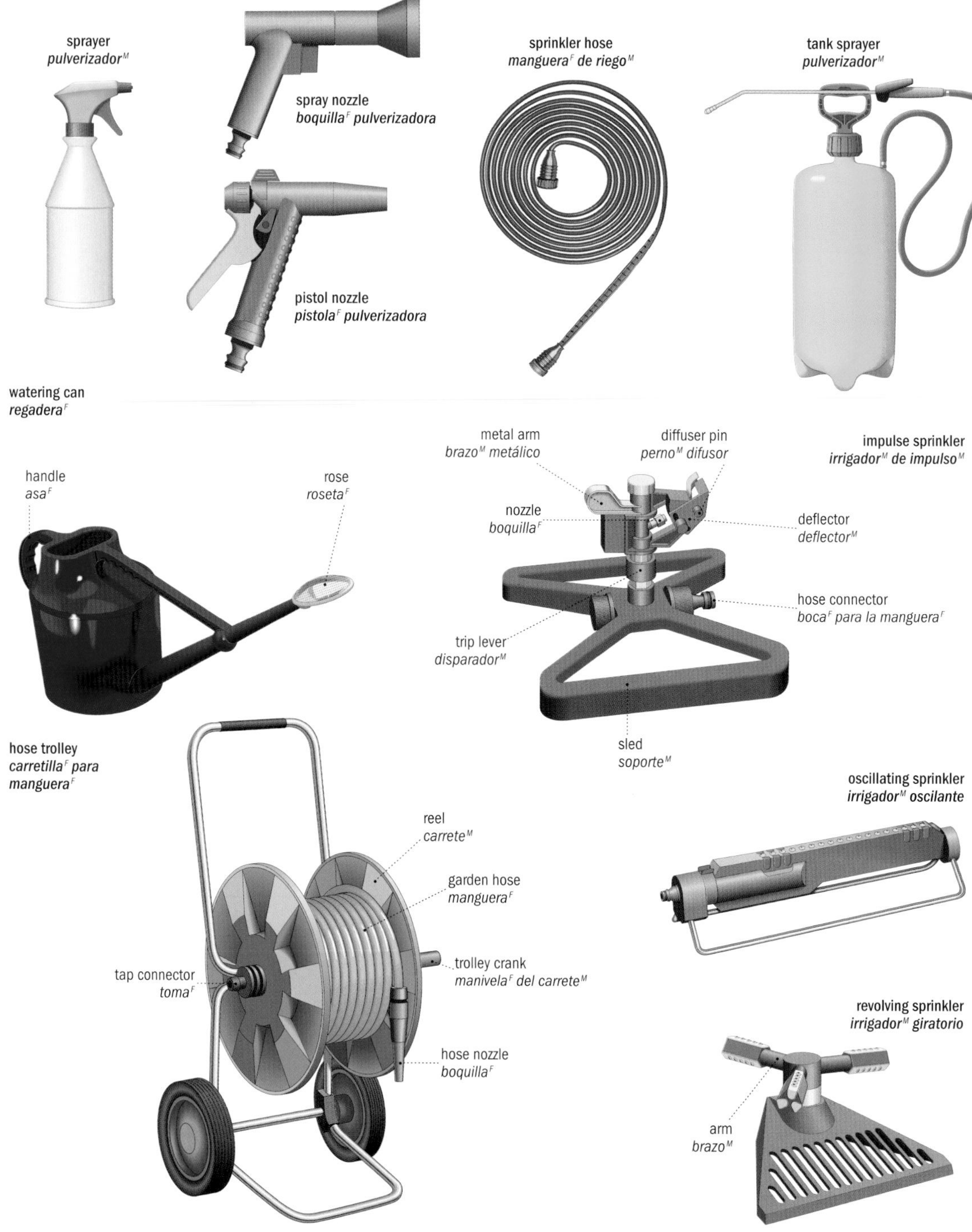
sprayer
pulverizador[M]
spray nozzle
boquilla[F] pulverizadora
pistol nozzle
pistola[F] pulverizadora
sprinkler hose
manguera[F] de riego[M]
tank sprayer
pulverizador[M]
watering can
regadera[F]
handle
asa[F]
rose
roseta[F]
metal arm
brazo[M] metálico
diffuser pin
perno[M] difusor
impulse sprinkler
irrigador[M] de impulso[M]
nozzle
boquilla[F]
deflector
deflector[M]
hose connector
boca[F] para la manguera[F]
trip lever
disparador[M]
sled
soporte[M]
hose trolley
carretilla[F] para manguera[F]
oscillating sprinkler
irrigador[M] oscilante
reel
carrete[M]
garden hose
manguera[F]
trolley crank
manivela[F] del carrete[M]
tap connector
toma[F]
hose nozzle
boquilla[F]
revolving sprinkler
irrigador[M] giratorio
arm
brazo[M]

lawn care

cuidado^M del césped^M

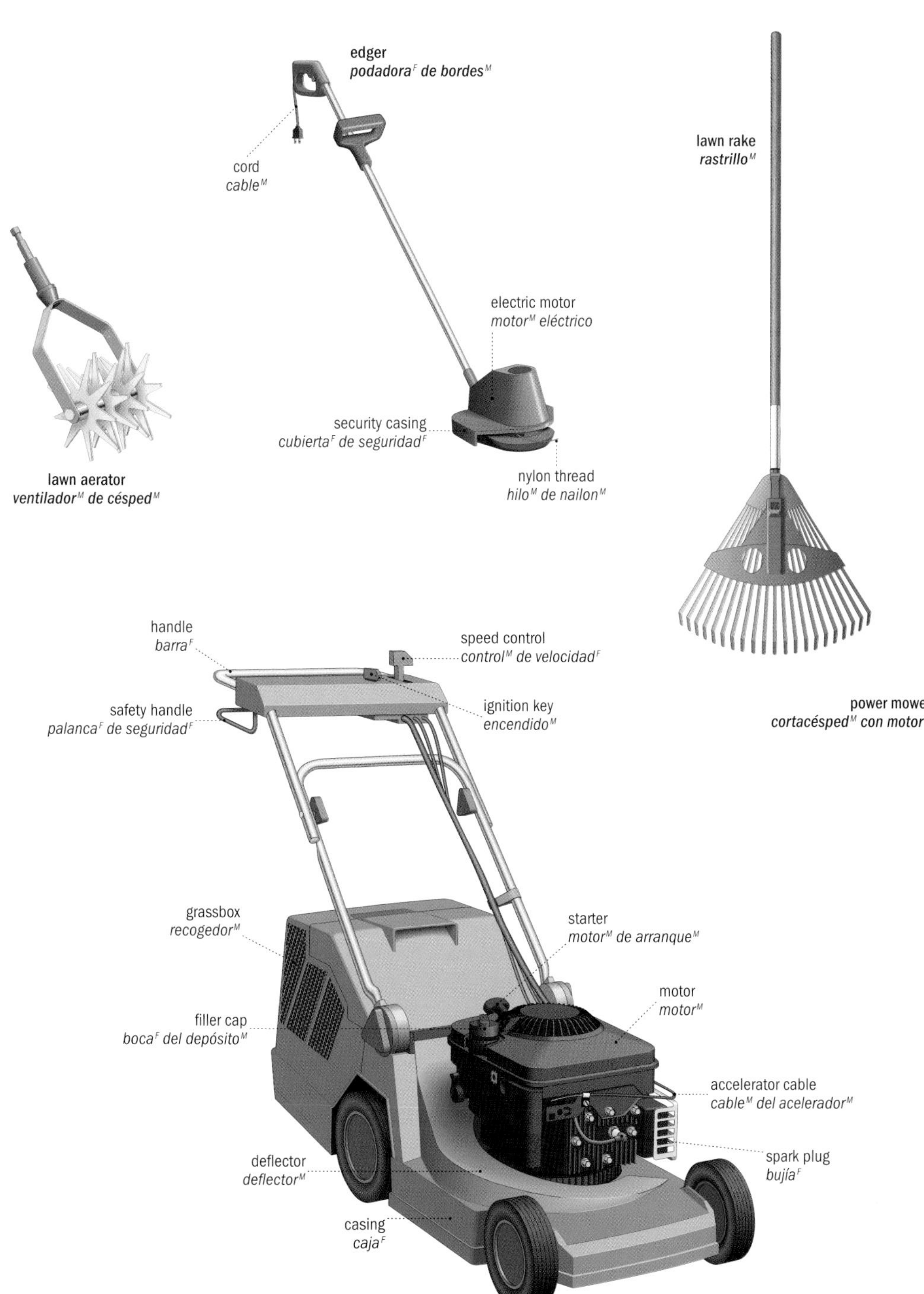
edger
podadora^F de bordes^M
cord
cable^M
electric motor
motor^M eléctrico
security casing
cubierta^F de seguridad^F
nylon thread
hilo^M de nailon^M
lawn rake
rastrillo^M
lawn aerator
ventilador^M de césped^M
handle
barra^F
speed control
control^M de velocidad^F
safety handle
palanca^F de seguridad^F
ignition key
encendido^M
power mower
cortacésped^M con motor^M
grassbox
recogedor^M
starter
motor^M de arranque^M
motor
motor^M
filler cap
boca^F del depósito^M
accelerator cable
cable^M del acelerador^M
spark plug
bujía^F
deflector
deflector^M
casing
caja^F

men's headgear
sombreros^M de hombre^M

women's headgear
sombreros[M] de mujer[F]

pillbox hat
sombrero[M] sin alas[F]

cartwheel hat
pamela[F]

cloche
sombrero[M] de campana[F]

toque
toca[F]

gob hat
gorro[M] de marinero[M]

crown
copa[F]

brim
ala[F]

turban
turbante[M]

sou'wester
sueste[M]

unisex headgear
sombreros[M] unisex

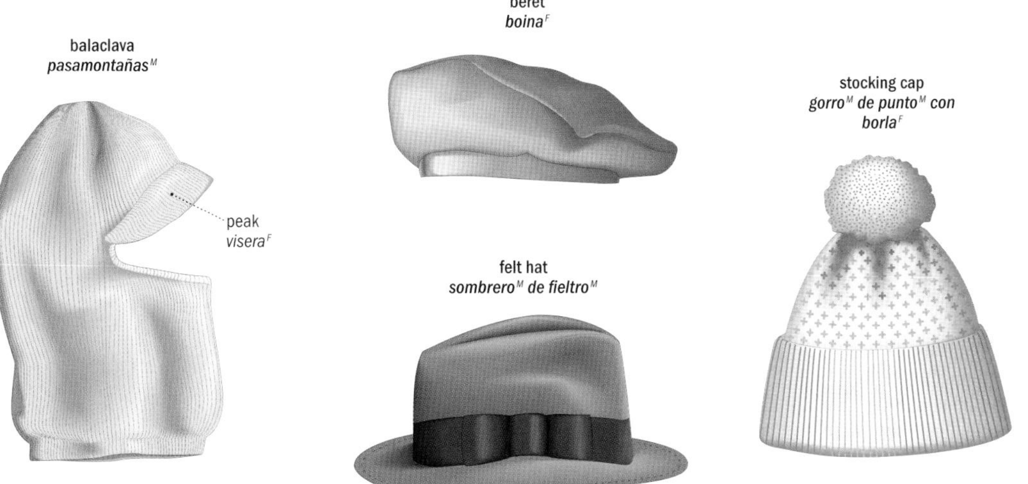

men's shoes
zapatos^M de hombre^M

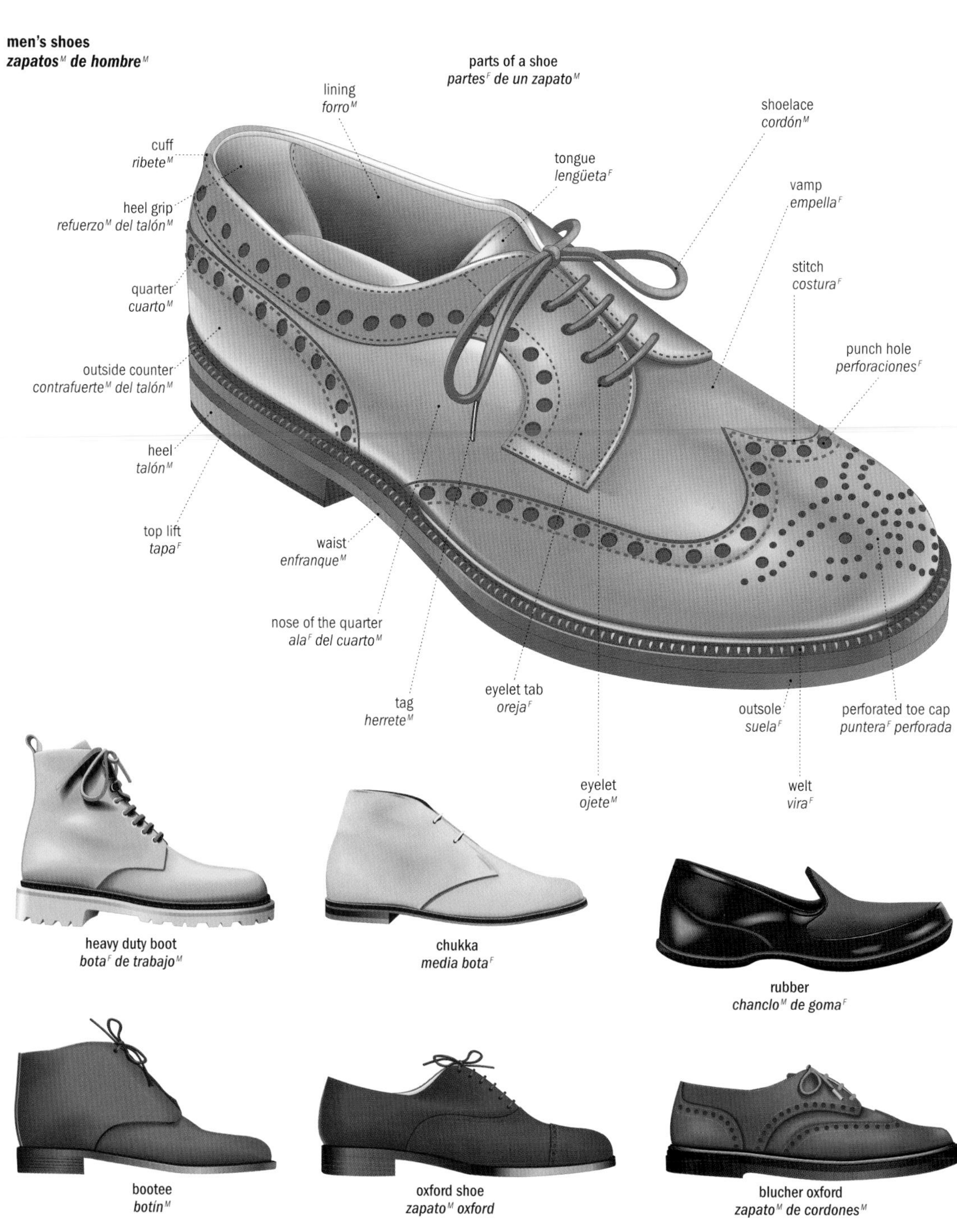
parts of a shoe
partes^F de un zapato^M
lining
forro^M
cuff
ribete^M
heel grip
refuerzo^M del talón^M
quarter
cuarto^M
outside counter
contrafuerte^M del talón^M
heel
talón^M
top lift
tapa^F
waist
enfranque^M
nose of the quarter
ala^F del cuarto^M
tag
herrete^M
eyelet tab
oreja^F
eyelet
ojete^M
tongue
lengüeta^F
shoelace
cordón^M
vamp
empella^F
stitch
costura^F
punch hole
perforaciones^F
outsole
suela^F
welt
vira^F
perforated toe cap
puntera^F perforada
heavy duty boot
bota^F de trabajo^M
chukka
media bota^F
rubber
chanclo^M de goma^F
bootee
botín^M
oxford shoe
zapato^M oxford
blucher oxford
zapato^M de cordones^M

women's shoes
zapatos[M] de mujer[F]

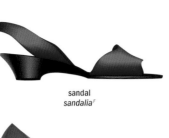

sandal
sandalia[F]

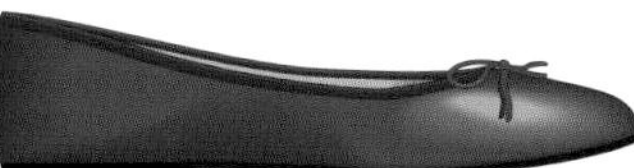

ballerina slipper
bailarina[F]

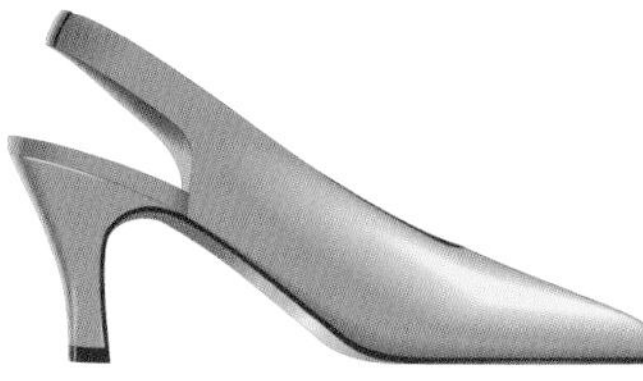

sling back shoe
zapato[M] de talón abierto

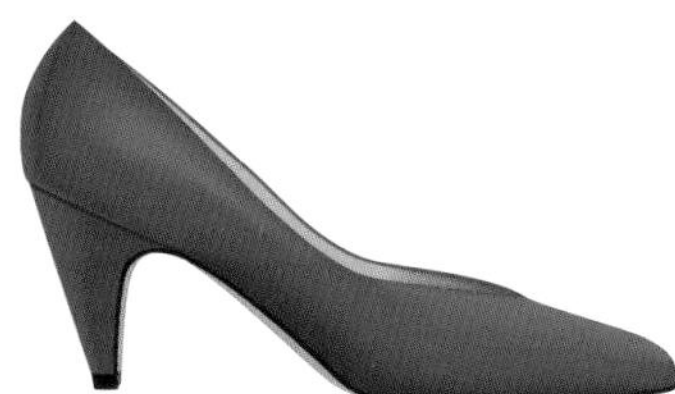

pump
zapato[M] de salón[M]

T-strap shoe
zapato[M] de correa[F]

one-bar shoe
zapato[M] de tacón[M] con correa[F]

casual shoe
zapato[M] con cordones[M]

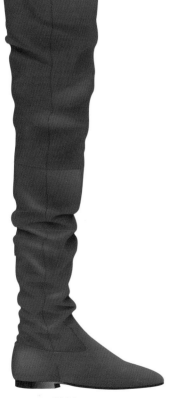

thigh-boot
bota[F] de medio muslo[M]

boot
bota[F]

ankle boot
botín[M]

unisex shoes
calzados*[M] *unisex

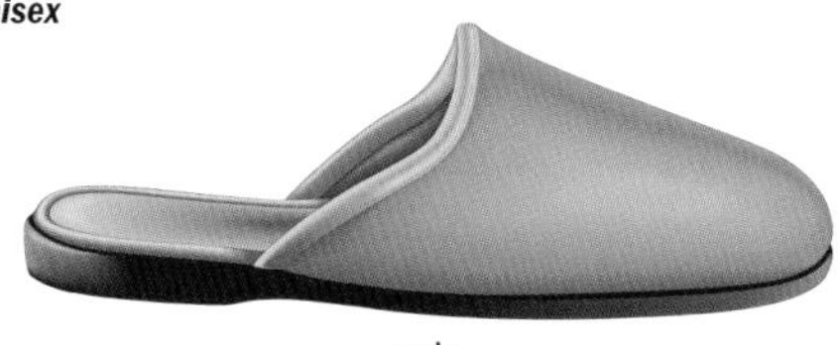

mule
pantufla[F]

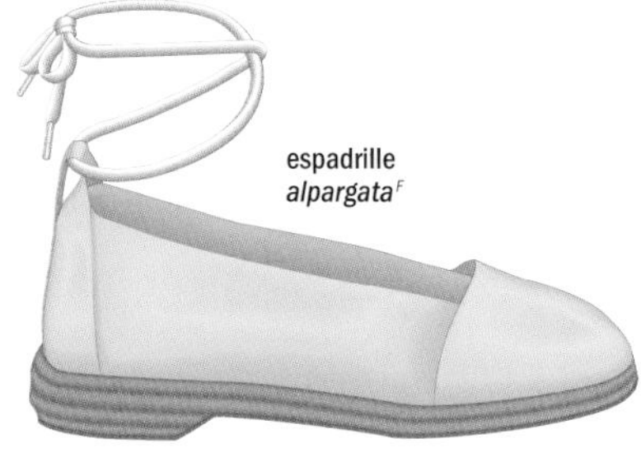

espadrille
alpargata[F]

tennis shoe
zapatilla[F] *de tenis*[M]

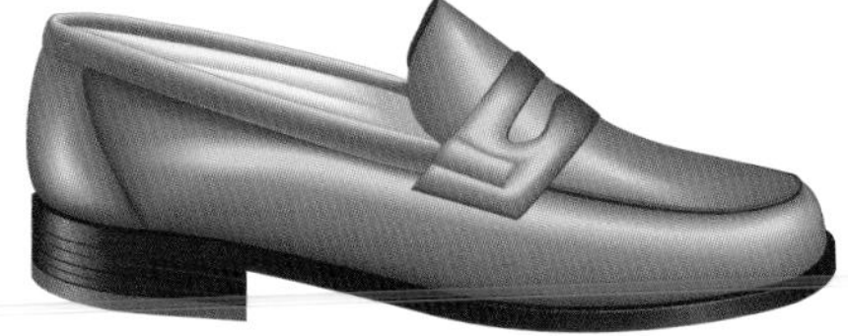

loafer
mocasín[M]

sandal
sandalia[F]

moccasin
mocasín[M]

thong
chancleta[F] *playera*

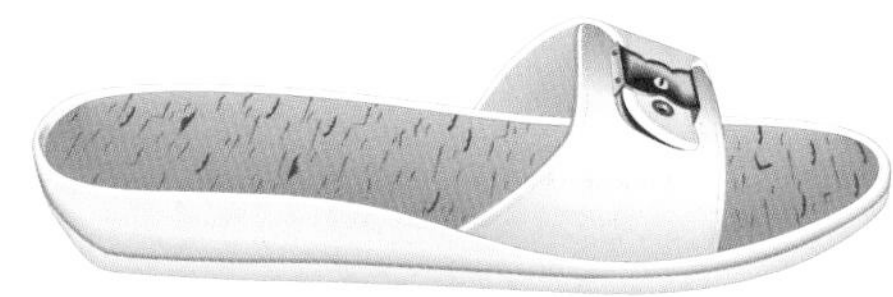

clog
chancleta[F]

sandal
sandalia[F]

hiking boot
bota[F] *de montaña*

men's gloves
guantes^M de hombre^M

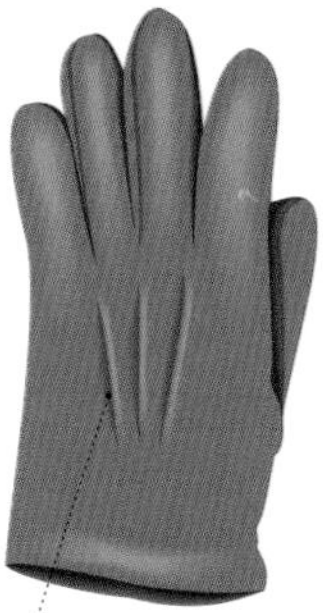

back of a glove
dorso^M de un guante^M

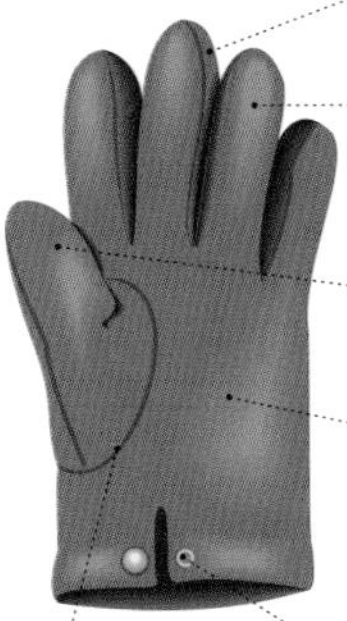

palm of a glove
palma^F de un guante^M

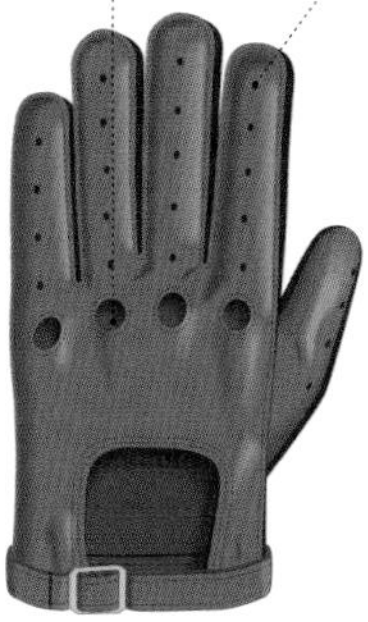

fourchette
horquilla^F

glove finger
dedo^M

thumb
pulgar^M

palm
palma^F

stitching
pespunte^M

seam
costura^F

snap fastener
botón^M de presión^F

opening
aberturas^F para los nudillos^M

perforation
perforaciones^F

driving glove
guante^M para conducir

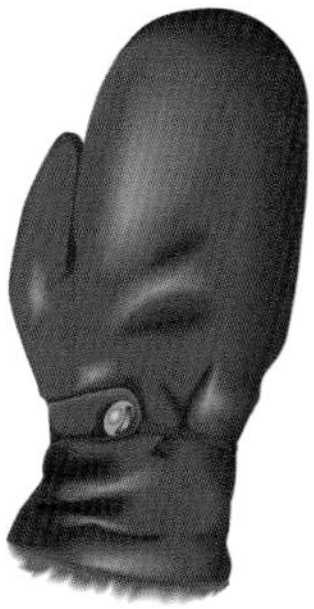

mitten
manopla^F

women's gloves
guantes^M de mujer^F

short glove
guante^M corto

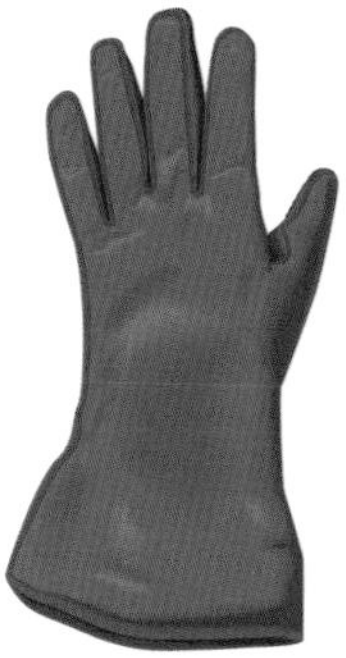

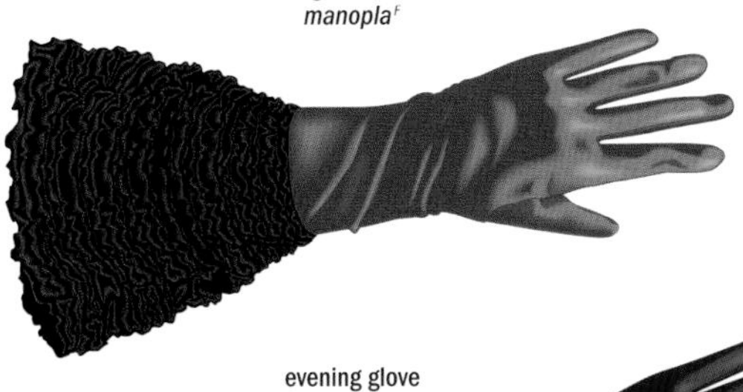

gauntlet
manopla^F

evening glove
guante^M largo

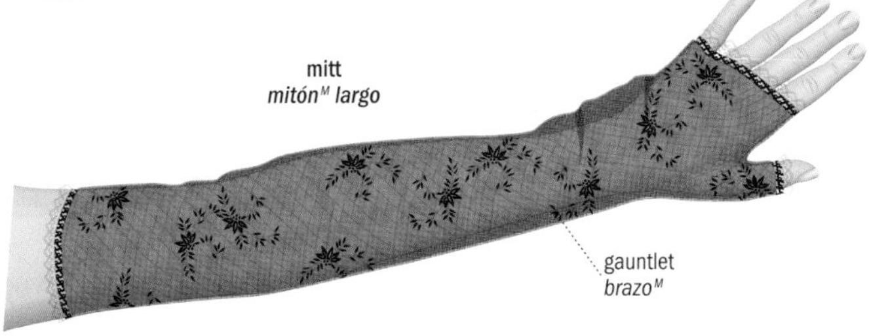

mitt
mitón^M largo

gauntlet
brazo^M

wrist-length glove
guante^M a la muñeca^F

jackets
chaquetas^F y chalecos^M

double-breasted jacket
chaqueta^F cruzada
collar
cuello^M
peaked lapel
solapa^F puntiaguda
lining
forro^M
breast welt pocket
bolsillo^M de ojal^M
sleeve
manga^F
flap
solapa^F
outside ticket pocket
bolsillo^M del cambio^M
patch pocket
bolsillo^M de parche^M
side back vent
abertura^F trasera lateral
vest
chaleco^M
V-neck
cuello^M en V
lining
forro^M
welt
ribete^M
front
delantero^M
seam
costura^F
welt pocket
bolsillo^M de ribete^M
adjustable waist tab
trincha^F
single-breasted jacket
chaqueta^F recta
lapel
solapa^F
notch
muesca^F
front
delantero^M
lining
forro^M
pocket handkerchief
pañuelo^M de bolsillo^M
flap pocket
bolsillo^M con cartera^F
back
espalda^F
sleeve
manga^F
center back vent
abertura^F trasera central

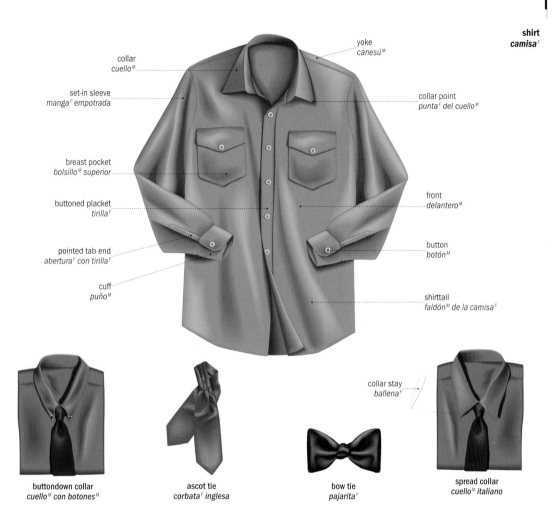

shirt
***camisa*[F]**

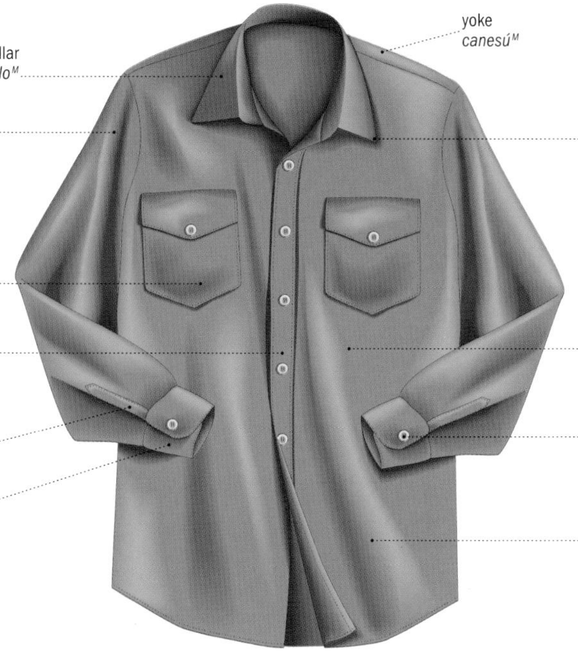

collar
cuello[M]
yoke
canesú[M]
set-in sleeve
manga[F] *empotrada*
collar point
punta[F] *del cuello*[M]
breast pocket
bolsillo[M] *superior*
buttoned placket
tirilla[F]
front
delantero[M]
pointed tab end
abertura[F] *con tirilla*[F]
button
botón[M]
cuff
puño[M]
shirttail
faldón[M] *de la camisa*[F]

buttondown collar
***cuello*[M] *con botones*[M]**

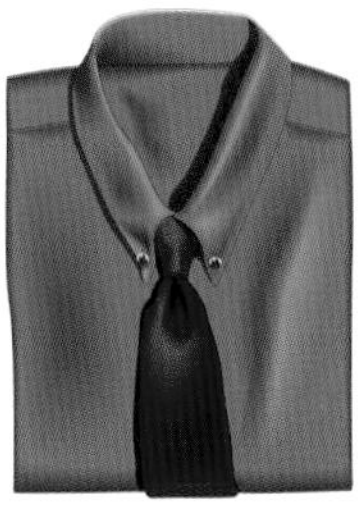

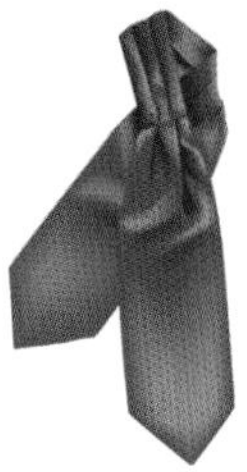

ascot tie
corbata*[F] *inglesa

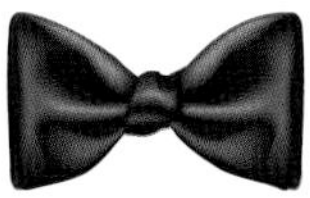

bow tie
***pajarita*[F]**

collar stay
ballena[F]

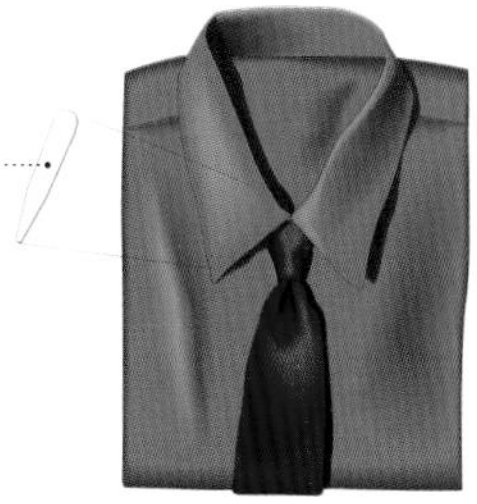

spread collar
cuello*[M] *italiano

necktie
corbata[F]

front apron
faldón[M] *delantero*
neck end
contorno[M] *del cuello*[M]
rear apron
faldón[M] *trasero*
lining
forro[M]
loop
presilla[F]
slip-stitched seam
costura[F] *invisible*

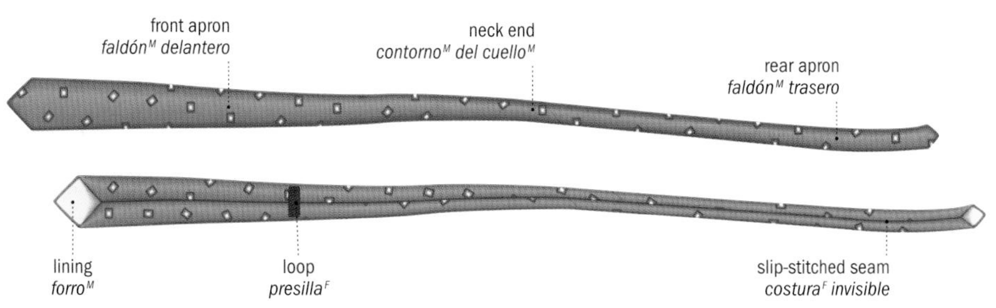

pants
pantalones[M]

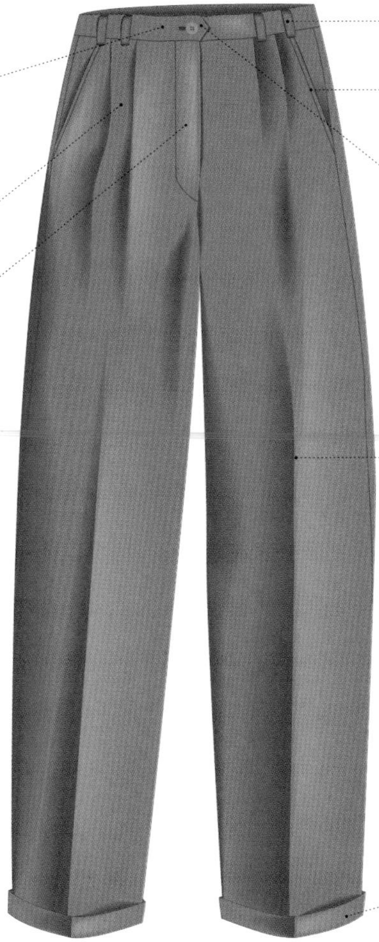

belt loop
trabilla[F]
waistband
pretina[F]
front top pocket
bolsillo[M] delantero
knife pleat
pinza[F]
waistband extension
trabilla[F] de la pretina[F]
fly
bragueta[F]
crease
raya[F]
cuff
vuelta[F]

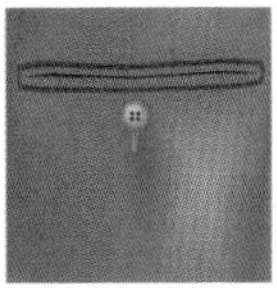

back pocket
bolsillo*[M] *trasero

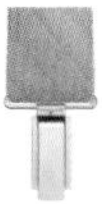

suspender clip
pinza[F]

suspenders
tirantes[M]

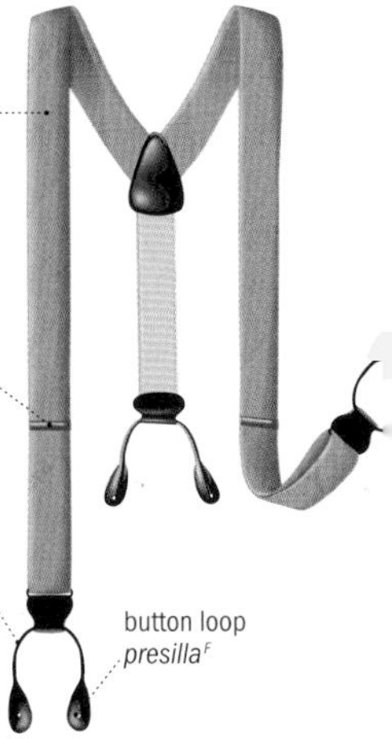

elastic webbing
banda[F] elástica
adjustment slide
corredera[F] de ajuste[M]
leather end
lengüeta[F] de cuero[M]
button loop
presilla[F]

belt
cinturón[M]

top stitching
pespunte[M]
panel
cuero[M]
tip
punta[F]
punch hole
ojete[M]
belt loop
trabilla[F]
tongue
pasador[M]
buckle
hebilla[F]

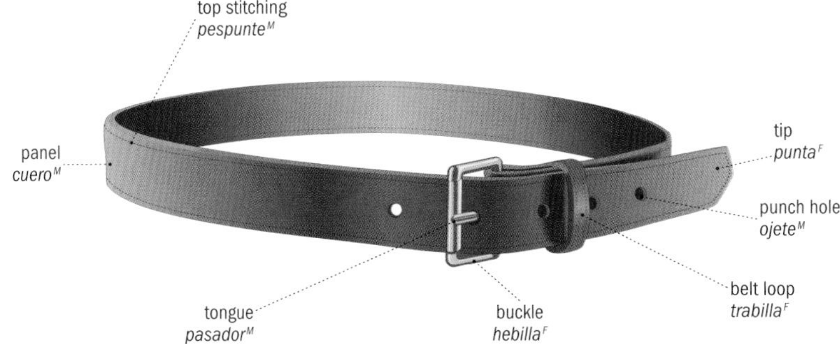

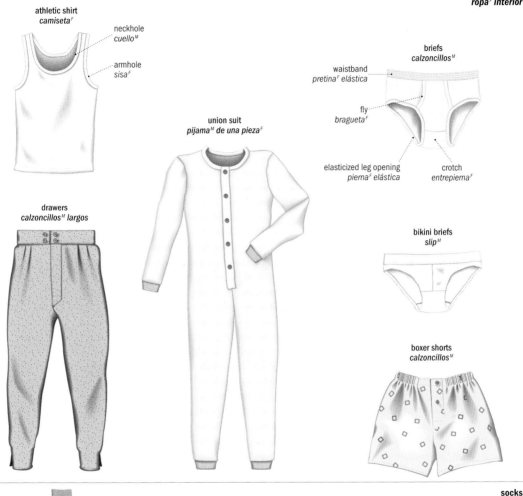

underwear
ropa^{F} interior

athletic shirt
camiseta^{F}

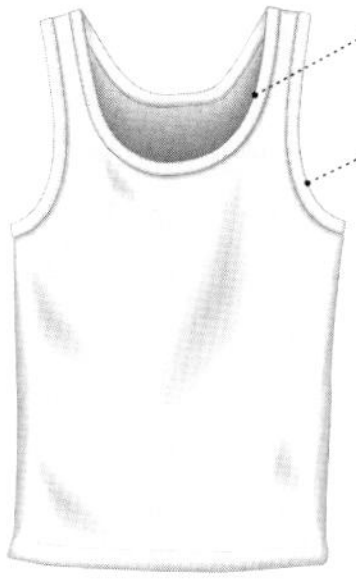

neckhole
cuello^{M}
armhole
sisa^{F}

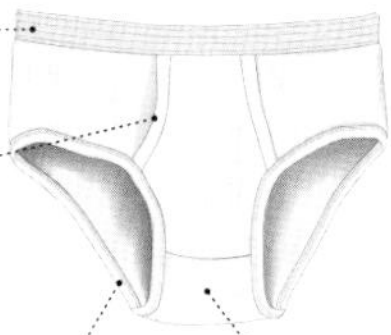

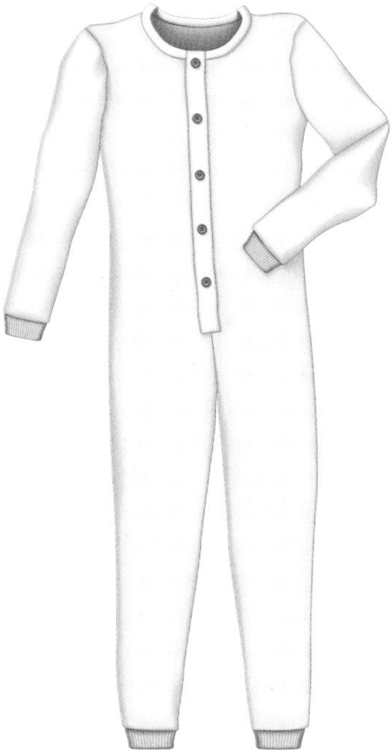

briefs
calzoncillos^{M}

waistband
pretina^{F} elástica
fly
bragueta^{F}
elasticized leg opening
pierna^{F} elástica
crotch
entrepierna^{F}

union suit
pijama^{M} de una pieza^{F}

drawers
calzoncillos^{M} largos

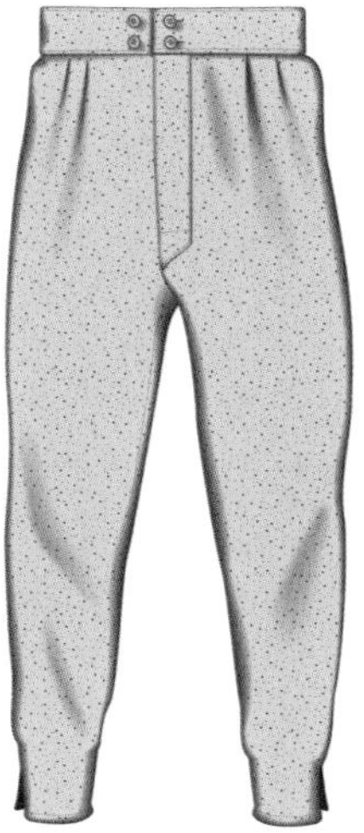

bikini briefs
slip^{M}

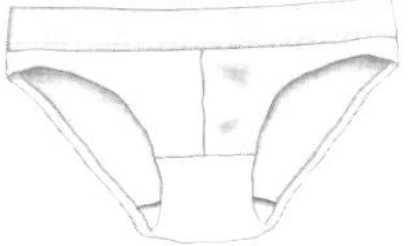

boxer shorts
calzoncillos^{M}

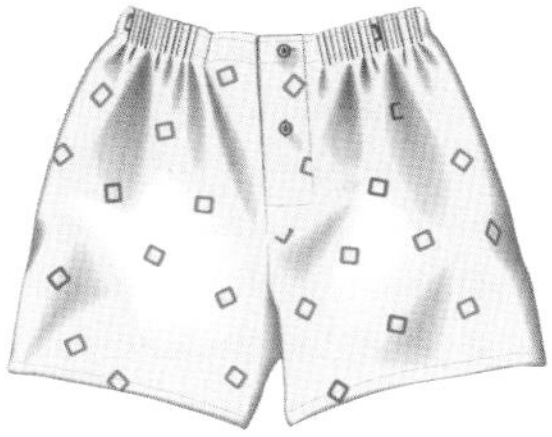

socks
calcetines^{M}

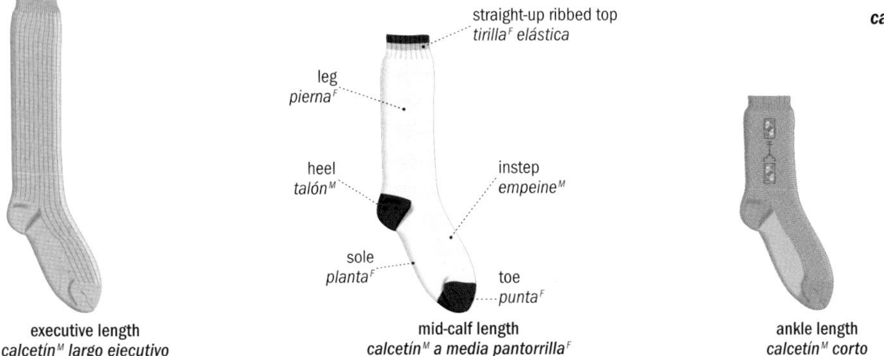

executive length
calcetín^{M} largo ejecutivo

straight-up ribbed top
tirilla^{F} elástica
leg
pierna^{F}
heel
talón^{M}
instep
empeine^{M}
sole
planta^{F}
toe
punta^{F}

mid-calf length
calcetín^{M} a media pantorrilla^{F}

ankle length
calcetín^{M} corto

coats
abrigos^M e impermeables^F

raincoat
impermeable^M
collar
cuello^M
raglan sleeve
manga^F raglán
notched lapel
solapa^F con ojal^M
tab
lengüeta^F
broad-welt side pocket
bolsillo^M de ribete^M ancho
buttonhole
ojal^M
side panel
paño^M lateral
overcoat
abrigo^M
notched lapel
solapa^F con ojal^M
breast pocket
bolsillo^M superior
breast dart
pinza^F
flap pocket
bolsillo^M con cartera^F
trench coat
trinchera^F
two-way collar
cuello^M de doble vista^F
epaulet
hombrera^F
raglan sleeve
manga^F raglán
gun flap
protector^M
sleeve strap loop
presilla^F de la manga^F
double-breasted buttoning
botonadura^F cruzada
belt
cinturón^M
sleeve strap
correa^F de la manga^F
belt loop
presilla^F del cinturón^M
broad-welt side pocket
bolsillo^M de ribete^M ancho
frame
hebilla^F
three-quarter coat
abrigo^M de tres cuartos

parka
parka[F]

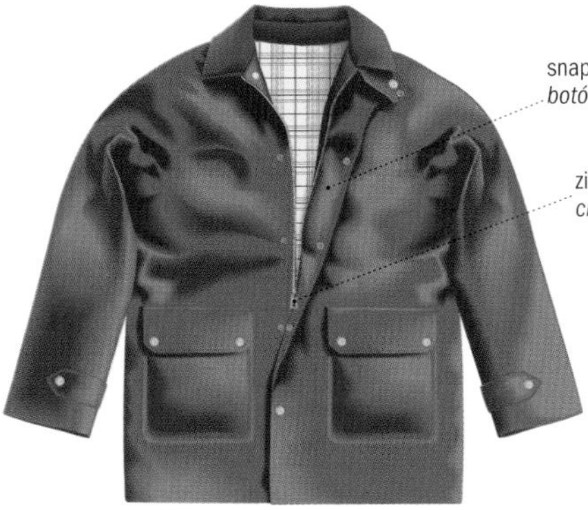

snap-fastening tab
botón[M] *de presión*[F]
zipper
cremallera[F]

sheepskin jacket
zamarra[F]

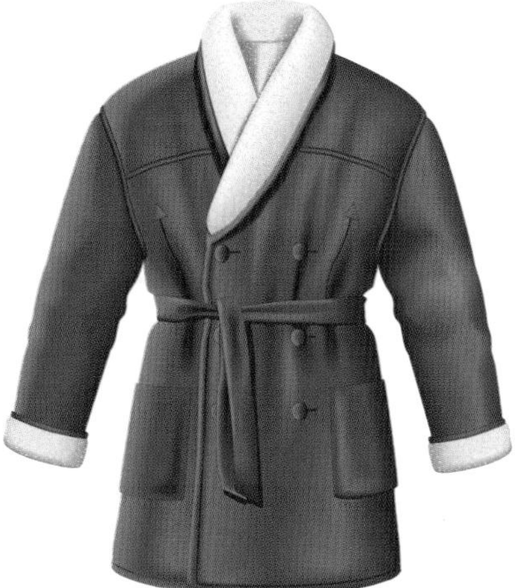

duffle coat
trenca[F]

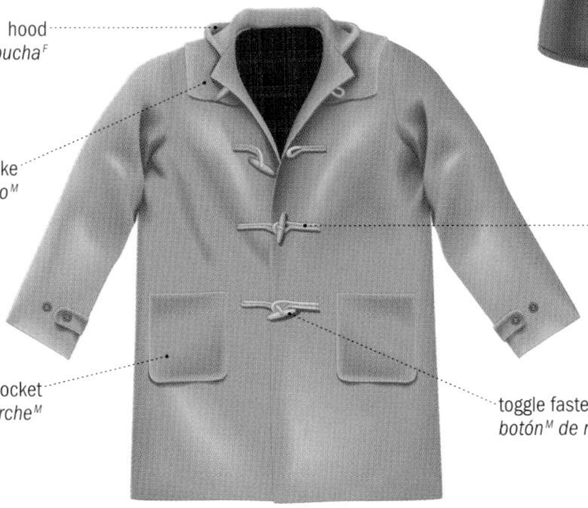

hood
capucha[F]
yoke
hombrillo[M]
frog
alamar[M]
patch pocket
bolsillo[M] *de parche*[M]
toggle fastening
botón[M] *de madera*[F]

jacket
cazadora[F]

snap fastener
botón[M] *de presión*[M]
hand-warmer pocket
bolsillo[M] *de ojal*[M]
elastic waistband
pretina[F] *elástica*

windbreaker
cazadora[F]

waistband
pretina[F]
drawstring
cordón[M]

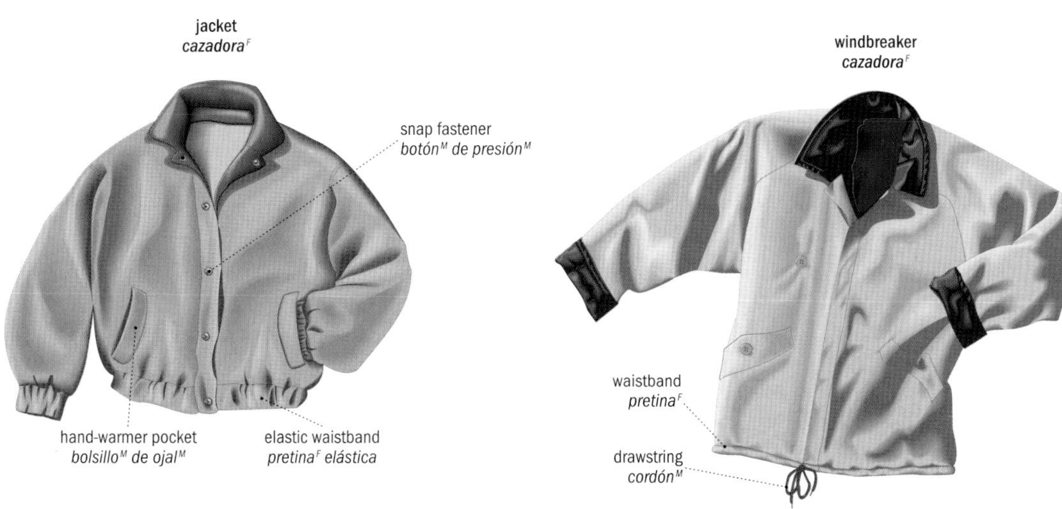

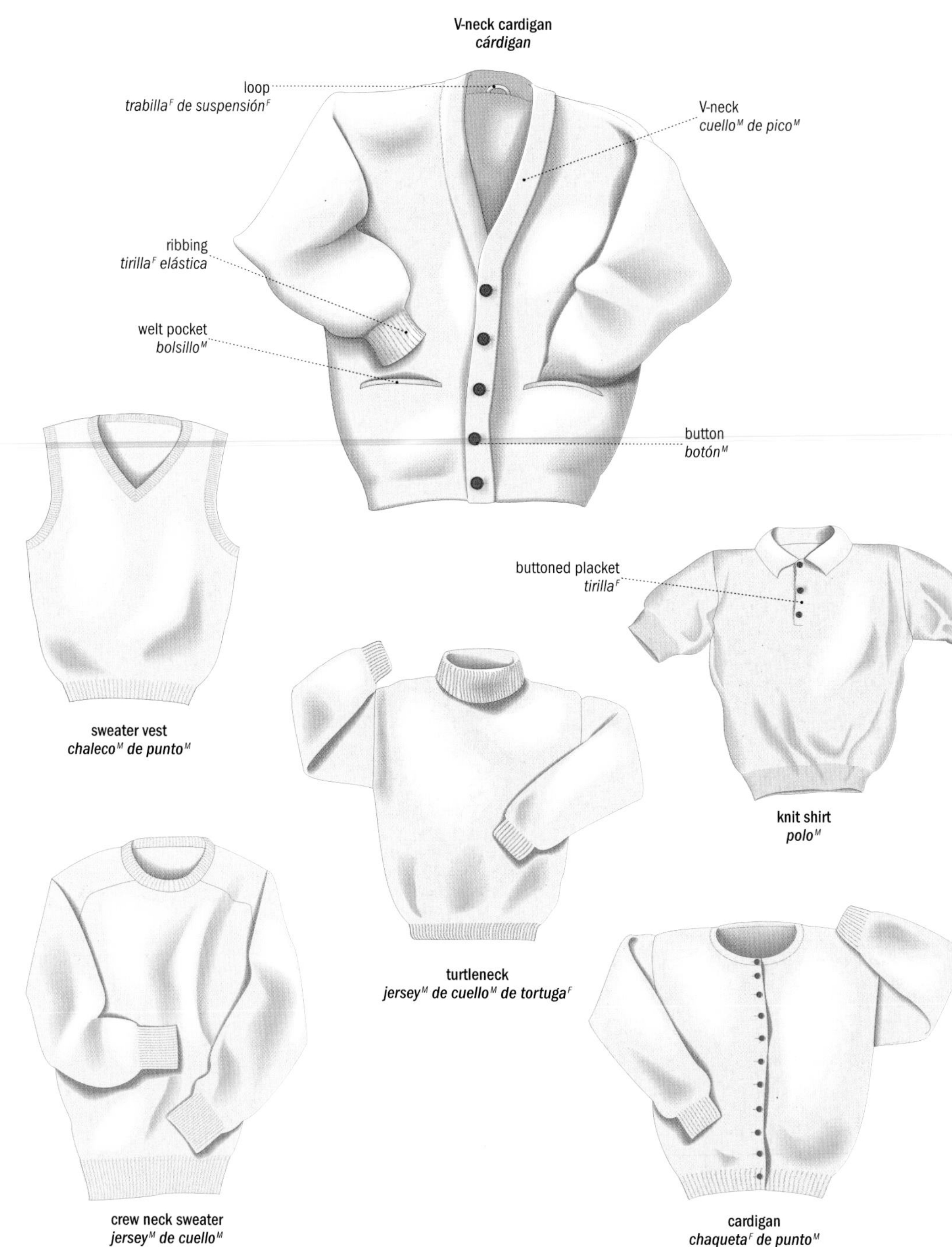

sweater vest
chaleco^M de punto^M

knit shirt
polo^M

turtleneck
jersey^M de cuello^M de tortuga^F

crew neck sweater
jersey^M de cuello^M redondo

cardigan
chaqueta^F de punto^M

coats
chaquetones[M] y abrigos[M]

suit
traje[M] de chaqueta[F]

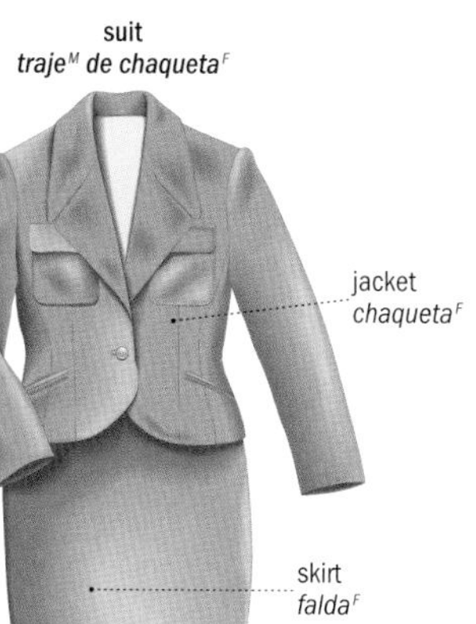

raglan
abrigo[M] raglán

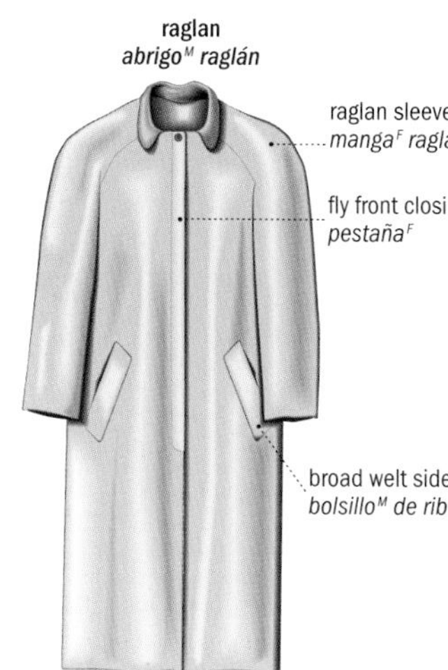

top coat
abrigo[M] redingote

pelerine
abrigo[M] con esclavina[F]

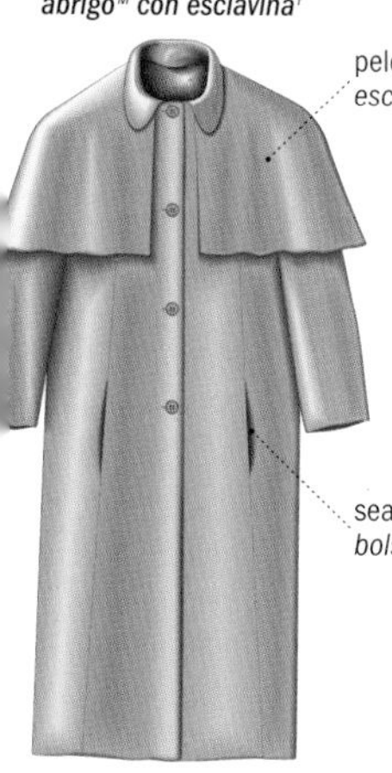

cape
capa[F]

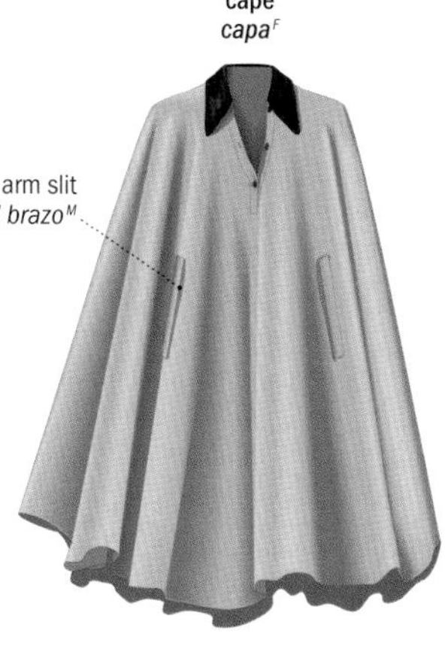

pea jacket
chaquetón[M] marinero

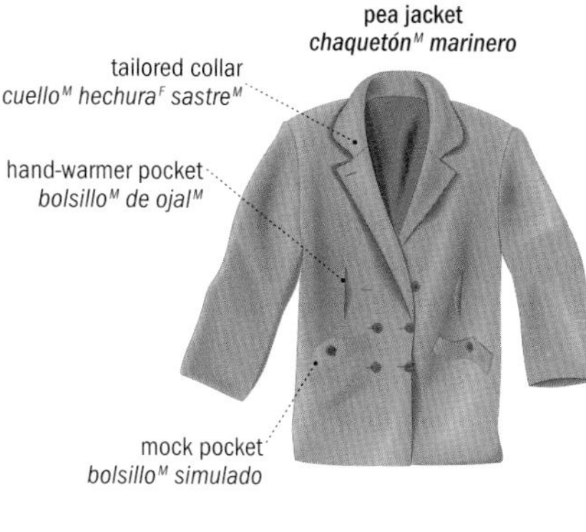

car coat
chaquetón[M] de tres cuartos

jacket
chaquetón[M]

poncho
poncho[M]

overcoat
abrigo[M]

CLOTHING

examples of dresses
ejemplos[M] de vestidos[M]

sheath dress
recto[M] entallado

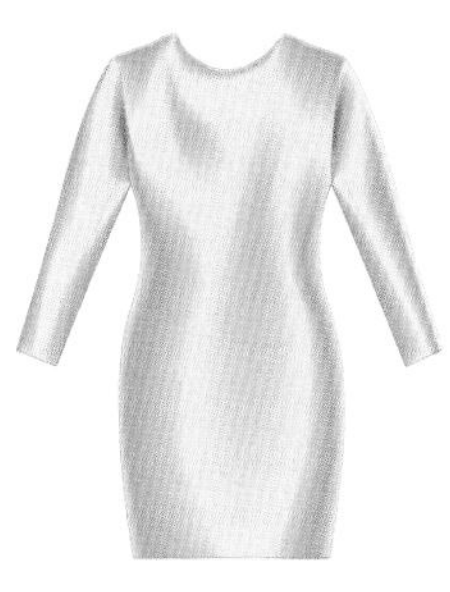

princess-seamed dress
corte[M] princesa[F]

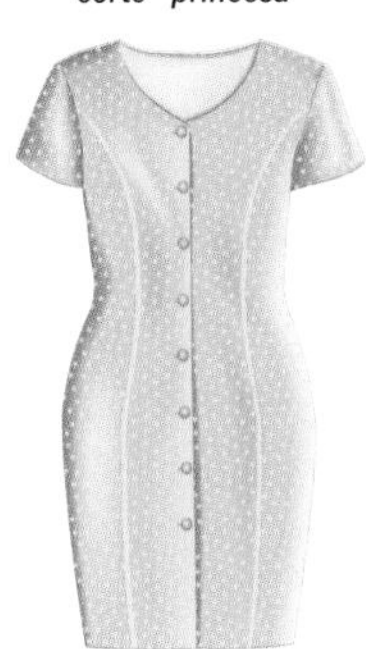

coat dress
traje[M] cruzado

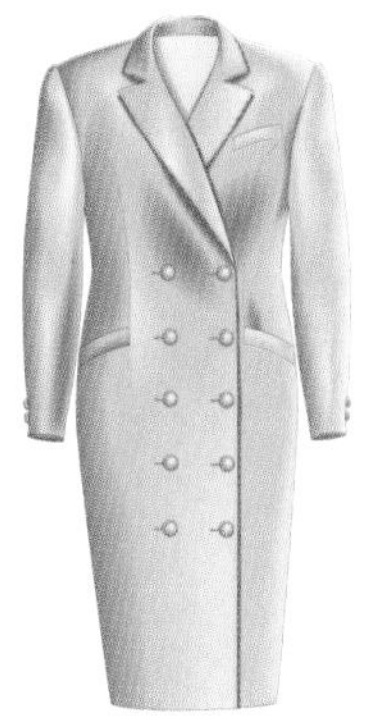

polo dress
vestido[M] de camiseta[F]

housedress
vestido[M] camisero sin mangas

shirtwaist dress
vestido[M] camisero

drop-waist dress
vestido de talle[M] bajo

trapeze dress
vestido[M] acampanado

sundress
vestido[M] de tirantes[M]

wraparound dress
vestido[M] cruzado

tunic dress
túnica[F]

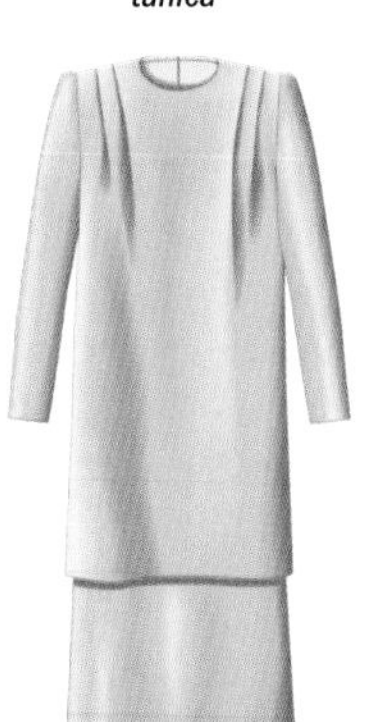

jumper
pichi[M]

examples of skirts
ejemplos[M] de faldas[F]

gored skirt
falda[F] de piezas[F]

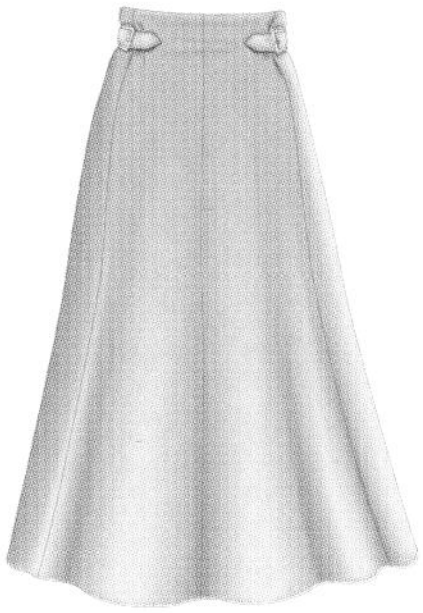

kilt
falda[F] escocesa

sarong
falda[F] sarong[M]

wraparound skirt
falda[F] cruzada

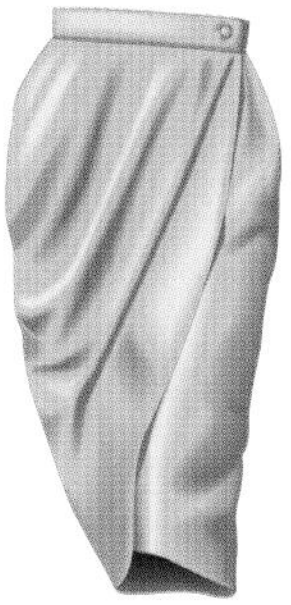

sheath skirt
falda[F] de tubo[M]

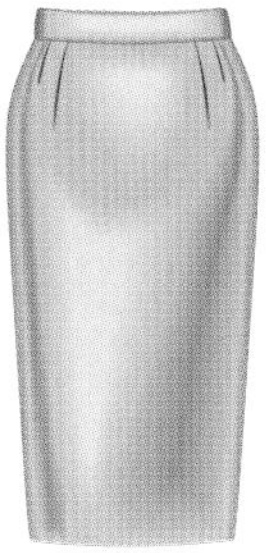

ruffled skirt
falda[F] de volantes[M]

straight skirt
falda[F] recta

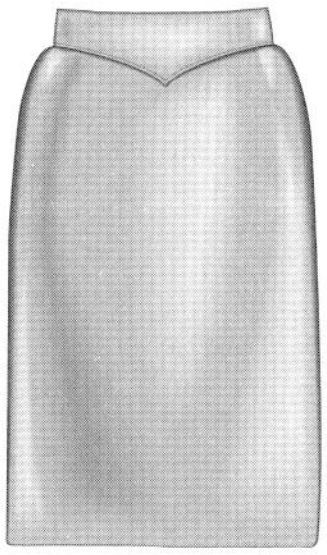

yoked skirt
falda[F] acampanada

gathered skirt
falda[F] fruncida

culottes
falda[F] pantalón[M]

examples of pleats
ejemplos[M] de tablas[F]

inverted pleat
tabla[F] delantera

kick pleat
tabla[F] abierta

accordion pleat
plisada

top-stitched pleat
pespunteada

knife pleat
tablas[F]

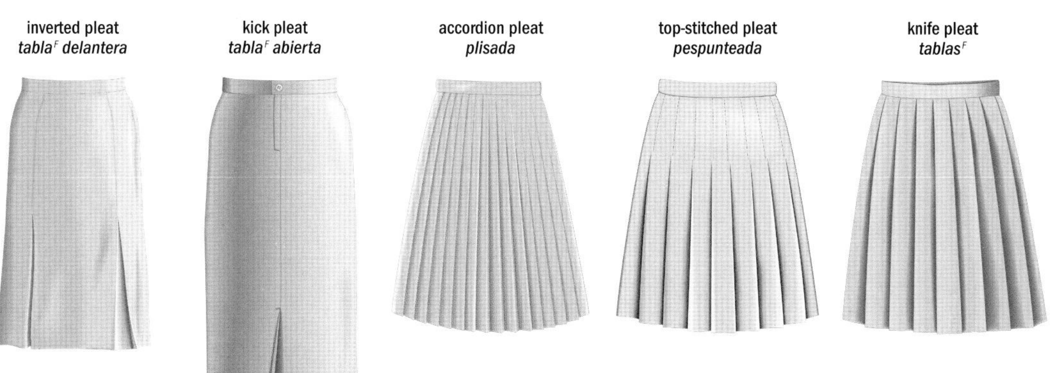

examples of pants
ejemplos[M] de pantalones[M]

shorts
pantalóns[M] cortos

Bermuda shorts
bermudas[M]

knickers
bombachos[M]

pedal pushers
pirata[M]

jeans
vaqueros[M]

ski pants
pantalones[M] de tubo[M]

footstrap
trabilla[F]

jumpsuit
buzo[M]

overalls
pantalón[M] peto[M]

bell bottoms
pantalones[M] acampanados

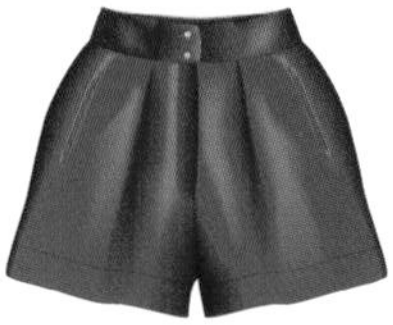

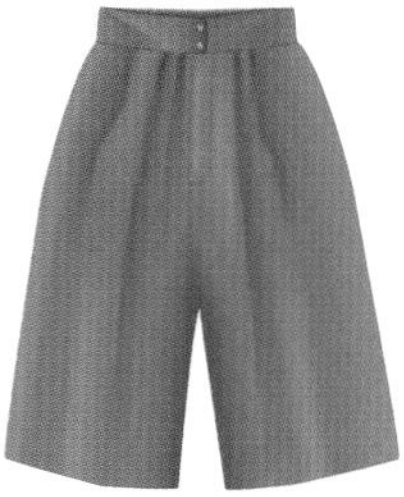

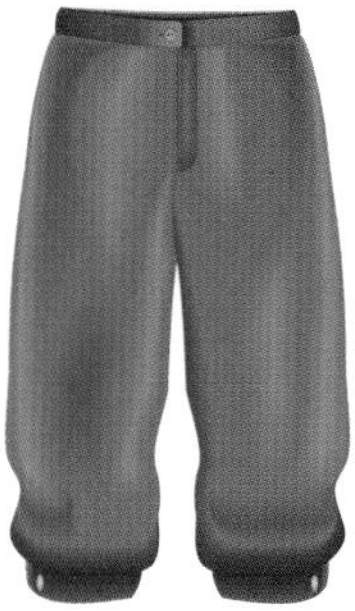

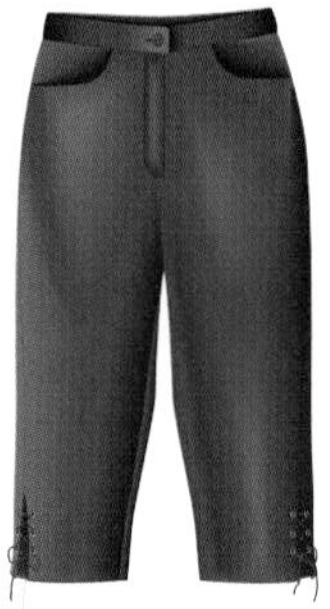

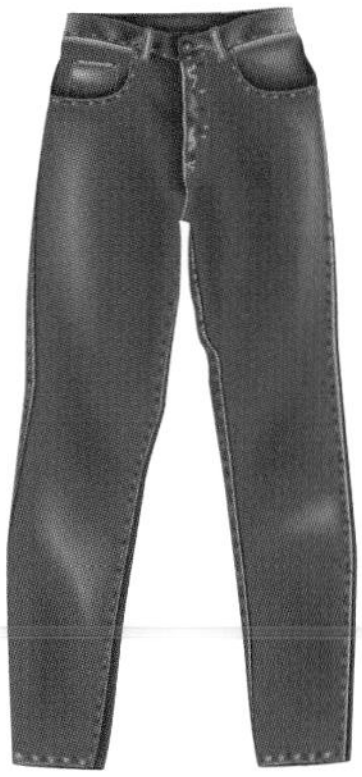

jackets, vest and sweaters
chaleco[M], jerseys[M] y chaquetas[F]

bolero
bolero[M]

spencer
bolero[M] con botones[M]

blazer
americana[F]

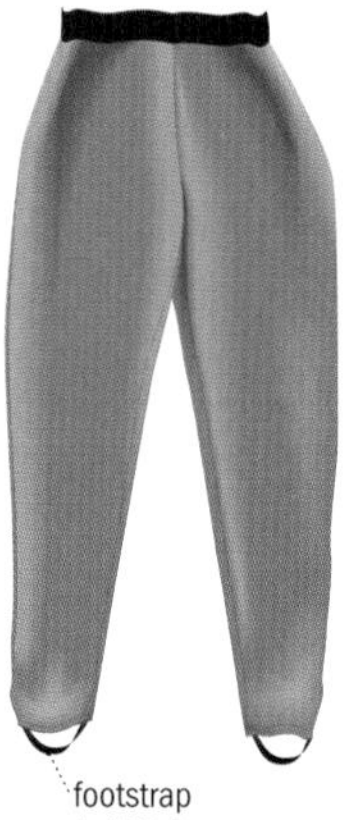

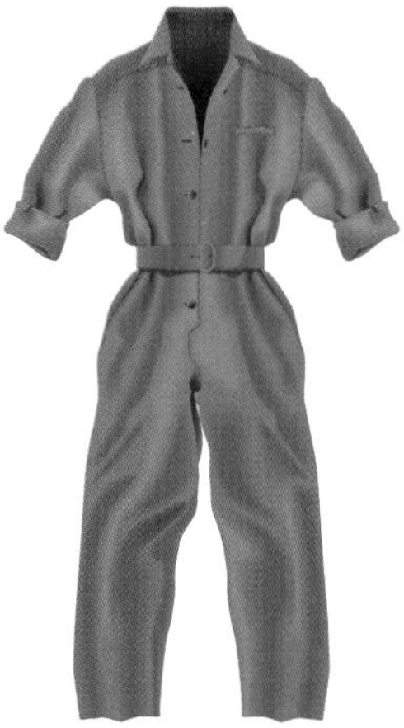

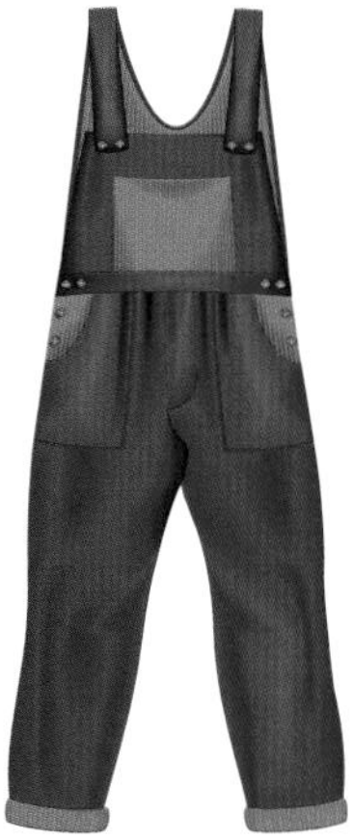

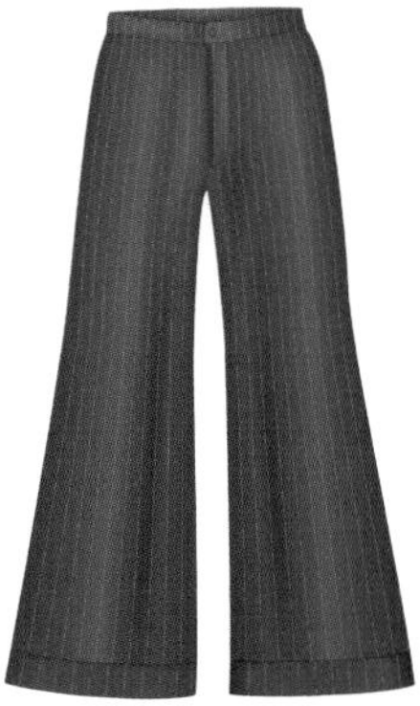

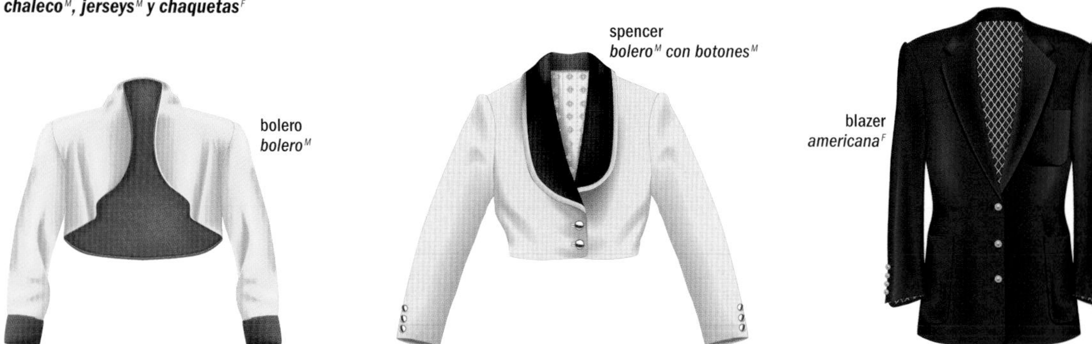

examples of shirts
ejemplos[M] *de blusas*[F] *y camisas*[F]

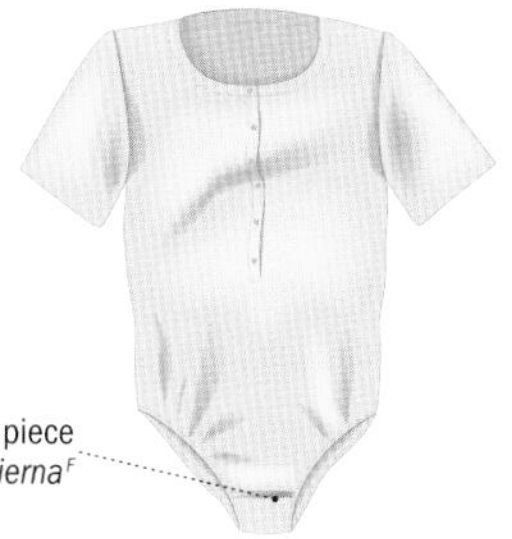

body suit
body[M]

crotch piece
entrepierna[F]

middy
camisa[F] *marinera*

yoke
canesú[M]

gather
fruncido[M]

shirttail
faldón[M]

oversized shirt
camisa[F]

classic blouse
camisera[F] *clásica*

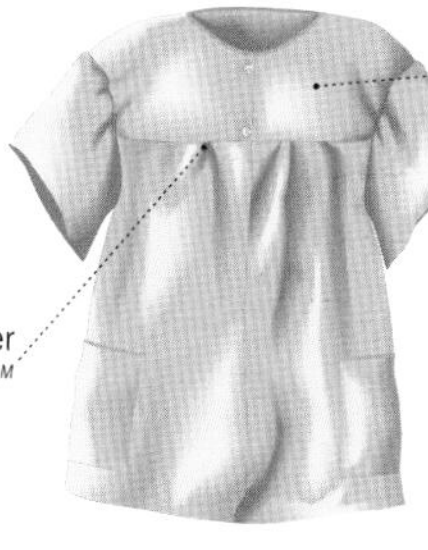

smock
blusón[M]

tunic
blusón[M] *con tirilla*[F]

wrapover top
chaqueta[F] *cruzada*

polo shirt
polo[M]

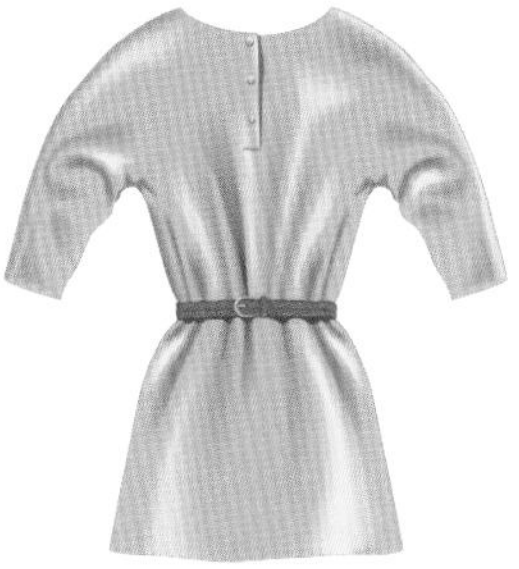

over-blouse
casaca[F]

CLOTHING

nightwear
lencería [F]

hose
medias[F]

knee-high sock
calcetín[M] largo

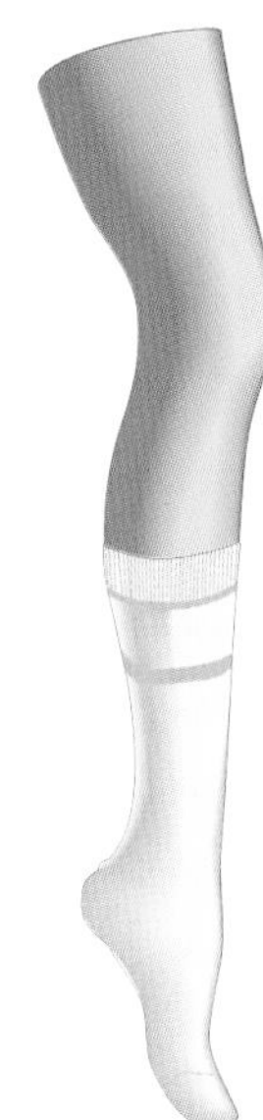

sock
calcetín[M]

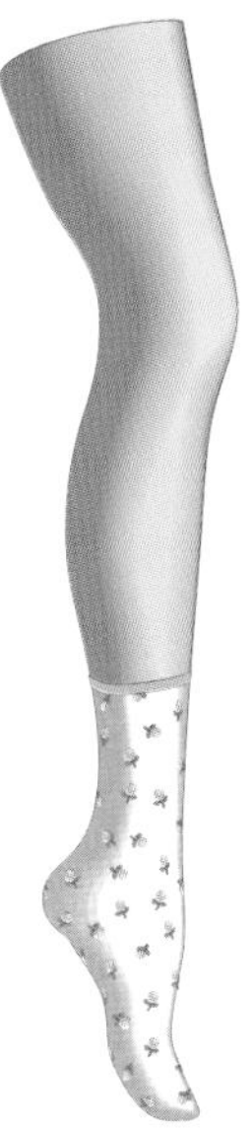

ankle sock
tobillera[F]

short sock
calcetín[M]

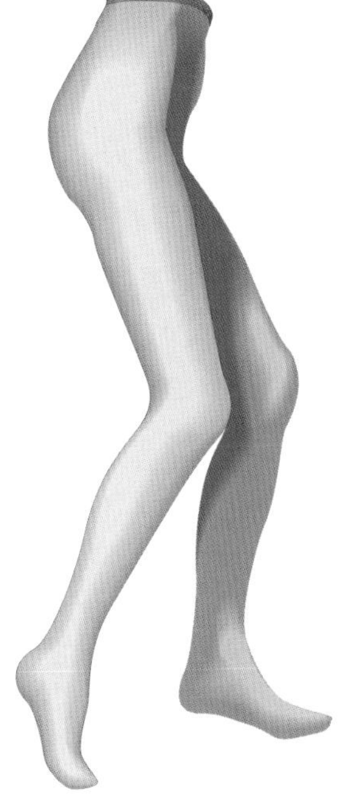

panty hose
pantis[M]/medias[F]

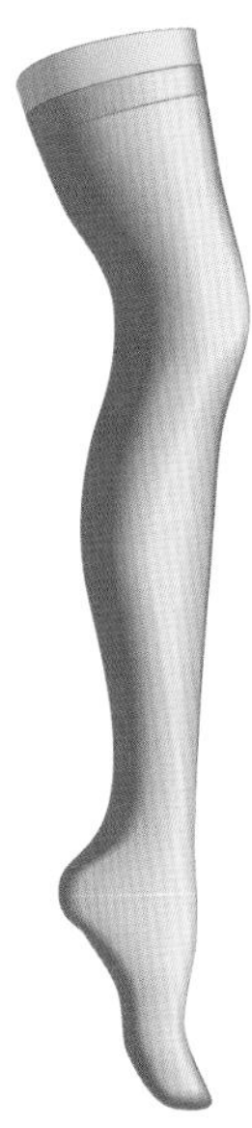

stocking
media[F]

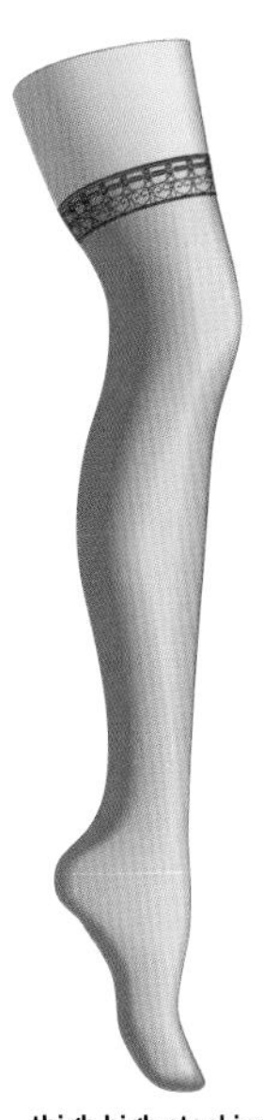

thigh-high stocking
media[F] antideslizante

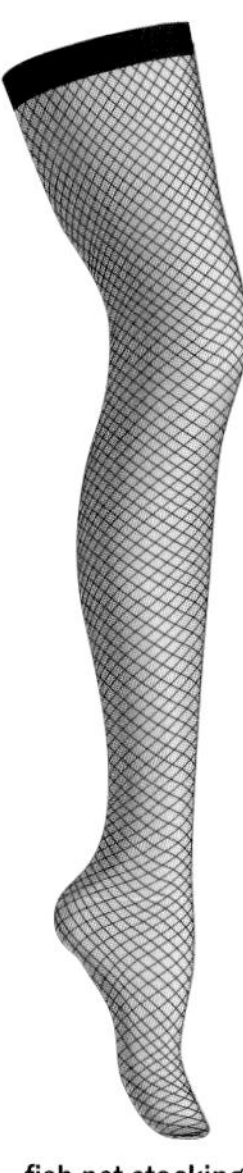

fish net stocking
media[F] de malla[F]

underwear
ropa*[F] *interior

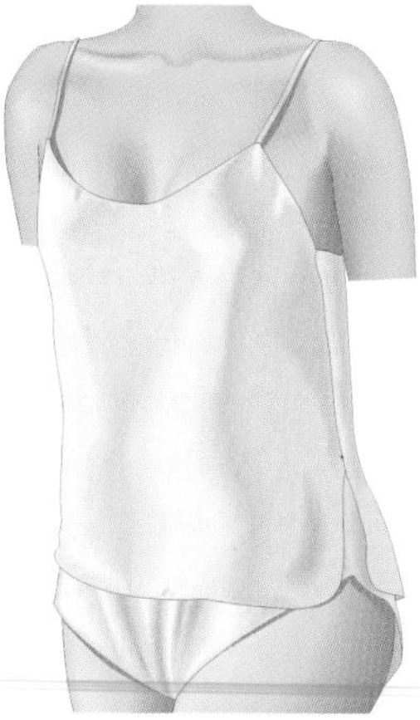

corselette
faja[F] *con sostén*[M]

camisole
camisola[F]

teddy
canesú[M]

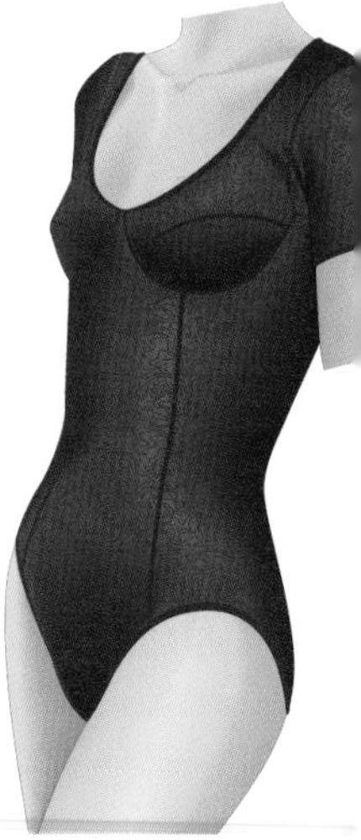

body suit
body[M]

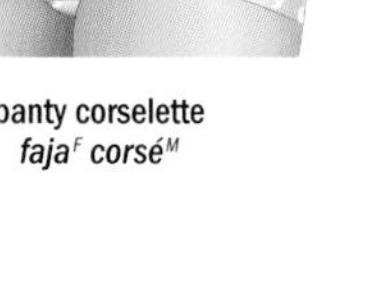

panty corselette
faja[F] *corsé*[M]

half-slip
falda[F] *combinación*[F]

foundation slip
combinación[F]

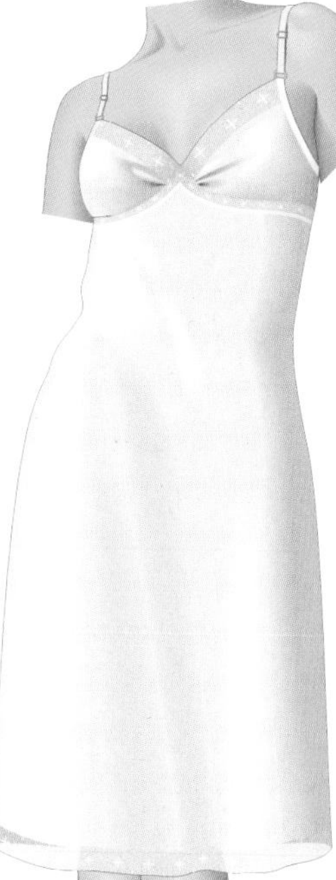

slip
combinación[F] *con sujetador*[M]

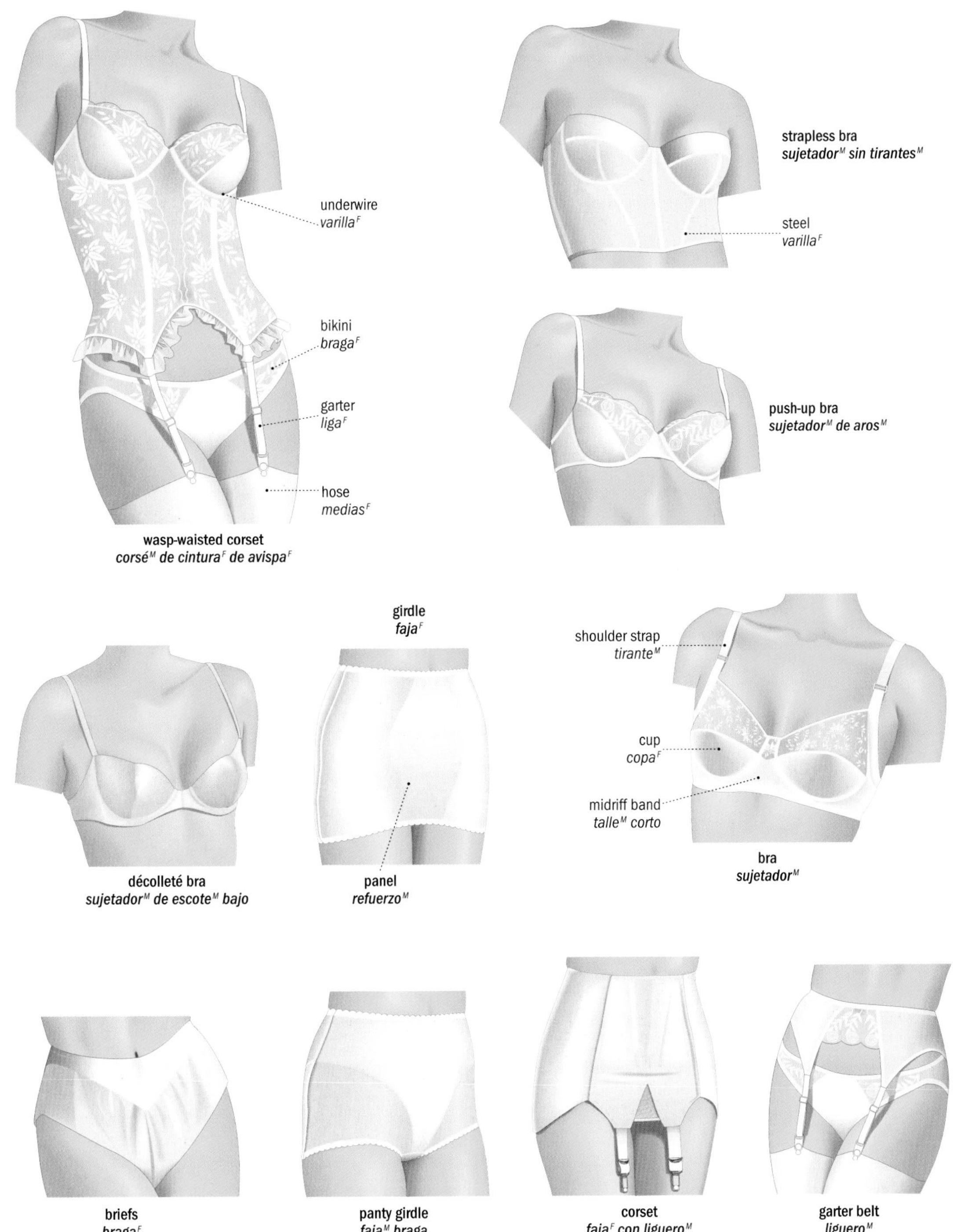
underwire
varilla^F
bikini
braga^F
garter
liga^F
hose
medias^F
wasp-waisted corset
corsé^M de cintura^F de avispa^F
strapless bra
sujetador^M sin tirantes^M
steel
varilla^F
push-up bra
sujetador^M de aros^M
décolleté bra
sujetador^M de escote^M bajo
girdle
faja^F
panel
refuerzo^M
shoulder strap
tirante^M
cup
copa^F
midriff band
talle^M corto
bra
sujetador^M
briefs
braga^F
panty girdle
faja^M braga
corset
faja^F con liguero^M
garter belt
liguero^M

newborn children's clothing

ropa[F] de bebé[M]

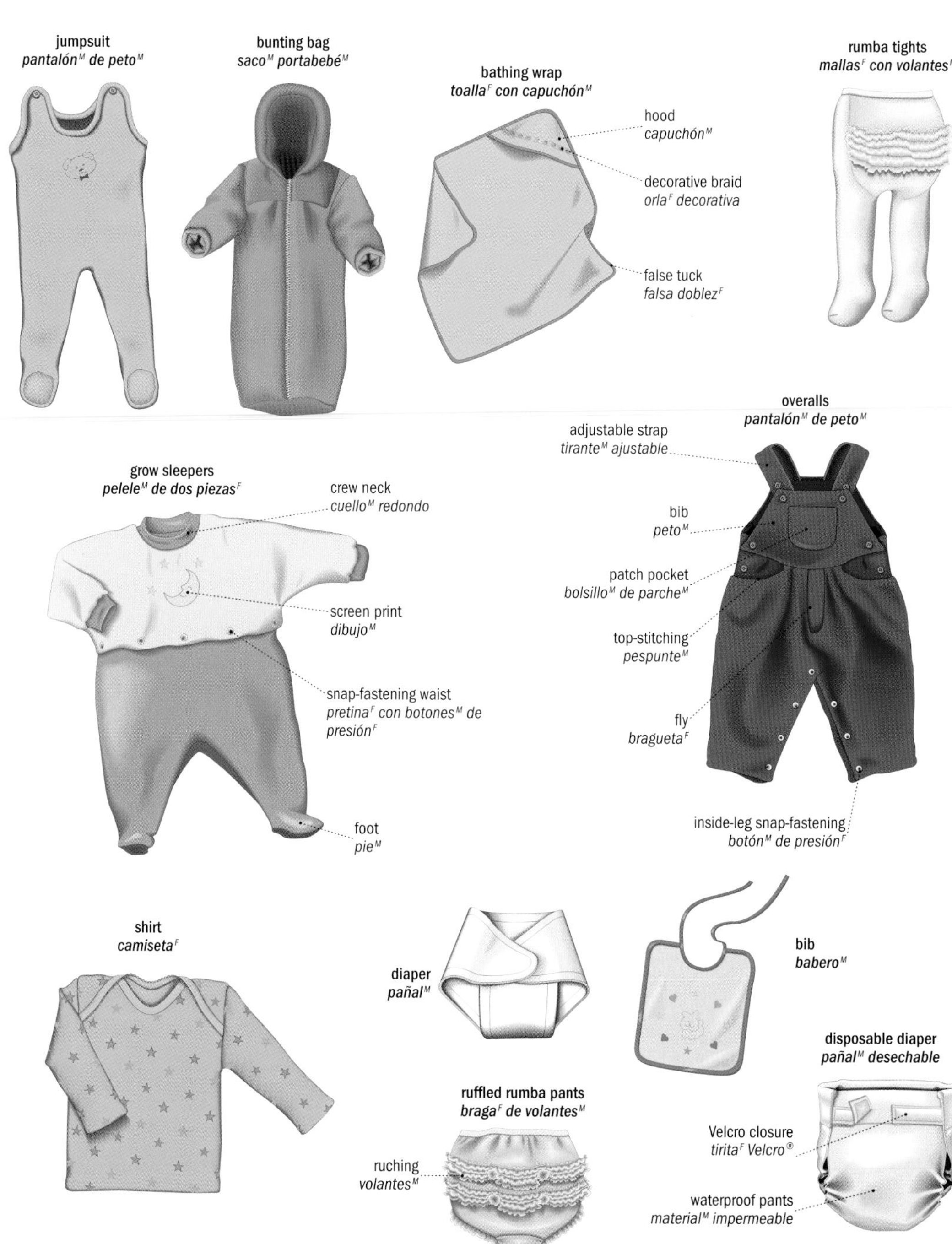

jumpsuit
pantalón[M] de peto[M]
bunting bag
saco[M] portabebé[M]
bathing wrap
toalla[F] con capuchón[M]
hood
capuchón[M]
decorative braid
orla[F] decorativa
false tuck
falsa doblez[F]
rumba tights
mallas[F] con volantes[M]
overalls
pantalón[M] de peto[M]
adjustable strap
tirante[M] ajustable
bib
peto[M]
patch pocket
bolsillo[M] de parche[M]
top-stitching
pespunte[M]
fly
bragueta[F]
inside-leg snap-fastening
botón[M] de presión[F]
grow sleepers
pelele[M] de dos piezas[F]
crew neck
cuello[M] redondo
screen print
dibujo[M]
snap-fastening waist
pretina[F] con botones[M] de presión[F]
foot
pie[M]
shirt
camiseta[F]
diaper
pañal[M]
bib
babero[M]
disposable diaper
pañal[M] desechable
ruffled rumba pants
braga[F] de volantes[M]
ruching
volantes[M]
Velcro closure
tirita[F] Velcro®
waterproof pants
material[M] impermeable

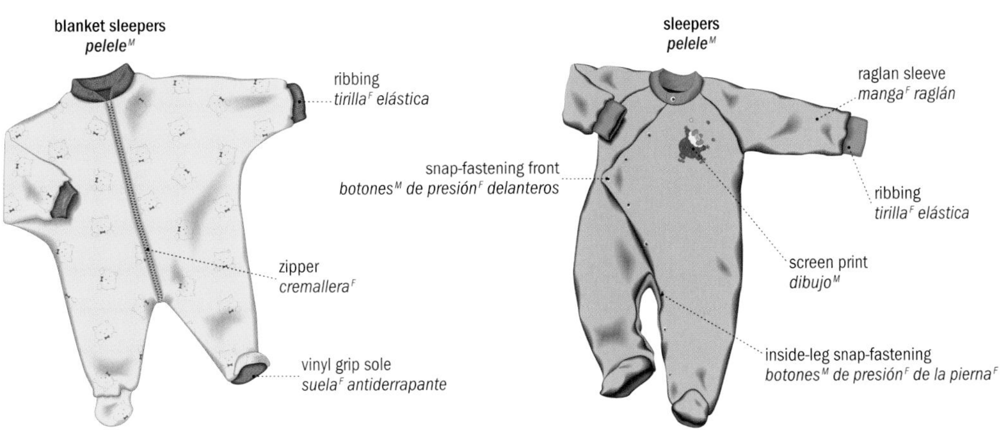

children's clothing

ropa^{F} de niños^{M}

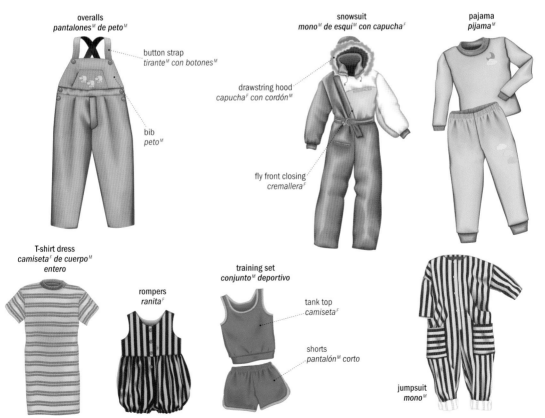

overalls
pantalones^{M} ***de peto***^{M}

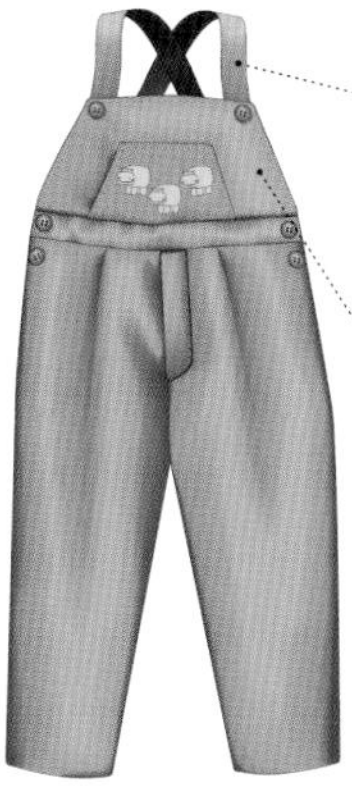

button strap
tirante^{M} *con botones*^{M}

bib
peto^{M}

snowsuit
mono^{M} ***de esquí***^{M} ***con capucha***^{F}

drawstring hood
capucha^{F} *con cordón*^{M}

fly front closing
cremallera^{F}

pajama
pijama^{M}

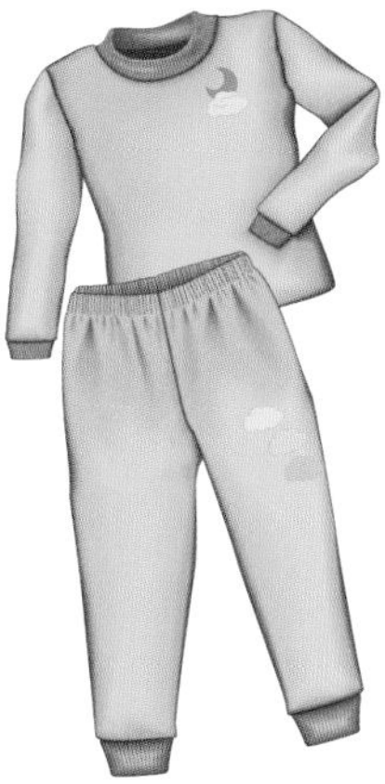

T-shirt dress
camiseta^{F} ***de cuerpo***^{M} ***entero***

rompers
ranita^{F}

training set
conjunto^{M} ***deportivo***

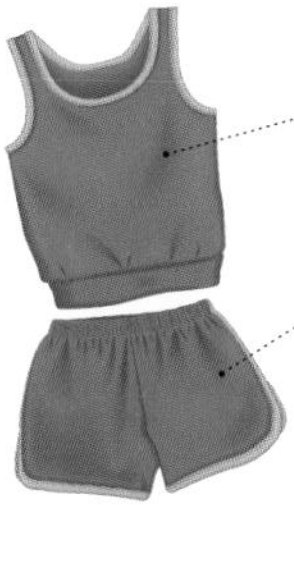

tank top
camiseta^{F}

shorts
pantalón^{M} *corto*

jumpsuit
mono^{M}

sportswear

ropa[F] deportiva

running shoe
zapatilla[F] deportiva

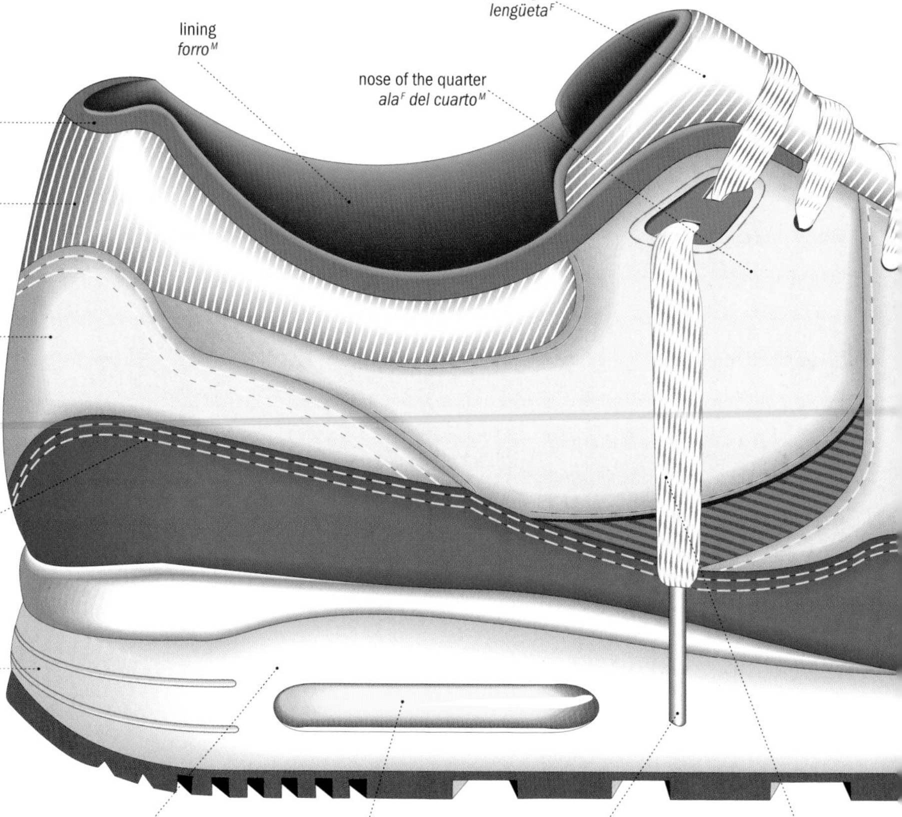

tongue
lengüeta[F]

lining
forro[M]

nose of the quarter
ala[F] del cuarto[M]

collar
ribete[M]

counter
contrafuerte[M]

quarter
cuarto[M]

stitch
pespunteado[M]

heel
talón[M]

middle sole
cambrillón[M]

air unit
cámara[F] de aire[M]

tag
herrete[M]

shoelace
cordón[M]

sweat suit
traje[M] de entrenamiento[M]

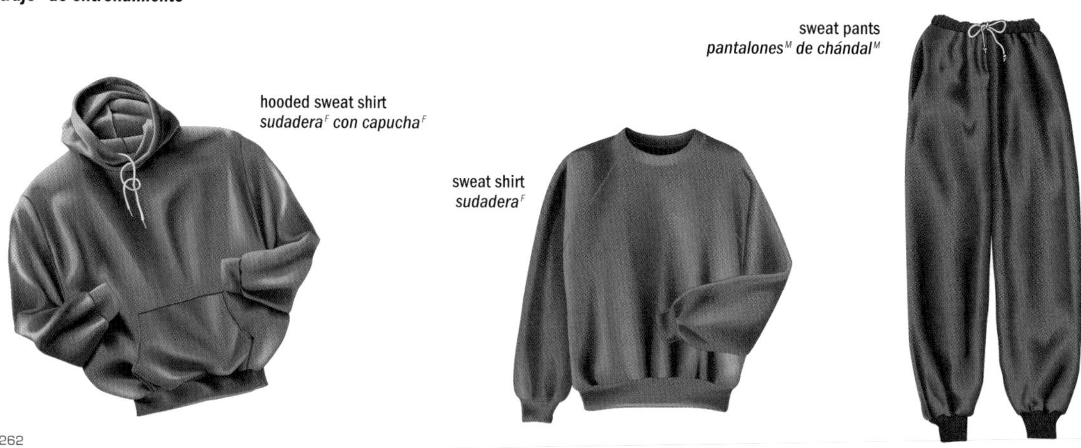

sweat pants
pantalones[M] de chándal[M]

hooded sweat shirt
sudadera[F] con capucha[F]

sweat shirt
sudadera[F]

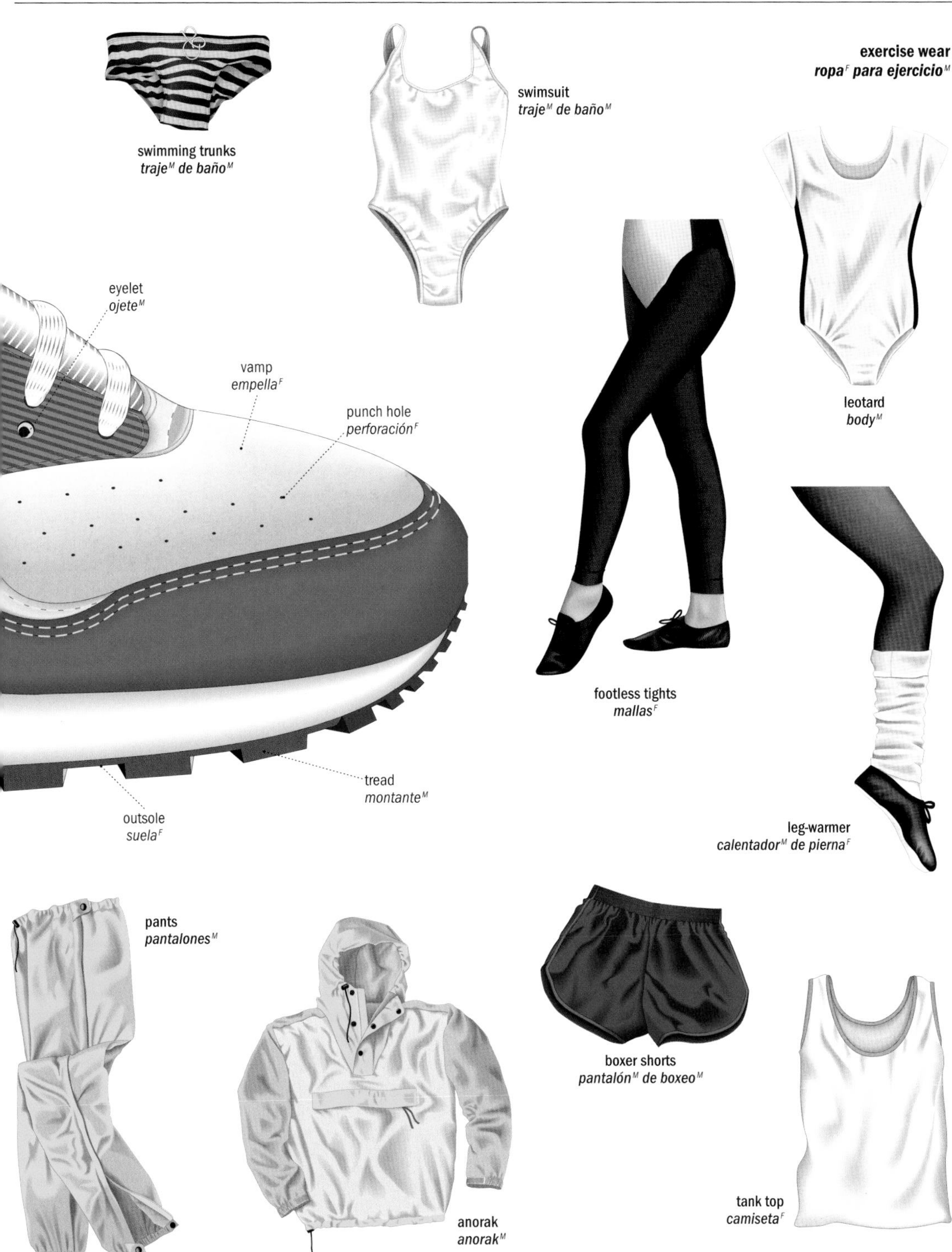
exercise wear
ropaF para ejercicioM
swimming trunks
trajeM de bañoM
swimsuit
trajeM de bañoM
eyelet
ojeteM
vamp
empellaF
punch hole
perforaciónF
tread
montanteM
outsole
suelaF
leotard
bodyM
footless tights
mallasF
leg-warmer
calentadorM de piernaF
pants
pantalonesM
anorak
anorakM
boxer shorts
pantalónM de boxeoM
tank top
camisetaF

jewelry
joyería[F]

earrings
***pendientes**[M]*

clip earrings
pendientes[M] de clip[M]

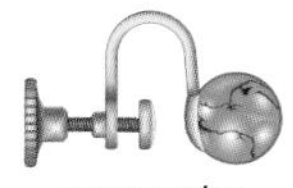
screw earring
pendientes[M] de tornillo[M]

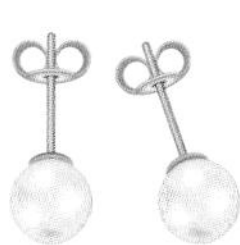
pierced earrings
pendientes[M] de espiga[F]

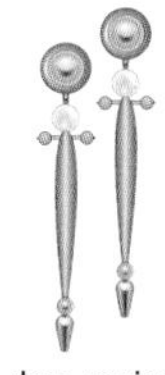
drop earrings
pendientes[M]

hoop earrings
pendientes[M] de aro[M]

necklaces
***collares**[M]*

matinee-length necklace
collar[M] de una vuelta[F], matinée[F]

velvet-band choker
gargantilla[F] de terciopelo[M]

pendant
pendiente[M]

rope necklace
lazo[M]

opera-length necklace
collar[M] de una vuelta[F], ópera[F]

bib necklace
collar[M] de 5 vueltas[M], peto[M]

choker
gargantilla[F]

locket
medallón[M]

bracelets
***brazaletes**[M]*

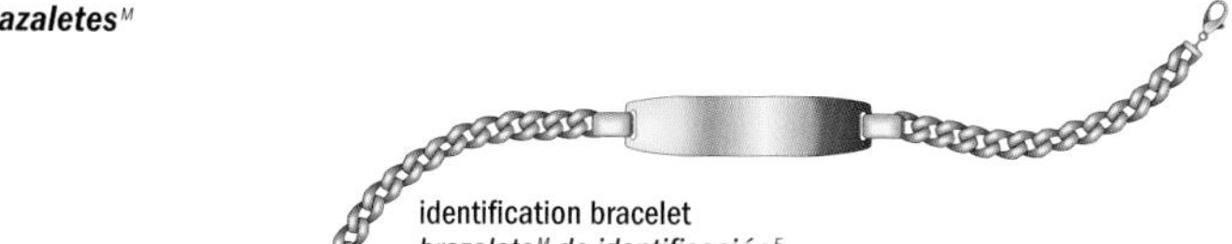
identification bracelet
brazalete[M] de identificación[F]

charm bracelet
pulsera[F] de dijes[M]

bangle
brazalete[M] tubular

rings
***anillos**[M]*

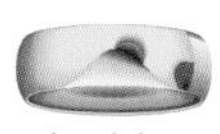
band ring
alianza[F]

signet ring
sortija[F] de sello[M]

solitaire ring
solitario[M]

engagement ring
anillo[M] de compromiso[M]

wedding ring
alianza[F]

nail care

manicura[F]

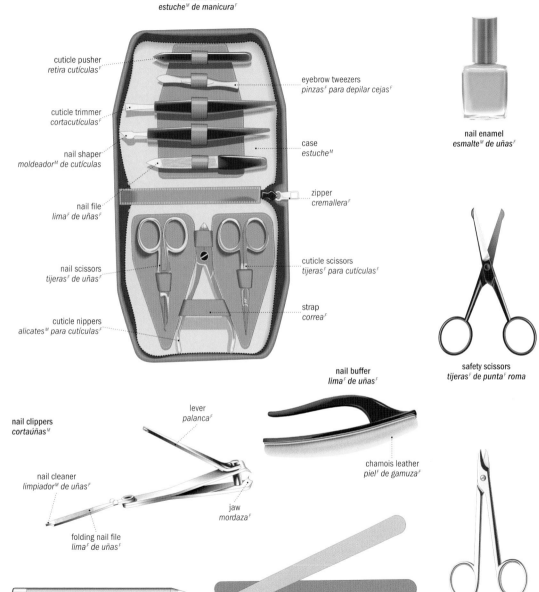

manicure set
estuche[M] de manicura[F]

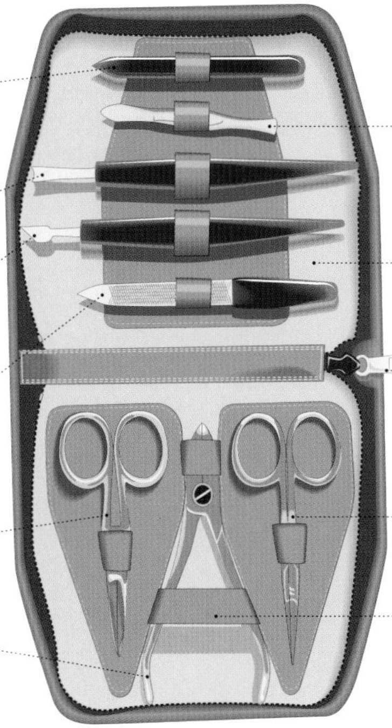

cuticle pusher
retira cutículas[F]

eyebrow tweezers
pinzas[F] para depilar cejas[F]

cuticle trimmer
cortacutículas[F]

nail shaper
moldeador[M] de cutículas

case
estuche[M]

zipper
cremallera[F]

nail file
lima[F] de uñas[F]

nail scissors
tijeras[F] de uñas[F]

cuticle scissors
tijeras[F] para cutículas[F]

strap
correa[F]

cuticle nippers
alicates[M] para cutículas[F]

nail enamel
esmalte[M] de uñas[F]

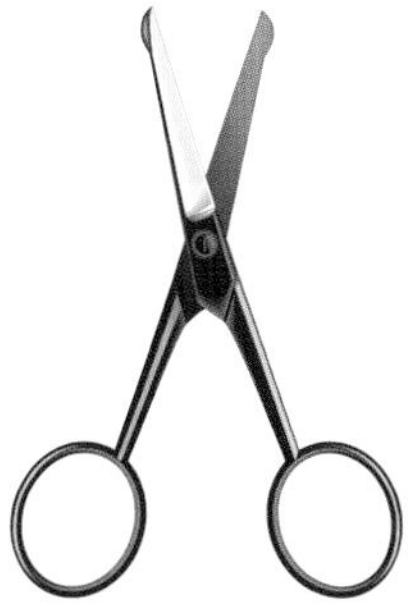

safety scissors
tijeras[F] de punta[F] roma

nail buffer
lima[F] de uñas[F]

chamois leather
piel[F] de gamuza[F]

nail clippers
cortaúñas[M]

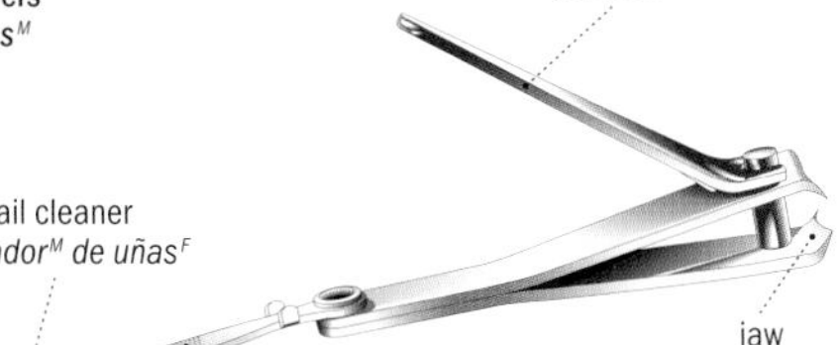

lever
palanca[F]

nail cleaner
limpiador[M] de uñas[F]

jaw
mordaza[F]

folding nail file
lima[F] de uñas[F]

nail whitener pencil
lápiz[M] blanco para uñas[F]

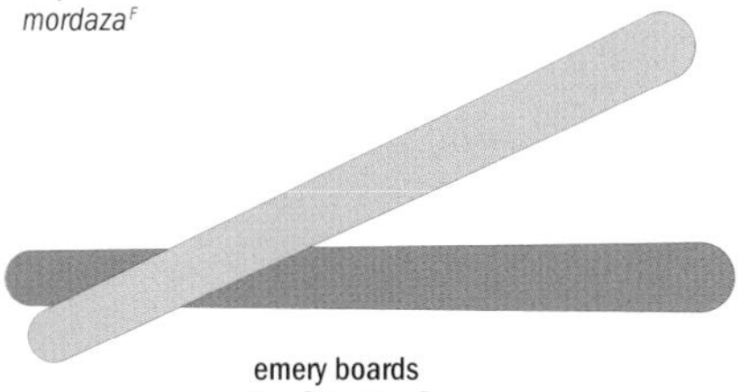

emery boards
lima[F] de uñas[F]

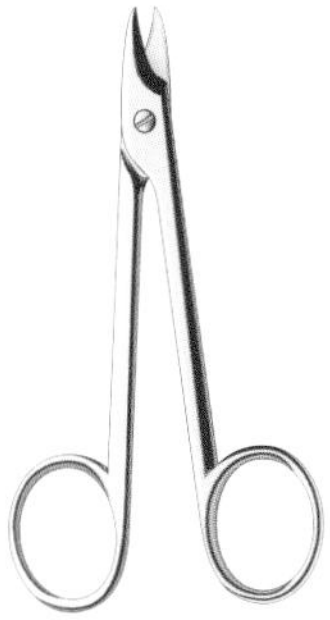

toenail scissors
tijeras[F] de pedicura[F]

makeup

maquillaje[M]

facial makeup
maquillaje[M] facial

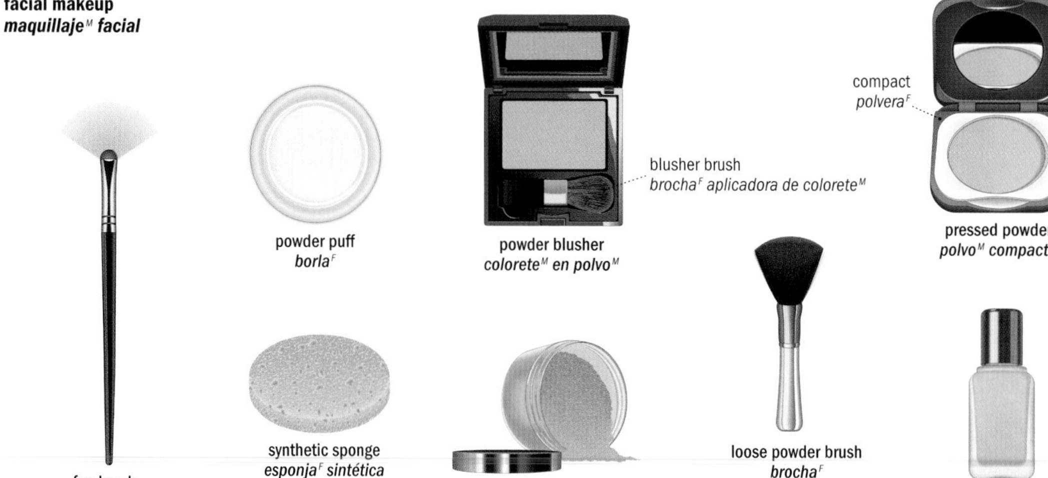

fan brush
brocha[F] en forma[F] de abanico[M]

powder puff
borla[F]

synthetic sponge
esponja[F] sintética

powder blusher
colorete[M] en polvo[M]

blusher brush
brocha[F] aplicadora de colorete[M]

loose powder
polvos[M] sueltos

loose powder brush
brocha[F]

compact
polvera[F]

pressed powder
polvo[M] compacto

liquid foundation
base[F] líquida

eye makeup
maquillaje[M] para ojos[M]

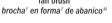

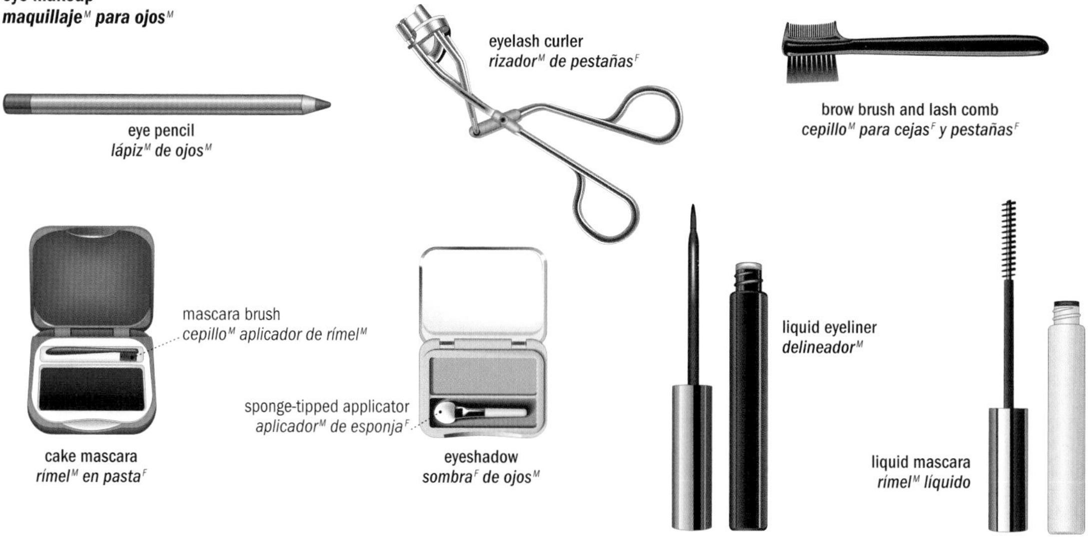

eye pencil
lápiz[M] de ojos[M]

eyelash curler
rizador[M] de pestañas[F]

brow brush and lash comb
cepillo[M] para cejas[F] y pestañas[F]

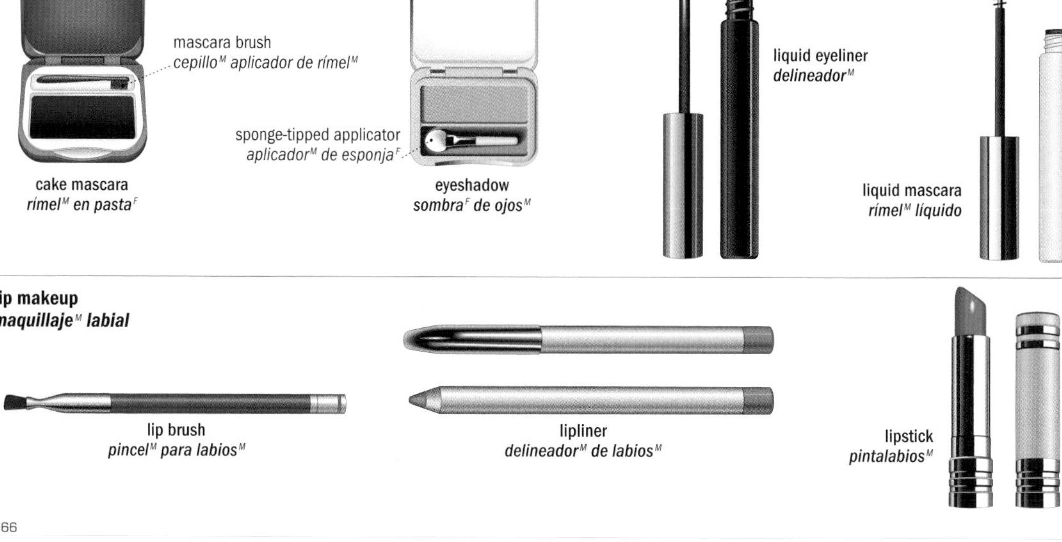

mascara brush
cepillo[M] aplicador de rímel[M]

cake mascara
rímel[M] en pasta[F]

sponge-tipped applicator
aplicador[M] de esponja[F]

eyeshadow
sombra[F] de ojos[M]

liquid eyeliner
delineador[M]

liquid mascara
rímel[M] líquido

lip makeup
maquillaje[M] labial

lip brush
pincel[M] para labios[M]

lipliner
delineador[M] de labios[M]

lipstick
pintalabios[M]

body care

cuidado[M] personal

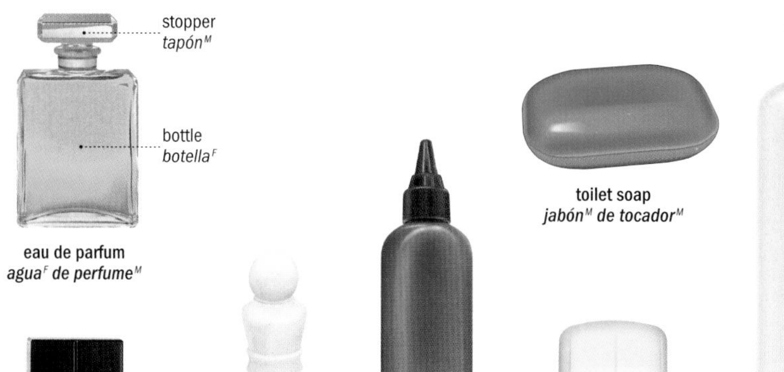

eau de parfum
agua[F] de perfume[M]

toilet soap
jabón[M] de tocador[M]

haircolor
tinte[M] para el cabello[M]

hair conditioner
acondicionador[M]

shampoo
champú[M]

deodorant
desodorante[M]

eau de toilette
agua[F] de colonia[F]

bubble bath
gel[M] de baño[M]

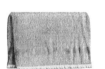

washcloth
manopla[F] de baño[M]

washcloth
toalla[F] para la cara[F]

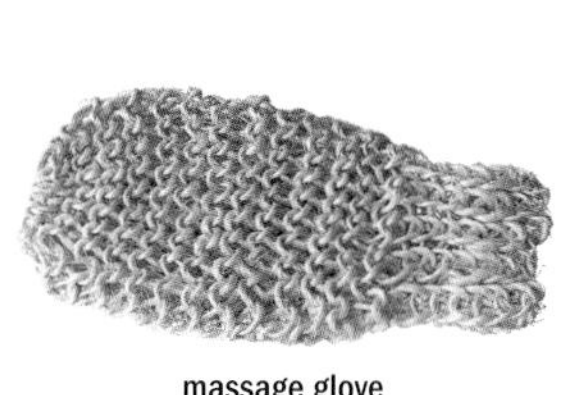

massage glove
guante[M] de crin[M]

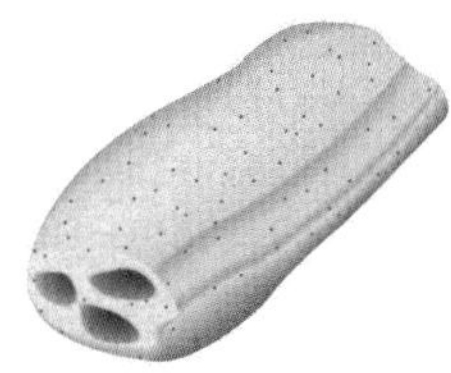

vegetable sponge
esponja[F] vegetal

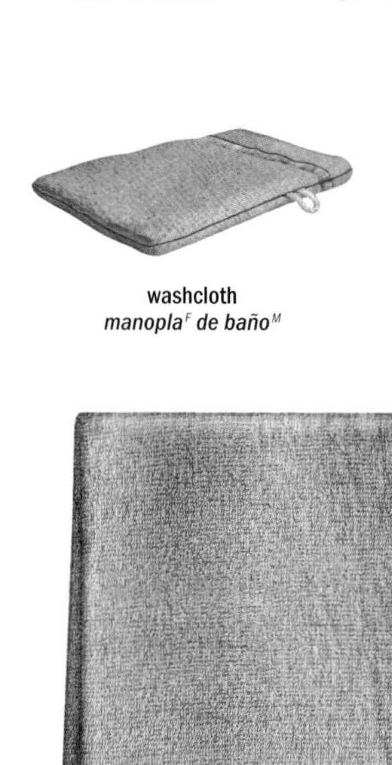

bath sheet
toalla[F] de baño[M]

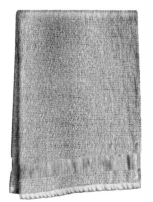

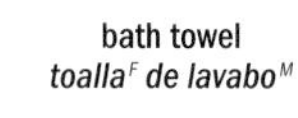

bath towel
toalla[F] de lavabo[M]

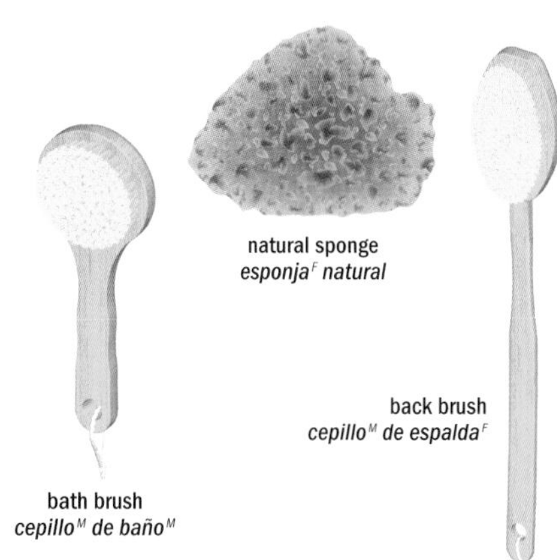

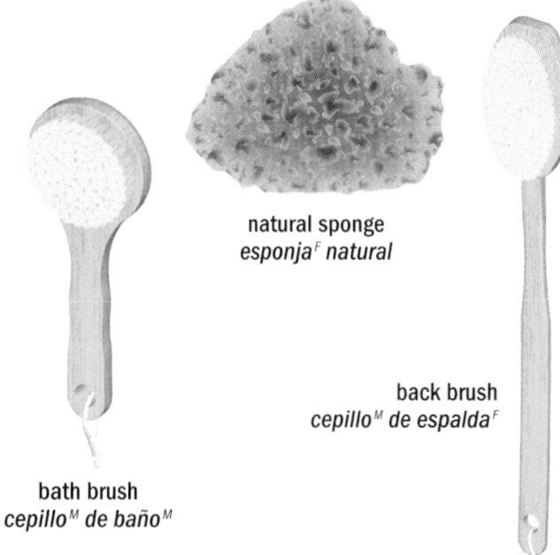

natural sponge
esponja[F] natural

back brush
cepillo[M] de espalda[F]

bath brush
cepillo[M] de baño[M]

hairdressing

peinado[M]

hairbrushes
cepillos[M]

flat-back brush
cepillo[M] con base[F] de goma[F]

round brush
cepillo[M] redondo

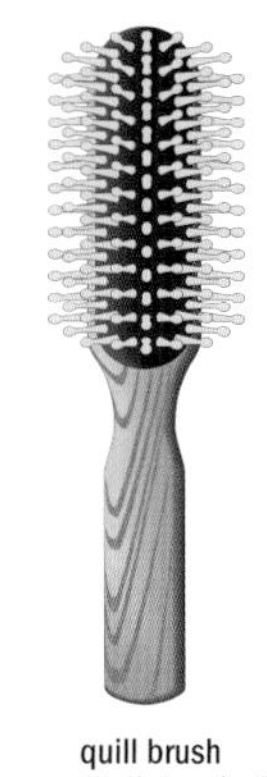
quill brush
cepillo[M] de púas[F]

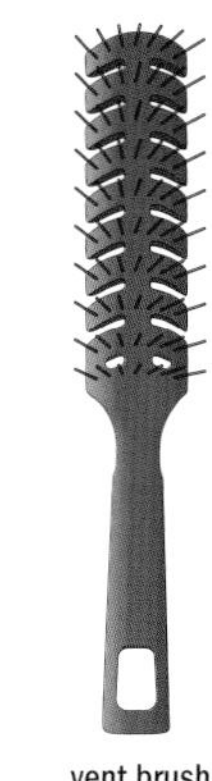
vent brush
cepillo[M] de esqueleto[M]

combs
peines[M]

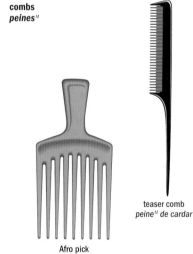

Afro pick
peine[M] afro

teaser comb
peine[M] de cardar

tail comb
peine[M] de mango[M]

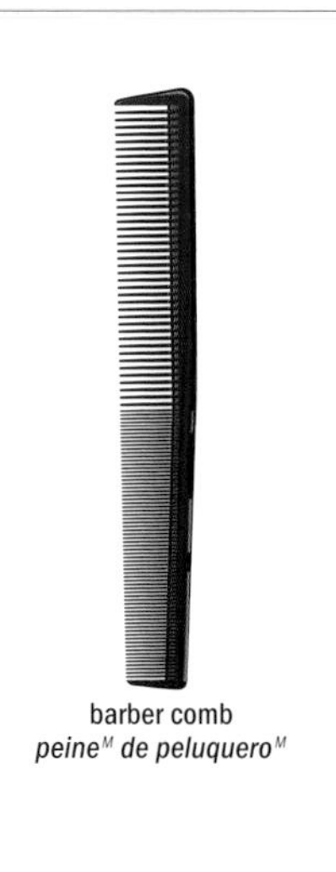
barber comb
peine[M] de peluquero[M]

pitchfork comb
peine[M] combinado

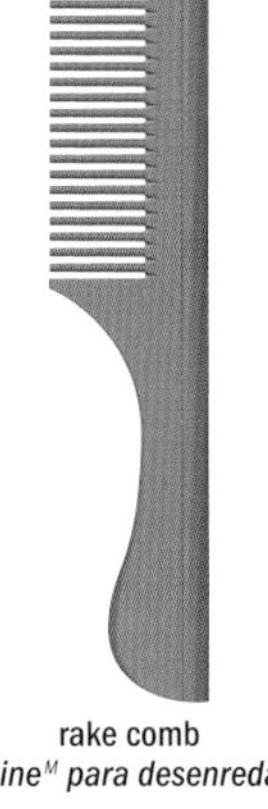
rake comb
peine[M] para desenredar

hair roller
rulo[M] para el cabello[M]

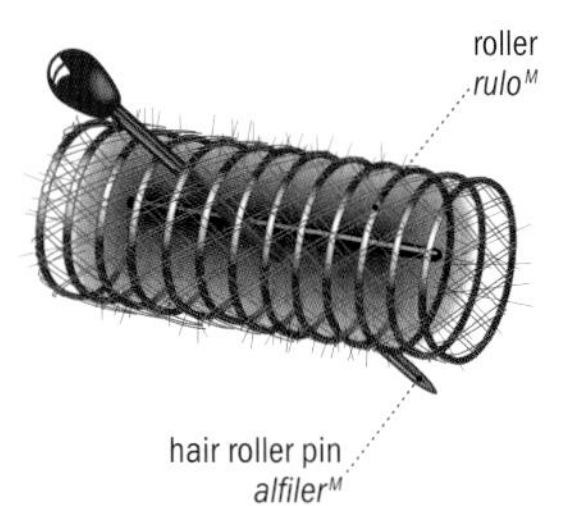
roller
rulo[M]

hair roller pin
alfiler[M]

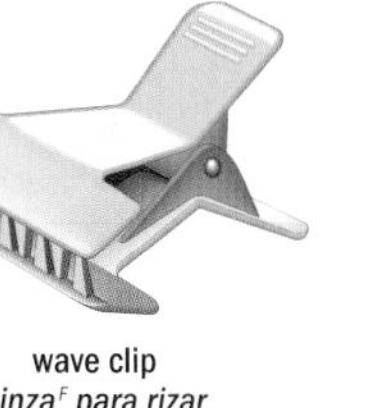
wave clip
pinza[F] para rizar

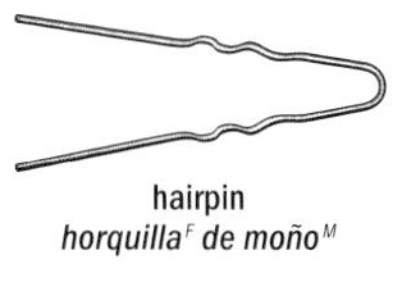
hairpin
horquilla[F] de moño[M]

bobby pin
horquilla[F]

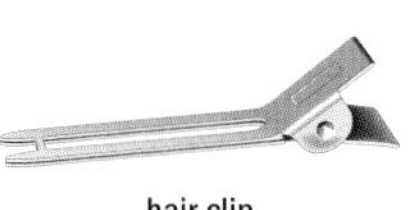

hair clip
pinza[F] para el cabello[M]

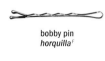

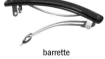

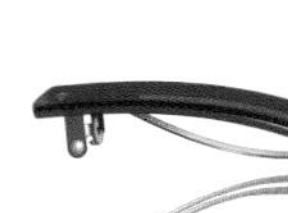
barrette
pasador[M]

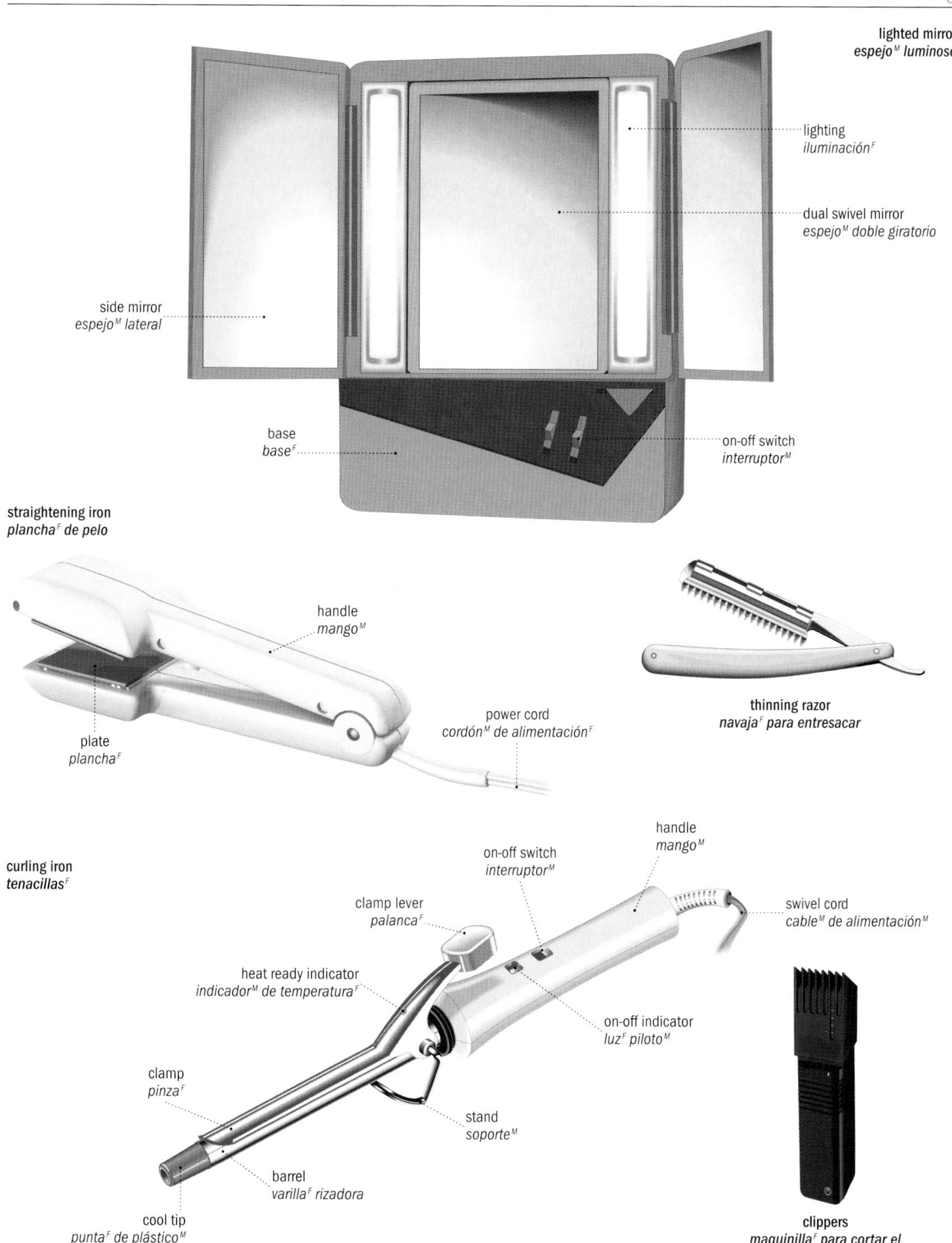
lighted mirror
espejo*^M *luminoso
lighting
iluminación^F
dual swivel mirror
espejo^M *doble giratorio*
side mirror
espejo^M *lateral*
base
base^F
on-off switch
interruptor^M
straightening iron
plancha*^F *de pelo
handle
mango^M
plate
plancha^F
power cord
cordón^M *de alimentación*^F
thinning razor
navaja*^F *para entresacar
curling iron
***tenacillas*^F**
handle
mango^M
on-off switch
interruptor^M
clamp lever
palanca^F
swivel cord
cable^M *de alimentación*^M
heat ready indicator
indicador^M *de temperatura*^F
on-off indicator
luz^F *piloto*^M
clamp
pinza^F
stand
soporte^M
barrel
varilla^F *rizadora*
cool tip
punta^F *de plástico*^M
clippers
***maquinilla*^F *para cortar el cabello*^M**

hairdressing

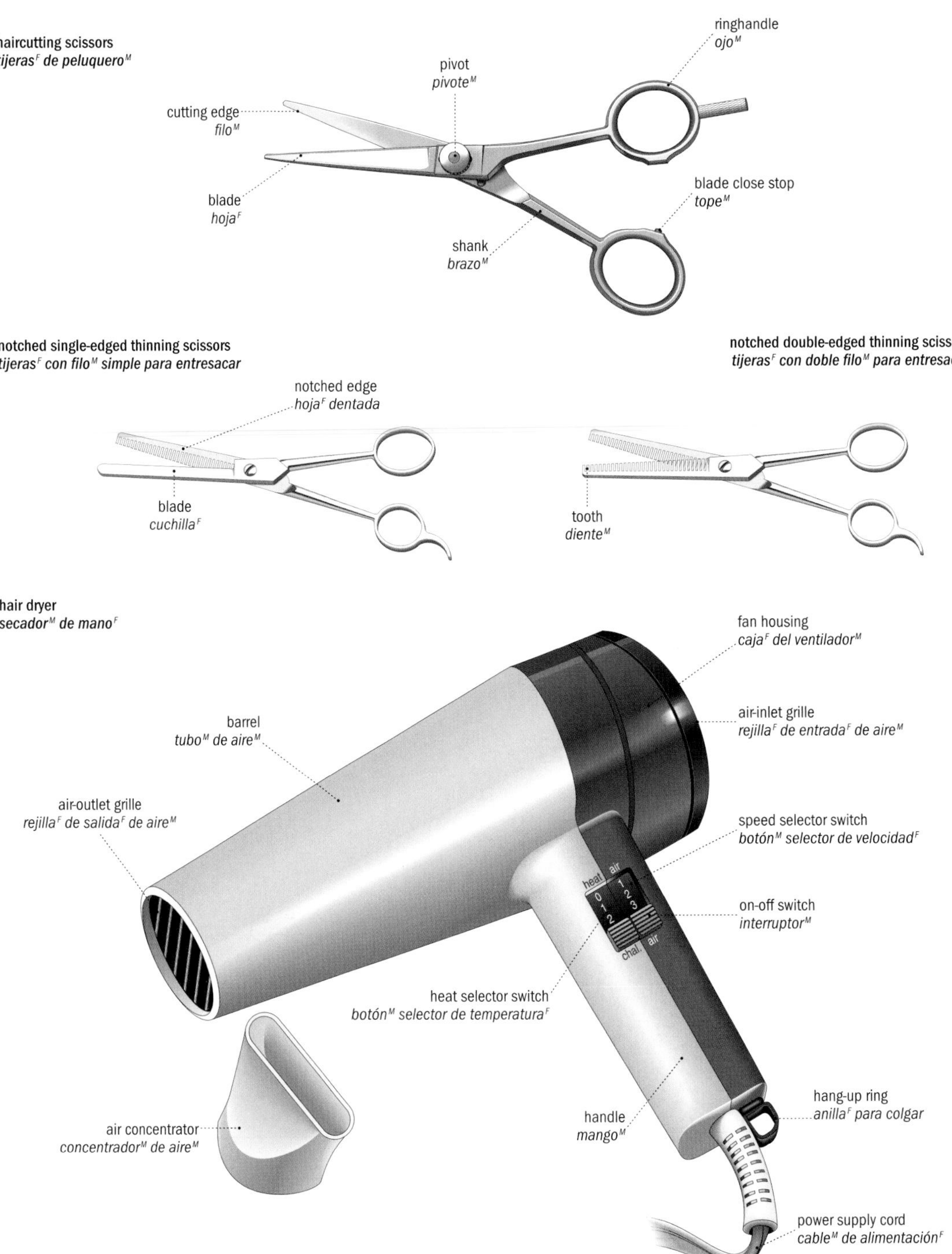
haircutting scissors
tijeras^F de peluquero^M
ringhandle
ojo^M
pivot
pivote^M
cutting edge
filo^M
blade
hoja^F
blade close stop
tope^M
shank
brazo^M
notched single-edged thinning scissors
tijeras^F con filo^M simple para entresacar
notched double-edged thinning scissors
tijeras^F con doble filo^M para entresacar
notched edge
hoja^F dentada
blade
cuchilla^F
tooth
diente^M
hair dryer
secador^M de mano^F
fan housing
caja^F del ventilador^M
barrel
tubo^M de aire^M
air-inlet grille
rejilla^F de entrada^F de aire^M
air-outlet grille
rejilla^F de salida^F de aire^M
speed selector switch
botón^M selector de velocidad^F
heat
air
0
1
2
1
2
3
chal.
air
on-off switch
interruptor^M
heat selector switch
botón^M selector de temperatura^F
hang-up ring
anilla^F para colgar
handle
mango^M
air concentrator
concentrador^M de aire^M
power supply cord
cable^M de alimentación^F

shaving

afeitado^M

shaving foam
espuma^F de afeitar

power cord
cable^M de alimentación^F

cleaning brush
escobilla^F limpiadora

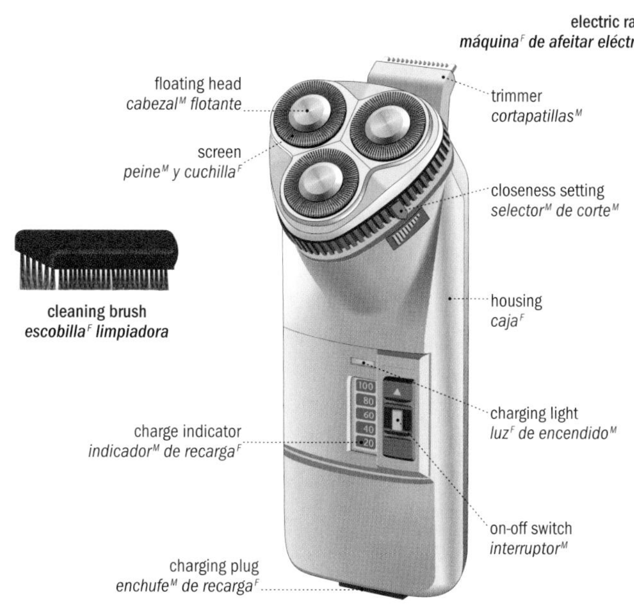

shaving brush
brocha^F de afeitar

plug adapter
adaptador^M

aftershave
loción^F para después del afeitado^M

straight razor
navaja^F de barbero^M

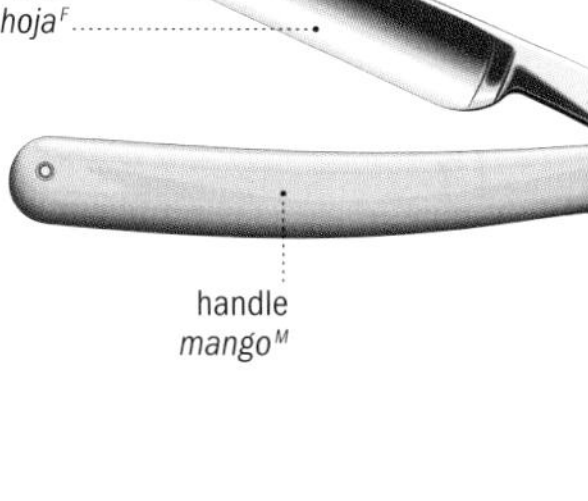

shaving mug
jabonera^F

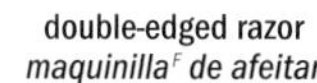

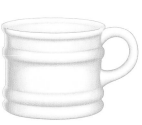

blade injector
distribuidor^M de hojas^F de afeitar

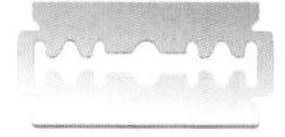

double-edged blade
hoja^F de afeitar

double-edged razor
maquinilla^F de afeitar

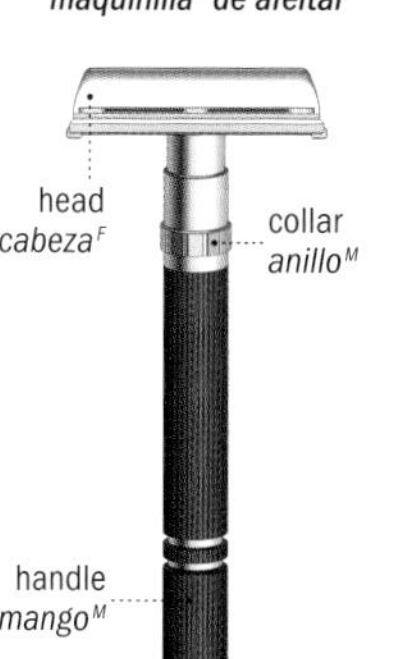

disposable razor
maquinilla^F desechable

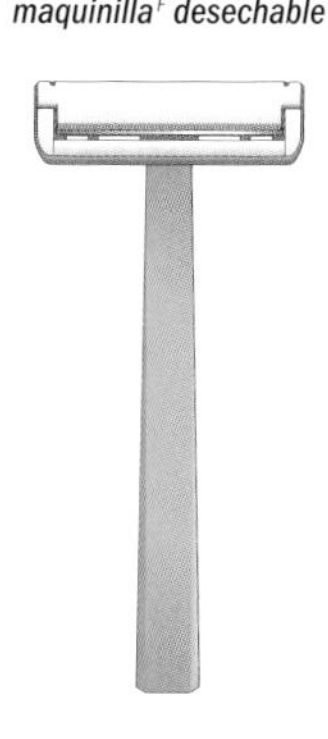

dental care

higiene[F] dental

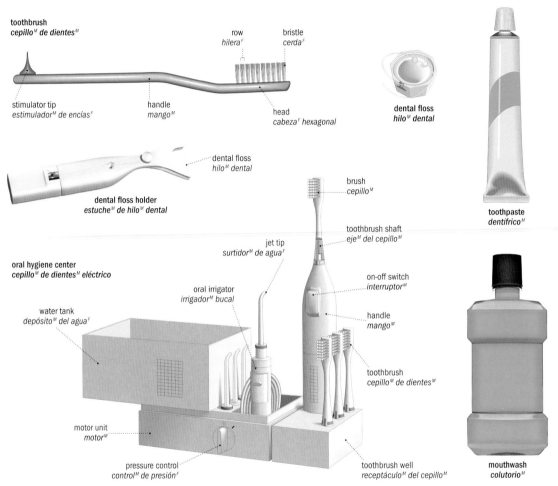

toothbrush
cepillo[M] de dientes[M]

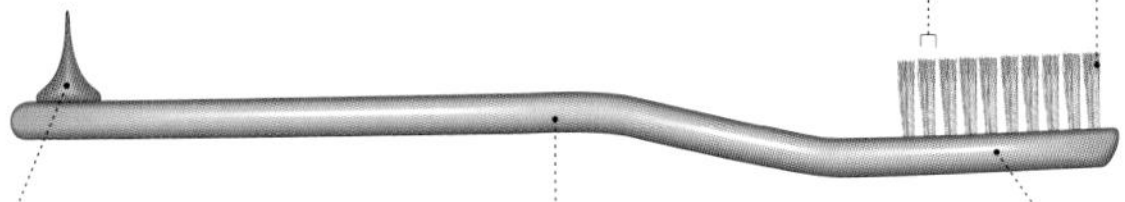

row
hilera[F]

bristle
cerda[F]

stimulator tip
estimulador[M] de encías[F]

handle
mango[M]

head
cabeza[F] hexagonal

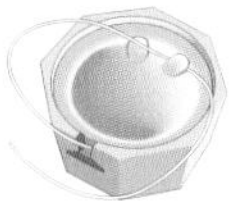

dental floss
hilo[M] dental

dental floss
hilo[M] dental

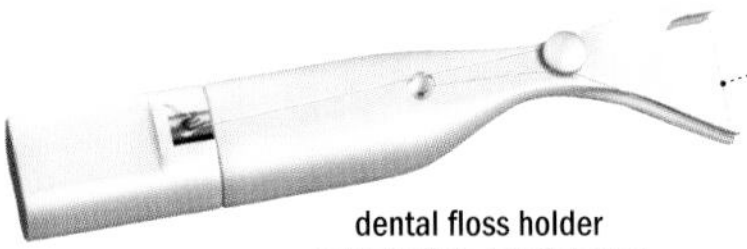

dental floss holder
estuche[M] de hilo[M] dental

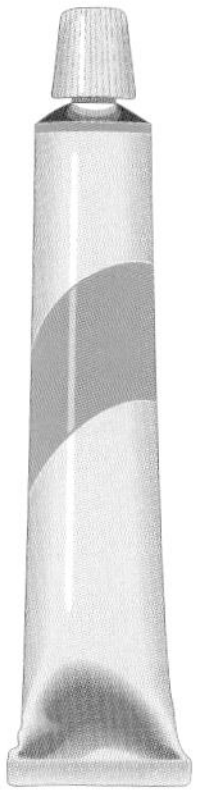

toothpaste
dentífrico[M]

brush
cepillo[M]

toothbrush shaft
eje[M] del cepillo[M]

jet tip
surtidor[M] de agua[F]

oral hygiene center
cepillo[M] de dientes[M] eléctrico

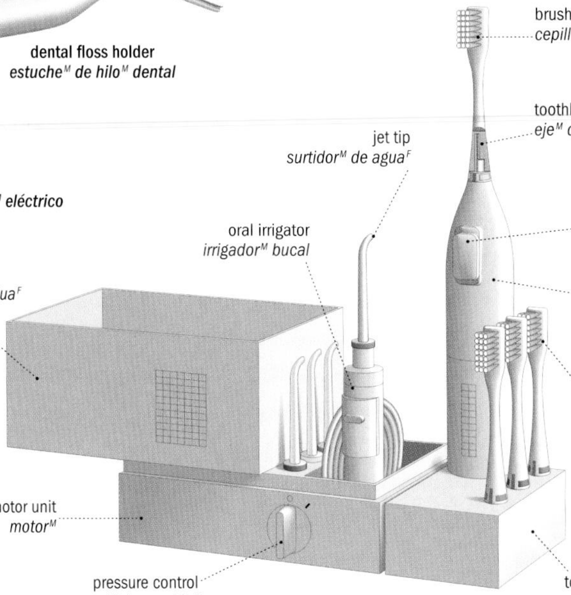

on-off switch
interruptor[M]

oral irrigator
irrigador[M] bucal

water tank
depósito[M] del agua[F]

handle
mango[M]

toothbrush
cepillo[M] de dientes[M]

motor unit
motor[M]

pressure control
control[M] de presión[F]

toothbrush well
receptáculo[M] del cepillo[M]

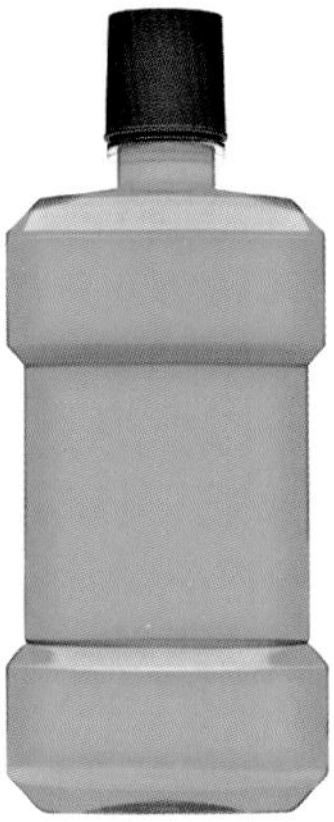

mouthwash
colutorio[M]

contact lenses

lentes[F] de contacto[M]

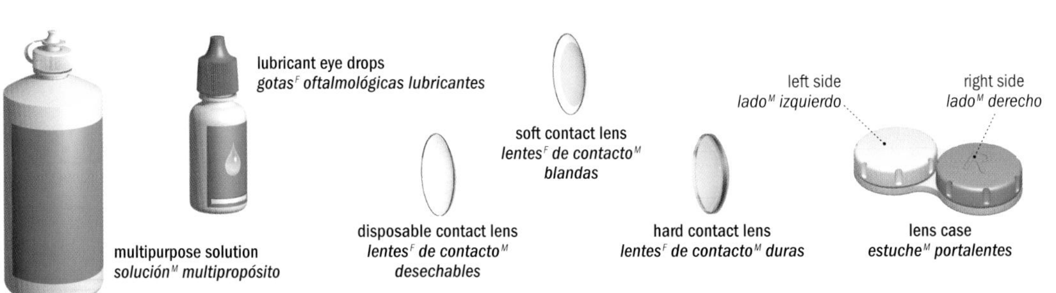

PERSONAL ADORNMENT AND ARTICLES

eyeglasses

gafas[F]

eyeglasses parts
gafas[F] : partes[F]

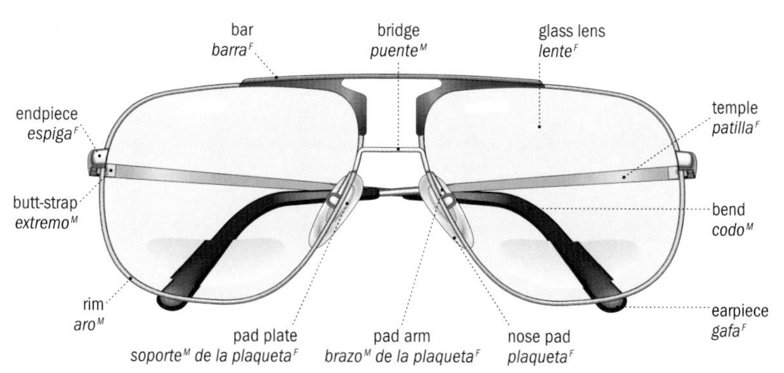

examples of eyeglasses
ejemplos[M] de gafas[F]

opera glasses
gemelos[M] de teatro[M]

sunglasses
gafas[F] de sol[M]

half-glasses
media luna[F]

umbrellas and stick

paraguas[M] y bastones[M]

umbrellas
paraguas[M]

umbrella stand
paragüero[M]

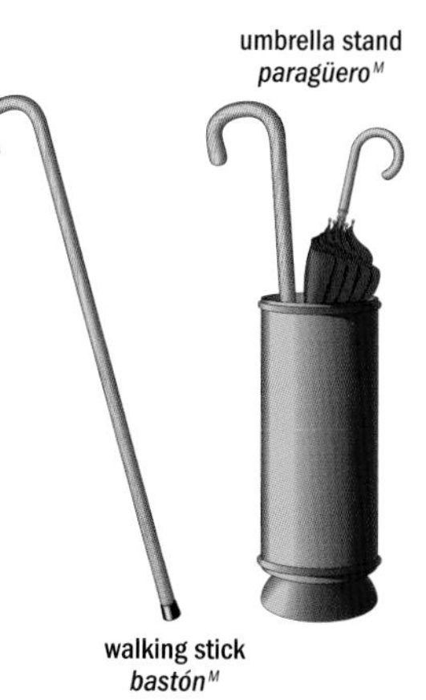

walking stick
bastón[M]

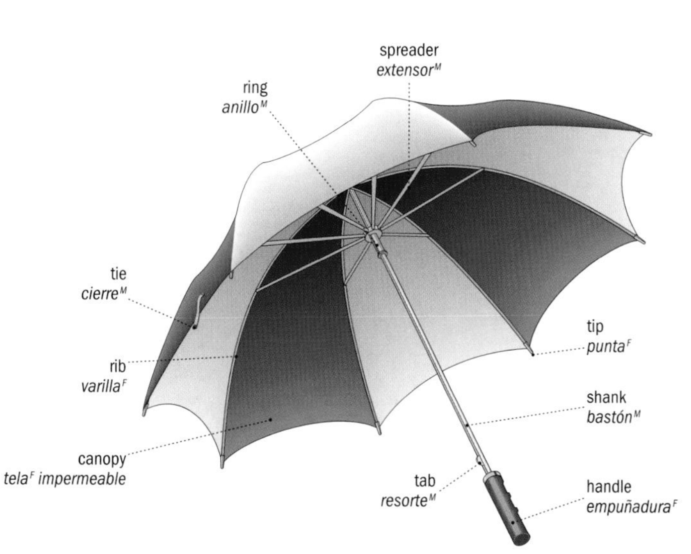

leather goods

artículos[M] de marroquinería

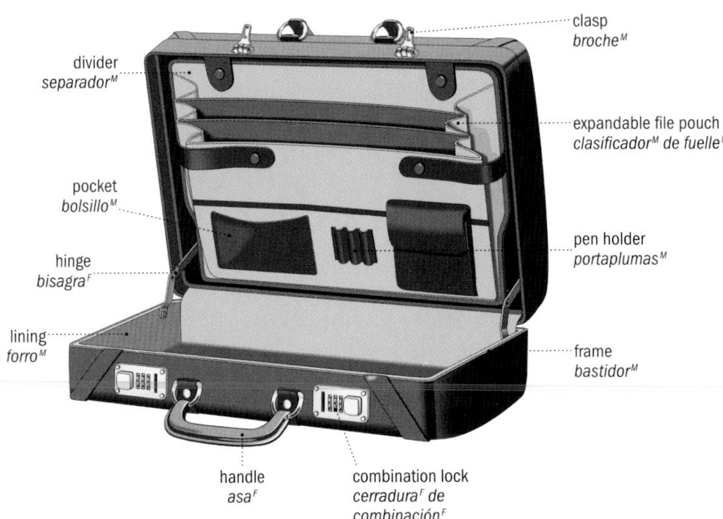

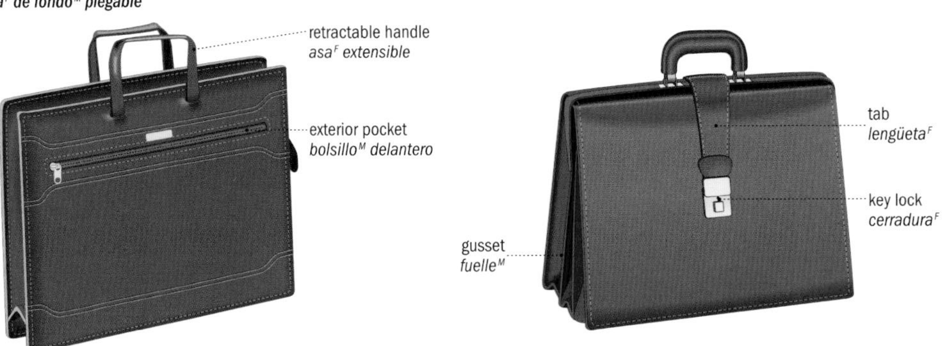

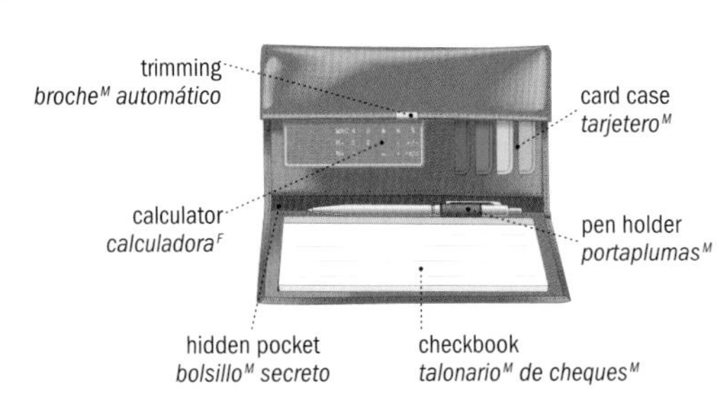

card case
tarjetero[M]

bill compartment
billetera[F]

windows
plásticos[M] transparentes

tab
lengüeta[F]

slot
ranura[F]

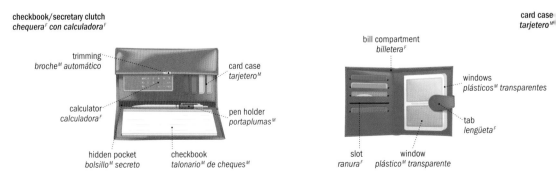

window
plástico[M] transparente

leather goods

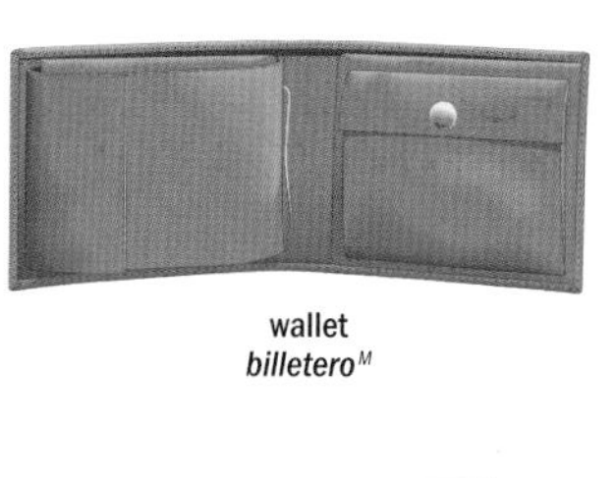

wallet
billetero[M]

coin purse
portamonedas[M]

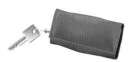

key case
llavero[M]

purse
monedero[M]

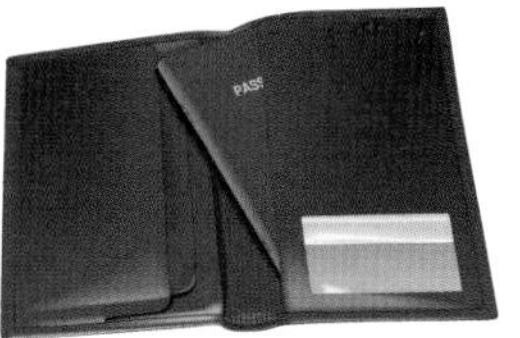

passport case
porta pasaportes[M]

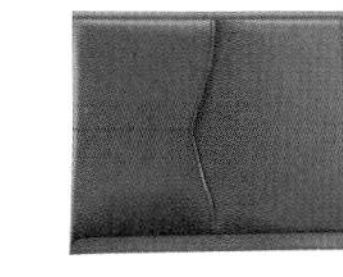

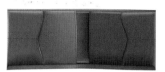

billfold
billetera[F]

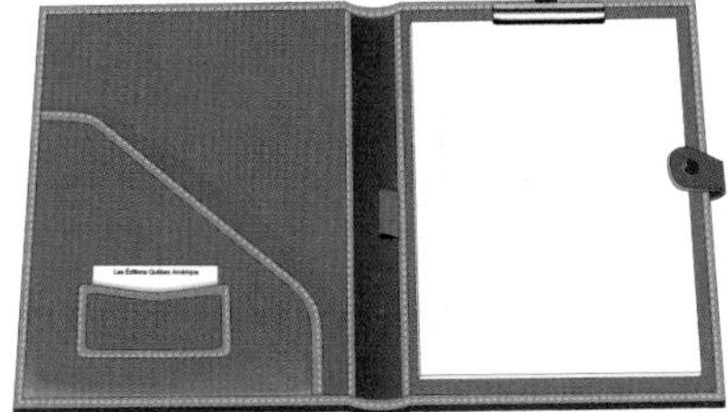

writing case
agenda[F]

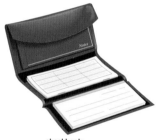

checkbook
talonario[M] *de cheques*[M]

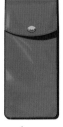

eyeglasses case
funda[F] *de gafas*[F]

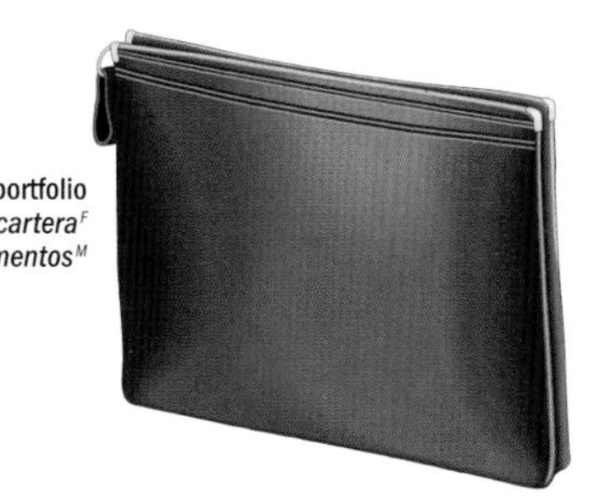

underarm portfolio
cartera[F]
portadocumentos[M]

handbags
bolsos[M]

drawstring bag
bolso[M] *tipo cubo*[M]

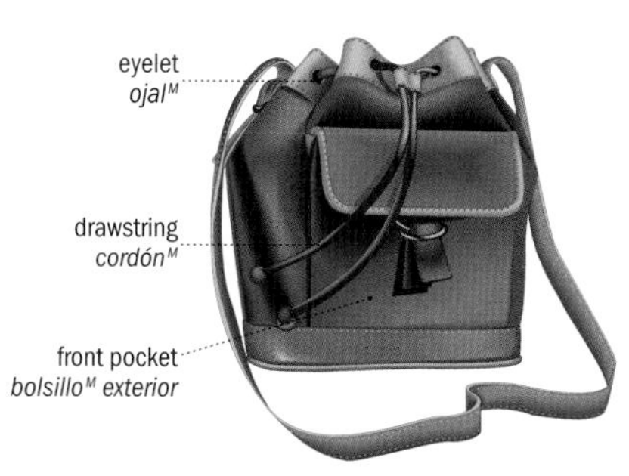

satchel bag
bolso[M] *clásico*

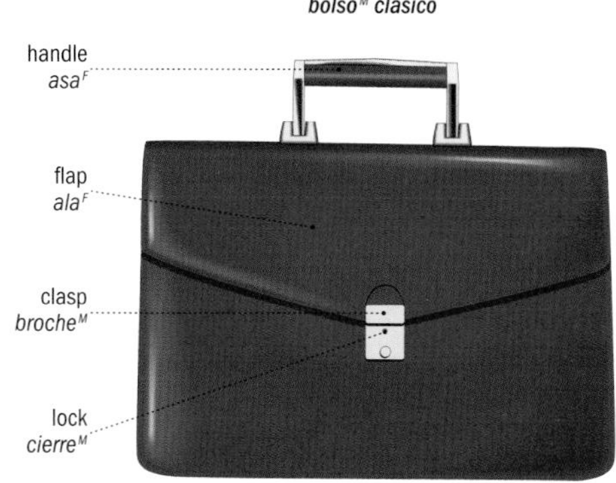

handbags

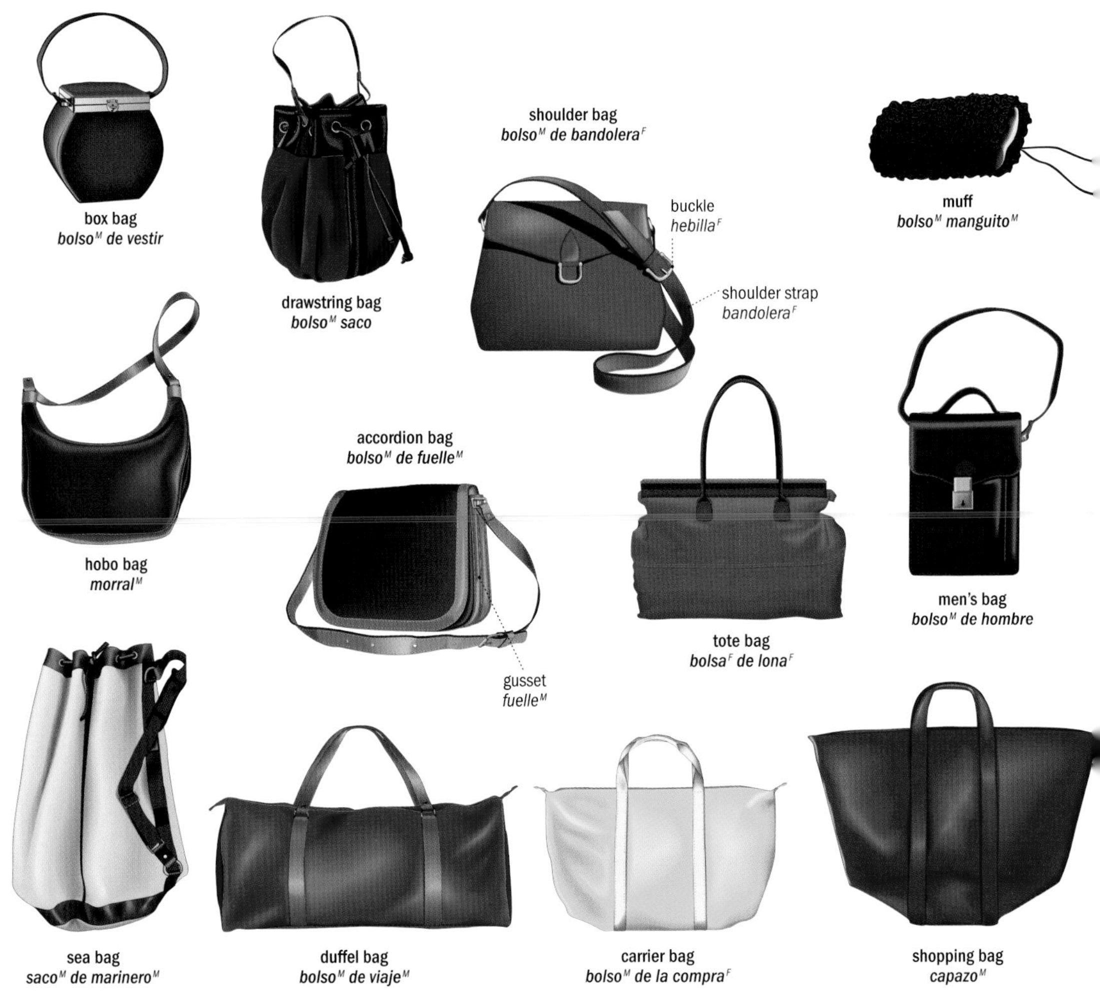

box bag
bolso[M] de vestir
drawstring bag
bolso[M] saco
shoulder bag
bolso[M] de bandolera[F]
buckle
hebilla[F]
shoulder strap
bandolera[F]
muff
bolso[M] manguito[M]
hobo bag
morral[M]
accordion bag
bolso[M] de fuelle[M]
gusset
fuelle[M]
tote bag
bolsa[F] de lona[F]
men's bag
bolso[M] de hombre
sea bag
saco[M] de marinero[M]
duffel bag
bolso[M] de viaje[M]
carrier bag
bolso[M] de la compra[F]
shopping bag
capazo[M]

luggage

equipaje[M]

utility case
neceser[M]
carry-on bag
bolso[M] de viaje[M]
handle
asa[F]
exterior pocket
bolsillo[M] exterior
shoulder strap
bandolera[F]
tote bag
maletín[M]

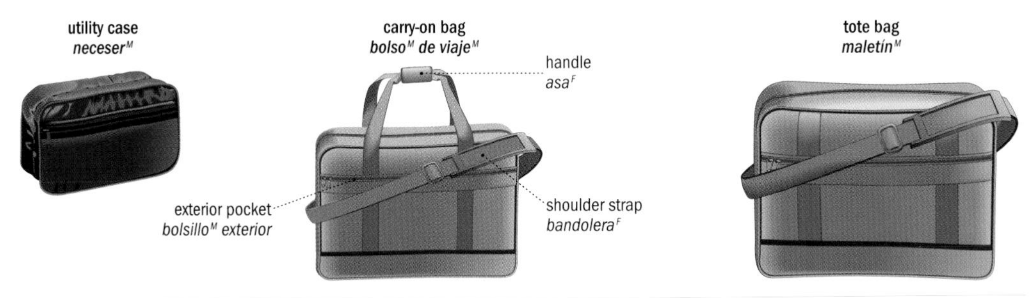

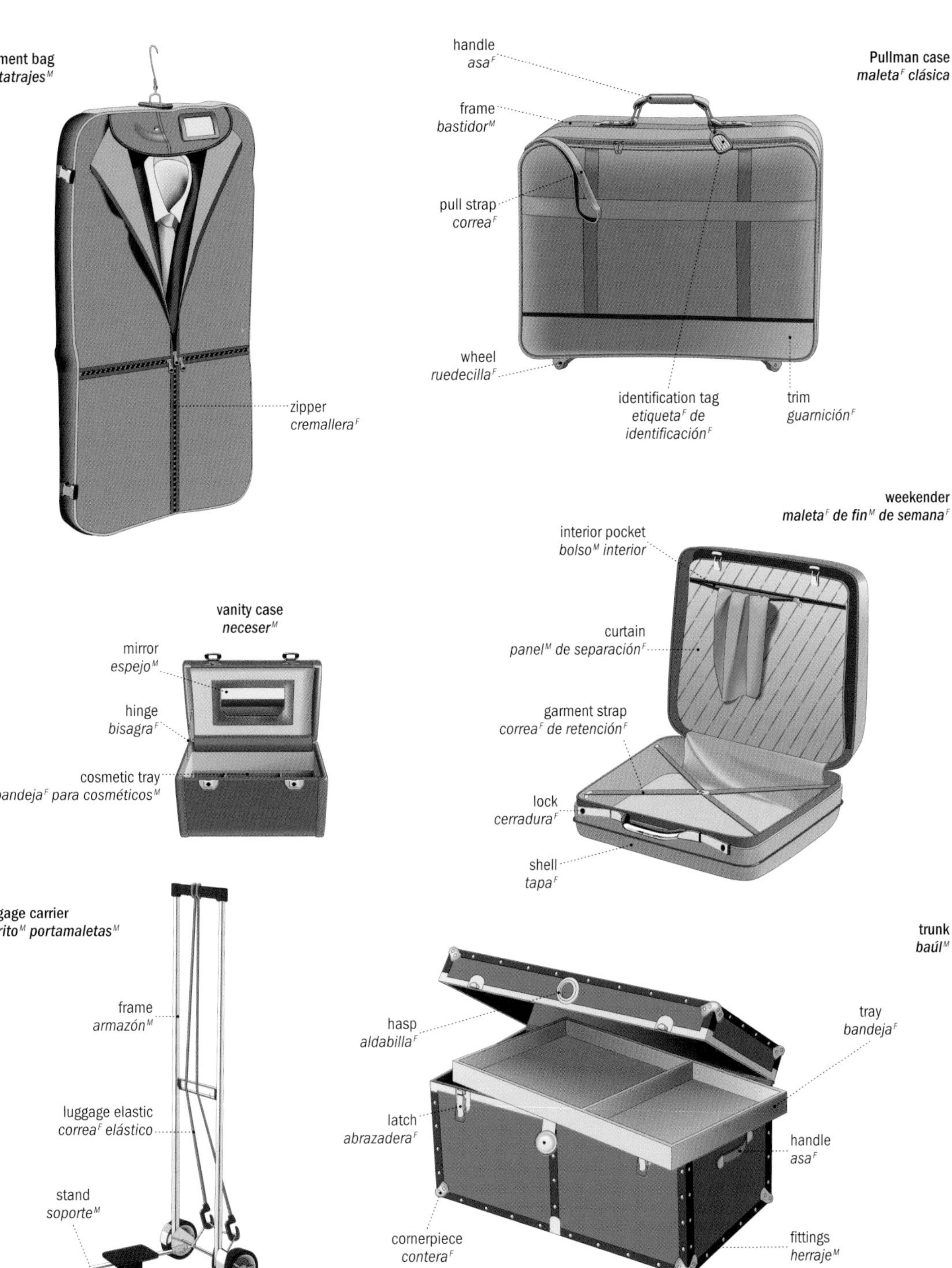
garment bag
portatrajes[M]
zipper
cremallera[F]
handle
asa[F]
frame
bastidor[M]
pull strap
correa[F]
wheel
ruedecilla[F]
identification tag
etiqueta[F] *de identificación*[F]
trim
guarnición[F]
Pullman case
maleta[F] *clásica*
weekender
maleta[F] *de fin*[M] *de semana*[F]
interior pocket
bolso[M] *interior*
curtain
panel[M] *de separación*[F]
garment strap
correa[F] *de retención*[F]
lock
cerradura[F]
shell
tapa[F]
vanity case
neceser[M]
mirror
espejo[M]
hinge
bisagra[F]
cosmetic tray
bandeja[F] *para cosméticos*[M]
luggage carrier
carrito[M] *portamaletas*[M]
frame
armazón[M]
luggage elastic
correa[F] *elástico*
stand
soporte[M]
trunk
baúl[M]
hasp
aldabilla[F]
tray
bandeja[F]
latch
abrazadera[F]
handle
asa[F]
cornerpiece
contera[F]
fittings
herraje[M]

pyramid

pirámide^F

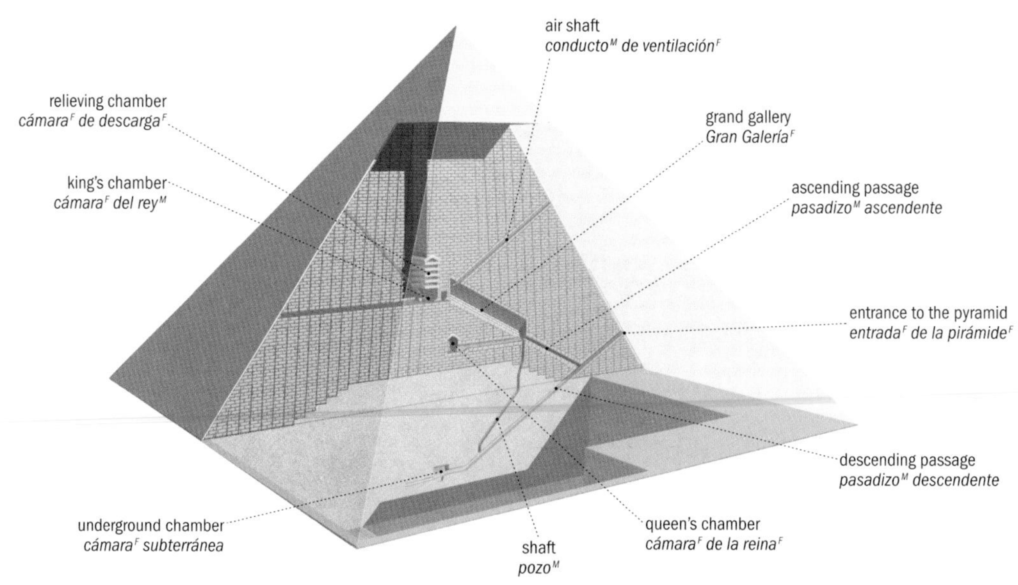
air shaft
conducto^M de ventilación^F
relieving chamber
cámara^F de descarga^F
grand gallery
Gran Galería^F
king's chamber
cámara^F del rey^M
ascending passage
pasadizo^M ascendente
entrance to the pyramid
entrada^F de la pirámide^F
descending passage
pasadizo^M descendente
underground chamber
cámara^F subterránea
queen's chamber
cámara^F de la reina^F
shaft
pozo^M

Greek theater

teatro^M griego

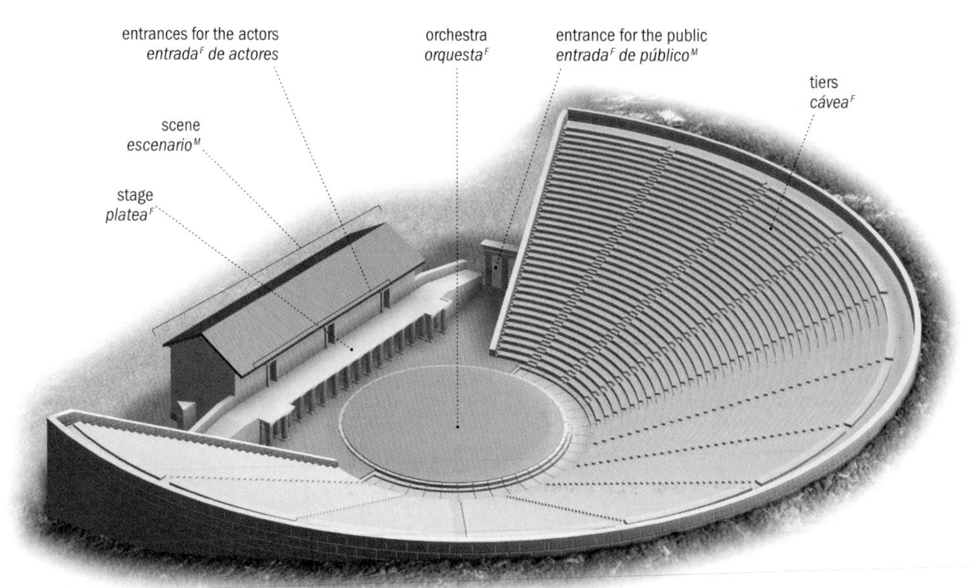
entrances for the actors
entrada^F de actores
orchestra
orquesta^F
entrance for the public
entrada^F de público^M
tiers
cávea^F
scene
escenario^M
stage
platea^F

Greek temple

templo^M griego

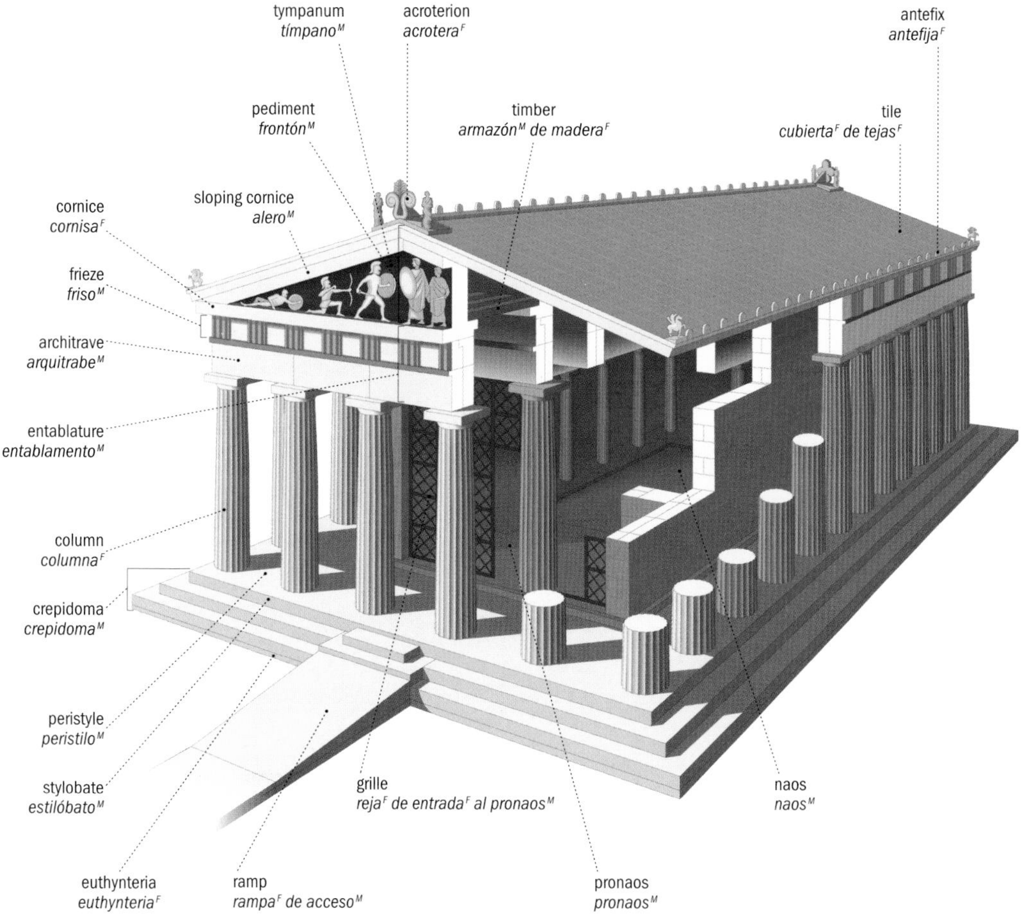

tympanum
tímpano^M
acroterion
acrotera^F
antefix
antefija^F
pediment
frontón^M
timber
armazón^M de madera^F
tile
cubierta^F de tejas^F
cornice
cornisa^F
sloping cornice
alero^M
frieze
friso^M
architrave
arquitrabe^M
entablature
entablamento^M
column
columna^F
crepidoma
crepidoma^M
peristyle
peristilo^M
stylobate
estilóbato^M
grille
reja^F de entrada^F al pronaos^M
naos
naos^M
euthynteria
euthynteria^F
ramp
rampa^F de acceso^M
pronaos
pronaos^M

plan
plano^M

naos
naos^M
location of the statue
ubicación^F de la estatua^F
opisthodomos
opistodomo^M
pronaos
pronaos^M
peristyle
peristilo^M
crepidoma
crepidoma^F
column
columna^F

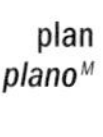

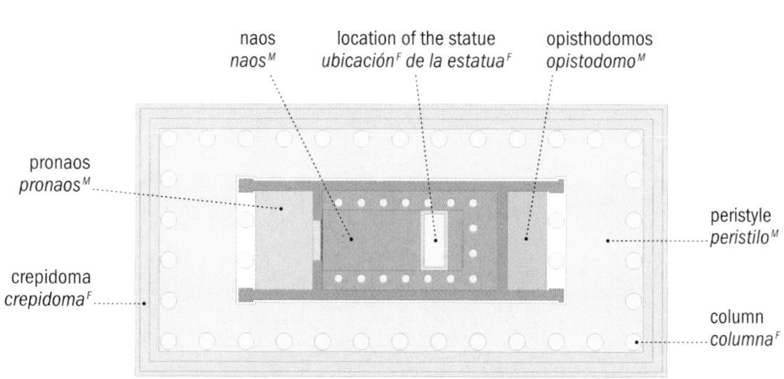

Roman house

casa[F] romana

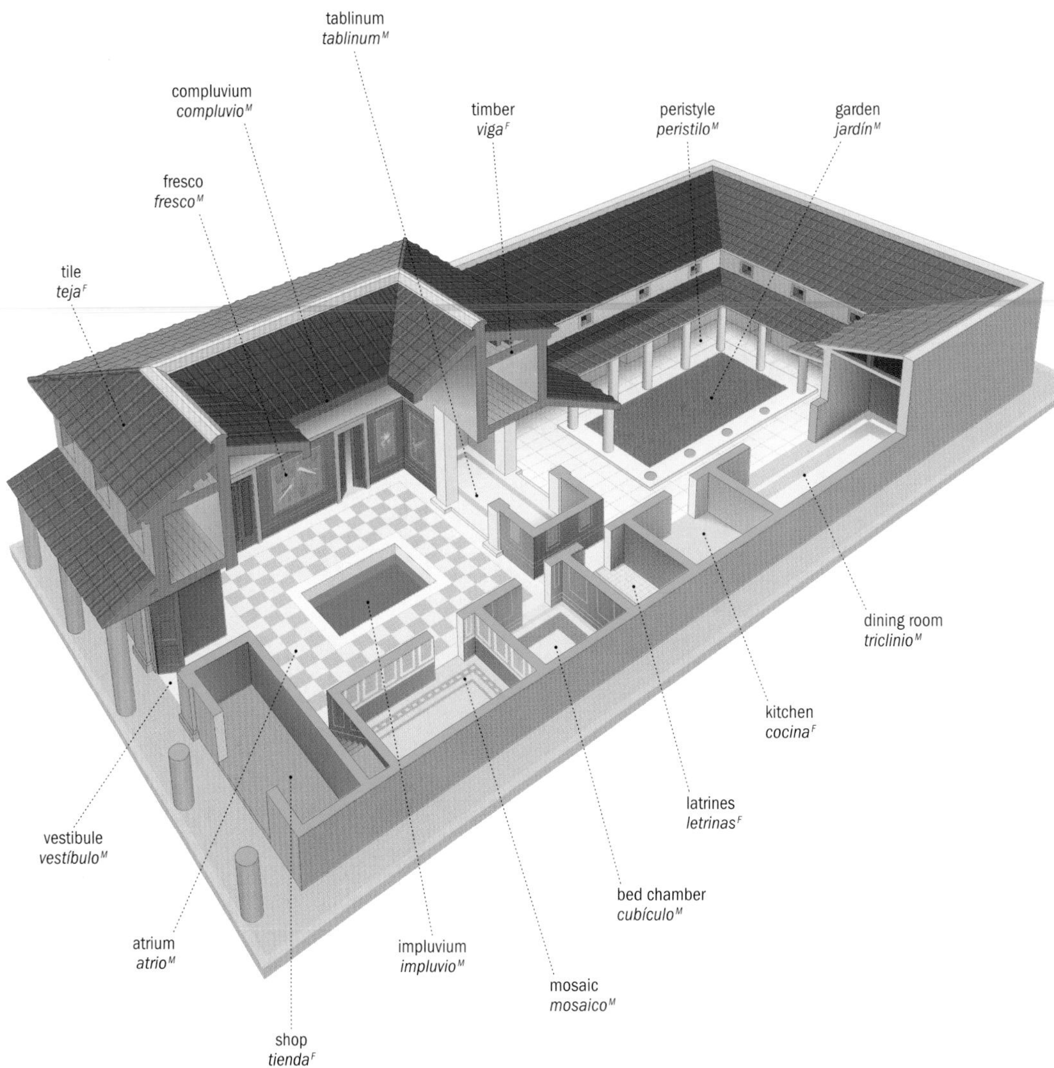
tablinum
tablinum[M]
compluvium
compluvio[M]
timber
viga[F]
peristyle
peristilo[M]
garden
jardín[M]
fresco
fresco[M]
tile
teja[F]
dining room
triclinio[M]
kitchen
cocina[F]
latrines
letrinas[F]
vestibule
vestíbulo[M]
bed chamber
cubículo[M]
atrium
atrio[M]
impluvium
impluvio[M]
mosaic
mosaico[M]
shop
tienda[F]

Roman amphitheater

anfiteatro^M romano

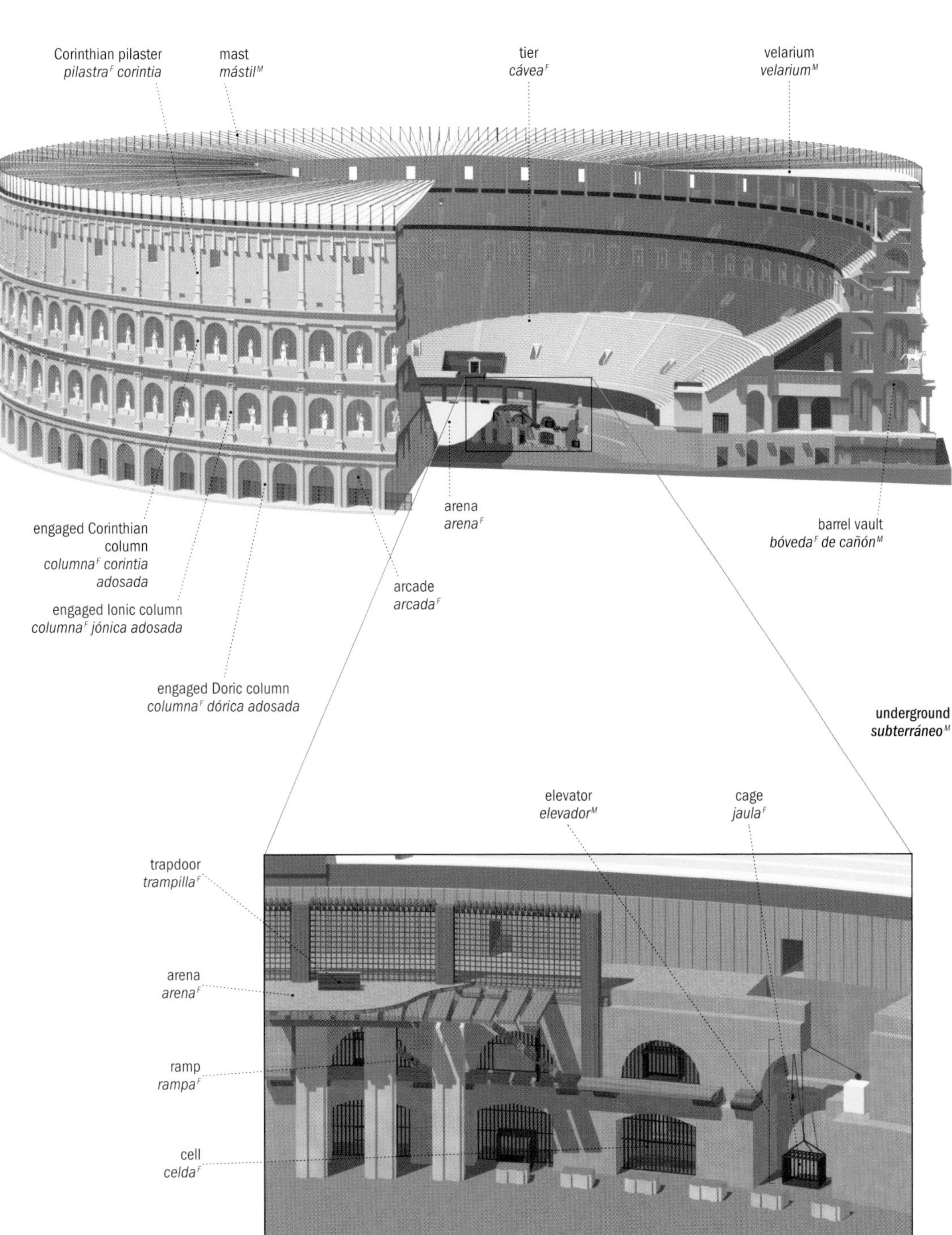
Corinthian pilaster
pilastra^F corintia
mast
mástil^M
tier
cávea^F
velarium
velarium^M
arena
arena^F
barrel vault
bóveda^F de cañón^M
engaged Corinthian column
columna^F corintia adosada
arcade
arcada^F
engaged Ionic column
columna^F jónica adosada
engaged Doric column
columna^F dórica adosada
underground
subterráneo^M
elevator
elevador^M
cage
jaula^F
trapdoor
trampilla^F
arena
arena^F
ramp
rampa^F
cell
celda^F

castle

castillo[M]

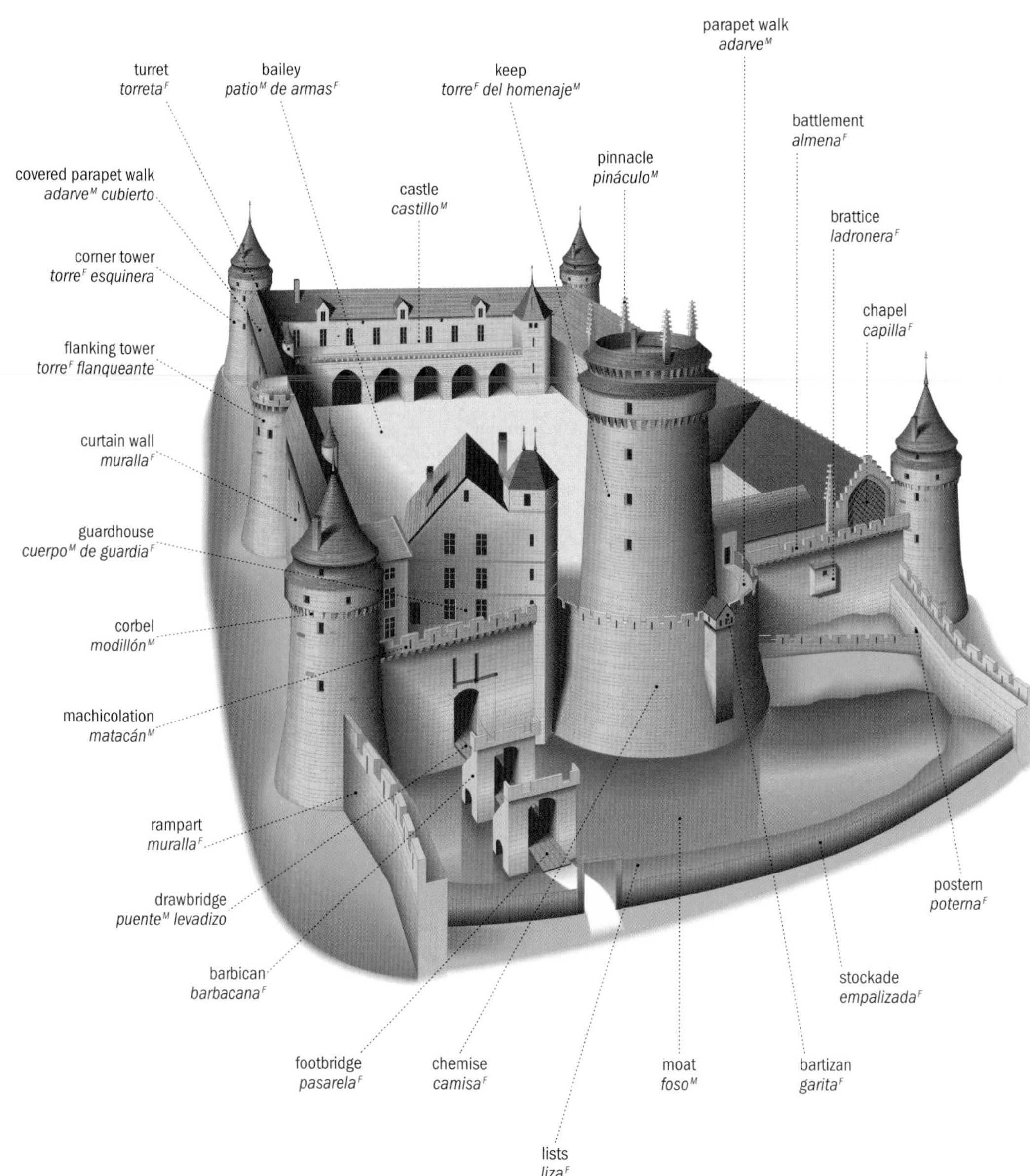
parapet walk
adarve[M]
turret
torreta[F]
bailey
patio[M] de armas[F]
keep
torre[F] del homenaje[M]
battlement
almena[F]
pinnacle
pináculo[M]
covered parapet walk
adarve[M] cubierto
castle
castillo[M]
brattice
ladronera[F]
corner tower
torre[F] esquinera
chapel
capilla[F]
flanking tower
torre[F] flanqueante
curtain wall
muralla[F]
guardhouse
cuerpo[M] de guardia[F]
corbel
modillón[M]
machicolation
matacán[M]
rampart
muralla[F]
drawbridge
puente[M] levadizo
postern
poterna[F]
barbican
barbacana[F]
stockade
empalizada[F]
footbridge
pasarela[F]
chemise
camisa[F]
moat
foso[M]
bartizan
garita[F]
lists
liza[F]

pagoda

pagoda[F]

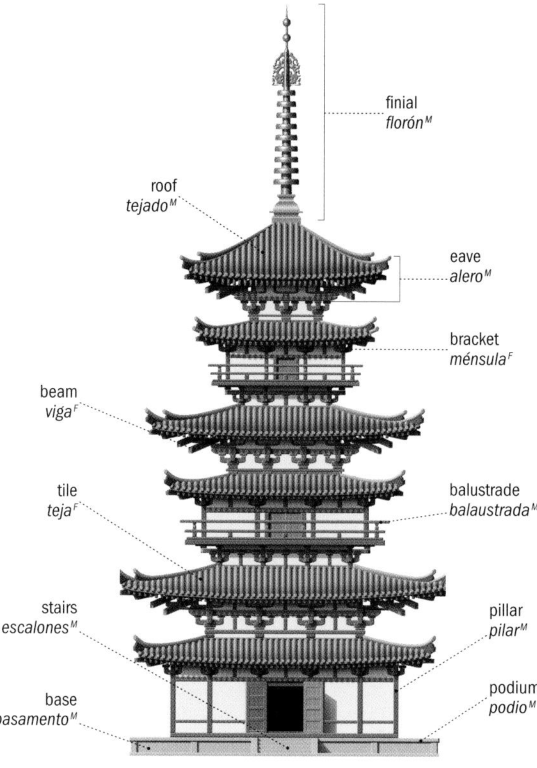

Aztec temple

templo[M] azteca

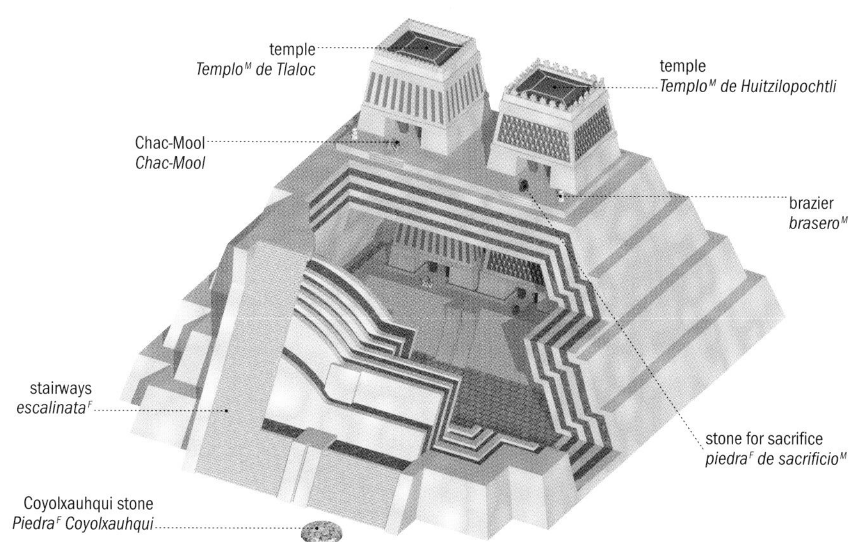

cathedral

catedral^F

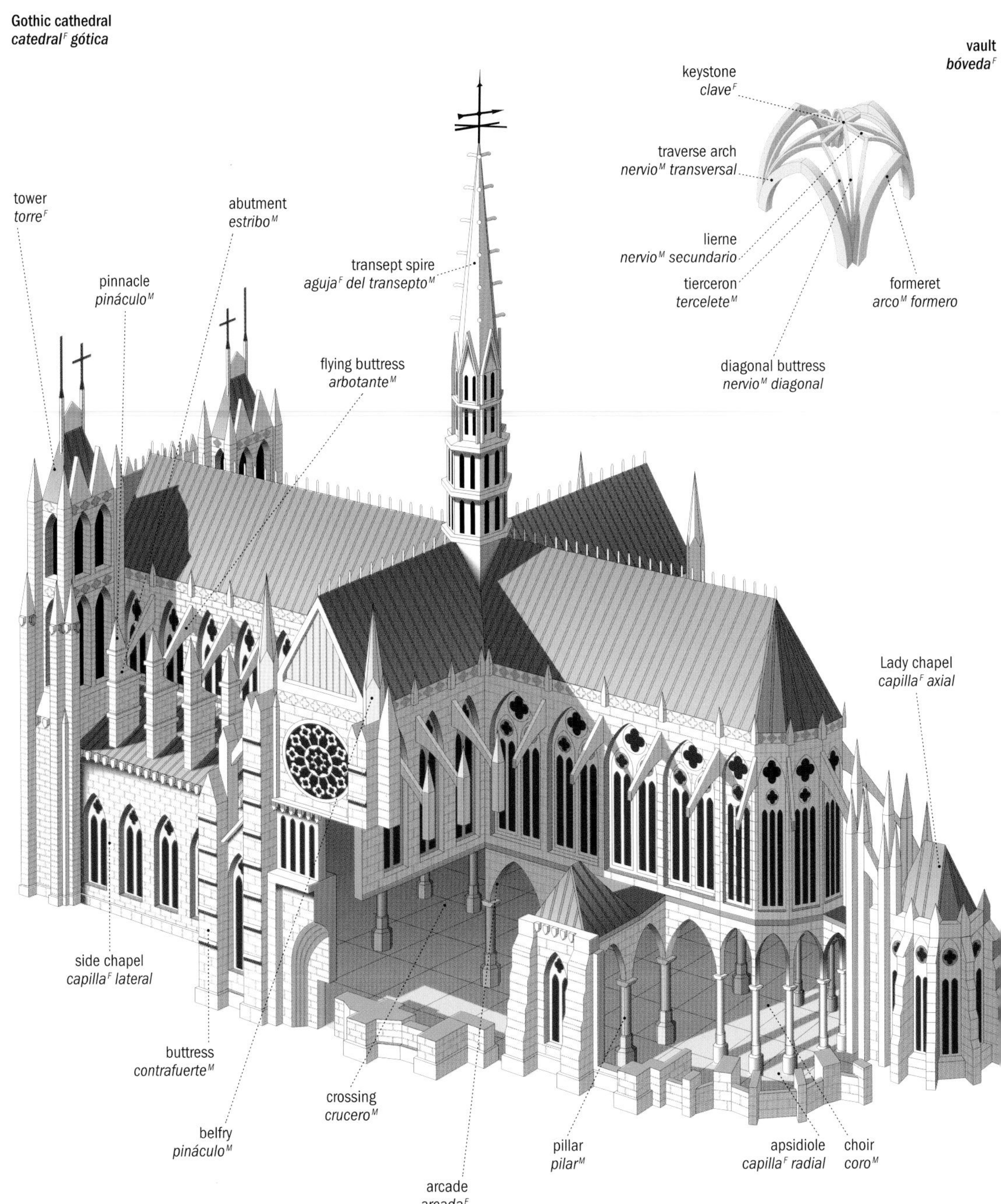
Gothic cathedral
catedral^F gótica
vault
bóveda^F
keystone
clave^F
traverse arch
nervio^M transversal
lierne
nervio^M secundario
tierceron
tercelete^M
formeret
arco^M formero
diagonal buttress
nervio^M diagonal
tower
torre^F
abutment
estribo^M
pinnacle
pináculo^M
transept spire
aguja^F del transepto^M
flying buttress
arbotante^M
Lady chapel
capilla^F axial
side chapel
capilla^F lateral
buttress
contrafuerte^M
crossing
crucero^M
belfry
pináculo^M
arcade
arcada^F
pillar
pilar^M
apsidiole
capilla^F radial
choir
coro^M

façade
***fachada**F*

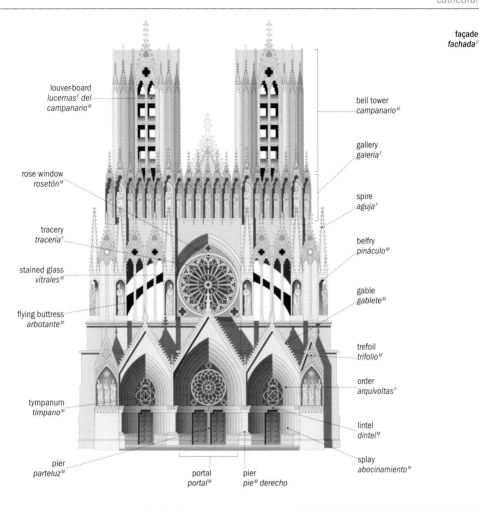

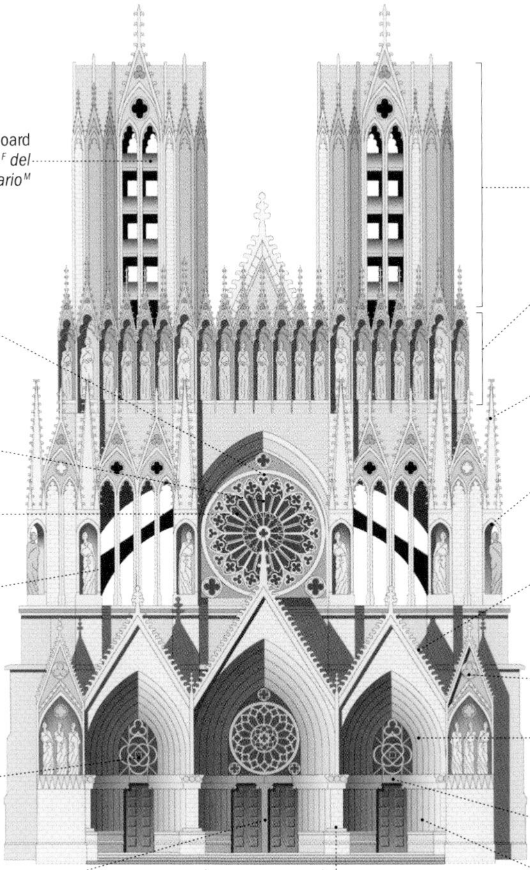

louver-board
*lucernas*F *del campanario*M
bell tower
*campanario*M
gallery
*galería*F
rose window
*rosetón*M
spire
*aguja*F
tracery
*tracería*F
belfry
*pináculo*M
stained glass
*vitrales*M
gable
*gablete*M
flying buttress
*arbotante*M
trefoil
*trifolio*M
order
*arquivoltas*F
tympanum
*tímpano*M
lintel
*dintel*M
splay
*abocinamiento*M
pier
*parteluz*M
portal
*portal*M
pier
*pie*M *derecho*

plan
***plano**M*

transept
*transepto*M
ambulatory
*deambulatorio*M
apsidiole
*capilla*F *radial*
aisle
*nave*F *lateral*
chevet
*cabecera*F
nave
*nave*F
Lady chapel
*capilla*F *axial*
porch
*pórtico*M
crossing
*crucero*M
choir
*coro*M
apse
*ábside*M

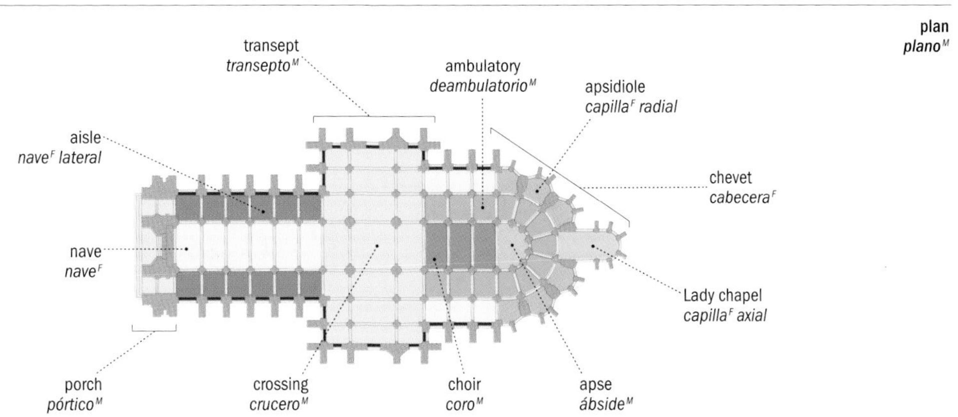

elements of architecture

elementos^M arquitectónicos

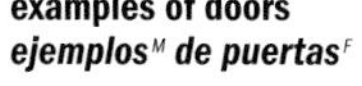

examples of doors
ejemplos^M de puertas^F

manual revolving door
puerta^F giratoria manual

canopy
tambor^M

wing
hoja^F

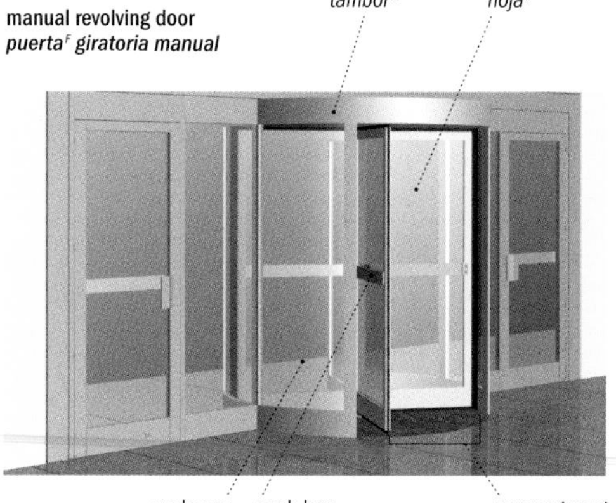

enclosure
estructura^F interior

push bar
tirador^M

compartment
compartimiento^M

automatic sliding door
puerta^F corredera automática

motion detector
sensor^M de movimiento

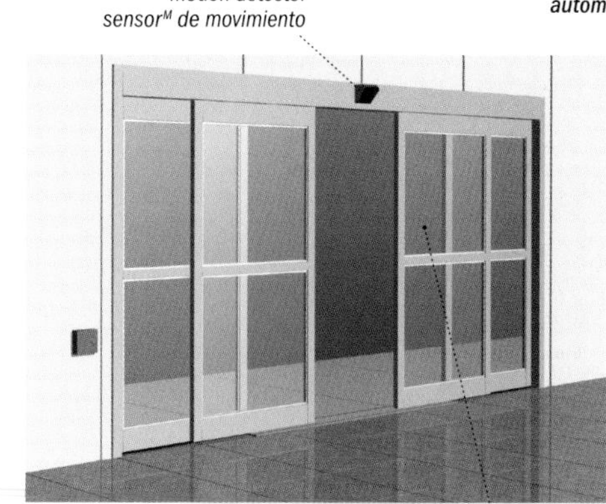

wing
hoja^F

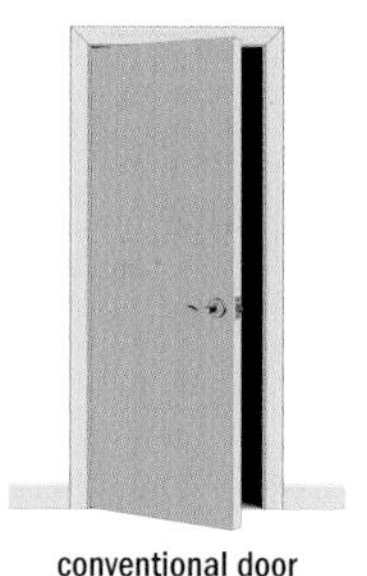

conventional door
puerta^F convencional

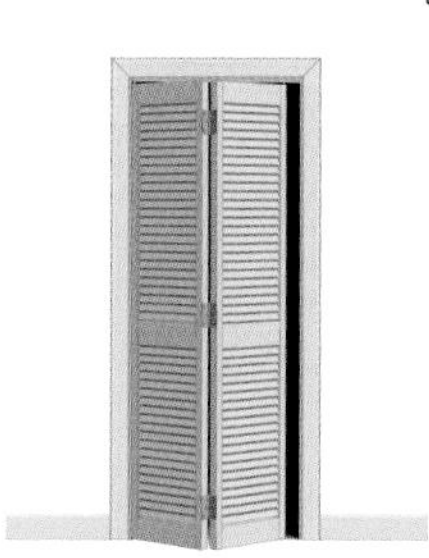

folding door
puerta^F plegable

strip
tira^F

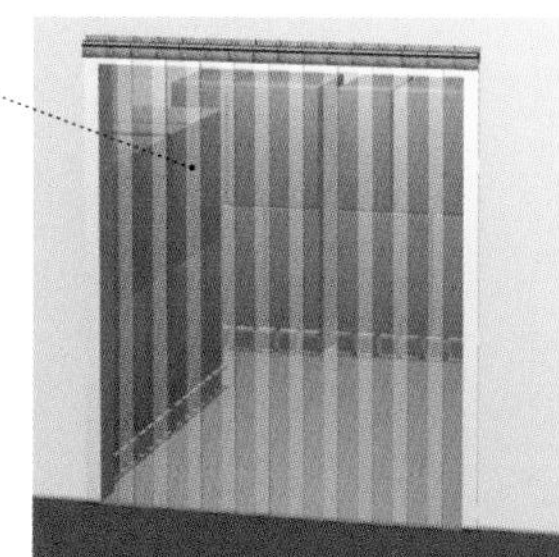

strip door
puerta^F de tiras^F

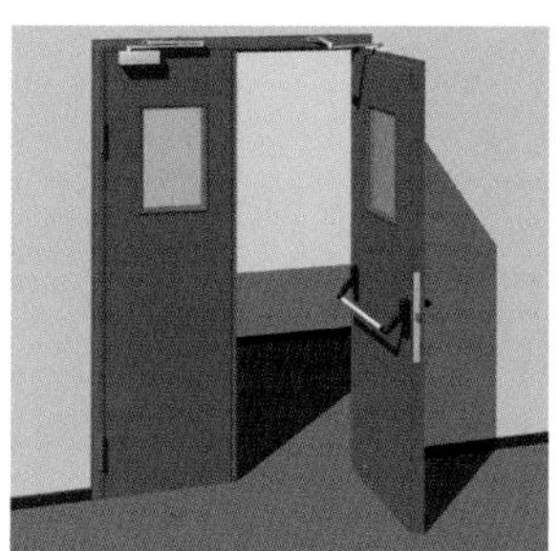

fire door
puerta^F cortafuego

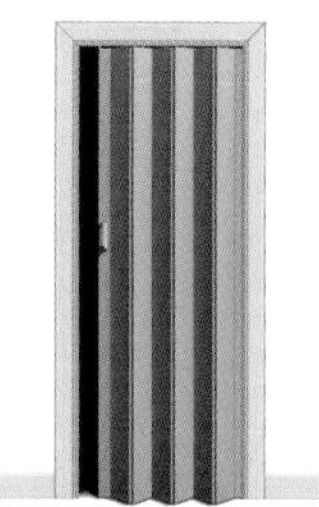

sliding folding door
puerta^F de librillo^M

sliding door
puerta^F corredera

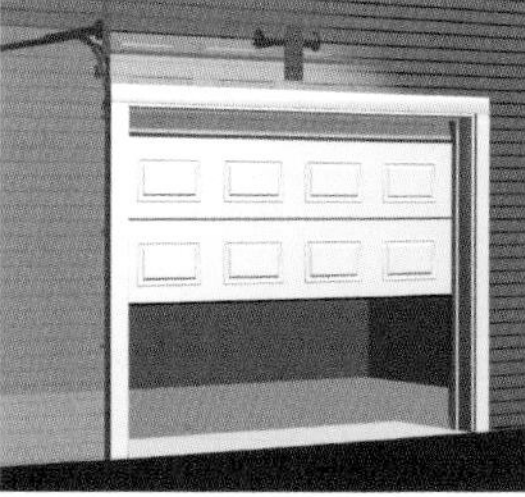

sectional garage door
puerta^F de garaje^M seccional

up and over garage door
puerta^F basculante de garaje^M

examples of windows
ejemplos[M] de ventanas[F]

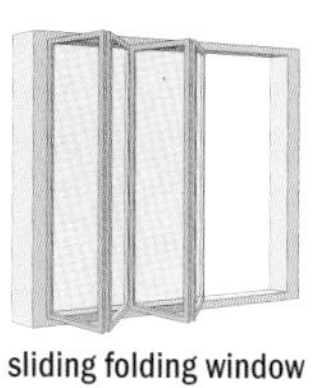

sliding folding window
ventana[F] de librillo[M]

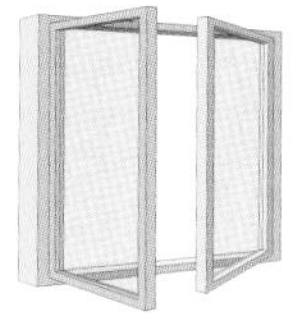

French window
ventana[F] a la francesa[F]

casement window
ventana[F] a la inglesa[F]

louvered window
ventana[F] de celosía[F]

sliding window
ventana[F] corredera

sash window
ventana[F] de guillotina[F]

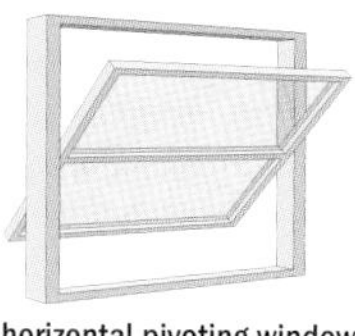

horizontal pivoting window
ventana[F] basculante

vertical pivoting window
ventana[F] pivotante

elevator

ascensor[M]

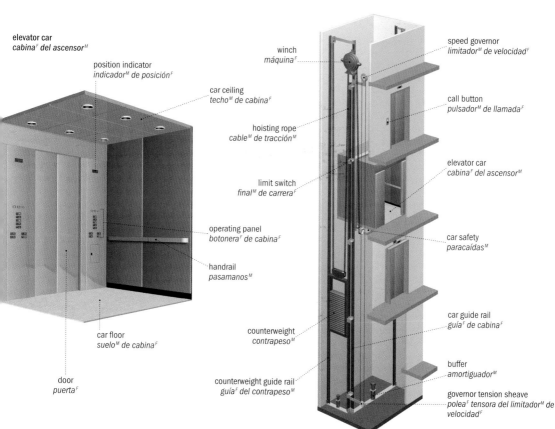

elevator car
cabina[F] del ascensor[M]

position indicator
indicador[M] de posición[F]

car ceiling
techo[M] de cabina[F]

operating panel
botonera[F] de cabina[F]

handrail
pasamanos[M]

car floor
suelo[M] de cabina[F]

door
puerta[F]

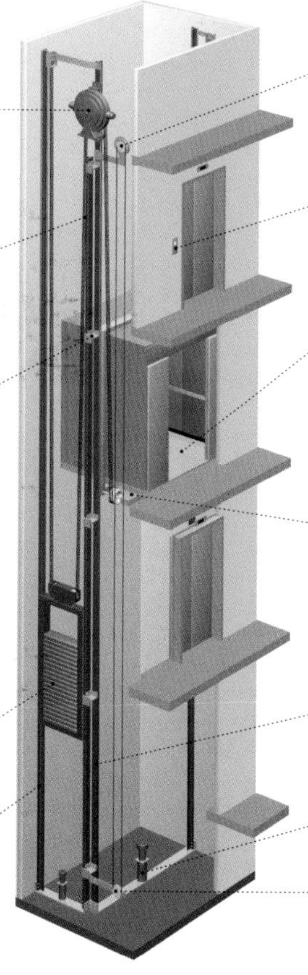

winch
máquina[F]

hoisting rope
cable[M] de tracción[M]

limit switch
final[M] de carrera[F]

counterweight
contrapeso[M]

counterweight guide rail
guía[F] del contrapeso[M]

speed governor
limitador[M] de velocidad[F]

call button
pulsador[M] de llamada[F]

elevator car
cabina[F] del ascensor[M]

car safety
paracaídas[M]

car guide rail
guía[F] de cabina[F]

buffer
amortiguador[M]

governor tension sheave
polea[F] tensora del limitador[M] de velocidad[F]

traditional houses

viviendas[F] tradicionales

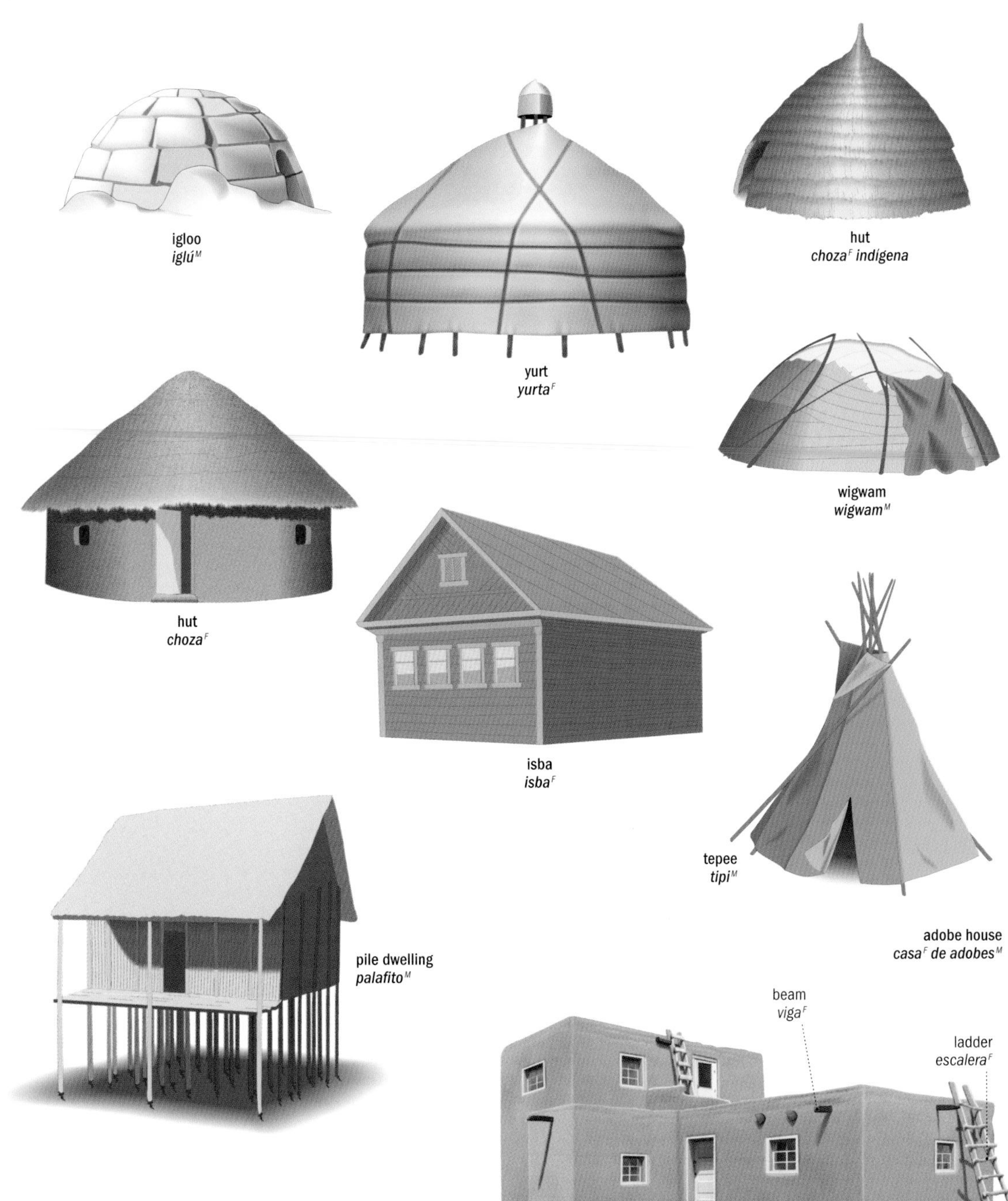

city houses

viviendas[F] urbanas

two-storey house
casa[F] de dos plantas[M]

one-storey house
casa[F] de una planta[F]

semi-detached cottage
casas[F] pareadas

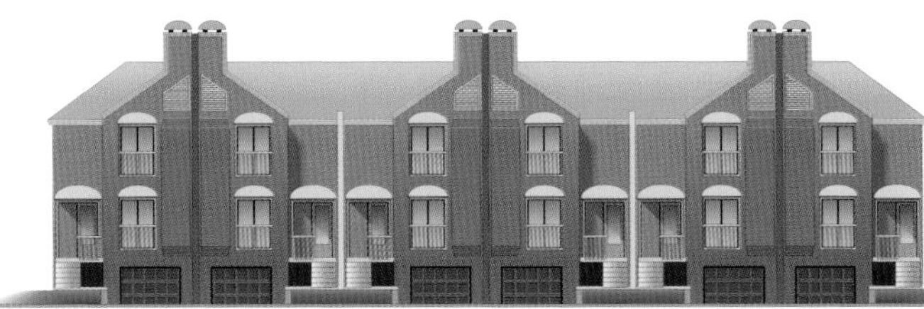

town houses
casas[F] adosadas

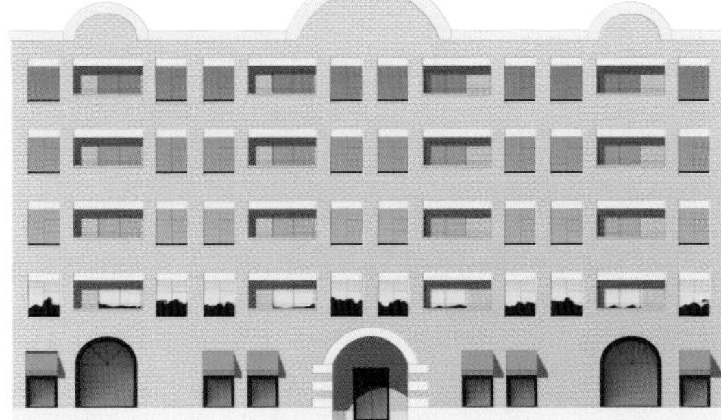

condominiums
viviendas[F] plurifamiliares

high-rise apartment
bloque[M] de apartamentos[M]

sound stage

platóᴹ de rodajeᴹ

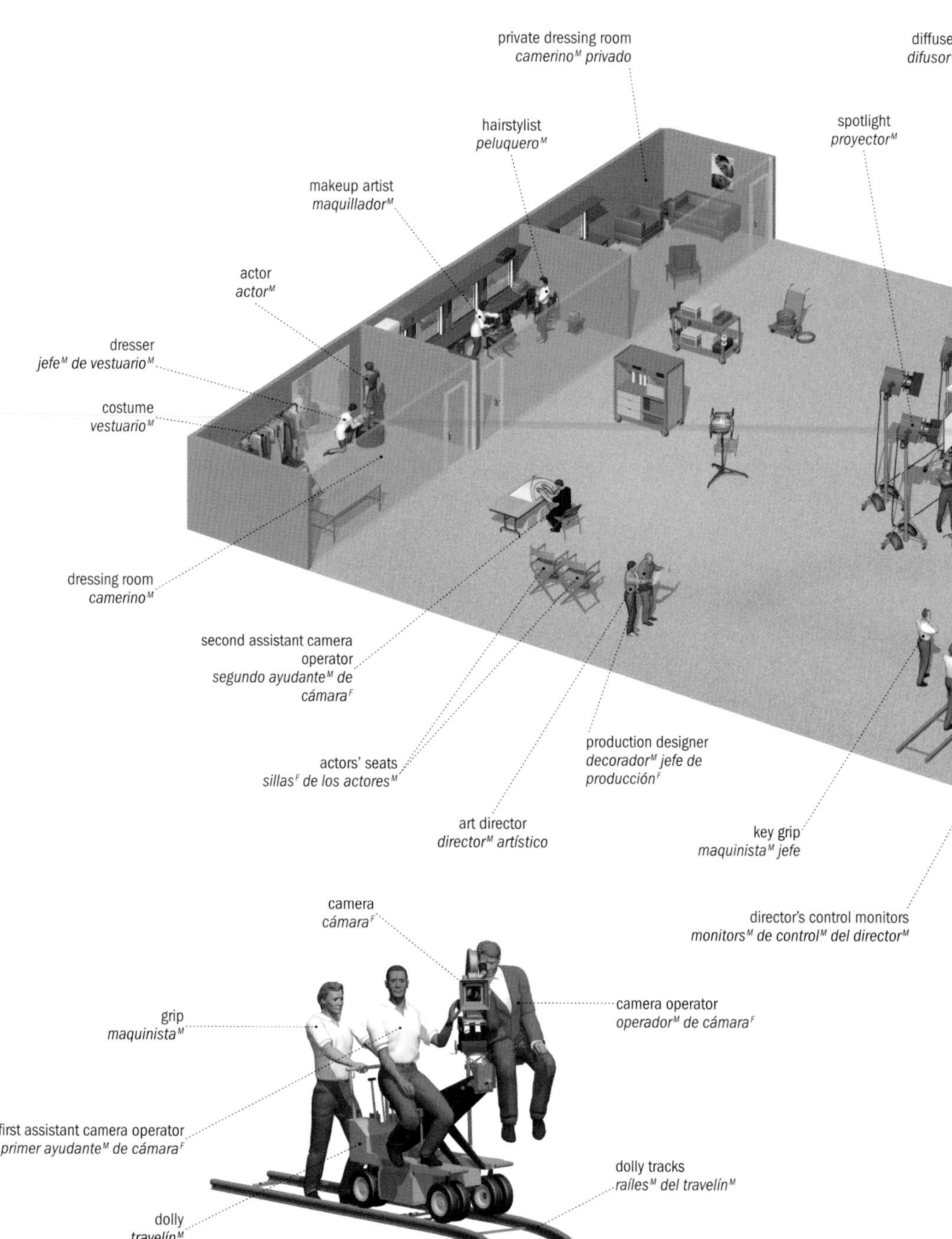
private dressing room
camerinoᴹ privado
diffuser
difusorᴹ
hairstylist
peluqueroᴹ
spotlight
proyectorᴹ
makeup artist
maquilladorᴹ
actor
actorᴹ
dresser
jefeᴹ de vestuarioᴹ
costume
vestuarioᴹ
dressing room
camerinoᴹ
second assistant camera operator
segundo ayudanteᴹ de cámaraᶠ
actors' seats
sillasᶠ de los actoresᴹ
production designer
decoradorᴹ jefe de producciónᶠ
art director
directorᴹ artístico
key grip
maquinistaᴹ jefe
director's control monitors
monitorsᴹ de controlᴹ del directorᴹ
camera
cámaraᶠ
camera operator
operadorᴹ de cámaraᶠ
grip
maquinistaᴹ
first assistant camera operator
primer ayudanteᴹ de cámaraᶠ
dolly tracks
railesᴹ del travelínᴹ
dolly
travelínᴹ

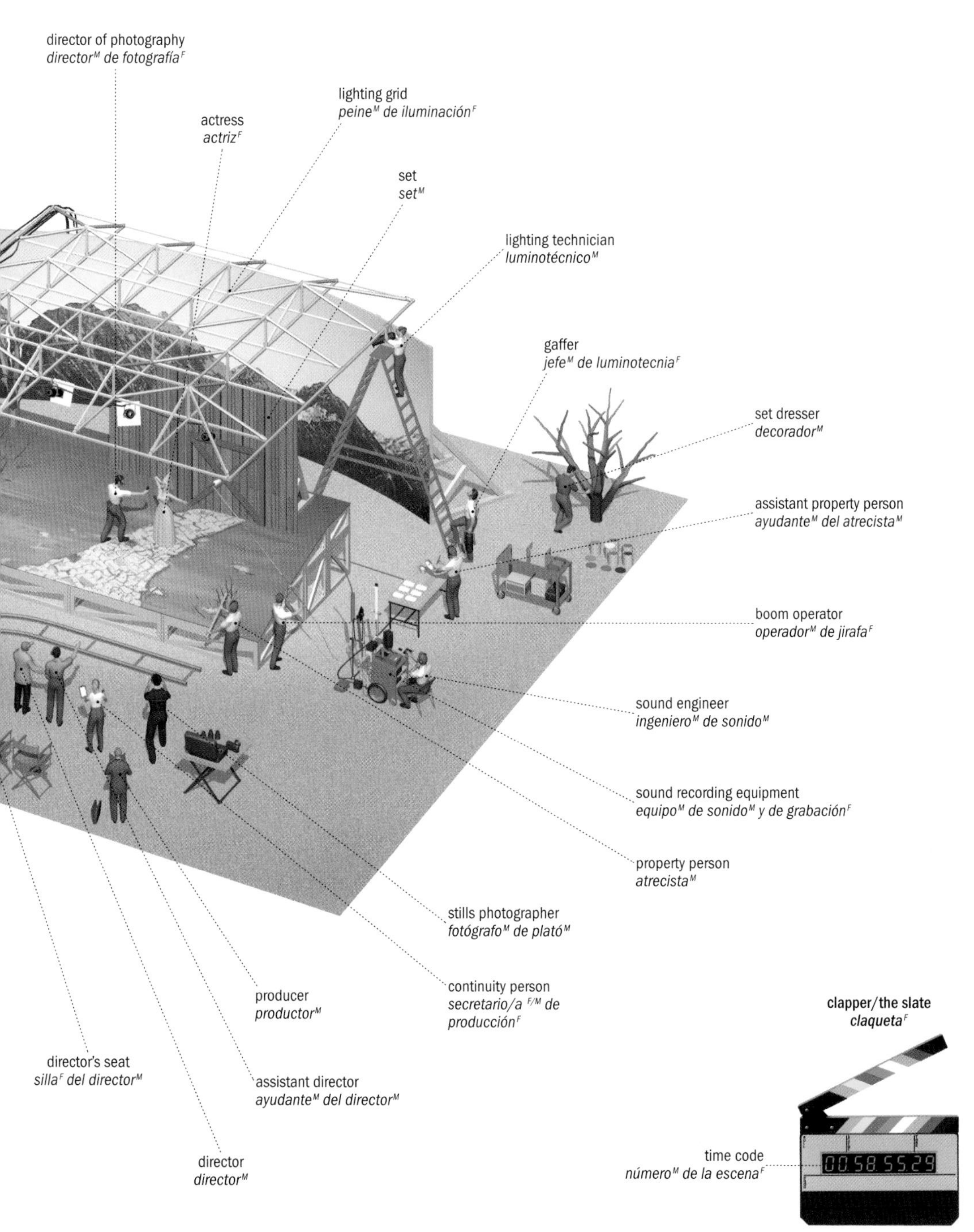
director of photography
directorᴹ de fotografíaᶠ
actress
actrizᶠ
lighting grid
peineᴹ de iluminaciónᶠ
set
setᴹ
lighting technician
luminotécnicoᴹ
gaffer
jefeᴹ de luminotecniaᶠ
set dresser
decoradorᴹ
assistant property person
ayudanteᴹ del atrecistaᴹ
boom operator
operadorᴹ de jirafaᶠ
sound engineer
ingenieroᴹ de sonidoᴹ
sound recording equipment
equipoᴹ de sonidoᴹ y de grabaciónᶠ
property person
atrecistaᴹ
stills photographer
fotógrafoᴹ de platóᴹ
continuity person
secretario/a ᶠ/ᴹ de producciónᶠ
producer
productorᴹ
director's seat
sillaᶠ del directorᴹ
assistant director
ayudanteᴹ del directorᴹ
director
directorᴹ
clapper/the slate
claquetaᶠ
time code
númeroᴹ de la escenaᶠ
00 58 55 29

theater

teatro[M]

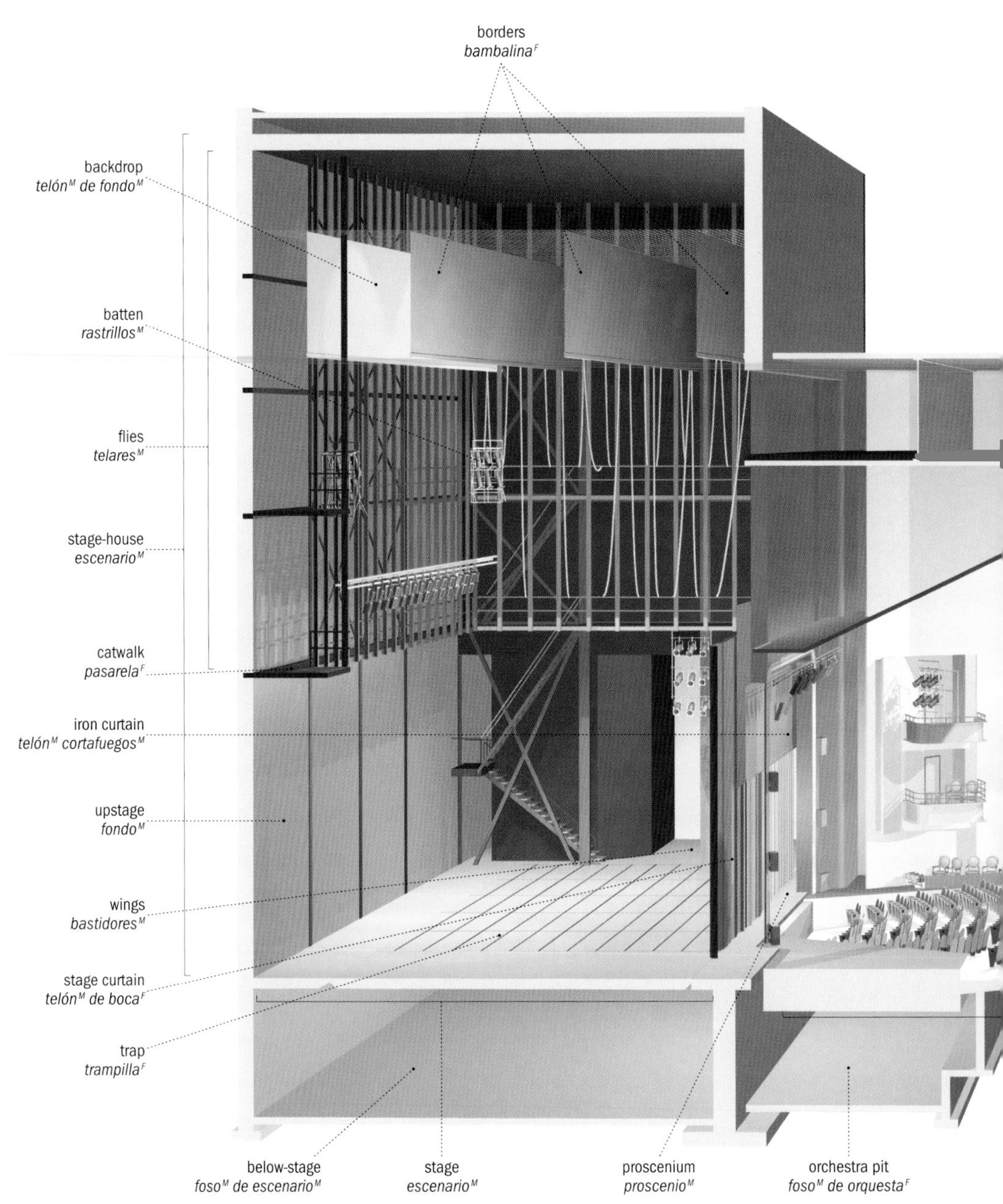
borders
bambalina[F]
backdrop
telón[M] de fondo[M]
batten
rastrillos[M]
flies
telares[M]
stage-house
escenario[M]
catwalk
pasarela[F]
iron curtain
telón[M] cortafuegos[M]
upstage
fondo[M]
wings
bastidores[M]
stage curtain
telón[M] de boca[F]
trap
trampilla[F]
below-stage
foso[M] de escenario[M]
stage
escenario[M]
proscenium
proscenio[M]
orchestra pit
foso[M] de orquesta[F]

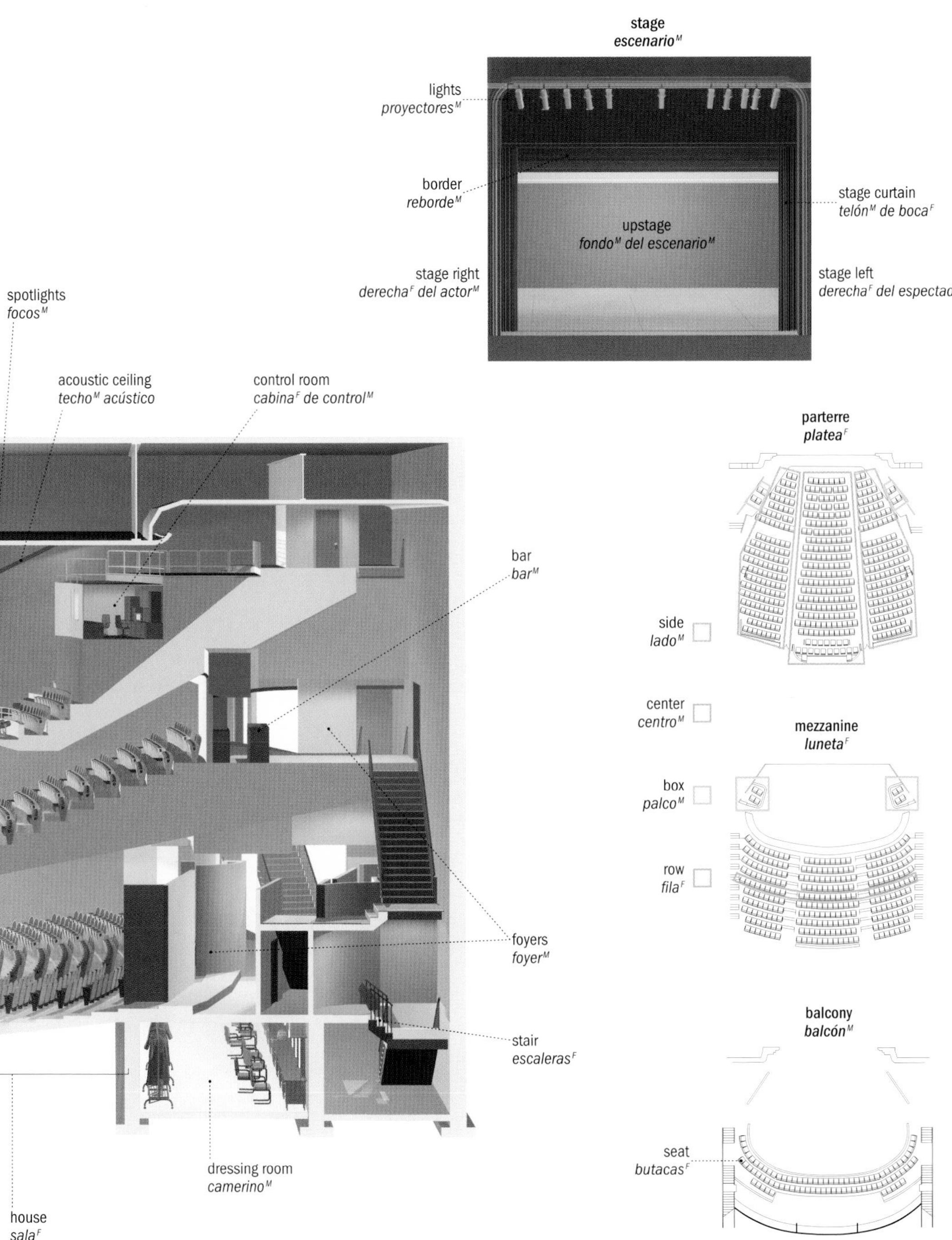
stage
escenario^M
lights
proyectores^M
border
reborde^M
stage curtain
telón^M de boca^F
upstage
fondo^M del escenario^M
stage right
derecha^F del actor^M
stage left
derecha^F del espectador^M
spotlights
focos^M
acoustic ceiling
techo^M acústico
control room
cabina^F de control^M
parterre
platea^F
bar
bar^M
side
lado^M
center
centro^M
mezzanine
luneta^F
box
palco^M
row
fila^F
foyers
foyer^M
balcony
balcón^M
stair
escaleras^F
seat
butacas^F
dressing room
camerino^M
house
sala^F

movie theater

cine^M

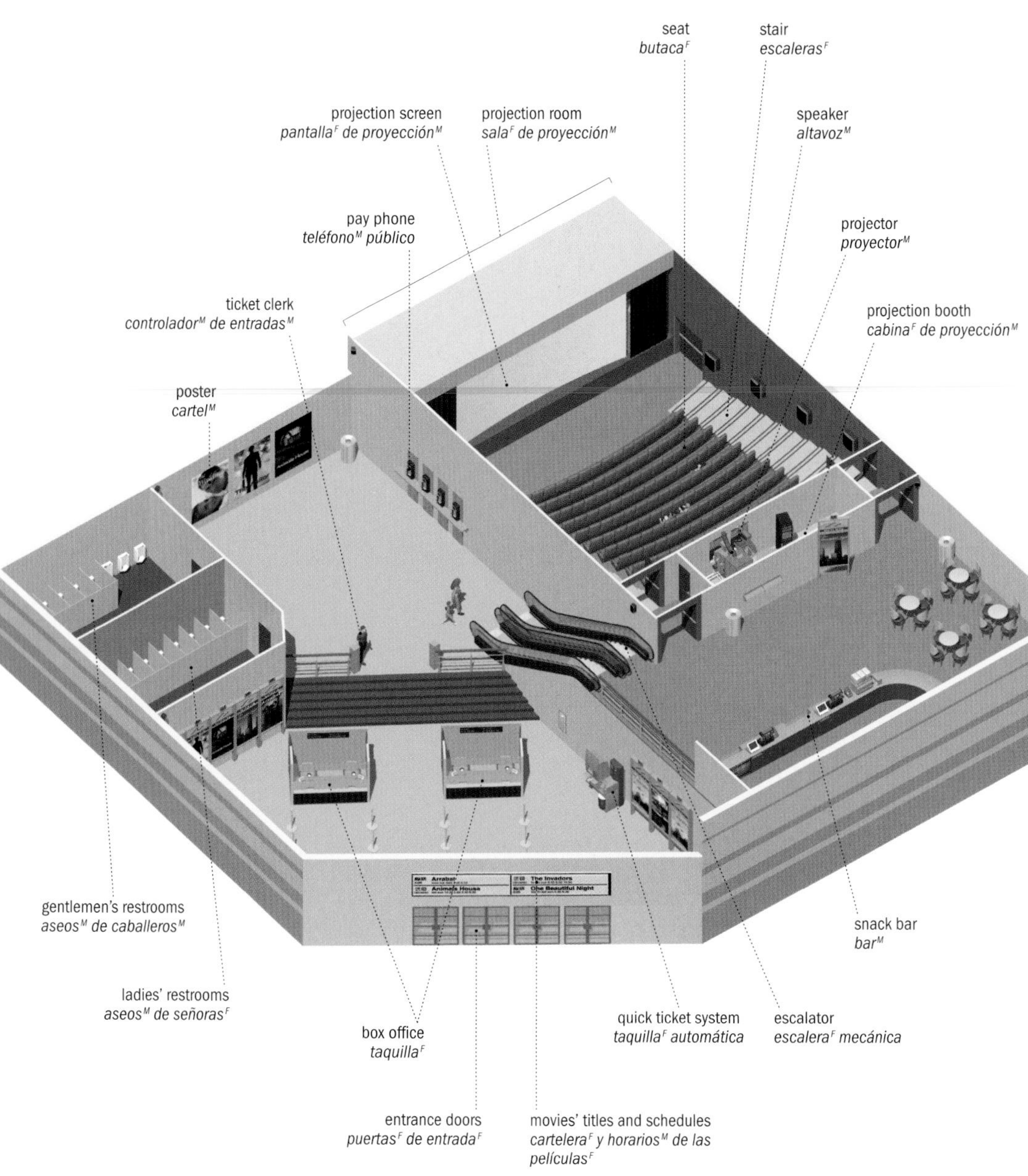
seat
butaca^F
stair
escaleras^F
projection screen
pantalla^F de proyección^M
projection room
sala^F de proyección^M
speaker
altavoz^M
pay phone
teléfono^M público
projector
proyector^M
ticket clerk
controlador^M de entradas^M
projection booth
cabina^F de proyección^M
poster
cartel^M
Arrabal
Animals House
The Invadors
One Beautiful Night
gentlemen's restrooms
aseos^M de caballeros^M
snack bar
bar^M
ladies' restrooms
aseos^M de señoras^F
box office
taquilla^F
quick ticket system
taquilla^F automática
escalator
escalera^F mecánica
entrance doors
puertas^F de entrada^F
movies' titles and schedules
cartelera^F y horarios^M de las películas^F

symphony orchestra

orquesta^{F} sinfónica

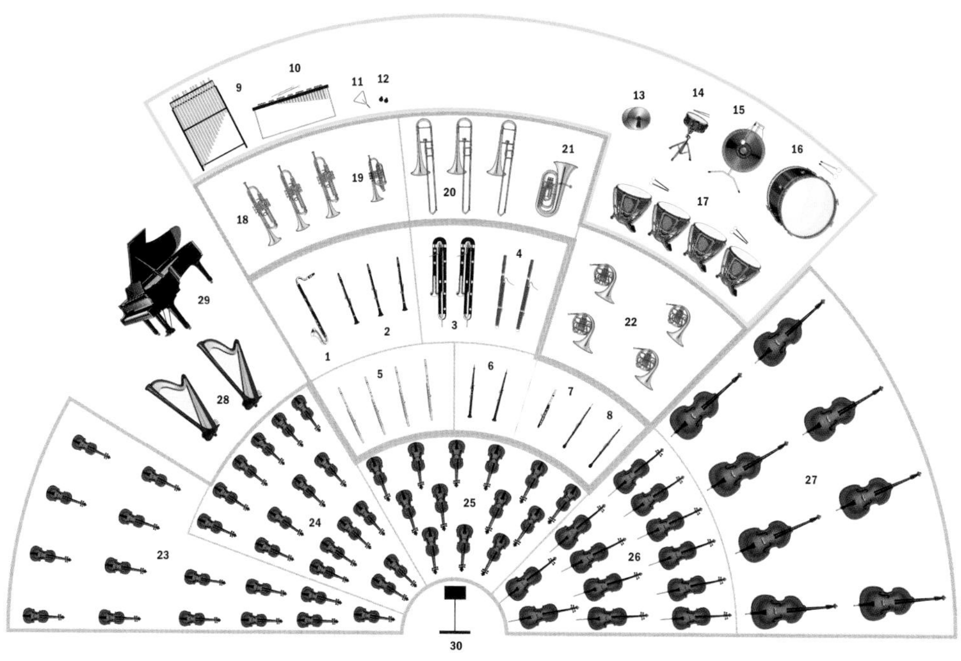

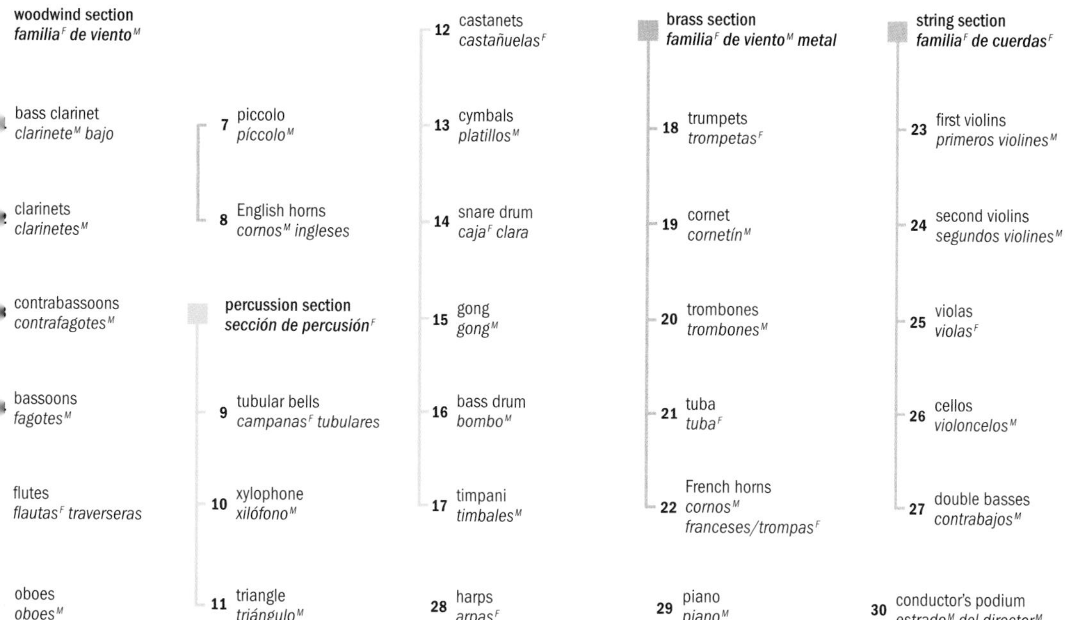

woodwind section
familia^{F} de viento^{M}

bass clarinet
clarinete^{M} bajo

clarinets
clarinetes^{M}

contrabassoons
contrafagotes^{M}

bassoons
fagotes^{M}

flutes
flautas^{F} traverseras

oboes
oboes^{M}

7 piccolo
píccolo^{M}

8 English horns
cornos^{M} ingleses

percussion section
sección de percusión^{F}

9 tubular bells
campanas^{F} tubulares

10 xylophone
xilófono^{M}

11 triangle
triángulo^{M}

12 castanets
castañuelas^{F}

13 cymbals
platillos^{M}

14 snare drum
caja^{F} clara

15 gong
gong^{M}

16 bass drum
bombo^{M}

17 timpani
timbales^{M}

28 harps
arpas^{F}

brass section
familia^{F} de viento^{M} metal

18 trumpets
trompetas^{F}

19 cornet
cornetín^{M}

20 trombones
trombones^{M}

21 tuba
tuba^{F}

22 French horns
cornos^{M} franceses/trompas^{F}

29 piano
piano^{M}

string section
familia^{F} de cuerdas^{F}

23 first violins
primeros violines^{M}

24 second violins
segundos violines^{M}

25 violas
violas^{F}

26 cellos
violoncelos^{M}

27 double basses
contrabajos^{M}

30 conductor's podium
estrado^{M} del director^{M}

traditional musical instruments

instrumentos^M musicales tradicionales

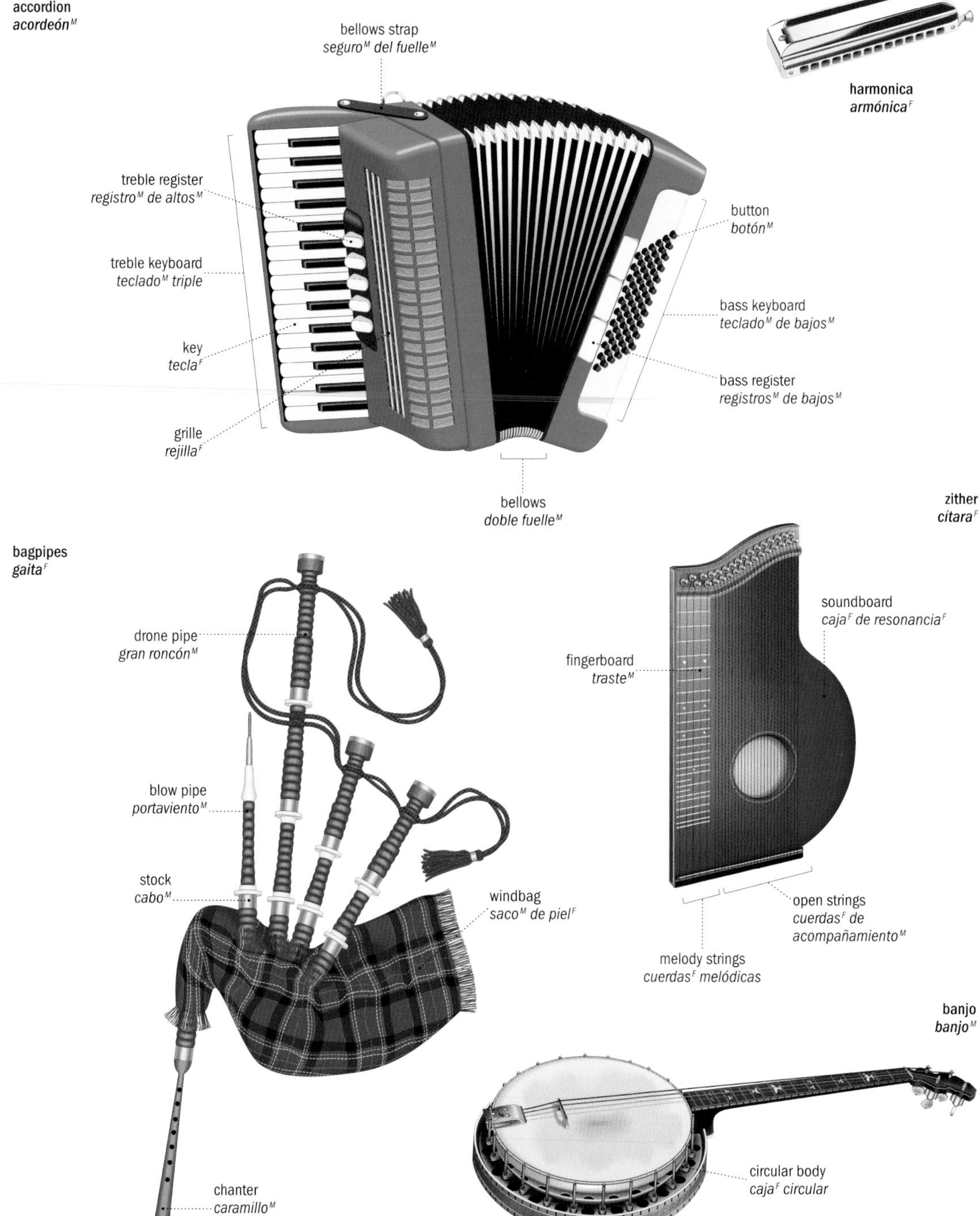

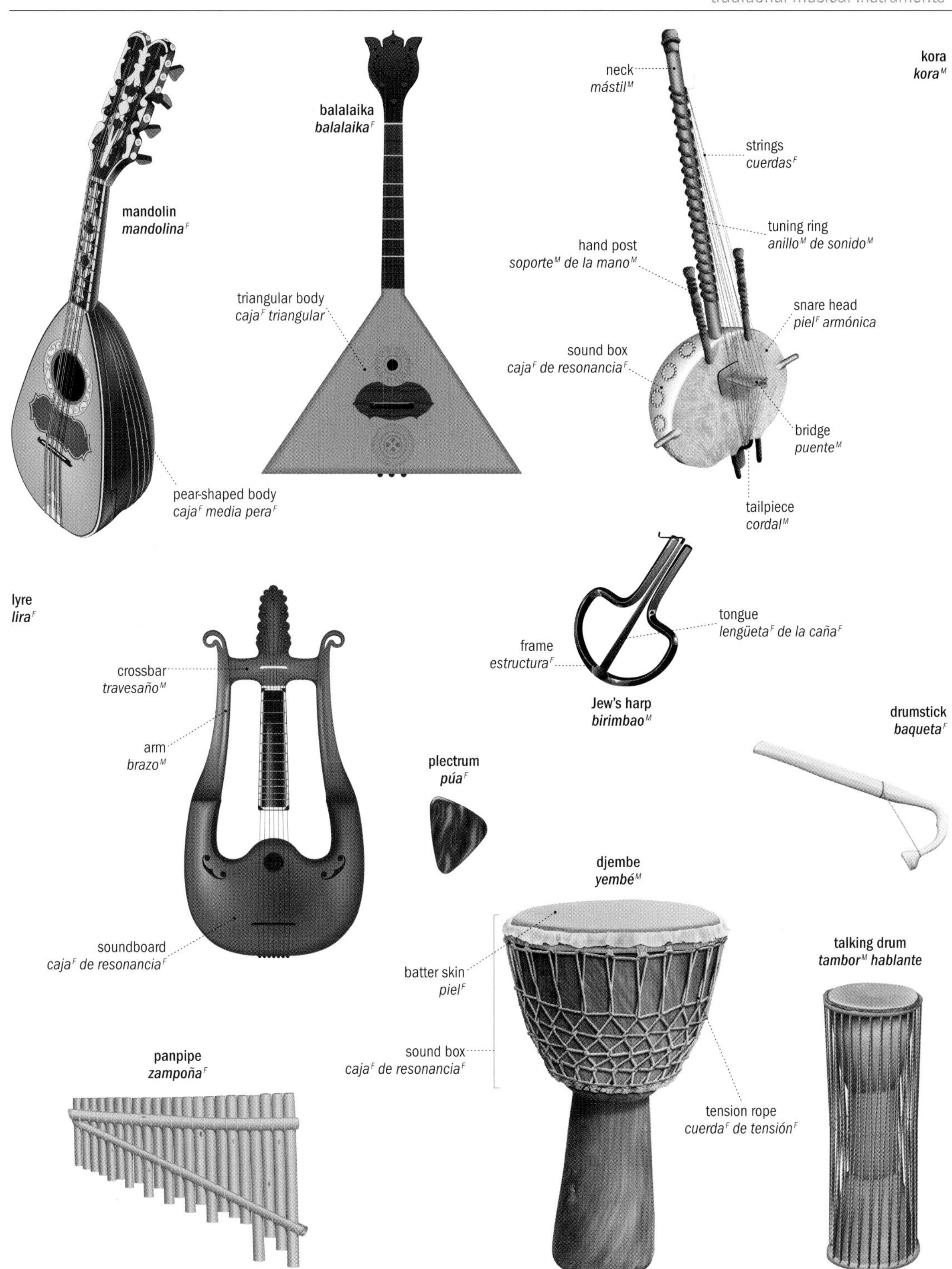
mandolin
mandolina[F]
pear-shaped body
caja[F] media pera[F]
balalaika
balalaika[F]
triangular body
caja[F] triangular
neck
mástil[M]
strings
cuerdas[F]
tuning ring
anillo[M] de sonido[M]
hand post
soporte[M] de la mano[M]
snare head
piel[F] armónica
sound box
caja[F] de resonancia[F]
bridge
puente[M]
tailpiece
cordal[M]
kora
kora[M]
lyre
lira[F]
crossbar
travesaño[M]
arm
brazo[M]
soundboard
caja[F] de resonancia[F]
plectrum
púa[F]
frame
estructura[F]
tongue
lengüeta[F] de la caña[F]
Jew's harp
birimbao[M]
drumstick
baqueta[F]
djembe
yembé[M]
batter skin
piel[F]
sound box
caja[F] de resonancia[F]
tension rope
cuerda[F] de tensión[F]
talking drum
tambor[M] hablante
panpipe
zampoña[F]

musical notation

notación[F] musical

staff
pentagrama[F]

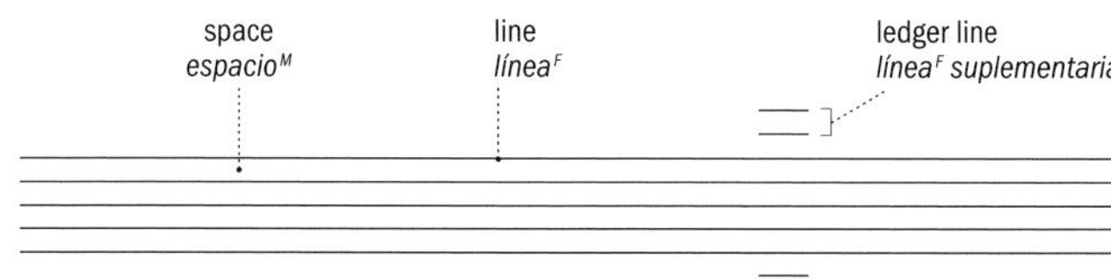

clefs
claves[F]

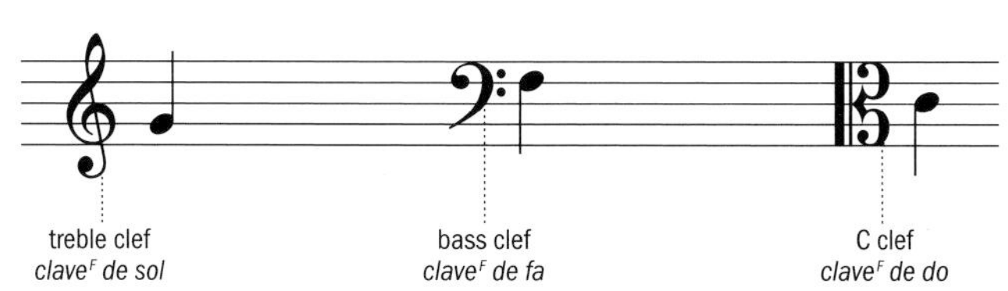

time signatures
compás[M]

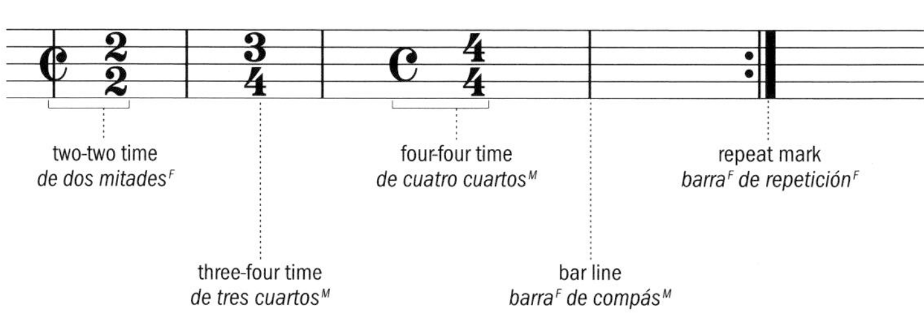

intervals
intervalos[M]

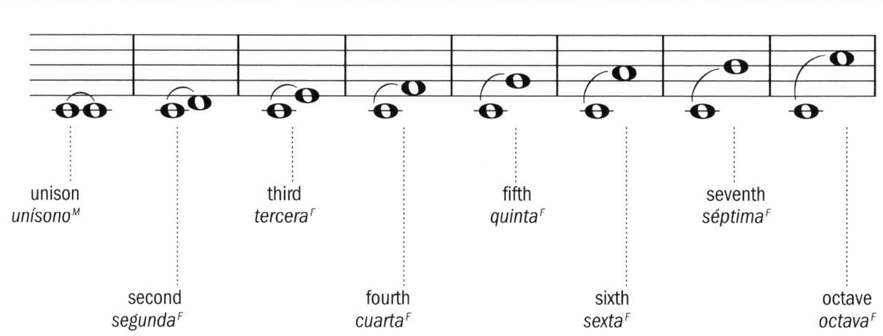

scale
escala[F]

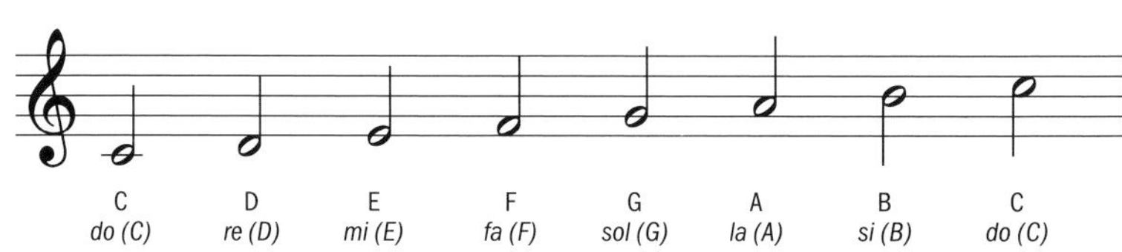

rest symbols
valores[M] de los silencios[M]

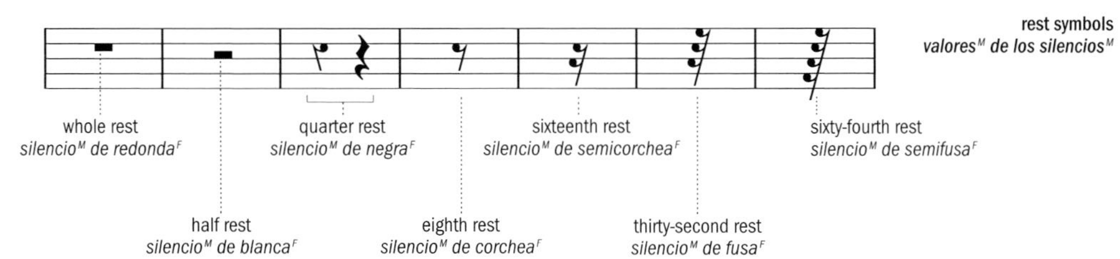

ornaments
adornos[M]

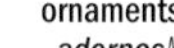

note symbols
valores[M] de las notas[F] musicales

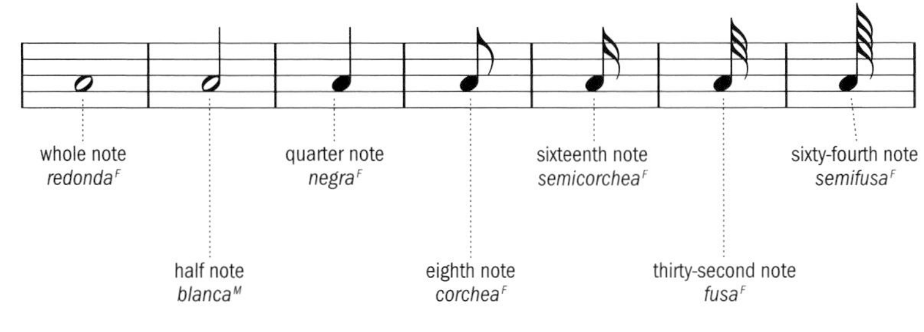

accidentals
accidentales[M]

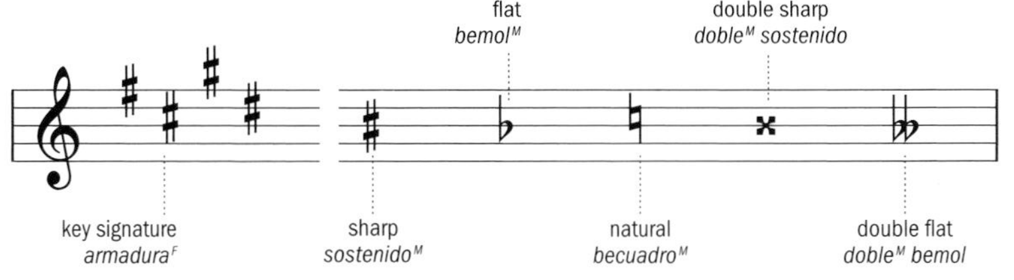

other signs
otros signos[M]

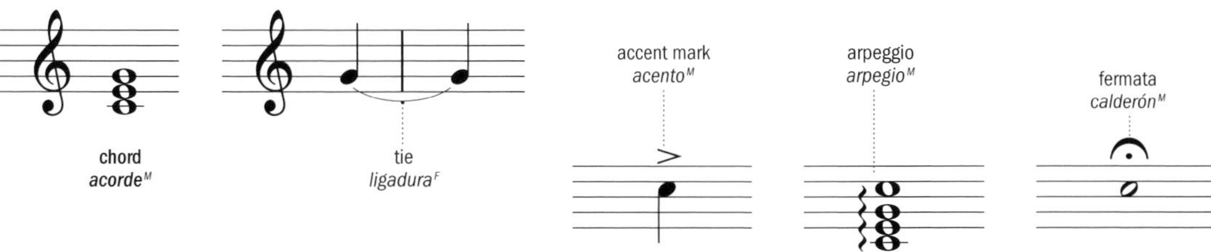

examples of instrumental groups

ejemplos^M de conjuntos^M instrumentales

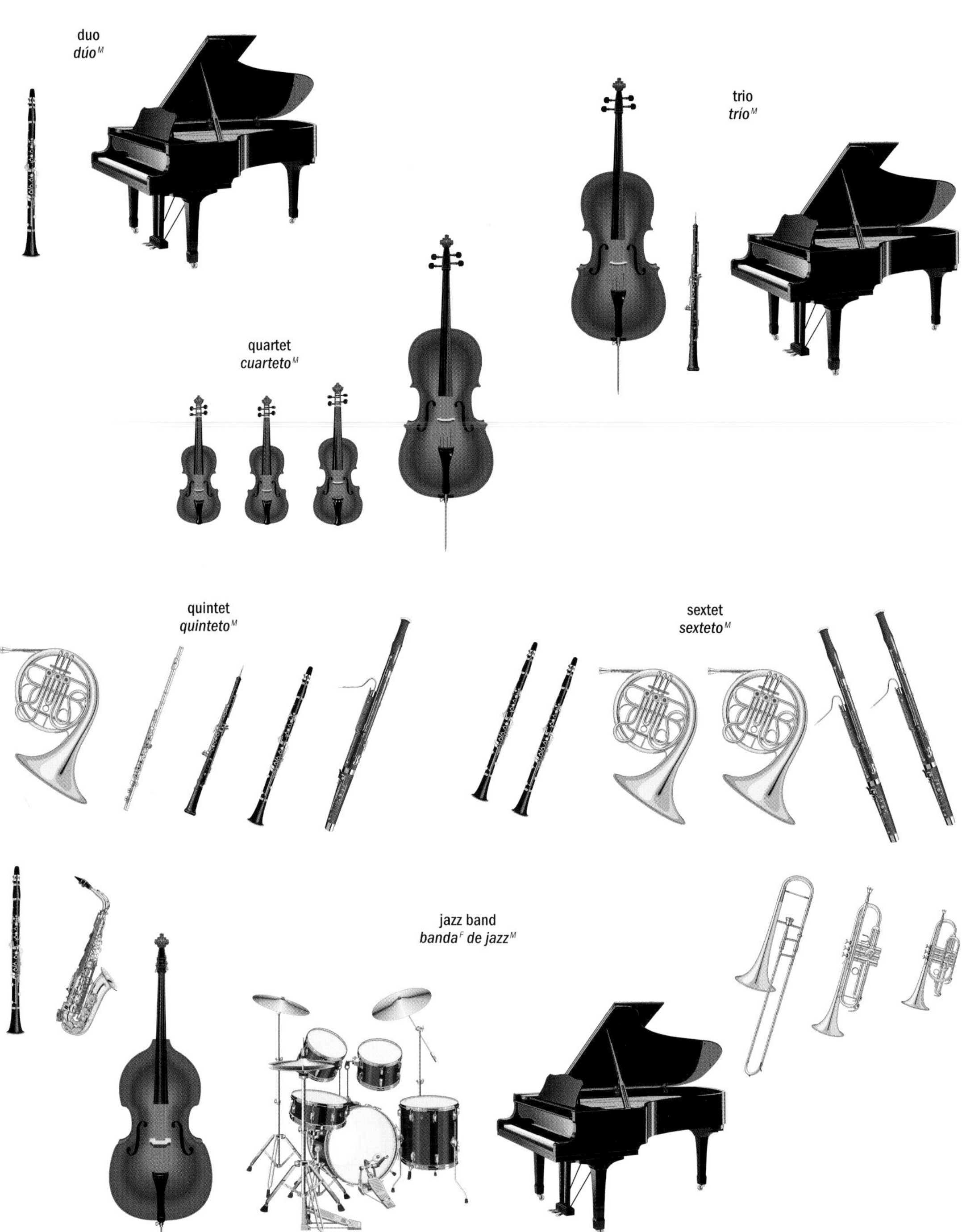

stringed instruments

instrumentos^M de cuerda^F

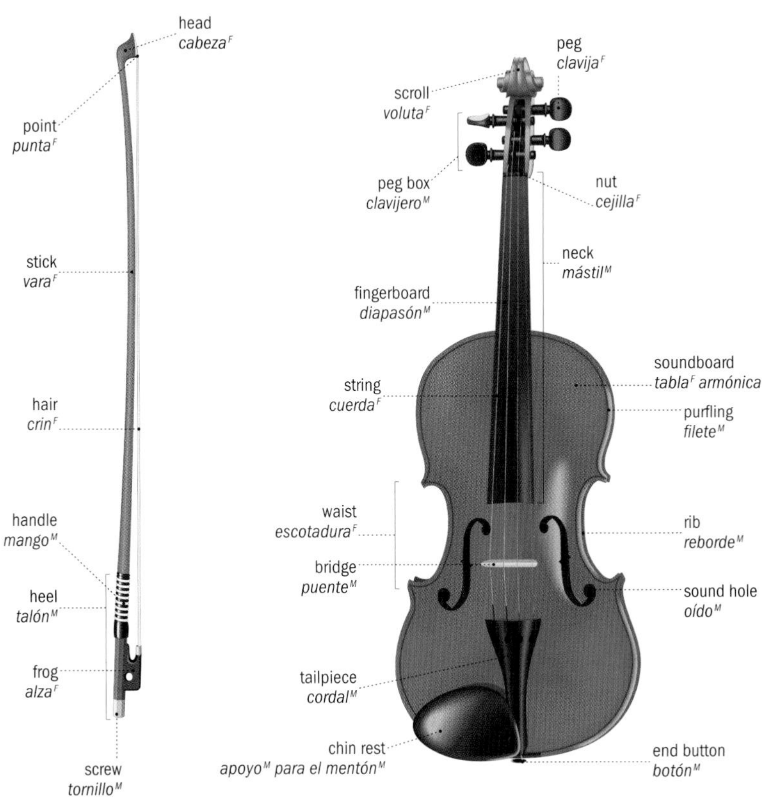

violin family
familia^F de los violines^M

stringed instruments

harp
arpa[F]

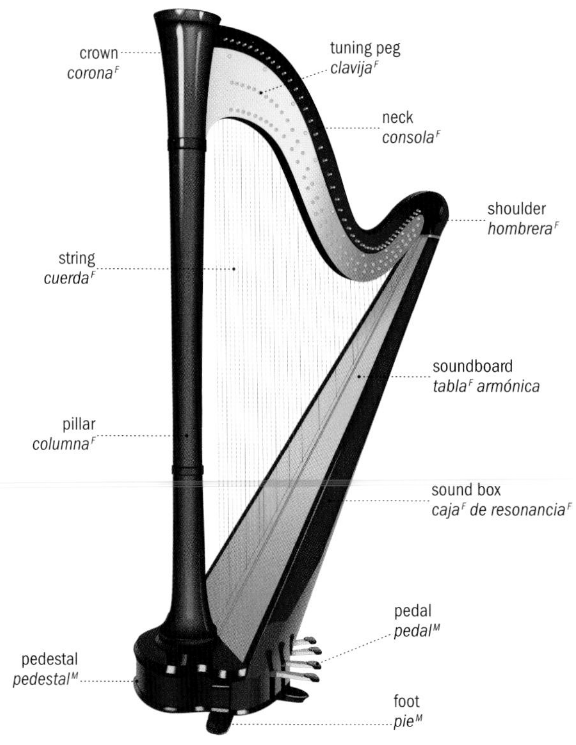

acoustic guitar
guitarra[F] *clásica*

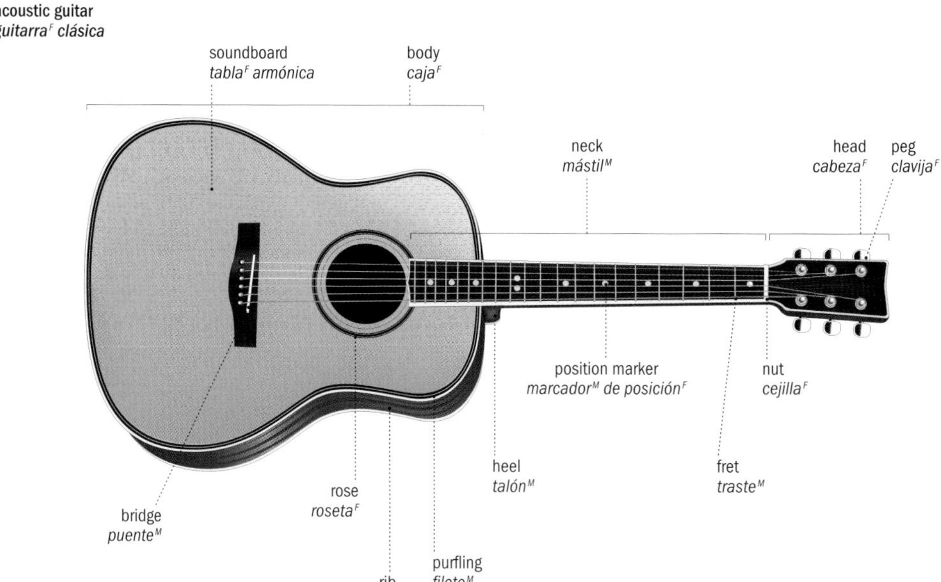

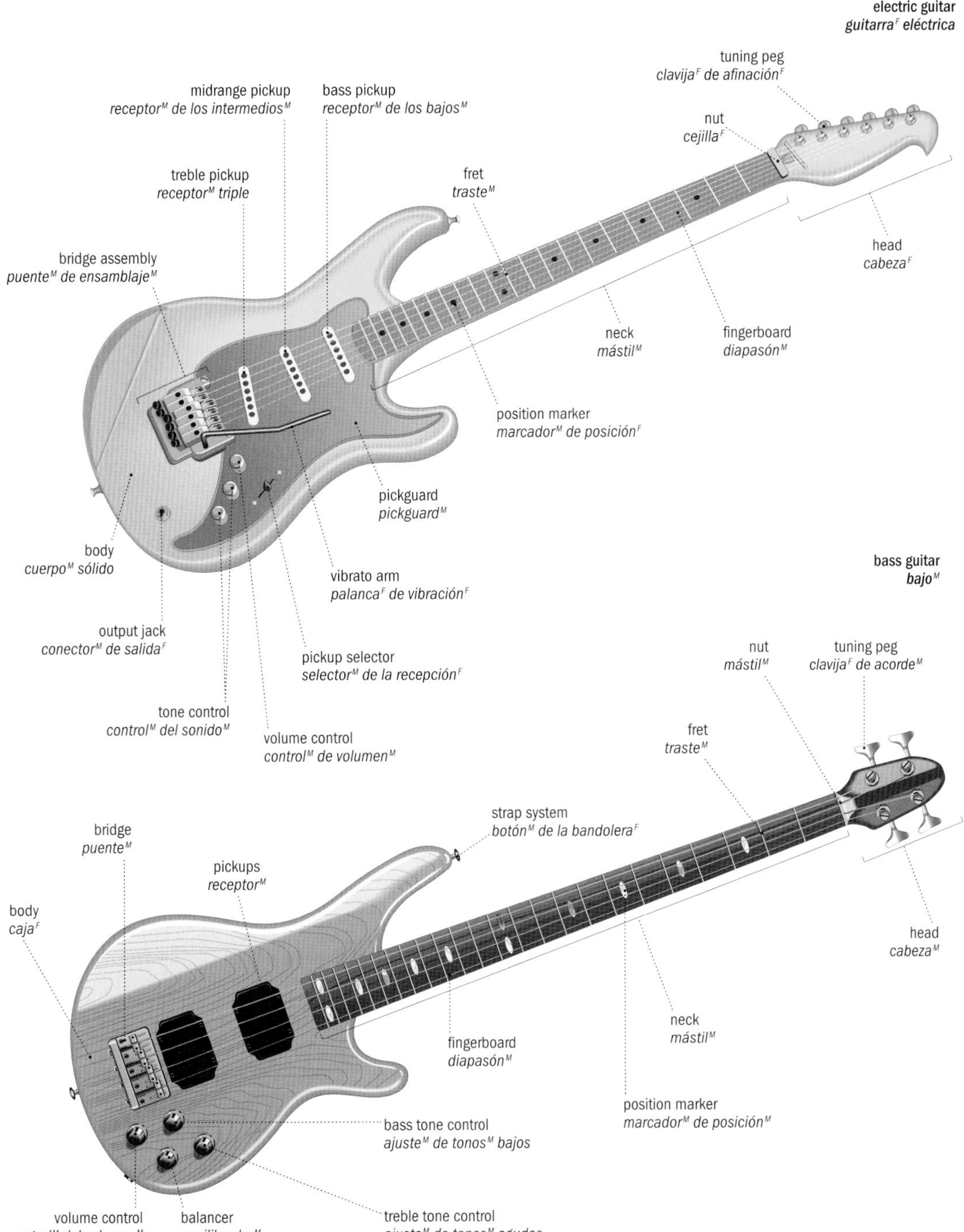
electric guitar
guitarra^F eléctrica
tuning peg
clavija^F de afinación^F
midrange pickup
receptor^M de los intermedios^M
bass pickup
receptor^M de los bajos^M
nut
cejilla^F
treble pickup
receptor^M triple
fret
traste^M
bridge assembly
puente^M de ensamblaje^M
head
cabeza^F
neck
mástil^M
fingerboard
diapasón^M
position marker
marcador^M de posición^F
pickguard
pickguard^M
body
cuerpo^M sólido
vibrato arm
palanca^F de vibración^F
output jack
conector^M de salida^F
pickup selector
selector^M de la recepción^F
tone control
control^M del sonido^M
volume control
control^M de volumen^M
bass guitar
bajo^M
nut
mástil^M
tuning peg
clavija^F de acorde^M
fret
traste^M
strap system
botón^M de la bandolera^F
bridge
puente^M
pickups
receptor^M
body
caja^F
head
cabeza^M
neck
mástil^M
fingerboard
diapasón^M
position marker
marcador^M de posición^M
bass tone control
ajuste^M de tonos^M bajos
volume control
control^M del volumen^M
balancer
equilibrador^M
treble tone control
ajuste^M de tonos^M agudos

keyboard instruments

instrumentos^M de teclado^M

upright piano
piano^M vertical

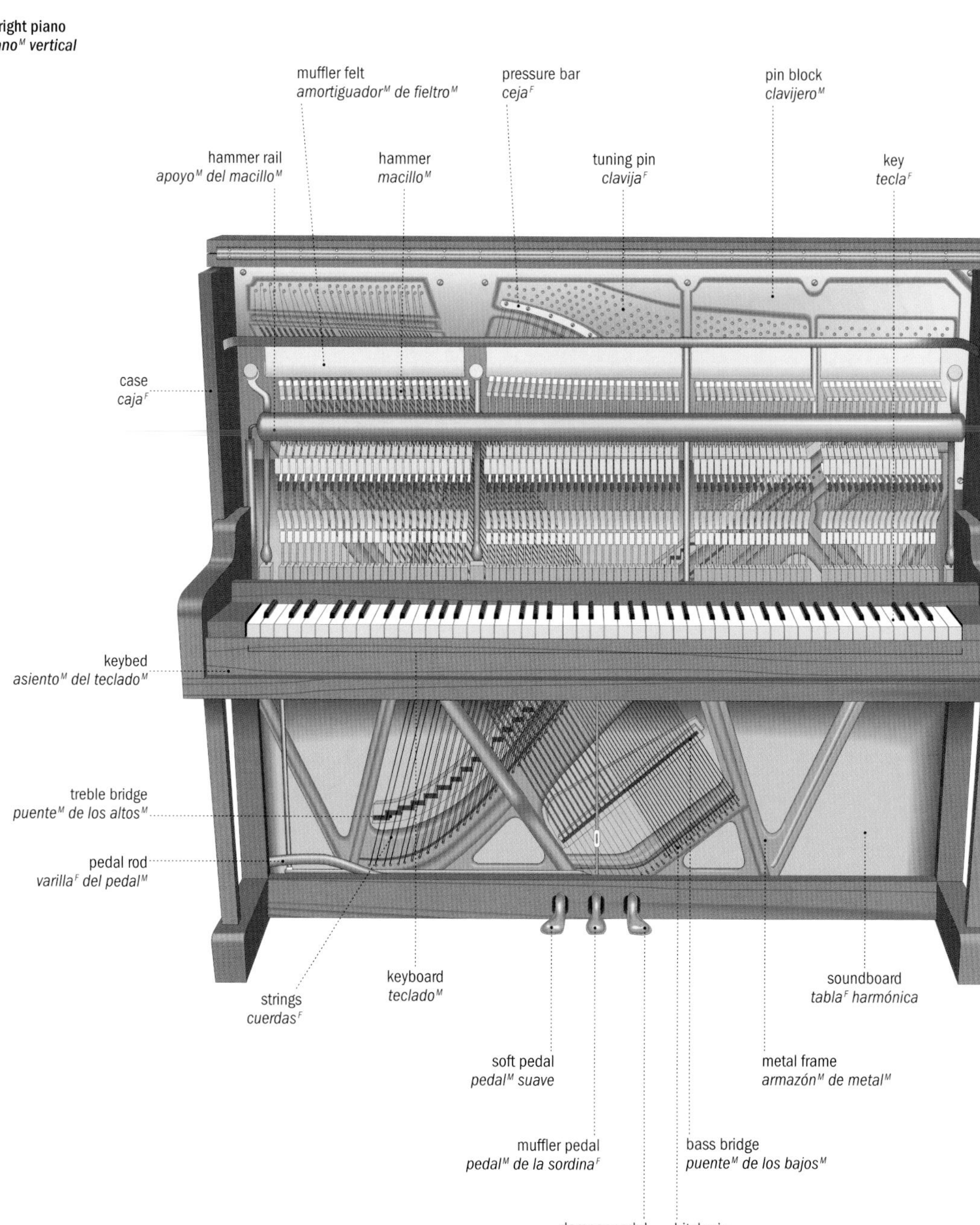

organ
órgano[M]

organ console
consola[F]

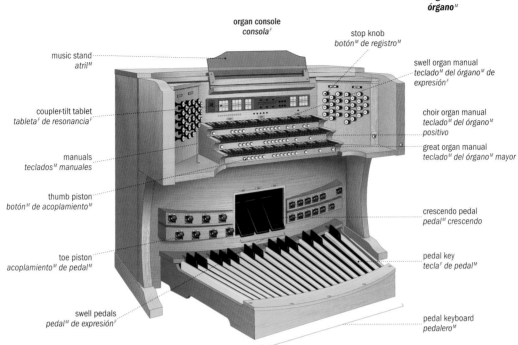

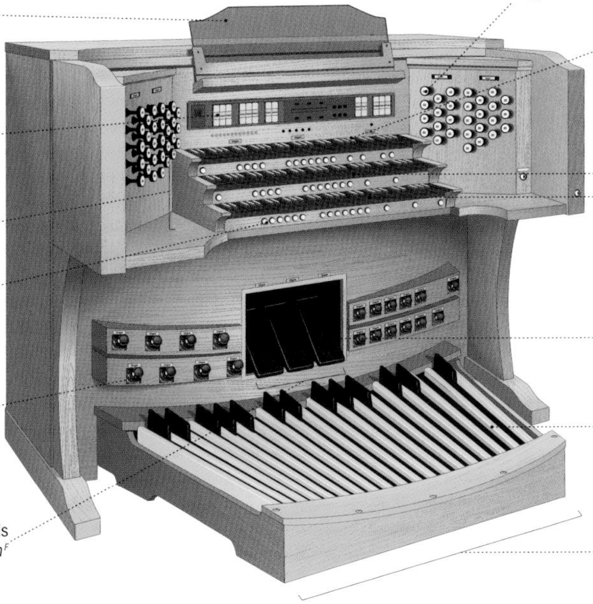

music stand
atril[M]

stop knob
botón[M] *de registro*[M]

swell organ manual
teclado[M] *del órgano*[M] *de expresión*[F]

coupler-tilt tablet
tableta[F] *de resonancia*[F]

choir organ manual
teclado[M] *del órgano*[M] *positivo*

great organ manual
teclado[M] *del órgano*[M] *mayor*

manuals
teclados[M] *manuales*

thumb piston
botón[M] *de acoplamiento*[M]

crescendo pedal
pedal[M] *crescendo*

toe piston
acoplamiento[M] *de pedal*[M]

pedal key
tecla[F] *de pedal*[M]

swell pedals
pedal[M] *de expresión*[F]

pedal keyboard
pedalero[M]

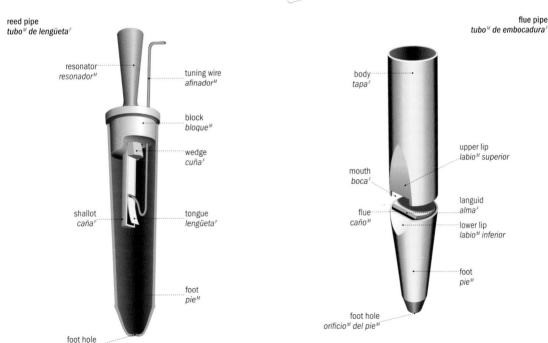

reed pipe
***tubo*[M] *de lengüeta*[F]**

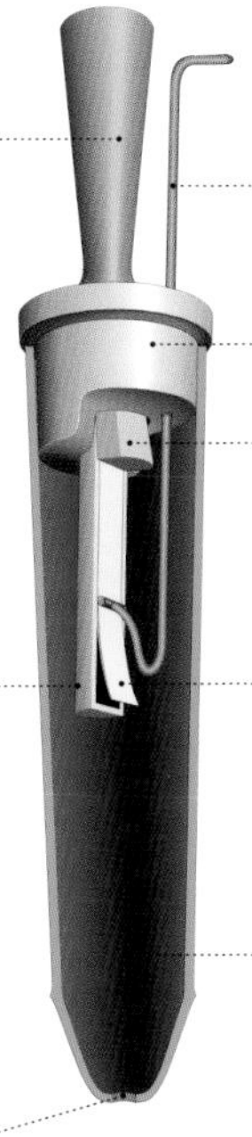

resonator
resonador[M]

tuning wire
afinador[M]

block
bloque[M]

wedge
cuña[F]

shallot
caña[F]

tongue
lengüeta[F]

foot
pie[M]

foot hole
orificio[M] *del pie*[M]

flue pipe
***tubo*[M] *de embocadura*[F]**

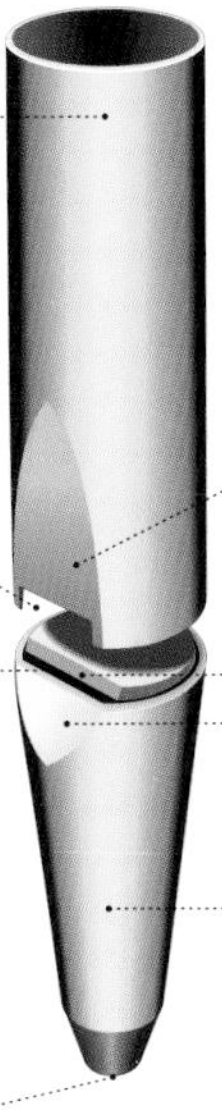

body
tapa[F]

upper lip
labio[M] *superior*

mouth
boca[F]

languid
alma[F]

flue
caño[M]

lower lip
labio[M] *inferior*

foot
pie[M]

foot hole
orificio[M] *del pie*[M]

wind instruments

instrumentos[M] de viento[M]

saxophone
saxofón^M

mouthpiece
boquilla^F

crook
embocadura^F

crook key
llave^F *de embocadura*^F

ligature
anillo^M *de ajuste*^M

reed
lengüeta^F

octave mechanism
mecanismo^M *para las octavas*^F

key lever
palanca^F

bell
pabellón^M

double reed
doble caña^F

single reed
caña^F *simple*

bell brace
sujetador^M *del pabellón*^M

key
llave^F

key guard
dispositivo^M *de protección*^F

body
cuerpo^M

key finger button
botón^M *de la llave*^F

thumb rest
gancho^M *del pulgar*^M

breech
culata^F

breech guard
protector^M *de la culata*^F

piccolo
píccolo^M

bassoon
fagot^M

clarinet
clarinete^M

oboe
oboe^M

tranverse flute
flauta^F

English horn
corno^M *inglés*

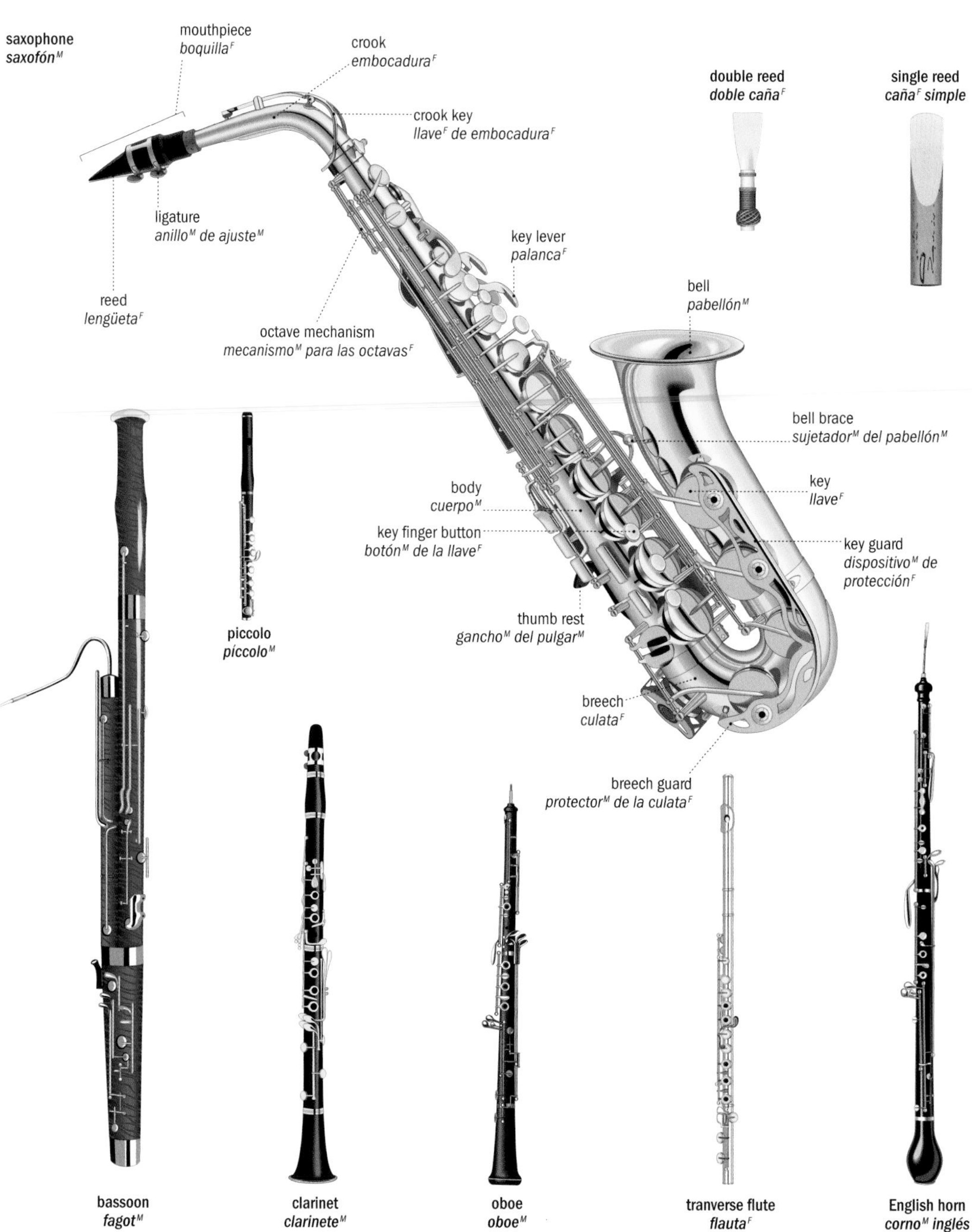

trumpet
trompeta
key
llave
little finger hook
gancho del meñique
bell
pabellón
mouthpipe
tubo
ring
anillo
mouthpiece receiver
empate de la boquilla
mouthpiece
boquilla
tuning slide
corredera de afinamiento
first valve slide
primer pistón móvil
spit valve
llave para agua
third valve slide
tercer pistón móvil
thumb hook
gancho del pulgar
valve
pistón
valve casing
tubo del pistón
second valve slide
segundo pistón móvil
mute
sordina
French horn
corno francés/trompa
cornet
cornetín
bugle
clarín
saxhorn
bombardino
trombone
trombón
tuba
tuba

percussion instruments

instrumentos[M] de percusión[F]

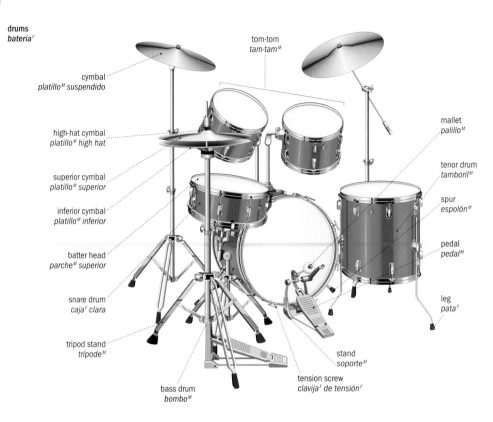

drums
batería[F]

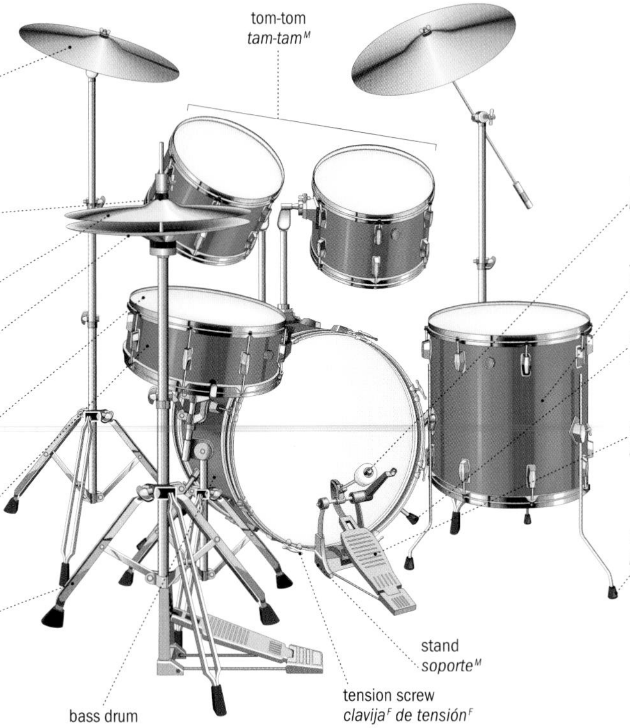

tom-tom
tam-tam[M]
cymbal
platillo[M] suspendido
high-hat cymbal
platillo[M] high hat
superior cymbal
platillo[M] superior
inferior cymbal
platillo[M] inferior
batter head
parche[M] superior
snare drum
caja[F] clara
tripod stand
trípode[M]
bass drum
bombo[M]
tension screw
clavija[F] de tensión[F]
stand
soporte[M]
mallet
palillo[M]
tenor drum
tamboril[M]
spur
espolón[M]
pedal
pedal[M]
leg
pata[F]

snare drum
caja[F] clara

lug
sujetador[M]
tension rod
varilla[F] de tensión[F]
snare strainer
tensor[M] de las cuerdas[F]
snare
cuerdas[F]
snare head
parche[M] inferior

kettledrum
timbal[M]

tie rod
barra[F] sujetadora
batter head
parche[M] superior
metal counterhoop
arco[M] tensor
tuning gauge
afinación[F]
shell
concha[F]
strut
puntal[M]
tension rod
varilla[F] de tensión[F]
crown
corona[F]
pedal
pedal[M]
caster
ruedecilla[F]
foot
pata[F]

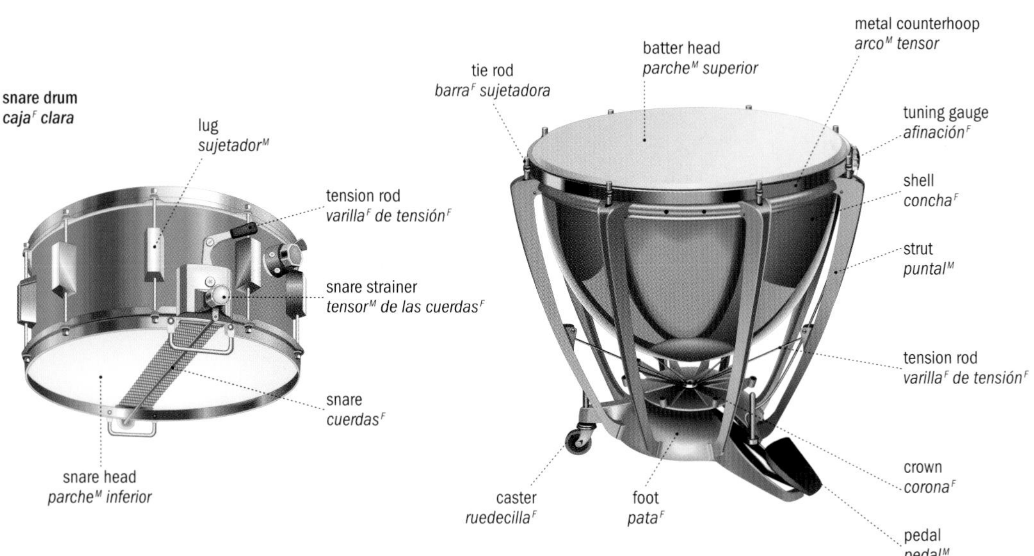

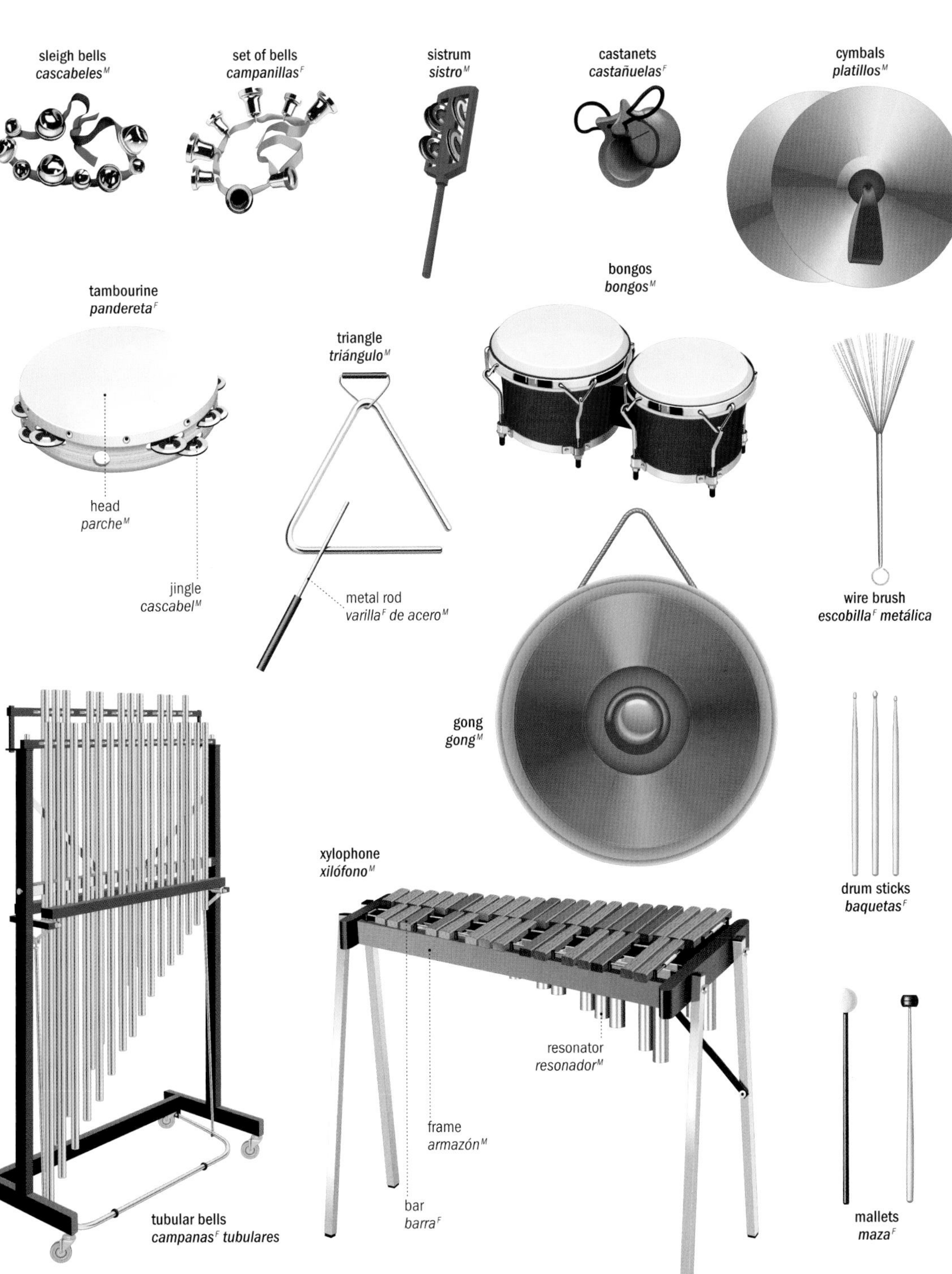
sleigh bells
cascabeles
set of bells
campanillas
sistrum
sistro
castanets
castañuelas
cymbals
platillos
tambourine
pandereta
head
parche
jingle
cascabel
triangle
triángulo
metal rod
varilla de acero
bongos
bongos
wire brush
escobilla metálica
gong
gong
drum sticks
baquetas
xylophone
xilófono
resonator
resonador
frame
armazón
bar
barra
tubular bells
campanas tubulares
mallets
maza

electronic instruments

instruments*M* electrónicos

sequencer
***secuenciador**M*

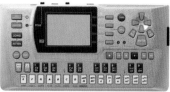

sampler
***muestreador**M*

headphone jack
toma F para auriculares M

function display
display M de las funciones M

disk drive
lector M de discos M

expander
***amplificador**M*

synthesizer
***sintetizador**M*

volume control
control M de volumen M

fine data-entry control
control M de entrada F de información F fina

disk drive
unidad F de discos M

system buttons
sistema M de botones M

function display
display M de funciones F

sequencer control
control M de secuencias F

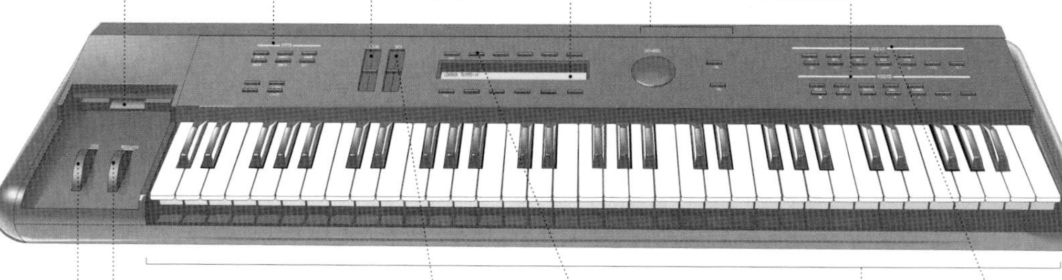

fast data-entry control
control M de entrada F de información F rápida

program selector
selector M de programa M

keyboard
teclado M

modulation wheel
rueda F de modulación F

voice edit buttons
botones M para editar la voz F

pitch wheel
rueda F para ajustar el tono M

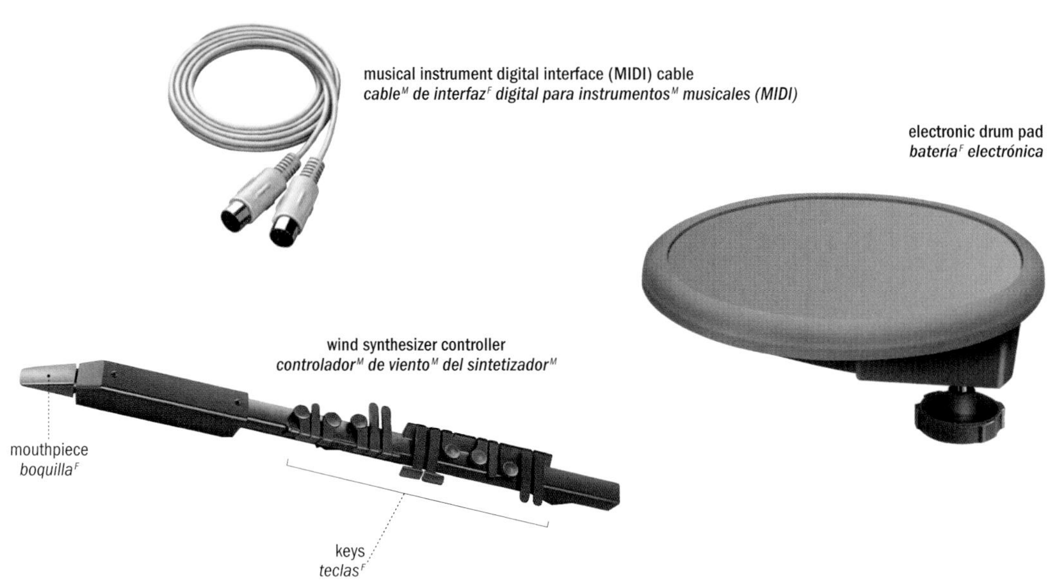

electronic piano
piano^M electrónico

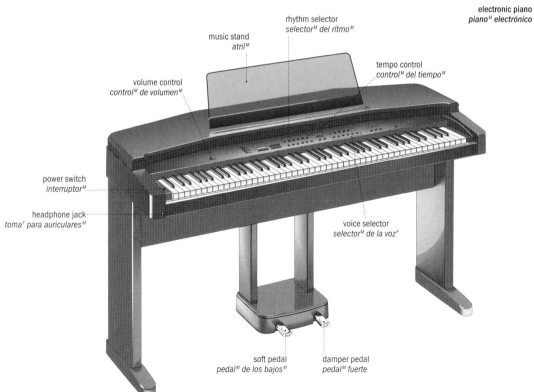

rhythm selector
selector^M del rítmo^M
music stand
atril^M
tempo control
control^M del tiempo^M
volume control
control^M de volumen^M
power switch
interruptor^M
headphone jack
toma^F para auriculares^M
voice selector
selector^M de la voz^F
soft pedal
pedal^M de los bajos^M
damper pedal
pedal^M fuerte

writing instruments

instrumentos^M para escribir

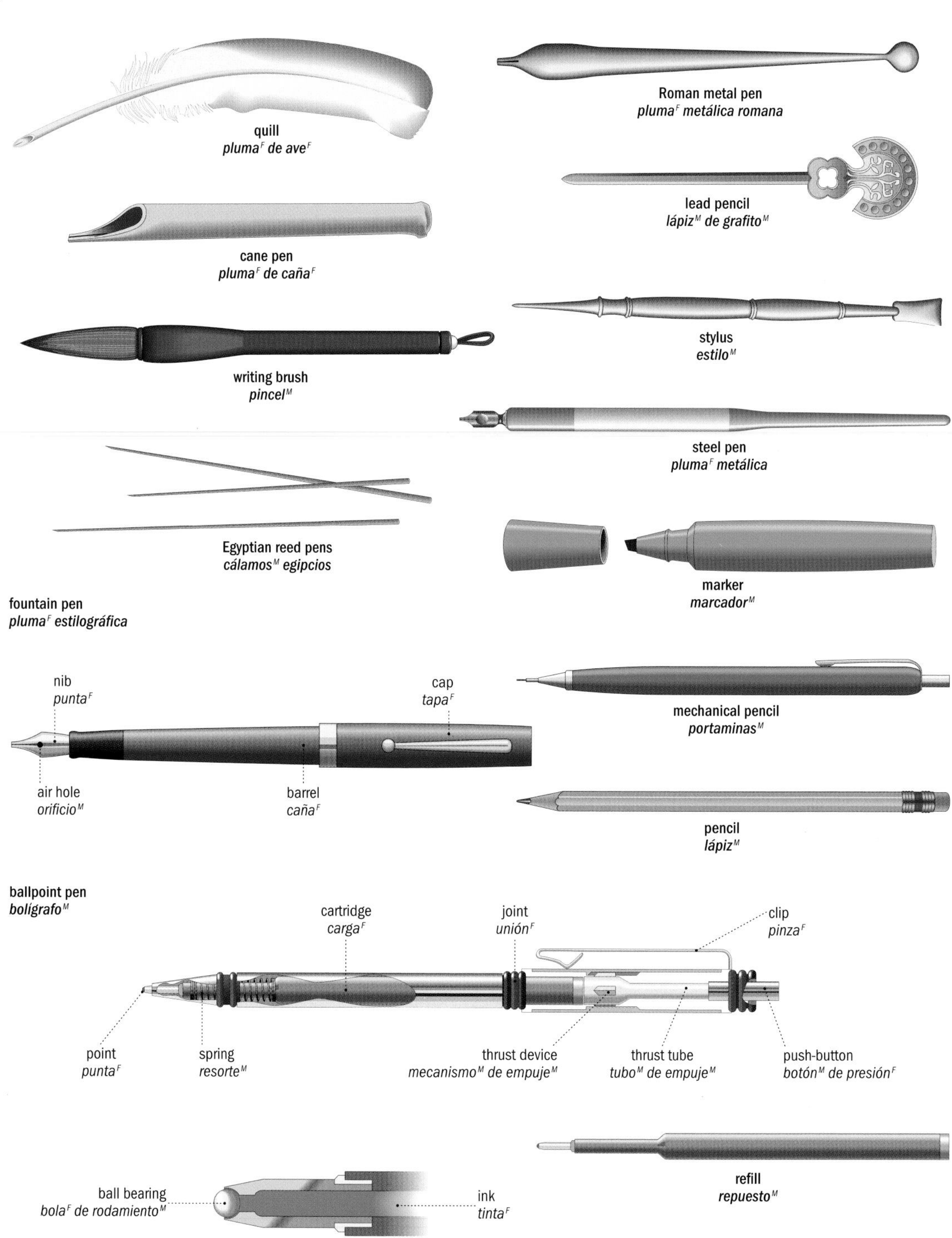
quill
pluma^F de ave^F
Roman metal pen
pluma^F metálica romana
lead pencil
lápiz^M de grafito^M
cane pen
pluma^F de caña^F
stylus
estilo^M
writing brush
pincel^M
steel pen
pluma^F metálica
Egyptian reed pens
cálamos^M egipcios
marker
marcador^M
fountain pen
pluma^F estilográfica
nib
punta^F
cap
tapa^F
air hole
orificio^M
barrel
caña^F
mechanical pencil
portaminas^M
pencil
lápiz^M
ballpoint pen
bolígrafo^M
cartridge
carga^F
joint
unión^F
clip
pinza^F
point
punta^F
spring
resorte^M
thrust device
mecanismo^M de empuje^M
thrust tube
tubo^M de empuje^M
push-button
botón^M de presión^F
refill
repuesto^M
ball bearing
bola^F de rodamiento^M
ink
tinta^F

newspaper

periódico[M]

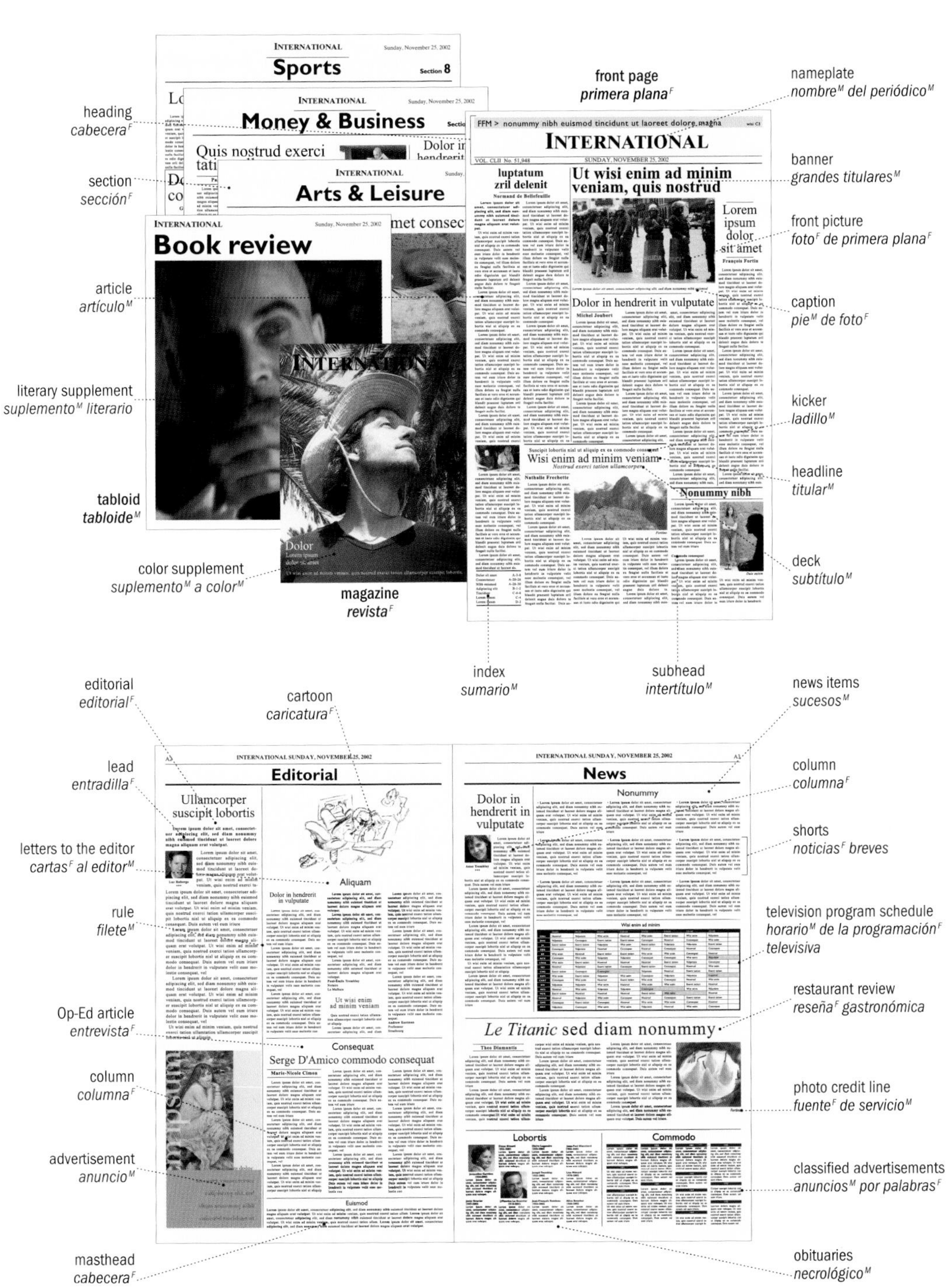

heading
cabecera[F]

section
sección[F]

article
artículo[M]

literary supplement
suplemento[M] *literario*

tabloid
tabloide[M]

color supplement
suplemento[M] *a color*[M]

magazine
revista[F]

Sports Section **8**

Money & Business

Arts & Leisure

Book review

front page
primera plana[F]

INTERNATIONAL

nameplate
nombre[M] *del periódico*[M]

banner
grandes titulares[M]

Ut wisi enim ad minim veniam, quis nostrud

front picture
foto[F] *de primera plana*[F]

caption
pie[M] *de foto*[F]

kicker
ladillo[M]

headline
titular[M]

deck
subtítulo[M]

index
sumario[M]

subhead
intertítulo[M]

news items
sucesos[M]

editorial
editorial[F]

cartoon
caricatura[F]

lead
entradilla[F]

letters to the editor
cartas[F] *al editor*[M]

rule
filete[M]

Op-Ed article
entrevista[F]

column
columna[F]

advertisement
anuncio[M]

masthead
cabecera[F]

Editorial

News

column
columna[F]

shorts
noticias[F] *breves*

television program schedule
horario[M] *de la programación*[F]
televisiva

restaurant review
reseña[F] *gastronómica*

photo credit line
fuente[F] *de servicio*[M]

classified advertisements
anuncios[M] *por palabras*[F]

obituaries
necrológico[M]

photography

fotografía[F]

single-lens reflex (SLR) camera: front view
cámara[F] réflex monocular: vista[F] frontal

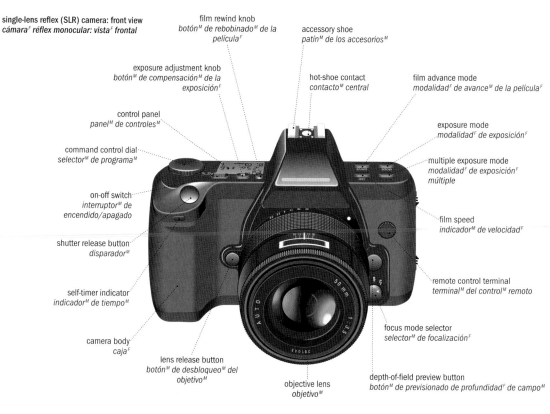

film rewind knob
botón[M] de rebobinado[M] de la película[F]

accessory shoe
patín[M] de los accesorios[M]

exposure adjustment knob
botón[M] de compensación[M] de la exposición[F]

hot-shoe contact
contacto[M] central

film advance mode
modalidad[F] de avance[M] de la película[F]

control panel
panel[M] de controles[M]

exposure mode
modalidad[F] de exposición[F]

command control dial
selector[M] de programa[M]

multiple exposure mode
modalidad[F] de exposición[F] múltiple

on-off switch
interruptor[M] de encendido/apagado

film speed
indicador[M] de velocidad[F]

shutter release button
disparador[M]

remote control terminal
terminal[M] del control[M] remoto

self-timer indicator
indicador[M] de tiempo[M]

focus mode selector
selector[M] de focalización[F]

camera body
caja[F]

lens release button
botón[M] de desbloqueo[M] del objetivo[M]

objective lens
objetivo[M]

depth-of-field preview button
botón[M] de previsionado de profundidad[F] de campo[M]

lenses
objetivos[M]

telephoto lens
teleobjetivo[M]

zoom lens
objetivo[M] zoom[M]

wide-angle lens
objetivo[M] gran angular[M]

macro lens
objetivo[M] macro

lens accessories
accesorios[M] para el objetivo[M]

lens cap
tapa[F] del objetivo[M]

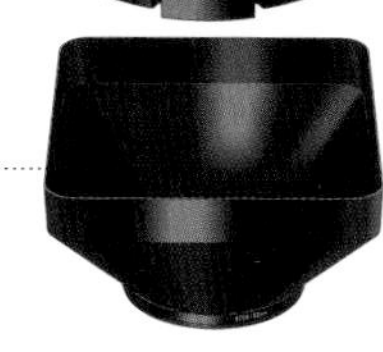

lens hood
capuchón[M]

polarizing filter
filtro[M] de polarización[F]

digital reflex camera: camera back
cámara[F] réflex digital: vista[F] posterior

menu button
botón[M] de selección[F] del menú[M]

settings display button
botón[M] de visualización[F] de ajustes[M]

strap eyelet
ojete[M] para la correa[F]

multi-image jump button
botón[M] de salto[M] de imágenes[F]

video and digital terminals
tomas[F] vídeo y digital

index/enlarge button
botón[M] de índice[M]/ampliación[F]

remote control terminal
botón[M] de control[M] remoto

power switch
conmutador[M] de alimentación[F]

viewfinder
visor[M]

cover
tapa[F]

compact memory card
tarjeta[F] de memoria[F]

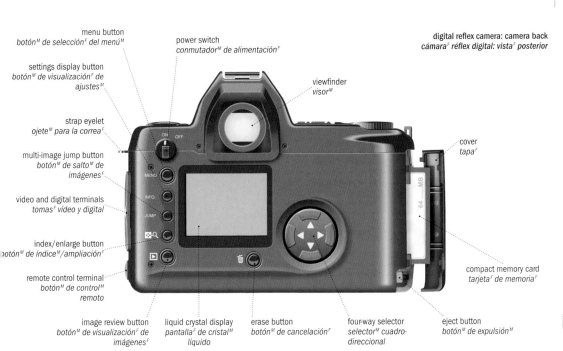

image review button
botón[M] de visualización[F] de imágenes[F]

liquid crystal display
pantalla[F] de cristal[M] líquido

erase button
botón[M] de cancelación[F]

four-way selector
selector[M] cuadro-direccional

eject button
botón[M] de expulsión[M]

still cameras
cámaras[F] fijas

Polaroid® camera
cámara[F] Polaroid Land

medium-format SLR (6 x 6)
cámara[F] reflex de formato[M] medio SLR (6x6)

rangefinder
telémetro[M]

digital camera
cámara[F] digital

disposable camera
cámara[F] desechable

view camera
cámara[F] de fuelle[M]

broadcast satellite communication

comunicación^F vía satélite

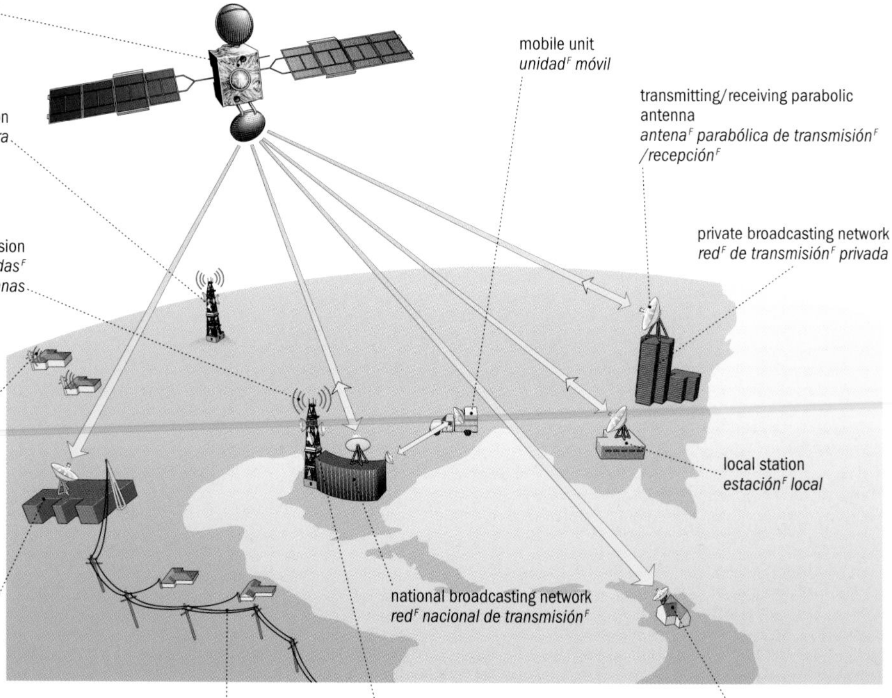

satellite
satélite^M
mobile unit
unidad^F móvil
transmitting/receiving parabolic antenna
antena^F parabólica de transmisión^F /recepción^F
relay station
estación^F repetidora
Hertzian wave transmission
transmisión^F de ondas^F hertzianas
private broadcasting network
red^F de transmisión^F privada
home antenna
antena^F doméstica
local station
estación^F local
national broadcasting network
red^F nacional de transmisión^F
cable distributor
cable^M distribuidor
distribution by aerial cable network
red^F de distribución^F por cable^M aéreo
transmitting tower
torre^F de transmisión^F /recepción^F
direct home reception
recepción^F directa en la casa^F

telecommunication satellites

satélites^M de telecomunicaciones^F

Eutelsat
Eutelsat^M

transmitting/receiving dish
antena^F de emisión^F /recepción^F
solar reflectors
reflectores^M solares
communication module
módulo^M de comunicación^F
service module
módulo^M de servicio^M
solar array
panel^M solar
propulsion module
módulo^M de propulsión^F
transmission dish
antena^F de emisión^F

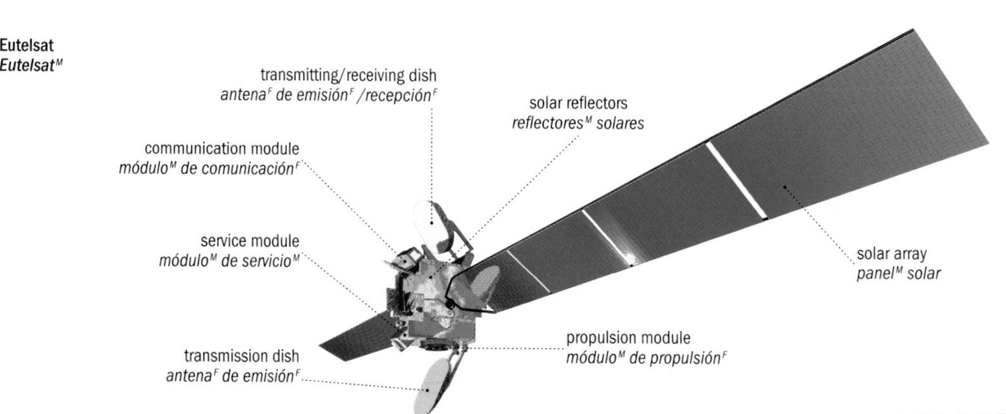

telecommunications by satellite

telecomunicaciones^{F} vía satélite^{M}

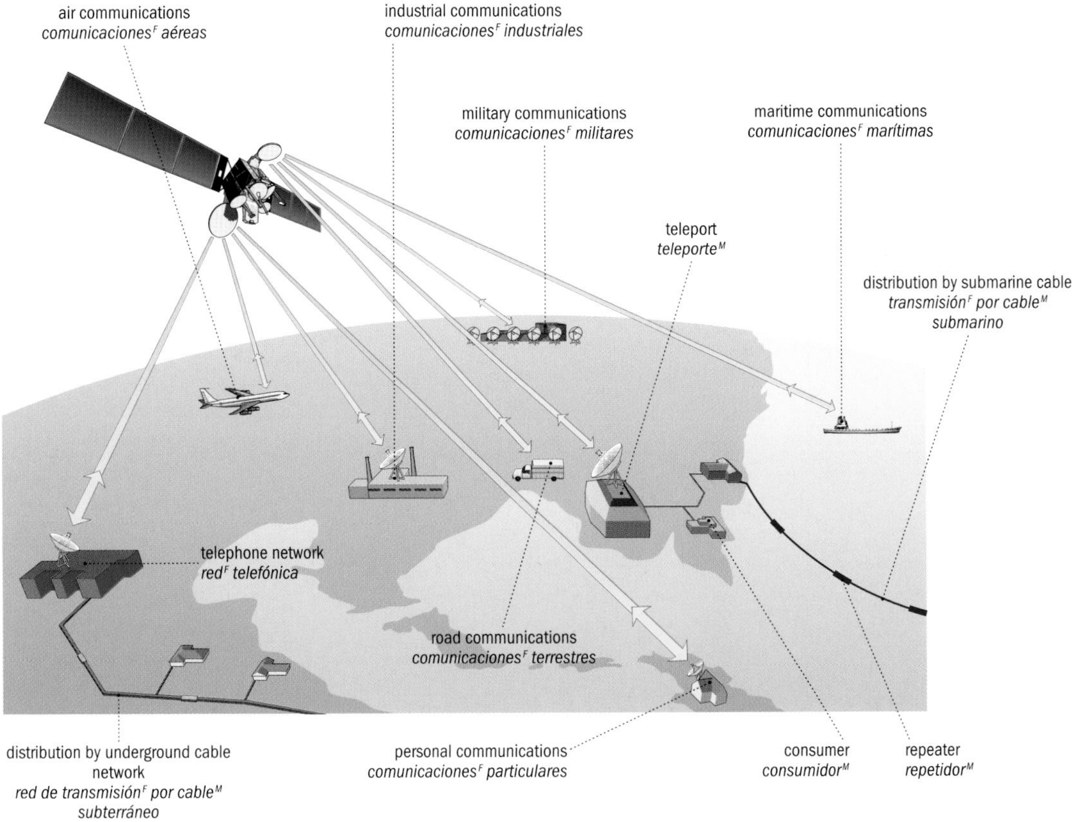

air communications
comunicaciones^{F} aéreas
industrial communications
comunicaciones^{F} industriales
military communications
comunicaciones^{F} militares
maritime communications
comunicaciones^{F} marítimas
teleport
teleporte^{M}
distribution by submarine cable
transmisión^{F} por cable^{M} submarino
telephone network
red^{F} telefónica
road communications
comunicaciones^{F} terrestres
distribution by underground cable network
red de transmisión^{F} por cable^{M} subterráneo
personal communications
comunicaciones^{F} particulares
consumer
consumidor^{M}
repeater
repetidor^{M}

telecommunication satellites

Anik
Anik^{M}

Intelsat
Intelsat^{M}

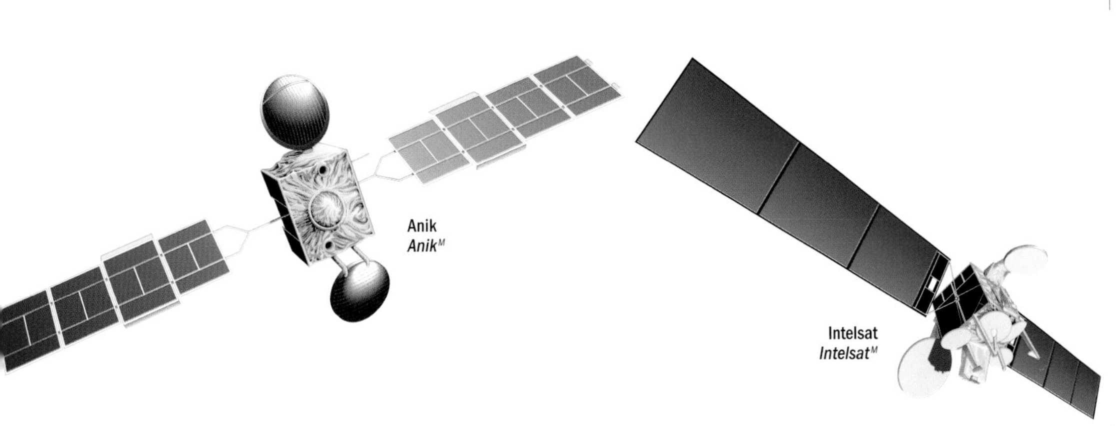

television

televisión^F

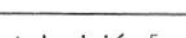

television set
televisor^M

picture tube
tubo^M de pantalla^F

electron gun
cañón^M de electrones^M

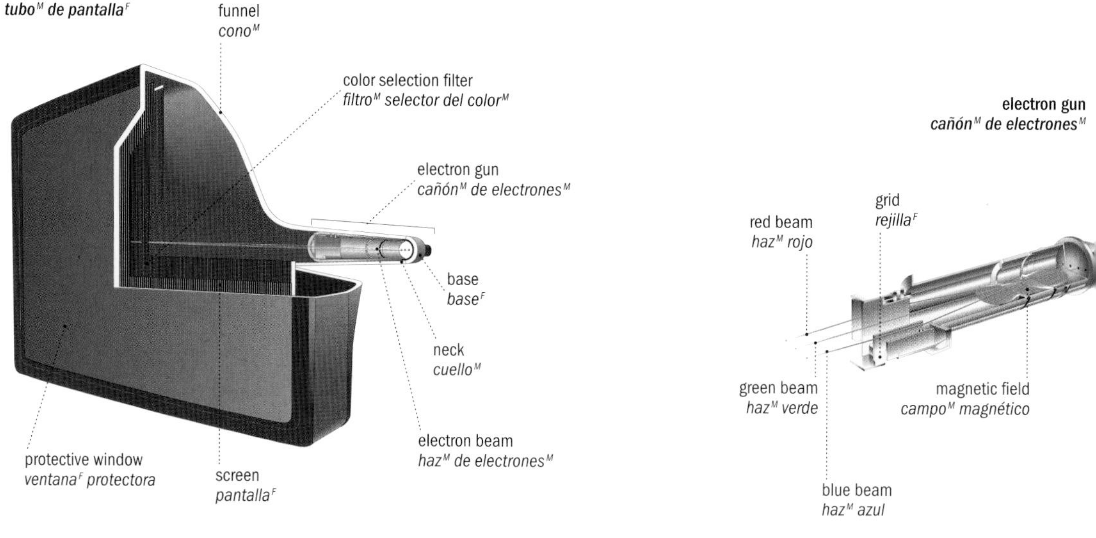

DVD player
reproductor^M DVD

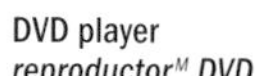

digital versatile disc (DVD)
disco^M versátil digital (DVD)

remote control
mando[M] a distancia[F]

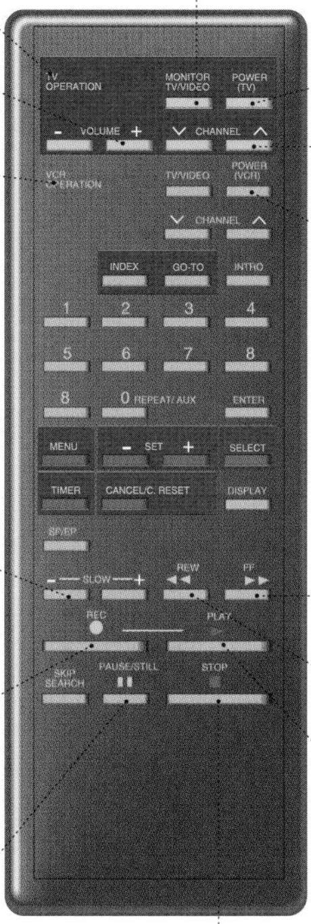

TV mode
modalidad[F] TV
TV/video button
botón[M] TV video[M]
volume control
control[M] de volumen[M]
TV power button
botón[M] de encendido TV
VCR mode
modalidad[F] VCR
channel scan button
botones[M] de búsqueda de canales[M]
channel selector controls
selector[M] de canales[M]
VCR power button
botón[M] de encendido VCR
preset buttons
botones[M] de ajuste[M]
slow-motion button
cámara[F] lenta
fast-forward button
avance[M] rápido
VCR controls
controles[M] VCR
rewind button
rebobinado[M]
record button
grabación[F]
play button
funcionamiento[M]
pause/still button
pausa[F] /imagen[F] fija
stop button
botón[M] de stop[M]

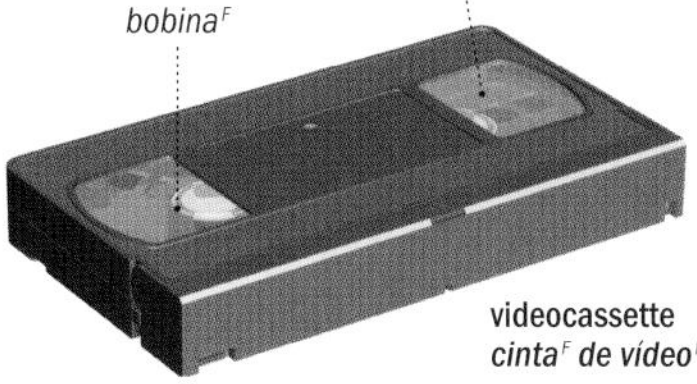

magnetic tape
cinta[F] magnética
reel
bobina[F]

videocassette
cinta[F] de vídeo[M]

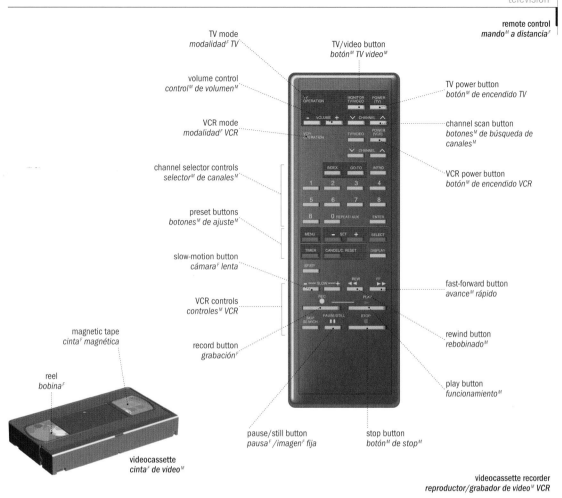

videocassette recorder
reproductor/grabador de video[M] VCR

cassette compartment
alojamiento[M] para la cinta[F]
data display
visualización[F] de la información[F]
play button
botón[M] de reproducción[F]
fast-forward button
botón[M] de avance[M] rápido
preset buttons
botones[M] de ajuste[M]
power button
interruptor[M]
reset button
botón[M] del contador[M] a cero
record button
botón[M] de grabación[F]
channel scan buttons
botones[M] para búsqueda[F] de canales[M]
cassette eject switch
botón[M] de expulsión[F]
stop button
botón[M] de stop[M]
rewind button
botón[M] de rebobinado[M]
pause/still button
pausa[F] /imagen[F] fija

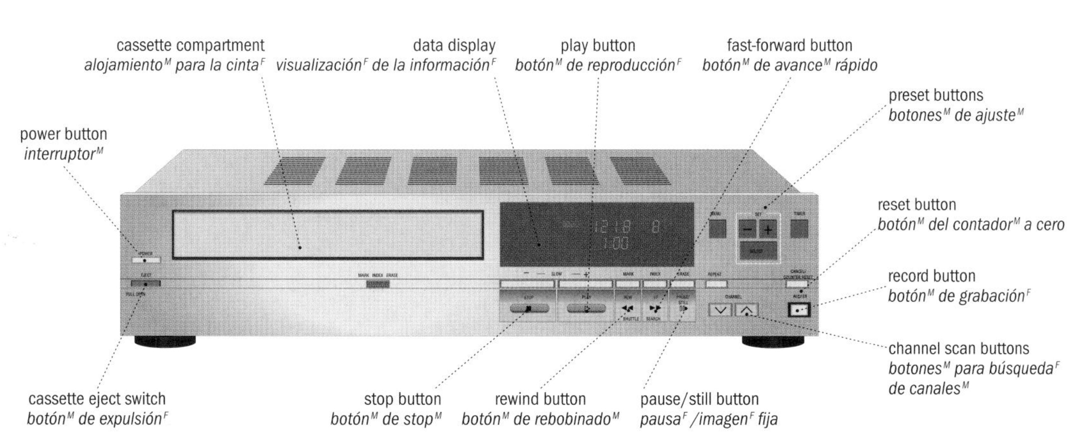

analog camcorder: front view
videocámara^{F} analógica: vista^{F} frontal

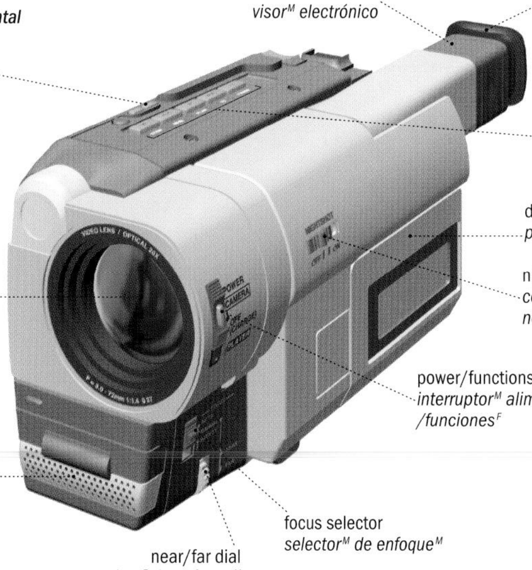

electronic viewfinder
visor^{M} electrónico
eyecup
ojera^{F}
edit search button
botón^{M} de selección^{M} y montaje^{M}
videotape operation controls
mandos^{M} de la cinta^{F} de vídeo^{M}
display panel
panel^{M} del display^{M}
nightshot switch
conmutador^{M} de grabación^{F} nocturna
zoom lens
objetivo^{M} zoom
power/functions switch
interruptor^{M} alimentación^{F} /funciones^{F}
microphone
micrófono^{M}
focus selector
selector^{M} de enfoque^{M}
near/far dial
ruleta^{F} de enfoque^{M} lejos/cerca

cassette compartment
alojamiento^{M} de la cinta^{F}

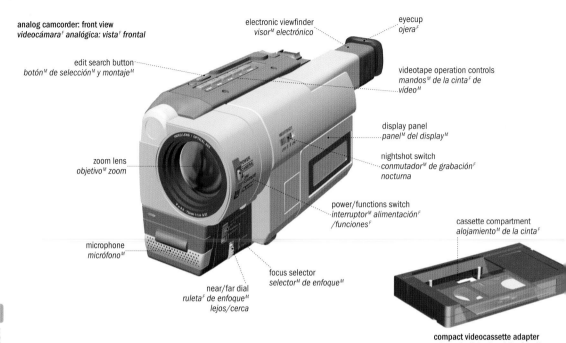

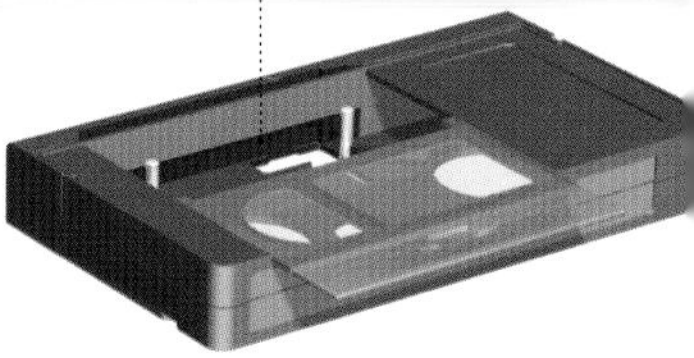

compact videocassette adapter
adaptador^{M} de cinta^{F} de vídeo^{M} compacto

analog camcorder: back view
videocámara^{F} analógica: vista^{F} posterior

eyepiece
ocular^{M}
power zoom button
botón^{M} del zoom^{M} eléctrico
recording start/stop button
tecla^{F} de inicio/stop de grabación^{F}
speaker
altavoz^{M}
rechargeable battery pack
pila^{F} recargable
image adjustment buttons
botones^{M} de ajuste^{M} de imagen^{F}
liquid crystal display
pantalla^{F} táctil LCD
indicators display button
tecla^{F} de fijación^{F} de pantalla^{F}
date display/recording button
botón grabación^{F} /visualización^{F} fecha^{F}
end search button
tecla^{F} de final^{M} de búsqueda^{F}
time display/recording button
botón grabación^{F} /visualización^{F} hora
special effects buttons
botones^{M} de efectos^{M} especiales
title display button
tecla^{F} de visualización^{F} del título^{M}
special effects selection dial
ruleta^{F} de selección^{F} de efectos^{M} especiales

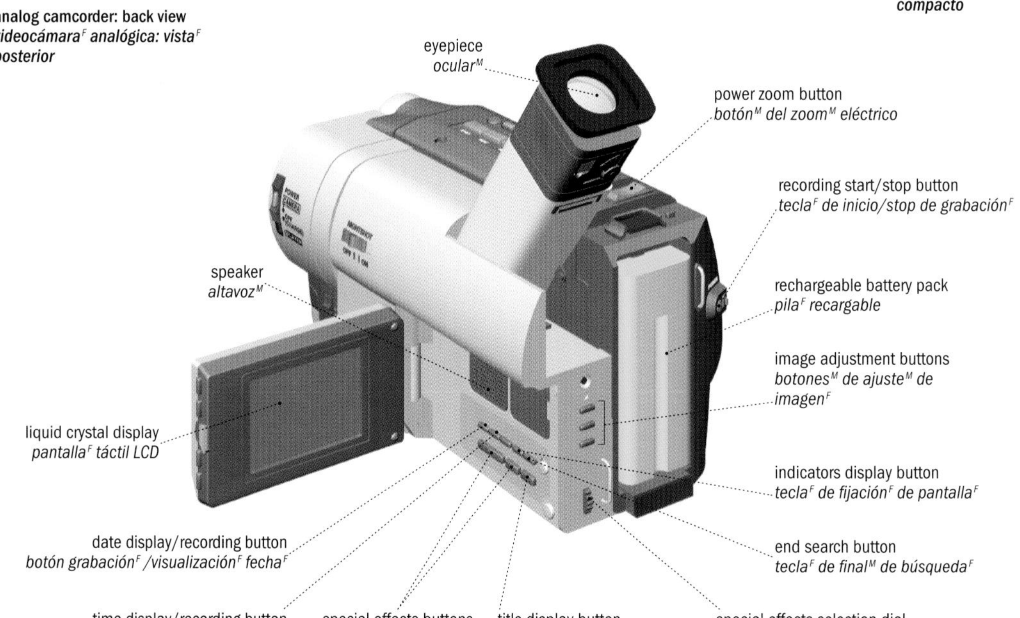

dish antenna
antena[F] parabólica

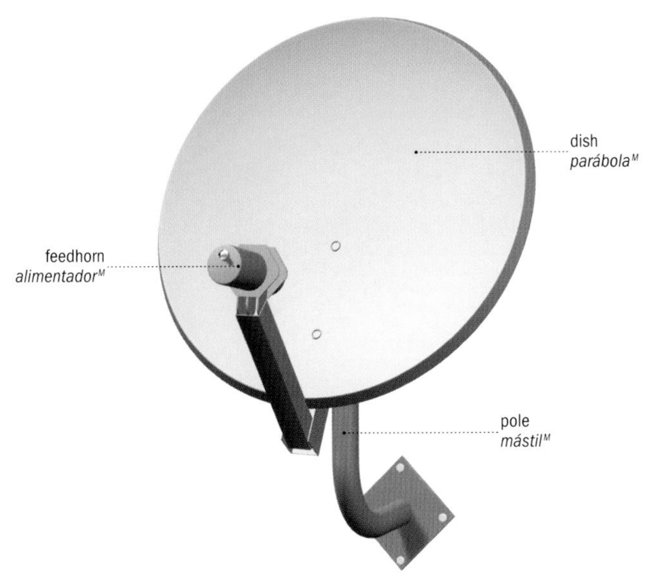

receiver
receptor[M]

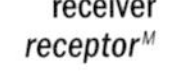

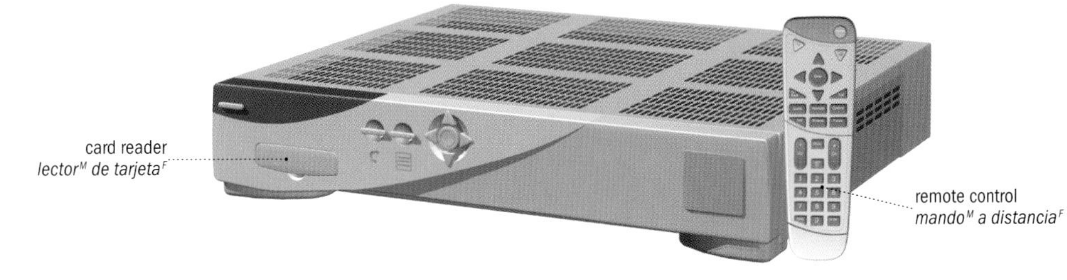

home theater
home[M] theatre

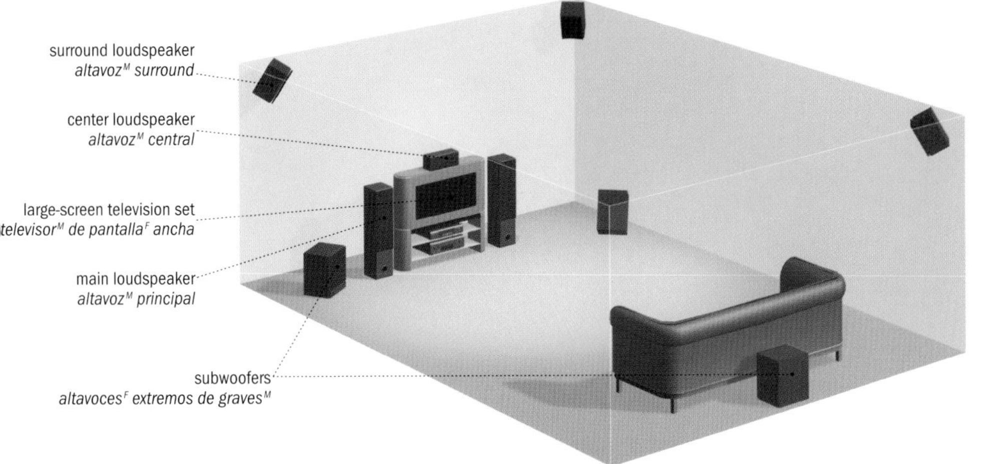

sound reproducing system

equipo^{M} de alta fidelidad^{F}

ampli-tuner: front view
amplificador^{M}/sintonizador^{M} : vista^{F} frontal

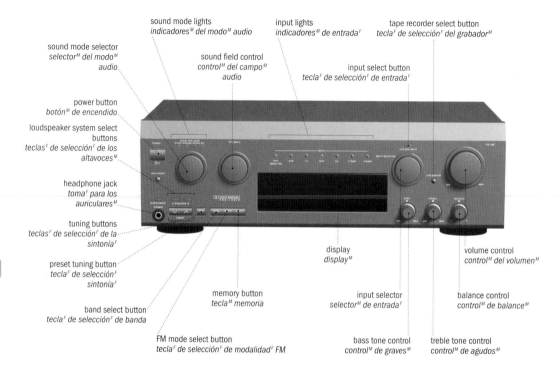

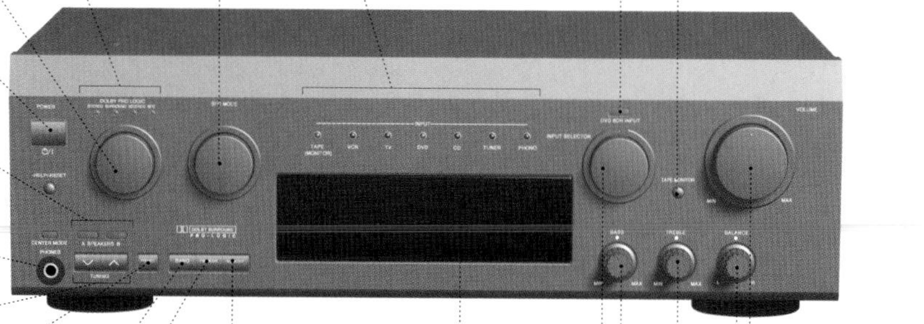

sound mode lights
indicadores^{M} del modo^{M} audio
input lights
indicadores^{M} de entrada^{F}
tape recorder select button
tecla^{F} de selección^{F} del grabador^{M}
sound mode selector
selector^{M} del modo^{M} audio
sound field control
control^{M} del campo^{M} audio
input select button
tecla^{F} de selección^{F} de entrada^{F}
power button
botón^{M} de encendido
loudspeaker system select buttons
teclas^{F} de selección^{F} de los altavoces^{M}
headphone jack
toma^{F} para los auriculares^{M}
tuning buttons
teclas^{F} de selección^{F} de la sintonía^{F}
preset tuning button
tecla^{F} de selección^{F} sintonía^{F}
display
display^{M}
volume control
control^{M} del volumen^{M}
memory button
tecla^{M} memoria
input selector
selector^{M} de entrada^{F}
balance control
control^{M} de balance^{M}
band select button
tecla^{F} de selección^{F} de banda
FM mode select button
tecla^{F} de selección^{F} de modalidad^{F} FM
bass tone control
control^{M} de graves^{M}
treble tone control
control^{M} de agudos^{M}

ampli-tuner: back view
amplificador^{M}/sintonizador^{M} : vista^{F} posterior

ground terminal
conector^{M} de puesta^{F} de tierra^{F}
cooling fan
ventilador^{M}
power cord
cable^{M} de alimentación^{F}
antenna terminals
conectores^{M} de antenas^{F}
CAUTION
SPEAKERS
HAUT-PARLEURS
input/output audio/video jacks
tomas^{F} entrada^{F}/salida^{F} video^{M}
loudspeaker terminals
conector^{F} de altavoces^{M}
switched outlet
conmutador^{M} de corriente^{F}

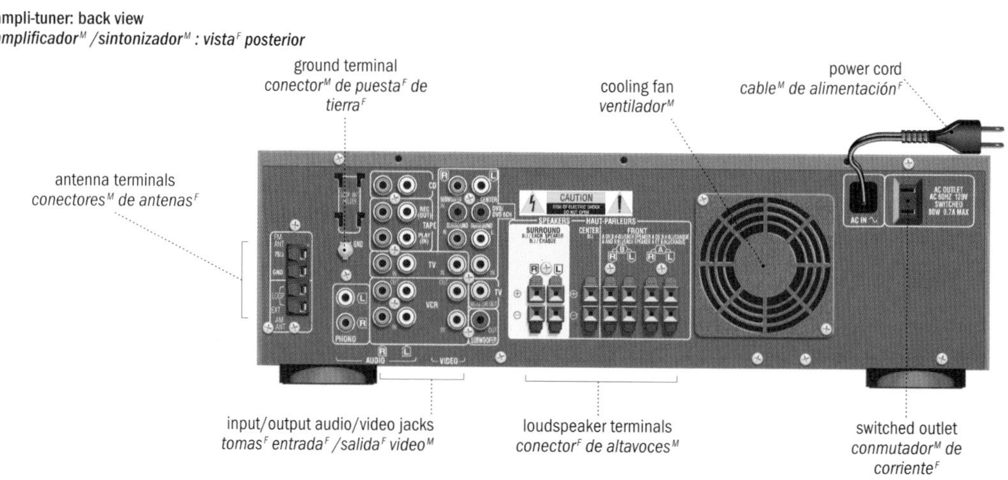

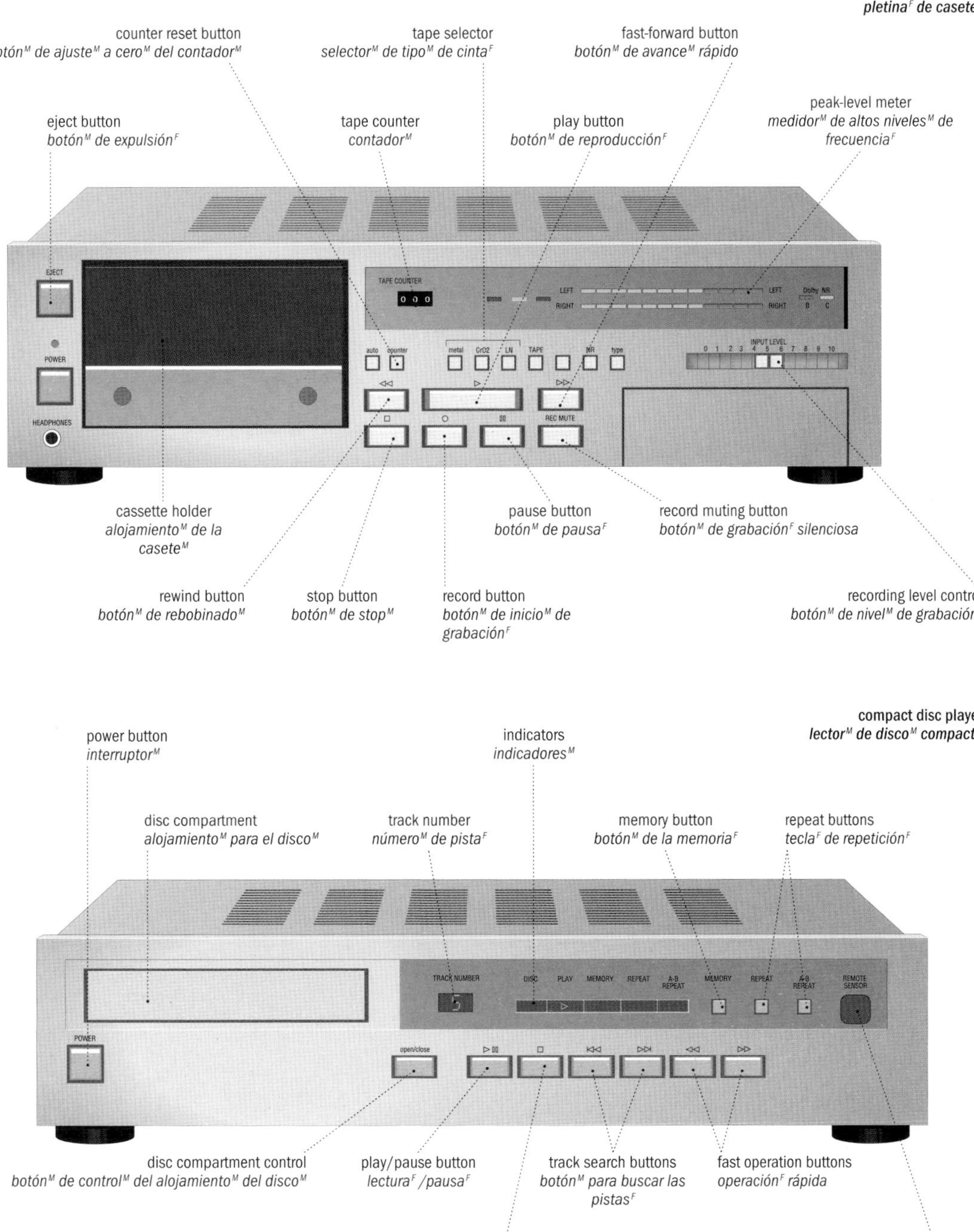
cassette tape deck
pletina^F de casete^F
counter reset button
botón^M de ajuste^M a cero^M del contador^M
tape selector
selector^M de tipo^M de cinta^F
fast-forward button
botón^M de avance^M rápido
eject button
botón^M de expulsión^F
tape counter
contador^M
play button
botón^M de reproducción^F
peak-level meter
medidor^M de altos niveles^M de frecuencia^F
cassette holder
alojamiento^M de la casete^M
pause button
botón^M de pausa^F
record muting button
botón^M de grabación^F silenciosa
rewind button
botón^M de rebobinado^M
stop button
botón^M de stop^M
record button
botón^M de inicio^M de grabación^F
recording level control
botón^M de nivel^M de grabación^F
compact disc player
lector^M de disco^M compacto
power button
interruptor^M
indicators
indicadores^M
disc compartment
alojamiento^M para el disco^M
track number
número^M de pista^F
memory button
botón^M de la memoria^F
repeat buttons
tecla^F de repetición^F
disc compartment control
botón^M de control^M del alojamiento^M del disco^M
play/pause button
lectura^F /pausa^F
track search buttons
botón^M para buscar las pistas^F
fast operation buttons
operación^F rápida
stop/clear button
botón^M para parar y borrar
remote control sensor
sensor^M del mando^M a distancia^F

sound reproducing system

headphones
auriculares[M]

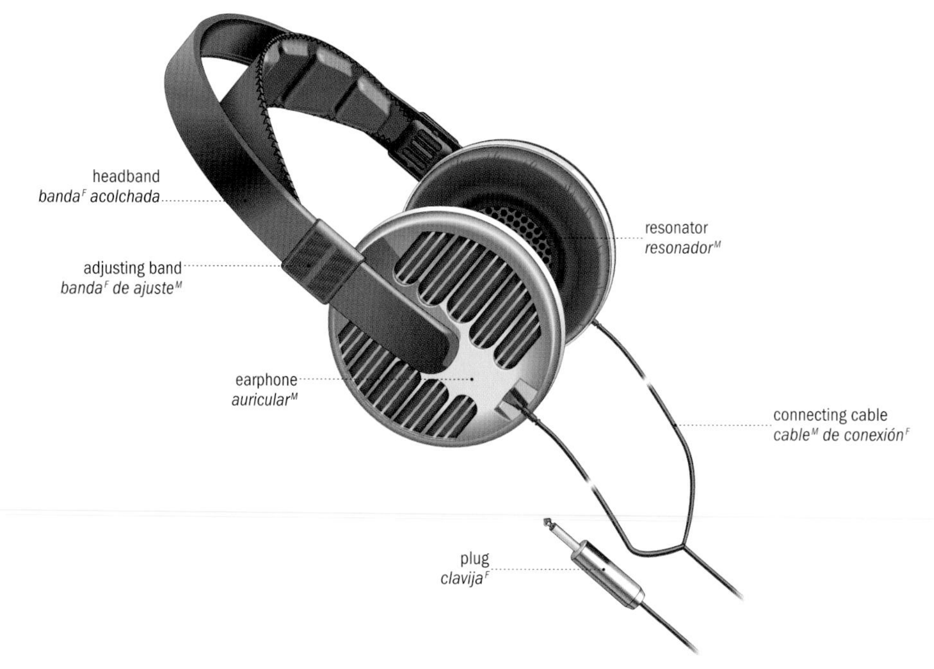

loudspeakers
altavoz[M]

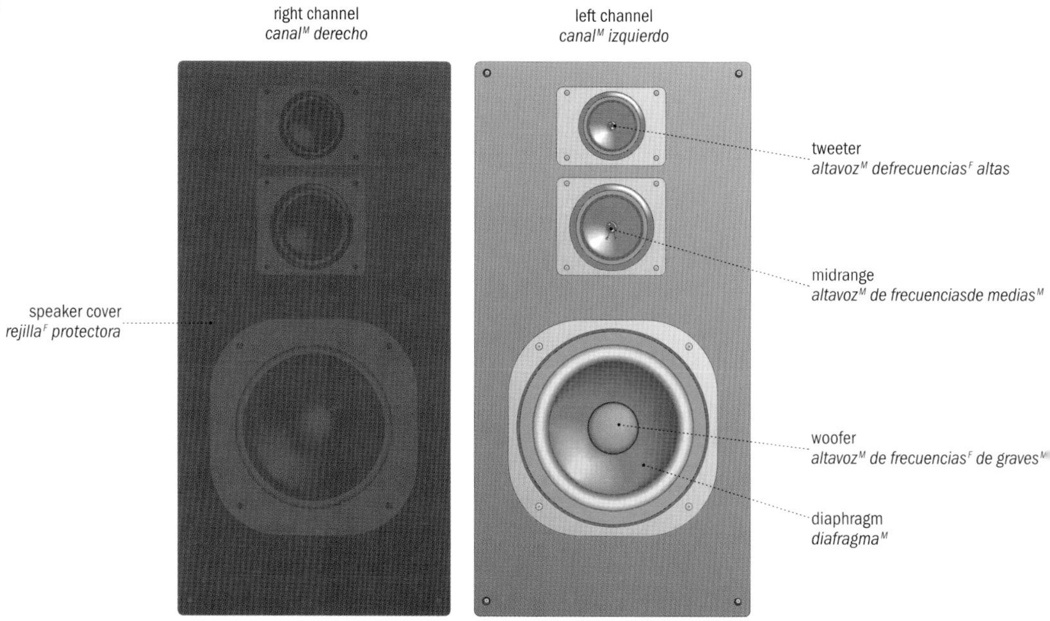

right channel
canal[M] derecho

left channel
canal[M] izquierdo

speaker cover
rejilla[F] protectora

tweeter
altavoz[M] defrecuencias[F] altas

midrange
altavoz[M] de frecuenciasde medias[M]

woofer
altavoz[M] de frecuencias[F] de graves[M]

diaphragm
diafragma[M]

mini stereo sound system

mini-cadena^F estéreo

compact disc player
lector de disco^M compacto
ampli-tuner
amplificador^M-sintonizador^M
loudspeaker
altavoz^M
compact disc recorder
reproductor^M de disco^M compacto
dual cassette deck
doble pletina^F de casete^F

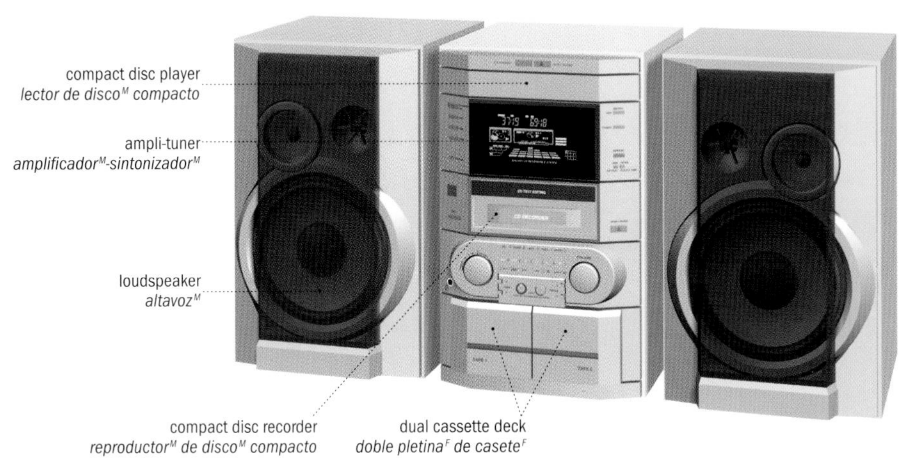

portable sound systems

sistemas^M de sonido^M portátiles

clock radio
radio^M despertador

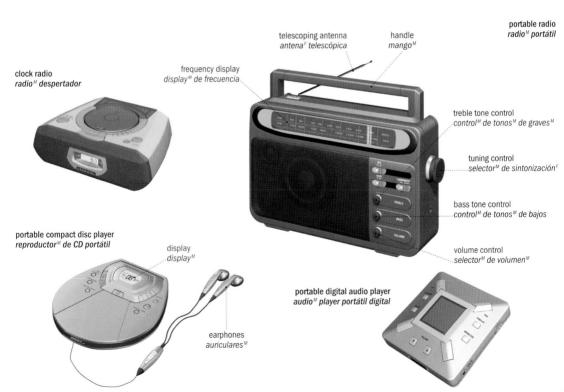

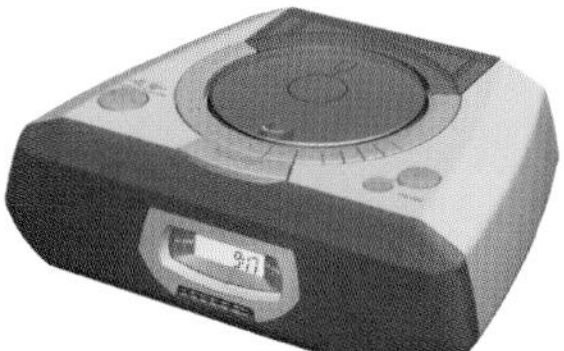

portable radio
radio^M portátil

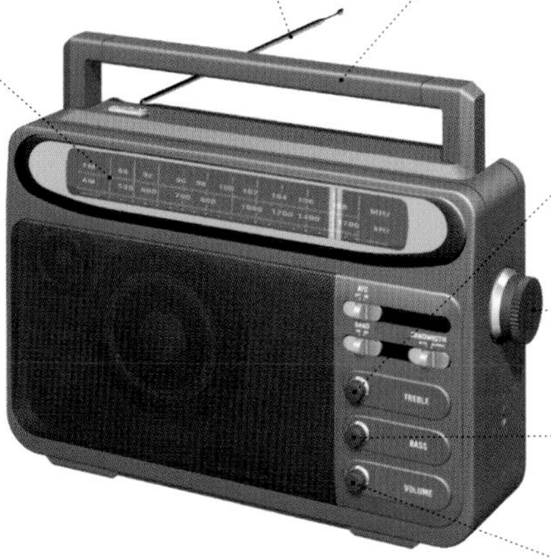

telescoping antenna
antena^F telescópica
handle
mango^M
frequency display
display^M de frecuencia
treble tone control
control^M de tonos^M de graves^M
tuning control
selector^M de sintonización^F
bass tone control
control^M de tonos^M de bajos
volume control
selector^M de volumen^M

portable compact disc player
reproductor^M de CD portátil

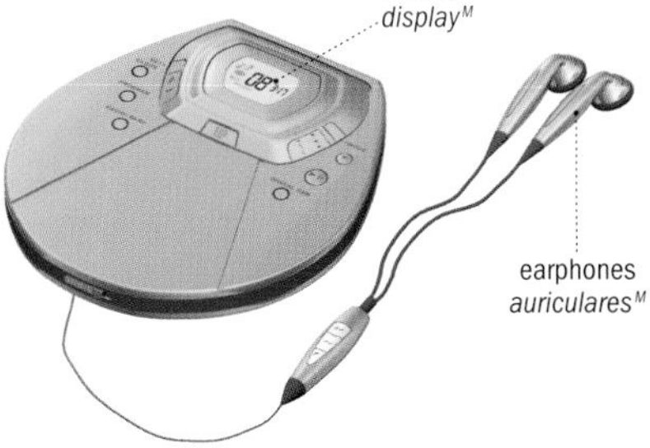

display
display^M
earphones
auriculares^M

portable digital audio player
audio^M player portátil digital

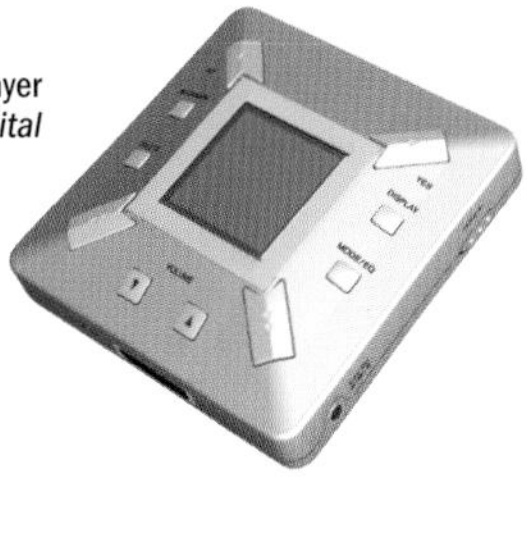

portable sound systems

personal radio cassette player
radiocasete[M] porttil personal (Walkman®)

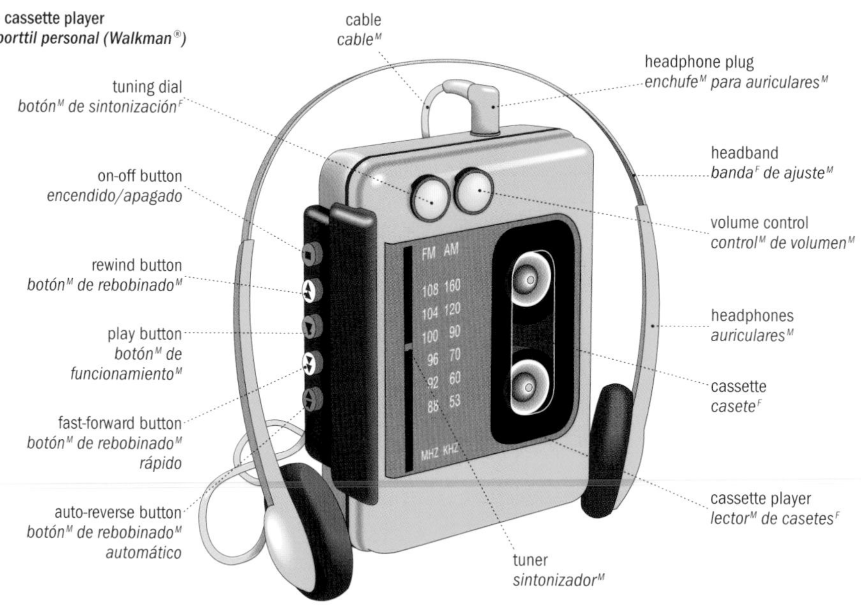

portable CD/radio/cassette recorder
radiocasete[M] con lector[M] de disco[M] compacto

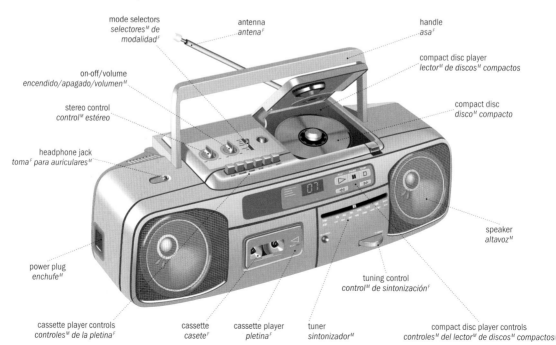

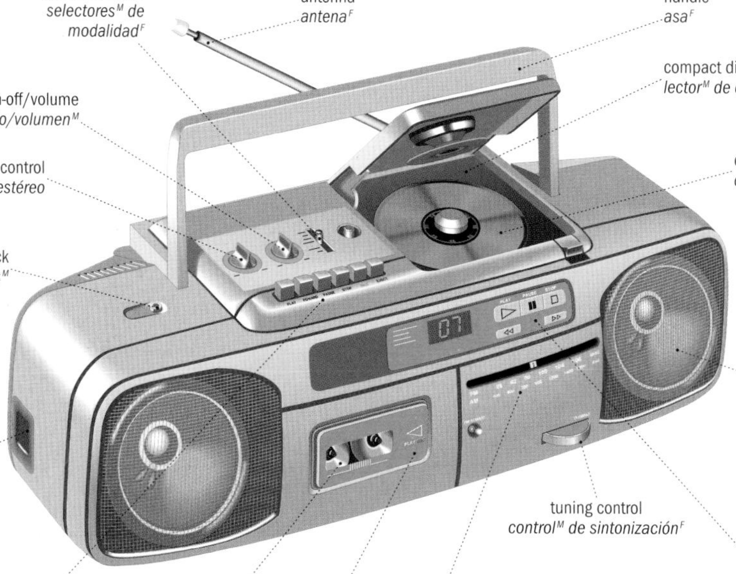

mode selectors
selectores[M] de modalidad[F]

antenna
antena[F]

handle
asa[F]

compact disc player
lector[M] de discos[M] compactos

on-off/volume
encendido/apagado/volumen[M]

compact disc
disco[M] compacto

stereo control
control[M] estéreo

headphone jack
toma[F] para auriculares[M]

speaker
altavoz[M]

power plug
enchufe[M]

tuning control
control[M] de sintonización[F]

cassette player controls
controles[M] de la pletina[F]

cassette
casete[F]

cassette player
pletina[F]

tuner
sintonizador[M]

compact disc player controls
controles[M] del lector[M] de discos[M] compactos

communication by telephone

comunicación[F] por teléfono[M]

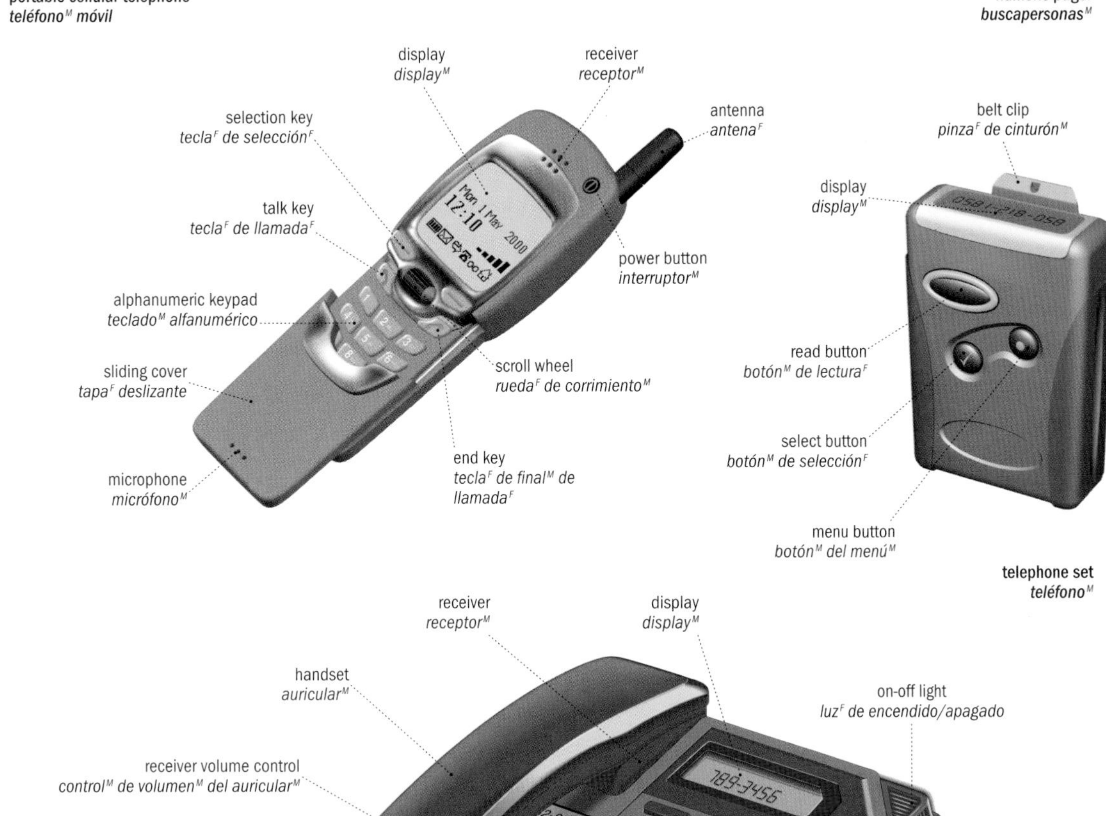

telephone set
teléfono[M]

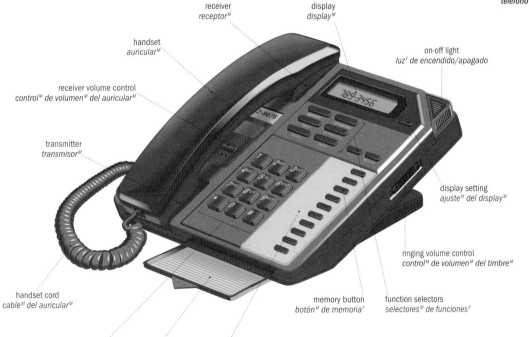

receiver
receptor[M]

display
display[M]

handset
auricular[M]

on-off light
luz[F] de encendido/apagado

receiver volume control
control[M] de volumen[M] del auricular[M]

transmitter
transmisor[M]

display setting
ajuste[M] del display[M]

ringing volume control
control[M] de volumen[M] del timbre[M]

handset cord
cable[M] del auricular[M]

memory button
botón[M] de memoria[F]

function selectors
selectores[M] de funciones[F]

push buttons
teclado[M]

telephone index
agenda[F] telefónica

automatic dialer index
marcador[M] automático

communication by telephone

telephone answering machine
contestador [M] ***automático***

calls indicator
indicador[M] de llamadas[F]
incoming message cassette
casete[F] para grabar los mensajes[M]
power-on light
luz[F] de encendido
outgoing announcement cassette
casete[F] con saludo[M]
auto answer indicator
indicador[M] de respuesta[F] automática
listen button
botón[M] de reproducción[F]
fast-forward button
botón[M] de avance[M] rápido
microphone
micrófono[M]
speaker
altavoz[M]
on/play button
botón[M] de encendido
stop button
botón[M] de stop[M]
record announcement button
botón[M] de grabación[F]
erase button
botón[M] para borrar
rewind button
botón[M] de rebobinado
volume control
control[M] del volumen[M]
power-on button
botón[M] de encendido

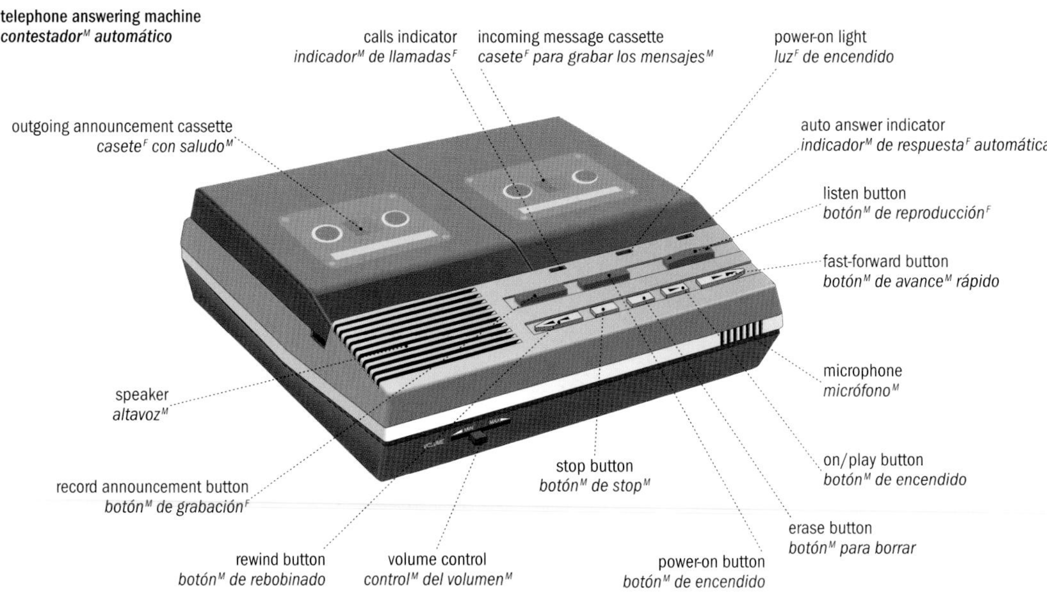

facsimile machine
fax [M]

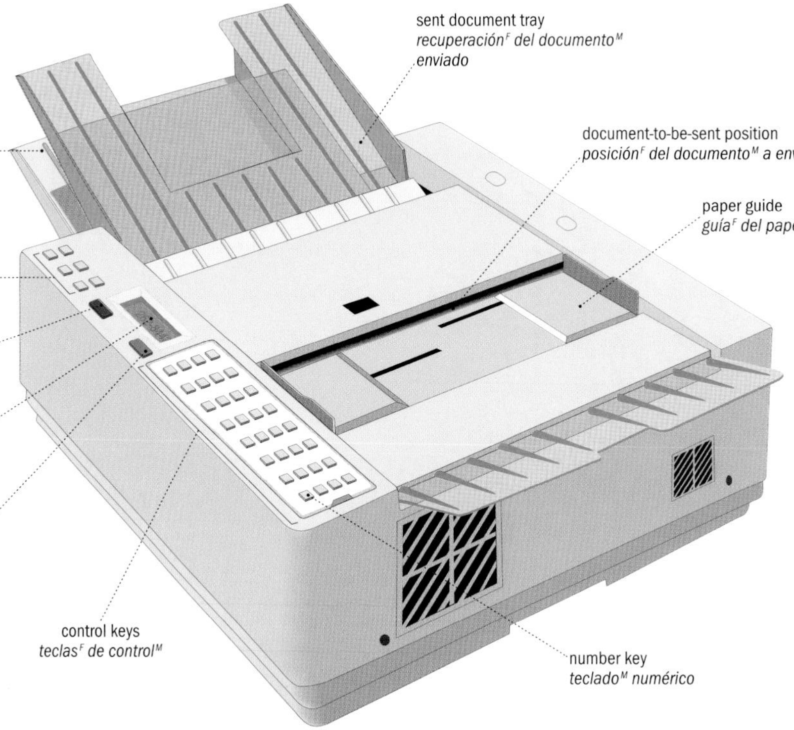

sent document tray
recuperación[F] del documento[M] enviado
receiving tray
recepción[F] de documentos[M]
document-to-be-sent position
posición[F] del documento[M] a enviar
paper guide
guía[F] del papel[M]
function keys
teclas[F] de función[F]
reset key
tecla[F] de reiniciación[F]
data display
visualización[F] de datos[M]
start key
tecla[F] de iniciación[M]
control keys
teclas[F] de control[M]
number key
teclado[M] numérico

personal computer

ordenador^{M} personal

video monitor
monitor^{M} de vídeo^{M}

vertical control
control^{M} vertical
horizontal control
control^{M} horizontal
centering control
control^{M} de centrado^{M}
contrast control
control^{M} de contraste^{M}
power indicator
indicador^{M} de encendido
power switch
interruptor^{M}
brightness control
control^{M} de brillo^{M}

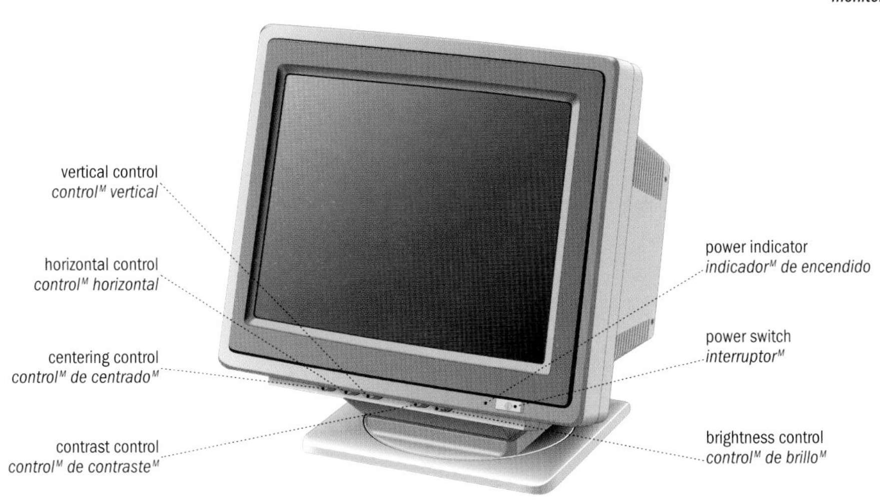

tower case: back view
ordenador^{M} : vista^{F} posterior

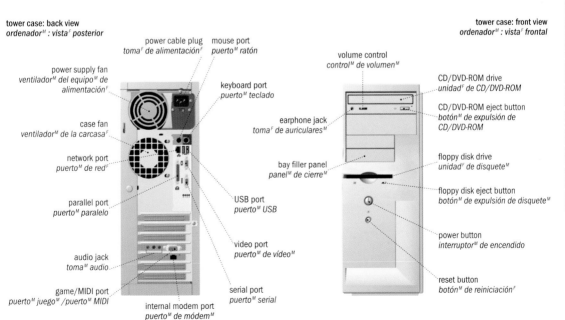

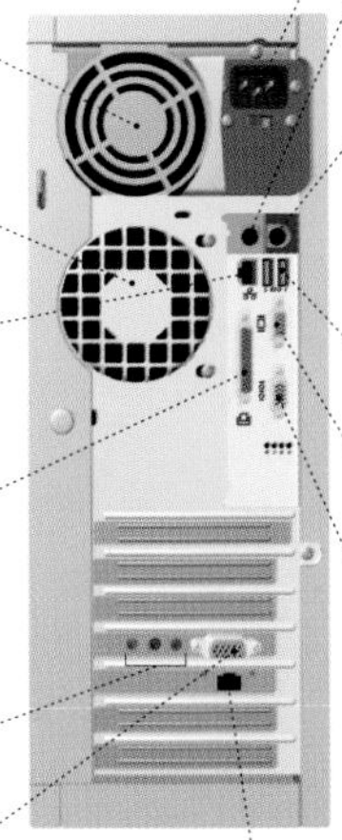

power cable plug
toma^{F} de alimentación^{F}
mouse port
puerto^{M} ratón
power supply fan
ventilador^{M} del equipo^{M} de alimentación^{F}
keyboard port
puerto^{M} teclado
case fan
ventilador^{M} de la carcasa^{F}
network port
puerto^{M} de red^{F}
parallel port
puerto^{M} paralelo
USB port
puerto^{M} USB
video port
puerto^{M} de vídeo^{M}
audio jack
toma^{M} audio
game/MIDI port
puerto^{M} juego^{M} /puerto^{M} MIDI
serial port
puerto^{M} serial
internal modem port
puerto^{M} de módem^{M} interno

tower case: front view
ordenador^{M} : vista^{F} frontal

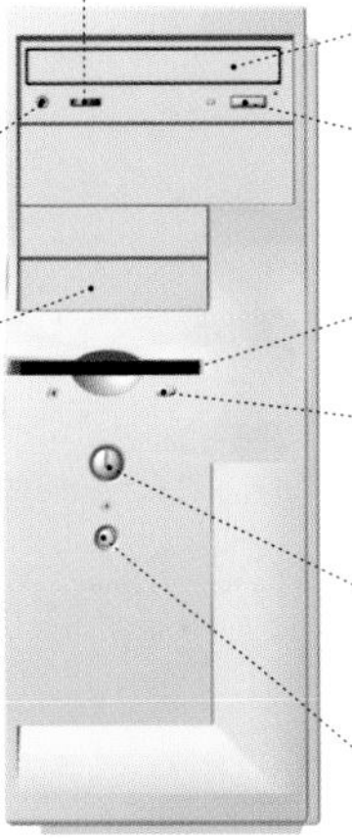

volume control
control^{M} de volumen^{M}
CD/DVD-ROM drive
unidad^{F} de CD/DVD-ROM
CD/DVD-ROM eject button
botón^{M} de expulsión de CD/DVD-ROM
earphone jack
toma^{F} de auriculares^{M}
bay filler panel
panel^{M} de cierre^{M}
floppy disk drive
unidad^{F} de disquete^{M}
floppy disk eject button
botón^{M} de expulsión de disquete^{M}
power button
interruptor^{M} de encendido
reset button
botón^{M} de reiniciación^{F}

input devices

unidades^F de entrada^F de información^F

keyboard and pictograms
teclado^M y pictogramas^M

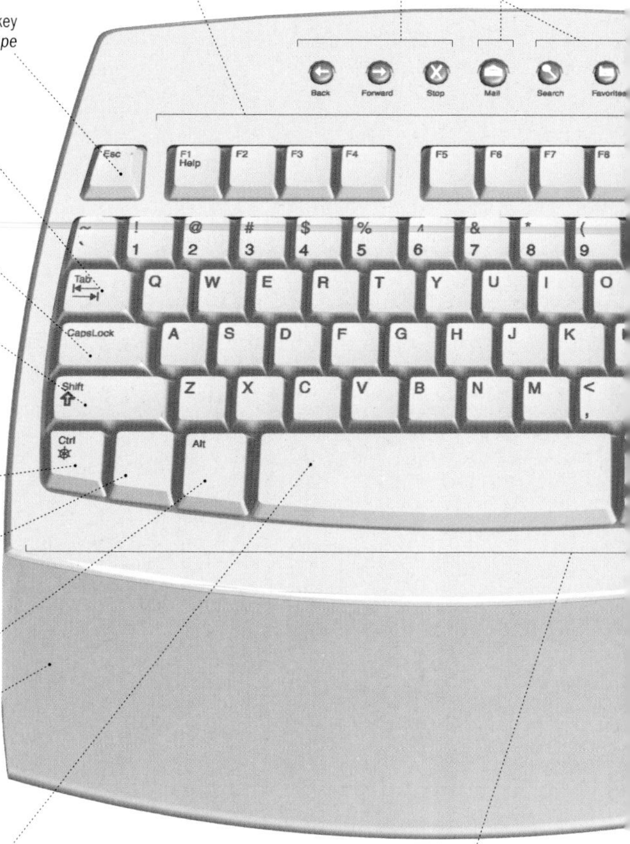
function keys
teclas^F de funciones^F
Internet keys
teclas^F Internet
e-mail key
tecla^F email
escape key
tecla^F escape
tabulation key
tecla^F tabulación
capitals lock key
tecla^F de bloqueo^M de mayúsculas
shift key
tecla^F de mayúsculas^F
control key
tecla^F de servicio^M
start key
tecla^F inicio
alternative key (Alt)
tecla^F alternativa
detachable palm rest
reposamanos^M
space bar
barra^F espaciadora
alphanumeric keypad
teclado^M alfanumérico
Back
Forward
Stop
Mail
Search
Esc
F1 Help
F2
F3
F4
F5
F6
F7
F8
Tab
CapsLock
Shift
Ctrl
Alt

escape
escape^M

tabulation left
tabulación^F a la izquierda^F

tabulation right
tabulación^F a la derecha^F

capitals lock
bloqueo^M mayúsculas^M

alternate: level 3 select
alternado: selección^F de nivel^M 3

shift: level 2 select
mayúscula^F : selección^F de nivel^M 2

control: group select
control^M : selección^F de grupo^M

control
control^M

alternate
alternativa^F

space
espacio^M

nonbreaking space
espacio^M sin pausa^F

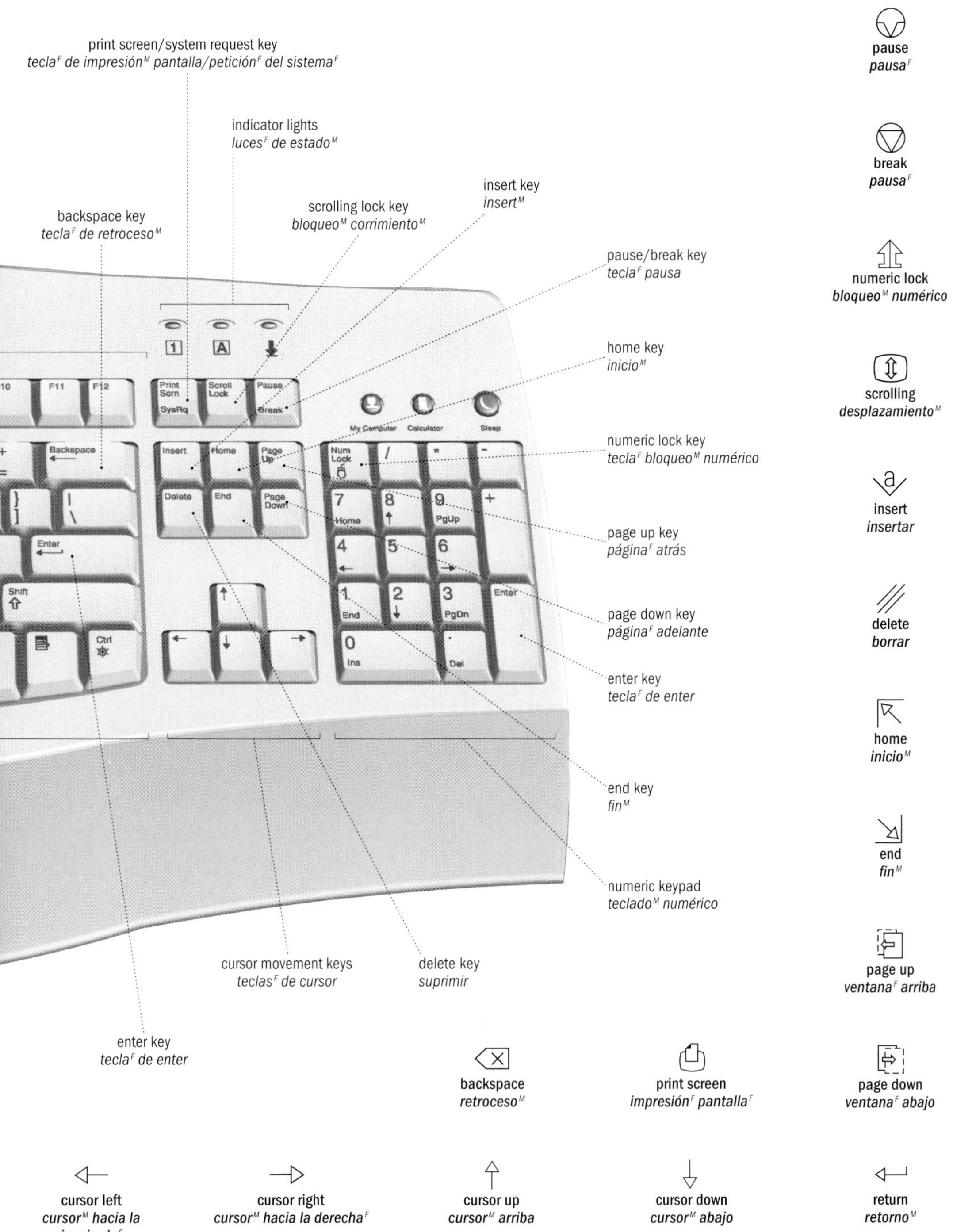
print screen/system request key
tecla[F] de impresión[M] pantalla/petición[F] del sistema[F]
indicator lights
luces[F] de estado[M]
insert key
insert[M]
scrolling lock key
bloqueo[M] corrimiento[M]
backspace key
tecla[F] de retroceso[M]
pause/break key
tecla[F] pausa
home key
inicio[M]
numeric lock key
tecla[F] bloqueo[M] numérico
page up key
página[F] atrás
page down key
página[F] adelante
enter key
tecla[F] de enter
end key
fin[M]
numeric keypad
teclado[M] numérico
cursor movement keys
teclas[F] de cursor
delete key
suprimir
enter key
tecla[F] de enter
F10
F11
F12
Print Scrn
SysRq
Scroll Lock
Pause
Break
My Computer
Calculator
Sleep
Backspace
Insert
Home
Page Up
Num Lock
Delete
End
Page Down
7 Home
8
9 PgUp
4
5
6
Enter
Shift
1 End
2
3 PgDn
Enter
Ctrl
0 Ins
. Del
pause
pausa[F]
break
pausa[F]
numeric lock
bloqueo[M] numérico
scrolling
desplazamiento[M]
insert
insertar
delete
borrar
home
inicio[M]
end
fin[M]
page up
ventana[F] arriba
backspace
retroceso[M]
print screen
impresión[F] pantalla[F]
page down
ventana[F] abajo
cursor left
cursor[M] hacia la izquierda[F]
cursor right
cursor[M] hacia la derecha[F]
cursor up
cursor[M] arriba
cursor down
cursor[M] abajo
return
retorno[M]

input devices

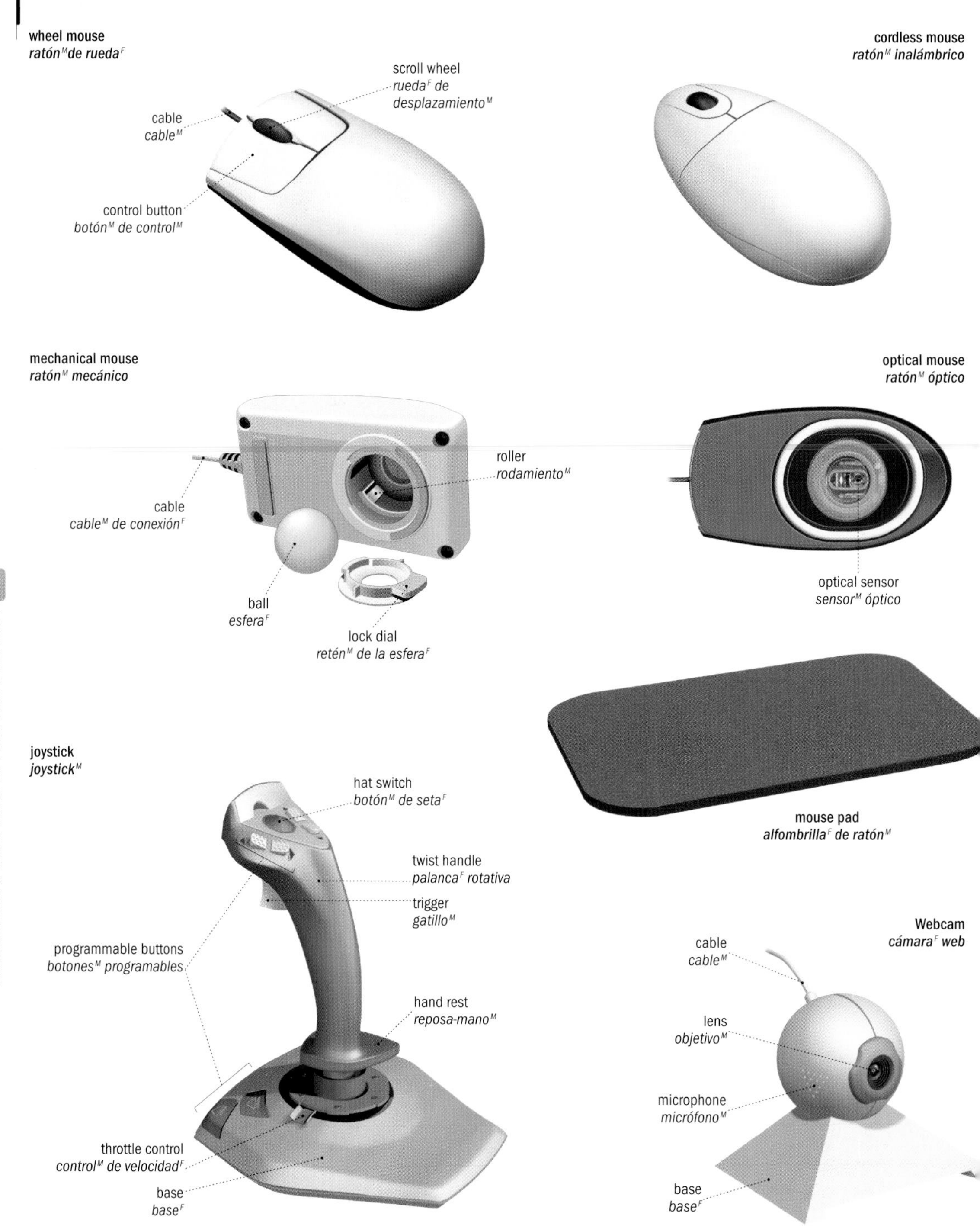
wheel mouse
ratón^M de rueda^F
scroll wheel
rueda^F de desplazamiento^M
cable
cable^M
control button
botón^M de control^M
cordless mouse
ratón^M inalámbrico
mechanical mouse
ratón^M mecánico
roller
rodamiento^M
cable
cable^M de conexión^F
ball
esfera^F
lock dial
retén^M de la esfera^F
optical mouse
ratón^M óptico
optical sensor
sensor^M óptico
mouse pad
alfombrilla^F de ratón^M
joystick
joystick^M
hat switch
botón^M de seta^F
twist handle
palanca^F rotativa
trigger
gatillo^M
programmable buttons
botones^M programables
hand rest
reposa-mano^M
throttle control
control^M de velocidad^F
base
base^F
Webcam
cámara^F web
cable
cable^M
lens
objetivo^M
microphone
micrófono^M
base
base^F

output devices

unidades[F] de salida[F] de información[F]

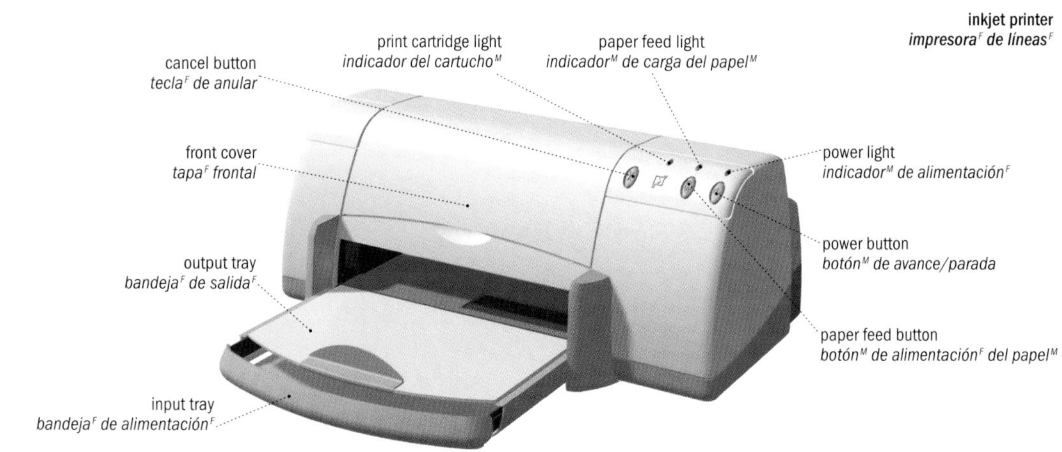

data storage devices

unidades[F] de almacenamiento[F] de información[F]

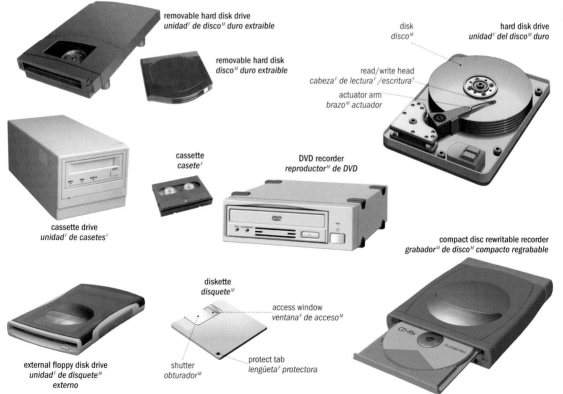

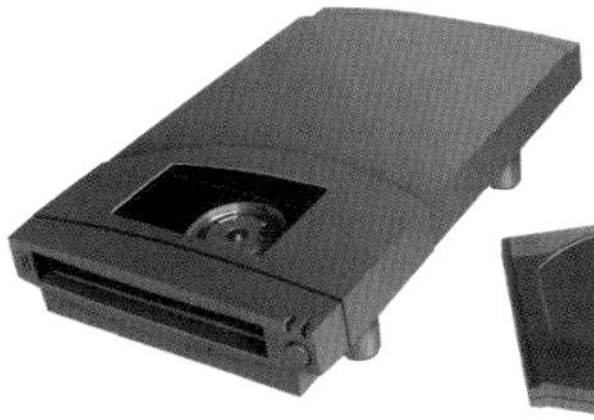

removable hard disk drive
unidad[F] de disco[M] duro extraíble

removable hard disk
disco[M] duro extraible

hard disk drive
unidad[F] del disco[M] duro

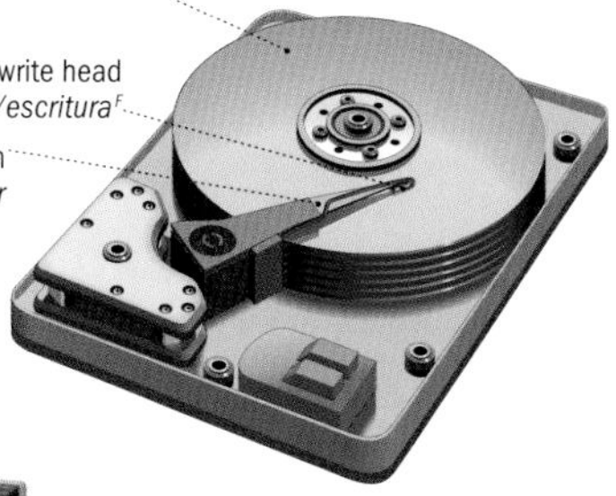

disk
disco[M]

read/write head
cabeza[F] de lectura[F]/escritura[F]

actuator arm
brazo[M] actuador

cassette drive
unidad[F] de casetes[F]

cassette
casete[F]

DVD recorder
reproductor[M] de DVD

compact disc rewritable recorder
grabador[M] de disco[M] compacto regrabable

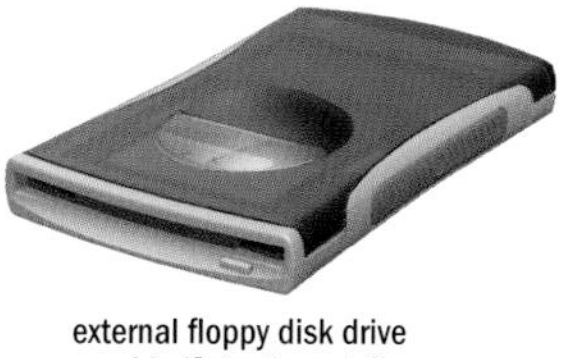

external floppy disk drive
unidad[F] de disquete[M] externo

diskette
disquete[M]

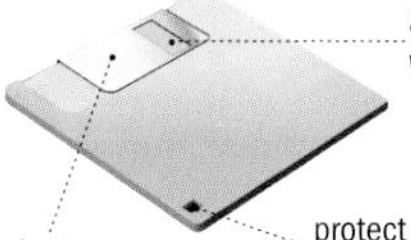

access window
ventana[F] de acceso[M]

shutter
obturador[M]

protect tab
lengüeta[F] protectora

Internet

Internet^M

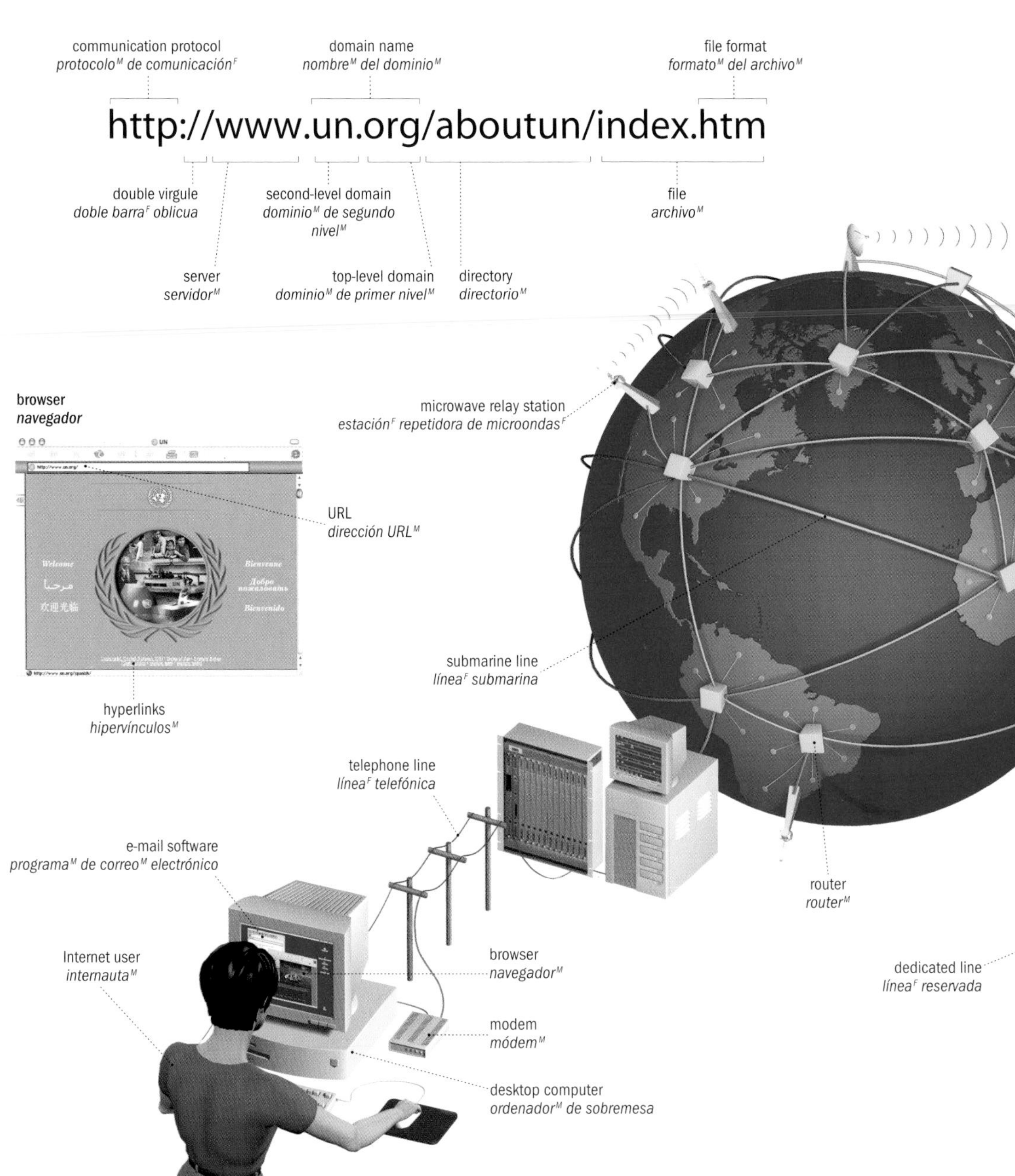
URL (uniform resource locator)
URL localizador universal de recursos
communication protocol
protocolo^M de comunicación^F
domain name
nombre^M del dominio^M
file format
formato^M del archivo^M
http://www.un.org/aboutun/index.htm
double virgule
doble barra^F oblicua
second-level domain
dominio^M de segundo nivel^M
file
archivo^M
server
servidor^M
top-level domain
dominio^M de primer nivel^M
directory
directorio^M
browser
navegador
microwave relay station
estación^F repetidora de microondas^F
URL
dirección URL^M
submarine line
línea^F submarina
hyperlinks
hipervínculos^M
telephone line
línea^F telefónica
e-mail software
programa^M de correo^M electrónico
router
router^M
Internet user
internauta^M
browser
navegador^M
dedicated line
línea^F reservada
modem
módem^M
desktop computer
ordenador^M de sobremesa

Internet uses

usos[M] de Internet[M]

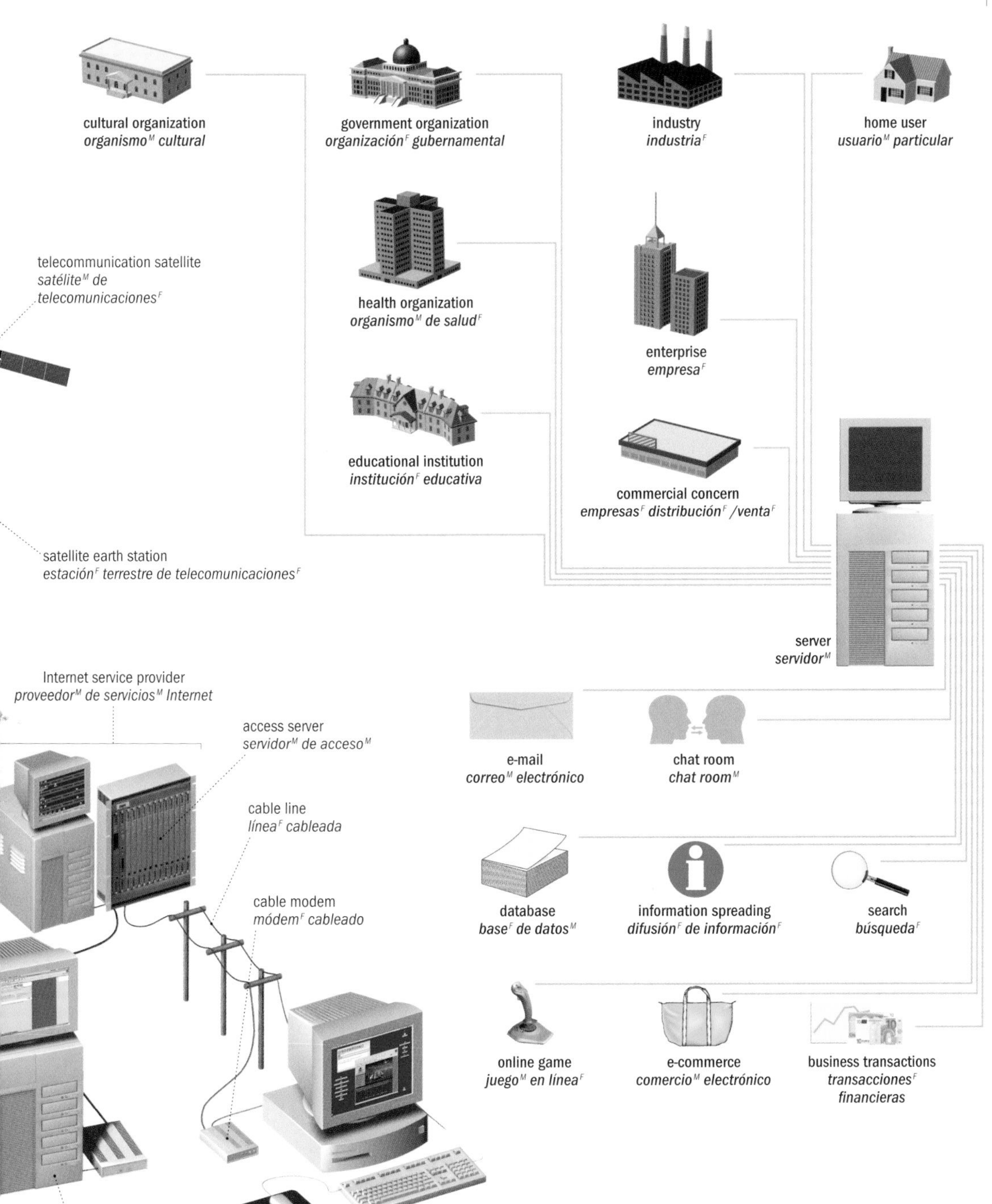
cultural organization
organismo[M] cultural
government organization
organización[F] gubernamental
industry
industria[F]
home user
usuario[M] particular
telecommunication satellite
satélite[M] de telecomunicaciones[F]
health organization
organismo[M] de salud[F]
enterprise
empresa[F]
educational institution
institución[F] educativa
commercial concern
empresas[F] distribución[F] /venta[F]
satellite earth station
estación[F] terrestre de telecomunicaciones[F]
server
servidor[M]
Internet service provider
proveedor[M] de servicios[M] Internet
access server
servidor[M] de acceso[M]
e-mail
correo[M] electrónico
chat room
chat room[M]
cable line
línea[F] cableada
cable modem
módem[F] cableado
database
base[F] de datos[M]
information spreading
difusión[F] de información[F]
search
búsqueda[F]
online game
juego[M] en línea[F]
e-commerce
comercio[M] electrónico
business transactions
transacciones[F] financieras
server
servidor[M]

laptop computer

ordenador^M portátil

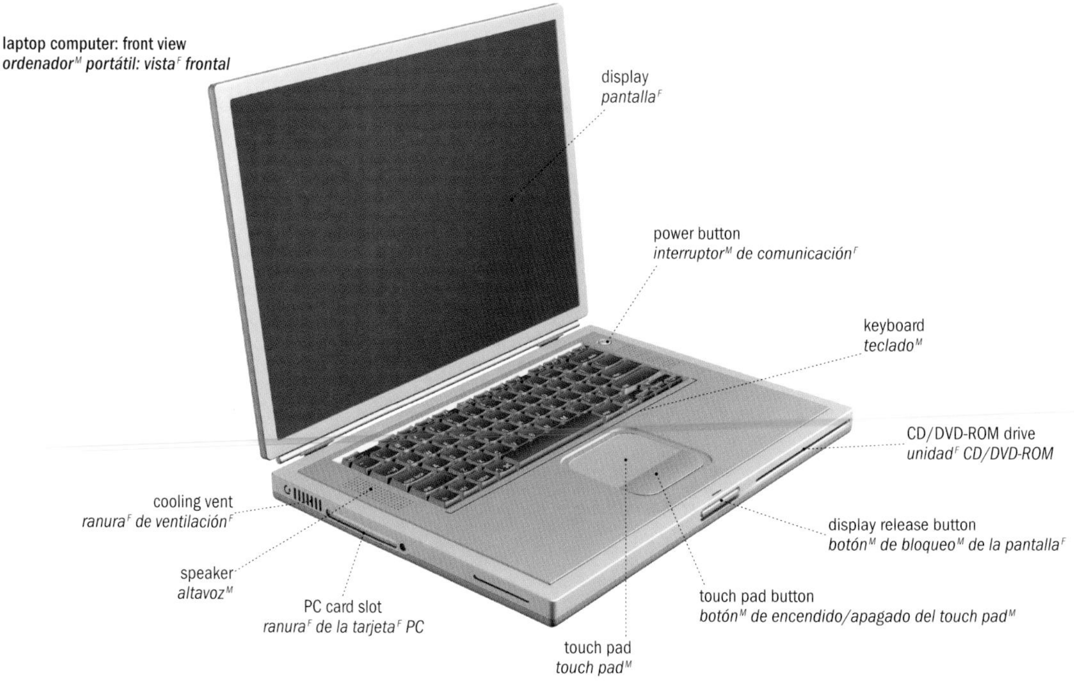

laptop computer: front view
ordenador^M portátil: vista^F frontal
display
pantalla^F
power button
interruptor^M de comunicación^F
keyboard
teclado^M
CD/DVD-ROM drive
unidad^F CD/DVD-ROM
cooling vent
ranura^F de ventilación^F
display release button
botón^M de bloqueo^M de la pantalla^F
speaker
altavoz^M
PC card slot
ranura^F de la tarjeta^F PC
touch pad button
botón^M de encendido/apagado del touch pad^M
touch pad
touch pad^M

laptop computer: rear view
ordenador^M portátil: vista^F posterior
power adapter
adaptador^M de corriente^F
direct-current power cord
cordón^M de alimentación^F de corriente^F continua
infrared port
puerto^M de infrarrojos^M
internal modem port
puerto^M de módem^M interno
alternating-current power cord
cordón^M de alimentación^F de corriente^F alterna
S-Video output
puerto^M de salida^F de S-video
cooling vent
ranura^F de ventilación^F
video port
puerto^M de salida^F de TV
power adapter port
conector^M de alimentación^F del adaptador^M
FireWire port
puerto^M FireWire
Ethernet port
puerto^M de Ethernet^M
USB port
puerto^M USB

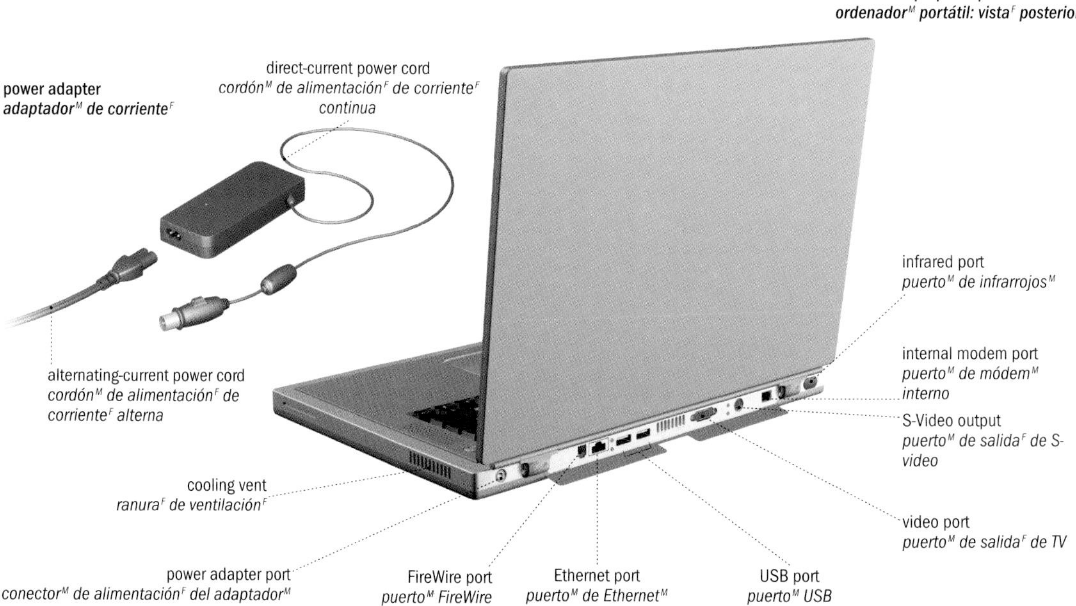

handheld computer/personal digital assistant (PDA)

ordenador[M] de bolsillo[M]

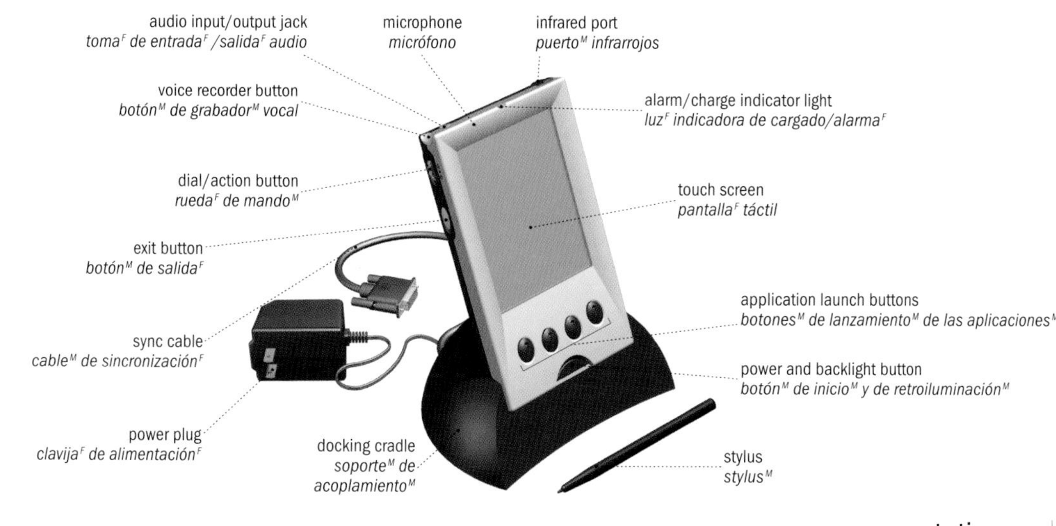

stationery

artículos[M] de escritorio[M]

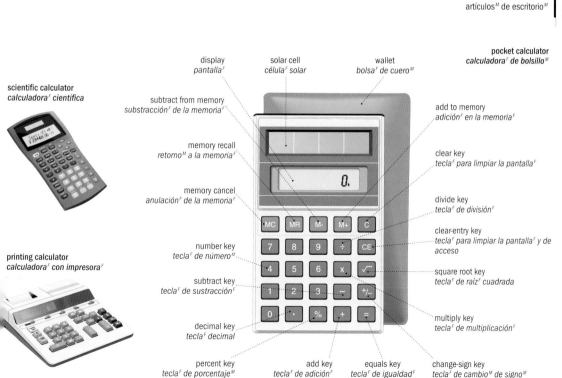

scientific calculator
calculadora[F] científica

printing calculator
calculadora[F] con impresora[F]

pocket calculator
calculadora[F] de bolsillo[M]

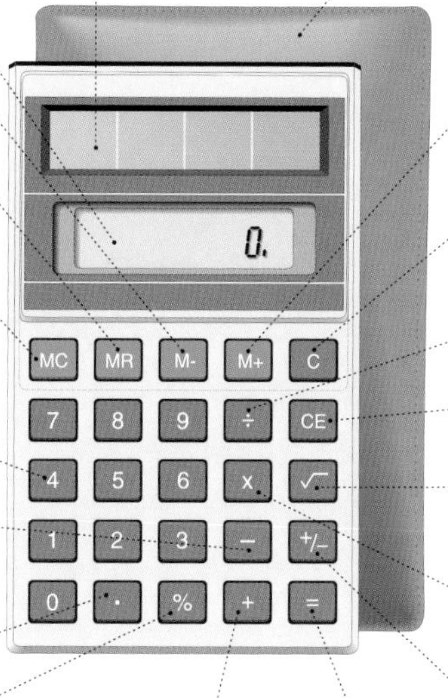

display
pantalla[F]

solar cell
célula[F] solar

wallet
bolsa[F] de cuero[M]

subtract from memory
substracción[F] de la memoria[F]

add to memory
adición[F] en la memoria[F]

memory recall
retorno[M] a la memoria[F]

clear key
tecla[F] para limpiar la pantalla[F]

memory cancel
anulación[F] de la memoria[F]

divide key
tecla[F] de división[F]

clear-entry key
tecla[F] para limpiar la pantalla[F] y de acceso

number key
tecla[F] de número[M]

square root key
tecla[F] de raíz[F] cuadrada

subtract key
tecla[F] de sustracción[F]

multiply key
tecla[F] de multiplicación[F]

decimal key
tecla[F] decimal

percent key
tecla[F] de porcentaje[M]

add key
tecla[F] de adición[F]

equals key
tecla[F] de igualdad[F]

change-sign key
tecla[F] de cambio[M] de signo[M]

MC MR M- M+ C
7 8 9 ÷ CE
4 5 6 x √
1 2 3 – +/–
0 . % + =

stationery

for time management
para el empleo ^M ***del tiempo*** ^M

tear-off calendar
calendario^M *de sobremesa*

calendar pad
calendario^M *de sobremesa*

electronic organizer
agenda^F *electrónica*

display
pantalla^F

alphabetical keypad
teclado^M *alfabético*

numeric keypad
teclado^M *numérico*

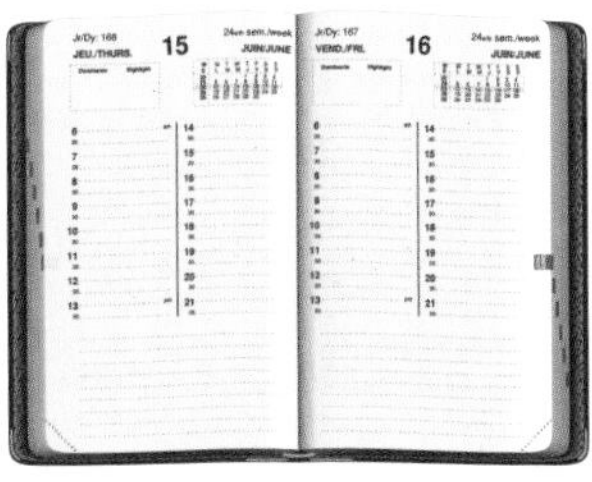

appointment book
agenda^F

memo pad
libreta^F

for correspondence
para la correspondencia ^F

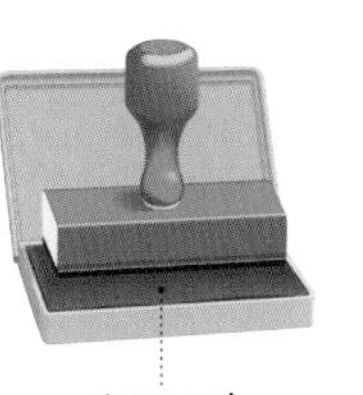

stamp pad
cojín^M *para sellos*^M

rubber stamp
sello^M *de goma*^F

numbering machine
foliador^M

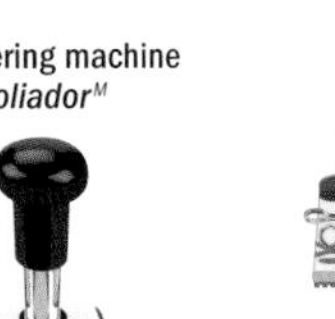

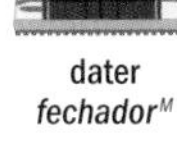

dater
fechador^M

desk tray
bandeja^F *de correspondencia*^F

rotary file
fichero^M *giratorio*

telephone index
agenda^F *telefónica*

padded envelope
sobre^{M} almohadillado

letter scale
balanza^{F} para cartas^{F}

finger tip
dedil^{M}

moistener
rueda^{F} humedecedora

letter opener
abrecartas^{M}

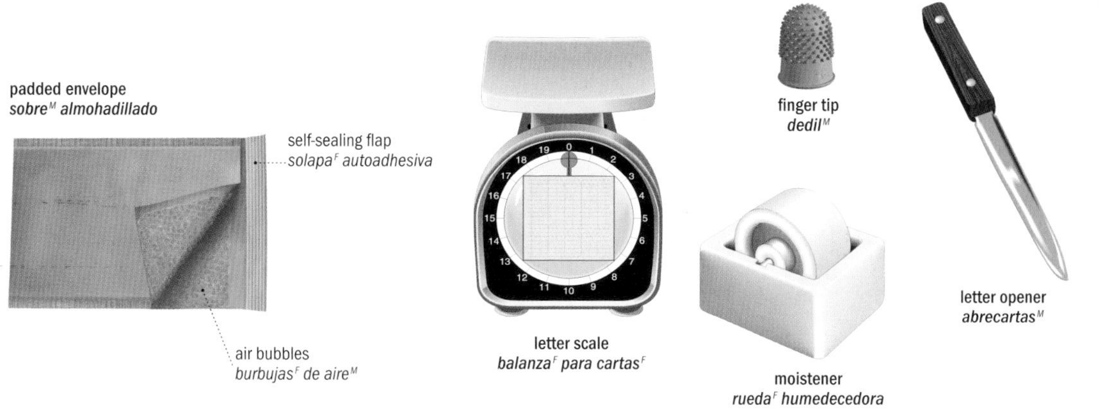

for filing
para archivar

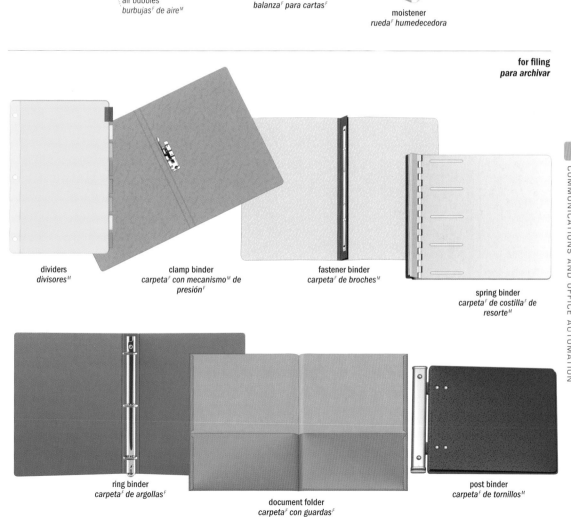

dividers
divisores^{M}

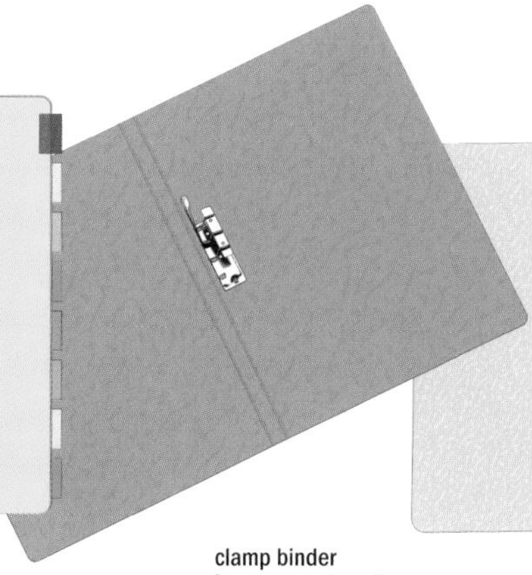

clamp binder
carpeta^{F} con mecanismo^{M} de presión^{F}

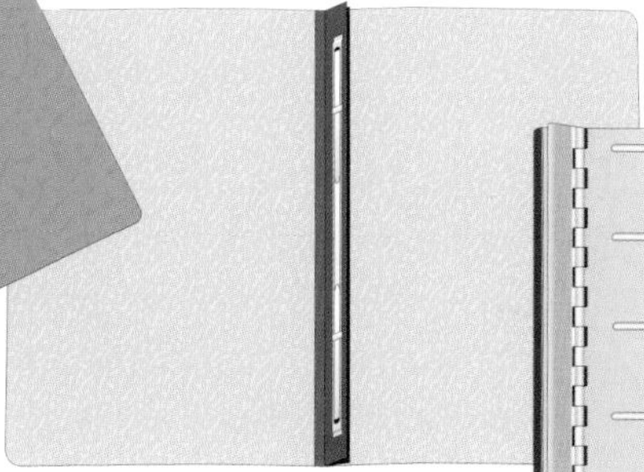

fastener binder
carpeta^{F} de broches^{M}

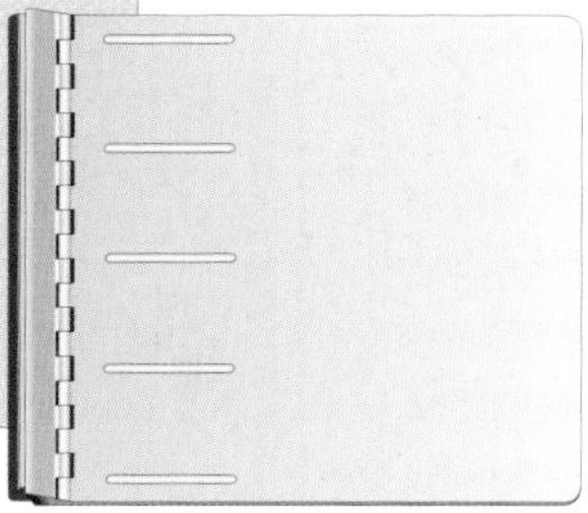

spring binder
carpeta^{F} de costilla^{F} de resorte^{M}

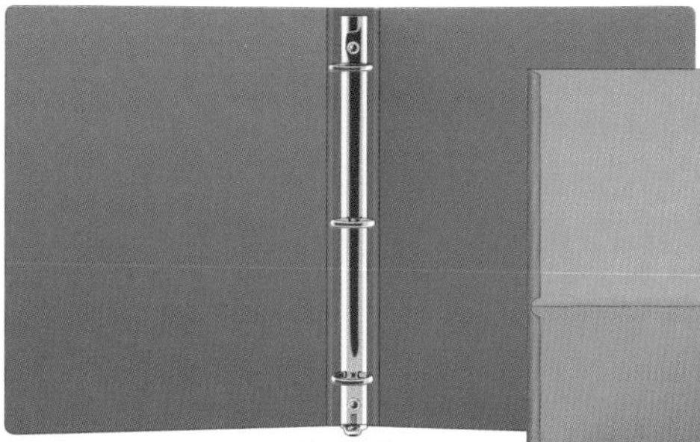

ring binder
carpeta^{F} de argollas^{F}

document folder
carpeta^{F} con guardas^{F}

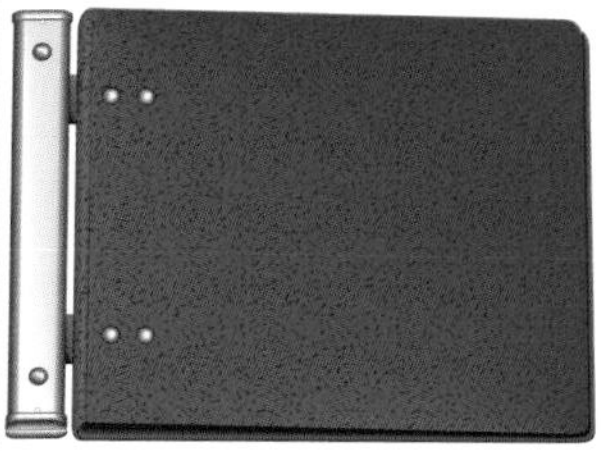

post binder
carpeta^{F} de tornillos^{M}

stationery

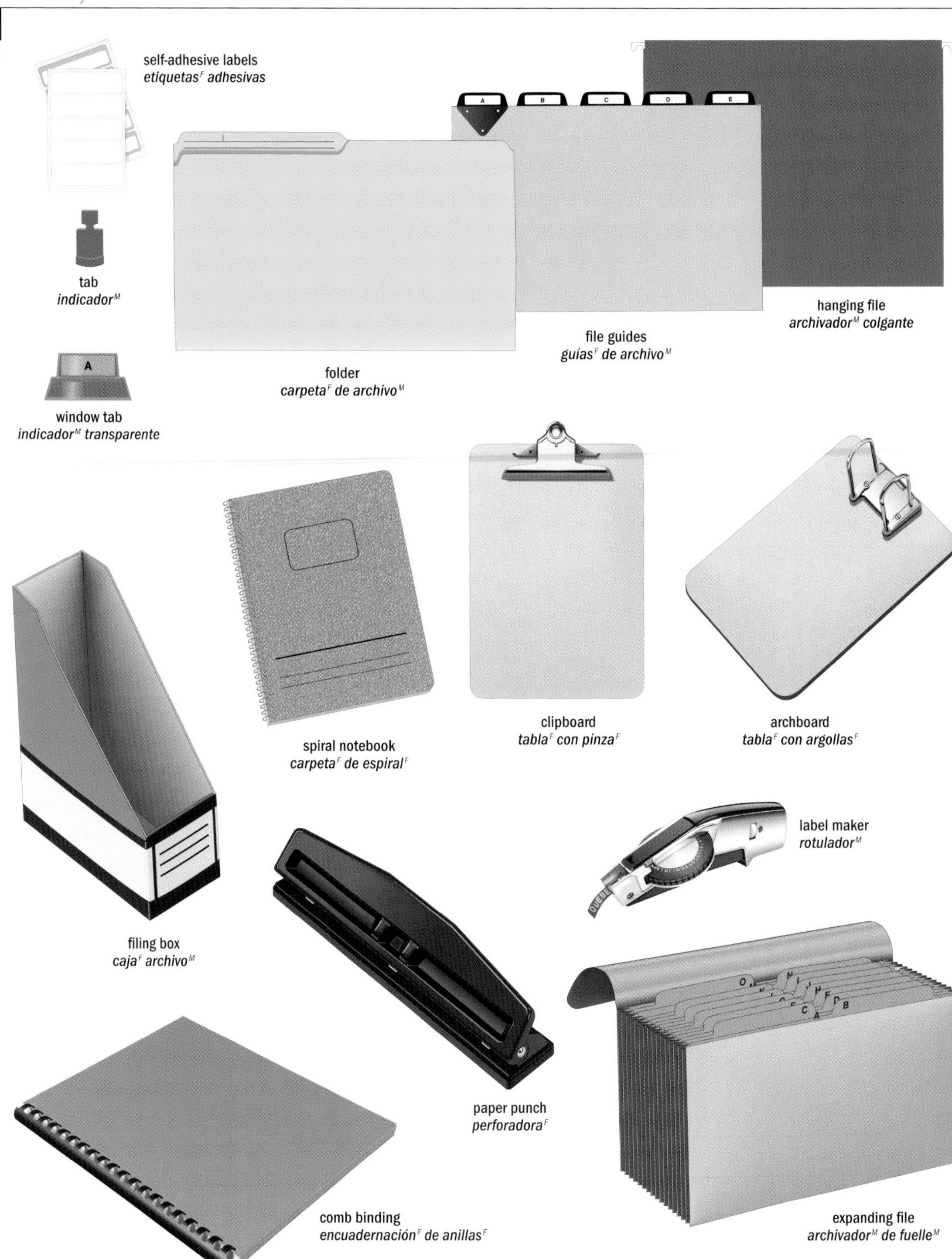
self-adhesive labels
etiquetas[F] *adhesivas*
tab
indicador[M]
window tab
indicador[M] *transparente*
folder
carpeta[F] *de archivo*[M]
file guides
guías[F] *de archivo*[M]
hanging file
archivador[M] *colgante*
spiral notebook
carpeta[F] *de espiral*[F]
clipboard
tabla[F] *con pinza*[F]
archboard
tabla[F] *con argollas*[F]
label maker
rotulador[M]
filing box
caja[F] *archivo*[M]
paper punch
perforadora[F]
comb binding
encuadernación[F] *de anillas*[F]
expanding file
archivador[M] *de fuelle*[M]

miscellaneous articles
artículos[M] varios

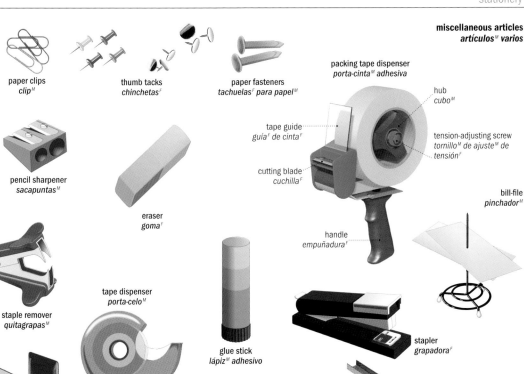

paper clips
clip[M]

thumb tacks
chinchetas[F]

paper fasteners
tachuelas[F] para papel[M]

packing tape dispenser
porta-cinta[M] adhesiva

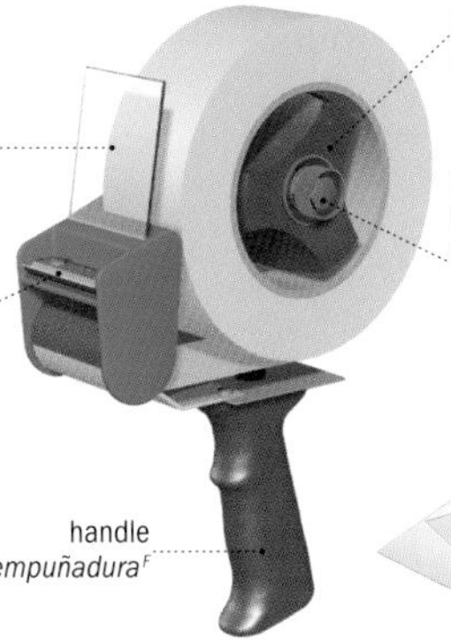

hub
cubo[M]

tape guide
guía[F] de cinta[F]

tension-adjusting screw
tornillo[M] de ajuste[M] de tensión[F]

cutting blade
cuchilla[F]

handle
empuñadura[F]

pencil sharpener
sacapuntas[M]

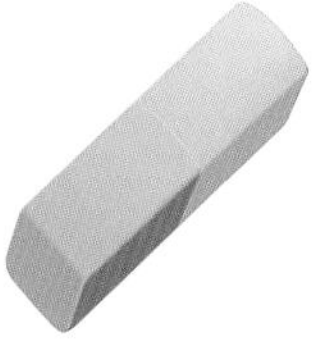

eraser
goma[F]

bill-file
pinchador[M]

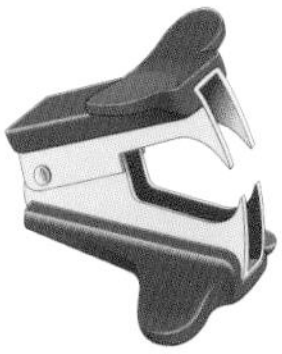

staple remover
quitagrapas[M]

tape dispenser
porta-celo[M]

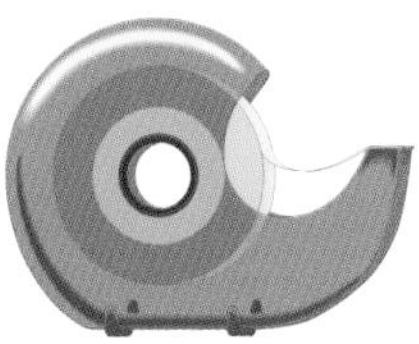

glue stick
lápiz[M] adhesivo

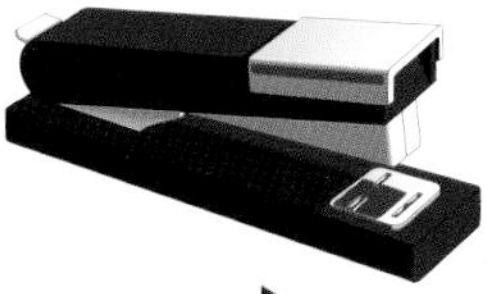

stapler
grapadora[F]

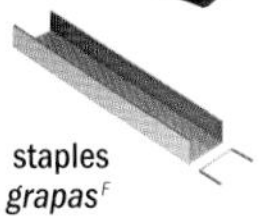

staples
grapas[F]

book ends
sujetalibros[M]

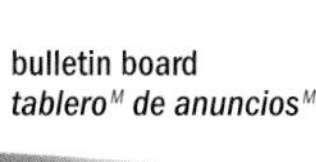

bulletin board
tablero[M] de anuncios[M]

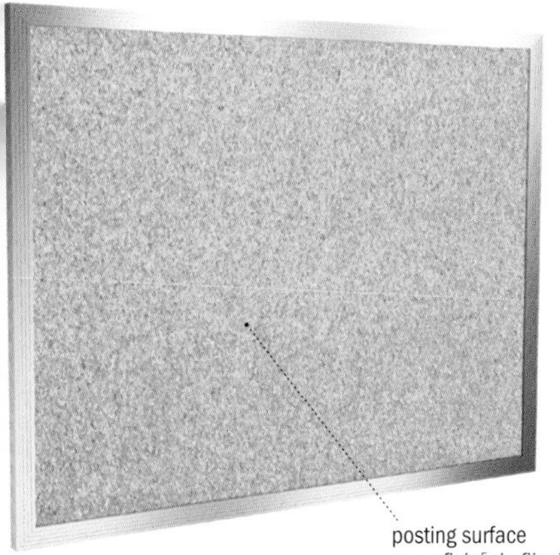

posting surface
superficie[F] de fijación[F]

paper clip holder
distribuidor[M] de clips[M]

magnet
imán[M]

cutting head
cabeza[F] cortadora

waste basket
papelera[F]

paper shredder
trituradora[F] de documentos[M]

pencil sharpener
sacapuntas[M]

waste basket
papelera

road system

sistema^M de carreteras^F

cross section of a road
sección^F transversal de una carretera^F

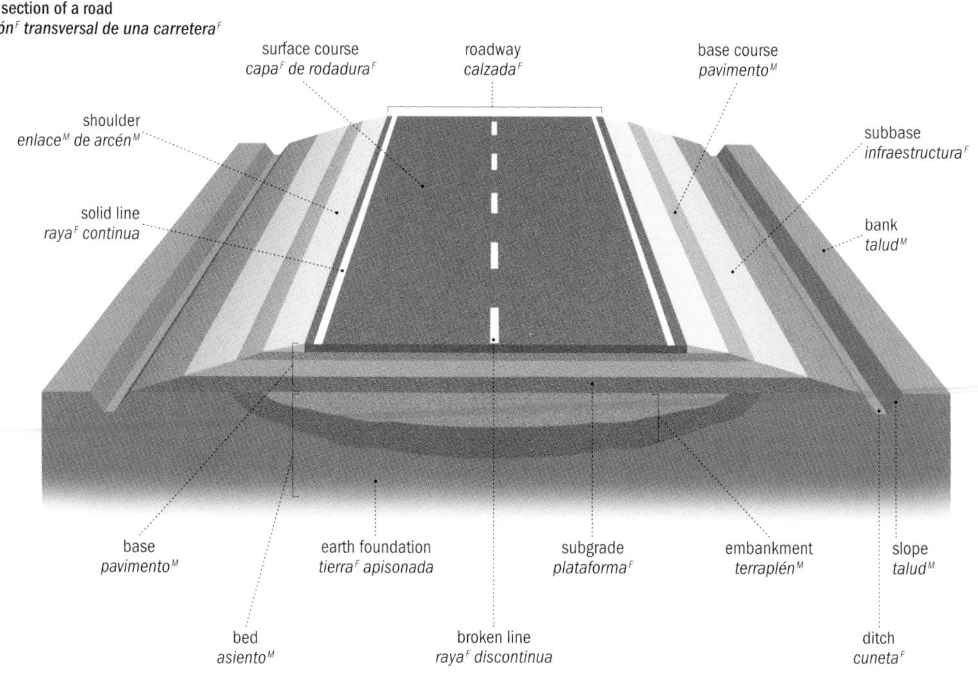

examples of interchanges
ejemplos^M de enlaces^M de carreteras^F

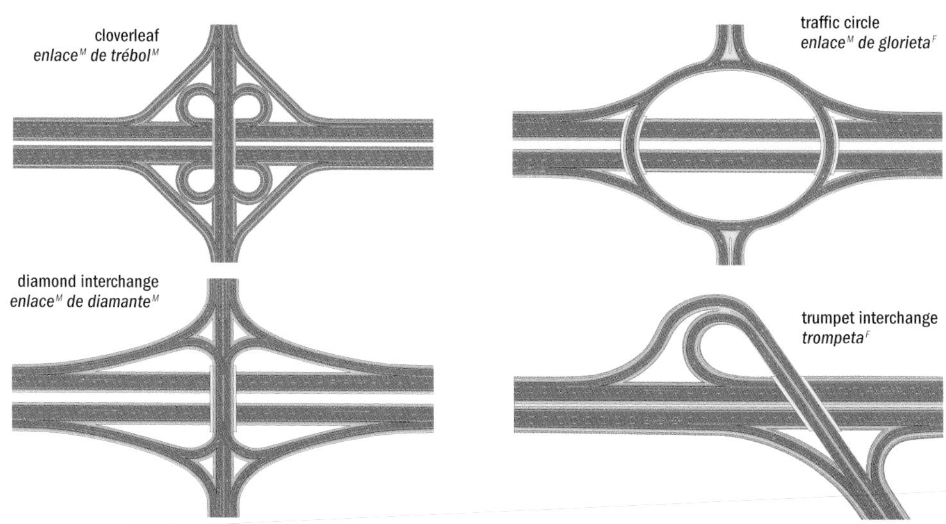

cloverleaf
***enlace**[M] **de trébol**[M]*

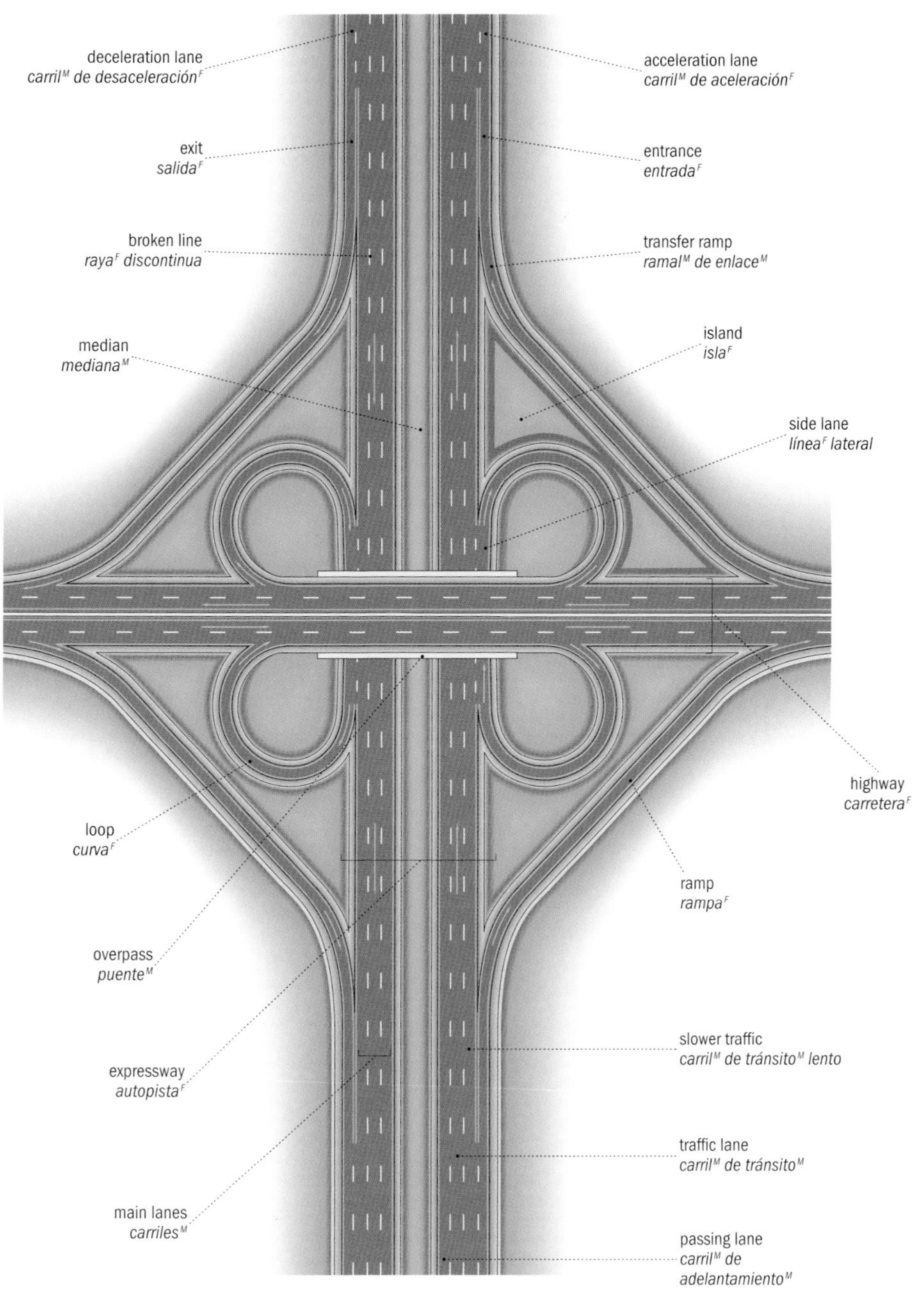
deceleration lane
carril[M] de desaceleración[F]
acceleration lane
carril[M] de aceleración[F]
exit
salida[F]
entrance
entrada[F]
broken line
raya[F] discontinua
transfer ramp
ramal[M] de enlace[M]
island
isla[F]
median
mediana[M]
side lane
línea[F] lateral
highway
carretera[F]
loop
curva[F]
ramp
rampa[F]
overpass
puente[M]
slower traffic
carril[M] de tránsito[M] lento
expressway
autopista[F]
traffic lane
carril[M] de tránsito[M]
main lanes
carriles[M]
passing lane
carril[M] de adelantamiento[M]

fixed bridges

puentes^M fijos

beam bridge
puente^M de viga^F

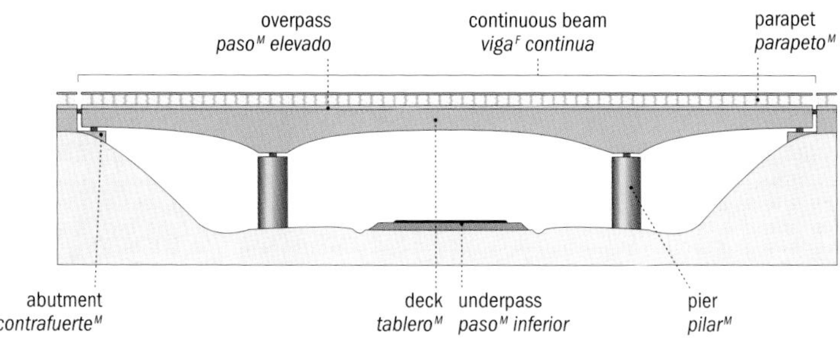

suspension bridge
puente^M colgante

cantilever bridge
puente^M cantilever

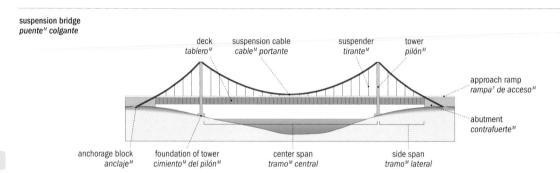

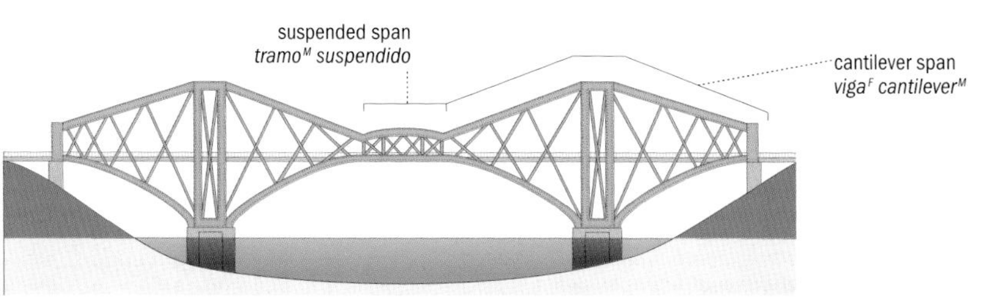

movable bridges

puentes^M móviles

swing bridge
puente^M giratorio

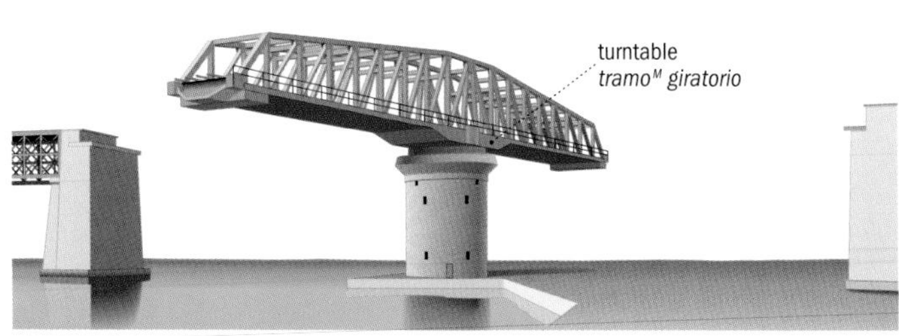

movable bridges

counterweight
contrapeso[M]

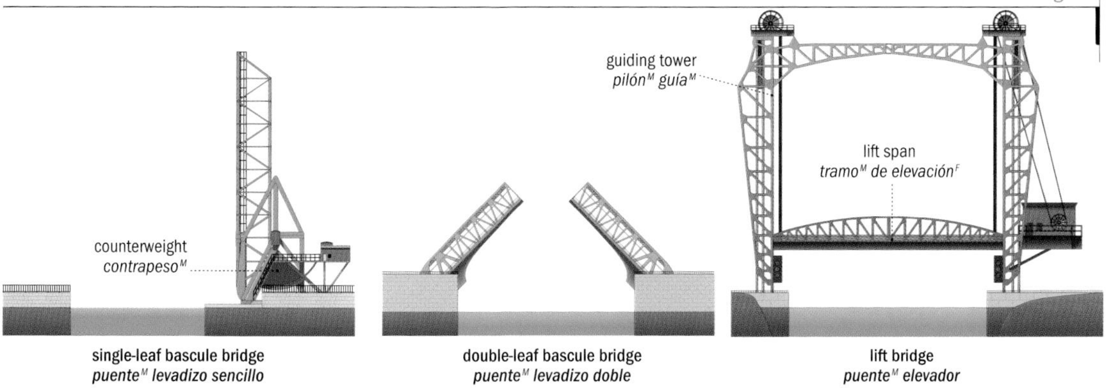

single-leaf bascule bridge
puente[M] levadizo sencillo

double-leaf bascule bridge
puente[M] levadizo doble

guiding tower
pilón[M] guía[M]
lift span
tramo[M] de elevación[F]

lift bridge
puente[M] elevador

road tunnel

túnel[M] de carretera[F]

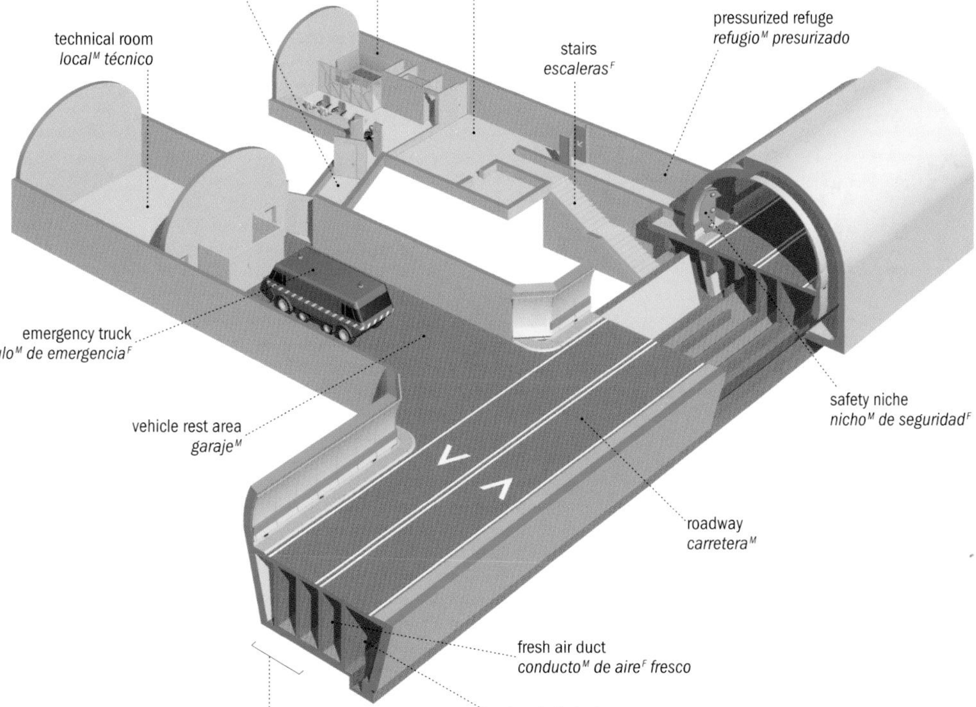

connecting gallery
galería[F] de conexión[F]
emergency station
estación[F] de emergencia[F]
shelter
refugio[M]
technical room
local[M] técnico
stairs
escaleras[F]
pressurized refuge
refugio[M] presurizado
emergency truck
vehículo[M] de emergencia[F]
vehicle rest area
garaje[M]
safety niche
nicho[M] de seguridad[F]
roadway
carretera[M]
fresh air duct
conducto[M] de aire[F] fresco
exhaust air duct
conducto[M] de aire[M] viciado
evacuation route
camino[M] de evacuación[F]

service station

estación[F] de servicio[M]

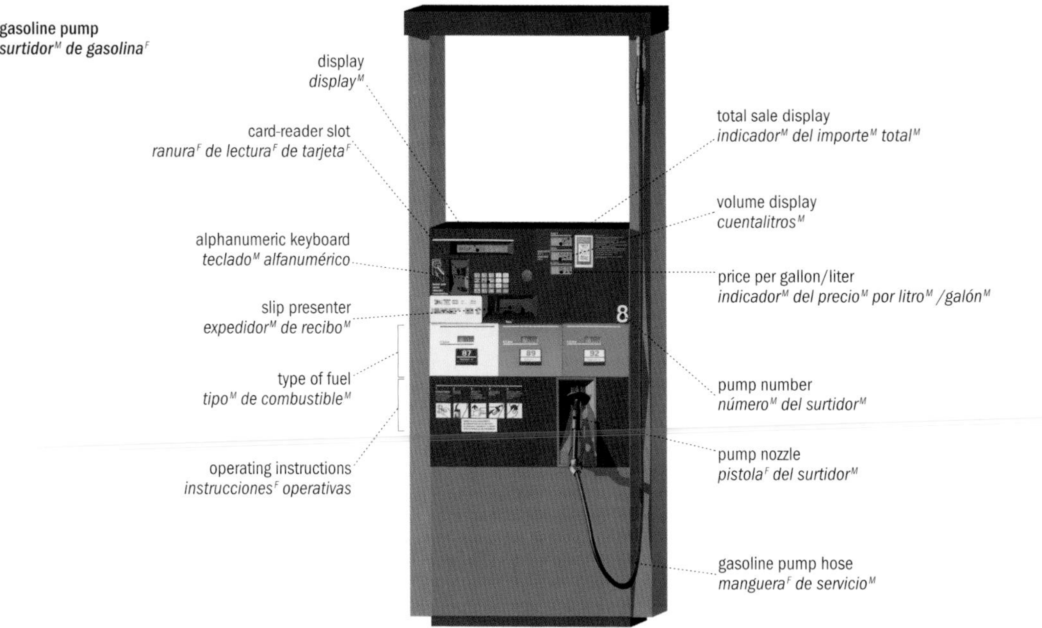
gasoline pump
surtidor[M] de gasolina[F]
display
display[M]
card-reader slot
ranura[F] de lectura[F] de tarjeta[F]
alphanumeric keyboard
teclado[M] alfanumérico
slip presenter
expedidor[M] de recibo[M]
type of fuel
tipo[M] de combustible[M]
operating instructions
instrucciones[F] operativas
total sale display
indicador[M] del importe[M] total[M]
volume display
cuentalitros[M]
price per gallon/liter
indicador[M] del precio[M] por litro[M] /galón[M]
pump number
número[M] del surtidor[M]
pump nozzle
pistola[F] del surtidor[M]
gasoline pump hose
manguera[F] de servicio[M]
8
87
89
92

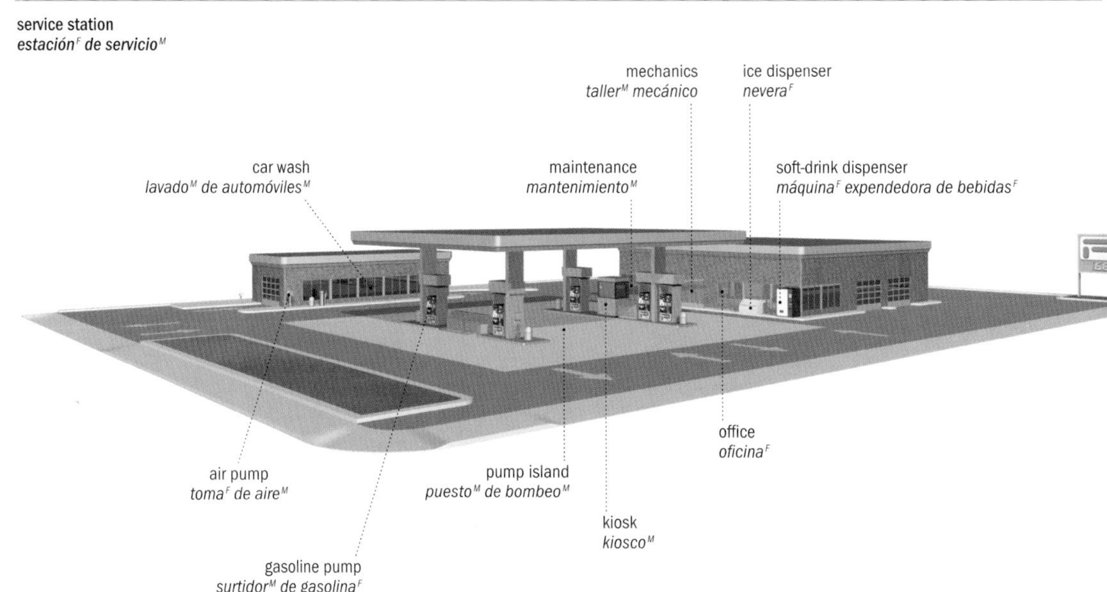
service station
estación[F] de servicio[M]
mechanics
taller[M] mecánico
ice dispenser
nevera[F]
car wash
lavado[M] de automóviles[M]
maintenance
mantenimiento[M]
soft-drink dispenser
máquina[F] expendedora de bebidas[F]
office
oficina[F]
air pump
toma[F] de aire[M]
pump island
puesto[M] de bombeo[M]
kiosk
kiosco[M]
gasoline pump
surtidor[M] de gasolina[F]

automobile

automóvil[M]

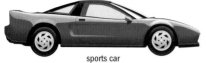

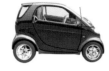

examples of bodies
ejemplos[M] de carrocerías[F]

sports car
deportivo[M]

micro compact car
automóvil[M] urbanita

hatchback
turismo[M] de tres puertas[F]

two-door sedan
cupé[M]

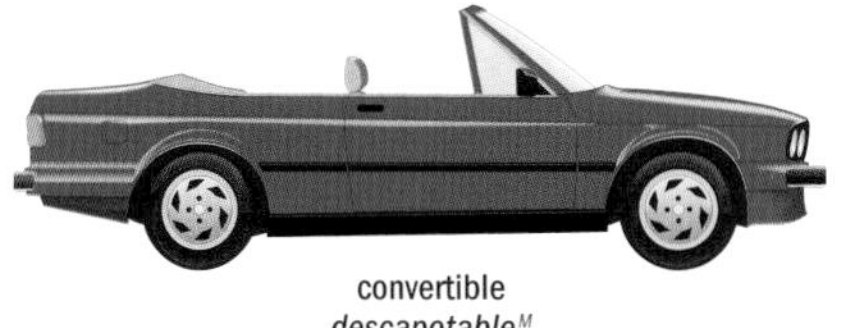

convertible
descapotable[M]

four-door sedan
berlina[F]

station wagon
coche[M] familiar

minivan
monovolumen[M]

sport-utility vehicle
vehículo[M] todo terreno[M]

pickup truck
camioneta[F]

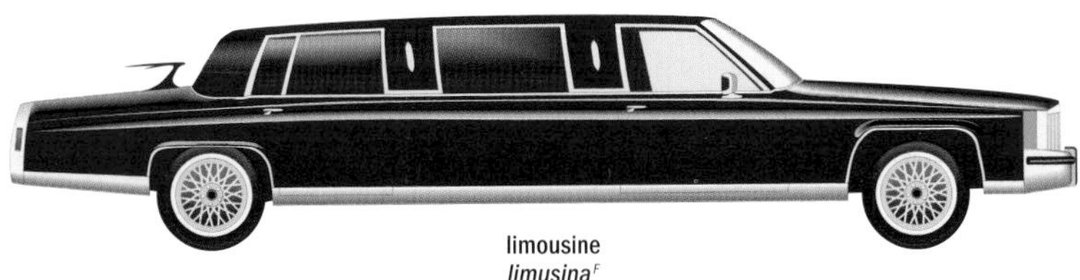

limousine
limusina[F]

automobile

body
carrocería[F]

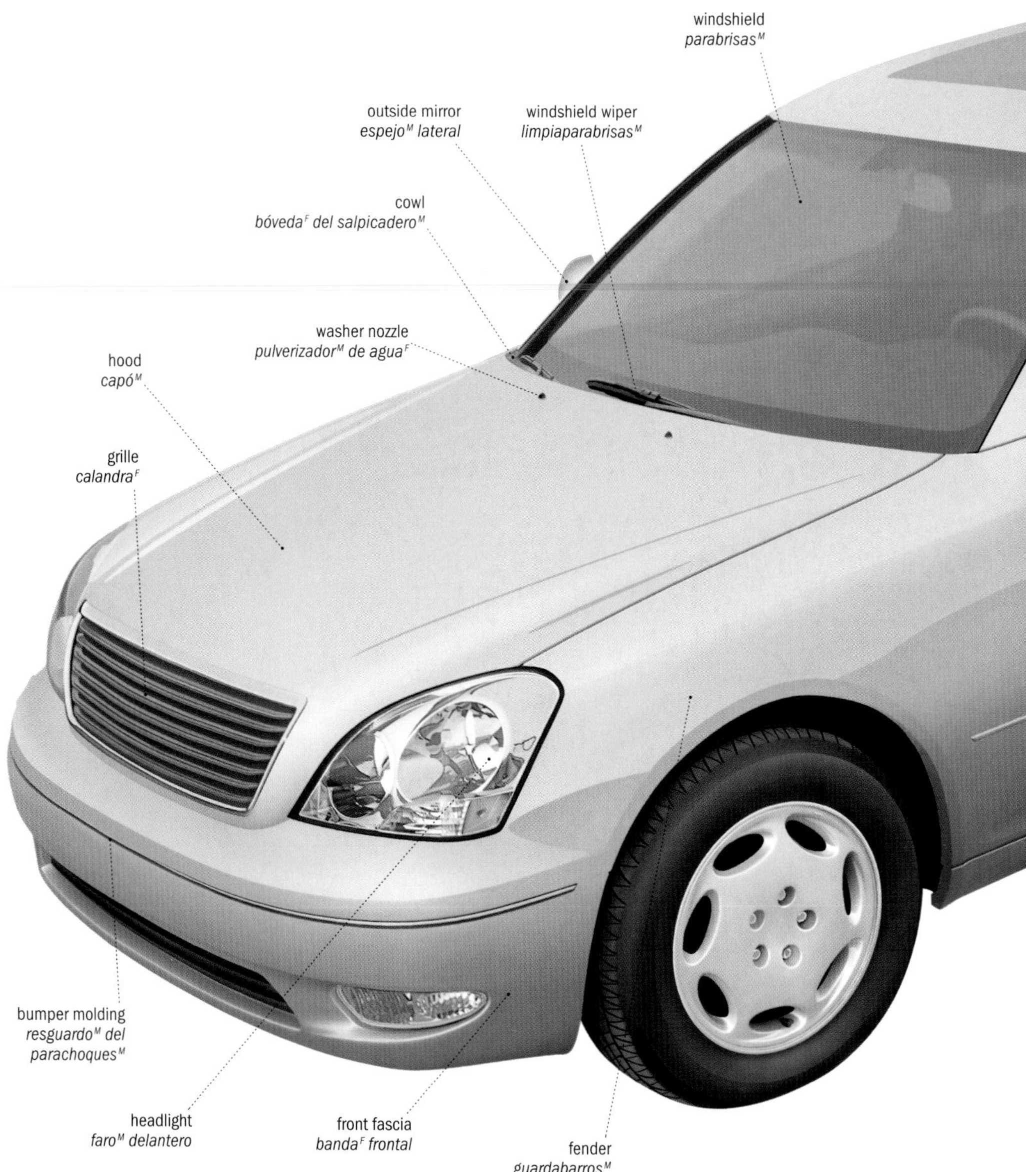
windshield
parabrisas[M]
outside mirror
espejo[M] lateral
windshield wiper
limpiaparabrisas[M]
cowl
bóveda[F] del salpicadero[M]
washer nozzle
pulverizador[M] de agua[F]
hood
capó[M]
grille
calandra[F]
bumper molding
resguardo[M] del parachoques[M]
headlight
faro[M] delantero
front fascia
banda[F] frontal
fender
guardabarros[M]

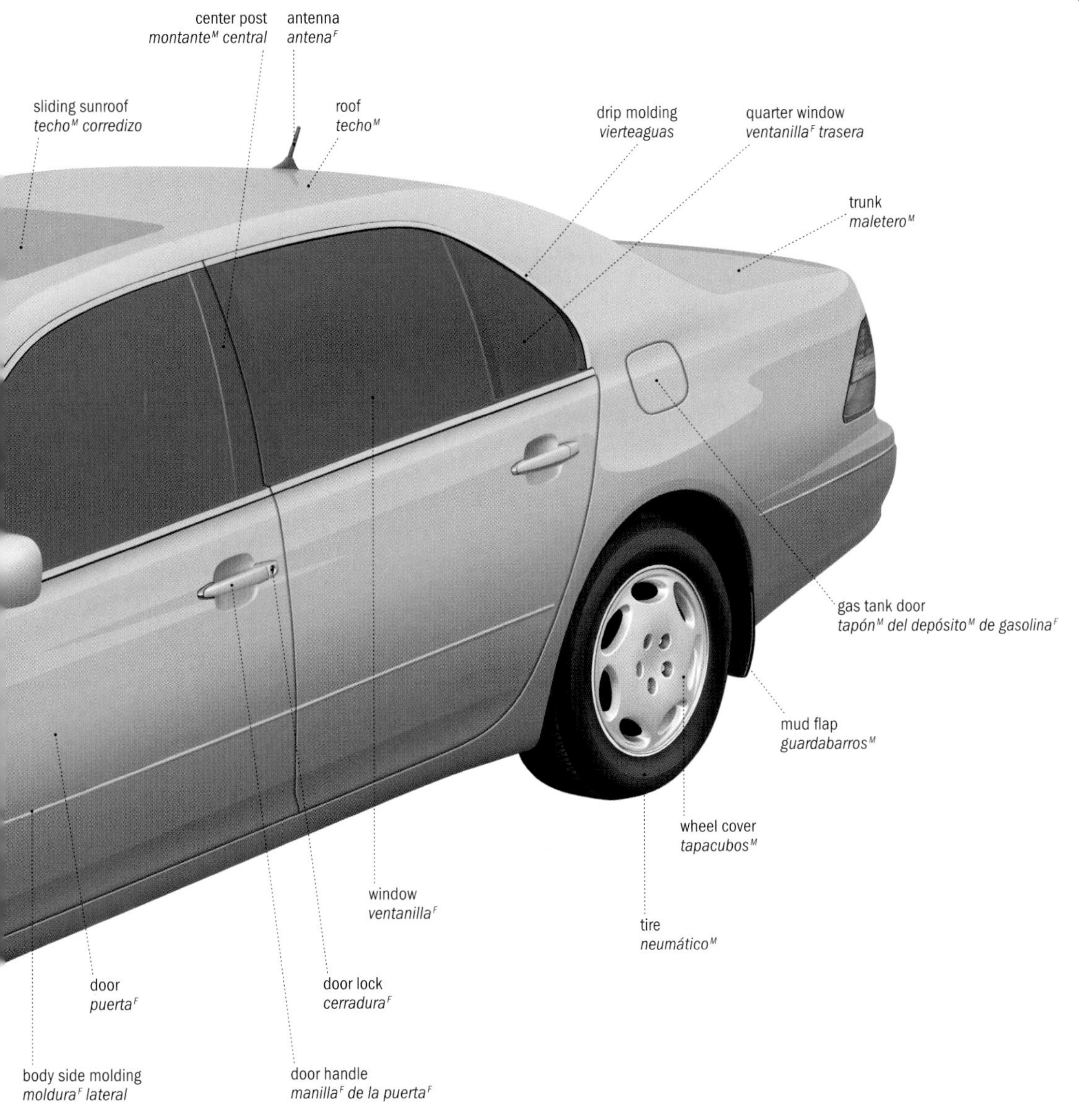
center post
montante^M central
antenna
antena^F
sliding sunroof
techo^M corredizo
roof
techo^M
drip molding
vierteaguas
quarter window
ventanilla^F trasera
trunk
maletero^M
gas tank door
tapón^M del depósito^M de gasolina^F
mud flap
guardabarros^M
wheel cover
tapacubos^M
window
ventanilla^F
tire
neumático^M
door
puerta^F
door lock
cerradura^F
body side molding
moldura^F lateral
door handle
manilla^F de la puerta^F

automobile systems: main parts
automóviles^{M} : componentes^{M} principales

clutch
embrague[M]

steering wheel
volante[M]

hand brake
freno[M] *de mano*[F]

distributor cap
delco[M]

steering column
barra[F] *de dirección*[F]

spark plug cable
cable[M] *de las bujías*[F]

gearshift lever
palanca[F] *de cambio*[M]

cylinder head cover
tapa[F] *de la culata*[F]

air filter
filtro[M] *del aire*[M]

battery
batería[F]

radiator
radiador[M]

cooling fan
ventilador[M]

alternator/fan belt
correa[F] *del ventilador*[M]

alternator
alternador[M]

exhaust manifold
colector[M] *de escape*[M]

front hydraulic brake line
circuito[M] *de frenado*[M]

disc brake
freno[M] *de disco*[M]

brake booster
servofreno[M]

gearbox
caja[F] *de cambios*[M]

exhaust pipe
tubo[M] *de escape*[M]

brake pedal
pedal[M] *del freno*[M]

TRANSPORT AND MACHINERY

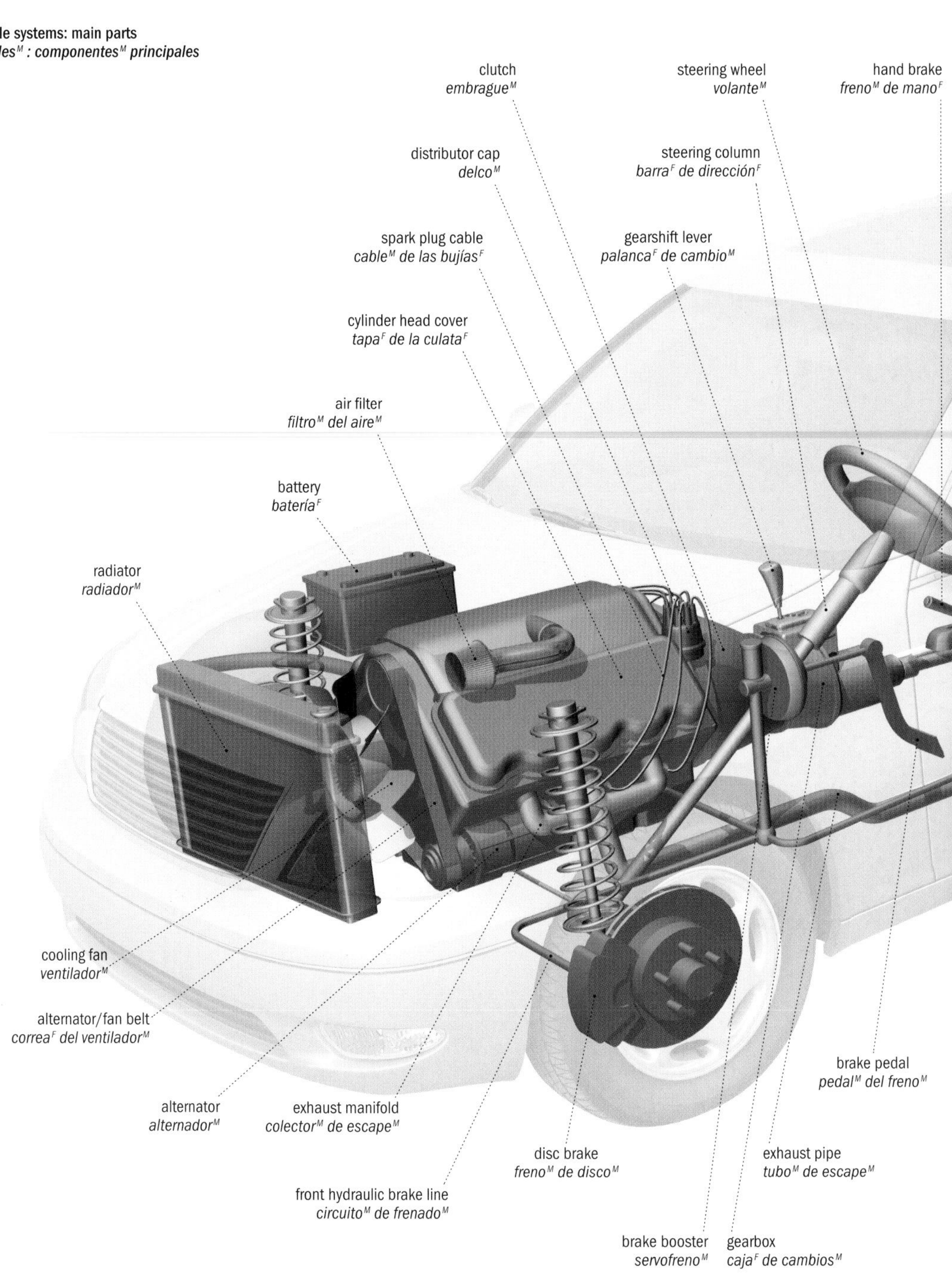

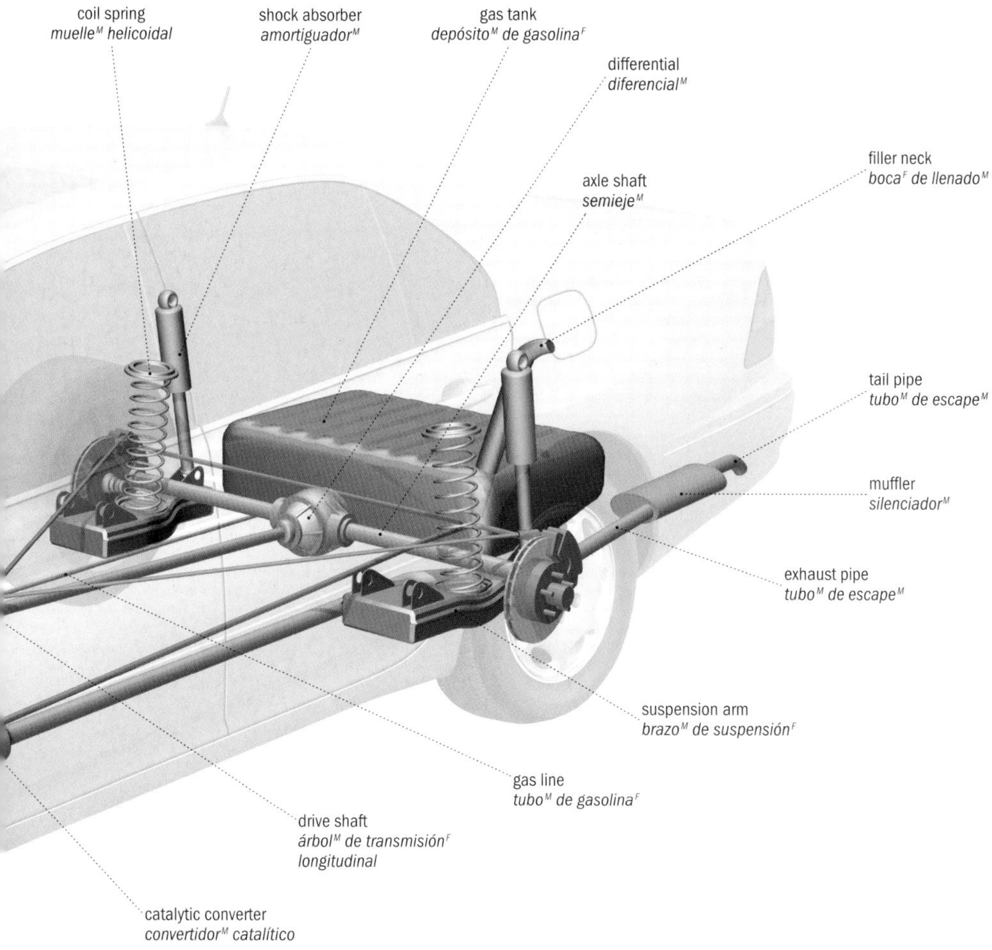

coil spring
muelle^{M} helicoidal
shock absorber
amortiguador^{M}
gas tank
depósito^{M} de gasolina^{F}
differential
diferencial^{M}
filler neck
boca^{F} de llenado^{M}
axle shaft
semieje^{M}
tail pipe
tubo^{M} de escape^{M}
muffler
silenciador^{M}
exhaust pipe
tubo^{M} de escape^{M}
suspension arm
brazo^{M} de suspensión^{F}
gas line
tubo^{M} de gasolina^{F}
drive shaft
árbol^{M} de transmisión^{F} longitudinal
catalytic converter
convertidor^{M} catalítico

automobile systems
sistemas^{M} del automóvil^{M}

suspension system
sistema^{M} de suspensión^{F}

transmission system
sistema^{M} de transmisión^{F}

gas supply system
sistema^{M} de alimentación^{F} de gasolina^{F}

steering system
sistema^{M} de dirección^{F}

braking system
sistema^{M} de frenado^{M}

electrical system
sistema^{M} eléctrico

exhaust system
sistema^{M} de escape^{M}

gasoline engine
motor^{M} de gasolina^{F}

cooling system
sistema^{M} de refrigeración^{F}

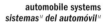

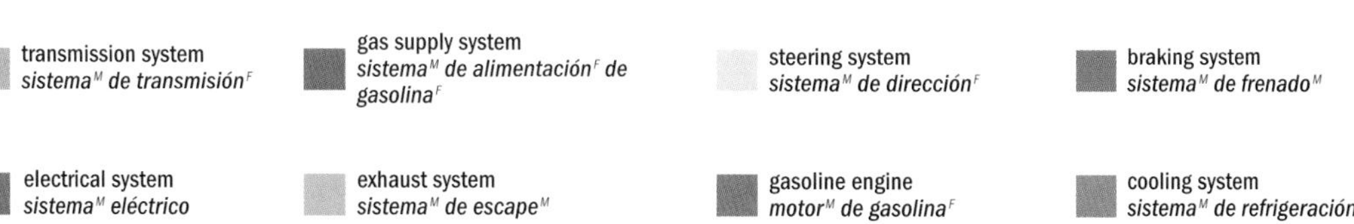

automobile

headlights
faros[M] delanteros

high beam
luz[F] larga
low beam
luz[F] de cruce[M]
fog light
luz[F] antiniebla
turn signal
intermitente[M]
side-marker light
luz[M] de posición[F]

taillights
luces[F] traseras

brake light
luz[F] de freno[M]
turn signal
intermitente[M]
brake light
luz[F] de freno[M]
license plate light
iluminación[F] de la placa[F] de matrícula[F]
reverse light
luz[F] de marcha[F] atrás
taillight
luz[F] trasera
side-marker light
luz[F] de posición[F]

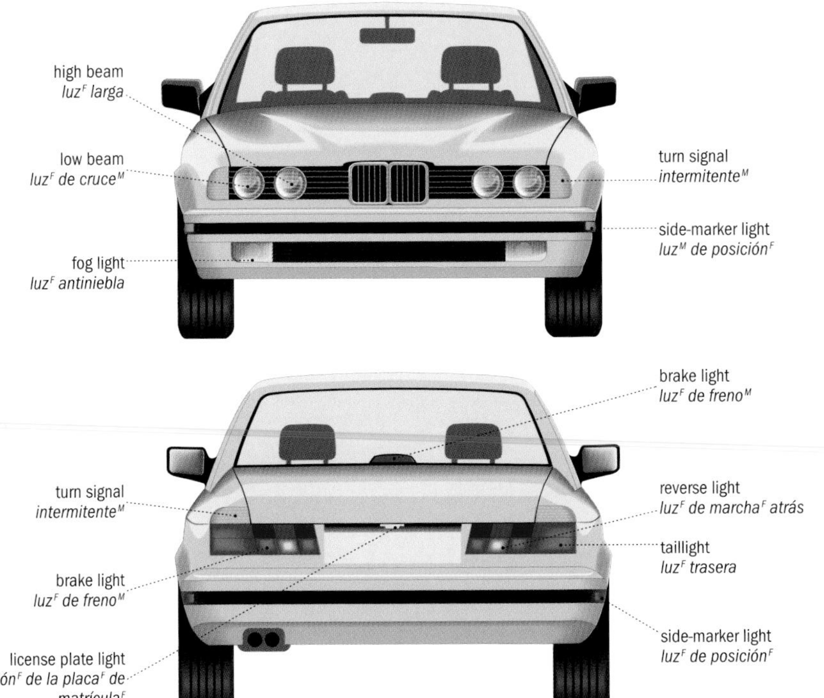

door
puerta[F]

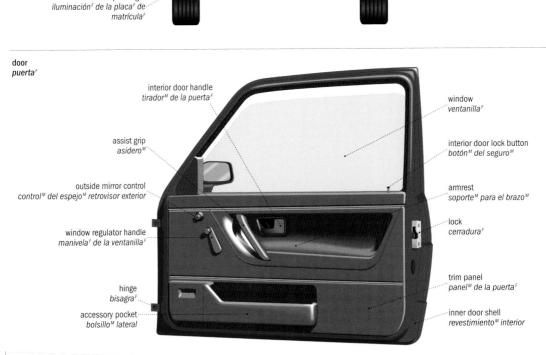

interior door handle
tirador[M] de la puerta[F]
assist grip
asidero[M]
outside mirror control
control[M] del espejo[M] retrovisor exterior
window regulator handle
manivela[F] de la ventanilla[F]
hinge
bisagra[F]
accessory pocket
bolsillo[M] lateral
window
ventanilla[F]
interior door lock button
botón[M] del seguro[M]
armrest
soporte[M] para el brazo[M]
lock
cerradura[F]
trim panel
panel[M] de la puerta[F]
inner door shell
revestimiento[M] interior

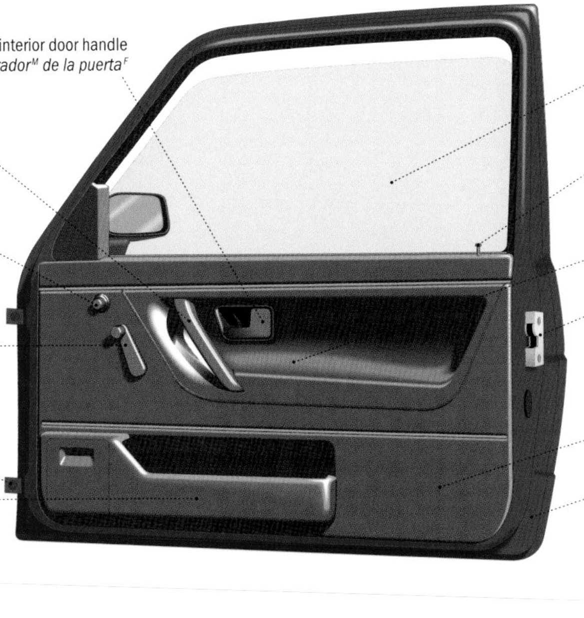

bucket seat: front view
asiento^M : vista^F frontal

bucket seat: side view
asiento^M : vista^F lateral

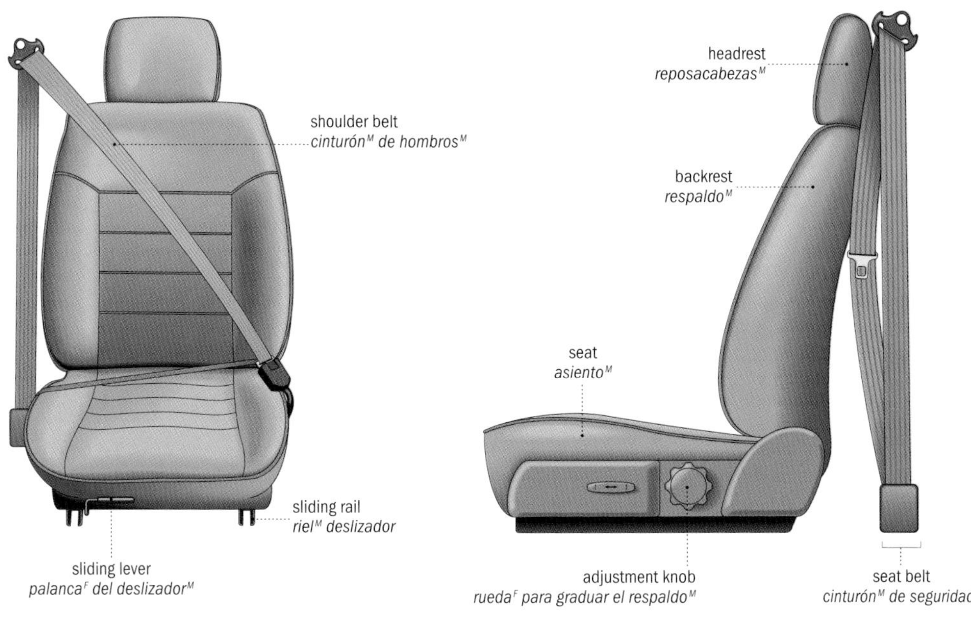

rear seat
asiento^M trasero

automobile

dashboard
***salpicadero**^M^*

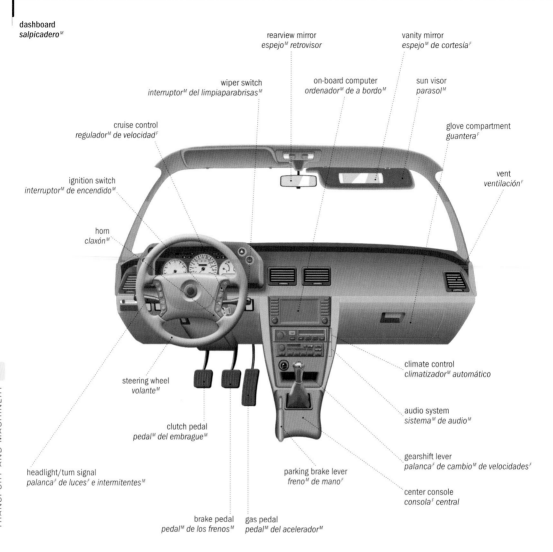

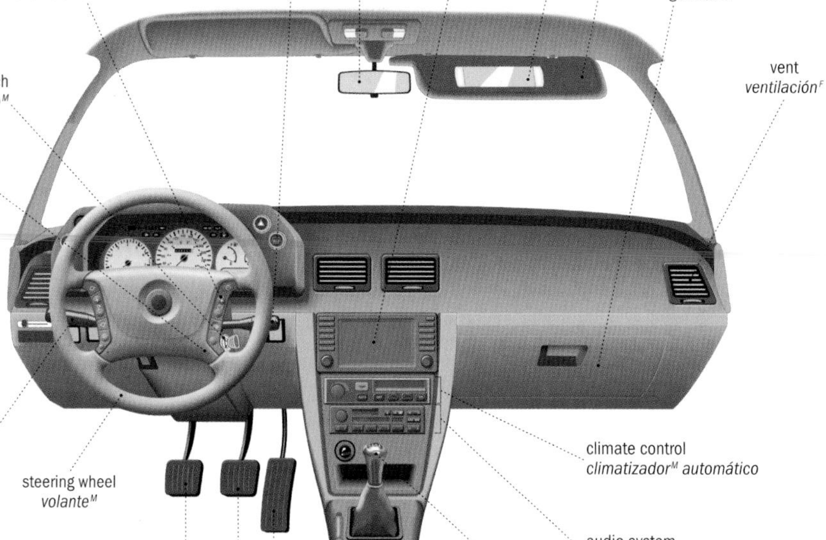

rearview mirror
espejo^M^ retrovisor
vanity mirror
*espejo^M^ de cortesía^F^*
wiper switch
*interruptor^M^ del limpiaparabrisas^M^*
on-board computer
*ordenador^M^ de a bordo^M^*
sun visor
*parasol^M^*
cruise control
*regulador^M^ de velocidad^F^*
glove compartment
*guantera^F^*
ignition switch
*interruptor^M^ de encendido^M^*
vent
*ventilación^F^*
horn
*claxón^M^*
climate control
climatizador^M^ automático
steering wheel
*volante^M^*
audio system
*sistema^M^ de audio^M^*
clutch pedal
*pedal^M^ del embrague^M^*
gearshift lever
*palanca^F^ de cambio^M^ de velocidades^F^*
headlight/turn signal
*palanca^F^ de luces^F^ e intermitentes^M^*
parking brake lever
*freno^M^ de mano^F^*
center console
consola^F^ central
brake pedal
*pedal^M^ de los frenos^M^*
gas pedal
*pedal^M^ del acelerador^M^*

air bag restraint system
sistema^M^ de restricción^F^ del airbag^M^

air bag
*airbag^M^*
safing sensor
*sensor^M^ de seguridad^F^*
primary crash sensor
sensor^M^ de colisión^F^ primario
electrical cable
cable^M^ eléctrico

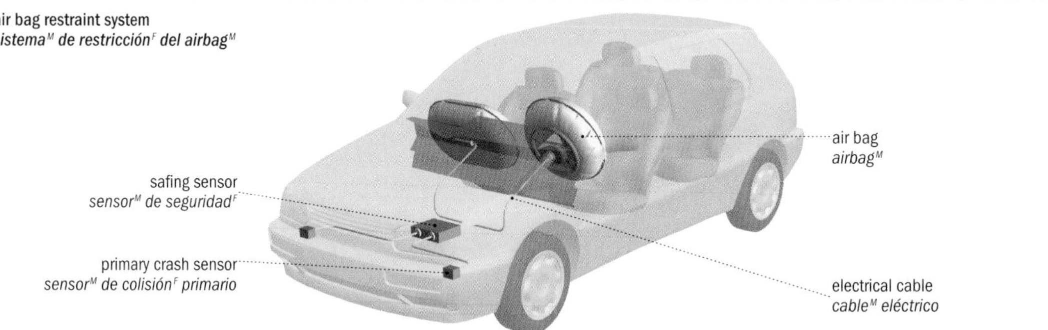

instrument panel
instrumentos[M] del salpicadero[M]

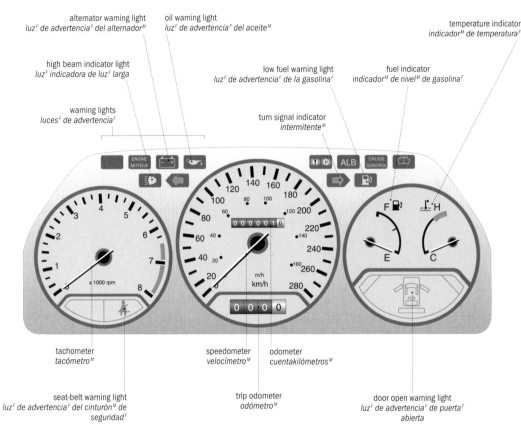

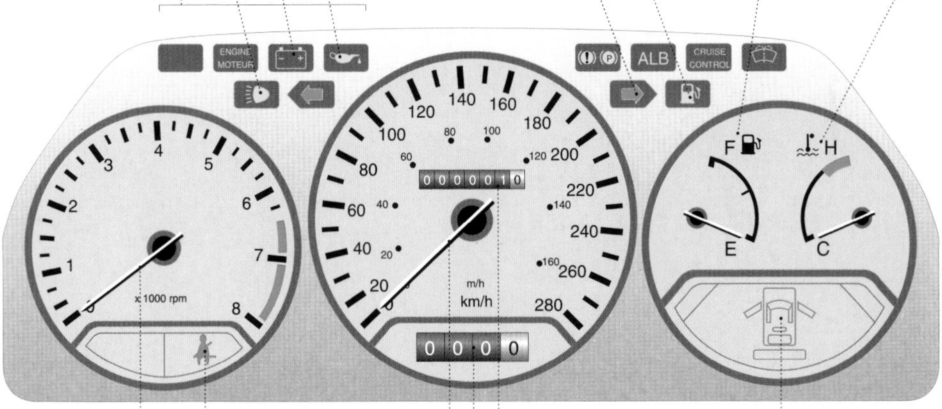

alternator warning light
luz[F] de advertencia[F] del alternador[M]
oil warning light
luz[F] de advertencia[F] del aceite[M]
temperature indicator
indicador[M] de temperatura[F]
high beam indicator light
luz[F] indicadora de luz[F] larga
low fuel warning light
luz[F] de advertencia[F] de la gasolina[F]
fuel indicator
indicador[M] de nivel[M] de gasolina[F]
warning lights
luces[F] de advertencia[F]
turn signal indicator
intermitente[M]
ENGINE MOTEUR
ALB
CRUISE CONTROL
x 1000 rpm
m/h
km/h
tachometer
tacómetro[M]
speedometer
velocímetro[M]
odometer
cuentakilómetros[M]
seat-belt warning light
luz[F] de advertencia[F] del cinturón[M] de seguridad[F]
trip odometer
odómetro[M]
door open warning light
luz[F] de advertencia[F] de puerta[F] abierta

windshield wiper
limpiaparabrisas[M]

windshield wiper blade
soporte[M]
articulation
articulación[F]
wiper
limpiador[M]
wiper arm
brazo[M]
tension spring
resorte[M] tensor
fluted shaft
tubo[M] articulado

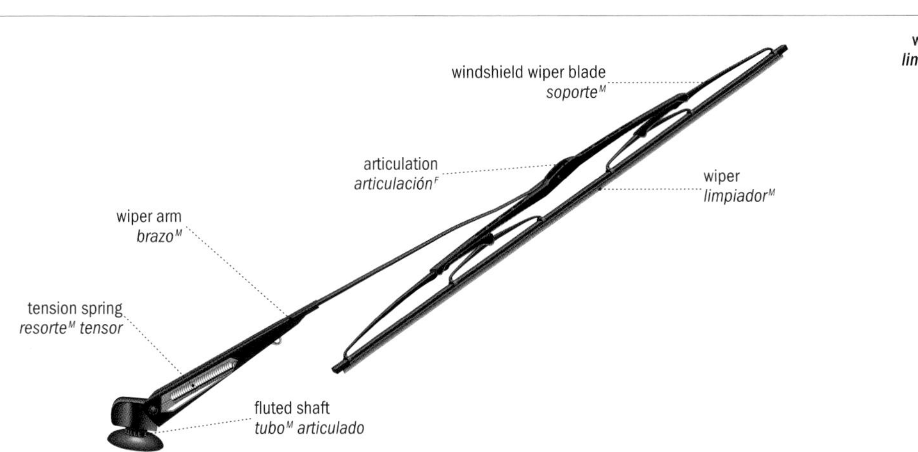

accessories
accesorios^M

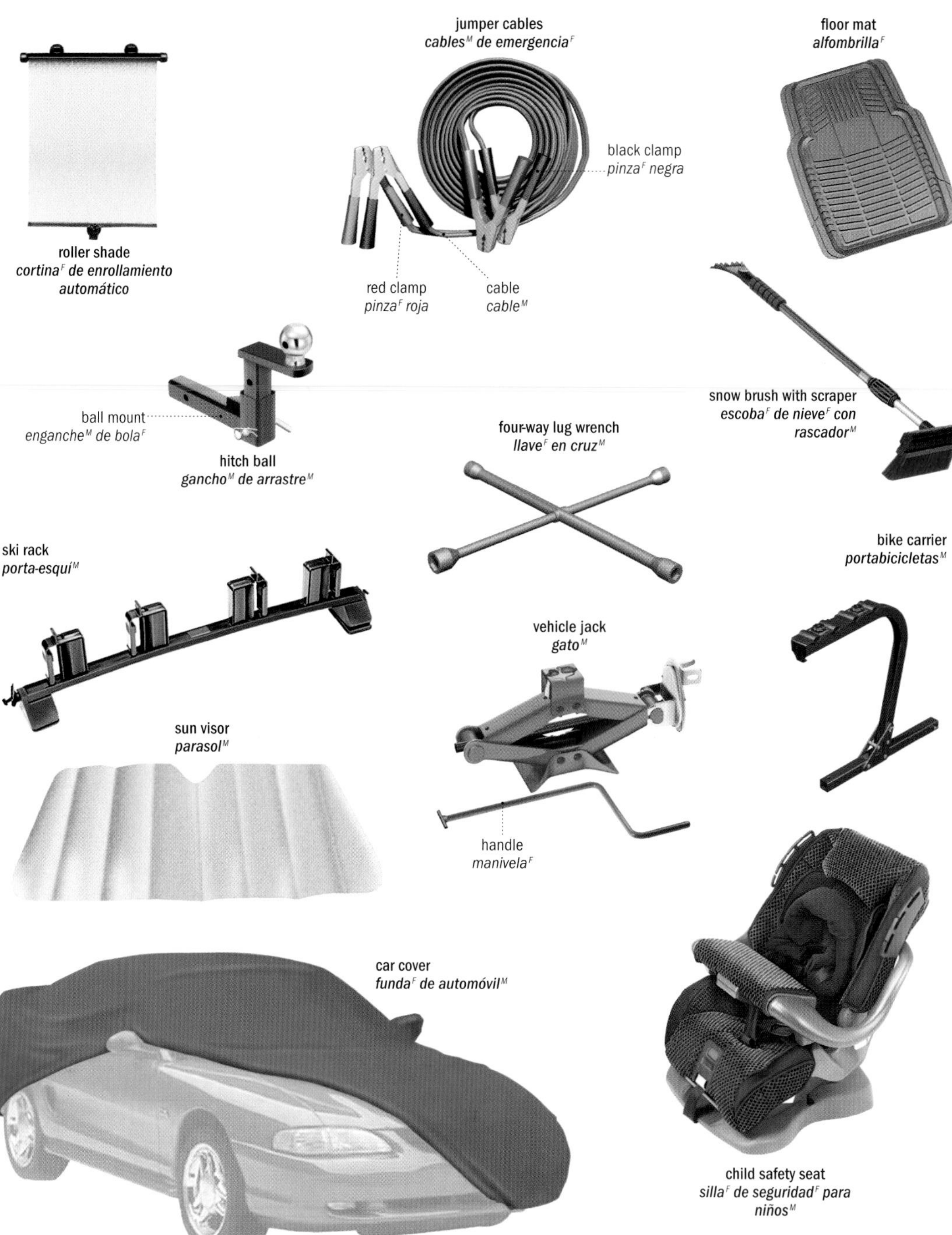
jumper cables
cables^M de emergencia^F
floor mat
alfombrilla^F
black clamp
pinza^F negra
roller shade
cortina^F de enrollamiento automático
red clamp
pinza^F roja
cable
cable^M
ball mount
enganche^M de bola^F
hitch ball
gancho^M de arrastre^M
snow brush with scraper
escoba^F de nieve^F con rascador^M
four-way lug wrench
llave^F en cruz^M
ski rack
porta-esquí^M
bike carrier
portabicicletas^M
vehicle jack
gato^M
sun visor
parasol^M
handle
manivela^F
car cover
funda^F de automóvil^M
child safety seat
silla^F de seguridad^F para niños^M

brakes

frenos[M]

disc brake
freno[M] de disco[M]

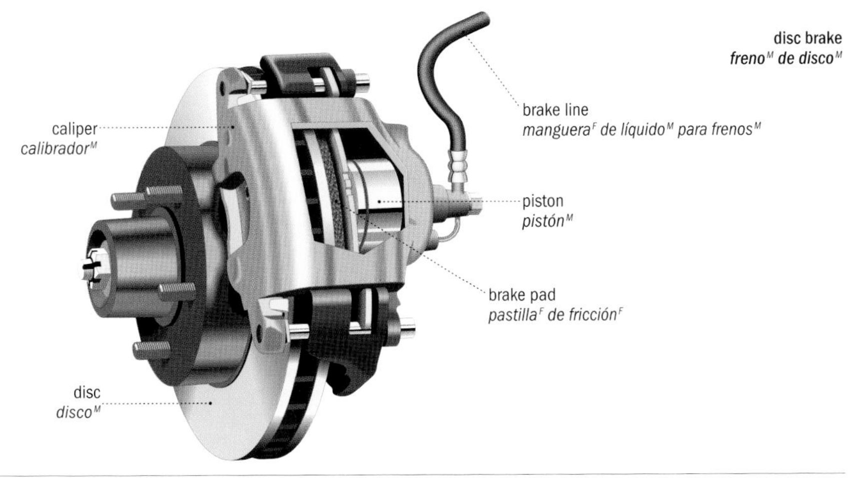

drum brake
freno[M] de tambor[M]

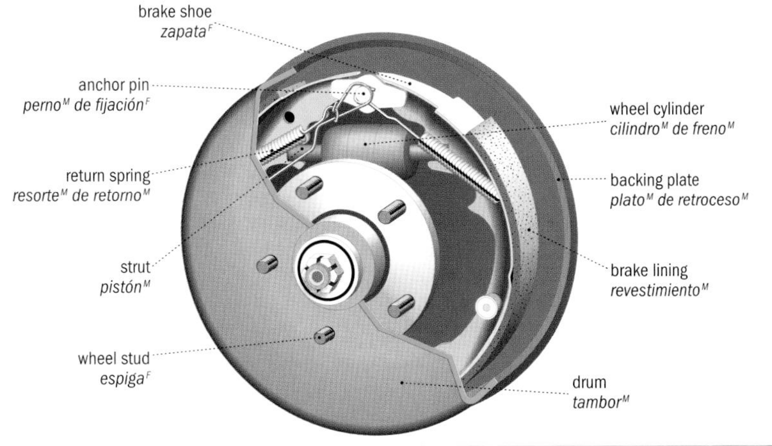

antilock braking system (ABS)
sistema[M] antibloqueo de frenos[M]

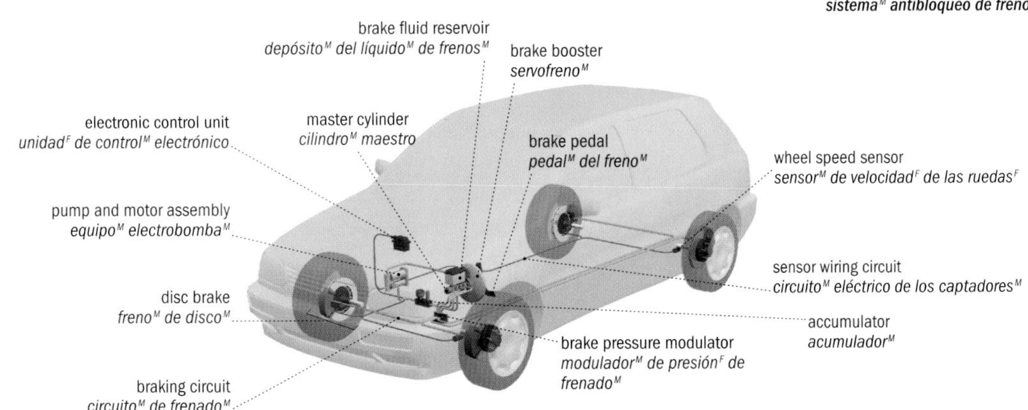

tire

neumático[M]

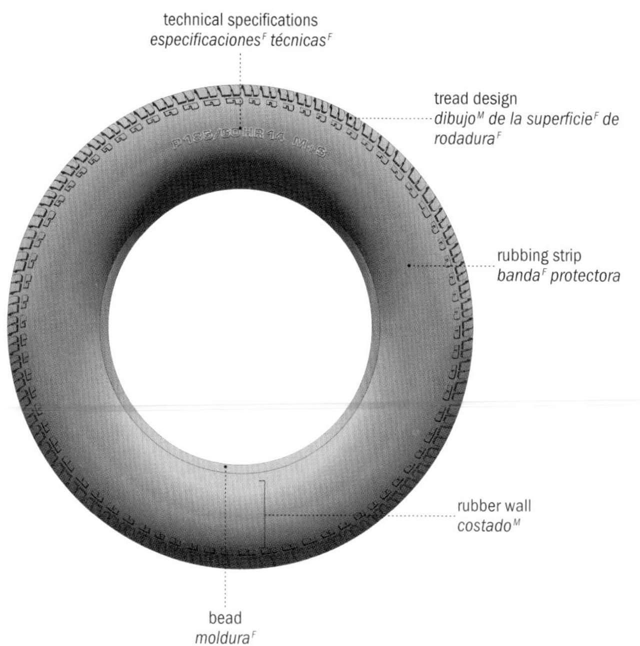

examples of tires
ejemplos[M] de neumáticos[M]

performance tire
neumático[M] de rendimiento[M]

all-season tire
neumático[M] de todas las estaciones[F]

winter tire
neumático[M] de invierno[M]

touring tire
neumático[M] de turismo[M]

radiator

radiador[M]

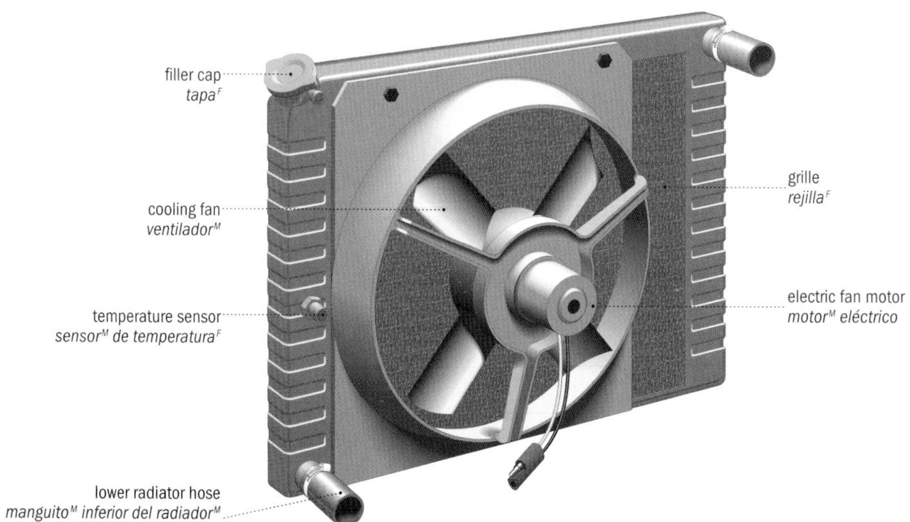

spark plug

bujía^F

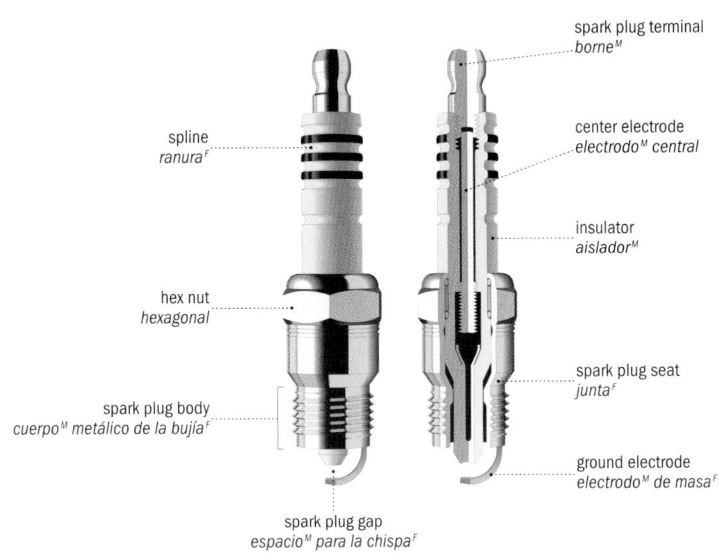
spark plug terminal
borne^M
spline
ranura^F
center electrode
electrodo^M central
insulator
aislador^M
hex nut
hexagonal
spark plug seat
junta^F
spark plug body
cuerpo^M metálico de la bujía^F
ground electrode
electrodo^M de masa^F
spark plug gap
espacio^M para la chispa^F

battery

batería^F

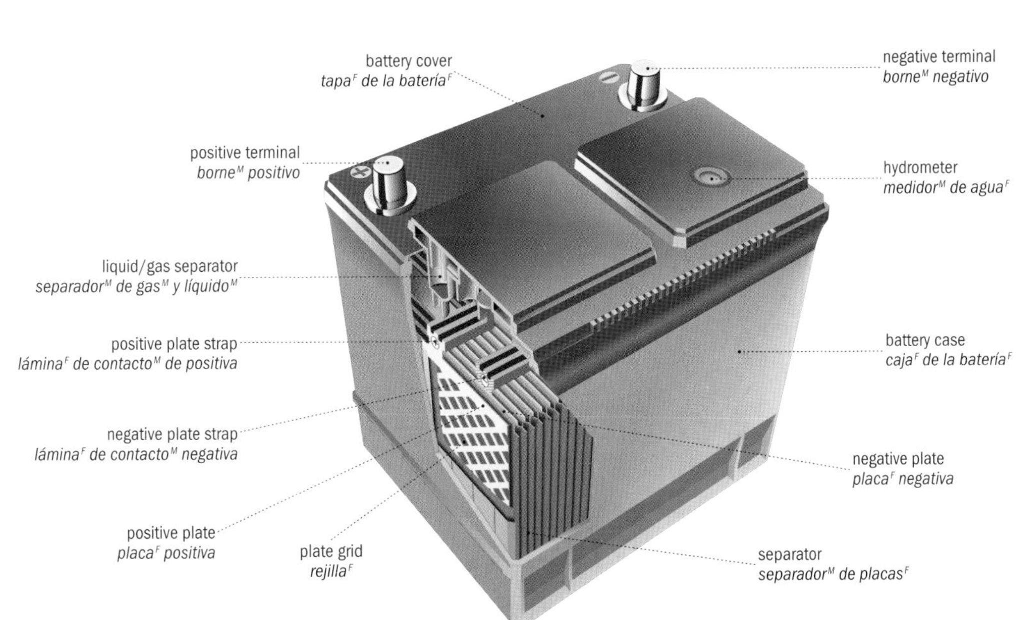
battery cover
tapa^F de la batería^F
negative terminal
borne^M negativo
positive terminal
borne^M positivo
hydrometer
medidor^M de agua^F
liquid/gas separator
separador^M de gas^M y líquido^M
positive plate strap
lámina^F de contacto^M de positiva
battery case
caja^F de la batería^F
negative plate strap
lámina^F de contacto^M negativa
negative plate
placa^F negativa
positive plate
placa^F positiva
plate grid
rejilla^F
separator
separador^M de placas^F

gasoline engine

motorM de gasolinaF

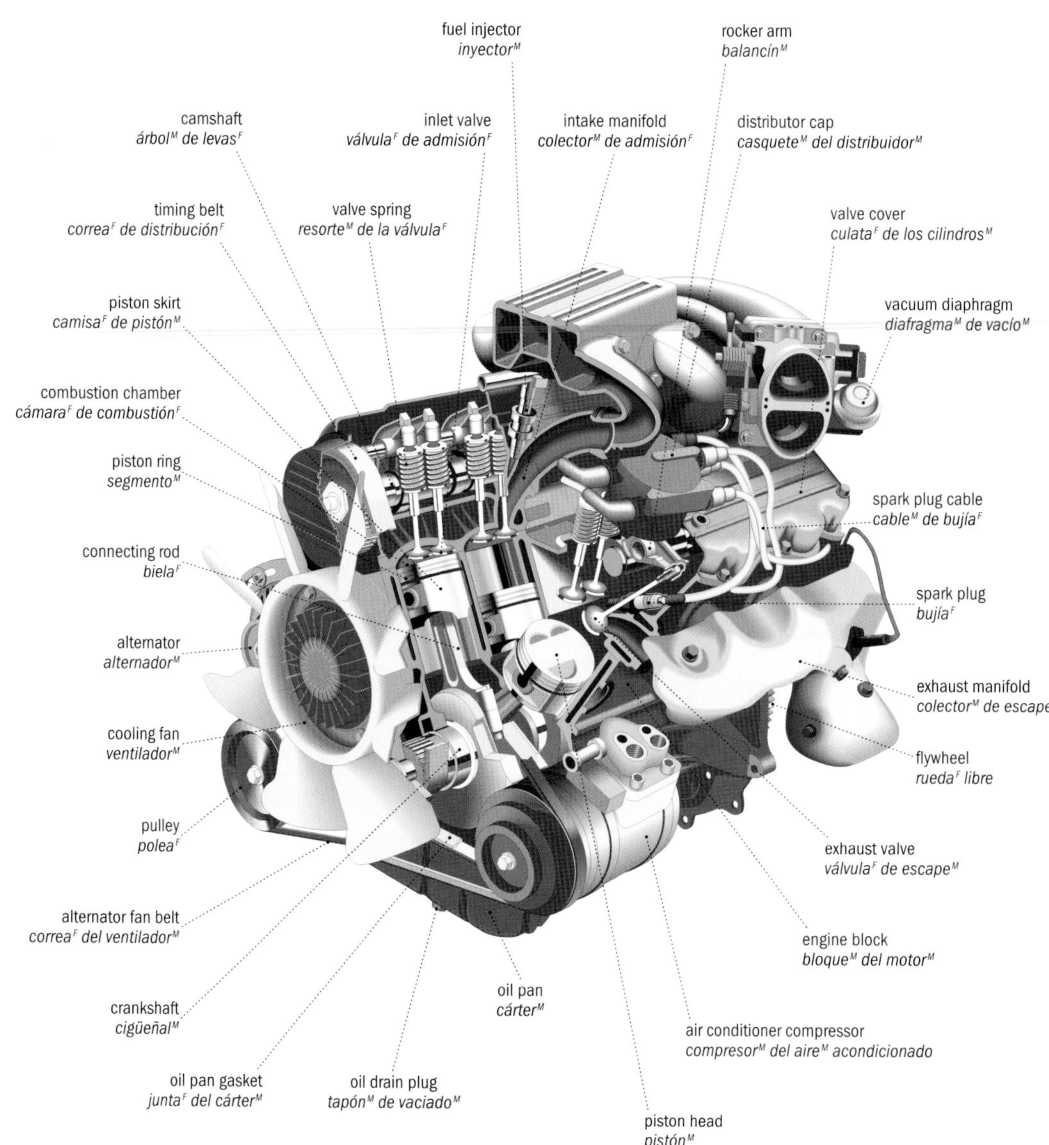
fuel injector
inyectorM
rocker arm
balancínM
camshaft
árbolM de levasF
inlet valve
válvulaF de admisiónF
intake manifold
colectorM de admisiónF
distributor cap
casqueteM del distribuidorM
timing belt
correaF de distribuciónF
valve spring
resorteM de la válvulaF
valve cover
culataF de los cilindrosM
piston skirt
camisaF de pistónM
vacuum diaphragm
diafragmaM de vacíoM
combustion chamber
cámaraF de combustiónF
piston ring
segmentoM
spark plug cable
cableM de bujíaF
connecting rod
bielaF
spark plug
bujíaF
alternator
alternadorM
exhaust manifold
colectorM de escapeM
cooling fan
ventiladorM
flywheel
ruedaF libre
pulley
poleaF
exhaust valve
válvulaF de escapeM
alternator fan belt
correaF del ventiladorM
engine block
bloqueM del motorM
oil pan
cárterM
crankshaft
cigüeñalM
air conditioner compressor
compresorM del aireM acondicionado
oil pan gasket
juntaF del cárterM
oil drain plug
tapónM de vaciadoM
piston head
pistónM

camping trailers

caravana[F]

trailer
remolque[M]

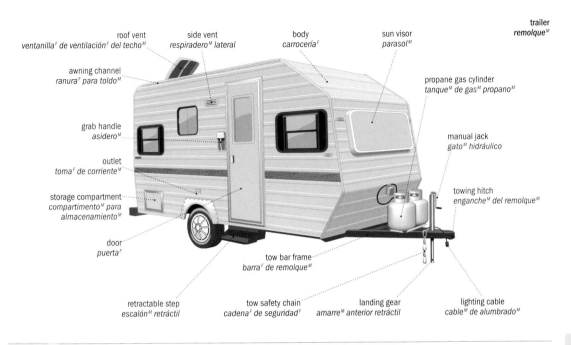

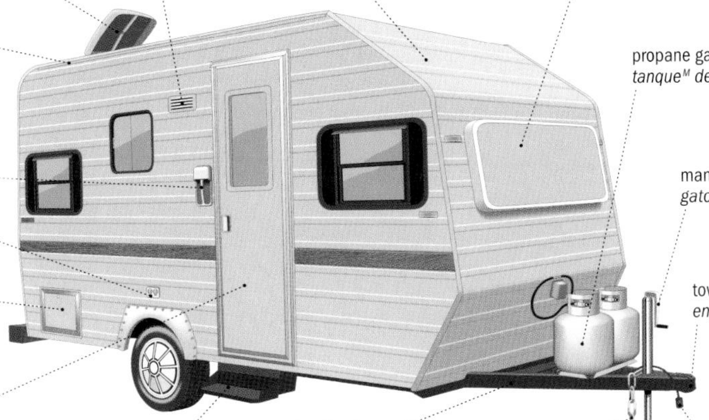

roof vent
ventanilla[F] de ventilación[F] del techo[M]
side vent
respiradero[M] lateral
body
carrocería[F]
sun visor
parasol[M]
awning channel
ranura[F] para toldo[M]
propane gas cylinder
tanque[M] de gas[M] propano[M]
grab handle
asidero[M]
manual jack
gato[M] hidráulico
outlet
toma[F] de corriente[M]
towing hitch
enganche[M] del remolque[M]
storage compartment
compartimento[M] para almacenamiento[M]
door
puerta[F]
tow bar frame
barra[F] de remolque[M]
retractable step
escalón[M] retráctil
tow safety chain
cadena[F] de seguridad[F]
landing gear
amarre[M] anterior retráctil
lighting cable
cable[M] de alumbrado[M]

tent trailer
caravana[F] plegable

roof
techo[M]
canopy
toldo[M]
window
ventana[F]
bunk
litera[F]
spare tire
rueda[F] de repuesto[M]
body
carrocería[F]
stabilizer jack
gato[M] estabilizador
screen door
puerta[F] mosquitera

motor home
autocaravana[M]

air conditioner
aire[M] acondicionado
luggage rack
portaequipajes[M]
ladder
escalerilla[F]

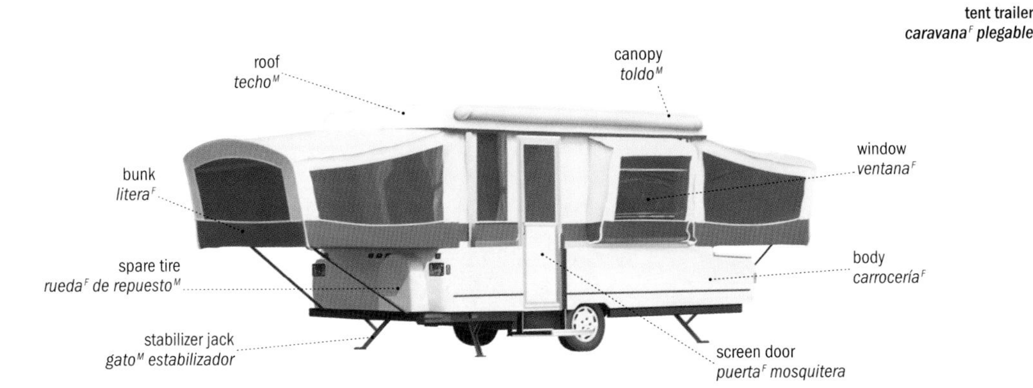

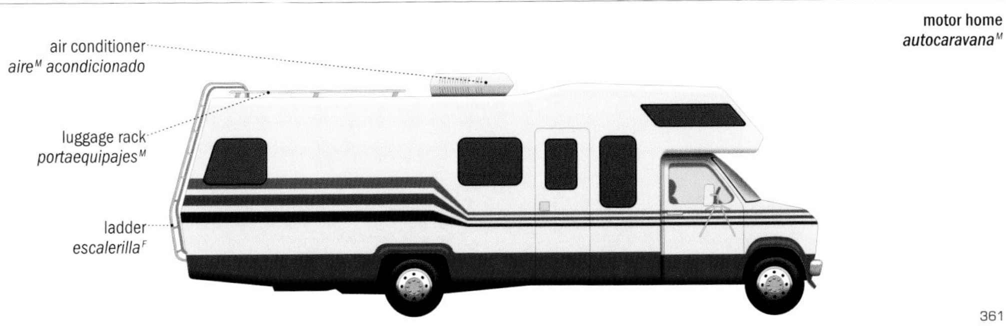

buses

autobúses^M

school bus
autobús^M escolar

blind spot mirror
retrovisor^M de gran angular^M

blinking lights
faros^M intermitentes

outside mirror
espejo^M retrovisor exterior

crossover mirror
espejo^M de cercanías^F

crossing arm
barra^F distanciadora

city bus
autobús^M urbano

air intake
toma^F de aire^M

two-leaf door
puerta^F de dos hojas^F

route sign
indicador^M de línea^F

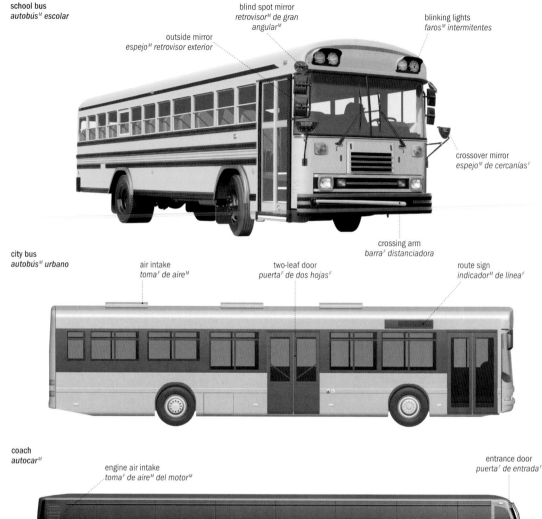

coach
autocar^M

entrance door
puerta^F de entrada^F

engine air intake
toma^F de aire^M del motor^M

engine compartment
compartimiento^M motor

baggage compartment
maletero^M

double-decker bus
***autocar*^M *de dos pisos*^M**

minibus
***minibús*^M**

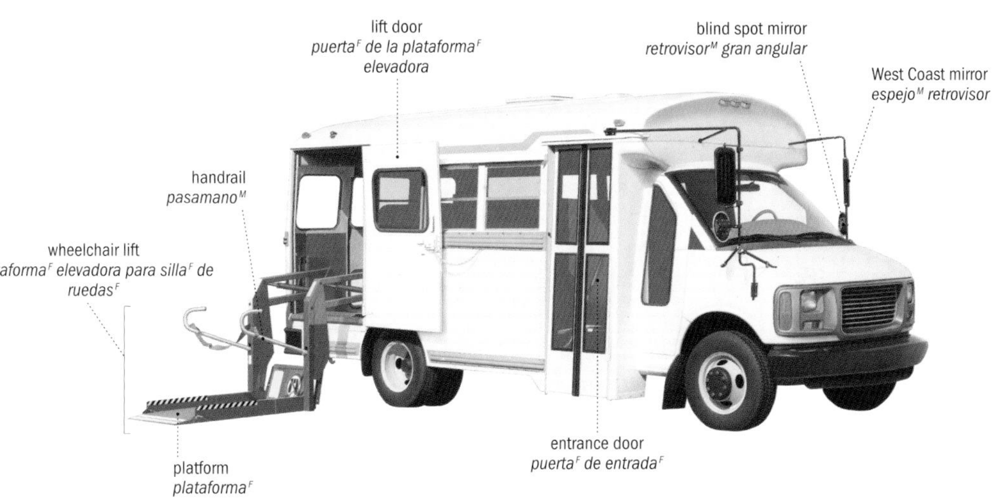

articulated bus
autobús*^M *articulado

trucking

camiones[M]

truck tractor
camión[M] tractor[M]

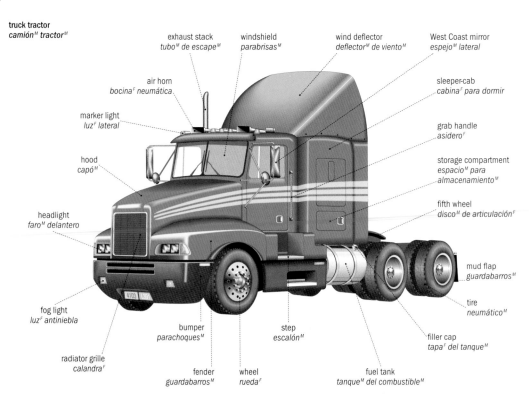

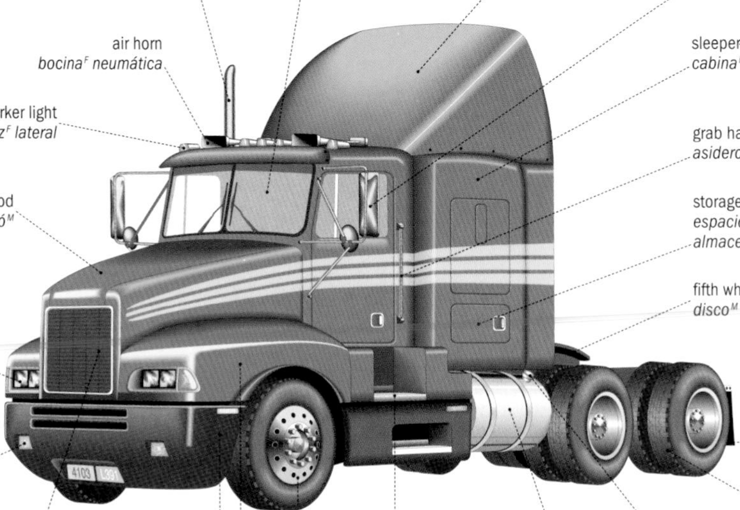

exhaust stack
tubo[M] de escape[M]
windshield
parabrisas[M]
wind deflector
deflector[M] de viento[M]
West Coast mirror
espejo[M] lateral
air horn
bocina[F] neumática
sleeper-cab
cabina[F] para dormir
marker light
luz[F] lateral
grab handle
asidero[F]
hood
capó[M]
storage compartment
espacio[M] para almacenamiento[M]
fifth wheel
disco[M] de articulación[F]
headlight
faro[M] delantero
mud flap
guardabarros[M]
tire
neumático[M]
fog light
luz[F] antiniebla
bumper
parachoques[M]
step
escalón[M]
filler cap
tapa[F] del tanque[M]
radiator grille
calandra[F]
fender
guardabarros[M]
wheel
rueda[F]
fuel tank
tanque[M] del combustible[M]

examples of trucks
ejemplos[M] de camiones[M]

tank body
cisterna[F]

tank truck
camión[M] cisterna[F]

garbage collection truck
compactadora[F]

loading hopper
tolva[F] de carga[F]
packer body
empaquetadora[F]

tow truck
grúa[F] remolque

boom
brazo[M] de elevación[F]
cable
cable[M]
hook
gancho[M]
towing device
dispositivo[M] de remolque[M]
winch controls
mandos[M] del cabestrante[M]
elevating cylinder
cilindro[M] elevador
winch
cabestrante[M]

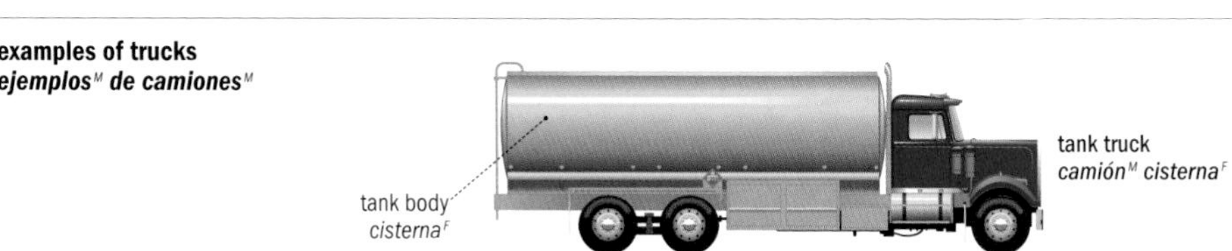

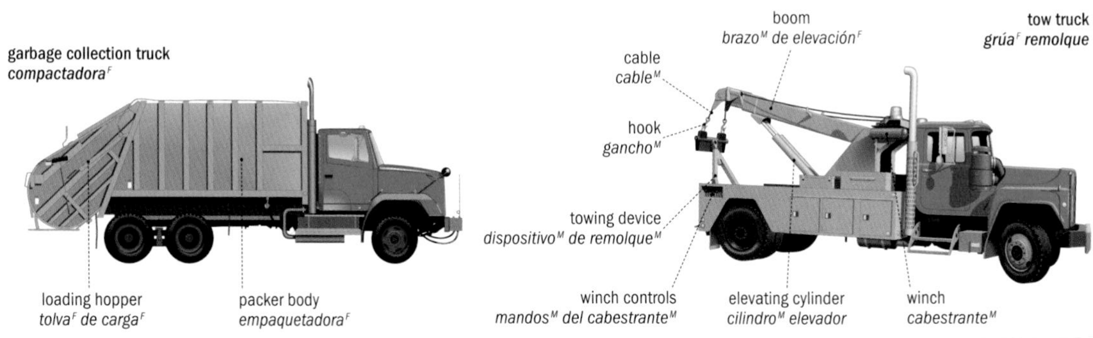

semitrailer
semirremolque[M] tipo[M] caja[F]

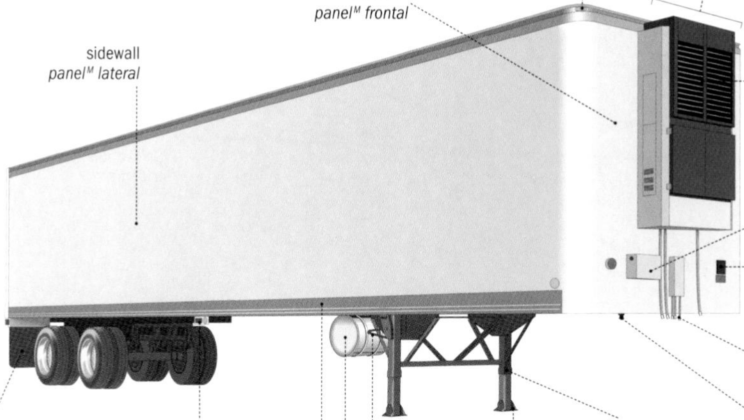

marker light
luz[F] lateral
refrigeration unit
unidad[F] de refrigeración[F]
frontwall
panel[M] frontal
sidewall
panel[M] lateral
vent door
ventilador[M]
battery box
caja[F] del acumulador[M]
partlow chart
regulador[M] de temperatura[F]
electrical connection
conexiones[F]
reflector
reflector[M]
landing gear
dispositivo[M] de amarre[M]
kingpin
perno[M] maestro
mud flap
guardabarros[M]
side rail
banda[F] lateral protectora
sand shoe
zapata[F]
auxiliary tank
tanque[M] auxiliar
landing gear crank
manivela[F]

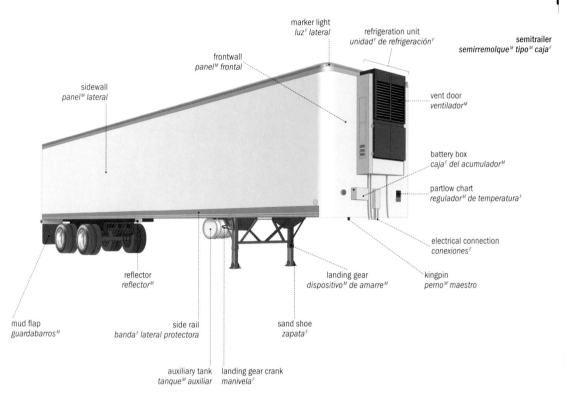

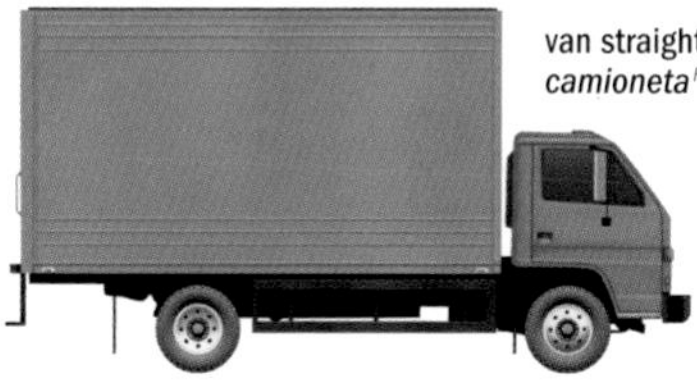

van straight truck
camioneta[F]

concrete mixer truck
hormigonera[F]

street sweeper
barredora[F]

collection body
cajón[M] de basura[F]
central brush
escoba[F] central
lateral brush
escoba[F] lateral
watering tube
tubo[M] de irrigación[F]

snowblower
quitanieves[M]

projection device
chimenea[F] de expulsión[F]
worm
tornillo[M] sin fin[M]

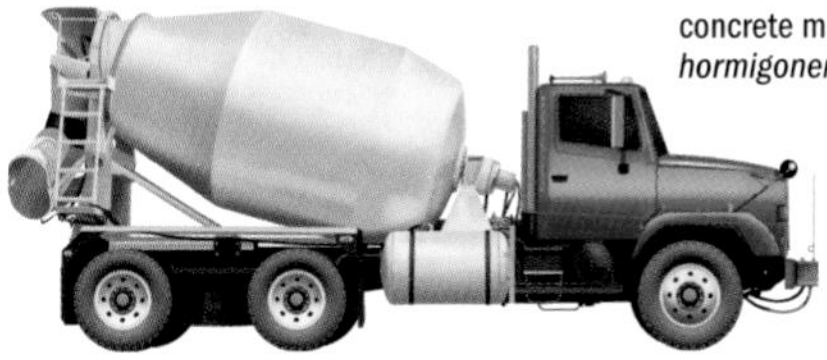

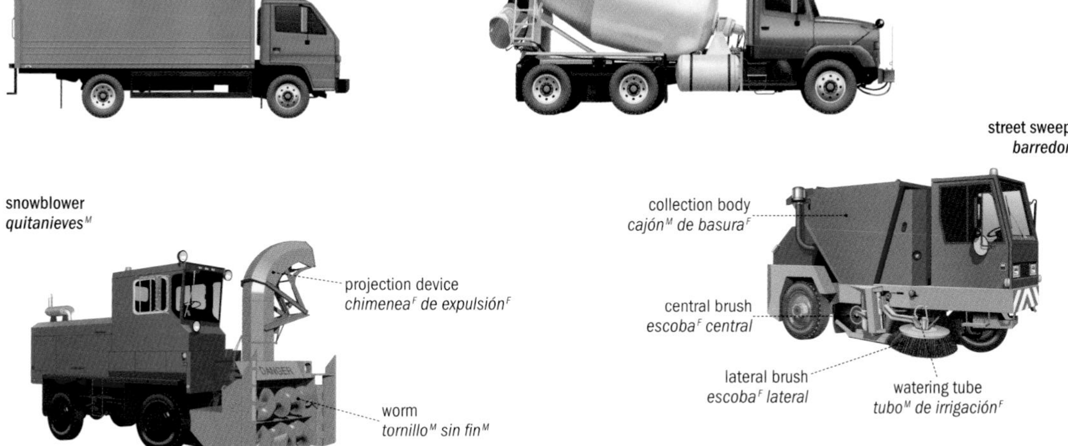

motorcycle

motocicleta[F]

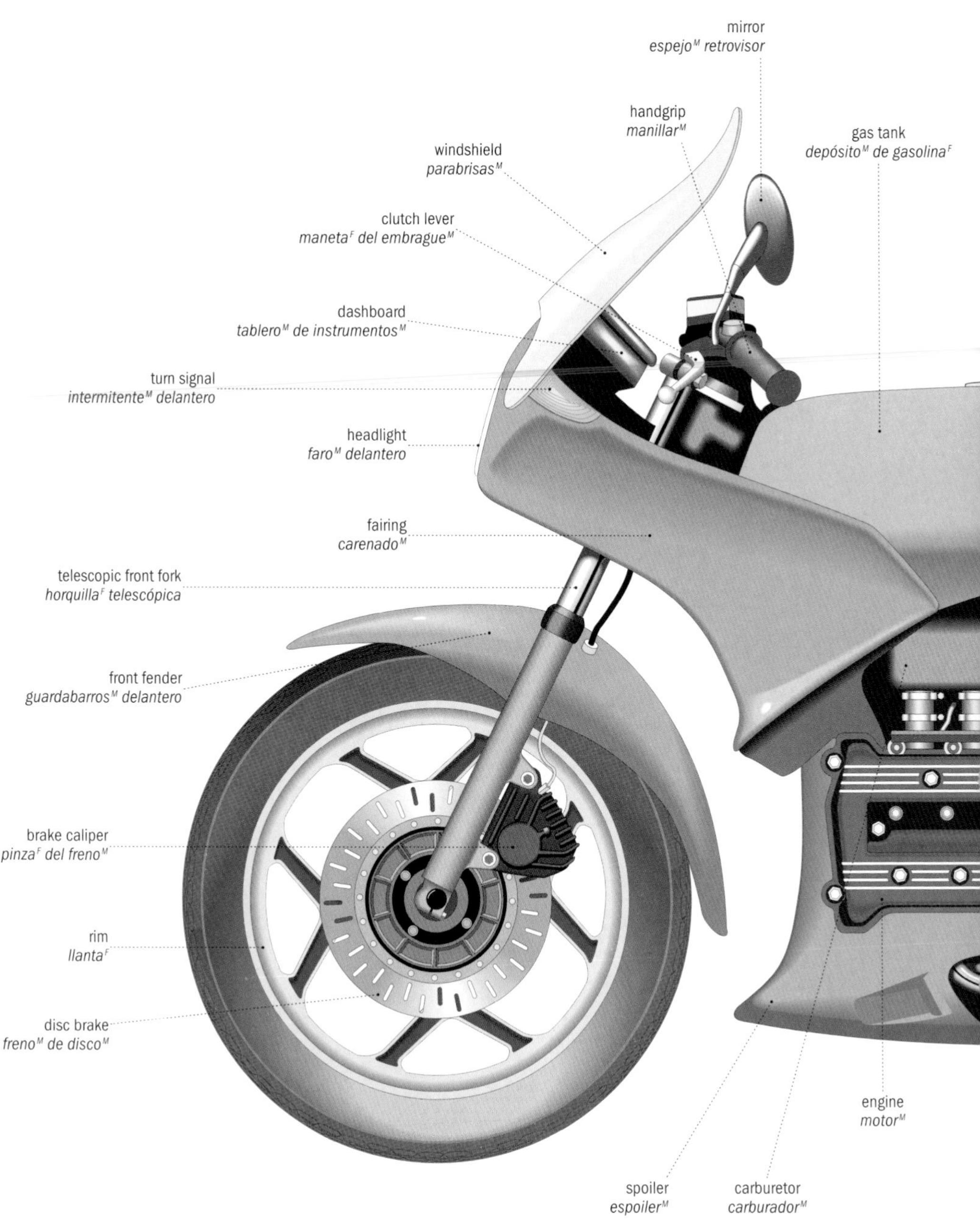
mirror
espejo[M] retrovisor
handgrip
manillar[M]
gas tank
depósito[M] de gasolina[F]
windshield
parabrisas[M]
clutch lever
maneta[F] del embrague[M]
dashboard
tablero[M] de instrumentos[M]
turn signal
intermitente[M] delantero
headlight
faro[M] delantero
fairing
carenado[M]
telescopic front fork
horquilla[F] telescópica
front fender
guardabarros[M] delantero
brake caliper
pinza[F] del freno[M]
rim
llanta[F]
disc brake
freno[M] de disco[M]
engine
motor[M]
spoiler
espoiler[M]
carburetor
carburador[M]

protective helmet
casco*^M *integral

bubble
casco^M
visor
visera^F
air inlet
respiradero^M
chin protector
protector^M *de la barbilla*^F
visor hinge
charnela^M *lateral*

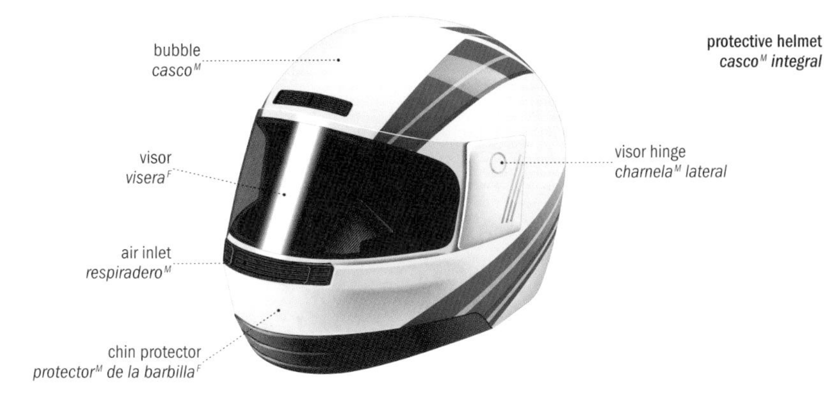

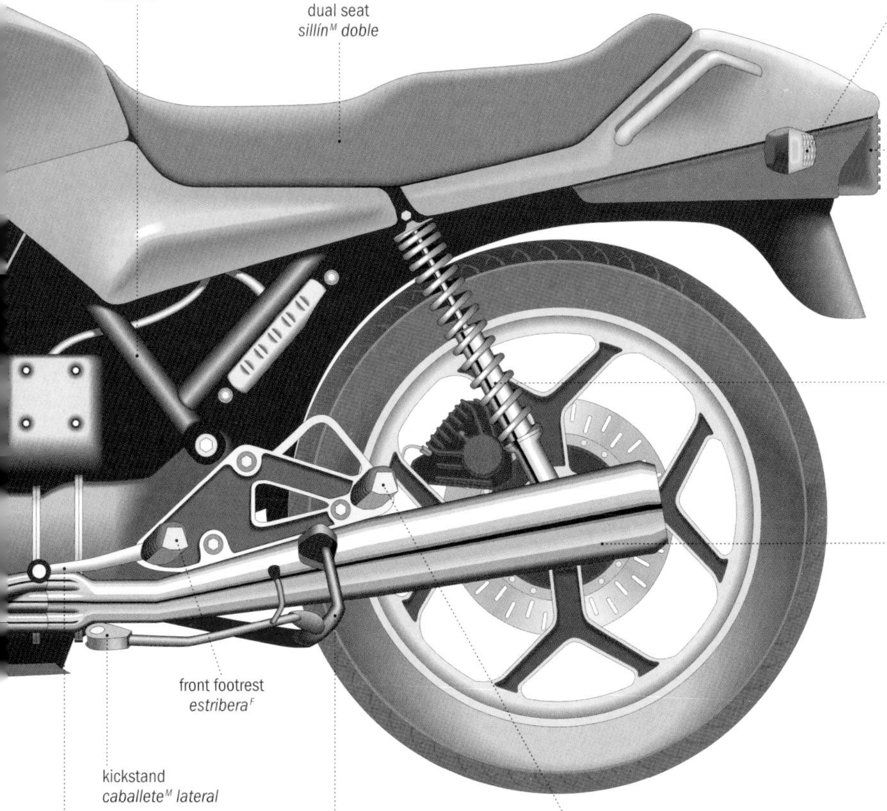

frame
bastidor^M
dual seat
sillín^M *doble*
turn signal
intermitente^M *trasero*
taillight
luz^F *trasera*
rear shock absorber
amortiguador^M
exhaust pipe
silenciador^M
front footrest
estribera^F
kickstand
caballete^M *lateral*
gearshift lever
palanca^F *de cambio*^M *de velocidades*^F
main stand
caballete^M *central*
pillion footrest
estribera^F *del pasajero*^M

TRANSPORT AND MACHINERY

motorcycle

motorcycle dashboard
tablero[M] de instrumentos[M]

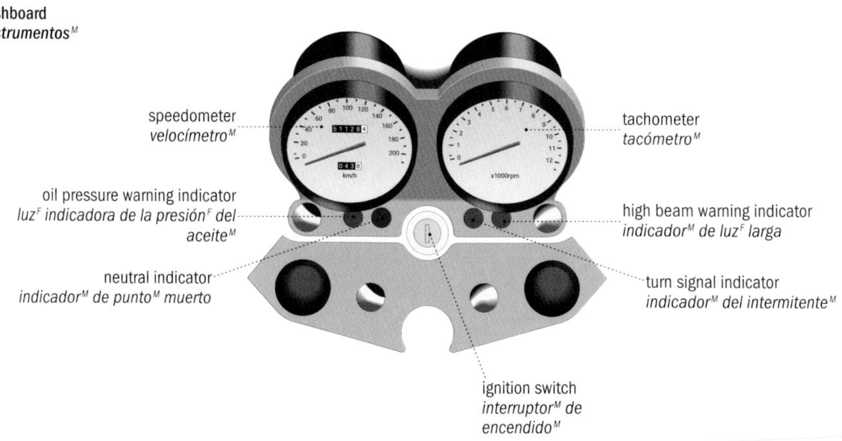

motorcycle: view from above
motocicleta[F] : vista[F] desde lo alto[M]

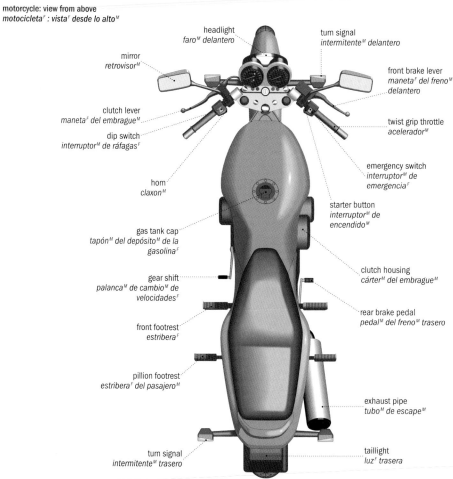

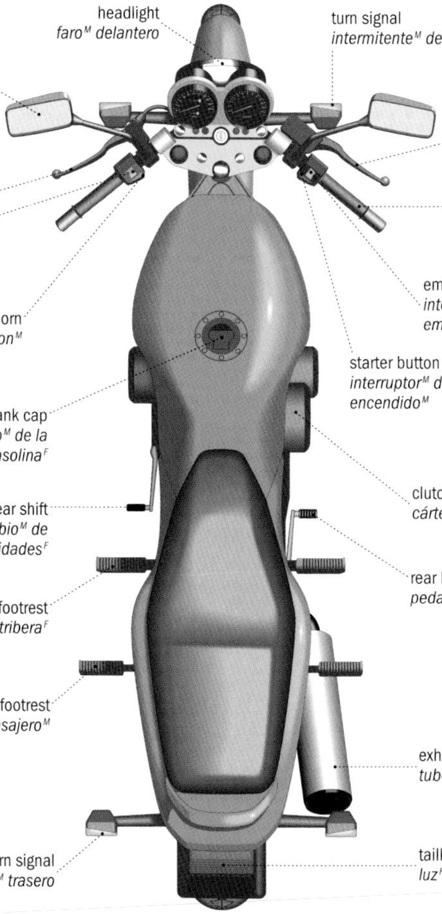

headlight
faro[M] delantero

turn signal
intermitente[M] delantero

mirror
retrovisor[M]

front brake lever
maneta[F] del freno[M] delantero

clutch lever
maneta[F] del embrague[M]

twist grip throttle
acelerador[M]

dip switch
interruptor[M] de ráfagas[F]

emergency switch
interruptor[M] de emergencia[F]

horn
claxon[M]

starter button
interruptor[M] de encendido[M]

gas tank cap
tapón[M] del depósito[M] de la gasolina[F]

clutch housing
cárter[M] del embrague[M]

gear shift
palanca[M] de cambio[M] de velocidades[F]

rear brake pedal
pedal[M] del freno[M] trasero

front footrest
estribera[F]

pillion footrest
estribera[F] del pasajero[M]

exhaust pipe
tubo[M] de escape[M]

turn signal
intermitente[M] trasero

taillight
luz[F] trasera

TRANSPORT AND MACHINERY

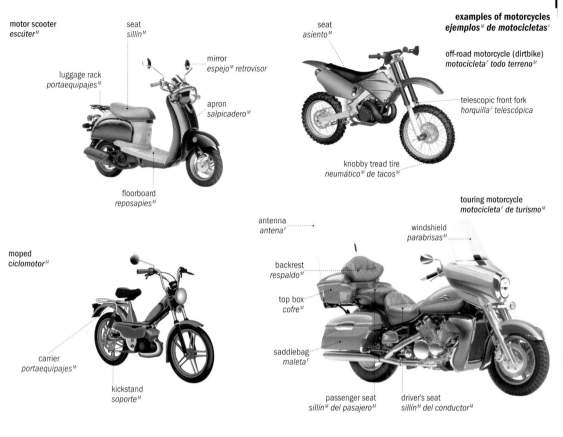

motor scooter
escúter[M]

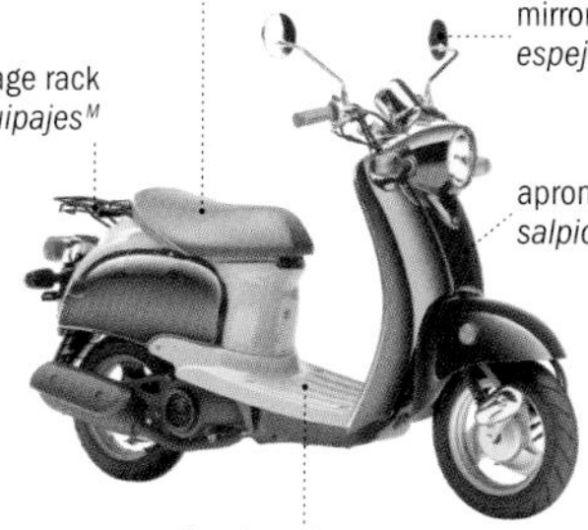

seat
sillín[M]
mirror
espejo[M] retrovisor
luggage rack
portaequipajes[M]
apron
salpicadero[M]
floorboard
reposapies[M]

examples of motorcycles
ejemplos[M] de motocicletas[F]

off-road motorcycle (dirtbike)
motocicleta[F] todo terreno[M]

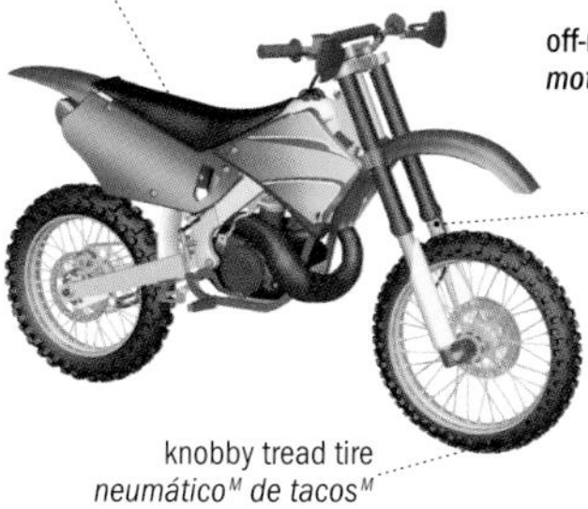

seat
asiento[M]
telescopic front fork
horquilla[F] telescópica
knobby tread tire
neumático[M] de tacos[M]

moped
ciclomotor[M]

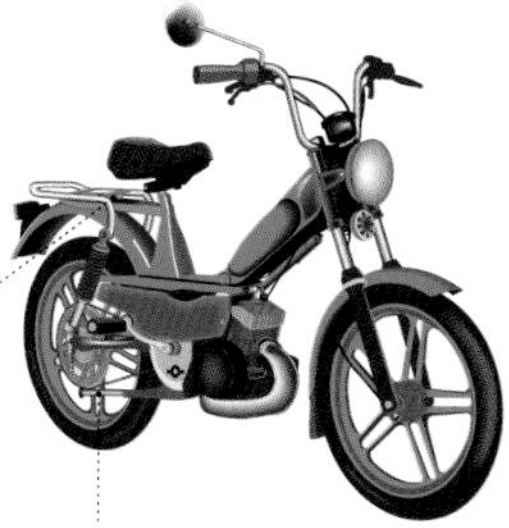

carrier
portaequipajes[M]
kickstand
soporte[M]

touring motorcycle
motocicleta[F] de turismo[M]

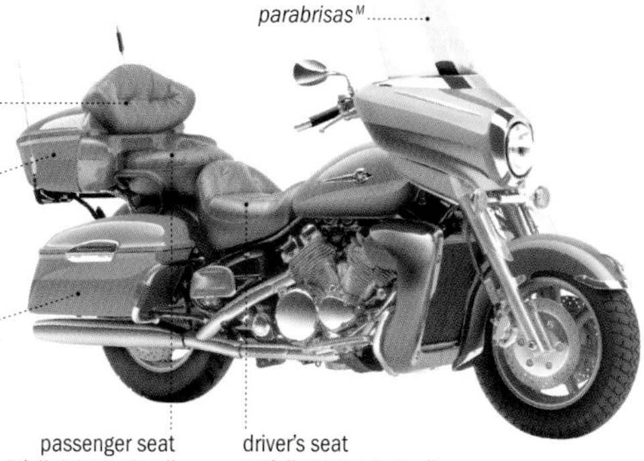

antenna
antena[F]
windshield
parabrisas[M]
backrest
respaldo[M]
top box
cofre[M]
saddlebag
maleta[F]
passenger seat
sillín[M] del pasajero[M]
driver's seat
sillín[M] del conductor[M]

4 X 4 all-terrain vehicle

quad[M]

rear cargo rack
portaequipajes[M] posterior
seat
sillín[M]
gas tank
depósito[M] de gasolina[F]
handgrip
manillar[M]
rear fender
parachoques[M] posterior
muffler
silenciador[M]
bumper
parachoques[M]
front shock absorber
amortiguador[M] delantero
gearshift lever
palanca[F] de cambio[M] de velocidades[F]

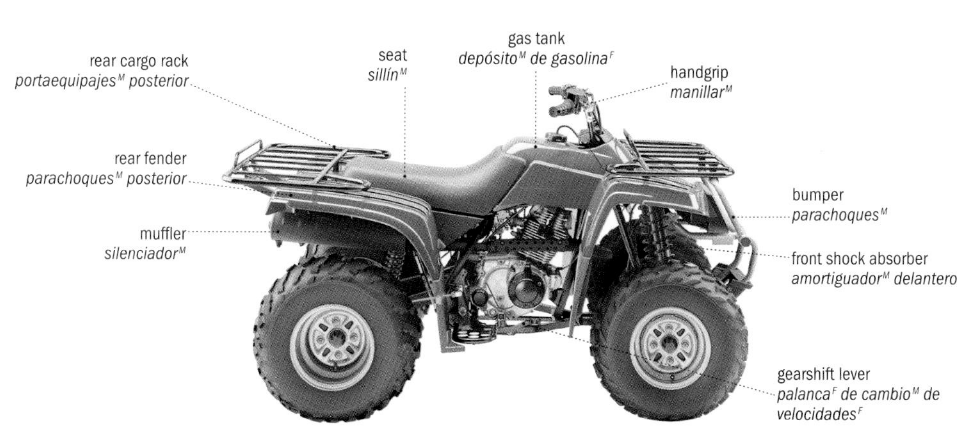

bicycle

bicicleta^F

parts of a bicycle
partes^F de una bicicleta^F

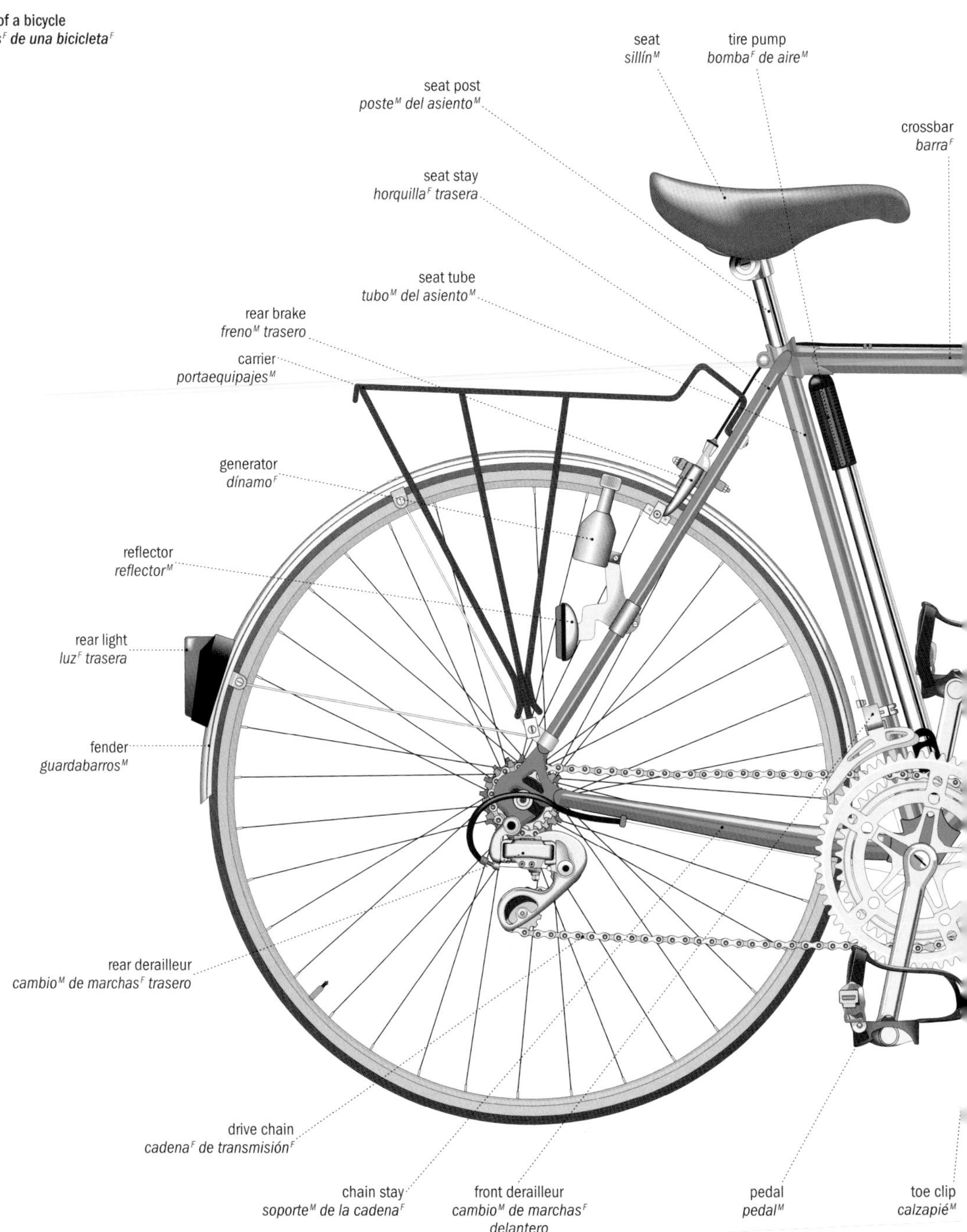

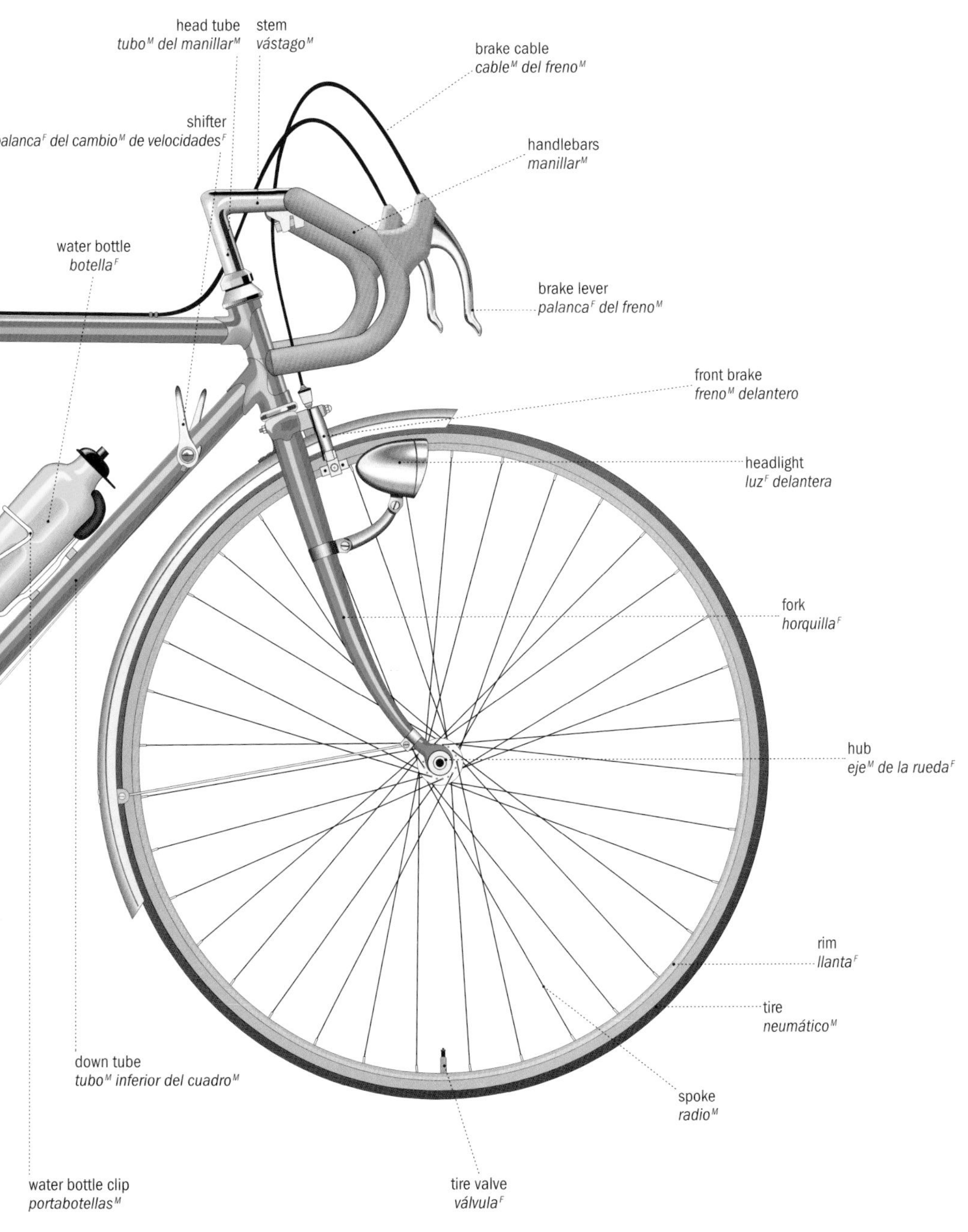
head tube
tuboᴹ del manillarᴹ
stem
vástagoᴹ
brake cable
cableᴹ del frenoᴹ
shifter
alancaᶠ del cambioᴹ de velocidadesᶠ
handlebars
manillarᴹ
water bottle
botellaᶠ
brake lever
palancaᶠ del frenoᴹ
front brake
frenoᴹ delantero
headlight
luzᶠ delantera
fork
horquillaᶠ
hub
ejeᴹ de la ruedaᶠ
rim
llantaᶠ
tire
neumáticoᴹ
down tube
tuboᴹ inferior del cuadroᴹ
spoke
radioᴹ
water bottle clip
portabotellasᴹ
tire valve
válvulaᶠ

bicycle

power train
***transmisión*[F] *de cadena*[F]**

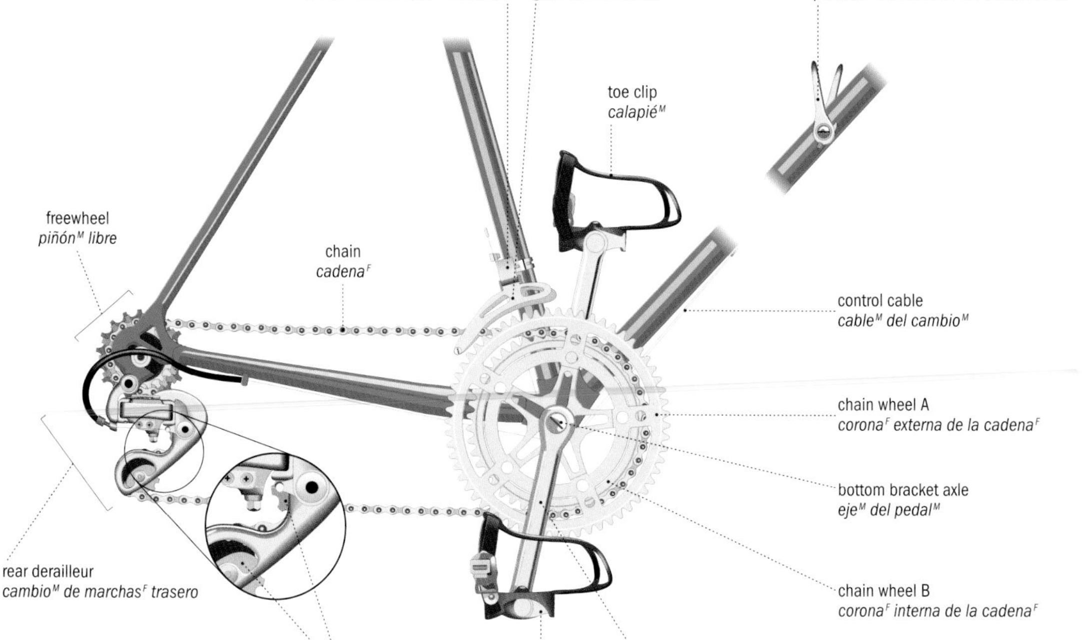

front derailleur
cambio[M] *de marchas*[F] *delantero*

chain guide
guía[F] *de la cadena*[F]

shifter
palanca[F] *del cambio*[M] *de velocidades*[F]

toe clip
calapié[M]

freewheel
piñón[M] *libre*

chain
cadena[F]

control cable
cable[M] *del cambio*[M]

chain wheel A
corona[F] *externa de la cadena*[F]

bottom bracket axle
eje[M] *del pedal*[M]

rear derailleur
cambio[M] *de marchas*[F] *trasero*

chain wheel B
corona[F] *interna de la cadena*[F]

jockey rollers
poleas[F] *de tensión*[F]

pedal
pedal[M]

crank
manivela[F]

accessories
***accesorios*[M]**

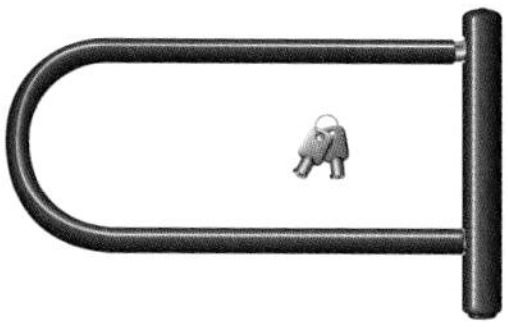

lock
***candado*[M] *para bicicleta*[F]**

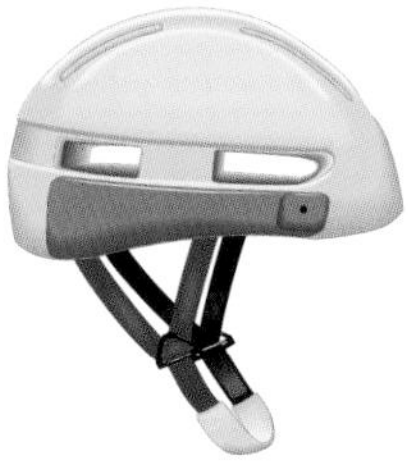

protective helmet
casco*[M] *protector

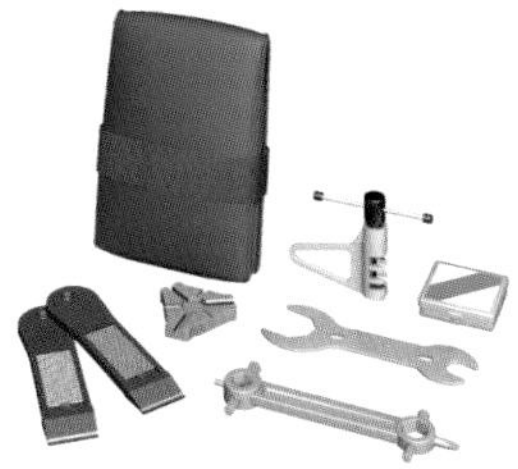

tool kit
***herramientas*[F]**

bicycle bag (pannier)
***cartera*[F]**

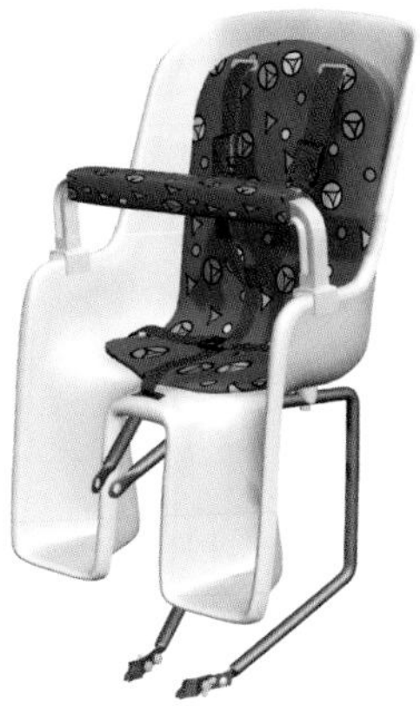

child carrier
***silla*[F] *porta-niño*[M]**

examples of bicycles
ejemplos^M de bicicletas^F
child's tricycle
triciclo^M
BMX bike
bicicleta^F BMX
Dutch bicycle
bicicleta^F holandesa
mountain bike
bicicleta^F todo terreno^M
city bicycle
bicicleta^F de ciudad^F
road bicycle
bicicleta^F de carretera^F
touring bicycle
bicicleta^F de turismo^M
tandem bicycle
tándem^M

passenger station

estación[F] de ferrocarril[M]

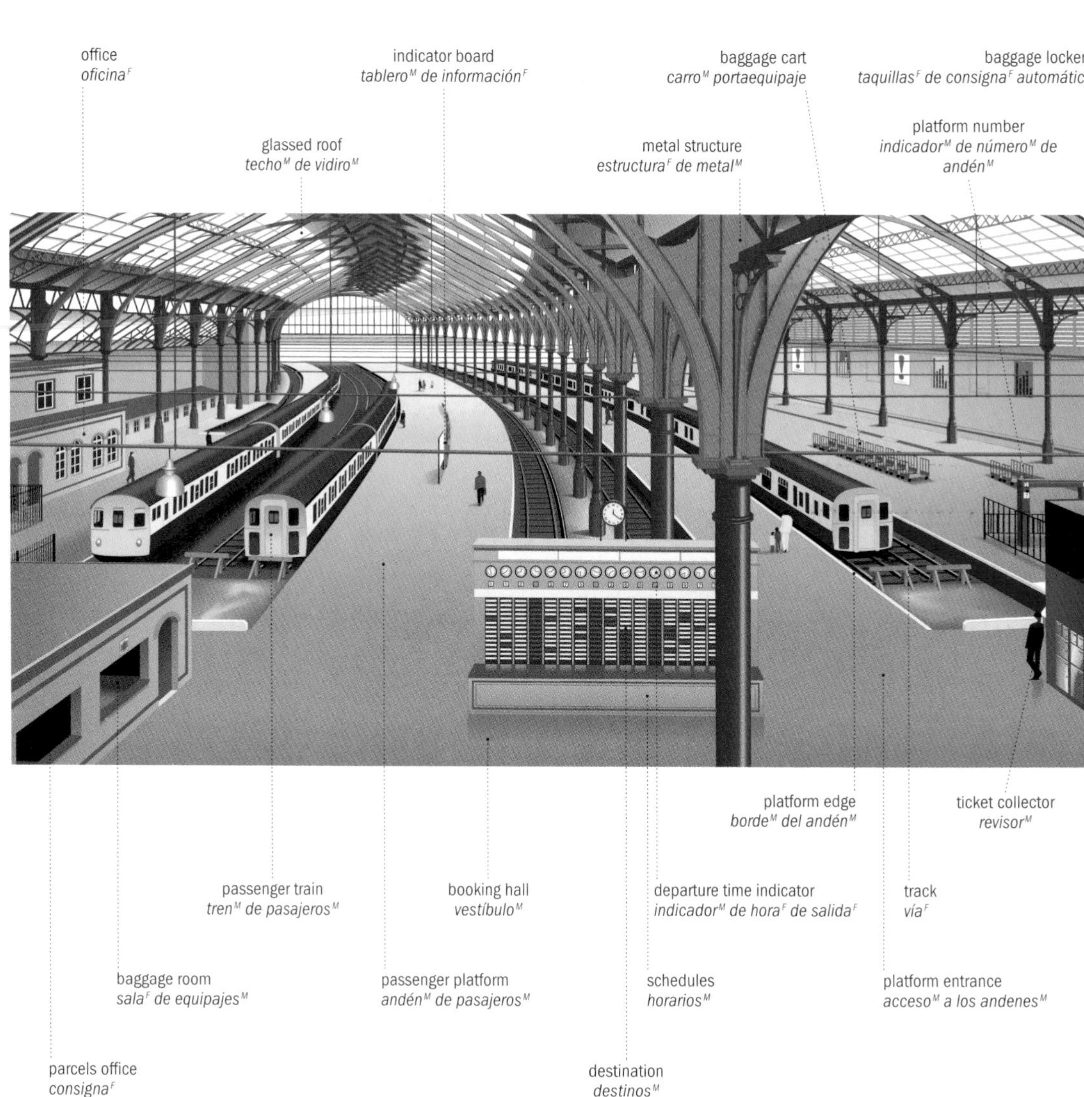
office
oficina[F]
indicator board
tablero[M] de información[F]
baggage cart
carro[M] portaequipaje
baggage lockers
taquillas[F] de consigna[F] automática
glassed roof
techo[M] de vidrio[M]
metal structure
estructura[F] de metal[M]
platform number
indicador[M] de número[M] de andén[M]
platform edge
borde[M] del andén[M]
ticket collector
revisor[M]
passenger train
tren[M] de pasajeros[M]
booking hall
vestíbulo[M]
departure time indicator
indicador[M] de hora[F] de salida[F]
track
vía[F]
baggage room
sala[F] de equipajes[M]
passenger platform
andén[M] de pasajeros[M]
schedules
horarios[M]
platform entrance
acceso[M] a los andenes[M]
parcels office
consigna[F]
destination
destinos[M]

railroad station

estación^F de ferrocarril^M

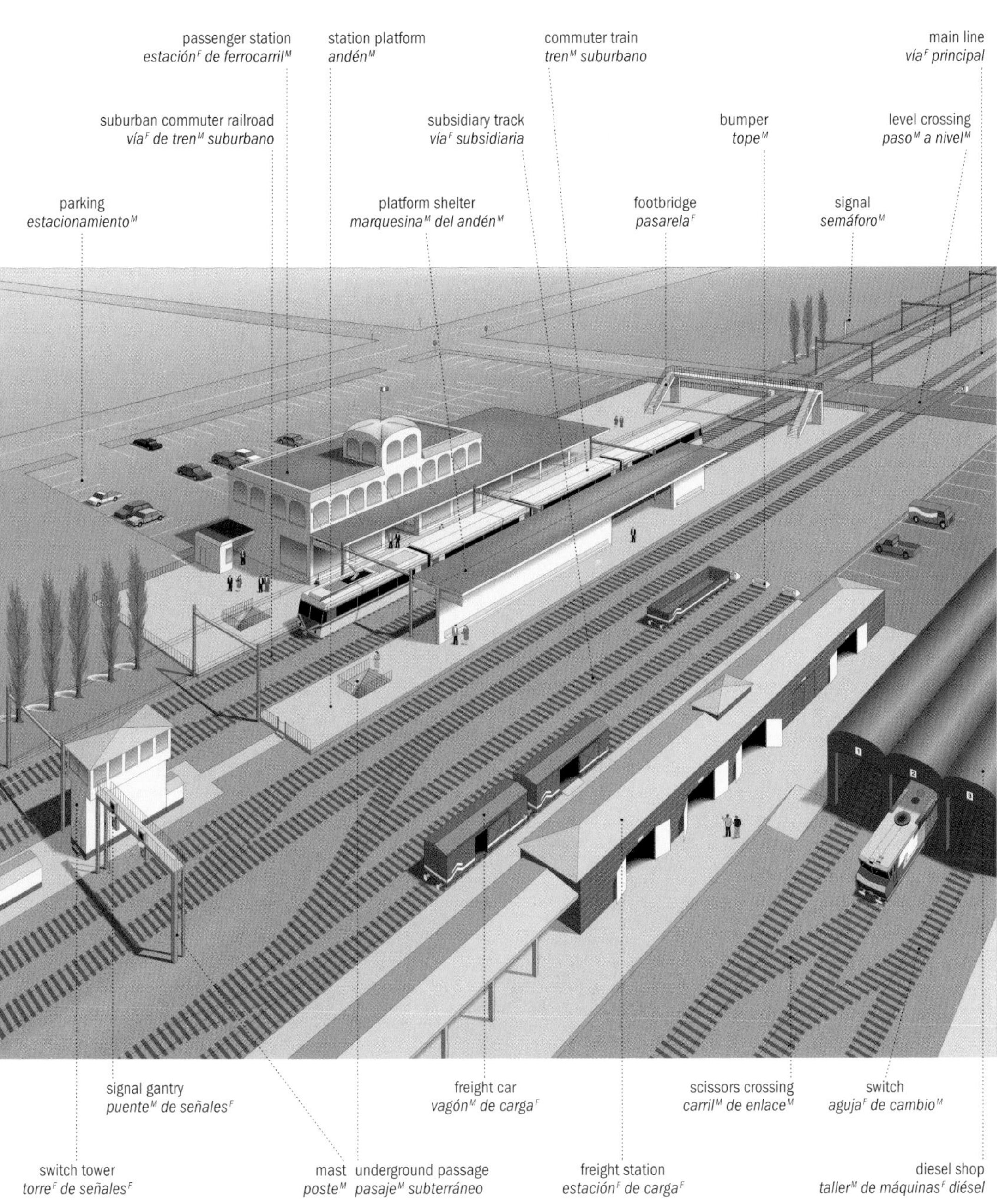
passenger station
estación^F de ferrocarril^M
station platform
andén^M
commuter train
tren^M suburbano
main line
vía^F principal
suburban commuter railroad
vía^F de tren^M suburbano
subsidiary track
vía^F subsidiaria
bumper
tope^M
level crossing
paso^M a nivel^M
parking
estacionamiento^M
platform shelter
marquesina^M del andén^M
footbridge
pasarela^F
signal
semáforo^M
signal gantry
puente^M de señales^F
freight car
vagón^M de carga^F
scissors crossing
carril^M de enlace^M
switch
aguja^F de cambio^M
switch tower
torre^F de señales^F
mast
poste^M
underground passage
pasaje^M subterráneo
freight station
estación^F de carga^F
diesel shop
taller^M de máquinas^F diésel

high-speed train

tren[M] de alta velocidad[F]

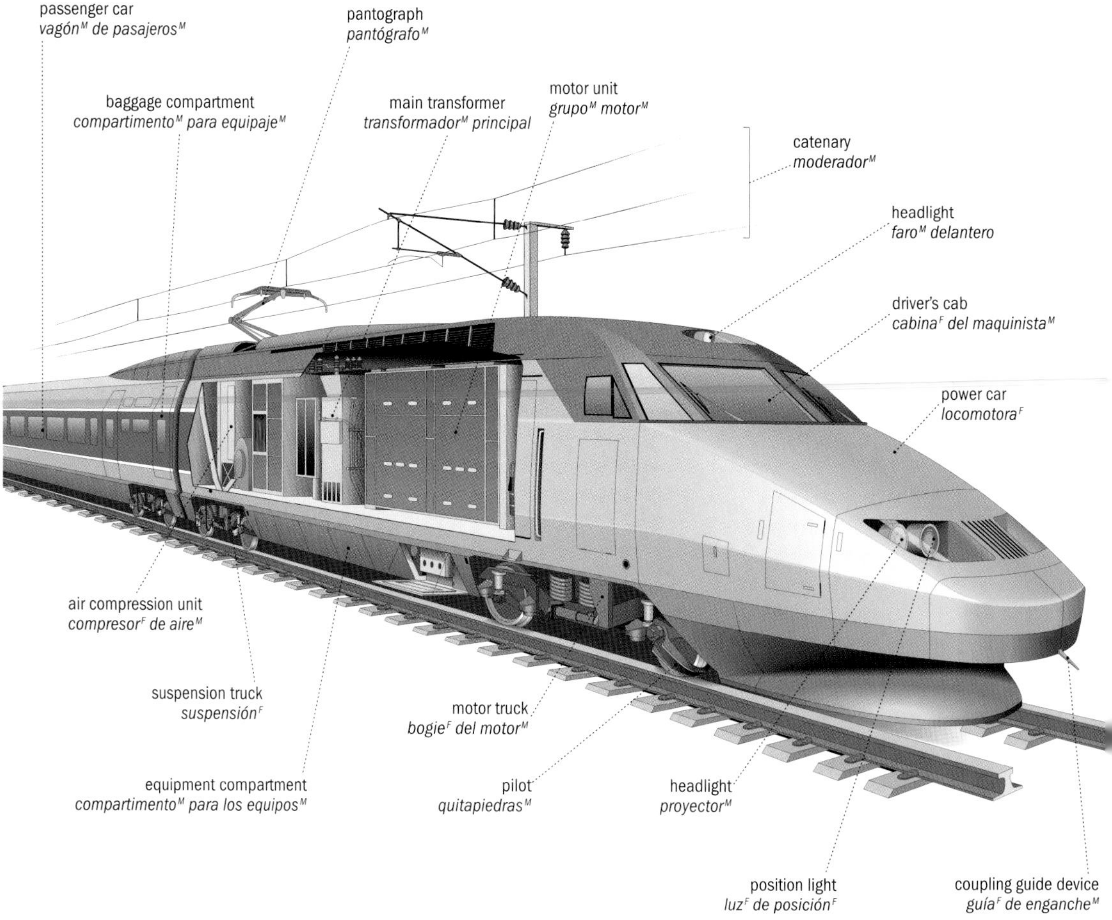

passenger car
vagón[M] de pasajeros[M]
pantograph
pantógrafo[M]
baggage compartment
compartimento[M] para equipaje[M]
main transformer
transformador[M] principal
motor unit
grupo[M] motor[M]
catenary
moderador[M]
headlight
faro[M] delantero
driver's cab
cabina[F] del maquinista[M]
power car
locomotora[F]
air compression unit
compresor[F] de aire[M]
suspension truck
suspensión[F]
motor truck
bogie[F] del motor[M]
equipment compartment
compartimento[M] para los equipos[M]
pilot
quitapiedras[M]
headlight
proyector[M]
position light
luz[F] de posición[F]
coupling guide device
guía[F] de enganche[M]

types of passenger cars

vagones[M] de pasajeros[M]

sleeping car
coche[M] cama[F]
dining car
vagón[M] comedor[M]
coach car
vagón[M] de pasajeros[M]

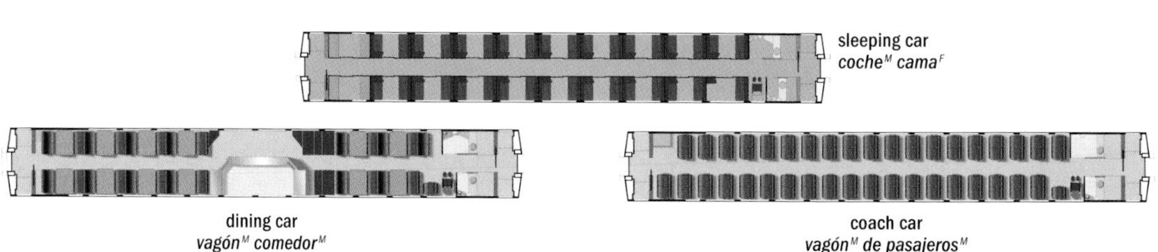

diesel-electric locomotive

locomotora[F] diésel eléctrica

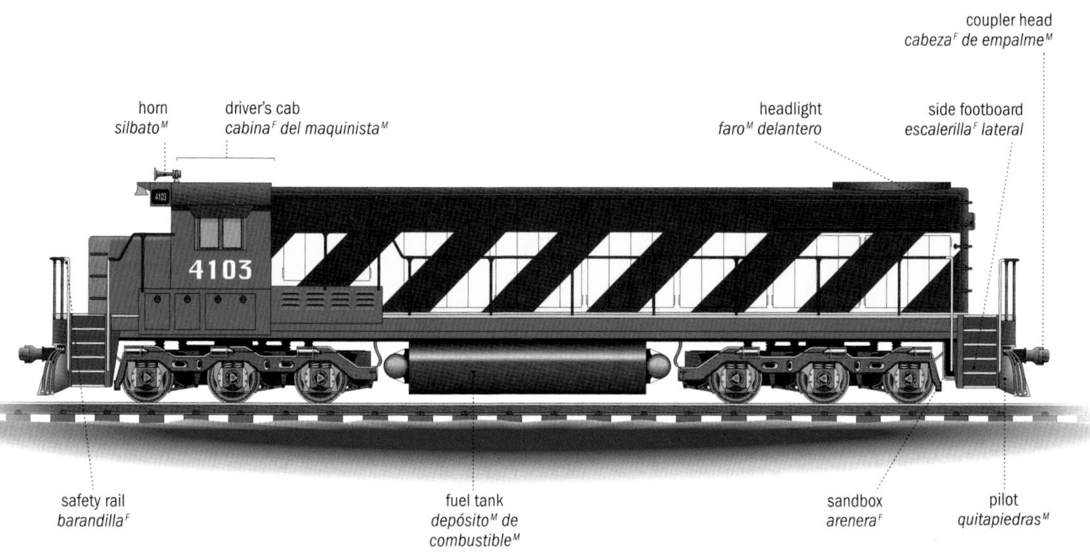

examples of freight cars

ejemplos[M] de vagones[M]

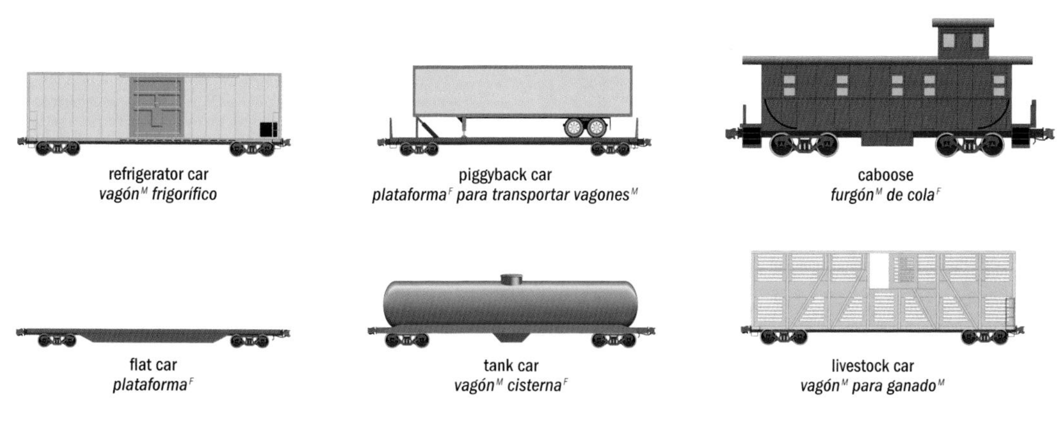

refrigerator car
vagón[M] frigorífico

piggyback car
plataforma[F] para transportar vagones[M]

caboose
furgón[M] de cola[F]

flat car
plataforma[F]

tank car
vagón[M] cisterna[F]

livestock car
vagón[M] para ganado[M]

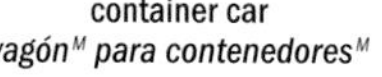

container car
vagón[M] para contenedores[M]

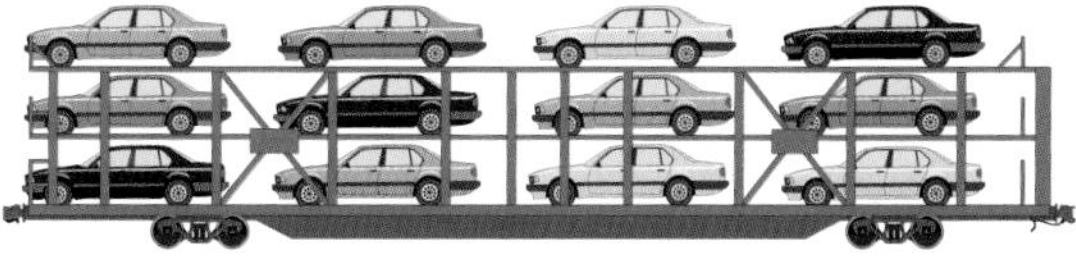

automobile car
vagón[M] para automóviles[M]

subway

metro[M]

subway station
estación[F] de metro[M]

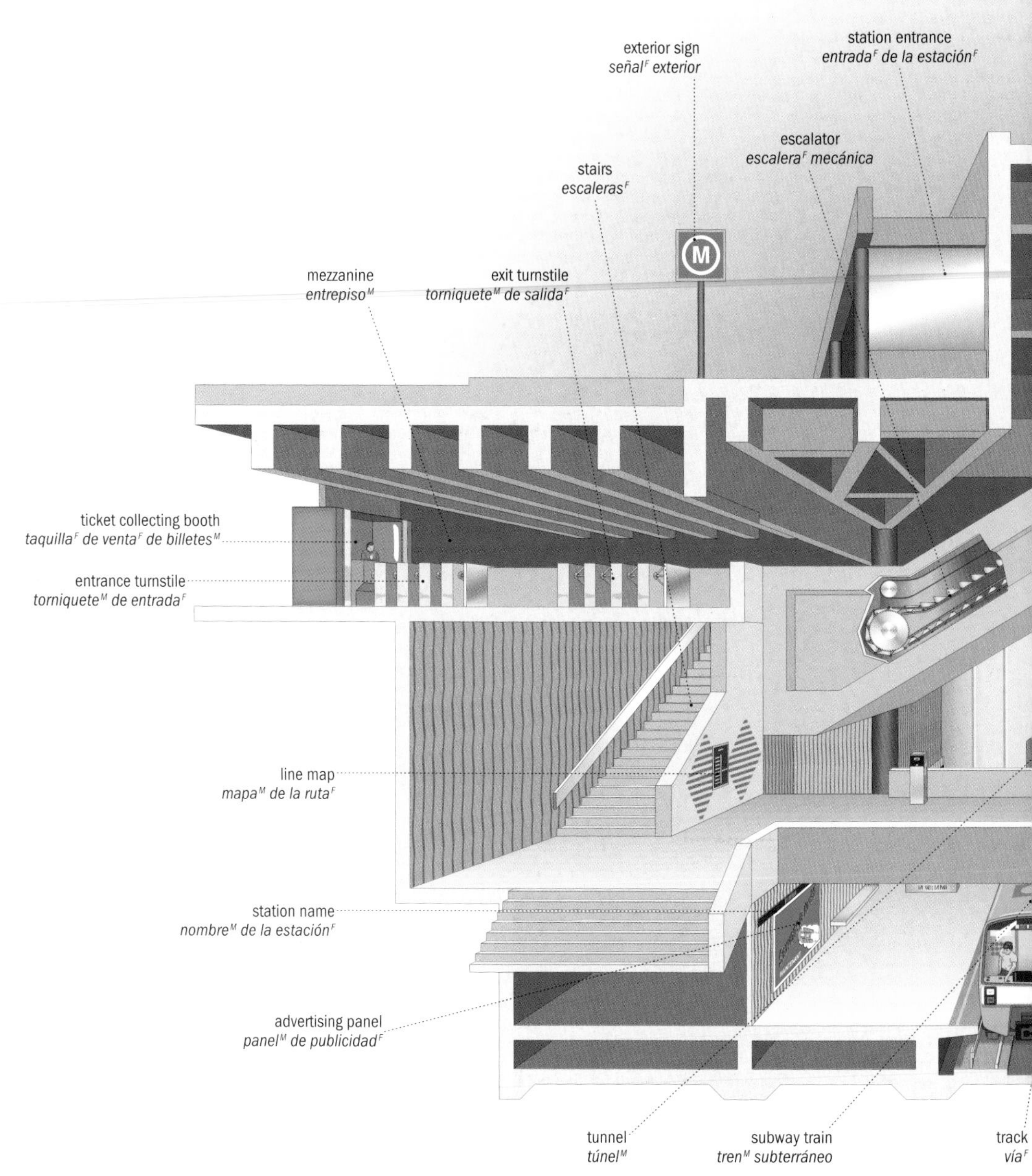
exterior sign
señal[F] exterior
station entrance
entrada[F] de la estación[F]
escalator
escalera[F] mecánica
stairs
escaleras[F]
mezzanine
entrepiso[M]
exit turnstile
torniquete[M] de salida[F]
ticket collecting booth
taquilla[F] de venta[F] de billetes[M]
entrance turnstile
torniquete[M] de entrada[F]
line map
mapa[M] de la ruta[F]
station name
nombre[M] de la estación[F]
advertising panel
panel[M] de publicidad[F]
tunnel
túnel[M]
subway train
tren[M] subterráneo
track
vía[F]

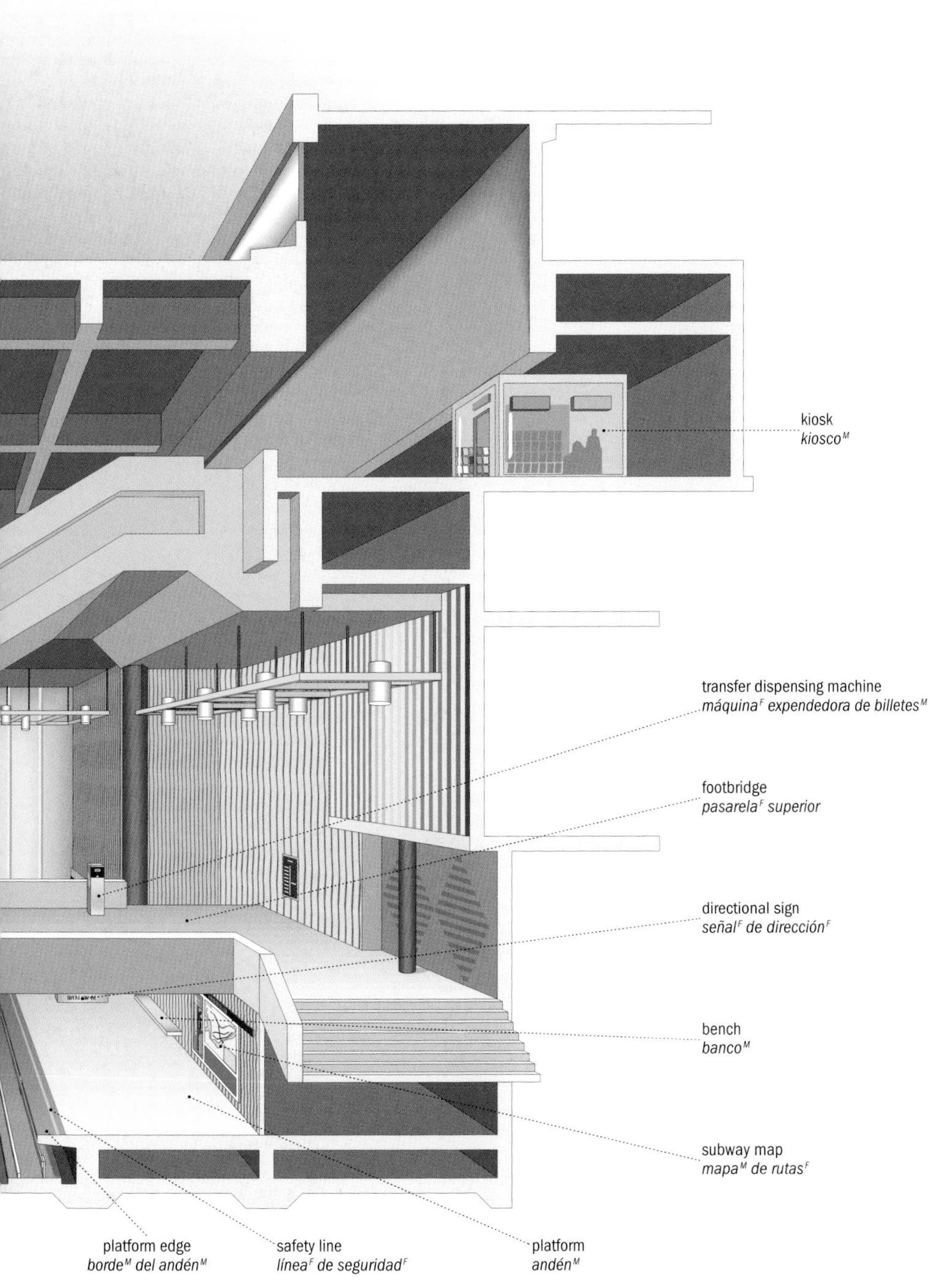
kiosk
kiosco[M]
transfer dispensing machine
máquina[F] *expendedora de billetes*[M]
footbridge
pasarela[F] *superior*
directional sign
señal[F] *de dirección*[F]
bench
banco[M]
subway map
mapa[M] *de rutas*[F]
platform edge
borde[M] *del andén*[M]
safety line
línea[F] *de seguridad*[F]
platform
andén[M]

subway

passenger car
***vagón*[M] *de pasajeros*[M]**

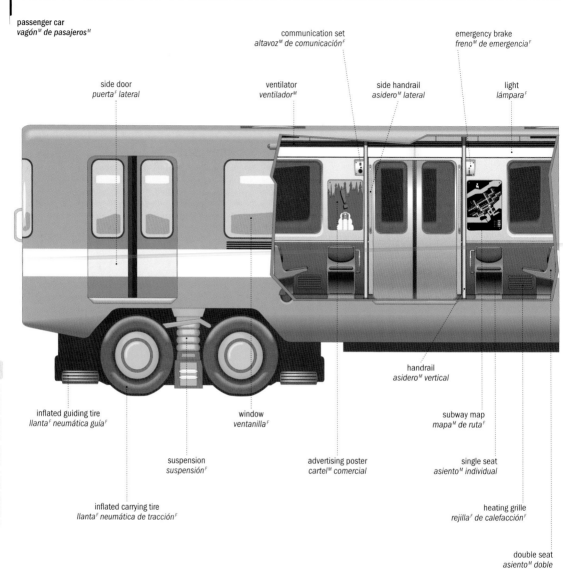

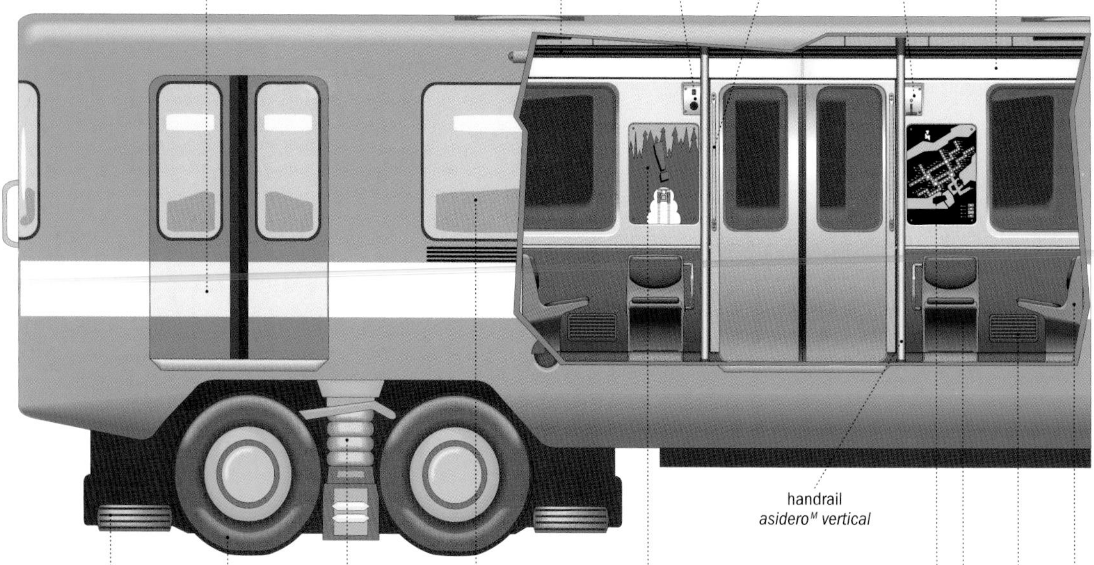

communication set
altavoz[M] *de comunicación*[F]
emergency brake
freno[M] *de emergencia*[F]
side door
puerta[F] *lateral*
ventilator
ventilador[M]
side handrail
asidero[M] *lateral*
light
lámpara[F]
handrail
asidero[M] *vertical*
inflated guiding tire
llanta[F] *neumática guía*[F]
window
ventanilla[F]
subway map
mapa[M] *de ruta*[F]
suspension
suspensión[F]
advertising poster
cartel[M] *comercial*
single seat
asiento[M] *individual*
inflated carrying tire
llanta[F] *neumática de tracción*[F]
heating grille
rejilla[F] *de calefacción*[F]
double seat
asiento[M] *doble*

subway train
tren*[M] *subterráneo

motor car
vagón[M] *máquina*[F]
trailer car
coche[M] *de tracción*[F]
motor car
vagón[M] *máquina*[F]

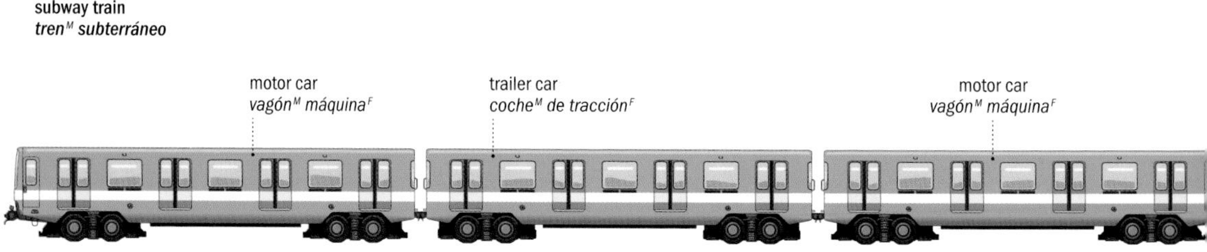

harbor

puerto[M]

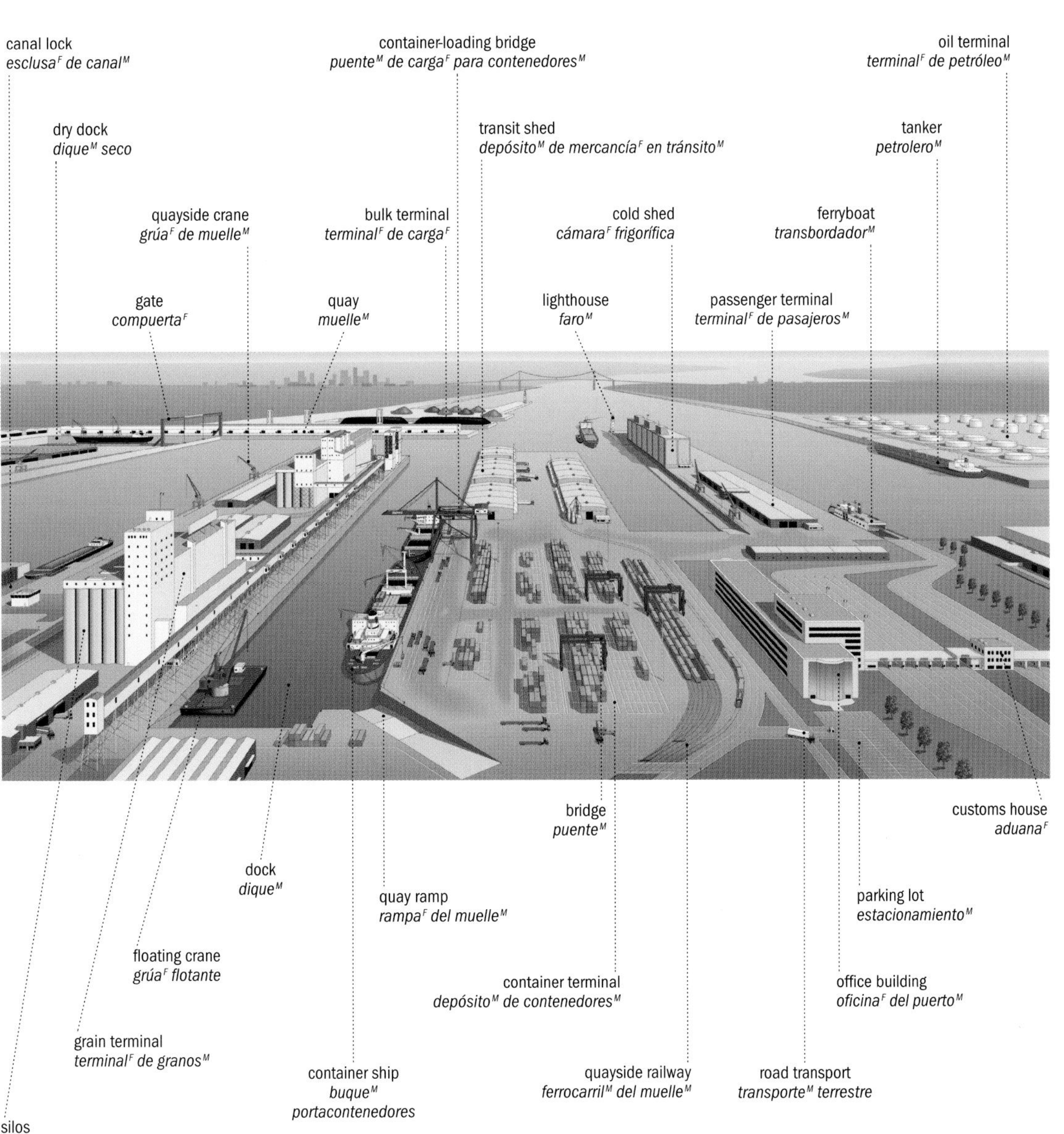
canal lock
esclusa[F] de canal[M]
container-loading bridge
puente[M] de carga[F] para contenedores[M]
oil terminal
terminal[F] de petróleo[M]
dry dock
dique[M] seco
transit shed
depósito[M] de mercancía[F] en tránsito[M]
tanker
petrolero[M]
quayside crane
grúa[F] de muelle[M]
bulk terminal
terminal[F] de carga[F]
cold shed
cámara[F] frigorífica
ferryboat
transbordador[M]
gate
compuerta[F]
quay
muelle[M]
lighthouse
faro[M]
passenger terminal
terminal[F] de pasajeros[M]
bridge
puente[M]
customs house
aduana[F]
dock
dique[M]
quay ramp
rampa[F] del muelle[M]
parking lot
estacionamiento[M]
floating crane
grúa[F] flotante
container terminal
depósito[M] de contenedores[M]
office building
oficina[F] del puerto[M]
grain terminal
terminal[F] de granos[M]
container ship
buque[M] portacontenedores
quayside railway
ferrocarril[M] del muelle[M]
road transport
transporte[M] terrestre
silos
silos[M]

examples of boats and ships

ejemplos^M de barcos^M y embarcaciones^F

drill ship
barco^M perforador

derrick
torre^F de perforación^F

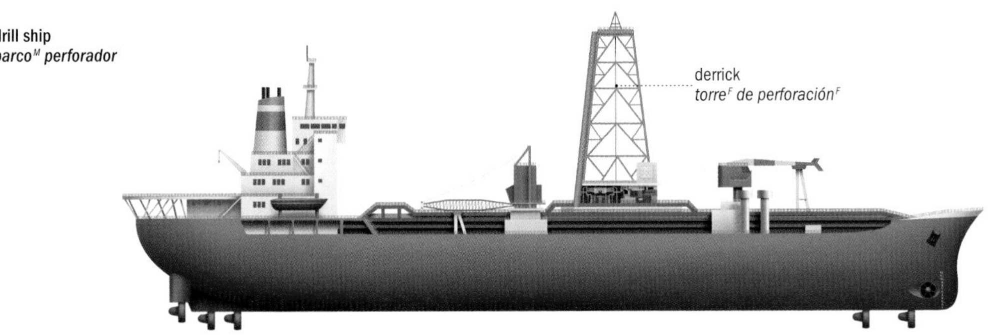

bulk carrier
buque^M de carga^F

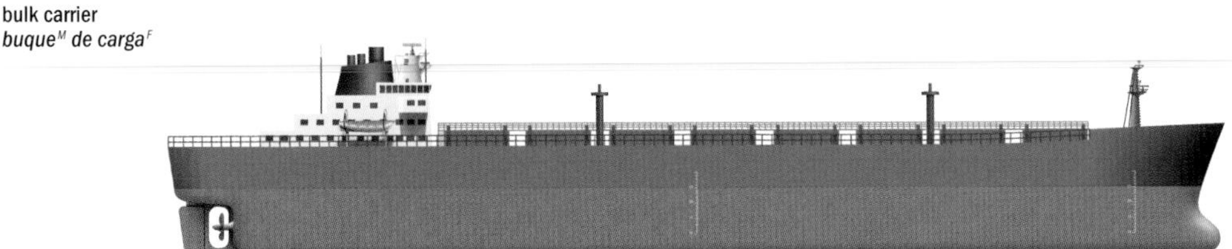

container ship
carguero^M portacontenedores

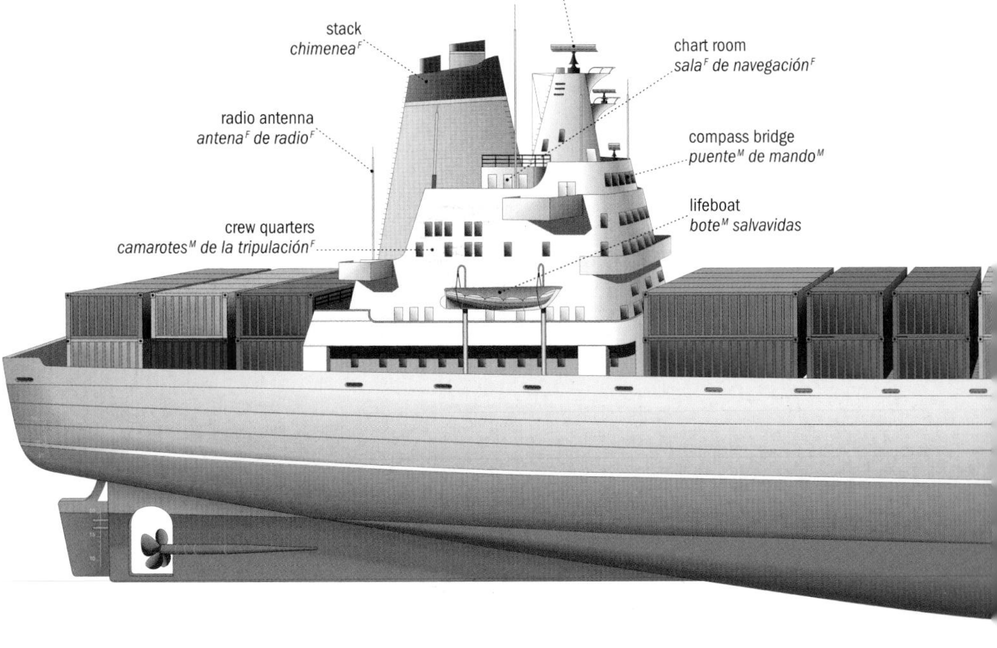

radar
radar^M
stack
chimenea^F
chart room
sala^F de navegación^F
radio antenna
antena^F de radio^F
compass bridge
puente^M de mando^M
lifeboat
bote^M salvavidas
crew quarters
camarotes^M de la tripulación^F

hovercraft
aerodeslizador**M **(hovercraft**M**)

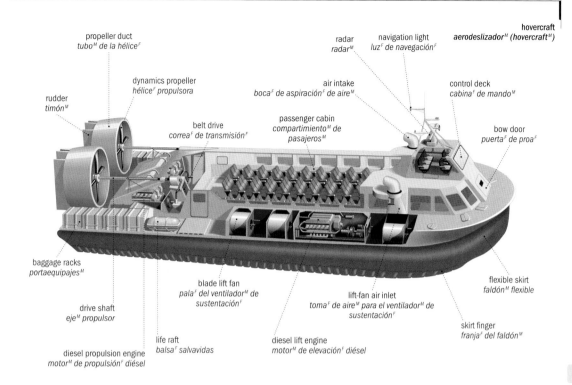

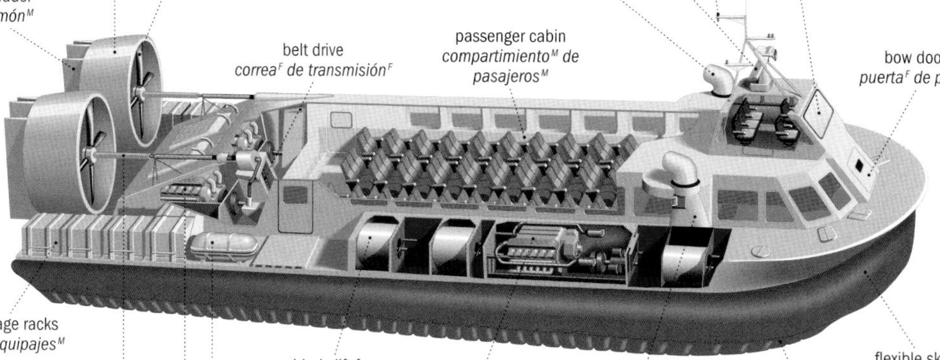

propeller duct
tuboM de la héliceF
radar
radarM
navigation light
luzF de navegaciónF
dynamics propeller
héliceF propulsora
air intake
bocaF de aspiraciónF de aireM
control deck
cabinaF de mandoM
rudder
timónM
passenger cabin
compartimientoM de pasajerosM
belt drive
correaF de transmisiónF
bow door
puertaF de proaF
baggage racks
portaequipajesM
flexible skirt
faldónM flexible
blade lift fan
palaF del ventiladorM de sustentaciónF
lift-fan air inlet
tomaF de aireM para el ventiladorM de sustentaciónF
drive shaft
ejeM propulsor
skirt finger
franjaF del faldónM
life raft
balsaF salvavidas
diesel lift engine
motorM de elevaciónF diésel
diesel propulsion engine
motorM de propulsiónF diésel

masthead light
luzF de topeM
container
contenedorM
container hold
bodegaF de contenedoresM
forecastle
castilloM de proaF
anchor-windlass room
escobénM

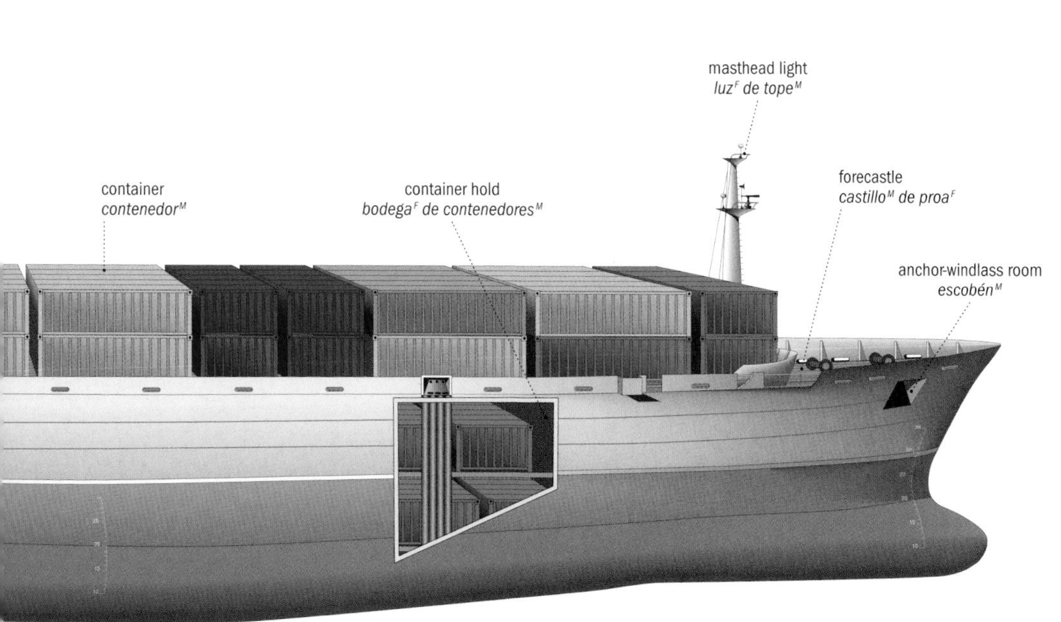

examples of boats and ships

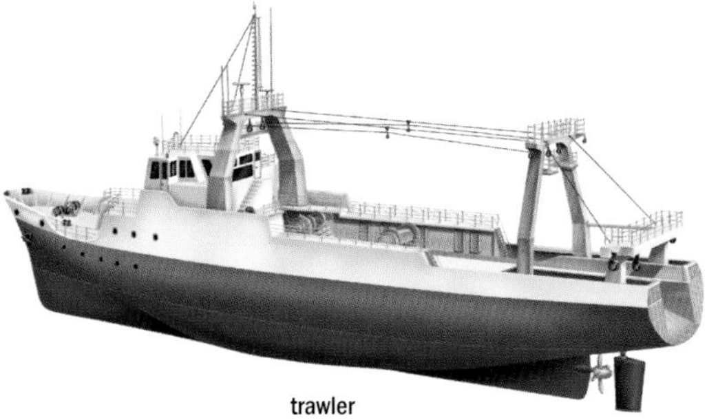

trawler
trainera[F]

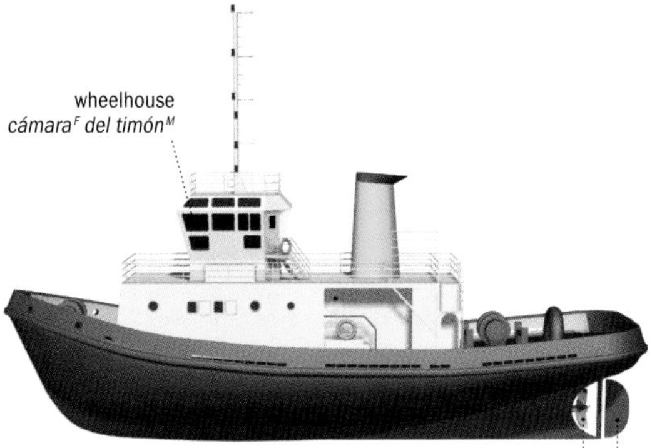

wheelhouse
cámara[F] del timón[M]
propeller
hélice[F]
rudder blade
pala[F] de timón[M]

tug
remolcador[M]

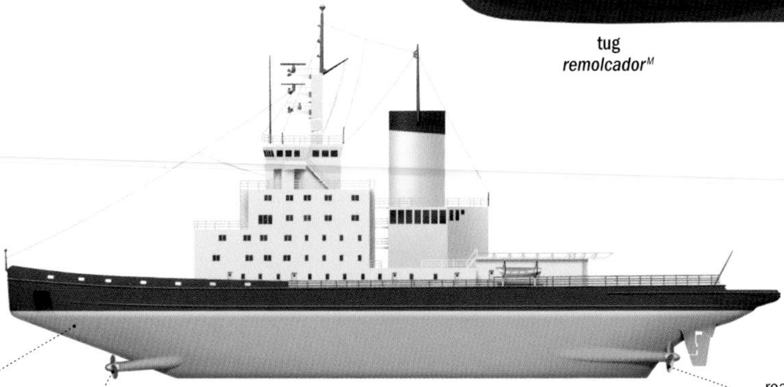

stem
proa[F]
stem propeller
hélice[F] de proa[F]
rear propeller
hélice[F] posterior

ice breaker
rompehielos[M]

tanker
petrolero[M]

radar mast
palo[M] del radar[M]
radio antenna
antena[F] de radio[F]
separator
separador[M]
davit
pescante[M]
gangway
pasarela[F]
engine control room
sala[F] de máquinas[F]
rudder
timón[M]
propeller
hélice[F]
pump room
sala[F] de bombeo[M]
transverse bulkhead
pared[F] transversal de contención[F]
lengthwise bulkhead
tabique[M] de contención[M] longitudinal

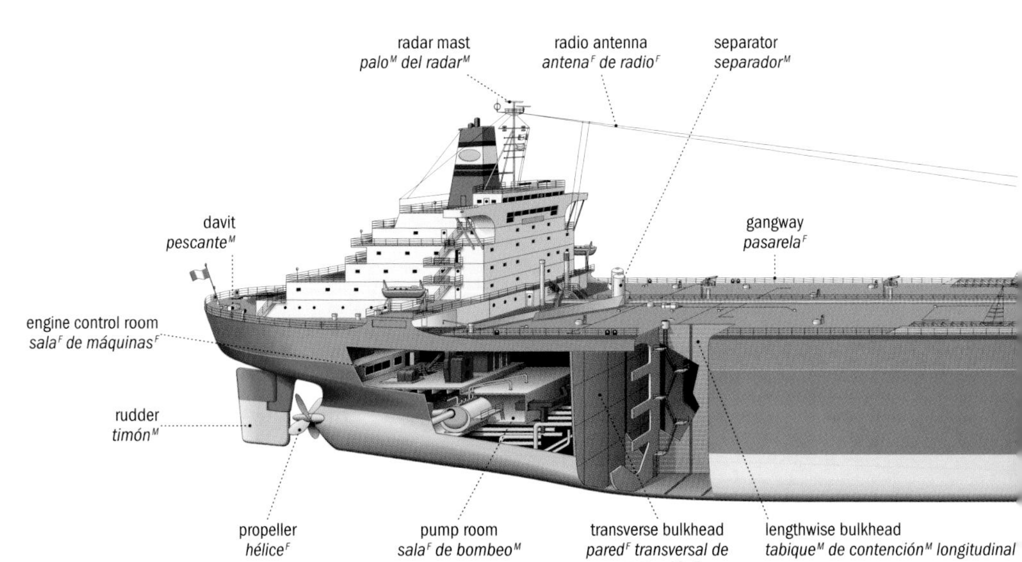

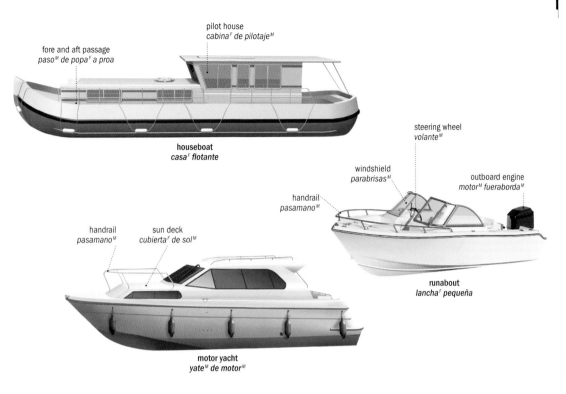

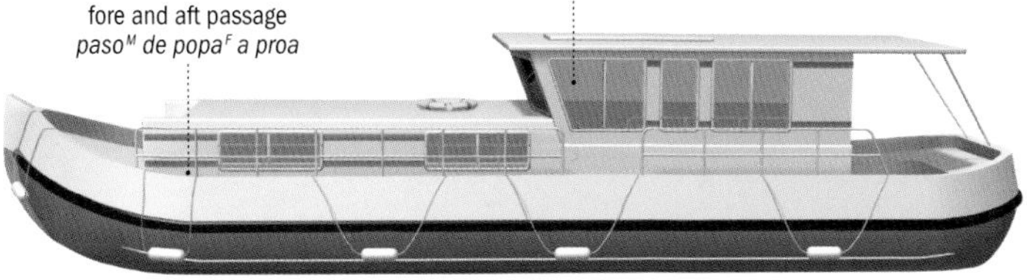

pilot house
cabina[F] de pilotaje[M]
fore and aft passage
paso[M] de popa[F] a proa

houseboat
casa[F] flotante

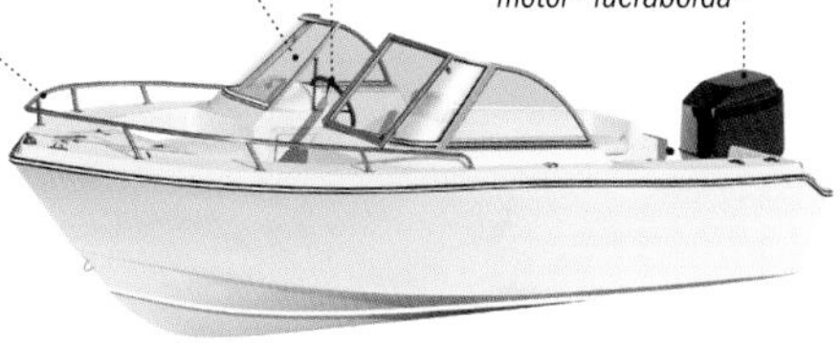

steering wheel
volante[M]
windshield
parabrisas[M]
outboard engine
motor[M] fueraborda[M]
handrail
pasamano[M]

runabout
lancha[F] pequeña

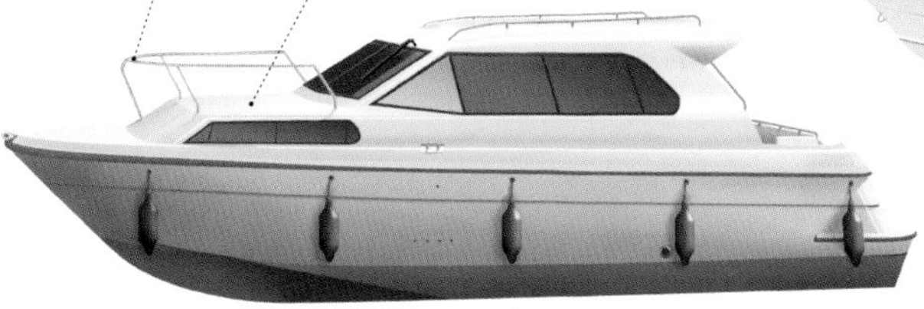

handrail
pasamano[M]
sun deck
cubierta[F] de sol[M]

motor yacht
yate[M] de motor[M]

derrick
grúa[F]
derrick mast
poste[M] de la grúa[F]
tank hatch
compuerta[F] de la cisterna[F]
air relief valve
válvula[F] de liberación[F] de aire[M]
foam monitor
cañón[M] expulsor de espuma[F]
foremast
palo[M] de proa[F]
mooring winch
amarra[F]
bitt
bita[F]
main deck
cubierta[F] principal
tank
tanque[M]
crossover cargo deck line
zona[F] de traspaso[M] de carga[F]
wall side
pared[F] lateral
web frame
cuaderna[F]
center keelson
contraquilla[F]
bulb
bulbo[M]

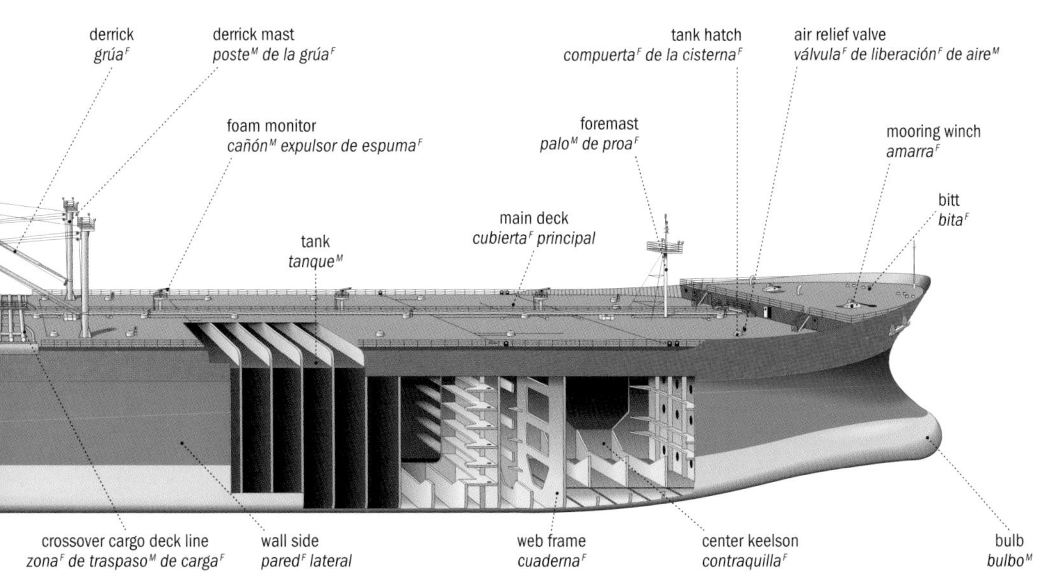

examples of boats and ships

ferry
transbordador[M]

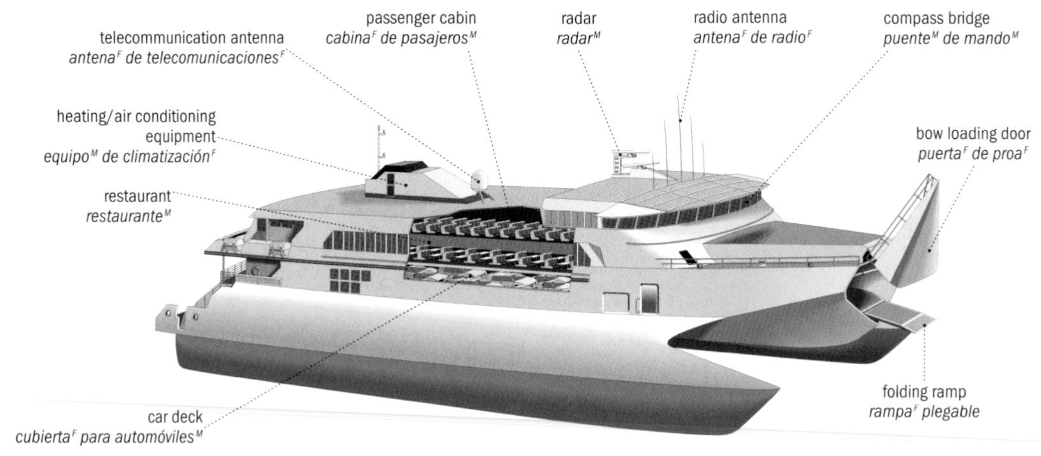

passenger liner
buque[M] trasatlántico

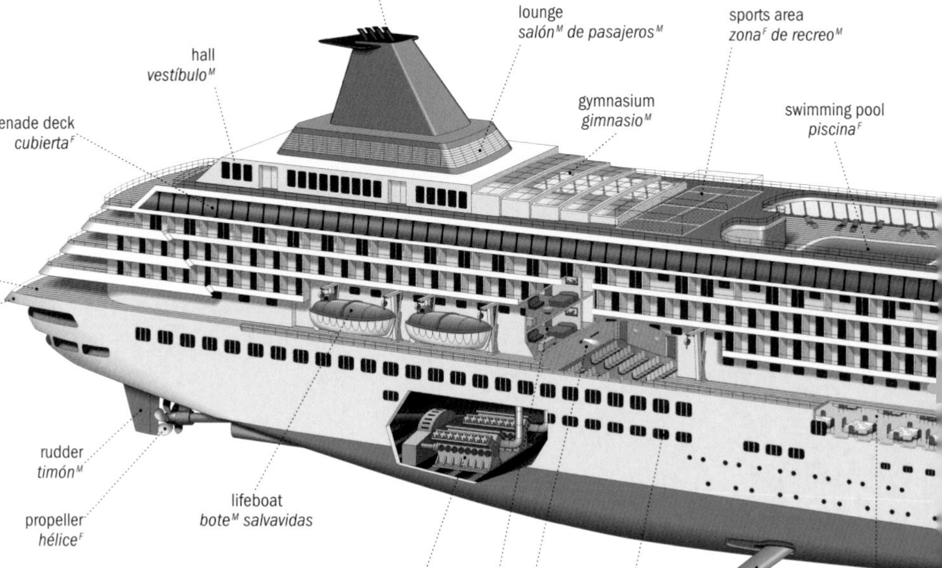

funnel
chimenea[F]

lounge
salón[M] de pasajeros[M]

sports area
zona[F] de recreo[M]

hall
vestíbulo[M]

gymnasium
gimnasio[M]

swimming pool
piscina[F]

promenade deck
cubierta[F]

quarter-deck
cubierta[F] de popa[F]

stern
popa[F]

rudder
timón[M]

propeller
hélice[F]

lifeboat
bote[M] salvavidas

engine room
sala[F] de máquinas[F]

porthole
ojo[M] de buey[M]

dining room
comedor[M]

cabin
camarote[M]

movie theater
sala[F] de cine[M]

stabilizer fin
aleta[F] estabilizadora

TRANSPORT AND MACHINERY

examples of boats and ships

hydrofoil boat
hidróptero [M]

radio antenna
antena[F] *de radio*[F]
radar
radar[M]
life buoy
salvavidas[M]
passenger cabin
cabina[F] *de pasajeros*[M]
compass bridge
puente[M] *de mando*[M]
strut
soporte[M]
propeller shaft
árbol[M] *de la hélice*[F]
surface-piercing foils
aleta[F] *de penetración*[F] *superficial*
rear foil
ala[F] *de popa*[F]
propeller
hélice[F]
front foil
aleta[F] *de proa*[F]

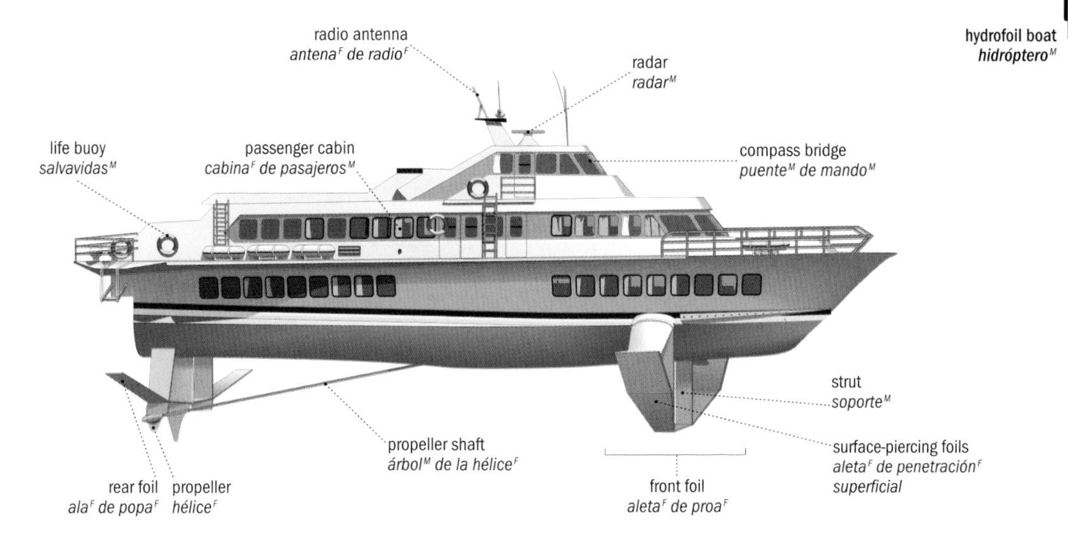

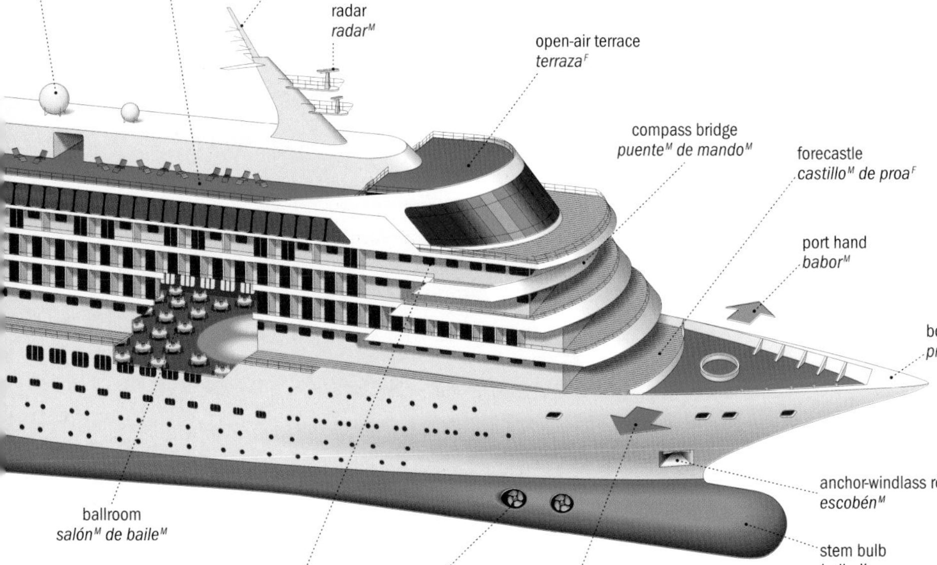

telecommunication antenna
antena[F] *de telecomunicaciones*[F]
radio antenna
antena[F] *de radio*[F]
sundeck
cubierta[F] *superior*
radar
radar[M]
open-air terrace
terraza[F]
compass bridge
puente[M] *de mando*[M]
forecastle
castillo[M] *de proa*[F]
port hand
babor[M]
bow
proa[F]
anchor-windlass room
escobén[M]
ballroom
salón[M] *de baile*[M]
stem bulb
bulbo[M]
captain's quarters
camarote[M] *del capitán*[M]
bow thruster
propulsor[M] *de proa*[F]
starboard hand
estribor[M]

airport

aeropuerto[M]

high-speed exit taxiway
salida[F] de la pista[F] de alta velocidad[F]
control tower cab
cabina[F] de la torre[F] de control[M]
control tower
torre[F] de control[M]
access road
carretera[F] de acceso[M]
taxiway
pista[F] de rodaje[M]
by-pass taxiway
pista[F] de enlace[M]
taxiway
pista[F] de rodaje[M]
apron
pista[F] de estacionamiento[M]
service road
ruta[F] de servicio[M]
apron
pista[F] de estacionamiento[M]

passenger terminal
terminal^F de pasajeros^M
maintenance hangar
hangar^M de mantenimiento^M
parking area
parque^M de estacionamiento^M
telescopic corridor
pasarela^F telescópico
service area
zona^F de servicio^M
boarding walkway
túnel^M de embarque^M
taxiway line
línea^F de pista^F
radial passenger-loading area
terminal^F satélite de pasajeros^M

airport

passenger terminal
terminal[M] de pasajeros[M]

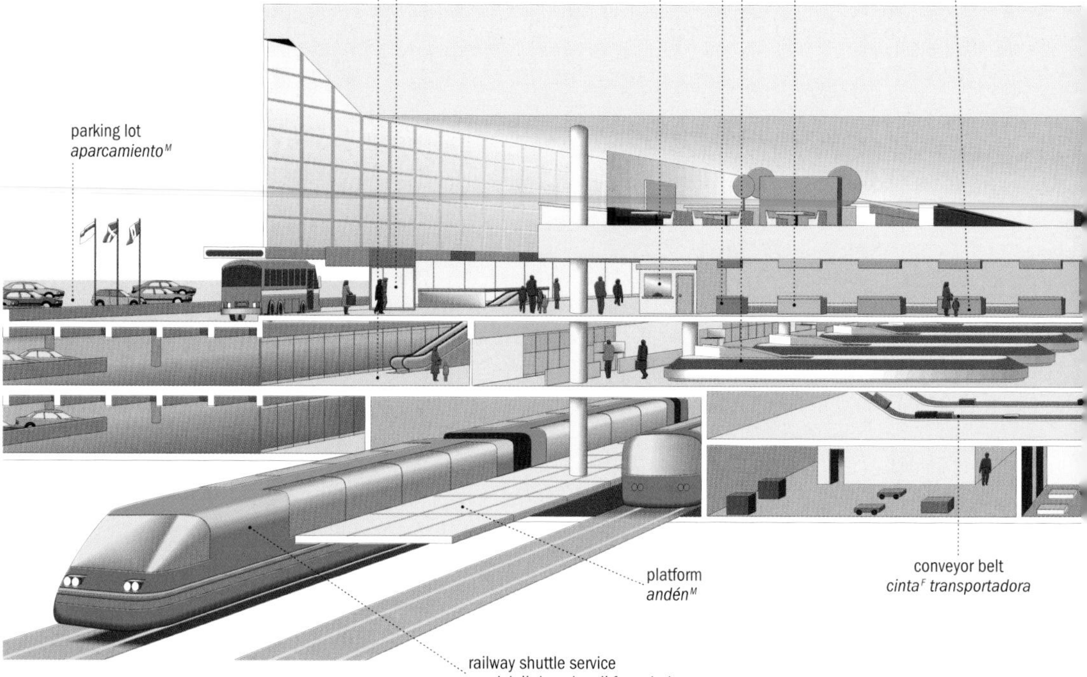

information counter
puesto[M] de información[F]
baggage claim area
entrega[F] de equipaje[M]
hotel reservation desk
oficina[F] de reservas[F] de hotel[M]
ticket counter
mostrador[M]
lobby
vestíbulo[M]
automatically controlled door
puerta[F] automática
baggage check-in counter
facturación[F] de equipaje[M]
parking lot
aparcamiento[M]
platform
andén[M]
conveyor belt
cinta[F] transportadora
railway shuttle service
servicio[M] de enlace[M] ferroviario

runway
pista[F] de aterrizaje[M] y despegue[M]

holding area marking
señal[F] de zona[F] de espera[F]
runway designation marking
señal[F] de identificación[F] de pista[F]
runway center line markings
señal[F] de eje[M] de pista[F]
runway side stripe markings
señales[F] laterales de pista[F]

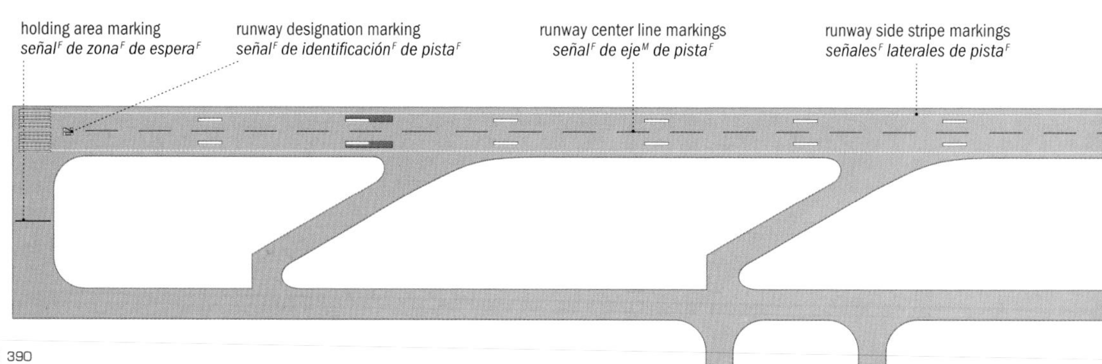

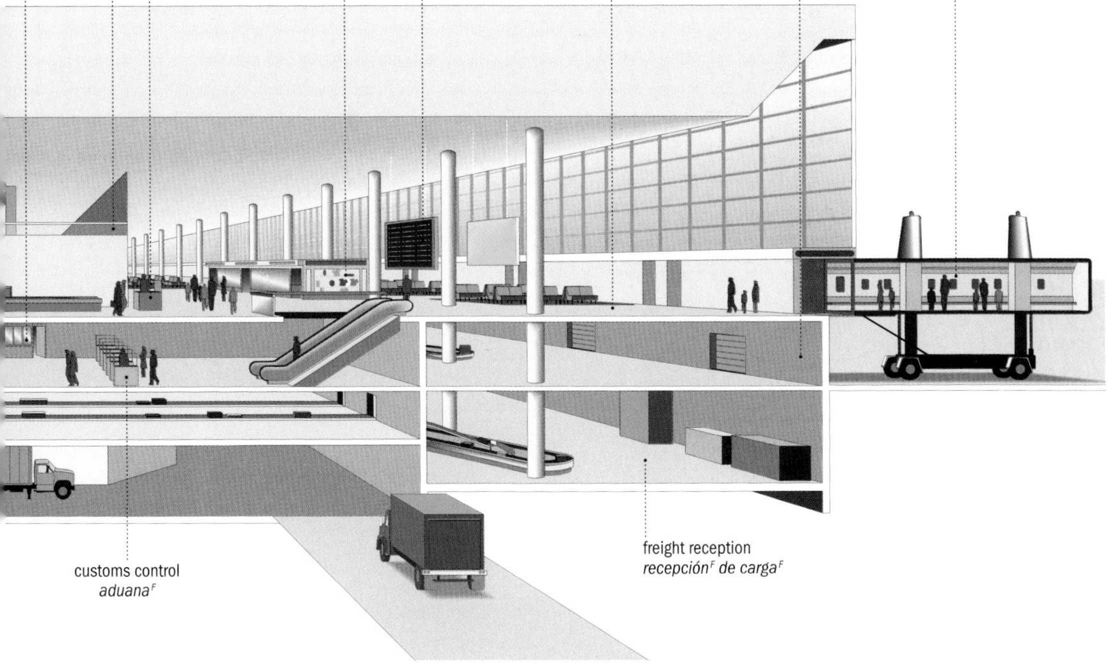

security check
control^M de seguridad^F
duty-free shop
tienda^F libre de impuestos^M
observation deck
mirador^M
flight information board
tablero^M de llegadas^F y salidas^F
freight expedition
expedición^F de carga^F
boarding room
sala^F de espera^F de embarque^M
passport control
control^M de pasaportes^M
passenger transfer vehicle
transbordador^M
freight reception
recepción^F de carga^F
customs control
aduana^F

exit taxiway
salida^F de la pista^F
runway touchdown zone marking
señal^F de zona^F de contacto^M de pista^F
runway threshold markings
señales^F de límite^M de la pista^F
fixed distance marking
señal^F de distancia^F fija

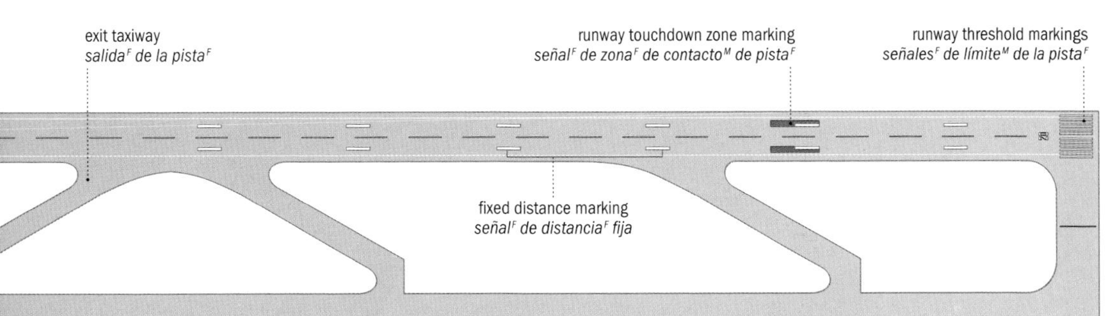

long-range jet

avión[M] turborreactor de pasajeros[M]

trailing edge
borde[M] de fuga[F]
aileron
alerón[M]
trailing-edge flap
aleta[F] del borde[M] de fuga[F]
spoiler
frenos[M]
antenna
antena[F]
upper deck
cubierta[F] superior
anticollision light
luz[F] anticolisión
flight deck
cabina[F] de mando[M]
windshield
parabrisas[M]
nose
morro[M]
door
puerta[F]
root rib
costilla[F] de encastre[M]
galley
cocina[F] de a bordo[M]
window
ventanilla[F]
wing rib
estructura[F] del ala[F]
weather radar
radar[M] de navegación[F]
first-class cabin
cabina[F] de primera clase[F]
nose landing gear
tren[M] de aterrizaje[M] delantero
spar
larguero[M]

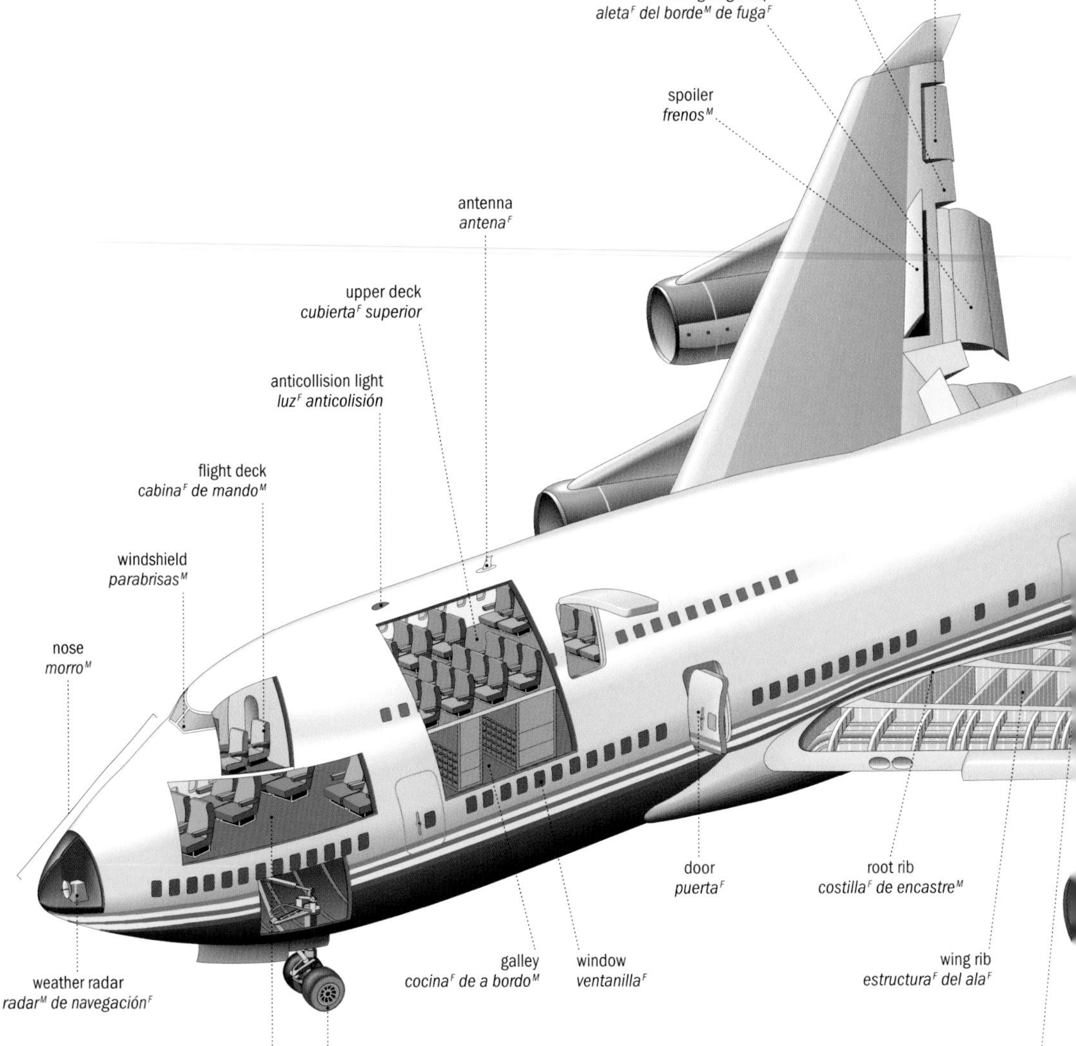

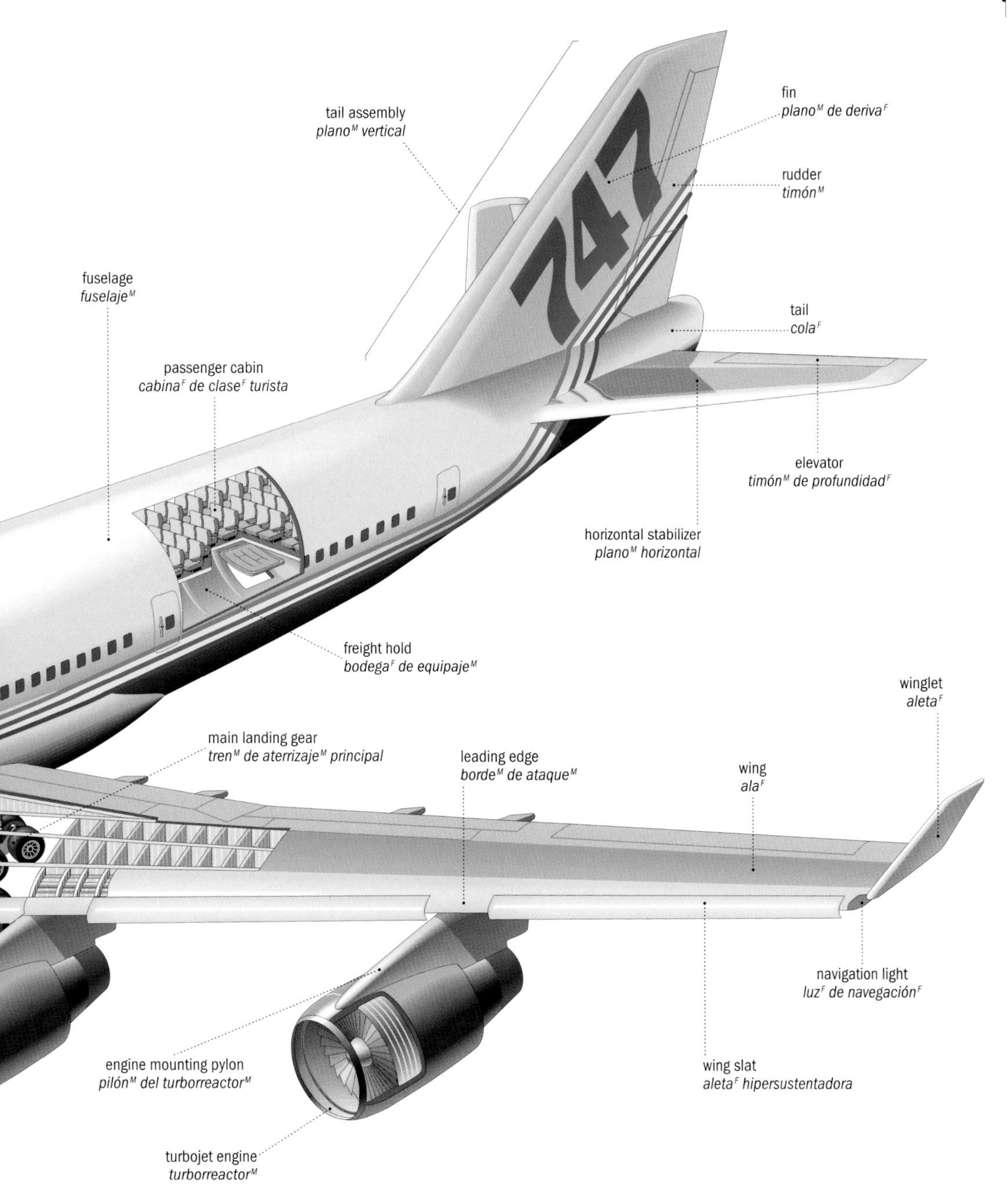
tail assembly
planoᴹ vertical
fin
planoᴹ de derivaᶠ
rudder
timónᴹ
fuselage
fuselajeᴹ
tail
colaᶠ
passenger cabin
cabinaᶠ de claseᶠ turista
elevator
timónᴹ de profundidadᶠ
horizontal stabilizer
planoᴹ horizontal
freight hold
bodegaᶠ de equipajeᴹ
winglet
aletaᶠ
main landing gear
trenᴹ de aterrizajeᴹ principal
leading edge
bordeᴹ de ataqueᴹ
wing
alaᶠ
navigation light
luzᶠ de navegaciónᶠ
engine mounting pylon
pilónᴹ del turborreactorᴹ
wing slat
aletaᶠ hipersustentadora
turbojet engine
turborreactorᴹ

examples of airplanes

ejemplos^M de aviones^M

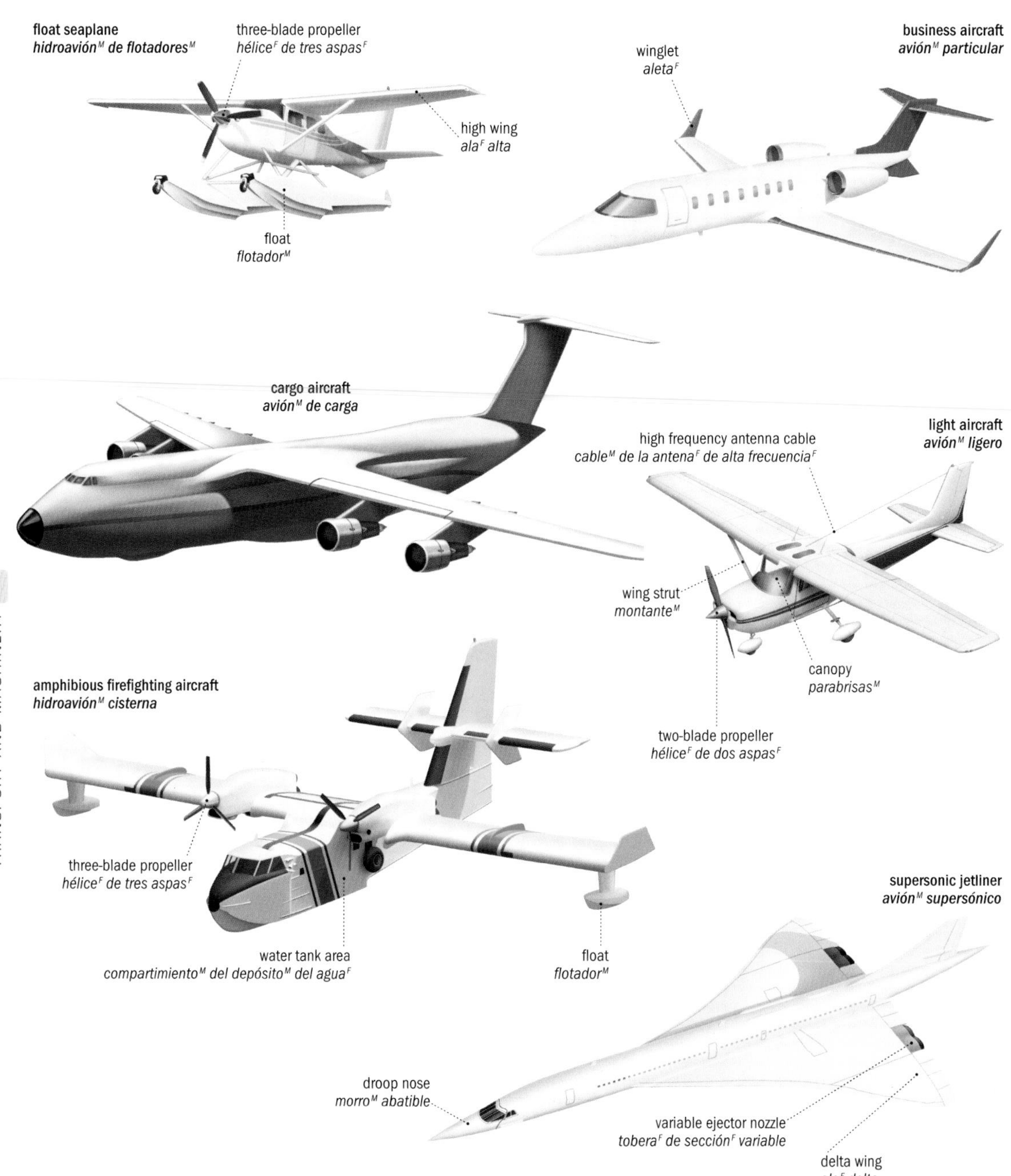
float seaplane
hidroavión^M de flotadores^M
three-blade propeller
hélice^F de tres aspas^F
high wing
ala^F alta
float
flotador^M
business aircraft
avión^M particular
winglet
aleta^F
cargo aircraft
avión^M de carga
light aircraft
avión^M ligero
high frequency antenna cable
cable^M de la antena^F de alta frecuencia^F
wing strut
montante^M
canopy
parabrisas^M
two-blade propeller
hélice^F de dos aspas^F
amphibious firefighting aircraft
hidroavión^M cisterna
three-blade propeller
hélice^F de tres aspas^F
water tank area
compartimiento^M del depósito^M del agua^F
float
flotador^M
supersonic jetliner
avión^M supersónico
droop nose
morro^M abatible
variable ejector nozzle
tobera^F de sección^F variable
delta wing
ala^F delta

TRANSPORT AND MACHINERY

movements of an airplane

movimientos^M de un avión^M

pitch
cabeceo^M
yaw
guiñada^F
roll
oscilación^M

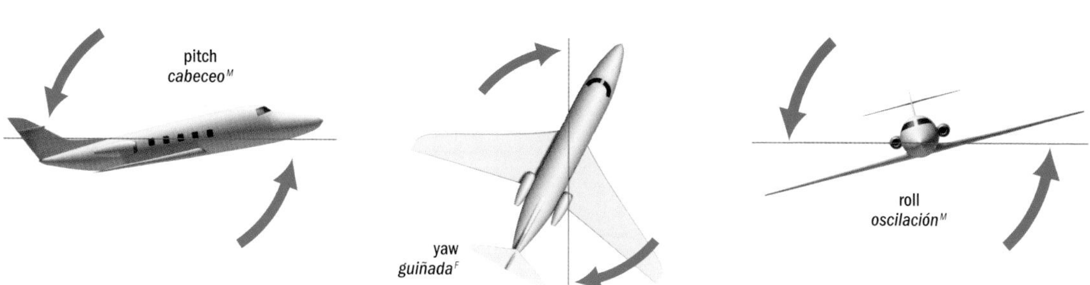

helicopter

helicóptero^M

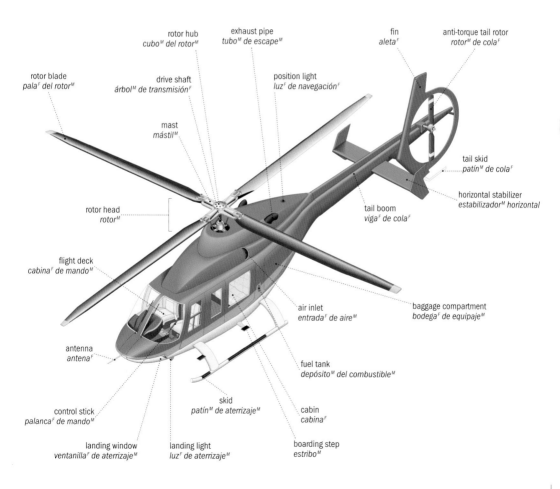

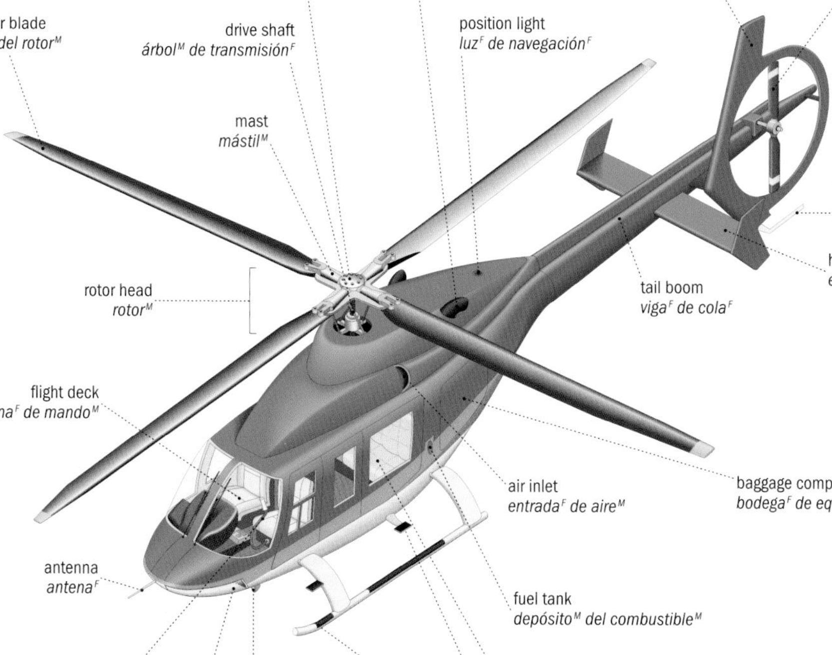

rotor hub
cubo^M del rotor^M
exhaust pipe
tubo^M de escape^M
fin
aleta^F
anti-torque tail rotor
rotor^M de cola^F
rotor blade
pala^F del rotor^M
drive shaft
árbol^M de transmisión^F
position light
luz^F de navegación^F
mast
mástil^M
tail skid
patín^M de cola^F
horizontal stabilizer
estabilizador^M horizontal
rotor head
rotor^M
tail boom
viga^F de cola^F
flight deck
cabina^F de mando^M
air inlet
entrada^F de aire^M
baggage compartment
bodega^F de equipaje^M
antenna
antena^F
fuel tank
depósito^M del combustible^M
skid
patín^M de aterrizaje^M
control stick
palanca^F de mando^M
cabin
cabina^F
landing window
ventanilla^F de aterrizaje^M
landing light
luz^F de aterrizaje^M
boarding step
estribo^M

material handling

manejo[M] de materiales[M]

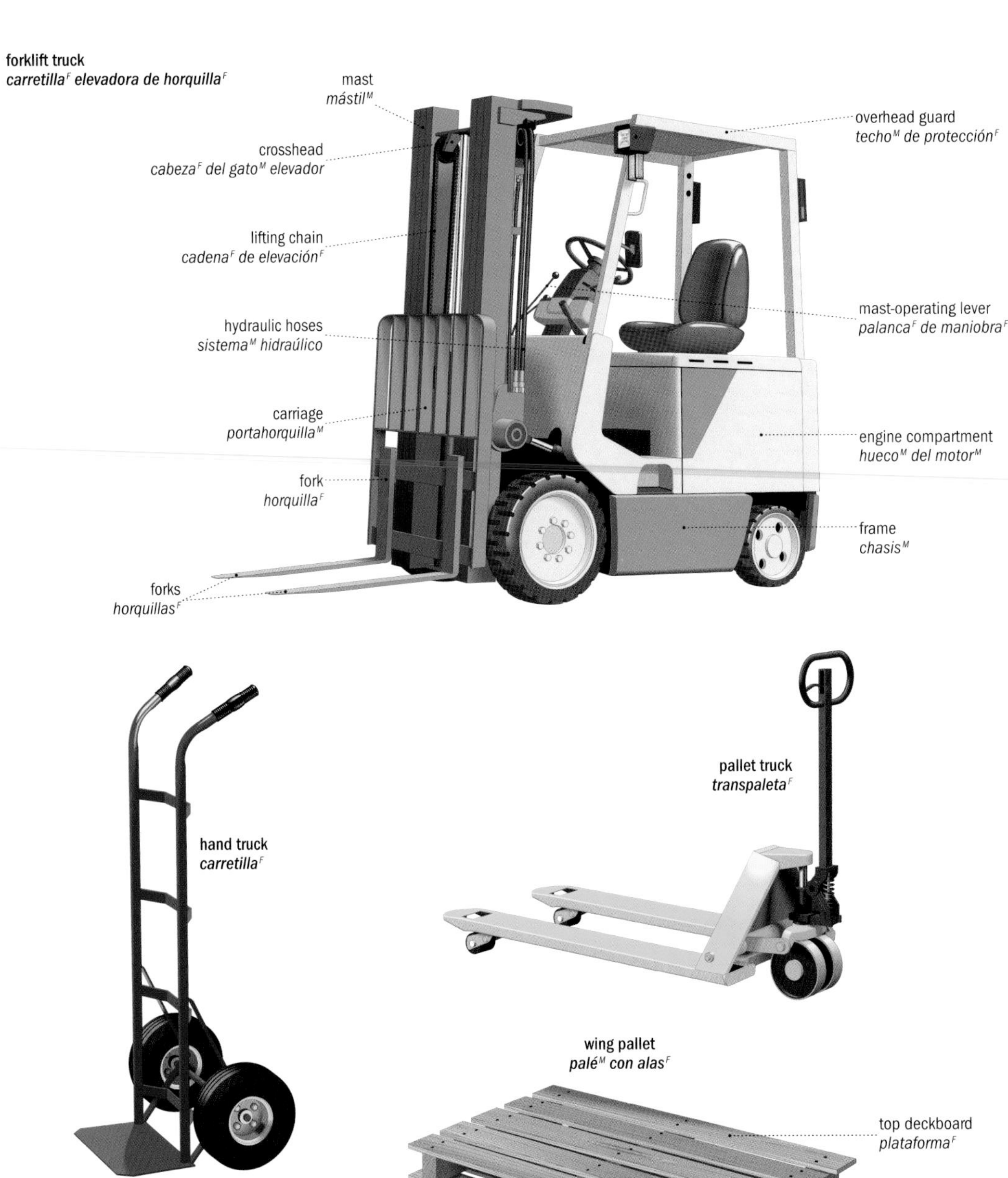
forklift truck
carretilla[F] elevadora de horquilla[F]
mast
mástil[M]
crosshead
cabeza[F] del gato[M] elevador
lifting chain
cadena[F] de elevación[F]
hydraulic hoses
sistema[M] hidraúlico
carriage
portahorquilla[M]
fork
horquilla[F]
forks
horquillas[F]
overhead guard
techo[M] de protección[F]
mast-operating lever
palanca[F] de maniobra[F]
engine compartment
hueco[M] del motor[M]
frame
chasis[M]
hand truck
carretilla[F]
pallet truck
transpaleta[F]
wing pallet
palé[M] con alas[F]
top deckboard
plataforma[F]
entry
entrada[F]
stringer
larguerillo[M]
bottom deckboard
plataforma[F] inferior

cranes
grúas^F

tower crane
grúa^F torre^F

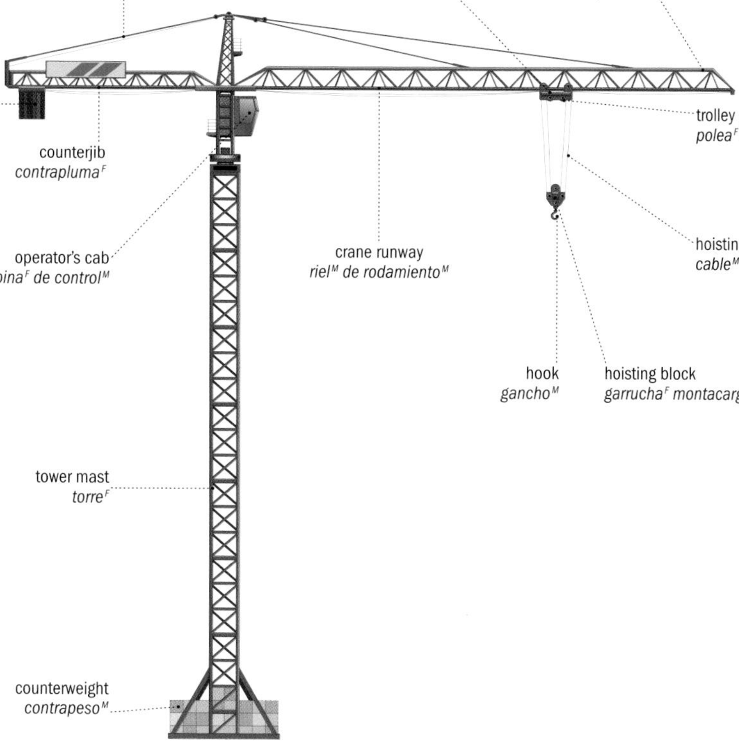

jib tie
tirante^M del pescante^M
trolley
montacargas^M
jib
pescante^M
counterjib ballast
contrapeso^M
trolley pulley
polea^F del montacargas^M
counterjib
contrapluma^F
operator's cab
cabina^F de control^M
crane runway
riel^M de rodamiento^M
hoisting rope
cable^M de elevación^F
hook
gancho^M
hoisting block
garrucha^F montacarga
tower mast
torre^F
counterweight
contrapeso^M

truck crane
grúa^F móvil

telescopic boom
brazo^M telescópico
elevating cylinder
cilindro^M elevador
operator's cab
cabina^F de mando^M
outrigger
estabilizador^M

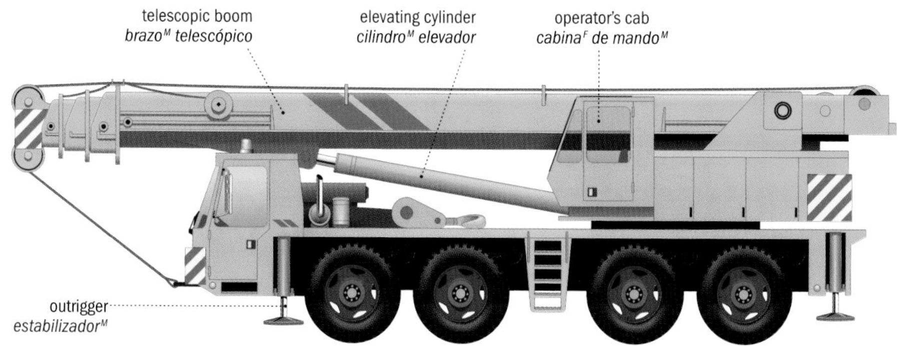

bulldozer

bulldozer[M]

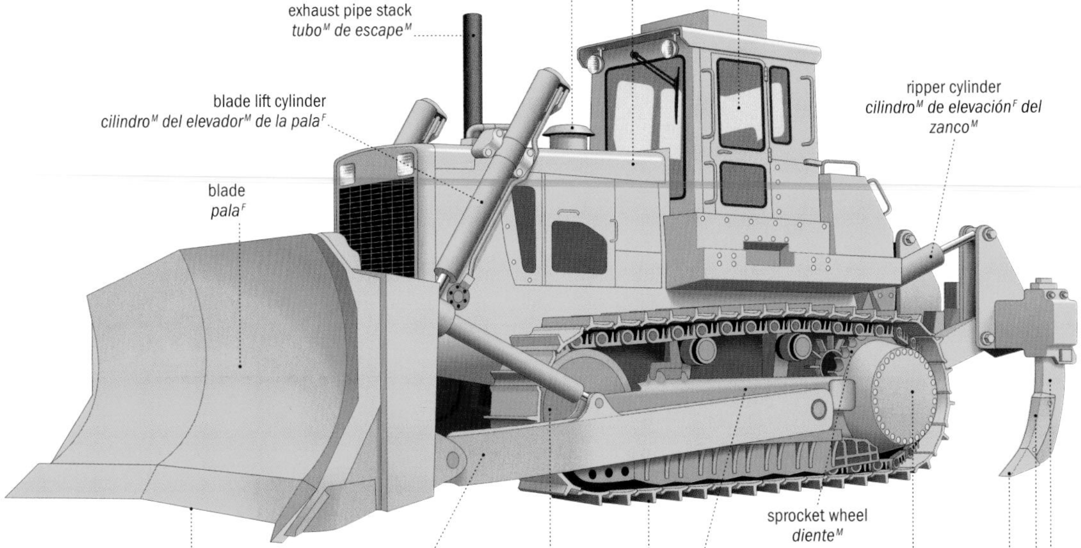

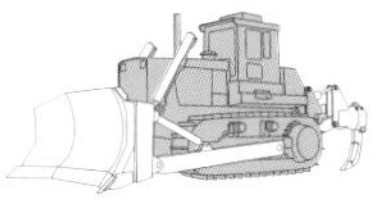

air pre-cleaner filter
filtro[M] de aire[M]

diesel motor compartment
motor[M] diésel

cab
cabina[F]

exhaust pipe stack
tubo[M] de escape[M]

blade lift cylinder
cilindro[M] del elevador[M] de la pala[F]

ripper cylinder
cilindro[M] de elevación[F] del zanco[M]

blade
pala[F]

cutting edge
cuchilla[F] de corte[M]

push frame
armazón[M] de empuje[M]

track idler
rueda[F] guía[F]

sprocket wheel
diente[M]

final drive
rueda[F] motriz

track
oruga[F]

ripper tip tooth
punta[F] del diente[M] de la desterronadora[F]

track roller frame
bastidor[M] de los rodillos[M]

shank protector
protector[M] del zanco[M]

ripper shank
diente[M] de la desterronadora[F]

crawler tractor
tractor[M] de orugas[F]

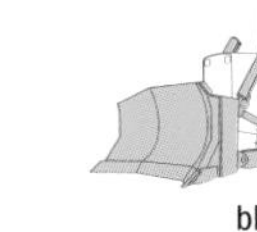

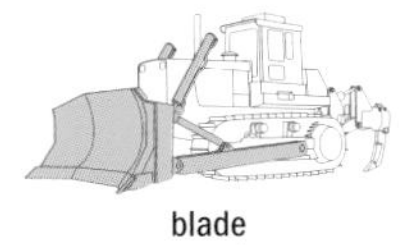

blade
pala[F]

ripper
zanco[M]

wheel loader

cargadora[F]-retroexcavadora[F]

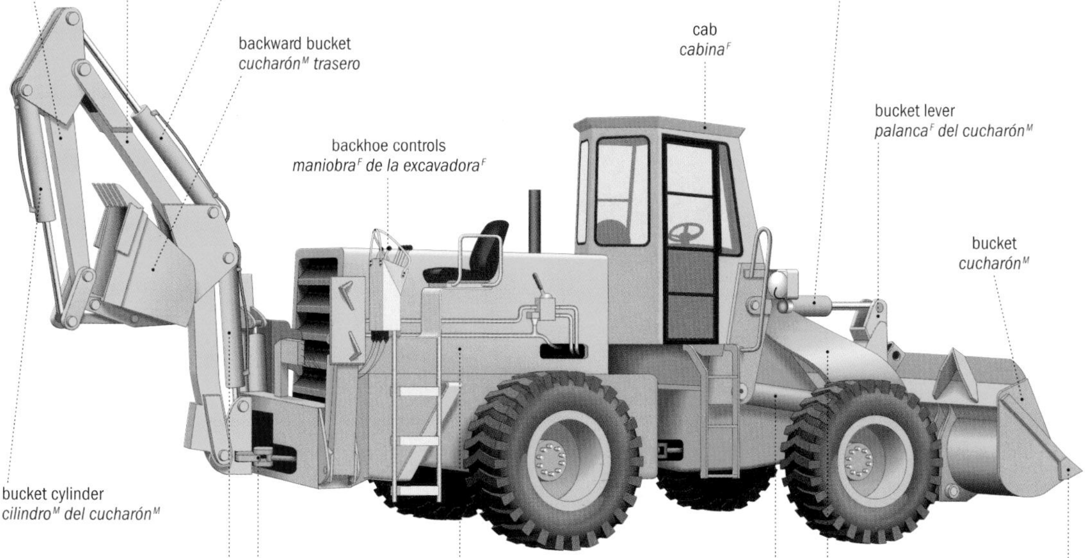

dipper arm
brazo[M] del cucharón[M]

dipper-arm cylinder
cilindro[M] del brazo[M] elevador

boom
elevador[M]

bucket cylinder
cilindro[M] del cucharón[M]

cab
cabina[F]

backward bucket
cucharón[M] trasero

bucket lever
palanca[F] del cucharón[M]

backhoe controls
maniobra[F] de la excavadora[F]

bucket
cucharón[M]

bucket cylinder
cilindro[M] del cucharón[M]

boom cylinder
cilindro[M] del elevador[M]

diesel engine compartment
motor[M] diesel

lift arm
brazo[M] elevador

boom swing hinge pin
perno[M] de articulación[F] del cucharón[M]

lift-arm cylinder
cilindro[M] del brazo[M] elevador

cutting edge
cuchilla[M] del cucharón[M]

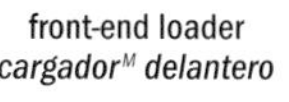

front-end loader
cargador[M] delantero

wheel tractor
tractor[M] de ruedas[F]

backhoe
excavadora[F]

scraper

raspador[M]

gooseneck
cuello[M] de ganso[M]
steering cylinder
cilindro[M] de dirección[F]
elevator
eyector[M]
tractor engine compartment
motor[M] del tractor[M]
draft tube
barra[F] de arrastre[M]
bowl
contenedor[M]
cutting edge
cuchilla[F] de corte[M]
draft arm
brazo[M] de arrastre[M]

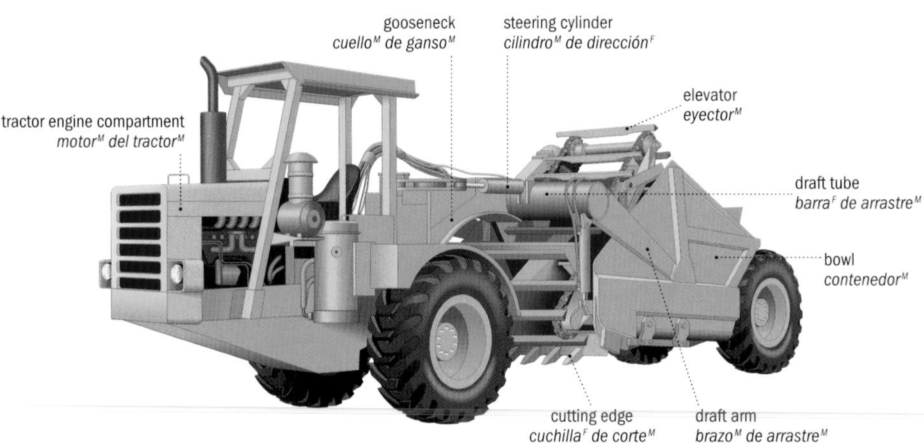

hydraulic shovel

pala[F] hidráulica

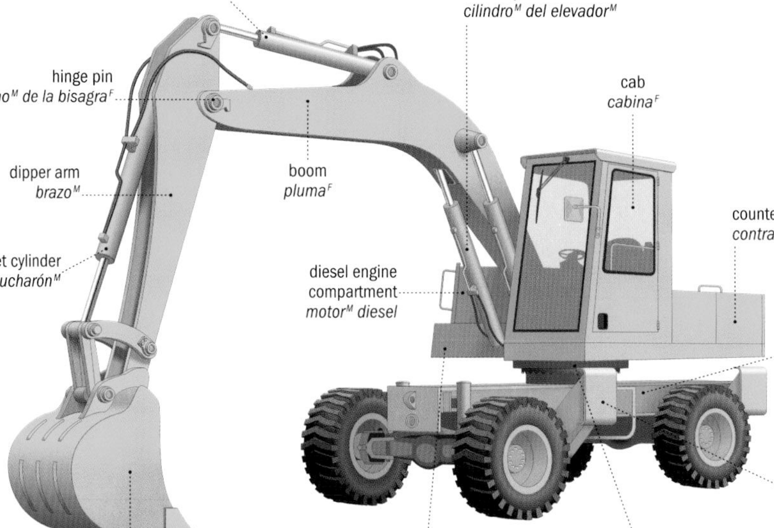

dipper-arm cylinder
cilindro[M] del brazo[M]
boom cylinder
cilindro[M] del elevador[M]
hinge pin
perno[M] de la bisagra[F]
cab
cabina[F]
dipper arm
brazo[M]
boom
pluma[F]
counterweight
contrapeso[M]
bucket cylinder
cilindro[M] del cucharón[M]
diesel engine compartment
motor[M] diesel
main frame
chasis[M]
outrigger
soporte[M] del plano[M] fijo
pivot cab upper structure
cabina[F] giratoria
turntable
plato[M] giratorio
dipper bucket
cucharón[M] excavador
tooth
diente[M]

grader

niveladora^F

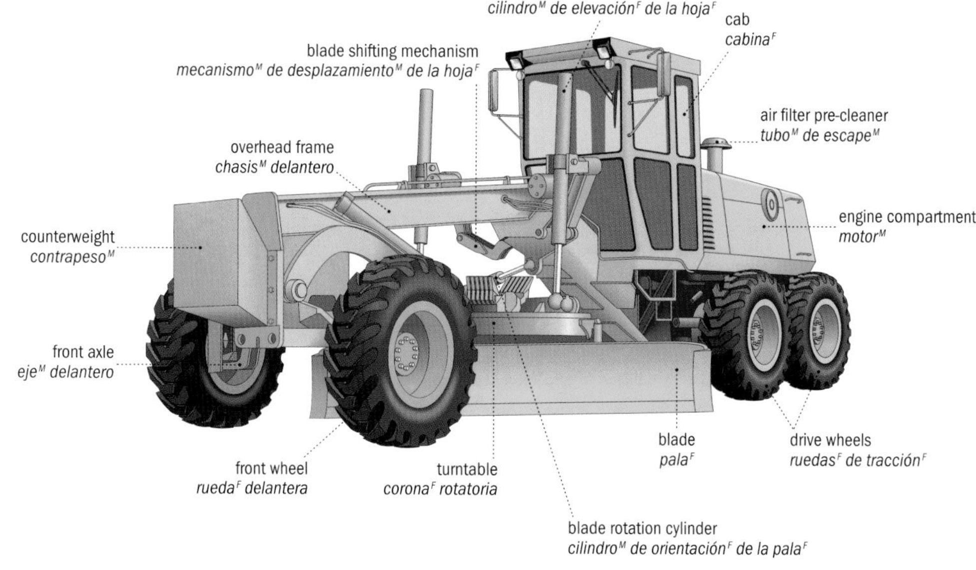
blade-lift cylinder
cilindro^M de elevación^F de la hoja^F
cab
cabina^F
blade shifting mechanism
mecanismo^M de desplazamiento^M de la hoja^F
air filter pre-cleaner
tubo^M de escape^M
overhead frame
chasis^M delantero
engine compartment
motor^M
counterweight
contrapeso^M
front axle
eje^M delantero
blade
pala^F
drive wheels
ruedas^F de tracción^F
front wheel
rueda^F delantera
turntable
corona^F rotatoria
blade rotation cylinder
cilindro^M de orientación^F de la pala^F

dump truck

volcadora^F

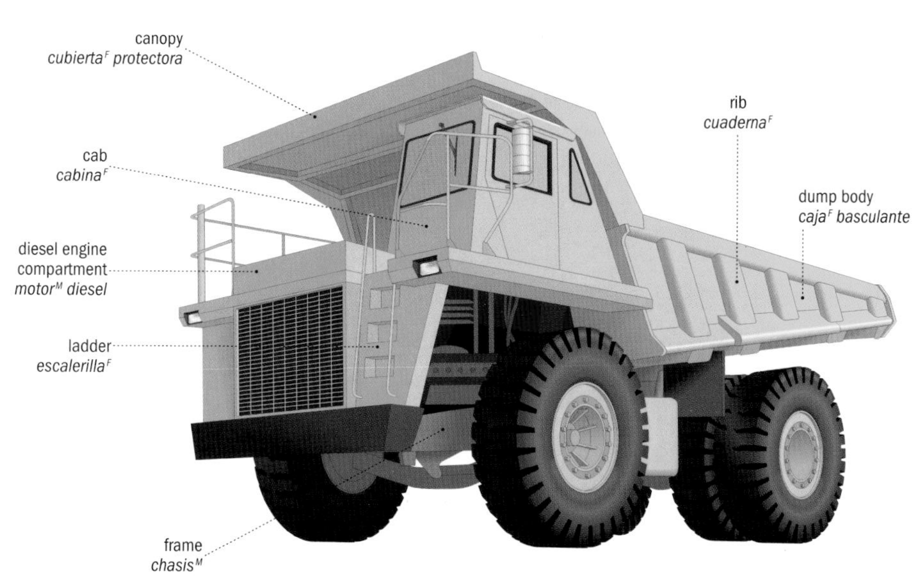
canopy
cubierta^F protectora
rib
cuaderna^F
cab
cabina^F
dump body
caja^F basculante
diesel engine compartment
motor^M diesel
ladder
escalerilla^F
frame
chasis^M

production of electricity from geothermal energy

producción[F] de electricidad[F] por energía[F] geotérmica

turbine
turbina[F]
generator
generador[M]
condenser
condensador[M]
high-tension electricity transmission tower
transporte[M] de electricidad[F] de alta tensión[M]
steam
vapor[M]
separator
separador[M]
transformer (voltage increase)
aumento[M] de la tensión[F]
water-steam mix
mezcla[F] de agua[F] y vapor[M]
cooling tower
torre[F] de refrigeración[F]
upper confining bed
capa[F] superior impermeable
water
agua[F]
geothermal field
campo[M] geotérmico
lower confining bed
sustrato[M] impermeable
production well
pozo[M] de producción
confined aquifer
acuífero[F] confinado
injection well
pozo[M] de inyección[M]
magma chamber
cámara[F] magmática

thermal energy

energía[F] térmica

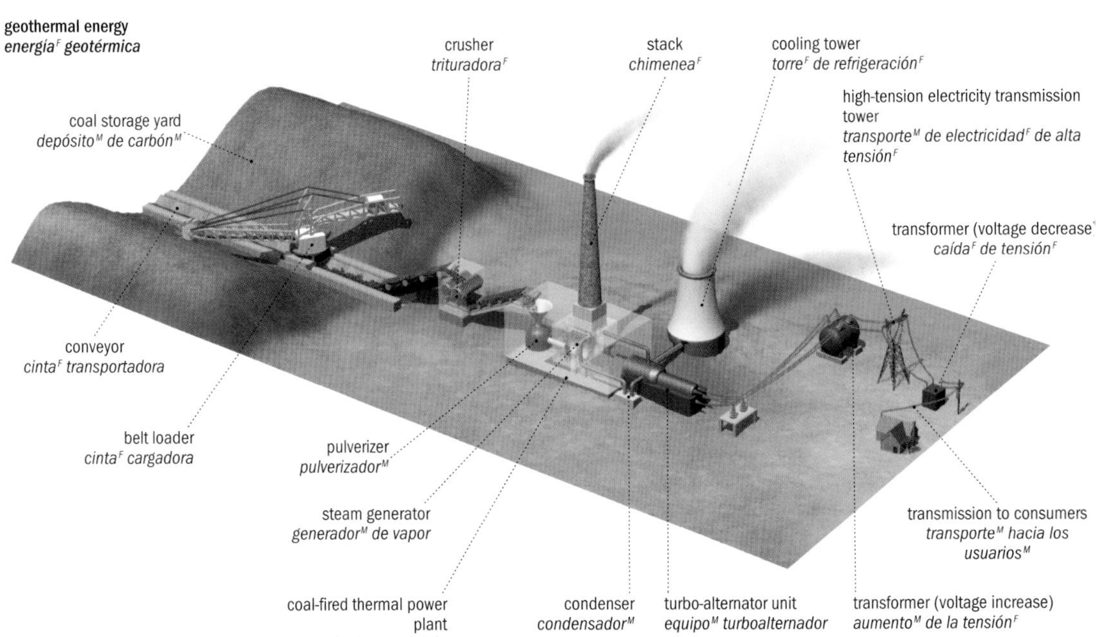

oil

petróleo^{M}

surface prospecting
prospección^{F} terrestre

seismographic recording
registro^{M} sísmico
shock wave
onda^{F} de choque^{M}
petroleum trap
trampa^{F} petrolífera

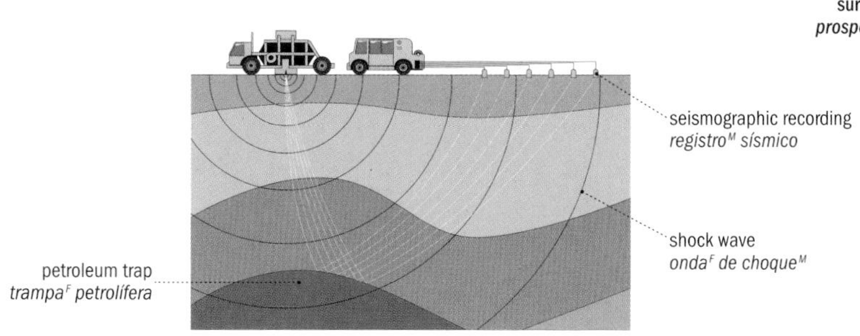

drilling rig
torre^{F} de perforación^{F}

crown block
caballete^{M} portapoleas
derrick
torre^{F} de perforación^{F}
swivel
cabeza^{F} de inyección^{F}
traveling block
polipasto^{M}
mud injection hose
manguera^{F} de inyección^{F} de lodo^{M}
lifting hook
gancho^{M} de tracción^{F}
rotary system
sistema^{M} rotativo
drilling drawworks
torno^{M} de perforación^{F}
kelly
vástago^{M} de arrastre^{M}
substructure
estructura^{F} inferior
rotary table
mesa^{F} rotatoria
vibrating mudscreen
tamiz^{M} vibratorio para lodos^{M}
anticline
anticlinal^{M}
drill pipe
tubo^{M} de perforación^{F}
mud pit
depósito^{M} de lodos^{M}
drill collar
collar^{M} de perforación^{F}
mud pump
bomba^{F} para lodos^{M}
bit
barrena^{F}
gas
gas^{M}
engine
motor^{M}
impervious rock
roca^{F} impermeable
oil
petróleo^{M}

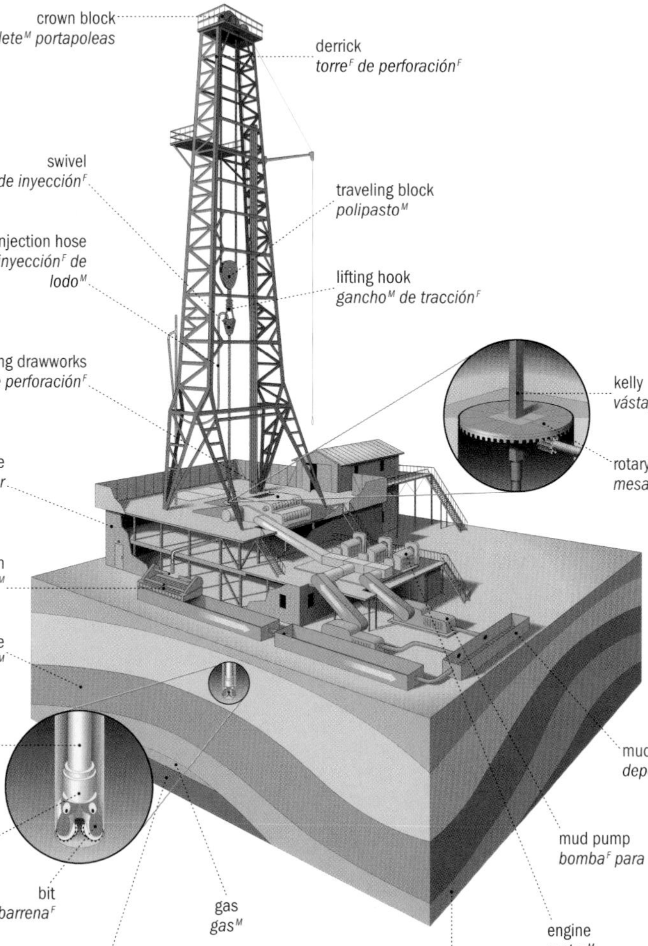

oil

floating-roof tank
tanque[M] *de techo*[M] *pontón*

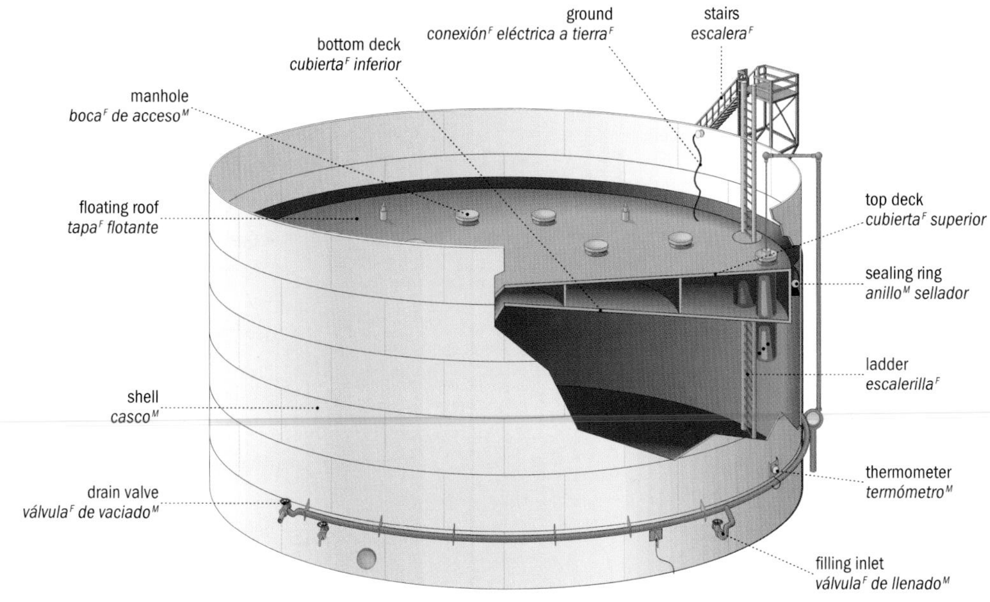
ground
conexión[F] eléctrica a tierra[F]
stairs
escalera[F]
bottom deck
cubierta[F] inferior
manhole
boca[F] de acceso[M]
floating roof
tapa[F] flotante
top deck
cubierta[F] superior
sealing ring
anillo[M] sellador
ladder
escalerilla[F]
shell
casco[M]
thermometer
termómetro[M]
drain valve
válvula[F] de vaciado[M]
filling inlet
válvula[F] de llenado[M]

crude-oil pipeline
oleoducto[M] *para crudo*[M]

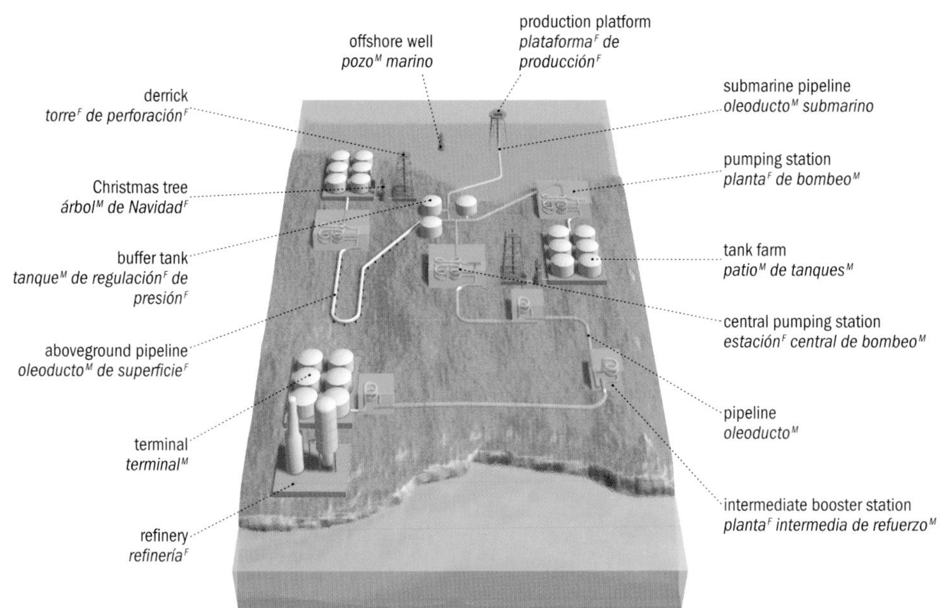
production platform
plataforma[F] de producción[F]
offshore well
pozo[M] marino
submarine pipeline
oleoducto[M] submarino
derrick
torre[F] de perforación[F]
pumping station
planta[F] de bombeo[M]
Christmas tree
árbol[M] de Navidad[F]
buffer tank
tanque[M] de regulación[F] de presión[F]
tank farm
patio[M] de tanques[M]
central pumping station
estación[F] central de bombeo[M]
aboveground pipeline
oleoducto[M] de superficie[F]
pipeline
oleoducto[M]
terminal
terminal[M]
intermediate booster station
planta[F] intermedia de refuerzo[M]
refinery
refinería[F]

refinery products
productos[M] del refinado[M]

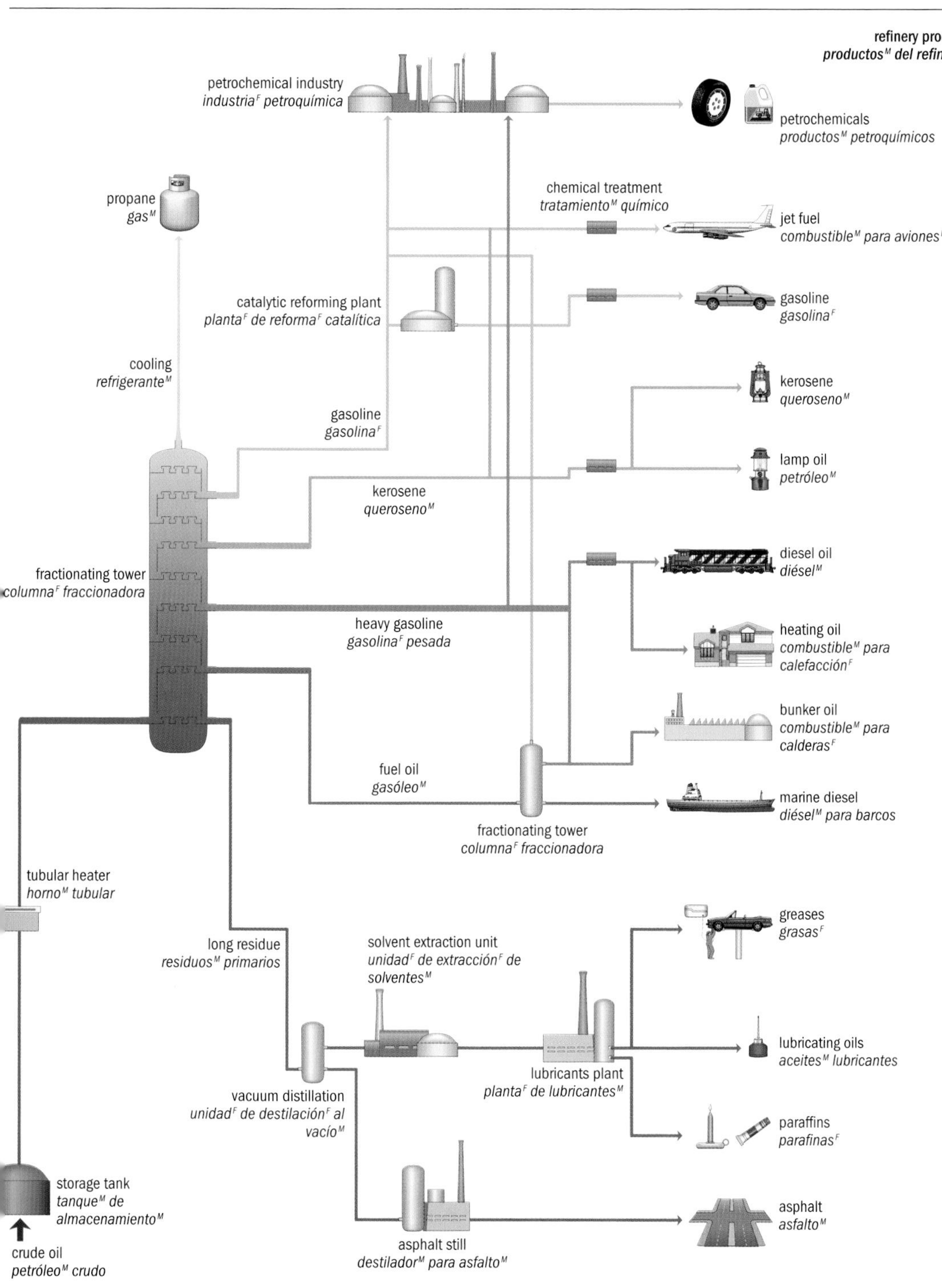
petrochemical industry
industria[F] petroquímica
petrochemicals
productos[M] petroquímicos
propane
gas[M]
chemical treatment
tratamiento[M] químico
jet fuel
combustible[M] para aviones[M]
catalytic reforming plant
planta[F] de reforma[F] catalítica
gasoline
gasolina[F]
cooling
refrigerante[M]
kerosene
queroseno[M]
gasoline
gasolina[F]
lamp oil
petróleo[M]
kerosene
queroseno[M]
diesel oil
diésel[M]
fractionating tower
columna[F] fraccionadora
heavy gasoline
gasolina[F] pesada
heating oil
combustible[M] para calefacción[F]
bunker oil
combustible[M] para calderas[F]
fuel oil
gasóleo[M]
marine diesel
diésel[M] para barcos
fractionating tower
columna[F] fraccionadora
tubular heater
horno[M] tubular
greases
grasas[F]
long residue
residuos[M] primarios
solvent extraction unit
unidad[F] de extracción[F] de solventes[M]
lubricating oils
aceites[M] lubricantes
lubricants plant
planta[F] de lubricantes[M]
vacuum distillation
unidad[F] de destilación[F] al vacío[M]
paraffins
parafinas[F]
storage tank
tanque[M] de almacenamiento[M]
asphalt
asfalto[M]
crude oil
petróleo[M] crudo
asphalt still
destilador[M] para asfalto[M]

hydroelectric complex

complejo^M hidroeléctrico

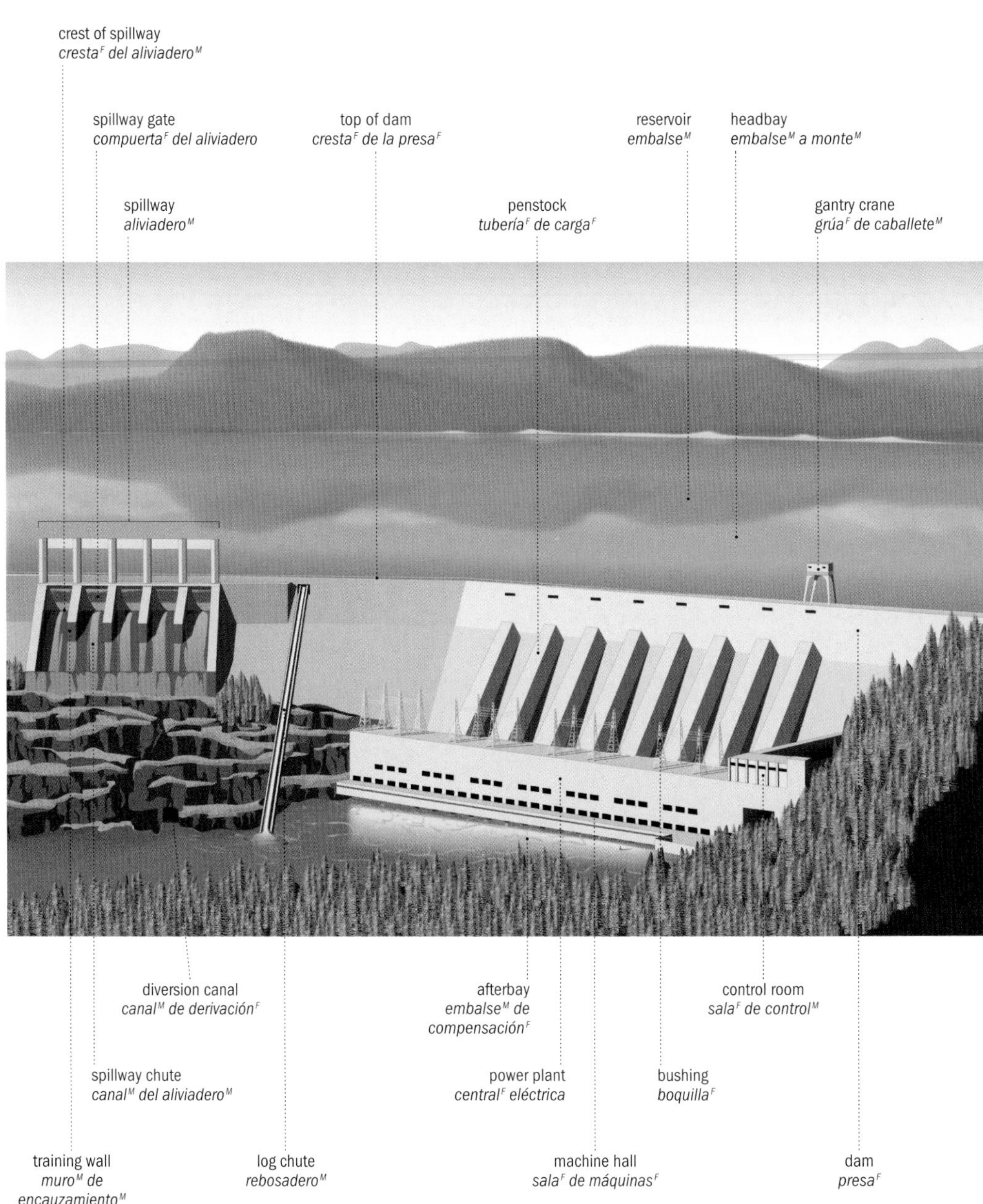
crest of spillway
cresta^F del aliviadero^M
spillway gate
compuerta^F del aliviadero
top of dam
cresta^F de la presa^F
reservoir
embalse^M
headbay
embalse^M a monte^M
spillway
aliviadero^M
penstock
tubería^F de carga^F
gantry crane
grúa^F de caballete^M
diversion canal
canal^M de derivación^F
afterbay
embalse^M de compensación^F
control room
sala^F de control^M
spillway chute
canal^M del aliviadero^M
power plant
central^F eléctrica
bushing
boquilla^F
training wall
muro^M de encauzamiento^M
log chute
rebosadero^M
machine hall
sala^F de máquinas^F
dam
presa^F

cross section of a hydroelectric power plant
secciónF transversal de una centralF hidroeléctrica

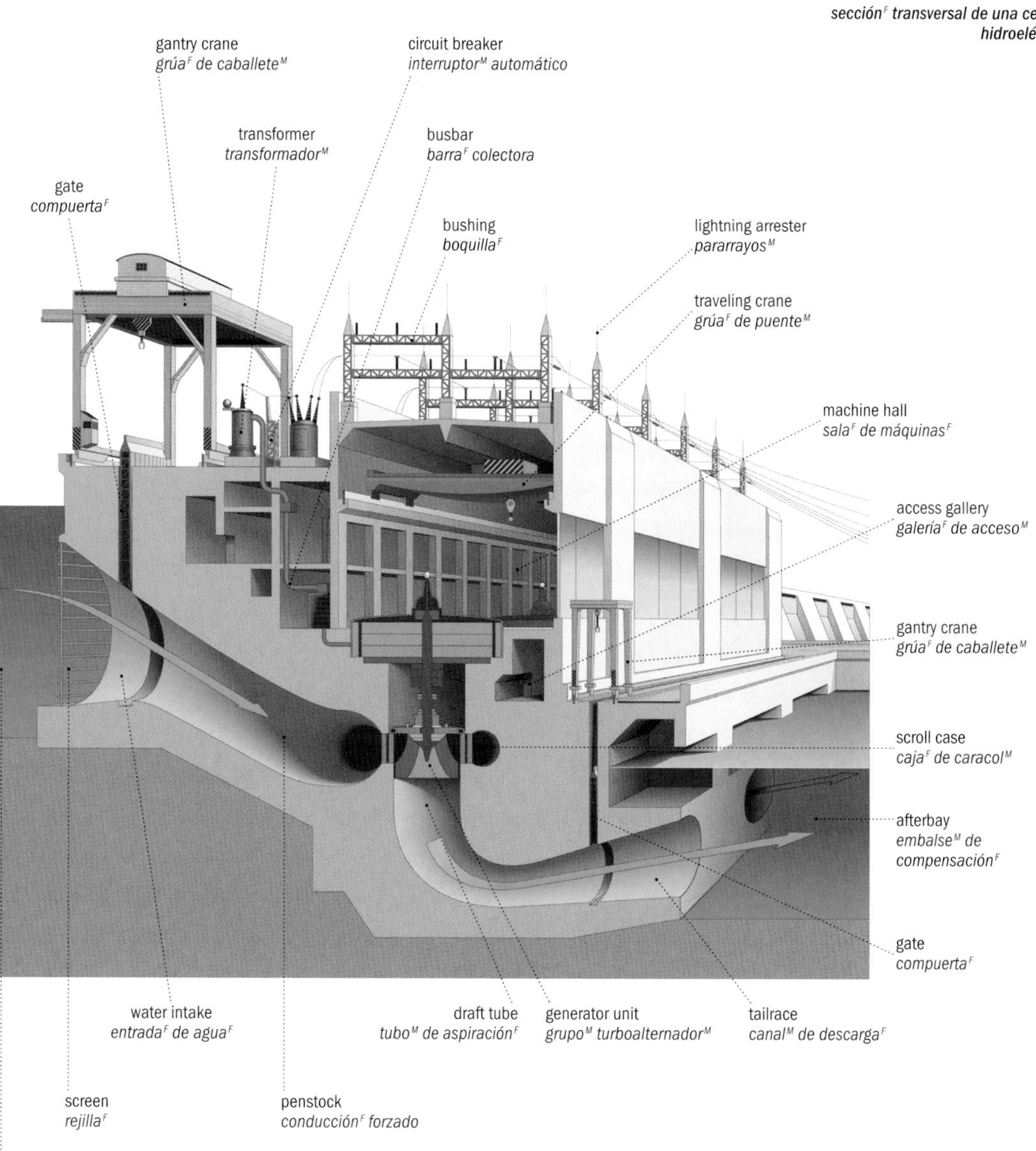

production of electricity from nuclear energy

producción[F] de electricidad[F] por energía[F] nuclear

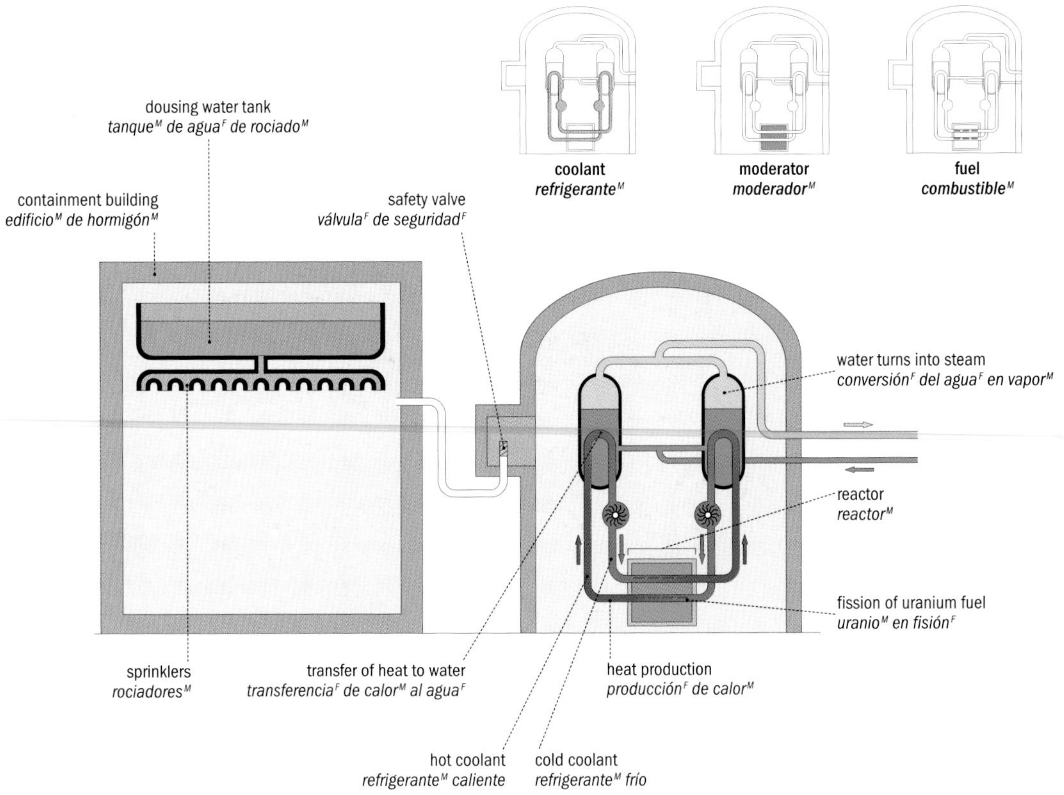

coolant
refrigerante[M]
moderator
moderador[M]
fuel
combustible[M]
dousing water tank
tanque[M] de agua[F] de rociado[M]
containment building
edificio[M] de hormigón[M]
safety valve
válvula[F] de seguridad[F]
water turns into steam
conversión[F] del agua[F] en vapor[M]
reactor
reactor[M]
fission of uranium fuel
uranio[M] en fisión[F]
sprinklers
rociadores[M]
transfer of heat to water
transferencia[F] de calor[M] al agua[F]
heat production
producción[F] de calor[M]
hot coolant
refrigerante[M] caliente
cold coolant
refrigerante[M] frío

steam pressure drives turbine
la presión[F] del vapor[M] impulsa las turbinas[F]
turbine shaft turns generator
el eje[M] de la turbina[F] hace girar el generador[M]
production of electricity by the generator
producción[F] de electricidad[F] por generador[M]
electricity transmission
transmisión[F] de electricidad[F]
voltage increase
ampliación[F] del voltaje[M]
water is pumped back into the steam generator
el agua[F] regresa al generador[M] de vapor[M]
condensation of steam into water
el vapor[M] se condensa en agua[F]
water cools the used steam
el agua[F] enfría el vapor[M] utilizado

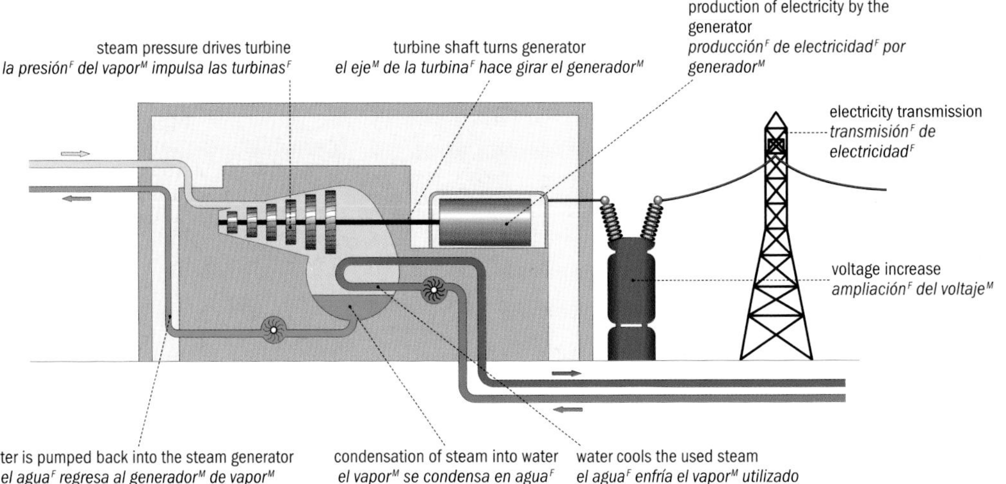

fuel bundle

elemento^M de combustible^M

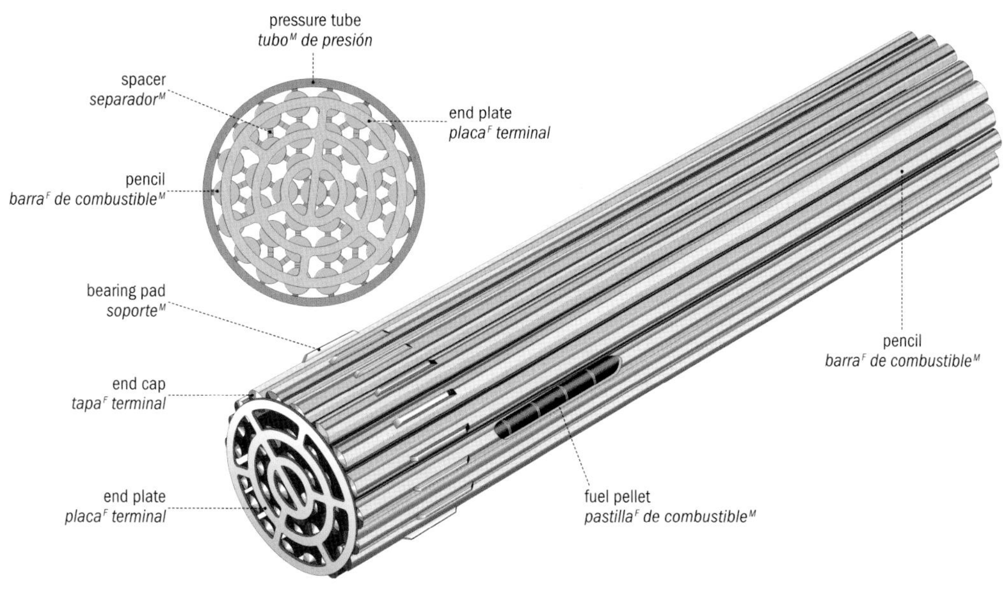

nuclear reactor

carga^F del reactor^M nuclear

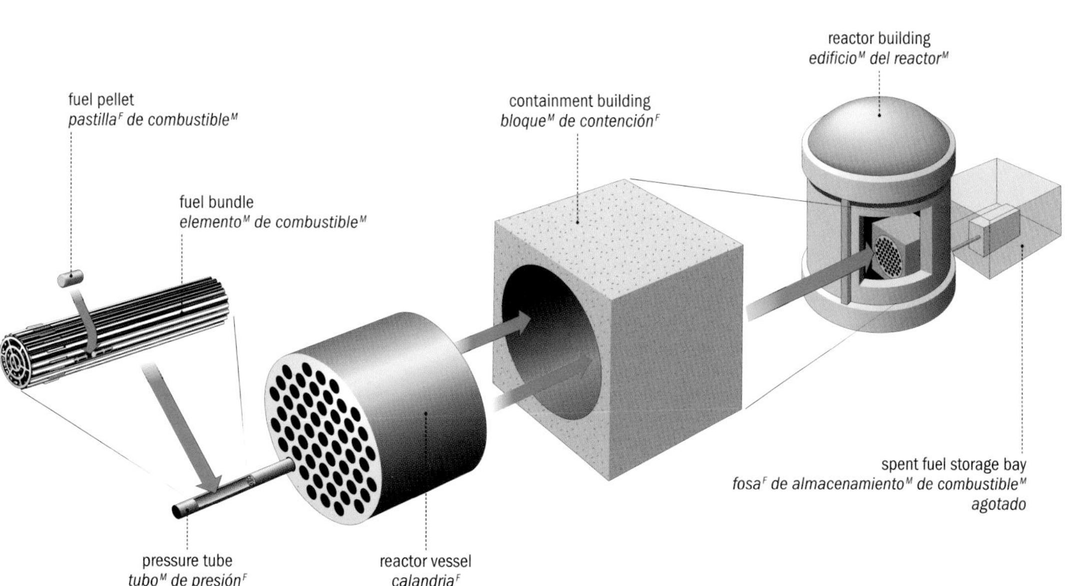

solar cell

célula^F solar

solar radiation
radiación^F solar
antireflection coating
recubrimiento^M antirreflectante
metallic contact grid
reja^F metálica de contacto^M
negative region
región^F negativa
negative contact
contacto^M negativo
positive/negative junction
junta^F positivo/negativo
positive region
región^F positiva
positive contact
contacto^M positivo

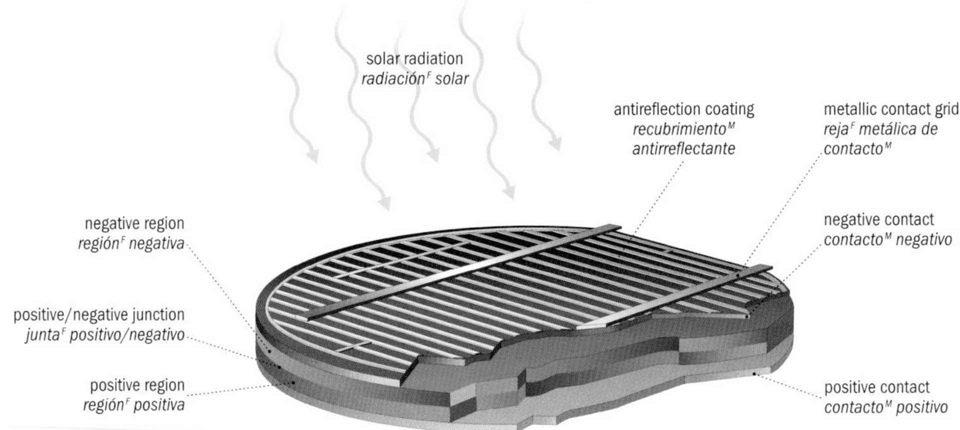

flat-plate solar collector

colector^M solar plano

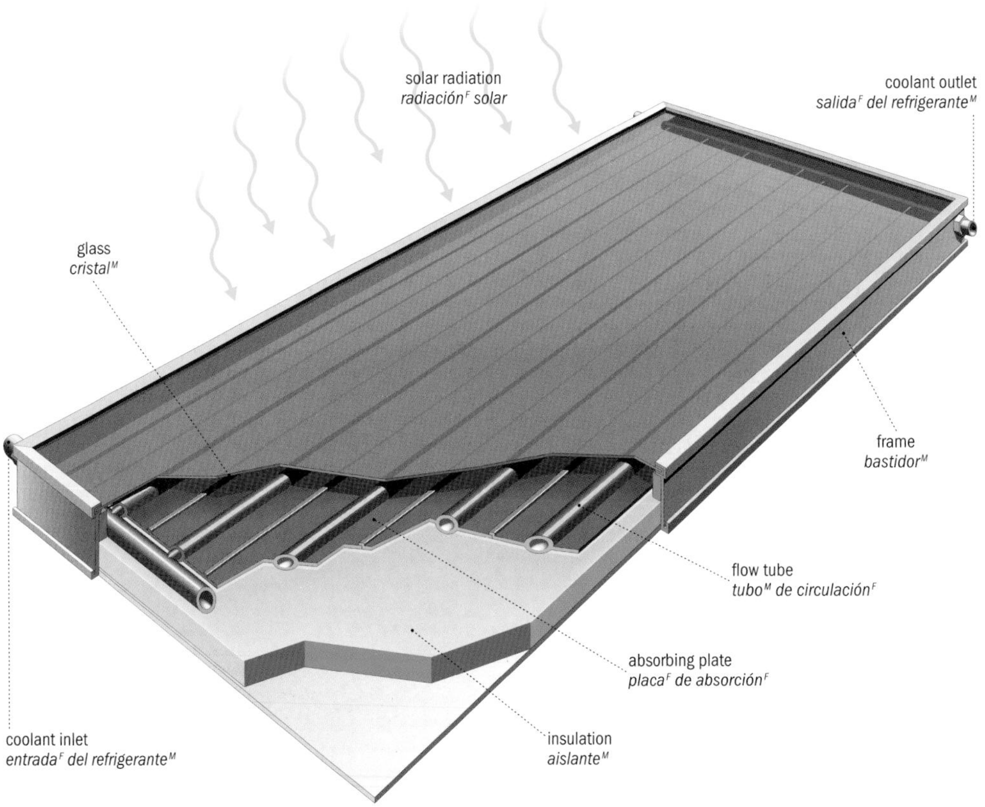

solar radiation
radiación^F solar
coolant outlet
salida^F del refrigerante^M
glass
cristal^M
frame
bastidor^M
flow tube
tubo^M de circulación^F
absorbing plate
placa^F de absorción^F
coolant inlet
entrada^F del refrigerante^M
insulation
aislante^M

solar-cell system

sistema^M de células^F solares

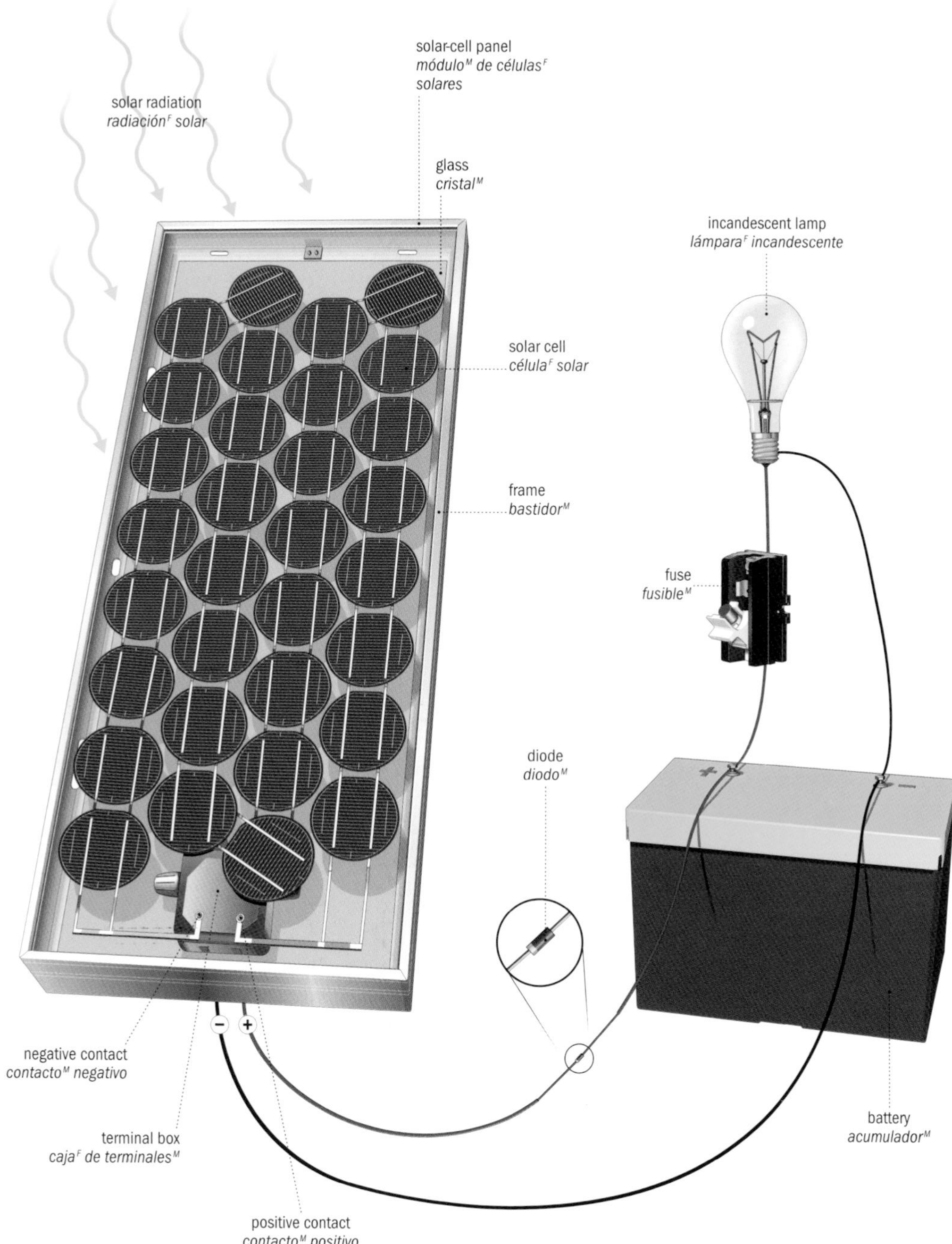

windmill

molino^M de viento^M

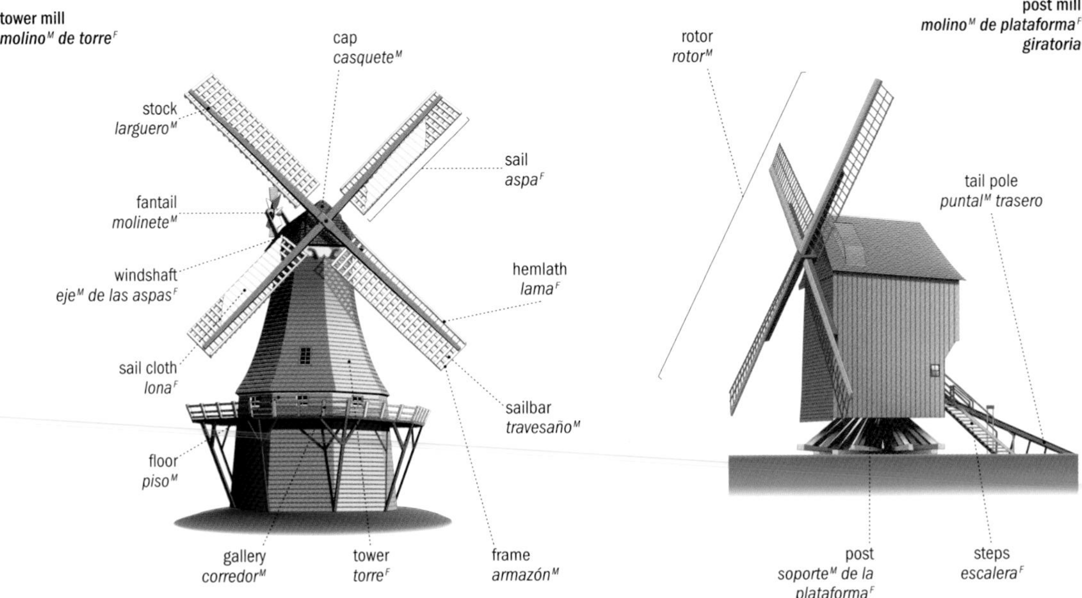

wind turbines and electricity production

turbinas^F de viento^M y producción^F eléctrica

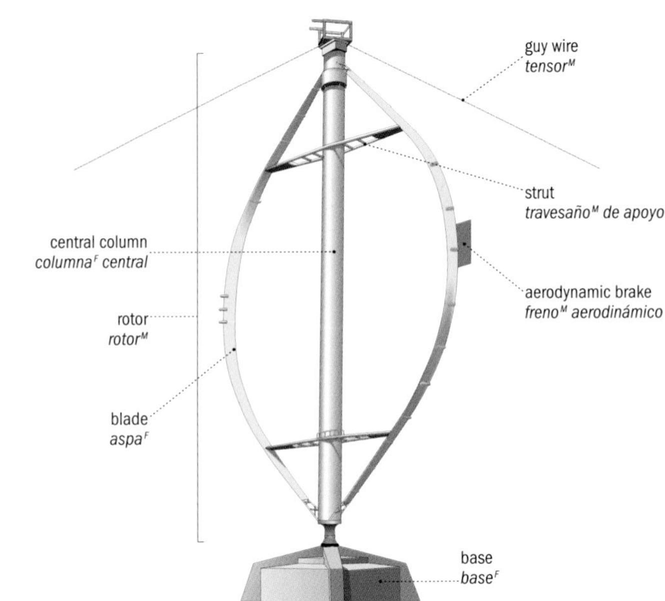

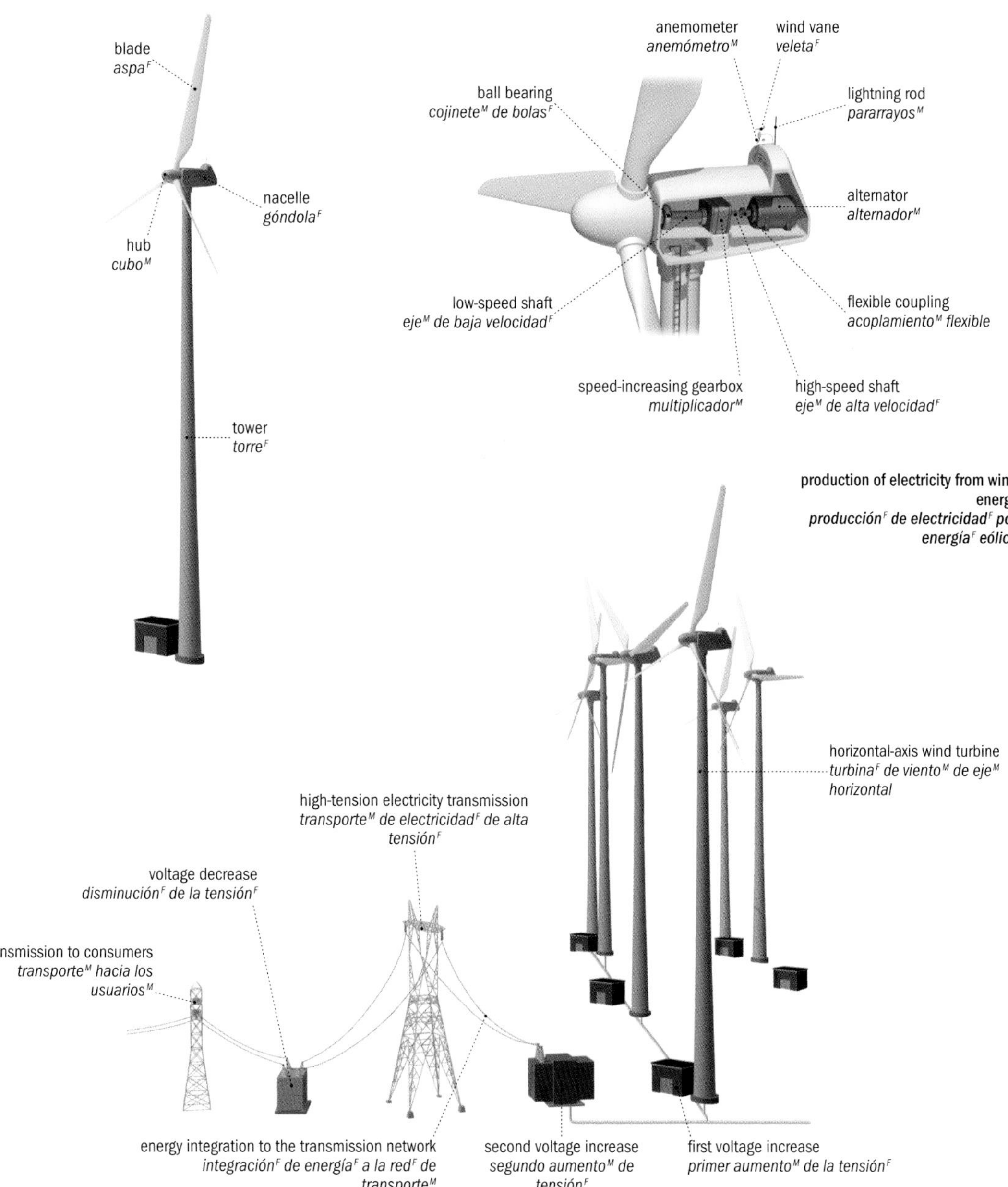
horizontal-axis wind turbine
turbina^F de viento^M de eje^M horizontal
blade
aspa^F
nacelle
góndola^F
hub
cubo^M
tower
torre^F
nacelle cross-section
sección^F transversal de la góndola^F
anemometer
anemómetro^M
wind vane
veleta^F
ball bearing
cojinete^M de bolas^F
lightning rod
pararrayos^M
alternator
alternador^M
low-speed shaft
eje^M de baja velocidad^F
flexible coupling
acoplamiento^M flexible
speed-increasing gearbox
multiplicador^M
high-speed shaft
eje^M de alta velocidad^F
production of electricity from wind energy
producción^F de electricidad^F por energía^F eólica
horizontal-axis wind turbine
turbina^F de viento^M de eje^M horizontal
high-tension electricity transmission
transporte^M de electricidad^F de alta tensión^F
voltage decrease
disminución^F de la tensión^F
transmission to consumers
transporte^M hacia los usuarios^M
energy integration to the transmission network
integración^F de energía^F a la red^F de transporte^M
second voltage increase
segundo aumento^M de tensión^F
first voltage increase
primer aumento^M de la tensión^F

matter

materia[F]

atom
átomo[M]

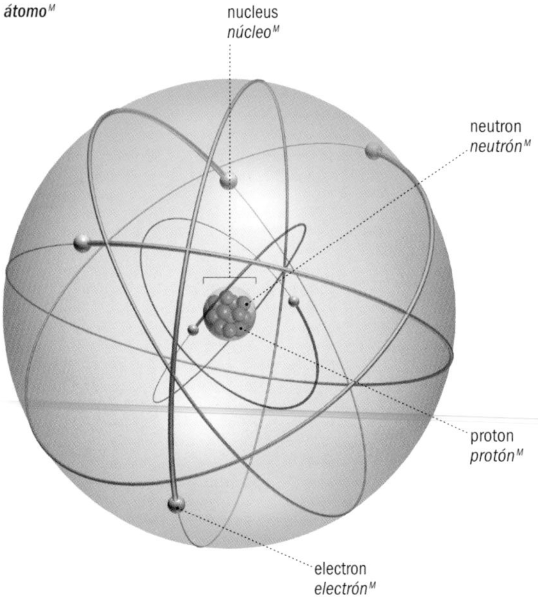

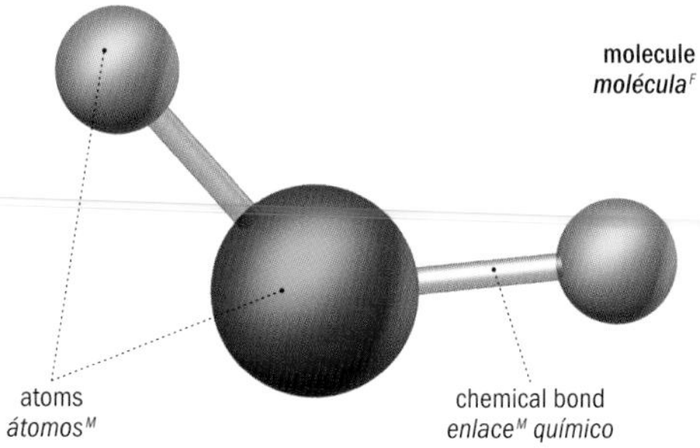

nucleus
núcleo[M]
neutron
neutrón[M]
proton
protón[M]
electron
electrón[M]

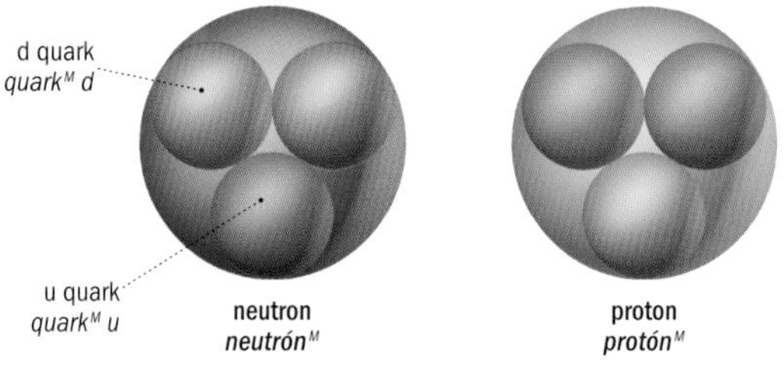

d quark
quark[M] d
u quark
quark[M] u
neutron
neutrón[M]
proton
protón[M]

molecule
molécula[F]
atoms
átomos[M]
chemical bond
enlace[M] químico

states of matter
estados[M] de la materia[F]

gas
gas[M]
condensation
condensación[F]
sublimation
sublimación[F]
evaporation
evaporación[F]
amorphous solid
sólido[M] amorfo
crystallization
cristalización[F]
supercooling
sobrefusión[F]
condensation
condensación[F]
liquid
líquido[M]
melting
fusión[F]
solid
sólido[M]
freezing
solidificación[F]

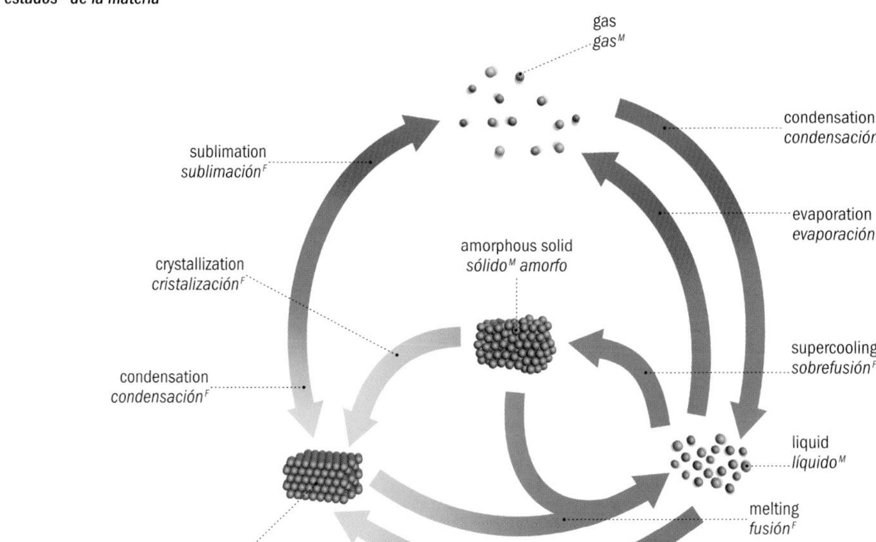

nuclear fission
fisión^M nuclear

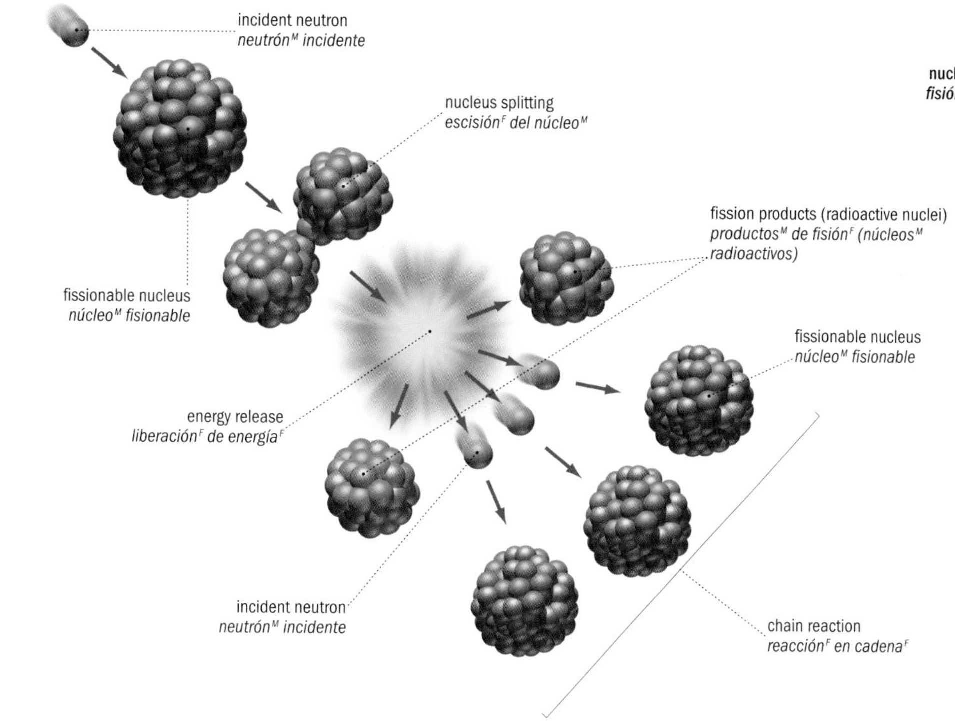

incident neutron
neutrón^M incidente
nucleus splitting
escisión^F del núcleo^M
fission products (radioactive nuclei)
productos^M de fisión^F (núcleos^M radioactivos)
fissionable nucleus
núcleo^M fisionable
fissionable nucleus
núcleo^M fisionable
energy release
liberación^F de energía^F
incident neutron
neutrón^M incidente
chain reaction
reacción^F en cadena^F

heat transfer
transmisión^F de calor^M

convection
convección^F
vapor
vapor^M
liquid
líquido^M
radiation
radiación^F
convection current
corriente^M de convección^M
solid
sólido^M
conduction
conducción^F
flame
llama^F

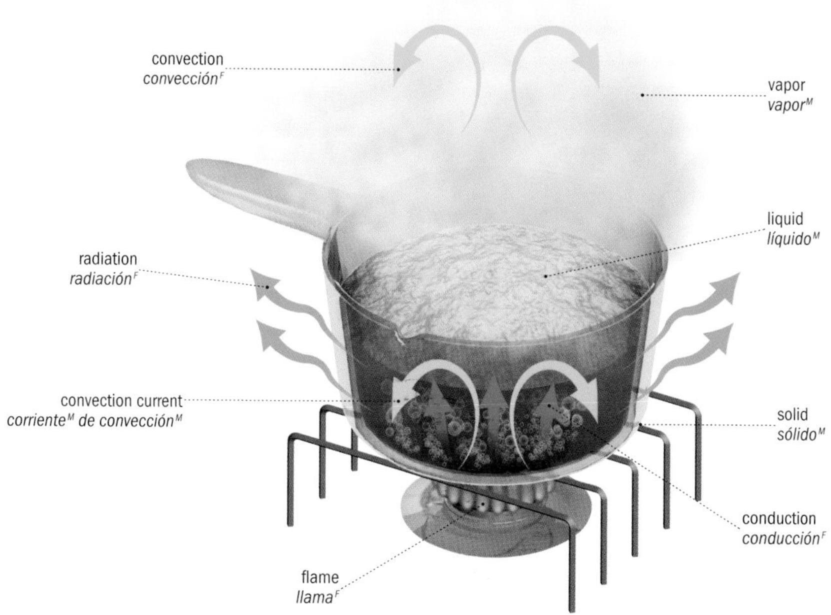

magnetism

magnetismo^M

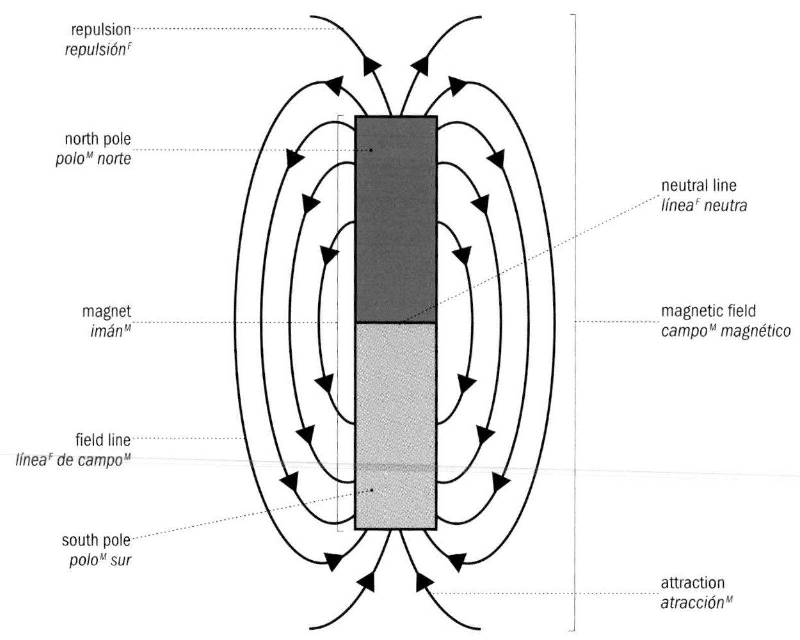

parallel electrical circuit

circuito^M eléctrico en paralelo^M

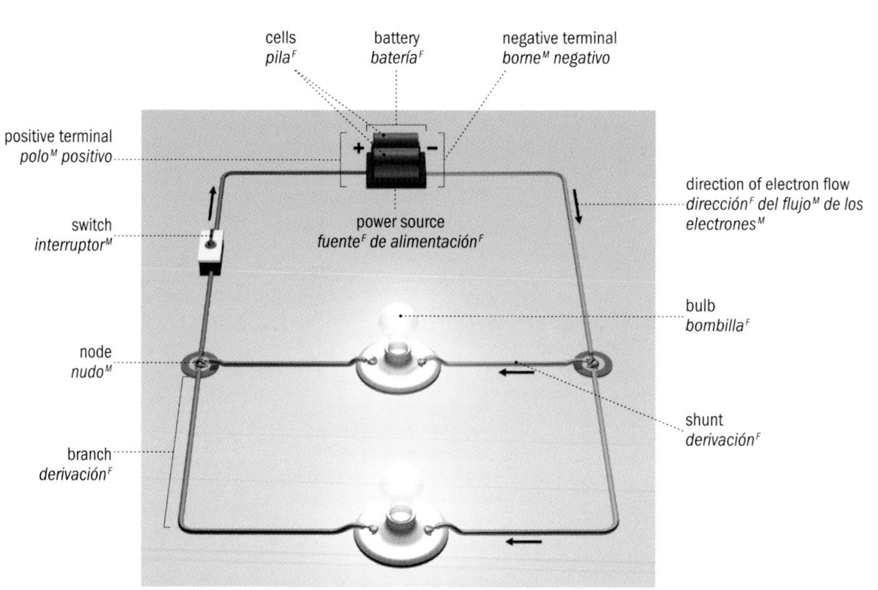

dry cells

pilas[F] secas

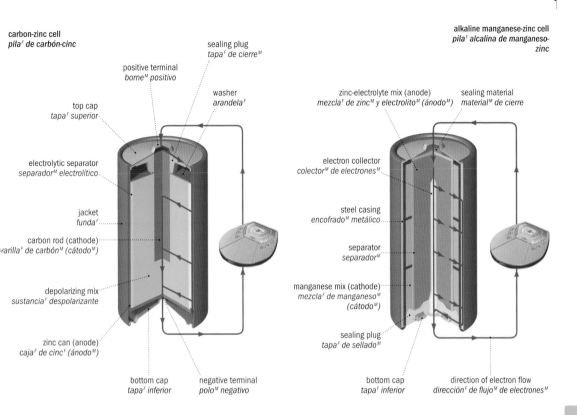

carbon-zinc cell
pila[F] de carbón-cinc

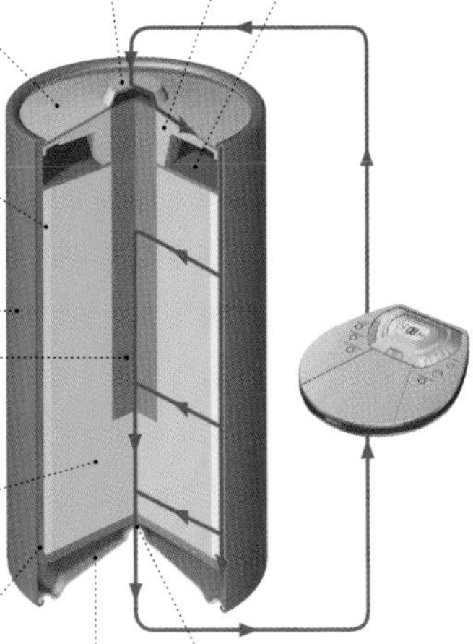

sealing plug
tapa[F] de cierre[M]

positive terminal
borne[M] positivo

washer
arandela[F]

top cap
tapa[F] superior

electrolytic separator
separador[M] electrolítico

jacket
funda[F]

carbon rod (cathode)
varilla[F] de carbón[M] (cátodo[M])

depolarizing mix
sustancia[F] despolarizante

zinc can (anode)
caja[F] de cinc[F] (ánodo[M])

bottom cap
tapa[F] inferior

negative terminal
polo[M] negativo

alkaline manganese-zinc cell
pila[F] alcalina de manganeso-zinc

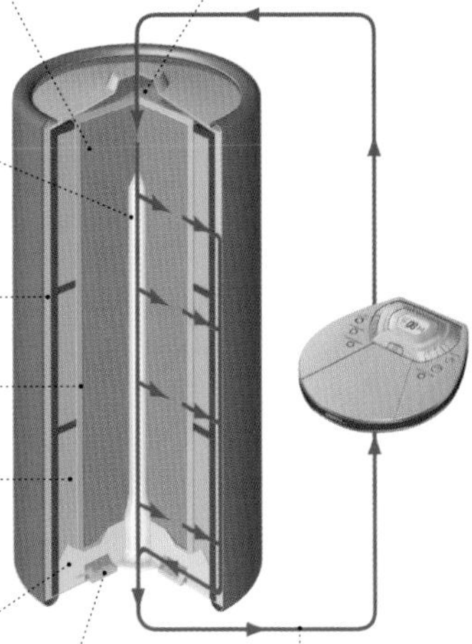

zinc-electrolyte mix (anode)
mezcla[F] de zinc[M] y electrolito[M] (ánodo[M])

sealing material
material[M] de cierre

electron collector
colector[M] de electrones[M]

steel casing
encofrado[M] metálico

separator
separador[M]

manganese mix (cathode)
mezcla[F] de manganeso[M] (cátodo[M])

sealing plug
tapa[F] de sellado[M]

bottom cap
tapa[F] inferior

direction of electron flow
dirección[F] de flujo[M] de electrones[M]

electronics

electrónica[F]

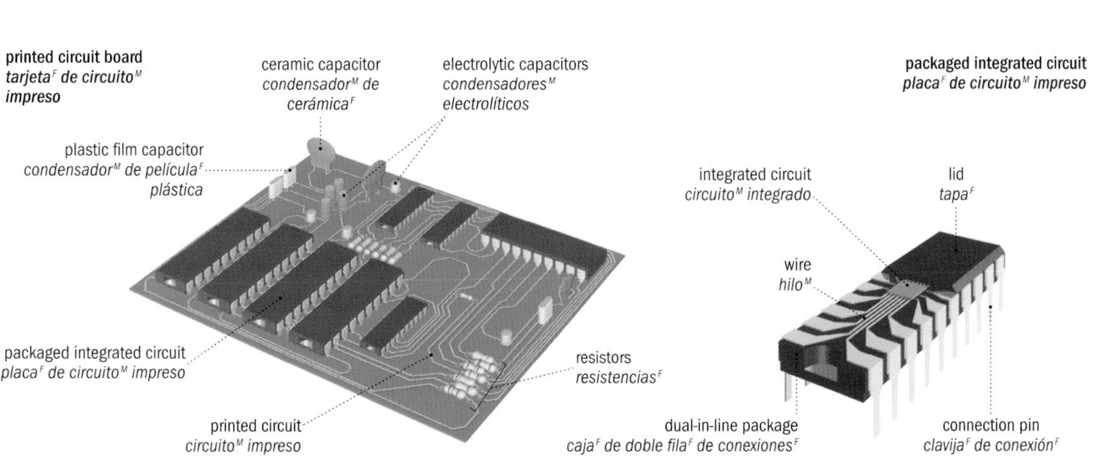

electromagnetic spectrum

espectro[M] electromagnético

microwaves
microondas[F]

ultraviolet radiation
radiación[F] ultravioleta

radio waves
ondas[F] radio

infrared radiation
radiación[F] infrarroja

X-rays
rayos[M] X

gamma rays
rayos[M] gamma

visible light
luz[F] visible

wave

onda[F]

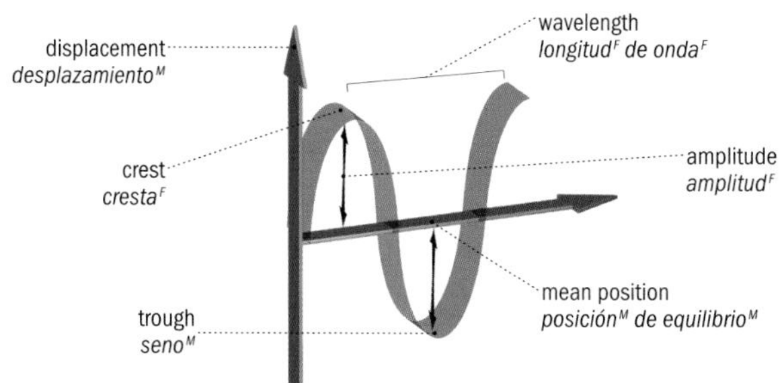

color synthesis

síntesis[F] de los colores[M]

additive color synthesis
síntesis[F] de los colores[M] aditivos

subtractive color synthesis
síntesis[F] de los colores[M] sustractivos

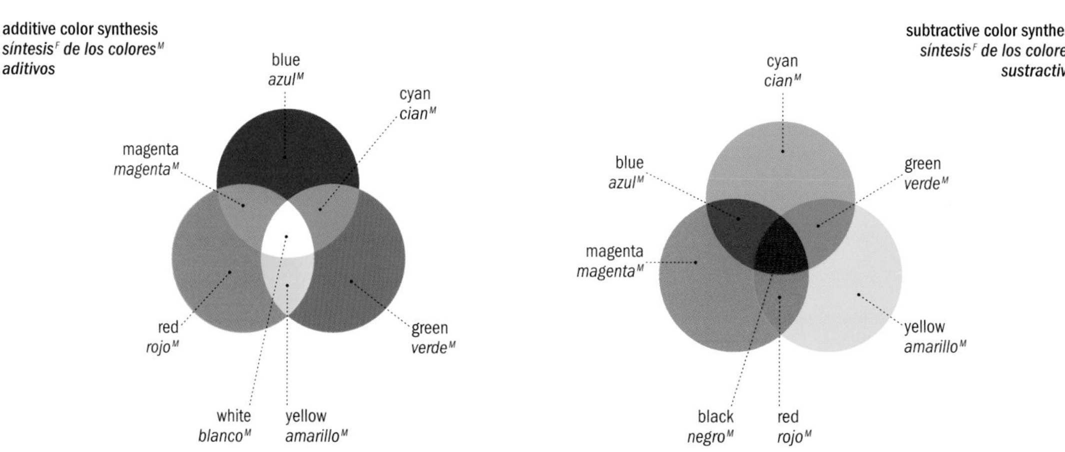

vision
visión[F]

normal vision
visión[F] normal

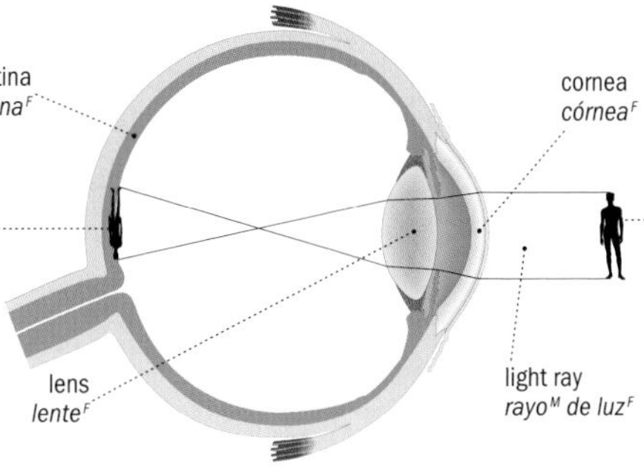

retina
retina[F]
cornea
córnea[F]
focus
enfoque[M]
object
objeto[M]
lens
lente[F]
light ray
rayo[M] de luz[F]

vision defects and corrective lenses
defectos[M] de la visión[F]

myopia
miopía[F]

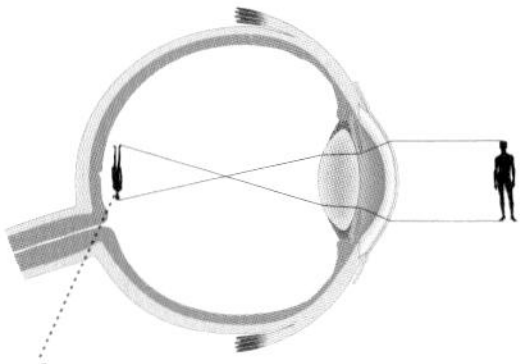

focus
enfoque[M]

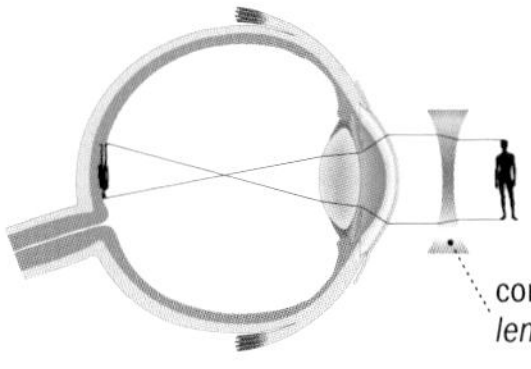

concave lens
lente[F] cóncava

hyperopia
hipermetropía[F]

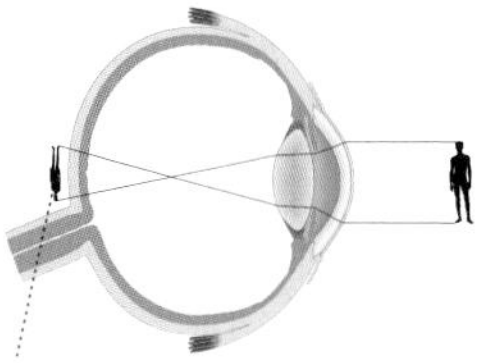

focus
enfoque[M]

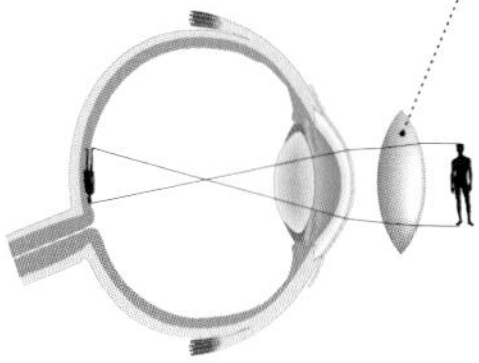

convex lens
lente[F] convexa

astigmatism
astigmatismo[M]

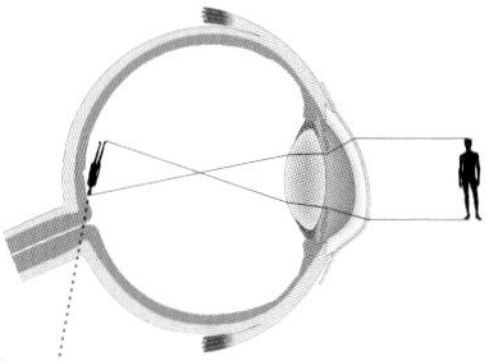

focus
foco[M]

toric lens
lente[F] tórica

lenses
lentes[F]

converging lenses
lentes[F] convergentes

biconvex lens
lente[F] biconvexa
positive meniscus
menisco[M] convergente
convex lens
lente[F] convexa
plano-convex lens
lente[F] convexo-plana

diverging lenses
lentes[F] divergentes

plano-concave lens
lente[F] cóncavo-plana
concave lens
lente[F] cóncava
biconcave lens
lente[F] bicóncava
negative meniscus
menisco[M] divergente

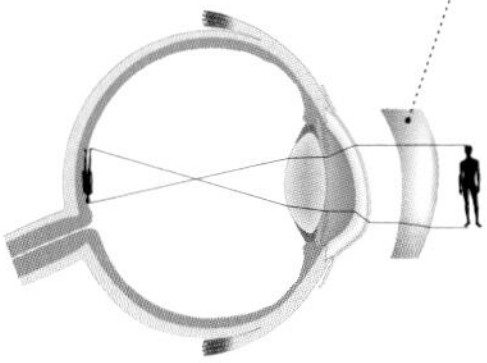

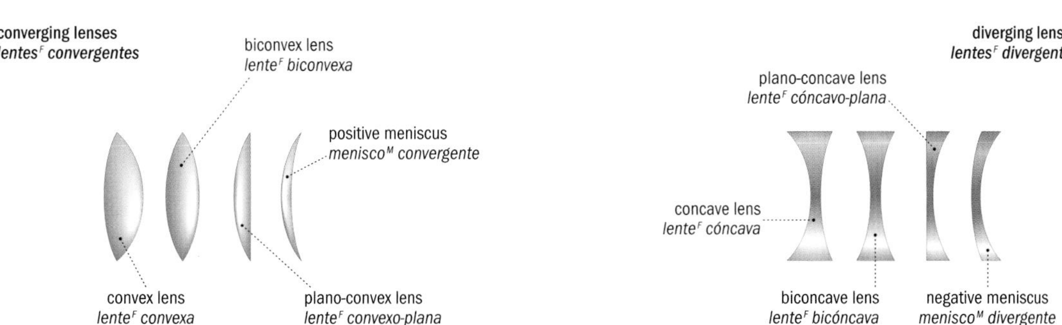

pulsed ruby laser

láser^M de rubí^M pulsado

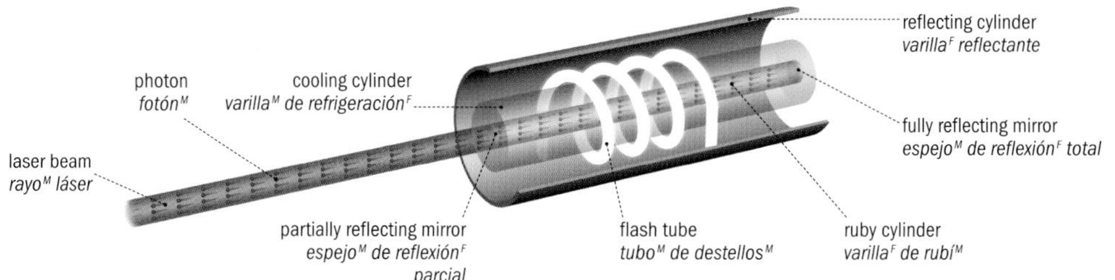

prism binoculars

prismáticos^M binoculares

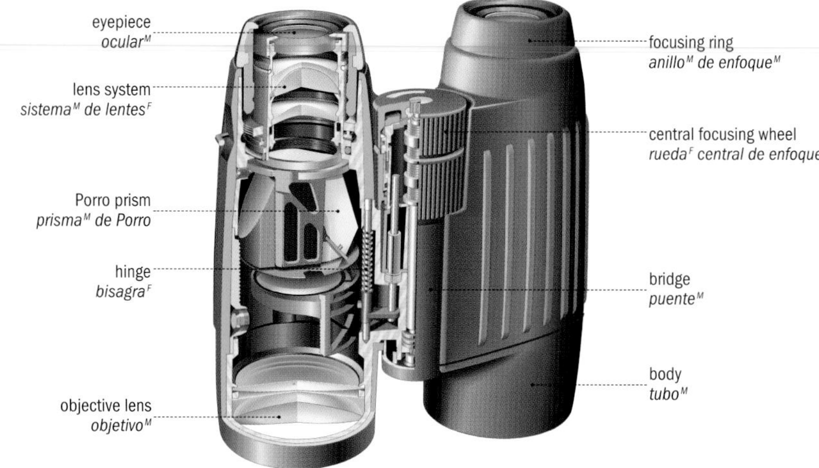

telescopic sight

visor^M telescópico

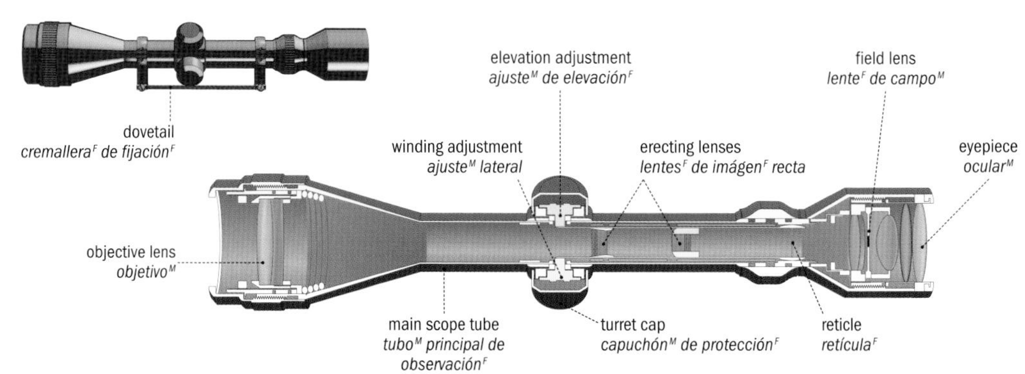

SCIENCE

magnifying glass and microscopes

lupa^F y microscopios^M

magnifying glass
lupa^F

eyepiece
ocular^M
revolving nosepiece
revólver^M *portaobjetivos*
stage clip
pinza^F *sujetamuestras*
draw tube
tubo^M *portaocular*
coarse adjustment knob
tornillo^M *macrométrico*^M
objective
objetivo^M
fine adjustment knob
tornillo^M *micrométrico*
glass slide
portaobjeto^M
stage
platina^F
arm
brazo^M
condenser
condensador^M
base
base^F
mirror
espejo^M

microscope
microscopio^M

draw tube
tubo^M *portaocular*
body tube
tubo^M *binocular*
eyepiece
ocular^M
revolving nosepiece
portaobjetivo^M *rotatorio*
limb top
portatubo^M
arm
brazo^M
objective
objetivo^M
mechanical stage
platina^F *mecánica*
stage clip
sujetador^M
stage
platina^F
glass slide
portaobjetos^M
fine adjustment knob
botón^M *de ajuste*^M *fino*
condenser adjustment knob
tornillo^M *de ajuste*^M *del condensador*^M
coarse adjustment knob
botón^M *de ajuste*^M *grueso*
field lens adjustment
ajuste^M *de la lente*^M *de campo*^M
mechanical stage control
control^M *de la plataforma*^F *corrediza*
base
pie^M
lamp
lámpara^F
condenser
condensador^M
condenser height adjustment
ajuste^M *de la altura*^F *del condensador*^M

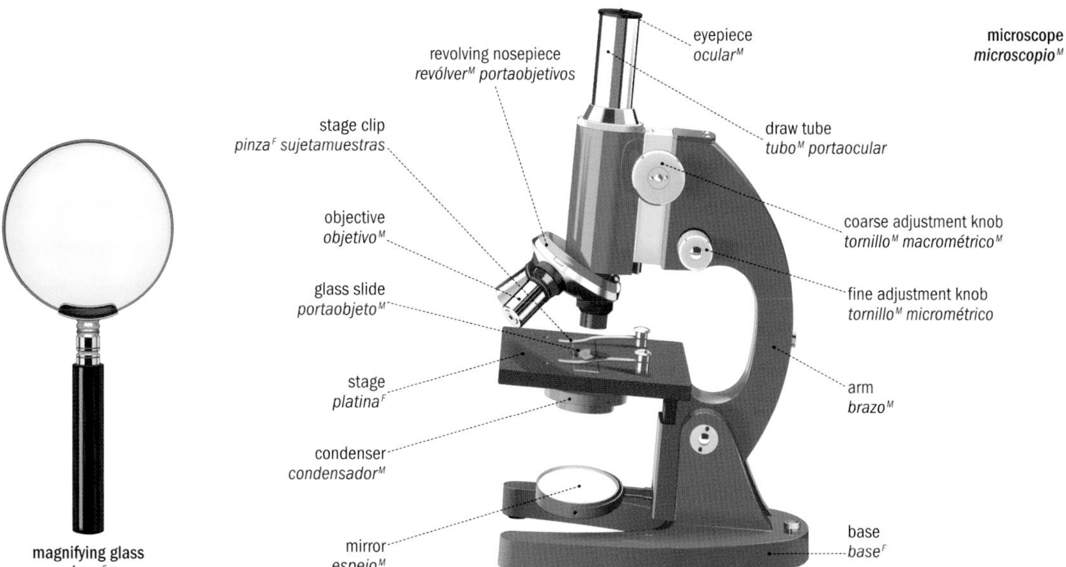

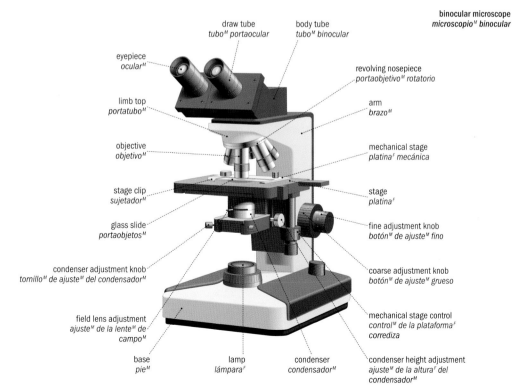

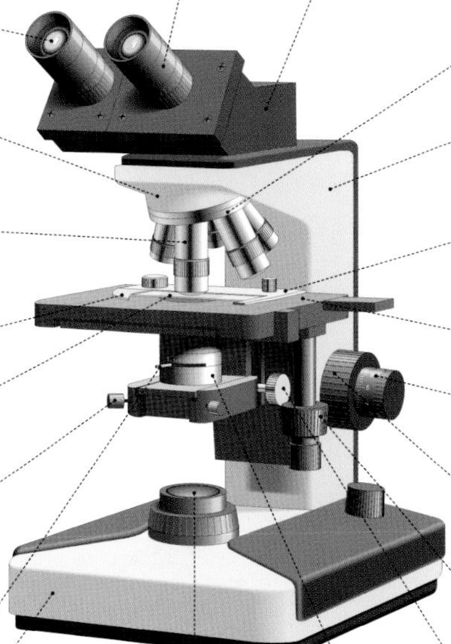

binocular microscope
microscopio^M ***binocular***

SCIENCE

measurement of weight

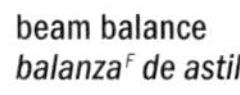

medición[F] del peso[M]

beam balance
balanza[F] de astil[M]

steelyard
báscula[F] romana

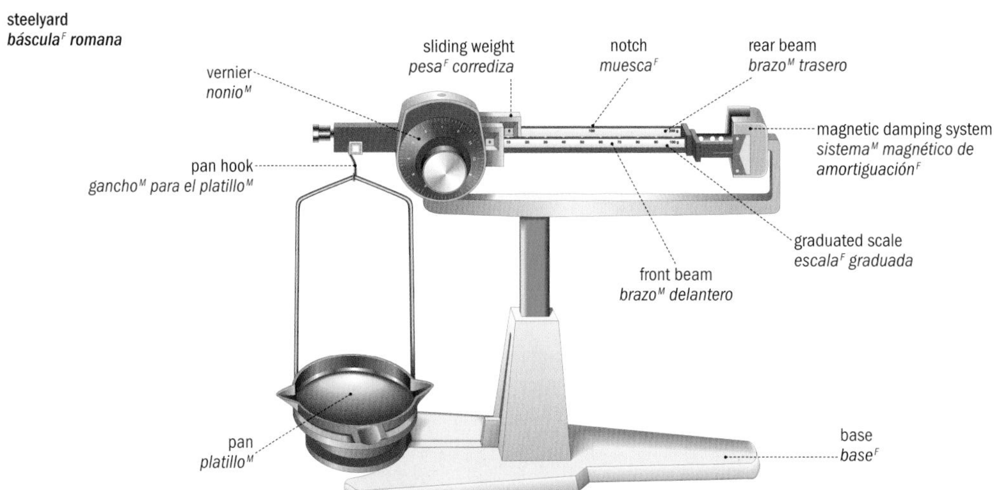

Roberval's balance
balanza[F] de Roberval

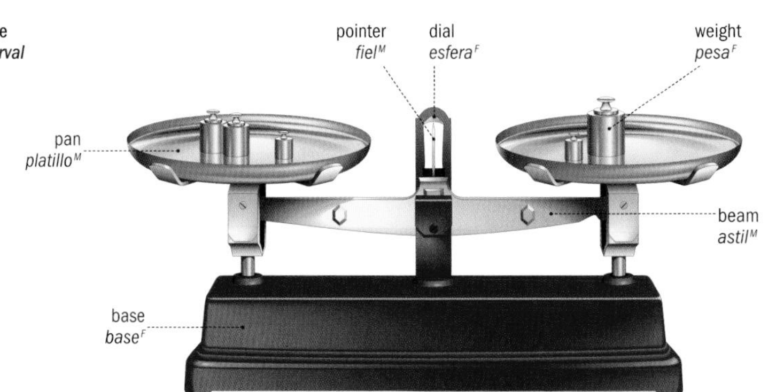

SCIENCE

measurement of weight

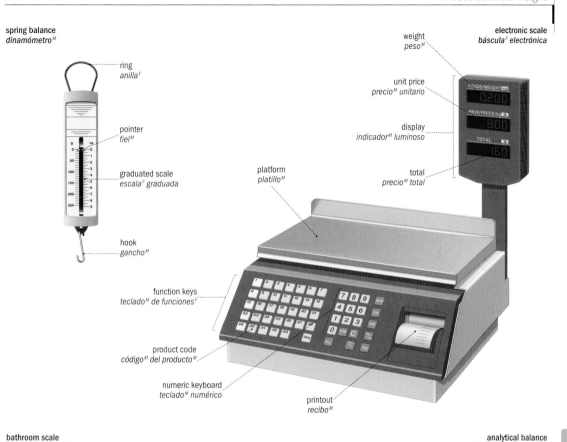

spring balance
***dinamómetro*[M]**

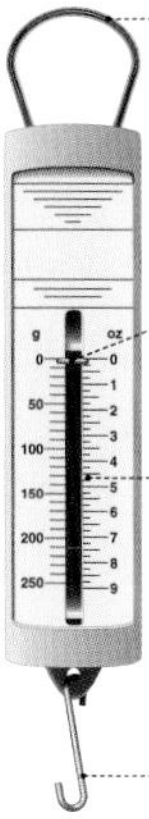

ring
anilla[F]
pointer
fiel[M]
graduated scale
escala[F] *graduada*
hook
gancho[M]

electronic scale
báscula*[F] *electrónica

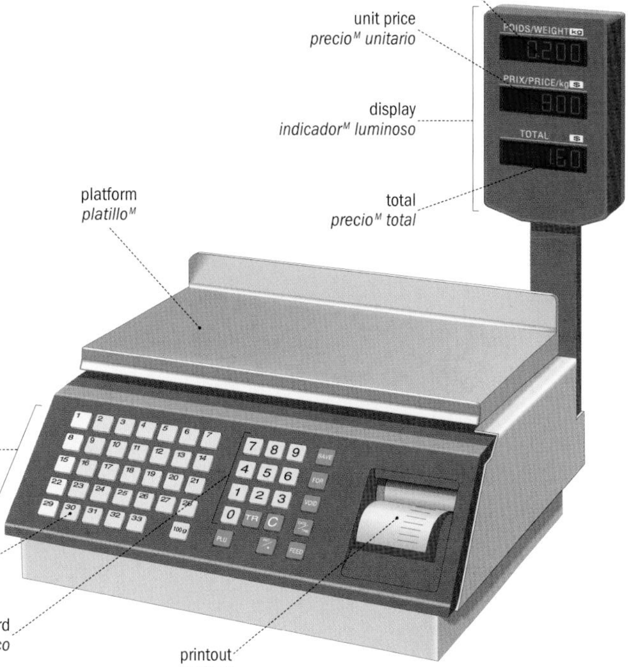

weight
peso[M]
unit price
precio[M] *unitario*
display
indicador[M] *luminoso*
total
precio[M] *total*
platform
platillo[M]
function keys
teclado[M] *de funciones*[F]
product code
código[M] *del producto*[M]
numeric keyboard
teclado[M] *numérico*
printout
recibo[M]

bathroom scale
***báscula*[F] *de baño*[M]**

digital display
indicador[M] *digital*
weighing platform
plataforma[F]

analytical balance
***balanza*[F] *de precisión*[F]**

glass case
urna[F]
access door
puerta[F]
pan
platillo[M]
leveling screw
tornillo[M] *nivelador*

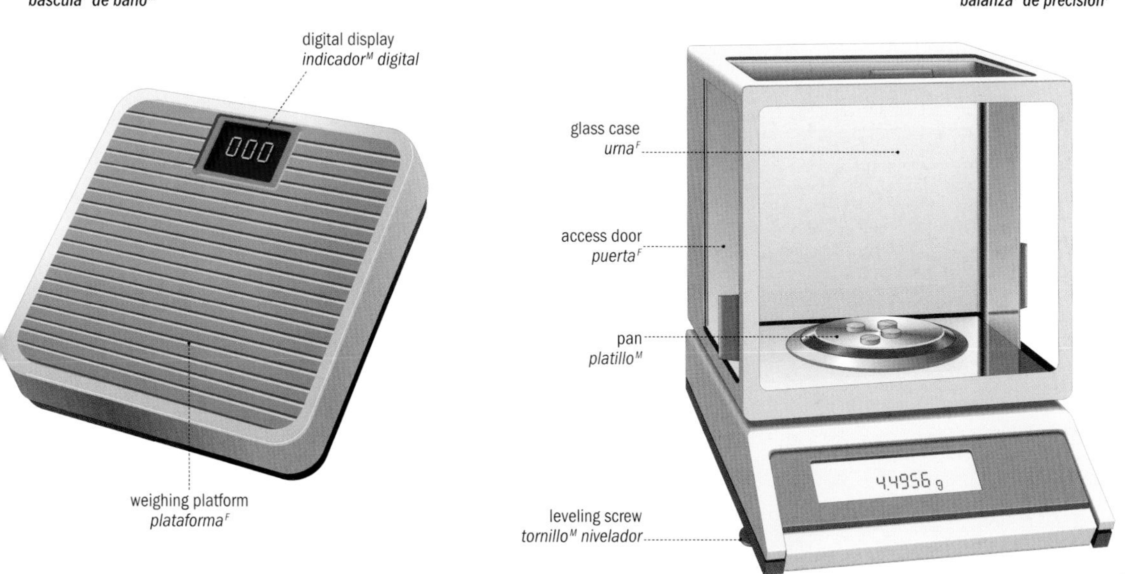

measurement of temperature

medición[F] de la temperatura[F]

thermometer
termómetro[M]

Fahrenheit scale
escala[F] Fahrenheit
temperature measured in Fahrenheit
grados[M] F
alcohol column
columna[F] de alcohol[M]
alcohol bulb
cubeta[F] de alcohol[M]
Celsius scale
escala[F] Celsius
temperature measured in Celsius
grados[M] C

clinical thermometer
termómetro[M] clínico

capillary bore
tubo[M] capilar
stem
tubo[M] de cristal[M]
mercury bulb
cubeta[F] de mercurio[M]
expansion chamber
cámara[F] de expansión[F]
scale
escala[F] de temperaturas[F]
column of mercury
columna[F] de mercurio[M]
constriction
estrechamiento[M]

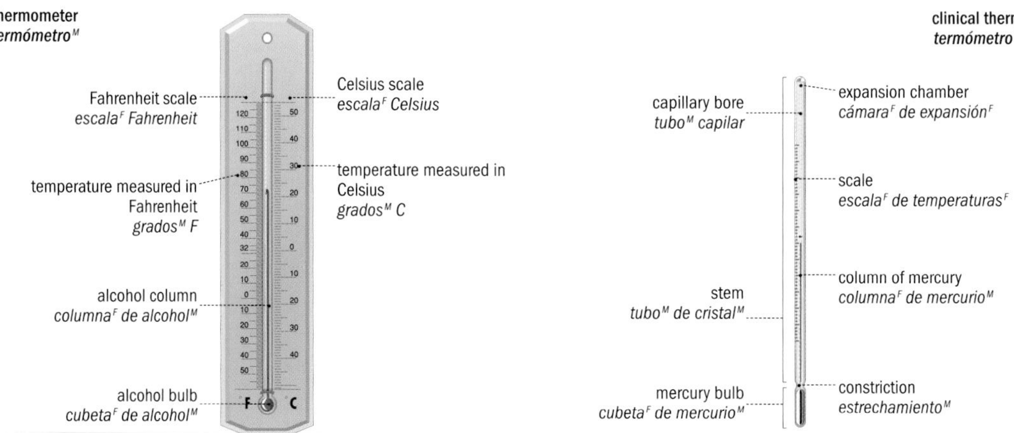

measurement of time

medición[F] del tiempo[M]

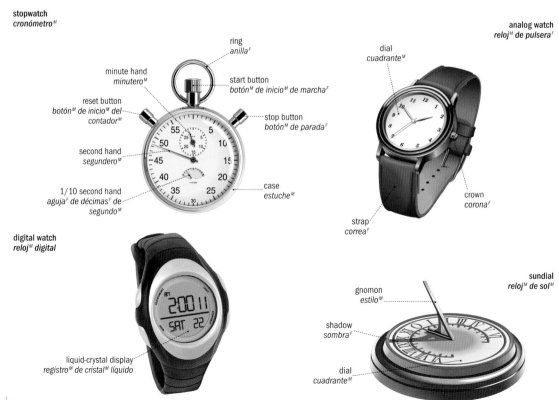

stopwatch
cronómetro[M]

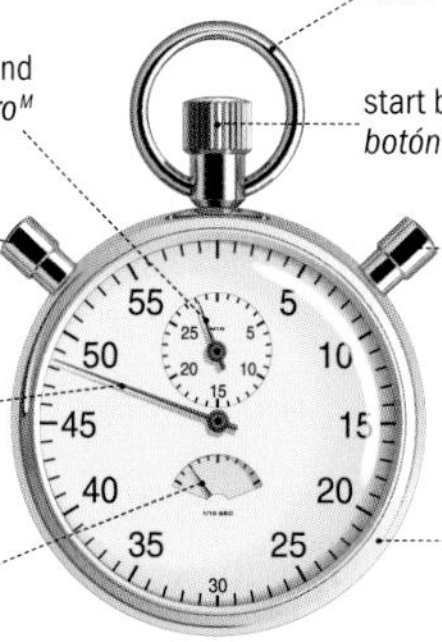

ring
anilla[F]
minute hand
minutero[M]
start button
botón[M] de inicio[M] de marcha[F]
reset button
botón[M] de inicio[M] del contador[M]
stop button
botón[M] de parada[F]
second hand
segundero[M]
1/10 second hand
aguja[F] de décimas[F] de segundo[M]
case
estuche[M]

analog watch
reloj[M] de pulsera[F]

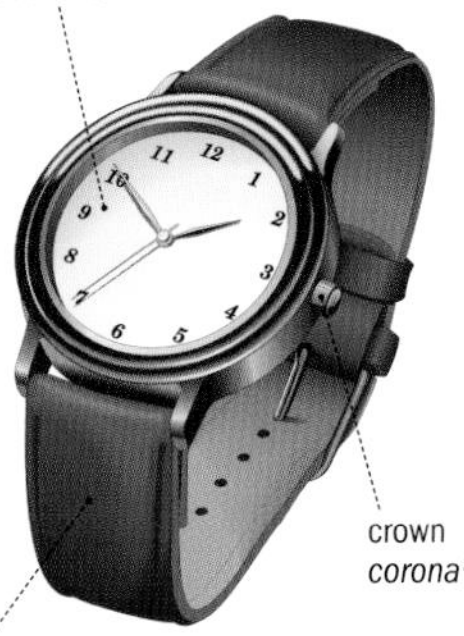

dial
cuadrante[M]
crown
corona[F]
strap
correa[F]

digital watch
reloj[M] digital

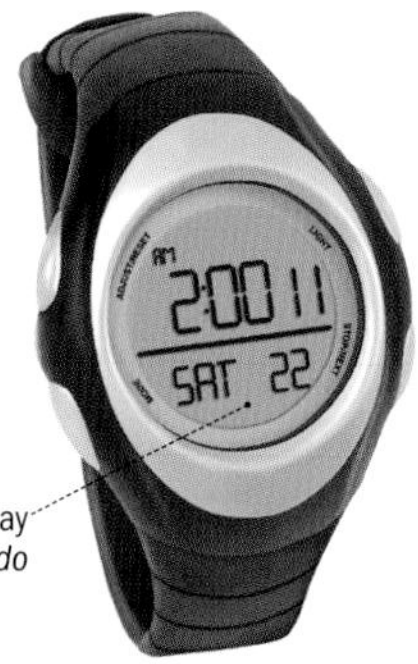

liquid-crystal display
registro[M] de cristal[M] líquido

sundial
reloj[M] de sol[M]

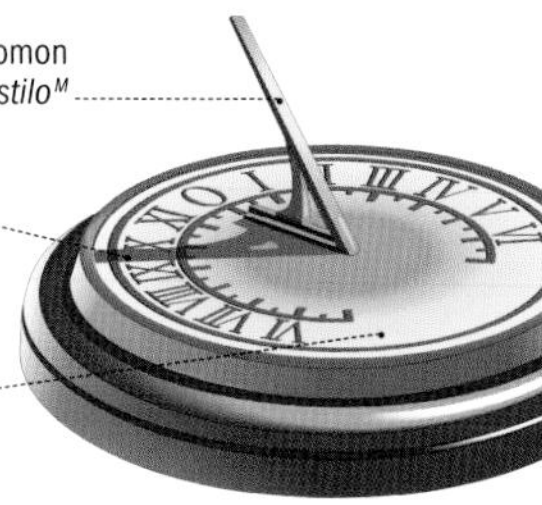

gnomon
estilo[M]
shadow
sombra[F]
dial
cuadrante[M]

SCIENCE

measurement of length

medición^F de la longitud^F

ruler
regla^F graduada

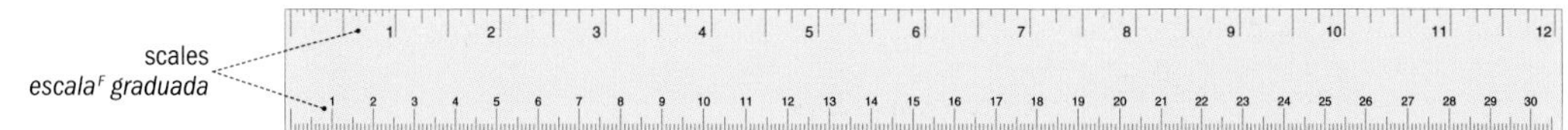

measurement of thickness

medición^F del espesor^M

vernier caliper
escala^F graduada de vernier^M, pico^M de rey^M

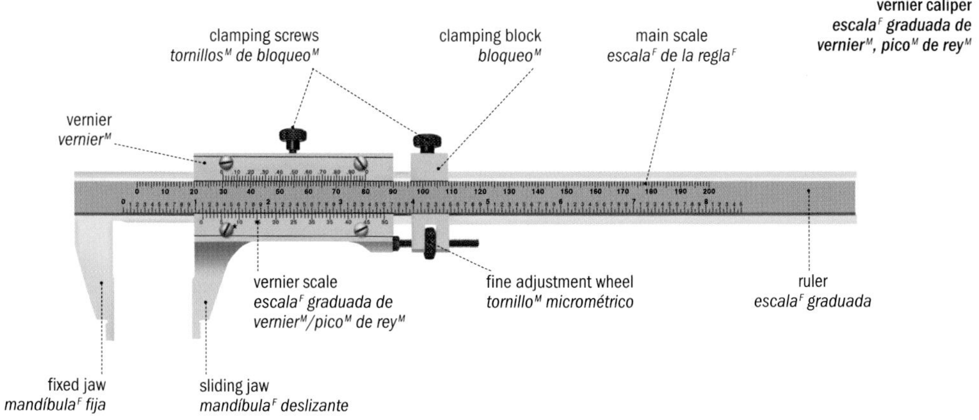

micrometer caliper
micrómetro^M

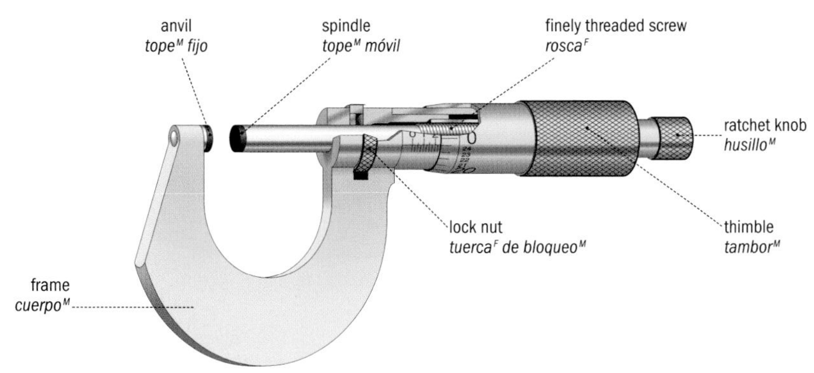

SCIENCE

international system of units

sistema[M] internacional de unidades[F] de medida[F]

unit of electric current
unidad[F] de medida[F] de corriente[F] eléctrica

ampere
amperio[M]

unit of electric potential difference
unidad[F] de medida[F] de la diferencia[F] de potencial[M] eléctrico

volt
voltio[M], volt[M]

unit of electric resistance
unidad[F] de medida[F] de resistencia[F] eléctrica

ohm
ohmnio[M]/ohm[M]

unit of electric charge
unidad[F] de medida[F] de carga[F] eléctrica

C

coulomb
culombio[M]

unit of power
unidad[F] de medida[F] de potencia[F] eléctrica

W

watt
vatio[M]

unit of frequency
unidad[F] de medida[F] de frecuencia[F]

Hz

hertz
hercio[M]

unit of luminous intensity
unidad[F] de medida[F] de intensidad[F] luminosa

cd

candela
candela[F]

unit of energy
unidad[F] de medida[F] de energía[F]

J

joule
julio[M]

unit of length
unidad[F] de medida[F] de longitud[F]

m

meter
metro[M]

unit of mass
unidad[F] de medida[F] de masa[F]

kg

kilogram
kilogramo[M]

unit of pressure
unidad[F] de medida[F] de presión[F]

Pa

pascal
pascal[M]

unit of force
unidad[F] de medida[F] de fuerza[F]

N

newton
newton[M]

unit of time
unidad[F] de medida[F] de tiempo[M]

s

second
segundo[M]

unit of amount of substance
unidad[F] de medida[F] de cantidad[F] de materia[F]

mol

mole
mole[M]

unit of radioactivity
unidad[F] de medida[F] de radioactividad[F]

Bq

becquerel
becquerel[M]

unit of temperature
unidad[F] de medida[F] de la temperatura[F]

°C

degree Celsius
grado[M] Celsius

unit of thermodynamic temperature
unidad[F] de medida[F] de temperatura[F] termodinámica

K

kelvin
kelvin[M]

biology

biología[F]

♂

male
masculino[M]

female
femenino[M]

Rh+

blood factor RH positive
factor[M] RH positivo

blood factor RH negative
factor[M] RH negativo

death
muerte[F]

*

birth
nacimiento[M]

SCIENCE

mathematics

matemáticas[F]

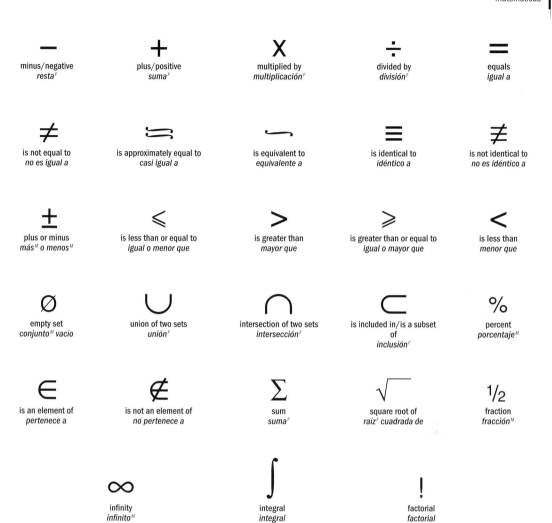

−
minus/negative
resta[F]

+
plus/positive
suma[F]

X
multiplied by
multiplicación[F]

÷
divided by
división[F]

=
equals
igual a

≠
is not equal to
no es igual a

≒
is approximately equal to
casi igual a

∽
is equivalent to
equivalente a

≡
is identical to
idéntico a

≢
is not identical to
no es idéntico a

±
plus or minus
más[M] *o menos*[M]

⩽
is less than or equal to
igual o menor que

>
is greater than
mayor que

⩾
is greater than or equal to
igual o mayor que

<
is less than
menor que

∅
empty set
conjunto[M] *vacío*

∪
union of two sets
unión[F]

∩
intersection of two sets
intersección[F]

⊂
is included in/is a subset of
inclusión[F]

%
percent
porcentaje[M]

∈
is an element of
pertenece a

∉
is not an element of
no pertenece a

Σ
sum
suma[F]

√
square root of
raíz[F] *cuadrada de*

½
fraction
fracción[M]

∞
infinity
infinito[M]

∫
integral
integral

!
factorial
factorial

Roman numerals
números[M] *romanos*

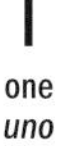
one
uno

five
cinco

X
ten
diez

L
fifty
cincuenta

C
one hundred
mil

five hundred
quinientos

M
one thousand
cien

SCIENCE

geometry

geometría[F]

°	'	"	π	⊥
degree *grado[M]*	**minute** *minuto[M]*	**second** *segundo[M]*	**pi** *pi[M]*	**perpendicular** *perpendicular[F]*

‖	∦	∟	obtuse	∠
is parallel to *es paralelo a*	**is not parallel to** *no es paralelo a*	**right angle** *ángulo[M] recto*	**obtuse angle** *ángulo[M] obtuso*	**acute angle** *ángulo[M] agudo*

geometrical shapes

formas[F] geométricas

examples of angles
ejemplos[M] de ángulos[M]

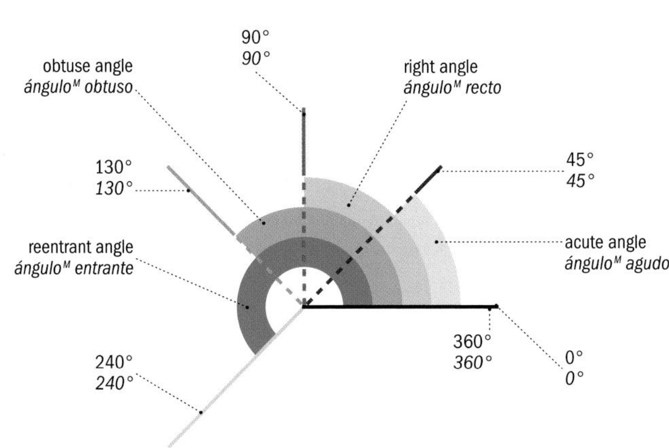

plane surfaces
superficies[F]

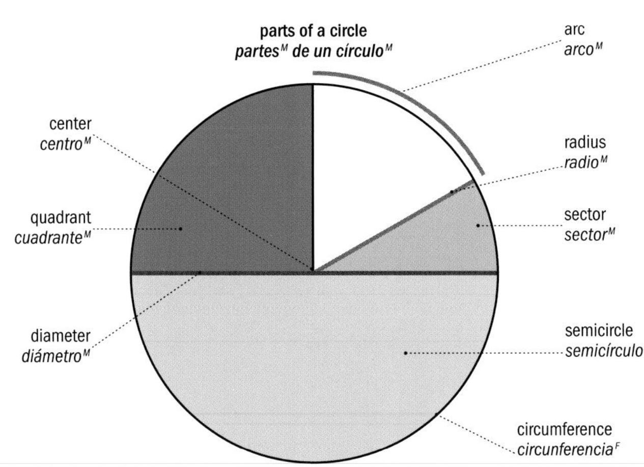

SCIENCE

polygons
polígonos[M]

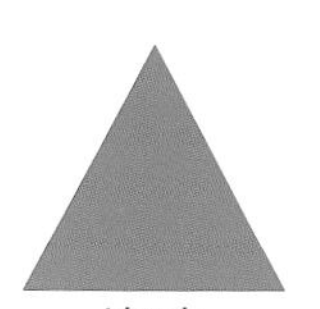
triangle
triángulo[M]

square
cuadrado[M]

rectangle
rectángulo[M]

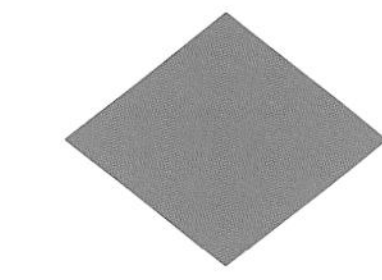

rhombus
rombo[M]

trapezoid
trapecio[M]

parallelogram
paralelogramo[M]

quadrilateral
cuadrilátero[M]

regular pentagon
pentágono[M] *regular*

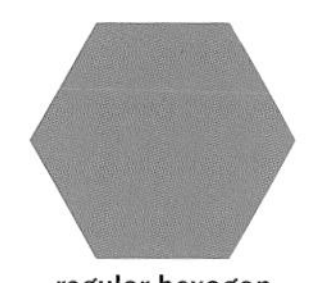
regular hexagon
hexágono[M] *regular*

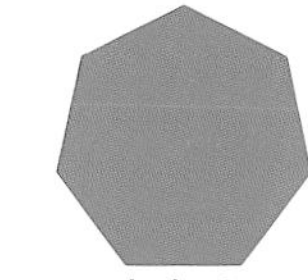
regular heptagon
heptágono[M] *regular*

regular octagon
octágono[M] *regular*

regular nonagon
nonágono[M] *regular*

regular decagon
decágono[M] *regular*

regular hendecagon
endecágono[M] *regular*

regular dodecagon
dodecágono[M] *regular*

solids
cuerpos[M] *sólidos*[M]

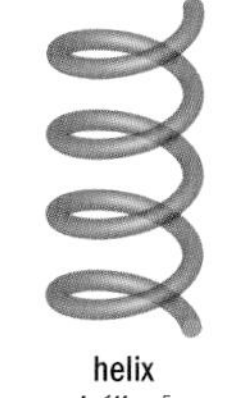
helix
hélice[F]

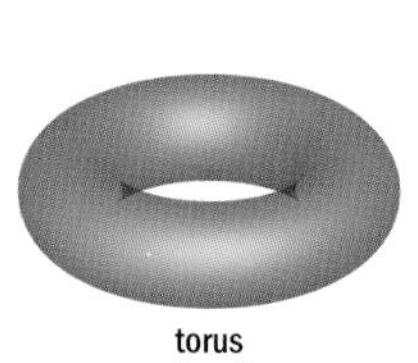
torus
toro[M]

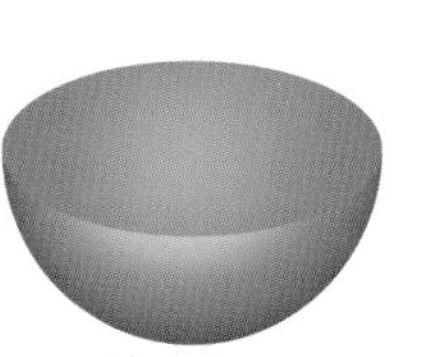
hemisphere
hemisferio[M]

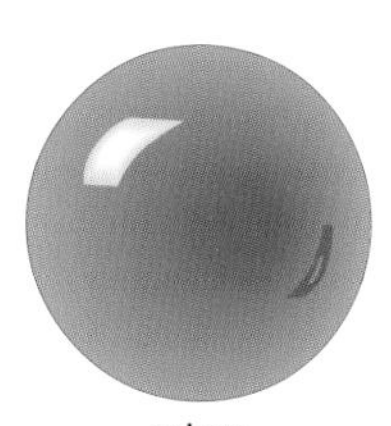
sphere
esfera[F]

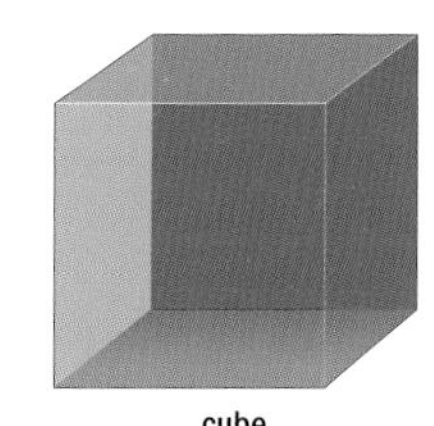
cube
cubo[M]

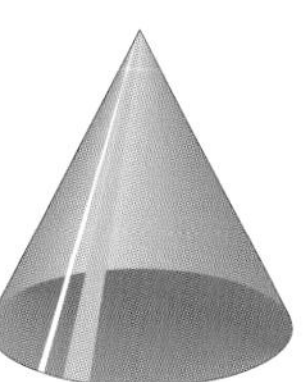
cone
cono[M]

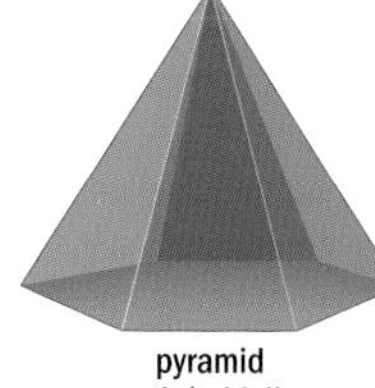
pyramid
pirámide[M]

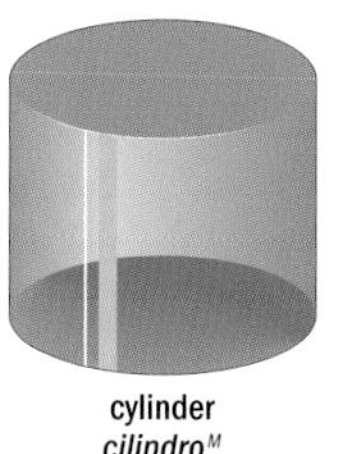
cylinder
cilindro[M]

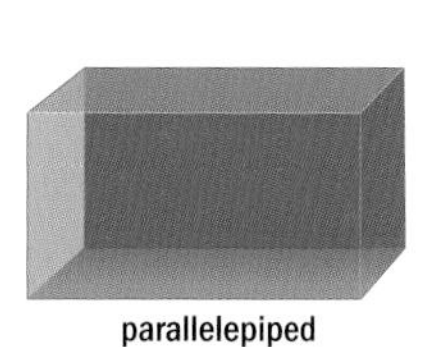
parallelepiped
paralelepípedo[M]

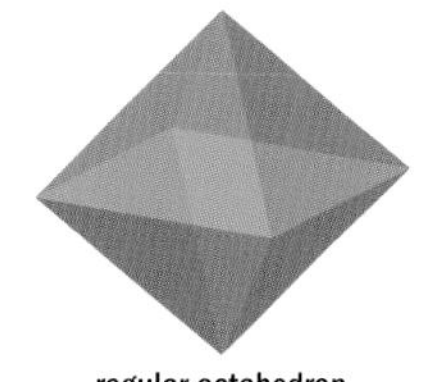
regular octahedron
octaedro[M] *regular*

agglomeration

conurbación[F]

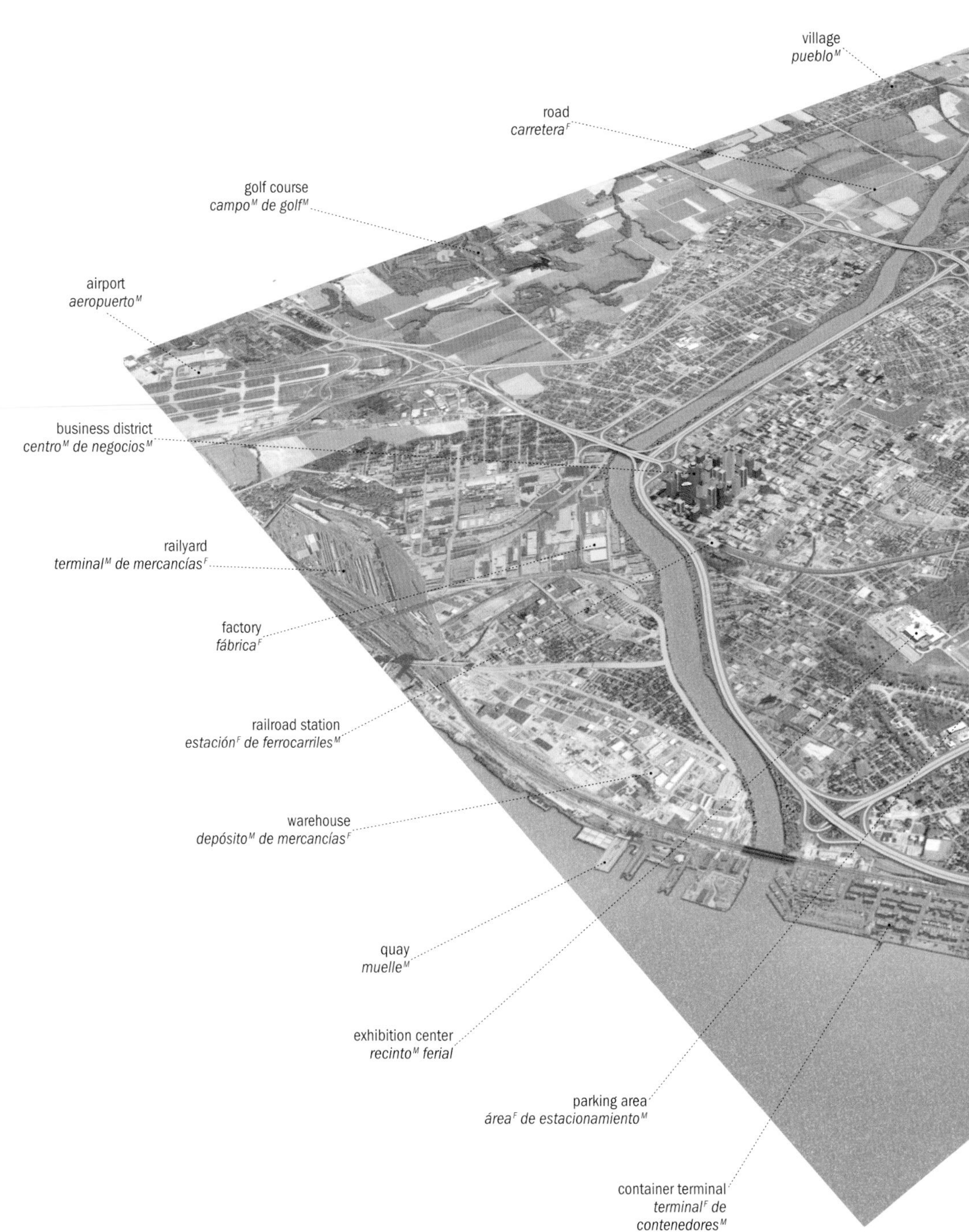
village
pueblo[M]
road
carretera[F]
golf course
campo[M] de golf[M]
airport
aeropuerto[M]
business district
centro[M] de negocios[M]
railyard
terminal[M] de mercancías[F]
factory
fábrica[F]
railroad station
estación[F] de ferrocarriles[M]
warehouse
depósito[M] de mercancías[F]
quay
muelle[M]
exhibition center
recinto[M] ferial
parking area
área[F] de estacionamiento[M]
container terminal
terminal[F] de contenedores[M]

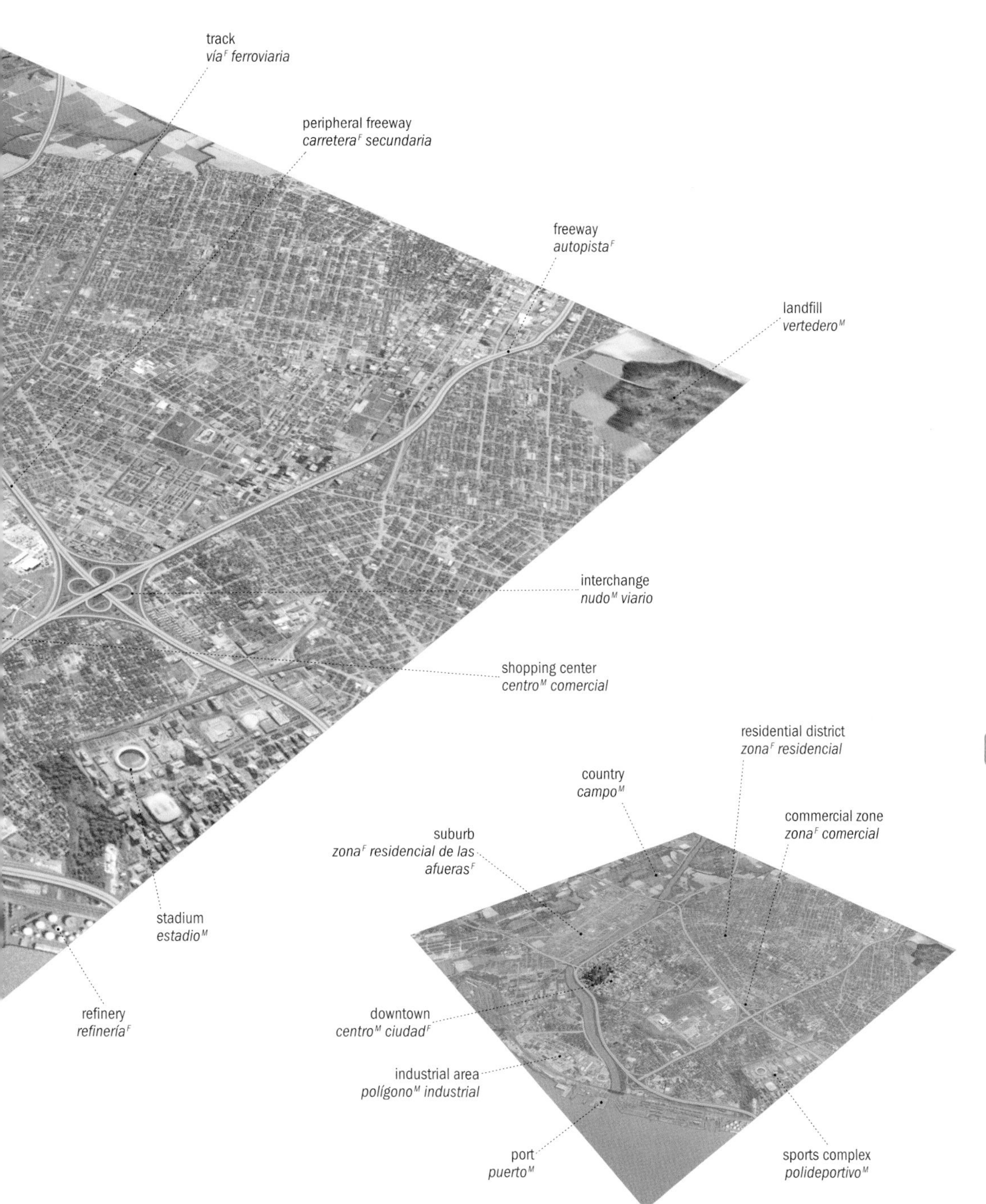
track
vía^F ferroviaria
peripheral freeway
carretera^F secundaria
freeway
autopista^F
landfill
vertedero^M
interchange
nudo^M viario
shopping center
centro^M comercial
residential district
zona^F residencial
country
campo^M
commercial zone
zona^F comercial
suburb
zona^F residencial de las afueras^F
stadium
estadio^M
refinery
refinería^F
downtown
centro^M ciudad^F
industrial area
polígono^M industrial
port
puerto^M
sports complex
polideportivo^M

downtown

centro[M] ciudad[F]

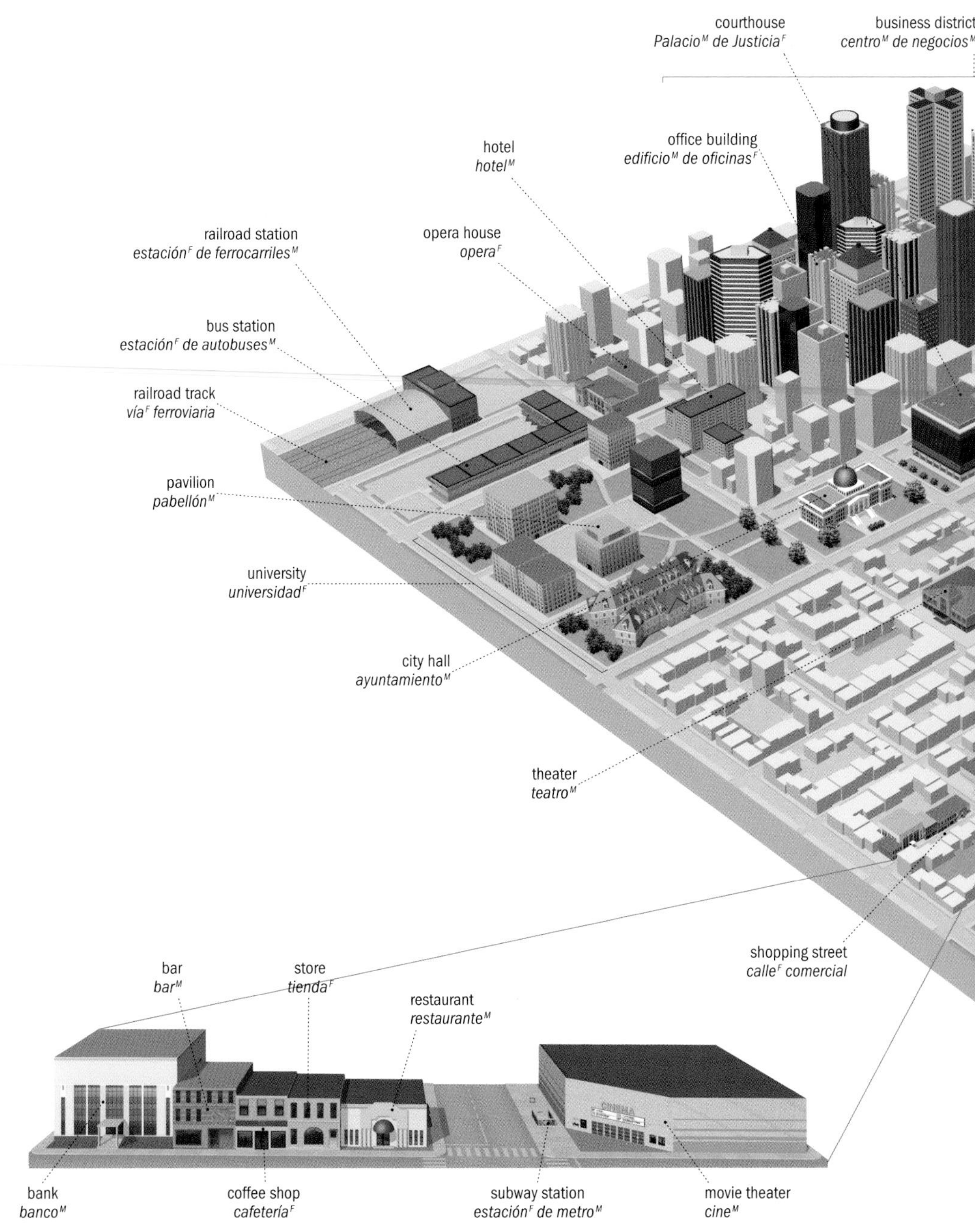
courthouse
Palacio[M] de Justicia[F]
business district
centro[M] de negocios[M]
hotel
hotel[M]
office building
edificio[M] de oficinas[F]
railroad station
estación[F] de ferrocarriles[M]
opera house
opera[F]
bus station
estación[F] de autobuses[M]
railroad track
vía[F] ferroviaria
pavilion
pabellón[M]
university
universidad[F]
city hall
ayuntamiento[M]
theater
teatro[M]
shopping street
calle[F] comercial
bar
bar[M]
store
tienda[F]
restaurant
restaurante[M]
bank
banco[M]
coffee shop
cafetería[F]
subway station
estación[F] de metro[M]
movie theater
cine[M]

SOCIETY

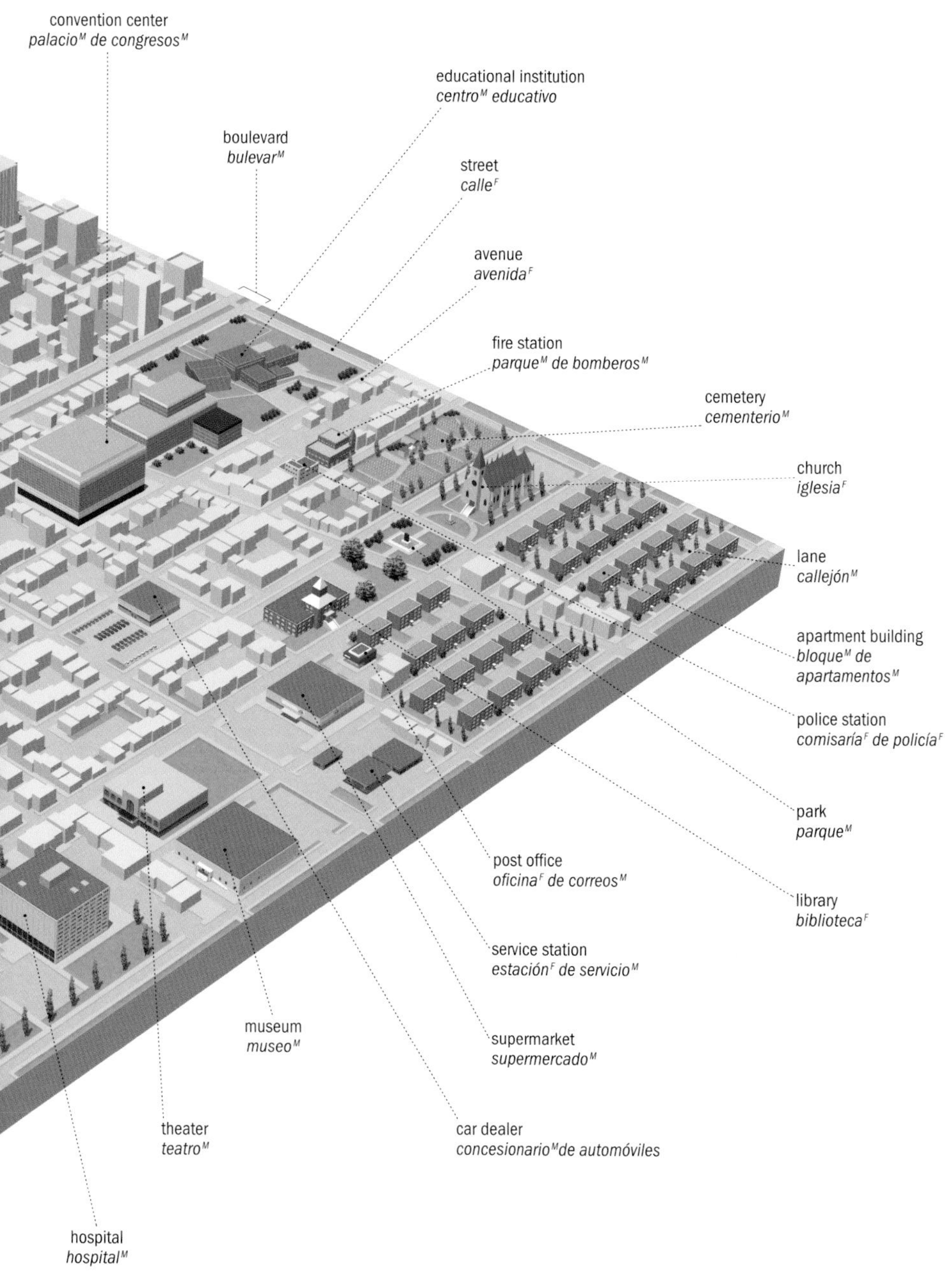
convention center
*palacio*M *de congresos*M
educational institution
*centro*M *educativo*
boulevard
*bulevar*M
street
*calle*F
avenue
*avenida*F
fire station
*parque*M *de bomberos*M
cemetery
*cementerio*M
church
*iglesia*F
lane
*callejón*M
apartment building
*bloque*M *de apartamentos*M
police station
*comisaría*F *de policía*F
park
*parque*M
post office
*oficina*F *de correos*M
library
*biblioteca*F
service station
*estación*F *de servicio*M
museum
*museo*M
supermarket
*supermercado*M
theater
*teatro*M
car dealer
*concesionario*M*de automóviles*
hospital
*hospital*M

cross section of a street

vista[F] transversal de una calle[F]

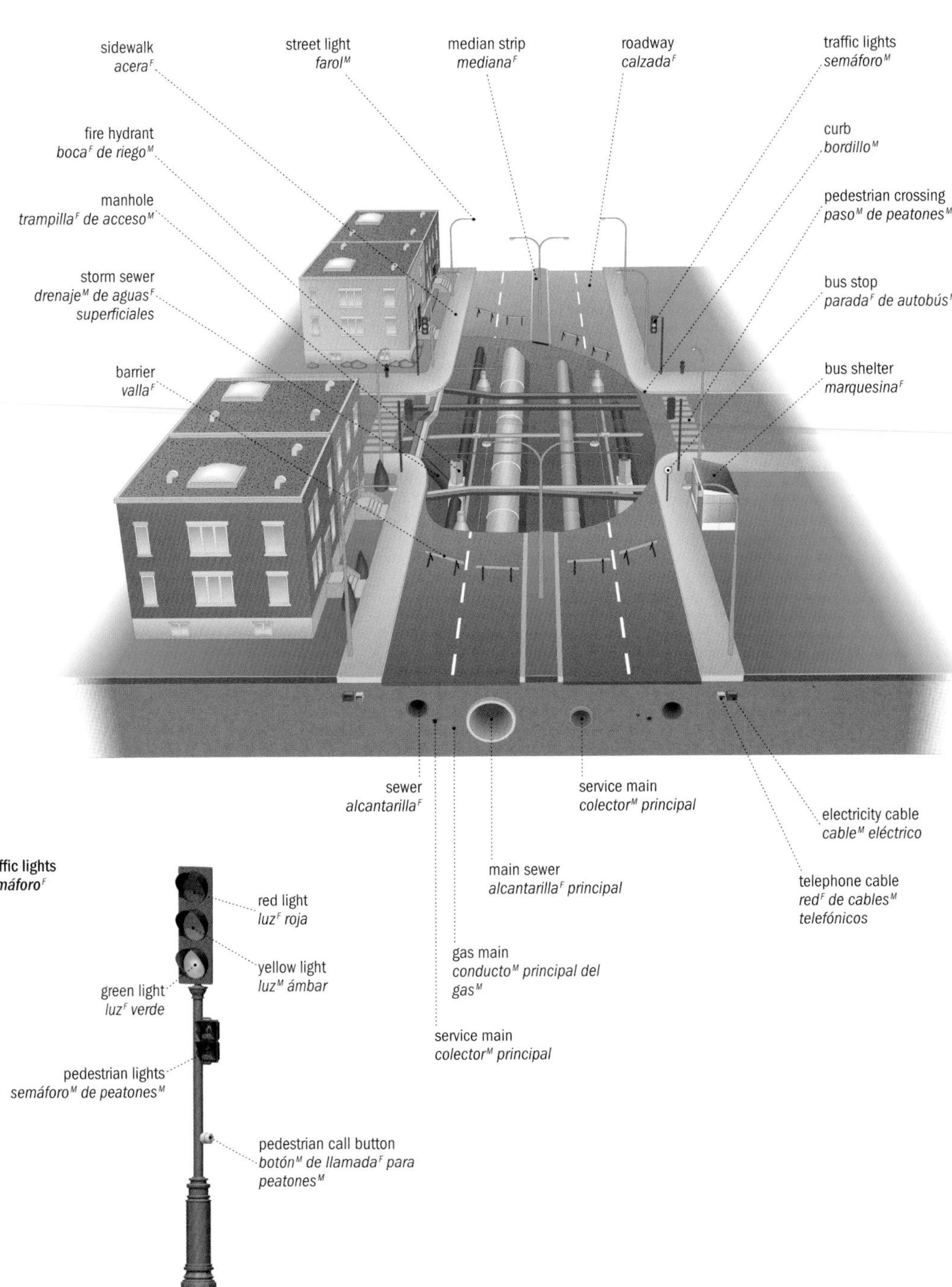
sidewalk
acera[F]
street light
farol[M]
median strip
mediana[F]
roadway
calzada[F]
traffic lights
semáforo[M]
fire hydrant
boca[F] de riego[M]
curb
bordillo[M]
manhole
trampilla[F] de acceso[M]
pedestrian crossing
paso[M] de peatones[M]
storm sewer
drenaje[M] de aguas[F] superficiales
bus stop
parada[F] de autobús[M]
barrier
valla[F]
bus shelter
marquesina[F]
sewer
alcantarilla[F]
service main
colector[M] principal
electricity cable
cable[M] eléctrico
main sewer
alcantarilla[F] principal
telephone cable
red[F] de cables[M] telefónicos
gas main
conducto[M] principal del gas[M]
service main
colector[M] principal
traffic lights
semáforo[F]
red light
luz[F] roja
yellow light
luz[M] ámbar
green light
luz[F] verde
pedestrian lights
semáforo[M] de peatones[M]
pedestrian call button
botón[M] de llamada[F] para peatones[M]

SOCIETY

office building

edificio^M de oficinas^F

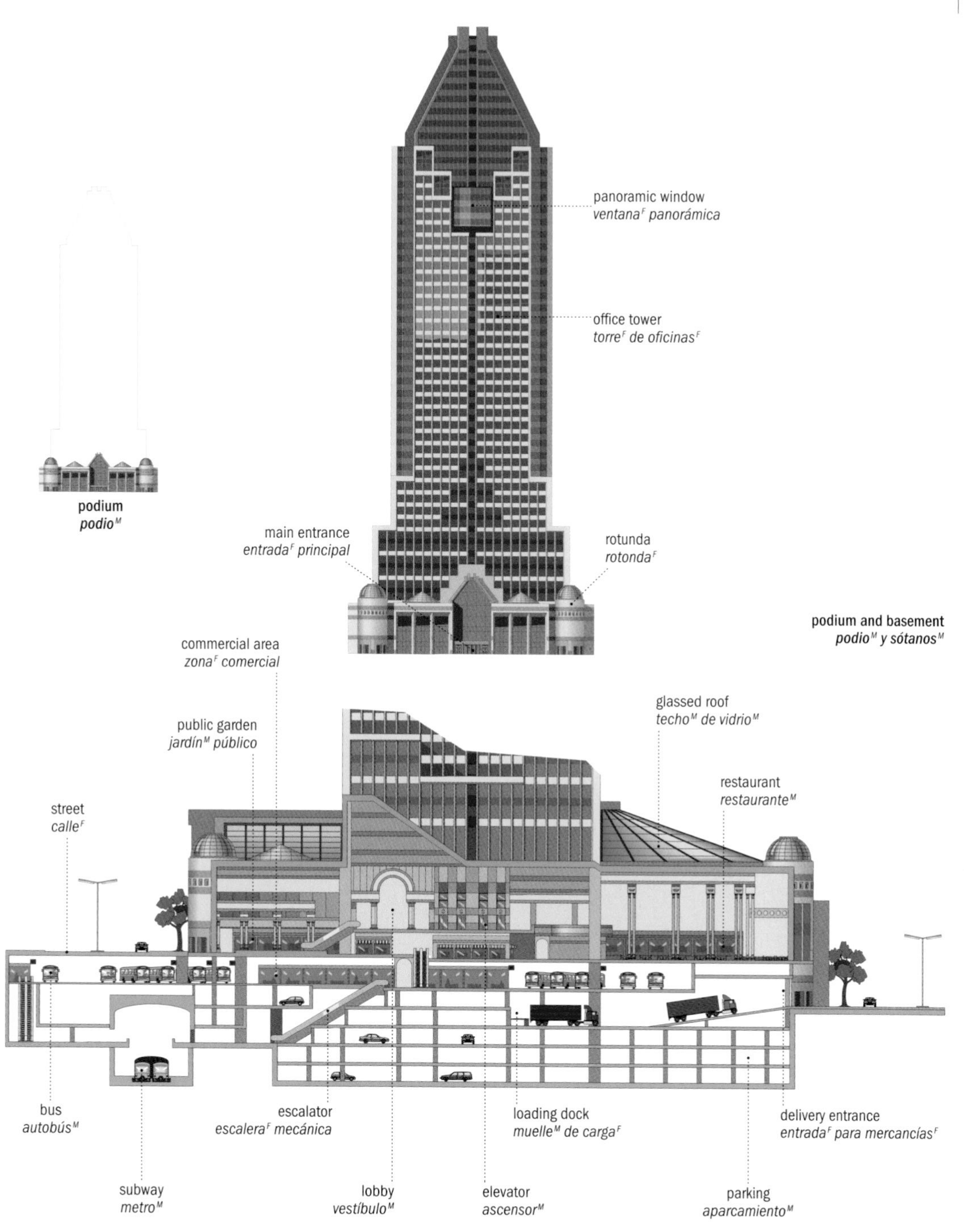
panoramic window
ventana^F panorámica
office tower
torre^F de oficinas^F
podium
podio^M
main entrance
entrada^F principal
rotunda
rotonda^F
podium and basement
podio^M y sótanos^M
commercial area
zona^F comercial
public garden
jardín^M público
glassed roof
techo^M de vidrio^M
restaurant
restaurante^M
street
calle^F
bus
autobús^M
escalator
escalera^F mecánica
loading dock
muelle^M de carga^F
delivery entrance
entrada^F para mercancías^F
subway
metro^M
lobby
vestíbulo^M
elevator
ascensor^M
parking
aparcamiento^M

SOCIETY

shopping center

centro[M] comercial

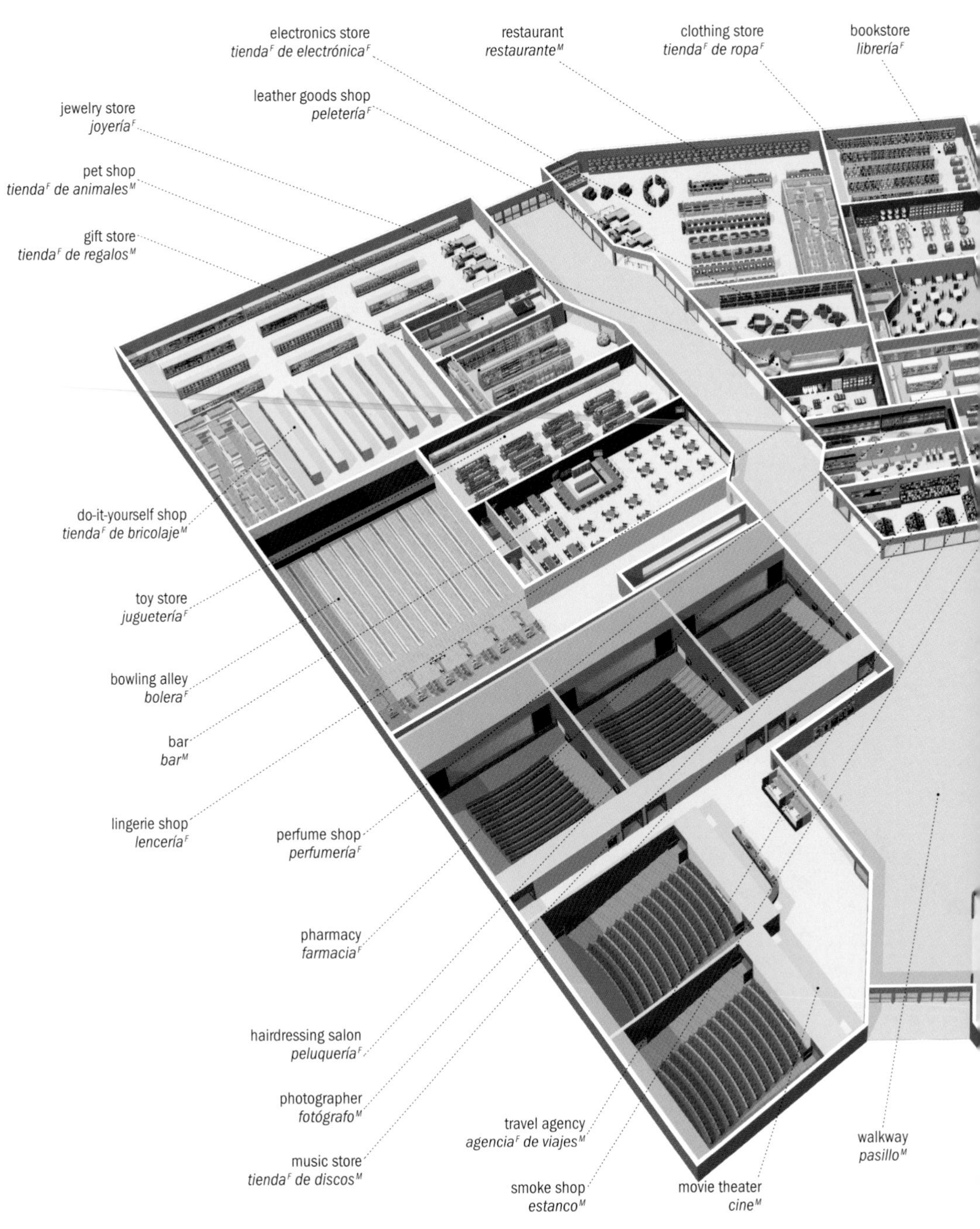
electronics store
tienda[F] de electrónica[F]
restaurant
restaurante[M]
clothing store
tienda[F] de ropa[F]
bookstore
librería[F]
leather goods shop
peletería[F]
jewelry store
joyería[F]
pet shop
tienda[F] de animales[M]
gift store
tienda[F] de regalos[M]
do-it-yourself shop
tienda[F] de bricolaje[M]
toy store
juguetería[F]
bowling alley
bolera[F]
bar
bar[M]
lingerie shop
lencería[F]
perfume shop
perfumería[F]
pharmacy
farmacia[F]
hairdressing salon
peluquería[F]
photographer
fotógrafo[M]
music store
tienda[F] de discos[M]
travel agency
agencia[F] de viajes[M]
smoke shop
estanco[M]
movie theater
cine[M]
walkway
pasillo[M]

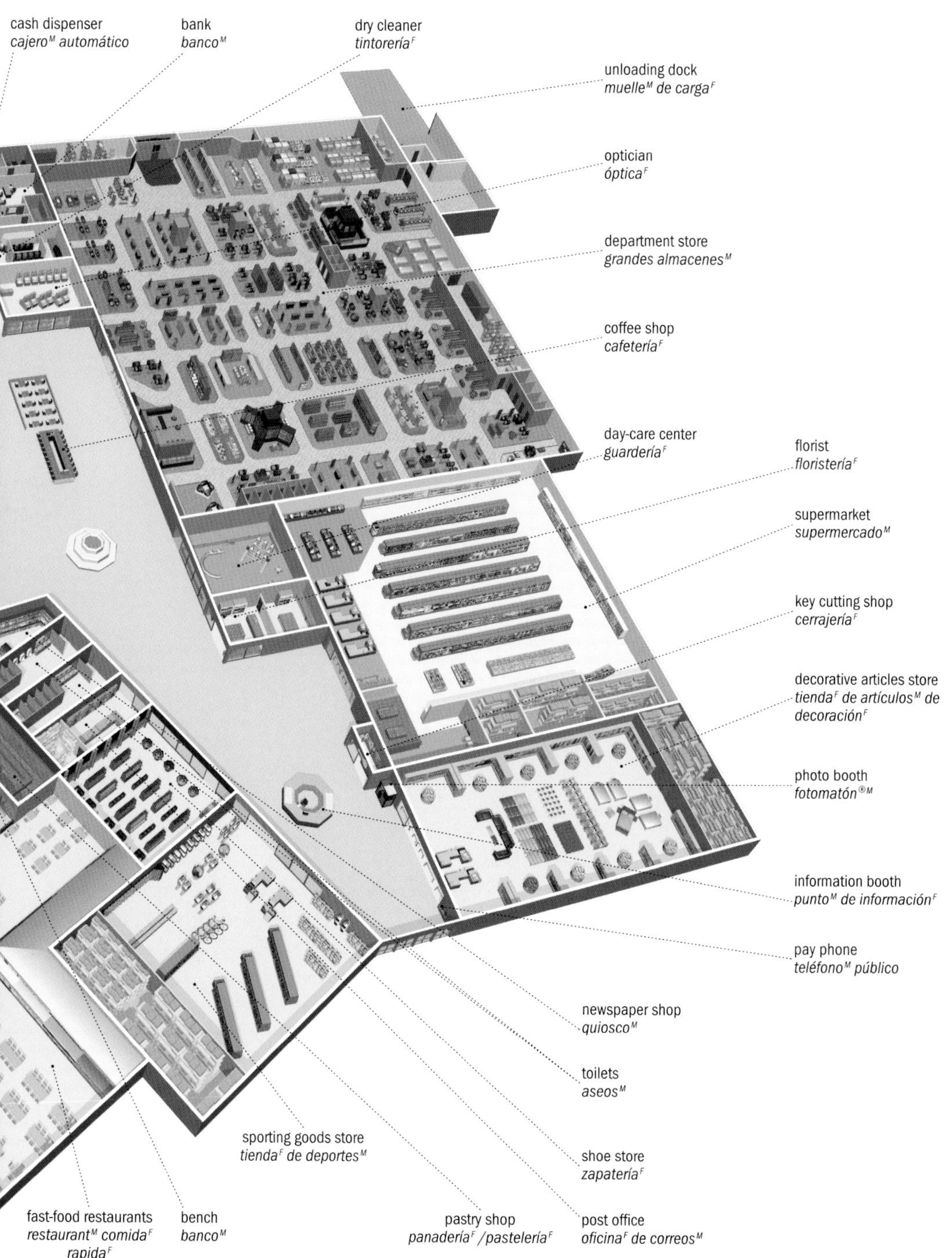
cash dispenser
cajero[M] automático
bank
banco[M]
dry cleaner
tintorería[F]
unloading dock
muelle[M] de carga[F]
optician
óptica[F]
department store
grandes almacenes[M]
coffee shop
cafetería[F]
day-care center
guardería[F]
florist
floristería[F]
supermarket
supermercado[M]
key cutting shop
cerrajería[F]
decorative articles store
tienda[F] de artículos[M] de decoración[F]
photo booth
fotomatón[®M]
information booth
punto[M] de información[F]
pay phone
teléfono[M] público
newspaper shop
quiosco[M]
toilets
aseos[M]
sporting goods store
tienda[F] de deportes[M]
shoe store
zapatería[F]
fast-food restaurants
restaurant[M] comida[F] rapida[F]
bench
banco[M]
pastry shop
panadería[F] /pastelería[F]
post office
oficina[F] de correos[M]

restaurant

restaurante[M]

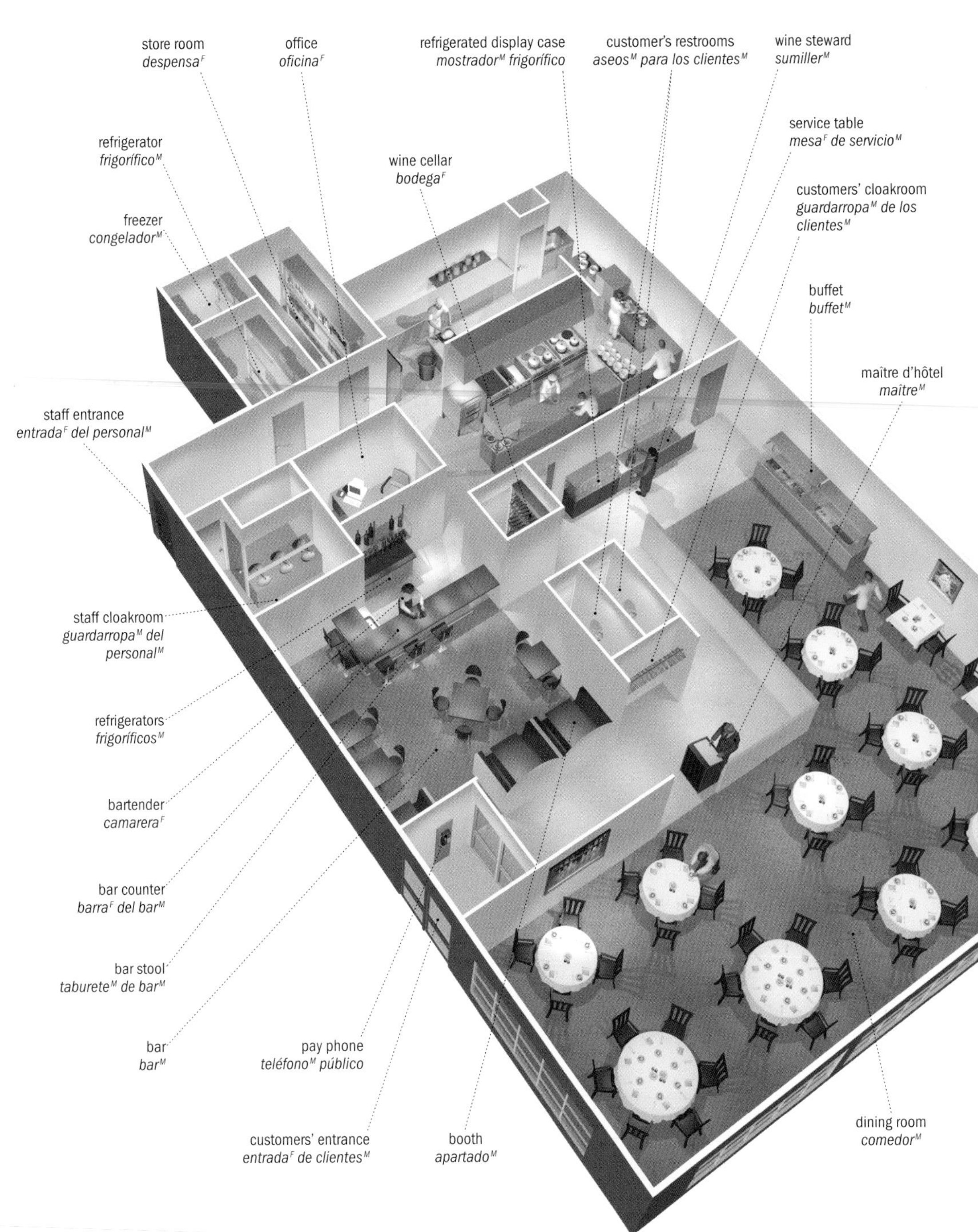
store room
despensa[F]
office
oficina[F]
refrigerated display case
mostrador[M] frigorífico
customer's restrooms
aseos[M] para los clientes[M]
wine steward
sumiller[M]
service table
mesa[F] de servicio[M]
refrigerator
frigorífico[M]
wine cellar
bodega[F]
customers' cloakroom
guardarropa[M] de los clientes[M]
freezer
congelador[M]
buffet
buffet[M]
maître d'hôtel
maître[M]
staff entrance
entrada[F] del personal[M]
staff cloakroom
guardarropa[M] del personal[M]
refrigerators
frigoríficos[M]
bartender
camarera[F]
bar counter
barra[F] del bar[M]
bar stool
taburete[M] de bar[M]
bar
bar[M]
pay phone
teléfono[M] público
customers' entrance
entrada[F] de clientes[M]
booth
apartado[M]
dining room
comedor[M]

hotel
hotel[M]

reception level
nivel[M] de la recepción[F]

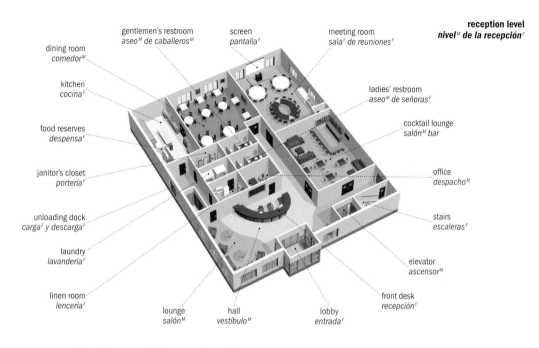

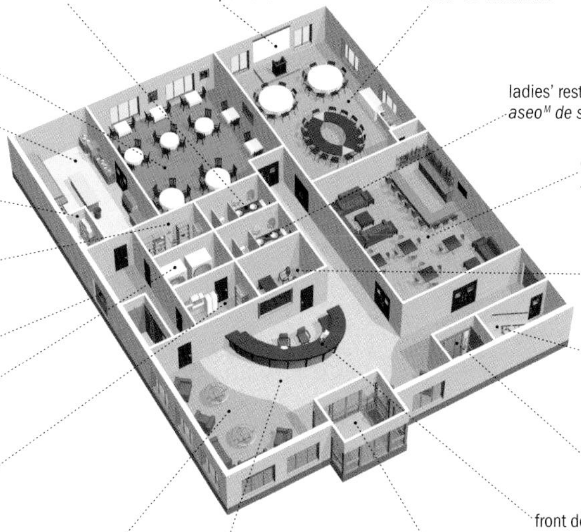

gentlemen's restroom
aseo[M] de caballeros[M]

screen
pantalla[F]

meeting room
sala[F] de reuniones[F]

dining room
comedor[M]

kitchen
cocina[F]

ladies' restroom
aseo[M] de señoras[F]

cocktail lounge
salón[M] bar

food reserves
despensa[F]

janitor's closet
portería[F]

office
despacho[M]

unloading dock
carga[F] y descarga[F]

stairs
escaleras[F]

laundry
lavandería[F]

elevator
ascensor[M]

linen room
lencería[F]

front desk
recepción[F]

lounge
salón[M]

hall
vestíbulo[M]

lobby
entrada[F]

hotel rooms
habitación[F] de hotel[M]

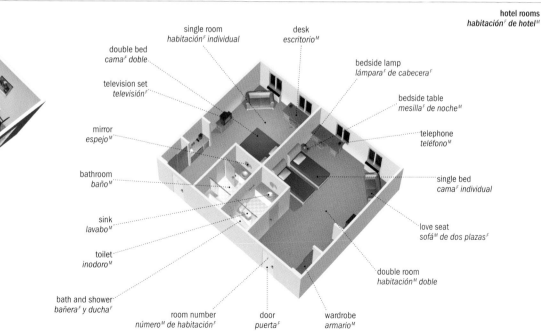

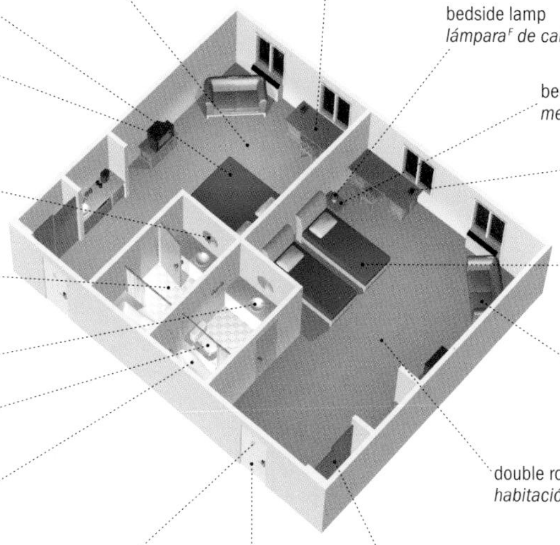

single room
habitación[F] individual

desk
escritorio[M]

double bed
cama[F] doble

bedside lamp
lámpara[F] de cabecera[F]

television set
televisión[F]

bedside table
mesilla[F] de noche[M]

mirror
espejo[M]

telephone
teléfono[M]

bathroom
baño[M]

single bed
cama[F] individual

sink
lavabo[M]

love seat
sofá[M] de dos plazas[F]

toilet
inodoro[M]

double room
habitación[M] doble

bath and shower
bañera[F] y ducha[F]

room number
número[M] de habitación[F]

door
puerta[F]

wardrobe
armario[M]

court

tribunal[M]

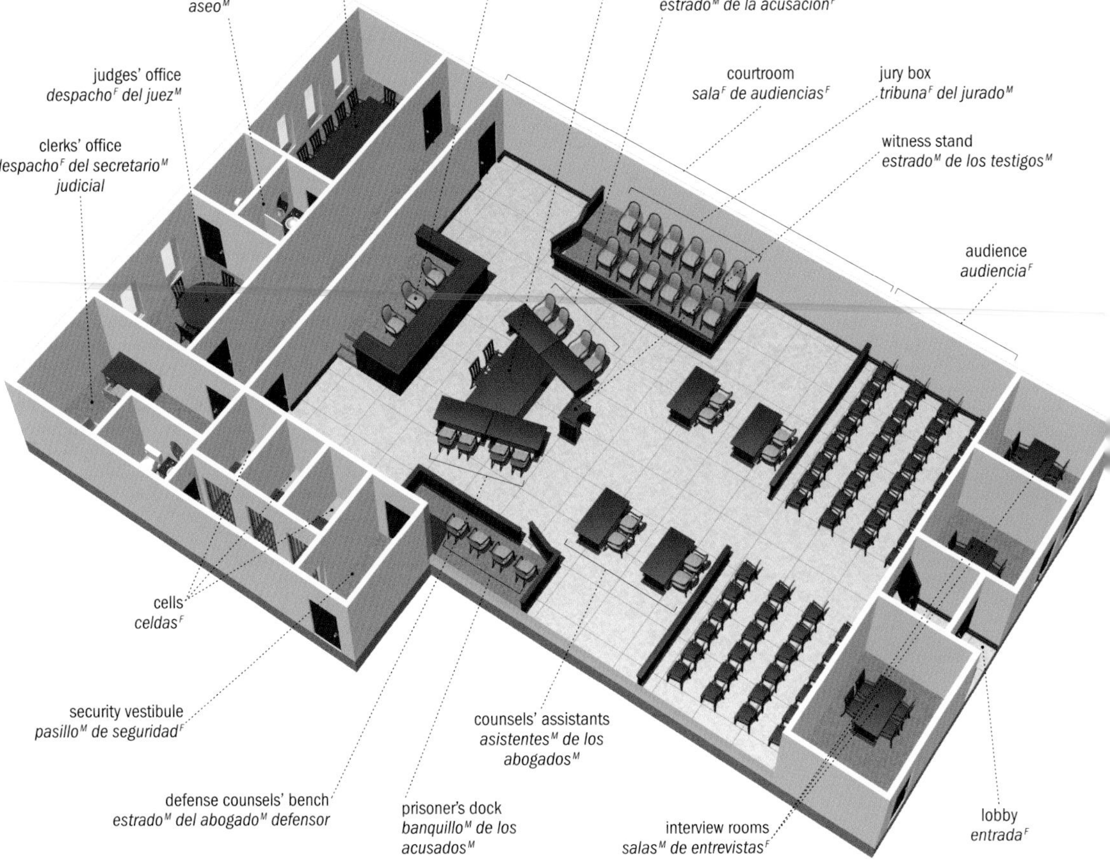

jurors' room
sala[F] del jurado[M]

judges' bench
estrado[M] de los jueces[M]

clerks' desk
estrado[F] de los secretarios[M] judiciales

restroom
aseo[M]

prosecution counsels' bench
estrado[M] de la acusación[F]

judges' office
despacho[F] del juez[M]

courtroom
sala[F] de audiencias[F]

jury box
tribuna[F] del jurado[M]

clerks' office
despacho[F] del secretario[M] judicial

witness stand
estrado[M] de los testigos[M]

audience
audiencia[F]

cells
celdas[F]

security vestibule
pasillo[M] de seguridad[F]

counsels' assistants
asistentes[M] de los abogados[M]

defense counsels' bench
estrado[M] del abogado[M] defensor

prisoner's dock
banquillo[M] de los acusados[M]

interview rooms
salas[M] de entrevistas[F]

lobby
entrada[F]

examples of currency abbreviations

ejemplos[M] de abreviaciones[F] de monedas[F]

dollar
dólar[M]

cent
centavo[M]

rupee
rupia[F]

euro
euro[M]

new shekel
nuevo shekel[M]

peso
peso[M]

yen
yen[M]

pound
libra[F]

money and modes of payment

dinero[M] y modos[M] de pago[M]

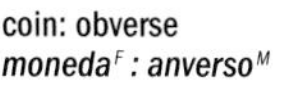

coin: obverse
moneda[F] : anverso[M]

date
fecha[F]

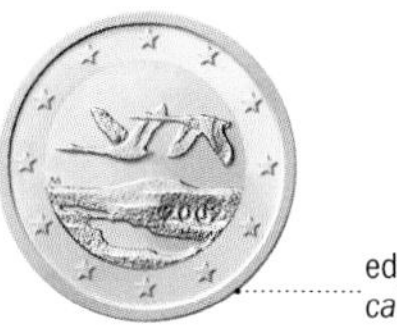

edge
canto[M]

banknote: front
billete[M]: recto[M]

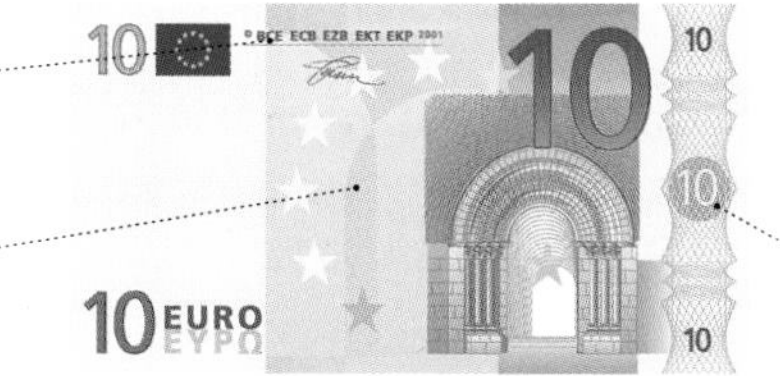

initials of the issuing bank
iniciales[F] del banco[M] emisor

security thread
hilo[M] de seguridad[F]

hologram foil strip
banda[F] holográfica metalizada

official signature
firma[F] oficial

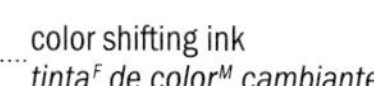

watermark
filigrana[F]

color shifting ink
tinta[F] de color[M] cambiante

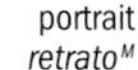

portrait
retrato[M]

serial number
número[M] de serie[F]

coin: reverse
moneda[F]: reverso[M]

outer ring
cordoncillo[M]

denomination
valor[M]

banknote: back
billete[M] : verso[M]

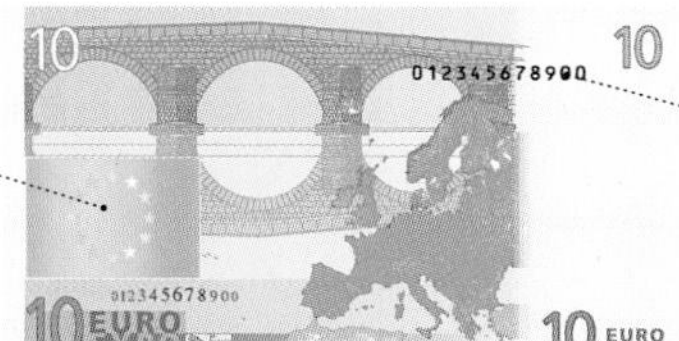

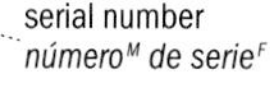

flag of the European Union
bandera[F] de la Unión[F] Europea

serial number
número[M] de serie[F]

motto
lema[M]

denomination
valor[M]

name of the currency
nombre[M] de la moneda[F]

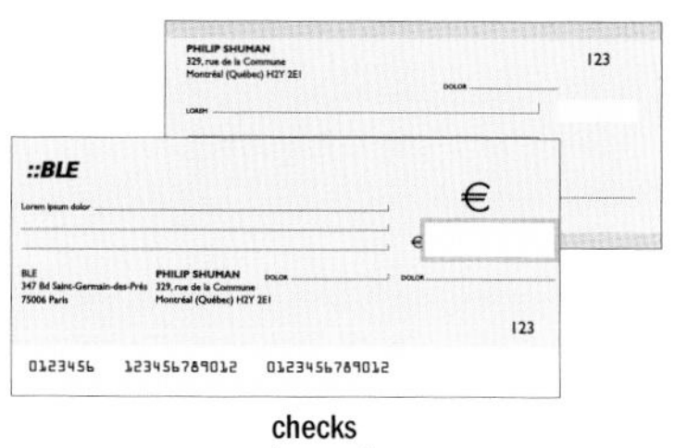

checks
cheques[M]

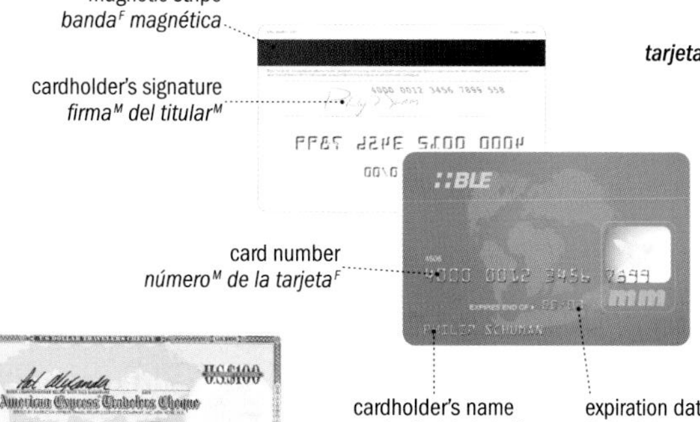

credit card
tarjeta[F] de crédito[M]

magnetic stripe
banda[F] magnética

cardholder's signature
firma[M] del titular[M]

card number
número[M] de la tarjeta[F]

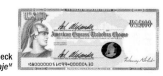

cardholder's name
nombre[M] del titular[M]

expiration date
fecha[F] de vencimiento[M]

traveler's check
cheque[M] de viaje[M]

SOCIETY

bank

banco^M

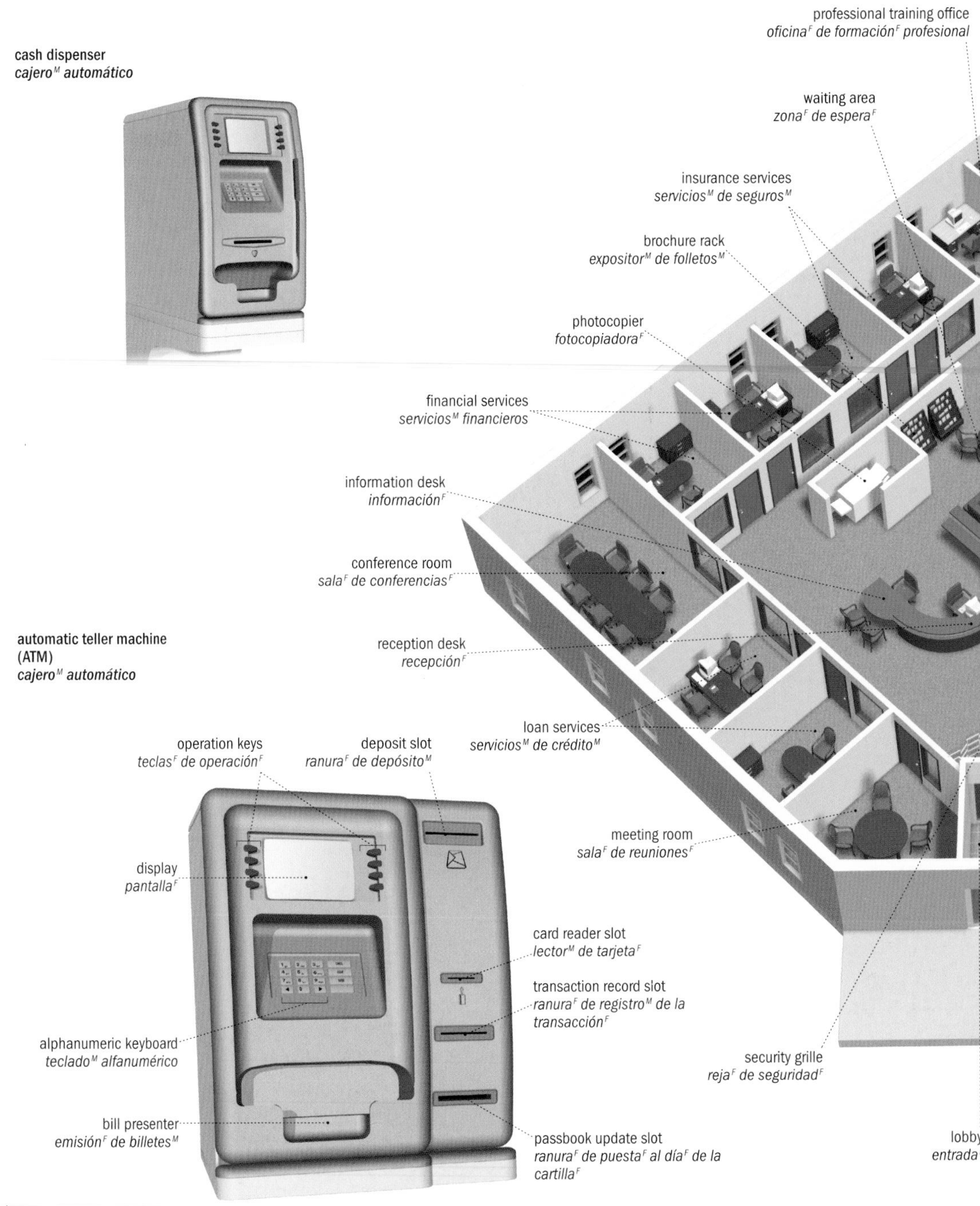
cash dispenser
cajero^M automático
professional training office
oficina^F de formación^F profesional
waiting area
zona^F de espera^F
insurance services
servicios^M de seguros^M
brochure rack
expositor^M de folletos^M
photocopier
fotocopiadora^F
financial services
servicios^M financieros
information desk
información^F
conference room
sala^F de conferencias^F
reception desk
recepción^F
automatic teller machine (ATM)
cajero^M automático
loan services
servicios^M de crédito^M
operation keys
teclas^F de operación^F
deposit slot
ranura^F de depósito^M
display
pantalla^F
meeting room
sala^F de reuniones^F
card reader slot
lector^M de tarjeta^F
transaction record slot
ranura^F de registro^M de la transacción^F
alphanumeric keyboard
teclado^M alfanumérico
security grille
reja^F de seguridad^F
bill presenter
emisión^F de billetes^M
passbook update slot
ranura^F de puesta^F al día^F de la cartilla^F
lobby
entrada^F

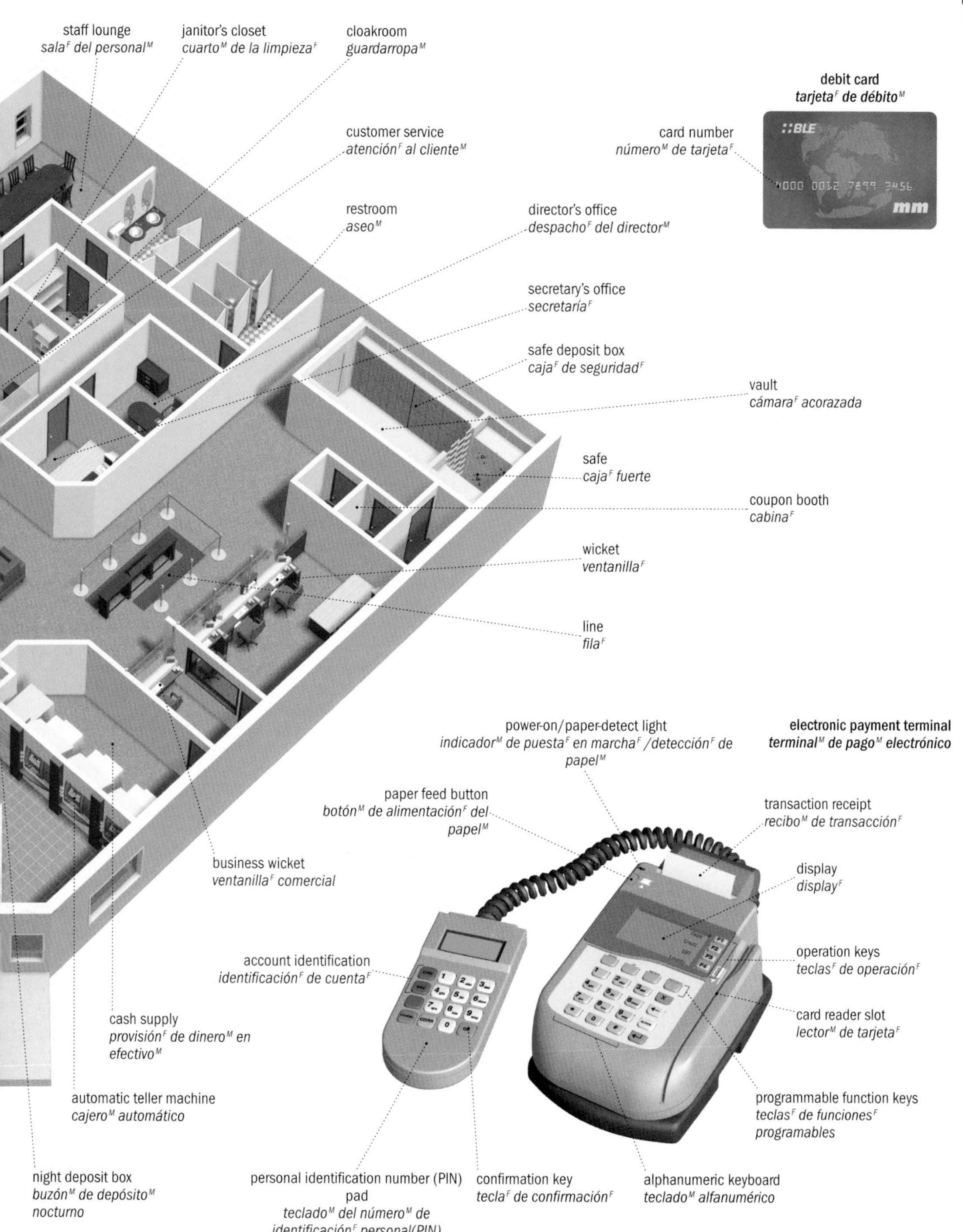
staff lounge
sala^F del personal^M
janitor's closet
cuarto^M de la limpieza^F
cloakroom
guardarropa^M
debit card
tarjeta^F de débito^M
customer service
atención^F al cliente^M
card number
número^M de tarjeta^F
::BLE
0000 0012 7899 3456
mm
restroom
aseo^M
director's office
despacho^F del director^M
secretary's office
secretaría^F
safe deposit box
caja^F de seguridad^F
vault
cámara^F acorazada
safe
caja^F fuerte
coupon booth
cabina^F
wicket
ventanilla^F
line
fila^F
power-on/paper-detect light
indicador^M de puesta^F en marcha^F/detección^F de papel^M
electronic payment terminal
terminal^M de pago^M electrónico
paper feed button
botón^M de alimentación^F del papel^M
transaction receipt
recibo^M de transacción^F
business wicket
ventanilla^F comercial
display
display^F
account identification
identificación^F de cuenta^F
operation keys
teclas^F de operación^F
cash supply
provisión^F de dinero^M en efectivo^M
card reader slot
lector^M de tarjeta^F
automatic teller machine
cajero^M automático
programmable function keys
teclas^F de funciones^F programables
night deposit box
buzón^M de depósito^M nocturno
personal identification number (PIN) pad
teclado^M del número^M de identificación^F personal(PIN)
confirmation key
tecla^F de confirmación^F
alphanumeric keyboard
teclado^M alfanumérico

SOCIETY

school

colegio^M

equipment storage room
depósito^M de de los utensilios^M
podium
estrado^M
art room
aula^F de artes^F plásticas
music room
aula^F de música^F
science room
aula^F de ciencias^F
change room
vestuarios^M
gym teachers' office
despacho^M del gimnasio^M
movable stands
gradas^F móviles
gymnasium
gimnasio^M
storeroom
almacén^M
computer science room
aula^F de informática^F
library
biblioteca^F
classroom for students with learning disabilities
aula^F para alumnos^M con dificultad de aprendizaje^M

classroom
clase^F

bulletin board
tablón^M de anuncios^M
geographical map
mapa^M geográfico
clock
reloj^M
globe
globo^M terráqueo
teacher
profesor^M
bookcase
librería^F
chalk board
pizarra^F
computer
ordenador^M
chair
sillón^M
armless chair
silla^F sin brazos^M
television set
televisior^M
teacher's desk
pupitre^M del profesor^M
student's desk
pupitre^M del alumno^M
student
alumno^M

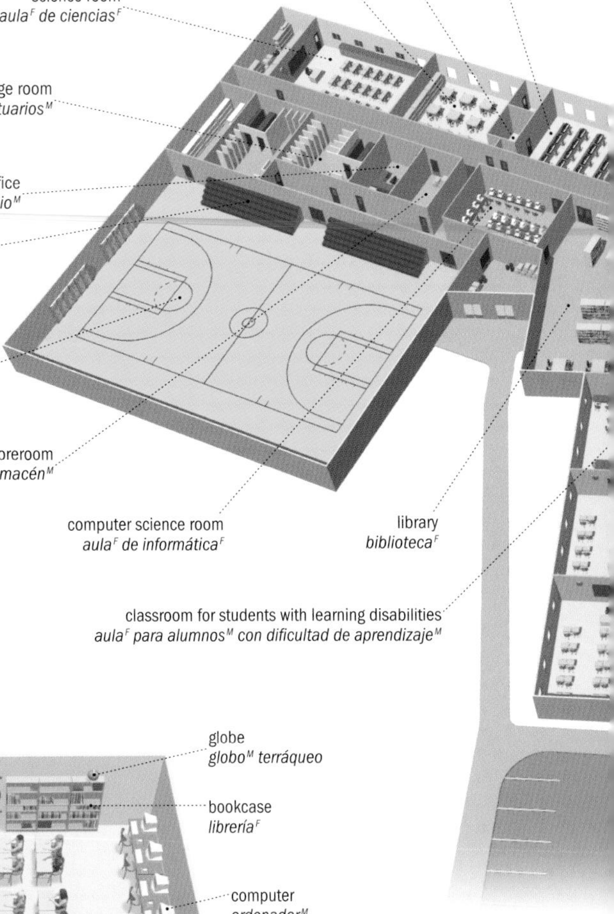

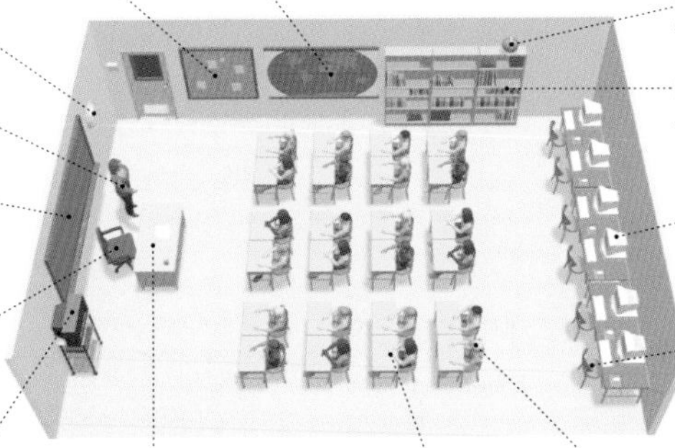

SOCIETY

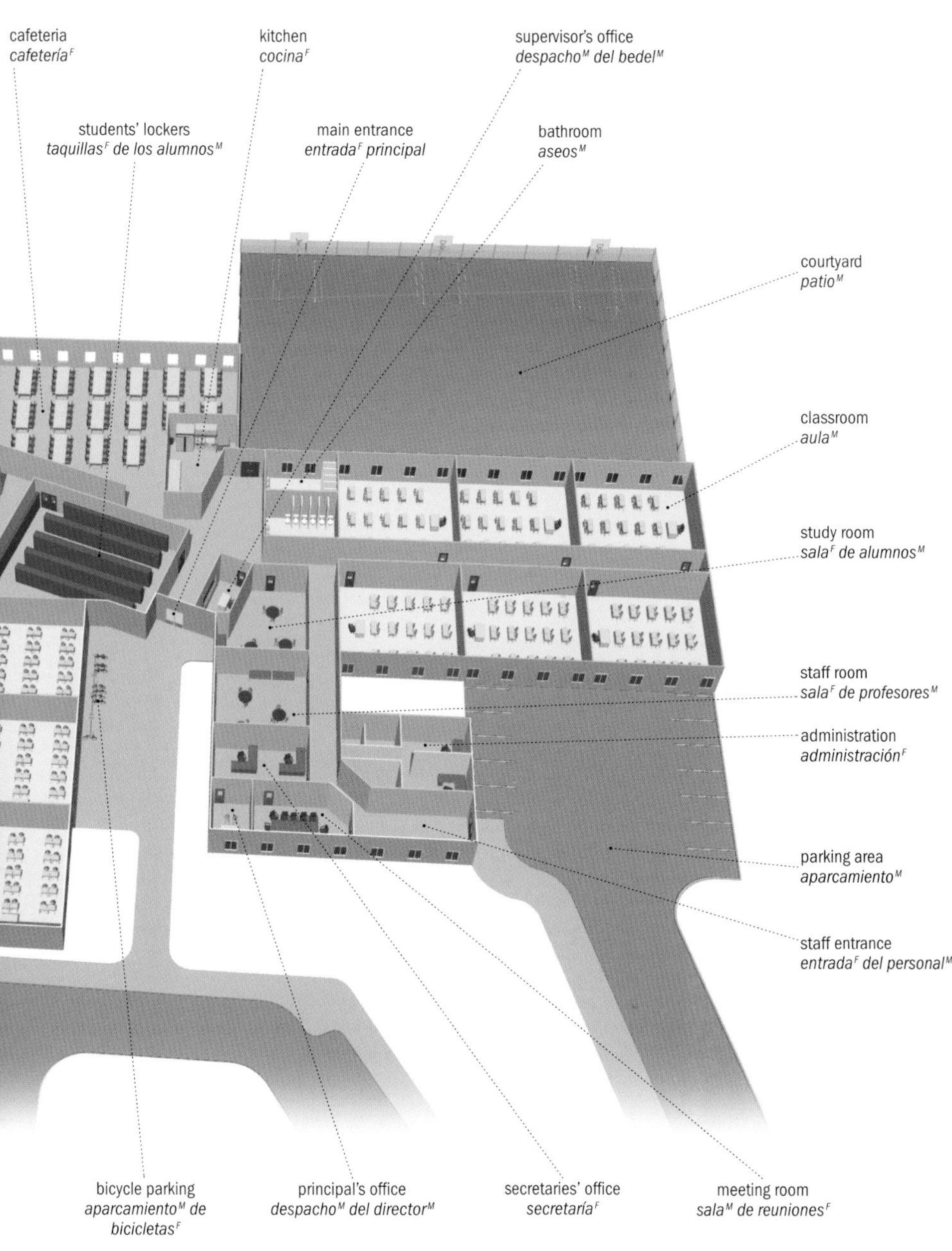
cafeteria
cafetería^F
kitchen
cocina^F
supervisor's office
despacho^M del bedel^M
students' lockers
taquillas^F de los alumnos^M
main entrance
entrada^F principal
bathroom
aseos^M
courtyard
patio^M
classroom
aula^M
study room
sala^F de alumnos^M
staff room
sala^F de profesores^M
administration
administración^F
parking area
aparcamiento^M
staff entrance
entrada^F del personal^M
bicycle parking
aparcamiento^M de bicicletas^F
principal's office
despacho^M del director^M
secretaries' office
secretaría^F
meeting room
sala^M de reuniones^F

Catholic church

iglesia[F]

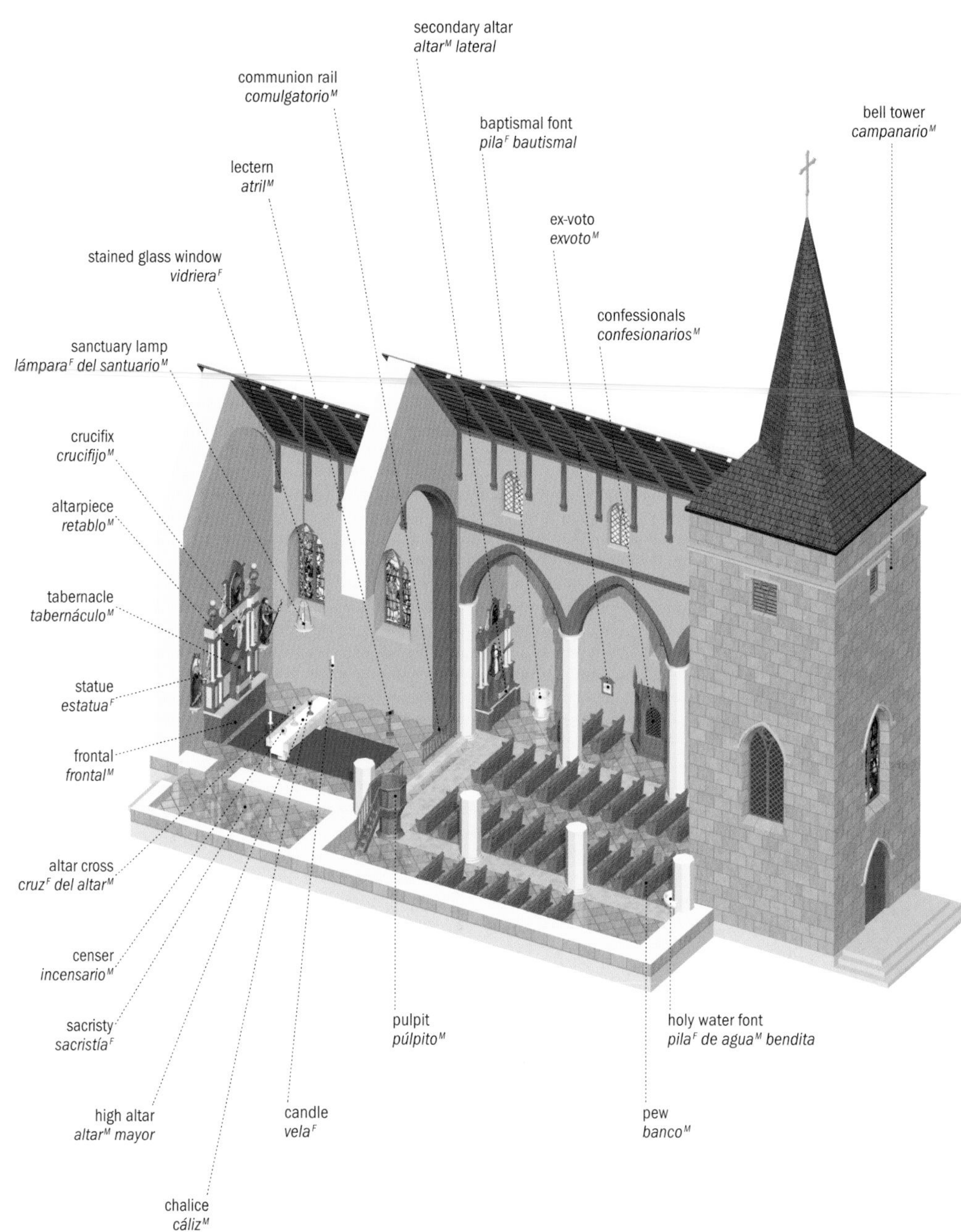

secondary altar
altar[M] lateral
communion rail
comulgatorio[M]
baptismal font
pila[F] bautismal
bell tower
campanario[M]
lectern
atril[M]
ex-voto
exvoto[M]
stained glass window
vidriera[F]
confessionals
confesionarios[M]
sanctuary lamp
lámpara[F] del santuario[M]
crucifix
crucifijo[M]
altarpiece
retablo[M]
tabernacle
tabernáculo[M]
statue
estatua[F]
frontal
frontal[M]
altar cross
cruz[F] del altar[M]
censer
incensario[M]
sacristy
sacristía[F]
pulpit
púlpito[M]
holy water font
pila[F] de agua[M] bendita
high altar
altar[M] mayor
candle
vela[F]
pew
banco[M]
chalice
cáliz[M]

synagogue

sinagoga[F]

menorah
menorah[F]
balcony
balcón[M]
memorial board
lápida[F] conmemorativa
pulpit
púlpito[M]
bimah
bimah[F]
eternal light
llama[F] perpetua
Torah scrolls
rollos[M] de la Torá[F]
Star of David
estrella[F] de David
Ten Commandments
diez mandamientos[M]
ark
arca[M]
rabbi's seat
asiento[M] del rabino[M]

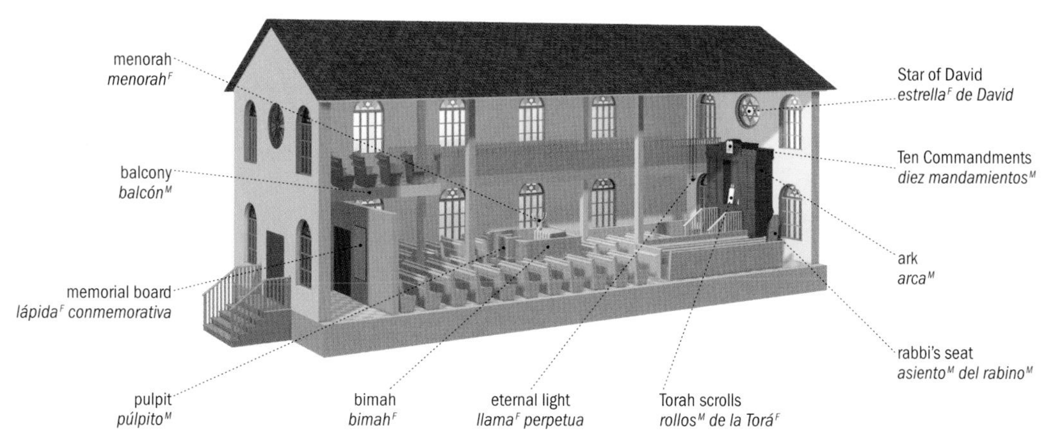

mosque

mezquita[F]

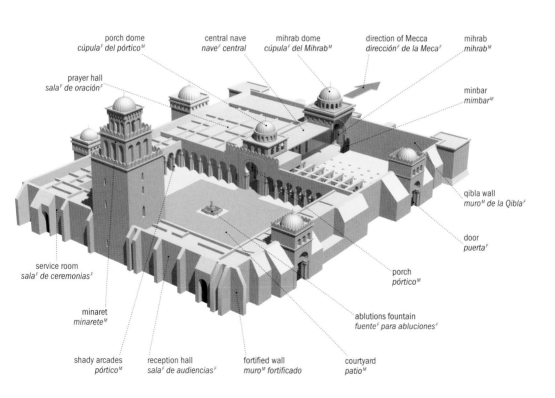

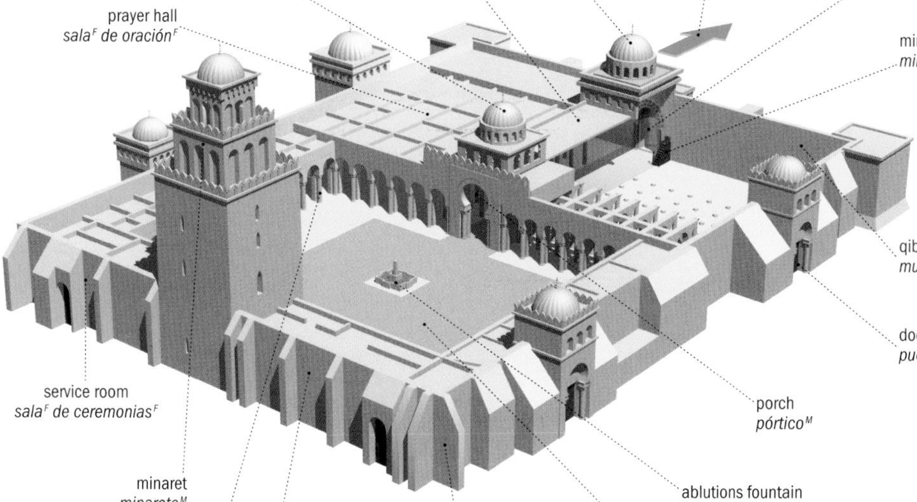

porch dome
cúpula[F] del pórtico[M]
central nave
nave[F] central
mihrab dome
cúpula[F] del Mihrab[M]
direction of Mecca
dirección[F] de la Meca[F]
mihrab
mihrab[M]
prayer hall
sala[F] de oración[F]
minbar
mimbar[M]
qibla wall
muro[M] de la Qibla[F]
door
puerta[F]
service room
sala[F] de ceremonias[F]
porch
pórtico[M]
minaret
minarete[M]
ablutions fountain
fuente[F] para abluciones[F]
shady arcades
pórtico[M]
reception hall
sala[F] de audiencias[F]
fortified wall
muro[M] fortificado
courtyard
patio[M]

flags

banderas^F

Americas
Américas^F

1 
Canada
Canadá^M

2
United States of America
Estados^M Unidos de América^F

3 
Mexico
México^M

4 
Honduras
Honduras^M

5
Guatemala
Guatemala^F

6 
Belize
Belice^M

7 
El Salvador
El Salvador^M

8 
Nicaragua
Nicaragua^F

9 

Costa Rica
Costa Rica^F

10 
Panama
Panamá^M

11 
Colombia
Colombia^F

12 

Venezuela
Venezuela^F

13
Guyana
Guyana^F

14 
Suriname
Surinam^M

15 
Ecuador
Ecuador^M

16 
Peru
Perú^M

17 
Brazil
Brasil^M

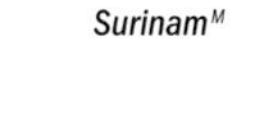
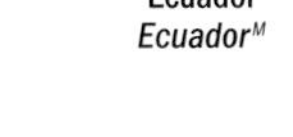

18 
Bolivia
Bolivia^F

19 
Paraguay
Paraguay^M

20 
Chile
Chile^M

21 
Argentina
Argentina^F

22
Uruguay
Uruguay^M

Caribbean Islands
islas^F del Caribe^M

23 
The Bahamas
Bahamas^F

24
Cuba
Cuba^F

25 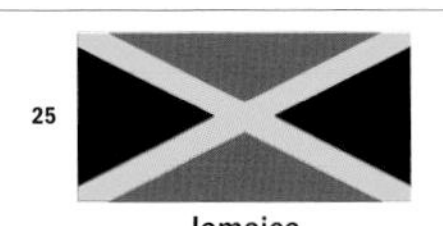
Jamaica
Jamaica^F

26
Haiti
Haití^M

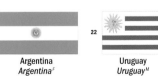

SOCIETY

27 

Saint Kitts and Nevis
Saint Kitts and Nevis[M]

28 

Antigua and Barbuda
Antigua[F] *y Barbuda*[F]

29 

Dominica
Dominica[F]

30 

Saint Lucia
Santa Lucía[F]

31 

Saint Vincent and the Grenadines
San Vicente y las Granadinas[F]

32 

Dominican Republic
República[F] *Dominicana*

33 

Barbados
Barbados[F]

34 

Grenada
Granada[F]

35 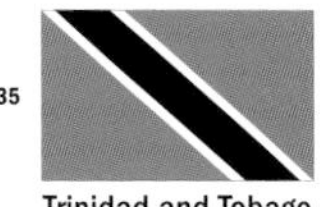

Trinidad and Tobago
Trinidad[F] *y Tobago*[M]

Europe
Europa[F]

36 

Andorra
Principado[M] *de Andorra*[F]

37 

Portugal
Portugal[M]

38 

Spain
España[F]

39 

United Kingdom
Reino[M] *Unido de Gran Bretaña*[F] *e Irlanda*[F] *del Norte*[M]

40 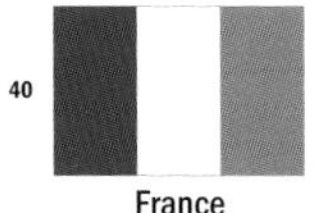

France
Francia[F]

41 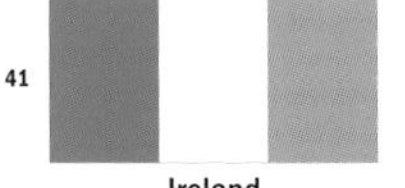

Ireland
Irlanda[F]

42 

Belgium
Bélgica[F]

43 

Luxembourg
Luxemburgo[M]

44 

Netherlands
Países[M] *Bajos*

flags

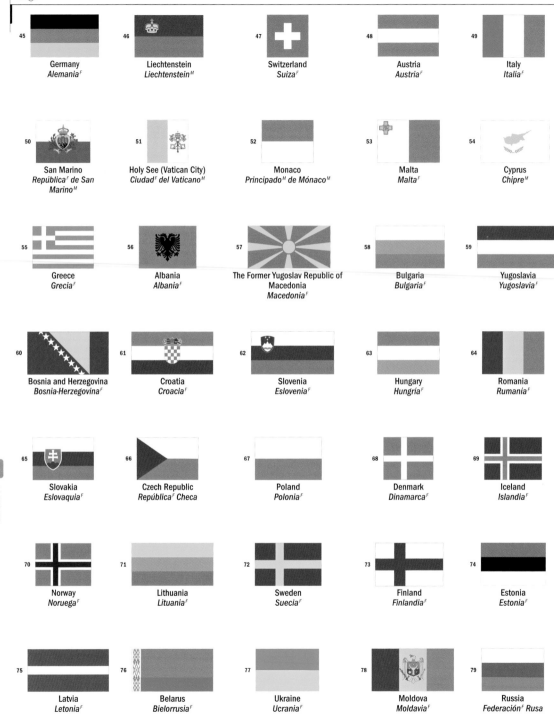

45  Germany — *Alemania[F]*

46  Liechtenstein — *Liechtenstein[M]*

47  Switzerland — *Suiza[F]*

48  Austria — *Austria[F]*

49 Italy — *Italia[F]*

50  San Marino — *República[F] de San Marino[M]*

51  Holy See (Vatican City) — *Ciudad[F] del Vaticano[M]*

52 Monaco — *Principado[M] de Mónaco[M]*

53 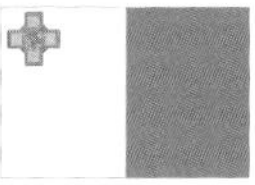 Malta — *Malta[F]*

54  Cyprus — *Chipre[M]*

55  Greece — *Grecia[F]*

56  Albania — *Albania[F]*

57  The Former Yugoslav Republic of Macedonia — *Macedonia[F]*

58 Bulgaria — *Bulgaria[F]*

59  Yugoslavia — *Yugoslavia[F]*

60  Bosnia and Herzegovina — *Bosnia-Herzegovina[F]*

61  Croatia — *Croacia[F]*

62  Slovenia — *Eslovenia[F]*

63  Hungary — *Hungría[F]*

64  Romania — *Rumanía[F]*

65  Slovakia — *Eslovaquia[F]*

66  Czech Republic — *República[F] Checa*

67 Poland — *Polonia[F]*

68  Denmark — *Dinamarca[F]*

69 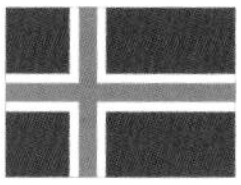 Iceland — *Islandia[F]*

70  Norway — *Noruega[F]*

71  Lithuania — *Lituania[F]*

72  Sweden — *Suecia[F]*

73  Finland — *Finlandia[F]*

74 Estonia — *Estonia[F]*

75  Latvia — *Letonia[F]*

76 Belarus — *Bielorrusia[F]*

77 Ukraine — *Ucrania[F]*

78  Moldova — *Moldavia[F]*

79 Russia — *Federación[F] Rusa*

Africa
***África*[F]**

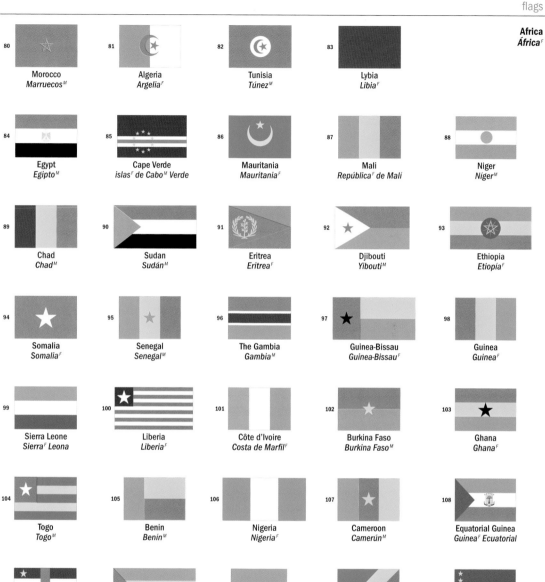

80  Morocco
Marruecos[M]

81  Algeria
Argelia[F]

82  Tunisia
Túnez[M]

83 Lybia
Libia[F]

84 Egypt
Egipto[M]

85  Cape Verde
islas[F] *de Cabo*[M] *Verde*

86  Mauritania
Mauritania[F]

87 Mali
República[F] *de Malí*

88  Niger
Níger[M]

89  Chad
Chad[M]

90  Sudan
Sudán[M]

91  Eritrea
Eritrea[F]

92 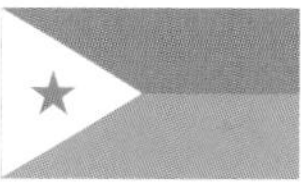 Djibouti
Yibouti[M]

93  Ethiopia
Etiopía[F]

94  Somalia
Somalia[F]

95  Senegal
Senegal[M]

96  The Gambia
Gambia[M]

97  Guinea-Bissau
Guinea-Bissau[F]

98 Guinea
Guinea[F]

99  Sierra Leone
Sierra[F] *Leona*

100  Liberia
Liberia[F]

101 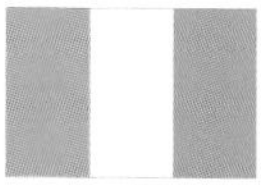 Côte d'Ivoire
Costa de Marfil[F]

102  Burkina Faso
Burkina Faso[M]

103  Ghana
Ghana[F]

104  Togo
Togo[M]

105  Benin
Benín[M]

106  Nigeria
Nigeria[F]

107  Cameroon
Camerún[M]

108  Equatorial Guinea
Guinea[F] *Ecuatorial*

109 Central African Republic
República[F] *Centroafricana*

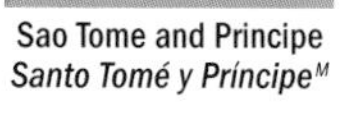

110 Sao Tome and Principe
Santo Tomé y Príncipe[M]

111 Gabon
Gabón[M]

112  Republic of the Congo
Congo[M]

113 Democratic Republic of the Congo
República[F] *Democrática del Congo*[M]

114  Rwanda
Ruanda[M]

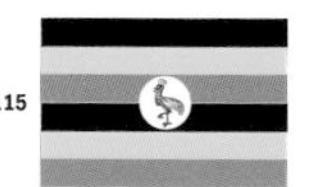

115 Uganda
Uganda[F]

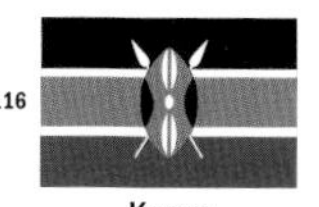

116 Kenya
Kenia[F]

117 Burundi
Burundi[M]

118 Tanzania
Tanzania[F]

SOCIETY

flags

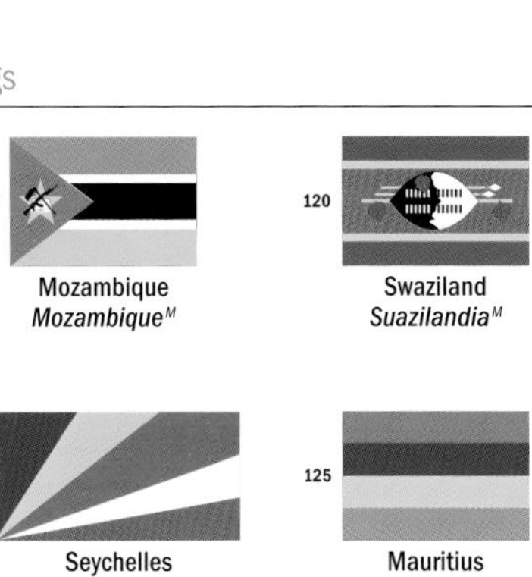

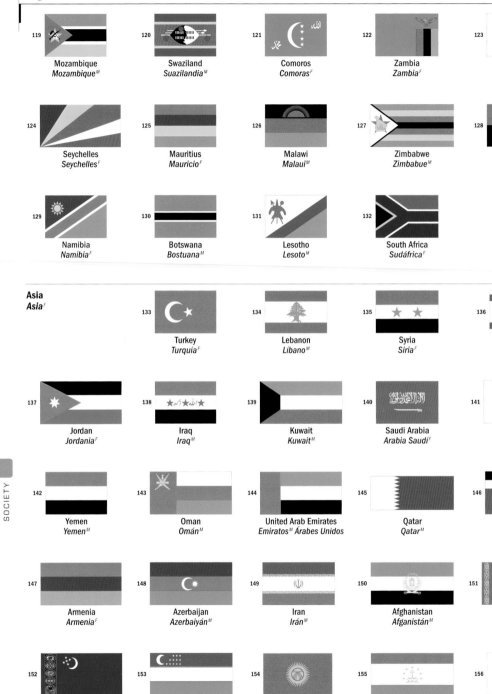

119 Mozambique *Mozambique*M

120 Swaziland *Suazilandia*M

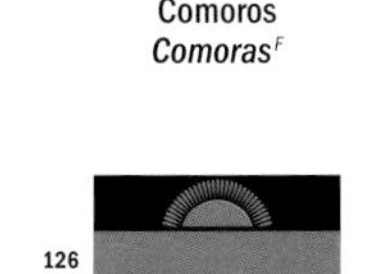

121 Comoros *Comoras*F

122 Zambia *Zambia*F

123 Madagascar *Madagascar*M

124 Seychelles *Seychelles*F

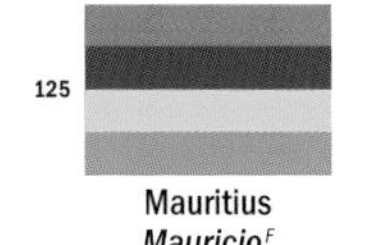

125 Mauritius *Mauricio*F

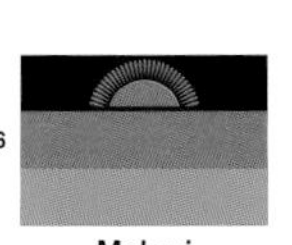

126 Malawi *Malaui*M

127 Zimbabwe *Zimbabue*M

128 Angola *Angola*F

129 Namibia *Namibia*F

130 Botswana *Bostuana*M

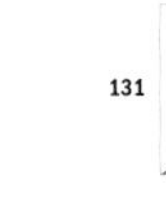

131 Lesotho *Lesoto*M

132 South Africa *Sudáfrica*F

Asia
*Asia*F

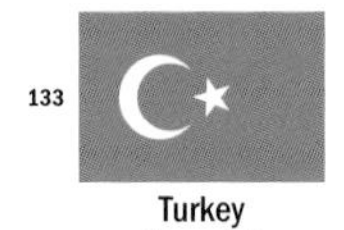

133 Turkey *Turquía*F

134 Lebanon *Líbano*M

135 Syria *Siria*F

136 Israel *Israel*M

137 Jordan *Jordania*F

138 Iraq *Iraq*M

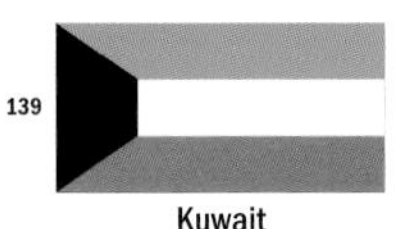

139 Kuwait *Kuwait*M

140 Saudi Arabia *Arabia Saudí*F

141 Bahrain *Bahrein*M

142 Yemen *Yemen*M

143 Oman *Omán*M

144 United Arab Emirates *Emiratos*M *Árabes Unidos*

145 Qatar *Qatar*M

146 Georgia *Georgia*F

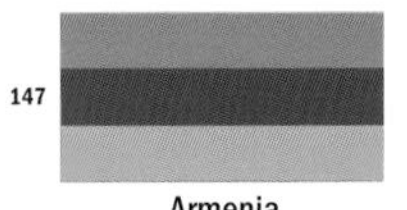

147 Armenia *Armenia*F

148 Azerbaijan *Azerbaiyán*M

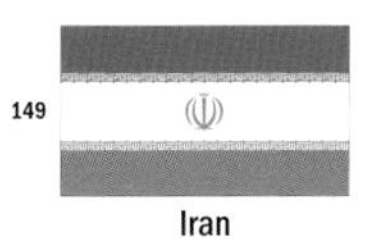

149 Iran *Irán*M

150 Afghanistan *Afganistán*M

151 Kazakhstan *Kazajistán*M

152 Turkmenistan *Turkmenistán*M

153 Uzbekistan *Uzbekistán*M

154 Kyrgyzstan *Kirguizistán*M

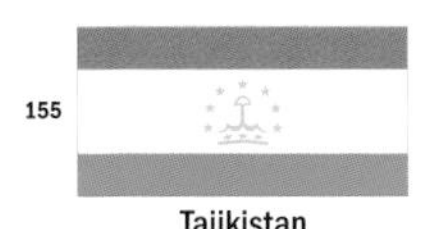

155 Tajikistan *Tajikistán*M

156 Pakistan *Pakistán*M

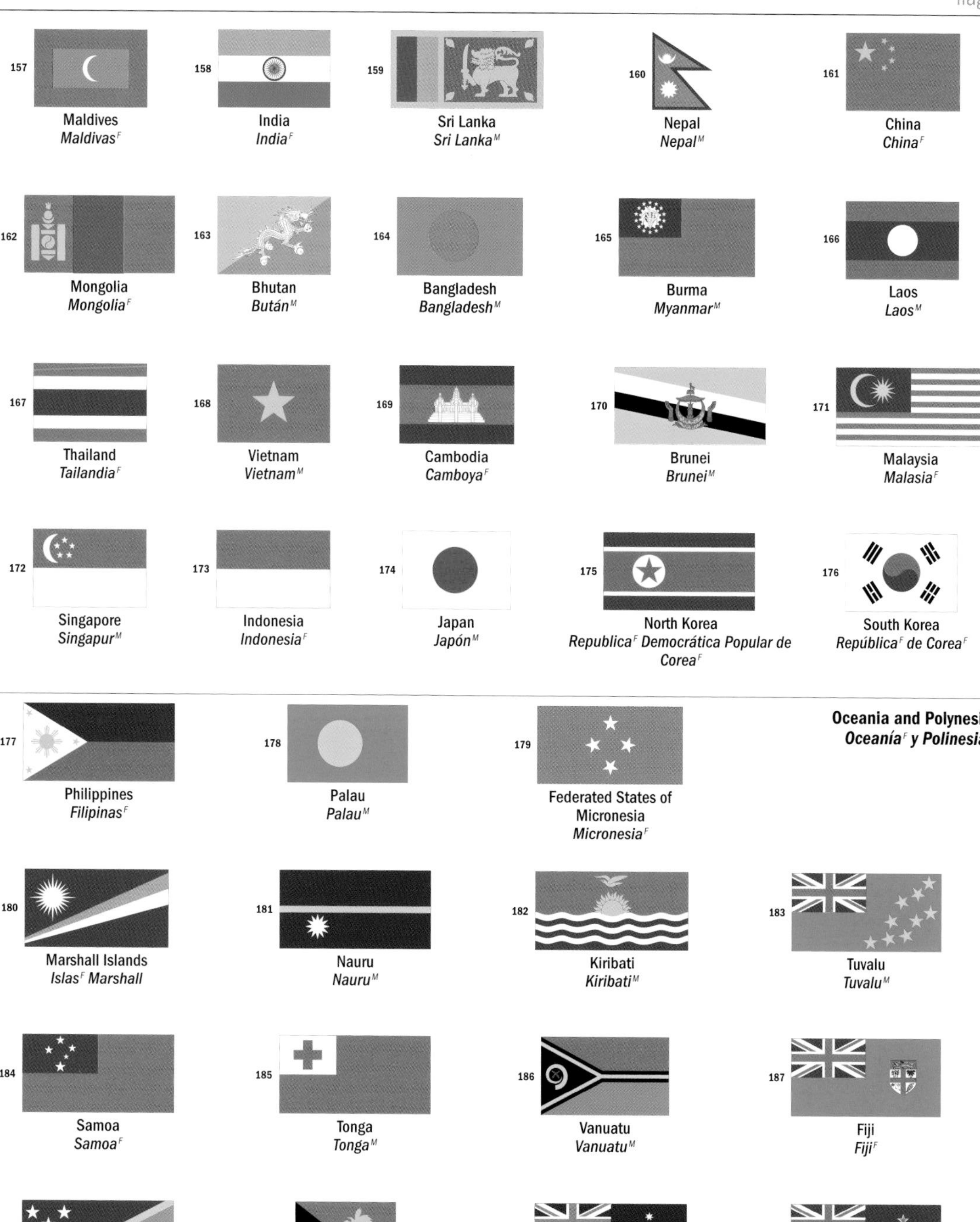
157 Maldives
Maldivas[F]
158 India
India[F]
159 Sri Lanka
Sri Lanka[M]
160 Nepal
Nepal[M]
161 China
China[F]
162 Mongolia
Mongolia[F]
163 Bhutan
Bután[M]
164 Bangladesh
Bangladesh[M]
165 Burma
Myanmar[M]
166 Laos
Laos[M]
167 Thailand
Tailandia[F]
168 Vietnam
Vietnam[M]
169 Cambodia
Camboya[F]
170 Brunei
Brunei[M]
171 Malaysia
Malasia[F]
172 Singapore
Singapur[M]
173 Indonesia
Indonesia[F]
174 Japan
Japón[M]
175 North Korea
Republica[F] Democrática Popular de Corea[F]
176 South Korea
República[F] de Corea[F]
Oceania and Polynesia
Oceanía[F] y Polinesia[F]
177 Philippines
Filipinas[F]
178 Palau
Palau[M]
179 Federated States of Micronesia
Micronesia[F]
180 Marshall Islands
Islas[F] Marshall
181 Nauru
Nauru[M]
182 Kiribati
Kiribati[M]
183 Tuvalu
Tuvalu[M]
184 Samoa
Samoa[F]
185 Tonga
Tonga[M]
186 Vanuatu
Vanuatu[M]
187 Fiji
Fiji[F]
188 Solomon Islands
Islas Salomón[F]
189 Papua New Guinea
Papua Nueva Guinea[F]
190 Australia
Australia[F]
191 New Zealand
Nueva Zelanda[F]

fire prevention

prevención[F] de incendios[M]

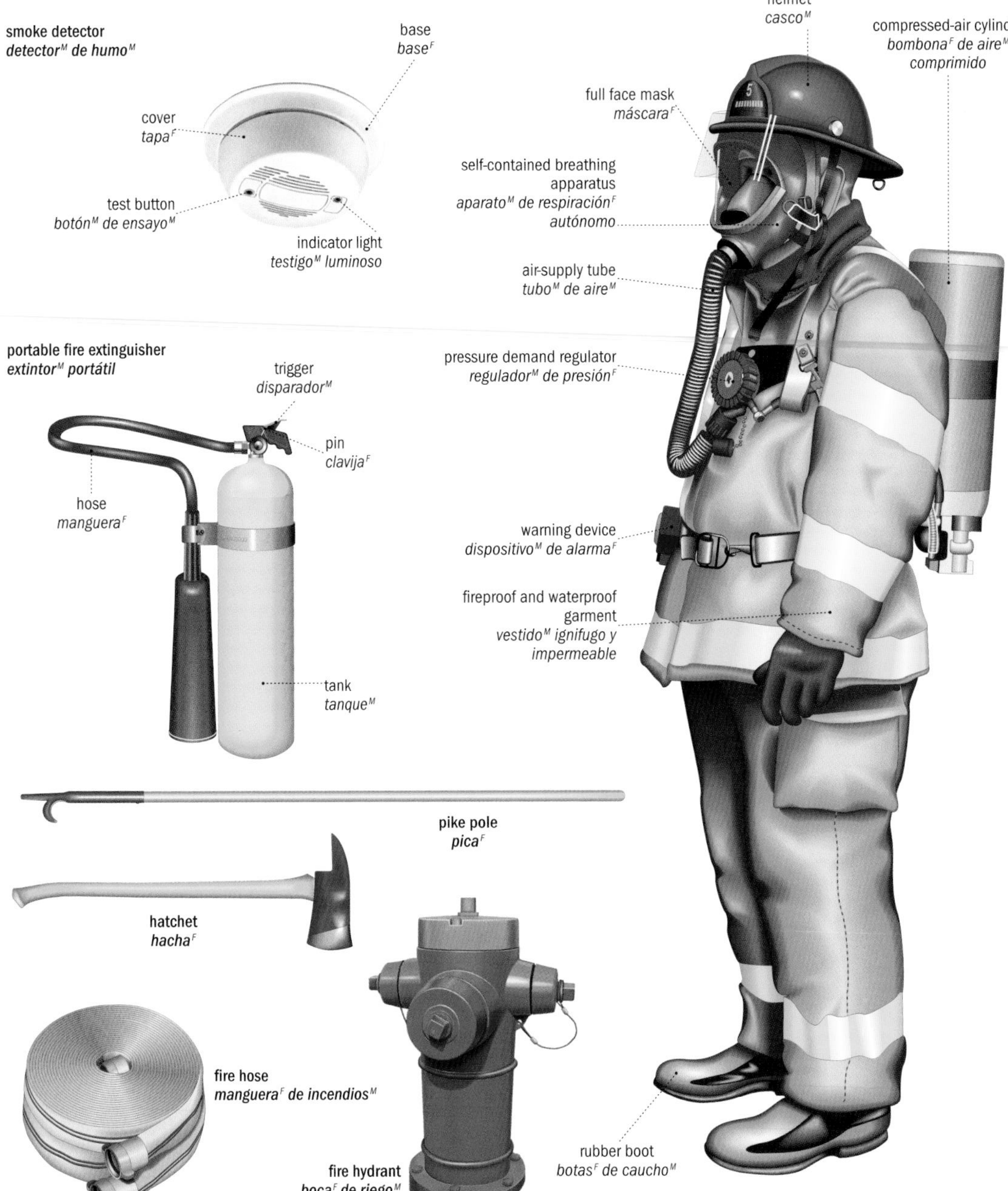
fire-fighting materials
material[M] de lucha[F] contra los incendios[M]
smoke detector
detector[M] de humo[M]
base
base[F]
cover
tapa[F]
test button
botón[M] de ensayo[M]
indicator light
testigo[M] luminoso
portable fire extinguisher
extintor[M] portátil
trigger
disparador[M]
pin
clavija[F]
hose
manguera[F]
tank
tanque[M]
pike pole
pica[F]
hatchet
hacha[F]
fire hose
manguera[F] de incendios[M]
fire hydrant
boca[F] de riego[M]
firefighter
bombero[M]
helmet
casco[M]
compressed-air cylinder
bombona[F] de aire[M] comprimido
full face mask
máscara[F]
self-contained breathing apparatus
aparato[M] de respiración[F] autónomo
air-supply tube
tubo[M] de aire[M]
pressure demand regulator
regulador[M] de presión[F]
warning device
dispositivo[M] de alarma[F]
fireproof and waterproof garment
vestido[M] ignífugo y impermeable
rubber boot
botas[F] de caucho[M]

fire engines
camiones[M] de bomberos[M]

pumper
autobomba[M] tanque

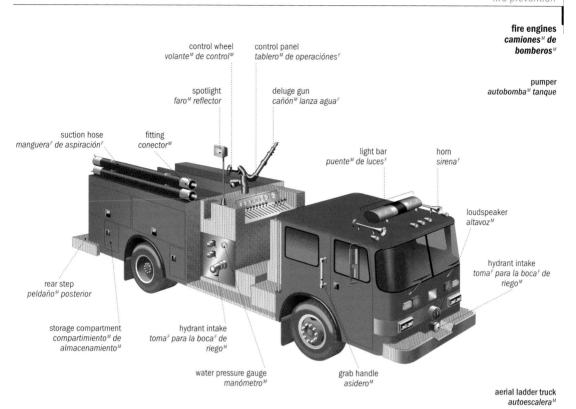

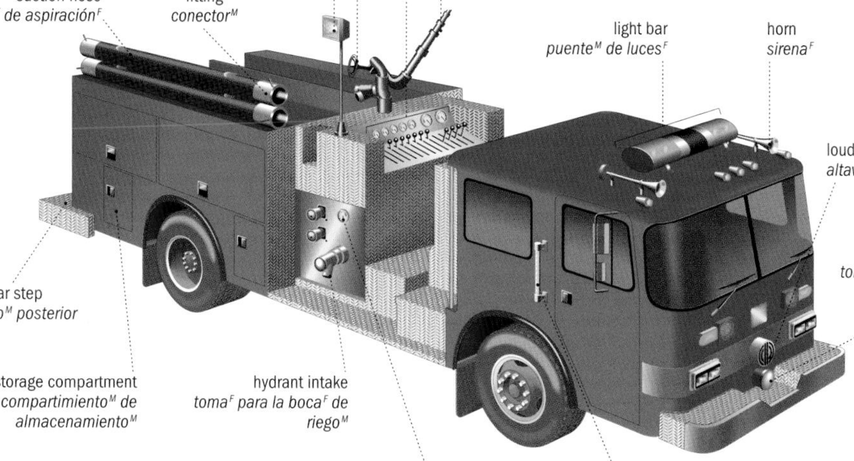

control wheel
volante[M] de control[M]
control panel
tablero[M] de operaciónes[F]
spotlight
faro[M] reflector
deluge gun
cañón[M] lanza agua[F]
suction hose
manguera[F] de aspiración[F]
fitting
conector[M]
light bar
puente[M] de luces[F]
horn
sirena[F]
loudspeaker
altavoz[M]
hydrant intake
toma[F] para la boca[F] de riego[M]
rear step
peldaño[M] posterior
storage compartment
compartimiento[M] de almacenamiento[M]
hydrant intake
toma[F] para la boca[F] de riego[M]
water pressure gauge
manómetro[M]
grab handle
asidero[M]

aerial ladder truck
autoescalera[M]

ladder pipe nozzle
escalera[F] con boquilla[F] telescópica
telescopic boom
elevador[M] telescópico
oscillating light
faro[M] de destello[M]
elevating cylinder
cilindro[M] elevador
turntable mounting
plataforma[F] giratoria
tower ladder
escalera[F] telescópica
top ladder
tope[M] de la escalera[F]
spotlight
faro[M] reflector
storage compartment
compartimiento[M] de almacenamiento[M]
outrigger
gato[M]

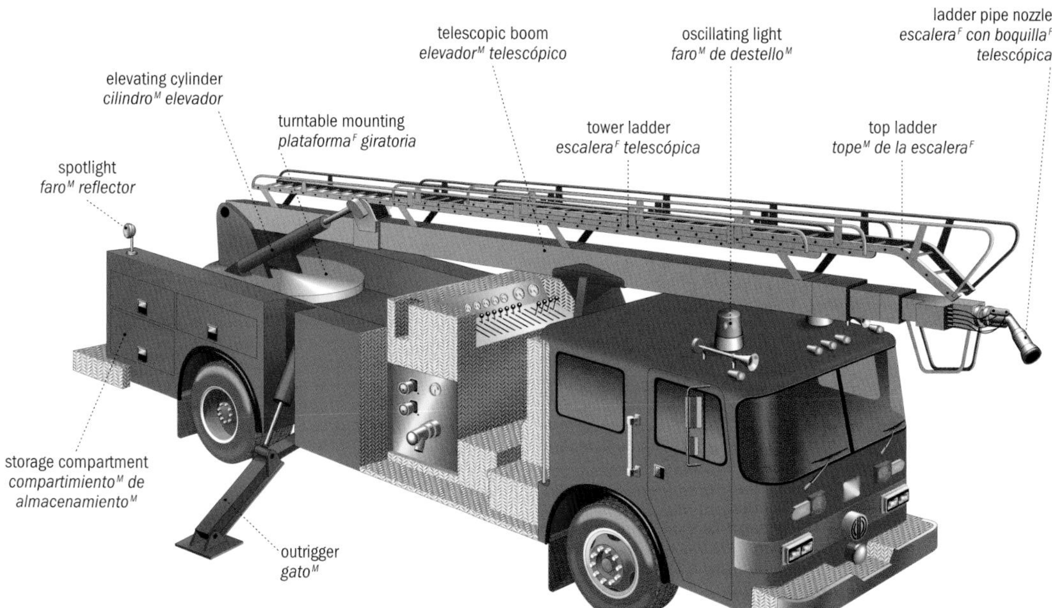

crime prevention

prevención^F de la criminalidad^F

police officer
agente^M de policía^F

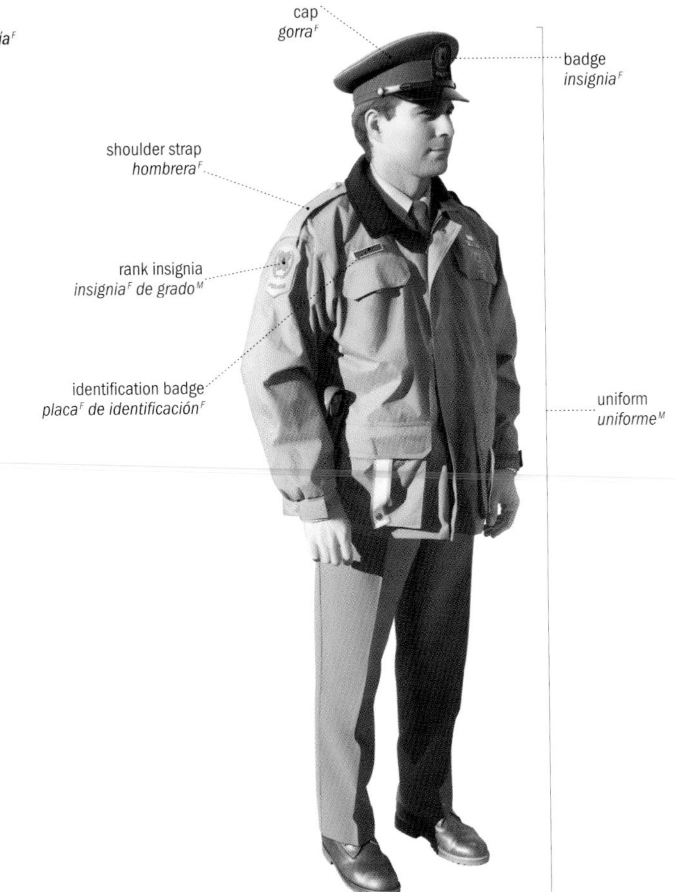

duty belt
cinturón^M de servicio^M

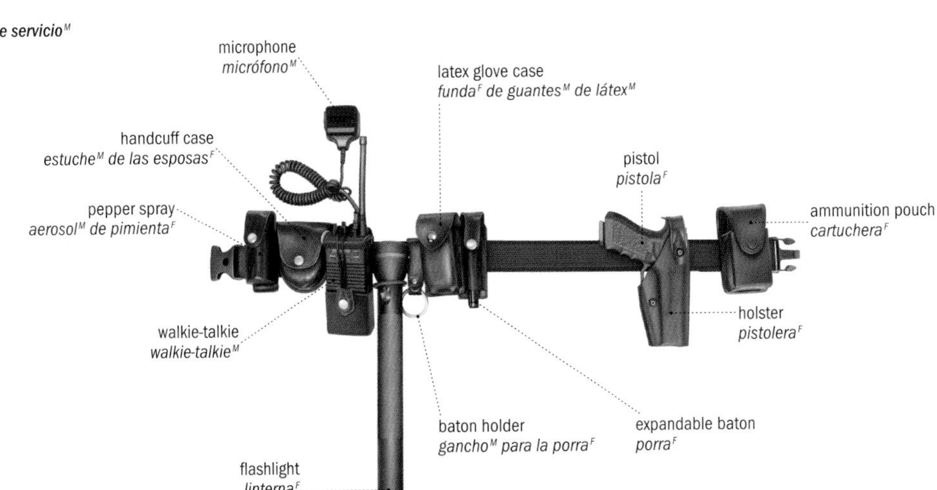

dashboard equipment
equipamiento ^{M} ***del salpicadero*** ^{M}

radar transceiver
transmisor^{M}-receptor^{M} radar^{M}
light bar controller
sistema^{M} de control^{M} del puente^{M} de luces^{F}
reading light
lámpara^{F} de lectura^{F}
microphones
micrófonos^{M}
dashboard computer
ordenador^{M} de a bordo
computer programs
programas^{M} informáticos
radar display
pantalla^{F} del radar^{M}
radio
radio^{F}

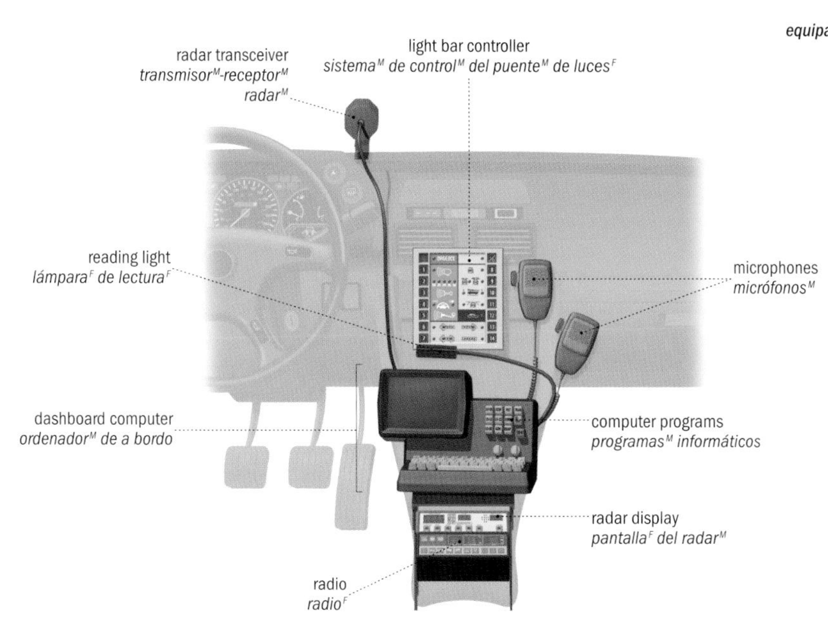

police car
coche ^{M} ***de policía*** ^{F}

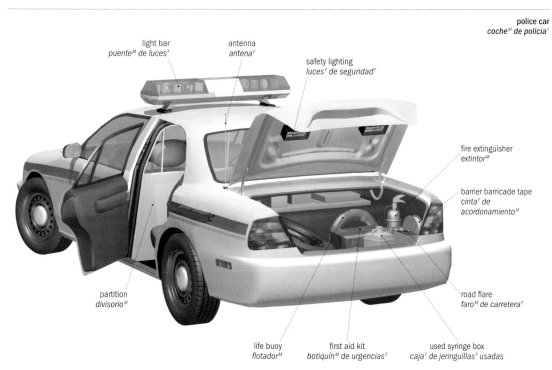

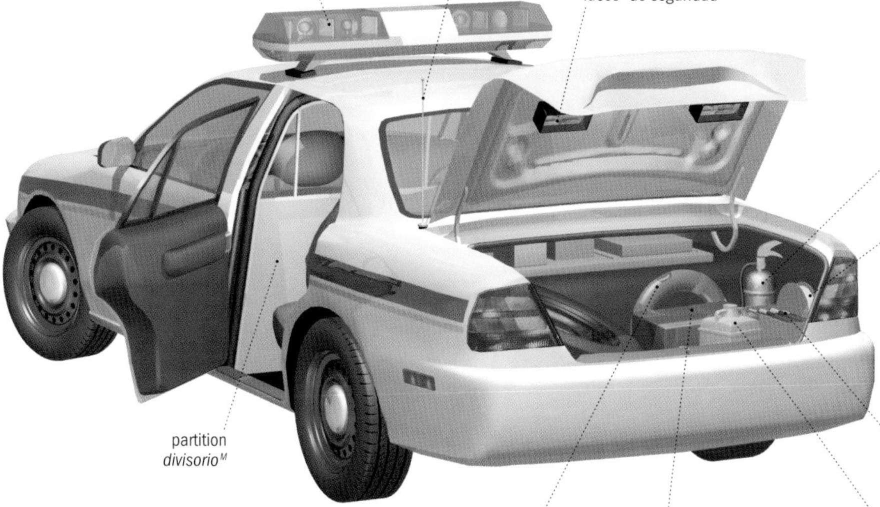

light bar
puente^{M} de luces^{F}
antenna
antena^{F}
safety lighting
luces^{F} de seguridad^{F}
fire extinguisher
extintor^{M}
barrier barricade tape
cinta^{F} de acordonamiento^{M}
partition
divisorio^{M}
road flare
faro^{M} de carretera^{F}
life buoy
flotador^{M}
first aid kit
botiquín^{M} de urgencias^{F}
used syringe box
caja^{F} de jeringuillas^{F} usadas

SOCIETY

ear protection

protección[F] para los oídos[M]

safety earmuffs
cascos[M] de seguridad[F]

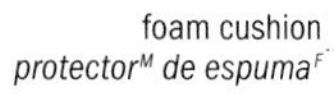

earplugs
tapones[M] para los oídos[M]

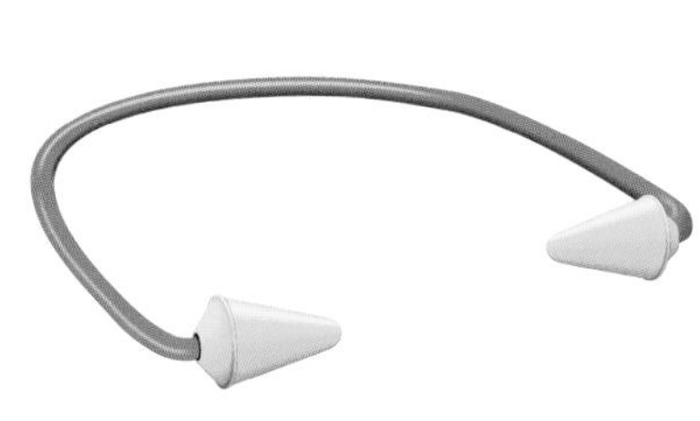

eye protection

protección[F] para los ojos[M]

safety glasses
gafas[F] de seguridad[F]

safety goggles
gafas[F] protectoras

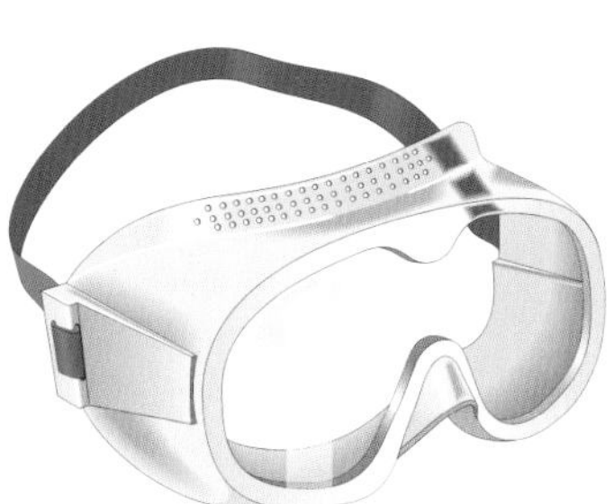

head protection

protección[F] para la cabeza[F]

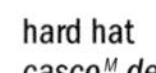

hard hat
casco[M] de seguridad[F]

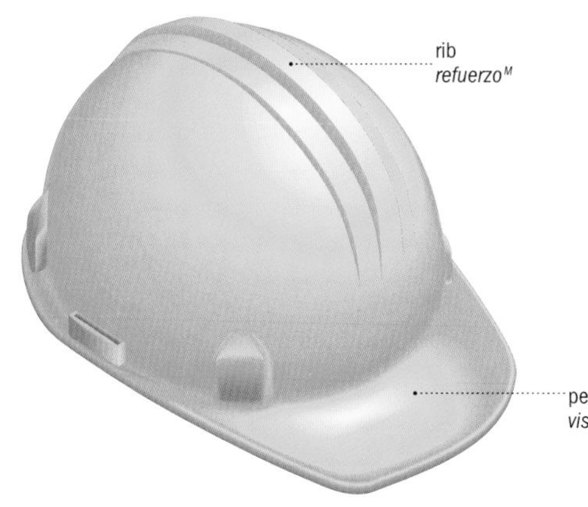

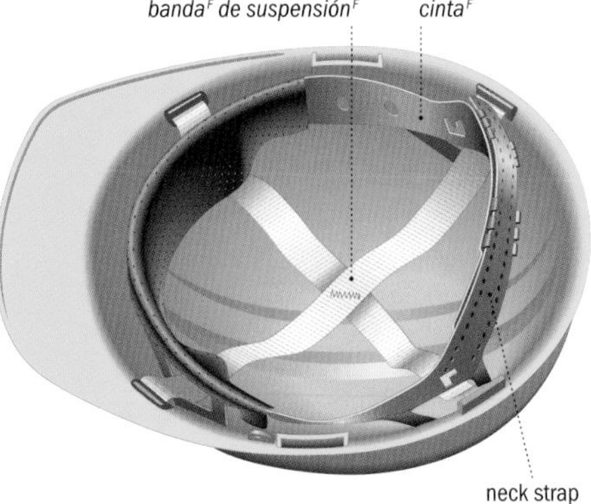

SOCIETY

respiratory system protection

protección[F] para el sistema[M] respiratorio[M]

respirator
máscara[F] antigás[M]

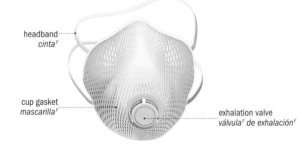

half-mask respirator
máscara[F] para el polvo[M]

foot protection

protección[F] para los pies[M]

safety boot
bota[F] de seguridad[F]

toe guard
puntera[F] protectora

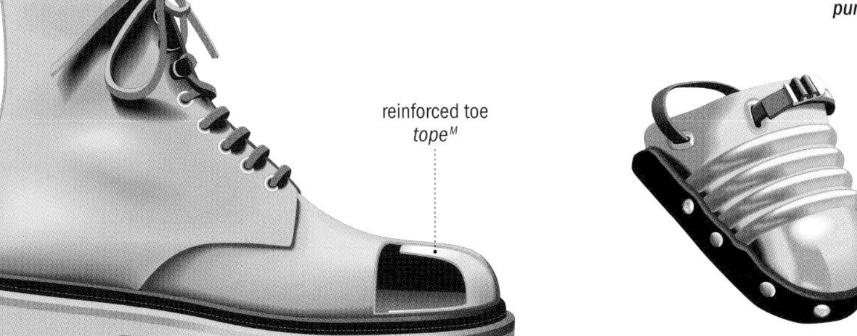

ambulance

ambulancia[F]

stethoscope
fonendoscopio[M]

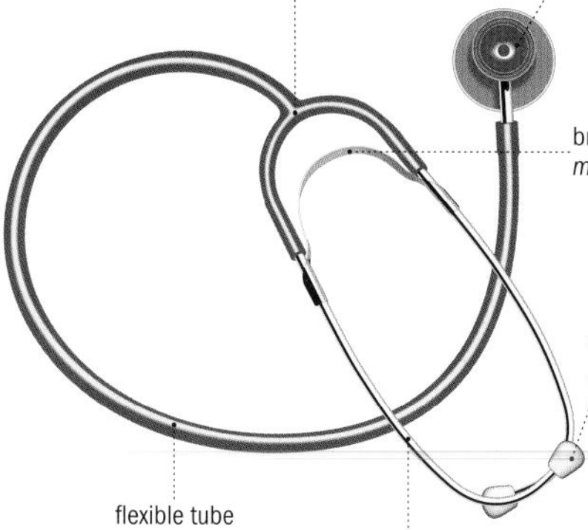

Y-tube
tubo[M] en Y

sound receiver
receptor[M] del sonido[M]

branch clip
muelle[M]

earpiece
auricular[M]

flexible tube
tubo[M] flexible

branch
rama[F]

syringe
jeringuilla[F]

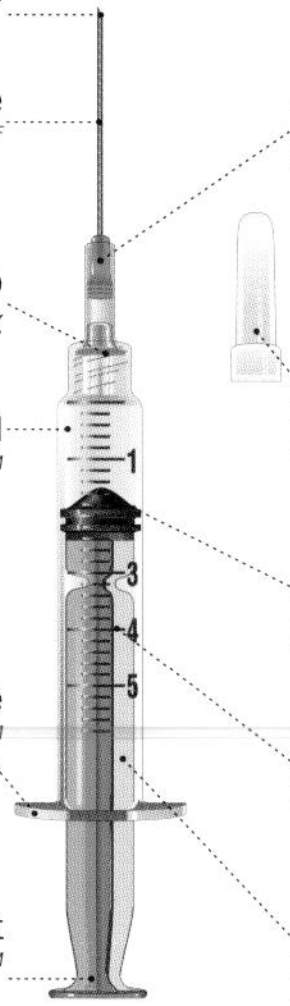

bevel
bisel[M]

needle
aguja[F]

needle hub
portaagujas[M]

Luer-Lock tip
jeringilla[F] de Luer-Lock

tip protector
capuchón[M]

hollow barrel
cilindro[M]

rubber bulb
pera[F] de goma[F]

finger flange
pestaña[F] de arrojo[M]

scale
escala[F]

thumb rest
apoyo[M] del pulgar[M]

plunger
émbolo[M]

latex glove
guantes[M] de látex[M]

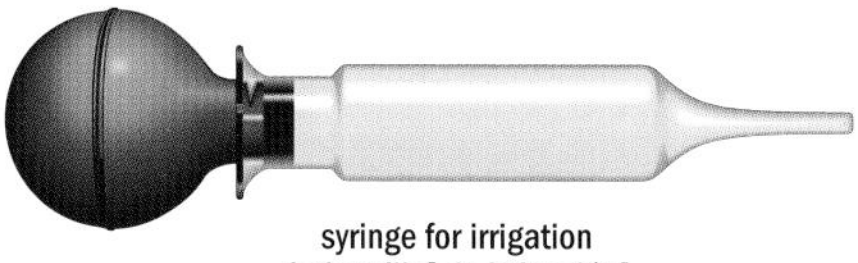

syringe for irrigation
jeringuilla[F] de irrigación[F]

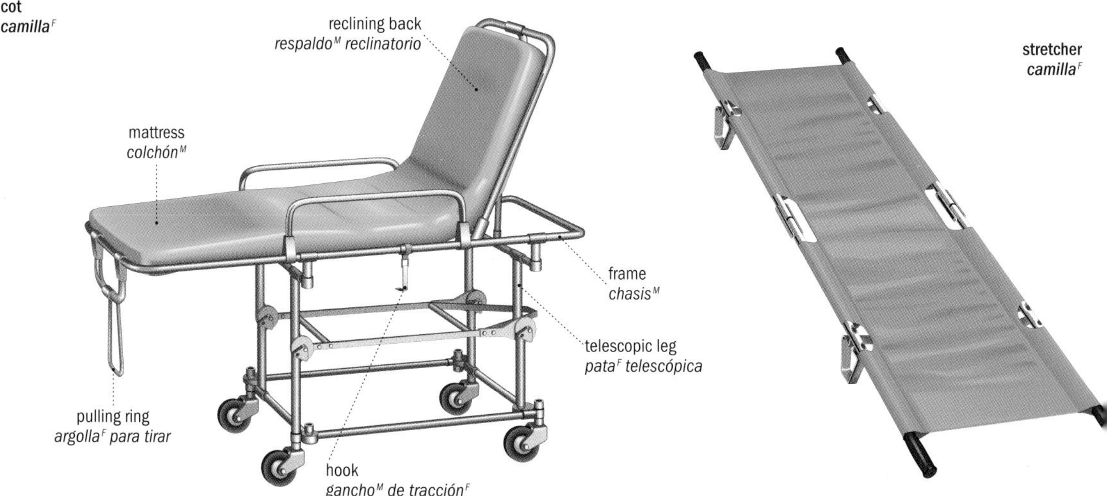

SOCIETY

first aid kit

botiquínM de primeros auxiliosM

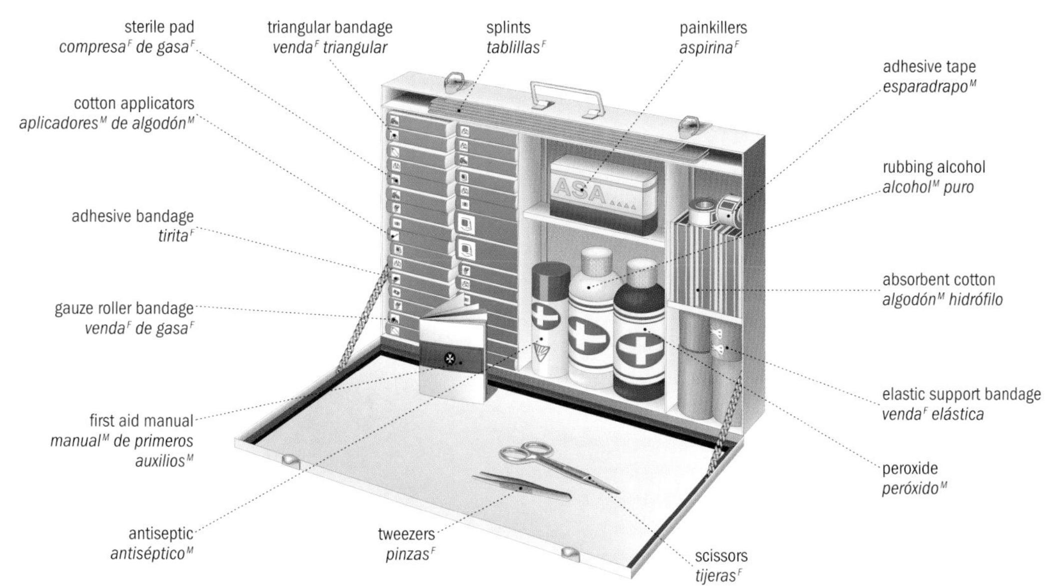

clinical thermometers

termómetrosM clínicos

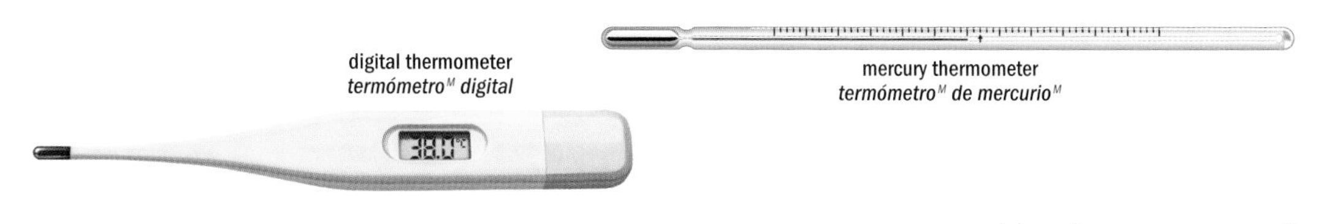

blood pressure monitor

tensiómetroM

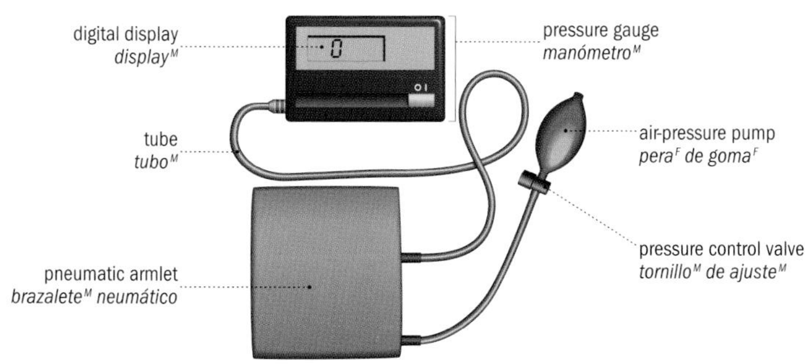

SOCIETY

hospital

hospital^M

emergency
urgencias^F

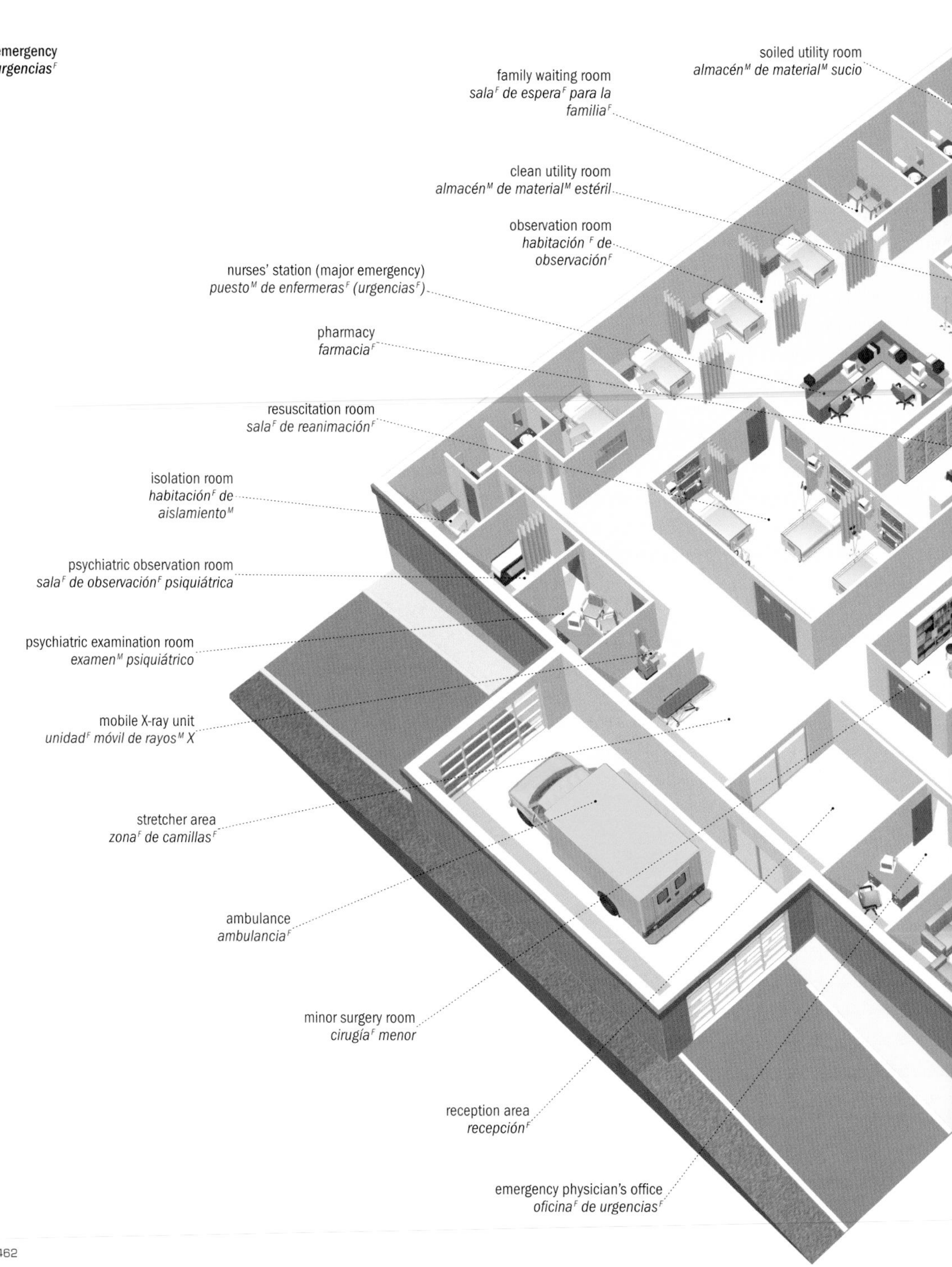

soiled utility room
almacén^M de material^M sucio
family waiting room
sala^F de espera^F para la familia^F
clean utility room
almacén^M de material^M estéril
observation room
habitación^F de observación^F
nurses' station (major emergency)
puesto^M de enfermeras^F (urgencias^F)
pharmacy
farmacia^F
resuscitation room
sala^F de reanimación^F
isolation room
habitación^F de aislamiento^M
psychiatric observation room
sala^F de observación^F psiquiátrica
psychiatric examination room
examen^M psiquiátrico
mobile X-ray unit
unidad^F móvil de rayos^M X
stretcher area
zona^F de camillas^F
ambulance
ambulancia^F
minor surgery room
cirugía^F menor
reception area
recepción^F
emergency physician's office
oficina^F de urgencias^F

SOCIETY

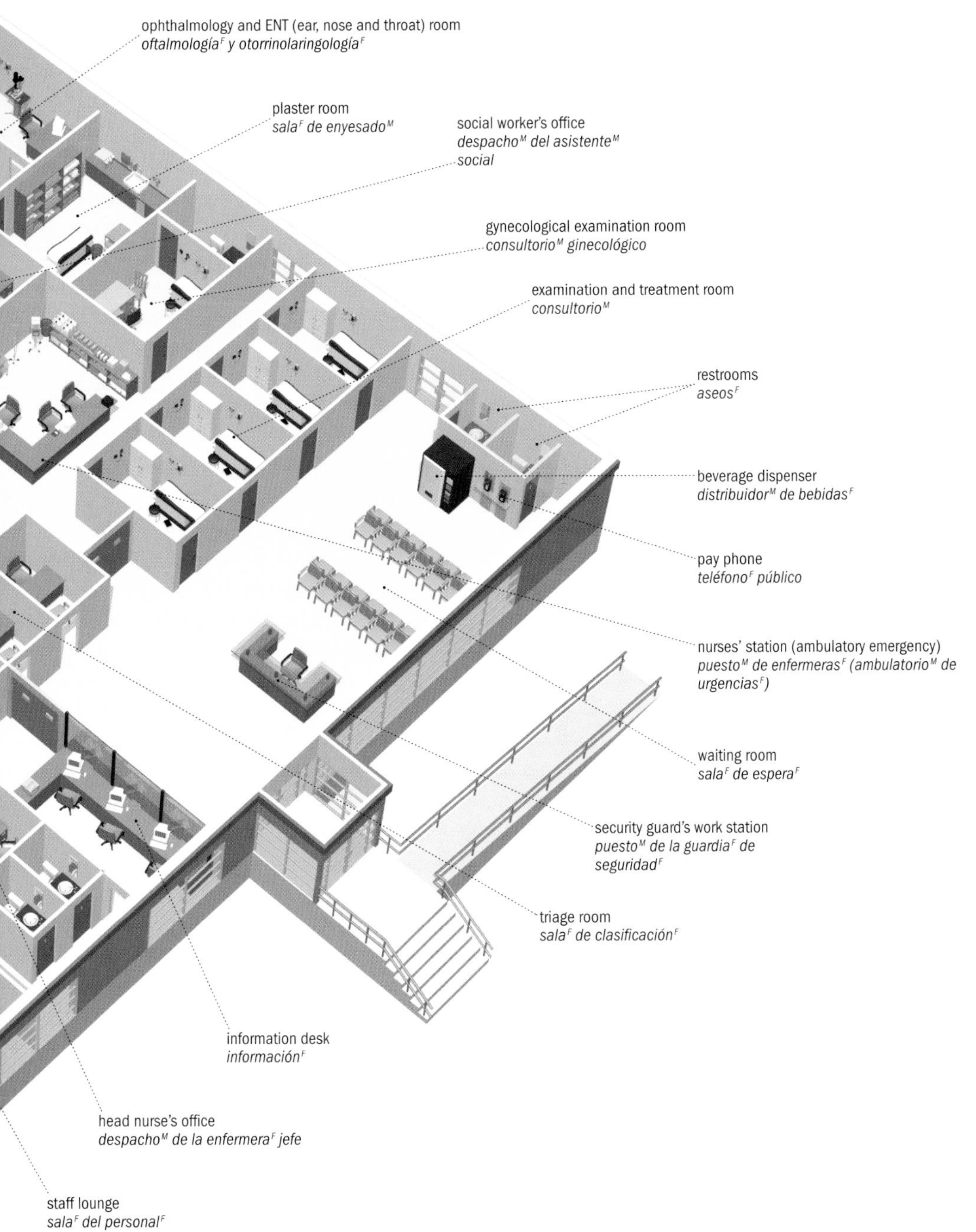
ophthalmology and ENT (ear, nose and throat) room
oftalmología^F y otorrinolaringología^F
plaster room
sala^F de enyesado^M
social worker's office
despacho^M del asistente^M social
gynecological examination room
consultorio^M ginecológico
examination and treatment room
consultorio^M
restrooms
aseos^F
beverage dispenser
distribuidor^M de bebidas^F
pay phone
teléfono^F público
nurses' station (ambulatory emergency)
puesto^M de enfermeras^F (ambulatorio^M de urgencias^F)
waiting room
sala^F de espera^F
security guard's work station
puesto^M de la guardia^F de seguridad^F
triage room
sala^F de clasificación^F
information desk
información^F
head nurse's office
despacho^M de la enfermera^F jefe
staff lounge
sala^F del personal^F

patient room
habitación[M] de un paciente[M]

bedside lamp
lámpara[F] de cabecera[F]
resident
médico[M] interno
intravenous stand
colgador[M] de intravenosos[M]
physician
médico[M]
oxygen outlet
toma[F] de oxígeno[M]
patient
paciente[M]
shower
ducha[M]
overbed table
mesa[F] de cama[M]
bedside table
mesilla[F] de cabecera[F]
privacy curtain
cortina[F] separadora
toilet
inodoro[M]
chair
sillón[M] de reposo[M]
bathroom
baño[M]
hospital bed
cama[F] de hospital[M]
nurse
enfermera[F]

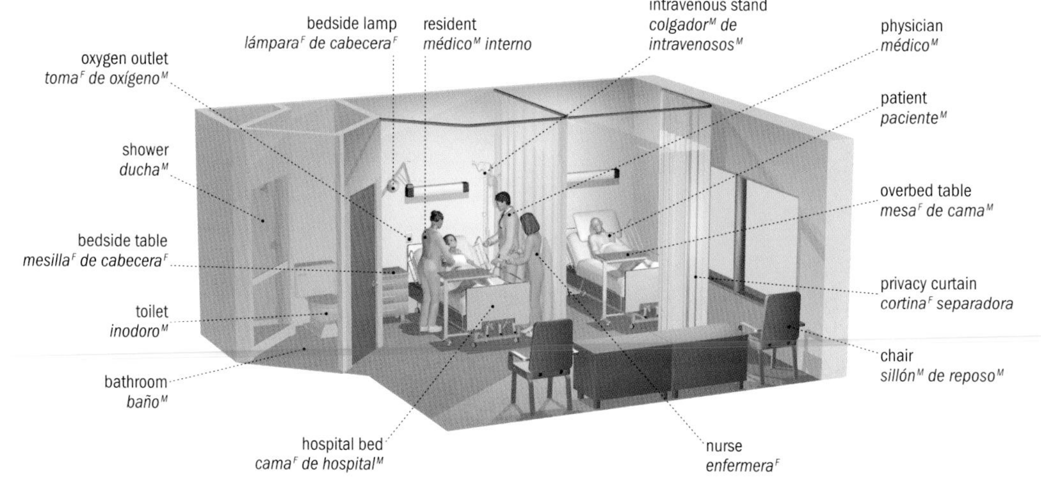

operating suite
bloque[M] de cirugía[F]

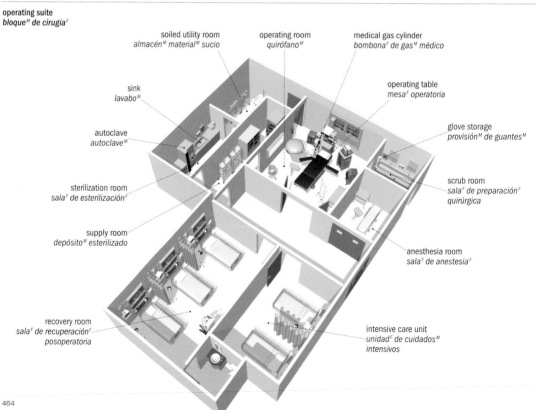

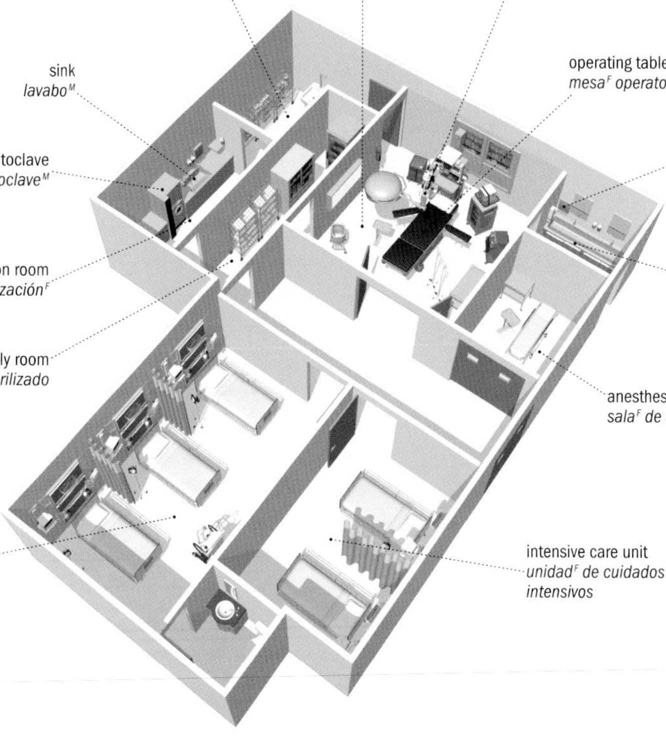

soiled utility room
almacén[M] material[M] sucio
operating room
quirófano[M]
medical gas cylinder
bombona[F] de gas[M] médico
operating table
mesa[F] operatoria
sink
lavabo[M]
glove storage
provisión[M] de guantes[M]
autoclave
autoclave[M]
scrub room
sala[F] de preparación[F] quirúrgica
sterilization room
sala[F] de esterilización[F]
supply room
depósito[M] esterilizado
anesthesia room
sala[F] de anestesia[F]
recovery room
sala[F] de recuperación[F] posoperatoria
intensive care unit
unidad[F] de cuidados[M] intensivos

SOCIETY

ambulatory care unit
ambulatorio[M]

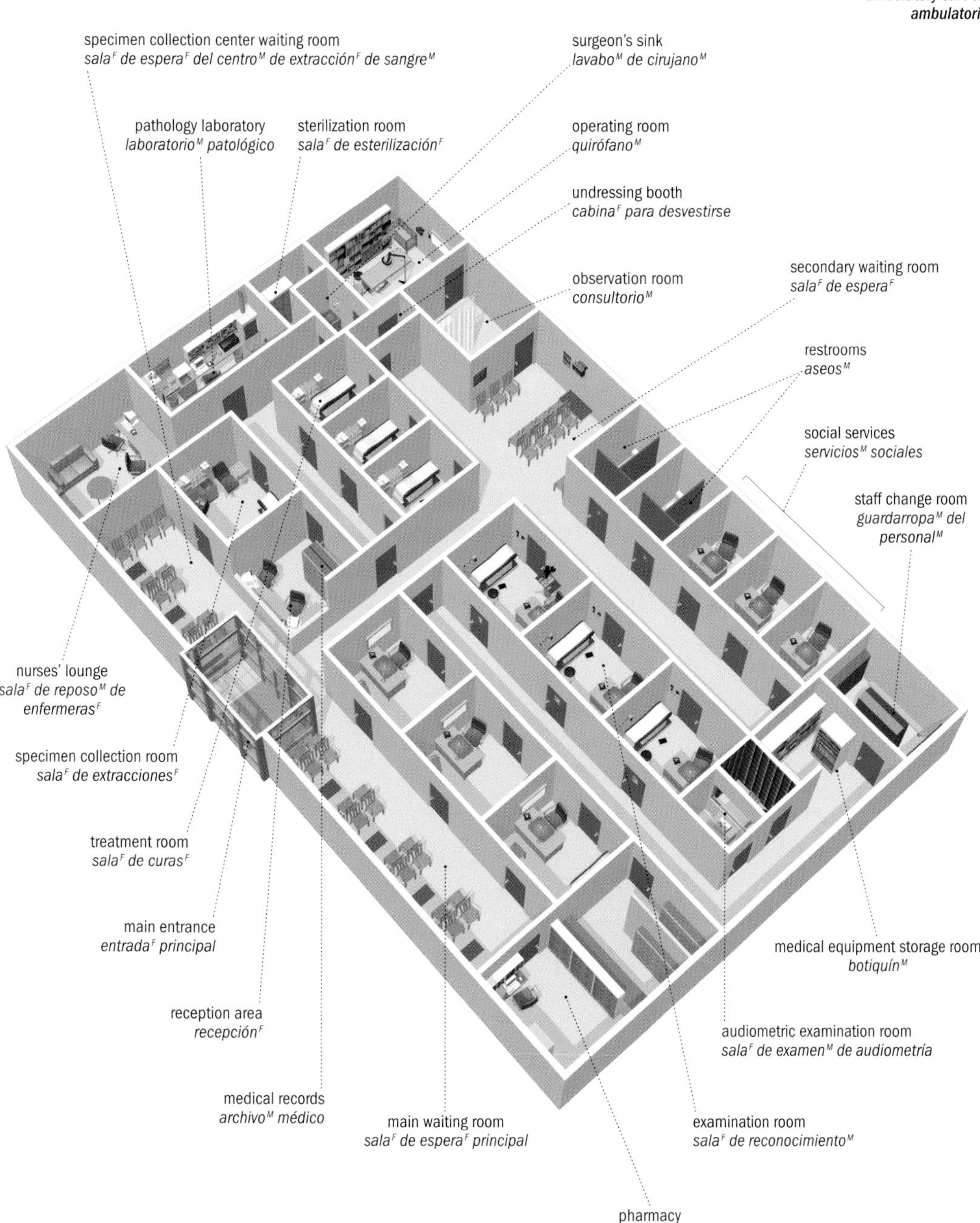
specimen collection center waiting room
sala[F] *de espera*[F] *del centro*[M] *de extracción*[F] *de sangre*[M]
surgeon's sink
lavabo[M] *de cirujano*[M]
pathology laboratory
laboratorio[M] *patológico*
sterilization room
sala[F] *de esterilización*[F]
operating room
quirófano[M]
undressing booth
cabina[F] *para desvestirse*
observation room
consultorio[M]
secondary waiting room
sala[F] *de espera*[F]
restrooms
aseos[M]
social services
servicios[M] *sociales*
staff change room
guardarropa[M] *del personal*[M]
nurses' lounge
sala[F] *de reposo*[M] *de enfermeras*[F]
specimen collection room
sala[F] *de extracciones*[F]
treatment room
sala[F] *de curas*[F]
main entrance
entrada[F] *principal*
medical equipment storage room
botiquín[M]
reception area
recepción[F]
audiometric examination room
sala[F] *de examen*[M] *de audiometría*
medical records
archivo[M] *médico*
main waiting room
sala[F] *de espera*[F] *principal*
examination room
sala[F] *de reconocimiento*[M]
pharmacy
farmacia[F]

walking aids

auxiliares[M] ortopédicos para caminar

forearm crutch
muleta[F] de antebrazo[M]

forearm support
soporte[M] para el antebrazo[M]

handgrip
empuñadura[F]

adjuster
tubo[M] ajustable

underarm crutch
muleta[F] de sobaco[M]

underarm rest
soporte[M] para el sobaco[M]

crosspiece
travesaño[M]

upright
montante[M]

rubber tip
contera[F] de caucho[M]

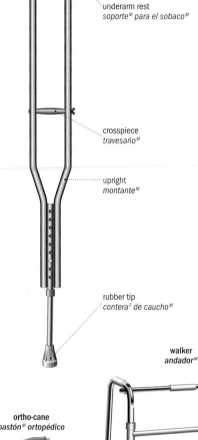

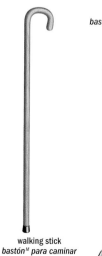

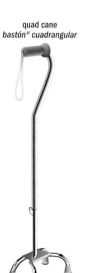

walking stick
bastón[M] para caminar

quad cane
bastón[M] cuadrangular

English cane
bastón[M] inglés

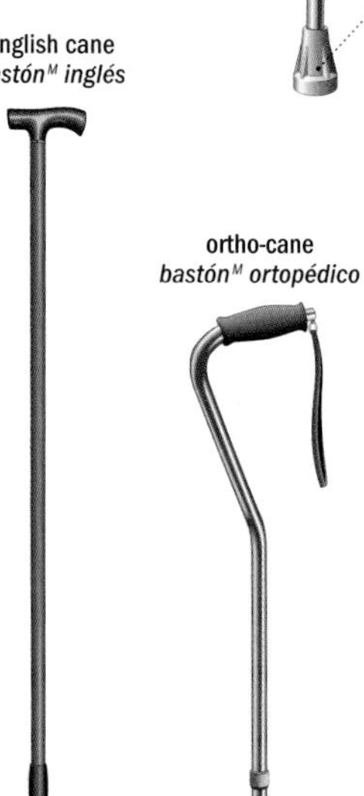

ortho-cane
bastón[M] ortopédico

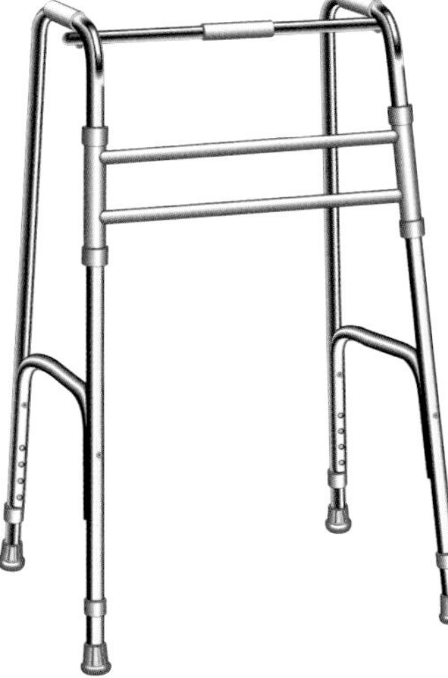

walker
andador[M]

wheelchair

silla[F] de ruedas[F]

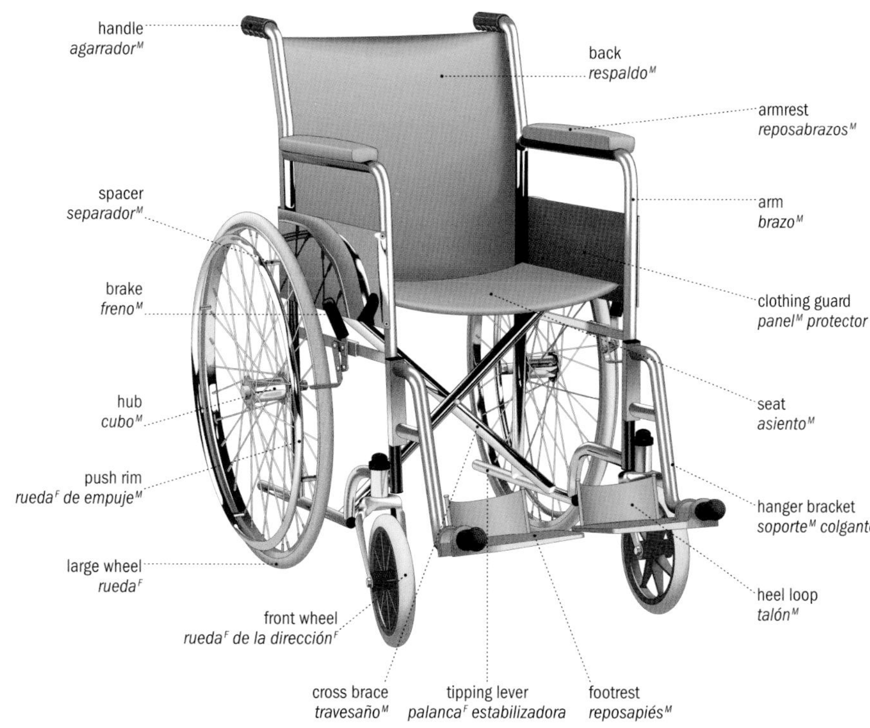

forms of medications

formas[F] farmacéuticas de medicamentos[M]

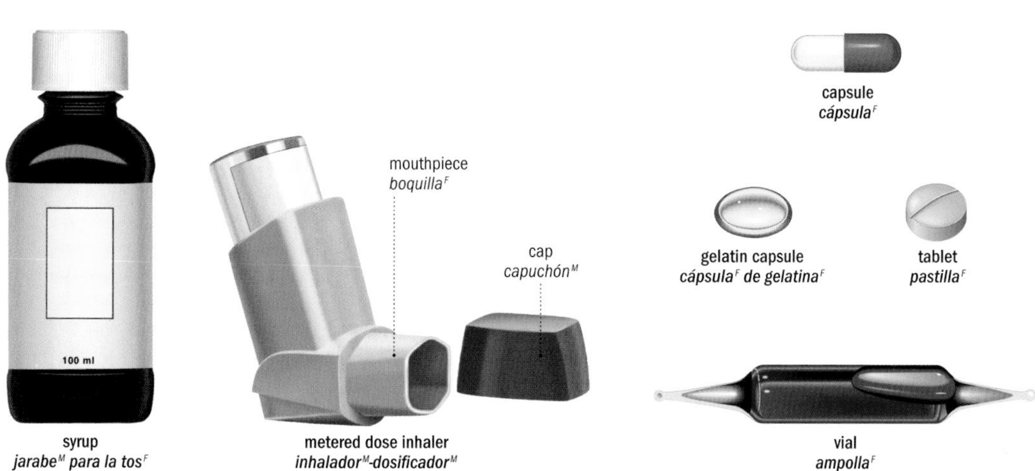

dice and dominoes

dados[M] y dominós[M]

ordinary die
dado[M] común

poker die
dado[M] de póquer[M]

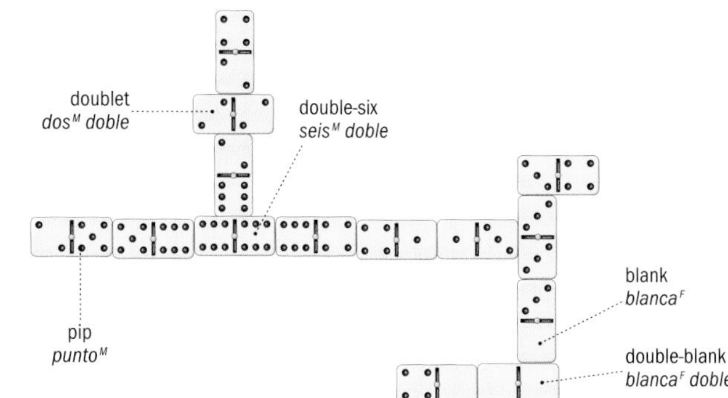

cards

baraja[F]

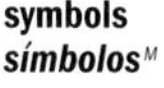

symbols
símbolos[M]

heart
corazón[M]

diamond
diamante[M]

club
trébol[M]

spade
espada[F]

joker
comodín[M]

ace
as[M]

king
rey[M]

queen
reina[F]

jack
jota[F]

standard poker hands
manos[F] de póquer[M]

high card
cartas[F] altas

one pair
un par[M]

two pairs
dos pares[M]

three-of-a-kind
trío[M]

straight
escalera[F]

flush
color[M]

full house
full[M]

four-of-a-kind
póquer[M]

straight flush
escalera[F] de color[M]

royal flush
escalera[F] real

board games

juegos[M] de mesa[F]

backgammon
backgammon[M]

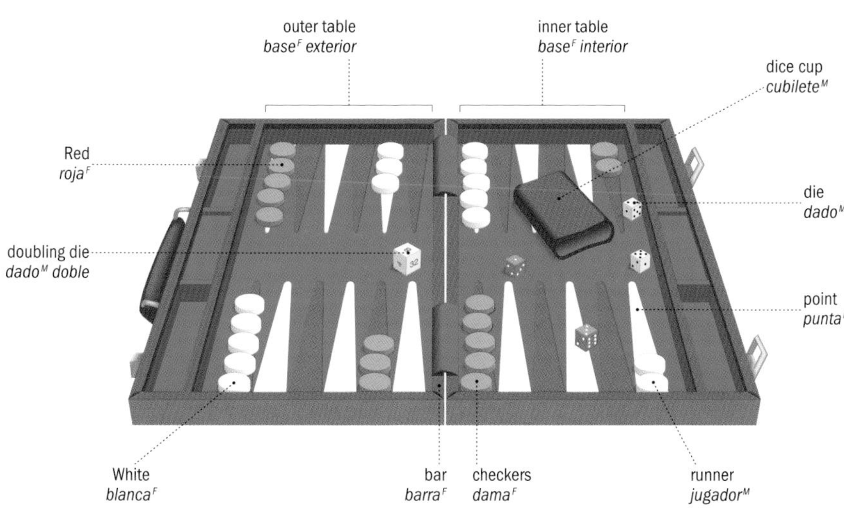

Monopoly®
Monopoly®[M]

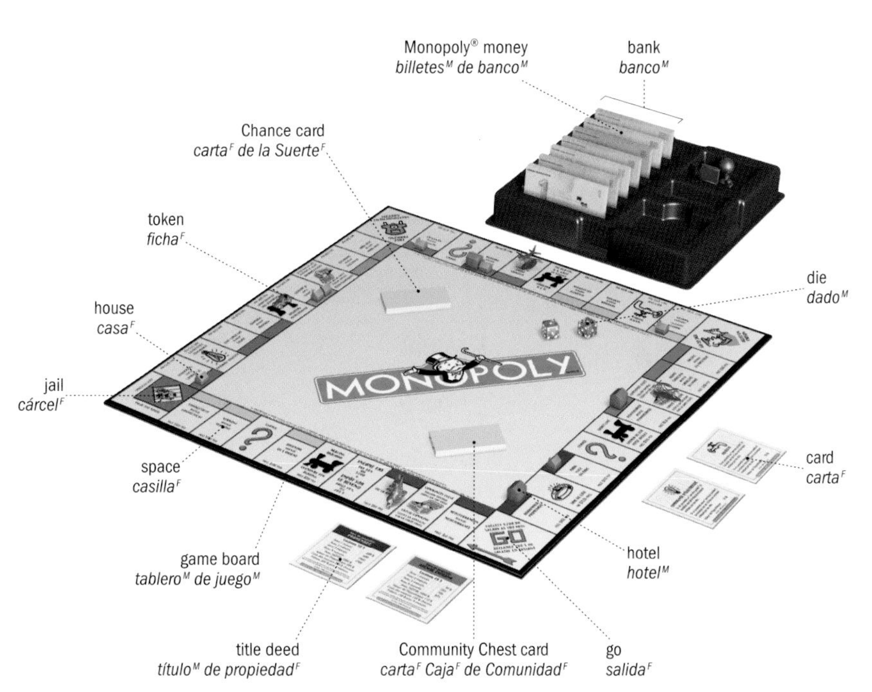

board games

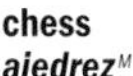

chess
ajedrez M

chessboard
tablero M *de ajedrez* M

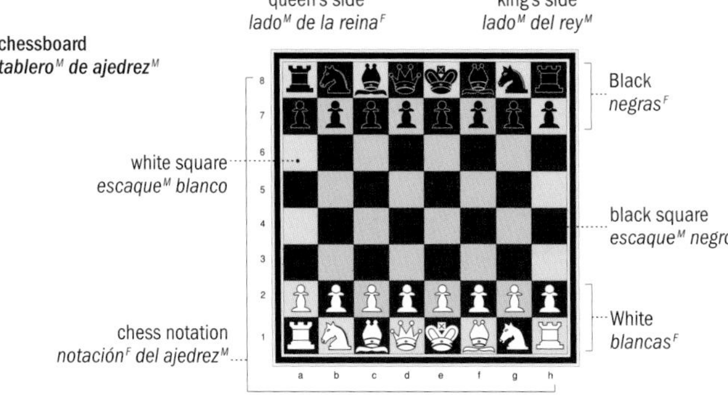

chess pieces
piezas F

pawn
peón M

rook
torre F

bishop
alfil M

knight
caballo M

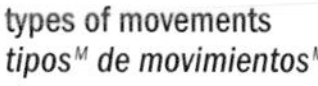

types of movements
tipos M *de movimientos* M

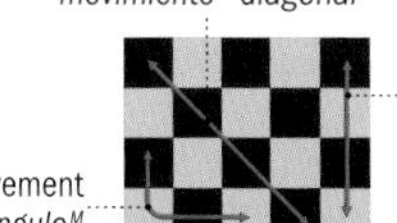

king
rey M

queen
reina F

go
go (sun-tse) M

board
tablero M

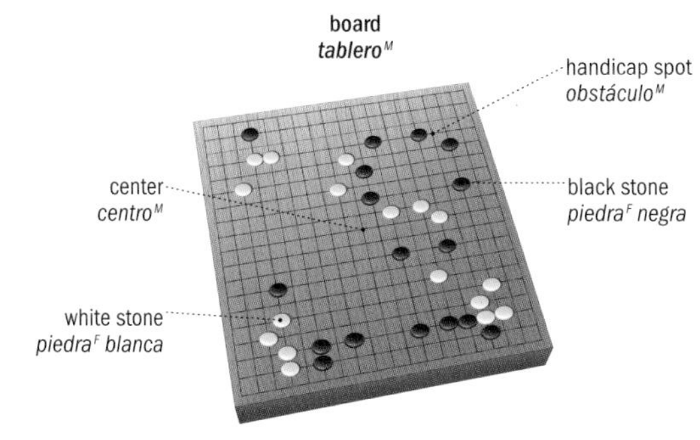

major motions
principales movimientos M

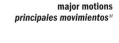

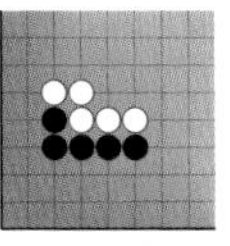

connection
conexión F

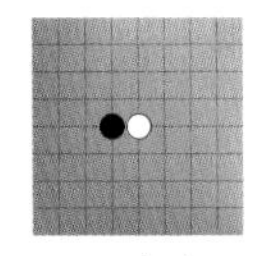

contact
contacto M

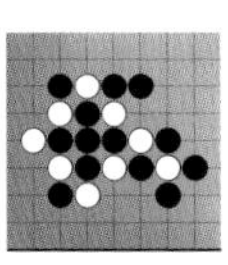

capture
captura F

checkers
damas F

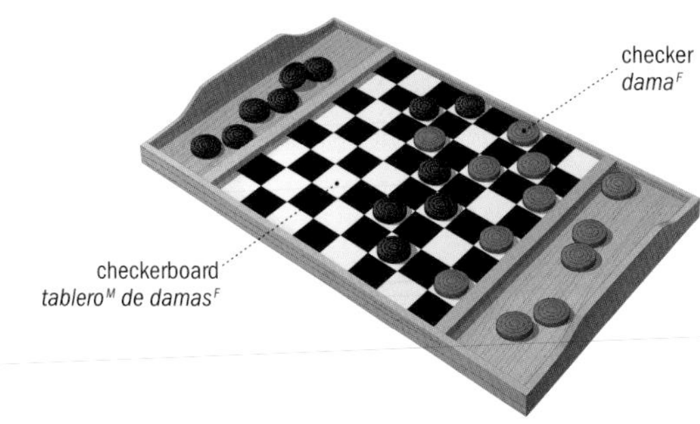

SPORTS AND GAMES

video entertainment system

videojuego[M]

game console
consola[F] de juego[M]
memory card slots
puertos[M] para tarjeta[F] de memoria[F]
CD/DVD player
lector[M] CD/DVD
action buttons
botones[M] de acción[F]
directional buttons
botones[M] de dirección[F]
controller
mando[M]
joysticks
joysticks[M]
visual display
pantalla[F]
controller ports
puertos[M] para el mando[M]
reset button
botón[M] de reset[M]
eject button
botón[M] de expulsión[F]

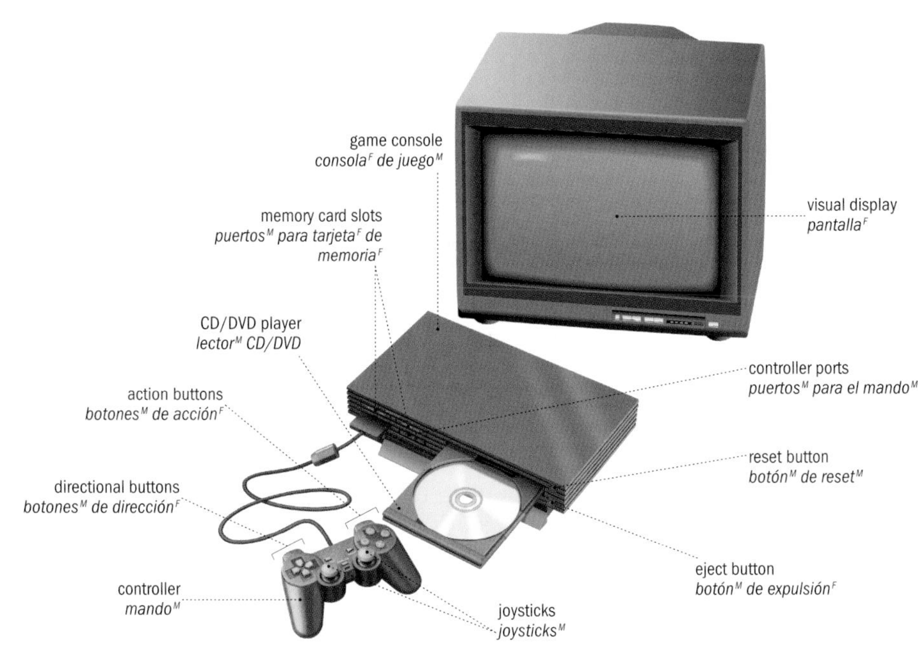

darts

juego[M] de dardos[M]

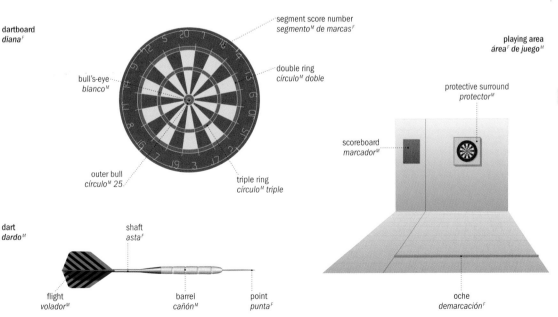

dartboard
diana[F]

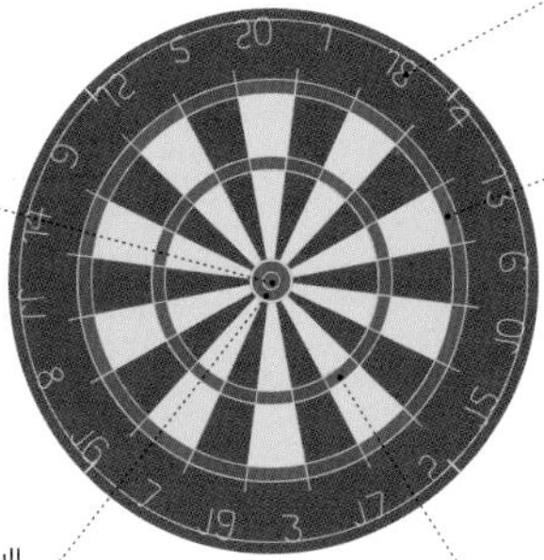

segment score number
segmento[M] de marcas[F]
double ring
círculo[M] doble
bull's-eye
blanco[M]
outer bull
círculo[M] 25
triple ring
círculo[M] triple

playing area
área[F] de juego[M]

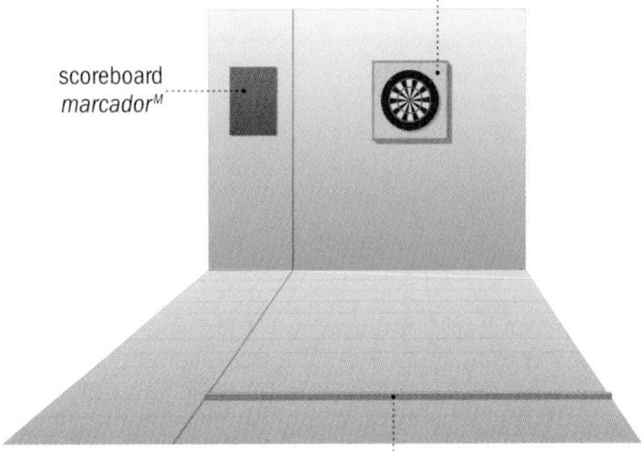

protective surround
protector[M]
scoreboard
marcador[M]
oche
demarcación[F]

dart
dardo[M]

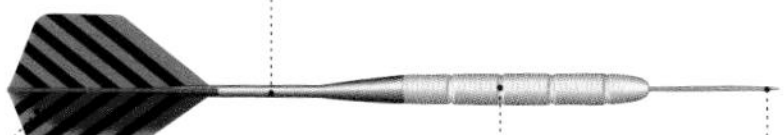

shaft
asta[F]
flight
volador[M]
barrel
cañón[M]
point
punta[F]

arena

estadio^{M}

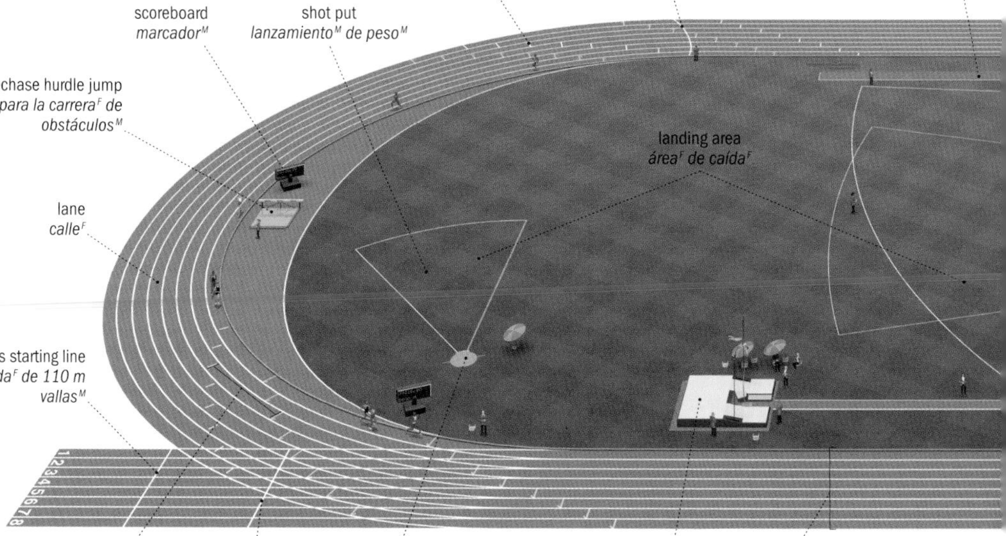

200 m starting line
línea^{F} de salida^{F} de 200 m
5,000 m starting line
línea^{F} de salida^{F} de 5.000 m
long jump and triple jump
salto^{M} de longitud^{F} y triple salto^{M}
scoreboard
marcador^{M}
shot put
lanzamiento^{M} de peso^{M}
steeplechase hurdle jump
ría^{F} para la carrera^{F} de obstáculos^{M}
landing area
área^{F} de caída^{F}
lane
calle^{F}
110 m hurdles starting line
línea^{F} de salida^{F} de 110 m vallas^{M}
takeover zone
zona^{F} de entrega^{F}
100 m and 100 m hurdles starting line
línea^{F} de salida^{F} de 100 m y 100 m vallas^{F}
throwing circle
círculo^{M} de lanzamiento^{M}
pole vault
salto^{M} de pértiga^{F}
track
pista^{F}

equipment
equipamiento^{M}

starting pistol
pistola^{F} de salida^{F}

shot
peso^{M}

baton
testigo^{M}

discus
disco^{M}

hammer
martillo^{M}

javelin
jabalina^{F}

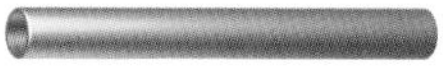

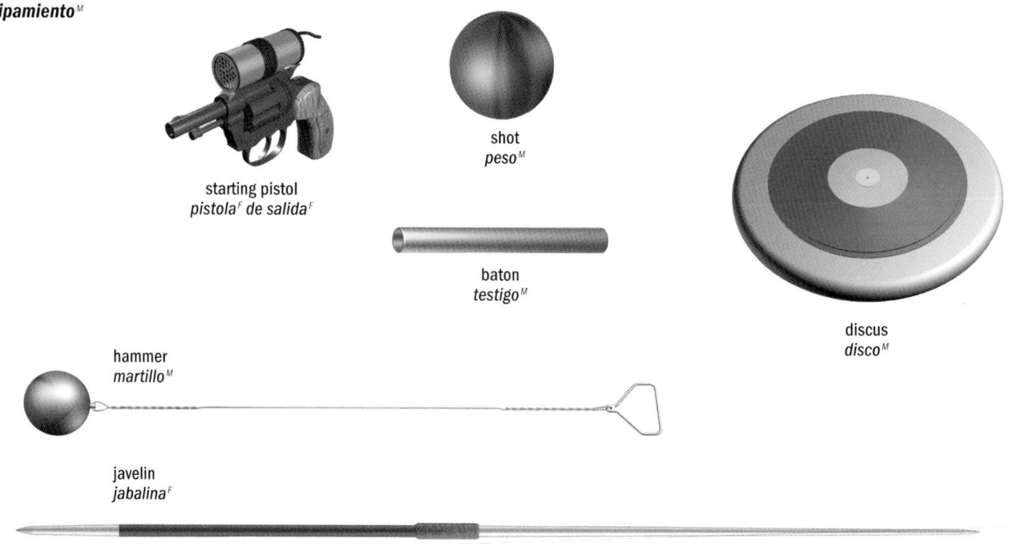

arena

discus and hammer throw
lanzamiento[M] de martillo[M] y disco[M]
1,500 m starting line
línea[F] de salida[F] de 1.500 m
safety cage
jaula[F] de protección[F]
throwing circle
círculo[M] de lanzamiento[M]
javelin throw
lanzamiento[M] de jabalina[F]
approach
pista[F] de salto[M]
high jump
salto[M] de altura[F]
400 m, 400 m hurdles, 4 x 100 m relay starting line
línea[F] de salida[F] de 400 m, 400 m vallas[F] y relevos[M] de 4x100 m
12345678
finish line
llegada[F]
10,000 m and 4 x 400 m relay starting line
línea[F] de salida[F] de 10.000 m y de relevos[M] de 4 x 400 m
800 m starting line
línea[F] de salida[F] 800 m

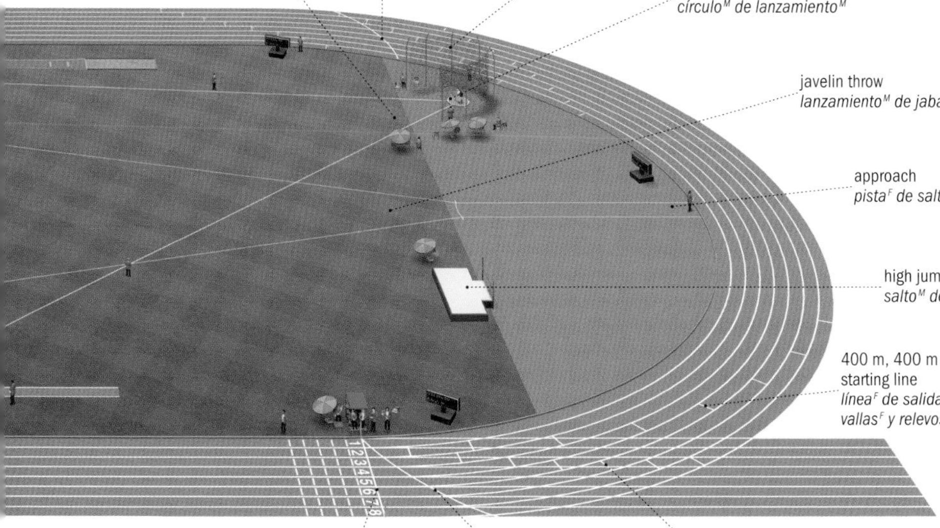

athlete: starting block
atleta[M] : taco[M] de salida[F]

singlet
camiseta[F]
number
número[M] dorsal
shorts
pantalón[M]
pedal
soporte[M] del pie[M]
track shoe
zapatilla[F]
notch
ranura[F]
starting line
línea[F] de salida[F]
anchor
tornillo[M] de anclaje[M]
lane line
línea[F] de la calle[F]
rack
cremallera[F]
spike
tacos[M]
block
taco[M]
base
pedestal[M]

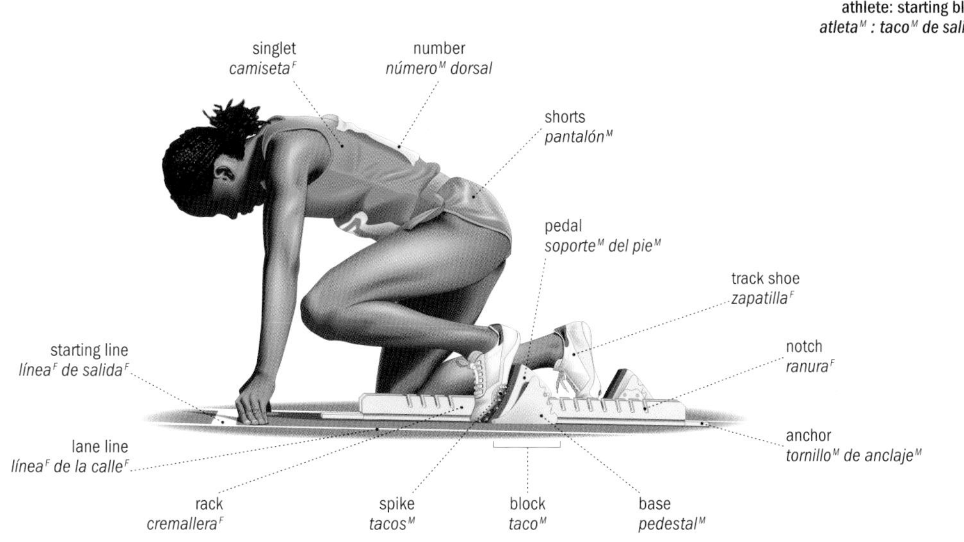

baseball

béisbol[M]

player positions
posición[F] de los jugadores[M]

left fielder
jugador[M] exterior izquierdo
center fielder
jugador[M] exterior central
shortstop
jugador[M] medio
right fielder
jugador[M] exterior derecho
third baseman
jugador[M] de tercera base[F]
second baseman
jugador[M] de segunda base[F]
catcher
receptor[M]
pitcher
lanzador[M]
first baseman
jugador[M] de primera base[F]

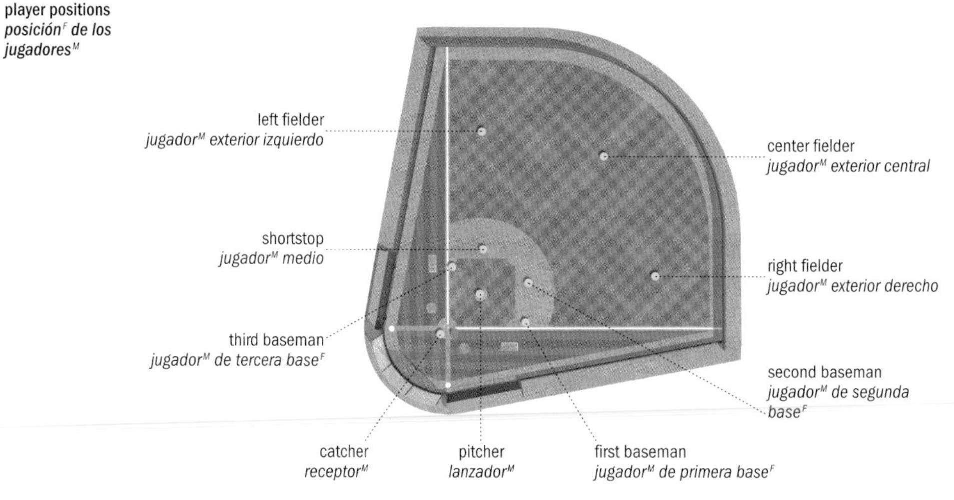

field
campo[M]

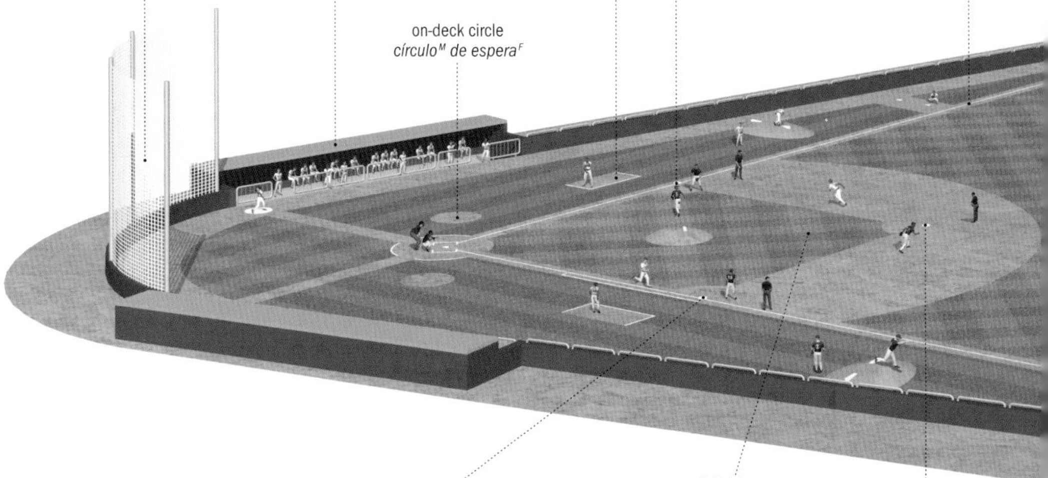

third base
tercera base[F]
coach's box
banquillo[M] del entrenador[M]
foul line
línea[F] de foul[M]
dugout
banquillo[M] de jugadores[M]
backstop
pantalla[F] de protección[F]
on-deck circle
círculo[M] de espera[F]
first base
primera base[F]
infield
diamante[M]
second base
segunda base[F]

SPORTS AND GAMES

pitch
lanzamiento^{M}

home-plate umpire
árbitro^M de base^F meta^F
batter
bateador^M
pitcher
lanzador^M
catcher
receptor^M
home plate
base^F meta^F
pitcher's mound
base^F de lanzamiento^M
pitcher's plate
plataforma^F de lanzamiento^M

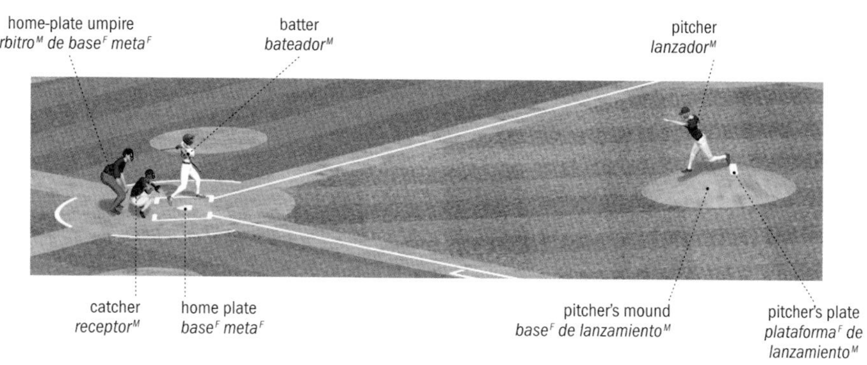

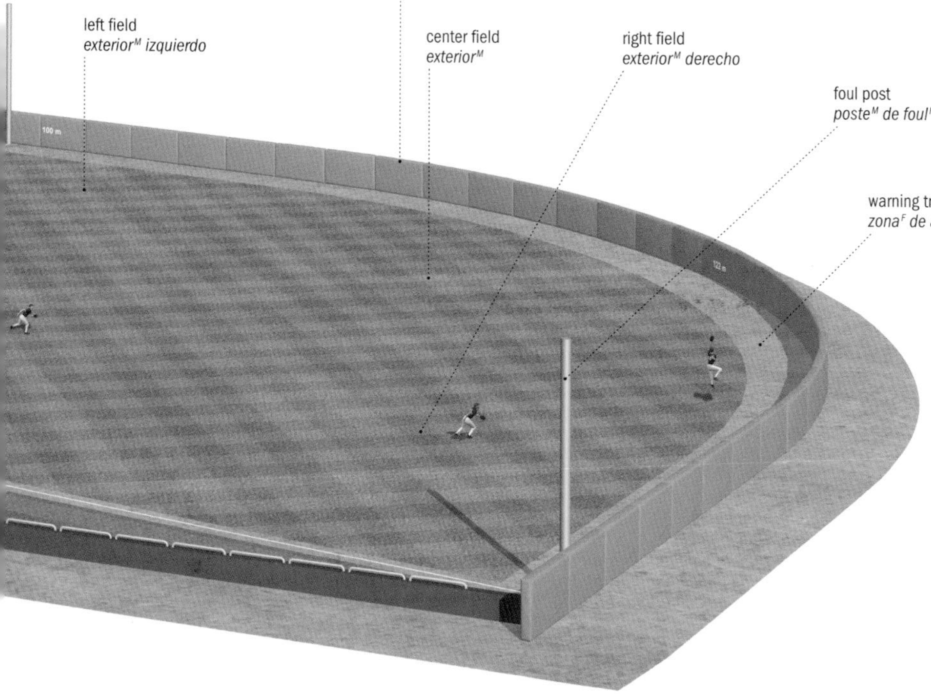

outfield fence
vallado^M del campo^M
left field
exterior^M izquierdo
center field
exterior^M
right field
exterior^M derecho
foul post
poste^M de foul^M
warning track
zona^F de atención^F
100 m
122 m

baseball

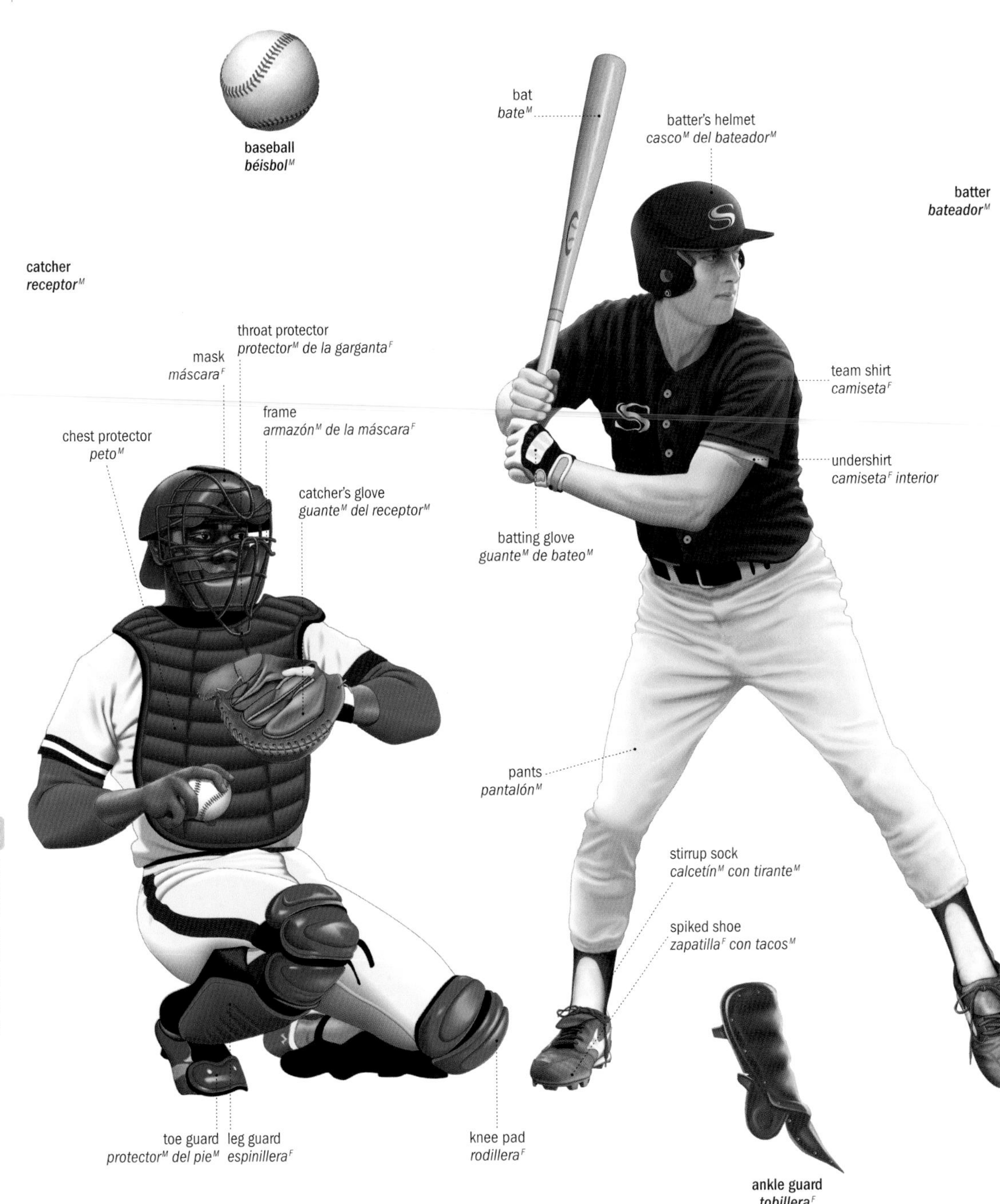
baseball
béisbol^M
bat
bate^M
batter's helmet
casco^M *del bateador*^M
batter
bateador^M
catcher
receptor^M
throat protector
protector^M *de la garganta*^F
mask
máscara^F
team shirt
camiseta^F
frame
armazón^M *de la máscara*^F
chest protector
peto^M
undershirt
camiseta^F *interior*
catcher's glove
guante^M *del receptor*^M
batting glove
guante^M *de bateo*^M
pants
pantalón^M
stirrup sock
calcetín^M *con tirante*^M
spiked shoe
zapatilla^F *con tacos*^M
toe guard
protector^M *del pie*^M
leg guard
espinillera^F
knee pad
rodillera^F
ankle guard
tobillera^F

baseball

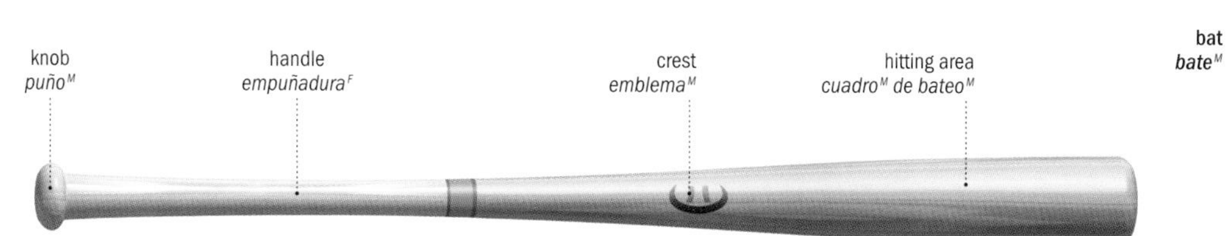

bat
bate[M]

cross section of a baseball
corte[M] ***de la pelota***[F] ***de béisbol***[M]

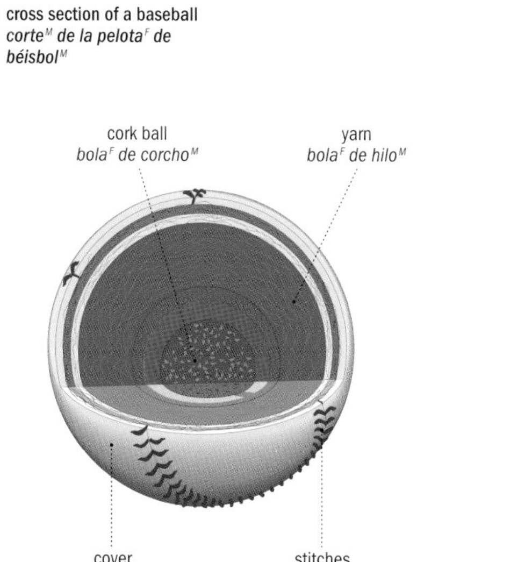

fielder's glove
guante[M] ***de recogida***[F]

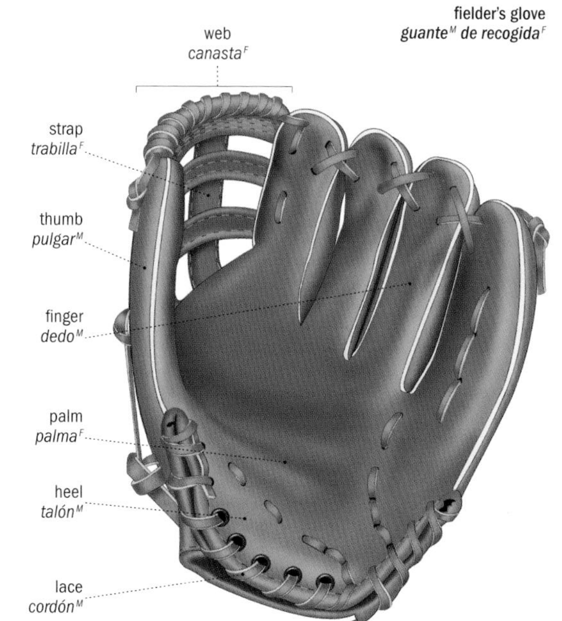

softball

softball[M]

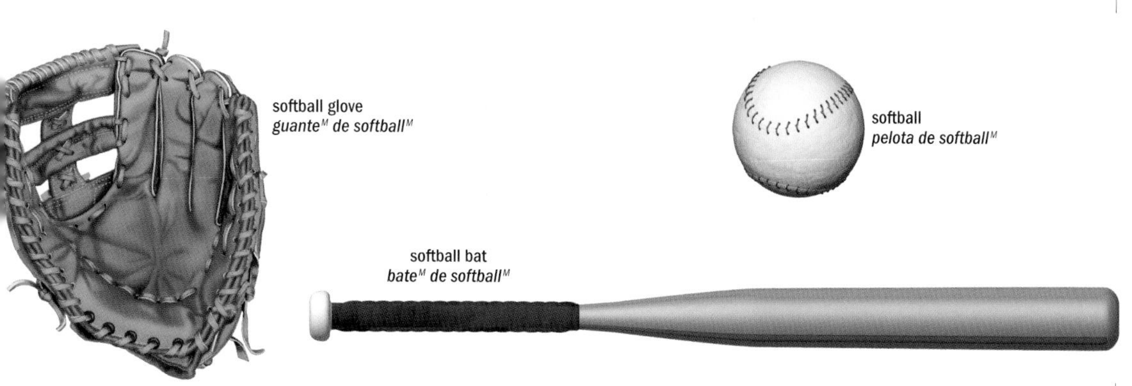

cricket

cricket[M]

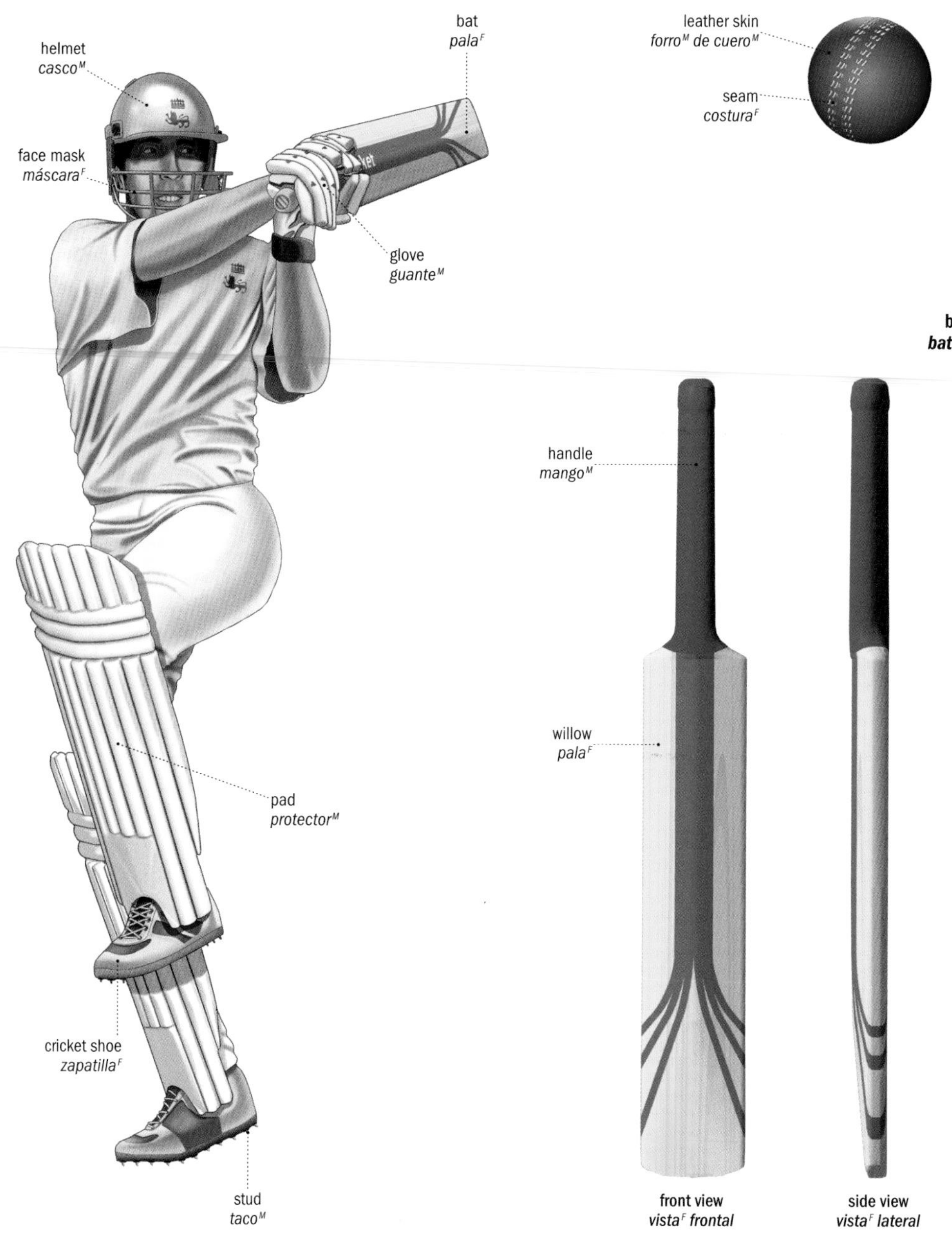
cricket player: batsman
jugador[M] de críquet[M] : bateador[M]
helmet
casco[M]
face mask
máscara[F]
bat
pala[F]
glove
guante[M]
pad
protector[M]
cricket shoe
zapatilla[F]
stud
taco[M]
cricket ball
pelota[F] de cricket[M]
leather skin
forro[M] de cuero[M]
seam
costura[F]
bat
bate[M]
handle
mango[M]
willow
pala[F]
front view
vista[F] frontal
side view
vista[F] lateral

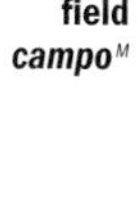

cricket

field
campo^{M}

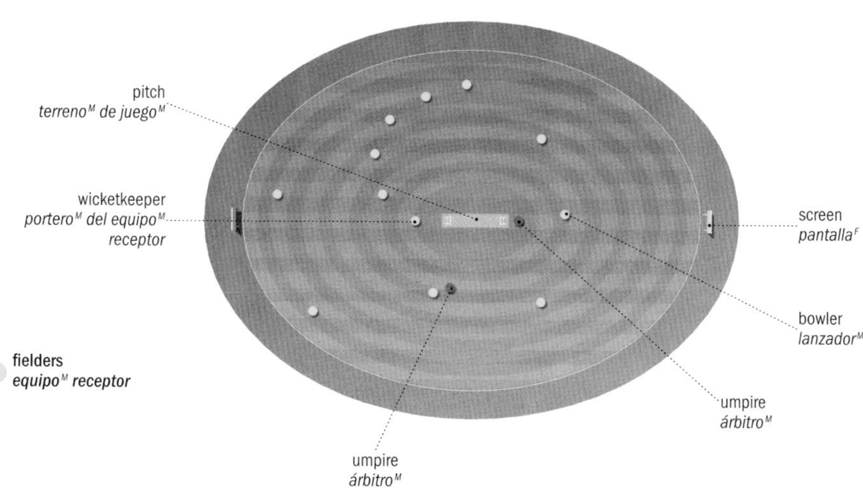

pitch
terreno^{M} *de juego*^{M}
wicketkeeper
portero^{M} *del equipo*^{M} *receptor*
screen
pantalla^{F}
bowler
lanzador^{M}
umpire
árbitro^{M}
umpire
árbitro^{M}
fielders
equipo^{M} ***receptor***

wicket
puerta^{F}

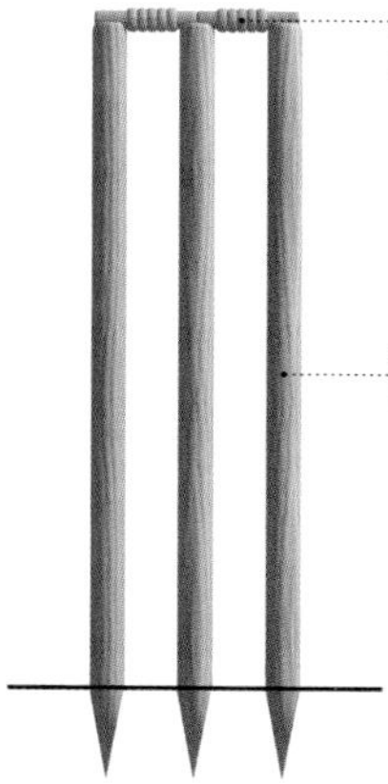

bail
travesaño^{M}
stump
estaca^{F}

pitch
terreno^{M} *de juego*^{M}

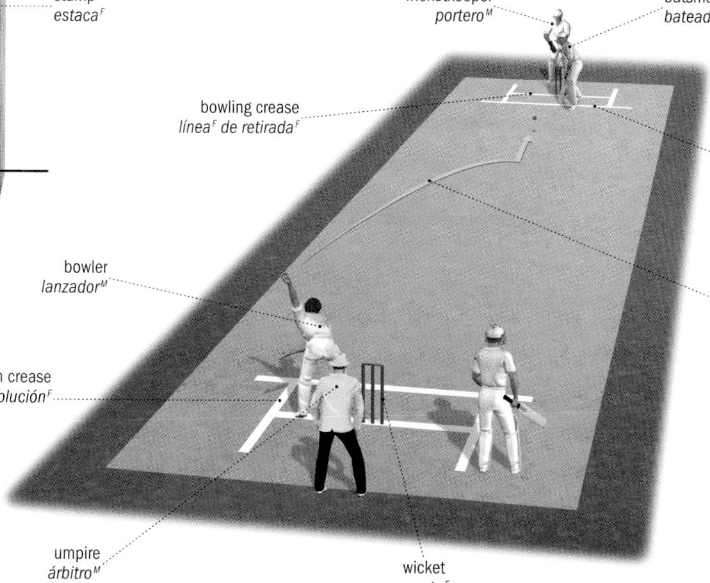

wicketkeeper
portero^{M}
batsman
bateador^{M}
bowling crease
línea^{F} *de retirada*^{F}
popping crease
línea^{F} *de lanzamiento*^{M}
bowler
lanzador^{M}
delivery
lanzamiento^{M}
return crease
línea^{F} *de devolución*^{F}
umpire
árbitro^{M}
wicket
puerta^{F}

soccer

fútbol[M]

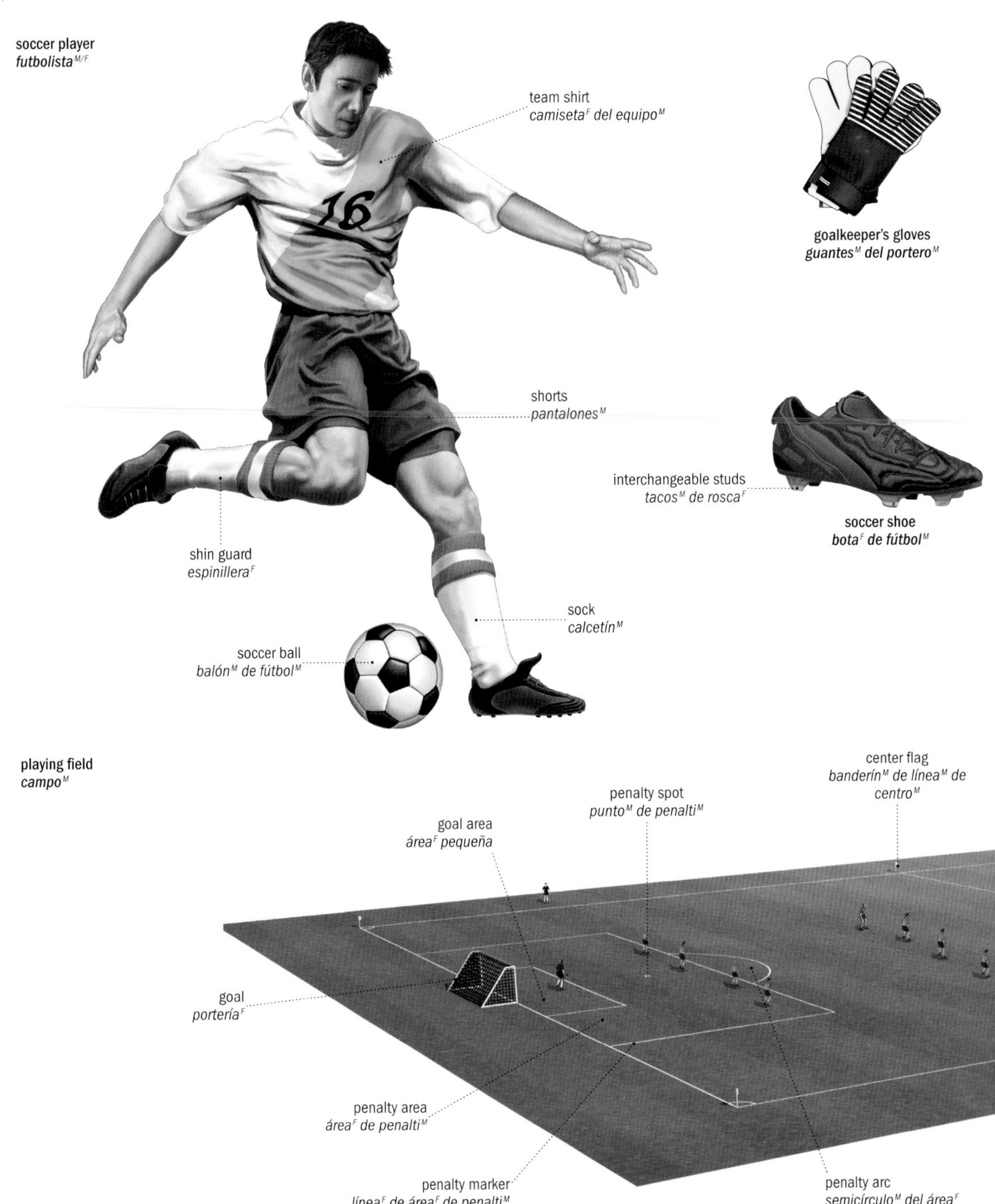

soccer player
futbolista[M/F]
team shirt
camiseta[F] del equipo[M]
goalkeeper's gloves
guantes[M] del portero[M]
shorts
pantalones[M]
interchangeable studs
tacos[M] de rosca[F]
soccer shoe
bota[F] de fútbol[M]
shin guard
espinillera[F]
sock
calcetín[M]
soccer ball
balón[M] de fútbol[M]
playing field
campo[M]
center flag
banderín[M] de línea[M] de centro[M]
penalty spot
punto[M] de penalti[M]
goal area
área[F] pequeña
goal
portería[F]
penalty area
área[F] de penalti[M]
penalty marker
línea[F] de área[F] de penalti[M]
penalty arc
semicírculo[M] del área[F]

SPORTS AND GAMES

player positions
***posición*[F] *de los jugadores*[M]**

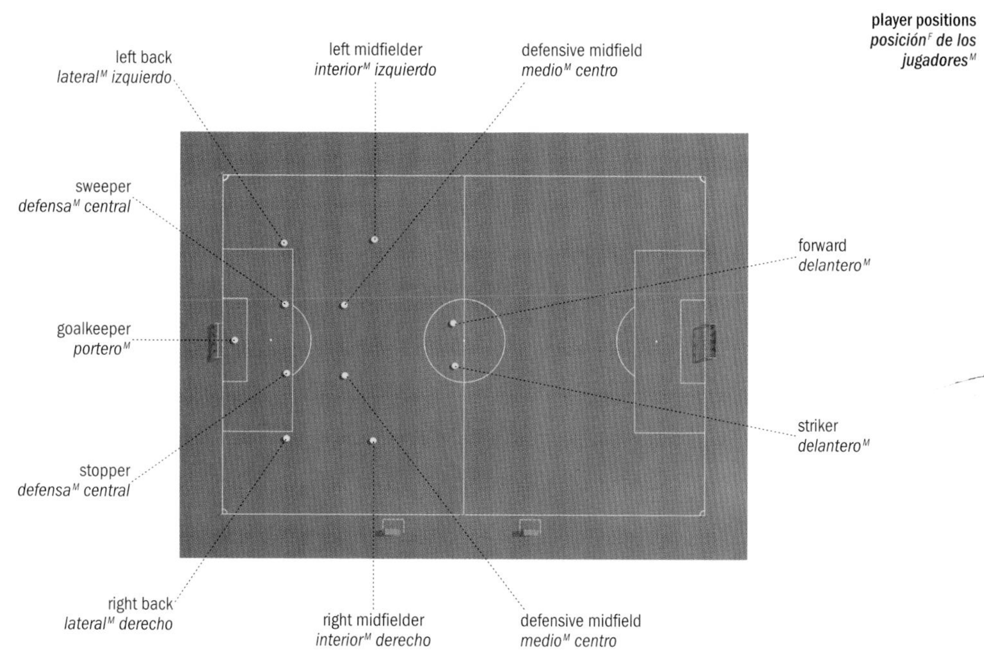
left back
lateral[M] *izquierdo*
left midfielder
interior[M] *izquierdo*
defensive midfield
medio[M] *centro*
sweeper
defensa[M] *central*
forward
delantero[M]
goalkeeper
portero[M]
striker
delantero[M]
stopper
defensa[M] *central*
right back
lateral[M] *derecho*
right midfielder
interior[M] *derecho*
defensive midfield
medio[M] *centro*

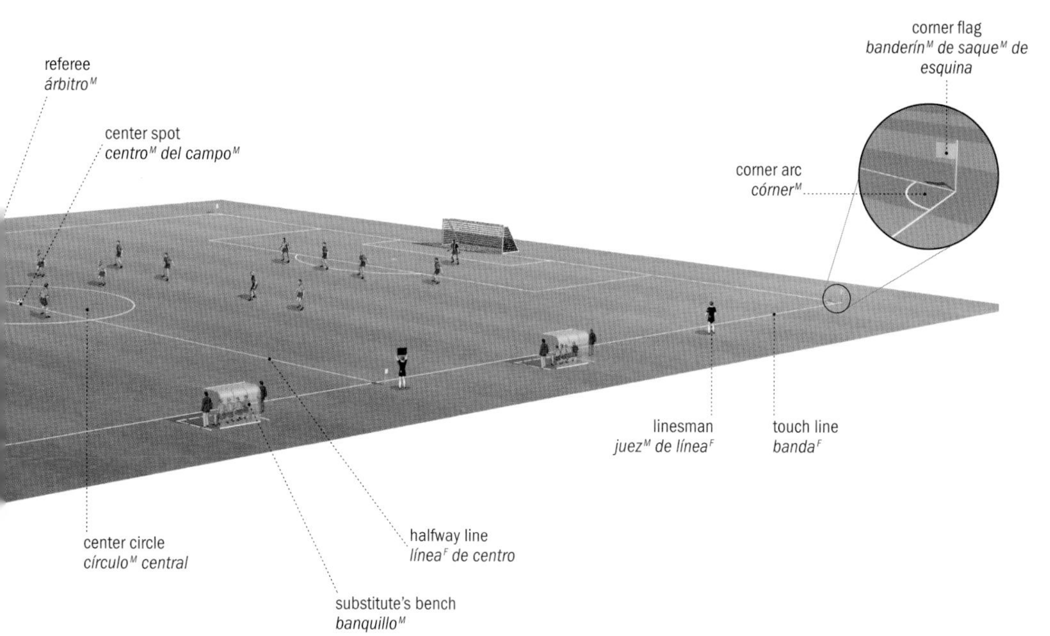
corner flag
banderín[M] *de saque*[M] *de esquina*
referee
árbitro[M]
center spot
centro[M] *del campo*[M]
corner arc
córner[M]
linesman
juez[M] *de línea*[F]
touch line
banda[F]
center circle
círculo[M] *central*
halfway line
línea[F] *de centro*
substitute's bench
banquillo[M]

rugby

rugby^M

players' positions
posición^F de los jugadores^M

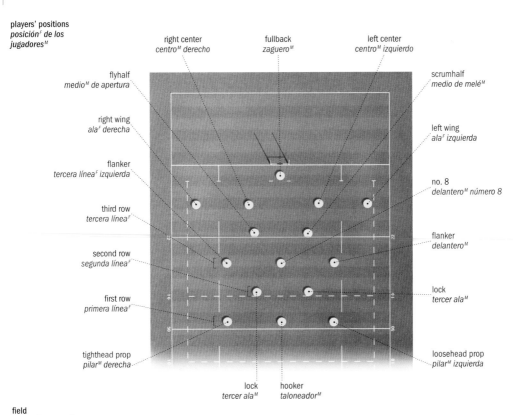

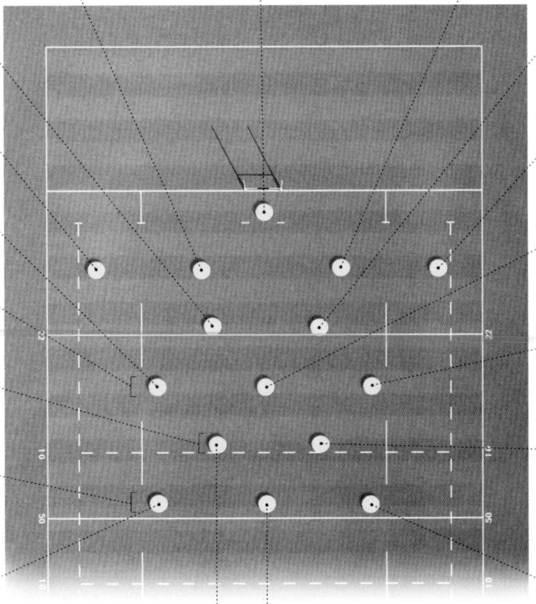

right center
centro^M derecho
fullback
zaguero^M
left center
centro^M izquierdo
flyhalf
medio^M de apertura
scrumhalf
medio de melé^M
right wing
ala^F derecha
left wing
ala^F izquierda
flanker
tercera línea^F izquierda
no. 8
delantero^M número 8
third row
tercera línea^F
flanker
delantero^M
second row
segunda línea^F
lock
tercer ala^M
first row
primera línea^F
tighthead prop
pilar^M derecha
loosehead prop
pilar^M izquierda
lock
tercer ala^M
hooker
taloneador^M

field
campo^M de juego^M

10 m line
línea^F de 10 m
flag
bandera^F
goal line
línea^F de marca^F
goalpost
palos^M
dead ball line
línea^F de fondo^M
22 m line
línea^F de 22 m

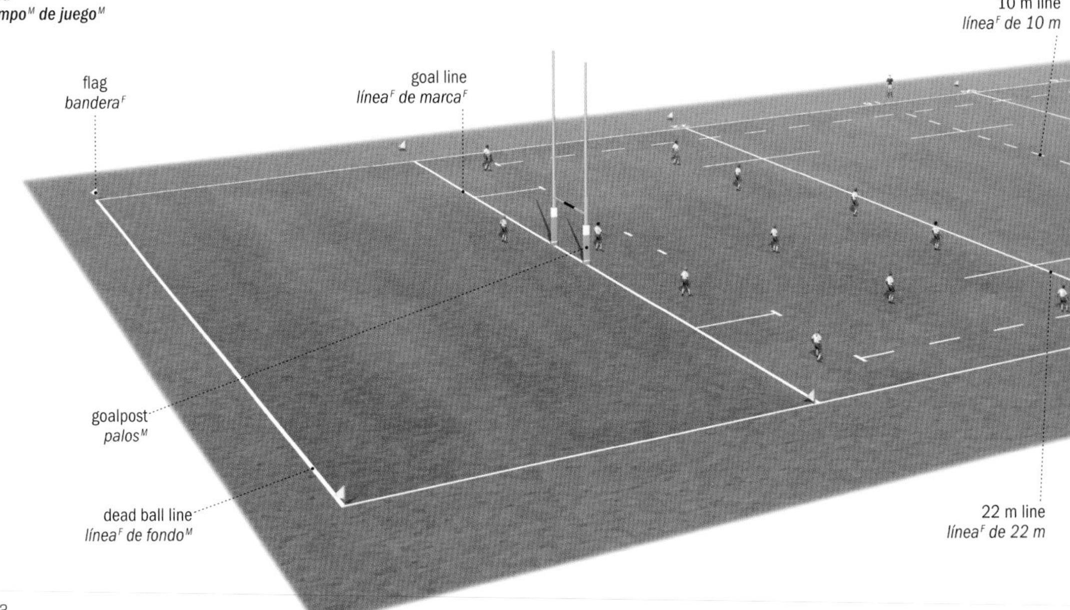

rugby

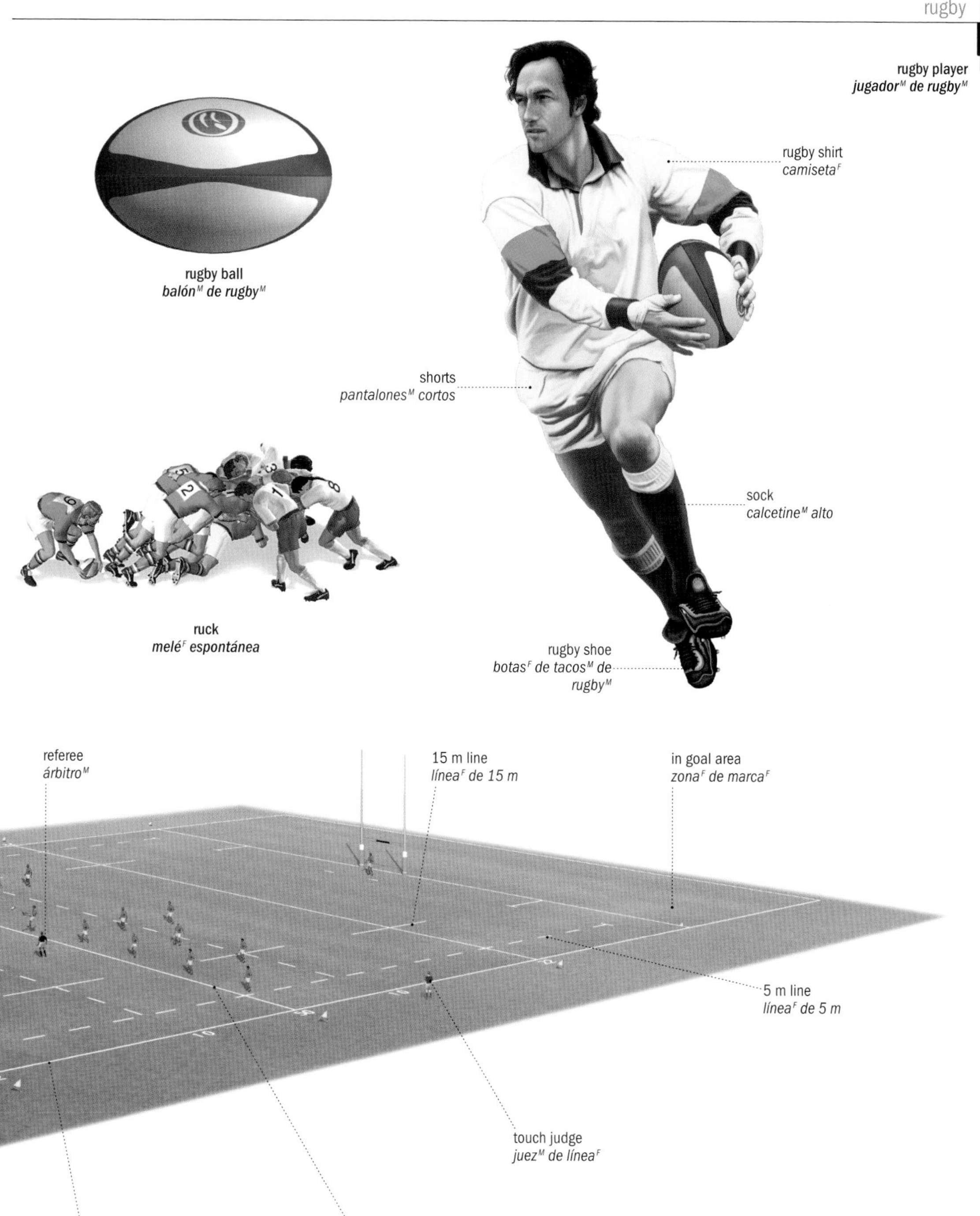
rugby player
jugador^M de rugby^M
rugby shirt
camiseta^F
rugby ball
balón^M de rugby^M
shorts
pantalones^M cortos
sock
calcetine^M alto
ruck
melé^F espontánea
rugby shoe
botas^F de tacos^M de rugby^M
referee
árbitro^M
15 m line
línea^F de 15 m
in goal area
zona^F de marca^F
5 m line
línea^F de 5 m
touch judge
juez^M de línea^F
touchline
línea^F de «touche»^{F}
halfway dash line
línea^F de medio campo^M

American football

fútbol^M americano

scrimmage: defense
melé^F: defensa^F

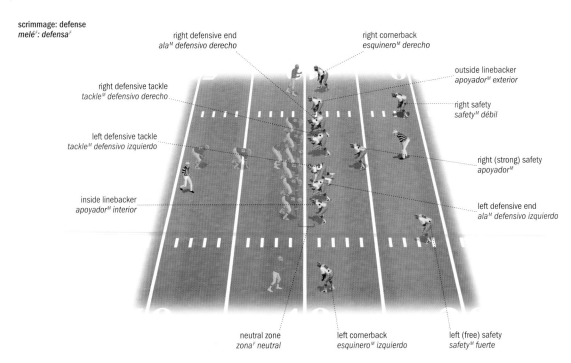

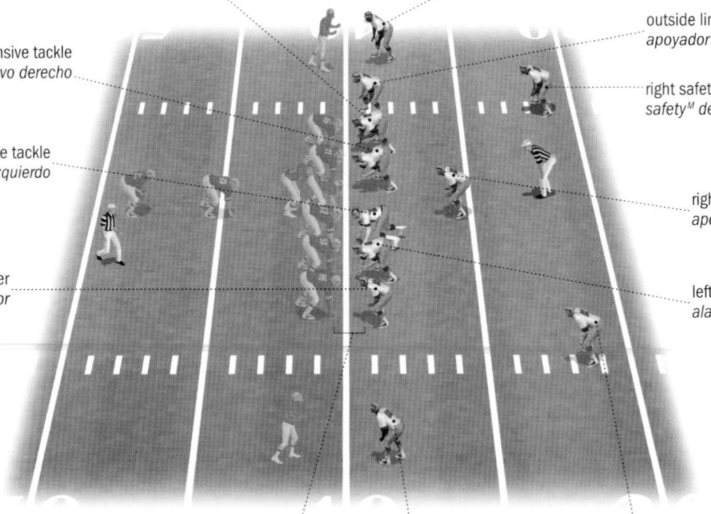

right defensive end
ala^M defensivo derecho
right cornerback
esquinero^M derecho
outside linebacker
apoyador^M exterior
right defensive tackle
tackle^M defensivo derecho
right safety
safety^M débil
left defensive tackle
tackle^M defensivo izquierdo
right (strong) safety
apoyador^M
inside linebacker
apoyador^M interior
left defensive end
ala^M defensivo izquierdo
neutral zone
zona^F neutral
left cornerback
esquinero^M izquierdo
left (free) safety
safety^M fuerte

playing field for American football
campo^M de juego^M de fútbol^M americano

inbounds line
línea^F límite^M de inicio^M de jugada^F
goal line
línea^F de gol^M
fifty-yard line
línea^F media
end zone
zona^F de anotación^F
end line
línea^F de fondo^M
10
20
30
40
yard line
línea^F yardas^F
sideline
banda^F

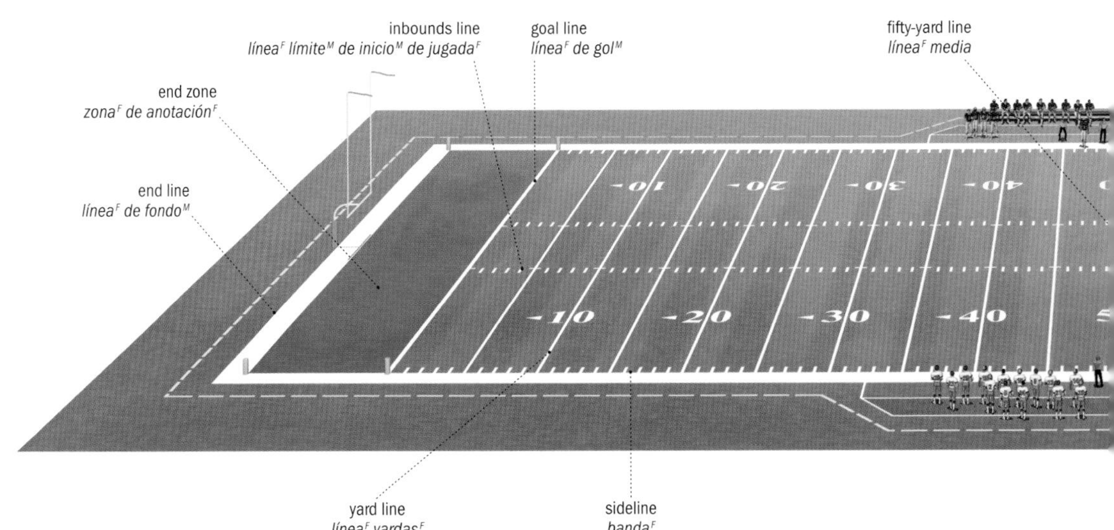

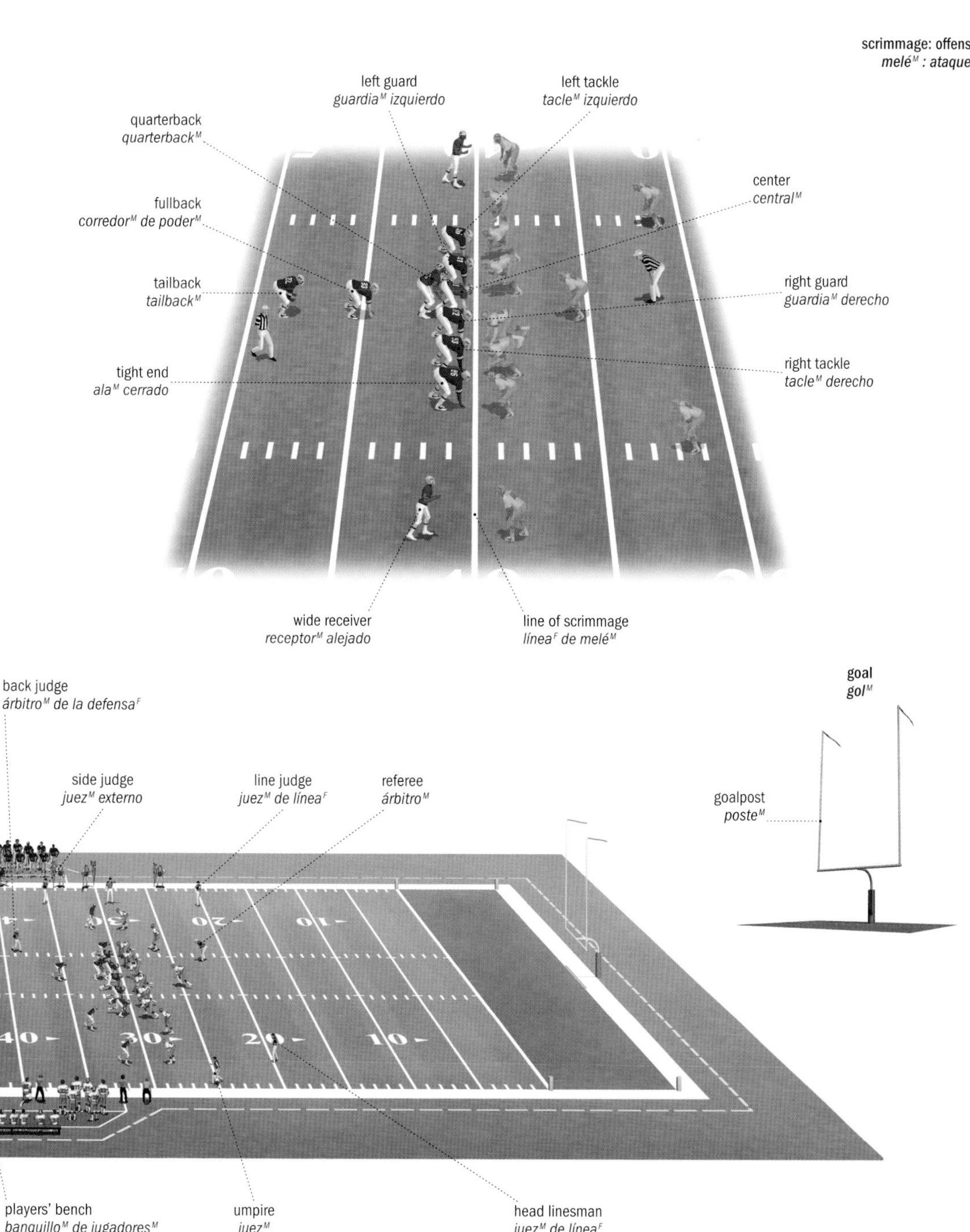
scrimmage: offense
meléM : ataqueM
left guard
guardiaM izquierdo
left tackle
tacleM izquierdo
quarterback
quarterbackM
center
centralM
fullback
corredorM de poderM
tailback
tailbackM
right guard
guardiaM derecho
tight end
alaM cerrado
right tackle
tacleM derecho
wide receiver
receptorM alejado
line of scrimmage
líneaF de meléM
back judge
árbitroM de la defensaF
goal
golM
side judge
juezM externo
line judge
juezM de líneaF
referee
árbitroM
goalpost
posteM
players' bench
banquilloM de jugadoresM
umpire
juezM
head linesman
juezM de líneaF

American football

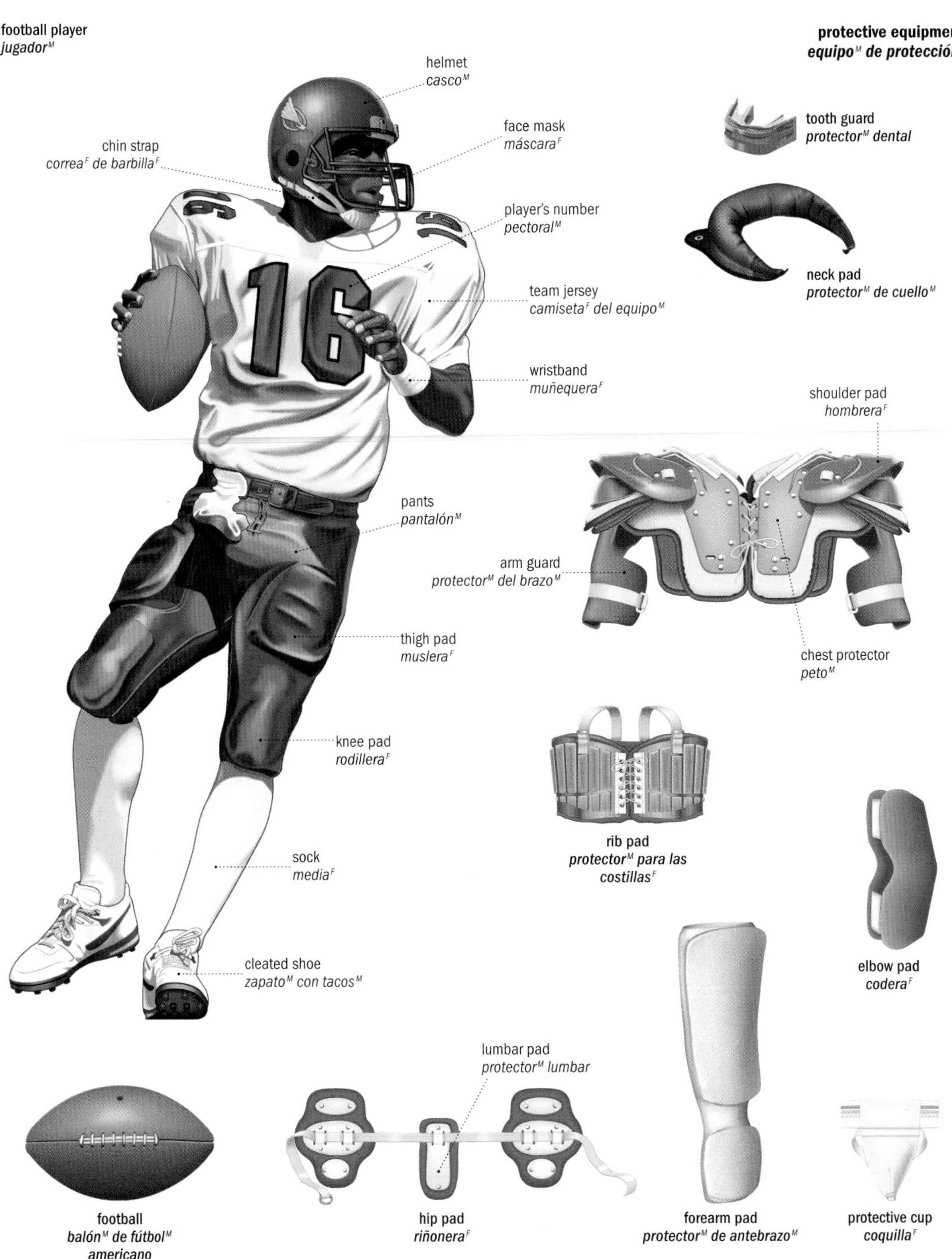
football player
jugadorM
helmet
cascoM
chin strap
correaF de barbillaF
face mask
máscaraF
player's number
pectoralM
team jersey
camisetaF del equipoM
wristband
muñequeraF
pants
pantalónM
thigh pad
musleraF
knee pad
rodilleraF
sock
mediaF
cleated shoe
zapatoM con tacosM
protective equipment
equipoM de protecciónF
tooth guard
protectorM dental
neck pad
protectorM de cuelloM
shoulder pad
hombreraF
arm guard
protectorM del brazoM
chest protector
petoM
rib pad
protectorM para las costillasF
elbow pad
coderaF
lumbar pad
protectorM lumbar
football
balónM de fútbolM americano
hip pad
riñoneraF
forearm pad
protectorM de antebrazoM
protective cup
coquillaF

volleyball

voleibol[M]

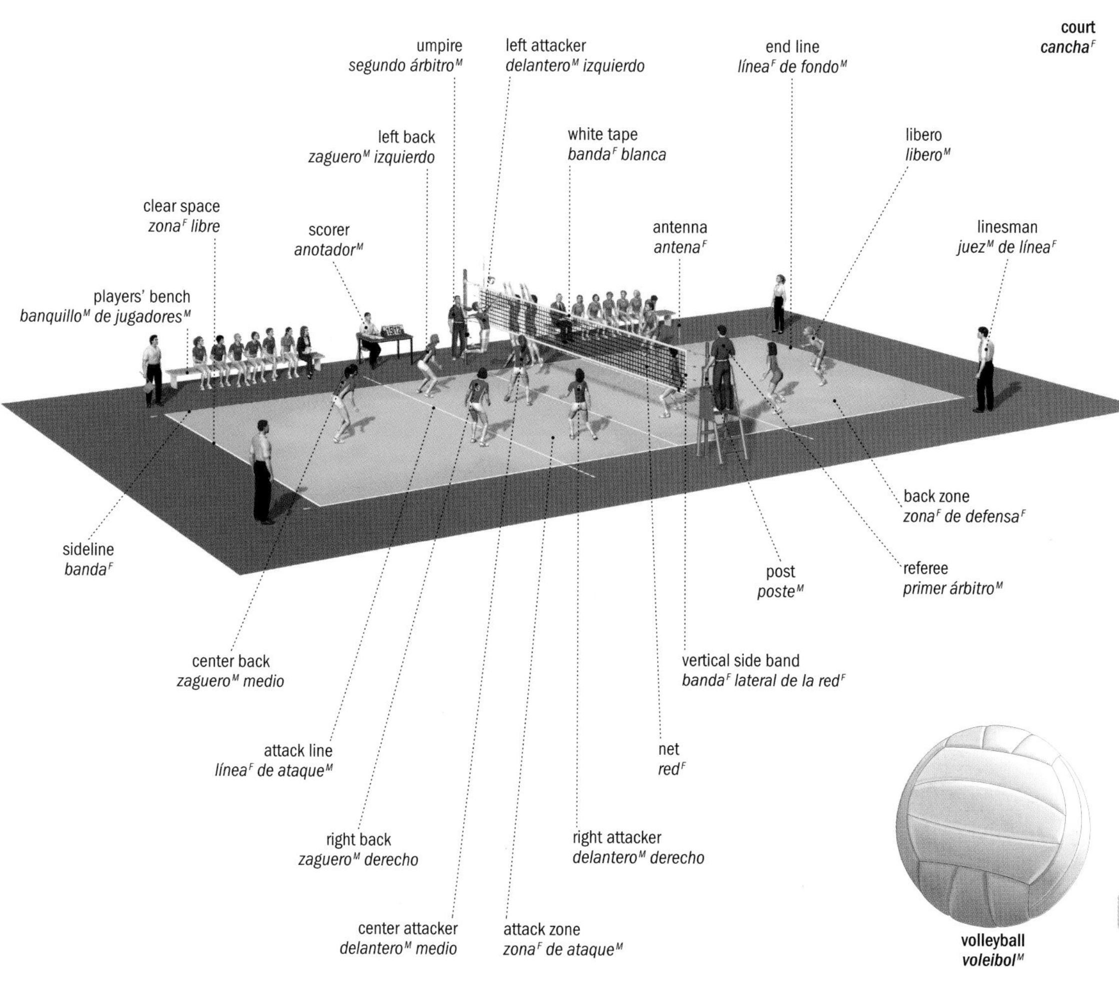

techniques

***técnicas*[F]**

tip
***toque*[M]**

bump
***rebote*[M]**

serve
***saque*[M]**

SPORTS AND GAMES

basketball

baloncesto[M]

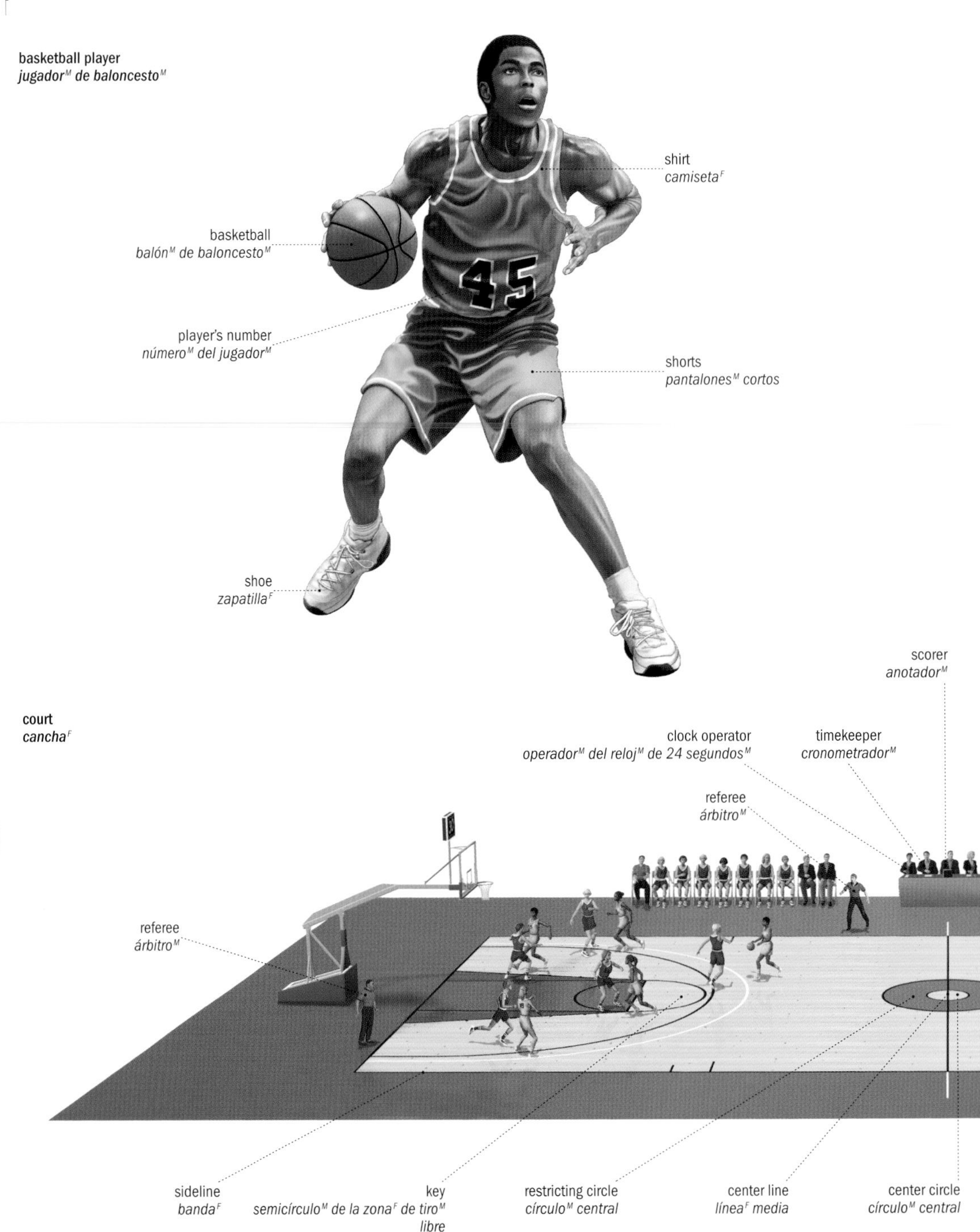

basketball player
jugador[M] de baloncesto[M]
shirt
camiseta[F]
basketball
balón[M] de baloncesto[M]
player's number
número[M] del jugador[M]
shorts
pantalones[M] cortos
shoe
zapatilla[F]
court
cancha[F]
scorer
anotador[M]
clock operator
operador[M] del reloj[M] de 24 segundos[M]
timekeeper
cronometrador[M]
referee
árbitro[M]
referee
árbitro[M]
sideline
banda[F]
key
semicírculo[M] de la zona[F] de tiro[M] libre
restricting circle
círculo[M] central
center line
línea[F] media
center circle
círculo[M] central

basketball

player positions
posiciones[M] de los jugadores[M]

point guard
base[M]
center
pívot[M]
guard
escolta[F]
left forward
alero[M] izquierdo
right forward
alero[M] derecho

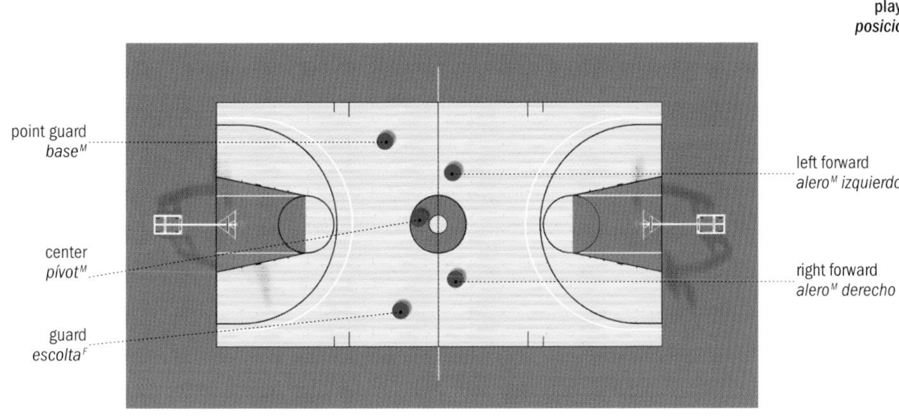

backstop
canasta[F]

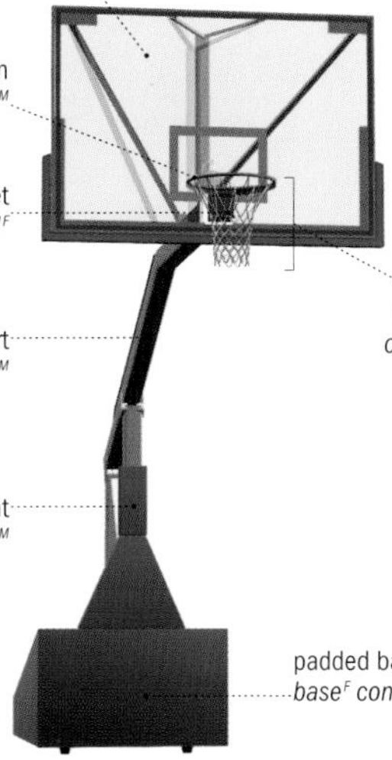

backboard
tablero[M]
rim
aro[M]
net
red[F]
basket
canasta[F]
backboard support
soporte[M] del tablero[M]
padded upright
poste[M] con protecciones[M]
padded base
base[F] con protecciones[F]

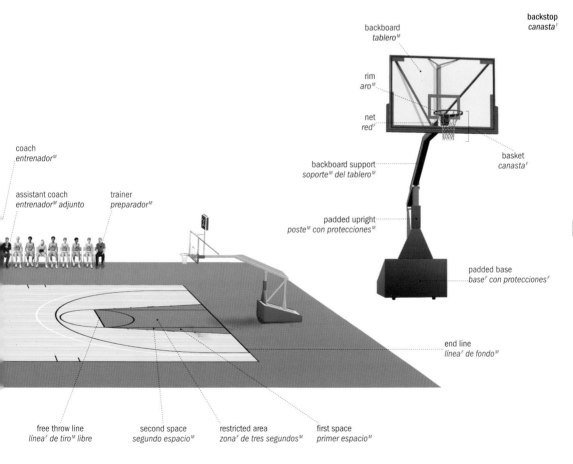

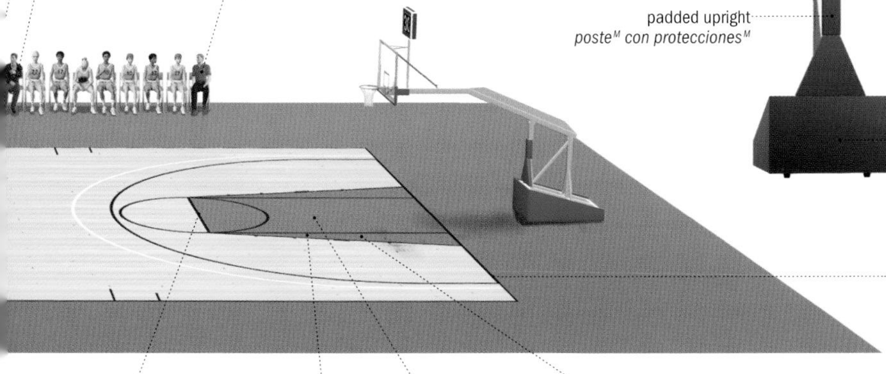

coach
entrenador[M]
assistant coach
entrenador[M] adjunto
trainer
preparador[M]
end line
línea[F] de fondo[M]
free throw line
línea[F] de tiro[M] libre
second space
segundo espacio[M]
restricted area
zona[F] de tres segundos[M]
first space
primer espacio[M]

tennis

tenis[M]

court
cancha[F]

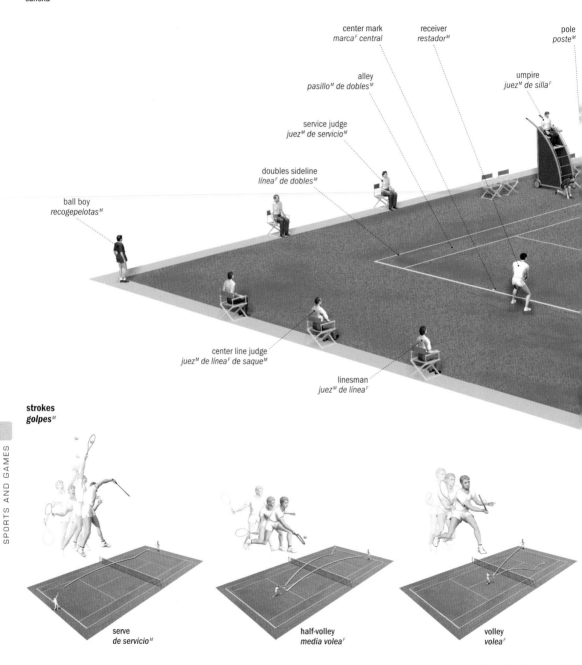

center mark
marca[F] central

receiver
restador[M]

pole
poste[M]

alley
pasillo[M] de dobles[M]

umpire
juez[M] de silla[F]

service judge
juez[M] de servicio[M]

doubles sideline
línea[F] de dobles[M]

ball boy
recogepelotas[M]

center line judge
juez[M] de línea[F] de saque[M]

linesman
juez[M] de línea[F]

strokes
golpes[M]

serve
de servicio[M]

half-volley
media volea[F]

volley
volea[F]

foot fault judge
juez^M de faltas^F de pie^M

center strap
cinta^F central

net band
cinta^F de la red^F

right service court
cuadro^M de saque^M derecho

server
jugador^M con el servicio^M

left service court
cuadro^M de saque^M izquierdo

service line
línea^F de servicio^M

baseline
línea^F de fondo^M

singles sideline
línea^F lateral de individuales^M

net judge
juez^M de red^F

net
red^F

forecourt
cuadro^M de saque^M

center service line
línea^F central de servicio^M

backcourt
cancha^F de fondo^M

lob
globo^M

drop shot
dejada^F

smash
smash^M

tennis

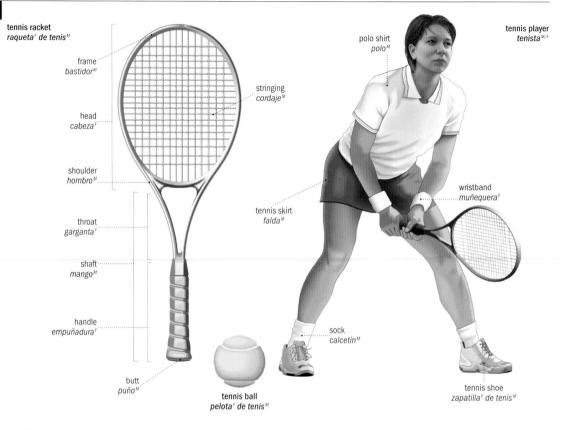

tennis racket
raqueta[F] de tenis[M]

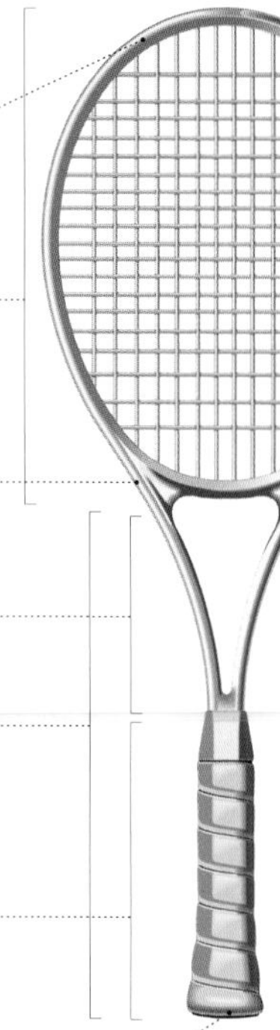

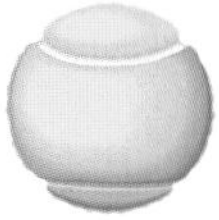

frame
bastidor[M]

stringing
cordaje[M]

head
cabeza[F]

shoulder
hombro[M]

throat
garganta[F]

shaft
mango[M]

handle
empuñadura[F]

butt
puño[M]

tennis ball
pelota[F] de tenis[M]

tennis player
tenista[M/F]

polo shirt
polo[M]

wristband
muñequera[F]

tennis skirt
falda[M]

sock
calcetín[M]

tennis shoe
zapatilla[F] de tenis[M]

scoreboard
marcador[M]

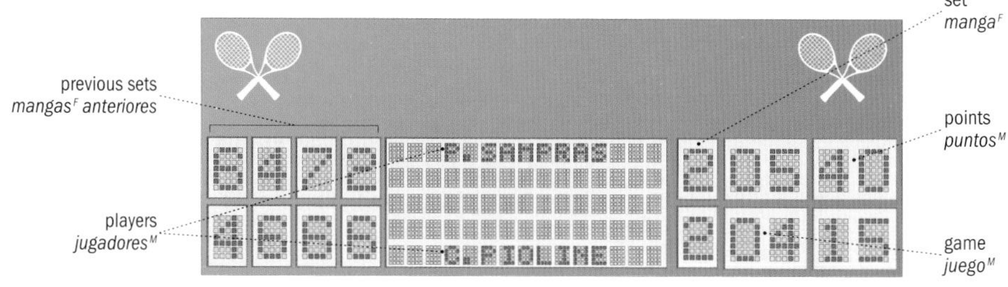

set
manga[F]

previous sets
mangas[F] anteriores

points
puntos[M]

players
jugadores[M]

game
juego[M]

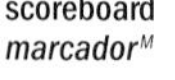

playing surfaces
superficies[F] de juego[M]

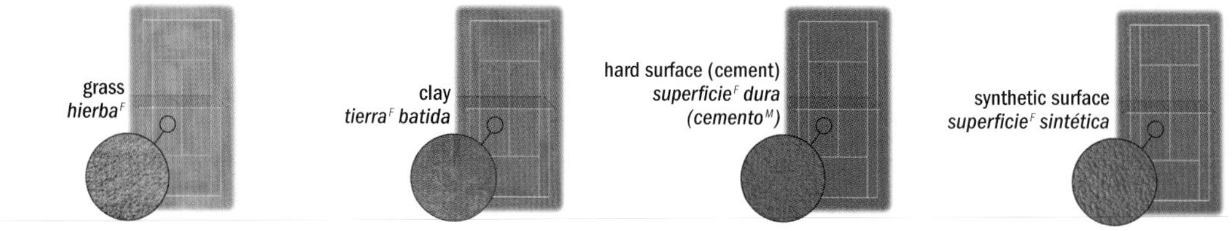

grass
hierba[F]

clay
tierra[F] batida

hard surface (cement)
superficie[F] dura (cemento[M])

synthetic surface
superficie[F] sintética

table tennis

tenis[M] de mesa[F]

table
mesa[F]

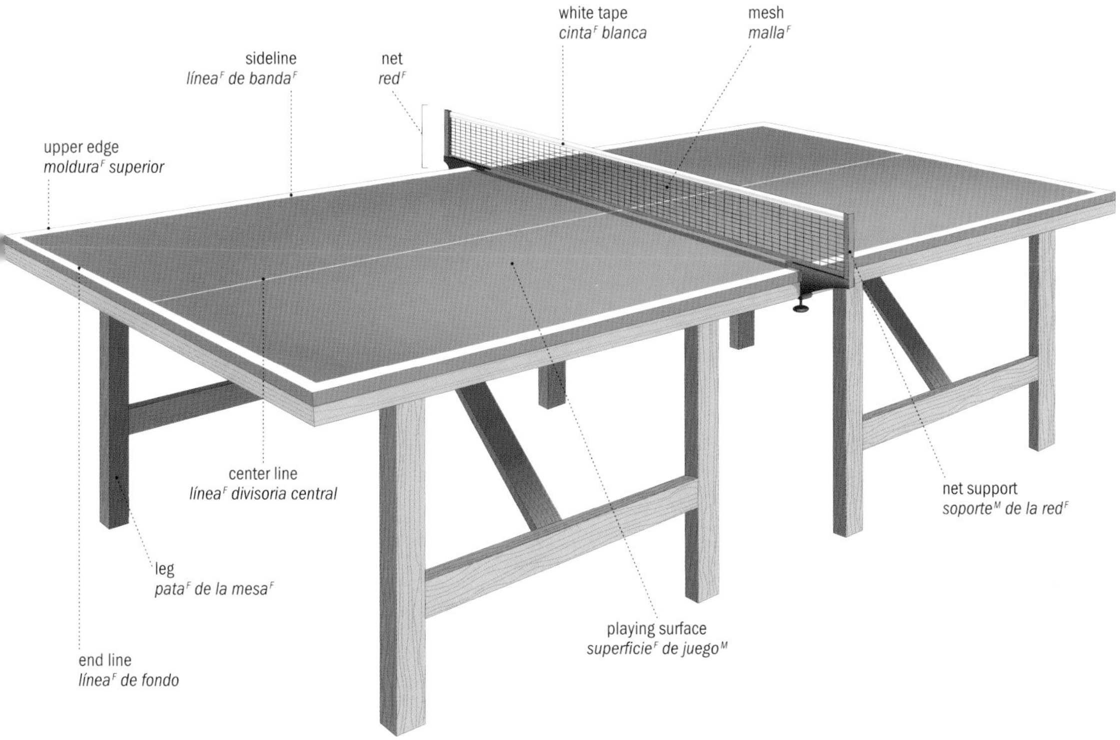

white tape
cinta[F] blanca
mesh
malla[F]
sideline
línea[F] de banda[F]
net
red[F]
upper edge
moldura[F] superior
center line
línea[F] divisoria central
net support
soporte[M] de la red[F]
leg
pata[F] de la mesa[F]
playing surface
superficie[F] de juego[M]
end line
línea[F] de fondo

table tennis paddle
pala[F]

handle
mango[M]
face
cara[F]
blade
paleta[F]
covering
revestimiento[M]

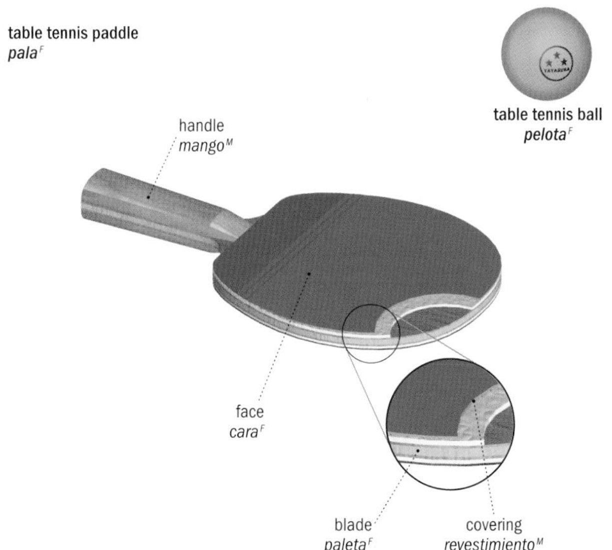

table tennis ball
pelota[F]

types of grips
formas[F] de agarrar la paleta[F]

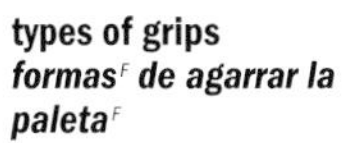

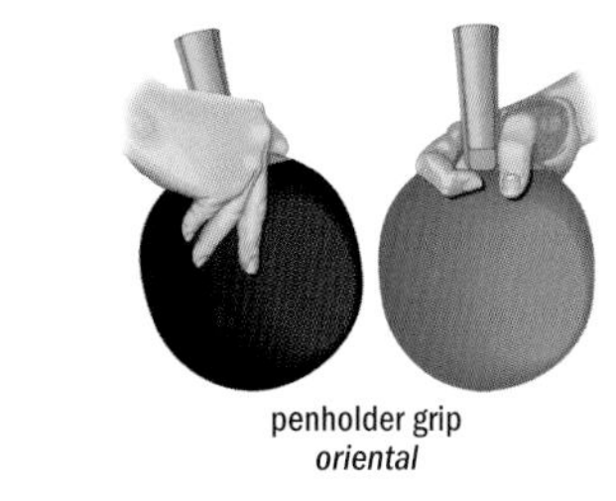

penholder grip
oriental

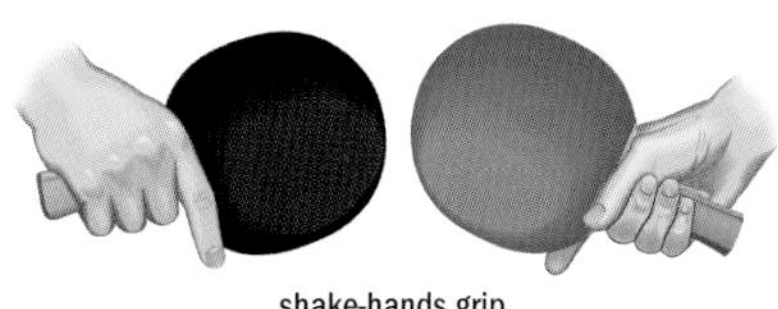

shake-hands grip
occidental

badminton

bádminton[M]

court
cancha[F]

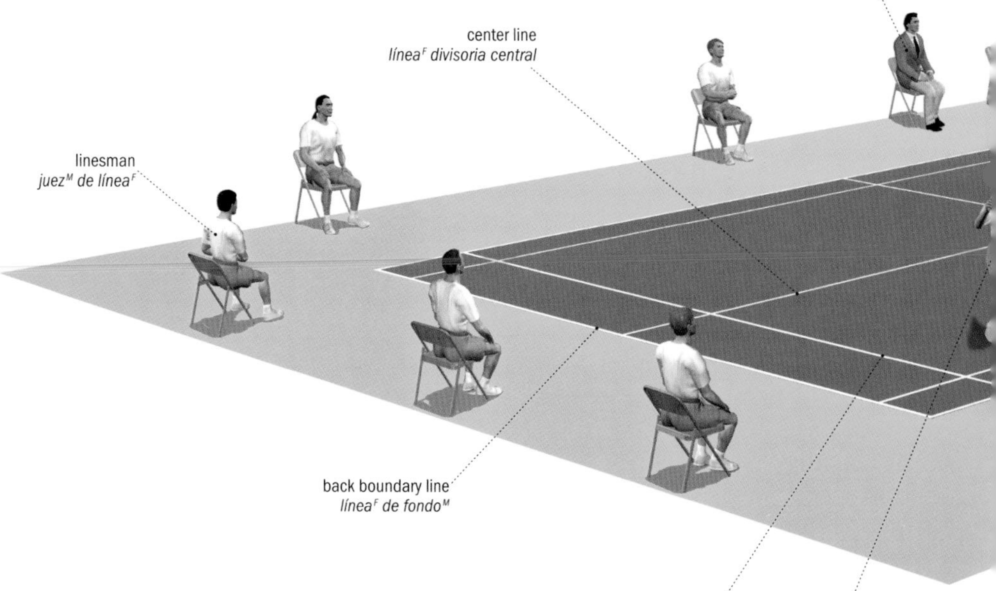

service judge
juez[M] de servicio[M]
center line
línea[F] divisoria central
linesman
juez[M] de línea[F]
back boundary line
línea[F] de fondo[M]
long service line
línea[F] de servicio[M] largo
server
jugador[M] de saque[M]

badminton racket
raqueta[F] de bádminton[M]

frame
bastidor[M]
handle
empuñadura[F]
stringing
cordaje[F]
shaft
mango[M]
butt
talón[M]
head
cabeza[F]

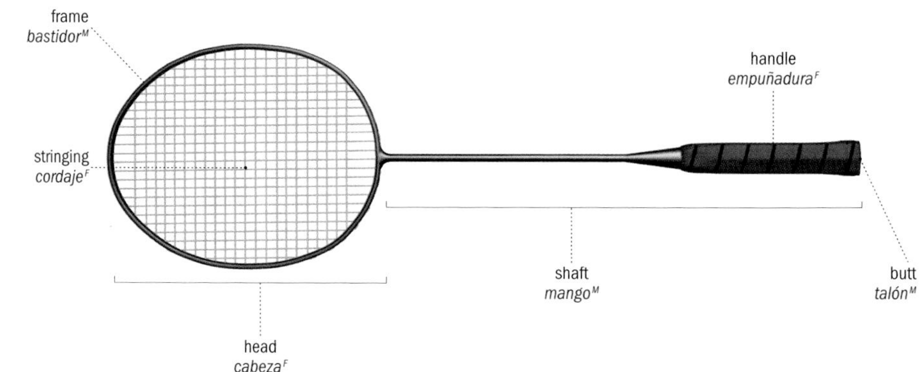

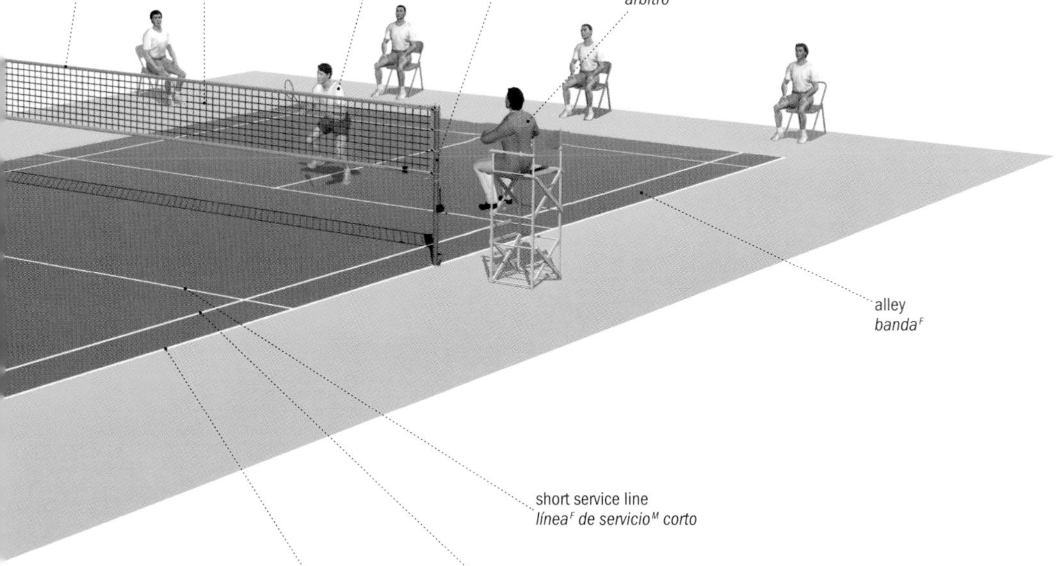

white tape
cinta^F blanca
receiver
restador^M
net
red^F
post
poste^M
umpire
árbitro^M
alley
banda^F
short service line
línea^F de servicio^M corto
singles sideline
línea^F lateral de individuales^M
doubles sideline
línea^F lateral de dobles^M

service zones
zona^F de saque

doubles service court
cuadro^M de servicio^M de dobles^M
singles service court
cuadro^M de servicio^M de individuales^M

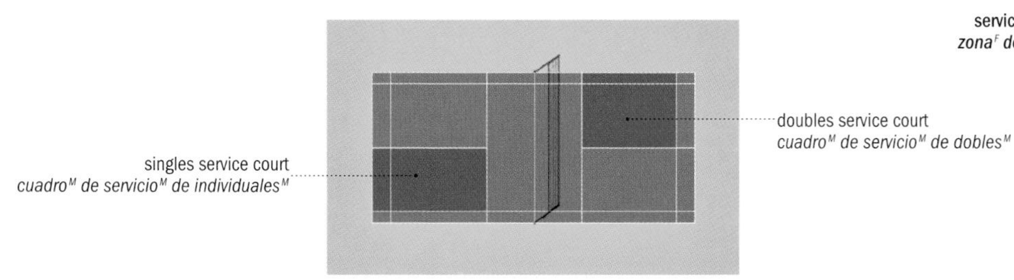

synthetic shuttlecock
volante^M sintético

feathered shuttlecock
volante^M de plumas^F

feather crown
penacho^M de plumas^F
cork tip
corcho^M

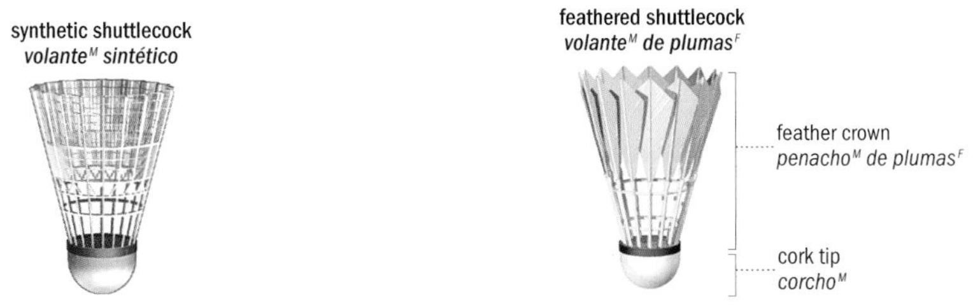

gymnastics

gimnasia^F

event platform
área^F de competición^F

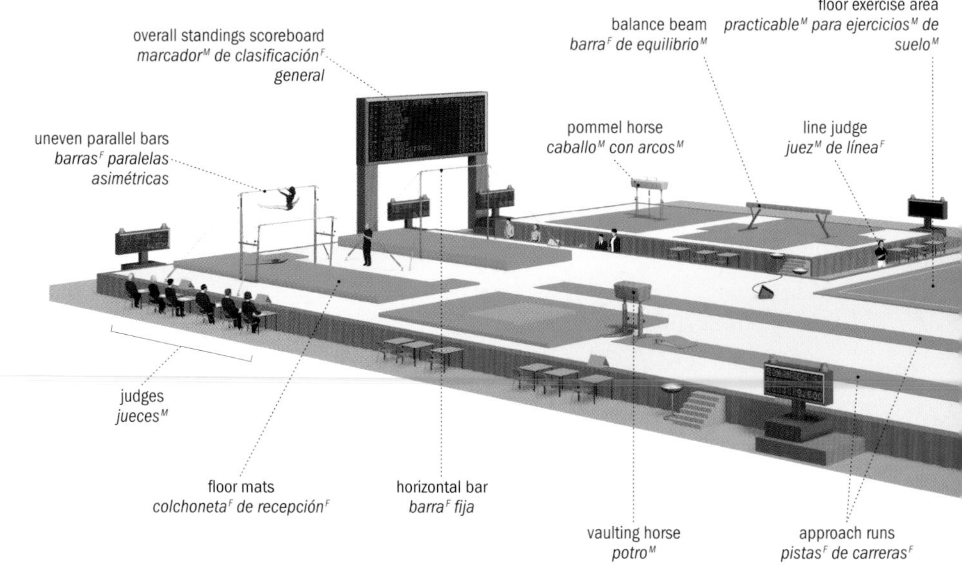

overall standings scoreboard
marcador^M de clasificación^F general
balance beam
barra^F de equilibrio^M
floor exercise area
practicable^M para ejercicios^M de suelo^M
uneven parallel bars
barras^F paralelas asimétricas
pommel horse
caballo^M con arcos^M
line judge
juez^M de línea^F
judges
jueces^M
floor mats
colchoneta^F de recepción^F
horizontal bar
barra^F fija
vaulting horse
potro^M
approach runs
pistas^F de carreras^F

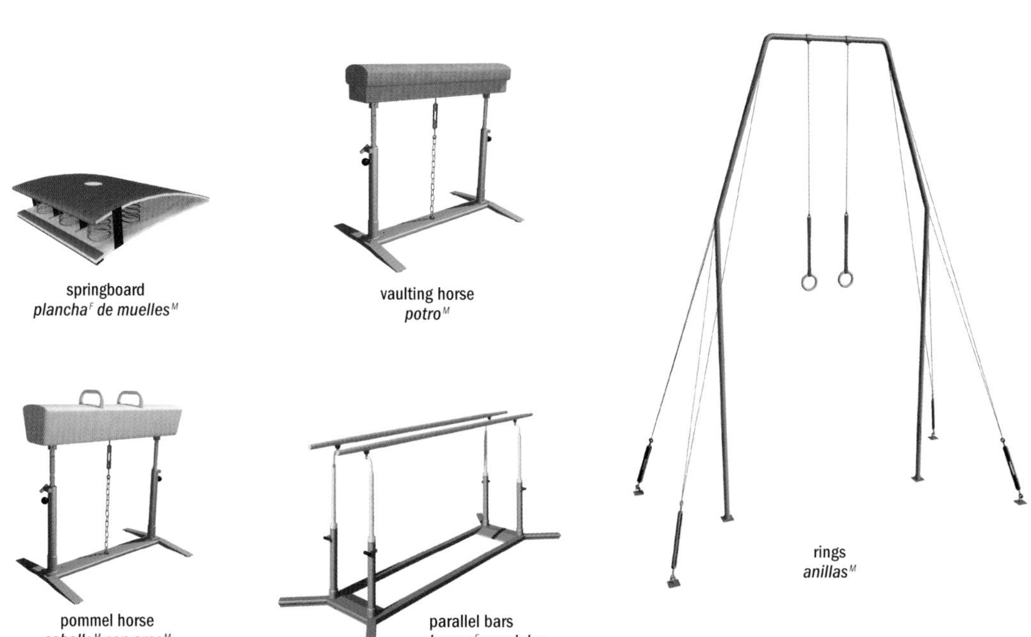

springboard
plancha^F de muelles^M
vaulting horse
potro^M
rings
anillas^M
pommel horse
caballo^M con aros^M
parallel bars
barras^F paralelas

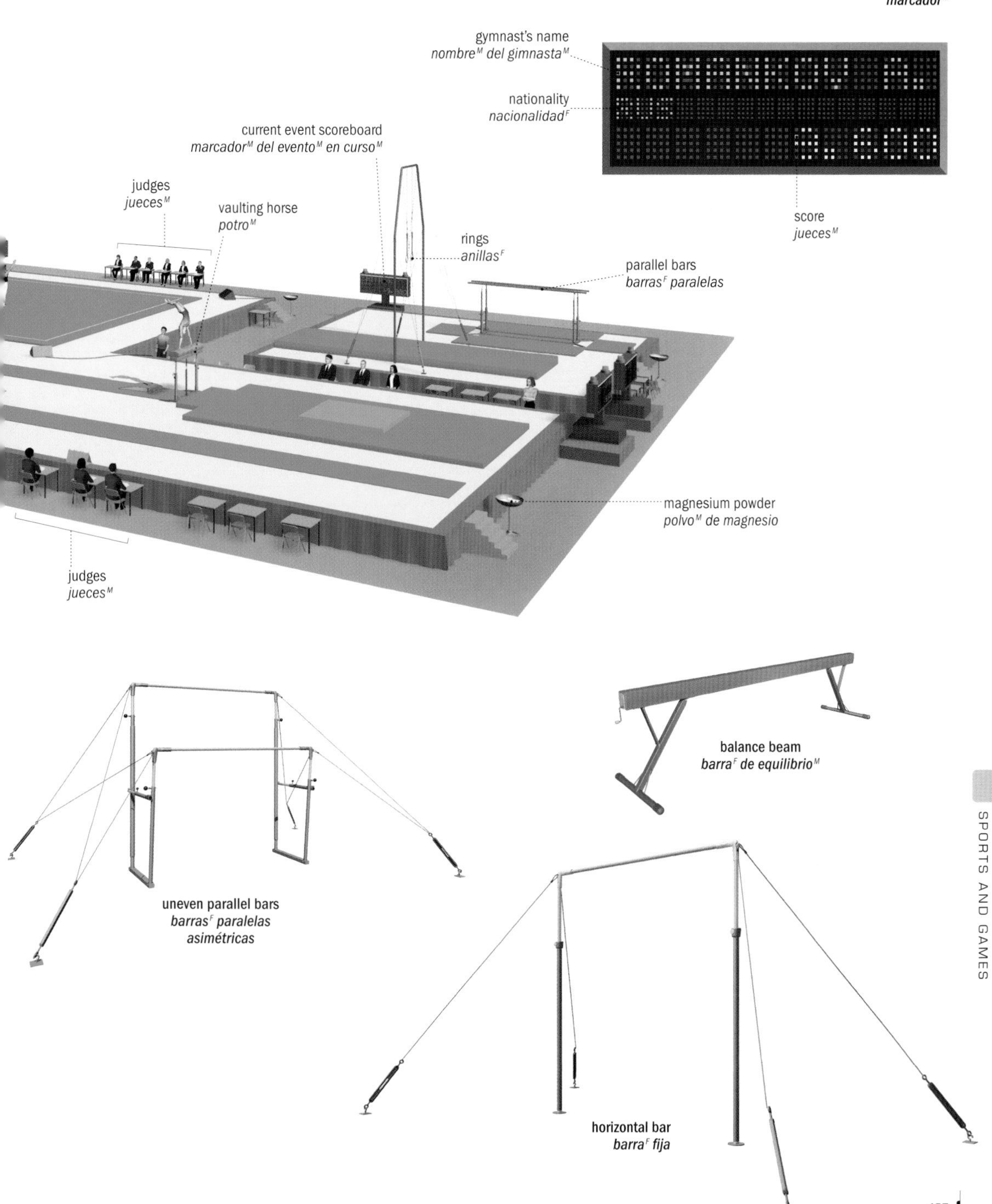
scoreboard
marcador[M]
gymnast's name
nombre[M] *del gimnasta*[M]
nationality
nacionalidad[F]
current event scoreboard
marcador[M] *del evento*[M] *en curso*[M]
judges
jueces[M]
vaulting horse
potro[M]
rings
anillas[F]
score
jueces[M]
parallel bars
barras[F] *paralelas*
magnesium powder
polvo[M] *de magnesio*
judges
jueces[M]
balance beam
barra[F] ***de equilibrio***[M]
uneven parallel bars
barras[F] ***paralelas asimétricas***
horizontal bar
barra[F] ***fija***

boxing

boxeo[M]

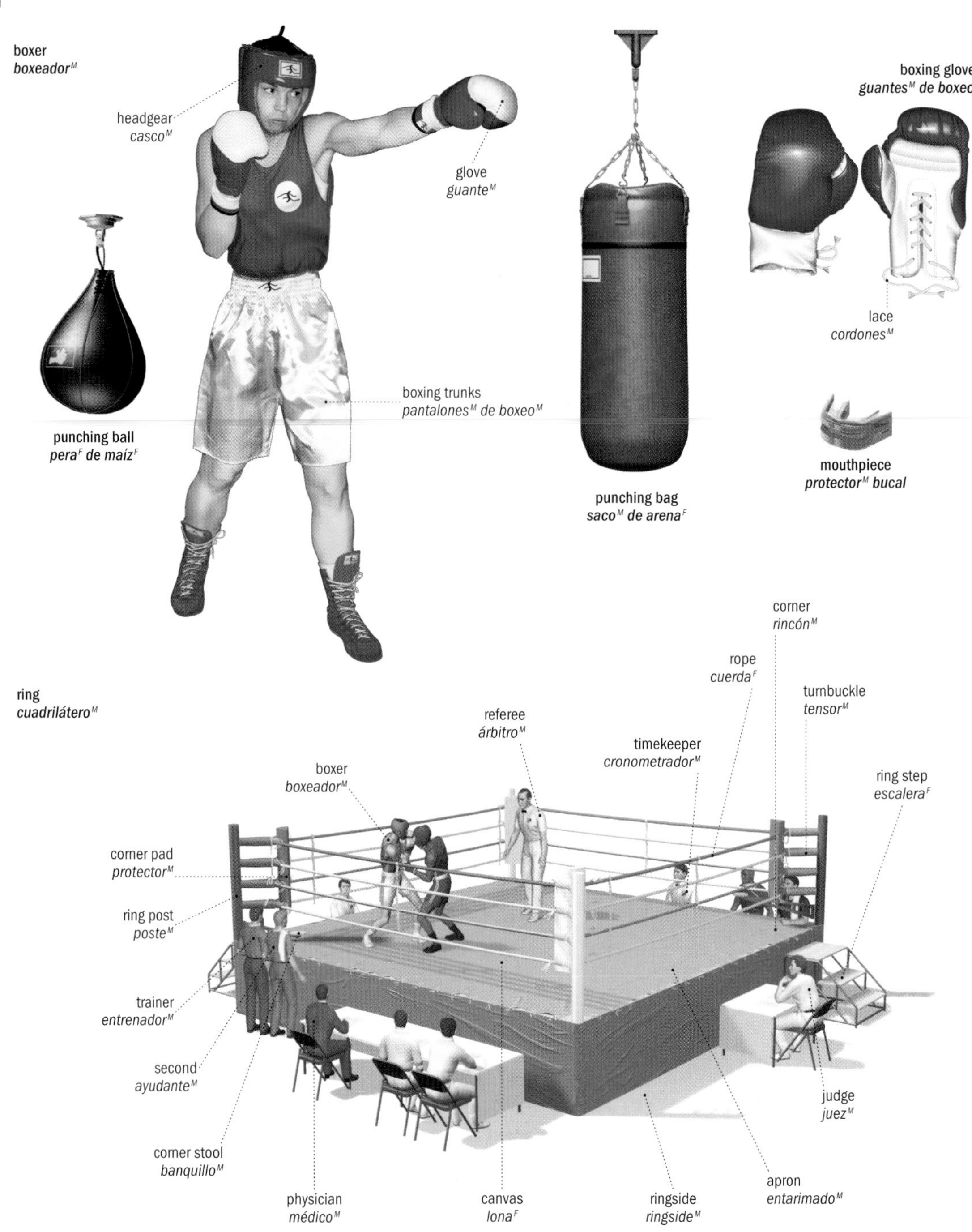
boxer
boxeador[M]
headgear
casco[M]
glove
guante[M]
boxing gloves
guantes[M] de boxeo[M]
lace
cordones[M]
boxing trunks
pantalones[M] de boxeo[M]
punching ball
pera[F] de maíz[F]
punching bag
saco[M] de arena[F]
mouthpiece
protector[M] bucal
ring
cuadrilátero[M]
corner
rincón[M]
rope
cuerda[F]
turnbuckle
tensor[M]
referee
árbitro[M]
timekeeper
cronometrador[M]
boxer
boxeador[M]
ring step
escalera[F]
corner pad
protector[M]
ring post
poste[M]
trainer
entrenador[M]
second
ayudante[M]
corner stool
banquillo[M]
physician
médico[M]
canvas
lona[F]
ringside
ringside[M]
apron
entarimado[M]
judge
juez[M]

judo

judo[M]

scorers and timekeepers
anotadores[M] y cronometradores[M]
mat
tatami[M]
medical team
equipo[M] médico
contestant
uke (defensor[M])
safety area
zona[F] de seguridad[F]
danger area
área[F] de peligro[M]
scoreboard
marcador[M]
contest area
zona[F] de combate[M]
referee
judoka[M] neutral
judge
juez[M]
examples of holds and throws
ejemplos[M] de llaves[F]
judogi
traje[M] de judo (judoji[M])
jacket
kimono[M]
holding
inmovilización[F]
stomach throw
proyección[F] en círculo[M]
sweeping hip throw
proyección[F] primera de cadera[F]
major outer reaping throw
osoto-gari (gran siega[F]) exterior
major inner reaping throw
gran siega[F] interior
naked strangle
estrangulación[F]
trousers
pantalón[M]
belt
cinturón[M]
arm lock
inmovilización[F] de brazo[M]
one-arm shoulder throw
proyección[F] por encima del hombro[M] con una mano[F]

weightlifting

halterofilia[F]

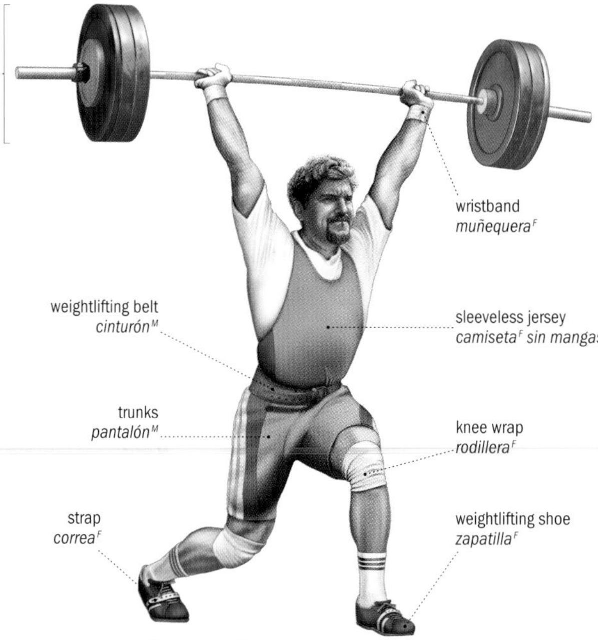

barbell
barra[F] con pesas[F]
wristband
muñequera[F]
weightlifting belt
cinturón[M]
sleeveless jersey
camiseta[F] sin mangas[F]
trunks
pantalón[M]
knee wrap
rodillera[F]
strap
correa[F]
weightlifting shoe
zapatilla[F]

clean and jerk
envión[M]

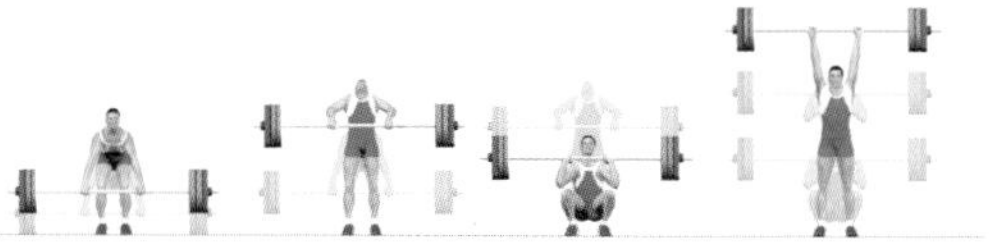

snatch
arranque[M]

fitness equipment

aparatos[M] de ejercicios[M]

dumbbells
pesas[F]

bar
barra[F]
weight
pesas[F]

handgrips
empuñaderas[F]

ankle/wrist weights
pesas[F] para muñecas[F] y tobillos[M]

jump rope
cuerda[F]

twist bar
barra[F] de torsión[F]

tension spring
resorte[M] de tensión[F]
grip
empuñadura[F]

chest expander
tensores[M] pectorales

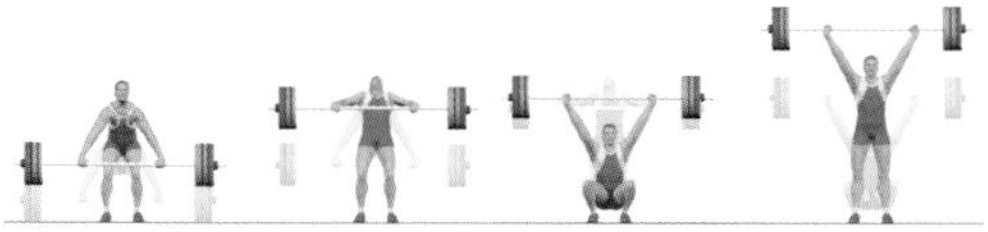

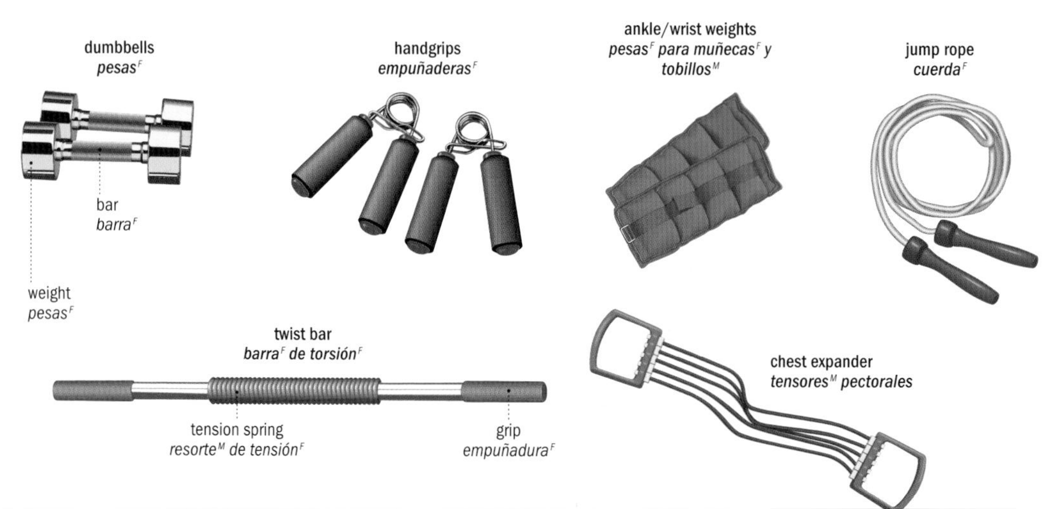

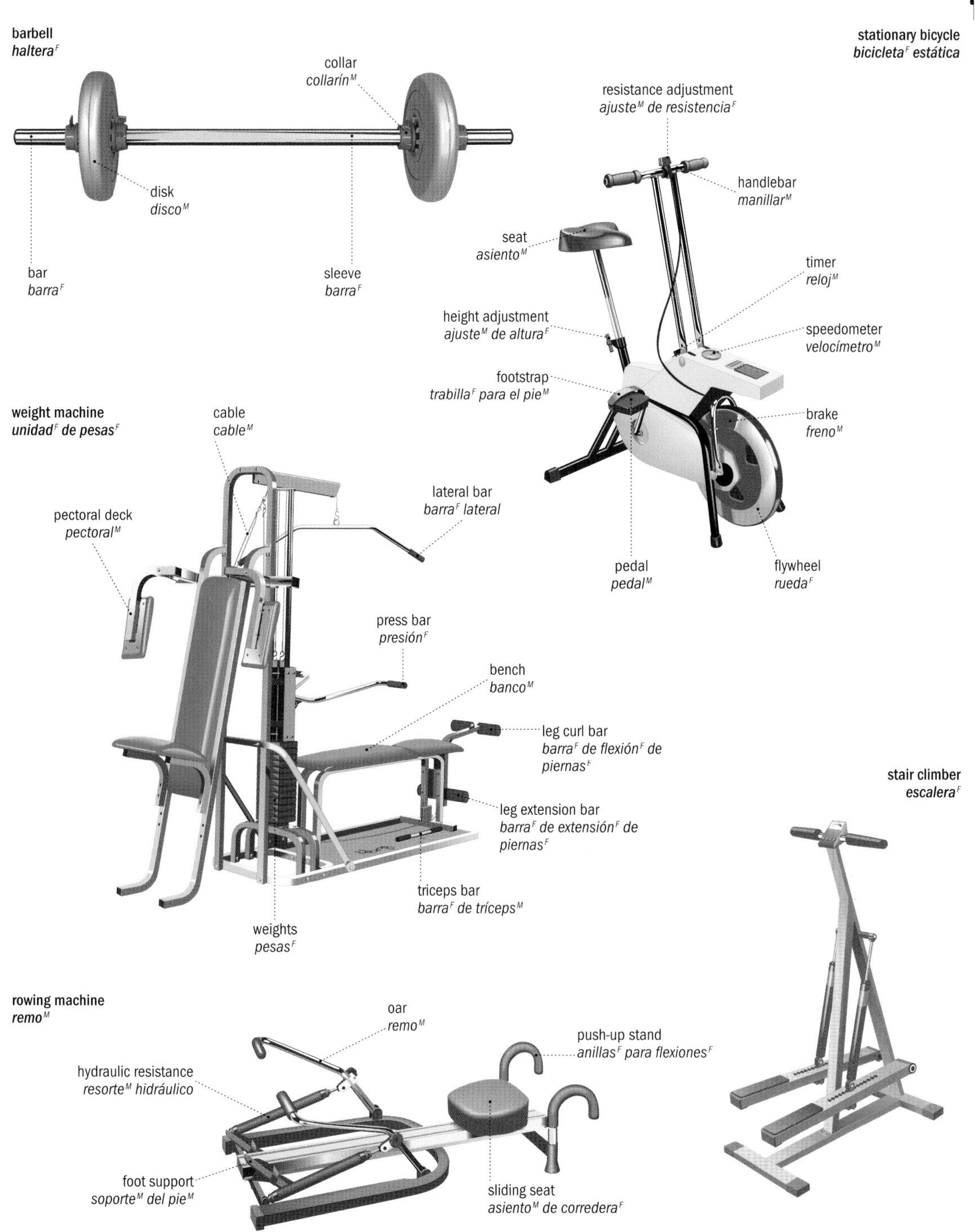
barbell
halteraF
collar
collarínM
disk
discoM
bar
barraF
sleeve
barraF
stationary bicycle
bicicletaF estática
resistance adjustment
ajusteM de resistenciaF
handlebar
manillarM
seat
asientoM
timer
relojM
height adjustment
ajusteM de alturaF
speedometer
velocímetroM
footstrap
trabillaF para el pieM
brake
frenoM
pedal
pedalM
flywheel
ruedaF
weight machine
unidadF de pesasF
cable
cableM
pectoral deck
pectoralM
lateral bar
barraF lateral
press bar
presiónF
bench
bancoM
leg curl bar
barraF de flexiónF de piernasF
leg extension bar
barraF de extensiónF de piernasF
triceps bar
barraF de trícepsM
weights
pesasF
stair climber
escaleraF
rowing machine
remoM
oar
remoM
push-up stand
anillasF para flexionesF
hydraulic resistance
resorteM hidráulico
foot support
soporteM del pieM
sliding seat
asientoM de correderaF

billiards

billar[M]

carom billiards
billar[M] francés

cue ball
bola[F] blanca
red ball
bola[F] roja
white object ball
bola[F] pinta

pool
pool[M]

object balls
bolas[F] numeradas
pocket
tronera[F]
cue ball
bola[F] blanca

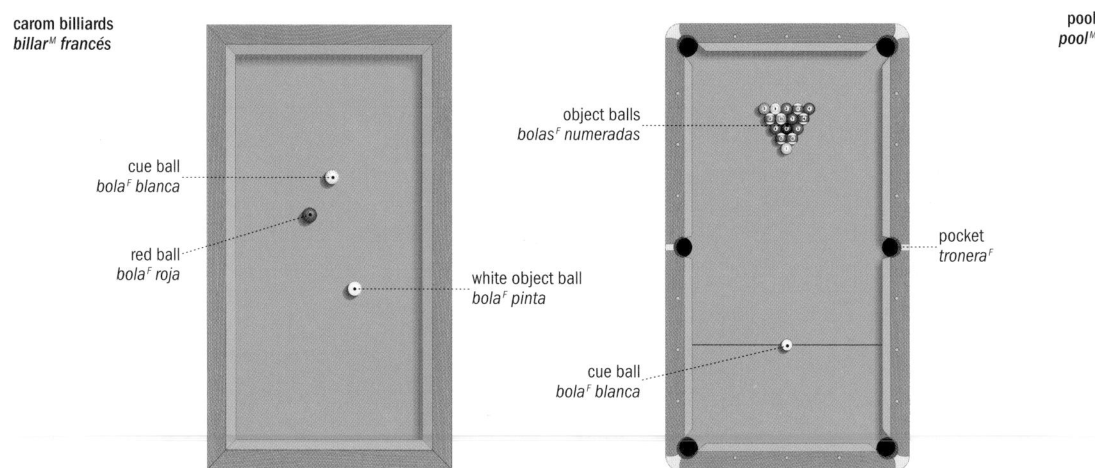

table
mesa[F]

«D»
D[F]
balk line spot
mosca[F] de la línea[F] de cuadro[M]
pyramid spot
mosca[F] superior
baize
tapete[M]
balk area
cuadro[M]
bottom pocket
bolsillo[M]
center spot
mosca[F] central
top pocket
tronera[F]
head cushion
banda[F] de goma[F]
balk line
línea[F] de cuadro[M]
hook
vástago[M]
billiard spot
mosca[F]
center pocket
tronera[F] central
rail
baranda[F]
foot cushion
banda[F] de la cabecera[F]

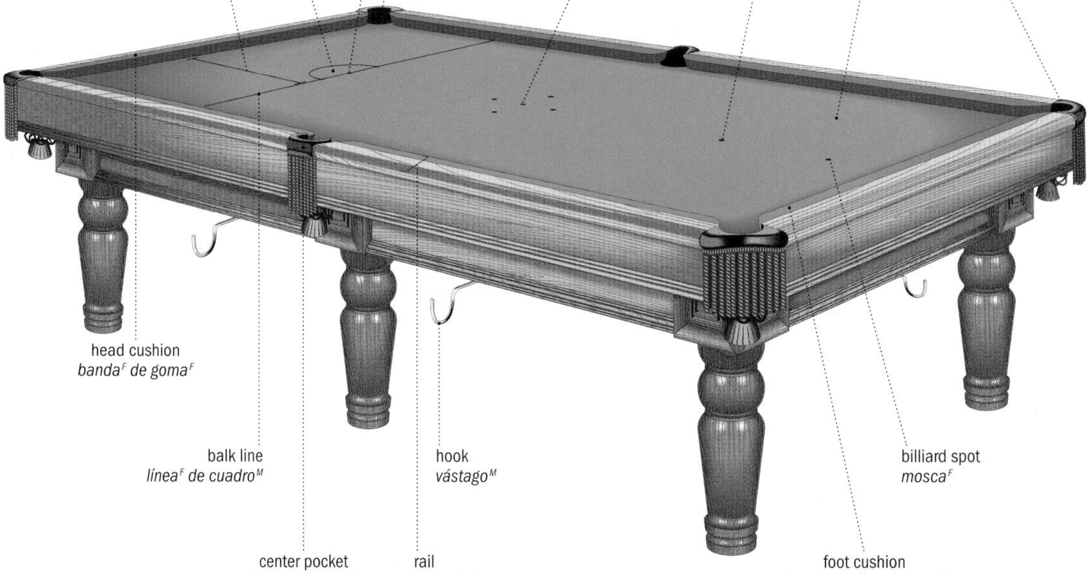

SPORTS AND GAMES

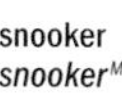

snooker
snooker[M]

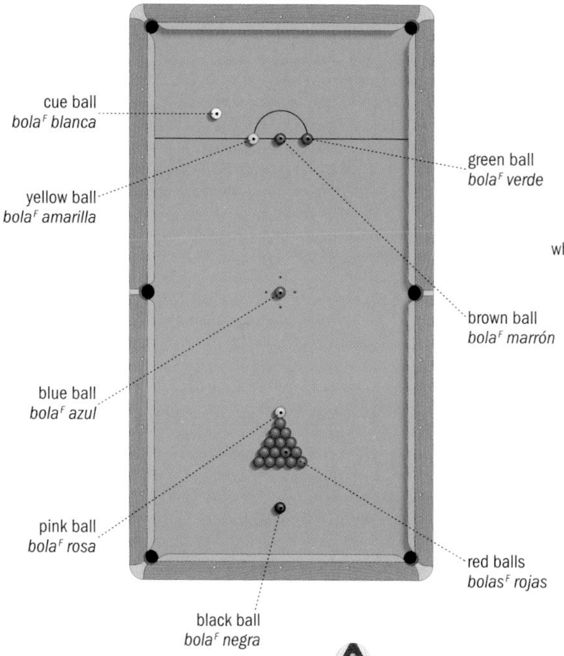

cue ball
bola[F] *blanca*

yellow ball
bola[F] *amarilla*

green ball
bola[F] *verde*

brown ball
bola[F] *marrón*

blue ball
bola[F] *azul*

pink ball
bola[F] *rosa*

red balls
bolas[F] *rojas*

black ball
bola[F] *negra*

English billiards
billar*[M] *inglés

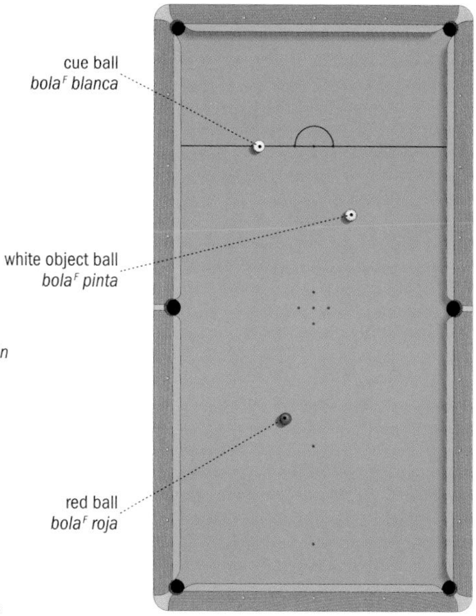

cue ball
bola[F] *blanca*

white object ball
bola[F] *pinta*

red ball
bola[F] *roja*

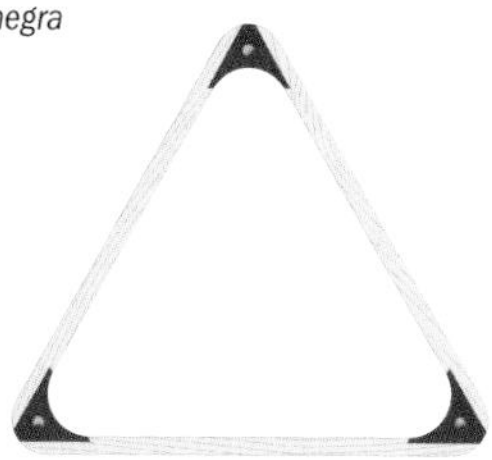

rack
***triángulo*[M]**

chalk
***tiza*[F]**

billiard cue
***taco*[M] *de billar*[M]**

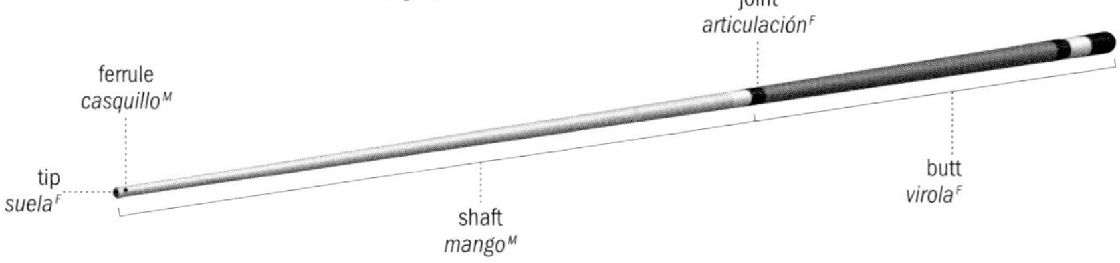

joint
articulación[F]

ferrule
casquillo[M]

tip
suela[F]

shaft
mango[M]

butt
virola[F]

bridge
***burra*[F]**

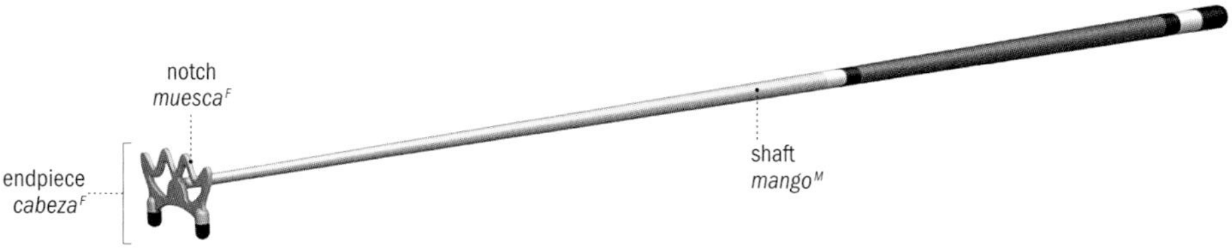

notch
muesca[F]

endpiece
cabeza[F]

shaft
mango[M]

golf

accesorios[M] de golf[M]

course
campo[M] de golf[M]

hole
zona[F] del hoyo[M]

clubhouse
casa[F] club[M]

practice green
green[M] de entrenamiento[M]

parking
aparcamiento[M]

sand bunker
foso[M] de arena[F]

rough
maleza[F]

teeing ground
punto[M] de salida[F]

water hazard
trampa[F] de agua[F]

green
green[M]

cart path
vereda[F]

fairway
pista[F]

pond
estanque[M]

trees
árboles[M]

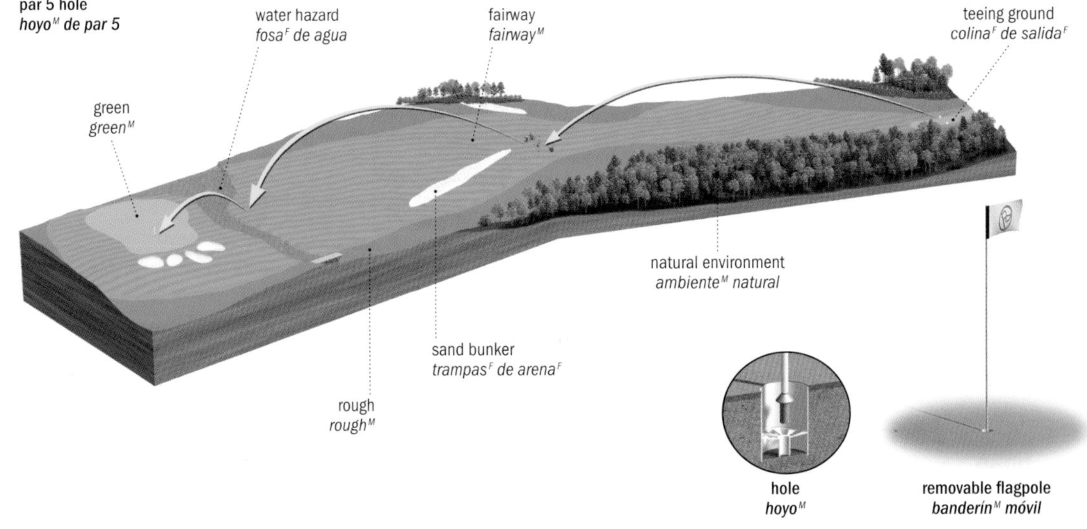

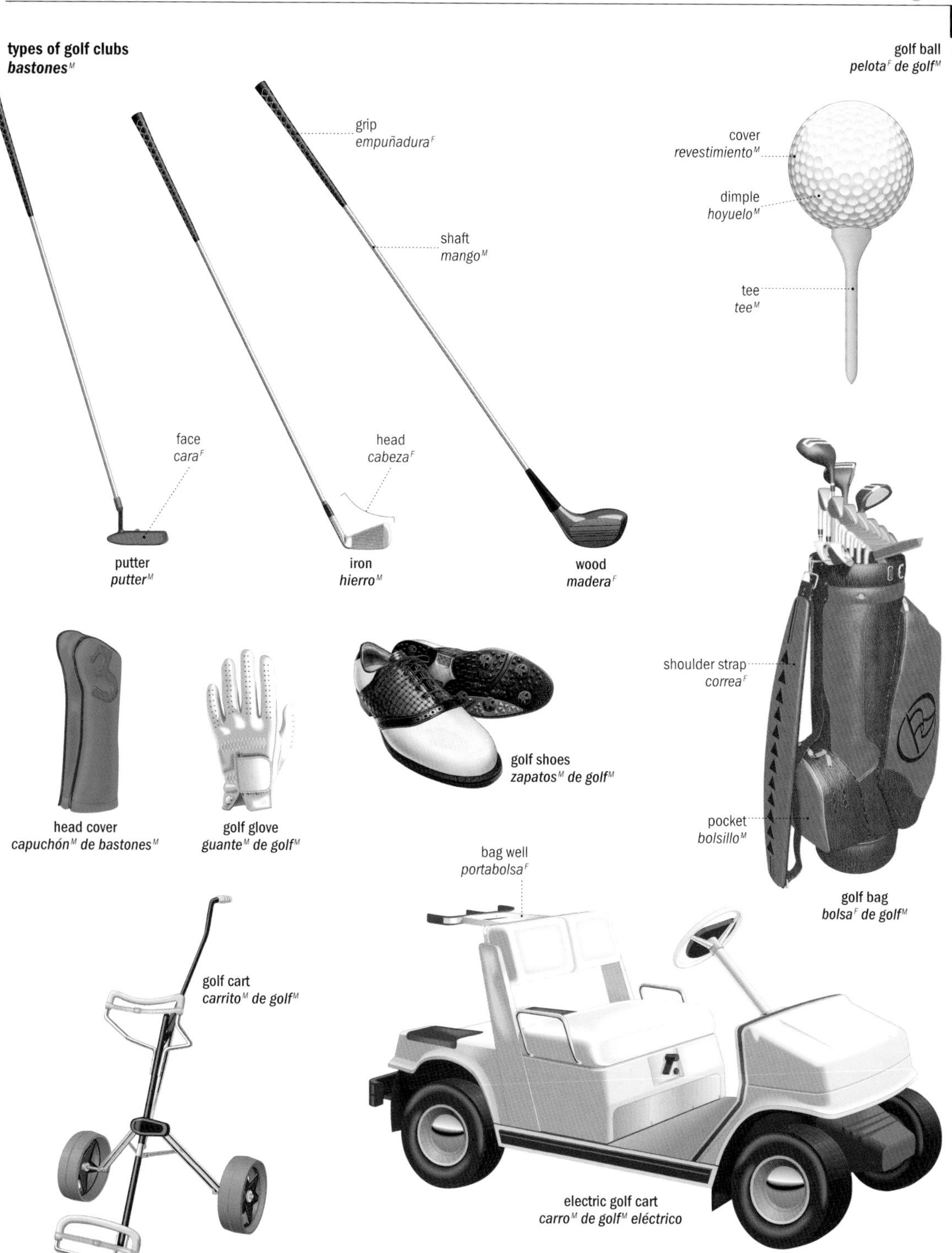
types of golf clubs
bastones^M
grip
empuñadura^F
shaft
mango^M
face
cara^F
head
cabeza^F
putter
putter^M
iron
hierro^M
wood
madera^F
golf ball
pelota^F de golf^M
cover
revestimiento^M
dimple
hoyuelo^M
tee
tee^M
shoulder strap
correa^F
pocket
bolsillo^M
golf bag
bolsa^F de golf^M
head cover
capuchón^M de bastones^M
golf glove
guante^M de golf^M
golf shoes
zapatos^M de golf^M
bag well
portabolsa^F
golf cart
carrito^M de golf^M
electric golf cart
carro^M de golf^M eléctrico

ice hockey

hockey[M] sobre hielo[M]

ice hockey player
jugador[M]

helmet
casco[M]

visor
visera[F]

player's number
número[M] del jugador[M]

team's emblem
emblema[M] del equipo[M]

glove
guante[M]

pants
pantalónes[M]

stocking
calcetines[M]

skate
bota[F]

blade
cuchilla[F]

player's stick
palo[M] del jugador[M]

butt end
pomo[M]

shaft
mango[M]

heel
talón[M]

blade
pala[F] del stick[M]

rink
pista[F]

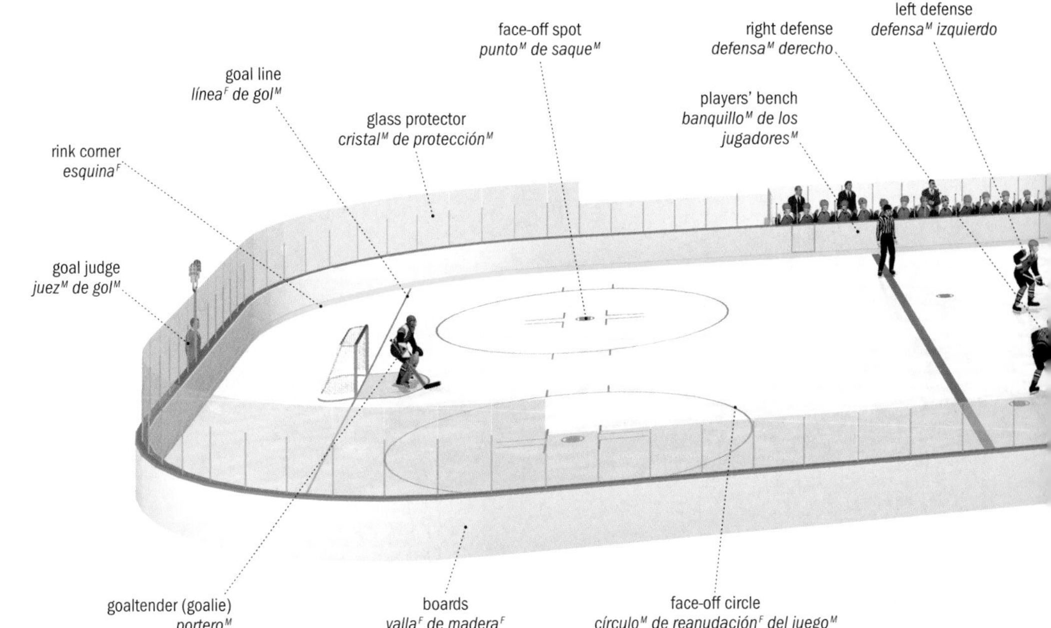

goaltender (goalie)
portero[M]
face mask
protector[M] facial
blocking glove
escudo[M]
catching glove
guante[M] rígido
goaltender's pad
protector[M] de piernas[F]
goaltender's stick
bastón[M] del portero[M]

protective cup
coquilla[F]

puck
disco[M]

goaltender's skate
patín[M] del portero[M]

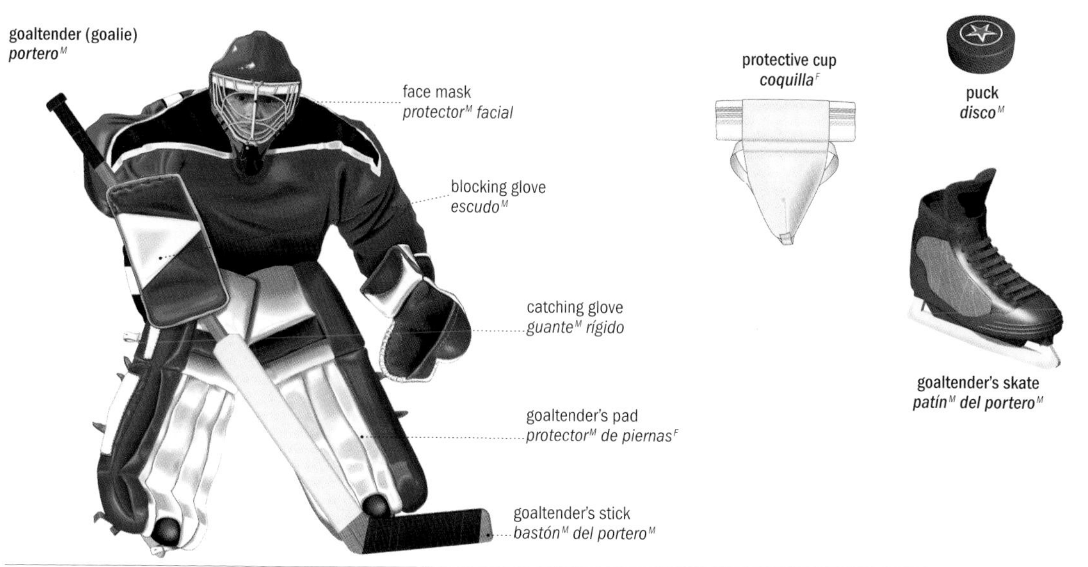

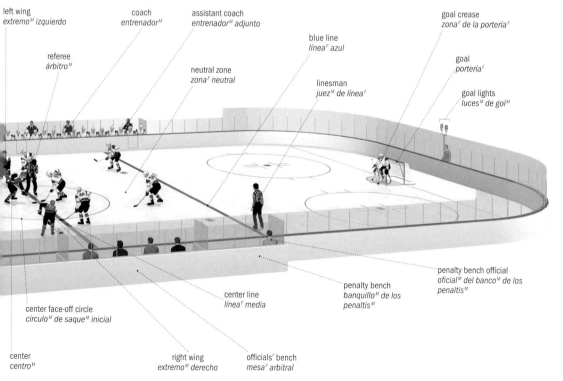

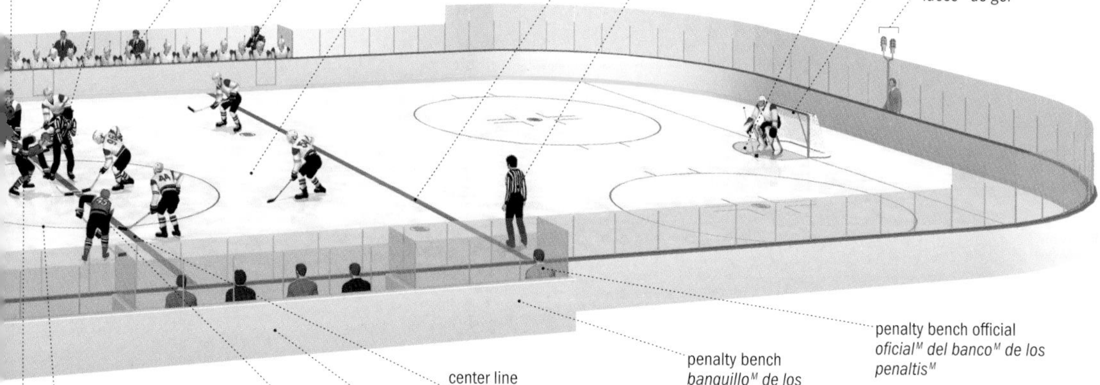

left wing
extremo[M] izquierdo
coach
entrenador[M]
assistant coach
entrenador[M] adjunto
goal crease
zona[F] de la portería[F]
referee
árbitro[M]
blue line
línea[F] azul
goal
portería[F]
neutral zone
zona[F] neutral
linesman
juez[M] de línea[F]
goal lights
luces[M] de gol[M]
penalty bench official
oficial[M] del banco[M] de los penaltis[M]
penalty bench
banquillo[M] de los penaltis[M]
center line
línea[F] media
center face-off circle
círculo[M] de saque[M] inicial
center
centro[M]
right wing
extremo[M] derecho
officials' bench
mesa[F] arbitral

speed skating

patinaje[M] de velocidad[F]

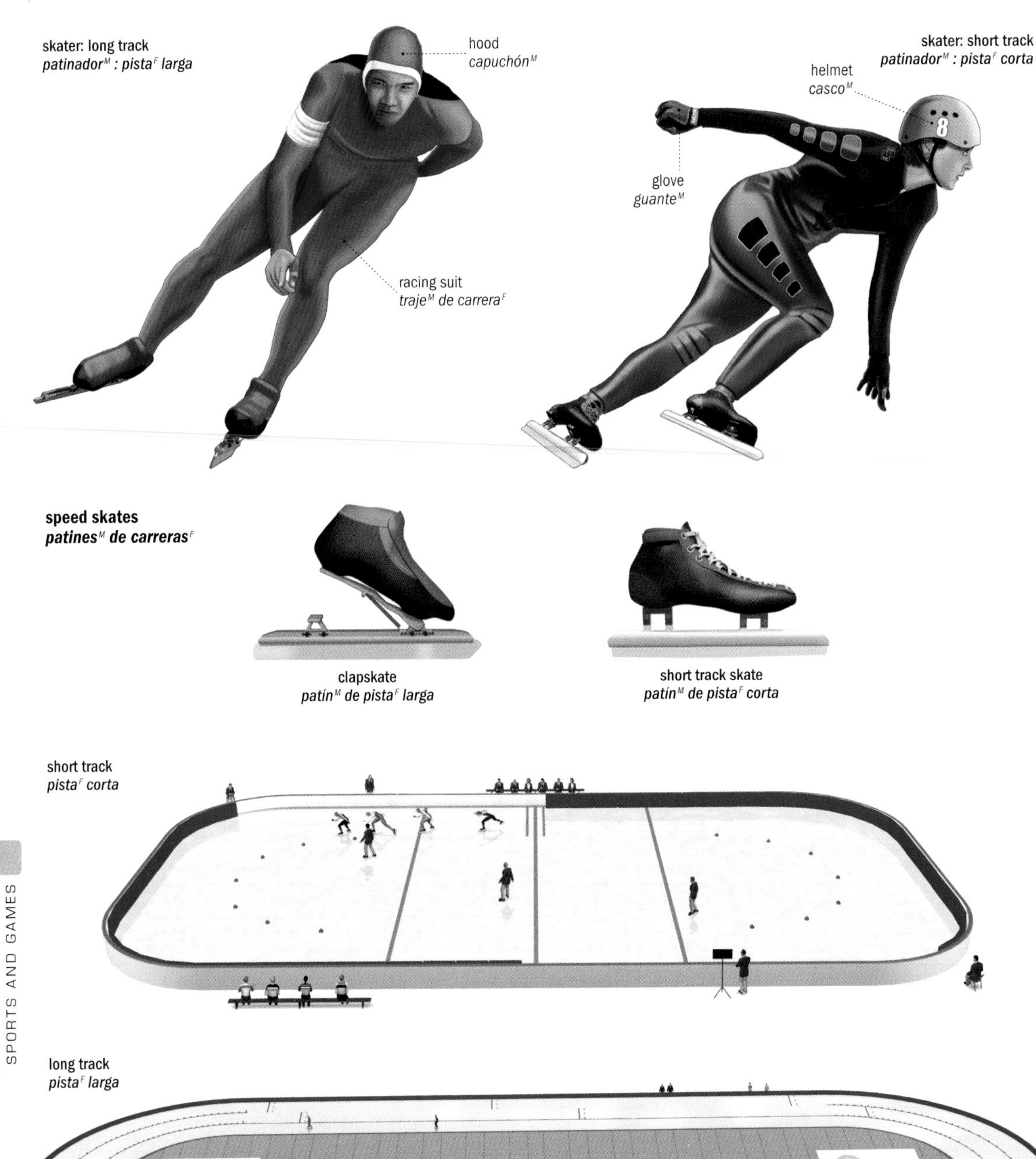

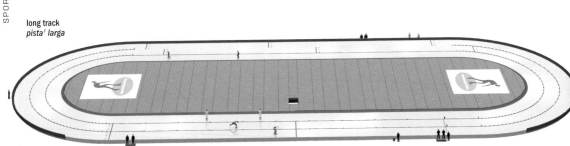

figure skating

patinaje[M] artístico

figure skate
patín[M] para figuras[F]

lining
forro[M]
hook
corchete[M]
tongue
lengüeta[F]
backstay
contrafuerte[M]
lace
cordón[M]
boot
bota[F]
eyelet
ojal[M]
heel
tacón[M]
sole
suela[F]
stanchion
montante[M]
edge
canto[M]
blade
hoja[F] de cuchilla[F]
toe pick
dientes[M]

dance blade
cuchilla[F] de baile[M]

free skating blade
cuchilla[F] de patinaje[M] artístico

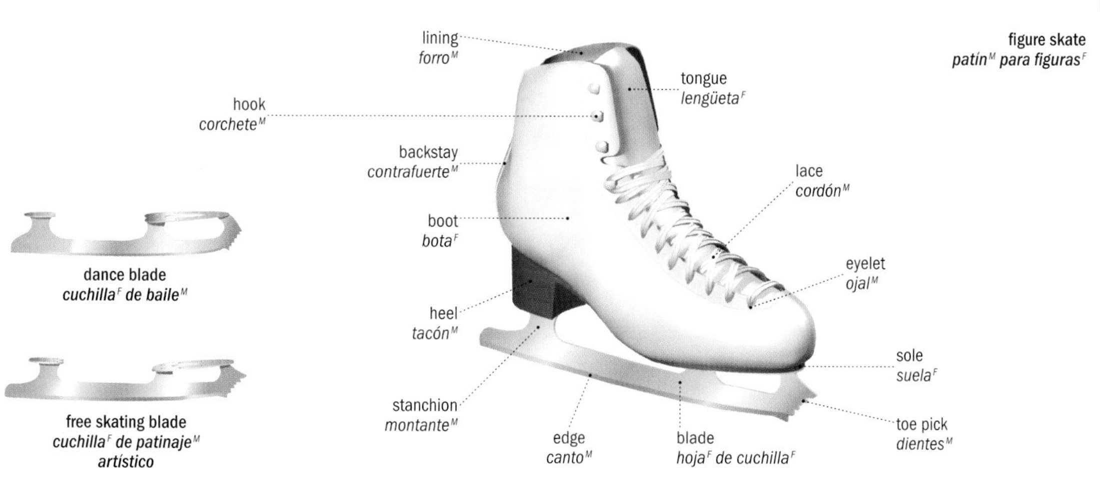

examples of jumps
ejemplos[M] de piruetas[F]

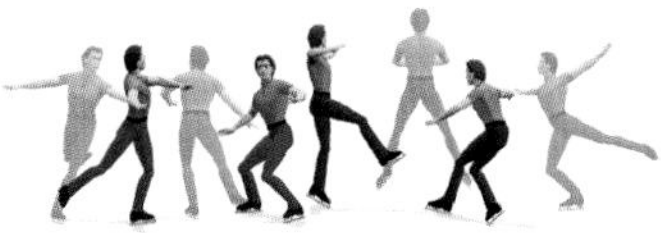

salchow
salchow[M]

axel
axel[M]

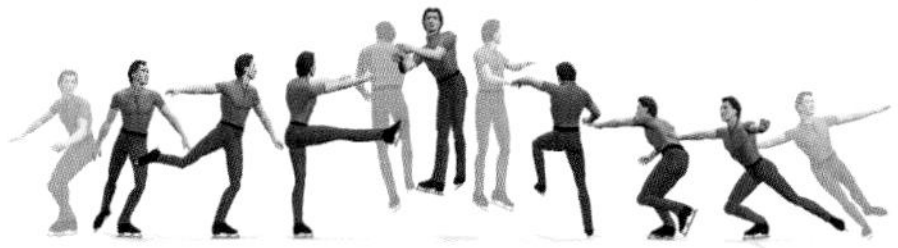

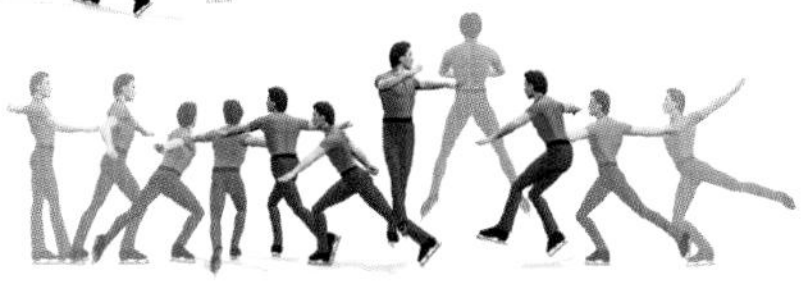

toe loop
loop[M] de puntera[F]

flip
flip[M]

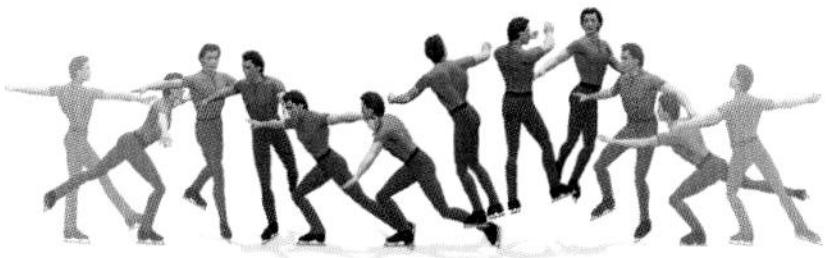

lutz
lutz[M]

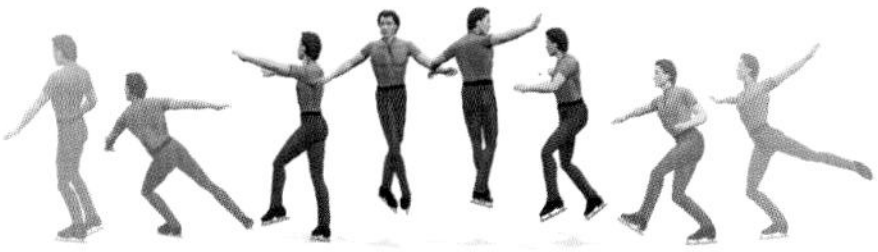

rink
pista[F] de patinaje[M] sobre hielo[M]

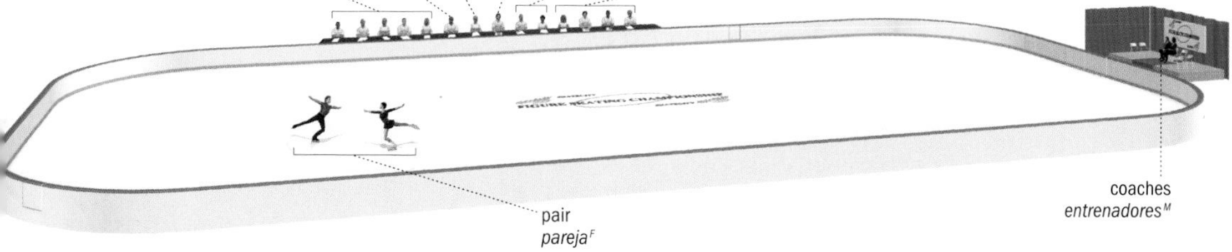

timekeeper
cronometrador[M]
referee
presidente[M] de jurado[M]
assistant referee
asistente[M] de presidente[M] del jurado[M]
technical delegates
delegados[M] técnicos
judges
jueces[M]
judges
jueces[M]
pair
pareja[F]
coaches
entrenadores[M]

SPORTS AND GAMES

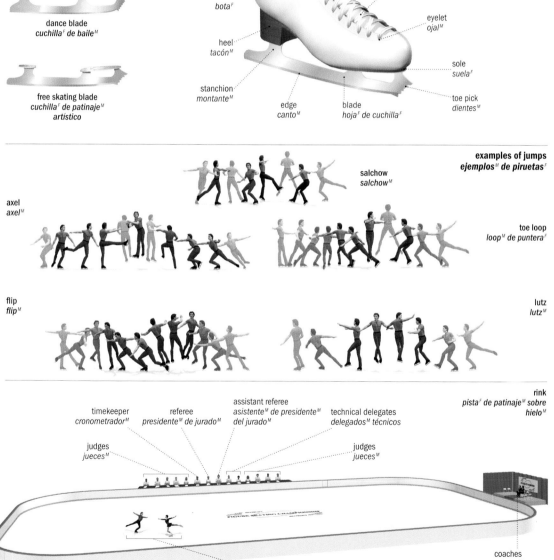

alpine skiing

esquí[M] alpino

alpine skier
esquiador[M] alpino

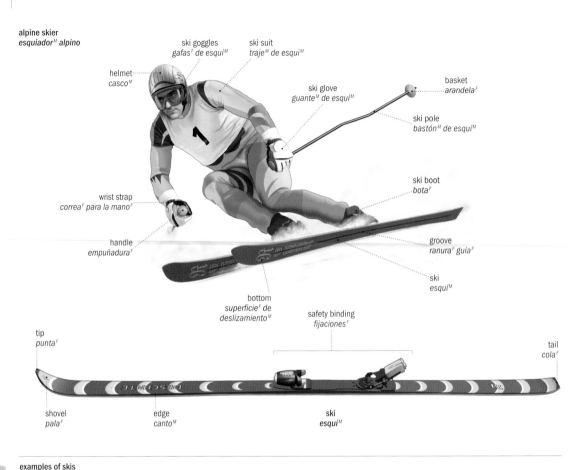

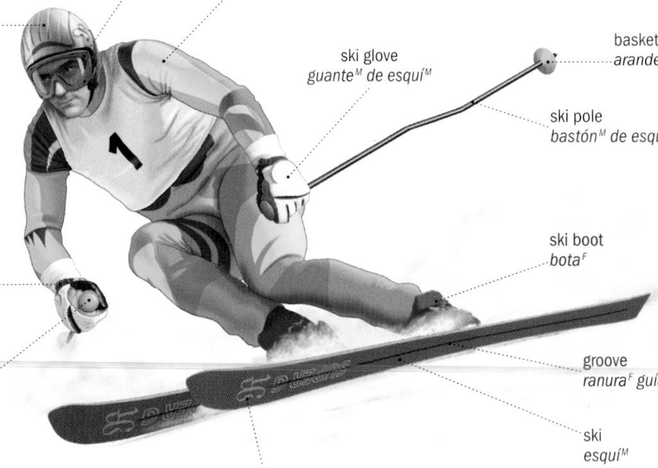

ski goggles
gafas[F] de esquí[M]
ski suit
traje[M] de esquí[M]
helmet
casco[M]
ski glove
guante[M] de esquí[M]
basket
arandela[F]
ski pole
bastón[M] de esquí[M]
ski boot
bota[F]
wrist strap
correa[F] para la mano[F]
handle
empuñadura[F]
groove
ranura[F] guía[F]
ski
esquí[M]
bottom
superficie[F] de deslizamiento[M]

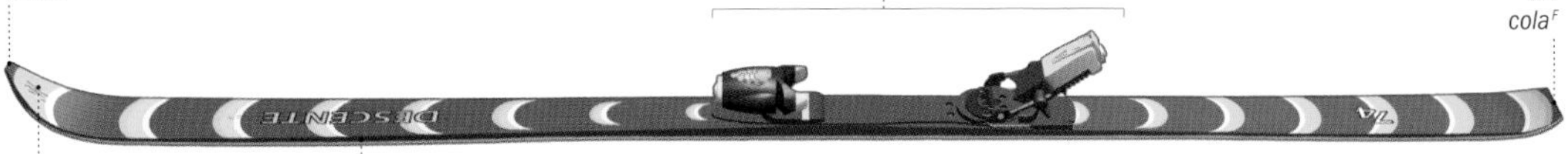

safety binding
fijaciones[F]
tip
punta[F]
tail
cola[F]
shovel
pala[F]
edge
canto[M]

ski
esquí[M]

examples of skis
ejemplos[M] de esquís[M]

slalom ski
esquí[M] de eslalon[M]

giant slalom ski
esquí[M] de eslalon[M] gigante

downhill and Super-G ski
esquí[M] de descenso[M] /eslalon[M]

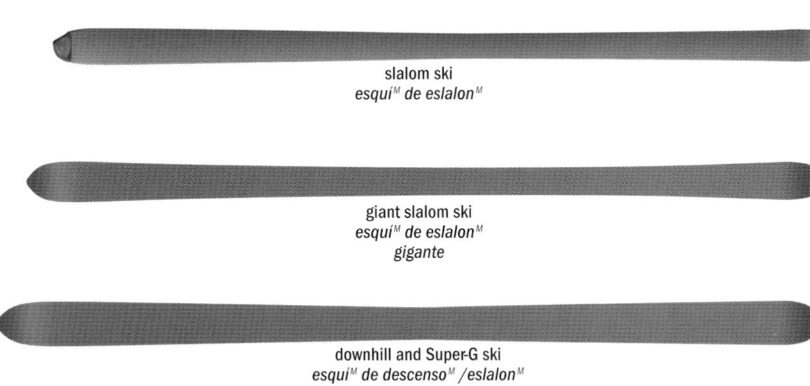

technical events
pruebas[F]

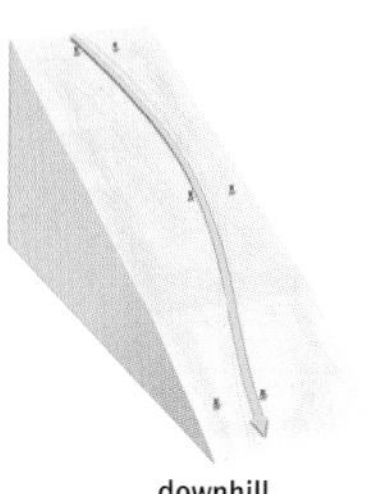
downhill
descenso[M]

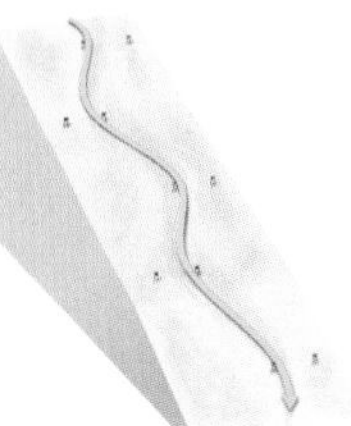
super giant (super-G) slalom
eslalon[M] *supergigante*

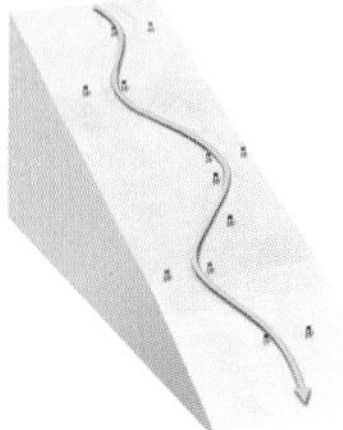
giant slalom
eslalon[M] *gigante*

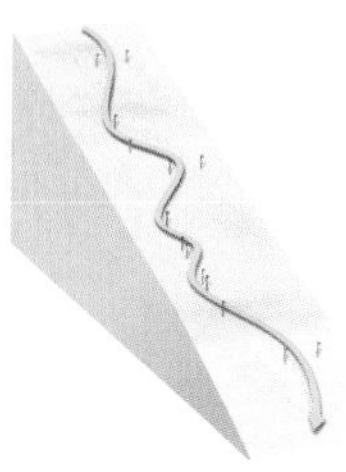
special slalom
eslalon[M] *especial*

ski boot
botas[F] ***para esquiar***

safety binding
fijación[F] ***de seguridad***[F] ***del esquí***[M]

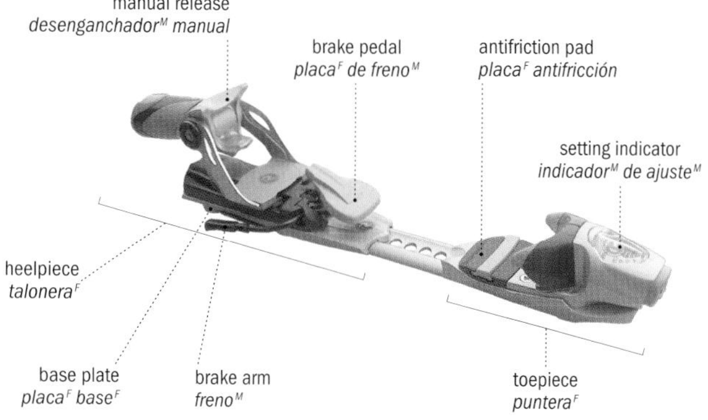

ski resort

estación[F] de esquí

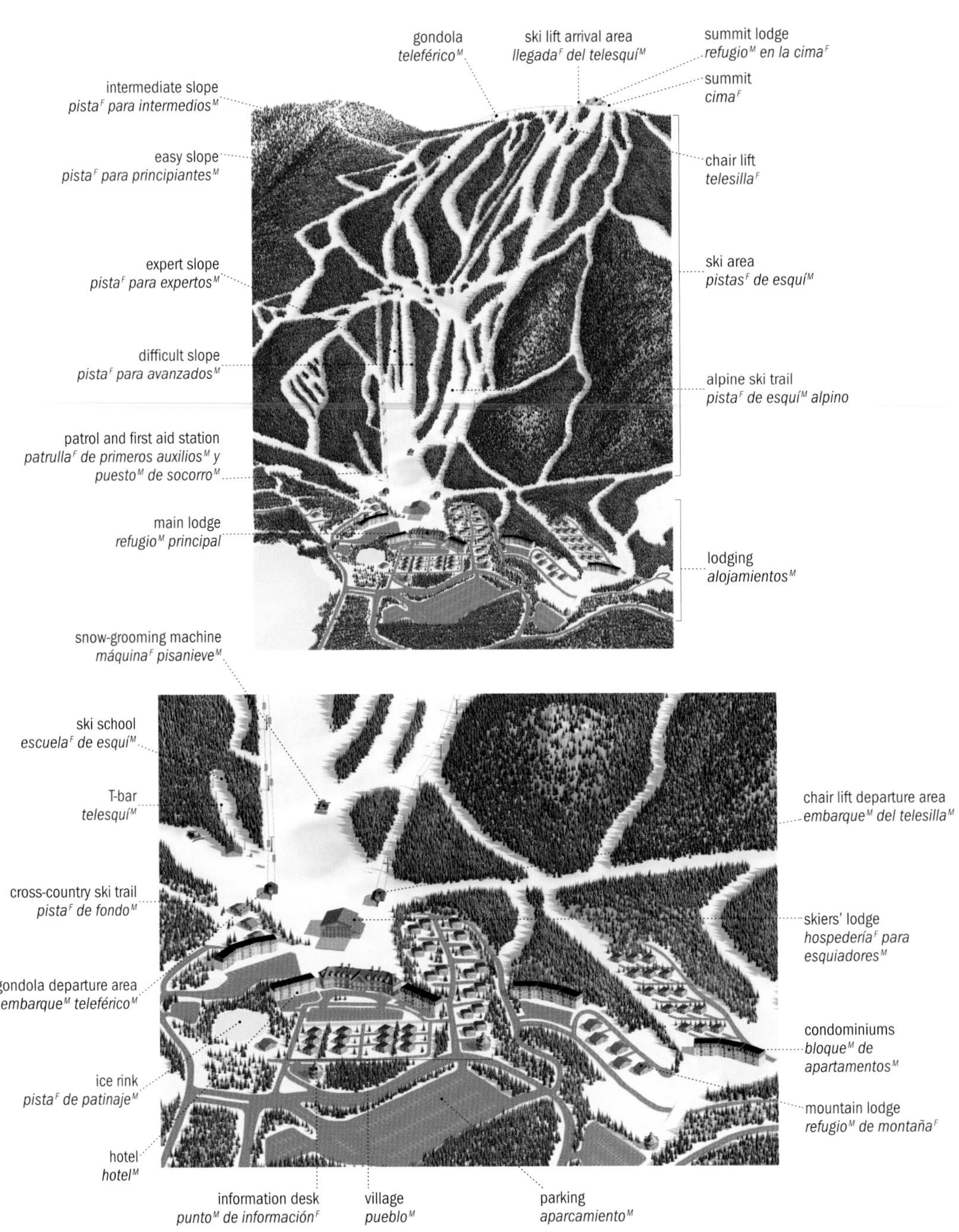
gondola
teleférico[M]
ski lift arrival area
llegada[F] del telesquí[M]
summit lodge
refugio[M] en la cima[F]
summit
cima[F]
intermediate slope
pista[F] para intermedios[M]
easy slope
pista[F] para principiantes[M]
chair lift
telesilla[F]
expert slope
pista[F] para expertos[M]
ski area
pistas[F] de esquí[M]
difficult slope
pista[F] para avanzados[M]
alpine ski trail
pista[F] de esquí[M] alpino
patrol and first aid station
patrulla[F] de primeros auxilios[M] y puesto[M] de socorro[M]
main lodge
refugio[M] principal
lodging
alojamientos[M]
snow-grooming machine
máquina[F] pisanieve[M]
ski school
escuela[F] de esquí[M]
T-bar
telesquí[M]
chair lift departure area
embarque[M] del telesilla[M]
cross-country ski trail
pista[F] de fondo[M]
skiers' lodge
hospedería[F] para esquiadores[M]
gondola departure area
embarque[M] teleférico[M]
condominiums
bloque[M] de apartamentos[M]
ice rink
pista[F] de patinaje[M]
mountain lodge
refugio[M] de montaña[F]
hotel
hotel[M]
information desk
punto[M] de información[F]
village
pueblo[M]
parking
aparcamiento[M]

SPORTS AND GAMES

snowboarding

snowboard^M

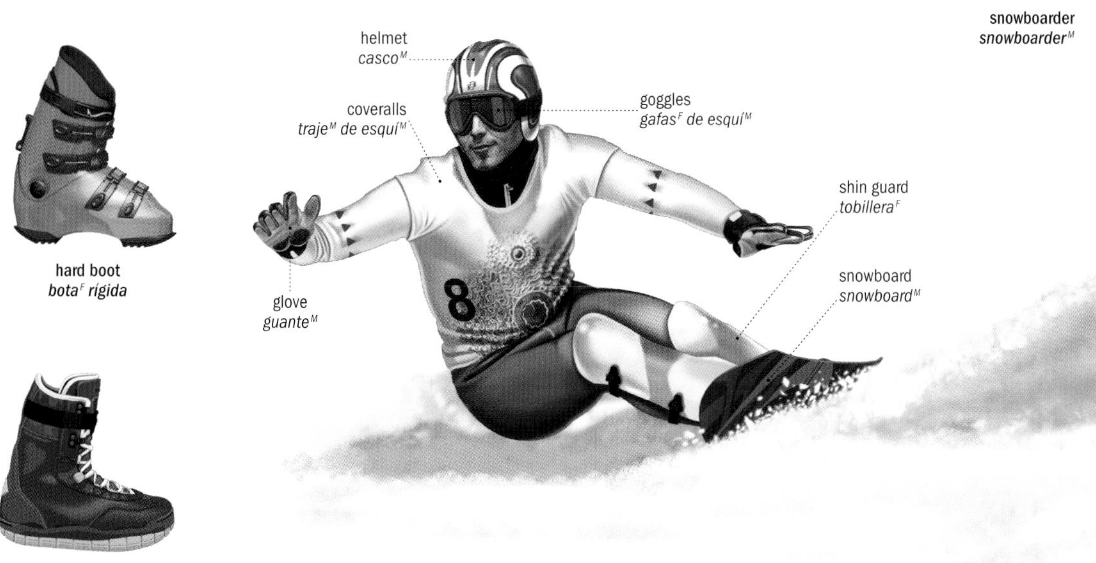

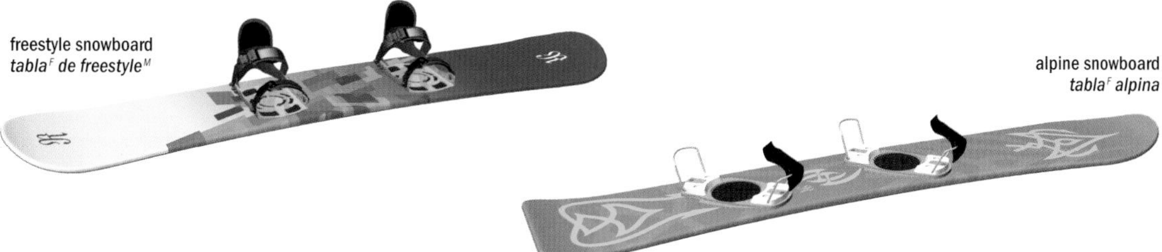

ski jumping

técnica^F de salto^M

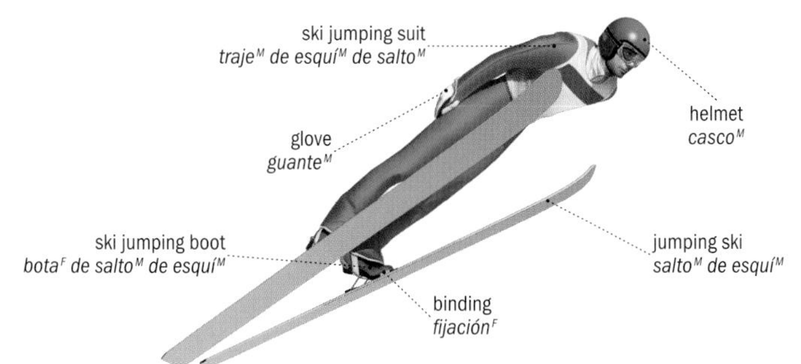

cross-country skiing

esquí[M] de fondo[M]

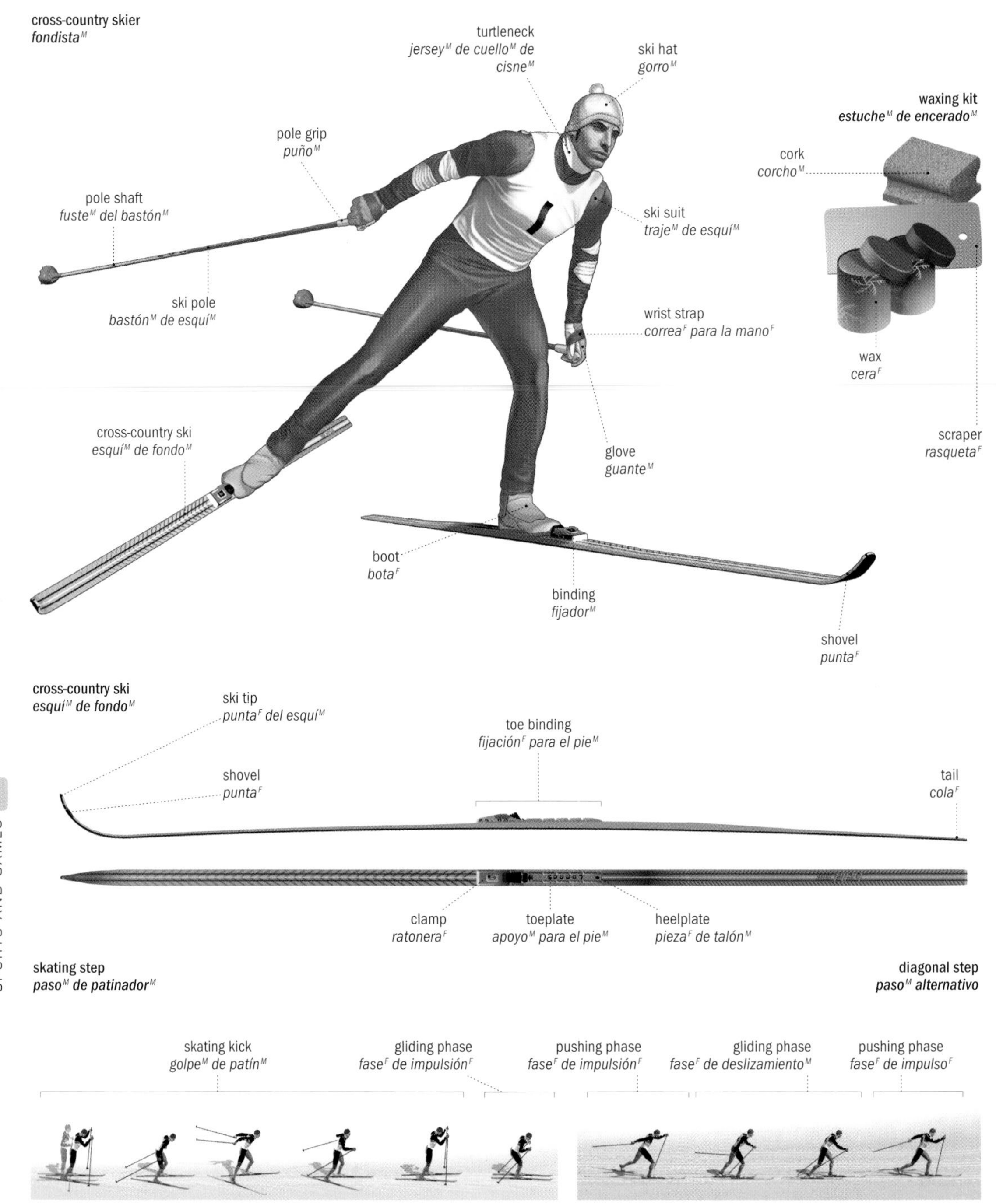
cross-country skier
fondista[M]
turtleneck
jersey[M] de cuello[M] de cisne[M]
ski hat
gorro[M]
waxing kit
estuche[M] de encerado[M]
pole grip
puño[M]
cork
corcho[M]
pole shaft
fuste[M] del bastón[M]
ski suit
traje[M] de esquí[M]
ski pole
bastón[M] de esquí[M]
wrist strap
correa[F] para la mano[F]
wax
cera[F]
cross-country ski
esquí[M] de fondo[M]
scraper
rasqueta[F]
glove
guante[M]
boot
bota[F]
binding
fijador[M]
shovel
punta[F]
cross-country ski
esquí[M] de fondo[M]
ski tip
punta[F] del esquí[M]
toe binding
fijación[F] para el pie[M]
shovel
punta[F]
tail
cola[F]
clamp
ratonera[F]
toeplate
apoyo[M] para el pie[M]
heelplate
pieza[F] de talón[M]
skating step
paso[M] de patinador[M]
diagonal step
paso[M] alternativo
skating kick
golpe[M] de patín[M]
gliding phase
fase[F] de impulsión[F]
pushing phase
fase[F] de impulsión[F]
gliding phase
fase[F] de deslizamiento[M]
pushing phase
fase[F] de impulso[F]

SPORTS AND GAMES

curling

curling^{M}

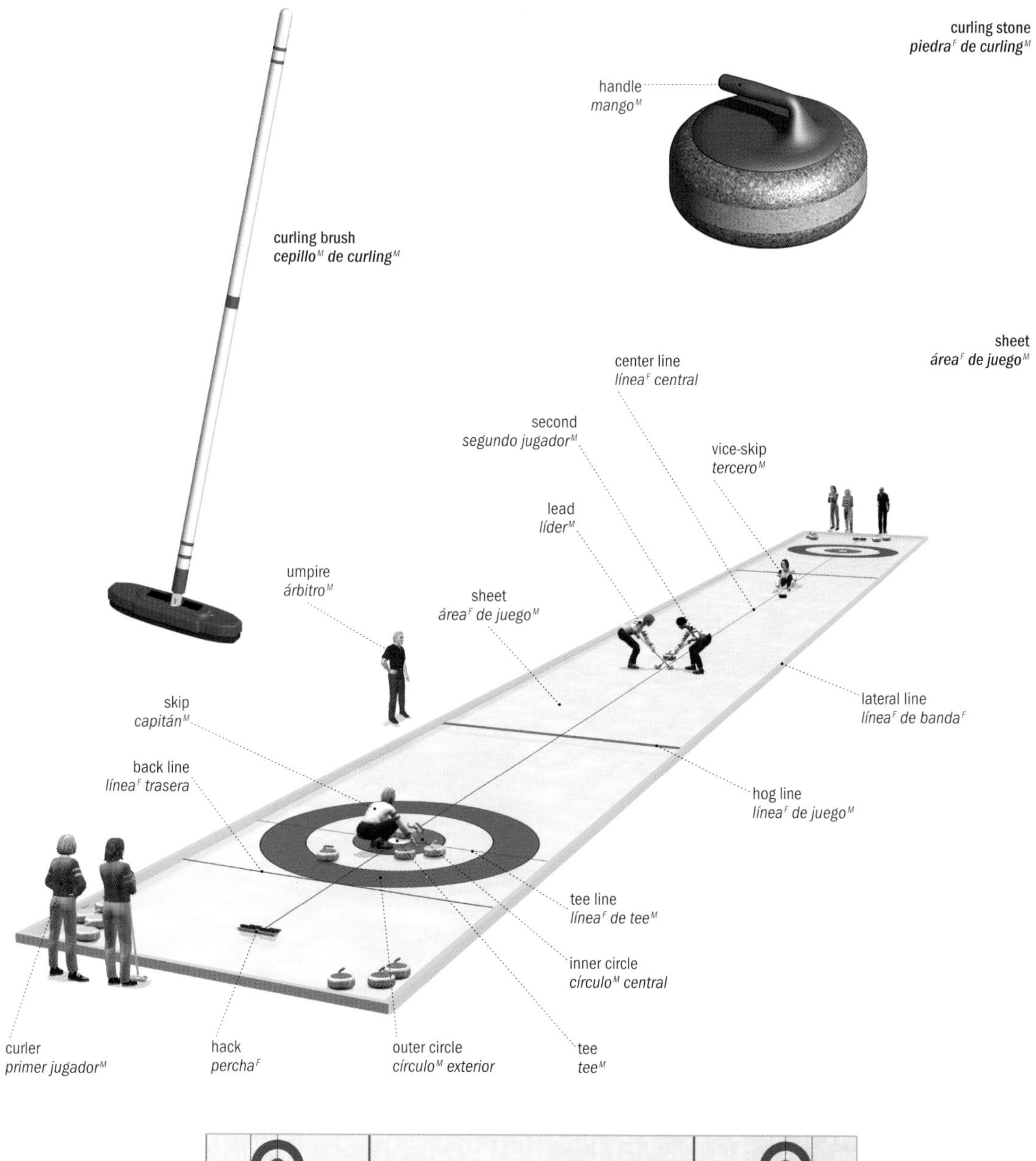
curling stone
piedra^{F} de curling^{M}
handle
mango^{M}
curling brush
cepillo^{M} de curling^{M}
sheet
área^{F} de juego^{M}
center line
línea^{F} central
second
segundo jugador^{M}
vice-skip
tercero^{M}
lead
líder^{M}
umpire
árbitro^{M}
sheet
área^{F} de juego^{M}
lateral line
línea^{F} de banda^{F}
skip
capitán^{M}
back line
línea^{F} trasera
hog line
línea^{F} de juego^{M}
tee line
línea^{F} de tee^{M}
inner circle
círculo^{M} central
curler
primer jugador^{M}
hack
percha^{F}
outer circle
círculo^{M} exterior
tee
tee^{M}
house
casa^{F}
free guard zone
zona^{F} de defensa^{F} protegida

swimming

natación[F]

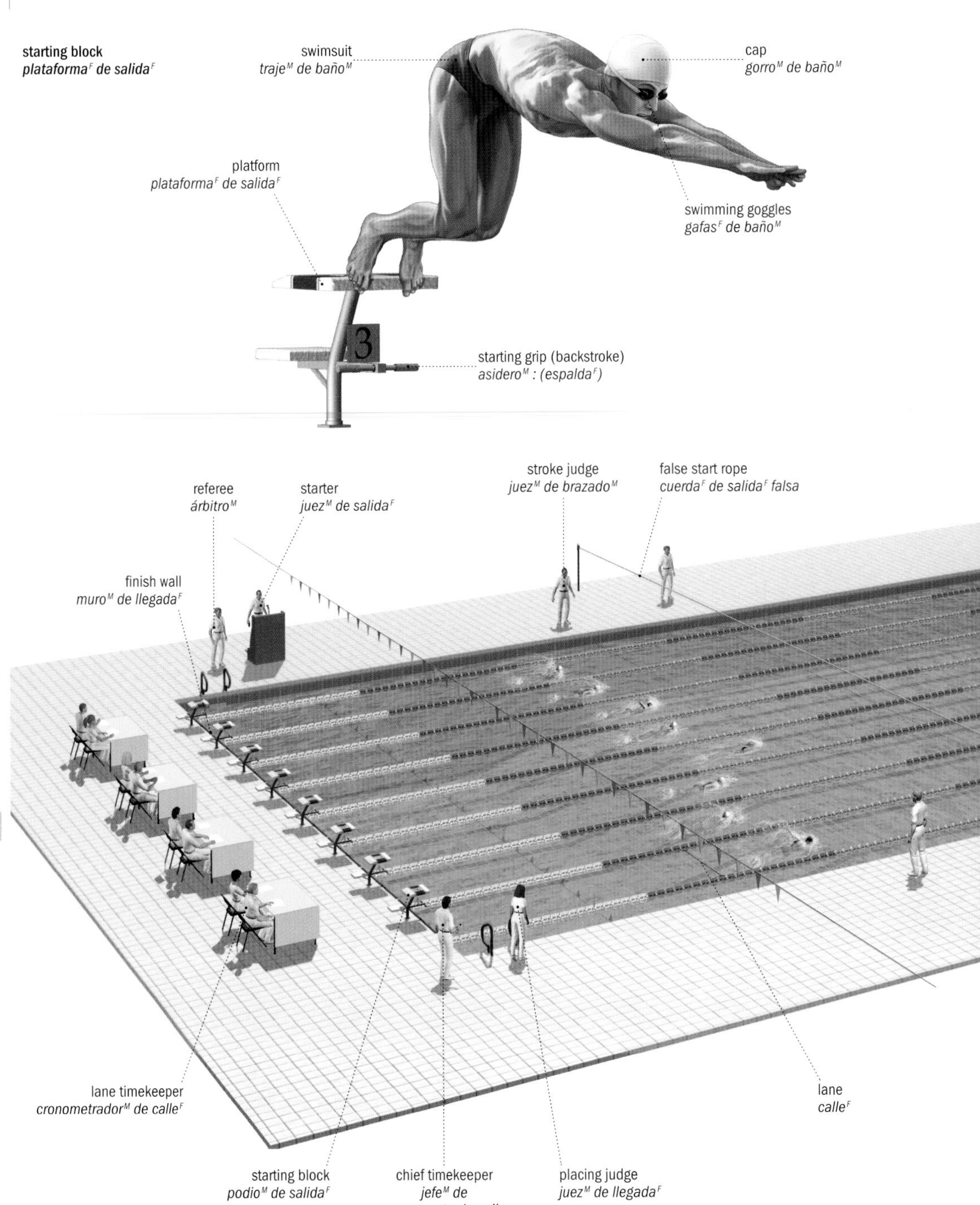

starting block
plataforma[F] de salida[F]
swimsuit
traje[M] de baño[M]
cap
gorro[M] de baño[M]
platform
plataforma[F] de salida[F]
swimming goggles
gafas[F] de baño[M]
3
starting grip (backstroke)
asidero[M] : (espalda[F])
referee
árbitro[M]
starter
juez[M] de salida[F]
stroke judge
juez[M] de brazado[M]
false start rope
cuerda[F] de salida[F] falsa
finish wall
muro[M] de llegada[F]
lane timekeeper
cronometrador[M] de calle[F]
lane
calle[F]
starting block
podio[M] de salida[F]
chief timekeeper
jefe[M] de cronometradores[M]
placing judge
juez[M] de llegada[F]

types of strokes
estilos[M] de natación[F]

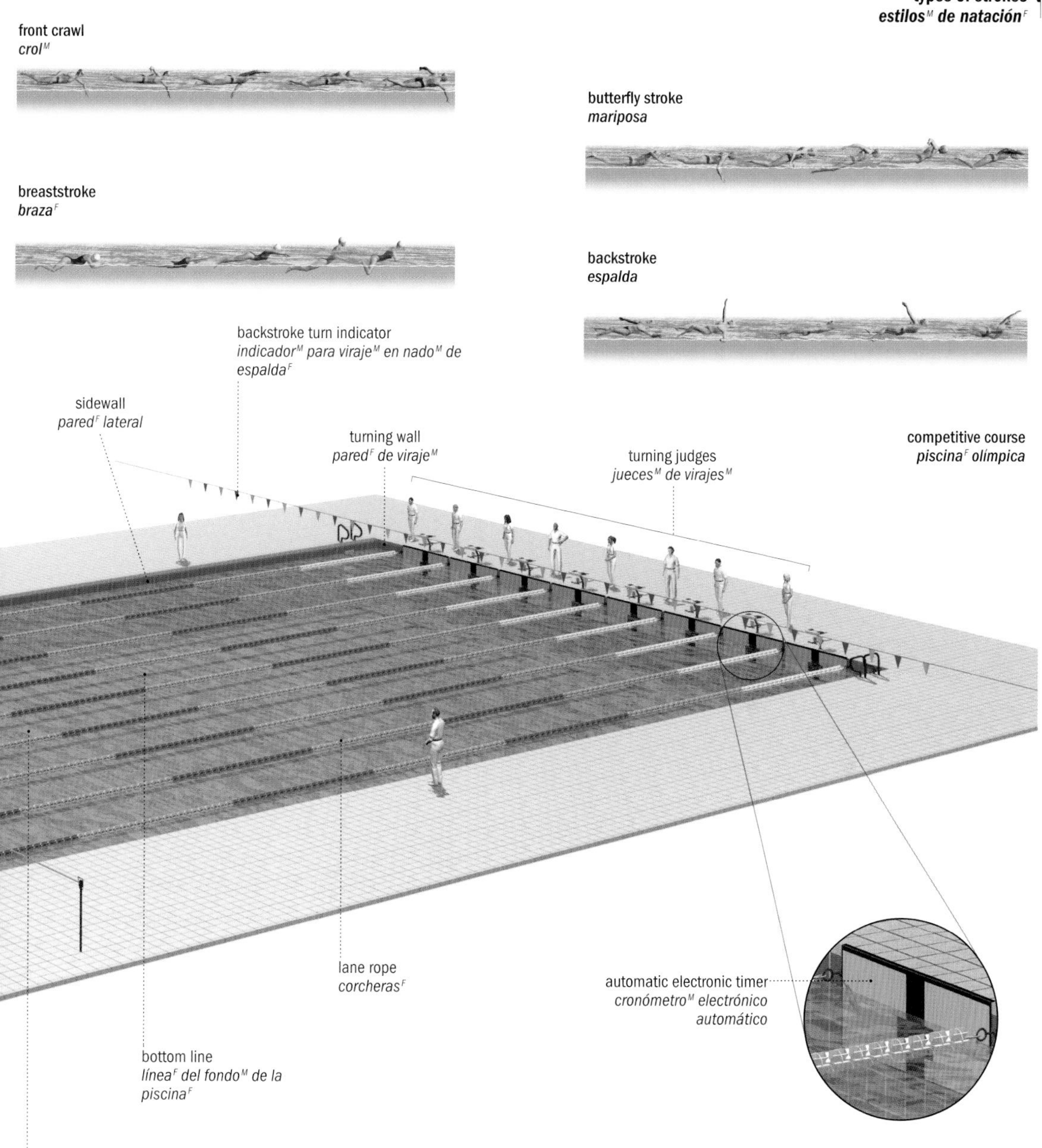
front crawl
crol[M]
butterfly stroke
mariposa
breaststroke
braza[F]
backstroke
espalda
backstroke turn indicator
indicador[M] para viraje[M] en nado[M] de espalda[F]
sidewall
pared[F] lateral
turning wall
pared[F] de viraje[M]
turning judges
jueces[M] de virajes[M]
competitive course
piscina[F] olímpica
lane rope
corcheras[F]
automatic electronic timer
cronómetro[M] electrónico automático
bottom line
línea[F] del fondo[M] de la piscina[F]
swimming pool
piscina[F]

diving

saltos[M]

starting positions
posiciones[F] de salto[M]

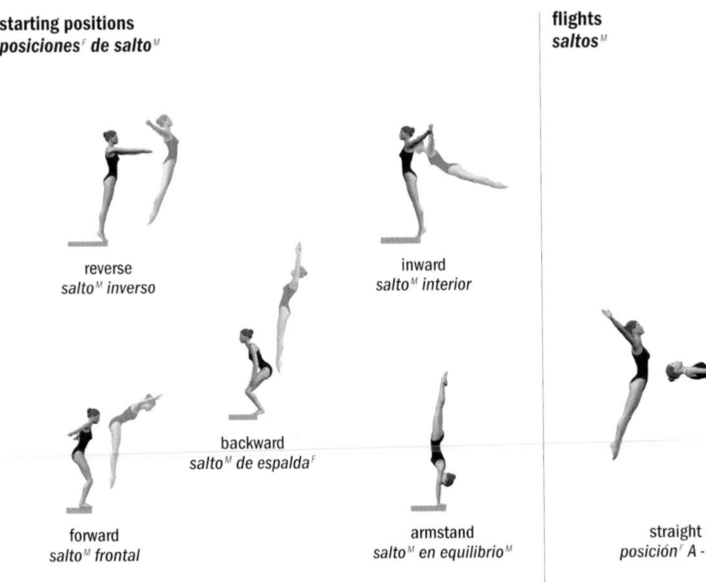

reverse
salto[M] inverso
inward
salto[M] interior
backward
salto[M] de espalda[F]
forward
salto[M] frontal
armstand
salto[M] en equilibrio[M]

flights
saltos[M]

tuck position
posición[F] C - cuerpo[M] encogido
straight position
posición[F] A - en plancha[F]
pike position
posición[F] B - hacer la carpa[F]

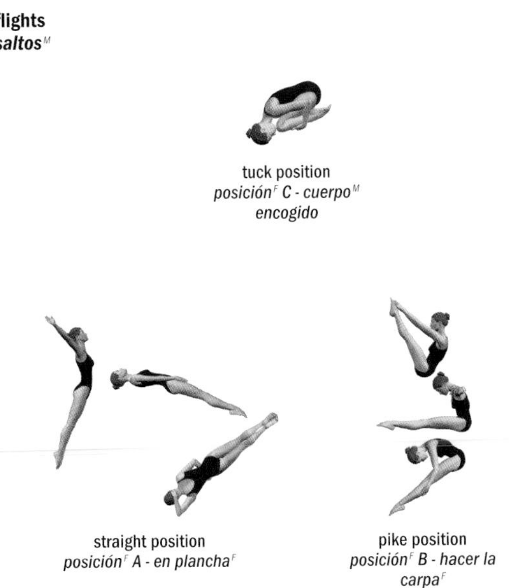

diving installations
torre[F] de saltos[M]

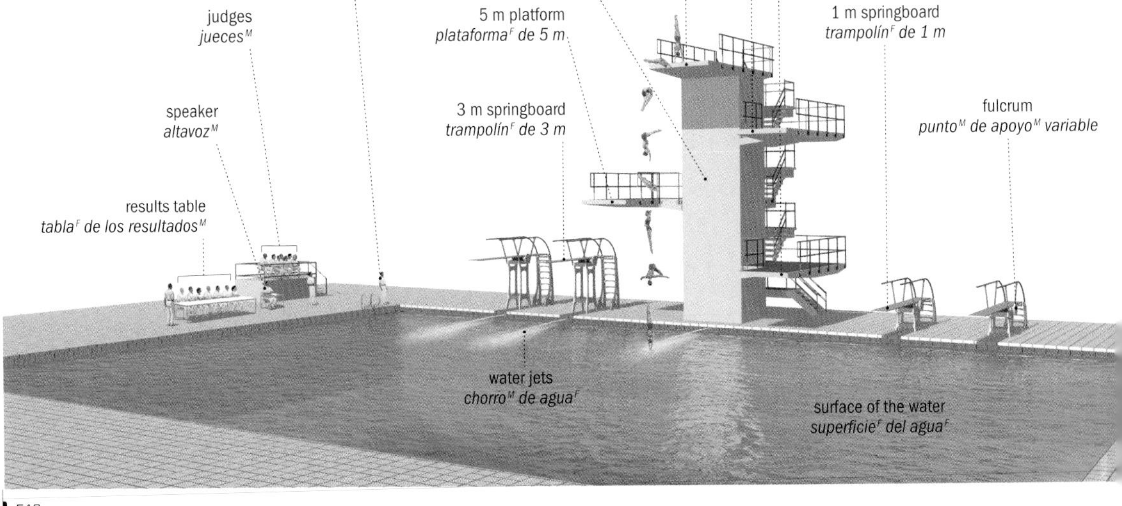

10 m platform
plataforma[F] de 10 m
7.5 m platform
plataforma[F] de 7,5 m
referee
juez-árbitro[M]
diving tower
torre[F] de saltos[M]
3 m platform
plataforma[F] de 3 m
judges
jueces[M]
5 m platform
plataforma[F] de 5 m
1 m springboard
trampolín[F] de 1 m
speaker
altavoz[M]
3 m springboard
trampolín[F] de 3 m
fulcrum
punto[M] de apoyo[M] variable
results table
tabla[F] de los resultados[M]
water jets
chorro[M] de agua[F]
surface of the water
superficie[F] del agua[F]

sailboard

windsurf^M

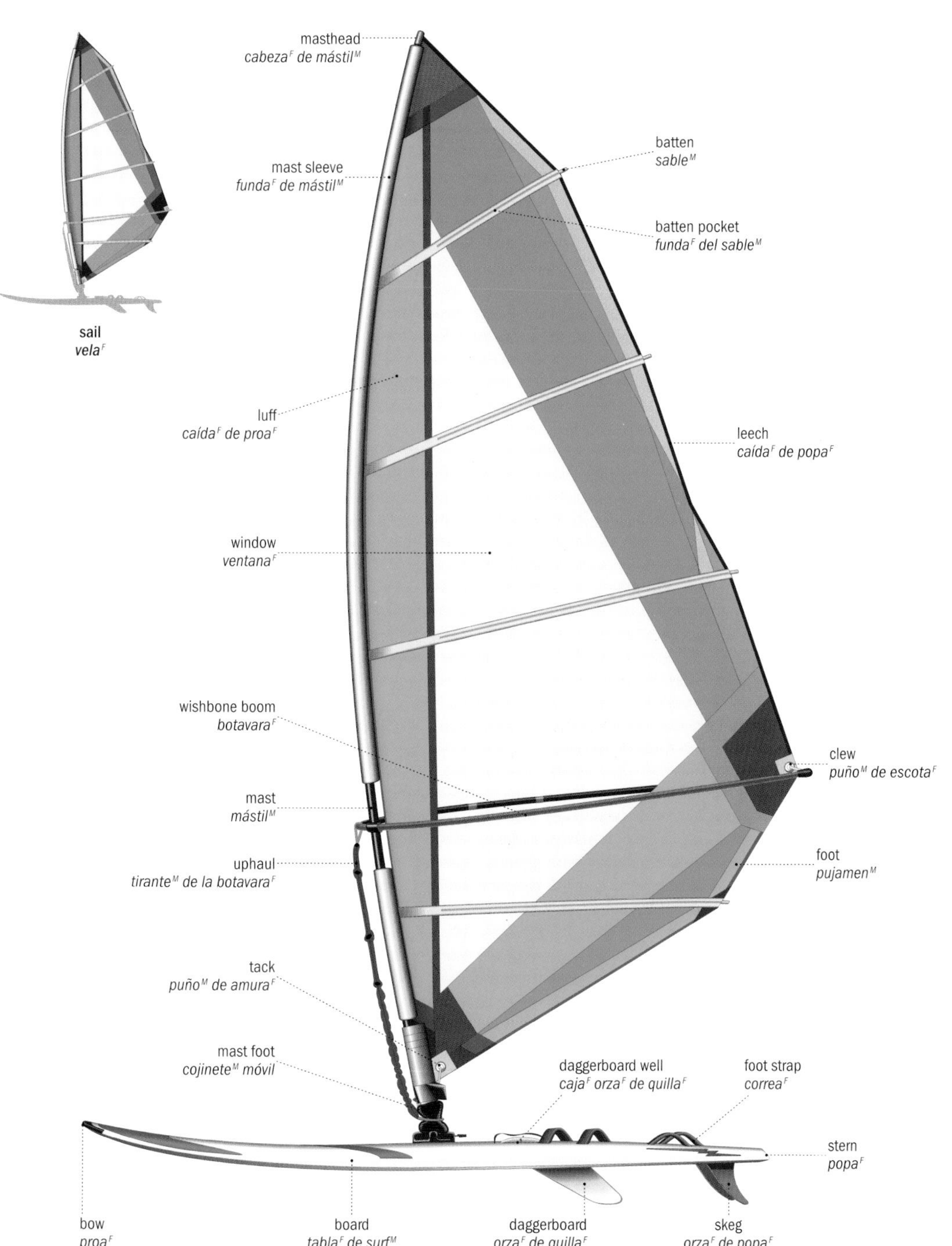
sail
vela^F
masthead
cabeza^F de mástil^M
batten
sable^M
mast sleeve
funda^F de mástil^M
batten pocket
funda^F del sable^M
luff
caída^F de proa^F
leech
caída^F de popa^F
window
ventana^F
wishbone boom
botavara^F
clew
puño^M de escota^F
mast
mástil^M
uphaul
tirante^M de la botavara^F
foot
pujamen^M
tack
puño^M de amura^F
mast foot
cojinete^M móvil
daggerboard well
caja^F orza^F de quilla^F
foot strap
correa^F
stern
popa^F
bow
proa^F
board
tabla^F de surf^M
daggerboard
orza^F de quilla^F
skeg
orza^F de popa^F

sailing

vela[F]

sailboat
velero[M]

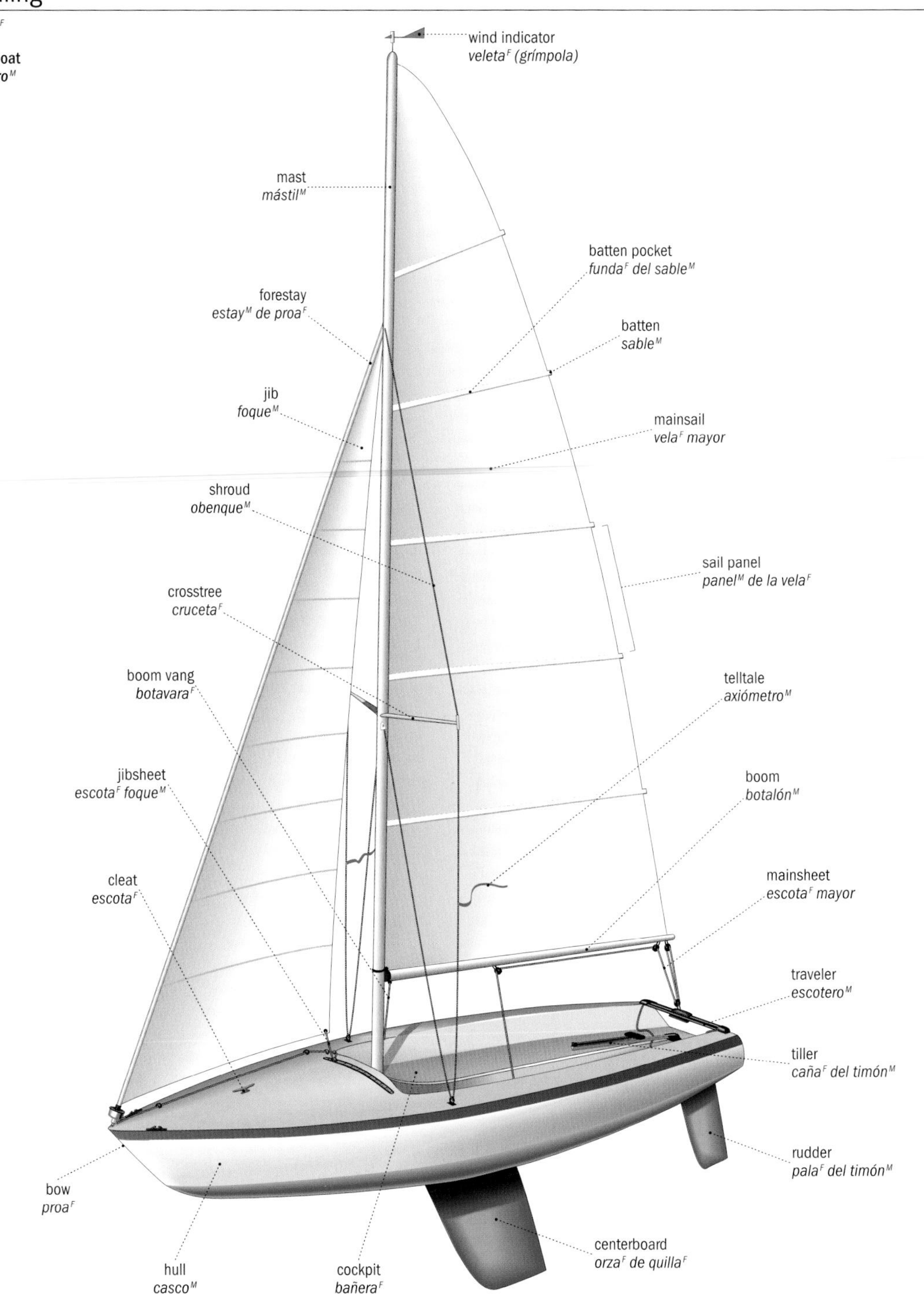
wind indicator
veleta[F] (grímpola)
mast
mástil[M]
batten pocket
funda[F] del sable[M]
forestay
estay[M] de proa[F]
batten
sable[M]
jib
foque[M]
mainsail
vela[F] mayor
shroud
obenque[M]
sail panel
panel[M] de la vela[F]
crosstree
cruceta[F]
boom vang
botavara[F]
telltale
axiómetro[M]
jibsheet
escota[F] foque[M]
boom
botalón[M]
cleat
escota[F]
mainsheet
escota[F] mayor
traveler
escotero[M]
tiller
caña[F] del timón[M]
rudder
pala[F] del timón[M]
bow
proa[F]
centerboard
orza[F] de quilla[F]
hull
casco[M]
cockpit
bañera[F]

multihulls
multicasco[M]

monohulls
monocascos[M]

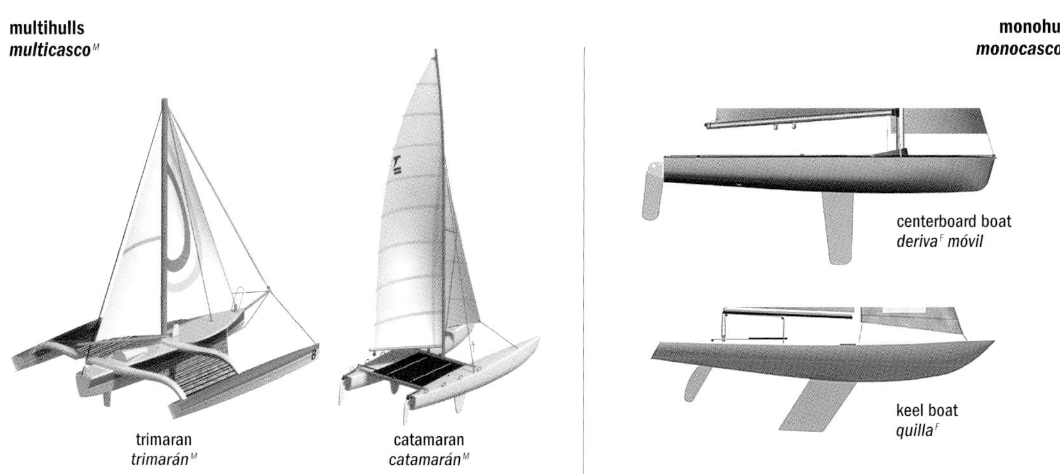

centerboard boat
deriva[F] *móvil*

keel boat
quilla[F]

trimaran
trimarán[M]

catamaran
catamarán[M]

upperworks
obra[F] ***muerta***

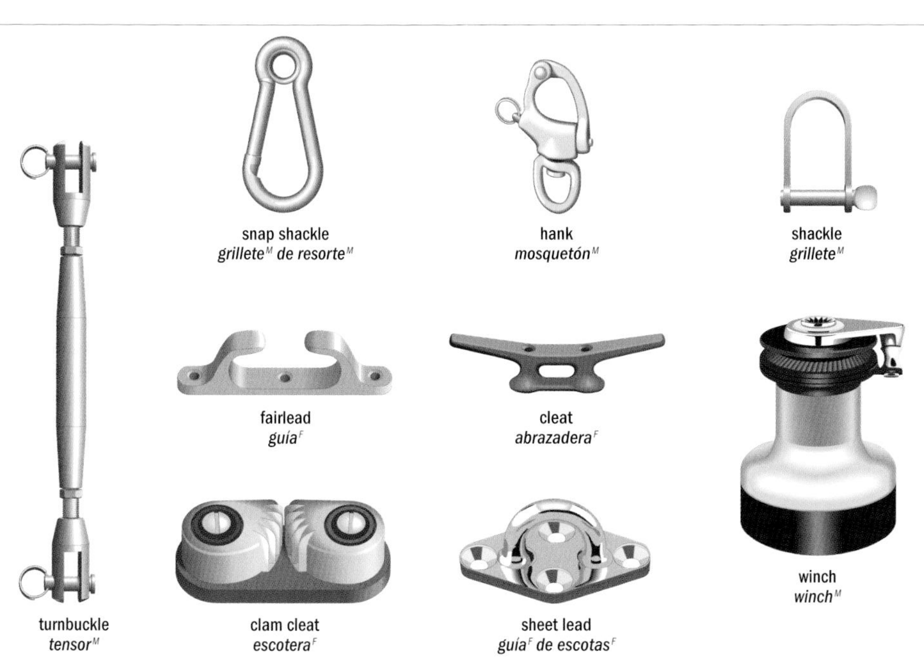

snap shackle
grillete[M] *de resorte*[M]

hank
mosquetón[M]

shackle
grillete[M]

fairlead
guía[F]

cleat
abrazadera[F]

winch
winch[M]

turnbuckle
tensor[M]

clam cleat
escotera[F]

sheet lead
guía[F] *de escotas*[F]

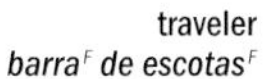

traveler
barra[F] *de escotas*[F]

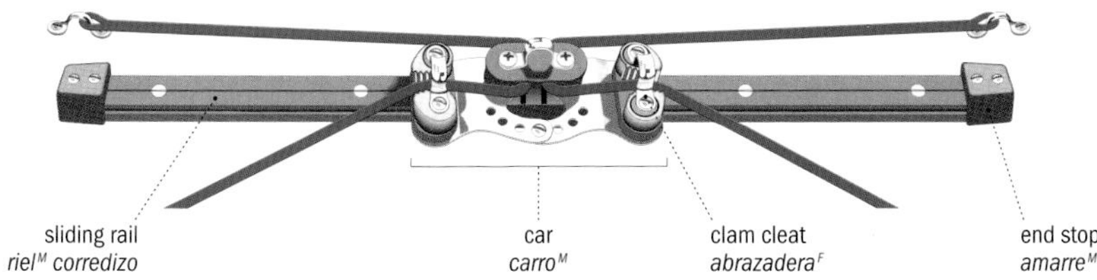

sliding rail
riel[M] *corredizo*

car
carro[M]

clam cleat
abrazadera[F]

end stop
amarre[M]

road racing

ciclismo^M por carretera^F

road-racing bicycle and cyclist
bicicleta^F de carreras^F y ciclista^M

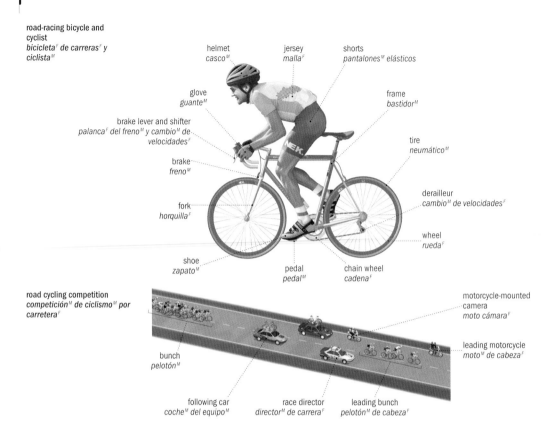

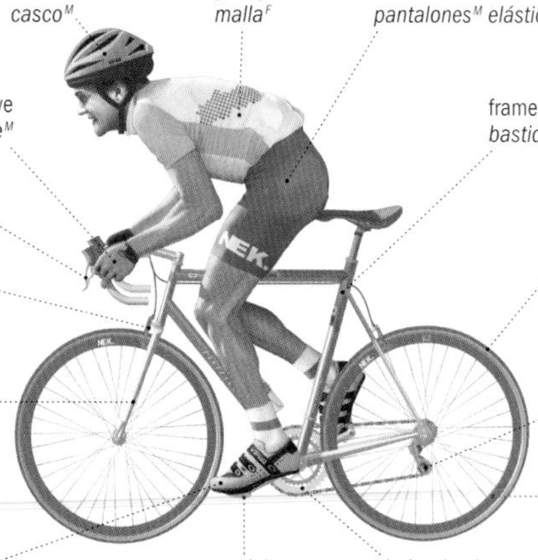

helmet
casco^M
jersey
malla^F
shorts
pantalones^M elásticos
glove
guante^M
frame
bastidor^M
brake lever and shifter
palanca^F del freno^M y cambio^M de velocidades^F
tire
neumático^M
brake
freno^M
derailleur
cambio^M de velocidades^F
fork
horquilla^F
wheel
rueda^F
shoe
zapato^M
pedal
pedal^M
chain wheel
cadena^F

road cycling competition
competición^M de ciclismo^M por carretera^F

motorcycle-mounted camera
moto cámara^F
leading motorcycle
moto^M de cabeza^F
bunch
pelotón^M
following car
coche^M del equipo^M
race director
director^M de carrera^F
leading bunch
pelotón^M de cabeza^F

mountain biking

ciclismo^M de montaña^F

cross-country bicycle and cyclist
bicicleta^F de cross^M y ciclista^M

goggles
gafas^F
back suspension
suspensión^F trasera
front fork
horquilla^F frontal
clipless pedal
pedal^M automático

downhill bicycle and cyclist
bicicleta^F de descenso^M y ciclista^F

protective goggles
gafas^F protectoras
chin strap
mentonera^F
raised handlebar
manillar^M
pedal with wide platform
pedal^M plano
hydraulic disc brake
freno^M de disco^M hidráulico

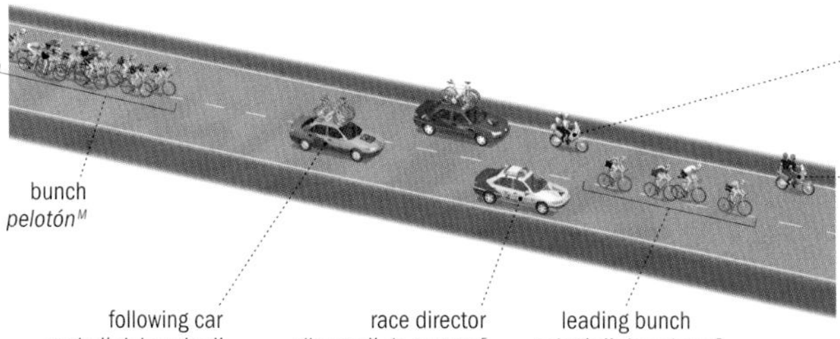

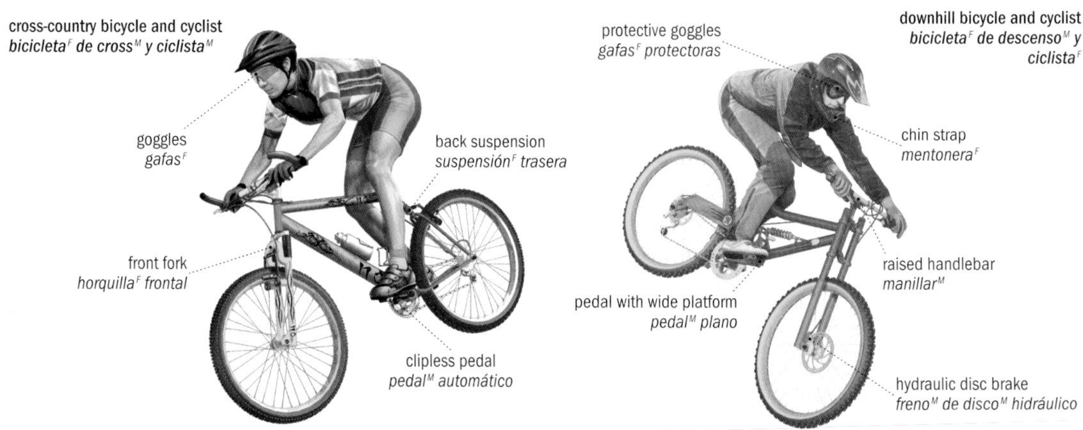

personal watercraft

motoF acuática

handlebar
manillarM
mirror
espejoM
seat
asientoM
sponson
estabilizadorM
hull
cascoM

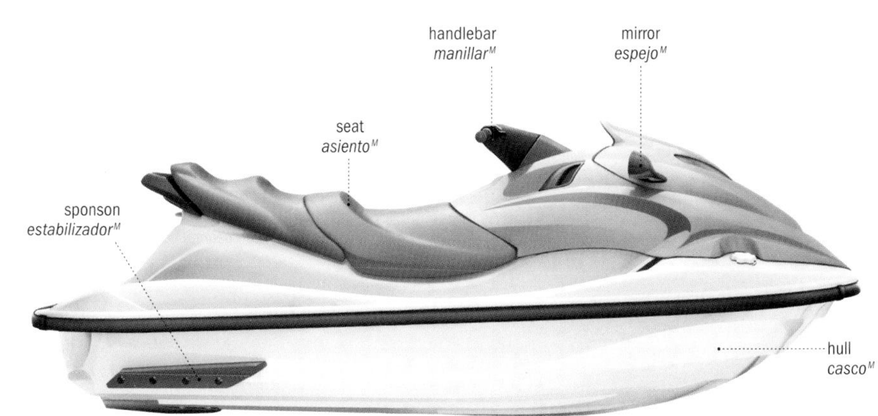

snowmobile

motoM nieve

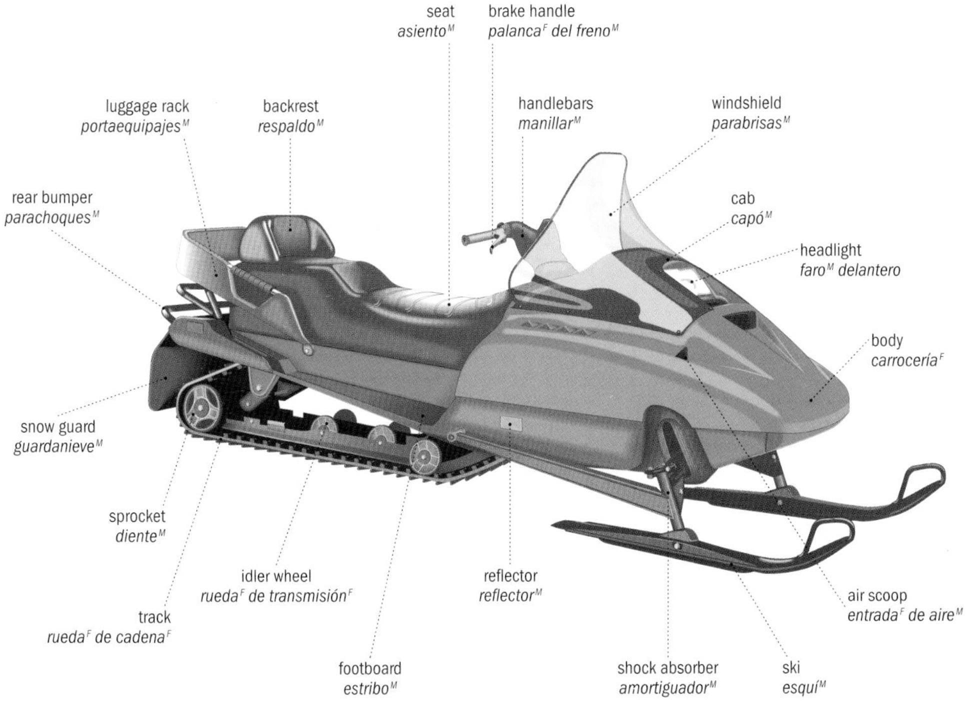

seat
asientoM
brake handle
palancaF del frenoM
luggage rack
portaequipajesM
backrest
respaldoM
handlebars
manillarM
windshield
parabrisasM
rear bumper
parachoquesM
cab
capóM
headlight
faroM delantero
body
carroceríaF
snow guard
guardanieveM
sprocket
dienteM
idler wheel
ruedaF de transmisiónF
reflector
reflectorM
air scoop
entradaF de aireM
track
ruedaF de cadenaF
footboard
estriboM
shock absorber
amortiguadorM
ski
esquíM

car racing

carreras[F] de coches[M]

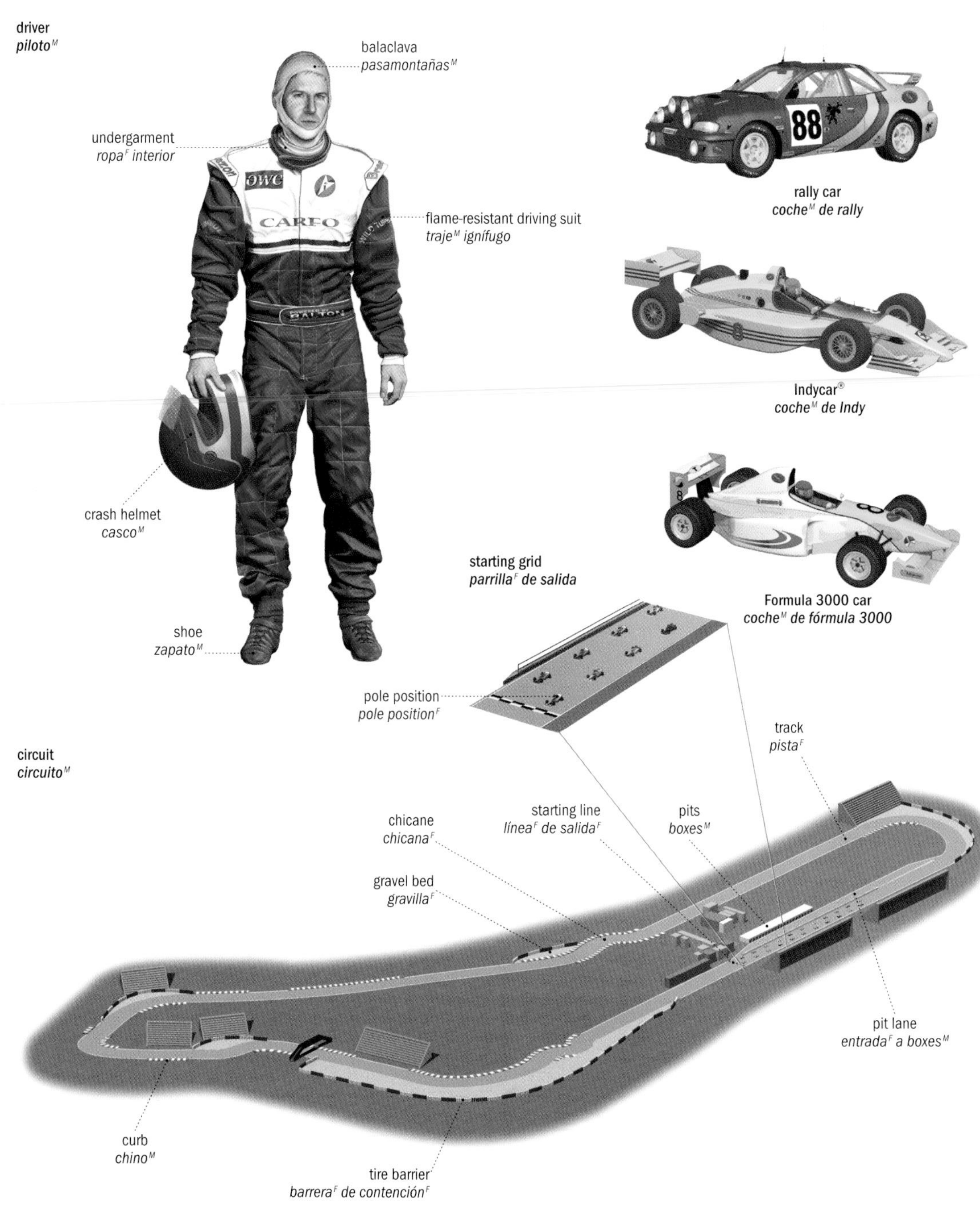
driver
piloto[M]
balaclava
pasamontañas[M]
undergarment
ropa[F] interior
flame-resistant driving suit
traje[M] ignífugo
crash helmet
casco[M]
shoe
zapato[M]
rally car
coche[M] de rally
Indycar®
coche[M] de Indy
Formula 3000 car
coche[M] de fórmula 3000
starting grid
parrilla[F] de salida
pole position
pole position[F]
track
pista[F]
circuit
circuito[M]
chicane
chicana[F]
starting line
línea[F] de salida[F]
pits
boxes[M]
gravel bed
gravilla[F]
pit lane
entrada[F] a boxes[M]
curb
chino[M]
tire barrier
barrera[F] de contención[F]

car racing

Formula 1® car
coche[M] de Fórmula[F] 1

roll structure
estructura[F] protectora
camera
cámara[F]
cockpit
habitáculo[M]
wing
alerón[M]
radio antenna
antena[F] de radio[F]
Pitot tube
tubo[M] de Pitot
safety belt
cinturón[M] de seguridad[F]
side fairings
alerón[M]
steering wheel
volante[M]

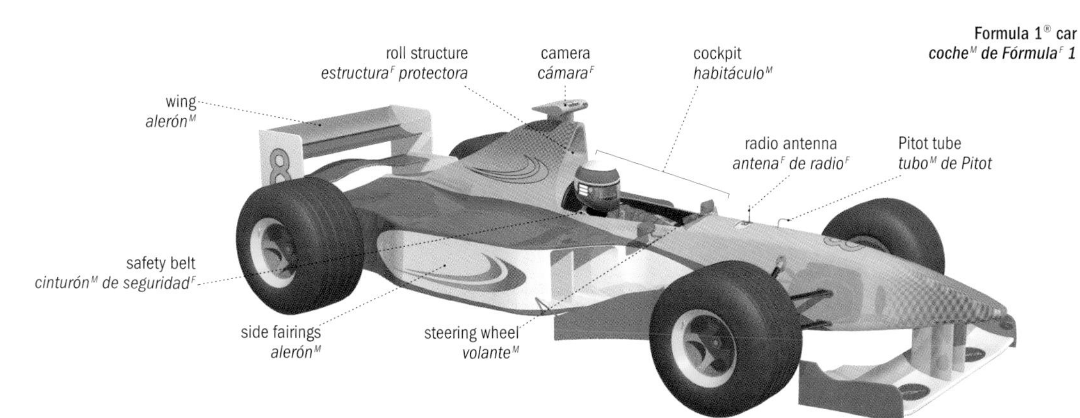

motorcycling

motocicleta[F]

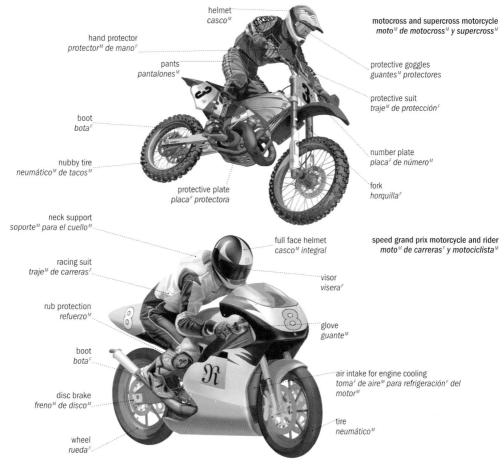

motocross and supercross motorcycle
moto[M] de motocross[M] y supercross[M]

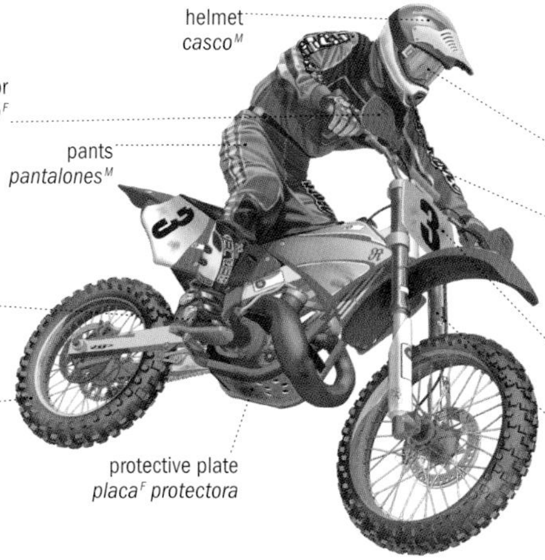

helmet
casco[M]
hand protector
protector[M] de mano[F]
pants
pantalones[M]
protective goggles
guantes[M] protectores
protective suit
traje[M] de protección[F]
boot
bota[F]
number plate
placa[F] de número[M]
nubby tire
neumático[M] de tacos[M]
fork
horquilla[F]
protective plate
placa[F] protectora

speed grand prix motorcycle and rider
moto[M] de carreras[F] y motociclista[M]

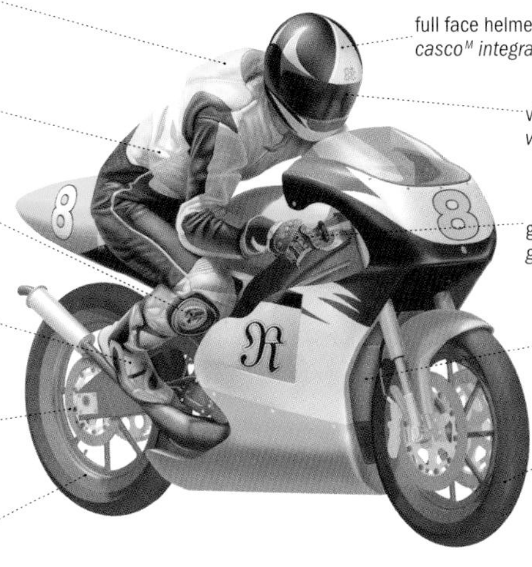

neck support
soporte[M] para el cuello[M]
full face helmet
casco[M] integral
racing suit
traje[M] de carreras[F]
visor
visera[F]
rub protection
refuerzo[M]
glove
guante[M]
boot
bota[F]
air intake for engine cooling
toma[F] de aire[M] para refrigeración[F] del motor[M]
disc brake
freno[M] de disco[M]
tire
neumático[M]
wheel
rueda[F]

skateboarding

skateboard^{M}

skateboard
monopatín^{M}

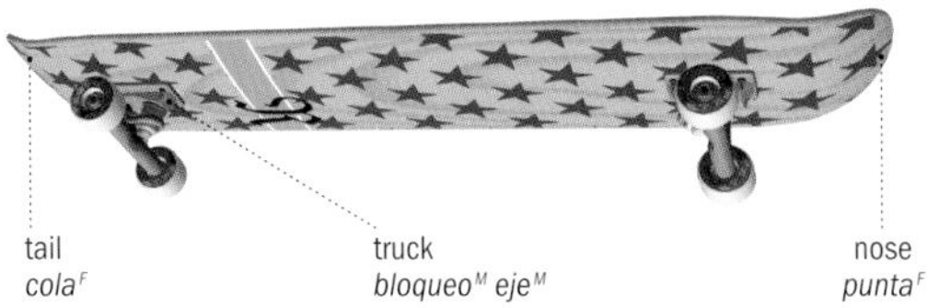

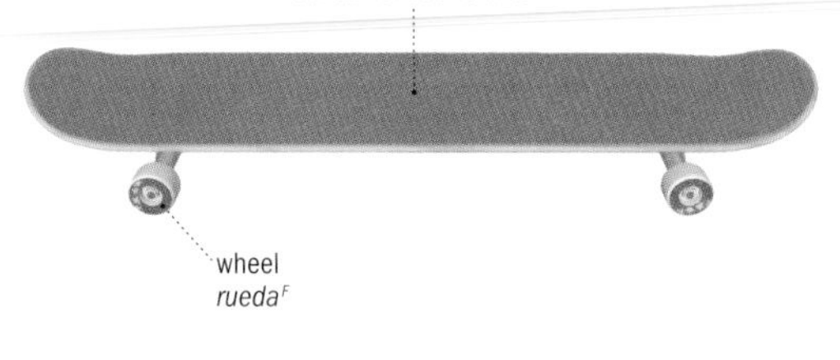

skateboarder
monopatín^{M}

ramp
medio tubo^{M}

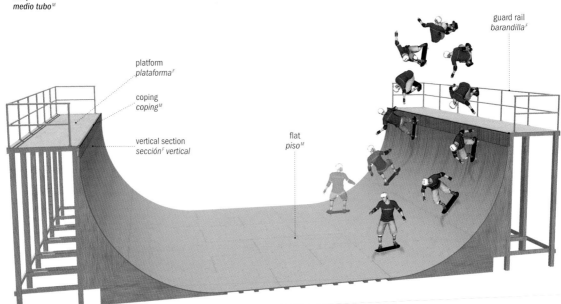

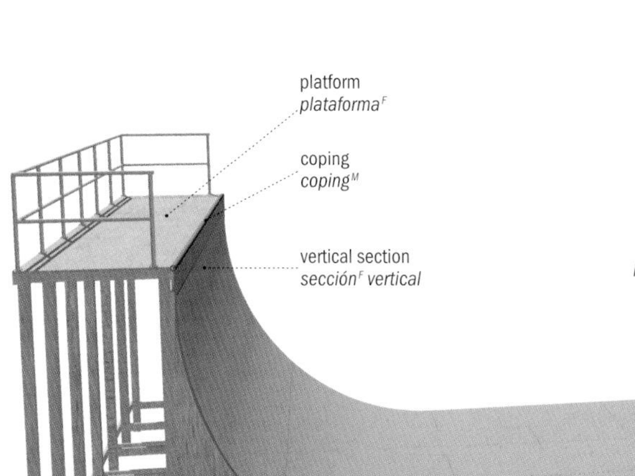

in-line skating

patinaje^M en línea^F

acrobatic skate
patinaje^M acrobático
inner boot
botín^M interior
upper shell
bota^F externa
frame
bastidor^M
wheel
rueda^F
skater
patinador^M
helmet
casco^M
elbow pad
codera^F
knee pad
rodillera^F
wrist guard
muñequera^F
in-line speed skate
patín^M en línea^F
in-line skate
patín^M en línea^F
inner boot
botín^F interior
upper shell
bota^F externa
in-line hockey skate
patín en línea^F de hockey^M
adjusting buckle
hebilla^F de ajuste^M
boot
bota^F
axle
eje^M
ROLLER
heel stop
freno^M trasero
wheel
rueda^F
truck
bogie^M

camping

acampada[F]

examples of tents
ejemplos[M] de tiendas[F] de campaña[F]

two-person tent
tienda[F] para dos

rainfly
doble techo[M]
door
puerta[F]
canopy
toldo[M] delantero
guy line
viento[M]
stake
estaquilla[F]
strainer
fiador[M]
zipper
cierre[M]
inner tent
tienda[F] interior
elastic strainer
fiador[M] elástico

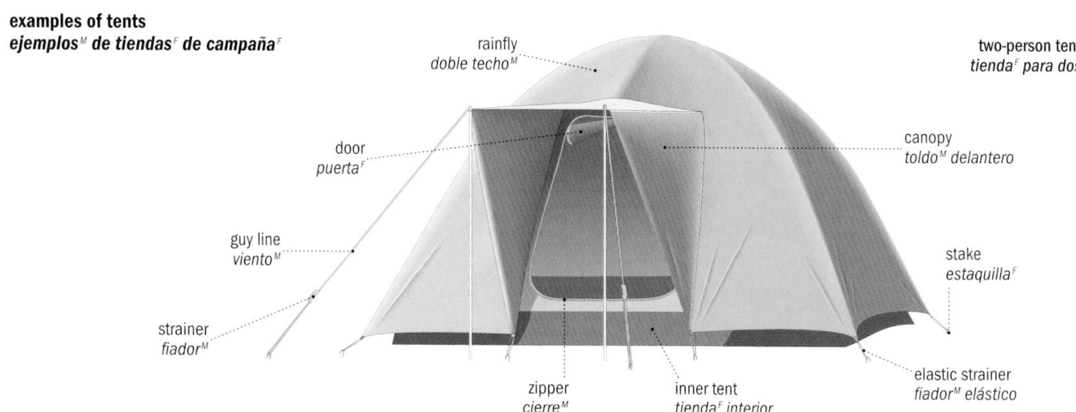

family tent
tienda[F] de campaña[F] tamaño[M] familiar

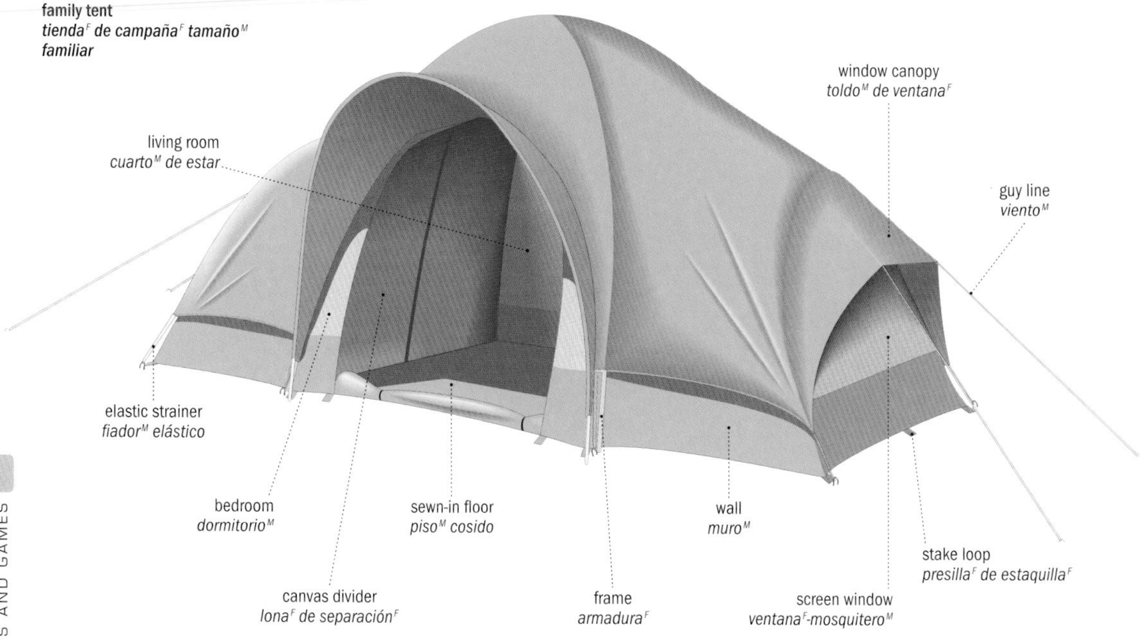

window canopy
toldo[M] de ventana[F]
living room
cuarto[M] de estar
guy line
viento[M]
elastic strainer
fiador[M] elástico
bedroom
dormitorio[M]
sewn-in floor
piso[M] cosido
wall
muro[M]
stake loop
presilla[F] de estaquilla[F]
canvas divider
lona[F] de separación[F]
frame
armadura[F]
screen window
ventana[F]-mosquitero[M]

wagon tent
tienda[F] tipo[M] vagón[M]

wall tent
tienda[F] rectangular

SPORTS AND GAMES

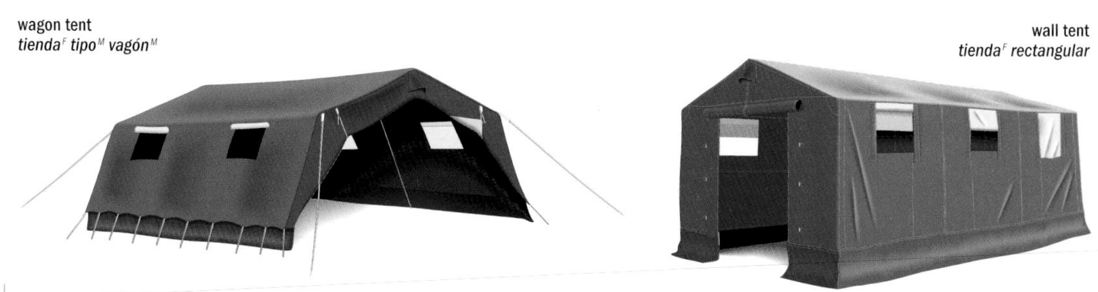

pup tent
tienda[F] de campaña[F] clásica

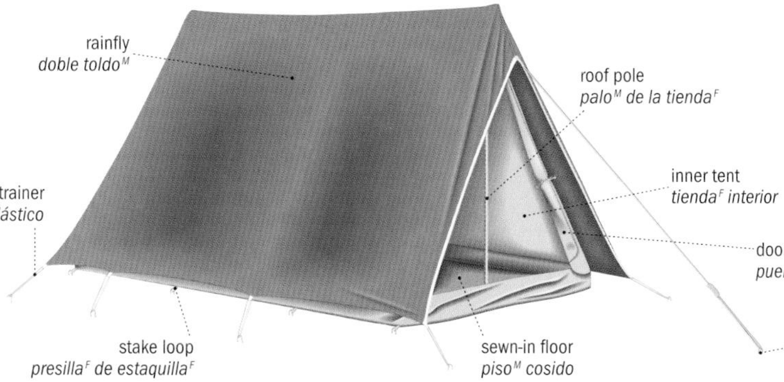

rainfly
doble toldo[M]

roof pole
palo[M] de la tienda[F]

inner tent
tienda[F] interior

elastic strainer
fiador[M] elástico

door
puerta[F]

stake loop
presilla[F] de estaquilla[F]

sewn-in floor
piso[M] cosido

stake
estaquilla[F]

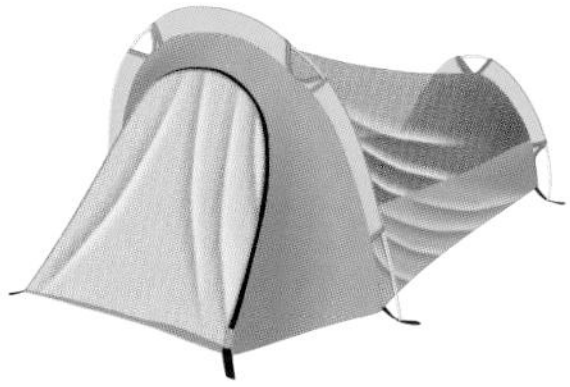

one-person tent
tienda[F] unipersonal

dome tent
tienda[F] tipo[M] domo[M]

pop-up tent
tienda[F] tipo[M] iglú[M]

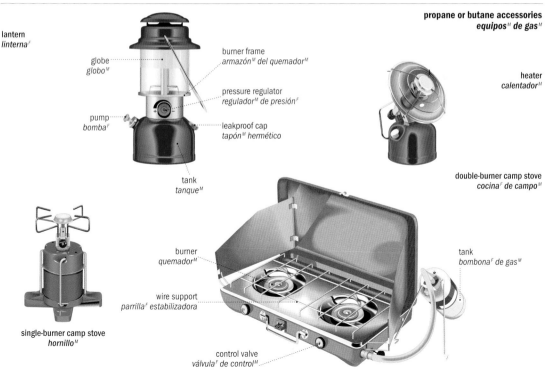

propane or butane accessories
equipos[M] de gas[M]

lantern
linterna[F]

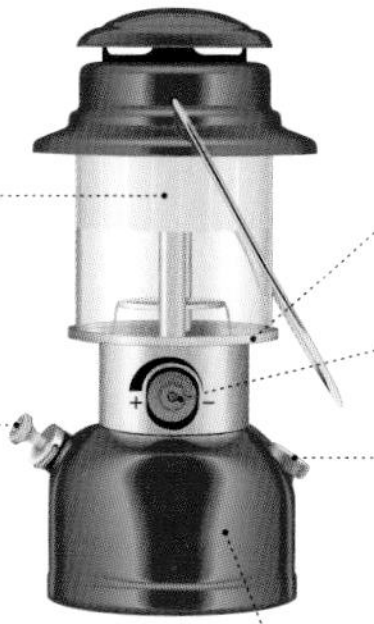

globe
globo[M]

burner frame
armazón[M] del quemador[M]

pressure regulator
regulador[M] de presión[F]

pump
bomba[F]

leakproof cap
tapón[M] hermético

tank
tanque[M]

heater
calentador[M]

double-burner camp stove
cocina[F] de campo[M]

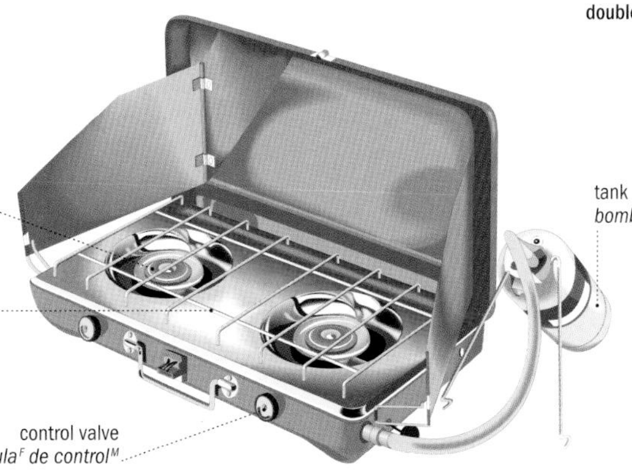

burner
quemador[M]

tank
bombona[F] de gas[M]

wire support
parrilla[F] estabilizadora

control valve
válvula[F] de control[M]

single-burner camp stove
hornillo[M]

camping

examples of sleeping bags
ejemplos^M de sacos^M de dormir

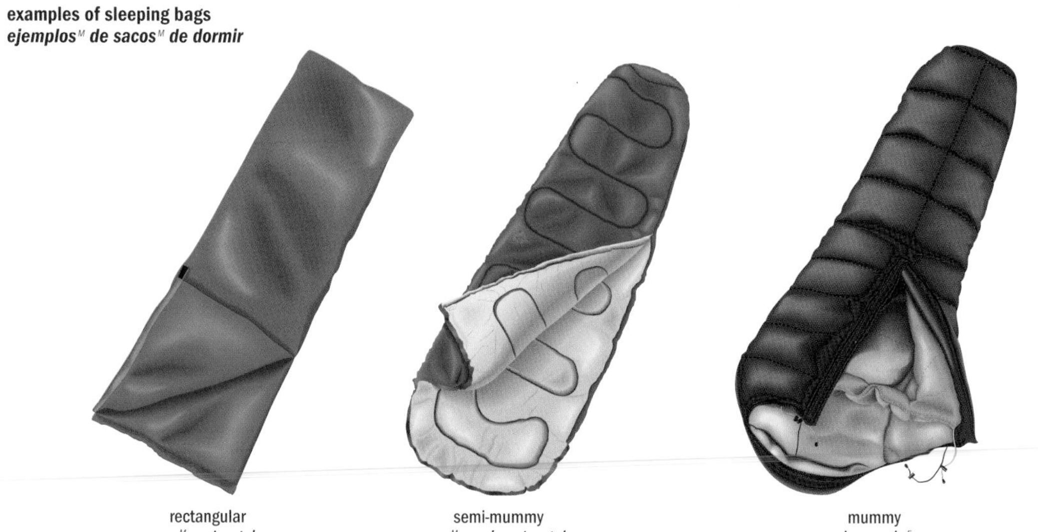

rectangular
saco^M rectangular

semi-mummy
saco^M semirrectangular

mummy
de momia^F

bed and mattress
camas^F y colchonetas^F

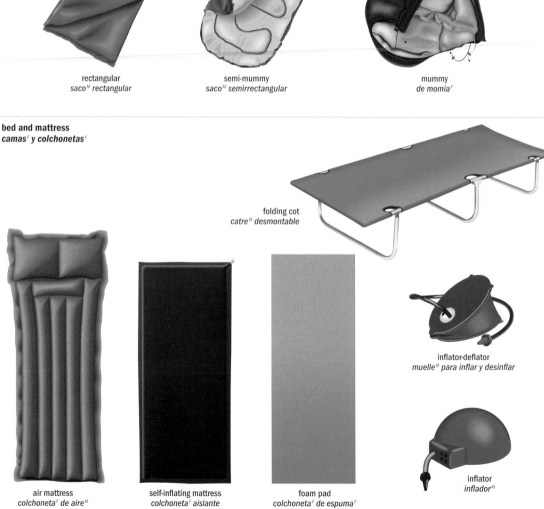

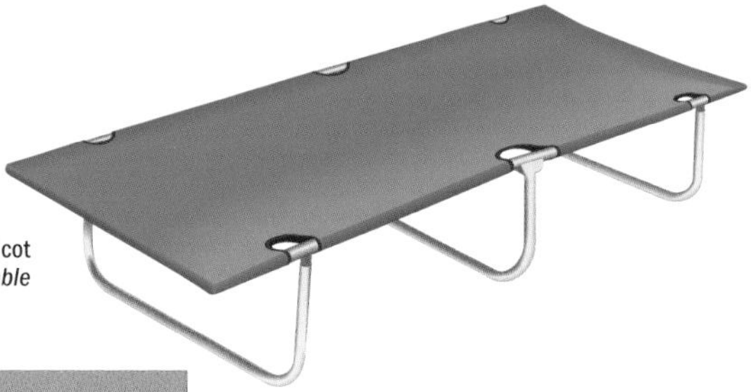

folding cot
catre^M desmontable

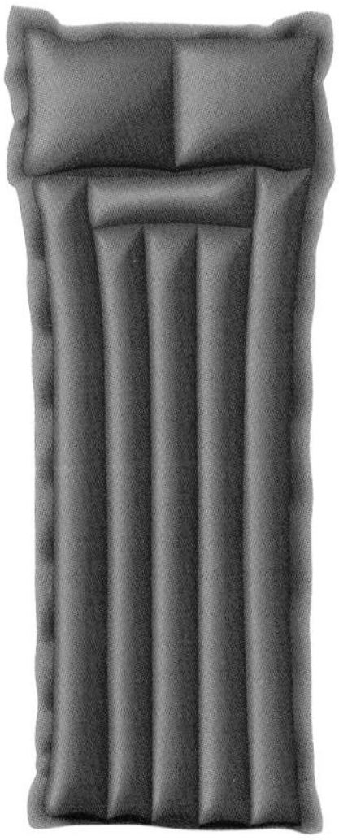

air mattress
colchoneta^F de aire^M

self-inflating mattress
colchoneta^F aislante

foam pad
colchoneta^F de espuma^F

inflator-deflator
muelle^M para inflar y desinflar

inflator
inflador^M

cutlery set
cubertería[F]

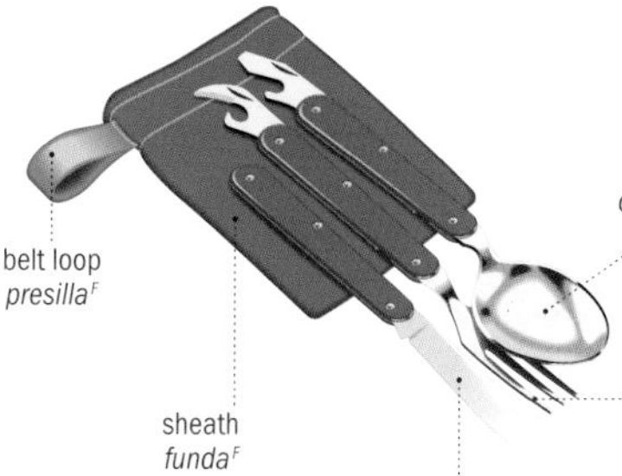

belt loop
presilla[F]

sheath
funda[F]

spoon
cuchara[F]

fork
tenedor[M]

knife
cuchillo[M]

cooking set
utensilios[M] de cocina[F]

plate
plato[M]

saucepan
cazuela[F]

handle
mango[M]

frying pan
sartén[F]

coffee pot
cafetera[F]

cup
taza[F]

camping equipment
equipamiento[M] para acampar

Swiss Army knife
navaja[F] multiusos suiza

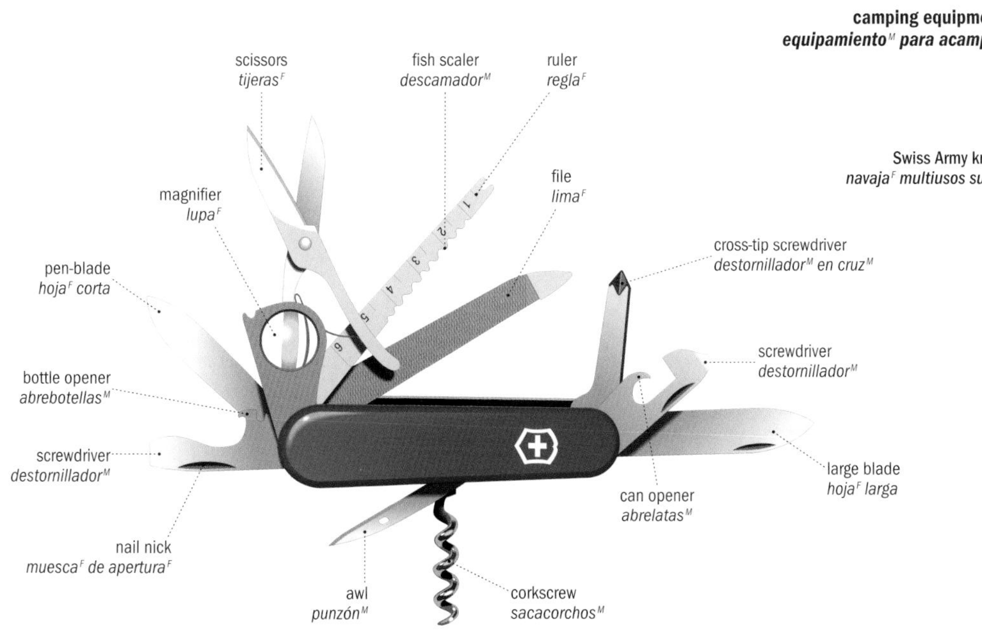

camping

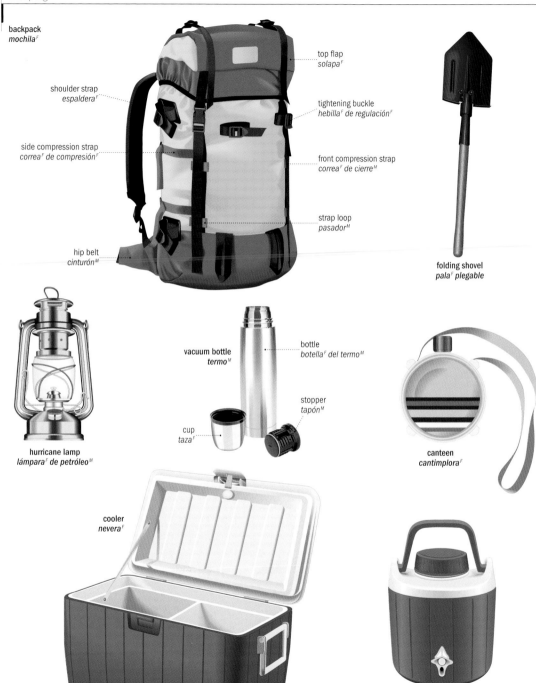

backpack
mochila[F]

top flap
solapa[F]

shoulder strap
espaldera[F]

tightening buckle
hebilla[F] *de regulación*[F]

side compression strap
correa[F] *de compresión*[F]

front compression strap
correa[F] *de cierre*[M]

strap loop
pasador[M]

hip belt
cinturón[M]

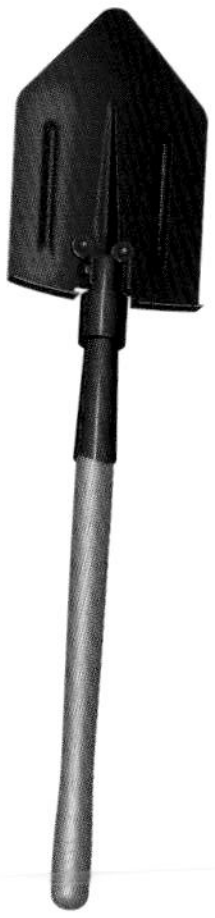

folding shovel
pala*[F] *plegable

hurricane lamp
***lámpara*[F] *de petróleo*[M]**

vacuum bottle
***termo*[M]**

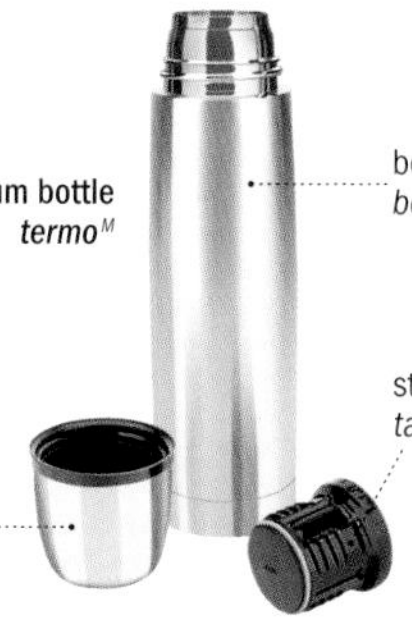

bottle
botella[F] *del termo*[M]

stopper
tapón[M]

cup
taza[F]

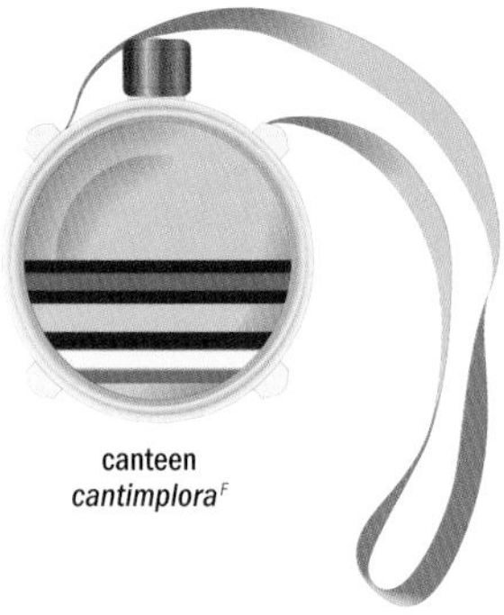

canteen
***cantimplora*[F]**

cooler
***nevera*[F]**

water carrier
***termo*[M] *con llave*[F] *de servicio*[M]**

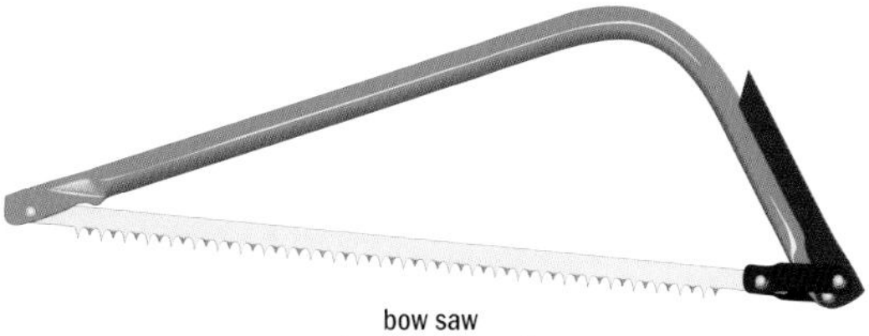

bow saw
sierra[F] de campo[M]

knife
cuchillo[M]

hatchet
hacha[F]

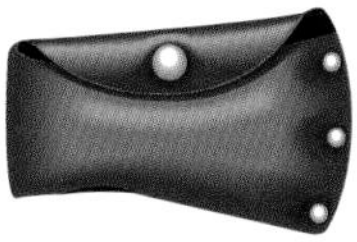

leather sheath
funda[F] de cuero[M]

sheath
funda[F]

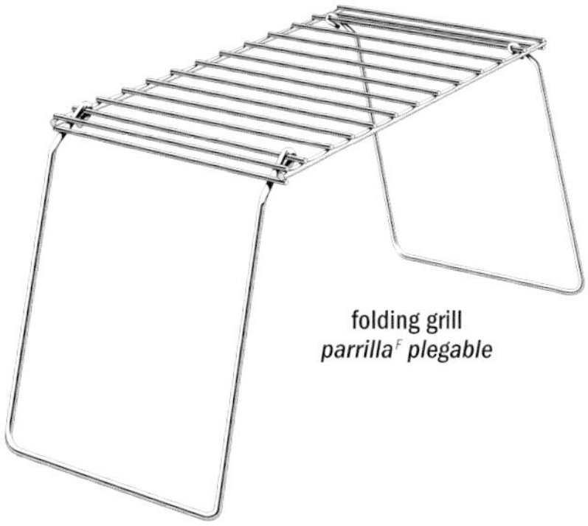

folding grill
parrilla[F] plegable

magnetic compass
brújula[F] magnética

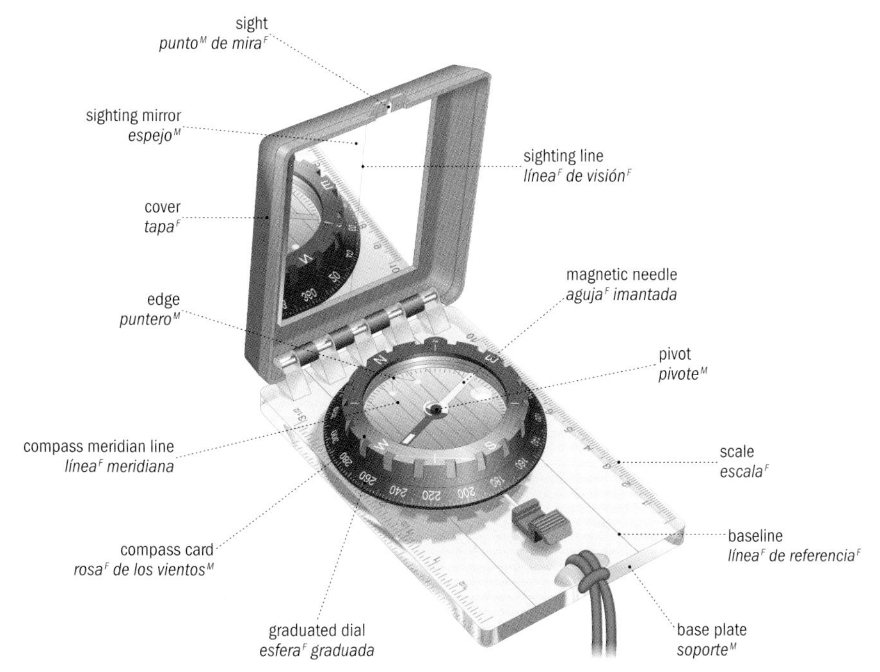

hunting

caza^F

rifle (rifled bore)
rifle^M

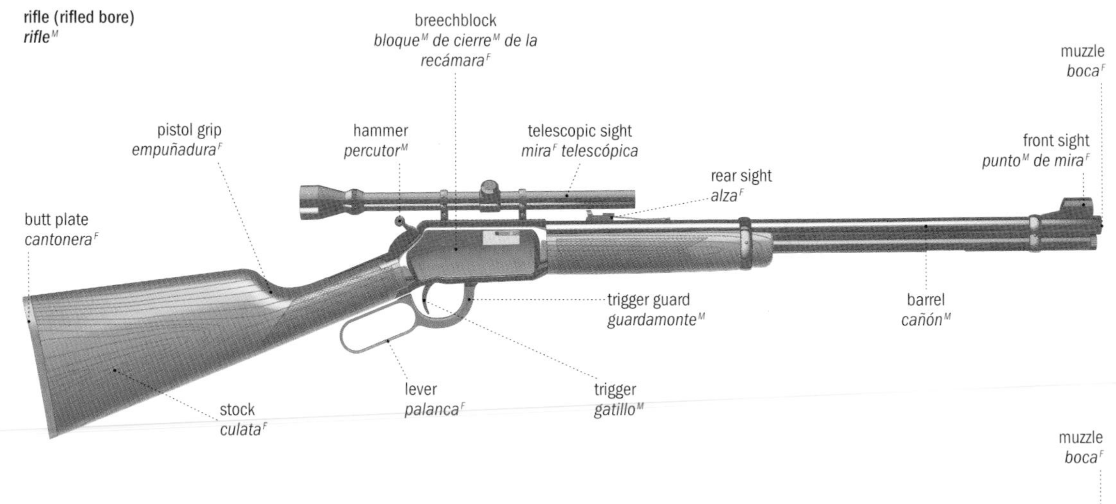
breechblock
bloque^M de cierre^M de la recámara^F
muzzle
boca^F
pistol grip
empuñadura^F
hammer
percutor^M
telescopic sight
mira^F telescópica
front sight
punto^M de mira^F
rear sight
alza^F
butt plate
cantonera^F
trigger guard
guardamonte^M
barrel
cañón^M
lever
palanca^F
trigger
gatillo^M
stock
culata^F
muzzle
boca^F
shotgun (smooth-bore)
escopeta^F
hammer
percutor^M
ventilated rib
banda^F de ventilación^F
front sight
punto^M de mira^F
pistol grip
empuñadura^F
butt plate
cantonera^F
barrel
cañón^M
breechblock
bloque^M de cierre^M de recámara^F
forearm
caña^F
trigger guard
guardamonte^M
trigger
gatillo^M
stock
culata^F

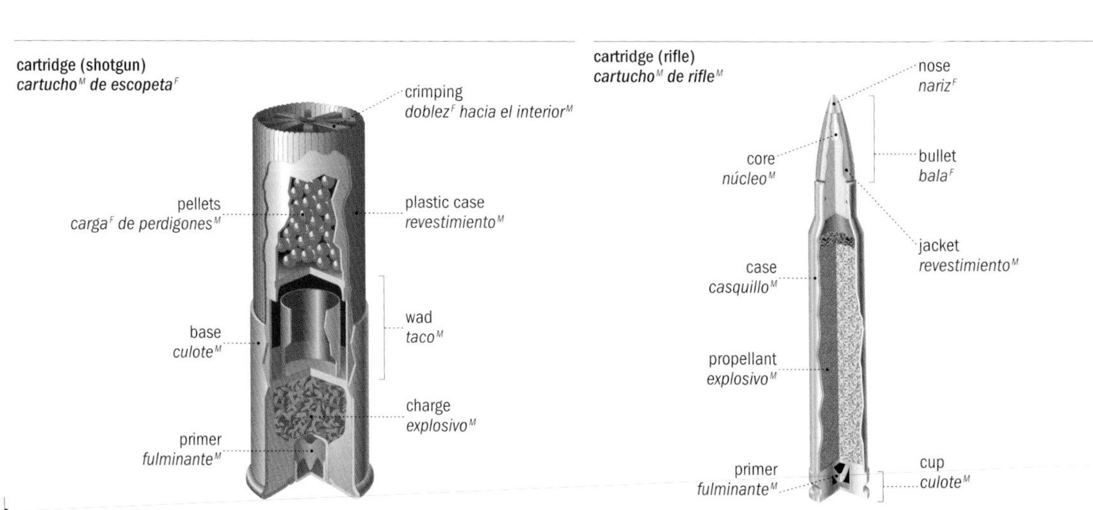
cartridge (shotgun)
cartucho^M de escopeta^F
crimping
doblez^F hacia el interior^M
pellets
carga^F de perdigones^M
plastic case
revestimiento^M
base
culote^M
wad
taco^M
charge
explosivo^M
primer
fulminante^M
cartridge (rifle)
cartucho^M de rifle^M
nose
nariz^F
core
núcleo^M
bullet
bala^F
jacket
revestimiento^M
case
casquillo^M
propellant
explosivo^M
primer
fulminante^M
cup
culote^M

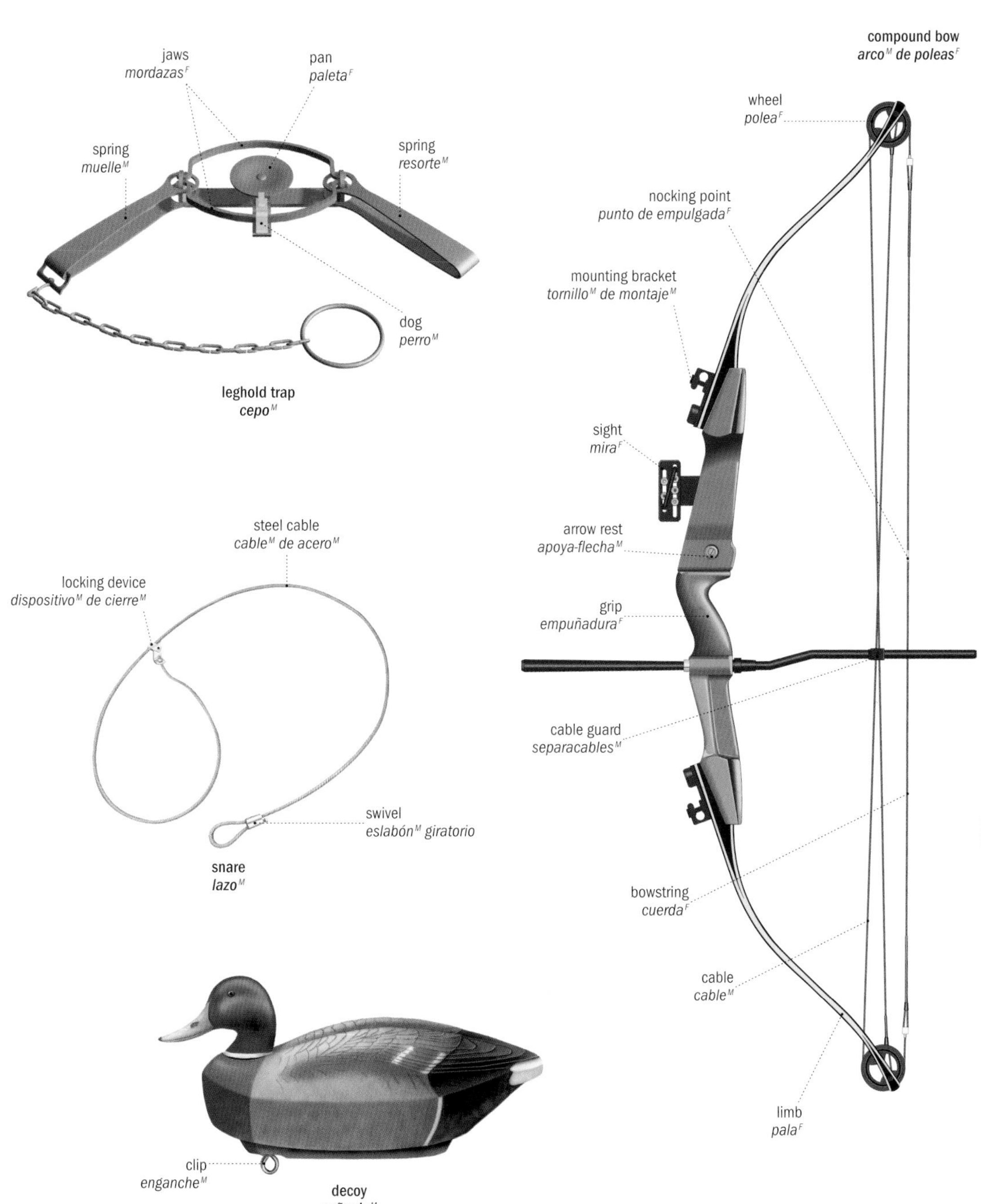
jaws
mordazas F
pan
paleta F
spring
muelle M
spring
resorte M
dog
perro M
leghold trap
cepo M
steel cable
cable M de acero M
locking device
dispositivo M de cierre M
swivel
eslabón M giratorio
snare
lazo M
clip
enganche M
decoy
señuelo M
compound bow
arco M de poleas F
wheel
polea F
nocking point
punto de empulgada F
mounting bracket
tornillo M de montaje M
sight
mira F
arrow rest
apoya-flecha M
grip
empuñadura F
cable guard
separacables M
bowstring
cuerda F
cable
cable M
limb
pala F

fishing

pesca[F]

flyfishing
pesca[F] con mosca[F]

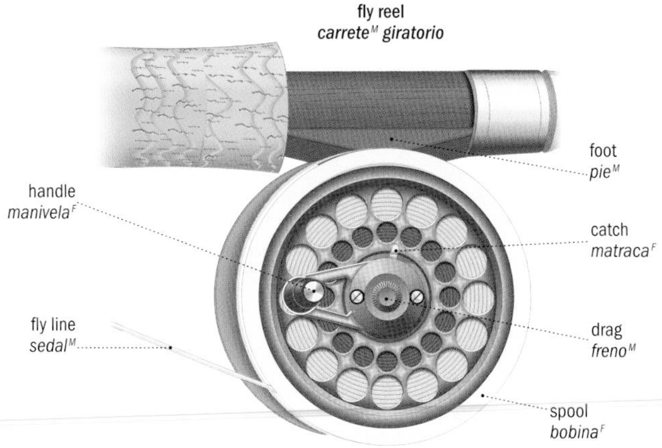

fly reel
carrete[M] giratorio
foot
pie[M]
handle
manivela[F]
catch
matraca[F]
fly line
sedal[M]
drag
freno[M]
spool
bobina[F]

fly rod
caña[F] para mosca[F]

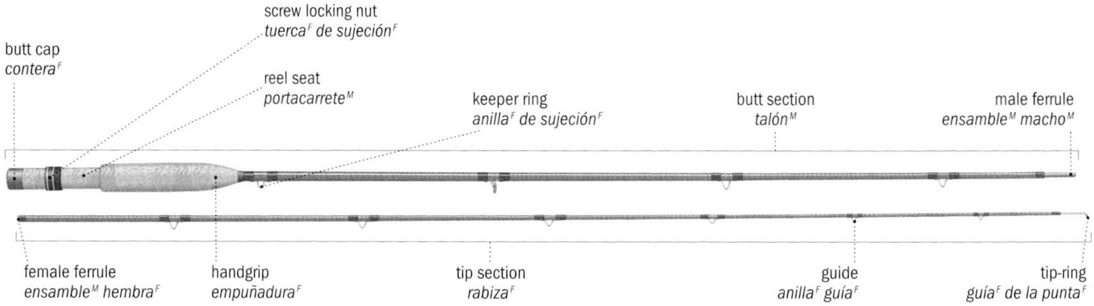

screw locking nut
tuerca[F] de sujeción[F]
butt cap
contera[F]
reel seat
portacarrete[M]
keeper ring
anilla[F] de sujeción[F]
butt section
talón[M]
male ferrule
ensamble[M] macho[M]
female ferrule
ensamble[M] hembra[F]
handgrip
empuñadura[F]
tip section
rabiza[F]
guide
anilla[F] guía[F]
tip-ring
guía[F] de la punta[F]

artificial fly
mosca[F] artificial

wing
ala[F]
topping
copete[M]
ribbing
costilla[F]
veil
velo[M]
cheek
carrillo[M]
tail
cola[F]
joint
articulación[F]
tip
cabo[M]
head
cabeza[F]
shoulder
hombro[M]
butt
talón[M]
body
cuerpo[M]
hackle
pelillo[M]
fishhook
anzuelo[M]

SPORTS AND GAMES

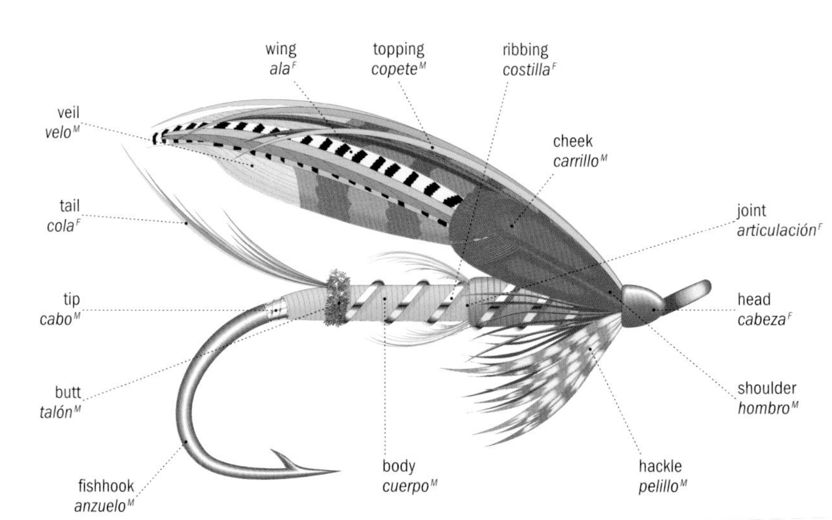

casting
***pesca*ᶠ *de lanzado*ᴹ**

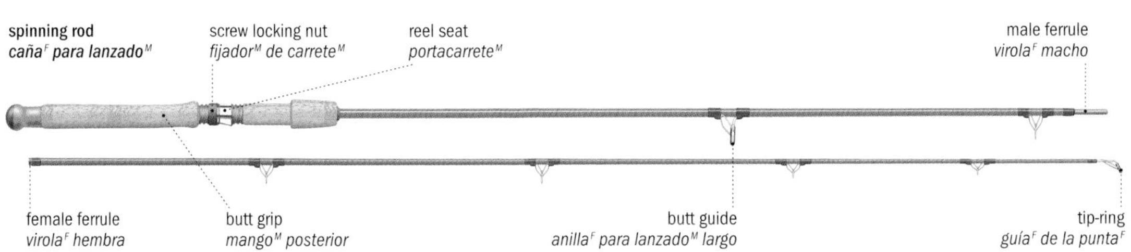

open-face spinning reel
carrete*ᴹ *de bobina*ᶠ *fija

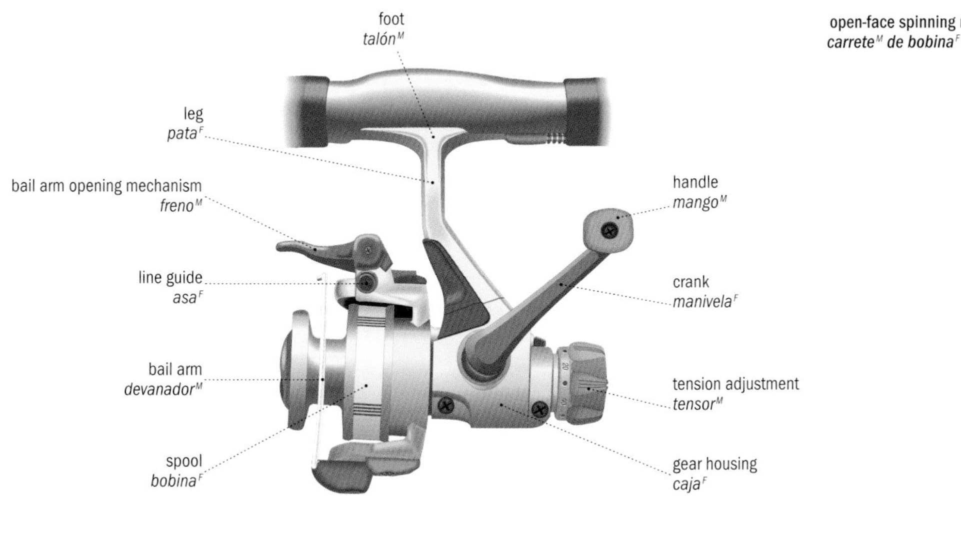

baitcasting reel
***carrete*ᴹ *de tambor*ᴹ**

fishing

fishhook
anzuelo[M]

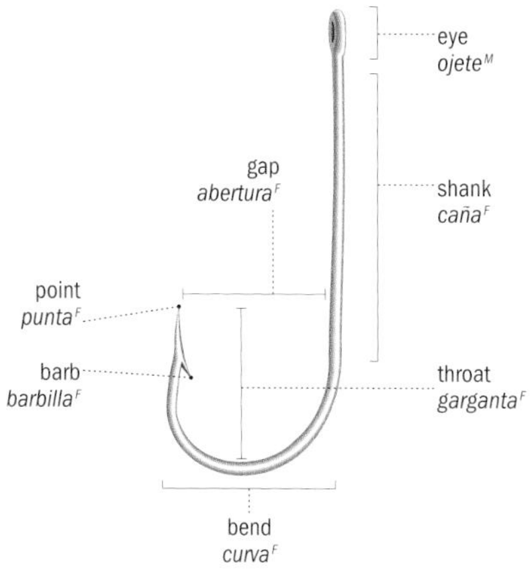

eye
ojete[M]

gap
abertura[F]

shank
caña[F]

point
punta[F]

barb
barbilla[F]

throat
garganta[F]

bend
curva[F]

float tackle
aparejo[M]

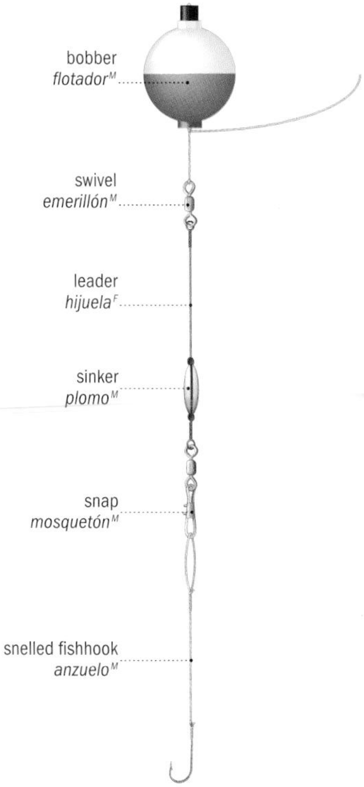

bobber
flotador[M]

swivel
emerillón[M]

leader
hijuela[F]

sinker
plomo[M]

snap
mosquetón[M]

snelled fishhook
anzuelo[M]

spinner
cuchara[F]

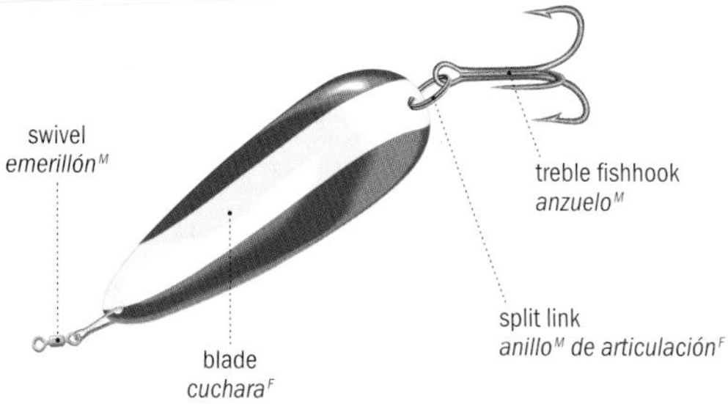

swivel
emerillón[M]

treble fishhook
anzuelo[M]

split link
anillo[M] *de articulación*[F]

blade
cuchara[F]

clothing and accessories
ropa[F] *y accesorios*[M]

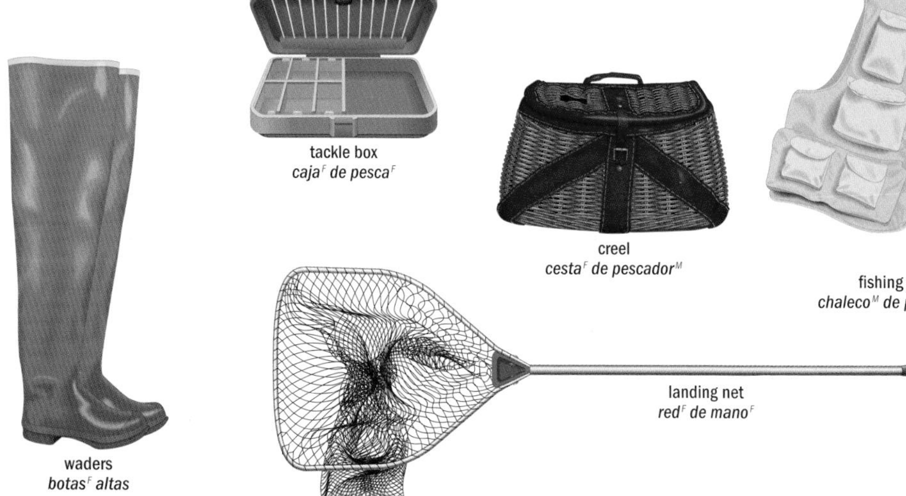

tackle box
caja[F] ***de pesca***[F]

creel
cesta[F] ***de pescador***[M]

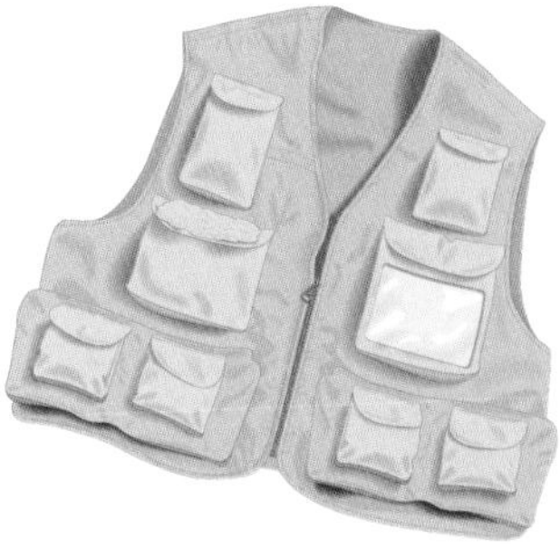

fishing vest
chaleco[M] ***de pescador***[M]

landing net
red[F] ***de mano***[F]

waders
botas[F] ***altas***

English Index

1 astronomical unit 3
1,500 m starting line 473
1/10 second hand 424
10 m line 482
10,000 m relay starting line 473
100 m hurdles starting line 472
100 m starting line 472
110 m hurdles starting line 472
15 m line 483
200 m starting line 472
22 m line 482
35 mm still camera 10
4 x 400 m relay starting line 473
5 m line 483
5,000 m starting line 472
50 astronomical units 2
50,000 astronomical units 2
800 m starting line 473

A

A 298
abalone 157
abdomen 67, 68, 70, 71, 78, 92, 94
abdominal aorta 102, 107
abdominal cavity 111, 112
abdominal segment 67
ablutions fountain 447
aboveground pipeline 404
aboveground swimming pool 184
abruptly pinnate 55
ABS 357
absorbed solar radiation 46
absorbent cotton 461
absorbing plate 410
absorption by clouds 46
absorption by Earth's surface 46
absorption of carbon dioxide 54
absorption of water and mineral salts 54
abutment 284, 344
abyssal hill 33
abyssal plain 33
Abyssinian 87
acanthus leaf 200
acceleration lane 343
accelerator cable 237
accelerator control 235
accent mark 299
access door 423
access gallery 407
access road 388
access server 335
access window 333
accessories 356, 372
accessory pocket 352
accessory shoe 314
accidentals 299
accordion 296
accordion bag 276
accordion pleat 253
account identification 443
accumulator 357
ace 468
achene 59, 60
acid rain 47, 48
acid snow 48
acorn nut 223
acorn squash 129
acoustic ceiling 293
acoustic guitar 302
acoustic meatus 115, 116
acrobatic skate 527
acromion 99
acroterion 279
action buttons 471
actor 290
actors' seats 290
actress 291
actuator arm 333
acute angle 428
Adam's apple 92
add key 337
add to memory 337
additive color synthesis 418
adductor longus 96
adductor magnus 97
Aden, Gulf 19, 20
adhesive bandage 461
adhesive disk 75
adhesive tape 461
adipose tissue 113, 114
adjustable channel 222
adjustable clamp 206
adjustable frame 226
adjustable lamp 206
adjustable strap 260
adjustable thermostat 179
adjustable waist tab 244
adjuster 466
adjusting band 324
adjusting buckle 527
adjusting catch 511
adjusting screw 222, 224
adjustment knob 353
adjustment slide 246
administration 445
adobe house 288
Adriatic Sea 18
adult skull, lateral view 100
adventitious roots 52
advertisement 313
advertising panel 378
advertising poster 380
adzuki beans 131
Aegean Sea 18
aerial cable network 316
aerial ladder truck 455
aerocyst 51
aerodynamic brake 412
affluent 32
Afghanistan 452
Africa 14, 20, 34, 451
African Plate 27
Afro pick 268
aft shroud 7
afterbay 406, 407
aftershave 271
agar-agar 123
agglomeration 430
agitator 212
agricultural pollution 47
aileron 392
air bag 354
air bag restraint system 354
air bubbles 339
air communications 317
air compression unit 376
air concentrator 270
air conditioner 361
air conditioner compressor 360
air conditioning equipment 386
air conditioning system 46
air filter 235, 350
air filter pre-cleaner 401
air hole 312
air horn 364
air inlet 367, 395
air inlet control 192
air intake 362, 383
air intake for engine cooling 525
air mass, type 39
air mattress 530
air pollutants 47
air pollution 47
air pre-cleaner filter 398
air pump 346
air relief valve 385
air scoop 523
air shaft 278
air space 79
air temperature 39
air transport 388
air unit 262
air vent 214
air-inlet grille 270
air-outlet grille 270
air-pressure pump 461
air-supply tube 454
aircraft weather station 38
airliner 37
airplane, movements 395
airport 25, 388, 430
aisle 120, 285
ajowan 139
ala 117
alarm/charge indicator light 337
Alaska, Gulf 16
Albania 450
albatross 80
albumen 79
alcohol bulb 424
alcohol column 424
Aleutian Islands 16
Aleutian Trench 34
alfalfa sprouts 130
alga, structure 51
algae 51
algae, examples 51
Algeria 451
alkaline manganese-zinc cell 417
alkekengi 132
all-purpose flour 144
all-season tire 358
all-terrain vehicle 369
alley 490, 495
alligator 77
allspice 138
alluvial deposits 32
almonds 133
alphabetical keypad 338
alphanumeric keyboard 346, 442, 443
alphanumeric keypad 327, 330
alpine ski trail 512
alpine skier 510
alpine skiing 510
alpine snowboard 513
Alps 18
Alsace glass 165
altar cross 446
altarpiece 446
alternate 330
alternate: level 3 select 330
alternating-current power cord 336
alternative key (Alt) 330
alternator 350, 360, 413
alternator fan belt 360
alternator warning light 355
alternator/fan belt 350
altitude clamp 8, 9
altitude fine adjustment 8, 9
altitude scale 37
altocumulus 42
altostratus 42
alula 78
aluminum foil 162
aluminum recycling container 49
alveolar bone 101
amaranth 143
Amazon River 17
ambulance 460, 462
ambulatory 285
ambulatory care unit 465
American bacon 156
American corn bread 145
American football 484
American football, playing field 484
American mustard 140
American outlet 198
American plug 198
Americas 448
Amery Ice Shelf 15
ammunition pouch 456
amoeba 66
amorphous solid 414
amount of substance, unit 426
ampere 426
amphibians, examples 75
amphibious firefighting aircraft 394
amphitheater, Roman 281
ampli-tuner 322, 325
amplitude 418
ampulla of fallopian tube 113
anal clasper 67
anal fin 74
analog camcorder 320
analog watch 424
analytical balance 423
anatomy 96
anatomy of a bivalve shell 73
anatomy of a male lobster 71
anatomy, human being 96
anchor 473
anchor pin 357
anchor point 70
anchor-windlass room 383, 387
anchorage block 344
anchovy 159
anconeus 97
Andes Cordillera 17
andirons 193
Andorra 449
andouillette 156
anemometer 413
anesthesia room 464
angles, examples 428
Angola 452
Anik 317
animal cell 66
animal dung 48
anise 142
ankle 92, 94
ankle boot 241
ankle guard 476

ankle length 247
ankle sock 257
ankle/wrist weights 500
annual ring 63
annular eclipse 4
anode 417
anorak 263
ant 69
Antarctic Circle 15, 21, 22
Antarctic Peninsula 15
Antarctic Plate 27
Antarctic Ridge 34
Antarctica 14, 15
antefix 279
antelope 84
antenna 7, 67, 68, 71, 326, 327, 349, 369, 392, 395, 457, 487
antenna terminals 322
antennule 71
anterior adductor muscle 73
anterior chamber 119
anterior end 73
anterior fontanelle 100
anterior horn 109
anterior nasal spine 100
anterior notch 115
anterior root 110
anterior tibial artery 102
anterior view 92, 94, 96, 98
anther 56
anti-torque tail rotor 395
anticline 403
anticollision light 392
antifriction pad 511
Antigua and Barbuda 449
antihelix 115
antilock braking system 357
antireflection coating 410
antiseptic 461
antislip shoe 219
antitragus 115
antivibration handle 235
anus 71, 73, 106, 111, 112
anvil 425
aorta 104, 105
aorta, arch 102, 103, 104
aortic valve 104
apartment building 433
aperture 73
aperture door 7
apex 72, 73, 101, 118
apical foramen 101
apocrine sweat gland 114
apothecium 50
Appalachian Mountains 16
apple 133
apple cider vinegar 141
apple corer 173
apple, section 58
application launch buttons 337
appoggiatura 299
appointment book 338
approach 473
approach ramp 344
approach runs 496
apricot 132
apron 200, 201, 202, 369, 388, 498
apse 285
apsidiole 284, 285
aquatic bird 79
aqueous humor 119
Arabian Peninsula 19
Arabian Sea 19
arachnids, examples 70
arachnoid 109
Aral Sea 19
arame 123
arbor 230
arc 428
arcade 281, 284
arch of aorta 102, 103, 104
arch of foot artery 102
archboard 340
archipelago 24
architecture 278
architecture, elements 286
architrave 279
Arctic 14
Arctic Circle 21, 22
Arctic Ocean 14
arena 281, 472
Arenberg parquet 190
areola 113
Argentina 448
Ariel 3
ark 447
arm 91, 93, 95, 200, 206, 236, 297, 421, 467
arm guard 486
arm lock 499
arm slit 251
arm stump 200
armchair 200
armchairs, examples 200
Armenia 452
armhole 247
armless chair 444
armoire 202
armpit 92, 94
armrest 205, 352, 353, 467
armstand 518
arpeggio 299
arrector pili muscle 114
arrow rest 535
art director 290
art room 444
arteries 102
artichoke 127
article 313
articulated bus 363
articulated joint 363
articulation 355
artificial fly 536
artificial lake 32
artificial satellite 37
arugula 127
asafetida 139
ascending aorta 103
ascending colon 106
ascending passage 278
ascot tie 245
ash layer 28
Asia 14, 19, 34, 452
Asian noodles 147
Asian pear 137
asparagus 125
asphalt 405
asphalt still 405
ass 84
assist grip 352
assistant camera operator 290
assistant coach 489, 507
assistant director 291
assistant property person 291
assistant referee 509
asteroid belt 3
asthenosphere 26
astigmatism 419
astronomical observatory 7
astronomical observatory, cross section 7
astronomical unit 3
astronomy 2
Atacama Desert 17
athlete 473
athletic shirt 247
Atlantic cod 161
Atlantic Ocean 14, 15, 18, 20
Atlantic salmon 161
atlas 99
atlas moth 69
Atlas Mountains 20
ATM 442, 443
atmosphere 44, 48
atoll 35
atom 414
atoms 414
atrium 280
attaché case 274
attachment storage area 209
attachments 209
attack line 487
attack zone 487
attitude control thrusters 12
attraction 416
audience 440
audio input/output jack 337
audio jack 329
audio system 354
audiometric examination room 465
auditory meatus, external 100
auditory ossicles 116
auger bit, solid center 228
auricle 116
auricle, ear 115
auriculars 78
Australia 14, 34, 453
Australian-Indian Plate 27
Austria 450
authorized landfill site 47
auto answer indicator 328
auto-reverse button 326
autoclave 464
automatic dialer index 327
automatic drip coffee maker 181
automatic electronic timer 517
automatic sliding door 286
automatic teller machine 443
automatic teller machine (ATM) 442
automatically controlled door 390
automobile 347
automobile car 377
automobile systems 350, 351
autotrophs 45
autumn 38
autumn squash 129
autumnal equinox 38
auxiliary handle 228
auxiliary tank 365
avenue 25, 433
avocado 128
awl 531
awning channel 361
axe 234
axel 509
axial rib 73
axillary artery 102
axillary bud 53
axillary nerve 108
axillary vein 102
axis 99
axle 527
axle shaft 351
axon 110
axon hillock 110
Azerbaijan 452
azimuth clamp 8, 9
azimuth fine adjustment 8, 9
Aztec temple 283

B

B 298
baboon 91
baby doll 256
back 78, 83, 86, 93, 95, 115, 167, 169, 201, 205, 226, 244, 467
back boundary line 494
back brush 267
back judge 485
back line 515
back of a glove 243
back pocket 246
back ribs 152
back suspension 522
back zone 487
backboard 489
backboard support 489
backcourt 491
backdrop 292
backgammon 469
backguard 210, 212, 213
backhoe 399
backhoe controls 399
backing plate 357
backpack 532
backrest 353, 369, 523
backspace 331
backspace key 331
backstay 509
backstop 474, 489
backstroke 517
backstroke turn indicator 517
backward 518
backward bucket 399
bacon 156
bactrian camel 85
badge 456
badger 88
badminton 494
badminton racket 494
Baffin Island 16
bag compartment 209
bag well 505
bagel 144
baggage cart 374
baggage check-in counter 390
baggage claim area 390
baggage compartment 362, 376, 395
baggage lockers 374
baggage racks 383
baggage room 374
bagger 121
bagpipes 296
baguette 144
Bahamas 448
Bahrain 452
Baikal, Lake 19
bail 479
bail arm 537
bail arm opening mechanism 537
bailey 282
baitcasting reel 537
baize 502
bakery 121
baking sheet 172
baking utensils 172
balaclava 239, 524
balalaika 297
balance beam 496, 497
balance control 322
balancer 303
balcony 189, 293, 447
balcony door 189
baling 49
balk area 502
balk line 502
balk line spot 502
Balkan Peninsula 18
ball 332
ball bearing 312, 413
ball boy 490
ball mount 356
ball peen 220
ball sports 474
ball-cock supply valve 196
ball-peen hammer 220
ballerina slipper 241
ballpoint pen 312
ballroom 387
balsamic vinegar 141
Baltic Sea 18
baluster 191
balustrade 283
bamboo shoot 125
banana 136
band ring 264
band select button 322
Bangladesh 453
bangle 264
banister 188, 189, 191
banjo 296
bank 342, 432, 437, 442, 469
banknote 441
banknote, back 441
banknote, front 441
banner 313
banquette 201
baptismal font 446
bar 273, 293, 309, 432, 436, 438, 469, 500, 501
bar counter 438
bar frame 207
bar line 298
bar nose 235
bar stool 201, 438
barb 538
Barbados 449
barbell 500, 501
barber comb 268
barbican 282
Barbuda 449
Barents Sea 18
bark 63
barley 61, 143
barley: spike 61
barn 122
barometric pressure 39
barometric tendency 39
barrel 269, 270, 312, 471, 534
barrel vault 281
barrette 268
barrier 205, 434
barrier barricade tape 457
barrier beach 35
bartender 438
bartizan 282
basaltic layer 26
base 54, 179, 180, 192, 199, 206, 227, 229, 269, 283, 318, 332, 342, 412, 421, 422, 454, 473, 534
base cabinet 164
base course 342
base of splat 200
base plate 227, 511, 533
baseball 474, 476
baseball, cross section 477
baseboard 191
baseline 491, 533
basement 182, 435
basement window 183
basic source of food 45
basil 142
basilic vein 102
basin wrench 216
basket 178, 181, 211, 212, 489, 510
basket weave pattern 190
basketball 488
basketball player 488
basmati rice 147
bass 160
bass bridge 304
bass clarinet 295
bass clef 298
bass drum 295, 308
bass guitar 303
bass keyboard 296
bass pickup 303
bass register 296
Bass Strait 15
bass tone control 303, 322, 325
bassoon 306
bassoons 295
baster 173
bat 476, 477, 478
bath 194, 439
bath brush 267
bath sheet 267
bath towel 267
bathing wrap 260
bathrobe 256
bathroom 188, 189, 195, 439, 445, 464
bathroom scale 423
bathroom skylight 189
bathtub 189, 195
baton 472
baton holder 456
batsman 478, 479
batten 292, 519, 520
batten pocket 519, 520
batter 475, 476
batter head 308
batter skin 297
batter's helmet 476
battery 221, 350, 359, 411, 416
battery box 365
battery case 359
battery cover 359
battery pack 228
batting glove 476

battlement 282
bay 5, 24
bay filler panel 329
Bay of Bengal 19
bayonet base 199
beach 35
bead 358
beak 90
beaker 171
beam 283, 288, 422
beam balance 422
beam bridge 344
bean bag chair 201
bean thread cellophane noodles 147
beans 130, 131
bearing pad 409
beater 176
beater ejector 176
beaters 176
Beaufort Sea 16
beauty care 121
beaver 82
becquerel 426
bed 204, 342, 530
bed chamber 280
bedrock 27, 54
bedroom 189, 528
bedside lamp 439, 464
bedside table 439, 464
beech 64
beechnut 133
beef cubes 152
beef, cuts 152
beer 120
beer mug 165
beet 129
begonia 56
Belarus 450
belfry 284, 285
Belgian endive 127
Belgium 449
Belize 448
bell 306, 307
bell bottoms 254
bell brace 306
bell tower 285, 446
bellows 296
bellows strap 296
bells 309
belly 83
below-stage 292
belt 225, 246, 248, 499
belt clip 327
belt drive 383
belt highway 25
belt loader 402
belt loop 246, 248, 531
bench 201, 379, 437, 501
bench seat 353
bend 273, 538
Bengal, Bay 19
Benin 451
beret 239
bergamot 134
bergère 200
bergschrund 30
Bering Sea 14
Bering Strait 16
Bermuda shorts 254
berries 132
berry fruit 59
bevel 460
bevel square 225
beverage can 163
beverage dispenser 463
Bhutan 453
bib 260, 261
bib necklace 264
biceps brachii 96
biceps femoris 97
biconcave lens 419
biconvex lens 419
bicycle 370
bicycle bag (pannier) 372
bicycle parking 445
bicycle, accessories 372
bicycle, parts 370
bicycles, examples 373
bidet 195
bike carrier 356
bikini 259
bikini briefs 247
bilberries 132
bill 78
bill compartment 274
bill presenter 442
bill-file 341
billfold 275
billhook 234
billiard cue 503
billiard spot 502
billiards 502
billiards, carom 502
billiards, English 503
bills, examples 79
bimah 447
binding 238, 513, 514
binocular microscope 421
biology 426
biosphere 44
biosphere, structure 44
biparous cyme 57
birch 64
bird 78
bird of prey 79
bird's eye chile 139
bird's nest fern 52
bird, morphology 78
birds 78
birds, examples 80
birth 426
bishop 470
bison 84
bit 221, 403
bits 228
bitt 385
bitter melon 128
bivalve shell 73
bivalve shell, anatomy 73
bivalve shell, morphology 73
Black 470
black 418
black ball 503
black beans 131
black bear 89
black clamp 356
black currants 132
black gram beans 131
black mustard 138
black pepper 138
black pollock 161
black radishes 129
black rye bread 144
black salsify 129
Black Sea 14, 18, 19
black square 470
black stone 470
black tea 148
black-eyed peas 130
blackberries 132
blade 52, 55, 167, 169, 177, 180, 198, 216, 219, 221, 226, 227, 229, 235, 270, 271, 398, 401, 412, 413, 493, 506, 509, 538
blade close stop 270
blade injector 271
blade lift cylinder 398
blade lift fan 383
blade locking bolt 227
blade rotation cylinder 401
blade shifting mechanism 401
blade tilting lock 227
blade tilting mechanism 227
blade-lift cylinder 401
blank 468
blanket 204
blanket sleepers 261
blastodisc 79
blazer 254
blender 176
blending 176
blending attachment 176
blind spot mirror 362, 363
blinking lights 362
block 215, 305, 473
blocking glove 507
blood circulation 102
blood circulation, schema 103
blood factor RH negative 426
blood factor RH positive 426
blood pressure monitor 461
blood sausage 156
blood vessel 104, 114
blood, composition 104
blow pipe 296
blowhole 90
blucher oxford 240
blue 418
blue ball 503
blue beam 318
blue line 507
blue mussels 157
blue-veined cheeses 151
blueberries 132
bluefish 160
blusher brush 266
BMX bike 373
boa 77
board 470, 519
board games 469
boarding room 391
boarding step 395
boarding walkway 389
boards 506
boater 238
boats 382
bobber 538
bobby pin 268
bobeche 207
bodies, examples 347
body 118, 180, 208, 228, 302, 303, 305, 306, 348, 361, 420, 523, 536
body care 267
body flap 13
body of fornix 109
body of nail 114
body side molding 349
body suit 255, 258
body temperature control unit 10
body tube 421
bok choy 126
bole 63
bolero 254
Bolivia 448
bolster 167, 169, 204
bolt 222, 223, 224
bolts 223
bongos 309
boning knife 169
bony fish 74
bony fishes 159
book ends 341
bookcase 444
booking hall 374
bookstore 436
boom 364, 399, 400, 520
boom cylinder 399, 400
boom operator 291
boom swing hinge pin 399
boom vang 520
booster parachute 12
booster seat 205
boot 241, 509, 514, 525, 527
bootee 240
booth 438
borage 142
bordeaux glass 165
border 182, 293
borders 292
boreal forest 44
Bosnia and Herzegovina 450
Bothnia, Gulf 18
Botswana 452
bottle 267, 532
bottle opener 170, 531
bottom 510
bottom bracket axle 372
bottom cap 417
bottom deck 404
bottom deckboard 396
bottom line 517
bottom pocket 502
bottom rail 185, 202
bottom-fold portfolio 274
boulevard 25, 433
bow 238, 301, 387, 519, 520
bow door 383
bow loading door 386
bow saw 533
bow thruster 387
bow tie 245
bow-winged grasshopper 69
bowl 167, 177, 180, 400
bowl with serving spout 177
bowler 479
bowling alley 436
bowling crease 479
bowstring 535
box 192, 293
box bag 276
box end wrench 223
box office 294
box spring 204
boxer 498
boxer shorts 247, 263
boxing 498
boxing gloves 498
boxing trunks 498
bra 259
brace 187, 219
bracelets 264
brachial artery 102
brachial plexus 108
brachialis 96
brachioradialis 96, 97
bracket 283
bracket base 202
bract 60
brain 71
brains 154
brake 467, 501, 522
brake arm 511
brake booster 350, 357
brake cable 371
brake caliper 366
brake fluid reservoir 357
brake handle 523
brake lever 371, 522
brake light 352
brake line 357
brake lining 357
brake pad 357
brake pedal 350, 354, 357, 511
brake pressure modulator 357
brake shoe 357
brakes 357
braking circuit 357
braking system 351
branch 62, 63, 65, 125, 194, 416, 460
branch clip 460
branches 63
branching, examples 197
brandy snifter 165
brass section 295
brattice 282
brazier 283
Brazil 448
Brazil nuts 133
bread 144
bread and butter plate 166
bread guide 178
bread knife 169
bread machine 179
break 331
breaker 33
breast 78, 92, 94, 113
breast dart 248
breast pocket 245, 248
breast welt pocket 244
breaststroke 517
breech 306
breech guard 306
breechblock 534
brick carton 163
bricklayer's hammer 216
bridge 25, 273, 297, 301, 302, 303, 381, 420, 503
bridge assembly 303
bridges 344
bridging 187
Brie 151
briefcase 274
briefs 247, 259
brightness control 329
brim 238, 239
bristle 271, 272
bristles 219
broad beans 130
broad ligament of uterus 113
broad welt side pocket 251
broad-welt side pocket 248
broadcast satellite communication 316
broadleaved trees, examples 64
broccoli 127
broccoli rabe 127
brochure rack 442
broken line 342, 343
brook 32
brook trout 161
broom 193, 215
brow brush and lash comb 266
brown alga 51
brown ball 503
brown rice 147
brown sugar 149
browser 334
Brunei 453
brush 61, 209, 215, 219, 272
brussels sprouts 126
bubble 367
bubble bath 267
bucket 399
bucket cylinder 399, 400
bucket lever 399
bucket seat 353
buckle 246, 276, 353, 511
buckwheat 61, 143
buckwheat: raceme 61
bud 54
buffalo 84
buffer 287
buffer tank 404
buffet 203, 438
bugle 307
building sewer 194
bulb 125, 199, 217, 385, 416
bulb dibble 231
bulb vegetables 124
bulb, section 54
bulbil 54
bulbocavernous muscle 111
Bulgaria 450
bulge 6
bulk carrier 382
bulk terminal 381
bull's-eye 471
bulldog 86
bulldozer 398
bullet 534
bulletin board 341, 444
bumblebee 69
bump 487
bumper 209, 364, 369, 375
bumper molding 348
bunch 522
bunch of grapes 62
bundle 125
bunk 361
bunker oil 405
bunker silo 122
bunting bag 260
buoy weather station 38
burdock 129
burgundy glass 165
burial 49
Burkina Faso 451
Burma 453
burner 174, 210, 529
burner control knobs 210
burner frame 529
burner ring 174

Burundi 451
bus 435
bus shelter 434
bus station 432
bus stop 434
busbar 407
buses 362
bush 230
bush-cricket 69
bushing 406, 407
business aircraft 394
business district 430, 432
business transactions 335
business wicket 443
butane accessories 529
butcher's counter 120
butt 492, 494, 503, 536
butt cap 536
butt end 506
butt grip 537
butt guide 537
butt plate 534
butt section 536
butt-strap 273
butte 36
butter 150
butter compartment 211
butter cup 163
butter curler 169
butter dish 166
butter knife 168
butter lettuce 126
butterfly stroke 517
butterfly, morphology 67
buttermilk 150
buttock 93, 95, 111, 112
button 199, 245, 250, 296
button loop 246
button strap 261
buttondown collar 245
buttoned placket 245, 250
buttonhole 248
buttress 284
by-pass taxiway 388

C

C 298
C clef 298
C-clamp 224
cab 398, 399, 400, 401, 523
cabbage 126
cabin 386, 395
cabinet 164, 211, 212, 213, 318
cable 228, 326, 332, 356, 364, 501, 535
cable distributor 316
cable guard 535
cable line 335
cable modem 335
cable sleeve 228
caboose 377
cabriole leg 200
cabriolet 200
cafeteria 445
cage 281
caiman 77
cajun spice seasoning 139
cake mascara 266
cake pan 172
calcaneus 99
calculator 274
calculator, pocket 337
calculator, printing 337
calendar pad 338
calf 84, 93, 95
California, Gulf 16
caliper 357
call button 287
Callisto 2
calls indicator 328
calyx 56, 59, 60, 107
cambium 63
Cambodia 453
camel 85
Camembert 151
camera 290, 525
camera body 314
camera operator 290
Cameroon 451
camisole 258
camp stove 529
camping 528
camping equipment 531
camping trailers 361
camshaft 360
can opener 170, 180, 531
Canada 448
Canadian bacon 156
canal lock 381
canary melon 135
cancel button 333
candela 426
candle 446
candy thermometer 171
cane pen 312
canine 101
canisters 162
canned goods 121
cannelloni 146
cannon 83
canopy 273, 286, 361, 394, 401, 528
cantaloupe 135
canteen 532
cantilever bridge 344
cantilever span 344
canvas 498
canvas divider 528
cap 52, 176, 191, 238, 312, 412, 456, 467, 516
cap iron 229
capacitor 417
cape 24, 251
Cape Horn 17
Cape of Good Hope 20
Cape Verde 451
capillary blood vessel 114
capillary bore 424
capital 23
capitals lock 330
capitals lock key 330
capitulum 57
capon 155
capped tee 193
capsule 51, 467
capsule, section 60
captain's quarters 387
caption 313
capture 470
car 521
car ceiling 287
car coat 251
car cover 356
car dealer 433
car deck 386
car floor 287
car guide rail 287
car racing 524
car safety 287
car wash 346
carafe 181
carambola 137
carapace 71, 76
caraway 138
carbon rod 417
carbon-zinc cell 417
carburetor 366
card 469
card case 274
card number 441, 443
card reader 321
card reader slot 442, 443
card-reader slot 346
cardamom 138
cardholder's name 441
cardholder's signature 441
cardiac stomach 71
cardigan 250, 255
cardinal 80
cardoon 125
cards 468
cargo aircraft 394
cargo bay 12
cargo bay door 13
Caribbean Islands 448
Caribbean Plate 27
Caribbean Sea 14, 16
caribou 84
carina 74
carnation 56
carnivores 45
carnivorous mammals 86
carnivorous mammals, examples 88
carom billiards 502
carp 160
Carpathian Mountains 18
Carpentaria, Gulf 15
carpenter's hammer 220
carpentry material 225
carpentry: drilling tools 228
carpentry: nailing tools 220
carpentry: sawing tools 226
carpentry: screw-driving tools 221
carpet 190
carriage 396
carrier 369, 370
carrier bag 276
carrot 129
carry-on bag 276
cart path 504
cartilaginous fish 74
cartilaginous fishes 158
cartography 21
carton 163
cartoon 313
cartridge 216, 312, 459
cartridge (rifle) 534
cartridge (shotgun) 534
cartwheel hat 239
carving fork 169
carving knife 169
casaba melon 135
case 225, 265, 304, 424, 534
case fan 329
casement 186
casement window 287
cash dispenser 437, 442
cash register 121
cash supply 443
cashews 133
cashier 121
casing 186, 237
Caspian Sea 14, 19
cassava 124
Cassegrain focus 7
cassette 326, 333
cassette compartment 319, 320
cassette drive 333
cassette eject switch 319
cassette holder 323
cassette player 326
cassette player controls 326
cassette tape deck 323
castanets 295, 309
caster 205, 209, 308
castes 68
casting 537
castle 282
casual shoe 241
cat 87
cat's head 87
catalytic converter 351
catalytic reforming plant 405
catamaran 521
catch 536
catcher 474, 475, 476
catcher's glove 476
catching glove 507
catenary 376
cathedral 284
cathedral ceiling 189
cathedral, plan 285
cathode 417
Catholic church 446
catwalk 292
caudal fin 74, 90
cauliflower 127
caulking gun 216
cave 31, 35
cavernous body 111
cayenne pepper 139
CD/DVD player 471
CD/DVD-ROM drive 329, 336
CD/DVD-ROM eject button 329
cecum 106
cedar of Lebanon 65
ceiling 193
ceiling collar 193
ceiling fixture 206
ceiling joist 187
celeriac 129
celery 125
celestial bodies 2
celiac trunk 103, 107
cell 67, 281
cell body 110
cell membrane 50, 66
cell wall 50
cello 301
cellos 295
cells 416, 440
cellular telephone, portable 327
Celsius 426
Celsius scale 424
celtuce 126
cement 492
cement screed 190
cementum 101
cemetery 25, 433
censer 446
cent 440
center 293, 428, 470, 485, 489, 507
center attacker 487
center back 487
center back vent 244
center circle 481, 488
center console 354
center electrode 359
center face-off circle 507
center field 475
center fielder 474
center flag 480
center keelson 385
center line 488, 493, 494, 507, 515
center line judge 490
center loudspeaker 321
center mark 490
center pocket 502
center post 202, 349
center service line 491
center span 344
center spot 481, 502
center strap 491
centerboard 520
centerboard boat 521
centering control 329
Central African Republic 451
Central America 14, 16
central brush 365
central column 412
central focusing wheel 420
central incisor 101
central nave 447
central nervous system 109
central pumping station 404
centrifuge module 11
centriole 66
cephalic vein 102
cephalothorax 70, 71
ceramic capacitor 417
cereal 61, 143
cereal products 144
cerebellum 109
cerebropleural ganglion 73
cerebrospinal fluid 110
cerebrum 109
cervical vertebrae 99
cervix of uterus 112
Chac-Mool 283
Chad 451
Chad, Lake 20
chain 372
chain brake 235
chain guide 372
chain of dunes 36
chain of neurons 110
chain reaction 415
chain stay 370
chain wheel 522
chain wheel A 372
chain wheel B 372
chainsaw 235
chainsaw chain 235
chair 444, 464
chair lift 512
chair lift departure area 512
chairs, examples 201
chaise longue 201
chalaza 79
chalice 446
chalk 503
chalk board 444
chalk line 225
challah 145
chameleon 77
chamois leather 265
chamomile 148
champagne flute 165
Chance card 469
chandelier 207
change room 444
change-sign key 337
changing table 205
changing table 205
channel scan button 319
channel scan buttons 319
channel selector controls 319
chanter 296
chanterelles 123
Chantilly parquet 190
chapati 145
chapel 282
chard 125
charge 534
charge indicator 271
charger 228
charging light 271
charging plug 271
charlotte mold 172
charm bracelet 264
Charon 3
chart room 382
chat room 335
chayote 129
checkbook 274, 275
checkbook/secretary clutch 274
checker 470
checkerboard 470
checkers 469, 470
checkout 121
checkouts 121
checks 441
cheek 83, 86, 94, 220, 536
cheese box 163
cheese counter 121
cheese grater, rotary 170
cheese knife 168
cheeses, blue-veined 151
cheeses, fresh 150
cheeses, goat's-milk 150
cheeses, soft 151
cheetah 89
chef's knife 169
cheliped 71
chemical bond 414
chemical treatment 405
chemise 282
chemistry 414
cherimoya 136
cherries 132
chervil 142
chess 470
chess notation 470
chess pieces 470
chessboard 470
chest 83
chest expander 500
chest freezer 211
chest protector 476, 486
chesterfield 200
chestnuts 133
chevet 285
chèvre cheese 150

chicane 524
chick peas 130
chicken 155
chief timekeeper 516
chiffonier 203
child carrier 372
child safety seat 356
child's skull, lateral view 100
child's tricycle 373
children's clothing 261
children's furniture 205
Chile 448
chile 139
Chile Trench 34
chili powder 139
chimney 183, 193
chimney connection 192
chimney pot 183
chimpanzee 91
chin 78, 94
chin protector 367
chin rest 301
chin strap 486, 522
China 453
China Sea, East 19
China Sea, South 19
Chinese dates 137
chinois 171
chip cover 227
chipmunk 82
chipolata sausage 156
chives 124
chloroplast 50
chocolate 148
choir 284, 285
choir organ manual 305
choker 264
chop 152, 153
chord 299
chorizo 156
choroid 119
Christmas tree 404
chromatin 66
chromosphere 4
chrysalis 67
chuck 221, 228
chuck key 228
chuck, keyless 228
chukka 240
church 433
church, Catholic 446
cicada 69
ciliary body 119
ciliate 55
cilium 66
cinnamon 138
circle, parts 428
circuit 524
circuit breaker 407
circuit vent 194
circular body 296
circular route 25
circular saw 227
circular saw blade 227
circumference 428
circumvallate papilla 118
cirque 5
cirque, glacial 30
cirrocumulus 42
cirrostratus 42
cirrus 42
citron 134
citrus fruit 58
citrus fruits 134
citrus juicer 170, 177
city 23, 430
city bicycle 373
city bus 362
city hall 432
city houses 289
clam 157
clam cleat 521
clamp 198, 226, 269, 514
clamp binder 339
clamp lever 269
clamp spotlight 206
clamping block 425
clamping screw 224
clamping screws 425
clams 157
clapper/the slate 291
clapskate 508
clarinet 306
clarinets 295
clasp 274, 275
classic blouse 255
classified advertisements 313
classroom 444, 445
classroom for students with learning disabilities 444
clavicle 98
claw 71, 76, 78, 82, 220
claw hammer 220
clay 492
clean and jerk 500
clean utility room 462
cleaner height adjustment knob 209
cleaning brush 271
cleanout 197
clear key 337
clear space 487
clear-entry key 337
cleat 520, 521
cleated shoe 486
cleaver 169
clefs 298
clerks' desk 440
clerks' office 440
clew 519
cliff 5, 29, 35
climate control 354
climates of the world 40
climbing plant 230
clinical thermometer 424
clinical thermometers 461
clip 312, 535
clip earrings 264
clipboard 340
clipless pedal 522
clippers 269
clitoris 112
cloakroom 443
cloche 239
clock 444
clock operator 488
clock radio 325
clock timer 178, 210
clog 242
closed stringer 191
closeness setting 271
closet 188, 189, 203
clothing and accessories 538
clothing guard 467
clothing store 436
cloud 37, 41
cloud of volcanic ash 28
clouds 42
clouds of vertical development 42
cloudwater 48
cloverleaf 342, 343
cloves 138
club 468
club chair 200
clubhouse 504
clump of flowers 230
clutch 350
clutch housing 368
clutch lever 366, 368
clutch pedal 354
coach 362, 489, 507
coach car 376
coach's box 474
coaches 509
coal storage yard 402
coal-fired thermal power plant 402
coarse adjustment knob 421
coarse salt 141
coastal features 35
coat dress 252
coats 248, 251
cob 61
cobra 77
coccyx 98
cochlea 116
cochlear nerve 116
cockchafer 69
cockles 157
cockleshell 200
cockpit 520, 525
cocktail cabinet 203
cocktail glass 165
cocktail lounge 439
cocoa 148
coconut 133
Cocos Plate 27
coffee 148
coffee beans 148
coffee maker 181
coffee makers 181
coffee mill 180
coffee mug 166
coffee pot 531
coffee shop 432, 437
coffee spoon 168
coil spring 351
coin 441
coin purse 275
coin, reverse 441
coin: obverse 441
cola nuts 133
colander 171
cold air 41
cold coolant 408
cold shed 381
cold storage chamber 120, 121
cold temperate climates 40
cold-water circuit 194
cold-water pipe 194
cold-water supply line 196, 197
collar 53, 244, 245, 248, 262, 271, 501
collar point 245
collar stay 245
collards 126
collateral 110
collection body 365
collet 229
collie 86
Colombia 448
color selection filter 318
color shifting ink 441
color supplement 313
color synthesis 418
color television camera 10
columella 73
columella fold 73
column 31, 207, 279, 313
column of mercury 424
coma 6
comb binding 340
combat sports 498
combination box and open end wrench 223
combination lock 274
combs 268
combustion chamber 360
comet 6
comforter 204
command control dial 314
commercial area 435
commercial concern 335
commercial zone 431
commissure of lips of mouth 116
common carotid artery 102
common coastal features 35
common frog 75
common hair cap moss 51
common iliac artery 102, 107
common iliac vein 107
common nail 220
common periwinkles 157
common peroneal nerve 108
common plaice 161
common polypody 52
common toad 75
communicating ramus 110
communication by telephone 327
communication module 316
communication protocol 334
communication set 380
communication tunnel 13
communications volume controls 10
communion rail 446
Community Chest card 469
commuter train 375
Comoros 452
compact 266
compact disc 326
compact disc player 323, 325, 326
compact disc player controls 326
compact disc player, portable 325
compact disc recorder 325
compact disc rewritable recorder 333
compact memory card 315
compact videocassette adapter 320
compacting 49
compartment 286
compass 533
compass bridge 382, 386, 387
compass card 533
compass meridian line 533
compass rose 23
compass saw 226
competitive course 517
complex dune 36
complexus 97
compluvium 280
composition of the blood 104
compost bin 231
compound bow 535
compound eye 67, 68
compound leaves 55
compressed-air cylinder 454
compression coupling 197
computer 329, 444
computer programs 457
computer science room 444
computer screen intensity controls 10
concave lens 419
concave primary mirror 9
concha 115
conchiglie 146
concrete mixer truck 365
condensation 45, 414
condensation of steam into water 408
condenser 402, 421
condenser adjustment knob 421
condenser height adjustment 421
condiments 140
condominiums 289, 512
condor 80
conduction 415
conductor's podium 295
cone 65, 119, 429
conference room 442
confessionals 446
configuration of the continents 14
confined aquifer 402
confirmation key 443
confluence 32
Congo 451
Congo River 20
conic projection 22
conical washer 196
conifer 65
coniferous forest 44
conifers, examples 65
conjunctiva 119
connecting cable 324
connecting gallery 345
connecting rod 360
connection 470
connection pin 417
connection point 198
connective tissue 114
constriction 424
consumer 317
contact 470
contact devices 198
contact lenses 272
contact lever 207
container 176, 383
container car 377
container hold 383
container ship 381, 382
container terminal 381, 430
container-loading bridge 381
containment building 408, 409
contest area 499
contestant 499
continent 33
continental crust 26
continental margin 33
continental rise 33
continental shelf 33
continental slope 33
continents, configuration 14
continuity person 291
continuous beam 344
contrabassoons 295
contractile vacuole 66
contrast control 329
control 330
control button 332
control cable 372
control deck 383
control key 330
control keys 328
control knob 210, 212, 213, 214
control panel 178, 179, 210, 212, 213, 314, 455
control panel: dishwasher 214
control room 293, 406
control stick 395
control tower 388
control tower cab 388
control valve 529
control wheel 455
control: group select 330
controller 471
controller ports 471
convection 415
convection current 415
convection zone 4
convective cell 43
convenience food 121
convenience outlet 217
convention center 433
conventional door 286
convergent plate boundaries 27
converging lenses 419
convertible 347
convex lens 419
conveyor 402
conveyor belt 49, 390
Cook Strait 15
cooked ham 156
cookie cutters 172
cooking 178
cooking dishes 179
cooking plate 179
cooking set 531
cooking surface 179
cooking utensils 174
cooktop 164, 210
cooktop edge 210
cool tip 269
coolant 408
coolant inlet 410
coolant outlet 410
cooler 532
cooling 405
cooling cylinder 420
cooling fan 322, 350, 358, 360
cooling system 351
cooling tower 402
cooling vent 336
coping 526
coping saw 226
Coral Sea 15
coral snake 77
corbel 282
corbel piece 192
cord 208, 209, 217, 235, 237
cord sleeve 218, 229
cordate 55
cordless drill 228
cordless mouse 332
cordless screwdriver 221
core 4, 58, 534
coriander 142
Corinthian column 281
Corinthian pilaster 281
cork 514
cork ball 477
cork tip 495
corkscrew 531
corn 61, 143

corn bread 145
corn flour 144
corn oil 149
corn salad 127
corn syrup 149
corn: cob 61
cornea 119, 419
corner 498
corner arc 481
corner cupboard 203
corner flag 481
corner pad 498
corner stool 498
corner stud 187
corner tower 282
cornerpiece 277
cornet 295, 307
cornice 183, 185, 202, 279
corolla 56
corona 4
corona radiata 112
coronal suture 100
coronet 83
corpus callosum 109
corrective lenses 419
correspondence 338
corselette 258
corset 259
cortex 107
corymb 57
cosmetic tray 277
Costa Rica 448
costal shield 76
costume 290
cot 460
Côte d'Ivoire 451
cottage cheese 150
cotton applicators 461
cotyledon 53
coudé focus 7
cougar 88
coulomb 426
Coulommiers 151
counsels' assistants 440
counter 262
counter reset button 323
counterjib 397
counterjib ballast 397
countertop 164
counterweight 8, 287, 345, 397, 400, 401
counterweight guide rail 287
country 23, 431
coupler head 377
coupler-tilt tablet 305
coupling guide device 376
coupon booth 443
course 504
court 440, 487, 488, 490, 494
courthouse 432
courtroom 440
courtyard 445, 447
couscous 144
couscous kettle 175
cover 180, 198, 315, 454, 477, 505, 533
coveralls 513
covered parapet walk 282
covering 493
cow 84
cowl 348
Cowper's gland 111
cowshed 122
Coyolxauhqui stone 283
crab 158
crab spider 70
cracked bread 145
cracked rye bread 145
cradle 8, 9
cranberries 132
crane runway 397
cranes 397
cranial nerves 108
crank 170, 224, 372, 537
crank handle 225
crankshaft 360
crash helmet 524
crate 162
crater 5, 28
crater ray 5
crawler tractor 398
crayfish 158
cream 150
cream cheese 150
cream cup 163
creamer 166
crease 246
credit card 441
creel 538
creep 31
crenate 55
crêpe pan 175
crepidoma 279
crescendo pedal 305
crescent wrench 223
crescentic dune 36
crest 29, 33, 418, 477
crest of spillway 406
crevasse 30
crevice tool 209
crew neck 260
crew neck sweater 250, 255
crew quarters 382
crew return vehicle 11
crib 205
cribriform plate of ethmoid 117
cricket 478
cricket ball 478
cricket player 478
cricket shoe 478
crimping 534
crisper 211
Croatia 450
crocodile 77
crocus 56
croissant 144
crook 306
crook key 306
crookneck squash 129
crosne 124
cross brace 467
cross head 221
cross rail 201
cross section of a baseball 477
cross section of a hydroelectric power plant 407
cross section of a molar 101
cross section of a reflecting telescope 9
cross section of a refracting telescope 8
cross section of a road 342
cross section of a street 434
cross section of an astronomical observatory 7
cross-country bicycle 522
cross-country cyclist 522
cross-country ski 514
cross-country ski trail 512
cross-country skier 514
cross-country skiing 514
cross-headed tip 221
cross-tip screwdriver 531
crossbar 297, 370
crosshead 396
crossing 284, 285
crossing arm 362
crossover cargo deck line 385
crossover mirror 362
crosspiece 202, 466
crosstree 520
crotch 247
crotch piece 255
Crottin de Chavignol 150
croup 83
crown 63, 78, 101, 238, 239, 302, 308, 424
crown block 403
crucifix 446
crude oil 405
crude-oil pipeline 404
cruise control 354
crus of helix 115
crushed chiles 139
crusher 49, 402
crustaceans 71, 158
crustose lichen 50
crutch 466
crystal button 207
crystal drop 207
crystallization 414
Cuba 448
cube 429
cucumber 128
cue ball 502, 503
cuff 240, 245, 246
culottes 253
cultivated mushrooms 123
cultural organization 335
cumin 138
cumulonimbus 42
cumulus 42
cup 163, 166, 259, 531, 532, 534
cup gasket 459
cupped Pacific oysters 157
cupule 60
curb 434, 524
curler 515
curling 515
curling brush 515
curling iron 269
curling stone 515
curly endive 127
curly kale 126
currant tomatoes 128
currants 132
currency abbreviations, examples 440
currency, name 441
current event scoreboard 497
curry 138
cursor down 331
cursor left 331
cursor movement keys 331
cursor right 331
cursor up 331
curtain 277
curtain wall 282
curved jaw 222
customer service 443
customer's restrooms 438
customer's service entrance 198
customers' cloakroom 438
customers' entrance 438
customs control 391
customs house 381
cut nail 220
cuticle nippers 265
cuticle pusher 265
cuticle scissors 265
cuticle trimmer 265
cutlery basket 214
cutlery set 531
cuts of beef 152
cuts of lamb 153
cuts of pork 153
cuts of veal 152
cutter link 235
cutting 177
cutting blade 176, 180, 341
cutting board 169
cutting edge 167, 169, 270, 398, 399, 400
cutting head 341
cutting tools 234
cuttlefish 157
cyan 418
cycling 522
cyclone 43
cyclone names 43
cylinder 429
cylinder head cover 350
cylinder vacuum cleaner 209
cylindrical projection 22
cymbal 308
cymbals 295, 309
cypress scalelike leaves 65
Cyprus 450
cytopharynx 66
cytoplasm 50, 66, 112
cytoproct 66
cytostome 66
Czech Republic 450

D

D 298
d quark 414
daffodil 56
daggerboard 519
daggerboard well 519
daikon 129
dairy 122
dairy compartment 211
dairy products 120, 150
dairy products receiving area 120
Dalmatian 86
dam 406
damper pedal 304, 311
dance blade 509
dandelion 127
danger area 499
Danish Blue 151
Danish rye bread 145
Danube River 18
dark chocolate 148
dart 471
dartboard 471
darts 471
dashboard 354, 366
dashboard computer 457
dashboard equipment 457
data display 319, 328
data processing 38
data storage devices 333
database 335
date 441
date display/recording button 320
dater 338
dates 132
davit 384
day-care center 437
dead ball line 482
dead bolt 186
deadly poisonous mushroom 52
death 426
debit card 443
debris 43
decagon 429
decanter 165
deceleration lane 343
deciduous forest 44
decimal key 337
deck 313, 344
declination setting scale 8, 9
décolleté bra 259
decomposers 45
decorative articles store 437
decorative braid 260
decoy 535
dedicated line 334
deep end 184
deep fryer 178
deep peroneal nerve 108
deep-sea floor 26
defense counsels' bench 440
defensive midfield 481
deferent duct 111
deflector 236, 237
deforestation 47
defrost drain 211
degree 428
degree Celsius 426
Deimos 2
delete 331
delete key 331
delicatessen 120, 156
delicious lactarius 123
delivery 479
delivery entrance 435
delta 32, 35
delta distributary 32
delta wing 394
deltoid 96
deluge gun 455
demitasse 166
Democratic Republic of the Congo 451
dendrite 110
Denmark 450
denomination 441
dental alveolus 101
dental care 272
dental floss 272
dental floss holder 272
dentate 55
dentin 101
deodorant 267
deoxygenated blood 104
department store 437
departure time indicator 374
depolarizing mix 417
deposit slot 442
depth adjustment 229
depth of focus 27
depth-of-cut adjustment knob 229
depth-of-field preview button 314
derailleur 370, 372, 522
derby 238
dermis 114
derrick 382, 385, 403, 404
derrick mast 385
descending aorta 103
descending colon 106
descending passage 278
desert 36, 40, 44
desk 439
desk lamp 206
desk tray 338
desktop computer 334
dessert fork 168
dessert knife 168
dessert spoon 168
destination 374
destroying angel 52
detachable control 179
detachable palm rest 330
detergent dispenser 214
dew 41
dew shield 8
diable 175
diagonal buttress 284
diagonal movement 470
diagonal step 514
dial 422, 424
dial/action button 337
diameter 428
diamond 468
diamond interchange 342
diamond point 202
diaper 260
diaphragm 105, 324
dibble 231
dice 468
dice cup 469
die 469
diesel engine compartment 399, 400, 401
diesel lift engine 383
diesel motor compartment 398
diesel oil 405
diesel propulsion engine 383
diesel shop 375
diesel-electric locomotive 377
differential 351
difficult slope 512
diffuser 290
diffuser pin 236
digestive gland 71, 73
digestive system 106
digit 75, 82
digital audio player, portable 325
digital camera 315
digital display 423, 461
digital nerve 108
digital pulp 114
digital reflex camera 315
digital thermometer 461
digital versatile disc 318
digital watch 424
Dijon mustard 140
dike 28
dill 142
dimmer switch 198
dimple 505
dinette 164
dining car 376

dining room 188, 280, 386, 438, 439
dinner fork 168
dinner knife 168
dinner plate 166
dinnerware 166
diode 411
Dione 3
dip switch 368
dipper arm 399, 400
dipper bucket 400
dipper-arm cylinder 399, 400
direct home reception 316
direct-current power cord 336
direction of electron flow 416, 417
direction of Mecca 447
directional buttons 471
directional sign 379
director 291
director of photography 291
director's chair 200
director's control monitors 290
director's office 443
director's seat 291
directory 334
disc 357
disc brake 350, 357, 366, 525
disc compartment 323
disc compartment control 323
disc tray 318
discharge outlet 184
discus 472
discus throw 473
dish 179, 321
dish antenna 321
dishwasher 164, 214
dishwasher, control panel 214
disk 6, 333, 501
disk drive 310
diskette 333
disks 177
displacement 418
display 318, 322, 325, 327, 336, 337, 338, 346, 423, 442, 443
display cabinet 203
display panel 320
display preparation area 120
display release button 336
display setting 327
disposable camera 315
disposable contact lens 272
disposable diaper 260
disposable fuel cylinder 218
disposable razor 271
distal phalanx 114
distributary, delta 32
distribution by aerial cable network 316
distribution by submarine cable 317
distribution by underground cable network 317
distribution panel 198
distributor cap 350, 360
distributor service loop 198
district 25
ditali 146
ditch 342
divergent plate boundaries 27
diverging lenses 419
diversion canal 406
divide key 337
divided by 427
divider 274
dividers 339
diving 518
diving board 184
diving installations 518
diving tower 518
djembe 297
Djibouti 451
Dnieper River 18
do-it-yourself shop 436
dock 381
docking cradle 337
document folder 339
document-to-be-sent position 328
dodecagon 429
dog 86, 535
dog, morphology 86
dolichos beans 130
dollar 440
dolly 290
dolly tracks 290
dolphin 90
dolphin, morphology 90
domain name 334
dome shutter 7
dome tent 529
domestic appliances 176, 180, 208
domestic pollution 47
Dominica 449
Dominican Republic 449
dominoes 468
door 178, 202, 210, 213, 287, 349, 352, 361, 392, 439, 447, 528, 529
door handle 349
door jamb 185
door lock 349
door open warning light 355
door panel 202
door shelf 211
door stop 211
door switch 213
doorknob 185, 186
doors, examples 286
Doric column 281
dormer window 182
dorsal abdominal artery 71
dorsal fin 90
dorsalis pedis artery 102
dorsum of nose 117
dorsum of tongue 118
dose inhaler 467
double bass 301
double basses 295
double bed 439
double boiler 175
double flat 299
double kitchen sink 194
double plate 187
double reed 306
double ring 471
double room 439
double seat 380
double sharp 299
double virgule 334
double-blank 468
double-breasted buttoning 248
double-breasted jacket 244
double-burner camp stove 529
double-decker bus 363
double-edged blade 271
double-edged razor 271
double-leaf bascule bridge 345
double-six 468
double-twist auger bit 228
doubles service court 495
doubles sideline 490, 495
doublet 468
doubling die 469
doubly dentate 55
dough hook 176
Douglas, pouch 112
dousing water tank 408
dovetail 420
down tube 371
downhill 511
downhill bicycle 522
downhill cyclist 522
downhill ski 510
downspout 182
downtown 431, 432
draft arm 400
draft tube 400, 407
drag 536
dragonfly 69
drain 194
drain hose 212, 214
drain valve 404
draining circuit 194
draining spoon 173
Drake Passage 15, 17
draw hoe 233
draw tube 421
drawbridge 282
drawer 164, 202, 203, 205, 210
drawers 247
drawstring 249, 275
drawstring bag 275, 276
drawstring hood 261
dredger 172
dresser 203, 290
dresses, examples 252
dressing room 290, 293
dried chiles 139
drill collar 403
drill pipe 403
drill ship 382
drilling drawworks 403
drilling rig 403
drilling tools 228
drills 228
drink box 163
drinks 120
drip bowl 210
drip molding 349
drip pan 179
drip tray 181
dripping pan 174
drive belt 212
drive chain 370
drive shaft 351, 383, 395
drive wheel 180
drive wheels 401
driver 524
driver's cab 376, 377
driver's seat 369
driveway 183
driving glove 243
dromedary camel 85
drone 68
drone pipe 296
droop nose 394
drop earrings 264
drop light 217
drop shot 491
drop-leaf 202
drop-waist dress 252
drum 170, 213, 308, 357
drum brake 357
drum sticks 309
drumlin 29
drums 308
drumstick 297
drupelet 59
dry cells 417
dry cleaner 437
dry climates 40
dry dock 381
dry fruits 60, 133
dry gallery 31
dryer 213
dual cassette deck 325
dual seat 367
dual swivel mirror 269
dual-in-line package 417
duck 81, 155
duck egg 155
duffel bag 276
duffle coat 249
dugout 474
dulse 123
dumbbells 500
dump body 401
dump truck 401
dune 35
dunes, examples 36
duo 300
duodenum 106
dura mater 109, 110
durian 137
dust canister 229
dust receiver 208
dust ruffle 204
dust tail 6
dusting brush 209
dustpan 215
Dutch bicycle 373
Dutch oven 175
duty belt 456
duty-free shop 391
DVD 318
DVD player 318
DVD recorder 333
dynamics propeller 383

E

E 298
e-commerce 335
e-mail 335
e-mail key 330
e-mail software 334
eagle 81
ear 92, 201
ear drum 116
ear flap 238
ear loaf 144
ear protection 458
ear, auricle 115
ear, structure 116
earphone 324
earphone jack 329
earphones 325
earpiece 273, 460
earplugs 458
earrings 264
Earth 2, 3, 4, 5, 14
Earth coordinate system 21
earth foundation 342
Earth's atmosphere, profile 37
Earth's crust 26, 27
Earth's crust, section 26
Earth's orbit 4, 5
Earth, structure 26
earthflow 31
earthquake 27
East 23
East China Sea 19
East Pacific Rise 34
East-Northeast 23
East-Southeast 23
Eastern hemisphere 21
Eastern meridian 22
easy slope 512
eau de parfum 267
eau de toilette 267
eave 283
eccrine sweat gland 114
echinoderms 66
eclipses, types 4, 5
Ecuador 448
edge 441, 509, 510, 533
edger 237
edging 230
edible boletus 123
edit search button 320
editorial 313
educational institution 335, 433
eel 159
effluent 32
effusive volcano 28
egg 79, 112
egg beater 172
egg carton 162
egg noodles 147
egg poacher 175
egg slicer 173
egg timer 171
egg tray 211
eggplant 128
eggs 155
Egypt 451
Egyptian reed pens 312
eighth note 299
eighth rest 299
ejaculatory duct 111
eject button 315, 323, 471
El Salvador 448
elastic 204
elastic strainer 528, 529
elastic support bandage 461
elastic waistband 249
elastic webbing 246
elasticized leg opening 247
elbow 83, 86, 93, 95
elbow pad 486, 526, 527
elbows 146
electric charge, unit 426
electric current, unit 426
electric drill 228
electric fan motor 358
electric golf cart 505
electric griddle 179
electric grill, indoor 179
electric guitar 303
electric knife 177
electric motor 235, 237
electric potential difference, unit 426
electric range 210
electric razor 271
electric resistance, unit 426
electric steamer 179
electrical box 198
electrical cable 354
electrical circuit, parallel 416
electrical connection 365
electrical system 351
electricity 198
electricity cable 434
electricity meter 198
electricity tools 217
electricity transmission 408
electrolytic capacitors 417
electrolytic separator 417
electromagnetic spectrum 418
electron 414
electron beam 318
electron collector 417
electron flow, direction 416, 417
electron gun 318
electronic ballast 199
electronic control unit 357
electronic drum pad 311
electronic instruments 310
electronic organizer 338
electronic payment terminal 121, 443
electronic piano 311
electronic scale 423
electronic viewfinder 320
electronics 417
electronics store 436
elements of a house 185
elements of architecture 286
elephant 85
elevating cylinder 364, 397, 455
elevation 182
elevation adjustment 420
elevation zones 44
elevator 281, 287, 393, 400, 435, 439
elevator car 287
elevon 13
embankment 342
emergency 462
emergency brake 380
emergency physician's office 462
emergency station 345
emergency switch 368
emergency truck 345
emery boards 265
Emmenthal 151
empty set 427
emptying hose 212
enamel 101
enclosure 286
end 331
end aisle display 121
end button 301
end cap 409
end joist 187
end key 327, 331
end line 484, 487, 489, 493
end moraine 30
end piece 111
end plate 409
end search button 320
end stop 226, 521
end zone 484
endocardium 104
endocarp 57, 58
endoplasmic reticulum 50, 66
endpiece 273, 503

energy 402
energy integration to the transmission network 413
energy release 415
energy, unit 426
energy-saving bulb 199
engaged Corinthian column 281
engaged Doric column 281
engaged Ionic column 281
engagement ring 264
engine 366, 403
engine air intake 362
engine block 360
engine compartment 362, 396, 401
engine control room 384
engine housing 235
engine mounting pylon 393
engine room 386
English billiards 503
English cane 466
English Channel 18
English horn 306
English horns 295
English Index 539
English loaf 145
English mustard 140
enhanced greenhouse effect 46
enoki 123
ENT room 463
entablature 185, 279
enter key 331
enterprise 335
entire 55
entrance 343
entrance door 362, 363
entrance doors 294
entrance for the public 278
entrance hall 188
entrance to the pyramid 278
entrance turnstile 378
entrances for the actors 278
entry 396
environment 44
epaulet 248
epicalyx 59
epicenter 27
epicondyle 99
epidermis 114
epididymis 111
epidural space 110
epiglottis 105, 118
epitrochlea 99
equals 427
equals key 337
Equator 17, 20, 21, 22, 43
Equatorial Guinea 451
equipment 472
equipment compartment 376
equipment storage room 444
erase button 315, 328
eraser 341
erecting lenses 420
Eritrea 451
escalator 294, 378, 435
escape 330
escape key 330
escarole 126
escutcheon 73, 186, 197
esophagus 105, 106
espadrille 242
espresso machine 181
espresso maker 181
Estonia 450
eternal light 447
Ethernet port 336
Ethiopia 451
ethmoid, cribriform plate 117
Eurasia 14
Eurasian Plate 27
euro 440
Europa 2
Europe 14, 18, 34, 449
European experiment module 11
European outlet 198
European plug 198
European robin 80
European Union, flag 441
Eustachian tube 116, 117
Eutelsat 316
euthynteria 279
evacuation route 345
evaporated milk 150
evaporation 45, 414
evening glove 243
event platform 496
ex-voto 446
examination room 463, 465
examples of airplanes 394
examples of algae 51
examples of amphibians 75
examples of angles 428
examples of arachnids 70
examples of armchairs 200
examples of bicycles 373
examples of bills 79
examples of birds 80
examples of bodies 347
examples of branching 197
examples of broadleaved trees 64
examples of carnivorous mammals 88
examples of cat breeds 87
examples of chairs 201
examples of conifers 65
examples of currency abbreviations 440
examples of dog breeds 86
examples of doors 286
examples of dresses 252
examples of dunes 36
examples of eyeglasses 273
examples of feet 79
examples of ferns 52
examples of flowers 56
examples of forks 168
examples of freight cars 377
examples of heads 221
examples of holds and throws 499
examples of insects 69
examples of instrumental groups 300
examples of interchanges 342
examples of jumps 509
examples of knives 168
examples of lagomorphs 82
examples of leaves 65
examples of lichens 50
examples of marine mammals 90
examples of mosses 51
examples of motorcycles 369
examples of nails 220
examples of pants 254
examples of pleats 253
examples of primates 91
examples of reptiles 77
examples of rodents 82
examples of shirts 255
examples of shorelines 35
examples of skirts 253
examples of skis 510
examples of sleeping bags 530
examples of spoons 168
examples of tables 202
examples of tents 528
examples of tips 221
examples of tires 358
examples of trucks 364
examples of ungulate mammals 84
examples of utensils for cutting 169
examples of volcanoes 28
examples of windows 287
executive length 247
exercise wear 263
exhalation valve 459
exhaust air duct 345
exhaust manifold 350, 360
exhaust pipe 350, 351, 367, 368, 395
exhaust pipe stack 398
exhaust stack 364
exhaust system 351
exhaust tube 199
exhaust valve 360
exhibition center 430
exit 343
exit button 337
exit taxiway 391
exit turnstile 378
exocarp 57, 58, 59
exosphere 37
expandable baton 456
expandable file pouch 274
expander 310
expanding file 340
expansion bolt 221
expansion chamber 424
expert slope 512
expiration date 441
explosive volcano 28
exposure adjustment knob 314
exposure mode 314
expressway 343
extension 202
extension ladder 219
extension pipe 209
extension table 202
extensor carpi radialis brevis 97
extensor carpi radialis longus 97
extensor carpi ulnaris 97
extensor digitorum 97
extensor digitorum brevis 96
extensor digitorum longus 96
exterior dome shell 7
exterior door 185
exterior of a house 182
exterior pocket 274, 276
exterior sign 378
external auditory meatus 100
external ear 116
external floppy disk drive 333
external fuel tank 12
external jugular vein 102
external nose 117
external oblique 96, 97
external tooth lock washer 222
eye 43, 70, 71, 72, 76, 90, 94, 119, 220, 538
eye makeup 266
eye pencil 266
eye protection 458
eye ring 78
eye wall 43
eyeball 75, 119
eyebrow stripe 78
eyebrow tweezers 265
eyecup 320
eyeglasses 273
eyeglasses case 275
eyeglasses parts 273
eyeglasses, examples 273
eyelahes 87
eyelash 119
eyelash curler 266
eyelashes 87
eyelet 240, 263, 275, 509
eyelet tab 240
eyelid 76
eyepiece 8, 9, 320, 420, 421
eyepiece holder 8
eyeshadow 266
eyestalk 72
Eyre, Lake 15

F

F 298
fabric guide 208
façade 285
face 91, 92, 220, 493, 505
face mask 478, 486, 507
face-off circle 506
face-off spot 506
facepiece 459
faceplate 186
facial makeup 266
facsimile machine 328
factorial 427
factory 430
faculae 4
Fahrenheit scale 424
fairing 366
fairlead 521
fairway 504
falcon 81
Falkland Islands 17
fall front 203
fallopian tube 112
fallopian tubes 113
fallow 122
false rib 99
false start rope 516
false tuck 260
family tent 528
family waiting room 462
fan 213
fan brush 266
fan housing 270
fan trellis 230
fang 70, 76
fantail 412
farmhouse 122
farmhouse bread 145
farmstead 122
farmyard 122
fast data-entry control 310
fast operation buttons 323
fast-food restaurants 437
fast-forward button 319, 323, 326, 328
fastener binder 339
fats and oils 149
faucet 195
fault 27
feather crown 495
feathered shuttlecock 495
Federated States of Micronesia 453
feed tube 177, 180
feedhorn 321
feet, examples 79
feijoa 137
felt hat 238, 239
female 426
female cone 65
female ferrule 536, 537
female reproductive organs 112
femoral artery 102
femoral nerve 108
femoral vein 102
femur 98
fence 122, 182, 226
fender 348, 364, 370
fennec 88
fennel 125
fenugreek 138
fermata 299
fern 52
fern, structure 52
ferns, examples 52
ferrule 219, 503
ferry 386
ferryboat 381
fertilizer application 47
fetlock 83
fetlock joint 83
fettucine 146
fibers 215
fibula 98
fibularis brevis 97
fiddlehead 52
fiddleheads 125
field 472, 474, 479, 482
field lens 420
field lens adjustment 421
field line 416
field mouse 82
fielder's glove 477
fielders 479
fifth 298
fifth wheel 364
fifty 427
fifty-yard line 484
fig 137
figure skate 509
figure skating 509
Fiji 453
Fiji Islands 15
filament 56, 199
Filchner Ice Shelf 15
file 229, 334, 531
file format 334
file guides 340
filiform papilla 118
filing box 340
fill opening 208
filler cap 237, 358, 364
filler neck 351
filler tube 196
filleting knife 169
filling inlet 404
film advance mode 314
film rewind knob 314
film speed 314
filter 178, 184, 210
filter cover 459
filter holder 181
fin 393, 395
final drive 398
financial services 442
finch 80
finderscope 8, 9
fine adjustment knob 421
fine adjustment wheel 425
fine data-entry control 310
fine guidance system 7
finely threaded screw 425
finger 114, 477
finger flange 460
finger tip 339
fingerboard 296, 301, 303
fingernail 115
finial 283
finish line 473
finish wall 516
finishing nail 220
Finland 450
fir 65
fir needles 65
fire box 192
fire door 286
fire engines 455
fire extinguisher 457
fire extinguisher, portable 454
fire hose 454
fire hydrant 434, 454
fire irons 193
fire station 433
fire-fighting materials 454
firebrick 192
firebrick back 192
firefighter 454
fireplace 188, 192
fireplace screen 193
fireproof and waterproof garment 454
firestopping 187
FireWire port 336
firn 30
first aid kit 457, 461
first aid manual 461
first aid station 512
first assistant camera operator 290
first base 474
first baseman 474
first dorsal fin 74
first floor 182, 188
first leaves 53
first molar 101
first premolar 101
first quarter 5
first row 482
first space 489
first valve slide 307
first violins 295
first voltage increase 413
first-class cabin 392
fish fork 168
fish knife 168
fish net stocking 257
fish platter 166
fish poacher 174
fish scaler 531
fishes 74

fishes, bony 159
fishes, cartilaginous 158
fishhook 536, 538
fishing 536
fishing vest 538
fission of uranium fuel 408
fission products 415
fissionable nucleus 415
fitness equipment 500
fitted sheet 204
fitting 455
fittings 277
five 427
five hundred 427
five spice powder 139
fixed base 224
fixed bridges 344
fixed distance marking 391
fixed jaw 223, 224, 425
fixture drain 194
fjords 35
flag 482
flag of the European Union 441
flageolets 131
flags 448
flame 415
flame spreader tip 218
flame-resistant driving suit 524
flamingo 81
flank 78, 83
flanker 482
flanking tower 282
flap 244, 275
flap pocket 244, 248
flare 4
flare nut wrench 223
flash tube 420
flashing 193
flashlight 456
flat 299, 526
flat car 377
flat head 221
flat mirror 7
flat oyster 157
flat sheet 204
flat tip 221
flat washer 222
flat-back brush 268
flat-plate solar collector 410
flea 69
flesh 57, 58, 59
fleshy fruit 58, 59
fleshy fruit: pome fruit 58
fleshy fruit: stone fruit 57
fleshy leaf 54
flews 86
flexible boot 513
flexible coupling 413
flexible hose 209
flexible skirt 383
flexible tube 460
flexor carpi ulnaris 96, 97
flies 292
flight 471
flight deck 12, 392, 395
flight information board 391
flight of stairs 191
flights 518
flint 218
flip 509
float 394
float ball 196
float seaplane 394
float tackle 538
floating crane 381
floating head 271
floating ribs 98
floating roof 404
floating-roof tank 404
floodplain 32
floor 193, 412
floor brush 209
floor coverings, textile 190
floor drain 194
floor exercise area 496
floor joist 187
floor lamp 206
floor mat 356
floor mats 496
floorboard 190, 369
floppy disk drive 329
floppy disk eject button 329
florist 437
flour 144
flow tube 410
flower 53, 56
flower bed 183, 230
flower bud 53
flower, inflorescences 57
flower, structure 56
flowering 62
flowers, examples 56
flue 305
flue pipe 305
fluorescent tube 199
flush 468
flush handle 196
flute 228
fluted land 228
fluted shaft 355
flutes 295
fly 69, 246, 247, 260
fly agaric 52
fly front closing 251, 261
fly line 536
fly reel 536
fly rod 536
flyfishing 536
flyhalf 482
flying buttress 284, 285
flywheel 360, 501
FM mode select button 322
foam 33
foam cushion 458
foam monitor 385
foam pad 530
focus 27, 419
focus mode selector 314
focus selector 320
focusing knob 8, 9
focusing ring 420
fodder corn 122
fog 41
fog light 352, 364
foie gras 156
foil, aluminum 162
folder 340
folding chairs 201
folding cot 530
folding door 286
folding grill 533
folding nail file 265
folding ramp 386
folding shovel 532
foliage 63
foliate papilla 118
foliose lichen 50
follicle 60
follicle, section 60
following car 522
fondue fork 168
fondue pot 174
fondue set 174
fontanelle 100
food 120
food and kitchen 120
food can 163
food chain 45
food mill 170
food processor 177
food reserves 439
food tray 162
food vacuole 66
food, basic source 45
foot 72, 73, 91, 92, 93, 94, 95, 202, 260, 302, 305, 308, 519, 536, 537
foot cushion 502
foot fault judge 491
foot hole 305
foot protection 459
foot strap 519
foot support 501
football 486
football player 486
football, American 484
footboard 204, 523
footbridge 282, 375, 379
footing 187
footless tights 263
footrest 205, 224, 467
footstool 201
footstrap 254, 501
for filing 339
for measuring 171
for opening 170
for time management 338
foramen cecum 118
force, unit 426
fore and aft passage 385
forearm 83, 86, 93, 95, 534
forearm crutch 466
forearm pad 486
forearm support 466
forecastle 383, 387
forecourt 491
forehead 78, 92
foreleg 67, 68
forelimb 75
forelock 83
foremast 385
forest 29
forest fire 47
forestay 520
forewing 67
fork 8, 167, 371, 396, 522, 525, 531
forked tongue 76
forklift truck 396
forks 396
forks, examples 168
Former Yugoslav Republic of Macedonia 450
formeret 284
forming food vacuole 66
forms of medications 467
Formula 1® car 525
Formula 3000 car 524
fortified wall 447
forward 481, 518
fossil fuel 46, 48
foul line 474
foul post 475
foundation 187
foundation of tower 344
foundation slip 258
fountain pen 312
four blade beater 176
four-door sedan 347
four-four time 298
four-of-a-kind 468
four-way lug wrench 356
four-way selector 315
fourchette 243
fourth 298
fovea 119
fox 88
foyers 293
fraction 427
fractionating tower 405
frame 187, 192, 202, 204, 219, 224, 226, 248, 274, 277, 297, 309, 367, 396, 401, 410, 411, 412, 425, 460, 476, 492, 494, 522, 527, 528
frame stile 202
framing square 225
France 449
frankfurters 156
free guard zone 515
free margin 114
free skating blade 509
free throw line 489
freestyle snowboard 513
freeway 431
freewheel 372
freezer 164, 211, 438
freezer bag 162
freezer bucket 180
freezer compartment 211
freezer door 211
freezing 414
freezing rain 41
freight car 375
freight cars, examples 377
freight expedition 391
freight hold 393
freight reception 391
freight station 375
French bread 144
French horn 307
French horns 295
French press 181
French window 287
frequency display 325
frequency, unit 426
fresco 280
fresh air duct 345
fresh cheeses 150
fret 302, 303
friction strip 218
frieze 202, 279
frog 75, 249, 301
frog, morphology 75
frog-adjustment screw 229
frond 52
front 244, 245
front apron 245
front axle 401
front beam 422
front brake 371
front brake lever 368
front compression strap 532
front cover 333
front crawl 517
front derailleur 370, 372
front desk 439
front door 188
front fascia 348
front fender 366
front foil 387
front footrest 367, 368
front fork 522
front hydraulic brake line 350
front leg 201
front page 313
front picture 313
front pocket 275
front rigid section 363
front shock absorber 369
front sight 534
front tip 208
front top pocket 246
front view 478
front wheel 401, 467
front-end loader 399
frontal 446
frontal bone 98, 100
frontal sinus 117
frontalis 96
frontwall 365
frost 41
frozen food storage 121
frozen foods 121
fruit 57
fruit branch 62
fruit tree 122
fruit vegetables 128
fruition 62
fruits 120, 132
fruits, tropical 136
fruticose lichen 50
fry basket 171
frying pan 175, 531
fuel 408
fuel bundle 409
fuel indicator 355
fuel injector 360
fuel oil 405
fuel pellet 409
fuel tank 235, 364, 377, 395
fulcrum 518
full face helmet 525
full face mask 454
full house 468
full moon 5
fullback 482, 485
fully reflecting mirror 420
fumarole 28
function display 310
function keys 328, 330, 423
function selectors 327
fungicide 47
fungiform papilla 118
funiculus 59, 60
funnel 171, 318, 386
funnel cloud 43
fur 82, 91
furrow 118
fuse 198, 411
fuselage 393
fusilli 146
futon 204

G

G 298
gable 182, 285
gable stud 187
gable vent 182
gabletop 163
Gabon 451
gaffer 291
Gai-lohn 127
gaits, horse 83
galaxy 6
gallbladder 106
gallery 285, 412
galley 392
gallop 83
Gambia 451
game 154, 492
game board 469
game console 471
game port 329
games 468
gamma rays 418
gangway 384
gantry crane 406, 407
Ganymede 2
gap 538
garage 182
garage door 286
garam masala 139
garbage can 215
garbage collection truck 364
garbage disposal sink 197
garbage disposal unit 197
garden 280
garden cress 127
garden fork 233
garden hose 236
garden line 231
garden path 182
garden sorrel 127
garden spider 70
garden, pleasure 230
garden, public 435
garden, vegetable 122
gardening 230
gardening gloves 232
garlic 124
garlic press 170
garment bag 277
garment strap 277
garrison cap 238
garter 259
garter belt 259
garter snake 77
gas 403, 414
gas line 351
gas main 434
gas pedal 354
gas range 210
gas supply system 351
gas tank 351, 366, 369
gas tank cap 368
gas tank door 349
gasket 214
gaskin 83

gasoline 405
gasoline engine 351, 360
gasoline pump 346
gasoline pump hose 346
gastrocnemius 96, 97
gate 381, 407
gate-leg 202
gate-leg table 202
gather 255
gathered skirt 253
gauntlet 243
gauze roller bandage 461
gear housing 537
gear shift 368
gearbox 350
gearshift lever 350, 354, 367, 369
gelatin capsule 467
general view 186
generator 370, 402
generator unit 407
Genoa salami 156
gentlemen's restroom 439
gentlemen's restrooms 294
geographical map 444
geography 14
geology 26
geometrical shapes 428
geometry 428
Georgia 452
geothermal and fossil energy 402
geothermal energy 402
geothermal field 402
germ 61
German mustard 140
German rye bread 145
German salami 156
German shepherd 86
Germany 450
germination 53
geyser 28
Ghana 451
ghee 150
gherkin 128
giant slalom 511
giant slalom ski 510
gibbon 91
Gibraltar, Strait 18
gift store 436
gill slits 74
gills 52, 73
ginger 139
ginkgo nuts 133
giraffe 85
girder 187
girdle 259
glacial cirque 30
glacial lake 32
glacier 30, 32, 44
glacier tongue 30
glans penis 111
glass 410, 411
glass bottle 163
glass case 423
glass collection unit 49
glass cover 211
glass lens 273
glass protector 506
glass recycling container 49
glass roof 188
glass slide 421
glass sorting 49
glass-fronted display cabinet 203
glassed roof 374, 435
glassware 165
gliding phase 514
global warming 46
globe 444, 529
globular cluster 6
glottis 76
glove 10, 478, 498, 506, 508, 513, 514, 522, 525
glove compartment 354
glove finger 243
glove storage 464
glove, back 243
glove, palm 243
gloves 243
glucose 54
glue 190
glue stick 341
gluteal nerve 108
gluteus maximus 97
gnocchi 146
gnomon 424
go 469, 470
goal 480, 485, 507
goal area 480
goal crease 507
goal judge 506
goal lights 507
goal line 482, 484, 506
goalkeeper 481
goalkeeper's gloves 480
goalpost 482, 485
goaltender (goalie) 506, 507
goaltender's pad 507
goaltender's skate 507
goaltender's stick 507
goat 84
goat's milk 150
goat's-milk cheeses 150
goatfish 159
gob hat 239
Gobi Desert 19
goggles 218, 513, 522
golf 504
golf bag 505
golf ball 505
golf cart 505
golf cart, electric 505
golf clubs, types 505
golf course 430
golf glove 505
golf shoes 505
Golgi apparatus 50, 66
gonad 73
gondola 121, 512
gondola departure area 512
gong 295, 309
goose 81, 155
goose egg 155
goose-neck 191
gooseberries 132
gooseneck 400
gored skirt 253
gorge 31, 32
Gorgonzola 151
gorilla, morphology 91
Gothic cathedral 284
gour 31
government organization 335
governor tension sheave 287
grab handle 361, 364, 455
gracilis 97
grade slope 182
grader 401
graduated dial 533
graduated scale 422, 423
grain of wheat, section 61
grain terminal 381
Grand Canyon 16
grand gallery 278
granitic layer 26
granivorous bird 79
granulated sugar 149
granulation 4
grape 62
grape leaf 62
grape leaves 126
grape, section 59
grapefruit 134
grapefruit knife 169
grapes 132
grass 492
grassbox 237
grasshopper 69
grassland 44
grate 210
grater 170
grating, utensils 170
gravel bed 524
gravy boat 166
gray matter 109, 110
grease well 179
greases 405
Great Australian Bight 15
Great Barrier Reef 15
Great Dane 86
Great Dividing Range 15
great green bush-cricket 69
great horned owl 81
Great Lakes 16
great organ manual 305
Great Sandy Desert 15
great saphenous vein 102
great scallop 157
Great Victoria Desert 15
greater alar cartilage 117
greater covert 78
greater trochanter 99
Greece 450
Greek bread 144
Greek temple 279
Greek temple, plan 279
Greek theater 278
green 418, 504
green alga 51
green ball 503
green beam 318
green bean 131
green cabbage 126
green coffee beans 148
green gland 71
green light 434
green onion 124
green peas 130
green pepper 138
green russula 123
green sweet pepper 128
green tea 148
green walnut 60
greenhouse 122
greenhouse effect 46
greenhouse effect, enhanced 46
greenhouse effect, natural 46
greenhouse gas 46
greenhouse gas concentration 46
Greenland 16
Greenland Sea 14
Grenada 449
Grenadines 449
grid 318
grid system 22
grille 279, 296, 348, 358
grinding, utensils 170
grip 290, 500, 505, 535
grip handle 226
grip tape 526
gripping tools 222
grips, types 493
grocery bags 121
groin 92, 94
groove 169, 510
ground 404
ground beef 152
ground electrode 359
ground lamb 153
ground moraine 30
ground pepper 139
ground pork 153
ground terminal 322
ground veal 152
ground wire 198
groundhog 82
grounding prong 198
grow sleepers 260
growth line 72, 73
Gruyère 151
guard 169, 217, 489
guard rail 191, 211, 526
guardhouse 282
Guatemala 448
guava 137
guide 536
guide bar 235
guide handle 229
guiding tower 345
Guinea 451
guinea fowl 81, 154
guinea pig 82
Guinea, Gulf 20
Guinea-Bissau 451
guitar 302, 303
gulf 24
Gulf of Aden 19, 20
Gulf of Alaska 16
Gulf of Bothnia 18
Gulf of California 16
Gulf of Carpentaria 15
Gulf of Guinea 20
Gulf of Mexico 16
Gulf of Oman 19
Gulf of Panama 17
gum 101, 116
gun 216
gun flap 248
gurnard 159
gusset 274, 276
gusset pocket 255
Gutenberg discontinuity 26
gutter 182
guy line 528
guy wire 412
Guyana 448
guyot 33
gym teachers' office 444
gymnasium 386, 444
gymnast's name 497
gymnastics 496
gynecological examination room 463

H

hack 515
hackle 536
hacksaw 226
haddock 161
hair 93, 95, 114, 301
hair bulb 114
hair clip 268
hair conditioner 267
hair dryer 270
hair follicle 114
hair roller 268
hair roller pin 268
hair shaft 114
hairbrushes 268
haircolor 267
haircutting scissors 270
hairdressing 268
hairdressing salon 436
hairpin 268
hairstylist 290
Haiti 448
half handle 169
half note 299
half rest 299
half-glasses 273
half-mask respirator 459
half-slip 258
half-volley 490
halfway dash line 483
halfway line 481
halibut 161
hall 188, 386, 439
halo 6
halogen desk lamp 206
ham knife 169
hammer 304, 472, 534
hammer loop 225
hammer rail 304
hammer throw 473
hamster 82
hand 91, 93, 95, 115
hand blender 176
hand brake 350
hand cultivator 232
hand fork 232
hand held vacuum cleaner 208
hand miter saw 226
hand mixer 176
hand post 297
hand protector 235, 525
hand rest 332
hand tools 232
hand truck 396
hand-warmer pocket 249, 251
handbags 275
handcuff case 456
handgrip 366, 369, 466, 536
handgrips 500
handheld computer/personal digital assistant (PDA) 337
handicap spot 470
handle 167, 170, 176, 177, 178, 179, 180, 192, 204, 208, 209, 210, 211, 215, 216, 217, 219, 220, 221, 222, 223, 224, 225, 226, 227, 229, 231, 235, 236, 237, 269, 270, 271, 272, 273, 274, 275, 276, 277, 301, 325, 326, 341, 356, 467, 477, 478, 492, 493, 494, 510, 515, 531, 536, 537
handlebar 501, 523
handlebars 371, 523
handling 396
handrail 287, 363, 380, 385
handsaw 226
handset 327
handset cord 327
hang-up ring 270
hanger bracket 467
hanging basket 230
hanging file 340
hanging glacier 30
hanging pendant 206
hanging stile 185, 186, 202
hank 521
hapteron 51
harbor 381
hard boot 513
hard contact lens 272
hard disk drive 333
hard hat 458
hard palate 116, 117
hard surface 492
hard-shell clams 157
hare 82, 154
harissa 141
harmonica 296
harp 302
harps 295
hasp 277
hastate 55
hat switch 332
hatband 238
hatch 13
hatchback 347
hatchet 454, 533
hawk 216
hayloft 122
hazelnut, section 60
hazelnuts 133
head 6, 67, 72, 78, 93, 95, 103, 111, 125, 220, 221, 223, 229, 271, 272, 301, 302, 303, 309, 492, 494, 505, 536
head cover 505
head cushion 502
head harness 459
head linesman 485
head nurse's office 463
head of femur 99
head of frame 186
head of humerus 99
head protection 458
head tube 371
head, bird 78
headband 324, 326, 458, 459
headbay 406
headboard 204, 205
header 185, 187
headgear 238, 239, 498
heading 313
headland 35
headlight 348, 364, 366, 368, 371, 376, 377, 523
headlight/turn signal 354
headlights 352

headline 313
headphone jack 310, 311, 322, 326
headphone plug 326
headphones 324, 326
headrest 353
heads, examples 221
health and beauty care 121
health organization 335
hearing 115
heart 71, 73, 104, 105, 154, 468
heartwood 63
heat deflecting disc 199
heat energy 46
heat gun 219
heat loss 46
heat production 408
heat ready indicator 269
heat selector switch 270
heat shield 12
heat transfer 415
heat-sealed film 163
heater 529
heating 192
heating duct 213
heating element 213, 214, 218
heating equipment 386
heating grille 380
heating oil 405
heavy duty boot 240
heavy gasoline 405
heavy machinery 398
heavy rainfall 43
hedge 183, 230
hedge shears 234
hedge trimmer 235
heel 93, 95, 169, 226, 229, 240, 247, 262, 301, 302, 477, 506, 509
heel grip 240
heel loop 467
heel rest 176, 208
heel stop 527
heelpiece 511
heelplate 514
height adjustment 501
height adjustment scale 227
helicopter 395
helix 115, 429
helmet 10, 454, 478, 486, 506, 508, 510, 513, 522, 525, 526, 527
helmet ring 10
hemisphere 429
hemispheres 21
hemlath 412
hen 81
hen egg 155
hen house 122
hendecagon 429
hepatic vein 103
heptagon 429
herbal teas 148
herbicide 47
herbivores 45
herbs 142
heron 80
herring 159
herringbone parquet 190
herringbone pattern 190
hertz 426
Hertzian wave transmission 316
Herzegovina 450
heterotrophs 45
hex nut 359
hexagon 429
hexagon nut 223
hidden pocket 274
high altar 446
high beam 352
high beam indicator light 355
high beam warning indicator 368
high card 468
high chair 205
high cloud, type 39
high clouds 42
high frequency antenna cable 394
high jump 473
high pressure area 43
high pressure center 39
high wing 394
high-hat cymbal 308
high-rise apartment 289
high-speed exit taxiway 388
high-speed shaft 413
high-speed train 376
high-tension electricity transmission 413
high-tension electricity transmission tower 402
highball glass 165
highland 5, 40
highland climates 40
highway 25, 343
highway number 25
hijiki 123
hiking boot 242
hill 29
Himalayas 19
hind leg 67
hind leg, honeybee 68
hind limb 75
hind toe 78, 79
hind wing 67
hinge 178, 185, 186, 202, 214, 274, 277, 352, 420, 511
hinge pin 400
hip 93, 95
hip belt 532
hip pad 486
hippopotamus 85
hitch ball 356
hitch pin 304
hitting area 477
hive 122
hobo bag 276
hock 83, 86, 153
hockey 506
hockey skate, in-line 527
hoe 233
hoe-fork 233
hog line 515
hoisin sauce 140
hoisting block 397
hoisting rope 219, 287, 397
holding 499
holding area marking 390
holds, examples 499
hole 504
hollow barrel 460
hologram foil strip 441
holster 456
Holy See (Vatican City) 450
holy water font 446
home 331
home antenna 316
home key 331
home plate 475
home theater 321
home user 335
home-plate umpire 475
homogenized milk 150
Honduras 448
honey 149
honeybee 68
honeybee, hind leg 68
honeybee, middle leg 68
honeybee, morphology 68
honeydew melon 135
hood 192, 209, 249, 260, 348, 364, 508
hooded sweat shirt 262
hoof 83
hook 186, 217, 225, 364, 397, 423, 460, 502, 509
hooker 482
hoop earrings 264
horizontal bar 496, 497
horizontal control 329
horizontal ground movement 27
horizontal movement 470
horizontal pivoting window 287
horizontal seismograph 27
horizontal stabilizer 393, 395
horizontal-axis wind turbine 413
horn 354, 368, 377, 455
horned melon 136
hornet 69
horny beak 76
hors d'oeuvre dish 166
horse 83, 85
horse, gaits 83
horse, morphology 83
horsefly 69
horseradish 129
horseshoe mount 7
hose 209, 257, 259, 454
hose connector 236
hose nozzle 236
hose trolley 236
hospital 433, 462
hospital bed 464
hot coolant 408
hot pepper 128
hot-air outlet 192
hot-shoe contact 314
hot-water circuit 194
hot-water heater 194
hot-water pipe 194
hot-water supply line 197
hotel 432, 439, 469, 512
hotel reservation desk 390
hotel rooms 439
hour angle gear 7
house 182, 293, 469, 515
house furniture 200
house, elements 185
house, elevation 182
house, exterior 182
house, frame 187
house, structure 188
houseboat 385
housedress 252
household equipment 215
household products 120
household waste 47, 48
houses, city 289
houses, traditional 288
housing 199, 218, 228, 229, 271
hovercraft 383
hub 70, 341, 371, 413, 467
Hubble space telescope 7, 37
Hudson Bay 16
hull 60, 520, 523
human being 92
human body 92
human denture 101
humerus 98
humid continental - hot summer 40
humid continental - warm summer 40
humid subtropical 40
hummingbird 80
hummus 140
humpback whale 90
Hungary 450
hunting 534
hunting cap 238
hurricane 43
hurricane lamp 532
husk 60, 61
hut 288
hydrant intake 455
hydraulic disc brake 522
hydraulic hoses 396
hydraulic resistance 501
hydraulic shovel 400
hydroelectric complex 406
hydroelectric power plant, cross section 407
hydroelectricity 406
hydrofoil boat 387
hydrologic cycle 45
hydrometer 359
hydrosphere 44
hyena 88
hyperlinks 334
hyperopia 419
hypha 52
hyssop 142

I

Iapetus 3
Iberian Peninsula 18
ice 45
ice breaker 384
ice cream maker 180
ice cream scoop 173
ice cube dispenser 164
ice cube tray 211
ice dispenser 346
ice hockey 506
ice hockey player 506
ice rink 512
iceberg lettuce 126
Iceland 18, 450
icing syringe 172
identification badge 456
identification bracelet 264
identification tag 277
idler wheel 523
igloo 288
igneous rocks 26
ignition key 237
ignition switch 354, 368
iguana 77
ileum 106
iliohypogastric nerve 108
ilioinguinal nerve 108
ilium 98
image adjustment buttons 320
image review button 315
impervious rock 403
impluvium 280
impulse sprinkler 236
in goal area 483
in-ground swimming pool 184
in-line hockey skate 527
in-line skate 527
in-line skating 527
in-line speed skate 527
inbounds line 484
incandescent lamp 411
incandescent lightbulb 199
incident neutron 415
incineration 49
incisors 101
incoming message cassette 328
incus 116
Index 539
index 313
index finger 115
index/enlarge button 315
India 453
Indian Ocean 14, 15, 19, 20
indicator board 374
indicator light 454
indicator lights 331
indicators 318, 323
indicators display button 320
Indonesia 19, 453
indoor electric grill 179
industrial area 431
industrial communications 317
industrial pollution 47
industrial waste 47, 48
industry 335
Indycar® 524
inert gas 199
inferior cymbal 308
inferior dental arch 116
inferior mesenteric artery 107
inferior nasal concha 117
inferior rectus muscle 119
inferior vena cava 102, 103, 104, 107
infield 474
infiltration 45
infinity 427
inflated carrying tire 380
inflated guiding tire 380
inflator 530
inflator-deflator 530
inflorescences, types 57
inflorescent vegetables 127
information booth 437
information counter 390
information desk 442, 463, 512
information spreading 335
infrared port 336, 337
infrared radiation 46, 418
infraspiatus 97
infundibulum of fallopian tube 113
infusions 148
inhalation valve 459
initials of the issuing bank 441
injection well 402
ink 312
inkjet printer 333
inlaid parquet 190
inlet valve 360
inner boot 511, 527
inner circle 515
inner core 26
inner door shell 352
inner hearth 192
inner lip 73
inner planets 3
inner table 469
inner tent 528, 529
inner toe 78
inorganic matter 45
input devices 330
input lights 322
input select button 322
input selector 322
input tray 333
input/output audio/video jacks 322
insectivorous bird 79
insects, examples 69
insert 331
insert key 331
inside 167
inside linebacker 484
inside-leg snap-fastening 260, 261
instant-read thermometer 171
instep 247
instrument panel 355
instrumental groups, examples 300
insulated blade 217
insulated handle 179, 217
insulating material 190, 214
insulation 410
insulator 359
insurance services 442
intake manifold 360
integral 427
integrated circuit 417
Intelsat 317
intensive care unit 464
intensive farming 46, 48
intensive husbandry 46, 47
interchange 431
interchangeable studs 480
interchanges, examples 342
intercostal nerve 108
interior dome shell 7
interior door handle 352
interior door lock button 352
interior pocket 277
intermediate booster station 404
intermediate slope 512
internal boundary 23
internal ear 116
internal filum terminale 109
internal iliac artery 102, 103, 107
internal iliac vein 103
internal jugular vein 102
internal modem port 329, 336
internal tooth lock washer 222
international boundary 23
international space station 11
international system of units 426
Internet 334
Internet keys 330
Internet service provider 335
Internet user 334
Internet uses 335
internode 53
interosseus plantaris 96
interrupted projection 22
intersection of two sets 427
intertragic notch 115
intervals 298

interventricular septum 104
interview rooms 440
intestine 71, 73, 103
intravenous stand 464
intrusive filtration 47
intrusive rocks 26
inverted pleat 253
inward 518
Io 2
ion tail 6
Ionic column 281
Iran 452
Iraq 452
Ireland 449
iris 119
Irish moss 123
Irish Sea 18
Irish soda bread 145
iron 505
iron curtain 292
is an element of 427
is approximately equal to 427
is equivalent to 427
is greater than 427
is greater than or equal to 427
is identical to 427
is included in/is a subset of 427
is less than 427
is less than or equal to 427
is not an element of 427
is not equal to 427
is not identical to 427
is not parallel to 428
is parallel to 428
isba 288
ischium 99
island 24, 164, 188, 343
island arc 33
isobar 39
isolation room 462
isoseismal line 27
Israel 452
ISS 11
issuing bank, initials 441
isthmus 24
isthmus of fallopian tube 113
isthmus of fauces 116
Isthmus of Panama 16
Italy 450

J

jaboticabas 137
jack 468
jacket 249, 251, 417, 499, 534
jackets 244, 254
jackfruit 136
jaguar 89
jail 469
jalapeño chile 139
jalousie 186
Jamaica 448
jamb 192
janitor's closet 439, 443
Japan 19, 453
Japan Trench 34
Japan, Sea 19
Japanese experiment module 11
Japanese persimmon 137
Japanese plums 133
Jarlsberg 151
Java Trench 34
javelin 472
javelin throw 473
jaw 217, 221, 224, 228, 265
jaws 224, 535
jay 80
jazz band 300
jeans 254
jejunum 106
jerboa 82
jersey 522
Jerusalem artichoke 124
jet fuel 405
jet tip 272
Jew's harp 297
jewelry 264
jewelry store 436
jib 397, 520
jib tie 397
jibsheet 520
jicama 124
jig saw 227
jingle 309
jockey rollers 372
John Dory 161
joint 312, 503, 536
joint filler 216
joist 190
joker 468
Jordan 452
joule 426
joystick 332
joysticks 471
judge 498, 499
judges 496, 497, 509, 518
judges' bench 440
judges' office 440
judo 499
judogi 499
juice sac 58
juicer 180
juicing 177
jump rope 500
jump, steeplechase hurdle 472
jumper 252
jumper cables 356
jumping ski 513
jumps, examples 509
jumpsuit 254, 260, 261
juniper berries 138
Jupiter 2
jurors' room 440
jury box 440

K

Kalahari Desert 20
Kamchatka Peninsula 19
Kazakhstan 452
keel boat 521
keep 282
keeper ring 536
kelly 403
kelvin 426
Kenya 451
Kermadec-Tonga Trench 34
kernel 61
kerosene 405
ketchup 141
kettle 29, 180
kettledrum 308
key 296, 304, 306, 307, 488
key case 275
key cutting shop 437
key finger button 306
key grip 290
key guard 306
key lever 306
key lock 274
key signature 299
keybed 304
keyboard 304, 310, 330, 336
keyboard instruments 304
keyboard port 329
keyless chuck 228
keys 311
keystone 284
kick pleat 253
kicker 313
kickstand 367, 369
kidney 73, 103, 154
kielbasa sausage 156
killer whale 90
kilogram 426
kilt 253
kimono 256
king 468, 470
king's chamber 278
king's side 470
kingfisher 80
kingpin 365
kiosk 346, 379
Kiribati 453
kitchen 162, 164, 188, 280, 439, 445
kitchen knife 169
kitchen scale 171
kitchen shears 173
kitchen timer 171
kitchen utensils 169
kiwi 136
knee 83, 86, 92, 94
knee pad 476, 486, 526, 527
knee wrap 500
knee-high sock 257
knickers 254
knife 167, 531, 533
knife pleat 246, 253
knight 470
knit shirt 250
knives, examples 168
knob 202, 229, 477
knob handle 227
knobby tread tire 369
knurled bolt 219
kohlrabi 125
Kola Peninsula 18
kombu 123
kora 297
Korea, North 453
Korea, South 453
Korean Peninsula 19
Kuiper belt 2
kumquat 134
Kuril Trench 34
Kuwait 452
Kyrgyzstan 452

L

label maker 340
labial palp 67, 73
labium majus 112, 113
labium minus 112, 113
lablab beans 130
laboratory 7
laccolith 28
lace 477, 498, 509
lachrymal canal 119
lachrymal duct 119
lachrymal gland 119
lactiferous duct 113
ladder 184, 288, 361, 401, 404
ladder pipe nozzle 455
ladders 219
ladies' restroom 439
ladies' restrooms 294
ladle 173
Ladoga, Lake 18
Lady chapel 284, 285
ladybird beetle 69
lagomorphs 82
lagomorphs, examples 82
lagoon 35
lake 5, 24, 29, 32
lake acidification 48
Lake Baikal 19
Lake Chad 20
Lake Eyre 15
Lake Ladoga 18
Lake Malawi 20
Lake Tanganyika 20
Lake Titicaca 17
Lake Victoria 20
lakes 32
lamb cubes 153
lamb, cuts 153
lambdoid suture 100
lamina 51
lamp 421
lamp oil 405
lamp socket 199
lamprey 159
lanceolate 55
land 228
land pollution 47
land station 38
landfill 431
landfill site 47
landing 189, 191
landing area 472
landing gear 361, 365
landing gear crank 365
landing light 395
landing net 538
landing window 395
landslides 31
lane 433, 472, 516
lane line 473
lane rope 517
lane timekeeper 516
languid 305
lantern 230, 529
Laos 453
lapel 244
lapiaz 31
laptop computer 336
laptop computer: front view 336
laptop computer: rear view 336
larch 65
lard 149
larding needle 173
large blade 531
large intestine 106
large wheel 467
large-screen television set 321
larger spotted dogfish 158
larva 67
larynx 105
lasagna 146
laser beam 420
last quarter 5
latch 178, 214, 277
latch bolt 186
lateral bar 501
lateral brush 365
lateral condyle of femur 99
lateral cutaneous nerve of thigh 108
lateral incisor 101
lateral line 74, 515
lateral moraine 30
lateral semicircular canal 116
lateral view of adult skull 100
lateral view of child's skull 100
lateral-adjustment lever 229
latex glove 460
latex glove case 456
latissimus dorsi 97
latrines 280
Latvia 450
laundry 439
laundry room 188
lava flow 28
lava layer 28
lawn 183, 230
lawn aerator 237
lawn care 237
lawn edger 233
lawn rake 237
leaching 48
lead 313, 515
lead pencil 312
lead screw 228
lead-in wire 199
leader 538
leading bunch 522
leading edge 393
leading motorcycle 522
leaf 51, 53, 54, 55, 125
leaf axil 55
leaf lettuce 126
leaf margins 55
leaf node 53
leaf vegetables 126
leaf, structure 55
leakproof cap 529
leather end 246
leather goods 274
leather goods shop 436
leather sheath 533
leather skin 478
leaves, examples 65
Lebanon 452
lectern 446
ledger 187
ledger line 298
leech 519
leeks 124
left (free) safety 484
left atrium 103, 104
left attacker 487
left back 481, 487
left center 482
left channel 324
left cornerback 484
left defense 506
left defensive end 484
left defensive tackle 484
left field 475
left fielder 474
left forward 489
left guard 485
left kidney 107
left lung 103, 105
left midfielder 481
left pulmonary vein 104
left service court 491
left side 272
left tackle 485
left ventricle 103, 104
left wing 482, 507
leg 70, 76, 91, 93, 95, 202, 204, 205, 231, 247, 308, 493, 537
leg curl bar 501
leg extension bar 501
leg guard 476
leg-warmer 263
leghold trap 535
legume, section 60
legumes 130
lemon 134
lemon balm 142
lemur 91
length, unit 426
lengthwise bulkhead 384
lens 119, 332, 419
lens accessories 314
lens cap 314
lens case 272
lens hood 314
lens release button 314
lens system 420
lenses 314, 419
lentils 130
leopard 89
leotard 263
Lesotho 452
lesser covert 78
letter opener 339
letter scale 339
letters to the editor 313
lettuce 126
leucoplast 50
level crossing 375
leveling foot 212, 213, 214
leveling screw 423
lever 178, 197, 222, 265, 534
lever cap 229
lever corkscrew 170
Liberia 451
libero 487
library 433, 444
license plate light 352
lichen 50
lichen, structure 50
lichens, examples 50
lid 174, 177, 178, 179, 180, 181, 210, 211, 212, 215, 225, 417
Liechtenstein 450
lierne 284
life buoy 387, 457
life raft 383
life support system 10
life support system controls 10
lifeboat 382, 386
lift arm 399
lift bridge 345
lift chain 196
lift door 363
lift span 345
lift-arm cylinder 399
lift-fan air inlet 383
lifting chain 396
lifting hook 403

ligament 73
ligature 306
light 7, 8, 9, 380
light aircraft 394
light bar 455, 457
light bar controller 457
light ray 419
light shield 7
lighted mirror 269
lighthouse 381
lighting 199, 269
lighting cable 361
lighting grid 291
lighting technician 291
lightning 41
lightning arrester 407
lightning rod 183, 413
lights 206, 293
lily 56
lily of the valley 56
lima beans 131
limb 63, 535
limb top 421
lime 134
limit switch 287
limousine 347
limpet 157
linden 148
line 225, 298, 443
line guide 537
line judge 485, 496
line map 378
line of scrimmage 485
linear 55
lineman's pliers 217
linen 204
linen chest 203
linen room 439
lines of latitude 22
lines of longitude 22
linesman 481, 487, 490, 494, 507
lingerie shop 436
lingual papilla 118
lingual tonsil 118
lining 240, 244, 245, 262, 274, 509
lint filter 212
lint trap 213
lintel 192, 285
lion 89
lip 83, 87
lip brush 266
lip makeup 266
lipid droplet 50
lipliner 266
lipstick 266
liqueur glass 165
liquid 414, 415
liquid crystal display 315, 320
liquid eyeliner 266
liquid foundation 266
liquid mascara 266
liquid-crystal display 424
liquid/gas separator 359
listen button 328
lists 282
litchi 137
literary supplement 313
lithosphere 26, 44
Lithuania 450
little finger 115
little finger hook 307
liver 103, 106, 154
livestock car 377
living room 188, 528
lizard 77
llama 84
loading dock 435
loading door 192
loading hopper 364
loaf pan 179
loafer 242
loan services 442
lob 491
lobate 55
lobate toe 79
lobby 390, 435, 439, 440, 442
lobe 79
lobe bronchus 105
lobster 71, 158
lobster, morphology 71
lobule 115
local station 316
location of the statue 279
lock 185, 186, 202, 211, 275, 277, 352, 372, 482
lock dial 332
lock nut 425
lock rail 185
lock washer 222
lock-on button 227, 229
locket 264
locking button 208
locking device 209, 219, 535
locking lever 224
locking pliers 222
locking ring 221
locknut 197
locomotive, diesel-electric 377
loculus 58
lodging 512
log carrier 193
log chute 406
log tongs 193
loin 83, 93, 95
loin chop 153
long jump 472
long residue 405
long service line 494
long track 508
long-range jet 392
longan 136
longitudinal dunes 36
loop 245, 250, 343
loose powder 266
loose powder brush 266
loosehead prop 482
lopping shears 234
lore 78
loudspeaker 325, 455
loudspeaker system select buttons 322
loudspeaker terminals 322
loudspeakers 324
lounge 386, 439
louse 69
louver-board 285
louvered window 287
lovage 142
love seat 200, 439
low beam 352
low cloud, type 39
low clouds 42
low fuel warning light 355
low pressure area 43
low pressure center 39
low-speed shaft 413
low-tension distribution line 198
lower blade guard 227
lower bowl 181
lower confining bed 402
lower eyelid 75, 87, 119
lower guard retracting lever 227
lower lateral lobe 62
lower lateral sinus 62
lower lip 116, 305
lower lobe 105
lower mandible 78
lower mantle 26
lower radiator hose 358
lower shell 511
lubricant eye drops 272
lubricants plant 405
lubricating oils 405
Luer-Lock tip 460
luff 519
lug 308
lug wrench 356
luggage 276
luggage carrier 277
luggage elastic 277
luggage rack 361, 369, 523
lumbar pad 486
lumbar plexus 108
lumbar vertebra 110
lumbar vertebrae 99
luminous intensity, unit 426
lunar eclipse 5
lunar features 5
lung 105
lungs 105
lunula 114, 115
lunule 73
lupines 130
lutz 509
Luxembourg 449
Lybia 451
lynx 88
lyre 297
lysosome 66

M

macadamia nuts 133
macaque 91
macaw 80
Macedonia 450
machicolation 282
machine hall 406, 407
machinery shed 122
Mackenzie River 16
mackerel 159
macro lens 314
macronucleus 66
macula 119
Madagascar 20, 452
magazine 313
magenta 418
magma 28, 33
magma chamber 28, 402
magnesium powder 497
magnet 341, 416
magnetic compass 533
magnetic damping system 422
magnetic field 318, 416
magnetic gasket 211
magnetic lid holder 180
magnetic needle 533
magnetic separation 49
magnetic stripe 441
magnetic tape 319
magnetism 416
magnifier 531
magnifying glass 421
main bronchus 105
main circuit vent 194
main cleanout 194
main deck 385
main drain 184
main engine 13
main entrance 435, 445, 465
main frame 400
main landing gear 393
main lanes 343
main line 375
main lodge 512
main loudspeaker 321
main rooms 188
main scale 425
main scope tube 420
main sewer 434
main stalk 62
main stand 367
main switch 198
main transformer 376
main tube 8, 9
main vent 28
main waiting room 465
Maine coon 87
mainsail 520
mainsheet 520
maintenance 346
maintenance hangar 389
maître d'hôtel 438
major inner reaping throw 499
major motions 470
major outer reaping throw 499
makeup 266
makeup artist 290
malanga 129
malar region 78
Malawi 452
Malawi, Lake 20
Malaysia 453
Maldives 453
male 426
male cone 65
male ferrule 536, 537
male reproductive organs 111
male urethra 111
Mali 451
mallet 220, 308
mallets 309
malleus 116
malt vinegar 141
Malta 450
mammary gland 113
man 92
mandarin 134
mandible 67, 74, 98, 100
mandolin 297
mandoline 170
mane 83
maneuvering engine 13
manganese mix 417
mango 137
mango chutney 141
mangosteen 136
manhole 404, 434
manicure set 265
manned maneuvering unit 10
mantel 192
mantel shelf 192
mantid 69
mantle 72, 73
manual jack 361
manual release 511
manual revolving door 286
manual sorting 49
manuals 305
Manx 87
map projections 22
map, physical 24
map, political 23
map, road 25
map, urban 25
map, weather 39
maple 64
maple syrup 149
maquis 44
margarine 149
margin 55
marginal shield 76
Mariana Trench 34
Marie Byrd Land 15
marinade spices 139
marine 40
marine diesel 405
marine mammals 90
marine mammals, examples 90
maritime communications 317
maritime transport 381
marker 312
marker light 364, 365
marking tools 225
marmoset 91
marrow 154
Mars 2, 3
Marshall Islands 453
marten 88
mascara brush 266
mask 476
mason's trowel 216
masonry drill 228
masonry nail 220
masonry tools 216
mass 27
mass, unit 426
massage glove 267
masseter 96
mast 281, 375, 395, 396, 519, 520
mast foot 519
mast sleeve 519
mast-operating lever 396
master bedroom 189
master cylinder 357
masthead 313, 519
masthead light 383
mastoid fontanelle 100
mastoid process 100
mat 499
material handling 396
mathematics 427
matinee-length necklace 264
mating adaptor 11
matter 414
mattress 204, 205, 460, 530
mattress cover 204
Mauritania 451
Mauritius 452
maxilla 74, 98, 100, 117
maxillary bone 101
meadow 122
mean position 418
meander 32
measurement of length 425
measurement of temperature 424
measurement of thickness 425
measurement of time 424
measurement of weight 422
measuring beaker 171
measuring cup 171
measuring cups 171
measuring devices 424
measuring spoons 171
measuring tools 225
measuring, utensils 171
meat 152
meat grinder 170
meat keeper 211
meat thermometer 171
Mecca, direction 447
mechanical mouse 332
mechanical pencil 312
mechanical stage 421
mechanical stage control 421
mechanics 346
medial condyle of femur 99
medial moraine 30
median 343
median lingual sulcus 118
median nerve 108
median strip 434
medical equipment storage room 465
medical gas cylinder 464
medical records 465
medical team 499
medications, forms 467
Mediterranean Sea 14, 18, 20
Mediterranean subtropical 40
medium-format SLR (6 x 6) 315
medium-tension distribution line 198
medulla 107
medulla oblongata 109
meeting room 439, 442, 445
Meissner's corpuscle 114
Melanesia 15
melody strings 296
melon 135
melon baller 173
melons 135
melting 414
meltwater 30
memo pad 338
memorial board 447
memory button 322, 323, 327
memory cancel 337
memory card slots 471
memory recall 337
men's bag 276
men's clothing 244
men's gloves 243
men's headgear 238
men's shoes 240
meninges 109
menorah 447
menu button 315, 327
Mercury 2, 3
mercury bulb 424
mercury thermometer 461
merguez sausages 156
méridienne 200
mesa 36
mesh 205, 493

mesh bag 162
mesh strainer 171
mesocarp 57, 58, 59
mesopause 37
mesosphere 37
metal arm 236
metal counterhoop 308
metal frame 304
metal rod 309
metal sorting 49
metal structure 374
metallic contact grid 410
metamorphic rocks 26
meteorological forecast 38
meteorology 37
meteorology, station model 39
meter 426
metered dose inhaler 467
Mexico 448
Mexico, Gulf 16
mezzanine 293, 378
mezzanine stairs 189
micro compact car 347
microfilament 66
micrometer caliper 425
Micronesia, Federated States 453
micronucleus 66
microphone 320, 327, 328, 332, 337, 456
microphones 457
microscope 421
microscope, binocular 421
microscopes 421
microtubule 66
microwave oven 164, 178
microwave relay station 334
microwaves 418
Mid-Atlantic Ridge 34
mid-calf length 247
Mid-Indian Ridge 34
mid-ocean ridge 33
middle cloud, type 39
middle clouds 42
middle covert 78
middle ear 116
middle finger 115
middle leg 67
middle leg, honeybee 68
middle lobe 105
middle nasal concha 117
middle panel 185
middle phalanx 114
middle piece 111
middle primary covert 78
middle sole 262
middle toe 78
middy 255
MIDI cable 311
MIDI port 329
midrange 324
midrange pickup 303
midrib 51, 55, 60
midriff band 259
mihrab 447
mihrab dome 447
military communications 317
milk 150
milk chocolate 148
milk cup 163
Milky Way 6
millet 61, 143
millet: spike 61
Mimas 3
minaret 447
minbar 447
mini stereo sound system 325
minibus 363
minivan 347
mink 88
minor surgery room 462
mint 142
minus/negative 427
minute 428
minute hand 424
Miranda 3
mirror 195, 277, 366, 368, 369, 421, 439, 523
miscellaneous articles 341
miscellaneous equipment 231
miscellaneous utensils 173
Mississippi River 16
mist 41
miter box 226
miter latch 226
miter saw, hand 226
miter scale 226
mitochondrion 50, 66
mitral valve 104
mitt 243
mitten 243
mixed forest 44
mixing 176
mixing bowl 176
mixing bowls 172
moat 282
mobile remote servicer 11
mobile unit 316
mobile X-ray unit 462
moccasin 242
mock pocket 251
mode selectors 326
modem 334
moderator 408
modes of payment 441
modulation wheel 310
Mohorovicic discontinuity 26
moistener 339
molar, cross section 101
molars 101
molasses 149
Moldova 450
mole 426
molecule 414
mollusks 72, 157
Monaco 450
money 441
Mongolia 453
mongoose 88
monitor lizard 77
monkfish 160
monohulls 521
Monopoly® 469
Monopoly® money 469
mons pubis 112
monument 25
Moon 2, 4, 5
Moon's orbit 4, 5
Moon, phases 5
moons 2
mooring winch 385
moose 85
mop 215
moped 369
moraine 30
mordent 299
morels 123
Morocco 451
morphology of a bird 78
morphology of a bivalve shell 73
morphology of a butterfly 67
morphology of a dog 86
morphology of a dolphin 90
morphology of a female shark 74
morphology of a frog 75
morphology of a gorilla 91
morphology of a honeybee: worker 68
morphology of a horse 83
morphology of a lobster 71
morphology of a perch 74
morphology of a rat 82
morphology of a snail 72
morphology of a spider 70
morphology of a turtle 76
morphology of a univalve shell 73
morphology of a venomous snake: head 76
morphology of an octopus 72
mortadella 156
mortar 170
mosaic 280
mosque 447
mosquito 69
moss 51
moss, structure 51
mosses, examples 51
motion detector 286
motocross motorcycle 525
motor 212, 213, 214, 227, 229, 237
motor car 380
motor end plate 110
motor home 361
motor neuron 110
motor root 109, 110
motor scooter 369
motor sports 524
motor truck 376
motor unit 176, 177, 180, 208, 272, 376
motor vehicle pollution 47
motor yacht 385
motorcycle 366, 368
motorcycle dashboard 368
motorcycle-mounted camera 522
motorcycles, examples 369
motorcycling 525
motto 441
mouflon 84
mountain 29
mountain bike 373
mountain biking 522
mountain lodge 512
mountain mass 24
mountain range 5, 24, 26
mountain slope 29
mountain torrent 29
mounting bracket 535
mounting plate 199
mouse pad 332
mouse port 329
mouse, mechanical 332
mouth 71, 72, 73, 75, 94, 116, 305
mouthparts 68
mouthpiece 306, 307, 311, 467, 498
mouthpiece receiver 307
mouthpipe 307
mouthwash 272
movable bridges 344
movable jaw 223, 224
movable maxillary 76
movable stands 444
movements of an airplane 395
movie theater 294, 386, 432, 436
movies' titles and schedules 294
Mozambique 452
Mozambique Channel 20
mozzarella 150
Mt Everest 37
mud flap 349, 364, 365
mud injection hose 403
mud pit 403
mud pump 403
mudflow 31
muff 276
muffin pan 172
muffler 351, 369
muffler felt 304
muffler pedal 304
mule 84, 242
mullet 160
multi-image jump button 315
multigrain bread 145
multihulls 521
multipack 163
multiple exposure mode 314
multiplied by 427
multiply key 337
multipurpose solution 272
multipurpose tool 217
mummy 530
mung beans 131
Munster 151
muntin 185, 186
muscle fiber 110
muscles 96
museum 433
mushroom 52
mushroom, structure 52
mushrooms 123
music 296
music room 444
music stand 305, 311
music store 436
musical instrument digital interface cable 311
musical instruments, traditional 296
musical notation 298
muskmelon 135
muslin 171
mustard 140
mute 307
muzzle 83, 86, 87, 534
mycelium 52
myelin sheath 110
myocardium 104
myopia 419

N

naan 145
nacelle 413
nacelle, cross-section 413
nail 220
nail bed 114
nail buffer 265
nail care 265
nail cleaner 265
nail clippers 265
nail enamel 265
nail file 265
nail matrix 114
nail nick 531
nail scissors 265
nail set 220
nail shaper 265
nail whitener pencil 265
nailing tools 220
nails, examples 220
naked strangle 499
name of the currency 441
name plate 228
nameplate 313
Namib Desert 20
Namibia 452
naos 279
nape 78, 93, 95
nasal bone 100, 117
nasal cavity 105
nasal fossae 117
nasopharynx 117
national broadcasting network 316
national park 25
nationality 497
natural 299
natural arch 35
natural environment 504
natural greenhouse effect 46
natural sponge 267
Nauru 453
nave 285
navel 92, 94
navigation light 383, 393
Nazca Plate 27
Neapolitan coffee maker 181
near/far dial 320
neck 76, 83, 93, 94, 95, 101, 111, 167, 297, 301, 302, 303, 318
neck end 245
neck of femur 99
neck pad 486
neck roll 204
neck strap 458
neck support 525
neckhole 247
necklaces 264
necktie 245
nectarine 132
needle 36, 460
needle hub 460
needle-nose pliers 217
negative contact 410, 411
negative meniscus 419
negative plate 359
negative plate strap 359
negative region 410
negative terminal 359, 416, 417
negligee 256
neon lamp 217
neon tester 217
Nepal 453
Neptune 2, 3
nerve 114
nerve fiber 114
nerve termination 114
nerve, olfactory 117
nervous system 108
nervous system, central 109
nervous system, peripheral 108
nest of tables 202
net 487, 489, 491, 493, 495
net band 491
net judge 491
net support 493
Netherlands 449
nettle 127
network connection 198
network port 329
neurons 110
neutral conductor 198
neutral indicator 368
neutral line 416
neutral zone 484, 507
neutron 414
Nevis 449
New Caledonia 15
new crescent 5
New Guinea 15, 453
new moon 5
new shekel 440
New Zealand 15, 453
newborn children's clothing 260
newel post 191
Newfoundland Island 16
news items 313
newspaper 313
newspaper shop 437
newt 75
newton 426
nib 312
Nicaragua 448
nictitating membrane 87
Niger 451
Niger River 20
Nigeria 451
night deposit box 443
nightgown 256
nightingale 80
nightshot switch 320
nightwear 256
Nile 20
nimbostratus 42
nipple 92, 94, 113
nitric acid emission 48
nitrogen oxide emission 48
no. 8 482
nocking point 535
node 416
node of Ranvier 110
non-biodegradable pollutants 47
non-reusable residue waste 49
nonagon 429
nonbreaking space 330
noodles 147
nori 123
normal vision 419
North 23
North America 14, 16, 34
North American Plate 27
North Korea 453
North Pole 21
north pole 416
North Sea 14, 18
North-Northeast 23
North-Northwest 23
Northeast 23
Northern hemisphere 21
Northern leopard frog 75
northern right whale 90
Northwest 23
Norway 450
Norwegian Sea 18
nose 82, 83, 94, 117, 392, 526, 534
nose landing gear 392
nose leather 87
nose of the quarter 240, 262
nose pad 273
nosing 191

nostril 74, 75, 76, 78, 83, 117
notation, musical 298
notch 244, 422, 473, 503
notched double-edged thinning scissors 270
notched edge 270
notched lapel 248
notched single-edged thinning scissors 270
note symbols 299
nozzle 12, 216, 219, 236
nubby tire 525
nuclear energy 408
nuclear energy, production of electricity 408
nuclear envelope 50, 66
nuclear fission 415
nuclear reactor 409
nuclear waste 48
nuclear whorl 73
nucleolus 50, 66, 112
nucleus 6, 50, 66, 110, 112, 414
nucleus splitting 415
number 473
number key 328, 337
number plate 525
numbering machine 338
numeric keyboard 423
numeric keypad 331, 338
numeric lock 331
numeric lock key 331
numeric pager 327
nurse 464
nurses' lounge 465
nurses' station (ambulatory emergency) 463
nurses' station (major emergency) 462
nut 222, 223, 301, 302, 303
nutcracker 170
nutmeg 138
nutmeg grater 170
nuts 223
nylon thread 237

O

oak 64
oar 501
oasis 32, 36
oat flour 144
oats 61, 143
oats: panicle 61
Oberon 3
obituaries 313
object 419
object balls 502
objective 421
objective lens 8, 314, 420
oblique fissure 105
oboe 306
oboes 295
observation deck 391
observation post 7
observation room 462, 465
observation window 13
observatory 7
obturator nerve 108
obtuse angle 428
occipital bone 99, 100
occipitalis 97
ocean 5, 24, 45
ocean floor 33
ocean ridges 34
ocean trenches 34
ocean weather station 38
Oceania 14, 15
Oceania and Polynesia 453
oceanic crust 26
oche 471
octave 298
octave mechanism 306
octopus 72, 157
octopus, morphology 72
odd pinnate 55
odometer 355
off-road motorcycle (dirtbike) 369
office 346, 374, 438, 439
office building 381, 432, 435
office tower 435
official signature 441
officials' bench 507
offshore well 404
Ogen melon 135
ohm 426
oil 403
oil drain plug 360
oil pan 235, 360
oil pan gasket 360
oil pollution 48
oil pressure warning indicator 368
oil spill 48
oil terminal 381
oil warning light 355
okapi 84
okra 128
old crescent 5
old-fashioned glass 165
olecranon 99
olfactory bulb 117
olfactory mucosa 117
olfactory nerve 117
olfactory tract 117
olive oil 149
olives 128
Oman 452
Oman, Gulf 19
on-board computer 354
on-deck circle 474
on-off button 180, 326
on-off indicator 269
on-off light 327
on-off switch 177, 181, 206, 208, 209, 218, 269, 270, 271, 272, 314
on-off/volume 326
on/off switch 209
on/play button 328
one 427
one hundred 427
one pair 468
one thousand 427
one-arm shoulder throw 499
one-bar shoe 241
one-person tent 529
one-storey house 289
one-way head 221
onion 124
online game 335
oolong tea 148
Oort cloud 2
Op-Ed article 313
open crate 162
open end wrench 223
open stringer 191
open strings 296
open-air terrace 387
open-face spinning reel 537
opening 243
opening, utensils 170
opera glasses 273
opera house 432
opera-length necklace 264
operating instructions 346
operating panel 287
operating room 464, 465
operating suite 464
operating table 464
operation keys 442, 443
operator's cab 397
operator's cab 397
operculum 74
ophthalmology room 463
opisthodomos 279
opposable thumb 91
optic chiasm 109
optic nerve 119
optical mouse 332
optical scanner 121
optical sensor 332
optical sorting 49
optician 437
optics 418
oral cavity 105, 106
oral hygiene center 272
oral irrigator 272
orange 134
orange, section 58
orangutan 91
orbicularis oculi 96
orbiculate 55
orbital-action selector 227
orbiter 12, 13
orchard 122
orchestra 278, 295
orchestra pit 292
orchid 56
order 285
ordinary die 468
oregano 142
organ 305
organ console 305
organ meat 154
Orinoco River 17
ornamental kale 126
ornamental tree 122, 182, 230
ornaments 299
ortho-cane 466
oscillating light 455
oscillating sprinkler 236
ostrich 81
ostrich egg 155
other signs 299
ottoman 201
outboard engine 385
outdoor leisure 528
outer bull 471
outer circle 515
outer core 26
outer lip 73
outer planets 2
outer ring 441
outer table 469
outer toe 78
outfield fence 475
outgoing announcement cassette 328
outlet 361
output devices 333
output jack 303
output tray 333
outrigger 397, 400, 455
outside counter 240
outside linebacker 484
outside mirror 348, 362
outside mirror control 352
outside ticket pocket 244
outsole 240, 263
outwash plain 30
oval head 221
ovary 56, 112, 113
ovate 55
oven 164, 210
oven control knobs 210
oven thermometer 171
over-blouse 255
overall standings scoreboard 496
overalls 254, 260, 261
overbed table 464
overcoat 248, 251
overflow 194, 195
overflow protection switch 214
overflow tube 196
overhead frame 401
overhead guard 396
overlay flooring 190
overpass 343, 344
oversized shirt 255
ovule 56
owl 81
ox 85
oxbow 32
oxbow lake 32
oxford shoe 240
oxygen outlet 464
oxygen pressure actuator 10
oxygenated blood 104
oyster 123
oyster fork 168
oyster knife 169
oysters, cupped Pacific 157
ozone layer 37

P

pace 83
Pacific Ocean 14, 15, 19
Pacific Plate 27
Pacific salmon 161
Pacific-Antarctic Ridge 34
Pacinian corpuscle 114
package 163
packaged integrated circuit 417
packaging 162
packaging products 120
packer body 364
packing tape dispenser 341
pad 478
pad arm 273
pad plate 273
padded base 489
padded envelope 339
padded upright 489
paddy field 47
page down 331
page down key 331
page up 331
page up key 331
pagoda 283
pail 215
painkillers 461
paint roller 219
painting 219
pair 509
pajama 261
pajamas 256
Pakistan 452
palatine tonsil 118
palatoglossal arch 116
Palau 453
paling fence 230
pallet truck 396
palm 115, 243, 477
palm grove 36
palm of a glove 243
palm tree 64
palmaris brevis 96
palmaris longus 96
palmate 55
palmette 200
pan 422, 423, 535
pan hook 422
Panama 448
panama 238
Panama, Gulf 17
Panama, Isthmus 16
pancetta 156
pancreas 106
pane 186
panel 185, 246, 259
panoramic window 435
panpipe 297
pantograph 376
pantry 164, 188
pants 246, 263, 476, 486, 506, 525
pants, examples 254
panty corselette 258
panty girdle 259
panty hose 257
papaya 137
paper clip holder 341
paper clips 341
paper collection unit 49
paper fasteners 341
paper feed button 333, 443
paper feed light 333
paper guide 328
paper punch 340
paper recycling container 49
paper separation 49
paper shredder 341
paper sorting 49
paperboard separation 49
paperboard sorting 49
papilla 114, 119
papillary muscle 104
paprika 139
Papua New Guinea 15, 453
par 5 hole 504
parabolic dune 36
paraffins 405
Paraguay 448
parallel 22
parallel bars 496, 497
parallel electrical circuit 416
parallel port 329
parallelepiped 429
parallelogram 429
paramecium 66
Paraná River 17
parapet 344
parapet walk 282
parboiled rice 147
parcels office 374
parchment paper 162
parietal bone 99, 100
parietal pleura 105
paring knife 169
park 25, 433
parka 249
parking 375, 435, 504, 512
parking area 389, 430, 445
parking brake lever 354
parking lot 381, 390
Parmesan 151
parquet 190
parsley 142
parsnip 129
parterre 293
partial eclipse 4, 5
partially reflecting mirror 420
partition 60, 457
partlow chart 365
partridge 80
parts 200, 201, 204
parts of a bicycle 370
parts of a circle 428
parts of a shoe 240
pascal 426
pass 29
passbook update slot 442
passenger cabin 383, 386, 387, 393
passenger car 376, 380
passenger cars, types 376
passenger liner 386
passenger platform 374
passenger seat 369
passenger station 374, 375
passenger terminal 381, 389, 390
passenger train 374
passenger transfer vehicle 391
passing lane 343
passion fruit 136
passport case 275
passport control 391
pasta 146
pasta maker 170
pastern 83
pastry bag and nozzles 172
pastry blender 172
pastry brush 172
pastry cutting wheel 172
pastry shop 437
Patagonia 17
patch pocket 244, 249, 260
patella 98
patera 200
path 230
pathology laboratory 465
patient 464
patient room 464
patio 182, 230
patio door 164, 188
patrol and first aid station 512
pattypan squash 129
pause 331
pause button 323
pause/break key 331
pause/still button 319
paver 230
pavilion 432
pawn 470
pay phone 294, 437, 438, 463
PC card slot 336
pe-tsai 126

pea 60
pea jacket 251
peach 132
peach, section 57
peacock 81
peak 29, 238, 239, 458
peak-level meter 323
peaked lapel 244
peanut 130
peanut oil 149
pear 133
pear-shaped body 297
peas 130
pecan nuts 133
peccary 84
pectoral deck 501
pectoral fin 74, 90
pectoral limb 103
pectoralis major 96
pedal 302, 308, 370, 372, 473, 501, 522
pedal key 305
pedal keyboard 305
pedal pushers 254
pedal rod 304
pedal with wide platform 522
pedestal 302
pedestrian call button 434
pedestrian crossing 434
pedestrian lights 434
pedicel 56, 57, 58, 59, 62
pediment 279
pedipalp 70
peeler 169
peg 202, 224, 301, 302
peg box 301
pelerine 251
pelican 80
pellets 534
peltate 55
pelvic fin 74
pelvic limb 103
pen 27, 122, 312
pen holder 274
pen-blade 531
penalty arc 480
penalty area 480
penalty bench 507
penalty bench official 507
penalty marker 480
penalty spot 480
pencil 312, 409
pencil sharpener 341
pencil-point tip 218
pendant 264
penguin 80
penholder grip 493
peninsula 24
penis 92, 111
penne 146
penstock 406, 407
pentagon 429
penumbra shadow 4, 5
pepino 137
pepper shaker 166
pepper spray 456
pepperoni 156
percent 427
percent key 337
perch 160
perch, morphology 74
perching bird 79
percolator 181
percussion instruments 308
percussion section 295
perforated toe cap 240
perforation 243
performance tire 358
performing arts 294
perfume shop 436
pergola 230
pericardium 105
pericarp 58, 60
periodontal ligament 101
peripheral freeway 431
peripheral nervous system 108
peristome 66
peristyle 279, 280
peritoneum 111, 112
permanent pasture 122
peroneus longus 96
peroxide 461
peroxisome 66
perpendicular 428
perpetual snows 29
Persian 87
Persian Gulf 19
personal adornment 264
personal articles 264, 271
personal communications 317
personal computer 329
personal identification number pad 443
personal radio cassette player 326
personal watercraft 523
Peru 448
Peru-Chile Trench 34
peso 440
pesticide 47, 48
pestle 170
pet food 121
pet shop 436
petal 56
petiolar sinus 62
petiole 52, 55
petrochemical industry 405
petrochemicals 405
petroleum trap 403
pew 446
pharmacy 436, 462, 465
pharynx 105, 106
phase conductor 198
phases of the Moon 5
pheasant 81, 154
pheasant egg 155
Philippine Plate 27
Philippine Trench 34
Philippines 19, 453
philtrum 117
phloem 63
Phobos 2
phosphorescent coating 199
photo booth 437
photo credit line 313
photocopier 442
photographer 436
photography 314
photon 420
photoreceptors 119
photosphere 4
photosynthesis 54
photovoltaic arrays 11
phyllo dough 145
physical map 24
physician 464, 498
physics 418
pi 428
pia mater 109
piano 295, 304
piccolo 295, 306
pick 233
pickguard 303
pickling onions 124
pickup selector 303
pickup truck 347
pickups 303
pictograms 330
picture tube 318
pie pan 172
pier 285, 344
pierce lever 180
pierced earrings 264
pig 84
pigeon 81, 154
piggyback car 377
pigsty 122
pika 82
pike 160
pike perch 160
pike pole 454
pike position 518
pile 190
pile carpet 190
pile dwelling 288
pillar 27, 283, 284, 302
pillbox hat 239
pillion footrest 367, 368
pillow 204
pillow protector 204
pillowcase 204
pilot 376, 377
pilot house 385
pin 199, 454
pin base 199
pin block 304
PIN pad 443
pinch 199
pine needles 65
pine nuts 133
pine seed 65
pineal body 109
pineapple 136
pink ball 503
pink pepper 138
pinna 52, 82
pinnacle 282, 284
pinnatifid 55
pinto beans 131
pip 58, 468
pipe 209, 224
pipe clamp 224
pipe section 193
pipe wrench 216
pipeline 404
pistachio nuts 133
pistil 56
pistol 456
pistol grip 534
pistol grip handle 218, 228
pistol nozzle 236
piston 357
piston head 360
piston lever 216
piston release 216
piston ring 360
piston skirt 360
pit 57, 76
pit lane 524
pita bread 145
pitch 395, 475, 479
pitch wheel 310
pitcher 474, 475
pitcher's mound 475
pitcher's plate 475
pitchfork comb 268
pith 63
Pitot tube 525
pits 524
pituitary gland 109
pivot 217, 270, 271, 533
pivot cab upper structure 400
placing judge 516
plaice 161
plain 24, 32
plan 279, 285
plane 229
plane projection 22
plane surfaces 428
planets 2
planets, inner 3
planets, outer 2
planisphere 14
plano-concave lens 419
plano-convex lens 419
plant 53
plant cell 50
plant litter 54
plant, structure 53
plantain 136
plantaris 97
planting tools 231
plasma 104
plasma membrane 66
plasmodesma 50
plaster room 463
plastic case 534
plastic film (cellophane) 162
plastic film capacitor 417
plastics sorting 49
plastron 76
plate 178, 269, 531
plate grid 359
plateau 24, 29
platelet 104
platform 219, 363, 379, 390, 423, 516, 526
platform edge 374, 379
platform entrance 374
platform ladder 219
platform number 374
platform shelter 375
platform, 10 m 518
platform, 3 m 518
platform, 5 m 518
platform, 7.5 m 518
platter 166
play button 319, 323, 326
play/pause button 323
player positions 474, 481, 489
player's number 486, 488, 506
player's stick 506
players 492
players' bench 485, 487, 506
players' positions 482
playing area 471
playing field 480
playing surface 493
playing surfaces 492
playpen 205
pleasure garden 230
pleats, examples 253
plectrum 297
pleural cavity 105
plexus of nerves 101
pliers 222
plug 198, 228, 324
plug adapter 198, 271
plum sauce 141
plumber's snake 216
plumbing 194
plumbing system 194
plumbing tools 216
plums 132
plums, Japanese 133
plunger 216, 460
plus or minus 427
plus/positive 427
Pluto 2, 3
pneumatic armlet 461
pocket 225, 274, 502, 505
pocket calculator 337
pocket handkerchief 244
podium 283, 435, 444
point 167, 169, 301, 312, 469, 471, 538
point guard 489
point of interest 25
pointed tab end 245
pointer 422, 423
points 492
poisonous mushroom 52
poker 193
poker die 468
Poland 450
polar axis 7
polar bear 89
polar climates 40
polar ice cap 40
polar lights 37
polar tundra 40
polarizing filter 314
Polaroid® camera 315
pole 321, 490
pole grip 514
pole position 524
pole shaft 514
pole vault 472
police car 457
police officer 456
police station 433
political map 23
pollen basket 68
pollutants, non-biodegradable 47
polluting gas emission 47
pollution, agricultural 47
pollution, air 47
pollution, domestic 47
pollution, industrial 47
pollution, land 47
pollution, motor vehicle 47
pollution, oil 48
pollution, water 48
polo dress 252
polo shirt 255, 492
polygons 429
Polynesia 453
pome fruits 133
pomegranate 136
pomelo 134
pommel horse 496
poncho 251
pond 230, 504
pons Varolii 109
Pont-l'Évêque 151
poodle 86
pool 184, 502
pop-up tent 529
poplar 64
popping crease 479
poppy 56
poppy seeds 139
porch 183, 285, 447
porch dome 447
porcupine 82
pore 50, 60, 114
pork, cuts 153
Porro prism 420
port 431
port glass 165
port hand 387
portable CD/radio/cassette recorder 326
portable cellular telephone 327
portable compact disc player 325
portable digital audio player 325
portable fire extinguisher 454
portable radio 325
portable shower head 195
portable sound systems 325
portal 285
portal vein 103
porthole 386
portrait 441
Portugal 449
position indicator 287
position light 376, 395
position marker 302, 303
positive contact 410, 411
positive meniscus 419
positive plate 359
positive plate strap 359
positive region 410
positive terminal 359, 416, 417
positive/negative junction 410
post 412, 487, 495
post binder 339
post lantern 207
post mill 412
post office 433, 437
poster 294
posterior adductor muscle 73
posterior chamber 119
posterior cutaneous nerve of thigh 108
posterior end 73
posterior fontanelle 100
posterior horn 109
posterior root 110
posterior rugae 93, 95
posterior semicircular canal 116
posterior view 93, 95, 97, 99, 113
postern 282
posting surface 341
potato masher 173
potatoes 124
pothole 31
pouch 162
pouch of Douglas 112
poultry 155
poultry shears 173
pound 440
pouring spout 215
powder blusher 266
powder puff 266
powdered milk 150

ASTRONOMY > 2-13; EARTH > 14-49; VEGETABLE KINGDOM > 50-65; ANIMAL KINGDOM > 66-91; HUMAN BEING > 92-119; FOOD AND KITCHEN > 120-181; HOUSE > 182-215; DO-IT-YOURSELF AND GARDENING > 216-237; CLOTHING > 238-263; PERSONAL ADORNMENT AND ARTICLES > 264-277; ARTS AND ARCHITECTURE > 278-311; COMMUNICATIONS AND OFFICE AUTOMATION > 312-341; TRANSPORT AND MACHINERY > 342-401; ENERGY > 402-413; SCIENCE > 414-429; SOCIETY > 430-467; SPORTS AND GAMES > 468-538

powdered mustard 140
powdered sugar 149
power adapter 336
power adapter port 336
power and backlight button 337
power button 318, 319, 322, 323, 327, 329, 333, 336
power cable plug 329
power car 376
power cord 177, 227, 229, 269, 271, 322
power indicator 329
power light 333
power mower 237
power plant 406
power plug 326, 337
power source 416
power supply cord 270
power supply fan 329
power switch 311, 315, 329
power train 372
power zoom button 320
power, unit 426
power-on button 328
power-on light 328
power-on/paper-detect light 443
power/functions switch 320
practice green 504
prairie 24
prayer hall 447
precipitation 45
precipitation area 39
prehensile digit 91
premaxilla 74
premolars 101
prepared foods 121
prepuce 111
present state of weather 39
preset buttons 319
preset tuning button 322
press bar 501
pressed cheeses 151
pressed powder 266
pressure bar 304
pressure change 39
pressure control 272
pressure control valve 461
pressure cooker 174
pressure demand regulator 454
pressure gauge 461
pressure regulator 174, 529
pressure tube 409
pressure, unit 426
pressurized refuge 345
prevailing wind 43
previous sets 492
price per gallon/liter 346
prickly pear 137
prickly sphagnum 51
primaries 78
primary consumers 45
primary covert 78
primary crash sensor 354
primary mirror 7
primary root 53
primates, examples 91
prime focus 7
prime focus observing capsule 7
prime meridian 22
primer 534
princess seams 258
princess-seamed dress 252
principal's office 445
Principe 451
print cartridge light 333
print screen 331
print screen/system request key 331
printed circuit 417
printed circuit board 417
printer, ink jet 333
printing calculator 337
printout 423
prism binoculars 420
prisoner's dock 440
privacy curtain 464
private broadcasting network 316
private dressing room 290
probe receptacle 178
proboscis 67
procedure checklist 10
producer 291
product code 423
production designer 290
production of electricity by the generator 408
production of electricity from geothermal energy 402
production of electricity from nuclear energy 408
production of electricity from wind energy 413
production platform 404
production well 402
professional training office 442
profile of the Earth's atmosphere 37
program selector 310
programmable buttons 332
programmable function keys 443
projection booth 294
projection device 365
projection room 294
projection screen 294
projector 294
proleg 67
promenade deck 386
prominence 4
pronaos 279
pronator teres 96
propane 405
propane accessories 529
propane gas cylinder 361
propellant 534
propeller 384, 386, 387
propeller duct 383
propeller shaft 387
property line 182
property person 291
propulsion module 316
proscenium 292
prosciutto 156
prosecution counsels' bench 440
prostate 111
protect tab 333
protection layer 10
protective cup 486, 507
protective equipment 486
protective goggles 522, 525
protective helmet 367, 372
protective plate 525
protective suit 525
protective surround 471
protective window 318
proton 414
protoneuron 110
province 23
pruning saw 234
pruning shears 234
pruning tools 234
pry bar 220
pseudopod 66
psychiatric examination room 462
psychiatric observation room 462
pubis 92, 94
public building 25
public garden 435
puck 507
Puerto Rico Trench 34
pull strap 277
pull tab 163
pulley 219, 360
pulling ring 460
Pullman case 277
pulmonary artery 102, 105
pulmonary trunk 104
pulmonary valve 104
pulmonary vein 102
pulp 58, 101
pulp chamber 101
pulpit 446, 447
pulsed ruby laser 420
pulverizer 402
pump 184, 212, 214, 241, 529
pump and motor assembly 357
pump island 346
pump nozzle 346
pump number 346
pump room 384
pumper 455
pumpernickel 145
pumping station 404
pumpkin 129
punch hole 240, 246, 263
punching bag 498
punching ball 498
pup tent 529
pupil 87, 119
purfling 301, 302
purse 275
purslane 127
push bar 286
push button 176, 214
push buttons 327
push frame 398
push rim 467
push-button 312
push-up bra 259
push-up stand 501
pusher 170, 177, 180
pushing phase 514
putter 505
pygal shield 76
pyloric stomach 71
pyramid 278, 429
pyramid spot 502
pyramid, entrance 278
Pyrenees 18
python 77

Q

Qatar 452
qibla wall 447
quad cane 466
quadrant 428
quadrilateral 429
quail 81, 154
quail egg 155
quark 414
quarter 240, 262
quarter note 299
quarter rest 299
quarter window 349
quarter-deck 386
quarterback 485
quartet 300
quay 381, 430
quay ramp 381
quayside crane 381
quayside railway 381
queen 68, 468, 470
Queen Maud Land 15
queen's chamber 278
queen's side 470
quiche plate 172
quick ticket system 294
quill 312
quill brush 268
quince 133
quinoa 143
quintet 300

R

rabbi's seat 447
rabbit 82, 154
raccoon 88
race director 522
raceme 57
racing suit 508, 525
rack 174, 178, 210, 214, 473, 503
racket sports 493
raclette 151
raclette with grill 179
radar 382, 383, 386, 387
radar display 457
radar mast 384
radar transceiver 457
radial nerve 108
radial passenger-loading area 389
radial thread 70
radiation 415
radiation zone 4
radiator 350, 358
radiator grille 364
radiator panel 13
radiators 11
radicchio 126
radicle 53, 63
radio 457
radio antenna 382, 384, 386, 387, 525
radio waves 418
radioactive nuclei 415
radioactivity, unit 426
radish 129
radius 98, 428
rafter 187
raglan 251
raglan sleeve 248, 251, 261
rail 202, 502
rail transport 374
railing 189
railroad line 25
railroad station 25, 375, 430, 432
railroad track 432
railway shuttle service 390
railyard 430
rain 41
rain cap 193
rainbow 41
raincoat 248
rainfly 528, 529
raining, utensils for 171
raised handlebar 522
rake 233
rake comb 268
rally car 524
rambutan 137
ramekin 166
ramp 279, 281, 343, 526
rampart 282
random orbit sander 229
range hood 164, 210
rangefinder 315
rank insignia 456
Ranvier, node 110
ras el hanout 139
raspberries 132
raspberry, section 59
rat 82
rat, morphology 82
ratchet 221
ratchet box end wrench 223
ratchet knob 425
ratchet socket wrench 223
rattlesnake 77
raven 80
ravioli 146
razor clam 157
reach-in freezer 120
reactor 408
reactor building 409
reactor vessel 409
read button 327
read/write head 333
reading lamp 206
reading light 457
reading mirror 10
reamer 177
rear apron 245
rear beam 422
rear brake 370
rear brake pedal 368
rear bumper 523
rear cargo rack 369
rear derailleur 370, 372
rear fender 369
rear foil 387
rear leg 201
rear light 370
rear propeller 384
rear rigid section 363
rear seat 353
rear shock absorber 367
rear sight 534
rear step 455
rearview mirror 354
récamier 200
receiver 321, 327, 490, 495
receiver volume control 327
receiving area 120
receiving tray 328
receptacle 51, 56, 59
receptacle analyzer 217
reception area 462, 465
reception desk 442
reception hall 447
reception level 439
rechargeable battery pack 320
recharging base 208
reclining back 460
record announcement button 328
record button 319, 323
record muting button 323
recording level control 323
recording start/stop button 320
recovery room 464
rectangle 429
rectangular 530
rectum 106, 111, 112
rectus abdominis 96
rectus femoris 96
recycling 49
recycling bin 49
recycling containers 49
Red 469
red 418
red alga 51
red ball 502, 503
red balls 503
red beam 318
red blood cell 104
red cabbage 126
red clamp 356
red kidney beans 131
red light 434
red onion 124
Red Sea 14, 19, 20
red sweet pepper 128
red whortleberries 132
red-kneed tarantula 70
redfish 161
reed 306
reed pipe 305
reel 236, 319
reel seat 536, 537
reentrant angle 428
referee 481, 483, 485, 487, 488, 498, 499, 507, 509, 516, 518
refill 312
refill tube 196
refinery 404, 431
refinery products 405
reflected solar radiation 46
reflecting cylinder 420
reflecting telescope 9
reflecting telescope, cross section 9
reflector 217, 365, 370, 523
refracting telescope 8
refracting telescope, cross section 8
refrigerated display case 438
refrigeration unit 365
refrigerator 164, 211, 438
refrigerator car 377
refrigerator compartment 211
refrigerators 438
regular decagon 429
regular dodecagon 429
regular hendecagon 429
regular heptagon 429
regular hexagon 429
regular nonagon 429
regular octagon 429
regular octahedron 429
regular pentagon 429
reinforced toe 459
relay starting line 473
relay station 316
release lever 222
release of oxygen 54
relieving chamber 278
remote control 319, 321
remote control sensor 318, 323
remote control terminal 314, 315
remote manipulator system 11, 12

removable flagpole 504
removable hard disk 333
removable hard disk drive 333
renal artery 102, 107
renal hilus 107
renal papilla 107
renal pelvis 107
renal vein 102, 107
reniform 55
repeat buttons 323
repeat mark 298
repeater 317
reproductive organs, female 112
reproductive organs, male 111
reptiles 76
reptiles, examples 77
Republic of the Congo 451
repulsion 416
reservoir 181, 406, 407
reset button 319, 329, 424, 471
reset key 328
resident 464
residential district 431
residue waste, non-reusable 49
resistance adjustment 501
resistors 417
resonator 305, 309, 324
respirator 459
respiratory system 105
respiratory system protection 459
rest area 25
rest symbols 299
restaurant 386, 432, 435, 436, 438
restaurant review 313
restaurant, fast-food 437
restricted area 489
restricting circle 488
restroom 440, 443
restrooms 463, 465
results table 518
resurgence 31
resuscitation room 462
reticle 420
retina 119, 419
retractable handle 274
retractable step 361
return 331
return crease 479
return spring 357
reverse 518
reverse light 352
reversing switch 221, 228
revolving nosepiece 421
revolving sprinkler 236
rewind button 319, 323, 326, 328
Rhea 3
rhinoceros 85
rhizoid 51
rhizome 52
rhombus 429
rhubarb 125
rhythm selector 311
rias 35
rib 125, 273, 301, 302, 401, 458
rib joint pliers 222
rib pad 486
rib roast 152
ribbing 250, 261, 536
ribosome 50, 66
ribs 98
rice 61, 143, 147
rice noodles 147
rice paper 147
rice vermicelli 147
rice vinegar 141
rice: spike 61
ricotta 150
ridge 29
riegel 30
rifle (rifled bore) 534
rigatoni 146
right (strong) safety 484
right angle 428
right ascension setting scale 8, 9
right atrium 103, 104
right attacker 487
right back 481, 487
right center 482
right channel 324
right cornerback 484
right defense 506
right defensive end 484
right defensive tackle 484
right field 475
right fielder 474
right forward 489
right guard 485
right kidney 107
right lung 103, 105
right midfielder 481
right pulmonary vein 104
right safety 484
right service court 491
right side 272
right tackle 485
right ventricle 103, 104
right wing 482, 507
rillettes 156
rim 273, 366, 371, 489
rim soup bowl 166
rime 41
rinceau 200
rind 58
ring 52, 273, 307, 423, 424, 498
ring binder 339
ring post 498
ring step 498
ringhandle 270
ringing volume control 327
rings 264, 496, 497
ringside 498
rink 506, 509
rink corner 506
rinse-aid dispenser 214
rip fence 227
ripeness 62
ripening 62
ripper 398
ripper cylinder 398
ripper shank 398
ripper tip tooth 398
rise 191
riser 191
rising warm air 43
river 24, 25, 32
river estuary 24, 35
river otter 88
rivet 169, 222
road 25, 430
road bicycle 373
road communications 317
road cycling competition 522
road flare 457
road map 25
road number 25
road racing 522
road system 342
road transport 342, 381
road tunnel 345
road, cross section 342
road-racing bicycle 522
road-racing cyclist 522
roadway 342, 345, 434
roast 152, 153
roasted coffee beans 148
roasting pans 174
Roberval's balance 422
robin 80
rock basin 30
rock candy 149
rock garden 230
rocker arm 360
rocking chair 200, 201
rockslide 31
rocky desert 36
rocky islet 35
Rocky Mountains 16
rod 119
rodent 82
rodents 82
rodents, examples 82
roll 395
roll structure 525
roller 268, 332
roller cover 219
roller frame 219
roller shade 356
rolling pin 172
romaine lettuce 126
Roman amphitheater 281
Roman house 280
Roman metal pen 312
Roman numerals 427
Romania 450
Romano 151
romano beans 131
rompers 261
roof 183, 193, 283, 349, 361
roof pole 529
roof vent 194, 361
rook 470
room number 439
rooms, main 188
rooster 81
root 54, 101, 118, 167
root canal 101
root cap 53
root hairs 53
root of nail 114
root of nose 117
root rib 392
root system 53, 62
root vegetables 129
root-hair zone 63
rope 498
rope necklace 264
Roquefort 151
rose 56, 186, 236, 302
rose window 285
rosemary 142
Ross Ice Shelf 15
rotary cheese grater 170
rotary file 338
rotary system 403
rotary table 403
rotating dome 7
rotating drum 27
rotini 146
rotor 412
rotor blade 395
rotor head 395
rotor hub 395
rotunda 435
rough 504
round brush 268
round head 221
route sign 362, 363
router 229, 334
row 272, 293
rowing machine 501
royal agaric 123
royal flush 468
rub protection 525
rubber 240
rubber boot 454
rubber bulb 460
rubber gasket 197
rubber stamp 338
rubber tip 219, 466
rubber wall 358
rubbing alcohol 461
rubbing strip 358
ruby cylinder 420
ruching 260
ruck 483
rudder 13, 383, 384, 386, 393, 520
rudder blade 384
Ruffini's corpuscle 114
ruffled rumba pants 260
ruffled skirt 253
rug 190
rug and floor brush 209
rugby 482
rugby ball 483
rugby player 483
rugby shirt 483
rugby shoe 483
rule 313
ruler 425, 531
rumba tights 260
rump 78
run 191
runabout 385
rung 219
runner 469
running shoe 262
runway 390
runway center line markings 390
runway designation marking 390
runway side stripe markings 390
runway threshold markings 391
runway touchdown zone marking 391
rupee 440
Russia 450
Russian module 11
Russian pumpernickel 145
rutabaga 129
Rwanda 451
rye 61, 143
rye bread 144
rye: spike 61
Ryukyu Trench 34

S

S-Video output 336
sacral plexus 108
sacristy 446
sacrum 98, 99
saddlebag 369
safari jacket 255
safe 443
safe deposit box 443
safety 454
safety area 499
safety belt 525
safety binding 510, 511
safety boot 459
safety cage 473
safety earmuffs 458
safety glasses 458
safety goggles 458
safety handle 237
safety lighting 457
safety line 379
safety niche 345
safety rail 219, 377
safety scissors 265
safety tether 10
safety thermostat 213
safety valve 174, 408
saffron 138
safing sensor 354
sage 142
sagittal section 111, 112
Sahara Desert 20
sail 412, 519
sail cloth 412
sail panel 520
sailbar 412
sailboard 519
sailboat 520
Saint Bernard 86
Saint Kitts and Nevis 449
Saint Lawrence River 16
Saint Lucia 449
Saint Vincent and the Grenadines 449
salad bowl 166
salad dish 166
salad fork 168
salad plate 166
salad spinner 171
salamander 75
salami 156
salchow 509
saline lake 36
salivary gland 118
salivary glands 106
salmon, Atlantic 161
salmon, Pacific 161
salsify 129
salt 141
salt shaker 166
sambal oelek 141
Samoa 453
sampler 310
San Marino 450
sanctuary lamp 446
sand bar 33
sand bunker 504
sand island 35
sand paper 229
sand shoe 365
sandal 241, 242
sandbox 377
sanding disc 229
sanding pad 229
sandy desert 36
Sao Tome and Principe 451
saphenous nerve 108
sapodilla 137
sapwood 63
sardine 159
sarong 253
sartorius 96
sash frame 186
sash window 287
satchel bag 275
satellite 316
satellite earth station 335
Saturn 2, 3
saucepan 175, 531
Saudi Arabia 452
sauté pan 175
savanna 44
savanna climate 40
savory 142
savoy cabbage 126
sawing tools 226
saxhorn 307
saxophone 306
scale 74, 76, 79, 225, 298, 424, 460, 533
scale leaf 54
scales 425
scallion 124
scallop 157
scampi 158
Scandinavian cracked bread 145
Scandinavian Peninsula 18
scapula 98, 99
scapular 78
scarlet runner beans 131
scatter cushion 204
scene 278
scenic route 25
schedules 374
schema of circulation 103
schnauzer 86
school 444
school bus 362
Schwann, sheath 110
sciatic nerve 108
science 414
science room 444
scientific air lock 13
scientific calculator 337
scientific instruments 7, 13
scientific symbols 426
scissors 461, 531
scissors crossing 375
sclera 119
score 497
scoreboard 471, 472, 492, 497, 499
scoreboard, current event 497
scoreboard, overall standings 496
scorer 487, 488
scorers 499
scorpion 70
Scotia Plate 27
scouring pad 215
scraper 219, 400, 514
screen 271, 318, 407, 439, 479
screen door 361
screen print 260, 261
screen window 528
screw 221, 301
screw base 199
screw cap 163
screw earring 264
screw locking nut 536, 537
screwdriver 221, 531
screwdriver bit 228

screwdriver, cordless 221
scrimmage: defense 484
scrimmage: offense 485
scroll 301
scroll case 407
scroll foot 200
scroll wheel 327, 332
scrolling 331
scrolling lock key 331
scrotum 92, 111
scrub room 464
scrumhalf 482
scuffle hoe 233
sea 5, 24, 32
sea bag 276
sea bass 160
sea bream 159
sea kale 126
sea lettuce 123
sea level 26, 33, 37
sea lion 90
Sea of Japan 19
sea salt 141
sea-level pressure 39
seafood 121
seal 90
sealing material 417
sealing plug 417
sealing ring 404
seam 243, 244, 478
seam pocket 251
seamount 33
search 335
seasons of the year 38
seat 195, 196, 200, 201, 205, 293, 294, 353, 369, 370, 467, 501, 523
seat belt 353
seat cover 196
seat post 370
seat stay 370
seat tube 370
seat-belt warning light 355
seats 201
seaweed 123
sebaceous gland 114
second 298, 426, 428, 498, 515
second assistant camera operator 290
second base 474
second baseman 474
second dorsal fin 74
second floor 182, 189
second hand 424
second molar 101
second premolar 101
second row 482
second space 489
second valve slide 307
second violins 295
second voltage increase 413
second-level domain 334
secondaries 78
secondary altar 446
secondary consumers 45
secondary mirror 7, 9
secondary road 25
secondary root 53
secondary waiting room 465
secretaries' office 445
secretary 203
secretary's office 443
section 313
section of a bulb 54
section of a capsule: poppy 60
section of a follicle: star anise 60
section of a grape 59
section of a hazelnut 60
section of a legume: pea 60
section of a peach 57
section of a raspberry 59
section of a silique: mustard 60
section of a strawberry 59
section of a walnut 60
section of an apple 58
section of an orange 58
section of the Earth's crust 26
sectional garage door 286
sector 428
security casing 237
security check 391
security grille 442
security guard's work station 463
security thread 441
security trigger 235
security vestibule 440
sedimentary rocks 26
seed 53, 57, 58, 59, 60
seed coat 57, 61
seed leaf 53
seeder 231
seeding tools 231
seedless cucumber 128
segment 58
segment score number 471
seismic wave 27
seismogram 27
seismograph, vertical 27
seismographic recording 403
seismographs 27
select button 327
selection key 327
selective sorting of waste 49
self-adhesive labels 340
self-contained breathing apparatus 454
self-inflating mattress 530
self-sealing flap 339
self-service meat counter 120
self-timer indicator 314
semi-detached cottage 289
semi-mummy 530
semicircle 428
semicircular canal, lateral 116
semicircular canal, posterior 116
semicircular canal, superior 116
semimembranosus 97
seminal vesicle 111
semitendinosus 97
semitrailer 365
semolina 144
Senegal 451
Senegal River 20
sense organs 114
sense receptor 110
sensitive root 109
sensor probe 178
sensor wiring circuit 357
sensory impulse 110
sensory neuron 110
sensory root 110
sent document tray 328
sepal 56, 58, 59
separate collection 49
separator 359, 384, 402, 417
septal cartilage of nose 117
septic tank 48
septum 60, 117
septum pellucidum 109
sequencer 310
sequencer control 310
serac 30
serial number 441
serial port 329
serve 487, 490
server 334, 335, 491, 494
service area 25, 389
service box 198
service judge 490, 494
service line 491
service main 434
service module 316
service provider, Internet 335
service road 388
service room 447
service station 346, 433
service table 438
service zones 495
serving cart 202
sesame oil 149
set 291, 492
set dresser 291
set of bells 309
set of utensils 173
set-in sleeve 245
setting indicator 511
settings display button 315
seventh 298
sewer 434
sewn-in floor 528, 529
sextet 300
Seychelles 452
shackle 521
shad 160
shade 206
shadow 424
shady arcades 447
shaft 278, 471, 492, 494, 503, 505, 506
shake-hands grip 493
shallot 124, 305
shallow root 63
sham 204
shampoo 267
shank 152, 153, 220, 221, 228, 270, 273, 538
shank protector 398
shapka 238
shark, morphology 74
sharp 299
sharpening steel 169
sharpening stone 169
shaving 271
shaving brush 271
shaving foam 271
shaving mug 271
sheath 55, 531, 533
sheath dress 252
sheath of Schwann 110
sheath skirt 253
sheathing 187
shed 182, 230
sheep 84
sheep barn 122
sheepskin jacket 249
sheet 515
sheet lead 521
shekel, new 440
shelf 203, 211, 219
shelf channel 211
shell 60, 72, 73, 79, 277, 308, 404
shell membrane 79
shelter 345
shield bug 69
shift key 330
shift: level 2 select 330
shifter 371, 372
shin guard 480, 513
ships 382
shirt 245, 260, 488
shirttail 245, 255
shirtwaist dress 252
shitake 123
shock absorber 351, 523
shock wave 403
shoe 488, 522, 524
shoe store 437
shoe, parts 240
shoelace 240, 262
shoes 240
shoot 53, 63
shooting star 37
shop 280
shopping bag 276
shopping carts 121
shopping center 431, 436
shopping street 432
shore 33
shore cliff 35
shorelines, examples 35
short glove 243
short service line 495
short sock 257
short track 508
short track skate 508
shortening 149
shorts 254, 261, 313, 473, 480, 483, 488, 522
shortstop 474
shot 472
shot put 472
shotgun (smooth-bore) 534
shoulder 83, 86, 92, 94, 223, 302, 342, 492, 536
shoulder bag 276
shoulder belt 353
shoulder blade 93, 95
shoulder bolt 223
shoulder pad 486
shoulder strap 259, 276, 456, 505, 532
shovel 193, 233, 510, 514
shower 189, 439, 464
shower and tub fixture 194
shower head 195
shower stall 195
shredding 49
shrimp 158
shroud 520
shunt 416
shut-off valve 194, 196, 197
shutter 186, 333
shutter release button 314
shutting stile 185
shuttlecock, synthetic 495
Siamese 87
sickle 234
side 167, 293
side back vent 244
side chair 201
side chapel 284
side compression strap 532
side door 380
side fairings 525
side footboard 377
side handrail 380
side hatch 12
side judge 485
side lane 343
side mirror 269
side panel 248
side rail 219, 365
side span 344
side vent 28, 361
side view 478
side-marker light 352
sideline 484, 487, 488, 493
sidewalk 183, 434
sidewall 365, 517
Sierra Leone 451
sieve 171
sifter 172
sight 119, 533, 535
sighting line 533
sighting mirror 533
sigmoid colon 106
signal 375
signal gantry 375
signal lamp 178, 179, 180, 181, 208, 210, 214
signal light 181
signet ring 264
silique, section 60
silk 61
sill 28
sill of frame 186
sill plate 187
silos 381
silverware 167
simple eye 67
simple leaves 55
simple organisms 66
Singapore 453
single bed 439
single reed 306
single room 439
single seat 380
single-breasted jacket 244
single-burner camp stove 529
single-handle kitchen faucet 197
single-leaf bascule bridge 345
single-lens reflex camera 314
singles service court 495
singles sideline 491, 495
singlet 473
sink 164, 194, 195, 197, 439, 464
sinker 538
sinkhole 31
siphon 72
siphonal canal 73
sistrum 309
site 182
site plan 183
sitting room 188
sixteenth note 299
sixteenth rest 299
sixth 298
sixty-fourth note 299
sixty-fourth rest 299
skate 158, 506, 509
skateboard 526
skateboarder 526
skateboarding 526
skater 527
skater: long track 508
skater: short track 508
skating kick 514
skating step 514
skeg 519
skeleton 98
skerry 35
ski 510, 523
ski area 512
ski boot 510, 511
ski glove 510
ski goggles 510
ski hat 514
ski jumper 513
ski jumping 513
ski jumping boot 513
ski jumping suit 513
ski lift arrival area 512
ski pants 254
ski pole 510, 514
ski rack 356
ski resort 512
ski school 512
ski suit 510, 514
ski tip 514
ski, giant slalom 510
ski, jumping 513
skid 395
skiers' lodge 512
skimmer 173, 184
skin 57, 58, 59, 110, 114
skin surface 114
skip 515
skirt 251
skirt finger 383
skirts, examples 253
skis, examples 510
skull 92
skullcap 238
skunk 88
sky coverage 39
skylight 183, 189
slalom ski 510
slat 205
sled 236
sleeper-cab 364
sleepers 261
sleeping bags, examples 530
sleeping car 376
sleet 41
sleeve 244, 501
sleeve strap 248
sleeve strap loop 248
sleeveless jersey 500
sleigh bells 309
slide 214
sliding cover 327
sliding door 195, 286
sliding folding door 286
sliding folding window 287
sliding jaw 425
sliding lever 353
sliding rail 353, 521
sliding seat 501
sliding sunroof 349
sliding weight 422
sliding window 287
sling back shoe 241
slip 258
slip joint 222
slip joint pliers 222

slip presenter 346
slip-stitched seam 245
slope 342
sloping cornice 279
slot 167, 178, 221, 274
Slovakia 450
Slovenia 450
slow-burning wood stove 192
slow-motion button 319
slower traffic 343
SLR camera 314
small carton 163
small crate 162
small decanter 165
small hand cultivator 232
small intestine 106
small open crate 162
small saucepan 175
smash 491
smell 116
smelt 159
smock 255
smog 47
smoke baffle 192
smoke detector 454
smoke shop 436
smoked ham 153
smooth hound 158
snack bar 294
snail 72, 157
snail dish 173
snail tongs 173
snail, morphology 72
snake 76
snap 538
snap fastener 243, 249
snap shackle 521
snap-fastening front 261
snap-fastening tab 249
snap-fastening waist 260
snare 308, 535
snare drum 295, 308
snare head 297, 308
snare strainer 308
snatch 500
snelled fishhook 538
snooker 503
snout 74, 75
snow 41
snow brush 356
snow guard 523
snow peas 130
snow-grooming machine 512
snowblower 365
snowboard 513
snowboard, alpine 513
snowboard, freestyle 513
snowboarder 513
snowboarding 513
snowmobile 523
snowsuit 261
soap dish 195
soba noodles 147
soccer 480
soccer ball 480
soccer player 480
soccer shoe 480
social services 465
social worker's office 463
society 430
sock 257, 480, 483, 486, 492
socket head 221
socket set 223
socket-contact 198
socks 247
sofa 200
sofa bed 204
soft cheeses 151
soft contact lens 272
soft palate 116, 117
soft pedal 304, 311
soft ray 74
soft shell clam 157
soft-drink dispenser 346
softball 477
softball bat 477
softball glove 477
soil 48
soil fertilization 47
soil profile 54
soiled utility room 462, 464
solar array 316
solar cell 337, 410, 411
solar collector 410
solar eclipse 4
solar energy 54, 410
solar panel 7
solar radiation 45, 46, 410, 411
solar reflectors 316
solar shield 10
solar system 2
solar-cell panel 411
solar-cell system 411
solder 218
soldering gun 218
soldering iron 218
soldering tools 218
soldering torch 218
sole 161, 229, 247, 509, 511
soleplate 208
soleus 96
solid 414, 415
solid center auger bit 228
solid line 342
solid rocket booster 12
solids 429
solitaire ring 264
Solomon Islands 453
solvent extraction unit 405
Somalia 451
somen noodles 147
sorghum 61
sorghum: panicle 61
sorting plant 49
sorus 52
sou'wester 239
soufflé dish 172
sound box 297, 302
sound engineer 291
sound field control 322
sound hole 301
sound mode lights 322
sound mode selector 322
sound receiver 460
sound recording equipment 291
sound reproducing system 322
sound stage 290
sound systems, portable 325
soundboard 296, 297, 301, 302, 304
sounding balloon 38
soup bowl 166
soup spoon 168
soup tureen 166
sour cream 150
South 23
South Africa 452
South America 14, 17, 34
South American Plate 27
South China Sea 14, 19
South Korea 453
South Pole 21
south pole 416
South Pole 15
South-Southeast 23
South-Southwest 23
Southeast 23
Southeast Indian Ridge 34
Southern hemisphere 21
Southwest 23
Southwest Indian Ridge 34
soy sauce 140
soybean sprouts 131
soybeans 131
space 298, 330, 469
space bar 330
space probe 37
space shuttle 12, 37
space shuttle at takeoff 12
space telescope 7, 37
spacelab 13
spacer 409, 467
spacesuit 10
spade 233, 468
spade bit 228
spadix 57
spaghetti 146
spaghetti squash 129
spaghetti tongs 173
spaghettini 146
Spain 449
spar 392
spare tire 361
spareribs 153
spark plug 237, 359, 360
spark plug body 359
spark plug cable 350, 360
spark plug gap 359
spark plug seat 359
spark plug terminal 359
sparkling wine glass 165
sparrow 80
spatula 173
spatulate 55
speaker 294, 320, 326, 328, 336, 518
speaker cover 324
spear 125
special effects buttons 320
special effects selection dial 320
special slalom 511
specimen collection center waiting room 465
specimen collection room 465
speed control 176, 237
speed governor 287
speed grand prix motorcycle 525
speed grand prix rider 525
speed selector 176, 177
speed selector switch 227, 228, 270
speed skate, in-line 527
speed skates 508
speed skating 508
speed-increasing gearbox 413
speedometer 355, 368, 501
spelt wheat 143
spencer 254
spent fuel storage bay 409
sperm whale 90
spermatozoon 111
sphenoid bone 100
sphenoidal fontanelle 100
sphenoidal sinus 117
sphere 429
sphincter muscle of anus 106
spices 138
spicules 4
spider 70
spider web 70
spider, morphology 70
spike 57, 473
spiked shoe 476
spillway 406
spillway chute 406
spillway gate 406
spinach 127
spinach tagliatelle 146
spinal cord 109, 110
spinal cord, structure 109
spinal ganglion 109, 110
spinal nerve 109, 110
spindle 177, 201, 425
spine of scapula 99
spinner 538
spinneret 70
spinning rod 537
spinous process 110
spiny lobster 158
spiny ray 74
spiracle 67
spiral 221
spiral arm 6
spiral beater 176
spiral cloud band 43
spiral nail 220
spiral notebook 340
spiral rib 73
spiral screwdriver 221
spiral thread 70
spire 285
spirit level 225
spirulina 123
spit 35
spit valve 307
splat 200
splay 285
spleen 103
splenius 97
spline 359
splints 461
split link 538
split peas 130
spoiler 366, 392
spoke 371
sponge-tipped applicator 266
sponson 523
spool 536, 537
spool axle 537
spool-release mechanism 537
spoon 167, 531
spoons, examples 168
spores 52
sport-utility vehicle 347
sporting goods store 437
sports area 386
sports car 347
sports complex 431
sports on wheels 526
sports, combat 498
sportswear 262
spot 207
spotlight 290, 455
spotlights 293
spout 180, 181
spout assembly 197
spray arm 214
spray button 208
spray control 208
spray head 197
spray hose 195, 197
spray nozzle 208, 236
sprayer 236
spread collar 245
spreader 273
spring 27, 32, 38, 206, 212, 222, 312, 535
spring balance 423
spring binder 339
spring wing 221
spring-form pan 172
springboard 496
springboard, 1 m 518
springboard, 3 m 518
sprinkler hose 236
sprinklers 408
sprocket 523
sprocket wheel 398
spruce 65
spur 29, 228, 308
squamous suture 100
square 429
square movement 470
square root key 337
square root of 427
square trowel 216
square-headed tip 221
squash 128
squid 157
squirrel 82
Sri Lanka 453
stabilizer fin 386
stabilizer jack 361
stack 35, 382, 402
stacking chairs 201
stadium 431
staff 298
staff change room 465
staff cloakroom 438
staff entrance 438, 445
staff lounge 443, 463
staff room 445
stage 278, 292, 293, 421
stage clip 421
stage curtain 292, 293
stage left 293
stage right 293
stage-house 292
stained glass 285
stained glass window 446
stair 293, 294
stair climber 501
stairs 188, 191, 283, 345, 378, 404, 439
stairways 283
stairwell 189
stairwell skylight 189
stake 230, 528, 529
stake loop 528, 529
stakes 231
stalactite 31
stalagmite 31
stalk 51, 125
stalk vegetables 125
stamen 56, 58
stamp pad 338
stanchion 509
stand 27, 174, 176, 206, 269, 277, 308, 537
standard poker hands 468
stapes 116
staple remover 341
stapler 341
staples 341
star diagonal 8
star drag wheel 537
Star of David 447
starboard hand 387
starch 61
starch granule 50
starling 80
start button 424
start key 328, 330
start switch 213
starter 237, 516
starter button 368
starter handle 235
starting block 473, 516
starting grid 524
starting grip (backstroke) 516
starting line 473, 524
starting pistol 472
starting positions 518
starting step 191
state 23
states of matter 414
station circle 39
station entrance 378
station model 39
station name 378
station platform 375
station wagon 347
stationary bicycle 501
stationery 337
statue 446
steak 152
steak knife 168
steam 402
steam control knob 181
steam generator 402
steam iron 208
steam nozzle 181
steam pressure drives turbine 408
steamer 175
steamer basket 175
steel 259
steel cable 535
steel casing 417
steel pen 312
steelyard 422
steeplechase hurdle jump 472
steering column 350
steering cylinder 400
steering system 351
steering wheel 350, 354, 385, 525
stem 51, 52, 53, 54, 57, 58, 59, 181, 199, 371, 384, 424
stem bulb 387
stem propeller 384
step 191, 219, 364
step chair 201

step groove 191
step stool 219
stepladder 219
stepladders 219
steppe 40
steps 183, 184, 188, 412
steps in maturation 62
stereo control 326
sterile pad 461
sterilization room 464, 465
stern 386, 519
sternal artery 71
sternomastoid 96
sternum 98
stethoscope 460
stick 301
stifle 83
stigma 56, 60
stile 201
stile groove of sash 186
stile tongue of sash 186
still cameras 315
still water level 33
stills photographer 291
Stilton 151
stimulator tip 272
sting 68
stipule 55
stirrup sock 476
stitch 240, 262
stitches 477
stitching 243
stock 296, 412, 534
stock pot 175
stockade 282
stocking 257, 506
stocking cap 239
stomach 73, 103, 106
stomach throw 499
stone 57
stone for sacrifice 283
stone fruits 132
stone marten 88
stone, curling 515
stoner 173
stool 164
stop 86
stop button 235, 319, 323, 328, 424
stop knob 305
stop/clear button 323
stopper 267, 481, 532
stopwatch 424
storage compartment 361, 364, 455
storage door 211
storage furniture 202
storage tank 405
store 432
store room 438
storeroom 444
stork 80
storm collar 193
storm sewer 434
stormy sky 41
straight 468
straight flush 468
straight jaw 222
straight position 518
straight razor 271
straight skirt 253
straight-up ribbed top 247
straightening iron 269
straightneck squash 129
strainer 177, 180, 528
strainer body 197
strainer coupling 197
straining, utensils for 171
strait 24
Strait of Gibraltar 18
strap 265, 424, 477, 500
strap eyelet 315
strap loop 532
strap system 303
strapless bra 259
stratocumulus 42
stratopause 37
stratosphere 37
stratum basale 114
stratum corneum 114
stratum granulosum 114
stratum lucidum 114
stratum spinosum 114
stratus 42
straw 163
strawberries 132
strawberry, section 59
street 25, 433, 435
street light 434
street sweeper 365
strength sports 500
stretcher 202, 460
stretcher area 462
striker 218, 481
string 301, 302
string section 295
stringed instruments 301
stringer 396
stringing 492, 494
strings 297, 304
strip 286
strip door 286
strip flooring with alternate joints 190
strip lights 207
stroke judge 516
strokes 490
strokes, types 517
structure 186
structure of a fern 52
structure of a flower 56
structure of a house 188
structure of a leaf 55
structure of a lichen 50
structure of a moss 51
structure of a mushroom 52
structure of a plant 53
structure of a tree 63
structure of an alga 51
structure of the biosphere 44
structure of the ear 116
structure of the Earth 26
structure of the spinal cord 109
structure of the Sun 4
strut 308, 357, 387, 412
stud 187, 478
studded tire 358
student 444
student's desk 444
students' lockers 445
study 189
study room 445
stump 63, 479
sturgeon 158
style 56, 57, 58, 59, 60
stylobate 279
styloid process 100
stylus 312, 337
subarctic 40
subbase 342
subclavian artery 102
subclavian vein 102
subcutaneous tissue 114
subduction 27
subfloor 187, 190
subgrade 342
subhead 313
sublimation 414
submarine cable 317
submarine canyon 33
submarine line 334
submarine pipeline 404
subsidiary track 375
subsiding cold air 43
subsoil 54
substitute's bench 481
substructure 403
subterranean stream 31
subtract from memory 337
subtract key 337
subtractive color synthesis 418
suburb 431
suburban commuter railroad 375
suburbs 25
subway 378, 435
subway map 379, 380
subway station 378, 432
subway train 378, 380
subwoofers 321
sucker 62, 72
suction hose 455
Sudan 451
sudoriferous duct 114
sugar 149
sugar bowl 166
suit 251
sulcus terminalis 118
sulfur dioxide emission 48
sulfuric acid emission 48
sum 427
sumac 139
summer 38
summer solstice 38
summer squash 128
summit 29, 512
summit lodge 512
Sun 2, 4, 5, 38
sun deck 385
sun visor 354, 356, 361
Sun, structure 4
sundae spoon 168
sundeck 387
sundial 424
sundress 252
sunflower 56
sunflower-seed oil 149
sunglasses 273
sunspot 4
super giant slalom 511
Super-G ski 510
super-G slalom 511
supercooling 414
supercross motorcycle 525
superficial peroneal nerve 108
superior cymbal 308
superior dental arch 116
superior mesenteric artery 102, 107
superior mesenteric vein 102
superior nasal concha 117
superior rectus muscle 119
superior semicircular canal 116
superior vena cava 102, 103, 104
supermarket 120, 433, 437
supersonic jet 37
supersonic jetliner 394
supervisor's office 445
supply line 194
supply point 198
supply room 464
supply tube 197
support 9, 199, 201
support thread 70
suprarenal gland 107
sural nerve 108
surface course 342
surface element 210
surface insulation 12
surface of the water 518
surface prospecting 403
surface runoff 45
surface-piercing foils 387
surgeon's sink 465
Suriname 448
surround loudspeaker 321
suspended span 344
suspender 344
suspender clip 246
suspenders 246
suspension 380
suspension arm 212, 351
suspension band 458
suspension bridge 344
suspension cable 344
suspension system 351
suspension truck 376
suspensory ligament 119
suture 60, 73
swallow 80
swallow hole 31
Swaziland 452
sweat pants 262
sweat shirt 262
sweat suit 262
sweater vest 250
sweaters 250, 254
Sweden 450
sweeper 481
sweeping hip throw 499
sweet bay 142
sweet pepper 128
sweet potato 124
sweetbreads 154
swell organ manual 305
swell pedals 305
swift 80
swimming 516
swimming goggles 516
swimming pool 386, 517
swimming pool, in-ground 184
swimming trunks 263
swimsuit 263, 516
swing bridge 344
Swiss Army knife 531
Swiss chard 125
switch 198, 211, 219, 229, 375, 416
switch lock 228
switch plate 198
switch tower 375
switched outlet 322
Switzerland 450
swivel 403, 535, 538
swivel base 224
swivel cord 269
swivel head 224
swivel lock 224
swivel wall lamp 207
swordfish 159
symbols 468
sympathetic ganglion 109
symphony orchestra 295
symphysis pubis 111, 112
synagogue 447
synapse 110
sync cable 337
synthesizer 310
synthetic shuttlecock 495
synthetic sponge 266
synthetic surface 492
Syria 452
syringe 460
syringe for irrigation 460
syrup 467
system buttons 310
system of units 426

T

T-bar 512
T-shirt dress 261
T-strap shoe 241
tab 248, 273, 274, 340
Tabasco® sauce 140
tabernacle 446
table 202, 493, 502
table lamp 206
table mixer 176
table salt 141
table tennis 493
table tennis ball 493
table tennis paddle 493
tables, examples 202
tablespoon 168
tablet 467
tablinum 280
tabloid 313
tabulation key 330
tabulation left 330
tabulation right 330
tachometer 355, 368
tack 220, 519
tackle box 538
tackless strip 190
tag 240, 262
tagine 174
tagliatelle 146
tahini 140
tail 71, 76, 82, 83, 86, 90, 111, 393, 510, 514, 526, 536
tail assembly 393
tail boom 395
tail comb 268
tail feather 78
tail of helix 115
tail pipe 351
tail pole 412
tail skid 395
tail stop 224
tailback 485
taillight 352, 367, 368
taillights 352
tailored collar 251
tailpiece 197, 297, 301
tailrace 407
Tajikistan 452
takeover zone 472
talk key 327
talking drum 297
talon 79
talus 99
tamarillo 136
tamarin 91
tamarind paste 140
tambourine 309
tamper 181
tandem bicycle 373
tang 167, 169, 216
Tanganyika, Lake 20
tank 13, 385, 454, 529
tank ball 196
tank body 364
tank car 377
tank farm 404
tank hatch 385
tank lid 196
tank sprayer 236
tank top 261, 263
tank truck 364
tanker 381, 384
Tanzania 451
tap connector 236
tape 225
tape counter 323
tape dispenser 341
tape guide 341
tape lock 225
tape measure 225
tape recorder select button 322
tape selector 323
taproot 63
tarantula 70
taro 124
tarragon 142
tarsus 78
Tasman Sea 15
Tasmania 15
taste 116
taste bud 118
taste receptors 118
tasting spoon 173
taxiway 388
taxiway line 389
tea 148
tea bag 148
tea ball 173
tea towel 215
teacher 444
teacher's desk 444
team jersey 486
team shirt 476, 480
team's emblem 506
teapot 166
tear-off calendar 338
teaser comb 268
teaspoon 168
technical delegates 509
technical events 511
technical room 345
technical specifications 358
technical terms 57, 58, 59
techniques 487
tectonic lake 32

tectonic plates 27
teddy 258
tee 505, 515
tee line 515
teeing ground 504
teeth 101
Teflon tape 216
telecommunication antenna 386, 387
telecommunication satellite 335
telecommunication satellites 316
telecommunications by satellite 317
telephone 439
telephone answering machine 328
telephone cable 434
telephone index 327, 338
telephone line 334
telephone network 317
telephone set 327
telephone, communication 327
telephoto lens 314
teleport 317
telescope 7
telescope base 7
telescopic boom 397, 455
telescopic corridor 389
telescopic front fork 366, 369
telescopic leg 460
telescopic sight 420, 534
telescoping antenna 325
television program schedule 313
television set 318, 439, 444
telltale 520
telson 71
temperate forest 44
temperature control 178, 208, 211
temperature indicator 355
temperature measured in Celsius 424
temperature measured in Fahrenheit 424
temperature of dew point 39
temperature scale 37
temperature selector 178, 212, 213
temperature sensor 358
temple 92, 273, 283
tempo control 311
temporal bone 98, 100
ten 427
Ten Commandments 447
tenderloin roast 152
tendril 62
tennis 490
tennis ball 492
tennis player 492
tennis racket 492
tennis shoe 242, 492
tennis skirt 492
tenor drum 308
tension adjustment 537
tension rod 308
tension rope 297
tension screw 308
tension spring 355, 500
tension-adjusting screw 341
tensor fasciae latae 96
tent trailer 361
tentacle 72
tents, examples 528
tepee 288
teres major 97
teres minor 97
terminal 198, 210, 404
terminal arborization 110
terminal box 411
terminal bronchiole 105
terminal bud 53
terminal filament 109
terminal lobe 62
terminal moraine 30
termite 69
terrine 174
tertial 78
tertiary consumers 45
test button 454
testicle 111
testis 71
Tethys 3
textile floor coverings 190
Thailand 453
thallus 50, 51
The Bahamas 448
The Gambia 451
theater 292, 432, 433
theater, Greek 278
thermal energy 402
thermodynamic temperature, unit 426
thermometer 404, 424
thermopause 37
thermosphere 37
thermostat 178
thermostat control 211
thigh 78, 83, 86, 93, 95, 111, 112
thigh pad 486
thigh-boot 241
thigh-high stocking 257
thimble 425
thinning razor 269
thinning scissors 270
third 298
third base 474
third baseman 474
third finger 115
third floor 182, 189
third molar 101
third row 482
third valve slide 307
thirty-second note 299
thirty-second rest 299
thong 242
thoracic legs 71
thoracic vertebrae 99
thorax 67, 68, 92, 94
thread 221
threaded rod 223
three-blade propeller 394
three-four time 298
three-of-a-kind 468
three-quarter coat 248
threshold 185
throat 78, 224, 492, 538
throat protector 476
throttle control 332
throwing circle 472, 473
thrust device 312
thrust tube 312
thruster 10
thumb 115, 243, 477
thumb hook 307
thumb piston 305
thumb rest 306, 460
thumb tacks 341
thumbscrew 223
thyme 142
tibia 98
tibial nerve 108
tibialis anterior 96
tick 70
ticket clerk 294
ticket collecting booth 378
ticket collector 374
ticket counter 390
tie 273, 299
tie beam 187
tie rod 308
tier 281
tierceron 284
Tierra del Fuego 17
tiers 278
tiger 89
tight end 485
tightening buckle 532
tightening tools 222
tighthead prop 482
tile 12, 279, 280, 283
tiller 520
tilt-back head 176
timber 279, 280
time code 291
time display/recording button 320
time signatures 298
time, unit 426
timed outlet 210
timekeeper 488, 498, 509
timekeepers 499
timer 178, 179, 501
timing belt 360
timpani 295
tine 167
tip 55, 125, 167, 216, 218, 220, 221, 227, 246, 273, 487, 503, 510, 536
tip cleaners 218
tip of nose 117
tip protector 460
tip section 536
tip-ring 536, 537
tipping lever 467
tips, examples 221
tire 349, 358, 364, 371, 522, 525
tire barrier 524
tire pump 370
tire valve 371
tires, examples 358
tissue holder 195
Titan 3
Titania 3
Titicaca, Lake 17
title deed 469
title display button 320
toad 75
toaster 178
Tobago 449
toe 79, 86, 92, 94, 226, 229, 247
toe binding 514
toe clip 370, 372
toe guard 459, 476
toe loop 509
toe pick 509
toe piston 305
toenail scissors 265
toepiece 511
toeplate 514
toggle bolt 221
toggle fastening 249
Togo 451
toilet 189, 194, 195, 196, 439, 464
toilet bowl 196
toilet soap 267
toilet tank 195
toilets 437
token 469
tom-tom 308
tomatillos 128
tomato 128
tomato paste 140
tomato sauce 140
tombolo 35
tone control 303
Tonga 453
Tonga Trench 34
tongs 173
tongue 106, 116, 117, 154, 240, 246, 262, 297, 305, 509, 511
tongue sheath 76
tongue, dorsum 118
tonsil 116
tool belt 225
tool box 225
tool holder 229
tool kit 372
tool shelf 219
tool tether 10
tools for loosening the earth 233
tools, electricity 217
tooth 74, 76, 226, 227, 235, 270, 400
tooth guard 486
toothbrush 272
toothbrush shaft 272
toothbrush well 272
toothed jaw 222
toothpaste 272
top 63, 202, 219
top box 369
top cap 417
top coat 251
top deck 404
top deckboard 396
top flap 532
top hat 238
top ladder 455
top lift 240
top of dam 406
top pocket 502
top rail 185, 201, 202, 205
top rail of sash 186
top stitching 246
top-level domain 334
top-stitched pleat 253
top-stitching 260
topping 536
topsoil 54
toque 239
Torah scrolls 447
toric lens 419
tornado 43
torque adjustment collar 228
torque converter 212
Torres Strait 15
tortellini 146
tortillas 145
torus 429
total 423
total eclipse 4, 5
total sale display 346
tote bag 276
toucan 80
touch 114
touch judge 483
touch line 481
touch pad 336
touch pad button 336
touch screen 337
touchline 483
Toulouse sausages 156
touring bicycle 373
touring motorcycle 369
touring tire 358
tow bar frame 361
tow safety chain 361
tow truck 364
towel bar 195
tower 284, 344, 412, 413
tower case 329
tower crane 397
tower ladder 455
tower mast 397
tower mill 412
tower silo 122
towing device 364
towing hitch 361
town houses 289
toy store 436
tracery 285
trachea 105
track 374, 378, 398, 431, 472, 523, 524
track idler 398
track lighting 207
track number 323
track roller frame 398
track search buttons 323
track shoe 473
tractor engine compartment 400
traditional houses 288
traditional musical instruments 296
traffic circle 25, 342
traffic lane 343
traffic lights 434
tragus 115
trailer 361
trailer car 380
trailing edge 392
trailing-edge flap 392
train 374
trainer 489, 498
training set 261
training wall 406
transaction receipt 443
transaction record slot 442
Transantarctic Mountains 15
transept 285
transept spire 284
transfer dispensing machine 379
transfer of heat to water 408
transfer ramp 343
transform plate boundaries 27
transformer 207, 407
transformer (voltage decrease) 402
transformer (voltage increase) 402
transit shed 381
transmission 212
transmission dish 316
transmission system 351
transmission to consumers 402, 413
transmitter 327
transmitting tower 316
transmitting/receiving dish 316
transmitting/receiving parabolic antenna 316
transpiration 45
transport and machinery 342
transport, air 388
transport, maritime 381
transverse bulkhead 384
transverse colon 106
transverse dunes 36
transverse process 110
tranverse flute 306
trap 194, 196, 197, 292
trap coupling 197
trapdoor 281
trapeze dress 252
trapezius 96, 97
trapezoid 429
travel agency 436
traveler 520, 521
traveler's check 441
traveling block 403
traveling crane 407
traverse arch 284
trawler 384
tray 203, 205, 219, 225, 231, 277
tread 191, 263
tread design 358
treatment room 463, 465
treble bridge 304
treble clef 298
treble fishhook 538
treble keyboard 296
treble pickup 303
treble register 296
treble tone control 303, 322, 325
tree 63
tree fern 52
tree frog 75
tree pruner 234
tree, structure 63
tree, trunk 63
trees 504
trefoil 285
trench 33
trench coat 248
triage room 463
triangle 295, 309, 429
triangular bandage 461
triangular body 297
triangular fossa 115
triceps bar 501
triceps brachii 97
tricuspid valve 104
trifoliolate 55
trigger 235, 332, 454, 534
trigger guard 534
trigger switch 227, 228, 229
trill 299
trim 277
trim panel 352
trim ring 210
trimaran 521
trimmer 271
trimming 274
Trinidad and Tobago 449
trio 300
trip lever 196, 236
trip odometer 355
tripe 154
triple jump 472
triple ring 471
tripod 8
tripod accessories shelf 8

tripod stand 308
triticale 143
Triton 3
trolley 397
trolley crank 236
trolley pulley 397
trombone 307
trombones 295
Tropic of Cancer 20, 21, 22
Tropic of Capricorn 20, 21, 22
tropical climates 40
tropical cyclone 43
tropical cyclone names 43
tropical forest 44
tropical fruits 136
tropical rain forest 40, 44
tropical wet-and-dry (savanna) 40
tropical yam 124
tropopause 37, 46
troposphere 37
trot 83
trough 33, 39, 418
trousers 499
trout 161
trowel 232
truck 526, 527
truck crane 397
truck tractor 364
trucking 364
trucks, examples 364
truffle 123
trumpet 307
trumpet interchange 342
trumpets 295
trunk 52, 62, 63, 75, 93, 95, 277, 349
trunk, cross section 63
trunks 500
truss structure 11
trussing needle 173
tsetse fly 69
tub 212, 214, 230
tub platform 195
tub rim 212
tuba 295, 307
tube 163, 461
tube retention clip 199
tuber vegetables 124
tubular bells 295, 309
tubular element 210
tubular heater 405
tuck position 518
tug 384
tulip 56
tuna 160
tundra 44
tuner 326
tungsten-halogen lamp 199
tunic 255
tunic dress 252
tuning buttons 322
tuning control 325, 326
tuning controls 318
tuning dial 326
tuning gauge 308
tuning peg 302, 303
tuning pin 304
tuning ring 297
tuning slide 307
tuning wire 305
Tunisia 451
tunnel 378
turban 239
turbine 402
turbine shaft turns generator 408
turbo-alternator unit 402
turbojet engine 393
turbot 161
Turkey 452
turkey 81, 155
Turkmenistan 452
turmeric 138
turn 299
turn signal 352, 366, 367, 368
turn signal indicator 355, 368
turnbuckle 498, 521
turner 173
turning judges 517
turning wall 517
turnip 129
turnstile 378
turntable 176, 344, 400, 401
turntable mounting 455
turret 282
turret cap 420
turtle 76
turtle, morphology 76
turtleneck 250, 514
Tuvalu 453
TV mode 319
TV power button 319
TV/video button 319
tweeter 324
tweezers 461
twig 53, 63
twin-set 255
twist 228
twist bar 500
twist bit 228
twist drill 228
twist grip throttle 368
twist handle 332
two pairs 468
two-blade propeller 394
two-door sedan 347
two-leaf door 362
two-person tent 528
two-storey house 289
two-two time 298
two-way collar 248
tympanum 75, 279, 285
type of fuel 346
type of high cloud 39
type of low cloud 39
type of middle cloud 39
type of the air mass 39
types of eclipses 4, 5
types of golf clubs 505
types of grips 493
types of movements 470
types of passenger cars 376
types of strokes 517
typhoon 43

U

u quark 414
U.S. habitation module 11
U.S. laboratory 11
udon noodles 147
Uganda 451
Ukraine 450
ulna 98
ulnar nerve 108
ultraviolet radiation 418
umbel 57
umbo 73
umbra shadow 4, 5
umbrella pine 65
umbrella stand 273
umbrellas 273
umbrellas and stick 273
Umbriel 3
umpire 479, 485, 487, 490, 495, 515
unbleached flour 144
under tail covert 78
underarm crutch 466
underarm portfolio 275
underarm rest 466
undergarment 524
underground 281
underground cable network 317
underground chamber 278
underground flow 45
underground passage 375
underground stem 54
underlay 190
underpass 344
undershirt 476
underwater light 184
underwear 247, 258
underwire 259
undressing booth 465
uneven parallel bars 496, 497
ungulate mammals 83
ungulate mammals, examples of 84
unicellulars 66
uniform 456
uniform resource locator 334
union of two sets 427
union suit 247
uniparous cyme 57
unisex headgear 239
unisex shoes 242
unison 298
unit of amount of substance 426
unit of electric charge 426
unit of electric current 426
unit of electric potential difference 426
unit of electric resistance 426
unit of energy 426
unit of force 426
unit of frequency 426
unit of length 426
unit of luminous intensity 426
unit of mass 426
unit of power 426
unit of pressure 426
unit of radioactivity 426
unit of temperature 426
unit of thermodynamic temperature 426
unit of time 426
unit price 423
United Arab Emirates 452
United Kingdom 449
United States of America 448
univalve shell 73
univalve shell, morphology 73
university 432
unleavened bread 145
unloading dock 437, 439
up and over garage door 286
uphaul 519
upholstery nozzle 209
upper 511
upper blade guard 227
upper bowl 181
upper confining bed 402
upper cuff 511
upper deck 363, 392
upper edge 493
upper eyelid 75, 87, 119
upper lateral lobe 62
upper lateral sinus 62
upper lip 116, 305
upper lobe 105
upper mandible 78
upper mantle 26
upper shell 511, 527
upper strap 511
upper tail covert 78
upperworks 521
upright 184, 466
upright piano 304
upright vacuum cleaner 209
upstage 292, 293
Ural Mountains 18
Uranus 2, 3
urban map 25
ureter 107
urethra 107, 112
urinary bladder 107, 111, 112
urinary meatus 111
urinary system 107
URL 334
uropod 71
Uruguay 448
USB port 329, 336
used syringe box 457
usual terms 57, 58, 59
utensils for cutting, examples 169
utensils, kitchen 169
utensils, set 173
uterovesical pouch 112
uterus 112, 113
utility case 276
uvula 116, 117
Uzbekistan 452

V

V-neck 244, 250
V-neck cardigan 250
vacuole 50, 66
vacuum bottle 532
vacuum cleaner attachments 209
vacuum cleaner, cylinder 209
vacuum cleaner, upright 209
vacuum coffee maker 181
vacuum diaphragm 360
vacuum distillation 405
vagina 112, 113
valley 29, 32
valve 60, 73, 307
valve casing 307
valve cover 360
valve seat shaft 196
valve spring 360
vamp 240, 263
van straight truck 365
vane 213
vanilla extract 140
vanity cabinet 195
vanity case 277
vanity mirror 354
Vanuatu 453
vapor 415
variable ejector nozzle 394
vastus lateralis 96, 97
vastus medialis 96
vault 284, 443
vaulting horse 496, 497
VCR controls 319
VCR mode 319
VCR power button 319
veal cubes 152
vegetable bowl 166
vegetable brush 173
vegetable garden 122, 182
vegetable kingdom 50
vegetable sponge 267
vegetables 120, 124
vegetables, bulb 124
vegetables, fruit 128
vegetables, inflorescent 127
vegetables, leaf 126
vegetables, root 129
vegetables, stalk 125
vegetables, tuber 124
vegetation 44
vegetation regions 44
vehicle jack 356
vehicle rest area 345
veil 536
vein 55
veins 102
velarium 281
Velcro closure 260
velvet-band choker 264
Venezuela 448
venom canal 76
venom gland 76
venom-conducting tube 76
venomous snake, morphology 76
vent 354
vent brush 268
vent door 365
ventilated rib 534
ventilating circuit 194
ventilating grille 209
ventilator 380
ventral abdominal artery 71
ventral nerve cord 71
Venus 2, 3
verbena 148
vermicelli 147
vermiform appendix 106
vernal equinox 38
vernier 422, 425
vernier caliper 425
vernier scale 425
Versailles parquet 190
vertebral body 110
vertebral column 98, 109
vertebral shield 76
vertical control 329
vertical cord lift 208
vertical ground movement 27
vertical movement 470
vertical pivoting window 287
vertical pupil 76
vertical section 526
vertical seismograph 27
vertical side band 487
vertical-axis wind turbine 412
vest 244, 255
vestibular nerve 116
vestibule 116, 280
vial 467
vibrating mudscreen 403
vibrato arm 303
vice-skip 515
Victoria, Lake 20
video and digital terminals 315
video entertainment system 471
video monitor 329
video port 329, 336
videocassette 319
videocassette recorder 319
videotape operation controls 320
Vietnam 453
view camera 315
viewfinder 315
village 430, 512
vine shoot 62
vine stock 62
vinyl grip sole 261
viola 301
violas 295
violet 56
violin 301
violin family 301
viper 77
visceral ganglion 73
visceral pleura 105
vise 224
visible light 418
vision 419
vision defects 419
visor 367, 459, 506, 525
visor hinge 367
Vistula River 18
visual display 471
vitelline membrane 79
vitreous body 119
vocal cord 105
voice edit buttons 310
voice recorder button 337
voice selector 311
volcanic bomb 28
volcanic island 33
volcanic lake 32
volcano 26, 28
volcano during eruption 28
volcanoes, examples 28
Volga River 18
volley 490
volleyball 487
volt 426
voltage decrease 413
voltage increase 408
voltage tester 217
volume control 303, 310, 311, 319, 322, 325, 326, 328, 329
volume display 346
volute 200
volva 52
vulture 80
vulva 94, 113

W

wad 534
waders 538
wadi 36
wading bird 79
waffle iron 178
wagon tent 528
waist 93, 95, 240, 301
waist belt 205
waistband 246, 247, 249
waistband extension 246
waiter's corkscrew 170
waiting area 442
waiting room 463

wakame 123
walk 83
walk-in closet 189
walker 466
walkie-talkie 456
walking aids 466
walking leg 67
walking stick 273, 466
walkway 436
wall 5, 58, 184, 528
wall cabinet 164
wall cloud 43
wall lantern 207
wall sconce 207
wall side 385
wall tent 528
wallet 275, 337
walnut 64, 133
walnut, section 60
waning gibbous 5
wapiti (elk) 84
wardrobe 189, 203, 439
warehouse 430
warm air 41
warm temperate climates 40
warm-air baffle 192
warming plate 181
warning device 454
warning lights 355
warning plate 228
warning track 475
wasabi 141
wash tower 214
washcloth 267
washer 194, 212, 417
washer nozzle 348
washers 222
wasp-waisted corset 259
Wassily chair 200
waste basket 341
waste layers 47
waste pipe 196
waste stack 194
waste water 48
waste, selective sorting 49
water 402
water bottle 371
water bottle clip 371
water carrier 532
water chestnut 124
water cools the used steam 408
water goblet 165
water hazard 504
water hose 214
water intake 407
water is pumped back into the steam generator 408
water jets 518
water level 181
water level indicator 179
water meter 194
water pitcher 166
water pollution 48
water pressure gauge 455
water service pipe 194
water spider 70
water strider 69
water table 31, 48
water tank 181, 272
water tank area 394
water turns into steam 408
water-level selector 212
water-level tube 208
water-steam mix 402
watercourse 32, 48
watercress 127
waterfall 31, 32
watering can 236
watering tools 236
watering tube 365
watermark 441
watermelon 135
waterproof pants 260
waterspout 43
watt 426
wave 33, 418
wave base 33
wave clip 268
wave height 33
wave length 33
wavelength 418
wax 514
wax bean 131
wax gourd (winter melon) 128
wax seal 196
waxed paper 162
waxing gibbous 5
waxing kit 514
weasel 88
weather map 38, 39
weather radar 38, 392
weather satellite 38
weatherboard 185, 186
web 75, 79, 477
web frame 385
webbed foot 75
webbed toe 79
webbing 353
Webcam 332
Weddell Sea 15
wedding ring 264
wedge 305
wedge lever 229
weeder 232
weeding hoe 233
weekender 277
weeping willow 64
weighing platform 423
weight 422, 423, 500
weight machine 501
weightlifting 500
weightlifting belt 500
weightlifting shoe 500
weights 501
welding tools 218
welt 240, 244
welt pocket 244, 250
West 23
West Coast mirror 363, 364
West Indies 16
West-Northwest 23
West-Southwest 23
Western hemisphere 21
Western meridian 22
whale 90
wheat 61, 143
wheat, grain 61
wheat: spike 61
wheel 231, 277, 364, 522, 525, 526, 527, 535
wheel cover 349
wheel cylinder 357
wheel loader 399
wheel mouse 332
wheel speed sensor 357
wheel stud 357
wheel tractor 399
wheelbarrow 231
wheelchair 467
wheelchair lift 363
wheelhouse 384
whelk 157
whipping cream 150
whisk 172
whisker 82, 87
whistle 180
White 469, 470
white 418
white blood cell 104
white bread 145
white cabbage 126
white chocolate 148
white matter 109, 110
white mustard 138
white object ball 502, 503
white onion 124
white pepper 138
white rice 147
white square 470
white stone 470
white tape 487, 493, 495
white wine glass 165
white-tailed deer 84
whiting 161
whole note 299
whole rest 299
whole-wheat flour 144
wholegrain mustard 140
wholemeal bread 145
whorl 72, 73
wicket 443, 479
wicketkeeper 479
wide receiver 485
wide-angle lens 314
wigwam 288
wild boar 84
wild rice 143
Wilkes Land 15
willow 478
winch 287, 364, 521
winch controls 364
wind 47, 48
wind action 45
wind deflector 364
wind direction 39
wind energy 412
wind indicator 520
wind instruments 306
wind speed 39
wind synthesizer controller 311
wind turbine, horizontal-axis 413
wind turbines 412
wind vane 413
windbag 296
windbreaker 249
winding adjustment 420
windmill 412
window 178, 179, 186, 189, 210, 274, 349, 352, 361, 380, 392, 519
window canopy 528
window regulator handle 352
window sill 187
window tab 340
windows 274
windows, examples 287
windshaft 412
windshield 348, 364, 366, 369, 385, 392, 523
windshield wiper 348, 355
windshield wiper blade 355
wine 120
wine cellar 438
wine steward 438
wine vinegar 141
wing 13, 68, 78, 286, 393, 525, 536
wing covert 78
wing nut 223
wing pallet 396
wing rib 392
wing slat 393
wing strut 394
wing vein 67
wing, bird 78
winglet 393, 394
wings 292
winter 38
winter precipitation 41
winter solstice 38
winter sports 515
winter tire 358
wiper 355
wiper arm 355
wiper switch 354
wire 417
wire beater 176
wire brush 309
wire cutter 217
wire nut 217
wire stripper 217
wire support 529
wishbone boom 519
withers 83, 86
witness stand 440
wok 174
wok set 174
wolf 88
woman 94
women's clothing 251
women's gloves 243
women's headgear 239
women's shoes 241
won ton skins 147
wood 505
wood burning 192
wood chisel 229
wood ear 123
wood flooring 190
wood flooring arrangements 190
wood flooring on cement screed 190
wood flooring on wooden structure 190
wood frog 75
wood ray 63
woodbox 192
woodpecker 80
woods 25
woodwind section 295
woofer 324
Worcestershire sauce 140
work bench and vise 224
work surface 224
worker 68
worm 365
wraparound dress 252
wraparound skirt 253
wrapover top 255
wrenches 216, 223
wrist 86, 93, 95, 115
wrist guard 527
wrist strap 510, 514
wrist-length glove 243
wristband 486, 492, 500
writing brush 312
writing case 275
writing instruments 312

X

X-ray unit, mobile 462
X-rays 418
xylophone 295, 309

Y

Y-tube 460
yak 85
yard line 484
yard-long beans 130
yarn 477
yaw 395
yellow 418
yellow ball 503
yellow light 434
yellow onion 124
yellow sweet pepper 128
yellowjacket 69
Yemen 452
yen 440
yogurt 150
yoke 245, 249, 255
yoked skirt 253
yolk 79
Yucatan Peninsula 16
Yugoslavia 450
yurt 288

Z

Zambia 452
zebra 84
zest 58
zester 169
Zimbabwe 452
zinc can 417
zinc-electrolyte mix 417
zipper 249, 261, 265, 277, 528
zither 296
zona pellucida 112
zoom lens 314, 320
zucchini 128
zygomatic bone 98, 100

Indice español

A

abdomen 67, 68, 70, 71, 78, 92, 94
abdomen, oblicuo mayor 96, 97
abdomen, recto 96
abedul 64
abeja 68
abejorro 69
abertura 538
abertura con tirilla 245
abertura para el brazo 251
abertura trasera central 244
abertura trasera lateral 244
aberturas branquiales 74
aberturas para los nudillos 243
abeto 65
abisinio 87
abocinamiento 285
abono compuesto, cajón 231
abrazadera 8, 9, 198, 277, 521
abrebotellas 170, 531
abrecartas 339
abrelatas 170, 180, 531
abreviaciones de monedas, ejemplos 440
abrigo 248, 251
abrigo con esclavina 251
abrigo de tres cuartos 248
abrigo raglán 251
abrigo redingote 251
abrigos 248, 251
ábside 285
absorción de agua y sales minerales 54
absorción de dióxido de carbono 54
absorción por el suelo 46
absorción por las nubes 46
acampada 528
acantilado 35
acceso a los andenes 374
accesorios 209, 356, 372, 538
accesorios de golf 504
accesorios para el objetivo 314
accesorios personales 264
accesorios, cajetín 209
accesorios, objetivos 314
accidentales 299
acción del viento 45
accionador de presión del oxígeno 10
acedera 127
aceite de cacahuete 149
aceite de girasol 149
aceite de maíz 149
aceite de oliva 149
aceite de sésamo 149
aceites 149
aceites lubricantes 405
aceitunas 128
acelerador 235, 368
acelga 125
acento 299
acera 183, 434
achicoria de Treviso 126
acicular 55
acidificación de los lagos 48
ácido nítrico, emisión 48
ácido sulfúrico, emisión 48
acondicionador 267
acoplamiento de pedal 305
acoplamiento flexible 413
acorazonada 55
acorde 299
acordeón 296
acromion 99
acrotera 279
actor 290
actores, entrada 278
actriz 291
acuífero confinado 402
acumulador 357, 411
adaptador 271
adaptador de acoplamiento 11
adaptador de cinta de vídeo compacto 320
adaptador de corriente 336
adaptador de enchufes 198
adarve 282
adarve cubierto 282
adición en la memoria 337
administración 445
adobes, casa 288
adormidera, semillas 139
adornos 299
aduana 381, 391
aductor del muslo 96
aductor mayor 97
aerocisto 51
aerodeslizador (hovercraft) 383
aeropuerto 25, 388, 430
aerosol de pimienta 456
afeitado 271
afeitado, loción 271
Afganistán 452
afilador 169
afinación 308
afinador 305
afluente 32
África 14, 20, 34, 451
agar-agar 123
agarrador 467
agencia de viajes 436
agenda 275, 338
agenda electrónica 338
agenda telefónica 327, 338
agente de policía 456
agitador de aspas 212
agricultura intensiva 46, 48
agu bendita, pila 446
agua 402
agua de colonia 267
agua de deshielo 30
agua de nubes 48
agua de perfume 267
agua, castaña 124
agua, corriente 32
agua, depósito 181
agua, sales minerales, absorción 54
aguacate 128
aguanieve 41
aguas residuales 48
aguaturma 124
aguijón 68
águila 81
aguja 36, 285, 460
aguja de cambio 375
aguja de coser 173
aguja de décimas de segundo 424
aguja del transepto 284
aguja imantada 533
aguja picadora 173
agujas del abeto 65
agujas del pino 65
agujero apical 101
agujero ciego 118
airbag 354
airbag, sistema de restricción 354
aire acondicionado 361
aire cálido ascendente 43
aire caliente 41
aire frío 41
aire frío subsidente 43
aire libre, ocio 528
aislador 359
aislante 214, 410
aislante de cera 196
ajedrea 142
ajedrez 470
ajo 124
ajowán 139
ajustador de la bota 511
ajuste de altura 501
ajuste de elevación 420
ajuste de la altura del condensador 421
ajuste de la lente de campo 421
ajuste de profundidad 229
ajuste de resistencia 501
ajuste de tonos agudos 303
ajuste de tonos bajos 303
ajuste del display 327
ajuste fino de la altura 8, 9
ajuste fino del acimut 8, 9
ajuste lateral 420
ala 13, 68, 78, 238, 239, 275, 393, 536
ala alta 394
ala cerrado 485
ala de la nariz 87
ala de popa 387
ala defensivo derecho 484
ala defensivo izquierdo 484
ala del cuarto 240, 262
ala delantera 67
ala delta 394
ala derecha 482
ala izquierda 482
ala trasera 67
alamar 249
álamo 64
alas, tarima 396
albahaca 142
Albania 450
albañilería 216
albaricoque 132
albatros 80
albornoz 256
albúmina 79
albura 63
alcachofa 127
alcachofa de la ducha 195
alcantarilla 434
alcantarilla principal 434
alcaravea 138
alce 85
alcohol puro 461
aldabilla 277
Alemania 450
alerce 65
alero 279, 283
alero derecho 489
alero izquierdo 489
alerón 13, 392, 525
aleta 213, 393, 394, 395
aleta abdominal 74
aleta anal 74
aleta caudal 74, 90
aleta de fuselaje 13
aleta de la nariz 117
aleta de penetración superficial 387
aleta de proa 387
aleta del borde de fuga 392
aleta dorsal 90
aleta estabilizadora 386
aleta hipersustentadora 393
aleta pectoral 74, 90
aleta pélvica 74
alfalfa 130
alféizar 186, 187
alfil 470
alfiler 268
alfombra 190
alfombrilla 356
alfombrilla de ratón 332
alforfón 61
alga 51
alga parda 51
alga roja 51
alga verde 51
alga, estructura 51
algas 123
algas, ejemplos 51
algodón hidrófilo 461
alheña 142
alianza 264
alicates 222
alicates de electricista 217
alicates de presión 222
alicates de punta 217
alicates para cutículas 265
alicates pico de loro 222
aligátor 77
alimentación, cordón 177, 269
alimentación, fuente 416
alimentador 321
alimentos para animales 121
alimentos selectos 120
alitán 158
aliviadero 406
alma 305
almacén 444
almacén de congelados 121
almacén de material estéril 462
almacén de material sucio 462
almacén material sucio 464
almacenamiento de información, unidades 333
almeja 157
almejas 157
almena 282
almendra 57
almendras 133
almidón 61
almidón, glóbulo 50
almirez 170
almohada 204
alojamiento de la casete 323
alojamiento de la cinta 320
alojamiento para el disco 323
alojamiento para la cinta 319
alojamientos 512
alpargata 242
Alpes 18
alquequenje 132
alta presión, área 43
alta velocidad, tren 376
altar lateral 446
altar mayor 446
altar, cruz 446
altavoces extremos de graves 321
altavoz 294, 320, 324, 325, 326, 328, 336, 455, 518
altavoz central 321
altavoz de comunicación 380
altavoz de frecuencias de graves 324

altavoz de frecuenciasde medias 324
altavoz defrecuencias altas 324
altavoz principal 321
altavoz surround 321
alternado: selección de nivel 3 330
alternador 350, 360, 413
alternativa 330
altitud 44
alto de caña 511
altocúmulos 42
altostratos 42
altramuz 130
altura de la ola 33
altura del peldaño 191
alubias 131
álula 78
alumno 444
alumno, pupitre 444
alveolo 198
alvéolo dental 101
alza 301, 534
alzado 182, 212
amanita virosa 52
amapola 56, 60
amaranto 143
amarillo 418
amarra 385
amarre 521
amarre anterior retráctil 361
amasadora 179
ambiente 44
ambiente natural 504
ambulancia 460, 462
ambulatorio 465
ameba 66
América Central 14, 16
América del Norte 14, 16, 34
América del Sur 14, 17, 34
americana 254
americano, clavija de tipo 198
Américas 448
amígdala 116
amígdala lingual 118
amígdala palatina 118
amortiguador 287, 351, 367, 523
amortiguador de fieltro 304
amortiguador delantero 369
amperio 426
ampliación del voltaje 408
amplificador 310
amplificador /sintonizador : vista frontal 322
amplificador /sintonizador : vista posterior 322
amplificador-sintonizador 325
amplitud 418
ampolla 199, 467
ampolla de la trompa uterina 113
ampolla de vidrio 199
anacardos 133
anaquel 203, 211
anatomía 96
anatomía de un árbol 63
anatomía de un bogavante macho 71
anatomía de un hongo 52
anatomía de una concha bivalva 73
anatomía de una planta 53
anclaje 344
ancóneo 97
andador 466
andaduras 83
andén 375, 379, 390
andén de pasajeros 374
andouillete 156
anemómetro 413
anfibios, ejemplos 75
anfiteatro romano 281
Angola 452
anguila 159
ángulo agudo 428
ángulo entrante 428
ángulo horario 7
ángulo obtuso 428
ángulo recto 428
ángulos, ejemplos 428
Anik 317
anilla 423, 424
anilla de sujeción 536
anilla guía 536
anilla para colgar 270
anilla para lanzado largo 537
anillas 496, 497
anillas para flexiones 501
anillo 52, 271, 273, 307
anillo de ajuste 221, 306
anillo de articulación 538
anillo de compromiso 264
anillo de crecimiento 63
anillo de enfoque 420
anillo de reglaje del par de apriete 228
anillo de sonido 297
anillo de unión del casco 10
anillo graduado de ascensión recta 8, 9
anillo graduado de declinación 9
anillo ocular 78
anillo sellador 404
anillos 264
anís 142
anís estrellado 60
anjova 160
ano 71, 73, 106, 111, 112
año, estaciones 38
ánodo 417
anorak 263
anotador 487, 488
anotadores 499
Antártica 14, 15
antebrazo 86, 93, 95
antefija 279
antehélix 115
antena 7, 67, 68, 71, 326, 327, 349, 369, 392, 395, 457, 487
antena de alta frecuencia, cable 394
antena de emisión 316
antena de emisión /recepción 316
antena de radio 382, 384, 386, 387, 525
antena de telecomunicaciones 386, 387
antena doméstica 316
antena parabólica 321
antena parabólica de recepción 316
antena parabólica de transmisión 316
antena telescópica 325
anténula 71
anteojo buscador 8, 9
antera 56
anticiclón 39
anticlinal 403
Antigua y Barbuda 449
Antillas 16
antílope 84
antiséptico 461
antitrago 115
anulación de la memoria 337
anuncio 313
anuncios por palabras 313
anuncios, tablero 341
anzuelo 536, 538
aorta 104, 105
aorta abdominal 102, 107
aorta ascendente 103
aorta descendente 103
aorta, cayado 102, 103, 104
aovada 55
aparador 203
aparador con vitrina 203
aparato de Golgi 50, 66
aparato de respiración autónomo 454
aparato digestivo 106
aparato respiratorio 105
aparato urinario 107
aparatos de ejercicios 500
aparatos de medición 424
aparatos electrodomésticos 176, 208
aparcamiento 390, 435, 445, 504, 512
aparcamiento de bicicletas 445
aparejo 538
apartado 438
apartamentos 512
apéndice vermiforme 106
apéndices bucales 68
apéndices torácicos 71
apertura terminal 73
ápice 72, 73, 101, 118
apio 125
apio nabo 129
aplicador de esponja 266
aplicadores de algodón 461
aplique 207
apófisis espinosa 110
apófisis estiloides 100
apófisis mastoides 100
apófisis trasversa 110
apotecio 50
apoya-flecha 535
apoyador 484
apoyador exterior 484
apoyador interior 484
apoyatura 299
apoyo del macillo 304
apoyo del pulgar 460
apoyo para el mentón 301
apoyo para el pie 514
apoyo, punto 70
aquenio 59, 60
Arabia Saudí 452
arácnidos, ejemplos 70
aracnoides 109
arame 123
araña 70, 207
araña cangrejo 70
araña de agua 70
araña, morfología 70
araña, tela 70
arándanos 132
arándanos agrios 132
arándanos negros 132
arándanos rojos 132
arandela 207, 210, 417, 510
arandela de presión 222
arandela de presión de dientes externos 222
arandela de presión de dientes internos 222
arandela plana 222
arandelas 222
árbitro 479, 481, 483, 485, 488, 495, 498, 507, 515, 516
árbitro de base meta 475
árbitro de la defensa 485
árbol 63
árbol de la hélice 387
árbol de levas 360
árbol de Navidad 404
árbol de transmisión 395
árbol de transmisión longitudinal 351
árbol frutal 122
árbol ornamental 122, 182, 230
árbol, anatomía 63
árboles 504
árboles latifoliados, ejemplos 64
arborización terminal 110
arbotante 284, 285
arbusto 230
arca 447
arcada 281, 284
arce 64
arce, jarabe 149
archipiélago 24
archivador colgante 340
archivador de fuelle 340
archivar 339
archivo 334
archivo médico 465
archivo, formato 334
arco 301, 428
arco compuesto 535
arco dentario inferior 116
arco dentario superior 116
arco formero 284
arco insular 33
arco iris 41
arco natural 35
arco tensor 308
arcón congelador 211
ardilla 82
ardilla listada 82
área de alta presión 43
área de baja presión 43
área de caída 472
área de competición 496
área de descanso 25
área de estacionamiento 430
área de juego 471, 515
área de peligro 499
área de penalti 480
área de servicio 25
área pequeña 480
arena 281
arenera 377
arenque 159
aréola 113
Argelia 451
Argentina 448
argolla para tirar 460
Ariel 3
armadura 299, 528
armario 164, 202, 439
armario alto 164
armario bajo 164
armario del lavabo 195
armazón 187, 192, 202, 204, 207, 208, 212, 213, 219, 229, 277, 309, 412
armazón de empuje 398
armazón de la máscara 476
armazón de madera 279
armazón de metal 304
armazón del quemador 529
Armenia 452
armónica 296
aro 273, 489
arpa 302
arpas 295
arpegio 299
arquitectura 278
arquitrabe 279
arquivoltas 285
arranque 500
Arrecife, Gran Barrera 15
arrendajo 80
arriate 182, 230
arroyo 32
arroz 61, 143, 147
arroz : espiga 61
arroz basmati 147
arroz blanco 147
arroz integral 147
arroz silvestre 143
arroz vaporizado 147
arroz, fideos 147
arroz, galletas 147
arroz, vermicelli 147
arrozal 47
arteria arcuata 102
arteria axilar 102
arteria braquial 102
arteria carótida primitiva 102
arteria dorsal del pie 102
arteria dorsoabdominal 71
arteria esternal 71
arteria femoral 102
arteria ilíaca común 102, 107
arteria ilíaca interna 102, 103, 107
arteria mesentérica inferior 107
arteria mesentérica superior 102, 107
arteria pulmonar 102, 104, 105
arteria renal 102, 107
arteria subclavia 102
arteria tibial anterior 102
arteria ventral 71
artes escénicas 294
Ártico 14
articulación 355, 503, 536
artículo 313
artículos de escritorio 337
artículos de limpieza 120, 215
artículos de marroquinería 274
artículos para animales 121
artículos personales 264, 271
artículos varios 341
as 468
asa 176, 177, 178, 179, 180, 204, 209, 210, 215, 225, 226, 227, 229, 236, 274, 275, 276, 277, 326, 537
asa aislante 179
asa extensible 274
asado 152
asado de cerdo 153
asadores 174
asafétida 139
ascensor 287, 435, 439
ascensor, cabina 287
aseo 188, 440, 443
aseo de caballeros 439
aseo de señoras 439
aseos 437, 445, 463, 465
aseos de caballeros 294
aseos de señoras 294
aseos para los clientes 438
asfalto 405
Asia 14, 19, 34, 452
asidero 352, 361, 364, 455
asidero : (espalda) 516
asidero lateral 380
asidero vertical 380
asidero, espalda 516
asiento 195, 196, 200, 201, 205, 342, 353, 369, 467, 501, 523
asiento : vista frontal 353
asiento : vista lateral 353
asiento de corredera 501
asiento del rabino 447
asiento del tapón 196
asiento del teclado 304
asiento doble 380
asiento individual 380
asiento trasero 353
asientos 201
asistente de presidente del jurado 509
asistentes de los abogados 440
asno 84
aspa 412, 413
aspirador 209
aspirador manual 208
aspirina 461
asta 471
astada 55
astenosfera 26
astigmatismo 419
astil 422
astil, balanza 422
astrágalo 99
astronomía 2
atención al cliente 443
aterrizaje y despegue, pista 390
atizador 193
atlas 99
atleta : taco de salida 473
atletismo 472
atmósfera 44, 48
atmósfera terrestre, corte 37
atolón 35
átomo 414
átomos 414
atracción 416
atrecista 291
atril 305, 311, 446
atrio 280
atún 160
audiencia 440
audio player portátil digital 325
aula 445
aula de artes plásticas 444
aula de ciencias 444
aula de informática 444
aula de música 444
aula para alumnos con dificultad de aprendizaje 444
aumento de la tensión 402
aumento del efecto invernadero 46
aurícula derecha 103, 104
aurícula izquierda 103, 104
auricular 324, 327, 460
auriculares 78, 324, 325, 326
aurora polar 37
Australia 14, 34, 453
Austria 450
autobomba tanque 455
autobús 435
autobús articulado 363
autobús escolar 362
autobús urbano 362
autobuses 362
autobuses, estación 432
autocar 362
autocar de dos pisos 363

autocaravana 361
autoclave 464
autoescalera 455
automóvil 347
automóvil urbanita 347
automóviles : componentes principales 350
automóviles, contaminación 47
autopista 25, 343, 431
autótrofos 45
auxiliares ortopédicos para caminar 466
avance rápido 319
ave 78
ave acuática 79
ave de rapiña 79
ave granívora 79
ave insectívora 79
ave zancuda 79
avellana, corte 60
avellanas 133
avena 61, 143
avena : panícula 61
avena, harina 144
avenida 25, 433
aves 78
aves acuáticas 79
aves de corral 155
aves de rapiña 79
aves paseriformes 79
avestruz 81
avión de carga 394
avión de línea 37
avión ligero 394
avión particular 394
avión supersónico 394
avión turborreactor de pasajeros 392
avión, movimientos 395
aviones, ejemplos 394
avispa 69
avispón 69
axel 509
axila 92, 94
axila de la hoja 55
axiómetro 520
axis 99
axón 110
ayudante 121, 498
ayudante del atrecista 291
ayudante del director 291
ayutamiento 432
azada 233
azada de doble filo 233
azadón 233
azafrán 138
Azerbaiyán 452
azúcar 149
azúcar candi 149
azúcar glas 149
azúcar granulado 149
azúcar moreno 149
azúcar, termómetro 171
azucarero 166
azucena 56
azuela 233
azul 418
azul danés 151

B

babero 260
babilla 83
babor 387
babuino 91
bacalao del Atlántico 161
backgammon 469
bacón americano 156
bacón canadiense 156
bádminton 494
baguette 144
Bahamas 448
bahía 5, 24
Bahía de Baffin 16
Bahía de Bengala 19
Bahía de Hudson 16
Bahrein 452
bailarina 241
baile, cuchilla 509
bajada de aguas 182
bajante 196
bajo 303
bala 534
balalaika 297
balancín 360
balanza de astil 422
balanza de precisión 423
balanza de Roberval 422
balanza para cartas 339
balaustrada 283
balaustre 191
balcón 189, 293, 447
baldosa 230
ballena 245
ballena boréale 90
balón de baloncesto 488
balón de fútbol 480
balón de fútbol americano 486
balón de rugby 483
baloncesto 488
balsa salvavidas 383
bambalina 292
bambú, brote 125
banana 136
banco 201, 379, 432, 437, 442, 446, 469, 501
banco de arena 33
banco de trabajo 224
banco emisor, iniciales 441
banda 481, 484, 487, 488, 495
banda acolchada 324
banda antiadherente 526
banda blanca 487
banda de ajuste 324, 326
banda de goma 502
banda de jazz 300
banda de la cabecera 502
banda de suspensión 458
banda de ventilación 534
banda elástica 246
banda frontal 348
banda holográfica metalizada 441
banda lateral de la red 487
banda lateral protectora 365
banda magnética 441
banda nubosa en espiral 43
banda protectora 358
bandeja 179, 205, 225, 277
bandeja de alimentación 333
bandeja de correspondencia 338
bandeja de pastelería 172
bandeja de pintura 219
bandeja de salida 333
bandeja de vidrio 211
bandeja del disco 318
bandeja para cosméticos 277
bandeja para cubitos de hielo 211
bandeja para herramientas 219
bandeja para los entremeses 166
bandera 482
bandera de la Unión Europea 441
banderas 448
banderín de línea de centro 480
banderín de saque de esquina 481
banderín móvil 504
bandolera 276
bañera 189, 194, 195, 439, 520
Bangladesh 453
banjo 296
baño 439, 464
banqueta 201
banquillo 481, 498
banquillo de jugadores 474, 485, 487
banquillo de los acusados 440
banquillo de los jugadores 506
banquillo de los penaltis 507
banquillo del entrenador 474
Banquisa de Ross 15
baqueta 297
baquetas 309
bar 293, 294, 432, 436, 438
bar, barra 438
bar, taburete 438
baraja 468
baranda 502
barandilla 188, 189, 191, 219, 377, 526
barbacana 282
Barbados 449
barbecho 122
barbilla 538
barco perforador 382
bardana 129
barján 36
barqueta 162
barra 35, 237, 273, 309, 370, 469, 500, 501
barra antivibración 235
barra colectora 407
barra con pesas 500
barra de arrastre 400
barra de combustible 409
barra de compás 298
barra de dirección 350
barra de equilibrio 496, 497
barra de escotas 521
barra de extensión de piernas 501
barra de flexión de piernas 501
barra de pan 144
barra de remolque 361
barra de repetición 298
barra de torsión 500
barra de tríceps 501
barra del bar 438
barra distanciadora 362
barra espaciadora 330
barra fija 496, 497
barra lateral 501
barra sujetadora 308
barras paralelas 496, 497
barras paralelas asimétricas 496, 497
barredora 365
barrena 403
barrena de muro 228
barrera 205
barrera de contención 524
barrote 205
basamento 283
báscula de baño 423
báscula de cocina 171
báscula electrónica 423
báscula romana 422
base 125, 179, 180, 206, 227, 229, 269, 318, 332, 412, 421, 422, 454, 489
base con protecciones 489
base de cemento 190
base de cemento, parqué sobre 190
base de datos 335
base de la ola 33
base de lanzamiento 475
base del bulbo 54
base del hogar 192
base del respaldo 200
base del telescopio 7
base del tronco 63
base del tubo 199
base exterior 469
base fija 224
base giratoria 224
base impermeable 190
base interior 469
base líquida 266
base meta 475
bastidor 224, 226, 274, 277, 367, 410, 411, 492, 494, 522, 527
bastidor de los rodillos 398
bastidores 292
bastón 273
bastón cuadrangular 466
bastón de esquí 510, 514
bastón del portero 507
bastón inglés 466
bastón ortopédico 466
bastón para caminar 466
bastoncillo 119
bastones 273, 505
basura, cubo 215
basura, separación selectiva 49
bata 256
batata 124
bate 476, 477, 478
bate de softball 477
bateador 475, 476, 478, 479
batería 221, 228, 308, 350, 359, 416
batería electrónica 311
batidor 172
batidor mecánico 172
batidora de mano 176
batidora de mesa 176
batidora de pie 176
batiente 186
batir 176
baúl 203, 277
baya 59
bayas 132
bayas de enebro 138
bayeta de cocina 215
bayeta, cocina 215
bazo 103
bebé, ropa 260
bebidas 120
becquerel 426
becuadro 299
begonia 56
béisbol 474, 476
belfo 83
belfos 86
Bélgica 449
Belice 448
bemol 299
Benín 451
berberechos 157
berenjena 128
bergamota 134
berlina 347
bermudas 254
berro 127
berros de jardín 127
berza 126
besuguera 174
biblioteca 433, 444
bíceps braquial 96
bíceps femoral 97
bicicleta 370
bicicleta BMX 373
bicicleta de carreras 522
bicicleta de carretera 373
bicicleta de ciudad 373
bicicleta de cross y ciclista 522
bicicleta de descenso 522
bicicleta de turismo 373
bicicleta estática 501
bicicleta holandesa 373
bicicleta todo terreno 373
bicicleta, partes 370
bicicletas, ejemplos 373
bidé 195
biela 360
Bielorrusia 450
bígaros 157
bigotes 87
billar 502
billar francés 502
billar inglés 503
billete : verso 441
billete, recto 441
billete, verso 441
billete: recto 441
billetera 274, 275
billetero 275
billetes de banco 469
billetes, emisión 442
bimah 447
biología 426
biosfera 44
biosfera, estructura 44
birimbao 297
bisagra 178, 185, 186, 202, 214, 274, 277, 352, 420
bisel 460
bisonte 84
bistec 152
bita 385
bizna 60
blanca 299, 468, 469
blanca doble 468
blancas 470
blanco 418, 471
blastodisco 79
bloque 305
bloque de apartamentos 289, 433, 512
bloque de cierre de la recámara 534
bloque de cierre de recámara 534
bloque de cirugía 464
bloque de contención 409
bloque del motor 360
bloqueo 425
bloqueo corrimiento 331
bloqueo eje 526
bloqueo mayúsculas 330
bloqueo numérico 331
bloqueo, tornillos 425
blusón 255
blusón con tirilla 255
boa 77
bobina 319, 536, 537
boca 71, 72, 73, 75, 90, 94, 116, 220, 224, 305, 534
boca de acceso 404
boca de aspiración de aire 383
boca de llenado 351
boca de riego 434, 454
boca del depósito 237
boca para la manguera 236
bocina neumática 364
bodega 438
bodega de carga 12
bodega de contenedores 383
bodega de equipaje 393, 395
body 255, 258, 263
bogavante 71, 158
bogavante, morfología 71
bogie 527
bogie del motor 376
boina 239
bol 177
bol mezclador 176
bol para ensalada 166
bola 220
bola amarilla 503
bola azul 503
bola blanca 502, 503
bola de corcho 477
bola de hilo 477
bola de rodamiento 312
bola marrón 503
bola negra 503
bola pinta 502, 503
bola roja 502, 503
bola rosa 503
bola verde 503
bolas numeradas 502
bolas rojas 503
bolera 436
bolero 254
bolero con botones 254
boles para batir 172
boleto comestible 123
bolígrafo 312
Bolivia 448
bolsa 162
bolsa de cuero 337
bolsa de golf 505
bolsa de lona 276
bolsa de malla 162
bolsa para congelados 162
bolsa, cajetín 209
bolsas 121
bolsillo 225, 250, 274, 502, 505
bolsillo con cartera 244, 248
bolsillo de fuelle 255
bolsillo de ojal 244, 249, 251
bolsillo de parche 244, 249, 260
bolsillo de ribete 244
bolsillo de ribete ancho 248, 251
bolsillo del cambio 244
bolsillo delantero 246, 274
bolsillo disimulado 251
bolsillo exterior 275, 276
bolsillo lateral 352
bolsillo secreto 274
bolsillo simulado 251
bolsillo superior 245, 248
bolsillo trasero 246
bolsita de té 148
bolso clásico 275
bolso de bandolera 276
bolso de fuelle 276
bolso de hombre 276
bolso de la compra 276
bolso de vestir 276
bolso de viaje 276
bolso interior 277
bolso manguito 276
bolso saco 276
bolso tipo cubo 275

bolsos 275
bomba 184, 212, 214, 529
bomba de aire 370
bomba para lodos 403
bomba volcánica 28
bombachos 254
bombardino 307
bombero 454
bombilla 217, 416
bombilla de bajo consumo 199
bombilla de bayoneta 199
bombilla de rosca 199
bombilla incandescente 199
bombo 295, 308
bombona de aire comprimido 454
bombona de gas 529
bombona de gas desechable 218
bombona de gas médico 464
bongos 309
boniato 124
boquerón 159
boquilla 196, 216, 219, 236, 306, 307, 311, 406, 407, 467
boquilla de llenado 208
boquilla de vertido 184
boquilla para concentrar la llama 218
boquilla para expandir la llama 218
boquilla para suelos y alfombras 209
boquilla para tapicería 209
boquilla pulverizadora 236
boquilla rinconera 209
borde 55, 205, 210, 526
borde 526
borde de ataque 393
borde de fuga 392
borde de la cuba 212
borde de la punta 228
borde del andén 374, 379
borde del lomo 228
borde, hoja 55
bordes, podadora 237
bordillo 230, 434
borla 266
borne 359
borne negativo 359, 416
borne positivo 359, 417
borraja 142
borrar 331
Bosnia-Herzegovina 450
bosque 29
bosque de coníferas 44
bosque de hoja caduca 44
bosque mixto 44
bosque templado 44
bosque tropical 44
bosque tropical húmedo 44
bosques 25
Bostuana 452
bota 241, 506, 509, 510, 514, 525, 527
bota blanda 513
bota de fútbol 480
bota de medio muslo 241
bota de montaña 242
bota de salto de esquí 513
bota de seguridad 459
bota de trabajo 240
bota externa 511, 527
bota rígida 513
botador 220
botalón 520
botas altas 538
botas de caucho 454
botas de tacos de rugby 483
botas para esquiar 511
botavara 519, 520
bote salvavidas 382, 386
botella 267, 371
botella de vidrio 163
botella del termo 532
botella, vidrio 163
botes herméticos 162
botín 240, 241
botín interior 511, 527
botiquín 465
botiquín de primeros auxilios 461
botiquín de urgencias 457
botón 199, 245, 250, 296, 301
botón de acoplamiento 305
botón de ajuste a cero del contador 323
botón de ajuste fino 421
botón de ajuste grueso 421
botón de alimentación del papel 333, 443
botón de apagado 235
botón de avance rápido 319, 323, 328
botón de avance/parada 333
botón de bloqueo 225, 227
botón de bloqueo de la pantalla 336
botón de cancelación 315
botón de cierre 208
botón de compensación de la exposición 314
botón de control 332
botón de control del alojamiento del disco 323
botón de control remoto 315
botón de desbloqueo del objetivo 314
botón de encendido 318, 322, 328
botón de encendido del touch pad 336
botón de encendido TV 319
botón de encendido VCR 319
botón de enclavamiento 229
botón de enfoque 8, 9
botón de ensayo 454
botón de expulsión 315, 319, 323, 471
botón de expulsión de CD/DVD-ROM 329
botón de expulsión de disquete 329
botón de funcionamiento 326
botón de grabación 319, 328
botón de grabación silenciosa 323
botón de grabador vocal 337
botón de índice/ampliación 315
botón de inicio 337
botón de inicio de grabación 323
botón de inicio de marcha 424
botón de inicio del contador 424
botón de la bandolera 303
botón de la llave 306
botón de la memoria 323
botón de lectura 327
botón de llamada para peatones 434
botón de madera 249
botón de mando 210
botón de memoria 327
botón de montaje 320
botón de nivel de grabación 323
botón de parada 424
botón de pausa 323
botón de presión 243, 249, 260, 312
botón de previsionado de profundidad de campo 314
botón de rebobinado 319, 323, 326, 328
botón de rebobinado automático 326
botón de rebobinado de la película 314
botón de rebobinado rápido 326
botón de registro 305
botón de reiniciación 329
botón de reproducción 319, 323, 328
botón de reset 471
botón de retroiluminación 337
botón de salida 337
botón de salto de imágenes 315
botón de selección 320, 327
botón de selección del menú 315
botón de seta 332
botón de sintonización 326
botón de stop 319, 323, 328
botón de velocidades 176
botón de visualización de ajustes 315
botón de visualización de imágenes 315
botón del contador a cero 319
botón del horno 210
botón del menú 327
botón del seguro 352
botón del vaporizador 208
botón del zoom eléctrico 320
botón grabación fecha 320
botón grabación hora 320
botón para borrar 328
botón para buscar las pistas 323
botón para parar y borrar 323
botón selector 214
botón selector de temperatura 270
botón selector de velocidad 270
botón TV video 319
botón visualización fecha 320
botón visualización hora 320
botonadura cruzada 248
botonera de cabina 287
botones de acción 471
botones de ajuste 319
botones de ajuste de imagen 320
botones de búsqueda de canales 319
botones de dirección 471
botones de efectos especiales 320
botones de lanzamiento de las aplicaciones 337
botones de presión de la pierna 261
botones de presión delanteros 261
botones para búsqueda de canales 319
botones para editar la voz 310
botones programables 332
bóveda 284
bóveda de cañón 281
bóveda del salpicadero 348
bóveda palatina 116, 117
boxeador 498
boxeo 498
boxes 524
boya 38
bráctea 60
braga 259
braga de volantes 260
bragueta 246, 247, 260
branquias 73
braquial anterior 96
brasero 283
Brasil 448
braza 517
brazalete de identificación 264
brazalete neumático 461
brazalete tubular 264
brazaletes 264
brazo 83, 91, 93, 95, 200, 206, 231, 236, 243, 270, 297, 355, 400, 421, 467
brazo actuador 333
brazo de arrastre 400
brazo de elevación 364
brazo de la plaqueta 273
brazo de la sierra 235
brazo de presión 224
brazo de suspensión 212, 351
brazo del cucharón 399
brazo delantero 422
brazo elevador 399
brazo espiral 6
brazo metálico 236
brazo muerto 32
brazo muerto, lago 32
brazo por control remoto 11
brazo telescópico 397
brazo trasero 422
brazos 205
brazos del delta 32
brécol 127
brécol chino 127
brick 163
brick pequeño 163
brie 151
broca 221
broca de atornillado 228
broca de pala 228
broca helicoidal 228
broca helicoidal central 228
broca salomónica de canal angosto 228
brocas, barrenas, ejemplos 228
brocha 61, 219, 266
brocha aplicadora de colorete 266
brocha de afeitar 271
brocha en forma de abanico 266
broche 274, 275
broche automático 274
bronquio lobular 105
bronquio principal 105
bronquiolo terminal 105
brote 53
brote de bambú 125
brotes de soja 131
brújula magnética 533
Brunei 453
buccino 157
buey 85
búfalo 84
bufete 203
buffet 438
búho real 81
buitre 80
bujía 237, 359, 360
bujías, cable 350
bulbillo 54
bulbo 6, 125, 385, 387
bulbo olfatorio 117
bulbo piloso 114
bulbo raquídeo 109
bulbo, base 54
bulbo, corte 54
bulbo, tallo 54
bulbos 124
buldog 86
bulevar 25, 433
Bulgaria 450
bulldozer 398
buque de carga 382
buque portacontenedores 381
buque trasatlántico 386
burbujas de aire 339
Burkina Faso 451
burra 503
Burundi 451
buscapersonas 327
búsqueda 335
butaca 200, 294
butacas 293
butacas, ejemplos 200
Bután 453
buzo 254
buzón de depósito nocturno 443

C

caballa 159
caballete 187
caballete central 367
caballete lateral 367
caballete portapoleas 403
caballo 83, 85, 470
caballo con arcos 496
caballo con aros 496
caballo, morfología 83
cabeceo 395
cabecera 204, 205, 285, 313
cabellera 6
cabello, tinte 267
cabestrante 364
cabeza 6, 67, 72, 78, 87, 93, 95, 103, 111, 169, 220, 221, 223, 229, 271, 301, 302, 303, 492, 494, 503, 505, 536
cabeza cortadora 341
cabeza de empalme 377
cabeza de inyección 403
cabeza de lectura /escritura 333
cabeza de mástil 519
cabeza del fémur 99
cabeza del gato elevador 396
cabeza del húmero 99
cabeza hexagonal 272
cabeza móvil 176
cabeza; tipos 221
cabezal 167, 187, 204
cabezal flotante 271
cabezuela 57
cabina 395, 398, 399, 400, 401, 443
cabina armario 189
cabina de clase turista 393
cabina de control 293, 397
cabina de la ducha 195
cabina de la torre de control 388
cabina de mando 12, 383, 392, 395, 397
cabina de pasajeros 386, 387
cabina de pilotaje 385
cabina de primera clase 392
cabina de proyección 294
cabina del ascensor 287
cabina del maquinista 376, 377
cabina en el foco primario 7
cabina giratoria 400
cabina para desvestirse 465
cabina para dormir 364
cabina, botonera 287
cabina, guía 287
cabina, suelo 287
cabina, techo 287
cabio alto 185
cabio bajo 185
cable 217, 228, 235, 237, 326, 332, 356, 364, 501, 535
cable de acero 535
cable de alimentación 227, 269, 270, 271, 322
cable de alumbrado 361
cable de bujía 360
cable de conexión 324, 332
cable de elevación 397
cable de interfaz digital para instrumentos musicales (MIDI) 311
cable de la antena de alta frecuencia 394
cable de las bujías 350
cable de sincronización 337
cable de tracción 287
cable del acelerador 237
cable del auricular 327
cable del cambio 372
cable del freno 371
cable distribuidor 316
cable eléctrico 354, 434
cable portante 344
cables de baja tensión 198
cables de conexión 198
cables de emergencia 356
cables de suministro 198
cables de tensión mediana 198
cabo 24, 296, 536
Cabo de Buena Esperanza 20
Cabo de Hornos 17
cabo de soporte 70
Cabo Verde, islas{f} de 451
cabra 84
cabra, quesos 150
cabrio 187
cacahuete 130
cacahuete, aceite 149
cacao 148
cacerola 175
cacerola para baño de María 175
cacerola para fondue 174
cacerola refractaria 175
cachalote 90
cadena 235, 372, 522
cadena alimentaria 45
cadena de dunas 36
cadena de elevación 396
cadena de neuronas 110
cadena de seguridad 361
cadena de transmisión 370
cadena, reacción 415
cadena, sierra 235
cadena, transmisión 372
cadenita del tapón 196
cadera 93, 95
café 148
café expres, máquina 181
café y infusionnes 148
café, granos torrefactos 148
café, granos verdes 148
cafetera 181, 531
cafetera de émbolo 181
cafetera de filtro automática 181
cafetera de infusión 181
cafetera italiana 181
cafetera napolitana 181
cafeteras 181
cafetería 432, 437, 445
caída de popa 519
caída de proa 519

ASTRONOMÍA > 2-13; **TIERRA** > 14-49; **REINO VEGETAL** >50-65; **REINO ANIMAL** > 66-91; **SER HUMANO** > 92-119; **PRODUCTOS ALIMENTARIOS Y DE COCINA** > 120-181; **CASA** > 182-215; **BRICOLAJE Y JARDINERÍA** > 216-237; **VESTIDO** > 238-263; **ACCESORIOS Y ARTÍCULOS PERSONALES** > 264-277; **ARTE Y ARQUITECTURA** > 278-311; **COMUNICACIONES Y AUTOMATIZACIÓN DE OFICINA** > 312-341; **TRANSPORTE Y VEHÍCULOS** > 342-401; **ENERGÍA** > 402-413; **CIENCIA** > 414-429; **SOCIEDAD** > 430-467; **DEPORTES Y JUEGOS** > 468-538

caída de tensión 402
caimán 77
caja 121, 218, 225, 231, 237, 271, 302, 303, 304, 314, 318, 537
caja abierta 162
caja archivo 340
caja basculante 401
caja circular 296
caja clara 295, 308
caja colectora de polvo 229
caja de cambios 350
caja de caracol 407
caja de cinc (ánodo) 417
caja de conexiones 198
caja de doble fila de conexiones 417
caja de herramientas 225
caja de ingletes 226
caja de jeringuillas usadas 457
caja de la batería 359
caja de pesca 538
caja de resonancia 296, 297, 302
caja de seguridad 443
caja de servicio 198
caja de terminales 411
caja del acumulador 365
caja del motor 235
caja del ventilador 270
caja fuerte 443
caja media pera 297
caja orza de quilla 519
caja para la ceniza 192
caja para queso 163
caja pequeña 162
caja registradora 121
caja triangular 297
caja, queso 163
cajas 121
cajas de cartón para huevos 162
cajas de cartón, huevos 162
cajera 121
cajero automático 437, 442, 443
cajetín de accesorios 209
cajetín portabolsa 209
cajón 164, 202, 203, 205
cajón calientaplatos 210
cajón de abono compuesto 231
cajón de basura 365
cajón para carnes 211
calabacín 128
calabaza bonetera 129
calabaza bonetera amarilla 129
calabaza común 129
calabaza de China 128
calabaza de cuello largo 129
calabaza de cuello retorcido 129
calabaza romana 129
calamar 157
cálamos egipcios 312
calandra 348, 364
calandria 409
calapié 372
calcáneo 99
calcetín 257, 480, 492
calcetín a media pantorrilla 247
calcetín con tirante 476
calcetín corto 247
calcetín largo 257
calcetín largo ejecutivo 247
calcetine alto 483
calcetines 247, 506
calculadora 274
calculadora científica 337
calculadora con impresora 337
calculadora de bolsillo 337
calderón 299
calefacción 192
calefacción de leña 192
calendario de sobremesa 338
calentador 529
calentador de agua 194
calentador de pierna 263
calibrador 357
calibre de ajuste de profundidad de corte 229
calículo 59
caliptra 53
Calisto 2
cáliz 56, 59, 60, 107, 446
calle 25, 433, 435, 472, 516
calle comercial 432
callejón 433
calor, transmisión 415
calzada 342, 434
calzados 240
calzados unisex 242
calzapié 370
calzoncillos 247
calzoncillos largos 247
cama 204
cama de hospital 464
cama doble 439
cama individual 439
cama, coche 376
camaleón 77
cámara 290, 525
cámara acorazada 443
cámara anterior 119
cámara de aire 79, 262
cámara de combustión 360
cámara de descarga 278
cámara de expansión 424
cámara de fuelle 315
cámara de la reina 278
cámara de magma 28
cámara de televisión en color 10
cámara del rey 278
cámara del timón 384
cámara desechable 315
cámara digital 315
cámara frigorífica 120
cámara frigorífica 121, 381
cámara lenta 319
cámara magmática 402
cámara Polaroid Land 315
cámara posterior 119
cámara pulpar 101
cámara reflex de formato medio SLR (6x6) 315
cámara réflex digital: vista posterior 315
cámara réflex monocular: vista frontal 314
cámara rígida de 35 mm 10
cámara subterránea 278
cámara web 332
cámaras fijas 315
camarera 438
camarote 386
camarote del capitán 387
camarotes de la tripulación 382
camas y colchonetas 530
cambiador 205
cambio de marchas delantero 370, 372
cambio de marchas trasero 370, 372
cambio de presión 39
cambio de velocidades 522
cambium 63
Camboya 453
cambrillón 262
camello 85
camembert 151
camerino 290, 293
camerino privado 290
Camerún 451
camilla 460
camino de evacuación 345
camión cisterna 364
camión tractor 364
camiones 364
camiones de bomberos 455
camiones, ejemplos 364
camioneta 347, 365
camisa 245, 255, 282
camisa de pistón 360
camisa marinera 255
camisera clásica 255
camiseta 247, 260, 261, 263, 473, 476, 483, 488
camiseta de cuerpo entero 261
camiseta del equipo 480, 486
camiseta interior 476
camiseta sin mangas 500
camisola 258
camisón 256
campana 192, 210
campana de cocina 164
campanario 285, 446
campanas tubulares 295, 309
campanillas 309
campo 431, 474, 479, 480
campo de golf 430, 504
campo de juego 482
campo de juego de fútbol americano 484
campo geotérmico 402
campo magnético 318, 416
campo, línea 416
caña 83, 305, 312, 534, 538
caña del timón 520
caña para lanzado 537
caña para mosca 536
caña simple 306
Canadá 448
canal 228
canal de ajuste 222
canal de derivación 406
canal de descarga 407
Canal de la Mancha 18
Canal de Mozambique 20
canal del aliviadero 406
canal del sifón 73
canal del veneno 76
canal derecho 324
canal izquierdo 324
canal lacrimal 119
canalón 182
canasta 477, 489
canastilla 178
cancha 487, 488, 490, 494
cancha de fondo 491
candado para bicicleta 372
candela 426
candelabro de siete braz 447
canela 138
canelones 146
cañería 194, 197
cañería del desagüe 194
cañerías 194
canesú 245, 255, 258
cangrejo de mar 158
cangrejo de río 158
caniche 86
caño 305
cañón 471, 534
cañón de electrones 318
cañón expulsor de espuma 385
cañón lanza agua 455
cañón submarino 33
canotier 238
cantidad de materia, unidad de medida 426
cantimplora 532
canto 226, 441, 509, 510
cantonera 534
capa 251
capa basáltica 26
capa de ozono 37
capa de rodadura 342
capa granítica 26
capa protectora 10
capa superficial del suelo 54
capa superior impermeable 402
caparazón 71
capas de residuos 47
capazo 276
caperuza 193
caperuza de la chimenea 183
capilla 282
capilla axial 284, 285
capilla lateral 284
capilla radial 284, 285
capital 23
capitán 515
capó 348, 364, 523
capón 155
cápsula 51, 60, 467
cápsula de gelatina 467
captura 470
capucha 249
capucha con cordón 261
capuchón 260, 314, 460, 467, 508
capuchón de bastones 505
capuchón de plástico 217
capuchón de protección 420
capullo 53
caqui 137
cara 91, 92, 167, 493, 505
caracol 72
caracol terrestre 157
caracol, morfología 72
carambola 137
caramillo 296
caravana 361
caravana plegable 361
carbonero 161
carburador 366
cárcel 469
cardamomo 138
cardenal 80
cárdigan 250
cardo 125
carena 74
carenado 366
careta 459
carga 312
carga de perdigones 534
carga del reactor nuclear 409
carga eléctrica, unidad de medida 426
carga y descarga 439
carga, muelle 437
cargador 208, 228
cargador delantero 399
cargadora, retroexcavadora 399
cargadora-retroexcavadora 399
carguero portacontenedores 382
Caribe, islas del 448
Caribe, Placa 27
caricatura 313
carlota, molde 172
carne 152
carne de cordero troceada 153
carne de ternera troceada 152
carne de vacuno troceada 152
carne picada 152
carne picada de cerdo 153
carne picada de cordero 153
carne picada de vacuno 152
carnívoros 45
Carón 3
carpa 160
carpeta con guardas 339
carpeta con mecanismo de presión 339
carpeta de archivo 340
carpeta de argollas 339
carpeta de broches 339
carpeta de costilla de resorte 339
carpeta de espiral 340
carpeta de tornillos 339
carpintería 225
carpintería 220, 221, 222, 225, 226, 228
carreras de coches 524
carrete 236
carrete de bobina fija 537
carrete de tambor 537
carrete giratorio 536
carretera 25, 343, 345, 430
carretera de acceso 388
carretera de circunvalación 25
carretera secundaria 25, 431
carretera, sección transversal 342
carretera, túnel 345
carreteras, mapa 25
carreteras, sistema 342
carretilla 231, 396
carretilla elevadora de horquilla 396
carretilla para manguera 236
carril de aceleración 343
carril de adelantamiento 343
carril de desaceleración 343
carril de enlace 375
carril de tránsito 343
carril de tránsito lento 343
carriles 343
carrillo 536
carrito de golf 505
carrito portamaletas 277
carritos del supermercado 121
carro 521
carro de golf eléctrico 505
carro portaequipaje 374
carrocería 348, 361, 523
carrocerías, ejemplos 347
carta 469
carta Caja de Comunidad 469
carta de la Suerte 469
cartas al editor 313
cartas altas 468
cartel 294
cartel comercial 380
cartelera 294
cárter 228, 360
cárter del embrague 368
cartera 274, 372
cartera de fondo plegable 274
cartera portadocumentos 275
cartílago alar mayor 117
cartílago nasal del tabique 117
cartilla, puesta al día 442
cartografía 21
cartón 163
cartón pequeño 163
cartuchera 456
cartucho 216, 459
cartucho de escopeta 534
cartucho de rifle 534
casa 182, 469, 515
casa club 504
casa de adobes 288
casa de dos plantas 289
casa de una planta 289
casa flotante 385
casa romana 280
casa, elementos 185
casa, estructura 188
casa, exterior 182
casaca 255
casas adosadas 289
casas pareadas 289
cascabel 309
cascabeles 309
cascada 32
cascanueces 170
cáscara 60, 61
cascarón 79
casco 10, 83, 367, 404, 454, 478, 486, 498, 506, 508, 510, 513, 520, 522, 523, 524, 525, 526, 527
casco de seguridad 458
casco del bateador 476
casco integral 367, 525
casco protector 372
cascos de seguridad 458
casete 326, 333
casete con saludo 328
casete para grabar los mensajes 328
casi igual a 427
casilla 469
casillero 203
casquete 412
casquete del distribuidor 360
casquillo 199, 503, 534
castaña de agua 124
castañas 133
castañuelas 295, 309
castas 68
castillo 282
castillo de proa 383, 387
castor 82
catamarán 521
catarata 31
catedral 284
catedral gótica 284
catedral, plano 285
cátodo 417
catre desmontable 530
cauda helicis 115
cávea 278, 281
cavidad abdominal 111, 112
cavidad bucal 105, 106
cavidad nasal 76, 105
cavidad pleural 105
cayado de la aorta 102, 103, 104
caza 154, 534
cazadora 249
cazo 173
cazuela 531
cazuela vaporera 175
cebada 61, 143
cebada : espiga 61
cebolla amarilla 124
cebolla blanca 124
cebolla roja 124
cebolla tierna 124
cebolletas 124

cebollino 124
cebra 84
cedro del Líbano 65
cefalotórax 70, 71
ceja 304
cejilla 301, 302, 303
celda 67, 281
celdas 440
celdilla 58
celosía veneciana 186
célula animal 66
célula convectiva 43
célula de Schwann 110
célula solar 337, 410, 411
célula vegetal 50
cementerio 25, 433
cemento 101
centavo 440
centeno 61, 143
centeno : espiga 61
central 485
central eléctrica 406
central hidroeléctrica, sección transversal 407
central térmica de carbón 402
centriolo 66
centro 293, 428, 470, 507
centro ciudad 431, 432
centro comercial 431, 436
centro de negocios 430, 432
centro del campo 481
centro derecho 482
centro educativo 433
centro izquierdo 482
cepa de vid 62
cepillo 209, 215, 229, 272
cepillo aplicador de rimel 266
cepillo con base de goma 268
cepillo de baño 267
cepillo de curling 515
cepillo de dientes 272
cepillo de dientes eléctrico 272
cepillo de espalda 267
cepillo de esqueleto 268
cepillo de púas 268
cepillo para cejas y pestañas 266
cepillo para suelos 209
cepillo para verduras 173
cepillo redondo 268
cepillo-plumero 209
cepillos 268
cepo 535
cera 514
cerámica, condensador 417
cerca 122
cercado 122
cerda 272
cerdas 215, 219, 271
cerdo 84
cerdo, asado 153
cerdo, carne picada 153
cerdo, cortes 153
cereales 61, 143, 144
cerebelo 109
cerebro 71, 109
cerezas 132
cerradura 185, 186, 202, 274, 277, 349, 352
cerradura de combinación 274
cerrajería 186, 437
cerveza 120
cerviz 78
césped 183, 230
cesta de freír 171
cesta de pescador 538
cestillo 68
cesto 211, 214
cesto de cocción al vapor 175
cesto para cubiertos 214
cesto para verdura 211
Chac-Mool 283
Chad 451
chalaza 79
chaleco 244, 255
chaleco de pescador 538
chaleco de punto 250
chaleco, jerseys y chaquetas 254
chalecos 244
chalote 124
champiñón 123
champú 267
chancleta 242
chancleta playera 242
chanclo de goma 240
chapa 186
chapka 238
chaqueta 251
chaqueta cruzada 244, 255
chaqueta de punto 250, 255
chaqueta recta 244
chaquetas 244
chaquetón 251
chaquetón de tres cuartos 251
chaquetón marinero 251
chaquetones 251
charcutería 156
charnela lateral 367
chasis 396, 400, 401, 460
chasis delantero 401
chateo 335
chayote 129
cheque de viaje 441
chequera con calculadora 274
cheques 441
chesterfield 200
chicana 524
chifonier 203
Chile 448
chile 128
chile jalapeño 139
chimenea 183, 188, 192, 193, 382, 386, 402
chimenea de expulsión 365
chimenea lateral 28
chimenea principal 28
chimenea, conexión 192
chimenea, utensilios 193
chimpancé 91
China 453
chinche de campo 69
chinchetas 341
chino 171, 524
Chipre 450
chirimoya 136
chirivía 129
chistera 238
chocolate 148
chocolate amargo 148
chocolate blanco 148
chocolate con leche 148
chorizo 156
chorro de agua 518
choza 288
choza indígena 288
chuleta 152, 153
chuletón 152
chutney de mango 141
chutney, mango 141
cian 418
ciclismo 522
ciclismo de montaña 522
ciclismo por carretera 522
ciclismo por carretera, competición 522
ciclista 522
ciclo hidrológico 45
ciclomotor 369
ciclón 43
ciclón tropical 43
ciclones tropicales, denominación 43
cidra cayote 129
ciego 106
cielo turbulento 41
cien 427
ciencia 414
ciere, tapa 417
cierre 211, 273, 275, 528
cierre en relieve 163
ciervo 84
ciervo de Virginia 84
cigala 158
cigarra 69
cigüeña 80
cigüeñal 360
cilantro 142
ciliada 55
cilindro 429, 460
cilindro de dirección 400
cilindro de elevación de la hoja 401
cilindro de elevación del zanco 398
cilindro de freno 357
cilindro de orientación de la pala 401
cilindro del brazo 400
cilindro del brazo elevador 399
cilindro del cucharón 399, 400
cilindro del elevador 399, 400
cilindro del elevador de la pala 398
cilindro elevador 364, 397, 455
cilindro maestro 357
cilio 66
cima 29, 63, 512
cima bípara 57
cima unípara 57
cimiento del pilón 344
cinco 427
cinco especias chinas 139
cincuenta 427
cine 294, 432, 436
cinta 225, 238, 458, 459
cinta adhesiva 190
cinta blanca 493, 495
cinta cargadora 402
cinta central 491
cinta de acordonamiento 457
cinta de la red 491
cinta de teflón 216
cinta magnética 319
cinta métrica 225
cinta transportadora 49, 390, 402
cintura 93, 95
cinturón 246, 248, 499, 500, 532
cinturón de asteroides 3
cinturón de herramientas 225
cinturón de hombros 353
cinturón de Kuiper 2
cinturón de seguridad 205, 353, 525
cinturón de servicio 456
cinturón subabdominal 353
circo 5
circo glaciar 30
circuito 524
circuito de agua caliente 194
circuito de agua fría 194
circuito de desagüe 194
circuito de frenado 350, 357
circuito de ventilación 194
circuito eléctrico de los captadores 357
circuito eléctrico en paralelo 416
circuito impreso 417
circuito impreso, placa 417
circuito integrado 417
circulación sanguínea 102
círculo 25 471
Círculo Antártico 15, 22
círculo central 481, 488, 515
círculo de espera 474
círculo de la estación 39
círculo de lanzamiento 472, 473
círculo de reanudación del juego 506
círculo de saque inicial 507
círculo doble 471
círculo exterior 515
círculo graduado de declinación 8
Círculo polar antártico 21
Círculo polar ártico 21
círculo polar ártico 22
círculo triple 471
círculo, partes 428
circunferencia 428
circunvalación 25
cirrocúmulos 42
cirros 42
cirrostratos 42
ciruelas 132
cirugía menor 462
cisterna 364
cisterna del inodoro 195
cisura oblicua 105
cítara 296
citofaringe 66
citoplasma 50, 66, 112
citoprocto 66
citostoma 66
cítricos 58, 134
ciudad 23, 430
Ciudad del Vaticano 450
cizallas para setos 234
claqueta 291
clarín 307
clarinete 306
clarinete bajo 295
clarinetes 295
clase 444
clasificación de plásticos 49
clasificación general, marcador 496
clasificador de fuelle 274
clave 284
clave de do 298
clave de fa 298
clave de sol 298
clavel 56
claves 298
clavícula 98
clavija 301, 302, 304, 324, 454
clavija de acorde 303
clavija de afinación 303
clavija de alimentación 337
clavija de conexión 417
clavija de tensión 308
clavija de tipo americano 198
clavija europea 198
clavijero 301, 304
clavo 220
clavo común 220
clavo cortado 220
clavo de albañil 220
clavo helicoidal 220
clavo sin cabeza 220
clavos 138
clavos, ejemplos 220
claxon 368
claxón 354
clientes, entrada 438
clientes, guardarropa 438
climas áridos 40
climas de alta montaña 40
climas de montaña 40
climas del mundo 40
climas polares 40
climas templados cálidos 40
climas templados fríos 40
climas tropicales 40
climatizador automático 354
clip 341
clip de ajuste 199
clips, distribuidor 341
clítoris 112
cloroplasto 50
cobaya 82
cobertera inferior de la cola 78
cobertera superior de la cola 78
coberteras 78
coberteras mayores 78
coberteras medias 78
coberteras menores 78
coberteras primarias 78
coberteras primarias medias 78
cobertizo 122, 182, 230
cobertizo para ovejas 122
cobra 77
cocción al vapor, cesto 175
cocción, placa 179
cocción, platos 179
cóccix 98
coche cama 376
coche de Fórmula 1 525
coche de fórmula 3000 524
coche de Indy 524
coche de policía 457
coche de rally 524
coche de tracción 380
coche del equipo 522
coche familiar 347
cocina 162, 164, 188, 280, 439, 445
cocina de a bordo 392
cocina de campo 529
cocina de gas 210
cocina eléctrica 210
cocina, tijeras 173
cocina, utensilios 169, 174
cocinar 178
cóclea 116
coco 133
cocodrilo 77
Cocos, Placa 27
codera 486, 526, 527
código del producto 423
codillo 83, 86, 153
codo 86, 93, 95, 273
codorniz 81, 154
cofre 369
cojín 204
cojín para sellos 338
cojinete de bolas 413
cojinete móvil 519
col 126
col china 126
col lombarda 126
col marina 126
col ornamental 126
col rizada 126
col rizada de otoño 126
col verde 126
cola 71, 76, 82, 83, 86, 90, 111, 190, 393, 510, 514, 526, 536
cola de ion 6
cola de polvo 6
colada de lava 28
colador 177, 180, 197
colador fino 171
coladores 171
colchón 205, 460
colchón de muelles 204
colchoneta aislante 530
colchoneta de aire 530
colchoneta de espuma 530
colchoneta de recepción 496
colector de admisión 360
colector de electrones 417
colector de escape 350, 360
colector de grasa 179
colector principal 434
colector solar plano 410
colegio 444
coles de Bruselas 126
colgador de intravenosos 464
colgante 207
colibrí 80
coliflor 127
colina 29
colina abisal 33
colina de salida 504
colinabo 125
collar 219
collar cortafuego 193
collar de 5 vueltas , peto 264
collar de perforación 403
collar de una vuelta , matinée 264
collar de una vuelta , ópera 264
collares 264
collarín 193, 223, 229, 501
colleja 127
collie 86
colmena 122
colmillo 76, 101
Colombia 448
colon ascendente 106
colon descendente 106
colon sigmoideo 106
colon transverso 106
colonia, agua de 267
color 468
colores aditivos síntesis 418
colores sustractivos, síntesis 418
colores, síntesis 418
colorete en polvo 266
columela 73
columna 31, 207, 279, 302, 313
columna central 412
columna corintia adosada 281
columna de alcohol 424
columna de mercurio 424
columna dórica adosada 281
columna fraccionadora 405
columna jónica adosada 281
columna vertebral 98, 109
colutorio 272
comadreja 88
combinación 258
combinación con sujetador 258
combustible 408
combustible fósil 46, 48
combustible para aviones 405
combustible para calderas 405

combustible para calefacción 405
comedor 188, 386, 438, 439
comedor, vagón 376
comercio electrónico 335
cometa 6
comino 138
comisaría de policía 433
comisura labial 116
cómoda 203
comodín 468
Comoras 452
compactadora 364
compartimento para almacenamiento 361
compartimento para equipaje 376
compartimento para los equipos 376
compartimiento 286
compartimiento de almacenamiento 455
compartimiento de pasajeros 383
compartimiento del depósito del agua 394
compartimiento motor 362
compartimiento para lácteos 211
compartimiento para mantequilla 211
compás 298
competición de ciclismo por carretera 522
complejo hidroeléctrico 406
complexo mayor 97
compluvio 280
composición de la sangre 104
compresa de gasa 461
compresión 49
compresor de aire 376
compresor del aire acondicionado 360
compuerta 381, 407
compuerta de la cisterna 385
compuerta del aliviadero 406
comulgatorio 446
comunicación por teléfono 327
comunicación vía satélite 316
comunicaciones aéreas 317
comunicaciones industriales 317
comunicaciones marítimas 317
comunicaciones militares 317
comunicaciones particulares 317
comunicaciones terrestres 317
concentración de gas de efecto invernadero 46
concentrado de tomate 140
concentrado, tomate 140
concentrador de aire 270
concesionariode automóviles 433
concha 72, 73, 115, 200, 308
concha bivalva 73
concha bivalva, anotomía 73
concha bivalva, morfología 73
concha univalva 73
concha univalva, morfología 73
conchitas 146
condensación 45, 414
condensador 402, 421
condensador de cerámica 417
condensador de película plástica 417
condensadores electrolíticos 417
cóndilo externo 99
cóndilo interno 99
condimento de especias cajún 139
condimentos 140
cóndor 80
conducción 415
conducción forzado 407
conducto de aire caliente 213
conducto de aire fresco 345
conducto de aire viciado 345
conducto de ventilación 278
conducto deferente 111
conducto del veneno 76
conducto eyaculador 111
conducto galactóforo 113
conducto lacrimal 119
conducto principal del gas 434
conducto radicular 101
conducto semicircular lateral 116
conducto semicircular posterior 116
conducto semicircular superior 116
conducto sudorífero 114
conductor de fase 198
conductor neutral 198
conector 455
conector de alimentación del adaptador 336
conector de altavoces 322
conector de puesta de tierra 322
conector de salida 303
conector de tierra macho 198
conector de tierra, macho 198
conector del desagüe 194
conectores de antenas 322
conejo 82, 154
conexión 198, 470
conexión a la red 198
conexión de la chimenea 192
conexión de tierra 198
conexión eléctrica a tierra 404
conexión, clavija 417
conexión, galería 345
conexiones 365
conexiones, ejemplos 197
confesionarios 446
configuración de los continentes 14
configuración del litoral 35
confirmación, tecla 443
confluente 32
congelador 164, 438
congelador incorporado 211
congelados 121
Congo 451
congresos, palacio 433
conífera 65
coníferas, ejemplos 65
conjuntiva 119
conjunto deportivo 261
conjunto vacío 427
conjuntos instrumentales, ejemplos 300
conmutador de alimentación 315
conmutador de corriente 322
conmutador de grabación nocturna 320
conmutador de intensidad 198
cono 119, 318, 429
cono de penumbra 4, 5
cono de sombra 4, 5
cono femenino 65
cono masculino 65
conservas 121
consigna 374
consola 302, 305
consola central 354
consola de juego 471
consultorio 463, 465
consultorio ginecológico 463
consumidor 317
consumidores primarios 45
consumidores secundarios 45
consumidores terciarios 45
contacto 198, 199, 470
contacto central 314
contacto de conexión a tierra 198
contacto negativo 410, 411
contacto positivo 410, 411
contacto, dispositivos 198
contador 323
contador de agua 194
contador eléctrico 198
contaminación agrícola 47
contaminación de automóviles 47
contaminación de petróleo 48
contaminación del agua 48
contaminación del aire 47
contaminación del suelo 47
contaminación doméstica 47
contaminación industrial 47
contaminantes del aire 47
contaminantes no biodegradables 47
contenedor 383, 400
contenedor de reciclado de aluminio 49
contenedor de reciclado de papel 49
contenedor de reciclado de vidrio 49
contenedor de recogida de papel 49
contenedor de recogida de vidrio 49
contenedores de reciclaje 49
contenedores, terminal 430
contera 277, 536
contera de caucho 466
contestador automático 328
continente 5, 33
continente húmedo 40
continentes, configuración 14
contorno del cuello 245
contrabajo 301
contrabajos 295
contrafagotes 295
contrafuerte 262, 284, 344, 509, 511
contrafuerte del talón 240
contrahoja 229
contrahuella 191
contrapeso 8, 287, 345, 397, 400, 401
contrapeso, guía 287
contrapiso 187, 190
contrapluma 397
contraquilla 385
contratuerca 197
contraventana 186
control 330
control : selección de grupo 330
control de agudos 322
control de balance 322
control de brillo 329
control de centrado 329
control de contraste 329
control de entrada de información fina 310
control de entrada de información rápida 310
control de graves 322
control de la entrada de aire 192
control de la plataforma corrediza 421
control de pasaportes 391
control de presión 272
control de secuencias 310
control de seguridad 391
control de sintonización 326
control de temperatura 208
control de tonos de bajos 325
control de tonos de graves 325
control de velocidad 237, 332
control de volumen 303, 310, 311, 319, 326, 329
control de volumen del auricular 327
control de volumen del timbre 327
control del campo audio 322
control del espejo retrovisor exterior 352
control del sonido 303
control del tiempo 311
control del vaporizador 208
control del volumen 303, 322, 328
control estéreo 326
control horizontal 329
control remoto, unidad móvil de servicio 11
control vertical 329
controlador de entradas 294
controlador de viento del sintetizador 311
controles de intensidad de la pantalla del ordenador 10
controles de la pletina 326
controles de sintonización 318
controles de volumen de comunicaciones 10
controles del lector de discos compactos 326
controles del sistema de soporte vital 10
controles VCR 319
conurbación 430
convección 415
convención, corriente 415
conversión del agua en vapor 408
convertidor catalítico 351
convertidor de tensión 212
coordenadas terrestres, sistema 21
copa 63, 163, 238, 239, 259
copa de agua 165
copa de champaña 165
copa de cóctel 165
copa de flauta 165
copa para brandy 165
copa para licores 165
copa para oporto 165
copa para vino blanco 165
copa para vino de Alsacia 165
copa para vino de Borgoña 165
copa para vino de Burdeos 165
copete 83, 536
coquilla 486, 507
coquina 157
corazón 58, 71, 73, 104, 105, 154, 468
corbata 245
corbata inglesa 245
corchea 299
corcheras 517
corchete 509
corcho 495, 514
cordaje 492, 494
cordal 297, 301
cordero, carne picada 153
cordero, carne troceada 153
cordero, cortes 153
cordero, pierna 153
cordillera 5, 24, 26
Cordillera de los Andes 17
Cordillera del Atlas 20
cordón 208, 209, 225, 240, 249, 262, 275, 477, 509
cordón de alimentación 177, 229, 269
cordón de alimentación de corriente alterna 336
cordón de alimentación de corriente continua 336
cordón de alimentación, corriente continua 336
cordón de trazar 225
cordón litoral 35
cordón nervioso ventral 71
cordoncillo 441
cordones 498
corimbo 57
córnea 119, 419
córner 481
cornete inferior 117
cornete medio 117
cornete superior 117
cornetín 295, 307
cornisa 183, 185, 202, 279
corno francés 295, 307
corno inglés 306
cornos ingleses 295
coro 284, 285
coroides 119
corola 56
corona 4, 83, 101, 302, 308, 424
corona externa de la cadena 372
corona interna de la cadena 372
corona radiata 112
corona rotatoria 401
corpúsculo de Meissner 114
corpúsculo de Pacini 114
corpúsculo de Ruffini 114
corral 122
corral, aves 155
correa 265, 277, 424, 500, 505, 519
correa de ajuste 511
correa de barbilla 486
correa de cierre 532
correa de compresión 532
correa de distribución 360
correa de la manga 248
correa de retención 277
correa de seguridad 10
correa de transmisión 383
correa del tambor 212
correa del ventilador 350, 360
correa elástico 277
correa para el cuello 458
correa para herramientas 10
correa para la mano 510, 514
correas 459
corredera de afinamiento 307
corredera de ajuste 246
corredor 412
corredor de poder 485
correo electrónico 335
correo electrónico, programa 334
correos 433
correos, oficina 437
correspondencia 338
corriente de agua 32, 48
corriente de convección 415
corriente eléctrica, unidad de medida 426
corriente subterránea 31
corrimiento 31
corsé de cintura de avispa 259
cortacésped con motor 237
cortacutículas 265
cortador de alambre 217
cortador de huevos duros 173
cortafuego 187
cortapastas 172
cortapatillas 271
cortar 177
cortasetos eléctrico 235
cortaúñas 265
corte de la atmósfera terrestre 37
corte de la corteza terrestre 26
corte de la pelota de béisbol 477
corte de un bulbo 54
corte de un grano de trigo 61
corte de un melocotón 57
corte de una avellana 60
corte de una frambuesa 59
corte de una fresa 59
corte de una manzana 58
corte de una naranja 58
corte de una nuez 60
corte de una uva 59
corte princesa 252
corte transversal de un molar 101
corte transversal de un tronco 63
cortes de cerdo 153
cortes de cordero 153
cortes de ternera 152
cortes de vacuno 152
corteza 58, 63
corteza continental 26
corteza cortical 107
corteza oceánica 26
corteza terrestre 26, 27
corteza terrestre, corte 26
cortina 200
cortina de enrollamiento automático 356
cortina separadora 464
corvejón 83, 86
costa 33
Costa de Marfil 451
Costa Rica 448
costado 358
costas, ejemplos 35
costilla 536
costilla axial 73
costilla de encastre 392
costilla espiral 73
costilla falsa 99
costilla flotante 98
costillar 152, 153
costillas 98
costura 240, 243, 244, 477, 478
costura de corte princesa 258
costura invisible 245
cotiledón 53
cotillo 220
coulommiers 151
Cowper, glándula 111
cráneo 92
cráter 5, 28
cráter, estela luminosa 5
cremallera 249, 261, 265, 277, 473
cremallera de fijación 420
crepidoma 279
cresta 29, 33, 418
cresta de la presa 406
cresta del aliviadero 406
cricket 478
crin 83, 301
crisálida 67
cristal 410, 411
cristal de protección 506
cristalería 165
cristalino 119
cristalización 414
Croacia 450
croco 56
crol 517

cromatina 66
cromosfera 4
cronometrador 488, 498, 509
cronometrador de calle 516
cronometradores 499
cronómetro 424
cronómetro electrónico automático 517
crosne 124
Crottin de Chavignol 150
cruasán 144
crucero 284, 285
cruces de carreteras, ejemplos 342
cruceta 520
crucifijo 446
crudo, oleoducto 404
crus hélix 115
crustáceos 71, 158
cruz 83, 86
cruz del altar 446
cuaderna 385, 401
cuadrado 429
cuadrante 424, 428
cuadrilátero 429, 498
cuadro 183, 502
cuadro de bateo 477
cuadro de saque 491
cuadro de saque derecho 491
cuadro de saque izquierdo 491
cuadro de servicio de dobles 495
cuadro de servicio de individuales 495
cuadro de temperaturas 208
cuarta 298
cuarteto 300
cuartilla 83
cuarto 240, 262
cuarto creciente 5
cuarto de baño 189, 195
cuarto de estar 528
cuarto de la limpieza 443
cuarto menguante 5
Cuba 448
cuba 211, 212
cuba de lavado 214
cubertería 167, 531
cubeta colectora de gotas 181
cubeta congeladora 180
cubeta de alcohol 424
cubeta de mercurio 424
cubículo 280
cubierta 180, 386
cubierta de popa 386
cubierta de seguridad 237
cubierta de sol 385
cubierta de tejas 279
cubierta exterior de la cúpula 7
cubierta inferior 404
cubierta interior de la cúpula 7
cubierta para automóviles 386
cubierta principal 385
cubierta protectora 401
cubierta superior 387, 392, 404
cubierta térmica 12
cubilete 469
cubital anterior 96, 97
cubital posterior 97
cúbito 98
cubitos de hielo, bandeja 211
cubo 215, 341, 413, 429, 467
cubo de basura 215
cubo de basura reciclable 49
cubo del rotor 395
cuchara 167, 531, 538
cuchara de degustación 173
cuchara de helado 168
cuchara de mesa 168
cuchara de postre 168
cuchara de sopa 168
cuchara de té 168
cuchara para servir helado 173
cucharas dosificadoras 171
cucharas, ejemplos 168
cucharita de café 168
cucharón 399
cucharón excavador 400
cucharón trasero 399
cuchilla 176, 177, 180, 226, 235, 270, 341, 506
cuchilla de baile 509
cuchilla de corte 398, 400
cuchilla de patinaje artístico 509
cuchilla del cucharón 399
cuchilla para delimitar el césped 233
cuchilla, mecanismo de desplazamiento 401
cuchillas para batir 176
cuchillo 167, 531, 533
cuchillo de carne 168
cuchillo de carnicero 169
cuchillo de cocina 169
cuchillo de mantequilla 168
cuchillo de mesa 168
cuchillo de pan 169
cuchillo de pelar 169
cuchillo de pescado 168
cuchillo de postre 168
cuchillo de queso 168
cuchillo de trinchar 169
cuchillo eléctrico 177
cuchillo filetero 169
cuchillo para deshuesar 169
cuchillo para jamón 169
cuchillo para ostras 169
cuchillo para pomelos 169
cuchillos de cocina, ejemplos 169
cuchillos, ejemplos 168
cuello 53, 76, 83, 93, 94, 95, 101, 111, 167, 244, 245, 247, 248, 318
cuello con botones 245
cuello de cisne 191
cuello de doble vista 248
cuello de ganso 400
cuello de pico 250
cuello del fémur 99
cuello del útero 112
cuello en V 244
cuello hechura sastre 251
cuello italiano 245
cuello redondo 260
cuello redondo, jersey 255
cuenca oceánica 33
cuenco 167
cuenco de queso blando 166
cuentakilómetros 355
cuentalitros 346
cuerda 231, 301, 302, 498, 500, 535
cuerda de elevación 219
cuerda de salida falsa 516
cuerda de tensión 297
cuerda vocal 105
cuerda, instrumentos 301
cuerdas 297, 304, 308
cuerdas de acompañamiento 296
cuerdas melódicas 296
cuerno anterior 109
cuerno posterior 109
cuero 246
cuerpo 180, 228, 306, 425, 536
cuerpo calloso 109
cuerpo cavernoso 111
cuerpo celular 110
cuerpo ciliar 119
cuerpo de guardia 282
cuerpo de la uña 114
cuerpo del fórnix 109
cuerpo humano 92
cuerpo metálico de la bujía 359
cuerpo sólido 303
cuerpo vertebral 110
cuerpo vítreo 119
cuerpos celestes 2
cuerpos de Nissl 110
cuerpos sólidos 429
cuervo 80
cueva 35
cuidado del césped 237
cuidado personal 267
culata 306, 534
culata de los cilindros 360
culombio 426
culote 534
cultivador 233
cultivador de mano 232
cúmulo globular 6
cumulonimbos 42
cúmulos 42
cuna 205
cuña 305
cuna plegable 205
cuneta 342
cupé 347
cúpula 60
cúpula del Mihrab 447
cúpula del pórtico 447
cúpula giratoria 7
cúrcuma 138
curling 515
curry 138
cursor abajo 331
cursor arriba 331
cursor hacia la derecha 331
cursor hacia la izquierda 331
curva 343, 538
cuscús 144

D

dado 469
dado común 468
dado de póquer 468
dado doble 469
dados 468
dálmata 86
dama 469, 470
damas 470
damas, tablero 470
dardo 471
dátiles 132
datos, tratamiento 38
David, estrella 447
de cuatro cuartos 298
de dos mitades 298
de momia 530
de servicio 490
de tres cuartos 298
deambulatorio 285
decágono regular 429
decantador 165
decorador 291
decorador jefe de producción 290
dedalitos 146
dedil 339
dedo 75, 79, 82, 114, 243, 477
dedo anular 115
dedo de pata lobulada 79
dedo de pata palmípeda 79
dedo del corazón 115
dedo del pie 92, 94
dedo externo 78
dedo índice 115
dedo interno 78
dedo medio 78
dedo meñique 115
dedo palmeado 75
dedo posterior 78, 79
dedos del pie, extensor largo 96
dedos prensiles 91
dedos, extensor común 97
defectos de la visión 419
defensa central 481
defensa derecho 506
defensa izquierdo 506
deflector 236, 237
deflector de viento 364
deforestación 47
degustación, cuchara 173
Deimos 2
dejada 491
delantero 244, 245, 481, 482
delantero derecho 487
delantero izquierdo 487
delantero medio 487
delantero número 8 482
delco 350
delegados técnicos 509
delfín 90
delfín, morfología 90
delineador 266
delineador de labios 266
delta 32, 35
delta, brazos 32
deltoides 96
demarcación 471
dendrita 110
denominación de los ciclones tropicales 43
dentada 55
dentadura humana 101
dentífrico 272
dentina 101
deportes de balón 474
deportes de combate 498
deportes de fuerza 500
deportes de invierno 515
deportes de motor 524
deportes de pelota 474
deportes de raqueta 493
deportes sobre ruedas 526
deportivo 347
depósito de aceite 235
depósito de agua 181
depósito de carbón 402
depósito de combustible 377
depósito de contenedores 381
depósito de de los utensilios 444
depósito de gasolina 351, 366, 369
depósito de gasolina, tapón 349
depósito de lodos 403
depósito de mercancía en tránsito 381
depósito de mercancías 430
depósito de polvo 208
depósito del agua 272
depósito del combustible 395
depósito del líquido de frenos 357
depósito esterilizado 464
depósito externo de combustible 12
depósito nocturno, buzón 443
depósitos aluviales 32
depresión 39
depresión barométrica 39
derecha del actor 293
derecha del espectador 293
deriva móvil 521
derivación 416
derivación de la toma de aire 194
dermis 114
derrubios 31
derrumbamiento 31
desagüe 194, 195
desagüe de fondo 184
desagüe principal 194
desatascador 216
descamador 531
descapotable 347
descarga, cámara 278
descenso 511
descomponedores 45
descorazonador 173
desenganchador 216
desenganchador manual 511
desértico 40
deshuesador 173
desierto 36, 44
desierto arenoso 36
Desierto de Atacama 17
Desierto de Gobi 19
Desierto de Kalahari 20
Desierto de Namibia 20
Desierto del Sahara 20
desierto rocoso 36
desmenuzamiento 49
desnivel 182
desodorante 267
despacho 189, 439
despacho de la enfermera jefe 463
despacho del asistente social 463
despacho del bedel 445
despacho del director 443, 445
despacho del gimnasio 444
despacho del juez 440
despacho del secretario judicial 440
despensa 188, 438, 439
desplantador 232
desplazamiento 331, 418
despojos 154
desprendimiento 31
desprendimientos de tierras 31
destellos, tubo 420
destilador para asfalto 405
destinos 374
destornillador 221, 531
destornillador de trinquete 221
destornillador en cruz 531
destornillador inalámbrico 221
desyerbador 232
detector de humo 454
detector de tensión 217
detritos 43
devanador 537
diadema 458
diafragma 105, 324
diafragma de vacío 360
diagrama de la circulación 103
diamante 468, 474
diámetro 428
diana 471
diapasón 301, 303
dibujo 260, 261
dibujo de la superficie de rodadura 358
diente 74, 76, 167, 226, 227, 235, 270, 398, 400, 523
diente de la desterronadora 398
diente de león 127
dientes 101, 509
dientes, cepillo 272
diésel 405
diésel para barcos 405
diez 427
diez mandamientos 447
diferencia de potencial eléctrico, unidad de medida 426
diferencial 351
difusión de información 335
difusor 290
digestivo, aparato 106
Dinamarca 450
dínamo 370
dinamómetro 423
dinero 441
dinero en efectivo, provisión 443
dintel 185, 192, 285
diodo 411
Dione 3
dióxido de carbono, absorción 54
dióxido de sulfuro, emisión 48
dique 28, 381
dique seco 381
dirección de flujo de electrones 417
dirección de la Meca 447
dirección del flujo de los electrones 416
dirección del viento 39
dirección URL 334
director 291
director artístico 290
director de carrera 522
director de fotografía 291
directorio 334
disco 6, 227, 333, 357, 472, 501, 507
disco abrasivo 229
disco compacto 326
disco compacto regrabable, grabador 333
disco compacto, lector 323
disco compacto, reproductor 325
disco de articulación 364
disco desviador de calor 199
disco duro extraible 333
disco giratorio 176
disco versátil digital (DVD) 318
discontinuidad de Gutenberg 26
discontinuidad de Mohorovicic 26
discos 177
disminución de la tensión 413
disparador 236, 314, 454
disparador del tambor 537
display 322, 325, 327, 346, 443, 461
display de frecuencia 325
display de funciones 310
display de las funciones 310
disposición 182
dispositivo de alarma 454
dispositivo de amarre 365
dispositivo de bloqueo 219
dispositivo de cierre 535
dispositivo de protección 306
dispositivo de remolque 364
dispositivos de contacto 198
disquete 333
disquete externo, unidad 333
distribución de la vegetación 44
distribución, tablero 198
distribuidor de bebidas 463

distribuidor de clips 341
distribuidor de hielos 164
distribuidor de hojas de afeitar 271
distrito 25
divanes, ejemplos 200
división 427
divisores 339
divisorio 457
do (C) 298
doble barra oblicua 334
doble bemol 299
doble caña 306
doble dentada 55
doble filo, tijeras para entresacar 270
doble fuelle 296
doble pletina de casete 325
doble sostenido 299
doble techo 528
doble toldo 529
doblez hacia el interior 534
dodecágono regular 429
dólar 440
dolichos 130
Dominica 449
dominio 334
dominio de primer nivel 334
dominio de segundo nivel 334
dominio, nombre 334
dominós 468
dorada 159
dormitorio 189, 528
dormitorio principal 189
dorsal ancho 97
Dorsal del Atlántico medio 34
Dorsal del Índico medio 34
Dorsal del Índico sureste 34
Dorsal del Índico suroeste 34
Dorsal del Pacífico oriental 34
Dorsal del Pacífico-Antártico 34
dorsal oceánica 33
dorsales oceánicas 34
dorso 115, 118
dorso de la nariz 117
dorso de un guante 243
dos doble 468
dos pares 468
dosificador 467
Douglas, saco 112
drenaje de aguas superficiales 434
dromedario 85
drumlin 29
drupa 57
drupas 132
drupéola 59
ducha 189, 439, 464
ducha de teléfono 195
ducha y bañera 194
ducha, bañera 194
dulse 123
duna 35
duna compleja 36
duna parabólica 36
dunas longitudinales 36
dunas transversales 36
dunas, ejemplos 36
dúo 300
duodeno 106
duramadre 109, 110
duramen 63
durión 137

E

eclipse anular 4
eclipse de Luna 5
eclipse parcial 4, 5
eclipse solar 4
eclipse total 4, 5
eclipses, tipos 4, 5
Ecuador 22, 448
ecuador 17, 20, 21, 43
edificio de hormigón 408
edificio de oficinas 432, 435
edificio del reactor 409
edificio público 25
editorial 313
edredón 204
efecto invernadero 46
efecto invernadero natural 46
efecto invernadero, aumento 46
efecto invernadero, gas 46
efluente 32
Egipto 451
eglefino 161
eje 177, 271, 527
eje de alta velocidad 413
eje de baja velocidad 413
eje de la rueda 371
eje de las aspas 412
eje del cepillo 272
eje del pedal 372
eje del tambor 537
eje delantero 401
eje horizontal, turbina de viento 413
eje polar 7
eje propulsor 383
eje vertical, turbina de viento 412
ejemplos de abreviaciones de monedas 440
ejemplos de algas 51
ejemplos de anfibios 75
ejemplos de ángulos 428
ejemplos de arácnidos 70
ejemplos de aviones 394
ejemplos de barcos 382
ejemplos de bicicletas 373
ejemplos de blusas y camisas 255
ejemplos de brocas y barrenas 228
ejemplos de camiones 364
ejemplos de carrocerías 347
ejemplos de clavos 220
ejemplos de conexiones 197
ejemplos de coníferas 65
ejemplos de conjuntos instrumentales 300
ejemplos de costas 35
ejemplos de cucharas 168
ejemplos de cuchillos 168
ejemplos de cuchillos de cocina 169
ejemplos de dunas 36
ejemplos de embarcaciones 382
ejemplos de enlaces de carreteras 342
ejemplos de esquís 510
ejemplos de faldas 253
ejemplos de flores 56
ejemplos de gafas 273
ejemplos de helechos 52
ejemplos de hojas 65
ejemplos de insectos 69
ejemplos de lagomorfos 82
ejemplos de latifolios 64
ejemplos de líquenes 50
ejemplos de llaves 499
ejemplos de mamíferos carnívoros 88
ejemplos de mamíferos marinos 90
ejemplos de mamíferos ungulados 84
ejemplos de mesas 202
ejemplos de motocicletas 369
ejemplos de musgos 51
ejemplos de neumáticos 358
ejemplos de pájaros 80
ejemplos de pantalones 254
ejemplos de patas 79
ejemplos de picos 79
ejemplos de piruetas 509
ejemplos de primates 91
ejemplos de puertas 286
ejemplos de reptiles 77
ejemplos de roedores 82
ejemplos de sacos de dormir 530
ejemplos de sillas 201
ejemplos de tablas 253
ejemplos de tenedores 168
ejemplos de tiendas de campaña 528
ejemplos de vagones 377
ejemplos de ventanas 287
ejemplos de vestidos 252
ejemplos de volcanes 28
el agua enfría el vapor utilizado 408
el agua regresa al generador de vapor 408
el eje de la turbina hace girar el generador 408
El Salvador 448
el vapor se condensa en agua 408
elástico 204
electricidad 198, 217
electrodo central 359
electrodo de masa 359
electrodomésticos, aparatos 176, 208
electrodos 199
electrón 414
electrones, cañón 318
electrones, colectores 417
electrones, dirección de flujo 417
electrónica 417
elefante 85
elemento de combustible 409
elementos arquitectónicos 286
elementos de la casa 185
elevación continental 33
elevación de la cuchilla, cilindro 401
elevador 281, 399
elevador telescópico 455
embalaje 49
embalse 406, 407
embalse a monte 406
embalse de compensación 406, 407
embarque del telesilla 512
embarque teleférico 512
emblema 477
emblema del equipo 506
embocadura 306
embocadura del cable 208
émbolo 460
embrague 350
embudo 171
emergencia, estación 345
emergencia, vehículo 345
emerillón 538
Emiratos Árabes Unidos 452
emisión de ácido nítrico 48
emisión de ácido sulfúrico 48
emisión de billetes 442
emisión de dióxido de sulfuro 48
emisión de gases contaminantes 47
emisión de óxido de nitrógeno 48
emmenthal 151
empalizada 230, 282
empaquetadora 364
empate de la boquilla 307
empeine 247
empella 240, 263
empleo del tiempo 338
empresa 335
empresas distribución /venta 335
empujador 170, 177, 180
empuñaderas 500
empuñadura 227, 229, 273, 341, 466, 477, 492, 494, 500, 505, 510, 534, 535, 536
encañado 230
encendedor 218
encendido 237
encendido/apagado 326
encendido/apagado/volumen 326
enchufe 210, 217, 228, 326
enchufe americano 198
enchufe con control de tiempo 210
enchufe de recarga 271
enchufe de tipo europeo 198
enchufe del termómetro 178
enchufe para auriculares 326
enchufe y selector desmontables 179
encía 101, 116
encimera 164, 210
encofrado metálico 417
encuadernación de anillas 340
endecágono regular 429
endivia 127
endocardio 104
endocarpio 57, 58
enebro, bayas 138
eneldo 142
energía 402
energía calorífica 46
energía eólica 412
energía eólica, producción de electricidad 413
energía fósil 402
energía geotérmica 402
energía nuclear 408
energía nuclear, producción de electricidad 408
energía solar 54, 410
energía térmica 402
energía, liberación 415
energía, unidad de medida 426
enfermera 464
enfoque 419
enfranque 240
enganche 353, 535
enganche de bola 356
enganche del remolque 361
engranaje de avance 180
engrasador 173
enlace de arcén 342
enlace de diamante 342
enlace de glorieta 342
enlace de trébol 342, 343
enlace químico 414
enlosado del jardín 182
enramada 230
enredadera 230
ensaladera 166
ensamble hembra 536
ensamble macho 536
entablado 187
entablamento 185, 279
entarimado 190, 498
entarimado sobre estructura de madera 190
entera 55
enterramiento 49
entrada 189, 343, 396, 439, 440, 442
entrada a boxes 524
entrada de actores 278
entrada de agua 407
entrada de aire 395, 523
entrada de clientes 438
entrada de corriente 199
entrada de la estación 378
entrada de la pirámide 278
entrada de público 278
entrada del garaje 183
entrada del personal 438, 445
entrada del refrigerante 410
entrada del suministro 198
entrada para mercancías 435
entrada principal 188, 435, 445, 465
entradas, taquilla 294
entradilla 313
entrecejo 86
entrediente 167
entrega de equipaje 390
entrenador 489, 498, 507
entrenador adjunto 489, 507
entrenadores 509
entrenudo 53
entrepaño 202, 219
entrepaño horizontal 185
entrepaño vertical 185
entrepierna 247, 255
entrepiso 378
entresuelo 182, 189
entrevista 313
envase 163
envases 162
envero 62
envión 500
epeira 70
eperlano 159
epicarpio 57, 58, 59
epicentro 27
epicóndilo 99
epidermis 114
epidídimo 111
epífisis 109
epiglotis 105, 118
epitróclea 99
equilibrador 303
equilibrio, posición 418
equinoccio de otoño 38
equinoccio de primavera 38
equinodermos 66
equipaje 276
equipamiento 472
equipamiento del salpicadero 457
equipamiento para acampar 531
equipamiento vario 231
equipo de alimentación, ventilador 329
equipo de alta fidelidad 322
equipo de climatización 386
equipo de grabación 291
equipo de protección 486
equipo de sonido 291
equipo electrobomba 357
equipo médico 499
equipo receptor 479
equipo turboalternador 402
equipos de gas 529
equivalente a 427
Eritrea 451
erupción 4
erupción, volcan 28
es paralelo a 428
escabel 201
escala 225, 298, 460, 533
escala Celsius 424
escala de altitud 37
escala de altura 227
escala de inclinación 227
escala de ingletes 226
escala de la regla 425
escala de temperaturas 37, 424
escala Fahrenheit 424
escala graduada 422, 423, 425
escala graduada de vernier 425
escala graduada de vernier/pico de rey 425
escalera 184, 191, 288, 404, 412, 468, 498, 501
escalera con boquilla telescópica 455
escalera de color 468
escalera de plataforma 219
escalera de tijera 219
escalera del entresuelo 189
escalera extensible 219
escalera mecánica 294, 378, 435
escalera real 468
escalera telescópica 455
escalera, hueco 189
escaleras 188, 293, 294, 345, 378, 439
escaleras de mano 219
escalerilla 361, 401, 404
escalerilla lateral 377
escalfador de huevos 175
escalinata 183, 283
escalón 364
escalón retráctil 361
escalones 184, 283
escama 74, 76, 79
escanda común 143
escáner óptico 121
escape 330
escápula 93, 95, 98, 99
escapulares 78
escaque blanco 470
escaque negro 470
escarabajo 69
escarcha 41
escarola 126
escarola rizada 127
escena, número 291
escenario 278, 292, 293
escisión del núcleo 415
esclavina 251
esclerótica 119
esclusa científica de aire 13
esclusa de canal 381
escoba 215
escoba central 365
escoba de nieve con rascador 356
escoba eléctrica 209
escoba lateral 365
escobén 383, 387
escobilla 193
escobilla limpiadora 271
escobilla metálica 309
Escocia, Placa 27
escollo 35
escolta 489
escopeta 534
escoplo 229
escorpión 70
escorrentía subterránea 45
escorrentía superficial 45

escorzonera 129
escota 520
escota foque 520
escota mayor 520
escotadura 301
escotadura intertrágica 115
escotera 521
escotero 520
escotilla 12, 13
escritorio 203, 439
escritorio, artículos 337
escroto 92, 111
escuadra 225
escudilla 166
escudo 507
escudo solar 7
escuela de esquí 512
escurridera 173
escurridor 171
escurridores 171
escúter 369
esfagno 51
esfera 332, 422, 429
esfera de té 173
esfera graduada 533
esfínter anal 106
eslabón de corte 235
eslabón giratorio 535
eslalon especial 511
eslalon gigante 511
eslalon supergigante 511
Eslovaquia 450
Eslovenia 450
esmalte 101
esmalte de uñas 265
esófago 105, 106
espacio 298, 330
espacio epidural 110
espacio interior 211
espacio para almacenamiento 364
espacio para la chispa 359
espacio sin pausa 330
espada 468
espádice 57
espagueti 146
espalda 83, 93, 95, 244, 517
espaldar 76
espaldera 532
España 449
esparadrapo 461
esparavel 216
esparcimiento de fertilizante 47
espárrago 125
espátula 173
espatulada 55
especias 138
especias para salmuera 139
especificaciones técnicas 358
espectro electromagnético 418
espejo 195, 277, 421, 439, 523, 533
espejo cóncavo primario 9
espejo de cercanías 362
espejo de cortesía 354
espejo de lectura 10
espejo de reflexión parcial 420
espejo de reflexión total 420
espejo doble giratorio 269
espejo lateral 269, 348, 364
espejo luminoso 269
espejo plano 7
espejo primario 7
espejo retrovisor 354, 363, 366, 369
espejo retrovisor exterior 362
espejo secundario 7, 9
espermatozoide 111
espesor, medición 425
espículas 4
espiga 57, 167, 169, 202, 216, 273, 357
espina escapular 99
espina nasal anterior 100
espinaca 127
espinacas, tallarines 146
espinillera 476, 480
espira 72
espiráculo 90
espiral 70, 73, 221
espiral central 70
espiral embrionaria 73
espirulina 123
esplenio 97
espoiler 366
espolón 83, 228, 308
espolvoreador 172
esponja natural 267
esponja sintética 266
esponja vegetal 267
esporas 52
espuma 33
espuma de afeitar 271
espumadera 173
esqueleto 98
esquí 510, 523
esquí alpino 510
esquí alpino, pista 512
esquí de descenso 510
esquí de eslalon 510
esquí de eslalon gigante 510
esquí de fondo 514
esquí supergigante 510
esquí, pista 512
esquí, salto 513
esquiador alpino 510
esquina 506
esquinero derecho 484
esquinero izquierdo 484
esquís, ejemplos 510
estabilizador 397, 523
estabilizador horizontal 395
establo 122
estaca 479
estación central de bombeo 404
estación de autobuses 432
estación de carga 375
estación de emergencia 345
estación de esquí 512
estación de ferrocarril 374, 375
estación de ferrocarriles 430, 432
estación de metro 378, 432
estación de servicio 346, 433
estación del ferrocarril 25
estación espacial internacional 11
estación local 316
estación meteorológica aeronaval 38
estación meteorológica de boya 38
estación meteorológica oceánica 38
estación repetidora 316
estación repetidora de microondas 334
estación terrestre 38
estación terrestre de telecomunicaciones 335
estación, metro 378
estación, modelo 39
estacionamiento 375, 381
estaciones del año 38
estadio 431, 472
estado 23
estado actual del tiempo 39
estados de la materia 414
Estados Unidos de América 448
estalactita 31
estalagmita 31
estambre 56, 58
estanco 436
estaño de soldar 218
estanque 230, 504
estaquilla 528, 529
estatua 446
estay de proa 520
Este 23
Este Noreste 23
Este Sudeste 23
estela luminosa del cráter 5
estepario 40
esternocleidomastoideo 96
esternón 98
estigma 56, 60, 67
estilo 56, 57, 58, 59, 60, 312, 424
estilóbato 279
estilos de natación 517
estimulador de encías 272
estípula 55
estómago 73, 103, 106
estómago cardiaco 71
estómago pilórico 71
Estonia 450
estornino 80
estrado 444
estrado de la acusación 440
estrado de los jueces 440
estrado de los secretarios judiciales 440
estrado de los testigos 440
estrado del abogado defensor 440
estrado del director 295
estragón 142
estrangulación 499
estrato basal 114
estrato córneo 114
estrato de cenizas 28
estrato de lava 28
estrato de Malpighi 114
estrato granuloso 114
estrato lúcido 114
estratocúmulos 42
estratopausa 37
estratos 42
estratosfera 37
estrechamiento 424
estrecho 24
Estrecho de Bass 15
Estrecho de Bering 16
Estrecho de Cook 15
Estrecho de Gibraltar 18
Estrecho de Torres 15
estrella de David 447
estrella de frenado 537
estrella fugaz 37
estribación 29
estribera 367, 368
estribera del pasajero 367, 368
estribo 116, 284, 395, 523
estribor 387
estropajo con esponja 215
estropajo, esponja 215
estructura 186, 297
estructura de la biosfera 44
estructura de la médula espinal 109
estructura de la Tierra 26
estructura de madera, entarimado sobre 190
estructura de metal 374
estructura de un alga 51
estructura de un helecho 52
estructura de un liquen 50
estructura de un musgo 51
estructura de una casa 188
estructura de una flor 56
estructura de una hoja 55
estructura del ala 392
estructura del oído 116
estructura del Sol 4
estructura inferior 403
estructura interior 286
estructura protectora 525
estuario 24, 35
estuche 225, 265, 424
estuche de encerado 514
estuche de hilo dental 272
estuche de las esposas 456
estuche de manicura 265
estuche portalentes 272
estufa de leña a fuego lento 192
esturión 158
etapas de la maduración 62
Etiopía 451
etiqueta de identificación 277
etiquetas adhesivas 340
etmoides, lámina cribosa 117
Eurasia 14
euro 440
Europa 2, 14, 18, 34, 449
europeo, clavija de tipo 198
Eustaquio, trompa 116, 117
Eutelsat 316
euthynteria 279
evaporación 45, 414
examen psiquiátrico 462
excavación vesicouterina 112
excavadora 399
excrementos de animales 48
exosfera 37
expedición de carga 391
expedidor de recibo 346
explosivo 534
expositor de final de pasillo 121
expositor de folletos 442
exprimidor 170, 177
exprimidor de cítricos 177
exprimir 177
extensión 202
extensión plegable 202
extensor 273
extensor común de los dedos 97
extensor corto de los dedos del pie 96
extensor largo de los dedos del pie 96
exterior 475
exterior de una casa 182
exterior derecho 475
exterior izquierdo 475
extintor 457
extintor portátil 454
extracto de vainilla 140
extracto, vainilla 140
extremo 273
extremo anterior 73
extremo del brazo 235
extremo derecho 507
extremo izquierdo 507
extremo libre 114
extremo posterior 73
exvoto 446
eyector 400
eyector de las varillas 176

F

fa (F) 298
fábrica 430
fachada 285
factor RH negativo 426
factor RH positivo 426
factorial 427
facturación de equipaje 390
fáculas 4
fagot 306
fagotes 295
fairway 504
faisán 81, 154
faja 259
faja braga 259
faja con liguero 259
faja con sostén 258
faja corsé 258
falangeta 114
falangina 114
falda 251, 492
falda acampanada 253
falda combinación 258
falda cruzada 253
falda de piezas 253
falda de tubo 253
falda de volantes 253
falda escocesa 253
falda fruncida 253
falda pantalón 253
falda recta 253
falda sarong 253
faldas, ejemplos 253
faldón 204, 255
faldón de la camisa 245
faldón delantero 245
faldón flexible 383
faldón trasero 245
falla 27
fallas transformantes 27
Falopio, istmo de la trompa 113
Falopio, pabellón de la trompa 113
Falopio, trompa 112
falsa doblez 260
falsa escuadra 225
falsa oronja 52
falso almohadón 204
familia de cuerdas 295
familia de los violines 301
familia de viento 295
familia de viento metal 295
farallón 35
faringe 105, 106
farmacia 436, 462, 465
faro 381
faro de carretera 457
faro de destello 455
faro delantero 348, 364, 366, 368, 376, 377, 523
faro reflector 455
farol 207, 230, 434
farola 207
faros delanteros 352
faros intermitentes 362
fascia lata, tensor 96
fase de deslizamiento 514
fase de impulsión 514
fase de impulso 514
fases de la Luna 5
fauces, itsmo 116
fax 328
fecha 441
fecha de vencimiento 441
fechador 338
Federación Rusa 450
feijoa 137
femenino 426
femeninos, órganos genitales 112
fémur 98
fémur, cabeza 99
fémur, cuello 99
fenec 88
fenogreco 138
ferrocarril del muelle 381
ferrocarril, estación 25, 374, 375
fertilización del suelo 47
fertilizante, esparcimiento 47
festoneada 55
fetuchinas 146
fiador 528
fiador elástico 528, 529
fibra muscular 110
fibra nerviosa 114
fíbula 98
ficha 469
fichero giratorio 338
fideos 146
fideos asiáticos 147
fideos de arroz 147
fideos de huevo 147
fideos de judías mungo 147
fideos de soba 147
fideos de somen 147
fideos de udon 147
fiel 422, 423
fijación 513
fijación de seguridad del esquí 511
fijación para el pie 514
fijaciones 510
fijador 514
fijador de carrete 537
Fiji 453
fila 293, 443
filamento 56, 199
filete 301, 302, 313
filigrana 441
Filipinas 19, 453
filmación, plató 290
filo 167, 169, 270
filo simple, tijeras para entresacar 270
filón-capa 28
filtro 178, 181, 184, 210
filtro de aire 235, 398
filtro de pelusa 212, 213
filtro de polarización 314
filtro del aire 350
filtro selector del color 318
filum terminal 109
filum terminal interno 109
fin 331
final de carrera 226, 287
Finlandia 450
fiordo 35
firma del titular 441
firma oficial 441
física : óptica 418
fisión nuclear 415
flamenco 81
flanco 78
flauta 306
flautas traverseras 295
flexo 206
flip 509
flor 53, 56
flor, anatomía de una 56
floración 62
flores, ejemplos 56
floristería 437
florón 283
flotador 196, 394, 457, 538

flujo de los electrones, dirección 416
Fobos 2
foca 90
foco 207, 419
foco Cassegrain 7
foco coudé 7
foco primario 7
foco subacuático 184
focos 293
fogón 192
foie-gras 156
foliador 338
folículo 60
folículo piloso 114
follaje 63, 200
fondista 514
fondo 292
fondo del escenario 293
fondo oceánico 33
fonendoscopio 460
fontanela anterior 100
fontanela esfenoidal 100
fontanela mastoidea 100
fontanela posterior 100
fontanería 194, 216
foque 520
formación profesional, oficina 442
formas de agarrar la paleta 493
formas farmacéuticas de medicamentos 467
formas geométricas 428
formato del archivo 334
fórnix, cuerpo 109
forro 240, 244, 245, 262, 274, 477, 509
forro de cuero 478
forro de la lengua 76
fosa abisal 33
fosa de agua 504
fosa de almacenamiento de combustible agotado 409
Fosa de Japón 34
Fosa de Java 34
Fosa de Kermadec-Tonga 34
Fosa de Kuril 34
Fosa de las Aleutianas 34
Fosa de las Filipinas 34
Fosa de las Marianas 34
Fosa de Puerto Rico 34
Fosa Perú-Chile 34
Fosa Ryukyu 34
fosa séptica 48
fosa triangular 115
fosas 34
fosas nasales 117
foso 282
foso de arena 504
foso de escenario 292
foso de orquesta 292
foto 313
fotocopiadora 442
fotografía 314
fotógrafo 436
fotógrafo de plató 291
fotomatón® 437
fotón 420
fotorreceptores 119
fotosfera 4
fotosíntesis 54
fóvea 119
foyer 293
fracción 427
frambuesa, corte 59
frambuesas 132
Francia 449
franja del faldón 383
frecuencia, unidad de medida 426
fregadero 164, 197
fregadero con triturador de basura 197
fregadero doble 194
fregona 215
freidora 178
freno 467, 501, 511, 522, 536, 537
freno aerodinámico 412
freno de disco 350, 357, 366, 525
freno de disco hidráulico 522
freno de emergencia 380
freno de la cadena 235
freno de mano 350, 354
freno de tambor 357
freno delantero 371
freno trasero 370, 527
frenos 357, 392
frente 78, 92
fresa, corte 59
fresadora 229
fresas 132
fresco 280
frigorífico 164, 211, 438
frigoríficos 438
frijoles 131
friso 202, 279
fronda 52
frontal 96, 446
frontera interna 23
frontera internacional 23
frontón 279
frotador 218
fructificación 62
fruncido 255
fruta 120
fruta de jack 136
fruta de la pasión 136
frutas 132
frutas pomo 133
frutas secas 133
frutas tropicales 136
fruto carnoso 58, 59
frutos 57
frutos secos 60
fuelle 274, 276
fuente 32
fuente básica de alimento 45
fuente de alimentación 416
fuente de servicio 313
fuente de servir 166
fuente de verdura 166
fuente para abluciones 447
fuente para pescado 166
fuertes lluvias 43
fuerza, unidad de medida 426
full 468
fulminante 534
fumarola 28
funcionamiento 319
funciones programables, teclas 443
funda 417, 531, 533
funda de almohada 204
funda de automóvil 356
funda de colchón 204
funda de cuero 533
funda de gafas 275
funda de guantes de látex 456
funda de la almohada 204
funda de mástil 519
funda del sable 519, 520
funguicida 47
funículo 59, 60
furgón de cola 377
fusa 299
fuselaje 393
fusible 198, 411
fusilli 146
fusión 414
fuste del bastón 514
fútbol 480
fútbol americano 484
futbolista 480
futón 204

G

gablete 285
Gabón 451
gafa 273
gafas 273, 522
gafas : partes 273
gafas de baño 516
gafas de esquí 510, 513
gafas de seguridad 458
gafas de sol 273
gafas protectoras 218, 458, 522
gafas, ejemplos 273
gaita 296
gajo 58
galaxia 6
galería 285
galería de acceso 407
galería de conexión 345
galería seca 31
galleta de centeno 145
galleta escandinava 145
galletas de arroz 147
gallina 81
gallinero 122
gallineta 161
gallo 81
galope 83
gamba 158
Gambia 451
ganadería intensiva 46, 47
gancho 217, 225, 364, 397, 423
gancho de arrastre 356
gancho de tracción 403, 460
gancho del meñique 307
gancho del pulgar 306, 307
gancho para el platillo 422
gancho para la porra 456
ganglio cerebropleural 73
ganglio espinal 109, 110
ganglio simpático 109
ganglio visceral 73
Ganimedes 2
garaje 182, 345
garaje, entrada 183
garaje, puerta basculante 286
garam masala 139
garbanzos 130
garduña 88
garganta 31, 32, 78, 492, 538
gargantilla 264
gargantilla de terciopelo 264
garita 282
garra 79, 82, 86
garrafa 165
garrapata 70
garrucha montacarga 397
garza 80
gas 403, 405, 414
gas de efecto invernadero 46
gas inerte 199
gases contaminantes, emisión 47
gasóleo 405
gasolina 405
gasolina pesada 405
gasolina, motor 360
gatillo 216, 235, 332, 534
gatillo de seguridad 235
gato 356, 455
gato doméstico 87
gato estabilizador 361
gato hidráulico 361
gatos, razas 87
géiser 28
gel de baño 267
gemelos 96, 97
gemelos de teatro 273
generador 402
generador de vapor 402
geografía 14
geología 26
geometría 428
Georgia 452
germen 61
germinación 53
Ghana 451
gibón 91
gimnasia 496
gimnasio 386, 444
girasol 56
girasol, aceite 149
glaciar 30, 32, 44
glaciar suspendido 30
glande 111
glándula de Cowper 111
glándula de veneno 76
glándula digestiva 71, 73
glándula lacrimal 119
glándula mamaria 113
glándula salival 118
glándula sebácea 114
glándula sudoripara apocrina 114
glándula sudoripara ecrina 114
glándula suprarrenal 107
glándulas salivales 106
globo 491, 529
globo ocular 75, 119
globo sonda 38
globo terráqueo 444
glóbulo blanco 104
glóbulo rojo 104
glotis 76
glucosa 54
glúteo mayor 97
go (sun-tse) 470
gofrera 178
gol 485
golfo 24
Golfo de Adén 19, 20
Golfo de Alaska 16
Golfo de Botnia 18
Golfo de California 16
Golfo de Carpentaria 15
Golfo de Guinea 20
Golfo de México 16
Golfo de Omán 19
Golfo de Panamá 17
Golfo Pérsico 19
Golgi, aparato 50, 66
golondrina 80
golpe de patín 514
golpes 490
goma 341
gombo 128
gónada 73
góndola 121, 413
góndola, sección transversal 413
gong 295, 309
gorgonzola 151
gorila, morfología 91
gorra 238, 456
gorra de cuartel 238
gorra noruega 238
gorrión 80
gorro 514
gorro de baño 516
gorro de marinero 239
gorro de punto con borla 239
gota 207
gotas oftalmológicas lubricantes 272
grabación 319
grabación nocturna, conmutador 320
grabador de disco compacto regrabable 333
gradas móviles 444
grado 428
grado Celsius 426
grados C 424
grados F 424
Gran Bahía australiana 15
Gran Barrera de Arrecifes 15
Gran Cañón 16
Gran Cordillera divisoria 15
gran danés 86
Gran Desierto de Arena 15
Gran Desierto Victoria 15
Gran Galería 278
gran roncón 296
gran siega interior 499
Granada 449
granada 136
grandes almacenes 437
Grandes Lagos 16
grandes titulares 313
granero 122
granja 122
grano 61
grano de almidón 50
grano de trigo, corte 61
granos torrefactos de café 148
granos verdes de café 148
granulación 4
gránulo de lípido 50
grapadora 341
grapas 341
grasa para cocinar 149
grasa, glóbulo 50
grasas 149, 405
grasera 174, 179
gravilla 524
Grecia 450
green 504
green de entrenamiento 504
grieta 30
grifo 195
grifo de cocina de tres vías 197
grillete 521
grillete de resorte 521
grillo campestre 69
Groenlandia 16
grosellas 132
grosellas espinosas 132
grosellas negras 132
grúa 385
grúa de caballete 406, 407
grúa de muelle 381
grúa de puente 407
grúa flotante 381
grúa móvil 397
grúa remolque 364
grúa torre 397
grúas 397
grupa 83
grupeto 299
grupo motor 376
grupo turboalternador 407
gruta 31
gruyère 151
guacamayo 80
guante 10, 478, 498, 506, 508, 513, 514, 522, 525
guante a la muñeca 243
guante corto 243
guante de bateo 476
guante de crin 267
guante de esquí 510
guante de golf 505
guante de recogida 477
guante de softball 477
guante del receptor 476
guante largo 243
guante para conducir 243
guante rígido 507
guante, dorso 243
guante, palmo 243
guantera 354
guantes 243
guantes de boxeo 498
guantes de hombre 243
guantes de jardinería 232
guantes de látex 460
guantes de mujer 243
guantes del portero 480
guantes protectores 525
guarda 169
guarda fija del disco 227
guarda móvil del disco 227
guardabarros 348, 349, 364, 365, 370
guardabarros delantero 366
guardamonte 534
guardanieve 523
guardarropa 188, 189, 203, 443
guardarropa de los clientes 438
guardarropa del personal 438, 465
guardería 437
guardia derecho 485
guardia izquierdo 485
guarnición 201, 202, 277, 511
Guatemala 448
guayaba 137
guepardo 89
guía 226, 521
guía de cabina 287
guía de cinta 341
guía de corte 227
guía de enganche 376
guía de escotas 521
guía de la cadena 372
guía de la punta 536, 537
guía del contrapeso 287
guía del papel 328
guías de archivo 340
guiñada 395
guindilla 139
guindilla molida 139
guindilla seca 139
guindilla triturada 139
Guinea 451
Guinea Ecuatorial 451
Guinea-Bissau 451
guisante 60
guisantes 130
guisantes mollares 130
guisantes partidos 130
guitarra clásica 302
guitarra eléctrica 303
gusto 116
Guyana 448
guyot 33

H

habas 130
habitación de observación 462
habitación de aislamiento 462
habitación de hotel 439
habitación de un paciente 464
habitación doble 439
habitación individual 439
habitaciones principales 188
habitáculo 525
hacha 234, 454, 533
hacha de cocinero 169
Haití 448
halcón 81
halibut 161
hall de entrada 188
halo 6
haltera 501
halterofilia 500
hamada 36
hámster 82
hangar de mantenimiento 389
hapterio 51
harina 144
harina común 144
harina de avena 144
harina de maíz 144
harina integral 144
harina sin blanquear 144
harissa 141
hastial 182
haya 64
hayuco 133
haz azul 318
haz de electrones 318
haz rojo 318
haz verde 318
hebilla 246, 248, 276, 511
hebilla de ajuste 527
hebilla de regulación 532
heladera 180
helecho 52
helecho arbóreo 52
helecho nido de pájaro 52
helecho, estructura 52
helechos canela 125
helechos, ejemplos 52
hélice 384, 386, 387, 429
hélice de dos aspas 394
hélice de proa 384
hélice de tres aspas 394
hélice posterior 384
hélice propulsora 383
helicóptero 395
hélix 115
hemisferio 429
hemisferio Norte 21
hemisferio occidental 21
hemisferio oriental 21
hemisferio Sur 21
hemisferios 21
henil 122
heptágono regular 429
herbicida 47
herbívoros 45
hercio 426
herraje 277
herramientas 216, 217, 372
herramientas de soldadura 218
herramientas para apretar 222
herramientas para clavar 220
herramientas para cortar 234
herramientas para plantar 231
herramientas para regar 236
herramientas para remover la tierra 233
herramientas para segar 226
herramientas para sembrar 231
herramientas percutoras 228
herramientas, caja 225
herramientas, cinturón 225
herramientaspara atornillar 221
herrete 240, 262
hervidero 29
hervidor 180
heterótrofos 45
hexagonal 359
hexágono regular 429
hidroavión cisterna 394
hidroavión de flotadores 394
hidrocarburos, vertido 48
hidroelectricidad 406
hidróptero 387
hidrosfera 44
hielo 41, 45
hielos perpetuos 40
hielos, distribuidor 164
hiena 88
hierba 492
hierbabuena 142
hierbas aromáticas 142
hierro 505
hifa 52
hígado 103, 106, 154
higiene dental 272
higiene personal 121
higo 137
higo chumbo 137
hijiki 123
hijuela 538
hilera 272
hileras 70
hilio renal 107
hilo 417
hilo de nailon 237
hilo de seguridad 441
hilo dental 272
Himalaya 19
hinojo 125
hipermetropía 419
hipervínculos 334
hipocentro 27
hipófisis 109
hipopótamo 85
hisopo 142
hocico 74, 86, 87
hockey sobre hielo 506
hogar 192
hogar, muebles 200
hoja 51, 53, 54, 55, 61, 125, 167, 169, 216, 219, 221, 226, 227, 229, 270, 271, 286
hoja corta 531
hoja de acanto 200
hoja de afeitar 271
hoja de cuchilla 509
hoja de la vid 62
hoja de parra 126
hoja dentada 270
hoja flexible 54
hoja larga 531
hoja, axila 55
hoja, estructura 55
hojaldre, pasta 145
hojas compuestas 55
hojas escamadas del ciprés 65
hojas simples 55
hojas, ejemplos 65
hojita enrollada 52
hombre 92
hombre, guantes 243
hombre, ropa de 244
hombre, sombreros 238
hombre, zapatos 240
hombrera 248, 302, 456, 486
hombrillo 249
hombro 92, 94, 492, 536
home theatre 321
Honduras 448
hongo 52
hongo mortal 52
hongo venenoso 52
hongo, anatomía 52
hongos 123
horario de la programación televisiva 313
horarios 374
horarios de las películas 294
horca 233
hormiga 69
hormigonera 365
hornear, utensilios para 172
hornillo 210, 529
horno 164, 210
horno microondas 164, 178
horno tubular 405
horno, termómetro 171
horquilla 8, 243, 268, 371, 396, 522, 525
horquilla de mano 232
horquilla de moño 268
horquilla frontal 522
horquilla telescópica 366, 369
horquilla trasera 370
horquilla, carretilla elevadora 396
horquillas 396
hortalizas 125
hortalizas de fruto 128
hortalizas de tallos 125
hospedería para esquiadores 512
hospital 433, 462
hotel 432, 439, 469, 512
hotel, habitación 439
hoyo 31, 504
hoyo de par 5 504
hoyuelo 505
hoz 234
Hubble, telescopio espacial 7
hueco de la escalera 189
hueco del motor 396
huella 191
huerta 122
huerto 122, 182
huesillos auditivos 116
hueso 57
hueso alveolar 101
hueso cigomático 100
hueso esfenoides 100
hueso frontal 98, 100
hueso ilíaco 98
hueso maxilar 101
hueso nasal 100, 117
hueso occipital 100
hueso parietal 100
hueso temporal 98, 100
huevera 211
huevo 79
huevo de avestruz 155
huevo de codorniz 155
huevo de faisán 155
huevo de gallina 155
huevo de oca 155
huevo de pato 155
huevo, fideos 147
huevos 155
Huitzilopochtli, templo 283
humano, cuerpo 92
húmero 98
húmero, cabeza 99
hummus 140
humor acuoso 119
humus 54
Hungría 450
huracán 43
husillo 425

I

idéntico a 427
identificación de cuenta 443
iglesia 433, 446
iglú 288
igual a 427
igual o mayor que 427
igual o menor que 427
iguana 77
ijar 83
íleon 106
iluminación 199, 269
iluminación de la placa de matrícula 352
imán 211, 341, 416
imparipinnada 55
impermeable 248
impermeables 248
impluvio 280
impresión pantalla 331
impresora de líneas 333
impresora, calculadora 337
impulso nervioso 110
impulso, irrigador 236
incendio forestal 47
incensario 446
incineración 49
incisivo central 101
incisivo lateral 101
incisivos 101
incisura angular 115
inclusión 427
India 453
indicador 340
indicador de ajuste 511
indicador de alimentación 333
indicador de carga del papel 333
indicador de encendido 329
indicador de hora de salida 374
indicador de línea 362, 363
indicador de llamadas 328
indicador de luz larga 368
indicador de nivel de gasolina 355
indicador de número de andén 374
indicador de posición 287
indicador de puesta en marcha de papel 443
indicador de punto muerto 368
indicador de recarga 271
indicador de respuesta automática 328
indicador de temperatura 269, 355
indicador de tiempo 314
indicador de velocidad 314
indicador dedetección de papel 443
indicador del cartucho 333
indicador del importe total 346
indicador del intermitente 368
indicador del nivel del agua 179
indicador del precio por litro /galón 346
indicador digital 423
indicador luminoso 179, 423
indicador para viraje en nado de espalda 517
indicador transparente 340
indicadores 318, 323
indicadores de entrada 322
indicadores del modo audio 322
Indice 539
Indice español 539
Indonesia 19, 453
industria 335
industria petroquímica 405
infiltración 45, 47
infinito 427
inflador 530
inflorescencias 127
inflorescencias, variedades 57
información 437, 442, 463
infraestructura 342
infraspinoso 97
ingeniero de sonido 291
ingle 92, 94
inhalador 467
iniciales del banco emisor 441
inicio 331
inmovilización 499
inmovilización de brazo 499
inodoro 189, 194, 195, 196, 439, 464
insectos, ejemplos 69
insert 331
insertar 331
insignia 456
insignia de grado 456
institución educativa 335
instrucciones operativas 346
instrumentos científicos 7, 13
instrumentos de cuerda 301
instrumentos de percusión 308
instrumentos de teclado 304
instrumentos de trazado y medición 225
instrumentos de viento 306
instrumentos del salpicadero 355
instrumentos electrónicos 310
instrumentos musicales tradicionales 296
instrumentos para escribir 312
integración de energía a la red de transporte 413
integral 427
Intelsat 317
intensidad luminosa, unidad de medida 426
interior derecho 481
interior izquierdo 481
intermitente 352, 355
intermitente delantero 366, 368
intermitente trasero 367, 368
internauta 334
Internet 334
Internet, usos 335
interóseos del pie 96
interruptor 177, 180, 181, 198, 206, 207, 208, 209, 211, 213, 218, 219, 229, 269, 270, 271, 272, 311, 319, 323, 327, 329, 416
interruptor alimentación 320
interruptor automático 407
interruptor de alimentación 318
interruptor de comunicación 336
interruptor de emergencia 368
interruptor de encendido 329, 354, 368
interruptor de encendido/apagado 314
interruptor de gatillo 227, 228, 229
interruptor de la puerta 213
interruptor de ráfagas 368
interruptor del limpiaparabrisas 354
interruptor funciones 320
interruptor on/off 209
interruptor principal 198
interruptor selector de velocidad 227
intersección 427
intertítulo 313
intervalos 298
intestino 71, 73, 103
intestino delgado 106
intestino grueso 106
inundación, llanura 32
invernadero 122
inversor 221, 228
invierno 38
inyector 360
Ío 2
Irán 452
Iraq 452
iris 119
Irish moss 123
Irlanda 449
irrigador bucal 272
irrigador de impulso 236
irrigador giratorio 236
irrigador oscilante 236
isba 288
isla 24, 164, 343
isla de arena 35
Isla de Terranova 16
isla volcánica 33
Islandia 18, 450
Islas Aleutianas 16
islas de Cabo Verde 451
islas del Caribe 448
Islas Fiji 15
Islas Malvinas 17
Islas Marshall 453
Islas Salomón 453
islote rocoso 35
isobara 39
isosista 27
isquion 99
Israel 452
istmo 24
istmo de la trompa de Falopio 113
istmo de las fauces 116
Istmo de Panamá 16
Italia 450

J

jabalí 84
jabalina 472
jabón de tocador 267
jabonera 195, 271
jaboticaba 137
jaguar 89
Jamaica 448
jamba 185, 192
jamón ahumado 153
jamón de York 156
jamón serrano 156
Jápeto 3
Japón 19, 453
jarabe de arce 149
jarabe de maíz 149
jarabe para la tos 467
jardín 230, 280
jardín de rocalla 230
jardín público 435
jardín, enlosado 182
jardinería 230
jardinería, guantes 232

jarlsberg 151
jarra de agua 166
jarra de cerveza 165
jarra medidora 171
jarra para café 166
jarrita de leche 166
jaula 281
jaula de protección 473
jefe de cronometradores 516
jefe de luminotecnia 291
jefe de vestuario 290
jengibre 139
jerbo 82
jeringa de decoración 172
jeringilla de Luer-Lock 460
jeringuilla 460
jeringuilla de irrigación 460
jersey de cuello de cisne 514
jersey de cuello de tortuga 250
jersey de cuello redondo 250, 255
jerseys 250
jerseys combinados 255
jet supersónico 37
jícama 124
jirafa 85
jojoba 137
Jordania 452
jota 468
joyería 264, 436
joystick 332
joysticks 471
judía amarilla 131
judía china larga 130
judía de Egipto 130
judía verde 131
judías adzuki 131
judías de Limas 131
judías de ojo 130
judías mungo 131
judías mungo negras 131
judías negras 131
judías pinta 131
judías rojas 131
judías romanas 131
judo 499
judoka neutral 499
jueces 496, 497, 509, 518
jueces de virajes 517
juego 492
juego de casquillos 223
juego de dardos 471
juego de mesas 202
juego de pequeñas herramientas 232
juego de utensilios 173
juego en línea 335
juegos 468
juegos de mesa 469
juez 485, 498, 499
juez de brazado 516
juez de faltas de pie 491
juez de gol 506
juez de línea 481, 483, 485, 487, 490, 494, 496, 507
juez de línea de saque 490
juez de llegada 516
juez de red 491
juez de salida 516
juez de servicio 490, 494
juez de silla 490
juez externo 485
juez-árbitro 518
jugador 469, 486, 506
jugador con el servicio 491
jugador de baloncesto 488
jugador de criquet 478
jugador de primera base 474
jugador de rugby 483
jugador de saque 494
jugador de segunda base 474
jugador de tercera base 474
jugador exterior central 474
jugador exterior derecho 474
jugador exterior izquierdo 474
jugador medio 474
jugadores 492
jugadores, posición 481, 482
juguetería 436
julio 426
junta 214, 359
junta cónica 196
junta de goma 197
junta del cárter 360
junta positivo/negativo 410
Júpiter 2
Justicia, Palacio 432

K

Kazajistán 452
kelvin 426
Kenia 451
ketchup 141
kilogramo 426
kimono 256, 499
kiosco 346, 379
Kirguizistán 452
Kiribati 453
kiwano 136
kiwi 136
kombu 123
kora 297
Kuiper, cinturón 2
Kuwait 452

L

la (A) 298
la hoja según su borde 55
la presión del vapor impulsa las turbinas 408
labio 83, 87
labio córneo 76
labio externo 73
labio inferior 116, 305
labio interno 73
labio mayor 112, 113
labio menor 112, 113
labio superior 116, 305
laboratorio 7
laboratorio americano 11
laboratorio espacial 13
laboratorio patológico 465
lacolito 28
ladera 29
ladillo 313
lado 293
lado de la reina 470
lado del rey 470
lado derecho 272
lado izquierdo 272
ladrillo refractario 192
ladrillos refractarios 192
ladronera 282
lagarto 77
lago 5, 24, 29, 32
lago artificial 32
Lago Baikal 19
Lago Chad 20
lago de brazo muerto 32
Lago Eyre 15
lago glaciar 32
Lago Ladoga 18
Lago Malawi 20
Lago Tanganyika 20
lago tectónico 32
Lago Titicaca 17
Lago Victoria 20
lago volcánico 32
lagomorfos 82
lagomorfos, ejemplos 82
lagos 32
lagos, acidificación 48
laguna 35
laguna salada 36
lama 412
lámina 51
lámina cribosa del etmoides 117
lámina de contacto de positiva 359
lámina de contacto negativa 359
laminillas 52
lámpara 380, 421
lámpara de cabecera 206, 439, 464
lámpara de despacho halógena 206
lámpara de escritorio 206
lámpara de lectura 457
lámpara de mesa 206
lámpara de neón 217
lámpara de petróleo 532
lámpara de pie 206
lámpara de pinza 206
lámpara de prueba de neón 217
lámpara de techo 206
lámpara del santuario 446
lámpara halógena 199
lámpara incandescente 411
lámpara orientable de pared 207
lámparas 206
lámparas en serie 207
lamprea 159
lanceolada 55
lancha pequeña 385
langosta marina 158
lanzador 474, 475, 479
lanzamiento 475, 479
lanzamiento de jabalina 473
lanzamiento de martillo y disco 473
lanzamiento de peso 472
Laos 453
lapa 157
lapiaz 31
lápida conmemorativa 447
lápiz 312
lápiz adhesivo 341
lápiz blanco para uñas 265
lápiz de grafito 312
lápiz de ojos 266
larguerillo 396
larguero 186, 201, 219, 392, 412
larguero de la bisagra 202
larguero del marco 202
laringe 105
lasañas 146
láser de rubí pulsado 420
lata 163
lata de conserva 163
latas 162
lateral derecho 481
lateral izquierdo 481
laurel 142
lavabo 194, 195, 439, 464
lavabo de cirujano 465
lavado de automóviles 346
lavadora 194, 212
lavandería 188, 439
lavavajillas 164, 214
laya 233
lazo 238, 264, 535
leche 150
leche de cabra 150
leche en polvo 150
leche evaporada 150
leche homogeneizada 150
leche, suero 150
lecho oceánico 26
lecho ungular 114
lechuga de cogollo 126
lechuga de tallo 126
lechuga iceberg 126
lechuga marina 123
lechuga rizada 126
lechuga romana 126
lector CD/DVD 471
lector de casetes 326
lector de disco compacto 323, 325
lector de discos 310
lector de discos compactos 326
lector de tarjeta 321, 442, 443
lectura /pausa 323
lectura de tarjeta, ranura 346
legumbre 60
legumbres 130
lema 441
lémur 91
lencería 256, 436, 439
leñera 192
lengua 106, 116, 117, 118, 154
lengua bífida 76
lengua glaciar 30
lenguado 161
lengüeta 240, 248, 262, 274, 305, 306, 509, 511
lengüeta de cuero 246
lengüeta de la caña 297
lengüeta protectora 333
lengüeta, tubo 305
lente 273, 419
lente bicóncava 419
lente biconvexa 419
lente cóncava 419
lente cóncavo-plana 419
lente convexa 419
lente convexo-plana 419
lente de campo 420
lente tórica 419
lentejas 130
lentes 419
lentes convergentes 419
lentes de contacto 272
lentes de contacto blandas 272
lentes de contacto desechables 272
lentes de contacto duras 272
lentes de imágen recta 420
lentes divergentes 419
león 89
leopardo 89
Lesoto 452
Letonia 450
letrinas 280
leucoplasto 50
Líbano 452
libélula 69
líber 63
liberación de energía 415
liberador del seguro 222
Liberia 451
libero 487
Libia 451
libra 440
librería 436, 444
libreta 338
lichi 137
licuadora 176, 180
líder 515
liebre 82, 154
Liechtenstein 450
liga 259
ligadura 299
ligamento 73
ligamento alveolo-dentario 101
ligamento ancho del útero 113
ligamento suspensorio 119
liguero 259
lija 229
lijadora excéntrica 229
lima 134, 229, 531
lima de uñas 265
limbo 52
limitador de velocidad 287
limitador de velocidad, polea tensora 287
limón 134
limpiador 355
limpiador de boquillas 218
limpiador de uñas 265
limpiaparabrisas 348, 355
limpieza 215
limusina 347
lince 88
lindero 182
línea 298
línea azul 507
línea cableada 335
línea central 515
línea central de servicio 491
línea de «touche» 483
línea de 10 m 482
línea de 15 m 483
línea de 22 m 482
línea de 5 m 483
línea de área de penalti 480
línea de ataque 487
línea de banda 493, 515
línea de campo 416
línea de centro 481
línea de crecimiento 72, 73
línea de cuadro 502
línea de devolución 479
línea de dobles 490
línea de fondo 482, 484, 487, 489, 491, 493, 494
línea de foul 474
línea de gol 484, 506
línea de juego 515
línea de la calle 473
línea de lanzamiento 479
línea de marca 482
línea de medio campo 483
línea de melé 485
línea de pista 389
línea de referencia 533
línea de retirada 479
línea de salida 473, 524
línea de salida 100 m 472
línea de salida 800 m 473
línea de salida de 1.500 m 473
línea de salida de 10.000 m 473
línea de salida de 100 m vallas 472
línea de salida de 110 m vallas 472
línea de salida de 200 m 472
línea de salida de 400 m 473
línea de salida de 400 m vallas, línea de relevos de 4x100 m 473
línea de salida de 5.000 m 472
línea de salida de relevos 4 x 400 m 473
línea de seguridad 379
línea de servicio 491
línea de servicio corto 495
línea de servicio largo 494
línea de tee 515
línea de tiro libre 489
línea de visión 533
línea del fondo de la piscina 517
línea divisoria central 493, 494
línea lateral 74, 343
línea lateral de dobles 495
línea lateral de individuales 491, 495
línea límite de inicio de jugada 484
línea media 484, 488, 507
línea meridiana 533
línea neutra 416
línea reservada 334
línea submarina 334
línea suplementaria 298
línea telefónica 334
línea trasera 515
línea yardas 484
líneas de latitud 22
líneas de longitud 22
linterna 456, 529
linterna movible 217
liquen 50
liquen custráceo 50
liquen foliáceo 50
liquen fruticuloso 50
liquen, estructura 50
líquenes, ejemplos 50
líquido 414, 415
líquido cerebroespinal 110
lira 297
lisosoma 66
lista de procedimientos 10
lista superciliar 78
listón 211
litera 361
litoral, configuración 35
litosfera 26, 44
Lituania 450
lixiviación 48
liza 282
llama 84, 415
llama perpetua 447
llana 216
llanta 366, 371
llanta neumática de tracción 380
llanta neumática guía 380
llanura 24, 32
llanura abisal 33
llanura de inundación 32
llave 306, 307
llave combinada 223
llave de apriete 224
llave de carraca 223
llave de embocadura 306
llave de estrella abierta 223
llave de estrella común 223
llave de estrella hexagonal 223
llave de fontanero 216
llave de paso 194, 196, 197
llave de tuercas española 223
llave del mandril 228
llave en cruz 356
llave inglesa 216, 223
llave para agua 307
llavero 275
llaves 216, 223
llegada 473
llegada del telesquí 512
lluvia 41

lluvia ácida 47, 48
lluvia helada 41
lobo 88
lobulada 55
lóbulo 79, 115, 117
lóbulo inferior 105
lóbulo lateral inferior 62
lóbulo lateral superior 62
lóbulo medio 105
lóbulo superior 105
lóbulo terminal 62
local técnico 345
loción para después del afeitado 271
locomotora 376
locomotora diésel eléctrica 377
lóculo 58
lomo 78, 83, 86, 152, 167, 169, 215
lomo con canal 228
lona 412, 498
lona de separación 528
longan 136
longitud de la ola 33
longitud de onda 418
longitud, medición 425
longitud, unidad de medida 426
loop de puntera 509
loseta 12
lubina 160
lucernario 183
lucernario del baño 189
lucernario del hueco de la escalera 189
lucernas del campanario 285
luces de advertencia 355
luces de estado 331
luces de gol 507
luces de seguridad 457
luces traseras 352
lucio 160
lucioperca 160
luminotécnico 291
Luna 2, 4, 5
Luna creciente 5
luna llena 5
Luna menguante 5
luna neuva 5
Luna, eclipse 5
Luna, fases 5
luneta 293
lúnula 73, 114, 115
lupa 421, 531
lutz 509
Luxemburgo 449
luz 7, 8, 9
luz ámbar 434
luz anticolisión 392
luz antiniebla 352, 364
luz de advertencia de la gasolina 355
luz de advertencia de puerta abierta 355
luz de advertencia del aceite 355
luz de advertencia del alternador 355
luz de advertencia del cinturón de seguridad 355
luz de aterrizaje 395
luz de cruce 352
luz de encendido 271, 328
luz de encendido/apagado 327
luz de freno 352
luz de marcha atrás 352
luz de navegación 383, 393, 395
luz de posición 352, 376
luz de tope 383
luz delantera 371
luz indicadora de cargado 337
luz indicadora de la presión del aceite 368
luz indicadora de luz larga 355
luz larga 352
luz lateral 364, 365
luz piloto 269
luz roja 434
luz trasera 352, 367, 368, 370
luz verde 434
luz visible 418

M

macaco 91
macarrones 146
Macedonia 450
maceta 230
maceta colgante 230
macillo 304
macizo 24
macizo de flores 230
macronúcleo 66
mácula lútea 119
Madagascar 20, 452
madera 505
madera, pisos de 190
maduración, etapas 62
madurez 62
magacín 313
magenta 418
magma 28, 33
magnetismo 416
Maine coon 87
maître 438
maíz 61, 143
maíz : mazorca 61
maíz forrajero 122
maíz, aceite 149
maíz, harina 144
maíz, jarabe 149
maíz, pelo 61
malanga 129
Malasia 453
Malaui 452
Maldivas 453
maleta 369
maleta clásica 277
maleta de fin de semana 277
maletero 349, 362
maletín 274, 276
maleza 504
malla 493, 522
mallas 263
mallas con volantes 260
Malpighi, estrato 114
Malta 450
mamíferos acuáticos 90
mamíferos carnívoros 86
mamíferos carnívoros, ejemplos 88
mamíferos marinos, ejemplos 90
mamíferos ungulados 83
mamíferos ungulados, ejemplos 84
mancha solar 4
mandarina 134
mandíbula 67, 74, 98, 100
mandíbula deslizante 425
mandíbula fija 425
mandíbula inferior 78
mandíbula superior 78
mandioca 124
mando 471
mando a distancia 319, 321
mandolina 170, 297
mandos de la videocinta 320
mandos de los quemadores 210
mandos del cabestrante 364
mandril 221, 228
manecilla de vapor 181
manejo de materiales 396
maneta del embrague 366, 368
maneta del freno delantero 368
manga 244, 492
manga empotrada 245
manga raglán 248, 251, 261
manga y boquillas 172
mangas anteriores 492
mango 137, 167, 169, 170, 208, 216, 217, 218, 219, 220, 221, 222, 223, 224, 226, 228, 235, 269, 270, 271, 272, 301, 325, 478, 492, 493, 494, 503, 505, 506, 515, 531, 537
mango aislado 217
mango aislante 217
mango auxiliar 228
mango posterior 537
mangosta 88
mangostán 136
manguera 195, 197, 236, 454
manguera de alimentación 214
manguera de aspiración 455
manguera de desagüe 212, 214
manguera de incendios 454
manguera de inyección de lodo 403
manguera de líquido para frenos 357
manguera de riego 236
manguera de servicio 346
manguera de vaciado 212
manguera del rebosadero 196
manguera, carretilla 236
manguito inferior del radiador 358
manicura 265
manicura, estuche 265
manilla 185, 186, 192, 211
manilla de la puerta 349
manillar 366, 369, 371, 501, 522, 523
maniobra de la excavadora 399
manipulación 396
manivela 170, 224, 356, 365, 372, 536, 537
manivela de enrollado 225
manivela de la ventanilla 352
manivela del carrete 236
mano 91, 93, 95, 115, 170
manojo 125
manómetro 455, 461
manopla 243
manopla de baño 267
manos de póquer 468
manta 204
manteca de cerdo 149
mantenimiento 346
mantenimiento de pinturas 219
mantequera 166
mantequilla 150
mantequilla clarificada 150
mantis 69
manto 72, 73, 192
manto externo 26
manto freático 48
manto interno 26
manual de primeros auxilios 461
Manx 87
manzana 133
manzana, corte 58
manzanilla 148
mapa de carreteras 25
mapa de la ruta 378
mapa de ruta 380
mapa de rutas 379
mapa físico 24
mapa geográfico 444
mapa meteorológico 38, 39
mapa político 23
mapa urbano 25
mapache 88
maquillador 290
maquillaje 266
maquillaje facial 266
maquillaje labial 266
maquillaje para ojos 266
máquina 287
máquina de afeitar eléctrica 271
máquina de café exprés 181
máquina expendedora de bebidas 346
máquina expendedora de billetes 379
máquina para hacer pasta italiana 170
máquina pisanieve 512
maquinaria pesada 398
maquinilla de afeitar 271
maquinilla desechable 271
maquinilla para cortar el cabello 269
maquinista 290
maquinista jefe 290
maquis 44
mar 5, 24, 32
Mar Adriático 18
Mar Arábigo 19
Mar Báltico 18
Mar Caribe 14
Mar Caspio 14, 19
Mar de Aral 19
Mar de Barents 18
Mar de Beaufort 16
Mar de Bering 14
Mar de Caribe 16
Mar de Coral 15
Mar de Groenlandia 14
Mar de Irlanda 18
Mar de Japón 19
Mar de la China Meridional 14, 19
Mar de la China Oriental 19
Mar de Noruega 18
Mar de Tasmania 15
Mar de Weddell 15
Mar del Norte 14, 18
Mar Egeo 18
Mar Mediterráneo 14, 18, 20
Mar Negro 14, 18, 19
Mar Rojo 14, 19, 20
marca central 490
marcador 312, 471, 472, 492, 497, 499
marcador automático 327
marcador de clasificación general 496
marcador de posición 302, 303
marcador del evento en curso 497
marco 186
marco ajustable 226
margarina 149
Marie Byrd, Tierra 15
mariposa 517
mariposa de resorte 221
mariposa, morfología 67
mariquita 69
marítimo 40
marmota 82
marquesina 434
marquesina del andén 375
marroquinería, artículos 274
Marruecos 451
marta 88
Marte 2, 3
martillo 116, 472
martillo de albañil 216
martillo de bola 220
martillo de carpintero 220
martillo de uña 220
martín pescador 80
más o menos 427
masa 27
masa de aire 39
masa inerte 27
masa, unidad de medida 426
máscara 454, 476, 478, 486
máscara antigás 459
máscara para el polvo 459
mascarilla 459
masculino 426
masculinos, órganos genitales 111
masetero 96
mástil 281, 297, 301, 302, 303, 321, 395, 396, 519, 520
matacán 282
matemáticas 427
materia 414
materia inorgánica 45
materia, estados 414
material aislante 190
material de cierre 417
material de lucha contra los incendios 454
material impermeable 260
materiales varios 225
materiales, manejo 396
matraca 536
matriz ungular 114
Mauricio 452
Mauritania 451
maxilar 74, 100, 117
maxilar separable 76
maxilar superior 98
mayor que 427
mayúscula 330
maza 309
mazo 220
mazorca 61
meandro 32
meato auditivo 115, 116
meato auditivo externo 100
meato urinario 111
mecanismo de desplazamiento de la hoja 401
mecanismo de empuje 312
mecanismo para las octavas 306
mecedora 200, 201
medallón 264
media 257, 486
media antideslizante 257
media bota 240
media de malla 257
media luna 273
media volea 490
mediana 343, 434
medias 257, 259
medicamentos, formas farmacéuticas 467
medición de la longitud 425
medición de la temperatura 424
medición del espesor 425
medición del peso 422
medición del tiempo 424
médico 464, 498
médico interno 464
medida instantánea, termómetro 171
medidor de agua 359
medidor de altos niveles de frecuencia 323
medio centro 481
medio de apertura 482
medio de melé 482
medio tubo 526
medir, utensilios 171
médula 63, 107, 154
médula espinal 109, 110
médula espinal, estructura 109
Meissner, corpúsculo 114
mejilla 94
mejillónes 157
Melanesia 15
melazas 149
melé espontánea 483
melé: 484, 485
melisa 142
melocotón 132
melocotón, corte 57
melón amarillo 135
melón cantalupo 135
melón de miel 135
melón de Ogen 135
melón escrito 135
melón invernal 135
melones 135
membrana 58, 75
membrana celular 50, 66
membrana de plasma 66
membrana del cascarón 79
membrana del tímpano 116
membrana interdigital 79
membrana nuclear 50, 66
membrana plásmica 66
membrana vitelina 79
membrillo 133
meninges 109
menisco convergente 419
menisco divergente 419
menor que 427
ménsula 192, 283
mentón 78, 94
mentonera 522
menudillo 83
Mercurio 2, 3
meridiana 200
meridiano occidental 22
meridiano oriental 22
meridiano principal 22
merlán 161
mesa 36, 164, 202, 493, 502
mesa arbitral 507
mesa de cama 464
mesa de hojas abatibles 202
mesa de servicio 438
mesa operatoria 464
mesa plegable 202
mesa rotatoria 403
mesas, ejemplos 202
meseta 24, 29
mesilla de cabecera 464
mesilla de noche 439
mesita de servicio 202
mesocarpio 57, 58, 59
mesopausa 37
mesosfera 37
metal, selección 49
meteorología 37

metro 378, 426, 435
México 448
mezcla de agua y vapor 402
mezcla de manganeso (cátodo) 417
mezcla de zinc y electrolito (ánodo) 417
mezclador de pastelería 172
mezclar 176
mezquita 447
mi (E) 298
micelio 52
microfilamento 66
micrófono 320, 327, 328, 332, 337, 456
micrófonos 457
micrómetro 425
Micronesia 453
micronúcleo 66
microondas 418
microscopio 421
microscopio binocular 421
microscopios 421
microtúbulo 66
miel 149
miembro inferior 103
miembro superior 103
migala 70
mihrab 447
mijo 61, 143
mijo : espiga 61
mil 427
Mimas 3
mimbar 447
minarete 447
mini-cadena estéreo 325
minibús 363
miniporción de leche /nata 163
miniporción, leche/nata 163
minutero 171, 179, 424
minuto 428
miocardio 104
miopía 419
mira 535
mira telescópica 534
mirador 391
Miranda 3
mitocondria 50
mitocondrio 66
mitón largo 243
mízcalo 123
mobiliario para el hogar 200
mocasín 242
mochila 532
modalidad de avance de la película 314
modalidad de exposición 314
modalidad de exposición múltiple 314
modalidad TV 319
modalidad VCR 319
modelo de estación 39
módem 334
módem cableado 335
moderador 376, 408
modillón 282
modos de pago 441
modulador de presión de frenado 357
módulo centrífugo 11
módulo de células solares 411
módulo de comunicación 316
módulo de habitación americano 11
módulo de propulsión 316
módulo de servicio 316
módulo para experimentos europeo 11
módulo para experimentos japonés 11
módulo ruso 11
mofeta 88
molar, corte transversal 101
molares 101
Moldavia 450
molde acanalado 172
molde de carlota 172
molde de pan 179
molde de soufflé 172
molde para bizcocho 172
molde para magdalenas 172
molde para tartas 172
molde redondo con muelles 172
moldeador de cutículas 265
moldes de pastas 172
moldura 358
moldura lateral 349
moldura superior 493
mole 426
molécula 414
moler 170
molinete 412
molinillo de café 180
molino de plataforma giratoria 412
molino de torre 412
molino de viento 412
mollejas 154
moluscos 72, 157
moneda : anverso 441
moneda, anverso 441
moneda, reverso 441
moneda: reverso 441
monedero 275
Mongolia 453
monitor de vídeo 329
monitors de control del director 290
mono 261
mono de esquí con capucha 261
monocascos 521
monopatín 526
monopatín 526
Monopoly® 469
monovolumen 347
montacargas 397
montaña 29, 512
montaña alta, climas 40
Montañas Rocosas 16
montante 184, 187, 263, 394, 466, 509
montante central 185, 186, 202, 349
montante de la bisagra 185
montante de la cerradura 185
montante embarbillado 186
montante esquinero 187
montante quicial 186
monte de Venus 112
Monte Everest 37
monte marino 33
Montes Apalaches 16
Montes Cárpatos 18
Montes transantárticos 15
Montes Urales 18
montura en herradura 7
monumento 25
moqueta 190
moras 132
morcilla 156
morcillo 152
mordaza 217, 221, 222, 224, 226, 228, 229, 265
mordaza curva 222
mordaza fija 223, 224
mordaza móvil 223, 224
mordaza recta 222
mordazas 224, 535
mordente 299
morfología de un bogavante 71
morfología de un caballo 83
morfología de un caracol 72
morfología de un delfín 90
morfología de un gorila 91
morfología de un pájaro 78
morfología de un perro 86
morfología de un pulpo 72
morfología de un tiburón hembra 74
morfología de una abeja trabajadora 68
morfología de una araña 70
morfología de una concha bivalva 73
morfología de una concha univalva 73
morfología de una mariposa 67
morfología de una perca 74
morfología de una rana 75
morfología de una rata 82
morfología de una serpiente venenosa: cabeza 76
morfología de una tortuga 76
morilla 123
morillos 193
morral 276
morrena central 30
morrena de fondo 30
morrena frontal 30
morrena lateral 30
morrena terminal 30
morro 392
morro abatible 394
mortadela 156
mosaico 280
mosca 69, 502
mosca artificial 536
mosca central 502
mosca de la línea de cuadro 502
mosca superior 502
mosca tsetsé 69
mosquetón 521, 538
mosquito 69
mostaza 60
mostaza alemana 140
mostaza americana 140
mostaza blanca 138
mostaza de Dijon 140
mostaza en grano 140
mostaza en polvo 140
mostaza inglesa 140
mostaza negra 138
mostrador 390
mostrador de carne de autoservicio 120
mostrador de carne fresca 120
mostrador de quesos 121
mostrador frigorífico 438
mostrador, carne 120
mostrador, quesos 121
moto acuática 523
moto cámara 522
moto de cabeza 522
moto de carreras y motociclista 525
moto de motocross 525
moto nieve 523
moto, motocilista 525
motocicleta 366, 525
motocicleta : vista desde lo alto 368
motocicleta de turismo 369
motocicleta todo terreno 369
motocicletas, ejemplos 369
motor 176, 177, 180, 208, 212, 213, 214, 227, 229, 237, 272, 366, 401, 403
motor de arranque 237
motor de elevación diésel 383
motor de gasolina 351, 360
motor de propulsión diésel 383
motor del tractor 400
motor diesel 399, 400, 401
motor diésel 398
motor eléctrico 235, 237, 358
motor fueraborda 385
motor principal 13
motor, bogie 376
movimiento diagonal 470
movimiento en ángulo 470
movimiento horizontal 470
movimiento horizontal del suelo 27
movimiento vertical 470
movimiento vertical del suelo 27
movimientos de un avión 395
Mozambique 452
mozzarella 150
mucosa olfatoria 117
mueble bar 203
muebles contenedores 202
muebles infantiles 205
muela del juicio 101
muelle 381, 430, 460, 535
muelle de carga 435, 437
muelle helicoidal 351
muelle para inflar y desinflar 530
muerte 426
muesca 244, 422, 503
muesca de apertura 531
muestreador 310
muflón 84
muguete 56
mujer 94
mujer, guantes 243
mujer, ropa 251
mujer, sombreros 239
mujer, zapatos 241
mújol 160
mula 84
muleta de antebrazo 466
muleta de sobaco 466
multicasco 521
multipack 163
multiplicación 427
multiplicador 413
mundo, climas 40
muñeca 93, 95, 115
muñequera 486, 492, 500, 527
munster 151
muralla 282
muro 5, 184, 528
muro de cimentación 187
muro de encauzamiento 406
muro de la Qibla 447
muro de llegada 516
muro de nubes 43
muro del ojo 43
muro fortificado 447
músculo aductor anterior 73
músculo aductor posterior 73
músculo bulbocavernoso 111
músculo erector del pelo 114
músculo papilar 104
músculo recto inferior 119
músculo recto superior 119
músculos 96
muselina 171
museo 433
musgo 51
musgo, estructura 51
musgos, ejemplos 51
música 296
muslera 486
muslo 78, 83, 86, 93, 95, 111, 112
muslo, aductor 96
muslo, recto interno 97
musola 158
Myanmar 453

N

nabiza 127
nabo 129
nabo sueco 129
nacimiento 426
nacionalidad 497
nalga 93, 95, 111, 112
Namibia 452
naos 279
naranja 134
naranja china 134
naranja, corte 58
narciso 56
narina 74, 75, 76, 78
nariz 82, 94, 117, 534
nariz, aleta 117
nariz, dorso 117
nariz, ventana 117
nasofaringe 117
nata 150
nata agria 150
nata de montar 150
natación 516
Nauru 453
navaja 157
navaja de barbero 271
navaja jardinera 234
navaja multiusos suiza 531
navaja para entresacar 269
nave 285
nave central 447
nave espacial 37
nave lateral 285
navegador 334
Nazca, Placa 27
neblina 41
neceser 276, 277
necrológico 313
nectarina 132
nefridio 71
negra 299
negras 470
negro 418
Nepal 453
Neptuno 2, 3
nervadura central 60
nervadura principal 55
nervadura secundaria 55
nervio 114
nervio abdominogenital mayor 108
nervio abdominogenital menor 108
nervio auditivo 116
nervio central 51
nervio ciático mayor 108
nervio ciático menor del muslo 108
nervio ciático poplíteo externo 108
nervio ciático poplíteo interno 108
nervio circunflejo 108
nervio crural 108
nervio cubital 108
nervio diagonal 284
nervio digital 108
nervio espinal 109
nervio femorocutáneo 108
nervio glúteo 108
nervio intercostal 108
nervio mediano 108
nervio musculocutáneo de la pierna 108
nervio obturador 108
nervio olfatorio 117
nervio óptico 119
nervio radial 108
nervio raquídeo 110
nervio safeno externo 108
nervio safeno interno 108
nervio secundario 284
nervio tibial anterior 108
nervio transversal 284
nervio vestibular 116
nervios craneales 108
nervioso, sistema 108
neumático 349, 358, 364, 371, 522, 525
neumático de invierno 358
neumático de rendimiento 358
neumático de tacos 358, 369, 525
neumático de todas las estaciones 358
neumático de turismo 358
neumáticos, ejemplos 358
neurona motora 110
neurona sensorial 110
neuronas, cadena 110
neutrón 414
neutrón incidente 415
neuzes del Brasil 133
nevera 346, 532
neviza 30
newton 426
Nicaragua 448
nicho de seguridad 345
niebla 41
nieve 41
nieve ácida 48
nieves perpetuas 29
Níger 451
Nigeria 451
Nilo 20
nimbostratos 42
niños, ropa 261
nísperos 133
Nissl, cuerpos 110
nivel de agua 181
nivel de aire 225
nivel de equilibrio del agua 33
nivel de la recepción 439
nivel del agua 208
nivel del mar 26, 33, 37
nivel del mar, presión barométrica 39
nivel el agua, indicador 179
nivel freático 31
nivelador 229
niveladora 401
no es idéntico a 427
no es igual a 427
no es paralelo a 428
no pertenece a 427
nódulo de Ranvier 110
nogal 64
nombre de la estación 378
nombre de la moneda 441
nombre del dominio 334
nombre del gimnasta 497
nombre del periódico 313
nombre del titular 441
nonágono regular 429
nonio 422

ñoquis 146
Nor Noroeste 23
Noreste 23
nori 123
Noroeste 23
Norte 23
Norte Noreste 23
Noruega 450
notación del ajedrez 470
notación musical 298
notas musicales, valores 299
noticias breves 313
nube 37, 41
nube alta, tipo 39
nube baja, tipo 39
nube de cenizas 28
nube de Oort 2
nube en forma de embudo 43
nube media, tipo 39
nubes 42
nubes altas 42
nubes bajas 42
nubes de desarrollo vertical 42
nubes medias 42
nubes, absorción 46
nuca 93, 95
núcleo 4, 6, 50, 66, 110, 112, 414, 534
núcleo externo 26
núcleo fisionable 415
núcleo interno 26
núcleo, escisión 415
nucléolo 50, 66, 112
núcleos radiactivos 415
nudo 53, 416
nudo viario 431
Nueva Caledonia 15
Nueva Zelanda 15, 453
nuevo shekel 440
nuez 92, 133
nuez moscada 138
nuez moscada, rallador 170
nuez verde 60
nuez, corte 60
nuezes de cola 133
nuezes de ginkgo 133
nuezes de macadamia 133
número de habitación 439
número de identificación personal (PIN), teclado 443
número de la autopista 25
número de la carretera 25
número de la escena 291
número de la tarjeta 441
número de pista 323
número de serie 441
número de tarjeta 443
número del jugador 488, 506
número del surtidor 346
número dorsal 473
números romanos 427
nutria de río 88

O

oasis 32, 36
obenque 520
Oberón 3
obispillo 78
objetivo 8, 314, 332, 420, 421
objetivo gran angular 314
objetivo macro 314
objetivo zoom 314, 320
objetivos 314
objeto 419
oblicuo mayor del abdomen 96, 97
oboe 306
oboes 295
obra muerta 521
obrera 68
observación, puesto 7
observatorio 7
observatorio astronómico 7
observatorio astronómico, sección transversal 7
obstáculo 470
obturador 333
obturador de la cúpula 7
oca 81, 155
occidental 493
occipital 97, 99
Oceanía 14, 15, 453
océano 5, 24, 45
Océano Atlántico 14, 15, 18, 20
Océano Glacial Ártico 14
Océano Índico 14, 15, 19, 20
Océano Pacífico 14, 15, 19
ocelo 67
ocio al aire libre 528
octaedro regular 429
octágono regular 429
octava 298
ocular 8, 9, 320, 420, 421
ocular acodado 8
odómetro 355
Oeste 23
Oeste Noroeste 23
Oeste Suroeste 23
office 188
oficial del banco de los penaltis 507
oficina 346, 374, 438
oficina de correos 433, 437
oficina de formación profesional 442
oficina de reservas de hotel 390
oficina de urgencias 462
oficina del puerto 381
oftalmología 463
ohmnio/ohm 426
oído 115, 301
oído interno 116
oído medio 116
oído, estructura 116
ojal 248, 275, 509
ojera 320
ojete 240, 246, 263, 538
ojete para la correa 315
ojo 43, 70, 71, 72, 76, 90, 94, 119, 220, 270
ojo compuesto 67, 68
ojo de buey 386
ojos, maquillaje 266
okapi 84
ola 33
olécrano 99
oleoducto 404
oleoducto de superficie 404
oleoducto para crudo 404
oleoducto submarino 404
olfato 116
oliva, aceite 149
olla 175
olla a presión 174
olla para cuscús 175
Omán 452
ombligo 30, 92, 94
omoplato 93, 95, 98, 99
onda 418
onda de choque 403
onda sísmica 27
onda, longitud 418
ondas hertzianas, transmisión 316
ondas radio 418
Oort, nube 2
opera 432
operación rápida 323
operación, teclas 442, 443
operador de cámara 290
operador de jirafa 291
operador del reloj de 30 segundos 488
opérculo 74
opilión 69
opistodomo 279
óptica 437
orangután 91
orbicular 55
orbicular de los párpados 96
órbita lunar 4, 5
órbita terrestre 4, 5
orbitador 12, 13
orca 90
ordenador 444
ordenador portátil 336
ordenador de a bordo 354, 457
ordenador de bolsillo 337
ordenador personal 329
ordenador portátil: vista frontal 336
ordenador portátil: vista posterior 336
ordenador: vista frontal 329
ordenador: vista posterior 329
orégano 142
oreja 92, 116, 240
oreja de Judas 123
oreja de mar 157
oreja, pabellón 82
orejera 238
orellana 123
organismo cultural 335
organismo de salud 335
organismos simples 66
organización gubernamental 335
órgano 305
órganos genitales femeninos 112
órganos genitales masculinos 111
órganos sensoriales 114
orientación de la cuchilla, cilindro 401
oriental 493
orificio 312
orificio del pie 305
orificio nasal 83
orla decorativa 260
oronja 123
orquesta 278
orquesta sinfónica 295
orquídea 56
ortiga 127
oruga 67, 398
oruga de polilla 69
orza de popa 519
orza de quilla 519, 520
oscilación 395
oso negro 89
oso polar 89
osoto-gari (gran siega) exterior 499
ostra 157
ostras 157
otaria 90
otoño 38
otorrinolaringología 463
otros signos 299
ovario 56, 112, 113
oveja 84
óvulo 56, 112
óxido de nitrógeno, emisión 48
oxígeno, producción 54

P

pabellón 306, 307, 432
pabellón auricular 115, 116
pabellón de la oreja 82
pabellón de la trompa de Falopio 113
paciente 464
Pacífico, Placa 27
Pacini, corpúsculo de 114
página adelante 331
página atrás 331
pago electrónico, terminal 443
pagoda 283
país 23
Países Bajos 449
pajarita 245
pájaro carpintero 80
pájaro, morfología 78
pájaros, ejemplos 80
pajita 163
pak-choi 126
Pakistán 452
pala 193, 233, 398, 401, 478, 493, 510, 535
pala de timón 384
pala del rotor 395
pala del stick 506
pala del timón 520
pala del ventilador de sustentación 383
pala hidráulica 400
pala plegable 532
palacio de congresos 433
Palacio de Justicia 432
paladar, velo 117
palafito 288
palanca 178, 197, 220, 265, 269, 306, 534
palanca de arranque 235
palanca de bloqueo 229
palanca de bloqueo de la altura 8, 9
palanca de bloqueo del acimut 8, 9
palanca de cambio 350
palanca de cambio de velocidades 354, 367, 368, 369
palanca de cierre 214
palanca de enclavamiento 224
palanca de la cisterna 196
palanca de la cuña 229
palanca de luces e intermitentes 354
palanca de mando 395
palanca de maniobra 396
palanca de perforación 180
palanca de regulación de altura 209
palanca de seguridad 237
palanca de vibración 303
palanca del cambio de velocidades 371, 372
palanca del cucharón 399
palanca del deslizador 353
palanca del freno 371, 522, 523
palanca del tapón 196
palanca estabilizadora 467
palanca retráctil de la guarda móvil 227
palanca rotativa 332
Palau 453
palco 293
palé con alas 396
paleta 152, 173, 493, 535
paleta de albañil 216
paleta de relleno 216
paletilla 86, 153
palillo 308
palma 115, 243, 477
palma de un guante 243
palmar 36
palmar mayor 96
palmar menor 96
palmeada 55
palmera 64
palmeta 200
palo 215
palo de la tienda 529
palo de proa 385
palo del jugador 506
palo del radar 384
paloma 81
palos 482
palpo 73
palpo labial 67
pamela 239
pan 144
pan ácimo 145
pan alemán de centeno 145
pan americano de maíz 145
pan blanco 145
pan campesino 145
pan danés de centeno 145
pan de centeno negro 144
pan de flor 145
pan de pita 145
pan espiga 144
pan griego 144
pan indio chapatí 145
pan indio naan 145
pan integral 145
pan irlandés 145
pan judío hallah 145
pan multicereales 145
pan negro ruso 145
pan, molde 179
panadería 121, 437
pañal 260
pañal desechable 260
Panamá 448
panamá 238
panceta 156
páncreas 106
pandereta 309
panel de cierre 329
panel de control 212, 213, 214
panel de controles 314
panel de la puerta 352
panel de la vela 520
panel de mandos 178, 179, 210, 213
panel de publicidad 378
panel de separación 277
panel del display 320
panel frontal 365
panel lateral 365
panel protector 467
panel radiador 13
panel solar 7, 316
paneles fotovoltaicos 11
paño lateral 248
pantalla 193, 199, 206, 318, 336, 337, 338, 439, 442, 471, 479
pantalla de cristal líquido 315
pantalla de protección 474
pantalla de proyección 294
pantalla del radar 457
pantalla tácti 320
pantalla táctil 337
pantalla, tubo 318
pantalón 473, 476, 486, 499, 500
pantalón corto 261
pantalón de boxeo 263
pantalón de peto 260
pantalón peto 254
pantalones 246, 263, 480, 525
pantalónes 506
pantalones acampanados 254
pantalones cortos 483, 488
pantalones de boxeo 498
pantalones de chándal 262
pantalones de peto 261
pantalones de tubo 254
pantalones elásticos 522
pantalones, ejemplos 254
pantalóns cortos 254
pantis 257
pantógrafo 376
pantorrilla 93, 95
pantufla 242
pañuelo de bolsillo 244
papaya 137
papel de aluminio 162
papel de celofán 162
papel encerado 162
papel para el horno 162
papelera 341
papila 114
papila filiforme 118
papila foliada 118
papila fungiforme 118
papila gustativa 118
papila lingual 118
papila óptica 119
papila renal 107
papilla circunvalada 118
Papua Nueva Guinea 15, 453
paquete 163
para abrir y descorchar 170
parábola 321
parabrisas 348, 364, 366, 369, 385, 392, 394, 523
paracaídas 287
paracaídas auxiliar 12
parachoques 364, 369, 523
parachoques posterior 369
parada de autobús 434
parafinas 405
paraguas 273
Paraguay 448
paragüero 273
paralelepípedo 429
paralelo 22
paralelogramo 429
paramecio 66
parapeto 344
pararrayos 183, 407, 413
parasol 8, 354, 356, 361
parche 309
parche inferior 308
parche superior 308
pared celular 50
pared de viraje 517
pared lateral 385, 517
pared transversal de contención 384
pareja 509
parietal 99
paripinnada 55
parka 249
parmesano 151
párpado 76
párpado inferior 75, 87, 119
párpado interno 87
párpado superior 75, 87, 119
párpados, orbicular 96

parque 25, 433
parqué 190
parqué alternado a la inglesa 190
parqué Arenberg 190
parqué Chantilly 190
parque de bomberos 433
parqué de cestería 190
parque de estacionamiento 389
parqué de mosaico 190
parqué en punta de Hungría 190
parqué espinapez 190
parque nacional 25
parqué sobre base de cemento 190
parqué sobrepuesto 190
parqué Versalles 190
parqué, tipos 190
parrilla 178, 210
parrilla de salida 524
parrilla eléctrica 179
parrilla estabilizadora 529
parrilla plegable 533
parte superior 219
parteluz 186, 285
partes 200, 201, 204
partes de un círculo 428
partes de un zapato 240
partes de una bicicleta 370
pasadizo ascendente 278
pasadizo descendente 278
pasador 186, 246, 268, 532
pasaje subterráneo 375
pasajeros, avión turborreactor 392
pasajeros, terminal 390
pasajeros, vagones 376
pasamano 363, 385
pasamanos 191, 287
pasamontañas 239, 524
pasapuré 173
pasapurés 170
pasarela 282, 292, 375, 384
pasarela superior 379
pasarela telescópico 389
pascal 426
paseo 230
pasillo 120, 436
pasillo de dobles 490
pasillo de seguridad 440
paso 29, 83
paso a nivel 375
paso alternativo 514
Paso de Drake 15, 17
paso de patinador 514
paso de peatones 434
paso de popa a proa 385
paso elevado 344
paso inferior 344
pasta 146
pasta de hojaldre 145
pasta won ton 147
pastelería 437
pastelería, bandeja 172
pastelería, mezclador 172
pastilla 467
pastilla de combustible 409
pastilla de fricción 357
pastor alemán 86
pata 76, 91, 199, 201, 202, 204, 205, 231, 308, 537
pata anal 67
pata curvada 200
pata de la mesa 493
pata de locomoción 70
pata delantera 67, 68, 75, 201
pata lobulada, dedo 79
pata media 67, 68
pata móvil 202
pata palmípeda, dedo 79
pata telescópica 460
pata torácica 67
pata trasera 67, 68, 75, 201
pata ventosa 67
Patagonia 17
patas, ejemplos 79
patatas 124
pátera 200
patilla 273
patín de aterrizaje 395
patín de cola 395
patín de los accesorios 314
patín de pista corta 508
patín de pista larga 508
patín del portero 507
patín en línea 527
patín en línea de hockey 527
patín en línea, 527
patín para figuras 509
patinador 508, 527
patinaje acrobático 527
patinaje artístico 509
patinaje artístico, cuchilla 509
patinaje de velocidad 508
patinaje en línea 527
patinaje sobre hielo, pista 509
patinaje, pista 512
patines de carreras 508
patio 230, 445, 447
patio de armas 282
patio de butacas 293
patio de tanques 404
pato 81, 155
patrulla de primeros auxilios y puesto de socorro 512
pausa 331
pausa /imagen fija 319
pavimento 342
pavo 81, 155
pavo real 81
PC 334
peatones, semáforo 434
pecanas 133
pécari 84
peces 74
peces cartilaginosos 158
peces óseos 159
pecho 83, 92
pechuga 78
pecíolo 52, 55
pecorino romano 151
pectoral 486, 501
pectoral mayor 96
pedal 302, 308, 370, 372, 501, 522
pedal automático 522
pedal crescendo 305
pedal de expresión 305
pedal de la sordina 304
pedal de los bajos 311
pedal de los frenos 354
pedal del acelerador 354
pedal del embrague 354
pedal del freno 350, 357
pedal del freno trasero 368
pedal fuerte 304, 311
pedal plano 522
pedal suave 304
pedalero 305
pedernal 218
pedestal 206, 302, 473
pedipalpo 70
pedúnculo 51, 56, 57, 58, 59, 62
peinado 268
peinazo 202
peinazo de la cerradura 185
peinazo inferior 201, 202
peinazo superior 201, 202
peine afro 268
peine combinado 268
peine de cardar 268
peine de iluminación 291
peine de mango 268
peine de peluquero 268
peine para desenredar 268
peine y cuchilla 271
peines 268
pelaje 82, 91
pelapatatas 169
peldaño 191, 219
peldaño de arranque 191
peldaño posterior 455
pelele 261
pelele de dos piezas 260
peletería 436
pelícano 80
película plástica, condensador 417
película termosaldada 163
pelillo 536
pelo 93, 95, 114, 190
pelo de maíz 61
pelos absorbentes 53
pelos absorbentes, zona 63
pelos radicales 53
pelota 493
pelota de béisbol, corte 477
pelota de cricket 478
pelota de golf 505
pelota de softball 477
pelota de tenis 492
pelotón 522
pelotón de cabeza 522
peltada 55
peluquería 436
peluquero 290
peluquero, tijeras 270
pelvis renal 107
penacho 78
penacho de plumas 495
pendiente 264
pendientes 264
pendientes de aro 264
pendientes de clip 264
pendientes de espiga 264
pendientes de tornillo 264
pene 92, 111
península 24
Península Antártica 15
Península de Arabia 19
Península de Corea 19
Península de Kamchatka 19
Península de Kola 18
Península de los Balcanes 18
Península del Yucatán 16
Península Escandinava 18
Península Ibérica 18
pentágono regular 429
pentagrama 298
peón 470
pepinillo 128
pepino 128
pepino amargo 128
pepino dulce 137
pepino sin pepitas 128
pepita 58, 59
pepperoni 156
pera 133
pera asiática 137
pera de goma 460, 461
pera de maíz 498
perca 160
perca, morfología 74
percha 515
percoladora 181
percusión, instrumentos 308
percutor 534
pérdida de calor 46
perdiz 80
perejil 142
perfil del suelo 54
perfil, suelo 54
perforación 263
perforación, torre 403
perforaciones 240, 243
perforadora 340
perfumería 121, 436
pérgola 230
pericardio 105
pericarpio 58, 60
perifollo 142
perilla 227
periódico 313
periódico, nombre 313
peristilo 279, 280
peristoma 66
peritoneo 111, 112
perno 222, 223, 224
perno con collarín 223
perno de articulación del cucharón 399
perno de expansión 221
perno de fijación 357
perno de la bisagra 400
perno difusor 236
perno maestro 365
perno para falso plafón 221
pernos 223
peroné 98
peroneo corto 97
peroneo largo 96
peróxido 461
peroxisoma 66
perpendicular 428
perro 86, 535
perro, morfología 86
perros, razas 86
persa 87
personal, entrada 438
personal, guardarropa 438
pertenece a 427
Perú 448
pesa 422
pesa corrediza 422
pesas 500, 501
pesas para muñecas y tobillos 500
pesca 536
pesca con mosca 536
pesca de lanzado 537
pescado 121
pescante 384, 397
peso 423, 440, 472
peso, medición 422
pespunte 243, 246, 260
pespunteada 253
pespunteado 262
pestaña 119, 251
pestaña de arrojo 460
pestañas 87
pesticida 47, 48
pestillo 186
pestillo de ingletes 226
pétalo 56
petición del sistema 331
petirrojo 80
peto 260, 261, 476, 486
petróleo 403, 405
petróleo crudo 405
petrolero 381, 384
pez cartilaginoso 74
pez de San Pedro 161
pez espada 159
pez óseo 74
pezón 92, 94, 113
pi 428
piamadre 109
piano 295
piano electrónico 311
piano vertical 304
pica 82, 454
picadora de carne 170
picardía 256
píccolo 295, 306
pícea 65
pichi 252
pichón 154
pickguard 303
pico 29, 78, 233
pico de rey 425
picos, ejemplos 79
pictogramas 330
pie 52, 72, 73, 91, 92, 93, 94, 95, 176, 199, 260, 302, 305, 421, 536, 537
pie ajustable 212, 213, 214
pie de foto 313
pie de la cama 204
pie de voluta 200
pie derecho 187, 285
pie, arteria dorsal 102
pie, dedo 92, 94
pie, interóseos 96
piedra blanca 470
Piedra Coyolxauhqui 283
piedra de afilar 169
piedra de curling 515
piedra de sacrificio 283
piedra negra 470
piel 57, 58, 59, 110, 114, 297
piel armónica 297
piel de gamuza 265
pierna 83, 93, 95, 247
pierna de cordero 153
pierna elástica 247
pieza de talón 514
piezas 470
pijama 256, 261
pijama de una pieza 247
pila 416
pila alcalina de manganeso-zinc 417
pila bautismal 446
pila de agua bendita 446
pila de carbón-cinc 417
pila recargable 320
pilar 27, 283, 284, 344
pilar anterior del velo del paladar 116
pilar derecha 482
pilar izquierda 482
pilas secas 417
pilastra corintia 281
pilón 344
pilón del turborreactor 393
pilón guía 345
piloto 178, 180, 181, 208, 210, 214, 524
pimentero 166
pimentón, 139
pimienta blanca 138
pimienta de cayena 139
pimienta de Jamaica 138
pimienta molida 139
pimienta negra 138
pimienta rosa 138
pimienta verde 138
pimiento dulce amarillo 128
pimiento dulce rojo 128
pimiento dulce verde 128
piña 65, 136
pináculo 282, 284, 285
pinatífida 55
pincel 312
pincel de repostería 172
pincel para labios 266
pinchador 341
pingüino 80
pinna 52
pino piñonero 65
piñón 65
piñón libre 372
piñones 133
pintada 81, 154
pintalabios 266
pinza 71, 246, 248, 269, 312
pinza de cinturón 327
pinza del freno 366
pinza negra 356
pinza para el cabello 268
pinza para rizar 268
pinza roja 356
pinza sujetamuestras 421
pinzas 173, 461
pinzas multiuso 217
pinzas para caracoles 173
pinzas para depilar cejas 265
pinzas para espagueti 173
pinzas pelacables 217
pinzas universales 222
pinzón 80
piojo 69
pirámide 278, 429
pirámide, entrad 278
pirata 254
Pirineos 18
piruetas, ejemplos 509
piscina 184, 386, 517
piscina elevada 184
piscina enterrada 184
piscina olímpica 517
piso 193, 412, 526
piso cosido 528, 529
piso superior 363
pisos de madera 190
pista 472, 504, 506, 524
pista corta 508
pista de aterrizaje y despegue 390
pista de enlace 388
pista de esquí alpino 512
pista de estacionamiento 388
pista de fondo 512
pista de patinaje 512
pista de patinaje sobre hielo 509
pista de rodaje 388
pista de salto 473
pista larga 508
pista para avanzados 512
pista para expertos 512
pista para intermedios 512
pista para principiantes 512
pistachos 133
pistas de carreras 496
pistas de esquí 512
pistilo 56
pistola 216, 456

pistola de calor 219
pistola de salida 472
pistola del surtidor 346
pistola para calafateo 216
pistola para soldar 218
pistola pulverizadora 236
pistolera 456
pistón 307, 357, 360
pitón 77
pitorro 181, 215
pívot 489
pivote 217, 270, 511, 533
pivote móvil 222
pizarra 444
placa 164, 197
placa africana 27
placa antártica 27
placa antifricción 511
placa base 511
placa calcárea 73
placa costal 76
placa de absorción 410
placa de advertencias 228
placa de circuito impreso 417
placa de cocción 179
placa de Cocos 27
placa de Escocia 27
placa de especificaciones 228
placa de Filipinas 27
placa de freno 511
placa de identificación 456
placa de instalación 199
placa de Nazca 27
placa de número 525
placa del Caribe 27
placa del interruptor 198
placa del Pacífico 27
placa eléctrica 210
placa euroasiática 27
placa indoaustraliana 27
placa marginal 76
placa motora 110
placa negativa 359
placa norteamericana 27
placa positiva 359
placa protectora 525
placa sudamericana 27
placa supracaudal 76
placa térmica 181
placa terminal 409
placa vertebral 76
placas convergentes 27
placas divergentes 27
placas tectónicas 27
plafón 206
plancha 179, 208, 269
plancha de muelles 496
plancha de pelo 269
plancha de vapor 208
plancha eléctrica 179
plancha superior 178
planetas 2
planetas externos 2
planetas internos 3
planicie 24
planicie fluvio-glaciar 30
planisferio 14
plano de deriva 393
plano de la catedral 285
plano del templo griego 279
plano del terreno 183
plano horizontal 393
plano vertical 393
planta 53, 247
planta alta 182, 189
planta baja 182, 188
planta de bombeo 404
planta de lubricantes 405
planta de reforma catalítica 405
planta de separación selectiva 49
planta intermedia de refuerzo 404
planta, anatomía 53
plantador 231
plantador de bulbos 231
plantar delgado 97
plaqueta 104, 273
plasma 104
plasmodesmo 50
plástico transparente 274
plásticos transparentes 274
plásticos, clasificación 49
plastrón 76
plataforma 27, 219, 342, 363, 377, 396, 423, 526
plataforma continental 33
plataforma de 10 m 518
plataforma de 3 m 518
plataforma de 5 m 518
plataforma de 7,5 m 518
Plataforma de hielo de Amery 15
Plataforma de hielo de Filchner 15
plataforma de lanzamiento 475
plataforma de producción 404
plataforma de salida 516
plataforma elevadora para silla de ruedas 363
plataforma giratoria 455
plataforma giratoria, molino 412
plataforma inferior 396
plataforma para transportar vagones 377
plátano 136
platea 278
platija 161
platillo 422, 423
platillo high hat 308
platillo inferior 308
platillo superior 308
platillo suspendido 308
platillos 295, 309
platina 421
platina mecánica 421
platito para el pan 166
plato 531
plato de postre 166
plato de retroceso 357
plató de rodaje 290
plato giratorio 224, 400
plato lijador 229
plato llano 166
plato para caracoles 173
plato sopero 166
platos de cocción 179
playa 35
pletina 326
pletina de casete 323
pleura parietal 105
pleura visceral 105
plexo braquial 108
plexo lumbar 108
plexo nervioso 101
plexo sacro 108
pliegue anal 93, 95
pliegue de la columela 73
pliegues, ejemplos 253
plisada 253
plomo 538
pluma 27, 400
pluma de ave 312
pluma de caña 312
pluma estilográfica 312
pluma metálica 312
pluma metálica romana 312
plumas timoneras 78
Plutón 2, 3
pocilga 122
podadera 234
podadera de árboles 234
podadora de bordes 237
podio 283, 435
podio de salida 516
podio y sótanos 435
pole position 524
polea 219, 360, 535
polea del montacargas 397
polea tensora del limitador de velocidad 287
poleas de tensión 372
polideportivo 431
polígono industrial 431
polígonos 429
Polinesia 453
polipasto 403
polipodio común 52
polítrico 51
pollo 155
polo 250, 255, 492
polo negativo 417
polo Norte 21
polo norte 416
polo positivo 416
Polo Sur 15
polo Sur 21
polo sur 416
Polonia 450
polvera 266
polvo compacto 266
polvo de magnesio 497
polvos sueltos 266
pomelo 134
pomo 201, 202, 229, 506
pomo carnoso 58
pómulo 98
poncho 251
Pont-l'Évêque 151
pool 502
popa 386, 519
póquer 468
porcentaje 427
porche 183
poro 50, 60, 114
porra 456
porta martillo 225
porta pasaportes 275
porta-celo 341
porta-cinta adhesiva 341
porta-esquí 356
porta-filtro 181
portaagujas 460
portabicicletas 356
portabolsa 505
portabotellas 371
portabrocas de sujeción 228
portacarrete 536, 537
portaequipajes 361, 369, 370, 383, 523
portaequipajes posterior 369
portahorquilla 396
portal 285
portalámparas 199
portaleños 193
portaminas 312
portamonedas 275
portante 83
portaobjetivo rotatorio 421
portaobjeto 421
portaobjetos 421
portaocular 8
portaplumas 274
portarrollos de papel higiénico 195
portatrajes 277
portatubo 421
portaviento 296
portería 439, 480, 507
portero 479, 481, 506, 507
portero del equipo receptor 479
pórtico 285, 447
Portugal 449
posición A - en plancha 518
posición B - hacer la carpa 518
posición C - cuerpo encogido 518
posición de equilibrio 418
posición de lanzamiento, transbordador espacial 12
posición de los jugadores 474, 481, 482
posición del documento a enviar 328
posiciones de los jugadores 489
posiciones de salto 518
poste 191, 375, 485, 487, 490, 495, 498
poste con protecciones 489
poste de foul 475
poste de la grúa 385
poste del asiento 370
potencia eléctrica, unidad de medida 426
potema 282
potro 496, 497
pozo 278
pozo de inyección 402
pozo de producción 402
pozo marino 404
practicable para ejercicios de suelo 496
pradera 122
praderas 44
prado 122
precio total 423
precio unitario 423
precipitación 45
precipitaciones invernales 41
precisión, balanza 423
precocinados 121
premaxilar 74
premolares 101
prensa en C 224
prensa-café 181
preparador 489
prepucio 111
presa 406
presidente de jurado 509
presilla 245, 246, 531
presilla de estaquilla 528, 529
presilla de la manga 248
presilla del cinturón 248
presión 501
presión barométrica 39
presión barométrica a nivel del mar 39
presión, unidad de medida 426
pretina 246, 249
pretina con botones de presión 260
pretina elástica 247, 249
previsión meteorológica 38
primates, ejemplos 91
primavera 38
primer árbitro 487
primer aumento de la tensión 413
primer ayudante de cámara 290
primer espacio 489
primer jugador 515
primer molar 101
primer pistón móvil 307
primer premolar 101
primera aleta dorsal 74
primera base 474
primera línea 482
primera plana 313
primera plana, foto 313
primeras hojas 53
primeros auxilios, puesto de socorro 512
primeros violines 295
Principado de Andorra 449
Principado de Mónaco 450
principales movimientos 470
principales venas y arterias 102
prisma de Porro 420
prismáticos binoculares 420
proa 384, 387, 519, 520
probador de contactos con tierra 217
probóscide 67
producción de calor 408
producción de electricidad por energía eólica 413
producción de electricidad por energía geotérmica 402
producción de electricidad por energía nuclear 408
producción de electricidad por generador 408
producción de oxígeno 54
producción eléctrica 412
productor 291
productos alimenticios 120
productos de cocina 120
productos de fisión 415
productos del refinado 405
productos en oferta 121
productos lácteos 120, 150
productos para envasar 120
productos petroquímicos 405
productos, oferta 121
profesor 444
profesor, pupitre 444
profundidad del hipocentro 27
programa de correo electrónico 334
programación televisiva, horario 313
programador 212, 213, 214
programas informáticos 457
promontorio 35
pronador redondo 96
pronaos 279
proporción de nubes 39
propulsor 10, 12
propulsor de maniobras 13
propulsor de proa 387
propulsor sólido 12
propulsores de control de actitud 12
proscenio 292
prospección terrestre 403
próstata 111
protección para el sistema respiratorio 459
protección para la cabeza 458
protección para los oídos 458
protección para los ojos 458
protección para los pies 459
protector 210, 235, 248, 471, 478, 498
protector bucal 498
protector contra virutas 227
protector de antebrazo 486
protector de cuello 486
protector de espuma 458
protector de la barbilla 367
protector de la culata 306
protector de la garganta 476
protector de mano 525
protector de piernas 507
protector del brazo 486
protector del cable 218, 228, 229
protector del pie 476
protector del zanco 398
protector dental 486
protector facial 507
protector lumbar 486
protector para las costillas 486
protector solar 10
protocolo de comunicación 334
protón 414
protoneurona 110
protuberancia 4
proveedor de servicios Internet 335
provincia 23
provisión de dinero en efectivo 443
provisión de guantes 464
proyección cilíndrica 22
proyección cónica 22
proyección en círculo 499
proyección interrumpida 22
proyección plana 22
proyección por encima del hombro con una mano 499
proyección primera de cadera 499
proyección, cabina 294
proyección, pantalla 294
proyección, sala 294
proyecciones cartográficas 22
proyector 290, 294, 376
proyectores 293
pruebas 511
pseudópodo 66
púa 297
pubis 92, 94
público, entrada 278
pueblo 430, 512
puente 25, 78, 273, 297, 301, 302, 303, 343, 381, 420
puente cantilever 344
puente colgante 344
puente de carga para contenedores 381
puente de ensamblaje 303
puente de la nariz 117
puente de los altos 304
puente de los bajos 304
puente de luces 455, 457
puente de luces, sistema de control 457
puente de mando 382, 386, 387
puente de señales 375
puente de Varolio 109
puente de viga 344
puente elevador 345
puente giratorio 344
puente levadizo 282
puente levadizo doble 345
puente levadizo sencillo 345
puentes fijos 344
puentes móviles 344
puerco espín 82
puerros 124
puerta 7, 178, 202, 210, 213, 287, 349, 352, 361, 392, 423, 439, 447, 479, 528, 529
puerta automática 390
puerta basculante de garaje 286

puerta convencional 286
puerta corredera 286
puerta corredera automática 286
puerta cortafuego 286
puerta de dos hojas 362
puerta de entrada 185, 362, 363
puerta de garaje seccional 286
puerta de la bodega de carga 13
puerta de la plataforma elevadora 363
puerta de librillo 286
puerta de proa 383, 386
puerta de tiras 286
puerta del congelador 211
puerta del fogón 192
puerta del refrigerador 211
puerta giratoria manual 286
puerta lateral 380
puerta mosquitera 361
puerta plegable 195, 286
puerta trasera 188
puerta ventana 164, 189
puertas de entrada 294
puertas, ejemplos 286
puerto 381, 431
puerto de Ethernet 336
puerto de infrarrojos 336
puerto de módem interno 329, 336
puerto de red 329
puerto de salida de S-video 336
puerto de salida de TV 336
puerto de vídeo 329
puerto FireWire 336
puerto infrarrojos 337
puerto juego 329
puerto MIDI 329
puerto paralelo 329
puerto ratón 329
puerto serial 329
puerto teclado 329
puerto USB 329, 336
puertos para el mando 471
puertos para tarjeta de memoria 471
puesto de bombeo 346
puesto de enfermeras (ambulatorio de urgencias) 463
puesto de enfermeras (urgencias) 462
puesto de información 390
puesto de la guardia de seguridad 463
puesto de observación 7
puf 201
pujamen 519
pulga 69
pulgar 115, 243, 477
pulgar oponible 91
pulmón derecho 103, 105
pulmón izquierdo 103, 105
pulmones 105
pulpa 57, 58, 59, 101
púlpito 446, 447
pulpo 72, 157
pulpo, morfología 72
pulsador de llamada 287
pulsera de dijes 264
pulverizador 214, 236, 402
pulverizador de agua 348
puma 88
puño 245, 477, 492, 514
puño de amura 519
puño de escota 519
punta 55, 125, 167, 169, 216, 218, 220, 221, 226, 227, 246, 247, 273, 301, 312, 469, 471, 510, 514, 526, 538
punta cruciforme 221
punta de caja cuadrada 221
punta de diamante 202
punta de hoja plana 221
punta de la plancha 208
punta de plástico 269
punta de sujeción 304
punta del cuello 245
punta del diente de la desterronadora 398
punta del esquí 514
puntal 308
puntal trasero 412
puntales de refuerzo 187
puntas; tipos 221
puntera 229, 511
puntera perforada 240
puntera protectora 459
puntero 533
punto 468
punto de apoyo 70
punto de apoyo variable 518
punto de empulgada 535
punto de información 437, 512
punto de interés 25
punto de mira 533, 534
punto de penalti 480
punto de salida 504
punto de saque 506
puntos 492
punzón 531
pupila 87, 119
pupila vertical 76
pupitre del alumno 444
pupitre del profesor 444
putter 505

Q

Qatar 452
quad 369
quark d 414
quark u 414
quarterback 485
quelícero 70
quemador 174, 210, 529
queroseno 405
queso chèvre 150
queso cottage 150
queso cremoso 150
queso, rallador cilíndrico 170
quesos azules 151
quesos blandos 151
quesos de cabra 150
quesos frescos 150
quesos prensados 151
quiasma óptico 109
quijada 83, 86
quilla 521
química 414
quingombó 128
quinientos 427
quinta 298
quinteto 300
quinto octante 5
quinua 143
quiosco 437
quirófano 464, 465
quitagrapas 341
quitanieves 365
quitapiedras 376, 377

R

rábano 129
rábano blanco 129
rábano daikon 129
rábanos negros 129
rabillo 57, 58, 59
rabiza 536
racimo 57
racimo de uvas 62
raclette 151
raclette-grill 179
radar 382, 383, 386, 387
radar de navegación 392
radar meteorológico 38
radiación 415
radiación infrarroja 46, 418
radiación solar 45, 46, 410, 411
radiación solar absorbida 46
radiación solar refleja 46
radiación ultravioleta 418
radiador 350, 358
radiador, manguito 358
radiadores 11
radial externo primero 97
radial externo segundo 97
radícula 53, 63
radio 70, 98, 371, 428, 457
radio blando 74
radio despertador 325
radio espinoso 74
radio medular 63
radio portátil 325
radioactividad, unidad de medida 426
radiocasete con lector de disco compacto 326
radiocasete porttil personal (Walkman®) 326
raíces 53, 62, 129
raíces adventicias 52
raíles del travelín 290
raíz 54, 101, 118, 167
raíz anterior 110
raíz cuadrada de 427
raiz de la uña 114
raíz motora 109, 110
raíz posterior 110
raíz primaria 53, 63
raíz principal 53
raíz secundaria 53
raíz sensitiva 109, 110
raíz superficiale 63
rallador 169, 170
rallador cilíndrico de queso 170
rallador de nuez moscada 170
rallar 170
rally, coche 524
rama 53, 63, 65, 460
rama comunicante 110
rama con fruto 62
rama madre 63
ramaje 63
ramal de enlace 343
rambután 137
ramificación 62
ramificación colateral 110
ramilla 63
rampa 281, 343
rampa de acceso 279, 344
rampa del muelle 381
rampa plegable 386
rana 75
rana arborícola 75
rana bermeja 75
rana de bosque 75
rana leopardo 75
rana, morfología 75
ranita 261
ranura 169, 221, 274, 359, 473
ranura de depósito 442
ranura de la tarjeta PC 336
ranura de lectura de tarjeta 346
ranura de puesta al día de la cartilla 442
ranura de registro de la transacción 442
ranura de ventilación 336
ranura guía 510
ranura para el pan 178
ranura para toldo 361
Ranvier, nódulo 110
rape 160
raqueta de bádminton 494
raqueta de tenis 492
ras el hanout 139
raspador 400
rasqueta 219, 514
rastrillo 233, 237
rastrillso 292
rata 82
rata, morfología 82
ratón de campo 82
ratón inalámbrico 332
ratón mecánico 332
ratón óptico 332
ratónde rueda 332
ratonera 514
raviolis 146
raya 158, 246
raya continua 342
raya discontinua 342, 343
rayo 41
rayo de luz 419
rayo láser 420
rayos gamma 418
rayos X 418
razas de gatos 87
razas de perros 86
re (D) 298
Rea 3
reacción en cadena 415
reactor 408
reactor nuclear, carga 409
rebajo de escalón 191
rebobinado 319
reborde 293, 301, 302
rebosadero 194, 196, 406
rebote 487
rebozuelo 123
recalentamiento global 46
recepción 439, 442, 462, 465
recepción de carga 391
recepción de documentos 328
recepción directa en la casa 316
recepción, nivel 439
receptáculo 51, 56, 59
receptáculo del cepillo 272
receptor 303, 321, 327, 475, 476
receptor 474
receptor alejado 485
receptor de los bajos 303
receptor de los intermedios 303
receptor del sonido 460
receptor sensorial 110
receptor triple 303
receptores gustativos 118
recibo 423
recibo de transacción 443
reciclado 49
reciclado de aluminio, contenedor 49
reciclado de papel, contenedor 49
reciclado de vidrio, contenedor 49
reciclaje, contenedores 49
recinto ferial 430
recipiente 180
recipiente con vertedor 177
recipiente del abrillantador 214
recipiente del detergente 214
recipiente inferior 181
recipiente superior 181
reclamo 535
recogedor 215, 237
recogepelotas 490
recogida de papel, contenedor 49
recogida de vidrio, contenedor 49
recogida diferenciada 49
rectángulo 429
recto 106, 111, 112
recto anterior 96
recto del abdomen 96
recto entallado 252
recto interno del muslo 97
recubrimiento aislante 12
recubrimiento antirreflectante 410
recuperación del documento enviado 328
red 205, 487, 489, 491, 493, 495
red de cables telefónicos 434
red de distribución por cable aéreo 316
red de mano 538
red de transmisión por cable subterráneo 317
red de transmisión privada 316
red nacional de transmisión 316
red telefónica 317
redonda 299
redondo mayor 97
redondo menor 97
refinado, productos 405
refinería 404, 431
reflector 217, 365, 370, 523
reflectores solares 316
reflexión parcial, espejo 420
reflexión total, espejo 420
refrigeración, torre 402
refrigeración, varilla 420
refrigerante 405, 408
refrigerante caliente 408
refrigerante frío 408
refuerzo 259, 458, 525
refuerzo del talón 240
refugio 345
refugio de montaña 512
refugio en la cima 512
refugio presurizado 345
refugio principal 512
regadera 236
región lumbar 93, 95
región malar 78
región negativa 410
región positiva 410
registro de altos 296
registro de cristal líquido 424
registro sísmico 403
registro, cilindro 27
registros de bajos 296
regla 531
regla graduada 425
regla, escala 425
regulador de entrada de agua 214
regulador de presión 174, 454, 529
regulador de temperatura 365
regulador de velocidad 354
reina 68, 468, 470
Reina Maud, Tierra 15
reina, cámara 278
Reino Unido de Gran Bretaña e Irlanda del Norte 449
reino vegetal 50
reja 217
reja de entrada al pronaos 279
reja de entrada, pronaos 279
reja de seguridad 442
reja metálica de contacto 410
rejilla 174, 178, 210, 211, 296, 318, 358, 359, 407
rejilla de calefacción 380
rejilla de entrada de aire 270
rejilla de salida de aire 270
rejilla de ventilación 214
rejilla del ventilador 209
rejilla protectora 324
rejilla, sistema 22
rellano 191
rellano de la escalera 189
reloj 178, 210, 444, 501
reloj de arena 171
reloj de pulsera 424
reloj de sol 424
reloj digital 424
reloj programador 178
remache 169, 222
remate 191
remate en T 193
remeras primarias 78
remeras secundarias 78
remeras terciarias 78
remo 501
remolacha 129
remolcador 384
remolque 361
remolque rígido trasero 363
reniforme 55
reno 84
repetidor 317
repisa 192
repisa para accesorios 8
repollo 126
repollo verde 126
reposa-mano 332
reposabrazo 353
reposabrazos 467
reposacabezas 353
reposamanos 330
reposapies 205, 369
reposapiés 224, 467
reproductor de CD portátil 325
reproductor de disco compacto 325
reproductor de DVD 333
reproductor DVD 318
reproductor/grabador de video VCR 319
reptación 31
reptiles 76
reptiles, ejemplos 77
República Centroafricana 451
República Checa 450
República de Corea 453
República de Malí 451
República de San Marino 450
República Democrática del Congo 451
Republica Democrática Popular de Corea 453
República Dominicana 449
repuesto 312
repulsión 416
reseña gastronómica 313
resguardo del parachoques 348

residuos industriales 47
residuos domésticos 47, 48
residuos industriales 47, 48
residuos no reciclables 49
residuos nucleares 48
residuos primarios 405
resistencia 210, 213, 214, 218
resistencia eléctrica, unidad de medida 426
resistencias 417
resonador 305, 309, 324
resorte 27, 206, 212, 222, 273, 312, 535
resorte de la válvula 360
resorte de retorno 357
resorte de tensión 500
resorte hidráulico 501
resorte tensor 355
respaldo 200, 201, 205, 353, 369, 467, 523
respaldo reclinatorio 460
respiradero 182, 367
respiradero lateral 361
resta 427
restador 490, 495
restaurant comida rapida 437
restaurante 386, 432, 435, 436, 438
resurgencia 31
retablo 446
retén de la esfera 332
retén imantado 180
retícula 420
retículo endoplasmático 50, 66
retina 119, 419
retira cutículas 265
retoño 63
retorno 331
retorno a la memoria 337
retrato 441
retroceso 331
retrovisor 368
retrovisor de gran angular 362
retrovisor gran angular 363
revestimiento 357, 493, 505, 534
revestimiento de fósforo 199
revestimiento de la popa 7
revestimiento interior 352
revestimientos textiles del suelo 190
revisor 374
revista sensacionalista 313
revólver portaobjetivos 421
rey 468, 470
rey, cámara 278
ría para la carrera de obstáculos 472
ría, carrera de obstáculos 472
rías 35
ribete 238, 240, 244, 262
ribosoma 50, 66
ricotta 150
riel corredizo 214, 521
riel de iluminación 207
riel de rodamiento 397
riel deslizador 353
riel para las rejillas 211
rifle 534
rigatoni 146
rillettes 156
rimaya 30
rímel en pasta 266
rímel líquido 266
rincón 498
rinconera 203
ringside 498
rinoceronte 85
riñón 73, 103
riñón derecho 107
riñón izquierdo 107
riñonera 486
riñones 83, 154
río 24, 25, 32
Río Amazonas 17
Río Congo 20
Río Danubio 18
Río Dniéper 18
Río Mackenzie 16
Río Mississippi 16
Río Níger 20
Río Orinoco 17
Río Paraná 17
Río San Lorenzo 16
Río Senegal 20
Río Vístula 18
Río Volga 18
risco 5, 29
rizador de mantequilla 169
rizador de pestañas 266
rizoide 51
rizoma 52
róbalo 160
Roberval, balanza 422
roble 64
robot de cocina 177
roca firme 27
roca impermeable 403
roca madre 54
rocas ígneas 26
rocas intrusivas 26
rocas metamórficas 26
rocas sedimentarias 26
rociador 197
rociadores 408
rocío 41
rodaballo 161
rodamiento 332
rodapié 202
rodilla 83, 86, 92, 94
rodillera 476, 486, 500, 526, 527
rodillo 172, 219
rodillo de pintor 219
rodrigón 230, 231
roedor 82
roedores 82
roedores, ejemplos 82
roja 469
rojo 418
rollos de la Torá 447
rombo 429
romero 142
rompehielos 384
rompiente 33
ropa 538
ropa de bebé 260
ropa de cama 204
ropa de hombre 244
ropa de mujer 251
ropa de niños 261
ropa deportiva 262
ropa interior 247, 258, 524
ropa para ejercicio 263
ropero 203
roquefort 151
rorcual 90
rosa 56
rosa de los vientos 23, 533
rosca 221, 223, 425
roseta 186, 236, 302
rosetón 285
rosquilla 144
rotonda 25, 435
rotor 395, 412
rotor de cola 395
rótula 98
rotulador 340
rough 504
router 334
Ruanda 451
rubí pulsado, láser 420
rubí, varilla 420
rubio 159
rueda 231, 364, 467, 501, 522, 525, 526, 527
rueda central de enfoque 420
rueda de cadena 523
rueda de corrimiento 327
rueda de desplazamiento 332
rueda de empuje 467
rueda de la dirección 467
rueda de mando 337
rueda de modulación 310
rueda de repuesto 361
rueda de transmisión 523
rueda delantera 401
rueda giratoria 205
rueda guía 398
rueda humedecedora 339
rueda libre 360
rueda motriz 398
rueda para ajustar el tono 310
rueda para graduar el respaldo 353
ruedas de tracción 401
ruedecilla 209, 277, 308
Ruffini, corpúsculo 114
rugby 482
rugby, botas de tacos 483
ruibarbo 125
ruiseñor 80
ruleta de enfoque lejos/cerca 320
ruleta de selección de efectos especiales 320
rulo 268
rulo para el cabello 268
Rumanía 450
rupia 440
ruqueta 127
rusula verde 123
ruta de servicio 388
ruta pintoresca 25

S

sábalo 160
sabana 40, 44
sábana 204
sábana ajustable 204
sable 519, 520
sacacorchos 146, 170, 531
sacacorchos con brazos 170
sacapuntas 341
saco de arena 498
saco de Douglas 112
saco de marinero 276
saco de piel 296
saco portabebé 260
saco rectangular 530
saco semirrectangular 530
sacos de dormir, ejemplos 530
sacrificio, piedra 283
sacristía 446
sacro 98, 99
safety débil 484
safety fuerte 484
sahariana 255
Saint Kitts and Nevis 449
sal de mesa 141
sal gorda 141
sal marina 141
sala 188, 293
sala de alumnos 445
sala de anestesia 464
sala de audiencias 440, 447
sala de bombeo 384
sala de ceremonias 447
sala de cine 386
sala de clasificación 463
sala de conferencias 442
sala de control 406
sala de curas 465
sala de enyesado 463
sala de equipajes 374
sala de espera 463, 465
sala de espera de embarque 391
sala de espera del centro de extracción de sangre 465
sala de espera para la familia 462
sala de espera principal 465
sala de estar 188
sala de esterilización 464, 465
sala de examen de audiometría 465
sala de extracciones 465
sala de máquinas 384, 386, 406, 407
sala de navegación 382
sala de observación psiquiátrica 462
sala de oración 447
sala de preparación quirúrgica 464
sala de profesores 445
sala de proyección 294
sala de reanimación 462
sala de reconocimiento 465
sala de recuperación posoperatoria 464
sala de reposo de enfermeras 465
sala de reuniones 439, 442, 445
sala del jurado 440
sala del personal 443, 463
salamandra 75
salami alemán 156
salami de Génova 156
salas de entrevistas 440
salchicha chipolata 156
salchicha de Frankfurt 156
salchicha de Toulouse 156
salchicha kielbasa 156
salchicha merguez 156
salchow 509
salero 166
salida 343, 469
salida de agua fría 197
salida de aire caliente 192
salida de humo 192
salida de la pista 391
salida de la pista de alta velocidad 388
salida del refrigerante 410
salmón del Atlántico 161
salmón del Pacífico 161
salmonete 159
salmuera, especias 139
salón 188, 439
salón bar 439
salón de baile 387
salón de pasajeros 386
salpicadero 354, 369
salpicadero, equipamiento 457
salsa de ciruelas 141
salsa de soja 140
salsa de tamarindo 140
salsa de tomate 140
salsa hoisin 140
salsa Tobasco® 140
salsa Worcertershire 140
salsa, ciruelas 141
salsa, soja 140
salsa, tamarindo 140
salsa, tomate 140
salsa, Worcertershire 140
salsera 166
salsifí 129
saltador 513
saltamontes verde 69
salto de altura 473
salto de espalda 518
salto de esquí 513
salto de longitud 472
salto de pértiga 472
salto en equilibrio 518
salto frontal 518
salto interior 518
salto inverso 518
saltos 518
salvavidas 387
salvelino 161
salvia 142
sambal oelek 141
Samoa 453
San Bernardo 86
San Vicente y las Granadinas 449
sandalia 241, 242
sandía 135
sangre desoxigenada 104
sangre oxigenada 104
sangre, composición 104
Santa Lucía 449
Santo Tomé y Príncipe 451
santuario. lámpara 446
sapo común 75
saque 487
sardina 159
sargento 224
sarmiento 62
sartén 175, 531
sartén doble 175
sartén honda 175
sartén para crepes 175
sartén pequeña 175
sartorio 96
satélite 316
satélite artificial 37
satélite de telecomunicaciones 335
satélite meteorológico 38
satélite, comunicación 316
satélite, telecomunicaciones 317
satélites 2
satélites de telecomunicaciones 316
Saturno 2, 3
sauce llorón 64
saxofón 306
schnauzer 86
Schwann, célula 110
secador de mano 270
secadora de ensalada 171
secadora de ropa 213
sección 313
sección articulada 363
sección de percusión 295
sección del cañón 193
sección frontal 459
sección rígida de tracción delantera 363
sección sagital 111, 112
sección transversal de la góndola 413
sección transversal de un observatorio astronómico 7
sección transversal de un telecopio reflector 9
sección transversal de un telescopio refractor 8
sección transversal de una carretera 342
sección transversal de una central hidroeléctrica 407
sección vertical 526
secretaría 443, 445
secretario/a de producción 291
sector 428
secuenciador 310
sedal 536
segmento 360
segmento abdominal 67
segmento de marcas 471
segmento intermedio 111
segmento terminal 111
segunda 298
segunda aleta dorsal 74
segunda base 474
segunda línea 482
segundero 424
segundo 426, 428
segundo árbitro 487
segundo aumento de tensión 413
segundo ayudante de cámara 290
segundo espacio 489
segundo jugador 515
segundo molar 101
segundo pistón móvil 307
segundo premolar 101
segundos violines 295
seguridad 454
seguro 178, 209, 222
seguro de inclinación del disco 227
seguro de la base 224
seguro del fuelle 296
seguro del interruptor 228
seis doble 468
selección de cartón 49
selección de metal 49
selección de nivel 2 330
selección de papel 49
selección de vidrio 49
selección manual 49
selección óptica 49
selector 178
selector cuadro-direccional 315
selector de canales 319
selector de corte 271
selector de enfoque 320
selector de entrada 322
selector de focalización 314
selector de la recepción 303
selector de la voz 311
selector de movimiento orbital 227
selector de nivel de agua 212
selector de programa 310, 314
selector de sintonización 325
selector de temperatura 178, 212, 213
selector de tipo de cinta 323
selector de tostado 178
selector de velocidad 176, 228
selector de velocidades 176, 177
selector de volumen 325
selector del modo audio 322
selector del ritmo 311
selectores de funciones 327
selectores de modalidad 326
sellado, tapa 417
sello de goma 338
selva 44

semáforo 375, 434
semáforo de peatones 434
sembradora de mano 231
semicírculo 428
semicírculo de la zona de tiro libre 488
semicírculo del área 480
semicorchea 299
semieje 351
semifusa 299
semilla 53, 57, 58, 59, 60
semilla, tegumento 57
semillas de adormidera 139
semillas de soja 131
semimembranoso 97
semirremolque tipo caja 365
semirremolque, caja, tipo 365
semisótano 182
semitendinoso 97
semola 144
sémola 144
señal de dirección 379
señal de distancia fija 391
señal de eje de pista 390
señal de identificación de pista 390
señal de zona de contacto de pista 391
señal de zona de espera 390
señal exterior 378
señales de límite de la pista 391
señales laterales de pista 390
Senegal 451
seno 33, 94, 113, 418
seno del pecíolo 62
seno esfenoidal 117
seno frontal 117
seno lateral inferior 62
seno lateral superior 62
sensor de colisión primario 354
sensor de movimiento 286
sensor de seguridad 354
sensor de temperatura 358
sensor de velocidad de las ruedas 357
sensor del mando a distancia 318, 323
sensor óptico 332
sépalo 56, 58, 59
separacables 535
separación cartón 49
separación magnética 49
separación papel 49
separación selectiva de residuos 49
separador 274, 384, 402, 409, 417, 467
separador de gas y líquido 359
separador de placas 359
separador electrolítico 417
sepia 157
séptima 298
septum 60
septum pellucidum 109
ser humano 92
serac 30
serie, número 441
serpiente 76
serpiente coral 77
serpiente de cascabel 77
serpiente de jarretera 77
serpiente venenosa, morfología, cabeza 76
serpollo 62
serrucho 226
serrucho de punta 226
servicio de enlace ferroviario 390
servicio de mesa 166
servicio para fondue 174
servicio, estación 346
servicios de crédito 442
servicios de seguros 442
servicios financieros 442
servicios sociales 465
servidor 334, 335
servidor de acceso 335
servofreno 350, 357
sésamo, aceite 149
sesos 154
set 291
seta enoki 123
seto 183, 230
setos, cizallas 234
sexta 298
sexteto 300
Seychelles 452
shiitake 123
si (B) 298
siamés 87
sien 92
sierra circular de mano 227
sierra de cadena 235
sierra de calar 227
sierra de campo 533
sierra de ingletes 226
sierra de marquetería 226
sierra de podar 234
Sierra Leona 451
sierra para metales 226
sifón 72, 194, 196, 197
silbato 180, 377
silenciador 351, 367, 369
silencio de blanca 299
silencio de corchea 299
silencio de fusa 299
silencio de negra 299
silencio de redonda 299
silencio de semicorchea 299
silencio de semifusa 299
silencios, valores 299
silicua 60
silla alzadora 205
silla cabriolé 200
silla cojín 201
silla de brazos 200
silla de ruedas 467
silla de seguridad para niños 356
silla del director 291
silla escalera 201
silla plegable de lona 200
silla poltrona 200
silla porta-niño 372
silla sin brazos 201, 444
silla Wassily 200
sillas apilables 201
sillas de los actores 290
sillas plegables 201
sillas, ejemplos 201
sillín 369, 370
sillín del conductor 369
sillín del pasajero 369
sillín doble 367
sillón 444
sillón de reposo 464
silo 122
silos 381
símbolos 468
símbolos científicos 426
sinagoga 447
sinapsis 110
sínfisis púbica 111, 112
Singapur 453
síntesis de los colores 418
síntesis de los colores aditivos 418
síntesis de los colores sustractivos 418
sintetizador 310
sintonizador 326
sirena 455
Siria 452
sisa 247
sismógrafo 27
sismógrafo horizontal 27
sismógrafo vertical 27
sismógrafos 27
sismograma 27
sistema antibloqueo de frenos 357
sistema de aire acondicionado 46
sistema de alimentación de gasolina 351
sistema de audio 354
sistema de botones 310
sistema de carreteras 342
sistema de células solares 411
sistema de control del puente de luces 457
sistema de coordenadas terrestres 21
sistema de dirección 351
sistema de escape 351
sistema de frenado 351
sistema de lentes 420
sistema de refrigeración 351
sistema de restricción del airbag 354
sistema de retícula 22
sistema de soporte vital 10
sistema de suspensión 351
sistema de transmisión 351
sistema eléctrico 351
sistema fino de guía 7
sistema hidraúlico 396
sistema internacional de unidades de medida 426
sistema magnético de amortiguación 422
sistema manipulador remoto 11, 12
sistema nervioso 108
sistema nervioso central 109
sistema nervioso periférico 108
sistema rotativo 403
sistema solar 2
sistemas de sonido portátiles 325
sistemas del automóvil 351
sistro 309
skateboard 526
skimmer 184
slip 247
smash 491
smog/niebla tóxica 47
snooker 503
snowboard 513
snowboarder 513
soba, fideos 147
sobre almohadillado 339
sobrefusión 414
sociedad 430
sofá 200
sofá cama 204
sofá de dos plazas 200, 439
sofá tipo imperio 200
softball 477
Sol 2, 4, 5, 38
sol (G) 298
Sol, estructura 4
solapa 244, 532
solapa autoadhesiva 339
solapa con ojal 248
solapa puntiaguda 244
soldador 218
soldadura, herramientas 218
sóleo 96
solera doble 187
solera inferior 187
solideo 238
solidificación 414
sólido 414, 415
sólido amorfo 414
solitario 264
solsticio de invierno 38
solsticio de verano 38
solución multipropósito 272
Somalia 451
sombra 424
sombra de ojos 266
sombrero 52
sombrero de campana 239
sombrero de fieltro 238, 239
sombrero de hongo 238
sombrero sin alas 239
sombreros 238
sombreros de hombre 238
sombreros de mujer 239
sombreros unisex 239
somen, fideos 147
somier 204
sonda destapacaños 216
sonda espacial 37
sonda térmica 178
sonido, sistemas portátiles 325
sopera 166
soplete 218
soporte 9, 174, 199, 227, 236, 269, 277, 308, 355, 369, 387, 409, 533
soporte colgante 467
soporte de acoplamiento 337
soporte de la cadena 370
soporte de la mano 297
soporte de la plaqueta 273
soporte de la plataforma 412
soporte de la red 493
soporte del brazo 200
soporte del pie 473, 501
soporte del plano fijo 400
soporte del tablero 489
soporte para el antebrazo 466
soporte para el brazo 352
soporte para el cuello 525
soporte para el sobaco 466
sordina 307
sorgo 61
sorgo : panícula 61
soro 52
sortija de sello 264
sostenido 299
soufflé, molde 172
Sri Lanka 453
stilton 151
stylus 337
Suazilandia 452
subártico 40
subducción 27
sublimación 414
substracción de la memoria 337
subsuelo 54
subterráneo 281
subtítulo 313
subtropical húmedo 40
subtropical mediterráneo 40
sucesos 313
sudadera 262
sudadera con capucha 262
Sudáfrica 452
Sudán 451
Sudeste 23
Suecia 450
suela 229, 240, 263, 503, 509
suela antiderrapante 261
suela rígida 511
suelo 48
suelo de cabina 287
suelo, absorción 46
suelo, capa superficial 54
suelo, fertilización 47
suelo, movimiento horizontal 27
suelo, movimiento vertical 27
suelo, revestimientos 190
suero de la leche 150
sueste 239
Suiza 450
sujetador 259, 308, 421
sujetador de aros 259
sujetador de escote bajo 259
sujetador del pabellón 306
sujetador sin tirantes 259
sujetalibros 341
suma 427
sumario 313
sumiller 438
supercross 525
superficie de cocción 179
superficie de deslizamiento 510
superficie de fijación 341
superficie de juego 493
superficie de la piel 114
superficie del agua 518
superficie dura (cemento) 492
superficie lunar 5
superficie sintética 492
superficies 428
superficies de juego 492
supermercado 120, 433, 437
supinador largo 96, 97
suplemento a color 313
suplemento literario 313
suprimir 331
Sur 23
Sur Sudeste 23
Sur Suroeste 23
surco 118
surco medio 118
surco nasolabial 117
surco terminal 118
Surinam 448
Suroeste 23
surtidor 197
surtidor de agua 272
surtidor de gasolina 346
suspensión 376, 380
suspensión trasera 522
suspensión, brazo 351
sustancia blanca 109, 110
sustancia despolarizante 417
sustancia gris 109, 110
sustrato impermeable 402
sutura 60, 73
sutura coronal 100
sutura escamosa 100
sutura lambdoidea 100

T

tábano 69
tabernáculo 446
tabique de contención longitudinal 384
tabique interventricular 104
tabique nasal 117
tabique, cartílago nasal 117
tabla abierta 253
tabla alpina 513
tabla armónica 301, 302
tabla con argollas 340
tabla con pinza 340
tabla de cortar 169
tabla de freestyle 513
tabla de los resultados 518
tabla de surf 519
tabla delantera 253
tabla harmónica 304
tablas 253
tablero 202, 224, 344, 470, 489
tablero de ajedrez 470
tablero de anuncios 341
tablero de damas 470
tablero de distribución 198
tablero de información 374
tablero de instrumentos 366, 368
tablero de juego 469
tablero de llegadas y salidas 391
tablero de operaciónes 455
tableta de resonancia 305
tablillas 461
tablinum 280
tablón de anuncios 444
tabulación a la derecha 330
tabulación a la izquierda 330
taburete 164, 201
taburete de bar 438
taburete escalera 219
tachuela 220
tachuelas para papel 341
tacita de café 166
tackle defensivo derecho 484
tackle defensivo izquierdo 484
tacle derecho 485
tacle izquierdo 485
taco 473, 478, 534
taco de billar 503
taco de salida, atleta 473
tacómetro 355, 368
tacón 509
tacos 473
tacos de rosca 480
tacto 114
Tailandia 453
tailback 485
Tajikistán 452
tajín 140
tajina 174
taladro eléctrico 228
taladro percutor inalámbrico 228
tallarines de espinacas 146
talle corto 259
taller de máquinas diésel 375
taller mecánico 346
tallo 51, 53, 54, 114, 125
tallo del bulbo 54
tallo principal 62
talo 50, 51
talón 93, 95, 226, 228, 229, 240, 247, 262, 301, 302, 467, 477, 494, 506, 536, 537
talón de apoyo 176, 208
talón de la hoja 169
talonario de cheques 274, 275
taloneador 482
talonera 511
talud 342
talud continental 33
tam-tam 308
tamarillo 136

tamarino 91
tambor 170, 212, 213, 286, 357, 425, 537
tambor giratorio 27
tambor hablante 297
tamboril 308
tamiz 171, 172
tamiz vibratorio para lodos 403
tándem 373
tanque 13, 385, 454, 529
tanque auxiliar 365
tanque de agua de rociado 408
tanque de almacenamiento 405
tanque de gas propano 361
tanque de regulación de presión 404
tanque de techo pontón 404
tanque del combustible 235, 364
Tanzania 451
tapa 174, 176, 177, 178, 179, 180, 181, 186, 198, 209, 210, 211, 212, 215, 225, 240, 277, 305, 312, 315, 358, 417, 454, 533
tapa de cierre 417
tapa de la batería 359
tapa de la cisterna 196
tapa de la culata 350
tapa de sellado 417
tapa del filtro 459
tapa del inodoro 196
tapa del objetivo 314
tapa del tanque 364
tapa deslizante 327
tapa flotante 404
tapa frontal 333
tapa inferior 417
tapa superior 417
tapa terminal 409
tapacubos 349
tapete 502
tapón 196, 267, 532
tapón de registro 194
tapón de rosca 163
tapón de vaciado 360
tapón del depósito de gasolina 349
tapón del depósito de la gasolina 368
tapón del sifón 197
tapón hermético 529
tapones para los oídos 458
taquilla 294
taquilla automática 294
taquilla de venta de billetes 378
taquillas de consigna automática 374
taquillas de los alumnos 445
tarjeta de circuito impreso 417
tarjeta de crédito 441
tarjeta de débito 443
tarjeta de memoria 315
tarjeta, número 441
tarjetero 274
taro 124
tarso 78
Tasmania 15
tatami 499
taza 166, 196, 531, 532
tazas medidoras 171
té 148
té negro 148
té oolong 148
té verde 148
té, bolsita 148
teatro 292, 432, 433
teatro griego 278
techo 193, 349, 361
techo a dos aguas 189
techo acústico 293
techo corredizo 349
techo de cabina 287
techo de protección 396
techo de vidiro 374
techo de vidrio 188, 435
techo ponton, tanque 404
tecla 296, 304
tecla alternativa 330
tecla bloqueo numérico 331
tecla de adición 337
tecla de anular 333
tecla de bloqueo de mayúsculas 330
tecla de cambio de signo 337
tecla de confirmación 443
tecla de división 337
tecla de enter 331
tecla de fijación de pantalla 320
tecla de final de búsqueda 320
tecla de final de llamada 327
tecla de igualdad 337
tecla de impresión pantalla 331
tecla de iniciación 328
tecla de inicio/stop de grabación 320
tecla de llamada 327
tecla de mayúsculas 330
tecla de multiplicación 337
tecla de número 337
tecla de pedal 305
tecla de porcentaje 337
tecla de raíz cuadrada 337
tecla de reiniciación 328
tecla de repetición 323
tecla de retroceso 331
tecla de selección 327
tecla de selección de banda 322
tecla de selección de entrada 322
tecla de selección de modalidad FM 322
tecla de selección del grabador 322
tecla de selección sintonía 322
tecla de servicio 330
tecla de sustracción 337
tecla de visualización del título 320
tecla decimal 337
tecla email 330
tecla escape 330
tecla inicio 330
tecla memoria 322
tecla para limpiar la pantalla 337
tecla para limpiar la pantalla y de acceso 337
tecla pausa 331
tecla tabulación 330
teclado 304, 310, 327, 330, 336
teclado alfabético 338
teclado alfanumérico 327, 330, 346, 442, 443
teclado de bajos 296
teclado de funciones 423
teclado del número de identificación personal(PIN) 443
teclado del órgano de expresión 305
teclado del órgano mayor 305
teclado del órgano positivo 305
teclado numérico 328, 331, 338, 423
teclado triple 296
teclado, instrumentos 304
teclados manuales 305
teclas 311
teclas de control 328
teclas de cursor 331
teclas de función 328
teclas de funciones 330
teclas de funciones programables 443
teclas de operación 442, 443
teclas de selección de la sintonía 322
teclas de selección de los altavoces 322
teclas Internet 330
técnica de salto 513
técnicas 487
tee 505, 515
tegumento de la semilla 57
teja 280, 283
tejado 183, 193, 283
tejido adiposo 113, 114
tejido conjuntivo 114
tejido subcutáneo 114
tejón 88
tela de araña 70
tela impermeable 273
telares 292
telecomunicaciones vía satélite 317
telecomunicaciones, satélites 316
teleférico 512
teléfono 327, 439
teléfono móvil 327
teléfono público 294, 437, 438, 463
teléfono, comunicación 327
telémetro 315
teleobjetivo 314
teleporte 317
telescopio 7
telescopio espacial Hubble 7, 37
telescopio reflector 9
telescopio reflector, sección transversal 9
telescopio refractor 8
telescopio refractor, sección transversal 8
telesilla 512
telesquí 512
televisión 439
televisior 444
televisor 318
televisor de pantalla ancha 321
telón cortafuegos 292
telón de boca 292, 293
telón de fondo 292
telson 71
temperatura ambiente 39
temperatura del punto de rocío 39
temperatura termodinámica, unidad de medida 426
temperatura, medición 424
temperatura, sensor 358
templo azteca 283
Templo de Huitzilopochtli 283
Templo de Tlaloc 283
templo griego 279
templo griego, plano 279
tenacillas 269
tenazas 193
tendencia barométrica 39
tenedor 167, 531
tenedor de ensalada 168
tenedor de fondue 168
tenedor de mesa 168
tenedor de ostras 168
tenedor de pescado 168
tenedor de postre 168
tenedor de trinchar 169
tenedores, ejemplos 168
tenis 490
tenis de mesa 493
tenista 492
tensiómetro 461
tensión, disminución 413
tensor 412, 498, 521, 537
tensor de la fascia lata 96
tensor de las cuerdas 308
tensores pectorales 500
tentáculo 72
tentáculo ocular 72
tentáculo táctil 72
tercelete 284
tercer ala 482
tercer octante 5
tercer pistón móvil 307
tercera 298
tercera base 474
tercera línea 482
tercera línea izquierda 482
tercero 515
terminación nerviosa 114
terminal 198, 404
terminal de carga 381
terminal de contenedores 430
terminal de granos 381
terminal de mercancías 430
terminal de pago electrónico 121, 443
terminal de pasajeros 381, 389, 390
terminal de petróleo 381
terminal de tierra 198
terminal del control remoto 314
terminal satélite de pasajeros 389
términos familiares 57, 58, 59
términos técnicos 57, 58, 59
termita 69
termo 532
termo con llave de servicio 532
termómetro 404, 424
termómetro clínico 424
termómetro de azúcar 171
termómetro de horno 171
termómetro de medida instantánea 171
termómetro de mercurio 461
termómetro digital 461
termómetro para carne 171
termómetros clínicos 461
termopausa 37
termosfera 37
termostato 178, 211
termostato de seguridad 213
termostato regulable 179
ternera, carne troceada 152
ternera, cortes 152
ternero 84
terraplén 342
terraza 182, 387
terremoto 27
terreno de juego 479
terrina 174
terrina para mantequilla 163
terrina, mantequilla 163
testículo 111
testículos 71
testigo 472
testigo luminoso 454
testuz 83
tetera 166
Tetis 3
tibia 98
tibial anterior 96
tiburones 146
tiempo, medición 424
tiempo, unidad de medida 426
tienda 280, 432
tienda de animales 436
tienda de artículos de decoración 437
tienda de bricolaje 436
tienda de campaña clásica 529
tienda de campaña tamaño familiar 528
tienda de deportes 437
tienda de discos 436
tienda de electrónica 436
tienda de regalos 436
tienda de ropa 436
tienda interior 528, 529
tienda libre de impuestos 391
tienda para dos 528
tienda rectangular 528
tienda tipo domo 529
tienda tipo iglú 529
tienda tipo vagón 528
tienda unipersonal 529
tiendas de campaña, ejemplos 528
Tierra 2, 3, 4, 5, 14
tierra apisonada 342
tierra batida 492
Tierra de la Reina Maud 15
Tierra de Marie Byrd 15
Tierra de Wilkes 15
Tierra del Fuego 17
Tierra, estructura 26
tifón 43
tigre 89
tijeras 461, 531
tijeras con doble filo para entresacar 270
tijeras con filo simple para entresacar 270
tijeras de cocina 173
tijeras de pedicura 265
tijeras de peluquero 270
tijeras de podar 234
tijeras de punta roma 265
tijeras de uñas 265
tijeras para aves 173
tijeras para cutículas 265
tila 148
timbal 308
timbales 295
timón 13, 383, 384, 386, 393
timón de profundidad 393
tímpano 75, 279, 285
tímpano, membrana 116
tinta 312
tinta de color cambiante 441
tinte para el cabello 267
tintorería 437
tipi 288
tipo de combustible 346
tipo de nube alta 39
tipo de nube baja 39
tipo de nube media 39
tipos de cabeza 221
tipos de eclipses 4, 5
tipos de movimientos 470
tipos de parqué 190
tipos de puntas 221
tipos de varillas 176
tira 286
tirador 163, 210, 286
tirador de la puerta 352
tirante 187, 219, 259, 344
tirante ajustable 260
tirante con botones 261
tirante de la botavara 519
tirante del pescante 397
tirantes 246
tirilla 245, 250
tirilla elástica 247, 250, 261
tirita 461
tirita Velcro® 260
tiro de aire caliente 192
tisanas 148
Titán 3
Titania 3
tití 91
titular 313
titular, firma 441
título de propiedad 469
tiza 503
toalla con capuchón 260
toalla de baño 267
toalla de lavabo 267
toalla para la cara 267
toallero 195
tobera de sección variable 394
tobillera 257, 476, 513
tobillo 92, 94
toca 239
tocón 63
Togo 451
toldo 361
toldo de ventana 528
toldo delantero 528
tolva de carga 364
toma 236
toma audio 329
toma de aire 346, 362
toma de aire del motor 362
toma de aire del tejado 194
toma de aire para el ventilador de sustentación 383
toma de aire para refrigeración del motor 525
toma de aire principal 194
toma de alimentación 329
toma de auriculares 329
toma de corriente 361
toma de entrada audio 337
toma de oxígeno 464
toma de salida audio 337
toma para auriculares 310, 311, 326
toma para la boca de riego 455
toma para los auriculares 322
tomas entrada /salida video 322
tomas vídeo 315
tomate 128
tomates en rama 128
tomatillos 128
tómbolo 35
tomillo 142
Tonga 453
tope 224, 270, 375, 459
tope amortiguador 209
tope de la escalera 455
tope de la puerta 211
tope fijo 425
tope móvil 425
toque 487
Torá, rollos 447
tórax 67, 68, 92, 94
torca 31
tornado 43
tornillo 219, 221, 223, 301
tornillo cruciforme (Phillips) 221
tornillo de ajuste 206, 222, 224, 461
tornillo de ajuste de ranilla 229
tornillo de ajuste de tensión 341
tornillo de ajuste del condensador 421
tornillo de anclaje 473
tornillo de apriete 224

tornillo de cabeza achaflanada 221
tornillo de cabeza avellanada 221
tornillo de cabeza redonda 221
tornillo de caja cuadrada 221
tornillo de montaje 535
tornillo de sujeción 227
tornillo de un solo sentido 221
tornillo guía 228
tornillo macrométrico 421
tornillo micrométrico 421, 425
tornillo nivelador 423
tornillo sin fin 365
tornillos de bloqueo 425
torniquete de entrada 378
torniquete de salida 378
torno de banco 224
torno de perforación 403
toro 429
toronja 134
torre 284, 397, 412, 413, 470
torre de control 388
torre de oficinas 435
torre de perforación 382, 403, 404
torre de recepción 316
torre de refrigeración 402
torre de saltos 518
torre de señales 375
torre de transmisión 316
torre del homenaje 282
torre esquinera 282
torre flanqueante 282
torre, grúa 397
torrecilla de lavado 214
torrente de montaña 29
torreta 282
torsión 228
tortellini 146
tortillas 145
tortuga 76
tortuga, morfología 76
tostador 178
touch pad 336
trabilla 246, 254, 477
trabilla de la pretina 246
trabilla de suspensión 250
trabilla para el pie 501
tracción, coche 380
tracería 285
tracto olfatorio 117
tractor de orugas 398
tractor de ruedas 399
tractor, motor 400
tragadero 31
tragaluz 182
trago 115
trainera 384
traje cruzado 252
traje de baño 263, 516
traje de carrera 508
traje de carreras 525
traje de chaqueta 251
traje de entrenamiento 262
traje de esqui 510
traje de esquí 513, 514
traje de esquí de salto 513
traje de judo (judoji) 499
traje de protección 525
traje espacial 10
traje ignífugo 524
tramo 191
tramo central 344
tramo de elevación 345
tramo giratorio 344
tramo lateral 344
tramo suspendido 344
trampa de agua 504
trampa petrolífera 403
trampas de arena 504
trampilla 281, 292
trampilla de acceso 434
trampolín 184
trampolín de 1 m 518
trampolín de 3 m 518
transacción, recibo 443
transacciones financieras 335
transbordador 381, 386, 391
transbordador espacial 12
transbordador espacial en posición de lanzamiento 12
transepto 285
transferencia de calor al agua 408
transformador 207, 407
transformador principal 376
transmisión 212
transmisión de cadena 372
transmisión de calor 415
transmisión de electricidad 408
transmisión de ondas hertzianas 316
transmisión longitudinal, árbol 351
transmisión por cable submarino 317
transmisor 327
transmisor-receptor radar 457
transpaleta 396
transpiración 45
transporte 342
transporte aéreo 388
transporte de electricidad de alta tensión 402, 413
transporte ferroviario 374
transporte hacia los usuarios 402, 413
transporte marítimo 381
transporte terrestre 342, 381
trapecio 96, 97, 429
tráquea 105
traste 296, 302, 303
tratamiento de datos 38
tratamiento químico 405
travelín 290
travelín, raíles 290
travesaño 187, 201, 202, 219, 297, 412, 466, 467, 479
travesaño de apoyo 412
travesaño superior 186
travesaño superior de la vidriera 186
trébol 468
tren de alta velocidad 376
tren de aterrizaje delantero 392
tren de aterrizaje principal 393
tren de pasajeros 374
tren subterráneo 378, 380
tren suburbano 375
trenca 249
triángulo 295, 309, 429, 503
tribuna del jurado 440
tribunal 440
tríceps braquial 97
triciclo 373
triclinio 280
trifoliada 55
trifolio 285
trigo 61, 143
trigo : espiga 61
trigo sarraceno 61, 143
trimarán 521
trincha 244
trinchera 248
Trinidad y Tobago 449
trino 299
trinquete 221
trío 300, 468
tripa 154
triple salto 472
trípode 8, 308
tripulantes, vehículo de emergencia 11
triticale 143
Tritón 3
tritón 75
triturador de ajos 170
triturador de basura 197
trituradora 49, 402
trituradora de documentos 341
trocánter mayor 99
troje 122
tromba marina 43
trombarina 43
trombón 307
trombones 295
trompa 75, 295, 307
trompa de Eustaquio 116, 117
trompa de Falopio 112
trompa uterina, ampolla 113
trompas de Falopio 113
trompeta 307, 342
trompetas 295
trona 205
tronco 52, 62, 63, 75, 93, 95
tronco celiaco 103, 107
tronco, corte transversal 63
tronera 502
tronera central 502
tropical húmedo y seco 40
tropical lluvioso 40
Trópico de Cáncer 20, 21, 22
Trópico de Capricornio 20, 21, 22
tropopausa 37, 46
troposfera 37
trote 83
trucha 161
trufa 123
tuba 295, 307
tubérculos 124
tubería de agua caliente 194, 197
tubería de agua fría 194, 196
tubería de carga 406
tubo 163, 199, 224, 307, 420, 461
tubo ajustable 466
tubo alimentador 180
tubo articulado 355
tubo binocular 421
tubo capilar 424
tubo de aire 270, 454
tubo de aspiración 407
tubo de circulación 410
tubo de cristal 424
tubo de destellos 420
tubo de embocadura 305
tubo de empuje 312
tubo de entrada 177
tubo de escape 199, 350, 351, 364, 368, 395, 398, 401
tubo de extensión 209
tubo de gasolina 351
tubo de irrigación 365
tubo de la hélice 383
tubo de lengüeta 305
tubo de pantalla 318
tubo de perforación 403
tubo de Pitot 525
tubo de presión 409
tubo de subida del agua 181
tubo de suministro de agua 194, 197
tubo de toma de agua 194
tubo de vapor 181
tubo del asiento 370
tubo del manillar 371
tubo del pistón 307
tubo en Y 460
tubo flexible 209, 460
tubo fluorescente 199
tubo inferior del cuadro 371
tubo portaocular 421
tubo principal 8, 9
tubo principal de observación 420
tubo rígido 209
tucán 80
tuerca 222, 223
tuerca cerrada 223
tuerca de ajuste 197
tuerca de bloqueo 425
tuerca de mariposa 223
tuerca de sujeción 536
tuerca hexagonal 223
tuercas 223
tulipán 56
tumbona 201
tundra 40, 44
túnel 378
túnel de carretera 345
túnel de comunicación 13
túnel de embarque 389
Túnez 451
túnica 252
turbante 239
turbina 402
turbina de viento de eje horizontal 413
turbina de viento de eje vertical 412
turbinas de viento 412
turbo-alternador 402
turborreactor 393
turión 125
turismo de tres puertas 347
turismo, neumático 358
Turkmenistán 452
Turquía 452
Tuvalu 453

U

uapití (elk) 84
ubicación de la estatua 279
Ucrania 450
udon, fideos 147
ued 36
Uganda 451
uke (defensor) 499
umbela 57
umbo 73
umbral 30, 185
Umbriel 3
un par 468
uña 76, 78, 115, 220
uña, cuerpo 114
uña, raíz 114
uñas, esmalte 265
uñas, lima 265
unicelulares 66
unidad astronómica 3
unidad CD/DVD-ROM 336
unidad de casetes 333
unidad de CD/DVD-ROM 329
unidad de control de la temperatura del cuerpo 10
unidad de control electrónico 357
unidad de cuidados intensivos 464
unidad de destilación al vacío 405
unidad de disco duro extraíble 333
unidad de discos 310
unidad de disquete 329
unidad de disquete externo 333
unidad de extracción de solventes 405
unidad de medida de cantidad de materia 426
unidad de medida de carga eléctrica 426
unidad de medida de corriente eléctrica 426
unidad de medida de energía 426
unidad de medida de frecuencia 426
unidad de medida de fuerza 426
unidad de medida de intensidad luminosa 426
unidad de medida de la diferencia de potencial eléctrico 426
unidad de medida de la temperatura 426
unidad de medida de longitud 426
unidad de medida de masa 426
unidad de medida de potencia eléctrica 426
unidad de medida de presión 426
unidad de medida de radioactividad 426
unidad de medida de resistencia eléctrica 426
unidad de medida de temperatura termodinámica 426
unidad de medida de tiempo 426
unidad de pesas 501
unidad de refrigeración 365
unidad del disco duro 333
unidad móvil 316
unidad móvil de rayos X 462
unidad móvil de servicio por control remoto 11
unidad para maniobras en el espacio 10
unidades astronómicas 2
unidades de almacenamiento de información 333
unidades de entrada de información 330
unidades de medida, sistema internacional 426
unidades de salida de información 333
uniforme 456
unión 312, 427
unísono 298
universidad 432
uno 427
uranio en fisión 408
Urano 2, 3
uréter 107
uretra 107, 111, 112
urgencias 462
urinario, aparato 107
URL localizador universal de recursos 334
urna 423
urópodo 71
Uruguay 448
usos de Internet 335
usuario particular 335
utensilios de cocina 169, 174, 531
utensilios diversos 173
utensilios para la chimenea 193
utensilios para medir 171
utensilios para repostería 172
útero 112, 113
útero, ligamento ancho 113
uva 62
uva, corte 59
uvas 132
uvas, racimo 62
úvula 116, 117
Uzbekistán 452

V

vaca 84
vaciador 173
vacuno, carne picada 152
vacuno, carne troceada 152
vacuno, cortes 152
vacuola 50, 66
vacuola contráctil 66
vacuola digestiva 66
vacuola digestiva en formación 66
vagina 112, 113
vagón cisterna 377
vagón comedor 376
vagón de carga 375
vagón de pasajeros 376, 380
vagón frigorífico 377
vagón máquina 380
vagón para automóviles 377
vagón para contenedores 377
vagón para ganado 377
vagones de pasajeros 376
vagones, ejemplos 377
vaina 55, 60
vaina de mielina 110
vajilla 166
valla 434
valla de madera 506
vallado 182
vallado del campo 475
valle 29, 32
valor 441
valores de las notas musicales 299
valores de los silencios 299
valva 73
válvula 371
válvula aórtica 104
válvula de admisión 360
válvula de control 529
válvula de drenaje 211
válvula de entrada 196
válvula de escape 360
válvula de exhalación 459
válvula de inhalación 459
válvula de liberación de aire 385
válvula de llenado 404
válvula de seguridad 174, 408
válvula de vaciado 404
válvula mitral 104
válvula pulmonar 104
válvula tricúspide 104
Vanuatu 453
vapor 402, 415
vapor, tubo 181
vaporera eléctrica 179
vaporizador 208
vaquería 122
vaqueros 254
vara 301
varano 77
variedades de inflorescencias 57
varilla 199, 259, 273
varilla circular 176
varilla de acero 309
varilla de aspas 176
varilla de batir 176

varilla de carbón (cátodo) 417
varilla de gancho 176
varilla de refrigeración 420
varilla de rubí 420
varilla de tensión 308
varilla del pedal 304
varilla en espiral 176
varilla reflectante 420
varilla rizadora 269
varillas, tipos de 176
varios aparatos electrodomésticos 180
Varolio, puente 109
vaso 184
vaso capilar 114
vaso corto 165
vaso largo 165
vaso medidor 171
vaso mezclador 176
vaso sanguíneo 104, 114
vástago 220, 221, 371, 502
vástago aislado 217
vástago de arrastre 403
vasto externo 96
vasto interno 96, 97
vatio 426
vegetación 44
vegetación, distribución 44
vehículo de emergencia 345
vehículo de emergencia para los tripulantes 11
vehículo todo terreno 347
vehículos 342
vejiga 107, 111, 112
vela 446, 519
vela mayor 520
velarium 281
velero 520
veleta 413
veleta (grímpola) 520
velo 536
velo del paladar 116, 117
velo del paladar, pilar anterior 116
velocidad del viento 39
velocidad, selector 176
velocímetro 355, 368, 501
vena alar 67
vena axilar 102
vena basílica 102
vena cava inferior 102, 103, 104, 107
vena cava superior 102, 103, 104
vena cefálica 102
vena femoral 102
vena hepática 103
vena ilíaca 103
vena ilíaca común 107
vena mesentérica superior 102
vena porta 103
vena pulmonar 102
vena pulmonar derecha 104
vena pulmonar izquierda 104
vena renal 102, 107
vena safena interna 102
vena subclavia 102
vena yugular externa 102
vena yugular interna 102
venas y arterias, principales 102
vencejo 80
venda de gasa 461
venda elástica 461
venda triangular 461
veneno, conducto 76
veneno, glándula 76
venera 157
Venezuela 448
venta de billetes, taquilla 378
ventalla 60
ventana 178, 179, 186, 189, 361, 519
ventana a la francesa 287
ventana a la inglesa 287
ventana abajo 331
ventana arriba 331
ventana basculante 287
ventana corredera 287
ventana de acceso 333
ventana de celosía 287
ventana de guillotina 287
ventana de la nariz 117
ventana de librillo 287
ventana del semisótano 183
ventana panorámica 435
ventana pivotante 287
ventana protectora 318
ventana-mosquitero 528
ventanas, ejemplos 287
ventanilla 349, 352, 380, 392, 443
ventanilla comercial 443
ventanilla de aterrizaje 395
ventanilla de observación 13
ventanilla de ventilación del techo 361
ventanilla trasera 349
ventilación 354
ventilador 213, 322, 350, 358, 360, 365, 380
ventilador de césped 237
ventilador de la carcasa 329
ventilador del equipo de alimentación 329
ventosa 72, 75
ventrículo derecho 103, 104
ventrículo izquierdo 103, 104
Venus 2, 3
verano 38
verano fresco 40
verano tórrido 40
verbena 148
verde 418
verdolaga 127
verdura 120
verdura 124
verduras de hojas 126
vereda 504
vermicelli de arroz 147
vernier 425
vértebra lumbar 110
vértebras cervicales 99
vértebras dorsales 99
vértebras lumbares 99
vertedero 431
vertedero autorizado 47
vertedor 180
vertido de hidrocarburos 48
vesícula biliar 106
vesícula seminal 111
vestíbulo 116, 188, 280, 374, 386, 390, 435, 439
vestido acampanado 252
vestido camisero 252
vestido camisero sin mangas 252
vestido cruzado 252
vestido de camiseta 252
vestido de talle bajo 252
vestido de tirantes 252
vestido ignífugo y impermeable 454
vestidos, ejemplos 252
vestuario 290
vestuarios 444
vía 374, 378
vía de tren suburbano 375
vía férrea 25
vía ferroviaria 431, 432
Vía Láctea 6
Vía Láctea (vista desde arriba) 6
Vía Láctea (vista lateral) 6
vía principal 375
vía subsidiaria 375
víbora 77
vibrisas 82
vid 62
vid, hoja 62
videocámara analógica: vista frontal 320
videocámara analógica: vista posterior 320
videocinta 319
videojuego 471
vidriera 446
vidrio 186
vidrio, selección 49
vieira 157
viento 47, 48, 528
viento dominante 43
viento, instrumentos 306
viento, molino 412
vientre 83
vierteaguas 349
vierteguas 185, 186, 193
Vietnam 453
viga 280, 283, 288
viga cantilever 344
viga continua 344
viga de cola 395
viga maestra 11, 187
viga, puente 344
vigueta 190
vigueta del piso 187
vigueta del techo 187
vigueta esquinera 187
vinagre balsámico 141
vinagre de arroz 141
vinagre de malta 141
vinagre de manzana 141
vinagre de vino 141
vinagre, arroz 141
vinagre, malta 141
vinagre, manzana 141
vinagre, vino 141
vino 120
viola 301
violas 295
violeta 56
violín 301
violines, familia 301
violoncelo 301
violoncelos 295
vira 240
virola 503
virola hembra 537
virola macho 537
visera 238, 239, 367, 458, 506, 525
visión 419
visión normal 419
visión, defecos 419
visón 88
visor 210, 315
visor electrónico 320
visor telescópico 420
vista 119
vista anterior 92, 94, 96, 98
vista frontal 478
vista general 186
vista lateral 478
vista lateral del cráneo adulto 100
vista lateral del cráneo de un niño 100
vista posterior 93, 95, 97, 99, 113
vista transversal de una calle 434
visualización de datos 328
visualización de la información 319
vitrales 285
vitrina 203
vitrinas refrigeradas 120
vivienda 122
viviendas plurifamiliares 289
viviendas tradicionales 288
viviendas urbanas 289
volador 471
volante 350, 354, 385, 525
volante de control 455
volante de plumas 495
volante sintético 495
volantes 260
volcadora 401
volcán 26, 28
volcán efusivo 28
volcán en erupción 28
volcán explosivo 28
volcanes, ejemplo 28
volea 490
voleibol 487
volt 426
voltio 426
voluta 200, 301
volva 52
vuelo del peldaño 191
vuelta 246
vulva 94, 113

W

wakame 123
walkie-talkie 456
wasabi 141
wigwam 288
Wilkes, Tierra 15
winch 521
windsurf 519
wok 174

xilófono 295, 309

yak 85
yate de motor 385
yema 54, 79, 114
yema axilar 53
yema terminal 53
yembé 297
Yemen 452
yen 440
yeyuno 106
Yibouti 451
yogur 150
Yugoslavia 450
yunque 116
yurta 288

Z

zaguero 482
zaguero derecho 487
zaguero izquierdo 487
zaguero medio 487
zamarra 249
Zambia 452
zampoña 297
zanahoria 129
zanca 191
zanca de contén 191
zanco 398
zángano 68
zapata 224, 357, 365
zapata antideslizante 219
zapata de goma 219
zapatería 437
zapatilla 473, 478, 488, 500
zapatilla con tacos 476
zapatilla de tenis 242, 492
zapatilla deportiva 262
zapato 522, 524
zapato con cordones 241
zapato con tacos 486
zapato de cordones 240
zapato de correa 241
zapato de salón 241
zapato de tacón con correa 241
zapato de talón abierto 241
zapato oxford 240
zapatos de golf 505
zapatos de hombre 240
zapatos de mujer 241
zapote 137
zarcillo 62
zarpa 187
Zimbabue 452
zócalo 191
zócalo de la bañera 195
zona comercial 431, 435
zona de anotación 484
zona de ataque 487
zona de atención 475
zona de camillas 462
zona de combate 499
zona de convección 4
zona de defensa 487
zona de defensa protegida 515
zona de entrega 472
zona de espera 442
zona de la portería 507
zona de marca 483
zona de pelos absorbentes 63
zona de precipitación 39
zona de preparación de productos 120
zona de radiación 4
zona de recepción de mercancías 120
zona de recepción productos lácteos 120
zona de recreo 386
zona de saque 495
zona de seguridad 499
zona de servicio 389
zona de traspaso de carga 385
zona de tres segundos 489
zona del hoyo 504
zona libre 487
zona neutral 484, 507
zona pelúcida 112
zona residencial 431
zona residencial (de las afueras) 25
zona residencial de las afueras 431
zorro 88
zumaque 139